none of them tests it by facts himself. The distinguishing mark of economic science, as illustrated by this debate, is that it is a science in which verification of generalisations by reference to facts is neglected as irrelevant.

. . . I do not see how . . . [members of the public who survey the controversy] can avoid the conclusion that economics is not a science concerned with phenomena, but a survival of medieval logic, and that economists are persons who earn their livings by taking in one another's definitions for mangling. . . .

I know that in speaking thus I make enemies. I challenge a tradition of a hundred years of political economy, in which facts have been treated, not as controls of theory, but as illustrations. I shall be told that in the Social Sciences verification can never be clean enough to be decisive. I may be told that, in these sciences, observation has been tried and has failed, has led to shapeless accumulations of facts which themselves lead nowhere. I do not believe for a moment that this charge of barrenness of past enquiries can be sustained; to make it is to ignore many achievements of the past and to decry much solid work that is being done at this School and elsewhere. But if the charge of barrenness of realistic economics in the past were justified completely, that would not be a reason for giving up observation and verification. It would only be a reason for making our observations more exact and more numerous. If, in the Social Sciences, we cannot

yet run or fly, we ought to be content to walk, or to creep on all fours as infants. . . . For economic and political theorising not based on facts and not controlled by facts assuredly does lead nowhere. . . .

There can be no science of society till the facts about society are available. Till 130 years ago we had no census, no knowledge even of the numbers and growth of the people; till fifteen years ago we had no comprehensive records about unemployment even in this country, and other countries are still where we were a generation or more ago; social statistics of every kind—about trade, wages, consumption—are everywhere in their infancy. . . .

From Copernicus to Newton is 150 years. To-day, 150 years from the *Wealth of Nations,* we have not found, and should not expect to find, the Newton of economics. If we have travelled as far as Tycho Brahe we may be content. Tycho was both a theorist and an observer. As a theorist, he believed to his last day in the year 1601 that the planets went round the sun and that the sun and the stars went round the earth as the fixed centre of the universe. As an observer, he made with infinite patience and integrity thousands of records of the stars and planets; upon these records Kepler, in due course, based his laws and brought the truth to light. If we will take Tycho Brahe for our example, we may find encouragement also. It matters little how wrong we are with our theories, if we are honest and careful with our observations.

Extracts from Lord William Beveridge's farewell address as Director of the London School of Economics, June 24, 1937. Published in POLITICA, September, 1937.

ECONOMICS
FIFTH EDITION

RICHARD G. LIPSEY
Queen's University

PETER O. STEINER
The University of Michigan

Harper & Row, Publishers
New York, Hagerstown, San Francisco, London

ECONOMICS, FIFTH EDITION

Copyright © 1978
by Richard G. Lipsey and Peter O. Steiner
Portions of this work were first published in the United
Kingdom as *An Introduction to Positive Economics,*
© 1963 by Richard G. Lipsey

Sponsoring Editor: John Greenman
Special Projects Editor: Mary Lou Mosher
Project Editor: Cynthia Hausdorff
Designer: Ben Kann
Production Supervisor: Kewal K. Sharma
Compositor: Progressive Typographers, Inc.
Printer and Binder: Kingsport Press
Art Studio: Danmark & Michaels Inc.

Library of Congress Cataloging in Publication Data

Lipsey, Richard G   Date-
    Economics.

    Includes bibliographical references and index.
    1. Economics.   I. Steiner, Peter Otto, Date-
joint author.   II. Title.
HB171.5.L733   1978   330   77-15782
ISBN 0-06-044016-3

CONTENTS

Preface   xiii

Suggested outline for a one-semester course   xix

To the student   xxi

Part ONE *The nature of economics*   *1*

1 THE ECONOMIC PROBLEM   2

Economic problems of the seventies   3
What is economics?   5
Scarcity, 6   Choice, 6   A classification of economic problems, 9   Economics: a working definition, 11
Economic analysis and economic policy   12
The pervasiveness of policy decisions, 12   The relation between ends and means, 12   Conflicts of policy, 14   Economic and political objectives, 14

2 ECONOMICS AS A SOCIAL SCIENCE   17

The distinction between positive and normative, 17 The scientific approach, 19   Is human behavior predictable? 20   The nature of scientific theories, 22   What is a theory and how is it tested? 22 Economics as a developing science, 25

3 THE ROLE OF STATISTICAL ANALYSIS   29

Techniques for testing theories, 29   The statistical testing of economic theories: an example, 30 Evaluating the evidence, 35

4 AN OVERVIEW OF THE ECONOMY   38

The nature of the market economy   38
The decision makers, 40   Markets, 41 Kinds of economies, 41
How individual markets work: an overview of microeconomics   42
The circular flow: from microeconomics to macroeconomics, 44
An overview of macroeconomics   46

Part TWO   *A general view of the price system*   *51*

5   DEMAND, SUPPLY, AND PRICE   52

The basic theory of demand   52
*The nature of quantity demanded, 53   What
determines quantity demanded? 54   The quantity
of a commodity demanded and its own price, 56
Shifts in the demand curve, 57*
The basic theory of supply   59
*What determines quantity supplied? 59
The quantity of a commodity supplied and its own
price, 61   Shifts in the supply curve, 62*
The determination of price by demand and supply   63
The "laws" of supply and demand, 65

6   ELASTICITY OF DEMAND AND SUPPLY   70

Demand elasticity   70
*Price elasticity: a measure of the responsiveness of
quantity demanded to price changes, 72   Other
demand elasticities, 76*
Elasticity of supply   80

**7   SUPPLY AND DEMAND IN ACTION: PRICE
     CONTROLS AND AGRICULTURAL PROBLEMS**   82

Price controls   83
*Setting maximum prices, 83   Setting minimum
prices, 88*
The problems of agriculture   89
*Fluctuations and trends in prices and incomes, 91
Agricultural stabilization and support plans, 97
Problems with agricultural stabilization and support
plans, 99   American farm policy since 1929, 100
Has the farm problem disappeared? 101*

Part THREE   *Demand*   *107*

8   HOUSEHOLD CONSUMPTION BEHAVIOR   108

*The relation between market and household demand
curves, 108*
The marginal utility theory of household behavior   109
*Marginal and total utility, 109   Maximizing
utility, 112   Applying the distinction between
marginal and total utility, 115*
Household choice: an alternative analysis   119
*The budget line, 119   Indifference curve
analysis, 122*

9   DEMAND THEORY IN ACTION   130

Measurement of demand   131
*Modern measures of demand, 131   Problems of
measurement, 134*
Criticisms of demand theory   136
*Does demand theory make unreasonable assumptions
about rational household decision making? 136
Is demand theory only an elaborate way of saying
anything can happen? 137*

Part FOUR   *Production and cost*   *147*

10   THE FIRM, PRODUCTION, AND COST   148

The organization of production   149
*Proprietorships, partnerships, and corporations, 149
The rise of the modern corporation, 151
The firm in economic theory, 152*
Cost and profit to the firm   155
*The meaning and measurement of cost, 155
The measurement of opportunity cost by the firm, 156
Profits: their meaning and significance, 160*

11   PRODUCTION AND COST IN THE SHORT RUN   165

Real choices open to the firm   166
*Time horizons for decision making, 166
Connecting the runs: the production function, 167*
Short-run choices   168

*Total, average, and marginal products, 168
The shape of the marginal product curve, 170
Short-run variations in cost, 171*

12   COST IN THE LONG RUN   177

*Input decisions in the long run, 177   Cost curves in
the long run, 180   The relation between long-run
and short-run costs, 182   Shifts in cost curves,
183   Isoquants: an alternative analysis of the
firm's input decisions, 184*

**13   THE VERY LONG RUN: PROGRESS AND
      POLLUTION**   192

Progress and productivity   192
*Productivity, 193   Sources of increasing
productivity, 194   Invention and innovation, 196*

Past and future productivity growth, 198
Social cost   199
Cost to whom? 200   Pollution, 200

Externalities, 202   Who is to blame? 204
The significance of divergencies between social and
private costs, 205

Part **FIVE** *Markets and pricing*   *209*

14 PRICING IN COMPETITIVE MARKETS   210

Firm behavior and market structure   210
The significance of market structure, 211
Behavioral rules for the profit-maximizing
firm, 212
The theory of perfect competition   213
The assumptions of perfect competition, 213
Demand and revenue curves for the perfectly
competitive firm, 216
Short-run equilibrium: firm and industry   217
Equilibrium output of a firm in perfect
competition, 217   Short-run supply curves, 218
The determination of short-run equilibrium price, 220
Short-run profitability of the firm, 220
Long-run equilibrium   221
The long run in outline, 221   A more
detailed analysis of the long run, 223

15 PRICING IN MONOPOLY MARKETS   236

A monopolist selling at a single price   236
The monopolist's revenue curves, 236
Profit maximization in a monopolized market, 239
Equilibrium of the firm and industry, 240
The nature and extent of monopoly power   241
Measuring monopoly power, 242
Price discrimination   243
Why price discrimination pays, 244   When is price
discrimination possible? 244   The positive effects
of price discrimination, 245   The normative aspects
of price discrimination, 246   Price discrimination:
systematic and unsystematic, 247

16 INDUSTRIAL ORGANIZATION AND THEORIES
     OF IMPERFECT COMPETITION   250

Structure of the American economy   250
Patterns of concentration in manufacturing, 252
The theory of monopolistic competition   253
The theory, 254   Predictions, 250
Monopolistic competition after forty years, 258
Competition among the few: the theory of oligopoly   258
Developing theoretical models by assuming how firms
react, 259   Generalizing from hypotheses about
observed behavior, 260   Barriers to entry, 262
Price inflexibility: is there a kinked demand
curve? 265   A final word, 266

17 PRICE THEORY IN ACTION   269

Boycotts and their effect on market price   269
The 1973 meat boycott, 269   Results of the
boycott, 270
The attempt to monopolize perfectly competitive
industries   272
The instability of producers' co-ops, 273   Milk
withholding in Wisconsin, 273   The price of
haircuts, 275   The decline and fall of a patent
monopoly, 277
Is oligopoly theory necessary?   279
Cigarettes, 279   Steam-turbine generators, 279
Mixtures of market structures, 280

18 MONOPOLY VERSUS COMPETITION   283

Comparisons between monopoly and competition   283
The effect of changes in cost on price and quantity
produced, 283   The monopolization of a
competitive industry, 285   Differences in
efficiency of competition and monopoly, 285
The noneconomic appeal of competition, 287
The effect of market structure on cost, 288
The incentive to innovate, 289
Public policy toward monopoly: antitrust   290
The nature of antitrust policy, 291   Who makes
our antitrust policies? 292   The success of antitrust
policy, 297   Economics and the law, 297
Public policy toward monopoly: public utility regulation   298
Natural monopoly, 298   The theory of natural
monopoly regulation, 299   Problems of
implementing the theory, 300   Evaluating public
utility regulation, 302

19 WHO RUNS THE FIRM AND FOR WHAT ENDS?   305

Does the firm manipulate the market?   306
The hypothesis that the firm controls the market, 306
The evidence for the hypothesis, 307
Doubts about the hypothesis, 308
Who controls the modern corporation?   311
The hypothesis of minority control, 312
The hypothesis of the separation of ownership from
control, 313   The hypothesis of intercorporate
control groups, 314
Criticism of the economist's concept of the firm   314
Information and the modern firm, 314
The organization of the firm, 316
The motivation of the firm, 316

Part **SIX**   *Factor pricing and the distribution of income*   *321*

20   THE DISTRIBUTION OF NATIONAL INCOME   322

Problems of distribution, 322   The theory of distribution, 325
The demand for factors   326
*What determines the demand curve for a factor?   326
The derivation of demand for factors, 327*
The supply of factors   329
The total supply of factors, 329   The supply of factors to particular uses, 333
The price of factors in competitive markets   335
Factor price differentials, 335   Transfer earnings and economic rent, 338   Policy implications of the distinction between rents and transfer earnings, 340

21   COLLECTIVE BARGAINING, DISCRIMINATION, AND THE DETERMINATION OF WAGES   344

Theoretical models of wage determination   345
*A union in a competitive labor market, 345
A monopsonistic labor market without a union, 346
A union in a monopsonistic market, 347*
Labor market institutions   348
The evolution of the modern union   351
*Requirements of a successful union, 352
The historical development of American unions, 353*
Methods and objectives of the modern union   356
*Restricting supply to increase wages, 356
Competing goals, 358*
Discrimination and wages   360
*Black-white differentials in labor markets, 360
Female-male differentials in labor markets, 361
Economic discrimination, 362
Is economic discrimination possible in competition? 364*

22   INTEREST AND THE RETURN ON CAPITAL   367

The productivity of capital   367
The return on capital, 368   The value of an asset, 371
The relation between interest and the return on capital   372
*The demand for additional capital by a firm, 372   The economy as a whole, 373
A complication: many rates of interest, 376*
Sources of funds for investment   377
*Financing the modern corporation, 379   Stock and stockholders, 379   Bonds and bondholders, 379
Loans from financial institutions, 380
Reinvested profits, 380   Securities markets (stock markets), 380   The relation between prices and earnings, 382*

23   POVERTY, INEQUALITY, AND MOBILITY   389

The distribution of income between rich and poor: the problem of poverty   389
Who are the poor? 391   Why are there poor? 392   Black poverty, 393   "Waging war" on poverty, 394   Scope and adequacy of present programs, 396
Is distribution theory relevant?   398
*Do market conditions determine factor earnings?   398
Do factors move in response to changes in earnings? 401*
General criticisms of distribution theory   403
The theory restated, 403   Two important misconceptions, 404   Does the theory explain the functional distribution of income? 405

Part **SEVEN**   *The market economy: problems and policies*   *409*

24   THE PRICE SYSTEM: MARKET SUCCESS AND MARKET FAILURE   410

The interdependent economy   410
When markets work well, 413   How the price system works: the notion of general equilibrium, 414
Market failure   417
*Sources of market failure, 417   Coping with market failure, 420   Pollution control, 424
Achievements of American environmental policy, 427*

25   PUBLIC FINANCE AND PUBLIC EXPENDITURE   430

Public finance and taxation   430
*Tax policy and the distribution of income, 431
Tax structure and the allocation of resources, 436*
Public expenditure as a tool of micro policy   441
Types of government expenditure, 441   Coping with the urban crisis, 446   Evaluating government expenditures, 450
An overview of microeconomic policy   453

Part EIGHT *National income and fiscal policy* 457

26 NATIONAL INCOME 458

The concept of national income 459
*The Spendthrift economy, 459   The Frugal
economy, 462   The Governed economy, 464
The Open economy, 466   The U.S. economy, 468
Related measures of national income, 473*
Interpreting national income measures 474
*Money values versus real values, 475   Total
output versus per capita output, 475   Omissions
from measured national income, 476   Which
measure is best? 479*

27 WHAT DETERMINES NATIONAL INCOME? 482

Background to the theory of national income 483
*Preliminary definitions and assumptions, 483
National income in the Spendthrift economy, 486*
National income in the Frugal economy 487
*Investment decisions, 487   Consumption-saving
decisions, 487   The consumption function, 488
The saving function, 491   The aggregate
demand function, 492   Equilibrium income, 493
A link between saving and investment?, 499*
A generalization of the theory of equilibrium national
income 499
*The withdrawals-injections approach in the general
case, 499   The income-expenditure approach in the
general case, 503   Equilibrium national income: a
general graphical approach, 503*

28 CHANGES IN NATIONAL INCOME 506

Why national income changes 506
*Movements along curves versus shifts of
curves, 506   A shift in the injection
schedule, 508   A shift in the withdrawal
schedule, 509   Compensating shifts in injections
and withdrawals, 512   An alternative method of
deriving the basic predictions, 513*
The multiplier: a measure of the magnitude of changes
in income 514
*The definition of the multiplier, 515
The multiplier: an intuitive statement, 515
The multiplier: a graphic representation, 517
How large is the multiplier in the United States
today? 519*
Inflationary and deflationary gaps 519

*The "gaps" defined, 521   Using the concepts of
the "gaps," 522*

**29 CYCLES AND FLUCTUATIONS IN NATIONAL
INCOME** 525

*The historical record, 525   Is there a principal
cause of cycles? 526*
Shifts in consumption 527
*Shifts in the relationship between consumption
and disposable income, 529   Shifts in the
relationship between disposable income and national
income, 532   Shifts in the consumption
function and business fluctuations, 532*
Investment and its determinants 532
*Why does investment change? 534   Investment in
inventories, 534   Investment in residential
construction, 536   Investment in plant and
equipment, 537   The accelerator theory of
investment, 540*
Elements of a theory of fluctuations 543
*The terminology of business fluctuations, 543
Cumulative movements and turning points, 544
The variety in cyclical fluctuations, 546
Fluctuations: a consensus view? 548*

30 THEORIES AND TOOLS OF FISCAL POLICY 550

The theory of fiscal policy 551
*Fiscal impact on the economy, 551   The effects of
taxes and government spending, 552   Comparative
effects of alternative fiscal policies, 557*
Objectives of fiscal policy 559
*Fine tuning, 559   The removal of persistent
gaps, 560*
Tools of fiscal policy 560
*Automatic tools of fiscal policy: built-in
stabilizers, 561   Discretionary fiscal
policy, 564*

31 FISCAL POLICY IN ACTION 569

Fiscal policy at work in the United States 570
*Before 1946, 570   After World War
II, 571   Fiscal policy in the future: secular
stagnation or boom? 575*
The opportunity cost of government activity 577
*Effects of alternative means of financing government
activities, 578   The national debt, 581*

Part NINE   *Money, banking, and monetary policy*   589

32 THE NATURE AND HISTORY OF MONEY   590

The importance of money   590
*The "real" and money parts of the
economy, 590   The experience of price level
changes, 592   Why inflations and deflations
matter, 592*
The nature of money   598
*What is money? 598   The origins and growth of
metallic money, 600   The evolution of paper
money, 602   Deposit money, 606   Near
money and money substitutes, 609   Changing
concepts of what is money, 610*

**33 THE BANKING SYSTEM AND THE SUPPLY OF
MONEY**   612

The commercial banks   613
*Interbank activities, 614   Commercial banks as
profit-seeking institutions, 615   Reserves, 617*
The creation and destruction of deposit money by the
commercial banks   618
*A monopoly bank, a single new deposit, 619
Many banks, a single new deposit, 621
Many banks, many deposits, 622
Excess reserves and cash drains, 624*
Central banks   625
*Basic functions of a central bank, 625   The Federal
Reserve system, 627*
Central banks and the money supply   629
*Changing the required reserve ratios, 629
Changes in the discount rate, 630
Open market operations   630*

34 THE IMPORTANCE OF MONEY   635

The classical link between the money supply and the
price level: the quantity theory   635
*The transactions demand for money, 636
Assumptions of the quantity theory, 637
Effects of changes in the money supply: full
employment, 637   Effects of changes in the
money supply: unemployment, 638
The modified quantity theory, 638*
A modern view of the role of money   640
*The demand for money, 641   The speculative
motive, 642   Interest rates and aggregate
demand, 645   How money supply affects
national income, 646   The impact of monetary
policy, 647*

35 MONETARY POLICY   651

Objectives and instruments of monetary policy   651
*Controlling the interest rate through monetary
policy, 652   Controlling national income through
monetary policy, 652   A conflict between
national income and the rate of interest as policy
variables, 653   A conflict between the
money supply and interest rates as instrumental
variables, 654*
Monetary policy in action   655
*The "accord," 655   The shift from interest rates to
the money supply as the main target variable, 657
The use of monetary policy since the accord, 657
Use of tools other than open market operations, 660
Monetary policy: some interim conclusions, 664*

Part TEN   *International trade and finance*   667

**36 THE BALANCE OF PAYMENTS AND
EXCHANGE RATES**   668

The nature of exchange rates   668
The balance of payments   670
*The balance of actual payments, 670
The balance of desired payments, 676*
The determination of exchange rates   676
*Price changes caused by exchange rate changes, 677
What determines the equilibrium exchange
rate? 678   Fixed exchange rates, 680
Fixed versus fluctuating exchange rates, 682*

37 THE GAINS FROM TRADE   685

*Interpersonal, interregional, and international trade,
685   Sources of the gains from trade, 686
Additional sources of the gains from trade: learning by*

*doing and economies of scale, 691   Terms of
trade, 691*

38 TARIFFS   695

The nature and purpose of tariffs   695
*The case for free trade, 696   The case for
protectionism, 696   Trade versus tariffs, 698*
Trade and tariffs in the world today   704
*Tariffs in the United States, 704   International
agreements concerning trade and tariffs, 705*

**39 TWENTIETH-CENTURY INTERNATIONAL
MONETARY SYSTEMS**   710

Before World War II   711
*The gold standard, 711   Actual experience of the
gold standard, 712   The 1930s: a period of*

experimentation, 712
The rise and fall of the Bretton Woods system, 1944–1972   713
The International Monetary Fund, 714
Problems of an adjustable peg system, 715

Collapse of the Bretton Woods system, 718
The present system   721
Current and future problems, 723   Survival of the IMF in a world of floating exchange rates, 724
A final word, 725

Part ELEVEN *Macroeconomic policy in action: the control of inflation and unemployment*   729

40 THE NATURE OF UNEMPLOYMENT AND INFLATION   730

The goals of macroeconomic policy, 730
Unemployment   731
Why policy makers are concerned, 731   Causes of unemployment, 732   Tools for control of unemployment, 735   Experience of unemployment, 735
Inflation   736
Why policy makers are concerned, 736   Causes of inflation, 736   The control of inflation: validated and unvalidated inflation, 739   Experience of inflation, 740

41 CONFLICTS AMONG POLICIES: MONETARISTS VERSUS NEO-KEYNESIANS   742

Views of macroeconomic policy   742
Two extreme views, 742   Monetarist and neo-Keynesian views of stabilization policy, 743
The nature of the problem (diagnoses)   743
Cyclical fluctuations, 744   Inflations, 747
Instruments of policy (the potency of various medicines)   747

The influence of interest rates, 747   Monetary policy, 750   Fiscal policy, 752
Recommended policies (prescriptions)   754
Monetarist policies, 754   Neo-Keynesian policies, 758
The significance of the debate   758

42 CONFLICTS AMONG GOALS: UNEMPLOYMENT VERSUS INFLATION   762

Conflicts arising from various types of inflation   763
Demand-pull inflation, 763   From demand-pull to expectational inflation: the Phelps-Friedman theory, 767   Implications of the Phelps-Friedman theory, 771   Cost-push, and price-push theories, 775
Wage-price controls   776
Wage-price controls to regulate demand-pull inflations, 776   Wage-price controls as a cure for expectational inflation, 777   Wage-price controls to combat cost-push and price-push inflations, 778
Stagflation   780
Alternative explanations of American stagflation, 780   An evaluation of stagflation, 782

Part TWELVE *Economic growth and comparative systems*   787

43 GROWTH IN DEVELOPED ECONOMIES   788

The nature of economic growth   788
The definition of economic growth, 789
The cumulative nature of growth, 790
Benefits of growth, 791   Costs of growth, 793
Growth as a goal of policy: do the benefits justify the costs? 796
Theories of economic growth   797
Growth in a world without learning, 797   Growth with learning, 799   A contemporary view of growth, 800   Are there limits to growth? 804

44 GROWTH AND THE UNDERDEVELOPED ECONOMIES   809

The uneven pattern of development   809

Barriers to economic development   812
Population growth, 813   Resource limitations, 814   Inefficiency in the use of resources, 816
Fostering economic development   818
Planning or laissez faire? 818   Educational policy, 819   Population control, 820
Acquiring capital, 821
Patterns of development   823
Comparative advantage: the case for unbalanced growth, 823   Agricultural development versus industrialization, 824   Import substitution, 825
Industrialization, 826

45 COMPARATIVE ECONOMIC SYSTEMS   830

Different economic systems   831
Ownership of resources, 831   The decision process

*(coordinating principles), 832   Whose values? 833
Incentive systems, 834   Ends and
means, 835   The characterization of particular
economies, 835*
The economy of the Soviet Union   836
*Ownership, 836   The organization of
production, 837   The distribution of goods and
household incentives, 839   Planning in the Soviet*

*Union, 840   Prices in the planning process, 841
Comparative performance: the United States versus
the Soviet Union, 842*
The economy of Yugoslavia   846
*The decollectivization of agriculture, 847
Labor-managed enterprises, 848   The scope and
role of planning, 849*
Comparative systems: a final word   849

APPENDIXES   *853*

**Appendix to Chapter 2   MORE ON FUNCTIONAL
RELATIONS**   854

*Functional relations: the general expression of
relations among variables, 854   Functional
forms: precise relations among variables, 855
Error terms in economic hypotheses, 855*

**Appendix to Chapter 3   GRAPHIC ECONOMIC
MAGNITUDES**   857

*Graphing economic observations, 857
Graphing functions, 861*

**Appendix to Chapter 6   ELASTICITY: A FORMAL
ANALYSIS**   865

Arc elasticity, 865   Point elasticity, 868

**Appendix to Chapter 8   INDEX NUMBERS AND
MORE ON INDIFFERENCE CURVES**   869

Index numbers
*Index numbers as summary measures, 869
Use of index numbers to measure changes in
real income, 872*
More on indifference curves   875
*Derivation of demand curves, 875   The slope
of the demand curve, 876*

**Appendix to Chapter 10   BALANCE SHEETS,
INCOME STATEMENTS, AND COSTS OF
PRODUCTION: TWO VIEWS**   880

*An example, 880   An accountant's balance
sheet and income statement, 881   An economist's balance sheet and income statement, 883*

**Appendix to Chapter 30   THE PERMANENT-INCOME
HYPOTHESIS AND THE LIFE-CYCLE HYPOTHESIS**   885

*Variables, 885   Assumptions, 886
Implications, 887   Conclusion,   889*

**Appendix to Chapter 34   MONEY IN THE
NATIONAL INCOME MODEL**   890

*The theory, 890   An analysis of fiscal and
monetary policy, 894*

**Appendix to Chapter 41   MORE ON MONETARY
VERSUS FISCAL POLICY**   896

*The representation of monetary and fiscal
policy, 896   The effects of fiscal and
monetary policy, 898*

Mathematical Notes   901

Glossary   910

Index

Preface

Our basic motivation in writing *Economics* always has been, and in this fifth edition still is, to provide a book that reflects the enormous changes in economics over the last forty years. Economics is always changing, but in the period since World War II, there has been a change of such importance that we do ourselves and our students a great disservice if we neglect it. During this period economics has moved very rapidly toward becoming a genuine science. We apply the term *science* neither to praise nor to castigate economics, but to describe its movement toward that characteristic distinguishing any science: the systematic confrontation of theory with observation.

The quotation from Lord William Beveridge on the front endpaper of this book is our text —in the preacher's sense of that word —and it describes the first of the three main themes we wish to mention here. Beveridge was scolding the profession in 1937, but things since then have clearly changed for the better. Today we all agree that economics is not a stage on which we parade our pet theories and ask to have them admired solely for their elegance or their conclusions, nor is it a container in which we collect quantities of unrelated institutional and statistical material about the economy. Economists are engaged in a serious attempt to push back the frontiers of ignorance about the economic environment in order both to understand it and to control it. Economists must therefore continually be concerned with the relations among theory, institutions, and facts and must regard every theory as subject to empirical challenge. At relevant stages in this book, therefore, we have attempted to indicate which data are relevant and to distinguish between those ideas and theories that have been reasonably well tested and those that have not.

A second major theme of this book concerns the relations between economic theory and economic policy. An appreciation of these relations is not new to economics. Indeed, many nineteenth-century economists expressed the modern view that although economic theory can show us some of the consequences of our actions, it can never show us what we ought to do. What is new today is the realization of how little can be said about policy on the basis of the purely qualitative theories, and the resulting successful application of the quantitative revolution of the last thirty years to matters of policy. Three decades of systematic observations have provided us with a much better idea of how things are related to one another quantitatively, and this knowledge has greatly increased the economist's power to say sensible and relevant things about public policy. This is not to deny that there are still great areas where economists' knowledge is painfully sparse, as the current debates about how best to cope with problems of unemployment and inflation and on the efficacy of fiscal policy remind us.

The third major feature of the book relates to the way we view modern students. We have tried in several different ways to be as honest with them as is possible within the confines of an introductory textbook. No subject worth studying is always easy, and we have not glossed over hard points just because they are hard. We have tried to follow Einstein's advice: make things as easy as possible, but not easier. We do not approve of slipping particularly hard bits of analysis past students without letting them see what is happening and what has been assumed, nor do we approve of teaching them things they will have to unlearn if they go on in economics (a practice sometimes justified on the grounds that it is important to get to the big issues quickly).

Every student who continues in economics soon learns that, although economics has many triumphs to its credit, there are areas where present knowledge is woefully inadequate. It is sometimes argued that in an elementary course such inadequacies should be played down or altogether suppressed so that beginning students will not lose faith in their subject. We reject this view. Both the students' education and our subject depend upon careful criticism. We have devoted some space to examining both sensible and foolish criticisms of economic theories. In doing this, we hope to give students some inkling of how it is possible to criticize effectively, and hence to improve, the existing body of economic theory. Effective criticism of existing ideas is the springboard to progress in science, and we believe that an introduction to economics should also introduce students to methods for testing, criticizing, and evaluating the present state of the subject. We do not accept the notion that if you suggest the possibility of criticism to students, they will make hasty and confused criticisms. Students will always make criticisms and evaluations of their courses, and their criticisms are much more likely to be informed and relevant if they are given both practice and instruction in how to go about challenging in an effective, constructive manner what they have been taught rather than reverting to mere dogmatic assertion of error or irrelevance.

MAJOR REVISIONS IN THIS EDITION

Applications

Some policy problems are hardy perennials that are with us year after year; others arise suddenly and fade rather quickly. The relative urgency of particular problems changes sharply, even over so short a span as the three years since we wrote the Fourth Edition. Examples of newly relevant issues on the macro side include the emergence of two-digit inflation in the United States, changes in the composition of the labor force and in living styles so significant that the concept of "full employment" as it has been defined for decades may no longer be attainable, and the stubborn coexistence of rapid inflation and heavy unemployment. Interest has faded in such problems as managing fixed exchange rates. At the same time the debate over the relative efficacy of monetary and fiscal policies continues to be as lively as it was five years earlier. On the micro side, the near bankruptcy of New York City and the OPEC oil embargo have given new prominence to urban problems and to the looming energy crisis. This same period witnessed a growing disenchantment with government processes and government officials, and has led economists and others to take a much more critical look at the effectiveness of government regulation of economic activities. But in spite of all the changes, the "old" problems of poverty, of coping with discrimination, and of agricultural booms and busts are as pressing as ever. Interest in the volunteer army versus the draft, however, is temporarily at least a thing of the past.

We have tried to revise our treatment to provide applications and illustrations that are relevant to the problems that seem likely to be at the forefront of the attention of students using this edition. The basic framework of economics does not change rapidly, and few theories are discarded over any three-year time span, but the most interesting current applications do change, and so does the data available. This edition reflects many of these changes.

Reorganizations

As the core of our loyal users grows, we receive ever more constructive criticism of the way in which the material in our book is organized. "Good stuff," our correspondents often say, "but why not put x *ahead of* y or use z *instead of* x?" (Unfortunately, our correspondents don't all agree with one another.) These suggestions, and our own experience, have led to some important changes.

Microeconomics. Chapters 9, 19, and 23 each give important applications of economic theory, along with some consideration of commonly voiced criticisms. In each case, the chapter has been reorganized to put material of most general interest first, making it easier if desired to assign only part of the material in each of the chapters. A similar reorganization of Chapters 24 and 25 has been made. The organization of the material on costs and supply in Chapters 11 to 14 has been revised and simplified. Chapters 11 and 12 have been reorganized so as to include only material on production and costs. They are now much easier than the corresponding Fourth Edition chapters, which many found difficult. The derivation of short- and long-run supply curves is now postponed until Chapter 14, where it is covered as part of the theory of perfect competition. In the process of reviewing this material we concluded that much of the Fourth Edition coverage of the long run was too advanced and we have eliminated the appendix on costs. Isoquants, formerly relegated to an appendix, are now in the text, in a new "optional" section at the end of Chapter 12.

Macroeconomics. The basic theory of macroeconomics has been reworked substantially to make it more easily accessible to students. The chapter, *More on Consumption* has been eliminated and the most basic material is now taken up at relevant points in earlier chapters, while the discussion of permanent income and life-cycle hypotheses is placed in an appendix. The chapters on fiscal policy have been rewritten, in part to reflect the declining confidence of economists in the possibilities of fine tuning. In Part Nine (Money) the order of chapters has been reversed so that the determinants of the money supply can be discussed before the importance of money is studied in detail. The chapter on monetary policy has been restructured—some of the material has been transferred to Chapter 33 on the money supply where it more logically belonged, while a major new section, Monetary Policy in Action, has been added to Chapter 35. Chapter 39 has been substantially reworked to reflect the continuing rapid developments in international finance as the Bretton Woods system recedes into history and more experience is gained with floating exchange rates. Part Eleven has seen the greatest changes in the macro half of the book. These changes have been made to reflect the rapid accumulations of empirical knowledge and theorizing on the problems of unemployment and inflation. The part now begins with a new chapter in which various types of inflation and unemployment are discussed. This material should be of interest in itself, and it also sets the stage for some of the policy controversies subsequently discussed. Chapter 41 revises and updates the monetarist-Keynesian controversy. Chapter 42 is almost wholly new. It discusses alternative theories of inflation including the Phelps-Friedman theory, which augments the Phillips curve with expectations about inflation. The chapter then goes on to consider causes and cures for so-called stagflation — the coexistence of high unemployment and high rates of inflation. The discussion leads students close to the modern frontier of debate on this most relevant of all macro issues.

Other Changes of Note

The number of appendixes has been reduced in this edition, and the remaining appendixes have been moved to the back of the book. The appendixes were "interruptions" in the flow of the book and can be omitted without destroying its continuity. It now seems desirable to emphasize this by "setting them to one side." Some of them are more advanced and are designed for the honors student; others (for example, principles of accounting) include related but tangential material; still others (Appendix to Chapter 3 on graphing) are designed to bridge gaps in the backgrounds of some students. The coverage of an appendix is always described in the

chapter. An appendix should never be assigned routinely, but most courses will want to use some of them.

A number of our readers called attention to our use of *man* and the male pronoun to refer to both sexes. We have sought to remove gratuitous "sexist" language (e.g., "man's ability to cope with the population problem") without giving up well-known concepts ("man-hours of labor") or ancient phrases ("man does not live by bread alone").

The glossary, new in the Fourth Edition, has been much praised. We have revised it to bring the definitions in the text and glossary into close conformity. Because some users treat micro and macro economics in that order, and others in reverse order, words in the glossary are printed in boldface type when they are first mentioned in *either half* of the text.

Tag lines, captions, titles, and figure coloring and labels have all been reviewed and many revised in an effort to improve the teachability of the text. We have tried to use color and shading in a more consistent way.

Teaching Aids

Tag lines and captions for figures and tables. The tag line below the figure or table indicates succinctly the central conclusion intended by the illustration; the caption (in blue) provides information needed to reach that conclusion. Titles, tag lines, and captions are, with the figure or table, a self-contained set, and many students find them a useful device for reviewing a chapter.

Boxes. The material in blue "boxes" contains examples or materials that are relevant extensions of the text narrative but need not be read in sequence.

End-of-chapter material. Each chapter contains a Summary, a list of Concepts for Review, and a newly revised set of Discussion Questions. The questions are particularly useful for class discussion or for "quiz sections." They are answered in the Instructor's Manual.

Mathematical notes. Mathematical notes to the body of the text are collected in a self-contained section at the end of the book. Since mathematical notation and derivation is not required to understand the principles of economics, but is helpful in more advanced work, this seems to us to be a sensible arrangement. It provides clues to the uses of mathematics for the increasing numbers of students who come to beginning economics with some background in math, without encumbering the text with notes that may appear formidable to those who find mathematics arcane or frightening. Students with a mathematical background have many times told us they find the notes helpful.

Supplements

Our book is accompanied by a workbook, *Study Guide and Problems,* prepared by Professor Dascomb R. Forbush, Mrs. Dorothy Forbush, and Professor Frederic C. Menz. The workbook is designed to be used either in the classroom or by the students working on their own.

Professor Kenneth G. Elzinga of the University of Virginia has collected an exciting set of readings in *Economics, A Reader, Third Edition,* which takes the students beyond the confines of the single text and introduces them to such interesting articles as "Does Advertising Raise or Lower Prices," by Robert L. Steiner, "The Economics of the New Unemployment," by Martin Feldstein, and "What the Radical Economists Are Saying," by Martin Bronfenbrenner.

An *Instructor's Manual,* prepared by us, and a *Test Bank* prepared under our supervision are available to instructors adopting the book.

USING THE BOOK

This textbook reflects to some extent the way its authors would teach their own courses.

Needs of students differ; some want to have material that goes beyond the average class level, but others have gaps in their backgrounds. To accommodate the former, we have included more material than we would assign to every student. Also, because there are many different kinds of first-year economics courses in colleges and universities, we have included more material than normally would be included in any single course. Requests and suggestions from users of previous editions have prompted us to include some additional alternative material.

Although teachers can best design their own courses, it may be helpful if we indicate certain views of our own as to how this book *might* be adapted to different courses.

Sequence

Because the choice of order between macro and micro is partly a personal one, it cannot be decided solely by objective criteria. We believe that in the 1970s there are good reasons for preferring the micro-macro order. Whereas in the immediate post-World War II years, the major emphasis was on the development of both the theory and the policy implications of Keynesian economics, the thrust over the last ten years has been to examine the micro underpinnings of macro functions and to erect macroeconomics on a firmer base of micro behavioral relations. Changes have occurred not only in economic theory but in the problems that excite students. Although macroeconomic problems such as inflation and unemployment are still of great concern, many of the problems that students find most challenging today—the plight of the cities, poverty, pollution, and managing wage and price controls—are microeconomic in character. The micro-macro order, moreover, reflects the historical evolution of the subject. A century of classical and neoclassical development of microeconomics preceded the Keynesian development of macroeconomics.

For those who prefer the macro-micro order and who wish to reverse the order of our book, we have attempted to make reversibility virtually painless in this edition. The overview chapter that ends Part One has been built up to provide an improved base on which to build either the microeconomics of Part Two or the macroeconomics of Part Eight. Where some microeconomic concepts were required—as in the macro investment chapter—we have added brief sections to make the treatment self-contained, while providing review material for those who have been through the microeconomic section.

One-Semester Courses

Thorough coverage of the bulk of the book supposes a two-semester course in economics. A great many first courses in economics are only one semester (or equivalent) in length and our book can be easily adapted to such courses. Suggestions for use of this book for such courses are given on pages xix–xx. We recognize that for any one-semester course a choice must be made among emphases. Most one-semester survey courses necessarily give some coverage to theory and to policy, to micro- and macroeconomics, but the relative weights vary. Instructors will wish to choose the topics to be included or excluded and to vary the order to suit their own preferences.

ACKNOWLEDGMENTS

So many teachers, colleagues, students, and friends contributed to the original book and to its continuing revision that it is impossible for us to acknowledge our debts to all of them individually. Hundreds of users, both teachers and students, have written to us with specific suggested improvements, and much of the credit for the fact that the book does become more and more teachable belongs to them. We can no longer list them individually but we thank them all, most sincerely. A few individuals provided reviews of the Fourth Edition that were most helpful in preparing the present edition. These are Jeff Blais, Holy Cross College; Tom Bonsor, Eastern Washington State College; Ira Castles, Delta State University; Frances Esposito, Southeastern Massachusetts Tech. Institute; Emily Hoffman, University of North Carolina; Edwin Nadel, Ulster County Community College; Joe Rabianski, SUNY, Brockport; Randolph Rice, Louisiana State University; Louis Rossiter, University of North Carolina; Courtenay Stone, California State College, Northridge; Captain John Throckmorton, Jr., United States Military Academy; and Gerald Visgilio, Connecticut College. We thank them all.

Patricia O. Steiner contributed greatly to the updating of the illustrative examples and to the end-of-chapter questions. Jon Epstein and Chi-Keung Woo provided significant research assistance. David Sandalow and Ann Anderson contributed to the revision of the instructor's aids accompanying the text. Gordon Sparks, our co-author for the Canadian edition of this book, and Douglas Auld and Kenneth Grant, who contributed to the Canadian supplements, have all contributed to this edition as well.

Donna Seale, Diane Centelli, and Diane Vader managed to cope with mountains of manuscript. Weidenfeld and Nicholson generously gave permission to use material first prepared for the Fourth Edition of *An Introduction to Positive Economics* by R. G. Lipsey.

Finally, this Fifth Edition is dedicated by both of the authors to Claudia.

Richard G. Lipsey
Peter O. Steiner

Suggested outline for a one-semester course[1]

Basic core chapters for courses covering both micro and macro

Chapter	Title
	INTRODUCTION
1	The Economic Problem
2	Economics as a Social Science
4	An Overview of the Economy
	MICROECONOMICS
5	Demand, Supply, and Price
6	Elasticity of Demand and Supply
10	The Firm, Production, and Cost
11	Production and Cost in the Short Run
14	Pricing in Competitive Markets
15	Pricing in Monopoly Markets
24	The Price System: Market Success and Market Failure
	MACROECONOMICS
26	National Income
27	What Determines National Income?
28	Changes in National Income
30	Theories and Tools of Fiscal Policy
32	The Nature and History of Money
33	The Banking System and the Supply of Money
35	Monetary Policy

[1] A full semester course can cover about 20 to 22 full chapters. The core consists of 17 chapters. Selections from other chapters, as listed below or according to the instructor's own preferences, can produce courses with various emphases.

Chapters that can be added to give different emphases to different courses[2]

Chapter	Title
	MICROECONOMICS
* 7	Supply and Demand in Action: Price Controls and Agricultural Problems
12	Cost in the Long Run
*13	The Very Long Run: Progress and Pollution
17	Price Theory in Action
18	(up to p. 290) Monopoly versus Competition
*18	(beyond p. 290) Monopoly versus Competition
20	The Distribution of National Income
*21	(from p. 348) Collective Bargaining, Discrimination, and the Determination of Wages
*23	(up to p. 397) Poverty, Inequality, and Mobility
*25	Public Finance and Public Expenditure
	MACROECONOMICS
*31	Fiscal Policy in Action
37	The Gains from Trade
*38	Tariffs
40	The Nature of Unemployment and Inflation
43	Growth in Developed Economies
*44	Growth and the Underdeveloped Economies
45	Comparative Economic Systems

[2]Chapters shown with an * are particularly appropriate for courses with a heavy policy orientation. Chapters not listed here or in the core seem to us to be of lower priority in a one-semester course, but they are not necessarily too difficult.

To the student

A good course in economics will give you some real insight into how an economy functions and into some of the policy issues that are currently the subject of serious debate. Like all rewarding subjects, economics will not be mastered without effort. A book on economics must be worked at. It cannot be read like a novel.

Each student must develop an individual technique for studying, but the following suggestions may prove helpful. It is usually a good idea to read a chapter quickly in order to get the general run of the argument. At this first reading you may want to skip the "boxes" of text material and any footnotes. Then, after reading the Concepts for Review and the Discussion Questions, reread the chapter more slowly, making sure that you understand each step of the argument. With respect to the figures and tables, be sure you understand how the conclusions stated in the brief tag lines below each table or figure have been reached. You should be prepared to spend time on difficult sections; occasionally, you may spend an hour on only a few pages. Paper and a pencil are indispensable equipment in your reading. It is best to follow a difficult argument by building your own diagram while the argument unfolds rather than by relying on the finished diagram as it appears in the book. It is often helpful to invent numerical examples to illustrate general propositions. The end-of-chapter questions require you to apply what you have studied. We advise you to outline answers to some of the questions. In short, you must seek to understand economics, not to memorize it.

After you have read each part in detail, reread it quickly from beginning to end. It is often difficult to understand why certain things are done when they are viewed as isolated points, but when you reread a whole part, much that did not seem relevant or entirely comprehensible will fall into place in the analysis.

We call your attention to the glossary at the end of the book. Any time you run into a concept that seems vaguely familiar but is not clear to you, check the glossary. The chances are that it will be there, and its definition will remind you of what you once understood. If you are still in doubt, check the index entry to find where the concept is discussed more fully. Incidentally, the glossary, along with the tag lines under figures and tables and the end-of-chapter summaries, may prove very helpful when reviewing for the final examination.

The bracketed blue numbers in the text itself refer to a series of about fifty mathematical notes that are found starting on page 901. For those of you who like mathematics or prefer mathematical argument to verbal or geometric exposition, these may prove useful. They are not in any sense a necessary part of the understanding of the text, however, and may be omitted with impunity.

We hope that you will find the book rewarding and stimulating. Students who used earlier editions made some of the most helpful suggestions for revision, and we hope you will carry on the tradition. If you are moved to write to us, please do.

ECONOMICS

PART ONE

THE NATURE OF ECONOMICS

1

The economic problem

Not all of the world's serious problems are primarily economic. Political, biological, social, cultural, and philosophic issues often are predominant. But no matter how "non-economic" a particular problem may seem, it will almost always have a significant economic dimension.

The crises that lead to wars often have economic roots. Nations fight for oil and rice and land to live on, although the rhetoric of their leaders evokes God and Glory and the Fatherland. Arabs and Israelis fight today for a homeland, to be sure, but also for pastures and farms and water and transportation routes. War takes an enormous toll of human life and of materials. It uses up the time and talents, and in some cases the lives, of those who otherwise might be in civilian jobs or pursuing higher education; it consumes steel, leather, paper, and ships which have other uses. Wars divert not only resources but attention from other pressing social and economic problems.

A population explosion threatens to engulf the world as a result of our spectacular ability to reduce mortality rates more rapidly than we are willing or able to reduce birth rates. The current rate of world population growth is 2.2 persons a second, or about 190,000 per day, or 70 million per year. The causes are mainly biological, medical, and cultural, but the economic consequences are tremendous. Unless the human race can find ways to expand its food supply as fast as its numbers, increasing millions will be doomed to starvation. Indeed, as growing population pressure overworks the land, once fertile areas turn to deserts. Since the early 1800s economists have worried about the race between population and food supply and about limitations on the possibilities of getting more and more food from the land.

Race is not primarily an economic phenomenon, but the problem of racial discrimination has important economic effects on individuals and on the whole economy. Discrimination can underutilize the talents of men and women and waste society's resources through loss of job opportunities, unemployment, and poverty. The children of poverty grow up undernourished, undereducated, qualified for only the lowest paying jobs, and hostile to an alien world. These things have many consequences that affect us all, including the loss involved when resources and energy must be diverted from other uses to coping with racial problems.

But economics is not *only* a backdrop for human activities. Many of the most compelling problems—of the 1970s and every other decade—are primarily economic. The dominant economic problem of the 1930s was the massive unemployment of workers and resources known as the Great Depression. The wartime economy of the 1940s solved that problem but created new ones, especially the question of how to reallocate scarce resources suddenly between military and civilian needs. By the 1950s, inflation was appearing as a major problem in many countries. It is still with us. Much attention in the 1960s was devoted to trying to understand and to combat a slowdown in the pace of economic growth. Problems do change from decade to decade, but there are always problems.

Economic problems of the seventies

Poverty and wealth

A third of the world's population suffers from malnutrition. Ten million Americans live in acute hunger today, and many thousands will starve to death this year. Poverty is a major problem in America despite the fact that Americans continue to be among the richest people in the world in income per person and are this year richer, on average, than ever before. How can such poverty survive in the midst of relative plenty? Who are the poor,

and what makes them so? Will poverty take care of itself as we continue to grow richer? Can poverty ever be eliminated in the United States? In the world? Why does the average standard of living rise rapidly in some countries, slowly in others, and not at all in still others? Is equality of income a desirable or attainable national goal?

These questions involve two basic economic issues: what determines the level of income and what determines how that income is distributed.

Pollution and progress

Without the automobile, the airplane, and electricity, ours would be a very different and less comfortable world. But because of them air pollution has become a major problem. Without steel and cement and factories and tractors, the industrial development of the past century would have been impossible; with them, the volume of wastes discharged into water and air has grown to alarming proportions. Insecticides have increased agricultural production manyfold and virtually eliminated the dread diseases of malaria and cholera, but they have all but extinguished the peregrine falcon, endangered other species, including *Homo sapiens,* in ways not yet fully known, and biologically destroyed many lakes and streams. Is large-scale pollution the inevitable companion of economic growth? If it is, how much growth do we really want? If it is not, how can we ensure growth with less pollution?

Are the problems of pollution confined to capitalist economies, or do they occur in socialistic economies too? Once the problems are identified, how are they best attacked? Should this be largely the responsibility of private citizens, of corporations, or of government?

These questions concern the use, and abuse, of society's resources. They are among the basic economic questions, and they involve understanding why markets sometimes fail to work satisfactorily and how to deal with such failures.

Urban and rural crises

Great commercial and industrial societies have shown increasing tendencies for population to be concentrated in bigger cities. Big cities have huge slums where the poor and the disadvantaged congregate. Are slums the inevitable result of the working of economic laws? Can cities cope with what appear to be ever-worsening problems of crime, filth, and poverty?

Is rural squalor preferable to urban blight? Why are farmers still lagging behind industrial workers in income even though food is a basic necessity of all life? Why did America all through the 1960s pay farmers *not* to produce food while over half the world lived under the specter of starvation?

These questions concern what is produced, where it is produced, and where and how comfortably those who produce it spend their lives. They concern the forces that lead to changes in the pattern of living—and some of the problems that accompany those changes.

Unemployment and inflation

Full employment and stable prices seem to be desired by almost everyone, yet we seldom have had both at the same time. Sometimes (as in the first half of the seventies) we have had neither. Unemployment in 1976 was about 8 percent of the labor force. What is an acceptable level of unemployment? Can we be sure we will never again experience the trauma of the 1930s, when up to a quarter of all those who sought work were unable to find it?

What is an acceptable amount of inflation? Will not any inflation ultimately get out of hand and wipe out the value of money and savings? Why do prices in some countries today rise 30 percent or 40 percent a year whereas in others they rise at a rate of 2 or 3 percent? Why did inflation accelerate dramati-

cally over most of the world in the early 1970s? Why did consumer prices in the United States rise by only 18 percent between 1955 and 1965 but by 71 percent between 1965 and 1975? Why in *one* year between 1973 and 1974 did they rise by over 10 percent? Can a country control inflation? Why do we sometimes have both high unemployment and inflation?

These questions concern the stability of the economy and the causes and consequences of depression and inflation. They also concern the ability of people, individually or through governments, to control and change their economic environment.

Growth and the energy crisis

Energy is vital to an industrial economy—energy to drive its factories, to fuel its cars, to heat and light its homes and offices, and to do a myriad of other tasks. Over the last 200 years American output has grown, and with it has grown America's demand for the earth's limited fossil fuels. The amount of energy used in the United States doubled between 1950 and 1970, and it is expected to double again by 1985.

Throughout most of American history the increase in energy consumption caused no serious problems since new supplies were discovered about as rapidly as old ones were exhausted. Around the middle of the 1960s, however, a dramatic turn of events occurred. Although historically energy consumption had grown at a slightly *less* rapid rate than had overall production, since 1965 output has increased at about 3 percent per year while energy consumption has risen by 5 percent per year. This rapidly increasing demand for energy has not been matched by a corresponding increase in the rate of discovery of new reserves. Even before the 1973 Arab-Israel war and the OPEC cartel reduced supplies of Middle Eastern oil coming to the United States, proven reserves had declined and outright shortages had sometimes developed. Proven reserves of petroleum in the United States, which were 12.3 times as large as annual production in 1960 (and thus were expressed as a 12.3-year reserve), were only 11.1 years in 1970 and 10.8 years in 1975. Natural gas reserves fell from 17.4 years in 1960 to 10.5 years in 1975. To what extent do these changes in reserves reflect the operation of normal market forces, and to what extent do they reflect public policies that have encouraged consumption and discouraged exploration?

Do these trends mean an inevitable exhaustion of our energy resources and thus a limit to the future growth of both our population and our standard of living, or are they a temporary and transitory phenomenon? Fuel shortages were real enough at the start of the 1970s, and prices rose sharply. A great debate has developed concerning the appropriate response. Some have argued that if the government does not force us to make major changes now in how we use fuel we will face disaster before the end of the century. Others, less alarmed, have argued that the price rises now occurring will lead to an automatic correction of the problem by decreasing the amount of energy we consume and at the same time making it profitable to discover or develop new sources of energy. They believe the problems are transitory—that they will exist only for the next ten or twenty years and then be solved. Which group is closer to the truth?

The United States, with one-twentieth of the world's population, accounts for a third of the world's energy consumption. To what extent are the *world's* supplies of oil and gas (e.g., in Alaska, in the USSR, in Saudi Arabia, and under the oceans) adequate to the world's demands for energy? If they are adequate, is the U.S. shortage only a problem in trade, transportation, or foreign policy? To what extent can nuclear energy render coal and oil and gas as unnecessary as oil and gas rendered whale oil?

These are questions that concern our ability to discover and bring to market the basic resources we need, our ability to make more resources available by trade with other countries, our ability to find new substitutes for depleted resources, and our ability to adapt to scarcities by changing our techniques of production. The questions also concern the roles of the free price system and of government intervention designed to influence the workings of our market economy.

The role of government

What things should the government do, and what things should it leave to private decision makers? Do we, as John Kenneth Galbraith charges, allocate too little to government expenditure on such valuable things as health and education, while growing sated with privately produced goods such as big cars and electric can openers? Do we instead, as Milton Friedman charges, have the government do badly many things private groups could do well? Or do we do both?

Is there an economic limit to government spending or to the national debt? What is the debt, and how does it arise? Why do economists insist that if one American gets more dollar bills he or she will be richer, but if all Americans simultaneously get more dollar bills they will not in aggregate be richer?

Government involvement in the economy affects the working of what is already a complex economic system. How the economy operates and how differently it would operate with different institutions are current and compelling concerns of economists.

What is economics?

We have listed a few of the issues that are important today and on which economic analysis is supposed to shed light. One way to define the scope of economics is to say that it is the social science that deals with such problems. Fifty years ago such all-embracing definitions were popular. Perhaps the best known was Alfred Marshall's: "Economics is a study of mankind in the ordinary business of life." Because economic problems have certain common features, one may, by looking at them, arrive at a more penetrating definition.

The problems of economics arise out of the use of scarce resources to satisfy human wants.

A society's resources consist not only of the free gifts of nature, such as land, forests, and minerals, but also of human resources, both mental and physical, and all sorts of man-made aids to further production, such as tools, machinery, and buildings. Economists call such resources **factors of production**[1] because they are used to *produce* those things that people desire. The things produced are called **commodities.** Commodities may be divided into goods and services. **Goods** are tangible (e.g., cars or shoes) and **services** are intangible (e.g., haircuts or education). This distinction, however, should not be exaggerated. Any good is valued because of the services it yields to its owner. In the case of an automobile, for example, the services consist of such things as transportation, mobility, and, possibly, status. Notice the implication of positive value contained in the terms "goods" and "services." (Compare the terms "bads" and "disservices.")

   Goods and services are the means by which people seek to satisfy some of their wants. The act of making goods and services is called **production** and the act of using them to satisfy wants is called **consumption.** For most people in most societies goods and services are not regarded as desirable in themselves; no great utility is attached to piling them up endlessly in warehouses, never to be consumed.

---

[1] The definitions of terms in **bold face** type are gathered together in the glossary at the end of the book.

SCARCITY

For all practical purposes, human wants may be regarded as limitless. An occasional individual may have everything, but human capacity to generate new wants as fast as old ones are satisfied is well known to psychologists. For the overwhelming preponderance of the world's 4 billion human beings, *scarcity* is real and ever present. In relation to the desires of individuals (for more and better food, clothing, housing, schooling, vacations, entertainment, etc.), the existing supply of resources is woefully inadequate; there are enough to produce only a small fraction of the goods and services that people desire.

   Is not America rich enough that scarcity is nearly banished? After all, we have been characterized as the affluent society. Whatever affluence may mean it does not end the problem of scarcity. Most households that spend $35,000 a year (a princely amount by worldwide standards) have no trouble spending it on things that seem useful to them. Yet it would take many times the present output of the American economy to produce enough to allow all American households to consume that amount.

CHOICE

Because resources are scarce, all societies face the problem of deciding what to produce and how to divide it among their members. In most societies, many different individuals and organizations make or influence these choices. One of the ways the economies of such countries as the United States, France, India, China, and the Soviet Union differ is in the amount of influence that different groups have upon the choices.

Opportunity cost

Scarcity implies a need to choose, and choice implies costs because a decision to have more of one thing requires a decision to have less of something else. The problem of choice arises over and over again in economics. We consider first a trivial example and then one that vitally affects all of us. Both examples involve precisely the same fundamental principles.

We shall start by considering the choice that must be made by a small boy who has 10¢ to spend and who is determined to spend it all on candy. For him there are only two kinds of candy in the world: gumdrops, which sell for 1¢ each, and chocolates, which sell for 2¢. The boy would like to buy 10 gumdrops and 10 chocolates, but he knows (or will soon discover) that this is not possible. (In technical language, it is not an *attainable combination* given his scarce resources.) There are, however, several attainable combinations that he might buy: 8 gumdrops and 1 chocolate, 4 gumdrops and 3 chocolates, 2 gumdrops and 1 chocolate, and so on. Some of these combinations leave him with money unspent, but he is not interested in them. Only six combinations (as shown in Figure 1–1) are both attainable and use all of his money.

After careful thought, the boy has almost decided to buy 6 gumdrops and 2 chocolates, but at the last moment he decides that he simply must have 3 chocolates. What will it cost him to get this extra chocolate? One answer to this question is 2 gumdrops. In order to get the extra chocolate he must sacrifice 2 gumdrops, as is seen in Figure 1–1. Economists say that the opportunity cost of the third chocolate is what he must sacrifice in order to get it, which in this case is 2 gumdrops.

Another answer is that the cost of the third chocolate is 2¢, but given the boy's budget and his intentions, this answer is less revealing than the first one. Where the real choice is between more of this and more of that, the cost of "this" is fruitfully looked at as what you must sacrifice of "that." The idea of **opportunity cost** is one of the central insights of economics.

Every time one is forced by scarcity to make a choice, one is incurring opportunity costs.

Figure 1–1   A choice between gumdrops and chocolates

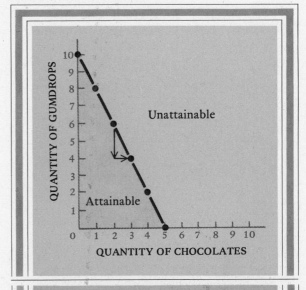

A limited amount of money forces a choice among alternatives. Six combinations of gumdrops and chocolates are attainable and use all of the boy's money. The downward-sloping line provides a boundary between attainable and unattainable combinations. The arrows show that the opportunity cost of 1 more chocolate is 2 gumdrops.

These costs are measured in terms of foregone alternatives.

Production possibilities

Although the previous example concerned a minor consumption decision, the essential nature of the decision is the same whatever the choice being considered.

Exactly the same problems arise, for example, in the important social choice between military and nonmilitary goods—between swords and plowshares. Throughout the 1960s and so far in the 1970s, about 10 percent of the total resources of the American economy has been devoted to the production

Figure 1–2 The choice between military goods and civilian goods

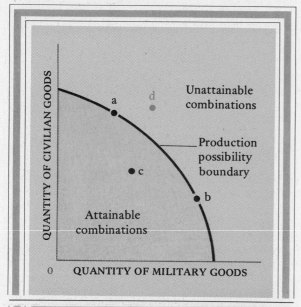

The downward-sloping boundary shows the combinations that are just attainable when all of the society's resources are efficiently employed. The quantity of military goods produced is measured along the horizontal axis, and the quantity of civilian goods along the vertical axis. Thus any point on the diagram indicates some amount of each kind of good produced. The production possibility boundary separates the attainable combinations of goods such as *a*, *b*, and *c* and unattainable combinations such as *d*. It slopes downward because resources are scarce, so that more of one good can be produced only if resources are freed by producing less of the other good.

of both arms and civilian goods. If we have full employment of resources and we wish to produce more arms, then we must produce less of all other goods, thereby reducing the quantity of goods available to satisfy civilian wants. The opportunity cost of more arms is foregone civilian goods, and somehow a choice must be made.

The choice is illustrated in Figure 1–2. Because resources are limited, some combinations—those that would require more than the total available supply of resources for their production—cannot be obtained. The downward-sloping curve on the graph divides the combinations that can be obtained from those that cannot be obtained. Points to the right of this curve cannot be obtained because there are not enough resources; points to the left of the curve can be obtained without using all of the available resources; and points on the curve can just be obtained if all of the available resources are used. The curve is called the **production-possibility boundary.** It slopes downward because, when all resources are being used, to get more of one kind of good some of the other kind must be sacrificed.[2]

The production-possibility curve illustrates three concepts: scarcity, choice, and opportunity cost. Scarcity is implied by the unattainable combinations; choice, by the need to choose among the attainable points; opportunity cost, by the downward slope of the boundary, which means that to get more of something one must accept less of something else.

These concepts have led many to this definition of economics: "Economics studies the problems of the allocation of scarce resources

of goods for military purposes. The American government has made a choice between the production of goods for civilian consumption and the production of arms. The choice is similar in form to the one facing the boy deciding what candies to buy with his dime. It is not possible to produce an unlimited quantity

[2] The curve will be *concave* downward, as in Figure 1–2, if more and more civilian goods must be given up to achieve successive increases in military goods. This shape implies that the opportunity cost grows larger and larger as we increase the amount of arms produced. Drawn as a straight line, as in Figure 1–1, the curve would imply that the opportunity cost of each good stayed constant, no matter how much of it was produced.

between alternative and competing ends." The issues emphasized by this definition are very important, but, as will be seen in the next section, there are other equally important issues in economics which the definition does not stress. Thus it no longer commands the support it did a generation ago, when it was widely regarded as *the* definition of economics.

A CLASSIFICATION OF ECONOMIC PROBLEMS

Modern economies involve thousands of complex production and consumption activities. While the complexity is important, many of the basic kinds of decisions that must be made are not very different from those made in a primitive economy in which people work with few tools and barter with their neighbors. Nor do capitalist, socialist, and communist economies differ in their need to solve these same basic problems, although they do differ, of course, in how they solve the problems. The great majority of the problems studied by economists fall within six problem areas.

1. What goods and services are being produced and in what quantities?

This question concerns the *allocation of scarce resources among alternative uses* (a shorter phrase, **resource allocation,** will usually be used hereafter). Any economy must have some mechanism for making decisions on the problem of resource allocation.

We are asking how choices are made between points such as *a* and *b* in Figure 1–2. In free-market economies, the majority of decisions about the allocation of resources is made through the price system. In other systems, more of the decisions are made by central planners. Economists are interested in the consequences of different kinds of decision making.

2. By what methods are goods and services produced?

Generally, there is more than one technically possible way in which a commodity can be made. Agricultural commodities, for example, can be produced by taking a small quantity of land and applying to it large quantities of fertilizer, labor, and machinery or by using a large quantity of land and applying only small quantities of fertilizer, labor, and machinery. Either method can be used to produce the same quantity of some crop. The first method is frugal with land but uses large quantities of other factors of production; the second uses large quantities of land but economizes on the other factors of production.

Which of the many alternative methods should be adopted? An often-cited criterion is the avoidance of inefficient methods. Production is said to be inefficient when it would be possible to reallocate resources and, as a result, produce more of at least one good without producing less of any other good.

Any scheme of production that uses all of society's resources but produces inefficiently leads to an output combination that falls *inside* the production-possibility boundary (at a point such as *c* in Figure 1–2). It would be possible to get more of either (or both) goods by using more efficient methods of production. Clearly, it is important that efficient rather than inefficient methods of production be used. Economists are interested both in distinguishing between efficient and inefficient methods and in how the choice of the method of production is made from among the methods that are efficient.

3. How is the supply of goods allocated among the members of the society?

Economists are interested in what determines how a nation's total income is distributed among such groups as landowners, laborers, and capitalists or among other groups such as farmers, union members, blacks, and the poor. They are interested also in the consequences of government intervention designed to change the distribution of income by using devices such as progressive income taxes, minimum-wage laws, and programs of social insurance.

These first three questions fall within what is called microeconomics. **Microeconomics**

Figure 1–3 The effect of unemployment on the production-possibility boundary

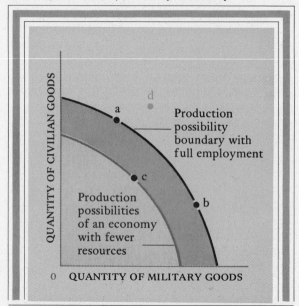

If some of an economy's resources are unused, the quantities of goods that can be produced are diminished and the economy is operating inside its full-employment production possibility boundary. The heavy black curve indicates the production possibility boundary if all of the society's resources are being used. If some of the resources lie idle, production will be at a point such as *c* inside the boundary—as if a smaller economy, with fewer resources, were operating efficiently at full employment. The effect of unemployment is the loss of the attainable combinations in the darker screened area.

concerns the allocation of resources and the distribution of income as they are affected by the workings of the price system and by some government policies.

4. Are the country's resources being fully utilized, or are some of them lying idle and thus going to waste?

It may seem strange that this question needs to be asked at all. Surely, if resources are so scarce that there are not enough of them to produce all urgently required goods, then available resources will not be left idle. Yet one of the most disturbing characteristics of free-market economies is that such waste sometimes occurs. Unemployed workers would like to have jobs, the factories in which they could work are available, the managers and owners would like to be able to operate their factories, raw materials are available in abundance, and the goods that could be produced by these resources are needed by individuals in the community. But for some reason nothing happens.

Massive unemployment occurred in the Great Depression of the 1930s. Although that disastrous experience—25 percent unemployment—has not been repeated, the problem is still with us in significant though lesser degree. The effect of unemployment on the production possibility boundary is illustrated in Figure 1–3.

Unemployment of resources is similar to an inefficient use of them (discussed above under question 2) in that both lead to production inside the full-employment production-possibility boundary. They are not the same problem, however, and the remedies are very different.

5. Is the purchasing power of money and savings constant, or is it being eroded because of inflation?

The world's economies have often experienced periods of prolonged and rapid changes in price levels. Over the long swing of history, price levels have sometimes risen and sometimes fallen. In recent decades, however, the course of prices has almost always been upward, sometimes faster, sometimes slower, but generally upward. The seventies has been a period of accelerating inflation in the United States and in most of the world. Thus today we are concerned with inflation and reduction in the purchasing power of money and savings.

Inflation is closely related to the amount of money in the economy. Money is the invention of human beings, not of nature, and the amount in existence can be controlled by them. Economists ask many questions about the causes and consequences of changes in the quantity of money and the effects of such changes on the price level.

6. Is the economy's capacity to produce goods growing or remaining the same over time?

Productive capacity grows rapidly in some countries and slowly in others, and in some countries it actually declines. Generally the most rapid growth in productive capacity has occurred in those countries that already have relatively high standards of living. As a result, living standards diverge more and more between the "have" and the "have not" countries. Growth in productive capacity can be represented in a production-possibility diagram as a pushing outward of the boundary, as shown in Figure 1–4. If the economy's capacity to produce goods and services is growing, combinations that are unattainable today become attainable tomorrow. Clearly, in an economy in which not nearly enough can be produced to satisfy all wants, growth will be important because growth makes it possible to have more of all goods.

Questions 4 to 6 fall within what is called macroeconomics. **Macroeconomics** is the study of the determination of economic aggregates such as total output, total employment, and the price level.

Figure 1–4 The effect of economic growth on the production possibility boundary

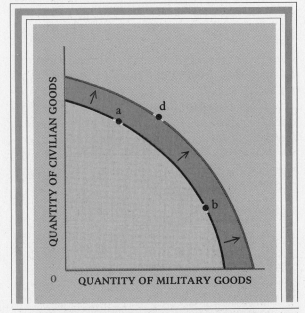

Economic growth shifts the boundary outward and makes it possible to have more of all commodities. Before growth in productive capacity, points *a* and *b* were on the production possibility boundary and point *d* was an unattainable combination. After growth, point *d* and many other previously unattainable combinations are attainable.

ECONOMICS: A WORKING DEFINITION

The six-way classification just discussed does not embrace all of the things that interest economists. Additional topics such as the problems of international trade or comparative economic systems might be included in one or more of those categories, or they might be treated separately. Similarly, the theory of economic policy might be regarded as affecting all of the problem areas mentioned, or it might be treated separately.

Our purpose in listing these problem areas

is to outline the scope of economics more fully than can be done with short definitions. Economics today is regarded much more broadly than it was even half a century ago. Earlier definitions stressed the alternative and competing uses of resources. Such definitions focused on choices between alternative points on a stationary production-possibility boundary. Important additional economic problems concern failure to achieve the boundary (problems of inefficiency or underemployment of resources) and the outward movement of the boundary over time (problems of growth and development).

Economics, broadly defined, concerns:

1. The ways in which a society uses its resources and distributes the fruits of production to individuals and groups in the society.
2. The ways in which production and distribution change over time.
3. The efficiencies and inefficiencies of economic systems.

Economic analysis and economic policy

Economics helps in understanding and predicting some aspects of human behavior. People, by nature curious about their environment, want to predict this behavior in order that they may control their environment and adapt it to their needs.

THE PERVASIVENESS OF POLICY DECISIONS

Governments derive their authority to form and carry out policy from their police power—indeed, the words "policy" and "police" come from the Greek word for state, *politeia.*

Some governments lean toward a policy of laissez faire, or non-interference; others toward a policy of attempting strict control over every facet of the economy.

All governments have economic policies. Even the decision not to act but to let nature take its course is a policy decision.

Whether to rely on market-place decision making or to replace it is as much a policy decision as is a government's decision to tax cigarettes.

Every year thousands of economic policy decisions are made by local, state, and federal governments. Most of them are never seriously debated. Nor is every facet of existing policy debated anew each year; indeed, many policy decisions now in force (such as giving unions the right to organize) were made decades ago. Only a few policy issues attract attention and become the subject of earnest and heated argument in a particular year.

THE RELATION BETWEEN ENDS AND MEANS

Any policy action has two aspects: the ends that the decision makers are attempting to achieve and the means by which the desired ends are to be achieved. The United States government simultaneously pursues many broad policy goals such as justice, progress, national security, and economic stability. To achieve its goal of justice, the government may decide to improve the economic status of disadvantaged groups.

Economics does not provide a "scientific" method for choosing between competing ends, but it does have a large role to play in policy formation. Suppose the government, in order to achieve its goal of stability, decides that unemployment and inflation must be controlled and that foreign exchange imbalances must be corrected. Once such a decision is made, these more specific goals require a number of specific policy actions. Forging the links between desired ends and feasible means is a most important aspect of policy formulation. The economist's training is well suited to help in determining whether a particular measure contributes to its goals and at what cost.

While each issue has its own special characteristics, there are also common concerns.

Four main questions need to be asked in every case: (1) What are the policy goals? (2) Do the proposed means achieve those goals? (3) Do they have adverse side effects? (4) Are there better alternative means?

Evaluating policies

Rent controls began in the United States during World War II. They are not only still with us, but they are growing in their coverage. Consider the position of a team of economists asked to examine the case for and against government's fixing the rents of private dwellings. How should they go about evaluating this policy proposal?

First, the economists would ask what goals rent control is meant to achieve. They might find that it is primarily intended to redistribute income from rich to poor.

Second, the economists would ask if rent control does in fact help to realize this policy goal. Rent control means that tenants pay less rent than they otherwise would and landlords receive less income than they otherwise would; thus rent control redistributes income from landlords to tenants. But do landlords tend to be richer than their tenants? If a survey shows that most tenants are, in fact, richer than their landlords, the economists can conclude that rent control does not achieve the redistributive goal for which it was being used. Then the case against rent control is clear, and that is the end of the story. If, however, the survey indicates that most tenants have lower incomes than their landlords, the economists will conclude that rent control *is* a means of obtaining the desired goal of income redistribution. Further study is then needed.

Third, the economists would ask if rent control has effects that conflict with other policy objectives. It may, for example, lead to the deterioration into slums of some areas where landlords do not find it economically worthwhile to maintain their property. It may also lead to a decrease in the total amount of rental housing as some owners shift their property out of rental uses and potential new investors do not find it worthwhile to construct apartment buildings and other rental units. When a policy action helps to achieve one goal but hinders the attainment of another, it is necessary to establish a trade-off between the goals. Usually there will be some rate at which people will trade a loss in one direction for a gain in another.

Fourth, the economists need to consider alternatives to see if there are other measures that will achieve the goals at a lower sacrifice in terms of setbacks to other policy objectives. It is probable, for example, that the progressive income tax redistributes income from rich to poor with more certainty and precision and with fewer undesired side effects than does rent control.

At any one of the four stages of their investigation, the economists may conclude that rent control is not a very effective means of achieving the policy makers' objectives. (In fact many economists have reached that conclusion about rent controls.) But suppose that the team of economists concludes that rent control *does* achieve the desired goals, that the undesirable effects in other directions are judged (by the policy makers) to be less important than the desirable effects in achieving the stated policy goals, and that there are no other practicable measures that would better achieve the goals? The team will then conclude that there is a strong case in favor of rent controls.[3]

Do not the views—and prejudices—of the

---

[3] People sometimes speak as if economic theory *justified* certain policy conclusions. For example, it is not uncommon to hear someone say that the policy of rent control is "economically unsound" or that it is "economic nonsense." Such viewpoints often represent an effort to dismiss a policy without thinking through to its consequence. Every time you encounter the catchphrase "economic nonsense" your suspicions should be aroused. What does this really mean? you should ask. Why is it dismissed as nonsense? Is the speaker basing his assertion on compelling evidence or simply asserting his own value judgment?

investigators have a great deal to do with the outcome of their investigation? A particular group of economists may have strong views on the particular measure it is attempting to assess. If the economists do not like the measure, they are likely to be relentless in searching out possible unwanted effects and somewhat less than thorough in discovering effects that help to achieve the desired goals. It is important though difficult to guard against an unconscious bias of this sort. Fortunately there are likely to be others with different biases. One advantage of publishing evaluations and submitting them to review and discussion is that it provides opportunities for those with different biases to discover arguments and evidence originally overlooked.

Proposing policies

It is frequently the role of the economist not only to analyze the consequences of a proposed policy (or to compare two or more policies) but to suggest policies. Given a statement of the objectives, economic analysis can be used to invent or publicize proposed policies that have not previously been under consideration. Economists in and out of government have clearly had a major impact on policy. The Employment Act of 1946 created a Council of Economic Advisers to advise the President on the state of the economy and on how the goal of full employment could best be achieved. Since 1960 the Council has played a large role in proposing policies. Other economists play major policy roles in the cabinet, on regulatory commissions and boards, and in many executive departments and administrative agencies. Congress, too, utilizes economic advisers. Nor is it necessary to be in government to affect government policy. Dozens of economists have significantly influenced economic policy from the sidelines. Milton Friedman, Paul Samuelson, James Tobin, Lawrence Klein, Arthur Okun, and Paul McCracken are examples of those whose statements are widely reported and help form the opinions of those who make policy decisions. John Kenneth Galbraith has had an enormous effect on public opinion about economic matters with his best-selling books, and Leonard Silk writes an influential column for *The New York Times.*

CONFLICTS OF POLICY

Governments have many policy goals. A particular policy that serves one goal may hinder another and have no effect on yet a third. Unemployment compensation, for example, may protect unemployed families from debilitating hardship; at the same time it may hinder the quickness with which labor moves from labor-surplus to labor-scarce occupations, thereby increasing the total unemployment in the country. Moreover, it will have no effect one way or the other on air pollution.

The significance of this point is too frequently overlooked. It is never enough to show that a proposed policy advances one of society's objectives. What must be shown about the policy is that it advances certain objectives sufficiently to overcome the cost in terms of the amount that it retards other objectives. In order to do this, it is necessary to determine *how much* of one must be given up to get how much more of the others. This involves the question of opportunity cost, on which the studies of economists can shed light. It is also necessary to decide whether the opportunity cost is worth incurring, and this is a matter of social valuation.

ECONOMIC AND POLITICAL OBJECTIVES

Actual policy making is more complicated than the previous discussion suggests, and a few of the many reasons policy issues get settled in a less systematic fashion deserve mention.

Decisions on interrelated issues of policy are made by many different bodies. Congress passes laws, the Supreme Court interprets laws, the Administration decides which laws to enforce with vigor and which to soft-pedal. The Treasury and the Federal Reserve System influence monetary factors, and a host of other agencies and semiautonomous bodies determine actions in respect to different aspects of policy goals. Merely because of the multiplicity of decision makers it would be truly amazing if fully consistent behavior resulted. The majority of Americans believe that there are major advantages to this separation of responsibilities, but one of its consequences is that inconsistent decisions will be made.

Furthermore, in a system such as ours, inconsistent decisions may result from political compromises between two or more interested groups, factions, or agencies. Such compromises are, of course, common in Congress, between Congress and the Executive, and among Executive departments.

Another problem arises from the fact that legislators in a democracy have their own and their party's reelection as one of their important goals. This means, for example, that any measure that imposes large costs and few benefits obvious to the electorate over the next few years is unlikely to find favor, no matter how large the long-term benefits are. There is a strong bias toward myopia in an elective system. Although much of this bias stems from shortsightedness and selfishness, another part reflects genuine uncertainty about the future. The further into the future the economist is calculating, the wider is the margin of possible error that must be attached to his statements. Thus it is not surprising that politicians who must worry about the next election often tend to worry less about the long-term effects of their actions: "After all," they may argue, "who can tell what will happen 20 years hence?"

These problems of political decision making are what George Bernard Shaw had in mind when he said that the only strong argument in favor of democracy is that all of its alternatives are even worse.

Summary

1. Economic problems are among the important concerns of every generation. Such problems have certain common features arising out of the fact that they concern the use of resources to satisfy human wants.

2. Scarcity is a fundamental problem faced by all economies. Not enough resources are available to produce all of the goods and services that people would like to consume. Scarcity makes it necessary to choose. All societies must have a mechanism for deciding what commodities will be produced and in what quantities.

3. The concept of opportunity cost emphasizes the problem of scarcity and choice by measuring the cost of obtaining a unit of one commodity in terms of the number of units of other commodities that could have been obtained instead.

4. Six basic questions faced by all economies are: What commodities are being produced and in what quantities? By what methods are the commodities produced and are those methods efficient? Who gets the commodities that are produced and in what quantities? Are the society's resources being fully utilized? What is happening to the purchasing power of money and savings? Is the economy's capacity to produce growing over time or remaining static?

5. Not all economies resolve these questions in the same ways or equally satisfactorily. Economists study how these questions are answered in various societies and the consequences of using one method rather than another to provide answers.

6. Governments, in varying degree, choose to intervene in the functioning of the economy. In so doing, they pursue economic policies.

7. It is necessary to distinguish between certain ends that are being sought and the means by which they will be achieved. Economics does not allow a "scientific" choice between alternative ends: It does not tell which of competing goals should be adopted. Economic analysis can help to determine if a particular measure contributes to stated goals and at what cost.

8. One of the main reasons particular policies will always be subject to debate and disagreement is that most policies that are effective in bringing us closer to some goals take us further away from others. This leads to policy conflicts, and it is necessary to judge how much of one objective is to be sacrificed in order to get more of another.

Concepts for review

Scarcity and the need for choice
Choice and opportunity cost
Production-possibility boundary
Resource allocation
Unemployed resources
Growth in productive capacity
Steps in evaluating economic policies
Conflicts of policies

Discussion questions

1. What does each of the following quotations tell you about the policy conflicts perceived by the person making the statement and about how he or she has resolved them?
  a. President Carter, January 1977: "We've got so many people out of work, and we've got so much unused industrial capacity, that I think if we carefully target employment opportunities around the country, we can decrease unemployment substantially before we start becoming equally concerned about inflation."
  b. Russell Baker, commenting on the decision of Nantucket Island residents to approve a Holiday Inn to cater to oil drillers: "Economics compels us all to turn things into slums. Although it will be too bad, it will be absolutely justifiable. An economic necessity. Another step down the ladder to paradise."
  c. *Time* magazine: "Considering our limited energy resources and the growing demand for electricity, the United States really has no choice but to use all of its possible domestic energy sources, including nuclear energy. Despite possible environmental and safety hazards, nuclear power is a necessity."
  d. King Khalid of Saudi Arabia: "Increasing oil production in order to lower oil prices would be the most damaging

thing that could happen to humanity. Experts say that if oil consumption continues to increase as it has, oil reserves will dry up by the end of this century."

2. When candidate Jimmy Carter was campaigning in October 1976 he said: "If I am elected I will take quick steps to make our postal service efficient and dependable again." To do so, the postal service estimates, would require an annual subsidy of $5 billion per year for five years. Are there opportunity costs to doing this? If so, what might they be? What alternatives to a subsidy might be used to achieve President Carter's objectives?

3. Consider the right to free speech in political campaigns. Suppose that the Flat Earth Society, the Socialist party, and the Republican party all demanded equal time on network TV in a presidential election. What economic questions are involved? Can there be freedom of speech without free access to the scarce resources needed to make one's speech heard?

4. The United States entered World War II with substantial unemployment of resources and gradually moved to full employment of available resources. Contrast the opportunity costs of fighting the war under these circumstances with the opportunity costs for an economy already at full employment.

5. Evidence accumulates that the use of chemical fertilizers, which increases agricultural production greatly, causes damage to water quality. Show the choice involved between more food and cleaner water in using such fertilizers. Use a production possibility curve with agricultural output on the vertical axis and water quality on the horizontal axis. In what ways does this production possibility curve reflect scarcity, choice, and opportunity cost? How would an improved fertilizer that increased agricultural output without further worsening water quality affect the curve? Suppose a pollution-free fertilizer were developed; would this mean there would no longer be any opportunity cost of using it?

6. What is the difference between scarcity and poverty? If everyone in the world had enough to eat, could we say that food was no longer scarce?

7. Does the United States government have a policy on old-age pensions? Did it have one before the Social Security Act was passed in 1935? Is there any defined issue on which the government can be said not to have a policy? Why or why not?

2

Economics as a social science

Economics is generally regarded as a social science. What exactly does it mean to be scientific? Can economics ever hope to be "scientific" in its study of those aspects of human behavior with which it is concerned? The first step in answering these questions is to be able to distinguish between positive and normative statements. The ability to make this distinction has been one of the reasons for the success of science in the last 300 years.

THE DISTINCTION BETWEEN POSITIVE AND NORMATIVE

Positive statements concern what is, was, or will be. **Normative statements** concern what ought to be.

Positive statements, assertions, or theories may be simple or complex, but they are basically about matters of fact.

Disagreements over positive statements are appropriately settled by an appeal to the facts.

Normative statements, because they concern what ought to be, are inextricably bound up with philosophical, cultural, and religious systems. A normative statement is one that makes, or is based on, a value judgment—a judgment about what is good and what is bad.

Disagreements over normative statements cannot be settled merely by an appeal to facts.

The distinction illustrated

The statement "It is impossible to break up atoms" is a positive statement that can quite definitely be (and of course has been) refuted by empirical observations, while the statement "Scientists ought not to break up atoms" is a normative statement that involves ethical judgments. The questions "What government policies will reduce unemployment?" and "What policies will prevent inflation?" are positive ones, while the question "Ought we to be more concerned about unemployment than about inflation?" is a normative one. The statement "A government deficit will reduce unemployment and cause an increase in prices" is a very simple hypothesis in positive economics, a hypothesis that can be tested by an appeal to empirical observation, while the statement "Because unemployment ought to matter more than inflation, a government deficit is sound policy" is a normative hypothesis that cannot be settled solely by an appeal to observation.

Having grasped this distinction, be careful not to turn it into an inquiry-stopping, dogmatic rule. From the fact that positive economics does not include normative questions (because its tools are inappropriate to them) it does *not* follow that the student of positive economics must stop her or his inquiry as soon as someone says the word "ought." Consider the statement "It is my value judgment that we *ought to have* rent control because controls are *good.*" It is quite in order for a practitioner of positive economics to ask "Why?" It may then be argued that controls have certain consequences and it is these consequences that are judged to be good. But the statements about the consequences of rent control will be positive testable statements. Thus the pursuit of what appears to be a normative statement will often turn up positive hypotheses on which the *ought* conclusion depends. There are, for example, probably few people who believe that government control of industry is in itself good or bad. Their advocacy or opposition will be based on certain beliefs about relations that can be stated as positive rather than normative hypotheses. For example: "Government control reduces (increases) efficiency, changes (does not change) the distribution of income, leads (does not lead) to an increase of state control in other spheres." A careful study of this emotive subject would reveal an agenda of positive economic questions that could keep a research team of economists occupied for many years.

The importance of the distinction

If we think something ought to be done, we can deduce other things that, if we wish to be consistent, ought to be done; but we can deduce nothing about what is done (i.e., is true). Similarly, if we know that two things are true, we can deduce other things that must be true, but we can deduce nothing about what is desirable (i.e., *ought* to be).

The distinction between positive and normative statement is critical because it is logically impossible to deduce normative statements from positive statements and vice versa.

First, consider an example involving both normative and positive statements. Suppose I believe (1) that it is a moral principle that one ought to be charitable to all human beings. Then if I am told (2) that the inhabitants of China are not Christians but are human beings, it follows (3) that one ought to be charitable toward Chinese. From (1) and (2) a normative rule has been deduced about how we ought to behave in a particular case. No positive statement about how we do behave can, however, be deduced from (1) and (2). Now suppose someone else comes along and says, "You ought not to be charitable toward the Chinese because moral principles dictate that you should be charitable only toward Christians." If an argument now arises about whether to be charitable toward the Chinese, this argument will turn on value judgments about how one ought to behave. These are questions on which reasonable people sometimes just have to agree to disagree. If both sides insist on holding to their views on charity, even if both are perfectly reasonable, there is no civilized way of forcing either to admit error.

Second, consider an example involving only positive statements. Assume I say (1) that capital punishment is a strong disincentive to murder and (2) that the Chinese abolished capital punishment after the Revolution, so that (3) the number of murders must have risen in China since the Revolution. The two factual statements, (1) and (2), and the deduction that follows from them are all positive statements. Nothing can be deduced about the moral desirability of abolishing capital punishment from statements (1) and (2), even if they are factually correct. Now suppose you say, "The number of murders has not risen in China since the Revolution; in fact, the number has fallen." If you hold to this view, you must deny one or the other of the first two positive statements. You could deny statement (1) by saying, for example, that capital punishment is actually an incentive to commit murder. You could deny statement (2) by saying, for example, that, although the Chinese pretended to abolish capital punishment as a propaganda move, they in fact retained it after the Revolution. In both cases the disagreement is over factual statements. If enough facts were gathered, and if both parties were reasonable, one party could be forced to admit being wrong.

The distinction between positive and normative has the value of allowing us to keep our views on how we would like the world to work separate from our views on how the world actually does work. We may be interested in both. It can only obscure the truth, however, if we let our views on what we would like to be bias our investigations of what actually is. It is for this reason that the separation of the positive from the normative is one of the foundation stones of science and that scientific inquiry, as it is normally understood, is usually confined to positive questions.

Positive and normative statements in economics

Economics, like other sciences, is concerned with questions, statements, and hypotheses that could conceivably be shown to be wrong (i.e., falsified) by actual observations of the world. It is not necessary to show them to be either consistent or inconsistent with the facts tomorrow or the next day; it is only necessary to be able to imagine evidence that could show them to be wrong. *Thus an appeal to the facts is an appropriate way in which to deal with them.* Other questions, including normative ones, cannot be settled by a mere appeal to empirical observation. This does not, of course, mean that they are unimportant. Such questions as "Should we subsidize higher education?" and "Should we send food to China?" must be decided by means other than a simple appeal to facts. In practice, such questions are usually settled by voting on them.

THE SCIENTIFIC APPROACH

Very roughly, the scientific approach, or scientific method as it is sometimes called, consists of relating questions to evidence. When presented with a controversial issue, scientists will ask what the evidence is both for and against it. They may then take a stand on the issue, with more or less conviction depending on the weight of the evidence. If there is little or no evidence, scientists will say that at present it is impossible to take a stand. They will then set about searching for relevant evidence. If they find that the issue is framed in terms that make it impossible to gather evidence for or against it, they will then usually try to recast the question so that it can be answered by an appeal to the evidence. This approach to a problem is what sets scientific inquiries off from other inquiries.

In some fields, the scientist, having reframed the question, is able to generate observations that will provide evidence for or against the hypothesis. Experimental sciences such as chemistry and some branches of psychology have an advantage because it is possible for them to produce relevant evidence through controlled laboratory experiments.

Other sciences such as astronomy and economics cannot do this. They must wait for natural events to produce observations that may be used as evidence in testing their theories.

The ease or difficulty with which one can collect evidence does not determine whether a subject is scientific or nonscientific.

How scientific inquiry proceeds and the ease with which it can be pursued do, however, differ substantially between fields in which laboratory experiment is possible and those in which it is not. Some of these differences will be discussed in Chapter 3. Until then we shall consider general problems more or less common to all sciences.

IS HUMAN BEHAVIOR PREDICTABLE?

Natural versus social sciences. Is it possible to conduct a scientific study in the field of human behavior? When considering whether it is possible to make a scientific study of such subjects as the causes of unemployment and the consequences of a large national debt, it is sometimes argued that natural sciences deal with inanimate matter that is subject to natural "laws" while the social sciences deal with man who has free will and cannot, therefore, be made the subject of natural laws.

This view implies that inanimate matter will show stable responses to certain stimuli, whereas animate matter will not. For example, if you put a match to a dry piece of paper, the paper will burn, whereas if you subject human beings to torture, some will break down and do what you want them to do and others will not. Even more confusing, the same individual may react differently to torture at different times.

Whether human behavior does or does not show sufficiently stable responses to factors influencing it as to be predictable within an acceptable margin of error is a positive question that can be settled only by an appeal to

evidence and not by *a priori* speculation. (**A priori** may be defined as the use of knowledge that is prior to actual experience.) The question itself might concern either the behavior of groups or that of isolated individuals.

Group versus individual behavior. It is a matter of simple observation that when a group of individuals is considered, they do not behave in a totally capricious way but do display stable responses to various stimuli that act on them. The warmer the weather, for example, the higher the number of people visiting the beach and the higher the sales of ice cream and Coca-Cola. It may be hard to say when or why one individual will buy an ice cream cone or a Coke, but a stable response pattern from a large group of individuals can be seen: the higher the temperature, the greater the sales of these two products at the beach.

There are many examples of situations in which group behavior can be predicted with great accuracy without being certain of individual behavior. No social scientist can predict, for example, when an apparently healthy individual is going to die, but death rates for large groups are stable enough to make life insurance a profitable business. This would not be so if group behavior were capricious. While social scientists cannot predict what particular individuals will be killed in auto accidents in the next holiday weekend, they can come very close to knowing how many will die in total. The more objectively measurable data they are given concerning, for example, the state of the weather on those days, and the increase in auto sales over the last year, the closer they will be able to predict total deaths.

The well-known fact that the pollsters can do a good job predicting elections on the basis of sample surveys provides evidence that people's behavior is predictable. If group human behavior were in fact capricious, there would be no point in trying to predict anything on the basis of sample surveys. The fact that 80 percent of the people sampled said they intended to vote for a certain candidate would give no information about the probable outcome of the election. Today's information would commonly be reversed tomorrow.

The difference between predicting individual and group behavior is illustrated by the fact that economists can predict with fair accuracy what households as a group will do when their take-home pay is increased. Some individuals may very well do surprising and, as far as we can see, unpredictable things, but the total response of all households to a permanent change in tax rates that leaves more money in their hands is predictable within quite a narrow margin of error. This stability in the response of households' spending to a change in their available income is the basis of economists' ability to predict successfully the outcome of major revisions in the tax laws.

This does not mean that people never change their minds or that future events can be foretold by a casual study of the past. People sometimes think in terms of a simple dichotomy: Either there are historical laws apparent to the casual observer or there is random behavior. They observe a prophet predicting that some change will take place in the future merely because it took place in the past and, upon seeing the prophet make an utterly mistaken prophecy, conclude that, because the prophet cannot prophesy, human behavior is random and thus unamenable to scientific study. The stability discussed here is a stable response to causal factors (e.g., next time it gets warm, ice cream sales will rise) and not merely inertia (e.g., ice cream sales will go on rising in the future because they have risen in the past).

The "law" of large numbers

Successful predictions about the behavior of large groups are made possible by the statistical "law" of large numbers. Very roughly, this law asserts that random movements of a large number of individual items tend to offset one another. This law is based on one of the most beautiful constants of behavior in the whole of science, natural and social, and yet it can be derived from the fact that human beings make errors! The law is based on the *normal curve of error,* which one encounters in elementary statistics.

What is implied by this law? Ask any one person to measure the length of a room and it will be almost impossible to predict in advance what sort of error of measurement he or she will make. Thousands of things will affect the accuracy of the measurement and, furthermore, the person may make one error today and quite a different one tomorrow. But ask a thousand people to measure the length of the same room and it can be predicted within a very small margin just how this *group* will make its errors! It can be asserted with confidence that more people will make small errors than will make large errors, that the larger the error, the fewer will be the number making it, that roughly the same number of people will overestimate as will underestimate the distance, and that the average error of all individuals will be zero.

If a common cause should act on each member of the group, it is possible to predict the average behavior of the group even though any one member may act in a surprising fashion. If, for example, each of the thousand individuals is given a tape measure that understates "actual" distances, it can be expected that, on the average, the group will now underestimate the length of the room. It is, of course, quite possible that one member, who had in the past been consistently undermeasuring distance because he was depressed psychologically, will now overestimate the distance because the state of his health has changed; but something else may happen to some other individual that will turn her from an overmeasurer into an undermeasurer. Individuals may do peculiar things for reasons that are inexplicable, but the group's behavior, when the inaccurate tape is substituted for the accurate one, will nonetheless be predictable precisely because the odd things that one individual does will tend to cancel out the odd things some other individual does.

Irregularities in individual behavior tend to cancel one another out, and the regularities tend to show up in repeated observations.

THE NATURE OF SCIENTIFIC THEORIES

There is abundant evidence of stable response patterns in human behavior. Some regularity between two or more things is observed, and someone asks why this should be so. A *theory* attempts to explain why. Once we have a theory it enables us to predict as yet unobserved events. Thus, for example, national income theory predicts that an increase in the government's budget deficit will reduce the volume of unemployment. The simple theory of market behavior predicts that, under certain specified conditions, the introduction of a sales tax will be accompanied by an increase in the price of the commodity concerned and that the price increase will be less than the amount of the tax. It also allows us to predict that if there is a partial failure of the potato crop, the total receipts earned by potato farmers will rise!

Theories are used in explaining observed phenomena. A successful theory enables us to predict in advance the consequences of various occurrences.

The pervasiveness of theories

Observations concern sequences of events. Any explanation whatsoever of how these events are linked together is a theoretical construct. Theories are what are used to impose order on observations, to explain how what is seen is linked together. Without theories there would be only a shapeless mass of meaningless observations.

The choice is not one between theory and observation but between better or worse theories to explain observations.

In a particular case one might see an increase in interest rates followed by a reduction in borrowing by corporations. The practical person may think the link is obvious, and indeed in some sense it may be, but nonetheless it requires a theoretical construction. Before these two events can be linked together, it is necessary to have a theory of what the managers are trying to do and how they try to do it, plus the assumption that the managers know what behavior will achieve their goals.

True in theory but not in practice

Misunderstanding about the place of theories in scientific explanation gives rise to many misconceptions. One of these is illustrated by the phrase "True in theory but not in practice." The next time you hear someone say this (or, indeed, the next time you say it yourself) you should immediately reply, "All right then, tell me what does happen in practice." Usually you will not be told mere facts, but you will be given an alternative theory—a different explanation of the facts. The speaker should have said, "The theory in question provides a poor explanation of the facts" (i.e., it is contradicted by some factual observations) and that the alternative theory is a better one.

WHAT IS A THEORY AND HOW IS IT TESTED?

A theory consists of (1) a set of definitions that clearly define the *variables* to be used, (2) a set of *assumptions* that outline the conditions under which the theory is to apply, (3) one or more *hypotheses* about how people behave, and (4) *predictions* that are deduced from the assumptions of the theory and can be tested against actual empirical observations.

Variables

Theories are concerned with how various things are related to each other. If we know how two things are related, then we know how one of them will change as the other changes. The things that we relate to each other are called variables. A **variable** is some magnitude that can take on different possible values. Variables are the basic elements of theories, and each one needs to be carefully defined.

Price is an example of an important economic variable. The price of a commodity is the amount of money that must be given up to purchase one unit of that commodity. To define a price we must first define the commodity to which it attaches. Such a commodity might be one dozen grade A large eggs. We could then enquire into the price of such eggs sold in, say, supermarkets in Fargo, North Dakota. This would define the variable. The particular values taken on by the variable might be 98¢ on July 1, 1977, $1.02 on July 8, 1977, and 99¢ on July 15, 1977. A series of observations on the values of a variable at different points in time, such as that just illustrated, is called a **time series.**

There are many distinctions between kinds of variables; two of the most important are discussed in the accompanying box.

Assumptions

Assumptions play a vital role in theorizing, and students are often greatly concerned about the justification of assumptions, particularly if they seem unrealistic. Suppose an economic theory starts out: "Assume that there is no government." Surely, says the reader, this assumption is totally unrealistic, and I cannot take seriously anything that comes out of the theory. But this assumption may merely be the economist's way of saying that, whatever the government does, even whether it exists, *is irrelevant for the purposes of this particular theory*. Now, put this way, the statement becomes an empirical assertion, and the only way to test it is to see if the predictions that follow from the theory do or do not fit the facts that the theory is trying to explain. If they do, then the theorist was correct in the assumption that the government could

be ignored for the particular purposes at hand. In this case the criticism that the theory is unrealistic because there really is a government is completely beside the point.

Another important use of an apparently unrealistic assumption may be to outline the set of conditions under which a theory is meant to hold. Consider a theory that assumes the government has a balanced budget. This may mean that the theorist intends that theory to apply only when there is a balanced budget; it may *not* mean that the size of the government's budget surplus or deficit is irrelevant to the theory.[1]

Usually it is not appropriate to criticize the simplifying assumptions of a theory only on the grounds that they are unrealistic. It is important to remember that all theory is an abstraction from reality. If it were not, it would merely duplicate the world and would add nothing to the understanding of it. A good theory abstracts in a useful and significant way; a poor theory does not. If one believes that the theorist has assumed away something important for the problem at hand, then one must believe, and try to show, that the conclusions of the theory are contradicted by the facts.

Hypotheses

Relations among variables. The critical step in formulating a theory is in making hypotheses. A hypothesis is a statement about how two or more variables are related to each other. It is, for example, a basic hypothesis of economics that the quantity produced of any commodity depends, among other things, on its price. Thus the two variables, the price of eggs and the quantity of eggs produced, are

---

[1] As the text illustrates, an assumption may mean many different things. When you encounter an assumption in economic theory, ask yourself whether it is being used to convey the idea that (1) the world actually behaves as assumed, (2) the factor under consideration is irrelevant to the theory, (3) the theory only holds when the condition specified in the assumption actually holds, or (4) a convenient fiction is being introduced to formalize some quite complex piece of behavior.

Kinds of variables

Endogenous and exogenous variables.
Endogenous variables are those that are explained within a theory. **Exogenous variables** are those that influence the endogenous variables but are themselves determined by considerations outside of the theory. Consider the theory that the price of apples in Seattle on a particular day is a function of several things, one of which was the weather in Wenatchee, Washington, during the previous apple-growing season. We can safely assume that the state of the weather is not determined by economic conditions. The price of apples in this case is an endogenous variable—something determined within the framework of the theory. The state of the weather in Wenatchee is an exogenous variable; changes in it influence apple prices because they affect the supply of apples, but the weather is uninfluenced by these prices.

Stock and flow variables.
A distinction between variables that is important in economics is that between stocks and flows. A flow variable has a time dimension; it is so much per unit of time. The quantity of grade A large eggs purchased in Cleveland is a flow variable. No useful information is conveyed if one is told that purchases were 2,000 dozen eggs unless we are told over what period of time these purchases occurred. Two thousand dozen per hour would indicate an active market in eggs, while 2,000 dozen per week would indicate a very sluggish market. A stock variable has no time dimension; it is just so much. Thus, if the egg producers' cooperative has 2 million dozen eggs in warehouses around the country, this quantity is a stock. All those eggs are there at one time. The stock variable is just a number, not a rate of flow of so much *per day* or *per month*.

Economic theories use both stock variables and flow variables, and it takes a little practice to keep them straight. The amount of income earned is a flow; there is so much per year or per month or per hour. The amount of a household's expenditure is also a flow—so much spent per week or per month. The amount of money in a bank account or a miser's hoard (earned, perhaps, in the past, but unspent) is a stock—just so many thousands of dollars. What of the interest earned by the miser who puts money into a savings bank? It is a flow. The key test is always whether a time dimension is required to give the variable significant meaning.

related to each other according to an economic hypothesis.

Functional relations. A **function,** or a functional relation, is a formal expression of a relation among variables.

The particular hypothesis that the quantity of eggs produced is related to the price of eggs is an example of a functional relation in economics. In its most general form, it merely says that quantity produced is related to price. More specifically, however, the hypothesis may be that as the price of eggs falls, the quantity produced will also fall. In other words, in this hypothesis price and quantity vary *directly* with each other. In the case of many hypotheses of this kind economists can be even more specific than this about the nature of the functional relation. On the basis of detailed factual studies, economists often have a pretty good idea of by *how much* quantity produced will change as a result of specified changes in price—i.e., about magnitude as well as about direction.[2]

Predictions
What is the nature of a scientific prediction? Is it the same thing as being able to prophesy the future?

A scientific prediction is a conditional statement that takes the form: *If* you do this, *then* such and such will follow.

If you mix hydrogen and oxygen under specified conditions, *then* water will be the result. *If* the government has a large budget deficit, *then* the volume of employment will be increased. It is most important to notice that this prediction is very different from the statement: "I prophesy that in two years' time there will be a large increase in employment because I believe the government will decide to have a large budget deficit." The government's decision to have a budget deficit or surplus in two years' time will be the outcome of many complex factors, emotions, objective circumstances, chance occurrences, and so on, few of which can be predicted by the economist. If the economist's prophecy about the level of employment turns out to be wrong because in two years' time the government does not have a large deficit, then all that has been learned is that the economist is not a good guesser about the behavior of the government. However, *if* the government does have a large deficit (in two years' time or at any other time) and *then* the volume of em-

[2] The appendix to this chapter (See page 854) gives for the interested reader a more detailed discussion of functional relations.

ployment does not rise, a conditional scientific prediction in the field of economic theory has been contradicted.

Testing theories
A theory is tested by confronting its predictions with evidence. It is necessary to discover if certain events are followed by the consequences predicted by the theory. For example, is an increase in the government's budget deficit followed by a reduction in unemployment? Testing is never easily accomplished (some of the problems involved are discussed in Chapter 3). As a generalization, it can be said that theories tend to be abandoned when they are no longer useful and that they cease to be useful when they cannot predict the consequences of actions in which one is interested better than the next best alternative. In an advanced science, the alternative will be another competing theory. If there is no competing theory there is the alternative of comparing the theory with predictions based on such naive views as "This year will be just like last year," "Any change observed in the past will go on in the future," and so on. When a theory fails consistently to predict better than the available alternatives, it is either modified or replaced by a superior alternative.

ECONOMICS AS A DEVELOPING SCIENCE
Economics is similar to other sciences in at least two respects. First, there are many observations of the world for which there are, at the moment, no fully satisfactory theoretical explanations. Second, there are many predictions that no one has yet satisfactorily tested. Serious students of economics must not expect to find a set of answers to all possible questions as they progress in their study. Very often they must expect to encounter nothing more than a set of problems that provides an agenda for further research. Even when they do find answers to problems, they

The interaction of deduction and measurement

The schematic diagram shows how deduction and measurement continuously interact. In any science, the sequence of theory and testing is continuous: Theories yield predictions that are tested; the tests yield new knowledge that allows theories to be changed and improved; the new theories yield new predictions—and the process goes on endlessly. The question of which came first, theory or observation, is like the debate over the chicken and the egg.

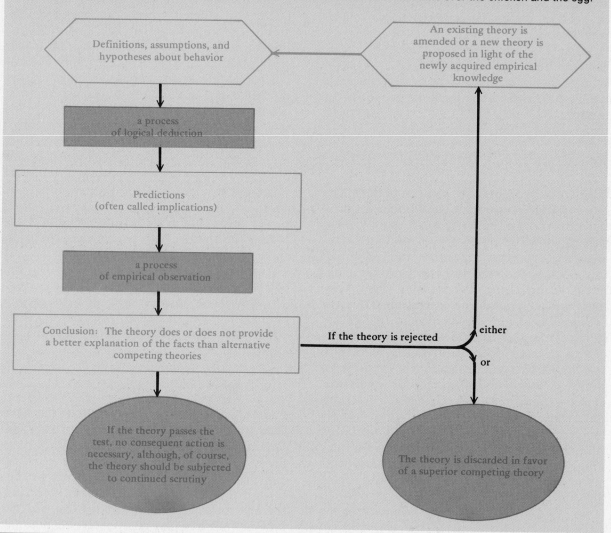

should accept these answers as tentative and ask even of the most time-honored theory, "What observations would be in conflict with this theory?"

Economics is still a very young science. On the one hand, economists do know a good deal about the behavior of the economy. On the other hand, many problems are almost untouched. Students who decide to specialize in economics may well find themselves only a few years from now, publishing a theory to account for some of the problems mentioned in this book; or they may find themselves making a set of observations that will refute some venerable theory described within these pages.

One final word of warning: Having counseled a constructive disrespect for the authority of accepted theory, it is necessary to warn against adopting an approach that is too cavalier. No respect attaches to the person who merely says, "This theory is for the birds, it is *obviously* wrong." This is too cheap. To criticize a theory effectively on empirical grounds, one must demonstrate, by a carefully made set of observations, that some aspect of the theory is contradicted by the facts. This is a task that is seldom easily accomplished.

Summary

1. It is possible, and fruitful, to distinguish between positive and normative statements. Positive statements concern what is, was, or will be, whereas normative statements concern what ought to be. Disagreements over positive statements are appropriately settled by an appeal to the facts. Disagreements over normative statements can never be settled by a mere appeal to factual evidence.

2. The success of scientific inquiry depends on separating positive questions about the way the world works from normative questions about how one would like the world to work. The scientific approach consists in formulating positive questions precisely enough so that they can be settled by an appeal to evidence and then finding means of gathering or producing the necessary evidence.

3. Some people feel that although natural phenomena can be subject to scientific inquiry and "laws" of behavior, human phenomena cannot. The evidence, however, is otherwise. Social scientists have observed many regular and stable human behavior patterns, and these form the basis for successful predictions of how people will behave under certain conditions.

4. The fact that some people sometimes act curiously, even capriciously, does not destroy the possibility of a scientific study of group behavior. Indeed, the odd and inexplicable things that one person does will tend to cancel out the odd and inexplicable things that another person does. Observation of group behavior often discloses fairly stable and predictable responses to things that exert a significant influence on the members of the group.

5. Observations reveal only sequences of events. Theories are designed to give meaning and coherence to these events. Theories thus pervade all attempts to explain events. A theory consists of a set of definitions of the variables to be employed, a set of assumptions giving the conditions under which the theory is meant to apply, and a set of hypotheses about how things behave. Any theory has certain logical implications that must be true if the theory is true.

6. A theory provides predictions of the type "*if* one event occurs, *then* another event will also occur." An important method of testing theories is to confront their predictions with evidence. When theories fail to predict better than the available alternatives, theories tend to be rejected. The progress of any science lies in finding better explanations of events than are now available. Thus, in any developing science, one must expect to discard present theories and replace them with demonstrably superior alternatives. Such a process improves the quality of the explanations.

7. The important concept of a functional relation is discussed in more detail in the appendix to this chapter, which begins on page 854.

Concepts for review

Positive and normative statements
The law of large numbers and the predictability of human
  behavior
The roles of variables, assumptions, and predictions in
  theorizing
Endogenous and exogenous variables
Stock and flow variables
Functional relations
Prediction versus prophecy
The scientific approach

Discussion questions

1. A baby doesn't "know" of the theory of gravity, yet in walking and eating he or she soon learns to use its principles. Distinguish between behavior and prediction of behavior. Does a business executive or a farmer have to understand economic theory to behave in a pattern consistent with economic theory?

2. "If human behavior were completely capricious and unpredictable, life insurance could not be a profitable business." Explain. Can you think of any businesses that do *not* depend on predictable human behavior?

3. Write five statements about inflation. (It does not matter whether the statements are correct, but you should confine yourself to those you think might be correct.) Classify each statement as positive or normative. If your list contains only one type of statement, try to add a sixth statement of the other type. Check the validity of your positive statements as well as you can against the data given in this text (see *Inflation* in the index). If this does not satisfy you about their validity, outline how you would go about completing the test of your statements.

4. Each of the following unrealistic assumptions is sometimes made. See if you can visualize situations in which each of them might be useful.
a. The earth is a plane.
b. There are no differences between men and women.
c. There is no tomorrow.
d. A bond will pay $100 interest a year forever.

5. "The following theory of wage determination proceeds on the assumption that labor unions do not exist." Of what use can such a theory be in the United States today?

6. Emotional statements can often be reworded so as to be tested by an appeal to evidence. How might you do that with respect to each of the following assertions?
a. The American economic system is the best in the world.
b. The provision of free medical care for the aged will inevitably end in socialized medicine for all, and socialized medicine will destroy our standards of medical practice by destroying the doctor's incentive to do his job well.
c. The natural gas shortage is a device by the gas producers to conceal their exploitations of the ordinary citizen by restricting output to gain profits.
d. Inflation is ruining the standard of living of the American worker and destroying the integrity of the family.

3

The role of statistical analysis

It is one thing for economists to theorize that two variables are somehow related to each other; it is quite another thing for them to be able to say *how* these things are related to each other. Economists might readily generalize on the basis of casual observation that when households receive more income they are likely to buy more of most commodities. But precisely how much will the consumption of a particular commodity rise as household incomes rise? Are there exceptions to the rule that the purchase of a commodity rises as income rises? For estimating precise magnitudes and for testing general rules or hypotheses, common sense, intuition, and casual observation do not often take us very far; more systematic statistical analysis is required.

Statistical analysis is required to test the hypothesis that two things are related and to estimate the numerical values of the function describing such a relation, if it exists.

In practice, of course, the same data can be used simultaneously to test whether a relationship exists and to provide a measure of it.

TECHNIQUES FOR TESTING THEORIES

The process of testing is complex. As a first step in seeing how to go about testing theories in economics, a distinction between laboratory and nonlaboratory methods must be made.

Laboratory sciences

In some sciences it is possible to obtain all observations required for testing theories from controlled experiments made under laboratory conditions. In these experiments, all the factors that are thought to affect the outcome of the process being studied are held constant. These factors are then varied one by one and the influence of each such variation is observed.

Suppose we have a theory that predicts that

the rate at which a substance burns is a function of (1) the rate at which oxygen is made available during the process of combustion and (2) the chemical properties of the substance. To test this theory we may take a number of identical pieces of some substance and burn them, varying the amount of oxygen made available in each case. This allows us to see how combustion varies with the quantity of oxygen supplied. We can then take a number of substances with different chemical compositions and burn them, making available identical amounts of oxygen in each case. This allows us to see how combustion varies with chemical composition.

In such an experiment we never have to use data that are generated when both chemical composition and the quantity of oxygen are varying simultaneously. Laboratory conditions are used to hold other things constant and to produce data for situations in which factors can be varied one at a time.

Nonlaboratory sciences

In many sciences factors cannot be isolated one at a time in laboratory experiments. In these sciences observations are still used to establish relationships and to test theories, but such observations appear in a relatively complex form because several things are happening at the same time.

Consider the hypothesis that one's health as an adult depends upon one's diet as a child. Clearly, all sorts of other factors affect the health of adults: heredity, conditions of childhood other than nutrition, and various aspects of adult environment. There is no acceptable way to examine this hypothesis in the manner of a controlled experiment, for it is unlikely that a group of adults could be found whose diet as children varied but for whom *all* other influences affecting health were the same. Are we to conclude that the hypothesis cannot be tested because other factors cannot be held constant? No, because to do so would be to deny many advances in medicine, biology,

and other sciences concerned with human beings—and, therefore, with fluctuating, unconstant factors—made during the last hundred years. Testing is more difficult where laboratory methods cannot be used, but, fortunately, it is still possible.

In a situation in which many things are varying at once, data must be used carefully. If only two people are being studied and it is found that the one with the better nutritional standards during youth has the poorer adult health record, this would not disprove the hypothesis that a good diet contributes to better health. It might well be that some other factor has exerted an overwhelming influence on these two individuals. The less healthy person may have lived most of his or her adult life in a disease-ridden area of the tropics, whereas the more healthy individual may have lived in a relatively pleasant part of temperate North America. Clearly, a single exception does not disprove the hypothesis of a relation between two things as long as we admit that other factors can also influence the outcome. But if a large number of people are studied with respect to childhood diet and adult health record, individual irregularities may be expected to cancel out and an underlying regularity to show up.

Contrast this strategy of basing decisions on a large number of observations with the practice in much ordinary conversation of acting as if a single contrary case disproved a theory. Notice how often a person advances a possible relation (e.g., between an education in law and some facet of character) and how someone else will "refute" this theory by citing a single counter-example (e.g., "Ralph Nader went to law school and did not turn out like that").

THE STATISTICAL TESTING OF ECONOMIC THEORIES: AN EXAMPLE

Economics is a nonlaboratory science. It is rarely possible to conduct controlled experiments with the economy. Millions of *uncontrolled experiments* are, however, going on every day. Householders are deciding what to purchase in the face of changing prices and incomes; firms are deciding what to produce and how to produce it; and governmental bodies are intervening in the economy with taxes, subsidies, and controls. All of these acts can be observed and recorded. Thus a mass of data is produced continually by the economy. Most things in which economists are interested, such as the volume of unemployment, the level of prices, and the distribution of income, are influenced by a large number of factors, all of which vary simultaneously. If economists are to test their theories about relations in the economy, they will have to use those statistical techniques that were designed for situations in which other things could not be held constant.

Consider the hypothesis that the quantity of beef purchased by low- and middle-income American households is an increasing function of their income. To begin with, observations should be made of household income and purchases of beef. It is impossible to enumerate the relevant households so a smaller number of observations (called a sample) must be taken in the hope that they are typical of the entire group.

The sample

We start by observing three households. The data are recorded in Table 3–1. These data may lead us to wonder if the hypothesis is wrong, but before we jump to that conclusion we note that "by chance" the three households selected may not be typical of all the households in the country. Expenditure on food, for example, is influenced by factors other than income, and possibly these other factors just happen to be the dominant forces in the three cases.

To check on this possibility, a large number of households should be selected in order to reduce the chances of consistently picking un-

Table 3–1 Three observations on beef purchases and income

Household	Household income	Beef purchases, pounds per week
1	$4,500	5.10
2	5,500	5.05
3	6,500	4.93

These three observations suggest that beef purchases go down as income rises, but a sample of three is too small to be persuasive.

typical households. Suppose this is done by selecting 100 households from among friends and acquaintances. A statistician points out, however, that the new group is a *biased sample,* for it contains households from only a limited geographical area, probably with only a limited occupational range, and possibly with incomes very similar to one another. (Since the way in which purchases of beef vary as income varies is of special interest, this last point is likely to be a very serious one.) As a result of these limitations, it is unlikely that this sample of households will be representative of all low- and middle-income households in the United States, which is the group in which we are interested.

The statistician suggests that a random sample of households be taken. A **random sample** is chosen according to a rigidly defined set of conditions that guarantees, among other things, that every household in which we are interested has an equal chance of being selected. Choosing the sample in a random fashion has two important consequences. First, it makes it unlikely that the sample will be very unrepresentative of all households; second (and more important), it allows us to calculate just how likely it is that the sample is unrepresentative in any given aspect by any stated amount. This second result is important because it allows us to make statements about the probability that the behavior of all households in the United States will differ by any quantitative amount from that of households in the sample. The reason this can be done is that the sample was chosen by chance and chance events are predictable.

That chance events are predictable may sound paradoxical at first. But if you pick a card from a deck of ordinary playing cards, how likely is it that you will pick a heart? an ace? an ace of hearts? You play a game in which you pick a card and win if it is a heart and lose if it is anything else; a friend offers you $5 if you win against $1 if you lose. Who will make money if the game is played a large number of times? The same game is played again, but now you get $3 if you win and pay $1 if you lose. Who will make money over a large number of draws? If you know the answers to these questions (and we will bet that most of you do), you must believe that chance events are predictable.

Table 3–2 Income class and average beef purchases

Annual household income	Average weekly beef purchases in pounds	Number of households
$0–999	2.13	532
1,000–1,999	2.82	647
2,000–2,999	3.70	692
3,000–3,999	4.25	867
4,000–4,999	4.86	865
5,000–5,999	5.16	513
6,000–6,999	5.20	371
7,000–7,999	5.30	159
8,000–8,999	5.52	121
9,000–9,999	5.90	60

Average beef purchases rise steadily as income rises. This sample of 4,827 U.S. households has been cross-classified according to income and average beef purchases. Thus, in the first row, the 532 households with incomes below $1,000 per year are grouped together and their average beef purchases calculated. In the second row, all households with incomes between $1,000 and $1,999 have been grouped together. This method reduces a mass of 4,827 pairs of observations to a mere 10.

In the present case suppose that a random sample of 4,827 households has been chosen. (How representative the sample is of all relevant households can be checked by comparing some characteristic of the households in it with a result that is known to hold for all American households.) Once the sample is chosen and checked for representativeness, the information required from it is collected. In this case, the information desired is the income of each household and its purchases of beef.

Analysis of the data

There are several ways in which the data may be used to evaluate the hypothesis. One of these is the use of a **scatter diagram.**[1] Figure 3–1 is a scatter diagram relating household income to purchases of beef. The pattern of the dots suggests that there is a strong tendency for purchases of beef to be higher, the higher is household income. It thus supports the hypothesis. There is *some* scattering of the dots because the relationship is "not perfect"; in other words, there is considerable variation in food purchases that cannot be associated with variations in household income. These "unexplained variations" in beef purchases occur for two main reasons: first, factors other than income influence beef purchases, and some of these other factors will undoubtedly have varied between the households in the sample; second, there will inevitably be some errors in measurement (e.g., a household might have incorrectly reported its beef purchases).

Another way to examine the hypothesis that beef purchases vary directly with income is to use a cross-classification table. Table 3–2 cross-classifies households by their income and their average beef purchases. At the loss of some considerable amount of detail, the

[1] The appendix to this chapter, which begins on page 857, outlines the elements of graphs and the graphical analysis of economic data and of functional relations between economic variables. Anyone who finds graphical analysis baffling should read this appendix now.

table makes clearer the general tendency for beef purchases to rise as income rises.

While both the scatter diagram and the cross-classification table reflect the general relationship between beef purchases and household income, neither concisely characterizes the specific relationship. **Regression analysis** is a widely used technique that provides quantitative measures of what the relationship is and how closely it holds. Regression analysis may be used if certain conditions are fulfilled.[2] A **regression equation** represents the best estimate of the *average* relationship between household income and beef purchases. Such an equation for our example will describe the tendency for higher household income to be associated with higher consumption of beef. (The equation of a straight line fitted to the data shown in Figure 3–1 is $B = 2.35 + 0.47Y$, where B is purchases of beef in pounds and Y is income in thousands of dollars per year. The equation shows that for every increase of \$1,000 in household income, beef consumption tends to increase by about one-half pound per week.)

A measure of how closely the relationship holds can be obtained by calculating the percentage of the variance[3] in household expenditure on beef that can be accounted for by variations in household income. This measure is called the **coefficient of determination** (r^2). It indicates, specifically in this case, the proportion of the variance in beef purchases that can be "explained" by associating it with variations in household incomes.

Third, a "significance test" can be applied to determine the chances that the relation discovered in the sample does not exist for the whole population and has arisen by chance because the households selected happen not to be representative of all households in the United States. It turns out (in this example)

[2] The detailed discussion of the techniques and conditions that must be met are left to courses in statistics and econometrics.

[3] *Variance* is a precise statistical measure of the amount of variability (dispersion) in a set of data.

Figure 3–1 A scatter diagram relating beef purchases to income

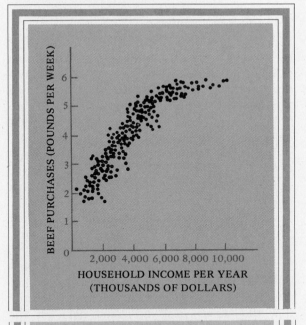

The scatter shows a clear tendency for beef consumption to rise with income. Household income is measured along the horizontal axis and purchases of beef along the vertical axis. Each dot shows the beef purchases and income of one household. The fact that the dots fall within a narrow, rising band suggests the existence of a systematic relationship. (There are 4,827 observations in the original sample, but only a random sample of these is shown in the figure because a scatter diagram with that number of points would be unintelligible.)

that if there were no increasing relation between income and beef purchases for U.S. households, there is less than one chance in 1 million that the rising pattern of dots shown in Figure 3–1 would have been observed. Since this chance is very small we prefer to believe the hypothesis that these two variables —beef purchases and household income—are in fact positively related in the United States.

Statistically the relationship is said to be "significant."

Extending the analysis

It is clear from the scatter diagram that *all* of the variation in households' purchases of beef cannot be accounted for by observed variations in household income. If it could, all the dots would lie on a line—which they do not. Some other factors clearly influence food expenditure. What could make one household with an income of $6,000 buy 20 percent more beef than another household with the same income? One possible factor is that households in different parts of the country may have been faced with very different prices of beef. Of course, there will be many other factors, such as size of family and religion, but price can be selected for the purpose of illustrating how to handle simultaneously more than one explanation. Assume that the survey also collected data on the prices of various cuts of beef in each city or town from which a household in the sample bought its meat. These data were then used to calculate the average price of beef facing each household.

There are now *three* observations for each one of the 4,827 households—their annual income, their weekly purchases of beef, and the average price of beef facing them. How should these data be handled? Unfortunately, the scatter-diagram technique is not available because the relation between three things cannot easily be shown on a two-dimensional graph. However, the data can be grouped in a fashion similar to the way they were grouped in Table 3–2. This time there are two variables that are thought to influence beef consumption, and the data have to be cross-classified in a more complicated manner, as shown in Table 3–3. (To prevent the table from becoming too large, households have been grouped into income groups of $2,000. This is only a matter of convenience; the classification can be made as detailed as required for the particular purpose at hand.)

This device of cross-classification as shown in Table 3–3 demonstrates clearly the sense in which we hold one variable constant while al-

Table 3–3 Average weekly beef purchases (in pounds) cross-classified by income and price

Household income	Average price of beef per pound			
	$.80–.99	$1.00–1.19	$1.20–1.39	$1.40–1.59
$0–1,999	2.65	2.59	2.51	2.43
2,000–3,999	4.14	4.05	3.94	3.88
4,000–5,999	5.11	5.00	4.97	4.84
6,000–7,999	5.35	5.29	5.19	5.07
8,000–9,999	5.79	5.77	5.60	5.53

Beef purchases vary directly with income and inversely with price. Each row in the table shows the effect of price on the purchases of beef for a given level of income. For example, reading across the second row, households with incomes between $2,000 and $3,999 bought an average of 4.14 pounds of beef when the price was between $.80 and $.99, 4.05 pounds when the price was between $1 and $1.19, and so on. The declining numbers across each row suggest that beef purchases decline as prices rise, for particular income groups. Each column of the table shows the effect of income on purchases of beef for a given price of beef.

lowing another to vary. Reading across any row, income is held constant within a specified range and price is being varied; reading down any column, price is held constant within a specified range and income is being varied.

To estimate a numerical relation between household income, average price, and beef purchases, the technique of multiple-regression analysis may be used.[4] It allows estimation of both the separate and joint effects on beef purchases of variations in the price of beef and variations in household income by fitting to the data an equation that "best" describes them. It also permits measurement of the proportion of the total variation in beef purchases that can be explained by associating it with variations both in income and in price. Finally, it permits use of significance tests to determine how likely it is that the relations found in the sample are the result of chance rather than an underlying relationship for all U.S. households. Chance enters because, by bad luck, an unrepresentative sample of households might have been chosen.

EVALUATING THE EVIDENCE

Statistical techniques can help to measure the nature and strength of economic relationships and show how probable it is that a certain result has occurred merely by chance. What they cannot do is prove that a hypothesis is either true or false. Nor can they tell us when the hypothesis should be accepted or rejected.

Can a hypothesis be proven true or false?

Most hypotheses in economics are what may be called universal hypotheses. They say that whenever certain specified conditions are fulfilled, cause X will always produce effect Y. Such universal hypotheses cannot be proven

[4] Where three or more variables are involved "multiple" rather than "simple" regression is used. The symbol R^2 (instead of r^2) is used for the coefficient of determination in a multiple-regression analysis.

to be correct because only a finite number of actual observations can be made and the possibility can never be ruled out that future observations will lead us eventually to discard the hypothesis.

By the same token, statistical measures cannot categorically disprove a hypothesis. Even if observations consistently conflict with the hypothesis, there is always the possibility that a very untypical set of observations has been used or that serious and systematic errors of measurement have been made. Even if the hypothesis is of the kind (rarely encountered in economics) that admits of no exceptions, it could not be regarded as absolutely refuted unless it was certain that the conflicting observations were not due to errors of measurement. We can never be certain of this. If, for example, the hypothesis is that all crows are black, surely the observation of one gray crow would refute it. But was that odd bird really a crow? Perhaps what looked like a gray crow was really a dusty black crow. Even if we satisfy ourselves fully that we saw a gray crow, future generations may not accept the evidence unless they go on observing the occasional gray crow. After all, the mass of well-documented evidence accumulated several centuries ago on the existence and power of witches is no longer accepted, even though it fully satisfied most contemporary observers. The existence of observational errors—even on a vast scale—has been shown to be possible, although (one fervently hopes) it is not very frequent.

Although categorical refutation is impossible, a large set of conflicting observations may make one dubious about the validity of a hypothesis—dubious enough to be prepared to discard it for all practical purposes.

The decision to reject or accept

Decision errors. We have seen that in general a hypothesis can never be proven or refuted conclusively, no matter how many observations are made. Nonetheless, since decisions have to be made, it is necessary to accept some hypotheses (acting as if they were proven) and reject some hypotheses (acting as if they were refuted). Just as a jury can make two kinds of errors (finding an innocent person guilty or letting a guilty one go free) so can statistical decision makers make two kinds of errors. They can reject hypotheses that are true, and they can accept hypotheses that are false. Luckily, like a jury, they can also make correct decisions—and indeed they expect to do so most of the time.

Because there can never be definitive proof or disproof, the decision to accept or to reject a hypothesis is always subject to error.

Decision rules. Although the possibility of error cannot be eliminated in statistics, it can be controlled. The method of control is to decide in advance how large a risk one is willing to take of rejecting a hypothesis if it is in fact correct.[5] Conventionally, in statistics this risk is often set at 5 percent or 1 percent. If the 5 percent cut-off point is used, we say that we will reject the hypothesis if there exists less than one chance in twenty that the same set of observations could have been made if the hypothesis were correct. Using the 1 percent decision rule gives the hypothesis a greater measure of reasonable doubt. A hypothesis is rejected only if the results that appear to contradict it could have happened by chance no more than one time in 100.

When action must be taken, some such rule of thumb is necessary. But it is important to understand, first, that no one can ever be *certain* about being right in rejecting a statistical hypothesis and, second, that there is nothing magical about arbitrary cut-off points. The

cut-off point is a device used whenever some decisions have to be made.

Finally, it should be remembered that the rejection of a hypothesis is seldom the end of inquiry. Decisions can be reversed should new evidence come to light. Often the result of a statistical test of a theory is to suggest a new hypothesis that "fits the facts" better than the previous one. Indeed, in some cases just looking at scatter diagrams (or making a regression analysis) uncovers apparent relations that no one anticipated and leads the economist to formulate a new hypothesis.

Summary

1. Theories are tested by checking their predictions against actual evidence. In some sciences, these tests can be conducted under laboratory conditions where only one thing changes at a time. In other sciences, testing must be done using the data produced by the world of ordinary events, where many factors are changing all at once. Modern statistical analysis is designed to test hypotheses where many variables are changing at once.

2. Sample data are often used in testing economic hypotheses. If the sample is a random one, the probability of the measured characteristics of the sample being misleading (because of the unlucky choice of a nonrepresentative sample) can be calculated.

3. Scatter diagrams are relatively simple devices for exploring the presence of systematic relationships between two variables. Regression analysis permits more specific measures of the relationship: what it is, how closely it holds, and whether or not it is "significant."

4. Hypotheses involving several variables require more sophisticated statistical techniques such as use of complex cross-classification tables and multiple-regression analysis, each of which attempts to identify the separate and joint effects of several variables on one another. These are extensions of the simpler techniques illustrated in the text.

5. While statistical tests allow us to assess the probability that what we observe is consistent with a particular hypothesis, they never allow determination of the truth or

[5] Return to the jury analogy: Our notion of a person being innocent unless the jury is persuaded of guilt "beyond a reasonable doubt" rests on our wishing to take only a small risk of rejecting the hypothesis of innocence if the person being tried is in fact innocent.

falsity of a hypothesis beyond any possible doubt. Because it is often necessary to act as if certain hypotheses are true and others false, decision rules may be required. Two frequently used cut-off points are 5 percent and 1 percent. Using a 5 percent decision rule, for example, a hypothesis is rejected only if observed results that appear to contradict the theory could have happened by chance no more than once in 20 times. Using a 1 percent rule, the hypothesis is given an even greater benefit of the doubt.

6. Methods of graphing economic observations and functional relations are further discussed in the appendix to this chapter, which begins on page 857.

Concepts for review

The twofold role of statistical analysis: measurement and testing
Cross-classification tables
Statistical techniques for nonlaboratory sciences
The difference between proving a hypothesis true and accepting the hypothesis
The difference between disproving a hypothesis and rejecting it

Discussion questions

1. According to a Senior Vice-President of Mellon Bank: "When it comes to forecasting the economy, the stock market has as good a record—if not better—than most economists." Can this hypothesis be tested? If so, how? If not, why not?

2. In 1974 the cost of automobile insurance rose sharply. The American Automobile Association said its increase was due not (as some charged) to the passage by many states of no-fault insurance laws in 1972 and 1973 but to the inflation in the cost of parts used in repairing cars. How might the AAA's hypothesis be tested?

3. "The simplest way to see that capital punishment is a strong deterrent to murder is to ask yourself whether you might be more inclined to commit murder if you knew in advance that you ran no risk of ending in the electric chair, the gas chamber, or on the gallows." Comment on the methodology of social investigation implied in this statement. What alternative approach would you suggest?

4. Can you think of examples of a single contradictory observation that would lead you to be sure that a theory was false? If your answer is yes, would you be willing to reject the theory on the basis of a report that someone else had made the same contradictory observation?

5. There are hundreds of eyewitnesses to the existence of flying saucers and other UFOs. There are films and eyewitness accounts of Nessie, the Loch Ness monster. Are you persuaded of their existence? If not, what would it take to persuade you? If so, what would it take to make you change your mind?

6. What is the role of the law of large numbers in making economic statements testable? Does not the fact that it depends on errors mean that any science that relies on it will be inviting errors?

7. A classic example of biased sampling was the attempt made by the Literary Digest in 1936 to predict the result of the presidential election. The magazine forecast a substantial Republican victory, and its subsequent demise has been attributed to this error. (Franklin D. Roosevelt won every state but Maine and Vermont from Republican Alfred Landon, and the political platitude "As Maine goes, so goes the nation" was reworded to "As Maine goes, so goes Vermont.") The Literary Digest poll was based on a random sample of names in telephone directories. Can you spot a potential flaw in this sample? Remember that this happened in 1936. Would the same bias have existed if the survey had been made in 1976? By 1948 the selection of the sample was much more sophisticated, but the Roper polls predicted Dewey over Truman by such a substantial margin that polling was discontinued after September 30. Truman, of course, won the election. What was the nature of the sampling error this time?

8. "A distinction between laboratory and nonlaboratory sciences is appropriate; a distinction between them as being exact or inexact in archaic." Do you agree?

4

An overview of the economy

The nature of the market economy

The economic problem as we know it today is a mere 10,000 or so years old, little more than an instant compared to the millions of years people have been on earth. It arose when the first agricultural revolution—dated somewhere this side of 10,000 B.C.—turned human beings from nomadic food gatherers into settled food producers who tended crops that they had planted and animals that they or their forebears had domesticated.

Surplus and specialization

Along with permanent settlement, the agricultural revolution brought surplus production: farmers could produce substantially more than they required to satisfy their own needs for survival. The agricultural surplus permitted the growth of many new specialized occupations, such as those followed by soldiers, priests, government officials, and skilled artisans. These people produced other goods and services while consuming the surplus food produced by farmers. Economists call this allocation of different jobs to different people **specialization of labor.** Specialization has proven extraordinarily efficient compared to a system in which everybody is self-sufficient, producing everything that they consume. The efficiency of specialization has at least two distinct sources. First, individual talents and abilities differ and specialization allows each person to do the thing she or he can do relatively best, while leaving everything else to be done by others. Not only do people do their own thing; they do their own best thing. Second, a person who concentrates on one job has a better chance of becoming efficient at it than does a jack-of-all-trades.

Specialization must be accompanied by trade. People who produce only one thing must trade most of it in return for all of the other things they require.

Voluntary agreements between those who wished to exchange goods with each other were possibly the most common way in which this exchange of produce took place in early societies. Naturally, trading became centered in particular gathering places. These places were called markets, and even today we use the term market economy to refer to economies in which people specialize in productive activities and meet most of their material wants through exchanges voluntarily agreed upon by the contracting parties.

Money

The earliest free-market economies depended on **barter,** which means that goods were traded directly for other goods. But barter can be very costly in terms of time spent searching out satisfactory exchanges. Thus money evolved to facilitate exchanges. The institution of money, eliminates the cumbrousness of barter by placing money between the two sides of each barter transaction. If a farmer has wheat and wants a hammer, he does not have to search for an individual who has a hammer and wants wheat; he merely has to find any individual who wants wheat. The farmer takes money in exchange for wheat and then finds another individual who wishes to trade a hammer—and gives up the money for the hammer.

Factor services

Market transactions in early economies involved mostly goods and services for consumption. An individual specialized in making some commodity and traded it for all the other products that he or she required. Most labor services were provided directly by the maker, by apprentices who were learning to become artisans themselves, and by slaves who did most of the domestic work. Over the last several hundred years many technical developments have encouraged specialization in the methods of production and made it efficient to organize agriculture and industry on a very large scale. Today the owner of a factory or large farm does not personally make the commodities that the farm or factory sells. Rather, the owner hires the labor services of others to do so. Similarly, the era of the small artisan who both made and sold a commodity is all but over.

Division of labor

Many of the technical developments over the last few hundred years have been based on what is called the **division of labor**—the specialization of tasks within the production process of a particular commodity. Each worker does not perform all the tasks involved in making a unit of the commodity. Instead the labor involved is divided into a series of tasks, and each individual does repetitively tasks that represent a small fraction of those necessary to produce the entire commodity. Indeed, it is possible today for an individual to spend years doing a production line job without ever knowing what commodity he or she is helping to produce!

Historically, the division of labor made it necessary to organize production in large and expensive factories. With this development individual workers lost their status as independent producers and became merely members of the "labor force"; they became dependent for their income on their ability to sell their labor to factory owners. For those who left the land for the factories there was moreover the loss of the plot of land that provided, at the minimum, the basis for subsistence.

Today's typical workers do not earn their incomes by selling goods that they themselves have produced; rather they sell their labor services to firms and receive money wages in return. They have increasingly become cogs in a machine that they do not fully understand or control.

Scarcity

All economies that have existed since the original agricultural revolution have been faced with the problem of scarcity because there are not enough resources to produce all of the goods and services that could be consumed. It is therefore necessary to allocate the available resources among their various possible uses and in so doing to choose what to produce and what not to produce.

In a market economy, the allocation of resources is the outcome of millions of independent decisions made by consumers and producers, all acting through markets.

Our main objective in this chapter is to provide an overview of this market mechanism.

THE DECISION MAKERS

There are three groups—households, firms, and central authorities—whose decisions determine market transactions. These are the *dramatis personae* of economic theory.

The household

A **household** is defined to be all the people who live under one roof and who make, or have others make for them, joint financial decisions. In the theory of demand, the household is the basic atom. The main assumption about the household is that it behaves consistently when faced with economic choices. As with all assumptions, the test of the value of this one is "Do the predictions that follow from it fit the facts?" We shall consider this in a later chapter. In the meantime, you should notice that when economists speak of "the consumer," they are in fact referring to the group of individuals comprising the household. Many interesting problems such as those concerning conflict within the family and parental control over the fate of minors are ignored when the household is taken as a basic unit. In their market behavior, households are assumed to behave with a singleness of purpose more usually associated with an individual. Thus the often-heard phrase "consumer sovereignty" really means not individual sovereignty but household sovereignty.

Households make two different kinds of decisions. The first concerns the spending of their money—which goods and services to buy and how much of each. The second concerns the selling of the services of the factors of production (including their own labor) that they control.

The firm

The **firm** is defined to be the unit that makes decisions regarding the employment of factors of production and the production of goods and services. It buys the services of factors of production from households and sells the goods and services that it produces to other firms, to households, and to the central authorities.

Firms, often referred to as producers, are assumed to make consistent decisions in relation to the choices open to them. The internal problems of who within the firm actually reaches particular decisions and of how they are reached are ignored. In short, the firm is taken as the atom of behavior on the supply side, just as the household is taken as the atom of behavior on the demand side. These and other assumptions concerning the firm are considered in more detail in Chapter 10.

It is assumed that the firm exists to make profits and that it tries to produce as much as it can. In other words, the firm seeks to maximize its profits. This assumption has come under serious attack, as is shown in Chapter 19, and a number of competing theories are considered in detail later. In the meantime, we can go quite a long way using the profit-maximizing assumption.

Central authorities

The **central authorities,** often called simply "the government," are defined to be all public agencies, government bodies, and other organizations belonging to or under the direct control of governments. State and local governments, as well as the federal government, are included. In the United States, the term "central authorities" includes the President, the Federal Reserve System, the city council, commissions and regulatory bodies, the legislature, the police force, and all other government bodies that exercise control over the behavior of firms and households. It is not important to draw up a comprehensive list of all central authorities, but one should have in mind a general idea of the organizations that have legal and political power to exert control over individual decision makers and over markets. It is *not* a basic assumption of economics that the central authorities always act in a consistent fashion or as if they were a single individual. Indeed, conflict between different central bodies is the subject of much of the theory of the control of the economy.

No single motive is assigned to the central authorities. They can have many objectives and, as is noted in Chapter 1, the objectives can be in conflict with each other. All that can be assumed is that the central authorities are motivated in their policies by a set of objectives that can be stated and used to evaluate the efficacy of their actions.

MARKETS

We have seen that the word "market" originally designated a place where goods were traded. The Fulton Fish Market in New York is a world-famous modern example of markets in the everyday sense, and most cities have produce markets where fresh produce is brought early in the morning and promptly sold. Much of early economic theory was based on an attempt to explain price behavior in just such markets. Why, for example, can you sometimes obtain tremendous bargains at the end of the day and at other times get what you want only at prices that appear exorbitant in relation to prices ruling a few hours before?

As theories of market behavior were developed, they were quickly extended to cover commodities such as wheat. Wheat produced anywhere in the world can be purchased almost anywhere else in the world, and the price of a given grade of wheat tends to be nearly uniform the world over. When we talk about the wheat market, the concept of a market has been extended well beyond the idea of a single place to which the producer, the storekeeper, and the homemaker go to sell and buy something.

To get a satisfactory definition of a market is not an easy task; some of the complications are discussed in Chapter 18. For present purposes, a **market** is defined as an area over which buyers and sellers negotiate the exchange of a well-defined commodity. The actual geographical area covered by a single market will vary greatly with the commodity. In the case of wheat, the market is very nearly the whole world; in the case of strawberries, it may be only a small area including and surrounding one city; in the case of haircuts, it may be only a few blocks within the city.

At this stage we shall distinguish between two kinds of markets: **product markets,** in which firms sell their outputs of goods and services, and **factor markets,** in which households sell the services of the factors of production they control.

In Part Two attention will be confined to so-called competitive markets in which there are so many buyers and sellers that no one of them can have any appreciable influence on price by varying the amount that he or she buys or sells. In Part Five we shall consider the behavior of markets more fully, discussing markets that do not meet the competitive requirements.

KINDS OF ECONOMIES

A market economy consists of individual markets. Such an economy is one in which the allocation of resources is determined by the production, sales, and purchase decisions made by firms, households, and central authorities. A **free-market economy** is defined to be an economy in which the decisions of individual households and firms (as distinct from the central authorities) exert the major influence over the allocation of resources.[1]

The opposite of a free-market economy is a **command economy,** in which the major decisions about the allocation of resources are made by the central authorities and in which firms and households produce and consume only as they are ordered.

The terms *free market* and *command economy* are used to describe tendencies that are apparent, even though no real economies rely solely either on free markets or on commands. Thus, in practice all economies are **mixed economies** in the sense that some decisions are made by firms and households and some by central authorities. In mixed economies it is common to distinguish between the **private sector,** in which decisions are principally made by households and firms, and the **public sector,** in which they are made by the central authorities. What does vary between economies is the degree of the mix. In some economies the size of the public sector is substantially smaller than it is in others.

How individual markets work: an overview of microeconomics

Early economists observed the market economy with wonder. They saw that most commodities were made by a large number of independent producers and yet in approximately the quantities that people wanted to purchase them. Natural disasters aside, there were neither vast surpluses nor severe shortages of products. They also saw that in spite

[1] Free-market economies are sometimes called capitalist economies; in fact, the term "capitalist" is often used as a synonym for "free market." The free-market economy, however, is the more descriptive of the two terms, since the amount of capital used is not closely related to the degree to which the economies are or are not centrally controlled.

of the ever-changing requirements in terms of geographical, industrial, and occupational patterns, most laborers were able to sell their services to employers most of the time.

How does the market produce this order in the absence of conscious coordination by the central authorities? It is one thing to have the same thing produced year in and year out when people's wants and incomes do not change; it is quite another thing to have production adjusting continually to changing wants, incomes, and techniques of production. Yet this *relatively* smooth adjustment is accomplished by the market—albeit with occasional, and sometimes serious, interruptions.

The great discovery of economists working in the eighteenth century was that the price system is a *social control mechanism.*

Adam Smith, whose classic *The Wealth of Nations,* published in 1776, was the high point of this development, spoke of the price system as "the invisible hand." It allows decision making to be decentralized under the control of millions of individual producers and consumers but nonetheless to be coordinated. Two examples may help to illustrate how this coordination occurs.

A change in demand

For the first example, assume that households wish to purchase more of some commodity than previously. To see the market's reaction to such a change, imagine a situation in which farmers find it equally profitable to produce either of two crops, carrots or brussels sprouts, and so are willing to produce some of both commodities, thereby satisfying the demands of households who wish to consume both. Now imagine that consumers develop a greatly increased desire for brussels sprouts and a diminished desire for carrots. This change might have occurred because of the discovery of hitherto unsuspected nutritive or curative powers of brussels sprouts, or it might have been the result of a successful advertising campaign on the part of the association of brussels sprout producers: "Eat brussels sprouts; they're grown *above* ground." Whatever the reason, there has been a major shift toward sprouts and away from carrots.

What will be the effects of this shift? When consumers buy more brussels sprouts and fewer carrots a shortage of brussels sprouts and a glut of carrots develop. In order to unload their surplus stocks of carrots, merchants reduce the price of carrots—in the belief that it is better to sell them at a reduced price than not to sell them at all. Sellers of brussels sprouts, however, find that they are unable to satisfy all their customer's demands for that product. Sprouts have become a scarce commodity, so the merchants charge more for them. As the price rises, fewer people are willing and able to purchase sprouts. Thus making them more expensive limits the demand for them to the available supply.

Farmers begin to observe a rise in the price of brussels sprouts and a fall in the price of carrots. Brussels sprout production has become more profitable than in the past: the costs of producing sprouts remain unchanged at the same time that their market price has risen. Similarly, carrot production will be less profitable than in the past because costs are unchanged but the price has fallen. Attracted by high profits in brussels sprouts and deterred by low profits or potential losses in carrots, farmers expand the production of sprouts and curtail the production of carrots. Thus the change in consumers' tastes, working through the price system, causes a reallocation of resources—land and labor—out of carrot production and into brussels sprout production.

As the production of carrots declines, the glut of carrots on the market diminishes and their price begins to rise. On the other hand, the expansion in brussels sprout production reduces the shortage and the price begins to fall. These price movements will continue until it no longer pays farmers to contract carrot production and to expand brussels sprout production. When the dust settles, the price of sprouts is higher than it was originally but lower than it was when the shortage sent the price soaring before output could be adjusted; and the price of carrots is lower than it was originally but higher than when the initial glut sent the price tumbling before output could be adjusted.

The reaction of the market to a change in demand leads to a transfer of resources. Carrot producers reduce their production; they will therefore be laying off workers and generally demanding fewer factors of production. Brussels sprout producers expand production; they will therefore be hiring workers and generally increasing their demand for factors of production.

Labor can probably switch from carrot to sprout production without much difficulty. If, however, there are other resources involved—say, a certain type of land that is better suited for sprout-growing than for carrot-growing—the demand for, and hence the price of, this land will be affected. On the one hand, when farmers increase their sprout production, their demands for those factors especially suited to sprout production also increase—and this creates a shortage of these resources and a consequent rise in their prices. On the other hand, with carrot production falling, the demand for land and other factors of production especially suited to carrot growing is reduced. A surplus results, and the prices of these factors are forced down.

Thus factors particularly suited to sprout production will earn more and will obtain a higher share of total national income than before. Factors particularly suited to carrot production, however, will earn less and will obtain a smaller share of the total national income than before.

Changes of this kind will be studied more fully later; the important thing to notice now is how a change in demand initiated by a change in consumers' tastes causes a reallocation of resources in the direction required to cater to the new set of tastes.

A change in supply

For a second example, consider a change originating with producers. Begin as before by imagining a situation in which farmers find it equally profitable to produce either sprouts or carrots and in which consumers are willing to buy, at prevailing market prices, the quantities of these two commodities that are being produced. Now imagine that, at existing prices, farmers become more willing to produce sprouts than in the past and less willing to produce carrots. This shift might be caused, for example, by a change in the costs of producing the two goods—a rise in carrot costs and a fall in sprout costs that would raise the profitability of sprout production and lower that of carrot production.

What will happen now? For a short time, nothing at all; the existing supply of sprouts and carrots on the market is the result of decisions made by farmers at some time in the past. But farmers now begin to plant fewer carrots and more sprouts, and soon the quantities on the market begin to change. The quantity of sprouts available for sale rises, and the quantity of carrots falls. A shortage of carrots and a glut of sprouts results. The price of carrots consequently rises, and the price of sprouts falls. As carrots become more expensive and sprouts become cheaper, fewer carrots and more sprouts will be bought. The rise in the price of carrots and the fall in the price of sprouts now act as incentives for farmers to move back into carrot production and out of sprout production.

This example began with a situation in which there was a shortage of carrots that caused the price of carrots to rise. The rise in the price of carrots removed the shortage in two ways: it reduced the quantity of carrots demanded and it increased the quantity of-

fered for sale (in response to the rise in the profitability of carrot production). Remember that there was also a surplus of brussels sprouts that caused the price to fall. The fall in price removed the surplus in two ways: it encouraged the consumers to buy more of this commodity and it reduced the quantity of sprouts produced and offered for sale (in response to a fall in the profitability of sprout production).

These examples illustrate a general point:

The price system is a mechanism that coordinates individual, decentralized decisions.

The existence of such a control mechanism is beyond dispute. How well it works in comparison with alternative coordinating systems has, however, been a matter of serious dispute for over a hundred years and remains today a major unsettled social question.

THE CIRCULAR FLOW: FROM MICROECONOMICS TO MACROECONOMICS

Figure 4–1 illustrates the two sets of markets, factor markets and product markets, through which the decisions of firms and households are coordinated. Consider households first. The members of households want commodities to keep them fed, clothed, housed, entertained, healthy, and secure; they also want them to educate, edify, beautify, stupefy, and otherwise amuse themselves. Households have, in varying amounts, resources with which to attempt to satisfy these wants. But their resources are insufficient to permit them to satisfy all of their wants. They are forced, therefore, to make choices as to what goods and services to buy in product markets that offer them myriad ways to spend their incomes.

The signals to which households respond are product-market prices; for each given set of prices, households make a set of choices. In

Figure 4–1   The circular flows of goods and services and money payments between firms and households

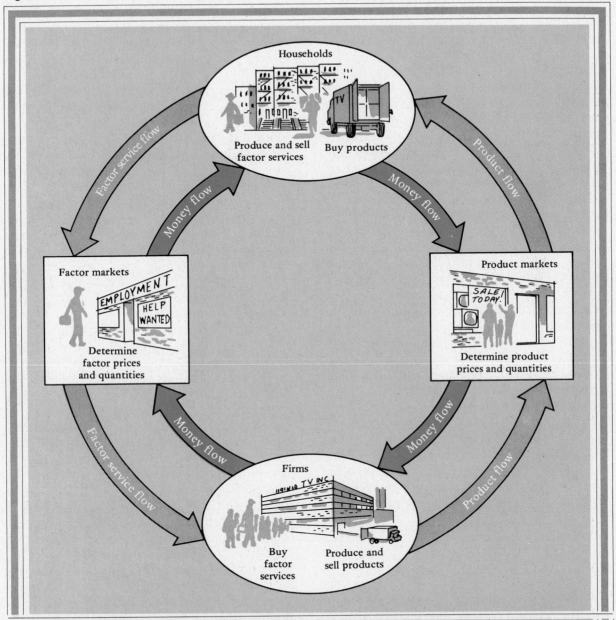

The interaction of firms and households in factor and product markets generates both real and money flows.   Factor services are sold through factor markets. The real flow is of factor services from households to firms and the money flow is of income from firms to households. Goods and services for consumption are sold through product markets. The real flow is of goods and services from firms to households and the money flow is of payments from households to firms.

so doing they also, in the aggregate, affect those prices. The prices also serve as signals to firms of what goods *they* may profitably provide. Given technology and the cost of factors, firms must choose among the products they might produce and sell, among the ways of producing them, and among the various quantities (and qualities) they can supply. By so doing, the firms too affect prices.

Firms must buy factors of production. The quantities demanded depend on the firms' production decisions, which in turn depend on consumers' demands. These demands for factors will in turn affect the prices of labor, managerial skill, raw materials, buildings, machinery, use of capital, land, and all other factors. The households who are owners of factors (or who possess the skills that can provide the factor services) respond to factor prices and make *their* choices about where to offer their services. These choices determine factor supplies and affect factor prices. Payments by firms to factor owners provide the owners of the factors with incomes. The recipients of these incomes are households whose members want commodities to keep them fed, clothed, housed entertained. . . . We have now come full circle!

The story we have told is one of firms and households being inextricably bound up with each other. Payments flow from households to firms and back to households again.

An overview of macroeconomics

The idea of payments and incomes flowing in a closed circuit, suggested in Figure 4–1, is basic to understanding macroeconomics. The figure shows the two main flows in the economy. The first is called the **real flow,** and it is the flow of goods and services from sellers to buyers. The second is called the **money flow,** and it is the flow of money payments from buyers to sellers. These money payments become the money incomes received by the sellers. Specifically, the money spent to purchase factor services becomes income to the households who sell the factor services, and the money spent by households to buy the goods produced by firms becomes the income of the firms. If households spent all the income they received on buying goods and services produced by firms, and if firms distributed all the income they received to households either by purchasing factor services or by distributing profits to their owners, then the circular flow would be very simple indeed. Everything that households received would be passed on to firms and everything that firms received would be passed on to households. The circular flow would be a completely closed system.

There are two main reasons why the circular flow is not a completely closed system. First, neither households nor firms spend all of the income they receive on purchasing goods and services from the other. Households, for example, have to pay income taxes and some of their after-tax income is saved. Some of the money that households do spend on purchasing goods and services goes to governments rather than firms because of sales taxes; only what is left becomes the receipts of firms. Furthermore, not all of the income received by firms is paid out to factors; some is paid to governments in the form of business taxes and some is saved by the firms. All of these examples may be gathered together under the general concept of withdrawals from the circular flow of income. **Withdrawals** consist of income received by households that is not passed on to firms in return for goods and services purchased and income received by firms that is not passed on to households either in return for factor services purchased or as distributed profits.

The second reason why the circular flow of income is not a completely closed system is that firms receive income that does not arise from the spending of households and households receive income that does not arise from the spending of firms. When governments spend money on goods and services that are produced by firms, for example, this creates income for the firms that does not arise directly out of the expenditure of private households. When governments hire the ser-vices of civil servants, mine inspectors, road builders, and other persons, they create in-come for households that does not arise directly out of the spending of firms. Simi-larly, if some firms purchase machines and equipment (say, out of funds borrowed from banks), this creates income for the other firms that manufacture the equipment (and for the households that supply the required factor services); but such income does not arise directly out of household spending. All of

Figure 4–2 Withdrawals and injections to the circular flow of income

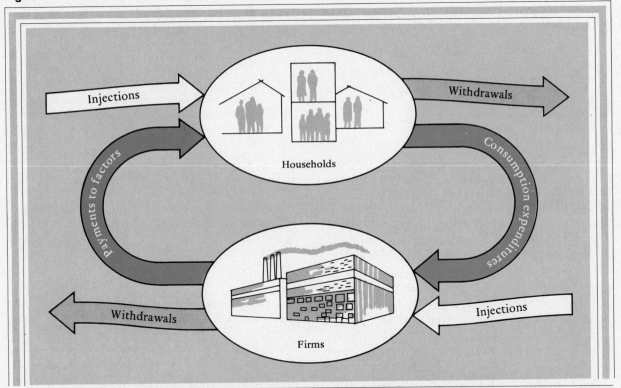

The circular flow is augmented by injections and diminished by withdrawals. Anything that creates income for households that does not arise out of the spending of firms, and anything that creates in-come for firms that does not arise out of the spending of households, is regarded as an injection. Any income received by firms or households that is not passed on to the other through the purchase of goods and services is a withdrawal.

these examples may be gathered together under the general concept of injections into the circular flow of income. **Injections** consist of income received by firms that does not arise out of the spending of households and income received by households that does not arise out of the spending of firms.

Figure 4–2 introduces both withdrawals from and injections into the circular flow of income. Of course, much detail remains to be filled in, but the main picture has already emerged.

There is a basic element of circularity in that much income received by households is passed on to firms and much income received by firms is passed on to households. But there are also withdrawals—income received by one group and not passed on to the other—and injections—income received by one group that does not arise out of the spending of the other.

It should be intuitively clear from this discussion that the size of the total incomes received by households and firms depends not only on their total purchases from one another but also on the size of the injections into and withdrawals from the circular flow. If your intuition further tells you that when withdrawals and injections are exactly equal there is no tendency for the total money flow either to rise or fall, then you have gained some insight into one of the basic propositions of macroeconomics.

Microeconomics, then, deals with the determination of prices and quantities in individual markets and with the relations between markets. Microeconomics thus looks at the details of the market economy. In contrast, macroeconomics suppresses much detail and paints the economy with a very broad brush. Macroeconomics deals with such aggregates as the total flow of payments from households to firms and the total flow of factor income from firms to households.

Microeconomics and macroeconomics look at different aspects of the circular flow of income. Both deal with important questions concerning the functioning of the economy. Whichever one studies first—microeconomics then macroeconomics, as this book is arranged, or macroeconomics then microeconomics, as it is possible to do by studying Parts Eight to Twelve before Parts Two to Seven—it is important to remember that they are complementary, not competing, theories and that both are needed for a full understanding of the functioning of a modern economy.

Summary

1. This chapter provides an overview of the workings of the market economy. All modern economies are based on specialization and division of labor, which necessitate the exchange of goods and services. Exchange takes place in markets and is facilitated by the use of money. Much of economics is devoted to a study of how free markets work to coordinate millions of individual, decentralized decisions.

2. In economic theory, three kinds of decision makers —households, firms, and central authorities—interact in markets. It is assumed that households seek to maximize their satisfaction (to the best of their ability) and that firms seek to maximize their profits, but that central authorities may have multiple objectives.

3. A market is defined, for the present, as an area over which buyers and sellers negotiate the exchange of a well-defined commodity. A free-market economy is one in which the allocation of resources is determined by the production, sales, and purchase decisions made by firms and households acting in response to such market signals as prices and profits.

4. The price system provides a set of signals that reflects changes in demand and supply and to which producers and consumers can react individually but in a nonetheless coordinated manner.

5. The interactions between households and firms through markets are illustrated in a circular-flow diagram

that traces both goods and money flows between households and firms. The real flows of goods and services from households to firms and from firms to households play a major role in generating the circular flow of income. This is the key concept of macroeconomics. At this stage only a very simplified version of these flows is discussed.

6. Because not all income received by households is spent for the output of firms and because some income received by firms is not paid out to households, there are withdrawals from the circular flow of income. There are also injections into the circular flow in the form of payments to firms that do not result from the spending of households and payments to households that do not result from the spending of firms. Some of the major concerns of macroeconomics involve the nature, significance, and determinants of various injections into and withdrawals from the circular flow.

7. Macroeconomics is largely concerned with what determines the size of the money flows in the economy as a whole. Microeconomics is concerned with the behavior in individual markets and the interrelations among markets. Microeconomics and macroeconomics are complementary parts of economic theory. They study different aspects of a single economic system, and both are needed for an understanding of the whole.

Concepts for review

Specialization and the division of labor
Economic decision makers
Markets and market economies
The private sector and the public sector
The price system as a social control mechanism
Linkages between firms and households
The circular flow of income
Real flows and money flows
Withdrawals and injections
The relation between microeconomics and macroeconomics

Discussion questions

1. There is a greater variety of specialists and specialty stores in large cities than in small cities having the same average income of the population. Explain this in economic terms.

2. Define the household of which you are a member. Consider your household's income last year. What proportion of it came from the sale of factor services to firms? Identify the other sources of income. Approximately what proportion of the expenditures by your household became income for firms?

3. "It is not from the benevolence of the butcher, the brewer, or the baker that we expect our dinner, but from their regard to their self-interest. We address ourselves, not to their humanity, but to their self-love, and never talk to them of our necessities, but of their advantages." Do you agree with this quotation from *The Wealth of Nations*? How are "their self-love" and "our dinner" related to the price system? What are assumed to be the motives of firms and of households?

4. Trace the effect of a sharp change in consumer demand away from cigarettes and toward chewing gum as a result of continuing reports linking smoking with lung cancer and heart disease. Can producers of cigarettes do anything to prevent their loss of profits?

5. Can you think of any decision makers in the U.S. economy today that do not fit into the categories of firm, household, and central authority?

6. Consider a major baby boom such as occurred following World War II. Trace out some significant microeconomic and macroeconomic effects of such a boom. Is there a clear line between them in every case?

7. Can you visualize one $20 bill being used in transactions that create $200 of income in one month? If so, how? If not, why not? Can you visualize it not being used in any transactions that create income in one month? If so, how? If not, why not? Do your answers imply that money and income are not related to one another?

PART TWO

A GENERAL VIEW OF THE PRICE SYSTEM

5

Demand, supply, and price

Some people believe that economics begins and ends with the "law" of supply and demand. It is, of course, too much to hope for "economics in one lesson." (An unkind critic of a book with that title commented that the author needed a second lesson.) The so-called laws of supply and demand are an important beginning in the attempt to answer vital questions about the workings of a market system. It is necessary to go beyond the overview of Chapter 4 and ask: How does the market work? How does it allocate resources? A first step is to understand what determines the demands for commodities, and the supplies of them, and how the price system allows the economy to reallocate resources in response to changes in demand and in supply. Under certain conditions the price system does this very efficiently. Of course, as we shall see subsequently, the price system sometimes works imperfectly, even badly, and may lead to the production of pollution, poverty, and inequality along with paper, tobacco, automobiles, and movies. Supply and demand prove to be helpful concepts in discussing both the price system's successes and its failures, and they also can be used to discuss the consequences of particular forms of government intervention such as price controls, minimum-wage laws, and sales taxes.

The basic theory of demand

The American consumer spent about $1 trillion on goods and services in 1975. What was it spent on, and why? Table 5–1 shows the composition of this expenditure and how it has changed in two decades. Economists ask many questions about the pattern of consumer expenditure: Why is it what it is at any moment of time? Why does it change in the way it does? Why did the fraction of total consumer expenditure for food decline from more than one-third in 1910 to only one-fifth

Table 5–1 Composition of personal consumption expenditures, 1955 and 1975 (percentages)

	1955		1975	
Durable goods		15.2		13.3
Motor vehicles and parts	7.0		5.3	
Furniture and household equipment	6.4		6.0	
Other	1.8		2.0	
Nondurable goods		48.5		42.6
Food	26.5		21.7	
Clothing and shoes	9.1		7.3	
Gasoline and oil	3.4		4.2	
Other	9.5		9.4	
Services		36.3		44.1
Housing and household operation	19.0		22.0	
Other	17.3		22.1	
Total		100.0		100.0

Source: *Economic Report of the President,* 1976.

The declining relative importance of food and clothing and the rising importance of gasoline and oil and services of all kinds stand out.

by 1975? Why did U.S. consumers allocate a negligible percentage of their total expenditure to automobiles in 1920, 4 percent in 1929, only 2 percent in 1932, 7 percent in 1972, and 5 percent in 1975? Why do Americans now heat their homes with electricity, oil, and natural gas when twenty-five years ago they used coal? Why do people who build houses in Norway and the American West rarely use brick while it is commonly used in England and the eastern United States? Why have the maid and the washerwoman been increasingly replaced by the vacuum cleaner and the washing machine?

We shall concentrate in this chapter not on the individual household but on the demand of *all* households for commodities. Of course, what all households do is only the sum of what each individual household does, and in Part Three we shall study the behavior of individual households in greater detail.

THE NATURE OF "QUANTITY DEMANDED"

The total amount of a commodity that all households wish to purchase is called the **quantity demanded** of that commodity. It is important to notice three things about this concept. First, quantity demanded is a *desired* quantity. It is how much households are willing to purchase, given the price of the commodity, other prices, their incomes, tastes, and so on. This may be a different amount than households actually succeed in purchasing. If sufficient quantities are not available, the amount households wish to purchase may exceed the amount they actually do purchase. To distinguish these two concepts, the term *quantity demanded* is used to refer to desired purchases, and phrases such as *quantity actually purchased* or *quantity exchanged* are used to refer to actual purchases.

Second, *desired* does not refer to idle dreams or future possibilities but to effective demands—that is, to the amounts people are willing to *buy* given the price they must pay for the commodity. For a person intending to spend $100 this year on a commodity whose price is $20, the quantity demanded is 5 units even though he or she would prefer to get 6 or 10 or even more units for the $100.

Third, quantity demanded is a flow; it does

not refer to a single isolated purchase but to a continuous flow of purchases. Quantity demanded must therefore be expressed as so much per period of time: 1 million oranges *per day,* 7 million *per week,* or 365 million *per year.* (The important distinction between stocks and flows was discussed in the box on page 24.)

WHAT DETERMINES QUANTITY DEMANDED?

Quantity demanded changes in response to a variety of circumstances, the most important of which we must now study.

1. *Quantity demanded varies with the tastes or preferences of the members of society.* Some consumers' tastes are passing fads, such as hula hoops and pet rocks; others are permanent (or at least long lasting), such as the American's preference for color television, the board game Monopoly, and a private car rather than public transportation.

Tastes do, to some extent, arise out of the basic wants and needs of human beings, and as such they are more nearly in the realm of the biologist and the psychologist than that of the economist. Changes in taste may, however, be the result of economic activities. One of the major purposes of advertising, on which more than $28 billion was spent in the United States in 1976, is not only to inform the household about what products will best suit its present wants but also to try to set fashions and to change tastes. There is little doubt that, at least within limits, the attempt is successful. Whatever the cause, whenever tastes do change, the quantity demanded will increase for commodities that have come into favor and decrease for those that have become less popular.

2. *Quantity demanded depends on the level of income of the average household.* In most cases, the larger is average income, the larger will be the quantity of a particular commodity demanded. As average income rises the demand

for all commodities does not increase in the same proportion. When the population is poor, much of its income must go to basic necessities: food, clothing, shelter. As it becomes richer, it will wish to buy more (and more expensive) food, clothing, and shelter, but it will also spend more on less basic items. In large part, the rise in income accounts for the *relative* decline in importance of food and other nondurable goods in the overall consumption pattern and the rise in importance of durable goods, housing, and, more recently, services.

3. *Quantity demanded depends on the size of the total population.* As the total population grows, more people need to be fed, clothed, housed, and entertained, and thus the quantity demanded increases as population increases. The relation is not quite so simple as it may seem at first. Just having more people is not sufficient; these people must have purchasing power before quantities demanded can increase. That is usually the case in developed countries since more population usually means more production, more employment, and more income earned. In some undeveloped countries, however, growth in population may occur with no corresponding growth in purchasing power.

4. *Quantity demanded depends on the distribution of income among households.* Imagine a society, an oil-rich shiekdom for example, in which the average income, though high, is the average of the very low incomes of the vast number of poor households and the very high incomes of the few enormously wealthy ones. This society would be expected to have a distribution of quantities demanded that was very different from that of a society in which the average income is the same but the actual income is distributed more equally. Income redistribution involves some groups gaining income and others losing income. The groups that gain income will usually prefer somewhat different goods from those preferred by

the groups that lose income; thus the quantity demanded of some goods will increase and that of others will decrease.

5. *Quantity demanded depends on the price of the commodity.* Goods and services are desired to satisfy wants and needs. Since there are always alternative ways to satisfy them, and since incomes are limited, a rise in the price of one commodity will cause some people to substitute other goods or services whose prices have not risen. The increase in the wages of domestic servants and the corresponding decrease in their use in the United States dramatically illustrates this hypothesis. The typical American household has had to make do without a servant, but it has substituted washing machines, vacuum cleaners, and frozen foods to lighten the housekeeping burden. The relevant aspect of a price change is that its price changes in relation to prices of other commodities. What matters is how cheap or expensive is a commodity *relative to* other commodities that could be used instead.

6. *Quantity demanded depends on the prices of many other commodities.* This is the other side of the coin of relative prices: A change in other prices also changes relative prices. Here the effect depends on whether the good whose price changes is a complement or a substitute commodity. A **substitute** for a particular commodity is one that satisfies similar needs or desires. Bricks and timber are substitutes in house construction. In the American West and in Norway, where wood is plentiful and thus relatively low priced, timber rather than brick provides the basic material for housing. In most of the American Northeast and in England, where lumber is scarce and relatively high priced, brick, which is relatively cheap, is used instead. In general, a decrease in the price of one commodity will decrease the quantity demanded of a good for which it is a substitute, and an increase in the substitute's price will increase the quantity demanded of the other commodity.

A **complement** is a commodity that tends to be used jointly with another commodity. Gasoline and automobiles are complements. When commodities are complements, a fall in the price of one will be expected to lead to an increase in the demand for the other. A fall in the price of automobiles, for example, would lead to a rise in the quantity of gasoline demanded. The reason is that a decrease in the price of automobiles relative to other goods will lead to greater use of automobiles—and hence of gasoline.

The six hypotheses just listed are not alternatives; they are a set of influences, all of which affect the quantity of a commodity demanded. [1]

Quantity demanded depends on and changes with taste and preference, average income, population, distribution of income, the price of the commodity, and the prices of other commodities.

To discover how quantity demanded is influenced by the factors just named, we let the factors vary one at a time (holding the others constant) and observe the effect that each has on quantity demanded. In this way we can study the influence of each variable in turn and come to understand its distinct influence.[2] Once we have done this we can aggregate the separate influences of two or more variables to discover what would happen if several

[1] Notes giving mathematical demonstrations of the concepts presented in the text are indicated by colored reference numbers. These notes can be found at the back of the book on pages 901–909.

[2] A relation in which many variables—average income, population, tastes, and many prices in this case—influence a single variable—quantity demanded in this case—is called a multivariate relation. The technique of studying the effect of each of the influencing variables one at a time, holding the other variables constant, is a common one in science and mathematics. Holding all other influencing variables constant is often described by the words "other things being equal" or by the equivalent Latin phrase **ceteris paribus**. Thus when economists speak of the influence of the price of wheat on the quantity of wheat demanded *ceteris paribus* they refer to what a change in the price of wheat would do to the quantity demanded if all other factors that influence the demand for wheat do not change. (This is such a common procedure in the sciences that there is a mathematical concept, the partial derivative, explicitly designed to accomplish this task.)

things changed at the same time—as of course they often do in practice. In this chapter we study the important influences of price and income on quantity demanded.

THE QUANTITY OF A COMMODITY DEMANDED AND ITS OWN PRICE

Assume first that everything that can affect quantity demanded other than the price of the commodity in question is held constant. The economist's hypothesis is that, for all commodities, quantity demanded increases as the price of the commodity falls, *ceteris paribus*. As its price falls, a commodity becomes cheaper relative to its substitutes and it is easier for the commodity to compete against these substitutes for the purchaser's expenditure. If, for example, brussels sprouts become very cheap, some shoppers will be induced, up to a point, to buy more sprouts and less of other vegetables whose prices are now high relative to the price of sprouts. If, however, brussels sprouts become very expensive, some (or all) shop-

pers will reduce their purchases of sprouts, possibly replacing them with some other vegetable.

The demand schedule and the demand curve

A **demand schedule** shows the relationship between the quantity of a commodity demanded and its price. A **demand curve** is a graphic representation of the demand schedule. Table 5–2 shows a hypothetical demand schedule for carrots. It shows the quantity of carrots that would be demanded at various prices in some geographical region that con-

Figure 5–1   A demand curve for carrots

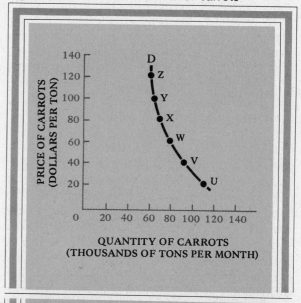

This demand curve relates quantity demanded to the price of carrots; its downward slope indicates that quantity demanded increases as price falls. There are six points corresponding to the price-quantity combinations shown in Table 5–2. Each row of the table defines a point on the demand curve. The smooth curve drawn through all of the points and labeled *D* is the demand curve.

Table 5–2   A demand schedule for carrots

	Price per ton p	Quantity demanded when average household income is $8,000 per year (thousands of tons per month) D
U	$ 20	110.0
V	40	90.0
W	60	77.5
X	80	67.5
Y	100	62.5
Z	120	60.0

The table shows the quantity of carrots that would be demanded at various prices, *ceteris paribus*. Row W indicates that if the price of carrots is $60 per ton, consumers will desire to purchase 77,500 tons of carrots per month, given the values of other variables that may affect quantity demanded (such as average household income).

stitutes a market for that commodity on the assumption that average household income is fixed at $8,000 (and that other variables do not change). It gives the quantities demanded for six selected prices; there is a separate quantity that would be demanded at each possible price. These six points can be plotted on a graph with price on the vertical axis and quantity on the horizontal one. Figure 5–1 shows such a graph. The smooth curve through these points is the demand curve. It shows the quantity of carrots that purchasers would like to buy at each price; a downward-sloping demand curve indicates that the quantity demanded increases as the price falls.

A single point on the demand curve indicates a single price-quantity combination. Notice that while any point on the demand curve represents a specific quantity demanded, the demand curve as a whole shows more.

The whole demand curve is a representation of the complete relation between quantity demanded and price, other things being equal.

When economists speak of the conditions of demand in a particular market as being given or known, they are referring not just to the particular quantity being demanded at the moment (i.e., not just to a particular point on the demand curve) but to the entire demand curve—to the complete functional relation whereby desired purchases are related to all the possible alternative prices of the commodity.

SHIFTS IN THE DEMAND CURVE

We have defined the demand curve using the assumption that other things remain equal. The influence of changes in variables other than price on the quantity demanded can now be studied by determining how they shift the demand curve. Any one of the five determinants of demand listed above (other than the commodity's own price) will have the ef-

fect of shifting the demand curve to the right if it increases the quantity demanded, other things remaining equal, and to the left if it decreases the quantity demanded, other things remaining equal.

Quantity demanded and average income

The basic hypothesis is that in the case of most commodities a rise in income, *ceteris paribus,* will cause an increase in the quantity demanded. Therefore, if the income of the average household rises, an increase is predicted in the amount that will be demanded at each price. Table 5–3 and Figure 5–2 show the effects of an increase in average household income on the hypothetical demand curve for carrots.[3] Notice that in the table we can examine the joint effect on quantity demanded of a change in price and a change in income. If, for example, income increases from $8,000 to $10,000 *and* price rises from $60 to $80 per ton, the quantity demanded will rise from 77.5 to 87.5 thousand tons per month.

Other causes of shifts in the demand curve

Earlier we defined a demand curve by looking at the *ceteris paribus* relation between the quantity demanded of a commodity and its own price. We then allowed average income to change and found that the effect of this on quantity demanded could be represented by *shifts* in the demand curve. Other variables can be treated in the same way. Anything that increases the quantity demanded of a commodity, its own price being held constant, shifts that commodity's demand curve to the right. Anything that decreases the quantity demanded of the commodity, its own price held constant, shifts the demand curve to the

---

[3] Here we are treating the change in income as a *shift* in the *ceteris paribus* relationship between price and quantity demanded. Another way of looking at the influence of income is to hold price constant and to look at the relationship of quantity demanded to level of income at a whole series of levels of income. This is done in the following chapter (see Figure 6–4).

Table 5–3 Two alternative demand schedules for carrots

	Price per ton p	Quantity demanded when average household income is 8,000 per year (thousands of tons per month) D	Quantity demanded when average income is $10,000 per year (thousands of tons per month) D_1	
U	$ 20	110.0	140.0	U'
V	40	90.0	116.0	V'
W	60	77.5	100.8	W'
X	80	67.5	87.5	X'
Y	100	62.5	81.3	Y'
Z	120	60.0	78.0	Z'

An increase in average income increases the quantity demanded at each price. When average income rises from $8,000 to $10,000 per year, quantity demanded at a price of $60 per ton rises from 77,500 tons per month to 100,800 tons per month. A similar rise occurs at every other price. Thus the demand schedule relating columns p and D is replaced by one relating columns p and D_1. The graphical representations of these two functions are labeled D and D_1 in Figure 5–2.

Figure 5–2 Two demand curves for carrots

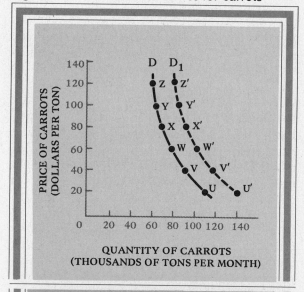

The rightward shift in the demand curve from D to D_1 indicates an increase in the quantity demanded at each price. The lettered points correspond to those in Table 5–3. A rightward shift in the demand curve indicates an increase in demand in the sense that more is demanded at the same price and that a higher price would be paid for the same quantity. In the example of Table 5–3, the increase in demand is due to an increase in income.

left. Figure 5–3 summarizes the major causes of shifts in the demand curve.

The distinction between changes in quantity demanded and changes in demand

We have so far used the phrase *quantity demanded*, rather than the shorter *demand*, because the latter has many meanings. Economists usually use the term **demand** to refer to the whole demand curve and the term *quantity demanded* to refer to a particular quantity being demanded (at a given level of the commodity's price and at given levels of all the other variables that influence demand).

It is vital to distinguish between a movement along a demand curve and a shift of the whole curve. A *movement along* a demand curve indicates that a different quantity will be demanded *because* the price has changed. An increase in the quantity demanded refers to a movement down the demand curve caused by a fall in price, while a decrease in the quantity demanded refers to a movement up the demand curve caused by a rise in price. A *shift* of a demand curve indicates that a different quantity will be demanded at each possible price because something else, such as income, tastes, or the price of some other good, has changed. *Increase in demand* and *decrease in demand* refer to such shifts in the whole demand curve—to changes in the quantity that will be demanded at *each* possible price.

To illustrate this terminology, look again at Table 5–3. When average income is $8,000, an increase in price from $60 to $80 decreases the *quantity demanded* from 77.5 to 67.5 thousand tons. An increase in average income from $8,000 to $10,000 increases *demand* from D to D_1.

The basic theory of supply

America's private industries produced goods and services worth more than $1 trillion in 1975. A broad classification of *what* was produced is given in Table 5–4. Economists have as many questions to ask about production and its changing composition as they do about consumption. The percentages shown in Table 5–4 reflect some of the changes in twenty years. Even more dramatic changes are visible in more detailed data. For example, the increase in output of the chemical industries was almost sixteen times that of the primary metals industries, seven times that of mining industries, and three times that of the petroleum industry between 1955 and 1975. Economists want to know why. Why did the aluminum industry grow faster than the steel industry? Why, even within a single industry, did some firms prosper and grow, others hold their own, and still others decline and fail? Why and how do firms and industries come into being? All of these questions and many others are aspects of a single question: *What determines the quantity of commodities actually supplied?*

A detailed discussion of these questions must wait until Part Four. At the moment, it is sufficient to develop only the basic relation between the price of a commodity and the quantity of it that will be produced and of-

Figure 5–3 Shifts in the demand curve

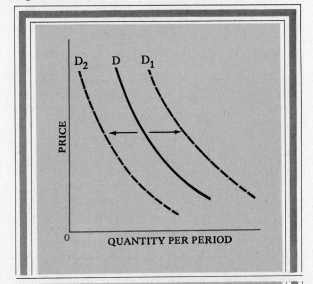

A shift in the demand curve from D to D_1 indicates an increase in demand; a shift from D to D_2 indicates a decrease in demand. An increase in demand means more is demanded at each price. Such a rightward shift can be caused by a rise in income, a rise in the price of a substitute, a fall in the price of a complement, a change in tastes in favor of the commodity, an increase in population, and a redistribution of income toward groups who favor the commodity.

A decrease in demand means less is demanded at each price. Such a leftward shift can be caused by a fall in income, a fall in the price of a substitute, a rise in the price of a complement, a change in tastes against the commodity, a decrease in population, and a redistribution of income away from groups who favor the commodity.

fered for sale by firms and to understand what forces might lead to shifts in this relationship.

WHAT DETERMINES QUANTITY SUPPLIED?

The amounts of some commodity that firms wish to sell is the **quantity supplied** of that

Table 5–4 Composition of national income by industry of origin, 1955 and 1975 (percentages)

Industry group[a]	1955	1975
Manufacturing	36.6	29.3
Mining and construction	7.7	7.2
Agriculture, forestry, fisheries	5.4	4.3
Transport, communications, utilities	9.4	9.2
Wholesale and retail trade	17.7	19.4
Finance, insurance, real estate	12.0	13.4
Other services	10.5	16.2
Other	0.7	1.0
	100.0	100.0

Source: *Survey of Current Business,* June 1976.

[a] Excluding government and government enterprises.

> Over two decades manufacturing, mining and construction, and agriculture have all declined in relative importance while services of all kinds have become more important.

commodity. It refers to what firms are willing and able to sell, not necessarily to what they succeed in selling. Quantity supplied is a flow; it is so much per unit of time—per day, per week, or per year.

Five factors are particularly important in influencing firms' willingness to supply a commodity.

1. *Quantity supplied depends on the goals of firms.* If all manufacturing companies prefer to engage in the production of medicines rather than rat poison because it makes them feel more important in society, more medicines and less rat poison will be produced than if producers held all commodities in equal regard. If producers of some commodity want to sell as much as possible, even if it costs them some profits to do so, more will be sold of that commodity than if they wanted to make maximum profits. If producers are reluctant to take risks, there will be a smaller production of goods whose production is risky. The usual assumption made by economists is that firms seek to maximize profits.

2. *Quantity supplied depends on the state of technology.* At any time, what is produced and

how it is produced depend on what is known. Over time, knowledge changes and so do the quantities supplied of individual commodities. The enormous increase in production per worker that has been going on in industrial societies for about 200 years is very largely due to improved methods of production. But the Industrial Revolution is more than a historical event; it is a present reality. Discoveries in chemistry have led to lower costs of production of well-established products, such as paints, and to a large variety of new products made of plastics and synthetic fibers. The invention of transistors and other miniaturized devices is currently revolutionizing production in television, high-fidelity equipment, computers, and guidance-control systems. Such things tend to increase the quantity supplied of some products and to reduce the quantity supplied of products that are displaced.

3. *Quantity supplied depends on the price of the commodity.* Other things being equal—in particular the prices of other commodities and of factors of production—the higher is the price of a commodity the greater will be the quantity of it the firms will wish to supply. This is

because the profits that can be earned from producing a commodity are almost certain to increase if the price of that commodity rises while the costs of factors used to produce it remain unchanged. Furthermore, if the prices of other commodities remain unchanged the profits that can be earned by producing them will be unchanged and as a result there will be a rise in *relative* profitability of producing the commodity whose price has risen. This will make firms, which are in business to earn profits, wish to produce more of the commodity whose price has risen and less of other commodities.

4. *Quantity supplied depends on the prices of other commodities.* Commodities may be substitutes or complements in production as well as in consumption. Land that grows wheat can also grow corn or be used to raise hogs. Suppose the price of corn falls and as a result corn is less profitable to produce. Some farmers will shift from corn to wheat production. Thus, from the point of view of wheat, an increase in the quantity supplied may be expected in response to a decrease in the price of corn if that leads to a substitution of wheat for corn production. What matters, of course, is relative prices. The relative price of wheat will rise if the price of wheat rises *or* if the price of corn falls.

In general, the change in the quantity supplied of one commodity is greater in response to a change in its own price than to a change in the price of another commodity. This is because, in the latter case, producers of the commodity whose price has declined can usually turn to several alternative products. Some corn farmers may shift to wheat production, but others may shift to hog or soybean production. The effect on wheat production is thus less than the effect on corn production.

5. *Quantity supplied depends on the costs of factors of production.* A change in factor prices is expected to affect supply by changing profits. A rise in the price of one factor will cause a larger increase in the costs of making those commodities that use a great deal of that factor than in the costs of producing those that use a relatively small amount of the factor. For example, a rise in the price of land will have a large effect on the costs of producing wheat and only a very small effect on the costs of producing automobiles. Thus a change in the price of one factor of production will cause changes in the *relative* profitability of different lines of production; this will cause producers to shift from one line to another and so cause changes in the quantities of different commodities supplied.

The five hypotheses are not alternatives; they are a set of influences all of which are thought to affect the quantity of a commodity supplied. [2]

Quantity supplied depends on and changes with the goals of firms, technology, prices of commodities, and the prices of factors of production.

THE QUANTITY OF A COMMODITY SUPPLIED AND ITS OWN PRICE

Assume first that everything that affects the quantity supplied other than the commodity's own price is held constant. An intuitively plausible hypothesis is that the quantity of a commodity produced and offered for sale will increase as the price of the commodity rises and decrease as the price falls (i.e., quantity and price will vary directly with each other). This hypothesis has a strong commonsense appeal because the higher the price of the commodity, the greater the profits that can be earned—and thus the greater the incentive to produce the commodity and offer it for sale. The hypothesis is known to be correct in a large number of cases. For the time being, we shall assume it to be generally correct.

The supply schedule and the supply curve

The **supply schedule** is analogous to the demand schedule, but it reflects the quantities producers wish to sell rather than the quan-

Table 5–5 A supply schedule for carrots

	Price per ton p	Quantity supplied (thousands of tons per month) S
u	$ 20	5.0
v	40	46.0
w	60	77.5
x	80	100.0
y	100	115.0
z	120	122.5

This table shows the quantities that producers wish to sell at various prices, other things being equal. Row y of the table indicates that if the price were $100 per ton, producers would wish to sell 115,000 tons of carrots per month.

Figure 5–4 A supply curve for carrots

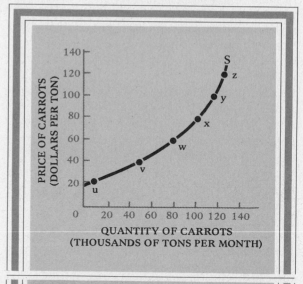

The supply curve relates quantity supplied to the price of the commodity; its upward slope indicates that quantity supplied increases as price increases. There are six points corresponding to the price-quantity combinations shown in Table 5–5. Each row in the table defines a point on the supply curve. The smooth curve drawn through all of the points and labeled S is the supply curve.

tities consumers wish to buy. Table 5–5 presents a hypothetical supply schedule for carrots. A **supply curve** is the graphic representation of the supply schedule and is illustrated in Figure 5–4. Once again, while each point on the supply curve merely represents a specific price-quantity combination, the whole curve shows more.

The whole supply curve is a representation of the complete relation between quantity supplied and price, other things being equal.

SHIFTS IN THE SUPPLY CURVE

As with demand, it is essential not to confuse a movement along the supply curve (caused by a change in price) and a shift in the entire curve (caused by a change in some influence other than price). To avoid confusion, the same terminology used with demand is adopted: **supply** refers to the whole relation between price and quantity supplied, and *quantity supplied* refers to a particular quantity actually supplied at a given price.

A shift in the supply curve means that at each price a different quantity will be supplied

than previously. An increase in the quantity supplied at each price is illustrated in Table 5–6 and graphed in Figure 5–5. This change appears as a rightward shift in the supply curve. In contrast, a decrease in the quantity supplied at each price would appear as a leftward shift. A shift in the supply curve must be the result of a change in one of the factors that influence the quantity supplied other than the commodity's own price. The major possible causes of such shifts are summarized in Figure 5–6.

An *increase or decrease in supply* refers to such shifts in the supply curve. In contrast an *in-*

Table 5–6 Two alternative supply schedules for carrots

	Price per ton p	Quantity supplied before cost-saving innovation (thousands of tons per month) S	Quantity supplied after the innovation (thousands of tons per month) S_1	
u	$ 20	5.0	28.0	u′
v	40	46.0	76.0	v′
w	60	77.5	102.0	w′
x	80	100.0	120.0	x′
y	100	115.0	132.0	y′
z	120	122.5	140.0	z′

A cost-saving innovation increases the quantity supplied at each price. As a result of the cost-saving innovation, quantity supplied at $100 per ton rises from 115,000 to 132,000 tons per month. A similar rise occurs at every price. Thus the supply schedule relating p and S is replaced by one relating p and S_1.

crease or decrease in quantity supplied refers to movements up or down the supply curve, respectively, in response to a change in the commodity's own price.

The determination of price by demand and supply

So far demand and supply have been considered separately. The next question is: How do these two forces interact to determine price in a competitive market? [3]

Table 5–7 brings together the demand and supply schedules from Tables 5–2 and 5–5. The quantities of carrots demanded and supplied at each price may now be compared; this is done in column 4 of Table 5–7.

Notice that there is only one price, $60 a ton, at which the quantity of carrots demanded equals the quantity supplied. At prices below $60 a ton there is a shortage of carrots because the quantity demanded exceeds the quantity supplied. This is often called a situation of **excess demand** or, what is the same thing, one of deficient supply. At

Figure 5–5 Two supply curves for carrots

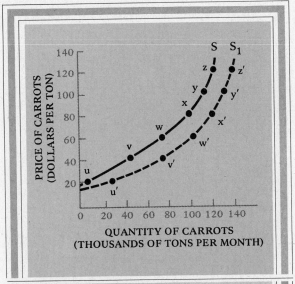

A rightward shift in the supply curve indicates an increase in the quantity supplied at each price. The points correspond to those in Table 5–6. A rightward shift in the supply curve indicates an increase in supply in the sense that more carrots are supplied at each price.

Figure 5–6 Shifts in the supply curve

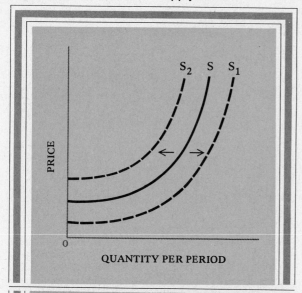

A shift in the supply curve from *S* to *S₁*, indicates an increase in supply; a shift from *S* to *S₂* indicates a decrease in supply. An increase in supply means more is supplied at each price. Such a rightward shift can be caused by some kinds of changes in producers' goals, improvements in technology, decreases in the prices of other commodities, and decreases in the prices of factors of production that are important in producing the commodity.

A decrease in supply means less is supplied at each price. Such a leftward shift can be caused by some kinds of changes in producers' goals, increases in the prices of other commodities, and increases in the prices of factors of production that are important in producing the commodity.

prices above $60 a ton there is a surplus of carrots because the quantity supplied exceeds the quantity demanded. This is called a situation of **excess supply** or one of deficient demand.

In order to discuss the determination of market price, suppose first that the price is $100 a ton. At this price, 115,000 tons would be offered for sale but only 62,500 tons would be demanded. There would be excess supply of 52,500 tons a month. It would not be surprising if sellers cut their prices in order to get rid of this surplus.

The tendency of sellers to cut prices when there is excess supply implies a downward pressure on prices.

Next consider the price of $20 a ton. At this price there is excess demand. The 5,000 tons produced each month get snapped up very quickly, and 105,000 tons of desired purchases cannot be made. Rivalry between would-be purchasers may lead to their offering more than the prevailing price in order to outbid other purchasers, and sellers, perceiving that they could have sold their available supplies many times over, may begin to ask a higher price for the quantities that they do have to sell.

The tendency for buyers to bid up prices when there is excess demand implies an upward pressure on prices.

Finally, consider a price of $60. At this price, producers wish to sell 77,500 tons a month and purchasers wish to buy that quantity. There is neither a shortage nor a surplus of carrots. There are no unsatisfied buyers to bid the price up, nor are there any unsatisfied sellers to force the price down. Once the price of $60 has been reached, therefore, there will be no tendency for it to change.

An equilibrium implies a state of rest, or balance, between opposing forces. The **equilibrium price** is the one toward which the actual market price will tend and the one that will persist once established, unless it is disturbed by some change in market conditions.

The price at which the quantity demanded equals the quantity supplied is called the equilibrium price.

This same story is told in graphic terms in Figure 5–7. The price of $60 is the equilib-

Table 5–7 Demand and supply schedules for carrots and equilibrium price

(1) Price per ton p	(2) Quantity demanded (thousands of tons per month) D	(3) Quantity supplied (thousands of tons per month) S	(4) Excess demand (+) Excess supply (−) (thousands of tons per month) D − S
$ 20	110.0	5.0	+105.0
40	90.0	46.0	+ 44.0
60	77.5	77.5	0.0
80	67.5	100.0	− 32.5
100	62.5	115.0	− 52.5
120	60.0	122.5	− 62.5

Equilibrium occurs where quantity demanded equals quantity supplied—where there is neither excess demand nor supply. These schedules are those of Tables 5–2 and 5–5. The equilibrium price is $60. For lower prices there is excess demand; for higher prices there is excess supply.

rium price because there is neither excess supply nor excess demand. All other prices are disequilibrium prices: They will not persist. If they do occur, the market will not be in a state of rest. At prices below the equilibrium, there will be shortages and rising prices; at prices above the equilibrium, there will be surpluses and falling prices.

The quantities demanded and supplied at any price can be read off the two curves, while the magnitude of the shortage or surplus is shown by the horizontal distance between the curves at each price. Inspection of the figure should make it clear visually that the equilibrium price occurs where the demand and supply curves intersect. Below that price there will be a shortage and hence an upward pressure on the existing price. Above it there will be a surplus and hence downward pressure on price. These pressures are represented by the colored vertical arrows in the figure.

THE "LAWS" OF SUPPLY AND DEMAND

Changes in any of the variables other than price that influence quantity demanded or supplied will cause a shift in either the supply curve or the demand curve (or both). There are four possible shifts: (1) a rise in demand (a

Figure 5–7 The determination of the equilibrium price of carrots

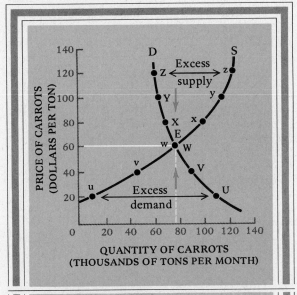

The equilibrium price corresponds to the point where demand and supply curves intersect. Point E indicates the equilibrium. At a price of $60, quantity demanded equals quantity supplied. At prices above equilibrium, there is excess supply and downward pressure on price. At prices below equilibrium, there is excess demand and upward pressure on price.

Laws, predictions, hypotheses

In what sense can the four propositions developed here be called "laws"? They are not like acts passed by Congress, interpreted by courts, and enforced by the police; they cannot be repealed if people do not like their effects. Nor are they like the laws of Moses, revealed to man by the voice of God. Are they "natural laws" similar to Newton's law of gravity? It was clearly this last sense that classical economists had in mind when they labeled them as laws, and it was Newton's laws that they had in mind as analogies.

The term *law* is used in science to describe a theory that has stood up to substantial testing. A law of this kind is not something that has been proven to be true for all times and all circumstances, nor is it regarded as immutable. As observations accumulate, laws may often be modified or the range of phenomena to which they apply may be restricted or redefined. Einstein's theory of relativity, for one example, forced such amendments and restrictions on Newton's laws.

The "laws" of supply and demand have stood up well to many empirical tests, but no one believes that they explain all market behavior. Indeed the range of markets over which they seem to meet the test of providing accurate predictions is now much smaller than it was 80 years ago. It is possible—though most economists would think it unlikely—that at some future time they would no longer apply to any real markets. They are thus laws in the sense that they predict certain kinds of behavior in certain situations and the predicted behavior occurs sufficiently often to lead people to continue to have confidence in the predictions of the theory. They are not laws—any more than are the laws of natural science—that are beyond being challenged by present or future observations that cast their predictions in doubt. Nor is it a heresy to question their applicability to any particular situation.

Laws, then, are hypotheses that have led to predictions that seem to account for observed behavior. They are theories that seem—in some circumstances at least—to have survived attempts to refute them and have proven useful. It is possible, in economics as in natural sciences, to be impressed both with the power of what we do know and with the awesome amount that we have yet to understand.

---

rightward shift in the demand curve); (2) a fall in demand (a leftward shift in the demand curve); (3) a rise in supply (a rightward shift in the supply curve); and (4) a fall in supply (a leftward shift in the supply curve).

To analyze the effects of any of these shifts we use the method known as **comparative statics.** We start from a position of equilibrium and then introduce the change to be studied. The new equilibrium position is determined and compared with the original one. The differences between the two positions of equilibrium must be due to the changes in the data that were introduced—for everything else has been held constant. The term is *comparative statics* because the method of analysis is to compare two positions of static equilibrium.

Figure 5–8 The "laws" of supply and demand

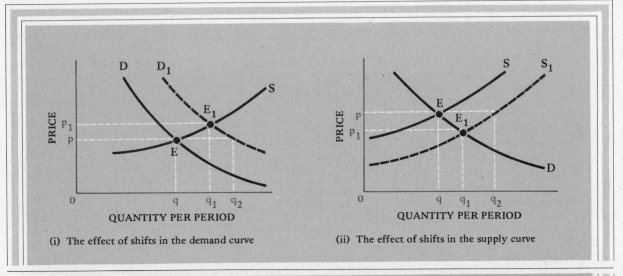

(i) The effect of shifts in the demand curve   (ii) The effect of shifts in the supply curve

The effects on equilibrium price and quantity of shifts in either demand or supply are called the laws of supply and demand.

A rise in demand. In (i) if demand rises from D to D_1, excess demand develops at price p. Price and quantity both rise to their new equilibrium values at E_1.

A fall in demand. In (i) if demand falls from D_1 to D, an excess supply develops at p_1. Price and quantity both fall to their new equilibrium values at E.

A rise in supply. In (ii) if supply rises from S to S_1, an excess supply develops at p. Price falls and quantity rises to their new equilibrium values at E_1.

A fall in supply. In (ii) if supply falls from S_1 to S, an excess demand develops at p_1. Price rises and quantity falls to their new equilibrium values at E.

Figure 5–8 shows the effects of these four shifts, which are the four so-called laws of supply and demand:[4]

1. A rise in demand causes an increase in both the equilibrium price and the equilibrium quantity bought and sold.

2. A fall in demand causes a decrease in both the equilibrium price and the equilibrium quantity bought and sold.

3. A rise in supply causes a decrease in the equilib-

rium price and an increase in the equilibrium quantity bought and sold.

4. A fall in supply causes an increase in the equilibrium price and a decrease in the equilibrium quantity bought and sold.

Summary

1. The amount of a commodity that households wish to purchase is called the quantity demanded. It is a flow expressed as so much per period of time. This quantity is determined by tastes, average household income, the size of population, the distribution of income among households, the price of the commodity, and the prices of other commodities.

[4] The detailed argument in each case follows that of pages 63–65 and Figure 5–7 as to what happens when supply does not equal demand. Be sure you understand the *market* behavior that gives rise to each of the four "laws" summarized here.

2. Quantity demanded is assumed to increase as the price of the commodity falls, *ceteris paribus.* The relationship between quantity demanded and price is represented graphically by a demand curve that shows how much will be demanded at each market price. A movement along a demand curve indicates a change in the quantity demanded in response to a change in the price of the commodity.

3. The demand curve shifts to the right (an increase in demand) if average income rises, if the price of a substitute rises, if the price of a complement falls, if population rises, or if there is a change in tastes in favor of the product. The opposite changes shift the demand curve to the left (a decrease in demand). A shift of a demand curve represents a change in the quantity demanded at each price and is referred to as a change in demand.

4. The amount of a commodity that firms wish to sell is called the quantity supplied. It is a flow expressed as so much per period of time. This quantity depends on the goals of firms, the state of technology, the price of the commodity, the prices of all other commodities, and the prices of factors of production.

5. Quantity supplied is assumed to increase as the price of the commodity increases, *ceteris paribus.* A movement along a supply curve indicates a change in the quantity supplied in response to a change in price.

6. The supply curve shifts to the right (an increase in supply) if the prices of other commodities fall, if the costs of producing the commodity fall, or if, for any reason, producers become more willing to produce the commodity. The opposite changes shift the supply curve to the left (a decrease in supply). A shift in the supply curve indicates a change in the quantity supplied at each price and is referred to as a change in supply.

7. The equilibrium price is the one at which the quantity demanded equals the quantity supplied. At any price below the equilibrium there will be excess demand while at any price above the equilibrium there will be excess supply. Graphically, equilibrium occurs where demand and supply curves cross.

8. Price is assumed to rise when there is a shortage and to fall when there is a surplus. Thus the actual market price will be pushed toward the equilibrium price, and when it is reached there will be neither shortage nor surplus and price will not change until either the supply curve or the demand curve shifts.

9. Using the method of comparative statics, the effects of a shift in either demand or supply can be predicted. A rise in demand raises both equilibrium price and quantity; a fall in demand lowers both. A rise in supply raises equilibrium quantity but lowers equilibrium price; a fall in supply lowers equilibrium quantity but raises equilibrium price. These are the so-called laws of supply and demand.

Concepts for review

Quantity demanded versus quantity exchanged
Demand schedules and demand curves
Quantity supplied versus quantity exchanged
Supply schedules and supply curves
Movements along a curve versus shifts in the curve
Changes in quantity demanded versus changes in demand
Changes in quantity supplied versus changes in supply
Equilibrium and equilibrium price
The determination of equilibrium
Comparative static analysis
The "laws" of supply and demand

Discussion questions

1. In the aftermath of the 1973 Arab-Israel war, the OPEC countries reduced production of oil by almost 10 percent. Show by supply and demand analysis the probable effect of this cutback on the price of oil. The subsequent gasoline shortage led to a decrease in demand for new gas-guzzling American cars and a surplus of them. What mechanisms operate to eliminate surpluses in a free market?

2. In July 1976 the Department of Agriculture predicted bumper crops of corn and wheat. But its chief economist, Don Paarlberg, warned consumers not to expect prices to decrease since the costs of production were rising and foreign demand for American crops was increasing. "The classic pattern of supply and demand won't work this time," Mr. Paarlberg said. Discuss his observation.

3. Explain each of the following in terms of changes in supply and demand.
a. DuPont increased the price of man-made fibers, although it acknowledged demand was weak.
b. Some of the first $10 Canadian Olympic coins were im-

perfectly stamped. Dealers and collectors are paying as much as $500 for these flawed pieces.

c. "Master Charge has replaced sugar-daddy," a Beverly Hills furrier said, explaining the rise in sales of mink coats.

d. The Edsel was a lemon when produced in 1958–1960 but is now a best seller among cars of its vintage.

e. When a frost hit the Florida citrus industry a spokesperson for the Israel citrus marketing board said Mediterranean producers would receive better prices for their crops everywhere in the world.

4. Suppose that tape recorder producers find that they are now able to sell more tape recorders at the same price than they did two years ago. Is this a shift of the demand curve or a movement along the curve? Suggest at least four separate reasons why this might occur.

5. What do you think would be the effect on the equilibrium price and quantity of marijuana of the legalization of its sale? What do you think would be the effect on the equilibrium prices of gold and paper if all the world's banks sold off their gold supplies and replaced them with paper certificates that were officially accepted as reserves?

6. The price of a color TV has dropped drastically over time. Would you explain this falling price in terms of demand or supply changes? What factors are likely to have caused the demand or supply shifts that did occur?

7. Classify the effect of each of the following as (a) a decrease in the demand for fish, (b) a decrease in the quantity of fish demanded, or (c) other. Illustrate each diagrammatically.

a. The government of Iceland bars fishermen of other nations from its waters.

b. People buy less fish because of a rise in fish prices.

c. The Roman Catholic Church relaxes its ban on eating meat on Fridays.

d. The price of beef falls and as a result households buy more beef and less fish.

e. In the interests of training marine personnel for national defense, the U.S. government decides to subsidize the American fishing industry.

f. It is discovered that eating fish is better for one's health than eating meat.

8. "The effect of price changes often eludes analysis. For example, two of the food groups that have shown absolute decreases in consumption per capita—flour and potatoes—have also shown decreases in price relative to the prices of all goods. Consumption of meat per capita has been rising in the face of an increase in relative prices." Do the changes elude your analysis? How would you reword the passage to make clear what you think did happen?

6

Elasticity of demand and supply

When flood damage led to major destruction of the onion crop, onion prices rose generally. In Hartford, Connecticut, they rose 42 percent in a week. Not surprisingly consumption fell. Very often it is not enough to know merely whether quantity rises or falls in response to a change in price; it is also important to know by how much. In this case, the press reported that the effect was to cause many consumers to stop using onions altogether and to substitute onion salt, sauerkraut, cabbage, and other products. Other consumers still bought onions but in reduced quantities. Overall consumption was down sharply. Were aggregate dollar sales of onions (price *times* quantity) higher or lower? The data above do not tell, but this is the sort of question that may matter a good deal. A government concerned with the effect of a partial crop failure on farm income will not be satisfied with being told that food prices will rise and quantities consumed will fall; it will need to know by approximately how much they will rise and fall if it is to assess the effects on farmers.

Demand elasticity

Consider a fall in the supply of carrots. The two parts of Figure 6–1 show the same leftward shift in the supply curve. Because the demand curves are different, the effects on equilibrium price and quantity are also different. In the first case, the quantity demanded varies greatly with price and a small rise in price restores equilibrium by removing the excess demand. In the second case, the quantity demanded is very insensitive to price changes and equilibrium is restored only when a large price rise has called forth the extra quantity necessary to satisfy the almost unchanged quantity demanded.

The difference may have great policy significance. Consider what would happen if the

Figure 6–1   The effect of the shape of the demand curve

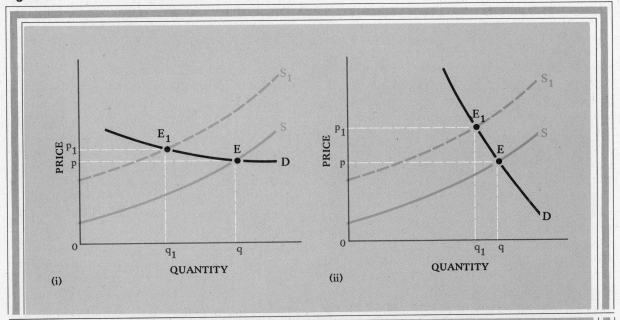

The flatter the demand curve, the less is the change in price and the greater is the change in quantity. Both parts of the figure show the same leftward shift in the supply curve. In each part, initial equilibrium is at price p and output q and the new equilibrium is at p_1 and q_1. In (i) the effect of the shift in supply from S to S_1 is a slight rise in the price and a large decrease in quantity. In (ii) the effect of the identical shift in the supply curve from S to S_1 is a large increase in the price and a relatively small decrease in quantity.

government persuaded farmers to produce more of a certain crop. (It might, for example, pay a subsidy to farmers for growing this crop.) If the government is successful, then at every possible price of the product there would be an increase in the quantity that farmers would be willing to produce. Thus the whole supply curve of the product would shift to the right. This may be illustrated in Figure 6–1 by assuming that the supply curve shifts from S_1 to S. Figure 6–1(i) illustrates a case in which the quantity that consumers demand is very sensitive to price changes. The extra production brings down price, but because the quantity demanded is very responsive, only a small change in price is necessary

in order to restore equilibrium. The effect of the government's policy, therefore, is to achieve a large increase in the production and sales of this commodity and only a small decrease in price. Figure 6–1(ii) illustrates a case in which the quantity demanded is quite unresponsive to price changes. As before, the increase in supply at the original price causes a surplus that brings price down. But this time the quantity demanded by consumers does not increase very much in response to the fall in price. Thus price continues to fall until, discouraged by lower and lower prices, farmers reduce the quantity supplied very nearly to the level attained before they received the increased incentive to produce. The effect of the government's policy is to bring about a large price fall and only a small increase in the quantity produced and sold.

In comparing the cases illustrated in Figure 6–1 it can be seen that the government's policy has exactly the same effectiveness as far as farmers' willingness to supply is concerned (the supply curve shifts are identical). But the effects on the equilibrium price and quantity are very different because of the different degrees to which the quantity demanded by consumers responds to price changes. If the purpose of the policy is to increase the quantity of this commodity produced and consumed, then the policy will be a great success when the demand curve is similar to the one shown in Figure 6–1(i) but it will be a failure when the demand curve is similar to the one shown in Figure 6–1(ii). If, however, the main purpose of the policy is to achieve a large reduction in the price of the commodity, the policy will be a failure when demand is as shown in (i) but it will be a great success when demand is as shown in (ii).

A shift in supply can have very different effects, depending on the shape of the demand curve.

PRICE ELASTICITY: A MEASURE OF THE RESPONSIVENESS OF QUANTITY DEMANDED TO PRICE CHANGES

When considering the responsiveness of the quantity demanded to changes in price, we may wish to make statements such as: "The demand for carrots was more responsive to price changes ten years ago than it is today," or "The demand for meat responds more to price changes than does the demand for green vegetables." In order to make such comparisons, a measure of the degree to which quantity demanded responds to changes in price is required.

In the previous examples it was possible to make comparisons between the two demand curves in Figure 6–1 on the basis of their geometrical steepness, because the curves were both drawn on the same scale. Thus, for any given price change, the quantity changes more on the flatter curve than it does on the steeper one. It can, however, be very misleading merely to inspect a *single* curve and to conclude from its general appearance something about the degree of responsiveness of quantity demanded to price changes. You can make a curve appear as steep or as flat as you like by changing the scales. For example, a curve that looks steep when the horizontal scale is 1 inch = 100 units will look much flatter when 1 inch = 1 unit if the same vertical scale is used in each case.

Instead of gaining a vague general impression from the shape of demand curves, one could note the actual change in quantity demanded in response to a certain price change. But it would still be impossible to compare degrees of responsiveness for different commodities.

Assume that we have the information shown in Table 6–1. Is it to be concluded that the demand for radios is not so responsive to price changes as the demand for beefsteak, because a cut in price of 20¢ gives quite a large increase in demand for beefsteak, whereas an equal price cut has very little effect on the demand for radios? There are two problems here. First, a reduction in price of 20¢ will be a large price cut for a low-priced commodity and an insignificant price cut for a high-priced commodity. The price reductions listed in

Table 6–1 Price reductions and corresponding increases in quantity demanded

Commodity	Reduction in price	Increase in quantity demanded
Beefsteak	$.20 per pound	7,500 pounds
Men's shirts	.20 per shirt	5,000 shirts
Radios	.20 per radio	100 radios

Table 6–2   Price and quantity information underlying data of Table 6–1

Commodity	Unit	Original price	New price	Average price	Original quantity	New quantity	Average quantity
Beefsteak	per pound	$ 1.70	$ 1.50	$ 1.60	116,250	123,750	120,000
Men's shirts	per shirt	8.10	7.90	8.00	197,500	202,500	200,000
Radio	per radio	40.10	39.90	40.00	9,950	10,050	10,000

These data provide the appropriate context of the data given in Table 6–1. The table relates the $.20 per unit price reduction of each commodity to the actual prices and quantities demanded.

Table 6–1 represent very different fractions of the total prices. Thus it is more revealing to know the percentage change in the price of the various commodities. Second, by an analogous argument, knowing the quantity by which demand changes is not very revealing unless the level of demand is also known. An increase of 7,500 tons is quite a significant reaction of demand if the quantity formerly bought was 15,000 tons, but it is only a drop in the bucket if the quantity formerly demanded was 10 million tons.

Table 6–2 shows the original and new levels of price and quantity. Changes in price and quantity expressed as percentages of the average prices and quantities are shown in the first two columns of Table 6–3.[1] **Elasticity of demand,** the measure of responsiveness of quantity demanded to price changes, is defined as

percentage change in quantity demanded
percentage change in price

When it is necessary to distinguish this

measure of elasticity from other related concepts it is sometimes referred to as "price elasticity of demand," since the variable causing the change in quantity demanded is the commodity's own price.

Interpreting numerical values of elasticity of demand

Because demand curves slope downward an *increase* in price is associated with a *decrease* in quantity demanded and vice versa. Thus, mathematically, the percentage changes in price and quantity have opposite signs and demand elasticity is a negative number. We shall follow the usual practice of ignoring the negative sign and speak of the measure as a positive number, as we have done in Table 6–3.

Table 6–3   The calculation of demand elasticities

Commodity	(1) Percentage decrease in price	(2) Percentage increase in quantity	(3) Elasticity of demand (2) ÷ (1)
Beefsteak	12.5	6.25	0.5
Men's shirts	2.5	2.5	1.0
Radios	0.5	1.0	2.0

Elasticity is the percentage change in quantity divided by the percentage change in price. The percentage changes are based on average prices and quantities shown in Table 6–2. For example, the $.20 per pound decrease in the price of beefsteak is 12.5 percent of $1.60. A $.20 change in the price of radios is only 0.5 percent of the average price of radios of $40.

[1] The use of averages is designed to avoid the ambiguity caused by the fact that, for example, the $.20 change in the price of beefsteak is a different percentage (11.8) of the original price, $1.70, than it is (13.3) of the new price, $1.50. We want the elasticity of demand between any two points (*A* and *B*) to be independent of whether we move from *A* to *B* or from *B* to *A*; as a result, using either "original" prices and quantities or "new" prices and quantities would be less satisfactory than using averages. In this illustration, $.20 is unambiguously 12.5 percent of $1.60 and applies to a price increase from $1.50 to $1.70, as well as to the decrease discussed in the text.

Thus, the more responsive the quantity demanded (radios relatively to beefsteak in the example), the greater the elasticity of demand

Figure 6–2   Elasticity along a straight-line demand curve

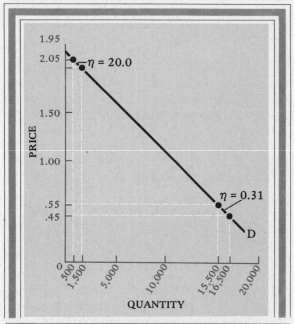

Moving down a straight-line demand curve, elasticity falls continuously. On this straight line, reduction in price of 10¢ always leads to the same increase (1,000 units) in quantity. Near the upper end of the curve, however, where price is $2 and quantity is 1,000 units, a reduction in price of 10¢ (from $2.05 to $1.95) is only a 5 percent reduction, but the 1,000-unit increase in quantity is a 100 percent increase. Elasticity, which is often symbolized by the Greek letter eta (η), is 20. At the price of 50¢ and quantity of 16,000 units, a price reduction of 10¢ (from 55¢ to 45¢) leads to the same 1,000-unit increase in demand. A 20 percent price decrease combines with a 6.25 percent quantity increase to give an elasticity of 0.31.

and the higher the measure (2.0 compared to 0.5). The numerical value of elasticity can vary from zero to infinity. Elasticity is zero if there is no change at all in quantity demanded when price changes, that is, when quantity demanded does not respond to a price change. The larger the elasticity, the larger is the percentage change in quantity for a given percentage change in price. As long as the elasticity of demand has a value of less than one, however, the percentage change in quantity is less than the percentage change in price. When elasticity is equal to one, then the two percentage changes are equal to each other. When the percentage change in quantity exceeds the percentage change in price, the value for the elasticity of demand is greater than one.

When the percentage change in quantity is less than the percentage change in price (elasticity less than one), the demand is said to be **inelastic.** When the percentage change in quantity is greater than the percentage change in price (elasticity greater than one), the demand is said to be **elastic.** This terminology is important, and you should become familiar with it.

A demand curve need not—and usually does not—have the same elasticity over every part of the curve. Figure 6–2 shows that a downward-sloping, straight-line demand curve does not have a constant elasticity. The only two cases in which a straight line does have constant elasticity are when it is vertical and when it is horizontal. Figure 6–3 illustrates three special cases.

Elasticity of demand and changes in total expenditure and total revenue

Money spent in purchasing a commodity is received by the sellers of the commodity. The total amount spent by purchasers is thus the gross revenue of the sellers. Often in economics it is vital to know how total expenditure by purchasers of a commodity or total gross receipts of sellers of the commodity (the same thing) reacts when the price of a product is changed.

What happens to total revenue depends on the relative size of the changes in price and quantity. The simplest example is sufficient to prove that total revenue may rise or fall in response to a price fall. Suppose 100 units of a commodity are being sold at a price of $1 and the price is then cut to 90¢. If the quantity sold rises to 101, the total revenue of the sellers falls from $100 to $90.90; but if quantity sold rises to 120, total revenue rises from $100 to $108.

In the example of radios, shirts, and beefsteak, note what happened in each case to total revenue when price fell. (These calculations are shown in Table 6–4.) In the case of beefsteak, the demand is inelastic and a cut in price lowered the revenue of sellers; in the case of radios, the demand is elastic and a cut in price raised the revenue earned by sellers. The borderline case is provided by men's shirts; here the demand elasticity is unity and the cut in price leaves total revenue unchanged.

These examples illustrate more general relationships:

1. If demand is elastic, a fall in price increases total expenditure and a rise in price reduces it.

Figure 6–3 Three demand curves

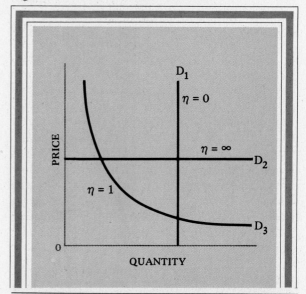

Each of these demand curves has constant elasticity. D_1 has *zero elasticity*: the quantity demanded does not change at all when price changes. D_2 has *infinite elasticity*: there exists a small price increase that decreases quantity demanded from an indefinitely large amount to zero. D_3 has *unit elasticity*: a given percentage increase in price brings an equal percentage decrease in quantity at all points on the curve.

Table 6–4 The changes in total revenue (total expenditure) for the example of Table 6–2

Commodity	Price × quantity originally	Price × quantity new prices and quantities	Change in revenue (expenditure)	Elasticity of demand from Table 6–3
Beefsteak	$ 197,625	$ 185,625	−$12,000	0.5
Men's shirts	1,599,750	1,599,750	0	1.0
Radios	398,995	400,995	+ 2,000	2.0

Whether revenue increases or decreases in response to a price cut depends on whether demand is elastic or inelastic. The $197,625 figure is the product of the original price of beefsteak ($1.70) and the original quantity (116,250 pounds). The $185,625 is the product of the new price ($1.50) and quantity (123,750), and so on.

2. If demand is inelastic, a fall in price reduces total expenditure and a rise in price increases it.

3. If elasticity of demand is unity, a rise or a fall in price leaves total expenditure unaffected.

Consider two real examples. When a bumper potato crop in the United States sent prices down 50 percent, quantity sold increased only 15 percent and potato farmers found their revenues falling sharply. Demand was clearly inelastic. When Salt Lake County's Utah Transit Authority cut its mass transit bus fares from 25 cents to 15 cents for the average journey, the volume of passenger traffic increased from 4.4 million to 14 million journeys within two years and revenues rose sharply. Demand was clearly elastic.

What determines elasticity of demand?

A great deal of work has been put into the measurement of demand elasticity, and in Chapter 9 we summarize some actual measurements. One of the most important determinants of elasticity is undoubtedly the degree of availability of close substitutes. Some commodities, such as margarine, cabbage, pork, and Fords, have quite close substitutes—butter, other green vegetables, beef, and similar makes of cars. A change in the price of these commodities, *the prices of the substitutes remaining constant,* can be expected to cause quite substantial substitution—a fall in price leading consumers to buy more of the commodity in question and a rise in price leading consumers to buy more of the substitute. Other commodities, such as salt, housing, and all vegetables taken together, have few, if any, satisfactory substitutes, and a rise in their price can be expected to cause a smaller fall in quantity demanded than would be the case if close substitutes were available.

To a great extent, elasticity depends on how widely or narrowly a commodity is being defined.

Food and shelter are necessities in the sense that life cannot go on without some min-imum quantity of them, and it is empirical fact that food as a whole has an inelastic demand over a large price range. It does not follow from this, however, that any one food, for example, white bread or cornflakes, is a necessity in the same sense. Thus there is no reason to believe that the quantity demanded for any one food cannot and will not fall greatly as a result of a rise in its price.

OTHER DEMAND ELASTICITIES

The purpose of measuring demand elasticity is to discover the degree to which the quantity demanded responds to a change in one of the factors that influence it. So far the response of the quantity of a commodity demanded to changes in the commodity's own price has been considered. It is also important to know how demand responds to changes in incomes and the prices of other goods.

Income elasticity of demand

The responsiveness of demand to changes in income is termed **income elasticity of demand** and is defined as

$$\frac{\text{percentage change in quantity demanded}}{\text{percentage change in income}}$$

For most goods, increases in income lead to increases in demand and income elasticity will be positive. These are called **normal goods.** Goods for which consumption decreases in response to a rise in income have negative income elasticities and are called **inferior goods.**

The income elasticity of normal goods may be less than unity (inelastic) or greater than unity (elastic), depending upon whether (say) a 10 percent increase in income leads to less than or more than a 10 percent increase in the quantity demanded. Not surprisingly, different commodities have different income elasticities (as the studies examined in Chapter 9 show). Goods that consumers at a given level of income regard as necessities tend to have lower income elasticities than do luxuries, for the obvious reason that as incomes rise it becomes possible for households to devote a smaller proportion of their income to meeting basic needs and a larger proportion to buying things they have always wanted but could not afford.

The reaction of demand to changes in income is extremely important. In most Western economies we know that economic growth is causing the level of total income to double every 20 to 30 years. This rise in income is shared to some extent by most of the households in the country. As they find their income increasing, they increase their demand for most commodities. But the demand for some commodities such as food and basic clothing will not increase very much as income rises, while the demand for other commodities increases rapidly as income rises. In much of western Europe the demand for durable goods is increasing most rapidly as household incomes rise, while in the United States it is the demand for services that is rising most rapidly. The uneven impact of the growth of income on the demand for different commodities has very important effects on the economy and groups in it, and these will be studied at several different points in this book.

The income elasticity of a particular good is expected to be different at widely different income levels. Consider how a family's diet may change as its income level rises. When incomes are very low, households may eat virtually no meat and consume lots of starchy foods such as bread and potatoes; at higher levels, they may eat the cheaper cuts of meat and more green vegetables along with their bread and potatoes; at yet higher levels they are likely to eat more (and more expensive) meat, to substitute frozen for canned vegetables, and to eat a greater variety of foods. In this sequence the income elasticity of hamburger may be high at low levels of income but decrease as income rises and steak replaces

hamburger. Different commodities will show different patterns. Potatoes are likely to exhibit low income elasticity while steak proves income-elastic over a wide range of income.[2] Figure 6–4 shows one particular pattern of income elasticity varying with income.[3]

Cross elasticity

The responsiveness of demand to changes in the prices of other commodities is called **cross elasticity of demand.** It is defined as

$$\frac{\text{percentage change in quantity demanded of one good, } X}{\text{percentage change in price of another good, } Y}$$

Cross elasticity can vary from minus infinity to plus infinity. Complementary goods will have negative cross elasticities and substitute goods will have positive cross elasticities. Bread and butter, for example, are complements; a fall in the price of bread will lead to an increase in the consumption of both commodities. The changes in the price of bread and the quantity of butter demanded will have opposite signs. Butter and margarine, on the other hand, are substitutes. A fall in the price of butter will increase the quantity of butter consumed but reduce the quantity of

---

[2] It is common to use the terms *income-elastic* and *income-inelastic* to refer to income elasticities of greater or less than unity. See the box on page 79.

[3] The curve in Figure 6–4, like the demand curve studied in Chapter 5, shows the relation of quantity demanded to *one* variable, *ceteris paribus*. This time the variable is income instead of price. (An increase in price of the commodity, incomes remaining constant, would shift downward the curve shown in Figure 6–4.)

In this chart, in contrast to the ordinary demand curve, quantity demanded is on the vertical axis. This follows the usual practice of putting the to-be-explained variable (called the dependent variable) on the vertical axis and the explanatory variable (called the independent variable) on the horizontal axis. It is the ordinary demand curve that has the axes "backwards." This practice dates back to Alfred Marshall's *Principles of Economics* (1890), the classic that is the foundation stone of modern price theory. [4] For better or worse Marshall's scheme is now used by everybody—although mathematicians never fail to wonder at this further example of the odd ways of economists.

Figure 6–4   An income-consumption curve relating quantity demanded to level of income

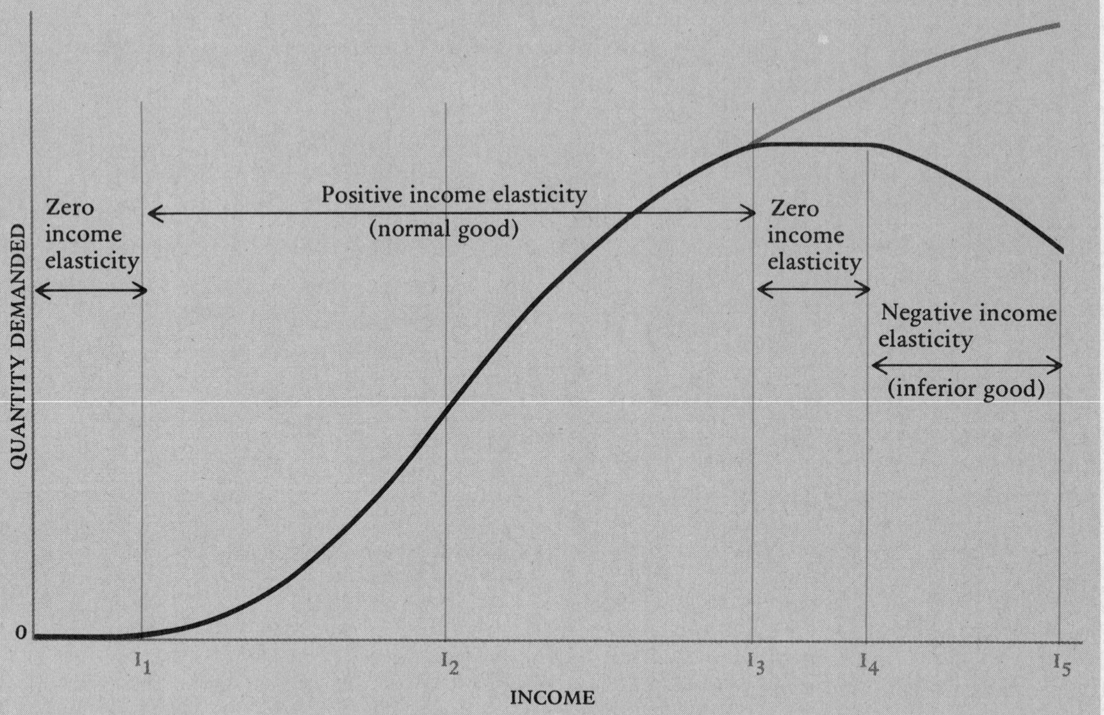

Different shapes of the curve relating quantity demanded to income correspond to different ranges of income elasticity.   The product whose income-consumption curve is shown by the heavy curve is a normal good for incomes up to I_4 and an inferior good above I_4. Whenever the curve is horizontal (from 0 to I_1 and from I_3 to I_4) income elasticity is zero. Between I_1 and I_2 quantity demanded is rising proportionally more rapidly than income (income elasticity greater than plus unity); between I_2 and I_3 quantity demanded is rising but less than proportionally (income elasticity greater than zero, less than unity). Different commodities will have different patterns: For example, if the income-consumption curve for some commodity was the heavy curve to I_3 and the screened curve thereafter, that commodity would not be an inferior good at any level of income.

margarine consumed. The changes in the price of butter and in the quantity of margarine will, therefore, have the same sign.

Measures of cross elasticity sometimes prove helpful in defining whether similar products should be considered to be in the same market. Some examples that have proved important in antitrust cases include glass bottles and metal cans for beer (high cross elasticity), men's shoes and women's shoes (low cross elasticity), coal and gas (high in some uses, low in others).

Nomenclature of elasticity

TERMINOLOGY	NUMERICAL MEASURE OF ELASTICITY	VERBAL DESCRIPTION
A. Price elasticity of demand [supply]		
Perfectly (or completely) inelastic	Zero	Quantity demanded [supplied] does not change as price changes
Inelastic	Greater than zero, but less than one	Quantity demanded [supplied] changes by a smaller percentage than does price
Unit elasticity	One	Quantity demanded [supplied] changes by exactly the same percentage as does price
Elastic	Greater than one, but less than infinity	Quantity demanded [supplied] changes by a larger percentage than does price
Perfectly (or infinitely) elastic	Infinity	Purchasers [sellers] are prepared to buy [sell] all they can at some price and none at all at an even slightly higher [lower] price
B. Income elasticity of demand		
Inferior Good	Negative	Quantity demanded decreases as income increases
Normal Good	Positive	Quantity demanded increases as income increases:
Income inelastic	Greater than zero, less than one	less than in proportion to income increase
Income elastic	Greater than one	more than in proportion to income increase
C. Cross elasticity of demand		
Substitute	Positive	Price increase of a substitute leads to an increase in quantity demanded of this good (and less of substitute)
Complement	Negative	Price increase of a complement leads to a decrease in quantity demanded of this good (and also less of the complement)

Elasticity of supply

The **elasticity of supply** measures the responsiveness of the quantity supplied to a change in price; it is defined as

percentage change in quantity supplied
percentage change in price

A rising supply curve has a positive elasticity of supply. If the supply curve is vertical—the quantity supplied does not change as price changes—elasticity of supply is zero. This would be the case, for example, if suppliers produced a given quantity and dumped it on the market for whatever it would bring. A horizontal supply curve has an infinitely high elasticity of supply: A small drop in price would reduce the quantity producers are willing to supply from an indefinitely large amount to zero. Between these two extremes elasticity of supply will vary with the shape of the supply curve.[4]

Supply elasticities are very important for many problems in economics. The brevity of the treatment here reflects two main facts: first, that much of the treatment of demand elasticity carries over to the case of supply and does not need repeating; second, that there will be more about the determinants of supply elasticity in Part Four. In the meantime it should be noted that supply elasticity depends to a great extent on how costs behave as output is varied. If costs of production rise rapidly as output rises, then the stimulus to expand production in response to a price rise will quickly be choked off by increases in costs. In this case supply will tend to be rather inelastic. If, however, costs rise only slowly as production increases, a rise in price that raises profits will call forth a large increase in quantity supplied before the rise in costs puts a halt to the expansion in output. In this case supply will tend to be rather elastic.

Summary

1. Elasticity of demand (also called *price elasticity*) is a measure of the extent to which the quantity demanded of a commodity responds to a change in its price. We define it as the percentage change in quantity divided by the percentage change in price that brought it about. Elasticity is here defined to be a positive number that varies from zero to infinity.

2. When the numerical measure of elasticity is less than one, demand is *inelastic.* This means that the percentage change in quantity is less than the percentage change in price that brought it about. When the numerical measure exceeds unity, demand is *elastic.* This means that the percentage change in quantity is greater than the percentage change in price that brought it about.

3. Elasticity and total revenue of sellers are related in this way: If elasticity is less than unity, a fall in price lowers total revenue; if elasticity is greater than unity, a fall in price raises total revenue; and if elasticity is unity, total revenue does not change as price changes.

4. The main determinant of the price elasticity of demand is the availability of substitutes for the commodity. The more and better the substitutes, the higher the elasticity.

5. Income elasticity is the percentage change in quantity demanded divided by the percentage change in income that brought it about. The income elasticity of demand for a commodity may well change as income varies. For example, a commodity that has a high income elasticity at a low income (because increases in income bring it within reach of the typical household) may have a low or negative income elasticity at higher incomes (because with further rises in incomes it can be replaced by a superior substitute).

6. Cross elasticity is the percentage change in quantity demanded divided by the percentage change in the price of some other commodity that brought it about.

7. Elasticity of supply is an important concept in economics. It measures the ratio of the percentage change in the quantity supplied of a commodity to the percentage change in its price. It is the analogue on the supply side of the elasticity of demand.

[4] Steepness, which relates to absolute rather than percentage changes, is *not* always a reliable guide. As is proven in the appendix to this chapter, which begins on page 865, any upward-sloping straight line through the origin has an elasticity of +1.0 over its entire range.

8. An appendix to this chapter, for students with some mathematical background, extends the analysis. It begins on page 865.

Concepts for review

Elasticity of demand
Significance of elastic and inelastic demands
Income elasticity of demand
Normal goods and inferior goods
Cross elasticity of demand
Elasticity of supply

Discussion questions

1. What, if anything, does each of the following newspaper quotations tell you about elasticity of demand?
a. "Ridership always went up when bus fares came down, but the increased patronage never was enough to prevent a decrease in overall revenue."
b. "Cutting air fares by use of the no-frills fare will be profitable only if it excludes the must-go-anyway traveler."
c. "When the Cincinatti Telephone Company started charging for directory-assistance calls, the number of [such] calls dropped 80 percent."
d. "The increase in postal rates from 8¢ to 13¢ has led us [The Naragansett Electric Co.] to have 60 percent of our bills hand delivered instead of mailed."
e. "Coffee to me is an essential—you've gotta have it."

2. It is being proposed to the Securities and Exchange Commission that brokerage commissions charged to investors be changed in order to help brokerage houses increase their revenues and thereby help avoid bankruptcy. In which direction should they be changed to meet the objective?

3. What would you predict about the relative price elasticity of demand of (a) food, (b) meat, (c) beef, (d) chuck roast, (e) Safeway chuck roast? What would you predict about their relative income elasticities?

4. The price of gasoline recently doubled and is expected to remain high.
a. How would you have expected demand to respond the first month or so after the price rise?
b. How would you expect demand to respond after several years?

5. If the elasticity of demand for railroad passenger travel is unity in the neighborhood of present prices and the railroads are losing money on their passenger traffic, how (if at all) can they make their passenger service profitable?

6. Consider the demand for margarine expressed in this quotation: "We always buy Fleischmann's now—I don't even have butter in the house. In the beginning it was the price, now I don't even consider that. We're very cholesterol conscious in our family." Interpret this in terms of elasticity of demand for butter and for margarine.

7. What elasticity measure or measures would be useful in answering the following questions?
a. Will cheaper transport into the central city help keep downtown shopping centers profitable?
b. Will raising the bulk-rate postage rate increase or decrease the postal deficit?
c. Are toothpaste and mouthwash in the same market?
d. Will an increase in gas field prices solve the natural gas shortage within a decade?

7

Supply and demand in action: price controls and agricultural problems

The spring of 1973 was one of the wettest in American history; the excessive rainfall and flooding diminished the size of many crops. The destruction of a large part of the California lettuce crop sent lettuce prices from about 39¢ a head to 69¢ in a two-week period; as a result, the quantity demanded was reduced to the available supply. Many shoppers who had ignored an earlier "political" boycott of lettuce now spent more on tomatoes and cottage cheese and refused to buy lettuce in the stores. Lettuce seed sales spurted as many American families planted their own lettuce in their backyards.

The winter and spring of 1976 were mild and warm, and the good weather generated bumper crops of fruits in California, where more than half of America's fruit crop—and virtually all of the crop used for canning—is grown. At prevailing prices the State Director of Food and Agriculture predicted 100,000 tons of unsold peaches, 50,000 tons of unsold pears, and similar surpluses of apricots, cherries, and nectarines. California's canneries would take the surplus fruit but only at sharply reduced prices, prices that meant lowered incomes for fruit growers.

While growers cursed a bountiful nature, consumers stood to benefit—until a trucker's strike made much of the crop undeliverable to the canneries and thus unsalable. A hastily organized coalition of fruit growers spent $1 million advertising fresh fruit in 47 cities. Growers were willing to incur both advertising and shipping costs in order to realize even a small net revenue from their surplus crops. Consumers lucky enough to live within driving distance of orchards could buy bushels of fruit at a small fraction of the prices they had paid a year earlier. These examples suggest why even the simple theory of supply and demand is so useful. Fluctuations in the supply of perishable products had just the effects economic theory predicts for products with inelastic demands.

The simple theory of supply and demand

also can explain more indirect and complex chains of effects. When weather conditions destroyed 80 percent of the U.S. soybean crop in a year when most other grains were also in somewhat short supply, a series of indirect but predictable results occurred. Soybeans have long been a primary ingredient of chicken feed for the mass-production broiler chicken industry. The decrease in supply of soybeans (a leftward shift of the supply curve) caused the price of soybeans to triple in a two-month period. Chicken farmers found the cost of a key input rising so fast that it did not pay to continue feeding baby chicks. Millions of them were simply killed and many more millions were not allowed to hatch. This led to a decrease in the supply of chickens (a leftward shift in the supply curve of chickens) and a rise in the price of chickens to households. In an attempt to increase the supply of soybeans available for chicken feed and thereby stem the rise in chicken prices, the U.S. government restricted exports of soybeans to Japan and other countries. This helped some—in the United States. In Japan, where imported soybeans are a staple of the human diet, a food shortage loomed and prices of soybeans soared. For many Japanese an already marginal diet became inadequate until alternative food supplies were secured. The failure of the U.S. soybean crop can be charted in the Japanese demographic statistics: a higher death rate and a lower marriage rate in the year of the failure and in the subsequent year.

In this chapter we use the laws of supply and demand and the method of comparative statics to derive predictions about some real-world problems and policies. The method, it will be recalled, is to start from a position of equilibrium—say, in the market for soybeans—and then introduce the change to be studied—for example, a shift to the left of the supply curve. Then we determine the new equilibrium position and compare it with the original one. The differences between the two positions of equilibrium (higher price, lower quantities actually exchanged) can be attributed to the change introduced, for that is the only change that has been allowed to occur.

This method will give correct predictions provided that in the real world prices and quantities move fairly quickly from one equilibrium toward another when some disturbing force, such as a crop failure, upsets the initial situation.

Price controls

SETTING MAXIMUM PRICES

It is common in wartime, and increasingly frequent in peacetime, for governments to fix maximum prices at which some goods and services may be sold. The Nixon administration, in its struggle with inflation, placed upper limits on prices and wages for a three-month period in 1971 and on prices for a two-month period in 1973. Although frequently referred to as fixed or frozen prices, most price controls specify the highest permissible price, often called the **price ceiling;** producers may legally charge that price or less.

If the ceiling price is set above the equilibrium price, the intervention will have no effect because the equilibrium price will still be attainable and the market equilibrium will in no way be inconsistent with the maximum-price law. If, however, the ceiling price is set at a level below the equilibrium one, the actual price must be reduced. The forced reduction of the price will cause a reduction in the quantity supplied, an increase in the quantity demanded, and a shortage of the commodity. This is illustrated in Figure 7–1. A first prediction of the effect of price control in a competitive market is:

If a maximum price is set below the equilibrium price, excess demand for the commodity will develop and the quantity exchanged will fall below its equilibrium amount.

Allocating a commodity in short supply

What happens to the excess demand that effective price ceilings produce? Price is not allowed to rise so as to allocate the available supply among the would-be purchasers, which is the normal free-market way of eliminating excess demand. It follows that some other method of allocation will have to be adopted. The theory does not predict what this other method will be, but experience has shown that certain alternatives are likely to arise. If stores sell their available supplies on a first-come-first-served basis, people are likely to rush to those stores that are rumored to have supplies of any commodity of which there is a severe shortage. In Europe during World War II, the rumor that a shop was selling supplies of some very scarce commodity could cause a local stampede. Buyers often spent days tracking down such a rumor and then hours in line, waiting to get into the shop. Usually the supplies were exhausted long before all were served.

Another system may develop if storekeepers themselves decide who will get the scarce commodities and who will not. Goods may be kept under the counter and sold only to regular customers. This happened in the fall of 1973 when gasoline supplies were cut short by the Arab oil embargo but prices were kept well below the equilibrium level. Gas station operators chose in many cases to sell only to regular customers. Given such power, sellers may do more than restrict sales to established customers; they might decide to sell only to people of a particular race or religion. All kinds of rules can be adopted. When sellers decide to whom they will sell and to whom they will not sell, allocation is by sellers' preferences.

If the government dislikes the somewhat arbitrary system of allocation that grows up, it can ration the good. Under rationing one must provide a ration coupon, along with money, to purchase the commodity. The government prints only enough coupons to match the available supplies and distributes them to households. The coupons might be distributed equally among the population, or they might be distributed on the basis of age, sex, marital status, number of dependents, or any other criterion that the authorities wish to adopt. Rationing substitutes the central authorities' preferences for the sellers' preferences in allocating the price-controlled commodity.

Figure 7–1   An effective price ceiling and black market pricing

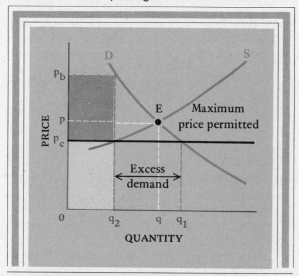

A ceiling price below the equilibrium price causes excess demand. Equilibrium price is at p. If a price ceiling is set at p_c, the quantity demanded will rise to q_1 and the quantity supplied will fall to q_2. Quantity q_1q_2 will be excess demand, but price may not legally rise. How many sellers allocate q_2 units among q_1 units demanded? If all of the output q_2 is sold on a black market, price to consumers would rise to p_b, with black marketeers earning illegal receipts shown by the darker shaded area.

Rationing commonly accompanies wartime price ceilings because of the tendency for other allocation schemes, such as first-come–first-served or allocation by sellers' preferences, to seem unfair and not in the spirit of wartime sharing of sacrifices.

Black markets

Ceiling prices, with or without rationing, are likely to give rise to black markets. A **black market** is one in which goods are sold illegally at prices above the legal maximum price. For many products there are only a few large producers but a great many retailers and, although it is easy to police the producers, it is difficult to locate all those who are, or could be, retailing the product, much less to police *them*. Although the central authorities may be able to control the price that producers get for their product, they may not be able effectively to control the price at which retailers sell to the public. What would you expect to happen in this case? The amount produced would remain unchanged because the producers would continue to receive the controlled price for their product. At the retail level, however, the opportunity for a black market would arise because purchasers would be willing to pay more than the ceiling price for the limited amounts of the commodity that were available. The theory of supply and demand leads to this prediction:

The potential for a profitable black market always exists when effective price ceilings are imposed because it will pay someone to buy at the controlled price and sell at the black-market price.

Figure 7–1 illustrates the limiting case in which all of the available supply is sold on a black market. The development of a black market depends on there being a few people willing to risk heavy penalties by running a black-market supply organization and a reasonably large number of persons prepared to purchase goods illegally on such a market. Because there are honest people in every society and because the central authorities usually have considerable power to enforce their price laws, it is more likely that some of the limited supplies would be sold at the controlled price and some, rather than all, at a black market price.

Actually predicting the existence or extent of a black market requires an assumption about people's willingness to break the law. It is an interesting comment on human nature that a case has never been documented in which effective price ceilings were not accompanied by the growth of a black market.

Does the development of a black market mean that the goals sought by imposing a price ceiling have been thwarted? This can be evaluated only when one knows what objectives the government hopes to achieve with its ceiling price. If the government is mainly concerned with an equitable division of a scarce product, it is likely that effective price control on manufacturers plus an effective black market at the retail level will produce the worst possible results. If, however, the government is interested mainly in restricting the total supply available for consumption in order to release resources for other more urgent needs such as war production, the policy works effectively although, many will feel, somewhat unfairly. Where the purpose is to keep prices down, the policy is a success to the extent that goods are sold at the controlled prices and a failure to the extent that they are sold at black-market prices.

There is much evidence confirming these predictions. Practically all belligerent countries in both World War I and World War II introduced schemes setting ceilings on prices well below free-market equilibrium levels. These schemes were always followed by shortages, then by either the introduction of rationing or the growth of some method of allocation such as allocation by sellers' preferences, and finally by the rise of a black market. These schemes were more effective in limiting consumption than in controlling prices, although they did restrain price increases because the patriotic response of many people to wartime controls led them to do without rather than patronize the black market.

Peacetime price controls, for the purpose of keeping prices down, have been much less successful in achieving their objective. The American experience with meat prices in 1973 is a dramatic case in point. Prices were con-

Rent control in Paris★

A dollar a month will pay a wage-earner's rent in Paris.† Such cheapness is amazing. Rent is reckoned as equal in cost to transport to and from work. To put it another way, a month's rent for a large family of six costs as much as eleven packets of cigarettes. Parisians spend on entertainment every month far more than they pay for three month's rent.

Even in a very modest budget such an expenditure absorbs but a small part of income. On average, rent makes up 1.4 percent of a wage-earner's expenditures. Such low rents are not a privilege confined to wage-earners. Rent seldom rises above 4 percent of any income; frequently it is less than 1 percent.

This may seem a very desirable state of affairs. It has its drawbacks. While you pay no more than these quite ridiculous prices if you are lucky enough to be in possession of a flat, if you are searching for lodgings you cannot find them at any price. *There are no vacant lodgings,* nor is anyone going to vacate lodgings which cost so little, nor can the owners expel anyone. Deaths are the only opportunity.

★ This account is excerpted from a longer paper entitled "No Vacancies" first published in the United States in 1948 and reprinted in F. A. Hayek, et al., *Rent Control—A Popular Paradox* (Vancouver B.C., The Fraser Institute, 1976) pp. 105–112. The author, Bertrand de Jouvenal, is a noted French author and journalist.

† All prices are in terms of 1946 dollars. To think of them in 1976 terms, multiply by three.

Young couples must live with in-laws, watching out for deaths. Tottering old people out to sun themselves will be shadowed back to their flat by an eager young wife who will strike a bargain with the *concierge,* so as to be first warned when the demise occurs. Other apartment-chasers have an understanding with the undertakers.

There are two ways of obtaining an apartment which death has made available. Legally, you may obtain from a public authority a requisition order: you will usually find that the same order for the same apartment has been given to other candidates. The illegal method is the surest: deal with the heir, and with his complicity immediately carry in some pieces of your furniture. As soon as you are in, you are king of the castle.

Buying one's way into an apartment will cost anything from $500 to $1,500 per room. At such prices wage-earners may as well give up hope of setting up house; they will have to stay with their families.

In short, rents are very low but there are no lodgings available. Nor are any being built—practically none have been built for the last 12 years.

There are some 84,000 buildings for habitation in Paris: 23,000 were built before 1850; 48,000 before 1880; 75,000 were built before World War I.

Sixteen thousand buildings are in such a state of disrepair that there is nothing that

trolled, but producers held beef off the market and a notable beef shortage occurred. Even professional football teams were forced to add lasagna to the training table menus. A black market in meat developed for those with money and a disposition to evade the law. Some of those without money, or at least not prepared to spend it on meat, engaged in what was reported as a great increase in illegal hunting for deer.

can be done but pull them down. Nor are the remainder altogether satisfactory. To go into sordid details, 82 percent of Parisians have no bath or shower, more than half must go out of their lodgings to find a lavatory, and a fifth do not even have running water. Little more than one in six of existing buildings is pronounced in good condition by the public inspectors. Lack of repair is ruining even these.

Owners can hardly be blamed. They are not in a financial position to keep up their buildings, let alone improve them. To take an example, here is a lady who owns three buildings containing 34 apartments, all inhabited by middle-class families. Her net loss from the apartments, after taxes and repairs, is $80 a year. Not only must her son put her up and take care of her, but he must also pay out the $80. She cannot sell; there are no buyers.

When the owner tries to cut down the repairs, he runs great risks. One postponed repairs on his roofs and rain filtering into an apartment spoiled a couple of armchairs. He was sued for damages and condemned to pay a sum amounting to three years of the tenant's paltry rent.

The miserable condition of owners is easily explained. While rents since 1914 have multiplied 6.8 times, taxes have grown 13.2 times and the cost of repairs has increased from 120 to 150 times the 1914 price!

A "right" has developed, the "right" to dig in. The French now have struck roots in their rented lodgings. One cannot allow the owner to dispossess tenants, because in that case he might so easily make an agreement secretly with a new tenant: rent control implied necessarily the denial of the owner's right to evict. The tenant's right to retain possession has been confirmed and the rent is raised slightly from time to time.

If a builder were now to put up flats similar to those in existence, these new apartments would have to be let for prices representing 10 times present rent ceilings, in order to reward the costs of construction and the capital invested. As long as the rents of existing buildings are held down artificially far below costs, it will be psychologically impossible to find customers at prices 10 times higher, and hence construction will not be undertaken.

Such is the differential between the legal and the economic price of lodgings that even the most fervent advocates of freedom are scared at the prospect of a return to it. They feel that if the right to dismiss tenants and the right to bargain and contract with them were restored, evictions could not be executed, the whole nation of tenants sitting down to nullify the decision. The thing, they say, has now gone too far, the price of rent is too far removed from the cost.

Figure 7–2 An effective price floor

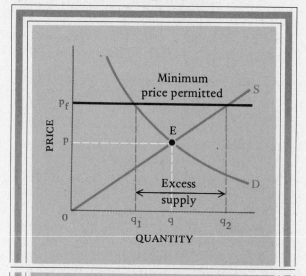

A minimum price above the equilibrium price causes excess supply. Equilibrium price is p. If a minimum price is set at p_f, there will be an excess of quantity supplied over the quantity demanded. Suppliers would like to sell q_2, but purchasers are only willing to buy q_1 at p_f. At the minimum price the actual quantity sold is only q_1. Sellers may seek ways to evade the minimum price and sell more at lower prices.

Perhaps the most extensively studied form of maximum price control concerns rentals of houses and apartments for private use. Such rent control schemes have usually produced shortages, private-allocation systems, and a black market. For example, in order to make up the difference between the controlled rent and the free-market rent, the landlord may charge the new tenant a grossly inflated sum for a few shabby sticks of furniture. When long continued, rent controls have tended to discourage building of new rental housing. (This rent-control-induced shortage led Professors Stigler and Friedman to point to the conflict between "ceilings" and "roofs.")

SETTING MINIMUM PRICES

Governments sometimes pass laws stating that certain goods and services cannot be sold below some minimum price, known as a **price floor.** In the United States there were once resale-price maintenance and fair-trade laws that limited the ability of retailers to sell below prices set by the manufacturers. Before reading on, ask yourself what the theory predicts about the effects of such minimum-price legislation.

This case is illustrated in Figure 7–2. If the minimum price is set below the equilibrium price, it has no effect on the market and the attainment of the free-market equilibrium and the fulfillment of the minimum-price law are perfectly compatible. But if the price floor is set above the equilibrium, the free-market equilibrium will be legally unattainable and the actual price will be higher. At that price there will be an excess of the quantity supplied over the quantity demanded. The prediction thus is:

If a minimum price is set above the equilibrium price, a surplus of the commodity will develop and the quantity exchanged will fall below its equilibrium level.

In this case there is a shortage of purchasers, not of the commodity, at the minimum price. Potential suppliers may compete in various ways for the available customers. Sellers will seek ways to cut prices; some will find loopholes in the law and others will merely flout it. In states that enforced fair-trade laws, discount houses became "buying clubs" in which one could purchase a life membership for a dollar. There is no opportunity for a set of black-market operators to take over the distribution of the product because there is nothing to be gained by buying at the controlled price and selling at the free-market price.

In 1975 Congress repealed the legislation authorizing fair-trade laws (minimum-price legislation) by the states, but legally established federal minimum prices survive today both in the form of minimum wage laws and in the form of agricultural policies to provide price supports.

Minimum wages

Most countries have minimum-wage laws. In the United States, federal minimum-wage legislation was introduced in the 1930s to cover the portion of the labor force that is engaged either directly in interstate commerce or in the production of goods for interstate commerce. In 1976 the federal minimum wage was $2.30 per hour and it covered over 75 percent of the labor force in the nongovernment sector; farm workers are also covered, but at a lower wage rate, $2.00 per hour in 1976. A minimum wage may be thought of as a price floor for a service. Assuming a competitive labor market with a downward-sloping demand curve and a rising supply curve, the analysis of Figure 7–2 can be used to illustrate the effects of a minimum wage.

Consider a minimum-wage law in an industry.

1. Where the law is effective, it will raise the wage rates of those who remain in employment.

2. It will lower the actual amount of employment in the industry.

3. It will create a surplus of labor that would like to but cannot obtain jobs in the industry affected.

4. It will create an incentive for some workers to try to evade the law by offering to work at wages below the legal minimum.

There is ample evidence confirming these predictions.[1]

Notice how many predictions the simple theory of demand and supply yields about the effects of price and wage controls. Most of these predictions have been shown to be accurate. It is interesting—and a little depressing,

too—to see how often legislators the world over are prepared to pass price-control laws without showing much appreciation of the likely effects of such measures.

There is, of course, nothing in the analysis to suggest that controls should never be used or that they will never work. But a strong possibility of unintended and undesired consequences may be difficult to guard against.

The problems of agriculture

The "farm problem" has been one of the most challenging (and troubling) for U.S. policy makers for half a century. Less than 9 million people—4.2 percent of the population—lived on farms in 1975, and they earned 3.6 percent of all personal income. Of this income, only 52 percent was from farm sources. Farm employment was 4 percent of national employment, but income earned by farmers from farming was only about 2 percent of personal income. Thus in 1975 farmers, farm operators, and farm workers lagged behind the rest of the population in earning power.

This situation alone makes the farmers' problems important. Farmers are a major political force in a large number of states. They wield a political influence (especially in the Senate) disproportionate to their numbers. Over the last three decades the government has tried a wide variety of farm policies: "parity," "production controls," "crop insurance," and "price supports" are terms that are constantly seen in the press.

The farm problem is interesting because of the importance of farmers in American life. It is also important because the key features of it—sharply fluctuating prices that are outside the producer's control, inelastic demand curves, and a low income elasticity of demand in a society that is exhibiting steady growth—are found singly and in various combinations in many of the economy's markets, farm and nonfarm alike.

---

[1] These predictions concern an individual industry. As an economy-wide matter there is a lively controversy about whether a minimum wage lowers overall employment. It need not if, for example, there are some uncovered occupations.

Figure 7–3   Wholesale price indexes, 1968–1975, quarterly averages (1967 = 100)

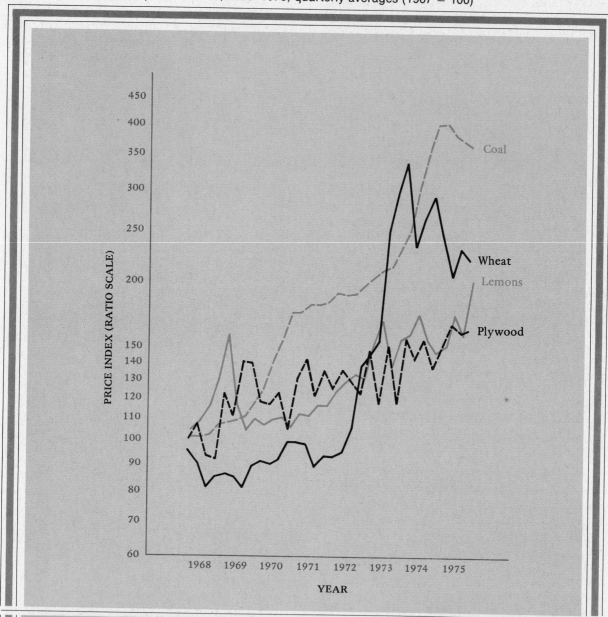

Variation in output leads to wide price fluctuations in many commodities.   Price fluctuations are characteristic of agricultural goods such as lemons and wheat, but they also occur in manufactured products such as plywood and in many raw materials such as coal. Notice both the seasonal (within the year) variations and the sharp year-to-year variations.

FLUCTUATIONS AND TRENDS IN PRICES AND INCOMES

The main causes of the farm problem are of three kinds: short-period fluctuations due to uncontrollable variations in supply; cyclical fluctuations due to variations in demand as the economy expands and contracts; and long-term trends in both demand and supply due to economic growth.

Short-term fluctuations

Figure 7–3 illustrates the extent to which prices of certain goods vary over the short period. This sort of pattern is typical of agricultural crops although it is not limited to them. Why do such fluctuations occur?

Farmers' crops are subject to variations in output because of many factors completely beyond their control. Some of the variation is simply a matter of season, but pests, floods, and lack of rain are capable of drastically reducing farm output, and exceptionally favorable conditions can cause production greatly to exceed expectations. By now you should not be surprised to hear that such unplanned fluctuations in output cause fluctuations in farm prices. Not only does price theory predict this obvious consequence, it also predicts some other less obvious ones that help in understanding some of the farmer's problems.

The basic behavior is illustrated in Figure 7–4. Because demand curves slope downward, variations in farm output placed on the market cause price fluctuations in the opposite direction to crop sizes. A bumper crop sends prices down, a small crop sends them up. The price change will be larger the less elastic the demand curve.

Because agricultural products tend to have inelastic demands, fluctuations in prices tend to be large in response to unplanned changes in production.

What are the effects on the receipts of farmers? If the commodity in question has an elasticity of demand greater than unity, increases in the quantity supplied will raise farmers' receipts and decreases will lower farmers' receipts. If the demand is inelastic, farmers' receipts will rise when price rises and fall when price falls.

If demands are inelastic, good harvests will bring reductions in total farm receipts and bad harvests will bring increases.

This result, which seems so paradoxical to most people unacquainted with economics, follows from the fact that when demand is inelastic, a given percentage change in the harvest will cause a much greater percentage change in price.

Because farm products do tend to have inelastic demands, farm receipts tend to vary inversely with crop size. When nature is bountiful and produces a bumper crop, farmers' receipts dwindle; when nature is moderately unkind and output falls unexpectedly, their receipts rise. The self-interests of the farmer and of the consumer are exactly opposed in such cases. This conflict was dramatically illustrated in 1972 and 1973 when worldwide grain failures sent grain prices skyrocketing and farm incomes up—and triggered the largest rise in consumer food prices in 25 years. In 1976 fair weather and bumper crops brought relief in the supermarkets but led to lower incomes in the farm belt.

Cyclical fluctuations in prices and incomes

Agricultural markets are subject not only to short-run instabilities due to uncontrolled output changes, but also, like many raw materials, to cyclical instability due to shifts in demand. In periods of prosperity, full employment prevails, incomes are high, and demands for all goods are high. In periods of depressed business activity, there is substantial unemployment, total incomes earned fall, and the demands for most goods fall as a result. As the tide of business prosperity ebbs and flows, demand curves for all goods rise and fall. What effect this will have on commodity prices depends upon the elasticity of *supply*. Industrial products typically have rather elastic supply curves, so shifts in demand cause fairly large changes in outputs but only small changes in prices. Agricultural commodities taken as a whole often have rather inelastic supplies. The very different patterns of response are illustrated in Figure 7–5.

For farm crops with inelastic supplies, a decrease in demand will lead to a sharp drop in prices and in farm receipts—as shown in Figure 7–5(i). Tables 7–1 and 7–2 show how this actually occurred in agriculture during the Great Depression.

To the public (and to many in Congress) the economic plight of farmers during the

Figure 7–4   The effect on price of unplanned variations in output depends upon elasticity of demand

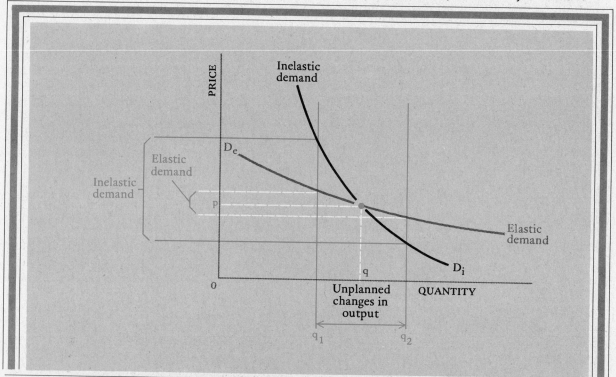

An unplanned fluctuation in output of a given size leads to a much sharper fluctuation in price if the demand curve is inelastic than if it is elastic.   Suppose the expected price is p and the planned output q. The two curves D_i and D_e are *alternative* demand curves. If actual production always equaled planned production, the equilibrium price and quantity would be p and q with either demand curve. Unplanned variations in output, however, cause quantity to fluctuate year by year between q_1 (a bad harvest) and q_2 (a good harvest). When demand is inelastic (shown by the heavy curve) prices will show large fluctuations. If demand is elastic (shown by the screened curve) price fluctuations will be much smaller.

Figure 7–5   The effect on receipts of a decrease in demand

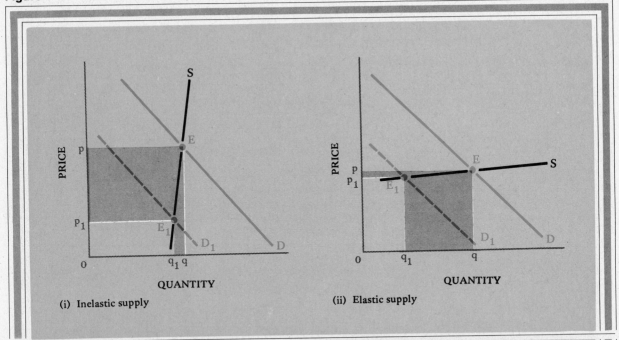

(i) **Inelastic supply**

(ii) **Elastic supply**

Either an inelastic or an elastic supply curve can lead to a sharp decrease in receipts, but the effect on prices is very different in the two cases.   When demand decreases from D to D_1, price and quantity decrease to p_1 and q_1 and total receipts decline by the shaded area. In (i) the cause is primarily the sharp decrease in price. In (ii) the cause is primarily the sharp decrease in quantity.

Great Depression seemed thus to be caused by the great fall in prices, which were themselves caused by the fall in demand for commodities with an inelastic supply curve. The notion of **price parity,** the ratio of the prices farms received for things they sold to the prices they paid for things they bought, was invoked to measure their hardship. Moreover, programs were proposed to restore price parity to farmers.

But this appealing diagnosis is incomplete. It is income received, not prices, that determines how much people have to spend. As Figure 7–5(ii) shows, a very elastic supply can be as much a curse as a very inelastic one in the face of a decrease in demand! The loss in

receipts in this case is primarily due to a decline in *quantity* sold rather than to a decline in *price,* but that does not make it less painful. This too is shown in Table 7–2. It is the ratio of farmers' incomes to others' incomes that matters in comparing the welfare of the two groups.[2]

[2] In Table 7–2 we label as an income parity index the ratio of agricultural receipts to industrial receipts. We use *receipts* instead of *profits* as a proxy for incomes in the sectors because most of the receipts in the sector become incomes earned in the sector. Thus farm income is not simply farm profits, because the wages paid to farm labor are also incomes attributable to farming. Similarly, the incomes earned in industry include the wages and salaries of workers as well as the profits of business. Of course some farm receipts are used to purchase industrial products, and some industrial receipts to purchase farm products.

Table 7–1 Agriculture and industry in the Great Depression: production and prices (index numbers 1929 = 100)

| Year | AGRICULTURE | | INDUSTRY | | PRICE PARITY INDEX P_A/P_I |
	Production	Prices P_A	Production	Prices P_I	
1929	100	100	100	100	100
1932	99	44	53	70	63
1937	108	83	103	85	97

Source: *Agriculture and the National Economy*, Temporary National Economic Committee, Monograph No. 23.

Agricultural prices fluctuated more sharply than industrial prices, but agricultural output was much more stable. The patterns shown here are roughly comparable to those of the two parts of Figure 7–5. The price parity index shows the ratio of agricultural prices to industrial prices.

What is clear is that both agriculture and industry suffered in the Great Depression but with different symptoms: farmers via low prices, industry via low production and high unemployment of workers and resources. While farmers clamored for the government to do something about prices, industry and industrial workers clamored for the government to do something to overcome unemployment of people and under-employment of factories. Each group had much to gain by the ending of the Depression; their interests are not always opposed. When President Herbert Hoover and the Republican Congress proved unresponsive to both pressures, they gave the Democrats and Franklin Roosevelt the opportunity to forge the farm–labor coalition that was to last for 20 years. The New Deal of 1933 was to include aid both to farmers and to industrial workers.

Long-term trends

Paradoxically, it is steady growth over time in the productive capacity and wealth of the American economy that has caused many long-term problems for American agriculture.

In the United States the actual increase in output per head has averaged between 2 and 3 percent per year over the last 50 years. The rise in production has been the result of the increased productivity of the working force. Workers can produce more per worker than they previously did. Such increases in production will lead to increases in the income of the

Table 7–2 Agriculture and industry in the Great Depression: total receipts (index numbers 1929 = 100)

Year	Agriculture total receipts	Industry receipts	Income parity index
1929	100	100	100
1932	44	37	119
1937	90	88	102

Either falling output or falling prices may lead to disastrous decreases in receipts and incomes. These data are derived from those in Table 7–1. The total receipts index is the price index multiplied by the production index. The income parity index shows the ratio of agricultural total receipts to industrial total receipts.

population, via rising wages and rising payments to other factors of production.

How will the people wish to consume their extra income? The relevant measure in this case is the income elasticity of demand, which measures the effect of increases in income on the demands for various goods. Income elasticities vary considerably among goods, and the income elasticity of most goods changes as income changes. At the levels of income existing in America and other advanced industrial nations, most foodstuffs have low income elasticities because most people are already well fed; when these people get extra income, they tend to spend much of it on consumers' durables, entertainment, and travel. As incomes grow well past subsistence levels, the demand for agricultural goods can be expected to increase relatively slowly with the passage of time, if population is relatively stable.

If productivity is expanding uniformly among industries and resources are not being shifted among industries, the demands for goods with low income elaticities will be expanding more slowly than output. In such industries excess supply will develop, prices and profits will be depressed, and it will be attractive for resources to move elsewhere. Exactly the reverse will happen for industries producing goods with high income elasticities. Demand will expand faster than supply, prices and profits will tend to rise, and resources will move into the industries producing these goods.

The need to transfer resources out of agricultural industries is even greater than would be required by their low income elasticities. The reason is that growth in agricultural productivity has been well above the average for the economy. Encouraged by government-financed research, by subsidies, and by a government-assured demand for farm output at a stable price, agricultural productivity has increased enormously in this century. American farm output per agricultural worker has grown at the rate of about 6 percent per year since 1930, nearly twice the rate of growth of industrial output per worker.

These productivity increases tend to shift the supply curves of agricultural goods to the right, indicating a greatly increased ability and willingness to produce at each price. In 1929 there were 12.8 million people employed on farms. The output they produced in 1929 could be produced today by 1.9 million people. If resources had not been reallocated out of farming, there would have been enormous increases in output which could hardly have been sold within the United States at any price. Fortunately, resources did move: actual employment on farms in 1976 was 4.3 million. The movement out of farming has not, however, been quite as fast as required. Adjusting for both productivity increases and population increases, 3.3 million farmers in 1976 could supply each of us with the same output of agricultural goods as each American consumed in 1929. This is 1 million fewer farmers than we had in 1976. Unless per capita consumption of all agricultural products had risen sharply there would necessarily be excess supplies of such products. For much of the past three decades such excesses have occurred.

Reallocations of resources in a free-market economy are expected to take place under the incentives of low prices, low wages, and depressed incomes in the declining sector and high prices, wages, and incomes in the expanding sector.

But incentives of this kind prove painful—indeed pain is the spur—to those who live and work on farms, especially if resources move slowly in response to depressed incomes. It is one thing for the farmer's son to move to the city; it may be quite another for the farmer and his father who are set in their ways. Because farmers are people—and voters—governments tend to respond to their cries for help in overcoming the depressed conditions in agriculture that free markets often produce.

How agricultural surpluses may become chronic, and agriculture a depressed sector

Imagine a simplified economy that has only two sectors, "agriculture" and "manufacturing," each of which grows at 6 percent per year. The income elasticity of demand is assumed to be 0.5 in agriculture and 1.5 in manufacturing. Assume that production is 50 units in each sector in "year zero." Supposing first that there is no movement of resources between the two sectors, the growth rate assures that output in each sector will double in 12 years, and thus that national income will double. Demand for agricultural goods increases by 50 percent, for manufacturing goods by 150 percent. The table below shows how, within the short space of 12 years, massive surpluses will appear in agriculture and shortages will occur in manufacturing.

Clearly, in such a case, resources need to be shifted out of agriculture and into manufacturing. Further, if the productivity increases are going on continuously, there will be a continual tendency toward excess supply of agricultural goods and excess demand for manufactured goods and a continuing need for resource reallocation.

But we have neglected prices and incomes so far. Because output is expanding faster than demand in the agricultural sector, prices will fall and incomes of producers will fall. In response to falling farm prices, there will be a decline in the demand for farm labor and the other factors of production used in agriculture, and the earnings of these factors will decline. At the same time, exactly the opposite tendencies will be observed in manufacturing. Here demand is expanding faster than output; prices will rise, incomes and profits of producers will be rising, and there will be a large demand for the factors of production used in manufacturing industries. So the price of these factors, and consequently the incomes that they earn, will be bid upward. In short, manufacturing will be a buoyant sector and agriculture a depressed sector. Now if resources move freely there will be a continuing flow of labor (and land and other factors of production) from agriculture to manufacturing. But if resources move too slowly, there will be a continuing depression in agriculture and chronic surpluses, whereas manufacturing will be buoyant with chronic scarcities.

	Agriculture	Manufacturing
Production in base year	50	50
Production in year 12	100	100
Assumed income elasticity of demand	.50	1.50
Quantity demanded in year 12	75	125
Therefore production in year 12 leads to a shortage or surplus of	25 (surplus)	25 (shortage)

AGRICULTURAL STABILIZATION AND SUPPORT PLANS

Governments throughout the world intervene in many agricultural markets in an attempt to deal with the problems just studied. They try to stabilize agricultural prices and incomes in the face of short-term and uncontrollable fluctuations in supply and cyclical fluctuations in demand. They also seek to support agricultural prices and incomes at levels sufficient to guarantee to farmers what is regarded as reasonable or decent living standards. In so doing they often weaken the incentives for resources to leave farming and thereby, if there is a long-run problem, make it worse.

Because income stabilization and price stabilization are not the same thing, there has been some confusion in what is intended in schemes designed to achieve "orderly agricultural marketing" or "farm parity"—phrases used in American legislation. We shall consider several schemes.

Suppose the supply curve in each case refers to planned (or average) production per year, but actual production fluctuates around that level. In a free market, as we have seen, this causes both prices and farmers' receipts to fluctuate widely from year to year.

The ever-normal granary

One method of preventing these fluctuations in prices and gross receipts is for the individual farmers to form a producers' association that tries to even out the supply *actually coming onto the market,* in spite of variations in production. It does this by storing a crop, say grain, in years of above-average production and selling out of its storage elevators in years of below-average production.

Since one farmer's production is an insignificant part of total production, there is no point in an individual farmer holding some production off the market in an effort to pre-

Figure 7–6 Stabilizing sales despite variable production: the ever-normal granary

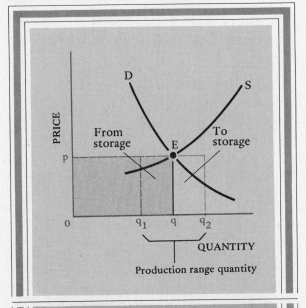

The ever-normal granary scheme sells the equilibrium quantity each year even though actual production varies. The planned supply curve is S; p and q are the equilibrium price and quantity. Actual production varies between q_1 and q_2. When production is q_2 the producers' association sells q and stores qq_2. When production is q_1 it still sells q, supplementing the current production by q_1q from its stored crops. Producers' revenue is stabilized at $p \cdot q$ (the shaded area) every year.

vent a fall in price in a year of bumper crops. But if all farmers get together and agree to vary the supply coming onto the market, then, collectively, they can have a major effect on price. The appropriate policy is illustrated in Figure 7–6.

Since revenues accrue to the producers when the goods are actually sold on the market, total revenues can be stabilized by

Figure 7–7 Government price supports
at the equilibrium price

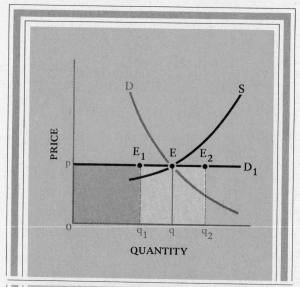

Government price supports at the equilibrium price stabilize prices and do not accumulate surpluses but cause revenues to
vary directly with production. Actual production varies around the equilibrium
level of q. When production is q_2 the government buys qq_2 and stores it. When production is q_1 the government sells q_1q from
storage. The quantity sold to the public is
always q, and this stabilizes price at p. The
government policy converts the demand
curve to D_1. If q is average production
there is no trend toward accumulation of
storage crops.

Farmers' revenue varies from pq_1 (the
darker shaded area) when production is q_1
to pq_2 (the entire shaded area) when production is q_2.

keeping sales constant at the equilibrium output even though production varies. This can
be accomplished by adding to or subtracting
from inventories the excesses or shortages of
production.

The fully successful ever-normal granary stabilizes
both prices and revenues of producers.

The costs of this scheme are those of providing storage and organizing and administering the program. A potential danger is that
the producers' association will sell on average
less than is produced (in order to get higher
prices) and will find itself with ever-
increasing stockpiles of the crop.

Government price supports at the equilibrium price

Because there are many difficulties in organizing and administering private stabilization
schemes such as the ever-normal granary,
why cannot the government do the same
thing, but do it more efficiently?

Suppose the government, instead of the
producers' association, enters the market itself, buying in the market and adding to its
own stocks when there is a surplus and selling
in the market—thereby reducing its stocks—
when there is a shortage. If it had enough
grain elevators and warehouses, and if its
support price was set at a realistic level, the
government could stabilize prices indefinitely. But, as Figure 7–7 illustrates, it would
not succeed in stabilizing farmers' revenues
and incomes, for farmers would find their
revenues high with a bumper crop and low
with a poor crop.

Government price supports at the equilibrium price
would not stabilize revenues. They would however
reverse the pattern of revenue fluctuation of a crop
with inelastic demand and a fluctuating supply.

In effect, the government policy imposes a
demand curve that is perfectly elastic at the
support price. This stabilizes price and expenditures by consumers but it does not
stabilize receipts to producers.

Government stabilization of farmers' revenues by open market purchases and sales

Obviously there is some governmental buying and selling policy that will stabilize
farmers' receipts. What are its characteristics?

As has been seen, too much price stability causes receipts to vary directly with production and too little price stability causes receipts to vary inversely with production. It appears that the government should aim at some intermediate degree of price stability. If the government allows prices to vary in inverse proportion to variations in production, then receipts will be stabilized. A 10 percent rise in production should be met by a 10 percent fall in price, and a 10 percent fall in production by a 10 percent rise in price.

The government wishing to stabilize farmers' receipts must make the demand curve facing the farmers one of unit elasticity. It must buy in periods of high output and sell in periods of low output, but only enough to let prices change in inverse proportion to farmers' output.

Government price supports above the free-market equilibrium level

Actual stabilization plans involving price supports usually set prices above the average free-market equilibrium level. This is partly due to the fact that stabilization is not the only goal, and there is a desire to assure farmers a standard of living comparable with that of city dwellers. This involves attempting to raise farm incomes in addition to stabilizing them.

The effects of such a support price are shown in Figure 7–8. The most important consequence is that it results in a situation in which over time the stabilizing authority buys more than it sells and unsold surpluses accumulate. The cost to the taxpayers includes any part of the outlay not ultimately recovered by sale of the crop, plus the costs of storage, handling, and administration.

PROBLEMS WITH AGRICULTURAL STABILIZATION AND SUPPORT PLANS

A first difficulty of plans that seek to raise farm income by raising prices above free-

market levels is the tendency to accumulate surpluses. Eventually, if agricultural surpluses persist, the stored crops will either have to be destroyed, given away, or dumped on the market for what they will bring. If the crops are thrown on the market and allowed to depress the price, then the original purposes

Figure 7–8 Price supports above the equilibrium price

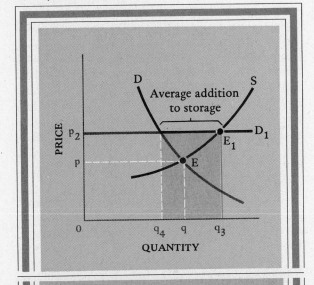

Price supports above the free-market equilibrium level lead to stable prices, growing inventories, and a subsidy to producers. The free-market equilibrium is at E. If the government will buy any quantity at p_2, the demand curve becomes the heavy black curve DD_1 and equilibrium shifts to E_1. Producers desire to produce the quantity q_3, but at the support price buyers wish to purchase only q_4; thus the government must expect to add q_4q_3 on average to its stockpile of the crop each year. It will of course add more in years of bumper crops than in years of poor crops. The size of the crop must fall below q_4 before the government can sell any of its accumulated surplus on the open market. The shaded area represents payments to producers by the government.

for which the crops were purchased—price stabilization and raising of farm incomes—are defeated. If the crops are destroyed or allowed to decay, the efforts of a large quantity of the country's scarce factors of production (the land, labor, and capital that went into producing the stored goods) will have been completely wasted.

Destroying crops is a vexing moral problem when millions are starving, but if the stored crops are given away or sold at a fraction of their cost to other countries, a political storm often results—as the sales of grain to the USSR by the United States in 1972 clearly showed. Furthermore, the government's plan will now show a deficit, for goods will have been purchased that cannot be sold except at a large loss. This deficit means that taxpayers generally will be paying farmers for producing goods that no one in the nation is willing to purchase at prices that come near to covering costs.

When support schemes begin to produce ever-growing surpluses the next step is often to try to limit each farmer's production. Quotas may be assigned to individual farmers and penalties imposed for exceeding the quotas. Or else, as has been done many times in the past, bonuses may be paid for leaving the land idle and for plowing crops under without harvesting them. Such measures waste resources because the output could be produced with fewer resources and the remaining resources used to produce goods elsewhere in the economy. All they dispense with is the visible symbol of trouble: the accumulating surpluses.

A second difficulty arises because the long period need to reallocate resources out of agriculture (a result of the low income elasticity of demand) will conflict with plans designed to stabilize farm incomes at a high level. A program that succeeds in giving the rural sector a high level of income will partially frustrate the market mechanism for inducing excess resources to move out of agri-culture. Indeed it may make matters worse. If the artificially profitable and stable market provides a stimulus for research and development that greatly increases productivity in the farm sector, it will shift the supply curve to the right, creating a further excess of quantity supplied over quantity demanded at the stabilized price.

AMERICAN FARM POLICY SINCE 1929

The American experience in trying to do something for the large, relatively poor, and politically influential farm population may be used to illustrate some of the theory just developed. In particular the twin difficulties noted above—surplus production and discouragement of sufficiently rapid shifting of resources out of agricultural production—have occurred. Moreover, as the statistics quoted on page 89 show, the farmer is still relatively poorer than other Americans.

The first serious intervention was in 1929, when the Federal Farm Board was set up to buy and sell farm produce in order to promote "orderly agricultural marketing." The Board's operations ended in complete failure when its attempt to support prices led to the accumulation of large stocks and a rapid exhaustion of the funds available.

The Roosevelt administration had learned the lesson that unless output can be restricted, holding prices above the market level requires unending injections of federal money to buy crops that can never be sold. It could not, however, politically or morally abandon the farmers, who were among the earliest victims of the Great Depression. The primary objective of the New Deal farm policy was to achieve some form of parity between farmers' incomes and other incomes in the nation. It was hoped (naively, perhaps) that income parity could be achieved by legislating for price parity. The relative prices of the things farmers sold (agricultural crops) and the things farmers bought (manufactured goods) were to be kept the same as they were in the period just before World War I. Since farm prices had fallen relative to the prices of manufactured goods, they were to be supported by the government at levels well above the free-market equilibrium levels.

A prominent feature of the New Deal program was designed to prevent the build-up of surplus output by paying farmers *not to produce* as well as paying them for what they did produce. The farm program also imposed acreage restrictions and marketing quotas on individual farmers.

But supported prices and guaranteed sales, government-financed research, and government loans for farm improvements were an enormous incentive to productivity, and output per acre and output per worker soared. Thus total output was not held down in spite of acreage limitations, and the federal costs for buying the resulting surplus crops or storing them and eventually destroying them, or selling them abroad at low prices, stayed at a very high level.

After World War II farm policy was modified but not basically changed. In the 1950s the notion of parity with pre-World War I relative prices was finally dropped, and the base for parity was made the average of prices ruling during the previous 10 years. Moreover actual prices were allowed to fall to a certain fraction of parity prices before the full price support was given. While this modification allowed a decline in relative prices over time, the permitted decline could occur only slowly and, at the same time, the effects of even these small price changes were mitigated by the introduction of other measures (such as the provision of subsidized water for irrigation and the Crop Storage and Loan Plan) that extended further assistance to farmers.[3]

Meanwhile, the so-called soil bank and

[3] The details of these plans need not concern us. What is important is that by giving a subsidy to farmers they reduce the incentives to shift resources out and encourage yet further research and development.

other programs continued to pay farmers not to produce commodities that consumers would not buy at the prevailing prices. Between 1968 and 1973 the federal government paid farmers over $15 billion for leaving 233 million acres unplanted. This acreage could have been used to increase grain output (say) by roughly 20 to 25 percent. But that would have either depressed prices or added to the hundred million tons already in storage.

HAS THE FARM PROBLEM DISAPPEARED?

Until five or ten years ago, most economists would have agreed that despite 40 years of government attempts—or perhaps because of them—the agricultural sector was still a major trouble spot in the economy and farm policy an expensive but predictable failure.

Yet few would have urged the government to cease its intervention altogether. For to leave to the price mechanism the task of reallocating resources out of farming would mean facing the prospect of a more or less permanently depressed sector of the community. It is doubtful if any American political party would be willing to accept the social and political consequences of leaving this sector to fend for itself.

Recent unexpected events have raised the possibility that our past policy has not been so disastrous after all and that by good luck if not by good judgment our accumulated surpluses have found an important use. Growing world population, growing world income, and some massive crop failures around the world have created the specter of a worldwide food shortage and of hunger and starvation. Devaluation of the dollar in the early 1970s and productivity gains have made American farm products cheaper abroad. The increasing demand for wheat, cotton, soybeans, and livestock has depleted stored reserves and in some cases led to shortages.

For one example, world reserves of wheat and feed grains, which were over 140 million tons in 1964 (90 percent of which were held in North America), were all but depleted by 1975. Predictably market prices have risen. An index of prices received by farmers (1967 = 100) that stood at 112 in 1971 was at 125 by June 1972 and at 202 in February 1975. This trend led in 1973 to a sharp reduction in subsidies. In that year, as the President signed a farm bill that reduced subsidies to farmers for nonproduction, the Secretary of Agriculture said, "We see the promised land—a land of full production and higher profit levels for our farmers . . . we face an expanded demand here and abroad for many years."

Not only were farmers prospering, but American agricultural technology appeared to

Farmers: small and large, rich and poor

Much of the motivation that has led to programs providing price supports and other subsidies to farmers was traditionally (and is still) based on the low income and hard life of average small family farmers. But they are not the only beneficiaries of support and subsidy programs. The rapid rise in agricultural productivity has stemmed from a technological revolution in agriculture. New and highly mechanized techniques have greatly increased the size at which a farm reaches lowest average cost of production. Not only has the government program supported small farmers who would otherwise have been displaced by larger units—in just the same way as the small grocery store is replaced by the supermarket—it has also entailed large payments to some very large, and already very rich, farmers. Payments for restricting acreage, for example, tend to be proportional to the number of acres owned, and the large payments thus go to the large farmers. Attempts to restrict government payments to $50,000 per farmer per year have so far been unsuccessful, although there is now a law restricting the annual payment to one farmer to $50,000 for *each* of his crops—although even here there are

exceptions! Clearly the support program is not being used exclusively to support the small farmer.

The New York Times not long ago reported on the extent to which the rich use farming to avoid paying taxes:

Corporate farms are big farms. Many consist of thousands of acres of the best land obtainable. Their owners often have backlogs of development capital and, if diversified, obtain numerous tax advantages. . . .

Federal tax records indicate that at least three out of every four people with annual incomes of $100,000 or more are involved in farming in some way, most of them reporting agricultural losses that can be written off against taxes on nonfarm income.

If Federal tax laws seem to help the city corporation that farms on the side more than the family farmer who farms full-time, they are not the only ways in which Federal programs tend to work against the little man.

The biggest farms receive the biggest subsidies, and also the most Government-supplied irrigation water.

Recently, Congress placed some limits on subsidies. And the courts are beginning to crack down on the big water users. But the gap between the rich and the poor still widened.

The newest phenomenon is the rise of corporate farming, representing in 1971

be the clue to increasing world food supplies. This technology has developed new seeds, new fertilizers, new methods, and, with these, opportunities for large-scale farming that produces vastly more output per acre than was produced a generation ago. Clearly, when hunger is a problem, more food becomes important. Much of the credit for in-

only 1 percent of all farms but a much higher percentage of farm output because they are large. The average farm in the United States is 400 acres; in contrast, Tenneco Oil Company owns or leases 135,000 acres in southern California for vegetable production. Some familiar corporate names now play a growing role in farming: ITT (hams), Greyhound (turkeys), Purex (lettuce), Ralston Purina (chickens), John Hancock (soybeans).

Whether large-scale corporate farming is a blessing or a curse depends on whether the efficient production and the low prices they bring are more important than the changes in the structure of rural life that accompanies them. A case in point concerns the broiler chicken. A generation ago most chickens were raised in small flocks in rural barnyards, and chicken was (along with ice cream) sufficiently expensive that it was the standard Sunday treat. By the 1960s chicken was close to the lowest priced form of meat, but the barnyard henhouse had been replaced by mass production of incubator chickens. Twenty large firms now dominate the industry. Chickens (like ice cream) became staples of the average family's diet, and kids complained about "having chicken again."

creases in agricultural productivity must be given to our past farm policies, not only for keeping farm prices higher than they otherwise would have been, but for direct and indirect government aid for agricultural research. The farm-agent, the agricultural experimental stations, and grants-in-aid to university researchers have been visible features of the American scene for decades. Sometimes cursed for the surpluses they encouraged, they may one day be regarded as vital steps in the amelioration of a serious worldwide food shortage.

Whether or not these developments portend the end of the "farm problem" and the beginning of a long-awaited era of farm prosperity in the United States is not yet clear. The farm prosperity of 1973 had largely faded by the time of the 1976 election campaign as a result of worldwide bumper crops, and both Democratic and Republican party platforms of that year promised more in the way of price and income supports.

There is no doubt that the *need* for food and other agricultural products throughout the world is high and rising because of the population explosion. Our reserves provided a needed cushion to a world that was willing to leave it to American and Canadian taxpayers to buy and store surplus commodities. But will these needs be translated into demand, in the sense of willingness to purchase at the prices required to bring forth supply? Will American agriculture, with its high wages and high expectations for farmers' incomes (based as they are on American standards of income), be able to compete successfully in world markets without government subsidy? Even American households are finding American food prices "out of sight"; American farm prices look still higher in New Delhi. If the answers to these questions are yes, all may be well; if no, the farm problem may soon be severe again.

Summary

1. The elementary theory of supply, demand, and price provides powerful tools for analyzing and understanding some real-world problems and policies. The chapter illustrates this with respect to price controls and agricultural policies.

2. When maximum prices, or price ceilings, are set below the equilibrium price, they cause shortages to appear, lead to allocation by sellers' or government's preferences, and provide a strong incentive for black marketeers to buy at the controlled price and sell at the higher free-market price.

3. When minimum prices, or price floors, are set above the equilibrium price, they cause surpluses to appear and provide a strong incentive for sellers to evade the law by selling below the legal price.

4. Agricultural commodities are subject to wide fluctuations in market prices, and these often lead to fluctuations of producers' incomes. This is because of year-to-year unplanned fluctuations in supplies combined with inelastic demands, and because of cyclical fluctuations in demands combined with inelastic supplies. Where demand is inelastic, large crops tend to be associated with low total receipts and small crops with high total receipts.

5. Fluctuations in farmers' gross receipts can be reduced by a producers' association that stores crops unsold when output is high and sells from inventories when output is low, or by appropriate government purchases and sales in the open market.

6. Price-stabilization schemes historically tend to involve stabilization above average free-market equilibrium levels. The result is a build-up of surpluses. To avoid these surpluses, attempts to stabilize prices at levels above the free-market equilibrium prices have tended to become associated with plans to restrict farmers' output. The tendency toward build-up of large unsold surpluses as well as later attempts to restrict output were both features of U.S. agricultural policy from 1930 to 1970.

7. The long-term problems of agriculture arise from a high rate of productivity growth on the supply side and a low income elasticity on the demand side. This means that, unless many resources are being transferred out of agriculture, quantity supplied will increase year after year faster than quantity demanded. If existing prices are maintained, and if farmers are guaranteed a market for all of their output at these prices, the yearly farm surplus will tend to increase.

8. A long-term solution to persistent surpluses requires a transfer of resources out of agriculture and into sectors where demand is growing faster than supply. In a free market, the incentive for this transfer would be provided by a continuing tendency for agricultural prices and incomes to be depressed. The political and social consequences of the hardships this would impose are not likely to appeal to any American political party.

9. Equitable and compassionate treatment of farmers is also part of farm policy. But the efforts of the government to maintain farm income at a level that compares favorably with incomes earned elsewhere tends to inhibit the reallocation mechanism and thus to increase farm surpluses above what they would otherwise be.

10. The early 1970s witnessed a worldwide food shortage and a boom in American agriculture. Whether this promises an end to our long-term farm problem depends on whether American farm products will remain competitive in world markets at prices that the world's growing population will pay after the effects of the great crop failures of 1972 wear off. The bumper crops of the mid 1970s suggest there is still a farm problem.

Concepts for review

Comparative statics
Maximum and minimum price controls
Black markets
Price supports at and above the level of free-market equilibrium
Price stabilization versus income stabilization
Price parity versus income parity
Income elasticity and long-period resource reallocation

Discussion questions

1. "When a controlled item is vital to everyone it is easier to start controlling the price than to stop controlling it. Such controls are popular with consumers, regardless of their uneconomic consequences. In this respect oil price controls resemble rent controls." Explain why it may be uneconomic to have such controls, why they may be popular, and why, if they are popular, the government might want to stop controlling them.

2. Journalist William Safire calls the energy crisis in natural gas "the unnatural shortage of natural gas." He writes: "Be angry at the real villians: the Washington-knows-best Congressmen, the self-anointed consumer 'protectors' and the regulatory bureaucracy. They thought they could protect the consumer by breaking the law of supply and demand, and as a result have made a classic case against government intervention." From these remarks what do you judge the policy to have been? Could *producers* have created the shortage of natural gas? If so, how? How would you define a "shortage"? Is there a valid distinction between a "natural shortage" and an "unnatural shortage"?

3. Medical and hospital care in Britain is provided free to individuals by the National Health Service, with the costs paid by taxation. Some British doctors complain that patients want "too much" medical care; patients complain that they have to wait "too long" in doctors' offices for the care they get and months or years for needed operations. Use the theory of supply and demand to discuss these complaints. Would you expect a private (pay) medical market to grow up alongside the National Health Service? Would you expect the government to welcome or discourage such a second service?

4. Predict the consequences of extending the legal minimum wage to the services of children, including those for mowing lawns and babysitting. Illegal use of alien farm workers in the United States ("wetbacks") is sometimes attributed to the fact that the U.S. minimum wage is above the average Mexican wage rate. Discuss whether the wetbacks are a phenomenon caused by the imposition of a minimum wage.

5. The Yarvard Law School, in Princetown, has 1,000 qualified applicants for 200 places in the first-year class. It is de-bating a number of alternative admission criteria: (a) a lottery, (b) date of initial application, (c) LSAT score, (d) recommendations from alumni, (e) place of residence of applicant. An economist on the faculty determines that if the tuition level is doubled, the excess demand will disappear. Argue for (or against) using the tuition rate to replace each of the other suggested criteria.

6. "The success of American agriculture has benefited everyone but the farmer." In the light of what you have learned in this chapter, explain the background of this quotation from a *Congressional Joint Economic Report*.

7. "This ought to be a time of rejoicing in the vineyards of California. The crop of wine grapes has rarely been richer, the harvest is nearly complete—and Americans are drinking more California wine than ever before." Why then are there falling profits and a record number of bankruptcies in the industry?

8. In 1974 the Kenya Meat Commission (KMC) decided it was undemocratic to allow meat prices to be out of the reach of the ordinary citizen. It decided to freeze meat prices. Six months later, in a press interview, the managing commissioner of the KMC made each of the following statements.
a. "The price of almost everything in Kenya has gone up but we have not increased the price of meat. The price of meat in this country is still the lowest in the world."
b. "Cattle are scarce in the country, but I do not know why."
c. "People are eating too much beef and unless they diversify their eating habits and eat other foodstuffs the shortage of beef will continue."
Do the facts alleged make sense given KMC's policy?

9. "If you are a farmer the weather is always bad." Discuss the sense in which this statement might be true.

PART THREE

DEMAND

8

Household consumption behavior

The early economists, struggling with the problem of what determined the relative prices of commodities, encountered what they came to call the **paradox of value:** necessary commodities such as water were observed to have prices that were low compared to the prices of many luxury commodities such as diamonds. Writing some 200 years ago, these early economists argued: Water is necessary to our very existence, whereas diamonds are a frivolous luxury that could disappear from the face of the earth tomorrow without causing any real upset. Does it not seem odd, therefore, that water is so cheap and diamonds are so expensive? It took a long time for economists to resolve this apparent paradox, and thus it is not surprising that even today the confusion persists in many quarters and clouds some current policy discussions.

We have already encountered one answer: It is supply and demand, not "necessity" or "luxury," that determine price in any competitive market, and the equilibrium price that equates supply and demand is relatively low for water and relatively high for diamonds. But why is the demand for a necessity not enough to assure that its price is high? After all, it is necessary to life itself. To address this more fundamental question we must go behind the market demand curve, which is the aggregate of all households' desired purchases at each possible price, and look to the behavior and motivation of the individual household. This involves first looking at the relation between the market demand curve and the demand curves of individual households and then looking into individual behavior.

THE RELATION BETWEEN MARKET AND HOUSEHOLD DEMAND CURVES

An example of the kind of information given by the market demand curves developed in Chapter 5 (see page 56) is that a total of 90,000 tons of carrots will be purchased each month when the price is $40 per ton. But this

Figure 8–1 The relation between household and market demand curves

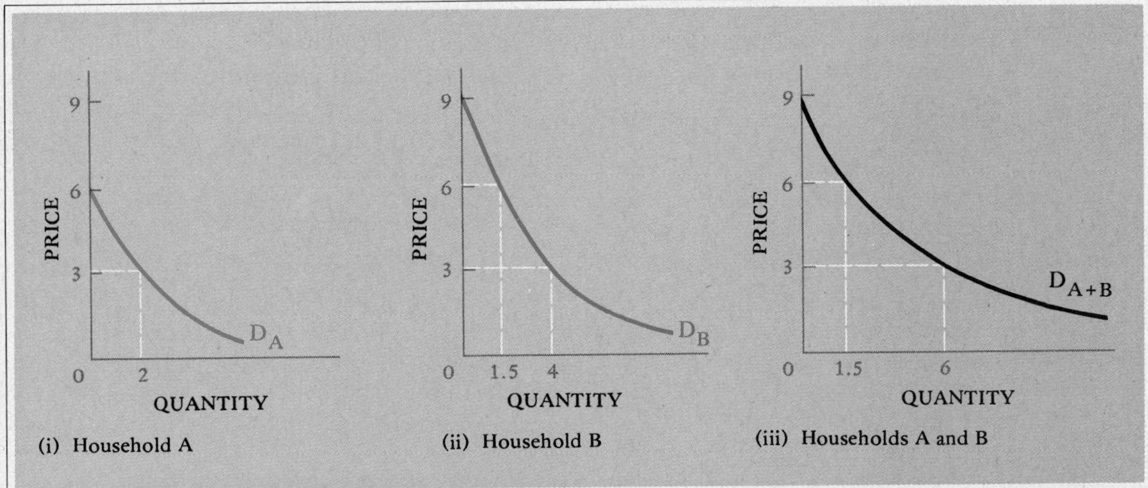

(i) Household A   (ii) Household B   (iii) Households A and B

An aggregate demand curve is the horizontal sum of the individual demand curves of all households in the market. The figure illustrates aggregation over only two households. At a price of $3, household A purchases 2 units and household B purchases 4 units; thus together they purchase 6 units. If there are thousands of households, the process is the same.

90,000 tons is the sum of the quantities demanded by millions of different households. It may be made up of 4 pounds for the McDaniels, 7 pounds for the Gonzaleses, 1.5 pounds for the Wilsons, and so on. The demand schedule for carrots in Chapter 5 also tells us that when the price rises to $60, aggregate quantity demanded falls to 77,500 tons per month. This quantity can also be traced back to individual households. The McDaniels perhaps would buy only 3 pounds, the Gonzaleses 6.5 pounds, and the Wilsons perhaps none at all. Notice that we have now described two points, not only on the market demand curve but on the demand curves of each of these households.

Aggregate behavior is merely the sum of the behavior of individual households. The market demand is the horizontal sum of the demand curves of the individual households.

It is the *horizontal* sum because we wish to add quantities demanded at a given price, and quantities are measured in the horizontal direction on a conventional demand curve graph. This process is illustrated in Figure 8–1.

The marginal utility theory of household behavior

MARGINAL AND TOTAL UTILITY

The satisfaction someone receives from consuming commodities is called his or her *utility*. The total utility obtained from consuming some commodity can be distinguished from the marginal utility of consuming one unit more or one unit less of it.

Total utility refers to the total satisfaction from consuming some commodity. **Marginal utility** refers to the change in satisfaction resulting from consuming a little more or a little less of the commodity. Thus, for example, the total utility of consuming ten units of some commodity is the total satisfaction that those ten units provide. The marginal utility of the tenth unit consumed is the satisfaction added by the consumption of that unit—or, in other words, the difference in total utility between consuming nine units and consuming ten units.[1]

The significance of this distinction can easily be seen by asking two questions: (1) If you had to give up the consumption of one of the following commodities completely, which would you choose: water or the movies? (2) If you had to choose between one of the following, which would you choose: increasing your consumption of water by 35 gallons a month (the amount required for an average bath) or attending one more movie each month?

In (1) you are comparing the value you place on your total consumption of water with the value you place on all your attendances at the movies. You are comparing the *total utility* of your water consumption with the *total utility* of your movie attendances. There is little doubt that everyone would answer (1) in the same way, revealing that the total utility derived from consuming water exceeds the total utility derived from attending the movies.

In (2) you are comparing the value you place on a small addition to your water consumption with the value you place on a small addition to your movie attendances. You are

comparing your *marginal utility* of water with your *marginal utility* of movie performances. The response to choice (2) is far less predictable than the response to choice (1). Some might select the extra movie; others might say that they have already seen all the movies they can stand (marginal utility of another visit to the movies, *zero*) and would select the extra water. Furthermore, their choice would depend on whether it was made at a time when water was plentiful, so that they had more or less all the water they wanted (marginal utility of a little more water, *low*), or when water was scarce, so that they might put quite a high value on obtaining a little more water (marginal utility of a little more water, *high*).

Choices of type (1) are encountered much less commonly than are choices of type (2). If our income rises a little, we have to decide to have some more of one thing or another. If we find that we are overspending, or if our income falls, we have to decide what to cut down on, to have a little less of this or a little less of that.

Real choices are rarely conditioned by total utilities; it is marginal utilities that are relevant in deciding choices concerning a little more or a little less.

The hypothesis of diminishing marginal utility

The basic hypothesis of utility theory, sometimes called the law of diminishing marginal utility, is:

The utility that any household derives from successive units of a particular commodity will diminish as total consumption of the commodity increases, the consumption of all other commodities being held constant.

Consider further the case of water. Some minimum quantity is absolutely necessary to sustain life, and a person would, if necessary, give up all his or her income and wealth to

---

[1] Here and elsewhere in elementary economics it is common to use interchangeably two concepts that mathematicians distinguish between. Technically, *incremental* utility is measured over a discrete interval, such as from nine to ten, whereas marginal utility is a rate of change measured over an infinitesimal interval. But common usage applies the word *marginal* when the last unit is involved, even if a one-unit change is not infinitesimal. [5]

obtain that quantity—the marginal utility of that quantity is extremely high. Much more than this bare minimum can be drunk, but the marginal utility of successive glasses of water drunk over some time period will decline steadily. Evidence for this hypothesis will be considered later, but you can convince yourself that it is at least a reasonable one by asking yourself a number of questions. How much money would induce you to cut your consumption of water by one glass per week? The amount will not be large. How much would induce you to cut it by a second glass? By a third glass? Back to only one glass consumed per week? The fewer glasses you are consuming already, the higher the marginal utility of one more or one less glass of water.

But water has many uses other than for drinking. A fairly high marginal utility will be attached to some minimum quantity for bathing, but much more than this minimum will be used for more frequent baths and for having a water level in the bath higher than is absolutely necessary. The last weekly gallon used for bathing is likely to have quite a low marginal utility. Again, some small quantity of water is necessary for brushing one's teeth, but many people leave the water running while brushing, and they can hardly pretend that the water so consumed between wetting and rinsing the brush has a high utility. When all the extravagant uses of water by the modern consumer are considered, it is certain that the marginal utility of the last, say, 30 percent of all units consumed is very low, even though the total utility of *all* the units consumed is extremely high.

Utility schedules and graphs

Assuming that utility can be measured, it is possible to illustrate the hypothesis. The schedule in Table 8–1 is a hypothetical one and is intended only to illustrate the assumptions that have been made about utility. It shows that total utility rises as the number of movies attended each month rises; everything

Table 8–1 Total and marginal utility schedules

Number of movies attended (attendances per month)	Total utility	Marginal utility
0	0	
1	30	30
2	50	20
3	65	15
4	75	10
5	83	8
6	89	6
7	93	4
8	96	3
9	98	2
10	99	1

Total utility rises but marginal utility declines as the consumption of this household increases. The marginal utility of 20, shown as the second entry in the last column, arises because total utility increased from 30 to 50—a difference of 20—with attendance at the second movie. Technically this is "incremental utility" over the interval from 1 to 2 units. When plotting marginal utility on a graph this value is plotted at the midpoint of the interval over which it is computed.

else being equal, the household gets more satisfaction, the more movies it consumes each month—at least over the range shown in the table. But the marginal utility of each additional movie per month is less than of the previous one (even though each one adds something to the household's satisfaction); thus the marginal utility schedule declines as quantity consumed rises. These same data are shown graphically in Figure 8–2.

Can marginal utility ever reach zero? With many commodities there is some maximum consumption after which additional units would confer no additional utility. If the individual were forced to consume more, the ad-

Figure 8–2   Total and marginal utility curves

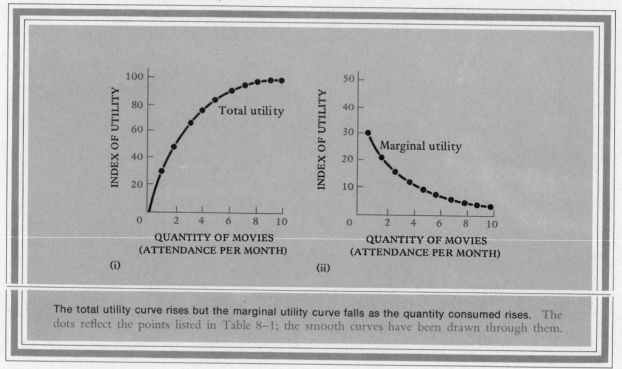

The total utility curve rises but the marginal utility curve falls as the quantity consumed rises.   The dots reflect the points listed in Table 8–1; the smooth curves have been drawn through them.

ditional units would actually reduce his or her total utility. Cigarettes provide an obvious example. There is some maximum number of cigarettes that most people would smoke per day, even if they did not have to worry about the cost. For nonsmokers that number is zero. Few smokers would want to go to the point of chain smoking from the second they awoke until the second they fell asleep. Long before consumption reached this point, additional cigarettes smoked would cease to add to utility and would begin to subtract from it; that is, additional cigarettes would have a negative marginal utility or, as it is sometimes called, a marginal *disutility*. The same is undoubtedly true of many other commodities such as food, alcoholic beverages, and most recreation. (Although some people might be happy to play golf from sunup to sunset seven days a week for the rest of their lives, most would not.)

MAXIMIZING UTILITY

A basic assumption of the economic theory of household behavior is that households consistently follow a particular rule.

The members of a household are assumed to maximize their total utility.

This is just another way of saying that the members of households try to make themselves as well off as they possibly can in the circumstances in which they find themselves. This assumption is sometimes taken to mean that households are assumed to be narrowly selfish and devoid of any altruistic motives. This is not so. If, for example, the household derives utility from giving its money away to others, this can be incorporated into the analysis, and the marginal utility that it gets from a dollar given away can be compared with the marginal utility that it gets from a dollar spent on itself.

The following can be predicted as a direct consequence of utility maximization: As long as a further unit consumed has a positive marginal utility, total utility can be increased by consuming more of the commodity. A **free good** is one for which no price needs to be paid. Thus consumption of any free good will be pushed to the point at which its marginal utility is zero.

The meaning of scarcity can now be reinterpreted:

Scarce goods have positive marginal utilities.

If all prices were zero, the total amounts that the population would want to consume would greatly exceed the amounts that could be produced with the available supplies of resources. Because households would get additional utility from consuming more goods than can be produced with the available resources, these goods are scarce.

The equilibrium of a household

How can a household adjust its expenditure so as to maximize the total utility of its members? Should it go to the point at which the marginal utility of each commodity is the same—i.e., the point at which it would equally value the last unit of each commodity consumed? This would make sense only if each commodity had the same price per unit. But if a household must spend $3 to buy an additional unit of one commodity and only $1 for a unit of another, the first commodity would represent a poor use of its money if the marginal utility of each were equal: It would be spending $3 to get satisfaction that it could have acquired for only $1.

The household maximizing its utility will allocate its expenditure between commodities so that the utility of the last dollar spent on each is equal.

Imagine that the household is in a position in which the utility of the last dollar spent on carrots yields three times the utility of the last dollar spent on brussels sprouts. In this case total utility can be increased by switching a dollar of expenditure from sprouts to carrots and gaining the difference between the utilities of a dollar spent on each.

The utility-maximizing household will continue to switch its expenditure from sprouts to carrots as long as a dollar spent on carrots yields more utility than a dollar spent on sprouts. But this switching reduces the quantity of sprouts that are consumed, and given the law of diminishing marginal utility, raises the marginal utility of sprouts; at the same time, it increases the quantity of carrots consumed and thereby lowers the marginal utility of carrots. Eventually the marginal utilities will have changed enough so that the utility of a dollar spent on carrots is just equal to the utility of a dollar spent on sprouts. At this point there is nothing to be gained by a further switch of expenditure from sprouts to carrots. If the household did persist in reallocation of its expenditure, it would further reduce the marginal utility of carrots (by consuming more of them) and raise the marginal utility of sprouts (by consuming less of them). Further reallocations would then lower total utility because the utility of a dollar spent on sprouts would now exceed the utility of a dollar spent on carrots.

Let us now leave carrots and sprouts and deal with commodities in general. Denote the marginal utility of the last unit of X by MU_x and its price by p_x. Let MU_y and p_y refer to a second commodity. The marginal utility per dollar of X will be MU_x/p_x. For example, if the last unit adds 30 units to utility and costs $2, then its marginal utility per dollar is $30/2 = 15$.

The condition required for a household to maximize its utility is, for any pair of commodities,

$$\frac{MU_x}{p_x} = \frac{MU_y}{p_y} \qquad [1]$$

This is just another way of writing the condition that the household will allocate its expenditure so that the utility gained from the last dollar spent on each commodity is equal.

This is the fundamental equation of the utility theory of demand. Each household demands each good (for example, movie attendances) up to the point at which the marginal utility per dollar spent on it is the same as the marginal utility of a dollar spent on another good (for example, water). When this condition is met the household cannot shift a dollar of expenditure from one commodity to another and increase its utility.

An alternative interpretation of household equilibrium

It is possible to rearrange the terms in equation [1] to gain an additional insight into household behavior.

$$\frac{MU_x}{MU_y} = \frac{p_x}{p_y} \qquad [2]$$

The right-hand side of this equation is given to the household by the market—it states the *relative* price of the two goods. It is determined by the market and is outside of the control of the individual household, which reacts to these market prices but is powerless to change them. The left-hand side concerns the ability of the goods to add to the household's satisfaction, and it is within the control of the household. By determining the quantities of different goods it buys, the household determines also their marginal utilities. (If you have difficulty seeing why, look again at Figure 8–2(ii).)

If the two sides of equation [2] are not equal, the household can increase its total satisfaction by rearranging its purchases. Assume, for example, that the price of a unit of X is twice the price of a unit of Y, ($p_x/p_y = 2$), while the marginal utility of a unit of X is three times that of a unit of Y, ($MU_x/MU_y = 3$). It will now pay the household to buy more X and less Y. If, for example, it reduces its purchases of Y by two units, it will free

enough purchasing power to buy a unit of X. Since one new unit of X bought yields 1.5 times the satisfaction of two units of Y foregone, this switch is worth making. What about a further switch of X for Y? As the household buys more X and less Y, the marginal utility of X will fall and the marginal utility of Y will rise. The household will go on rearranging its purchases—reducing Y consumption and increasing X consumption—until, in this example, the marginal utility of X is only twice that of Y. At this point there is no further room to increase total satisfaction by rearranging purchases between the two commodities.

Now consider what the household is doing. It is faced with a set of prices that it cannot change. The household responds to these prices, and maximizes its satisfaction, by adjusting the things it can change—the quantities of the various goods it purchases—until equation [2] is satisfied for all pairs of commodities.

This sort of equation—one side representing the choices the outside world gives decision makers and the other side representing the effect of those choices on their welfare—recurs in economics over and over again. It reflects the equilibrium position reached when decision makers have made the best adjustment they can to the external things that limit their choices.

When all households are fully adjusted to a given set of market prices, each and every household will have identical ratios of its marginal utilities for each pair of goods. This is because each household faces the same set of market prices. Of course a rich household may consume more of each commodity than will a poor household. The rich and the poor households (and every other household) will, however, adjust their *relative* purchases of each commodity so that the relative marginal utilities are the same for each household. Thus, if the price of X is twice the price of Y, each household will purchase X and Y to the point at which the household's marginal utility of X is twice its marginal utility of Y.

The derivation of the household's demand curve[2]

To derive the household's demand curve for a commodity, it is only necessary to ask what happens when there is a change in the price of that commodity. To do this for candy, take equation [2] and let X stand for candy and Y for all other commodities. Assume that candy involves such a small proportion of the consumer's total expenditure that the marginal utilities of all other goods are unaffected when the household spends a little more or a little less on candy. If total expenditure on candy rises from $1 a month to $2 in response to a 10 percent fall in the price of candy, this represents a large increase in candy consumption, and the marginal utility of candy must fall. But the extra dollar spent on candy may mean only 1¢ less spent on each of a hundred different commodities, and this reduction in the consumption of each of them is so small that it will have a negligible effect on their marginal utilities.

What will happen if, with all other prices constant, the price of candy rises? The household that started from a position of equilibrium will now find itself in a situation in which[3]

$$\frac{MU \text{ of candy}}{MU \text{ of } Y} < \frac{\text{price of candy}}{\text{price of } Y} \qquad [3]$$

To restore equilibrium, it must buy less candy, thereby raising its marginal utility until once again equation [2] is satisfied (where X is

candy). The common sense of this is that the marginal utility of candy *per dollar* falls when its price rises. If the household began with the utility of the last dollar spent on candy equal to the utility of the last dollar spent on all other goods, the rise in candy prices makes this no longer true. The household must buy less candy (and more of other goods) until the marginal utility of candy has risen enough that the utility of a dollar spent on candy is the same as it was before. Thus, if candy prices have doubled, the quantity purchased must be reduced until the marginal utility of candy has doubled.

This analysis leads to the basic prediction of demand theory.

A rise in the price of a commodity (with income and the prices of all other commodities held constant) will lead to a decrease in the quantity of the commodity demanded by each household.

If this prediction is valid for each household, it is also true for all households taken together. Thus the theory predicts a downward-sloping market demand curve.

APPLYING THE DISTINCTION BETWEEN MARGINAL AND TOTAL UTILITY

The paradox of value revisited

The paradox, stated in the first paragraph of this chapter, represented to Adam Smith a conflict between "value in use" and "value in exchange." It took the better part of a century of debate and analysis before the apparent paradox was satisfactorily resolved.

The paradoxical aspect arose because the intuitively appealing hypothesis that the market values of two commodities ought to be related to their total utilities was repeatedly refuted by any number of day-to-day observations. The early economists believed that expensive goods should be ones with high total utilities and cheap goods ones with low total utilities. They were thus arguing that market values (values in exchange) should be related to total utilities (values in use). Their

[2] This section may be omitted without loss of continuity. It derives the theoretical prediction that demand curves slope downward. This conclusion may instead be taken as an empirical observation so often confirmed that it may be assumed instead of derived.

[3] The inequality sign (<) always points to the smaller of two magnitudes. Since the price of candy rose, the right-hand side of equation [2] increased and the left-hand side stayed the same. Thus equation [2] was replaced by the inequality shown in equation [3].

Figure 8–3 The relation of elasticity of demand to utility

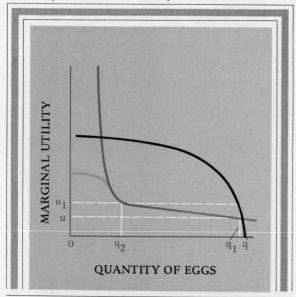

QUANTITY OF EGGS

Elasticity of demand is determined by marginal utilities in the relevant range, not total utilities. The household originally consumes q dozen eggs per month, and the last egg consumed has a marginal utility of u. The price of eggs now doubles. To achieve a new equilibrium the household must cut its egg consumption until the marginal utility of eggs doubles, rising from u to u_1. If the black line is the household's marginal utility curve, consumption only falls to q_1 and the household will have a very inelastic demand curve for eggs. If, however, the colored line is the household's marginal utility curve, consumption falls to q_2 and the household will have a very elastic demand curve. While the shape of the marginal utility curve in the relevant range is thus important, its shape outside of this range is irrelevant. To see this, let the colored curve have two alternative shapes in the range above u_1. The dark curve indicates a much higher total utility of the first units consumed than does the light curve, yet these alternative shapes have no influence on the household's behavior when it seeks to raise the marginal utility of eggs from u to u_1.

hypothesis compares the total market values (i.e., price *times* quantity) of two commodities with their total utilities.[4] A precise statement of it would be the relationship

$$\frac{p \times q \text{ of diamonds}}{p \times q \text{ of water}}$$

$$= \frac{\text{total utility of diamonds}}{\text{total utility of water}} \quad [4]$$

Unfortunately for the hypothesis, this relation does not hold in the real world. The total utility of water exceeds the total utility of diamonds, while in many places the total value of diamonds traded exceeds that of water traded.

The reason for this is that utility-maximizing market behavior depends on *marginal* utilities and their relationships to prices (as shown in equation [2]), not total utilities (as hypothesized in equation [4]). The paradox of value is thus explained by saying that equation [4] is not a valid deduction from the classical economists' own assumption that households were utility maximizers.

To see this intuitively, remember that water is cheap because there is enough of it that people consume it to the point at which its *marginal* utility is very low; thus they are not prepared to pay a high price to obtain a little more of it. Diamonds are very expensive because they are scarce (the owners of diamond mines keep diamonds scarce by limiting output), and people have to stop consuming them at a point where marginal utility is still high. Thus those who buy diamonds are prepared to pay a high price for an additional diamond.

Elasticity of demand, necessities and luxuries

Closely related to the paradox of value is a notion that might be expressed this way: Cer-

[4] The total utilities of two commodities cannot be simply related to their relative market *prices,* since the latter can be made anything we want by choosing the units appropriately. For example, one barrel of diamonds is expensive relative to one barrel of water, but a one-carat diamond is cheap relative to one reservoir full of water.

tain commodities, called luxuries, have low total utilities. They can be dispensed with altogether if circumstances require. Other commodities, called necessities, are essential to life and have high total utilities because certain minimum quantities of them are essential indeed.

It is quite reasonable to define necessities and luxuries in terms of total utilities, but proponents of this view go further. They attempt to use commonsense knowledge about luxuries and necessities to predict demand elasticities and to dispense with the need for measurement. They argue that since luxuries can easily be dispensed with, they will have highly elastic demands because when their prices rise consumers can stop purchasing them; on the other hand, necessities have almost completely inelastic demands because when prices rise the consumer has no choice but to continue to buy them.

If it worked, this approach would save time, for one would only have to determine whether a particular commodity was a necessity or a luxury to be able to predict its elasticity of demand. But elasticity of demand depends on marginal utilities, not total utilities, as we shall now see.

Demand theory leads to the prediction that when the price of a commodity—say, eggs—rises, the household will reduce its purchase of eggs enough to increase their *marginal* utility to the point where the marginal utility per dollar spent on eggs is the same as for other commodities whose prices did not rise. But will the reduction in quantity required to raise the marginal utility be a little or a lot? This depends on the shape of the marginal utility curve in the range that is relevant. If the marginal utility curve is flat, a large change in quantity is required and demand will be elastic. If the curve is steep, a small change will suffice and demand will be inelastic. Figure 8–3 considers several possibilities in response to a doubling in the price of eggs. It leads to these important conclusions:

The response of quantity demanded to a change in

price (i.e., the elasticity of demand) depends on the marginal utility over the relevant range and has no necessary relation to the total utility of the good.

"Just" prices

The emotional reaction to goods is often a response to their total utilities rather than to their marginal ones. We often hear an argument such as this: Water is a necessity of life of critical importance to rich and poor; it is wrong, therefore, to make people pay for so necessary a commodity. Such views often produce curious results. If, for example, water is provided free instead of at a modest cost,

Figure 8–4 A hypothetical marginal utility curve for water

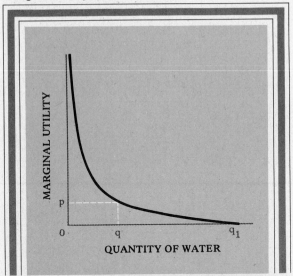

The imposition of a modest price may greatly reduce the quantity of water consumed without causing a large total sacrifice in the utility derived from water consumption. If water is priced at p, consumers will consume q units per month. Lowering the price to zero would increase consumption to q_1. Much of the water that a household would consume at a zero price has a very low marginal utility.

What do attitude surveys measure?

Consider a type of survey that is popular in both the daily newspapers and in sociology and political science. These surveys take the form of asking such questions as:

Do you like the Republicans more than the Democrats?

In deciding to live in area A rather than B, what factors influenced your choice? List the following in order of importance: neighbors, schools, closeness to swimming area, price and quality of housing available, play areas for children, general amenities.

In choosing a university, what factors were important to you? List in order of importance: environment, academic excellence, residential facilities, parents' opinion, school opinion, athletic facilities, tuition.

You should be able to add other examples to this list (which was drawn from real cases). *All of the above survey questions, and most of those you will be able to add, attempt to measure total rather than marginal utilities.* There is of course nothing illegal or immoral about this. People are free to measure anything that interests them, and in some cases knowledge of total utilities may be of practical value. But in many cases actual behavior will be determined by marginal utilities, and if one attempts to predict such behavior from a (correct) knowledge of total utilities, one will be hopelessly in error.

Where the behavior being predicted involves an either-or decision, such as a vote for the Democratic or the Republican candidate, the total utility that is attached to each choice will indeed be what matters be-

cause the voters are choosing one or the other. Where the decision is a marginal one between a little more or a little less, however, total utility is not what will determine behavior.

A recent newspaper poll in a large midwestern city showed that two-thirds of the city's voters rated its excellent school system as one of its important assets. Yet in a subsequent election the voters turned down a school bond issue. Is this irrational behavior, as the newspaper editorials charged? Does it show a biased sample in the poll? It demonstrates neither. The poll measured the people's assessment of the total utility derived from the school system, while the bond-issue vote depended on the people's assessments of the marginal utility of a little more money spent on the school system. There is nothing contradictory in anyone's feeling that the total utility of the city's fine school system is very large but that the city has other needs that have a higher marginal utility than further money spent on school construction.

A recent survey showed—paradoxically, it claimed—that many Americans are getting more pleasure from their families just at the time that they are electing to have smaller families. There is nothing paradoxical about a shift in tastes that increases the marginal utility of the first two or three children and reduces the marginal utility of each further child. Nor is there any paradox in a parent's getting a high total utility from the total time spent with the children but assigning a low marginal utility to the prospect of spending a little additional time with them each evening.

the extra consumption that will occur will be for many uses that yield a relatively low utility (such as letting the water run while brushing one's teeth). The relevant question when deciding between a zero price and a modest price for water is not "Is water so necessary that we do not want to deprive anyone of *all* of it?" but rather "Are the marginal uses of water such that we do not want to discourage anyone from using water for these purposes?" Clearly, these two questions can be given different answers.

Evidence concerning the consumption of water at various prices suggests that the marginal utility curve for water is shaped somewhat like the curve in Figure 8–4. The difference between providing water free and charging a modest price for it may mean a great deal in the quantity of water consumed. This additional water is costly to provide, and its provision requires scarce resources that could have been used to produce other things. If the utility of the commodities foregone is higher than the utility of the extra water consumed, then people are worse off as a result of receiving water free. A charge for water would release resources from water production to produce goods that yield a higher utility. Of course one might wish to provide some minimum quantity of water free to every household, but the effects of this would be very different from those of making water generally free.

Household choice: an alternative analysis

The marginal utility approach to household behavior came first historically and is still valued because of the great insights that the concept of marginal utility opened up. With the publication in 1939 of Sir John R. Hicks's classic *Value and Capital,* an alternative approach often called indifference curve analysis

became popular in English-language economics.[5] This is not a competing theory but a slightly different way of looking at choices by households. Its major innovation was that it did not invoke the notion of a *measurable* concept of utility.

THE BUDGET LINE

Consider a household faced with the choice between only two goods, food (F) and clothing (C). (Such choices between two goods reveal everything necessary for elementary theory.) Assume that the household has a certain money income, say $120 a month, and that the prices for food and clothing are fixed—at the outset at $4 a unit for food and $2 a unit for clothing. The household cannot afford to save; its only choice is in deciding how much of its $120 to spend on food and how much to spend on clothing.

The household's problem is illustrated by the line *ab* in Figure 8–5, which shows the combinations of food and clothing available to it. The household could spend all its income on clothing and obtain 60C and no F per month. Or it could decide to have 1F each month, at a cost of $4, and only 58$C$. It could also go to the other extreme and purchase only food, buying 30F and no C.

When all of the points indicating combinations that are just available to the household if it spends all its income are joined, the result is

[5] Hicks, whose career has been spent mainly at Oxford, was the first (and so far the only) British recipient of the Nobel prize in economics, for the contributions to economics that he made in *Value and Capital* and elsewhere. He did not invent indifference curve analysis; he took over, popularized, and extended the use of a concept developed by the great Italian economist Vilfredo Pareto in the first decade of this century. As is so often true in science, it is not the discoverer or the inventor, but the one who makes the timely and insightful application, who has the major impact. Thus it was Hicks, not Pareto, who led to the almost universal use of indifference analysis by economists in the 1940s and 1950s. Pareto in his time was following "hints" given in 1896 by the American economist Irving Fisher and in a slim volume published in 1886 by the Italian engineer Giovanni Antonelli. Such is the history of ideas.

Figure 8–5   Budget lines

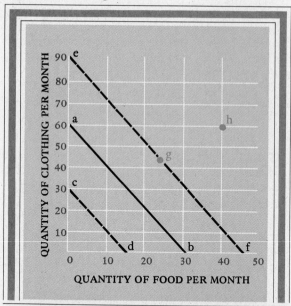

The budget line shows the quantities of goods available to a household given its money income and the prices of the goods it buys. Any point indicates a combination (or *bundle*) of so much food and so much clothing. Point *h*, for example, indicates 60 units of clothing and 40 units of food per month. With an income of $120 a month and prices of $4 for food and $2 for clothing, the household's budget line is *ab*. This line shows all the combinations of *F* and *C* just available to the household with that income and those prices.

An increase in money income from $120 to $180, with money prices of *F* and *C* constant, shifts the budget line outward, parallel to itself, to *ef*. A decrease in money income to $60 shifts the budget line to *cd*.

called the household's **budget line.** (It is also sometimes called an "iso-cost" line since all points on the line represent bundles of goods with the same total cost of purchase.)

Among the important properties of the budget line are the following. (You should

check enough examples against Figure 8–5 to satisfy yourself that they are true.)

1. Points on the budget line represent bundles of commodities that exactly use up the household's income. (Try, for example, the point 20*C* and 20*F*.)

2. Points between the budget line and the origin represent bundles of commodities that use up less than the household's income. (Try, for example, the point 20*C* and 10*F*.)

3. Points above the budget line represent combinations of commodities costing more to purchase then the household's present income. (Try, for example, the point 30*C* and 40*F*.)

The budget line shows all combinations of commodities that are available to the household given its money income and the prices of the goods that it purchases, if it spends all of its income on them.

Changes in money income

What happens to the budget line when money income changes? If the household's money income is halved from $120 to $60 per month, prices being unchanged, then the amount of goods it can buy will also be halved. If it spends all its income on clothing, it will now get 30*C* and no *F* (point *c* in Figure 8–5); if it spends all its income on food, it will get 15*F* and no *C* (point *d*). All possible combinations now open to the household appear on budget line *cd,* which is closer to the origin than the original budget line.

If the household's income rises to $180, it will be able to buy more of both commodities than it could previously. The budget line shifts outward. If it buys only clothing, it can now have 90*C*; if it buys only food, it can have 45*F*; if it divides its income equally between the two goods, it can have 45*C* and 22.5*F*.

Variations in the household's money income, with prices constant, shift the budget line parallel to itself.

Proportional changes in prices of both goods

Changing both prices in the same proportion shifts the budget line parallel to itself in the same way that a money income change shifted it. Doubling both prices with money income constant halves the amount of goods that can be purchased and thus has exactly the same effect on the household's budget line as halving money income with money prices constant. In both cases the household's original budget line is shifted inward.

It is now apparent that it is possible to have exactly offsetting changes in prices and money incomes. A change in money income and a *proportional* change of the same amount in all money prices leaves the position of the budget line—and hence the real choices available to the household—unchanged.

Changes in relative prices

Absolute price or *money price* or merely *price* of a commodity means the amount of money that must be spent to acquire 1 unit of the commodity. A **relative price** is the ratio of two absolute prices. The statement "the price of F is \$2" refers to an absolute price; "the price of F is twice the price of C" refers to a relative price.

A change in a relative price can be accomplished either by changing both of the prices in different proportions or by holding one price constant and changing the other. It is useful for our purposes to do the latter. The effects of such a change are shown in Figure 8–6. The basic conclusion that emerges is

A change in one price, with the other price held constant, changes the slope of the budget line.

The economic significance of the slope of the budget line for food and clothing (which we have just seen to be related to the relative prices of the two commodities) is that it reflects the opportunity cost of food in terms of clothing. To increase food consumption with expenditure constant, one must move

along the budget line consuming less clothing. Suppose the price of food (p_F) is \$2 and the price of clothing (p_C) is \$1. With income fixed, it is necessary to forego the purchase of 2 units of clothing to acquire 1 unit extra of food. The opportunity cost of food in terms of clothing is thus 2 units of clothing. But it can also be stated as p_F/p_C, which is the relative price. Notice that this relative price

Figure 8–6 The effect on the budget line of changes in the price of food

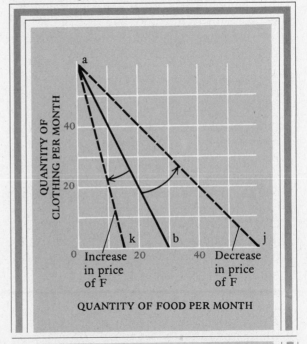

A change in the price of one commodity changes relative prices and thus changes the slope of the budget line. The original budget line *ab* arose from a money income of \$120 and prices of C of \$2 and of F of \$4. A fall in the price of F to \$2 doubles the quantity of F obtainable for any given quantity of C purchased and pivots the budget line outward to *aj*. A rise in the price of F to \$8 reduces the quantity of F obtainable and pivots the budget line inward to *ak*.

$(p_F = 2p_c)$ is consistent with an infinite number of absolute prices. If $p_F = \$40$ and $p_C = \$20$, it still takes the sacrifice of 2 units of clothing to acquire 1 unit of food. This shows that it is relative, not absolute, prices that determine opportunity cost. The general conclusion is that the opportunity cost of F in terms of C is measured by the slope of the budget line or (equivalently) by the relative price ratio. [6]

The basic conclusions restated

It may be helpful to restate the earlier conclusions in terms of absolute and relative prices. (You should reread what has gone before if you cannot prove them yourself.)

1. A change in money income, with absolute prices constant, shifts the budget line parallel to itself—inward toward the origin when income falls and outward away from the origin when income rises.

2. An equal proportional change in all absolute prices leaves relative prices unchanged. Multiplying all money prices by the same constant, with money income constant, has exactly the same effect on the budget line as dividing money income by the same constant with money prices constant.

3. An equal percentage change in all absolute prices and money income leaves the budget line exactly where it was before the changes occurred.

4. A change in relative prices causes the budget line to change its slope.

Real and money income

A household's **money income** is its income measured in money units, so many dollars and cents per month or per year. A household's **real income** is the purchasing power of its money income, i.e., the quantity of goods and services that can be purchased with its money income.

If money prices remain constant, any change in money income will cause a corresponding change in real income. If the house-

hold's money income rises by 10 percent (say from \$10,000 to \$11,000), the household can if it wishes buy 10 percent more of all commodities—its real income has also risen by 10 percent.

If prices change, however, real and money incomes will not change in the same proportion—indeed, they can easily change in opposite directions. Consider a situation in which all money prices rise by 10 percent. If money income falls, or rises by any amount less than 10 percent, real income falls. If money income also rises by 10 percent, real income will be unchanged. Only if money income rises by more than 10 percent will real income also rise.[6]

Changes in real income are shown graphically by shifts in the budget line. When the budget line in Figure 8–5 shifts outward, away from the origin, real income rises. When the line shifts inward, toward the origin, real income falls.

If we are interested in the household's potential standard of living, we are interested in its ability to purchase goods and services; this is appropriately measured by real income and not by money income.

INDIFFERENCE CURVE ANALYSIS[7]

What the household does is determined by both what it can do and what it would like to do. The budget line shows what the household *can do:* the choices that it can make given its money income and the prices of the commodities that it buys. What the household *wants to do* is determined by its tastes.

An indifference curve

Take an imaginary household and give it some quantity of each of the two goods, say

---

[6] Measurement of changes in real income is more complex if prices change in different proportions. The difficulties that then arise are discussed in the first part of the appendix to this chapter, which begins on page 865.

[7] The remainder of this chapter may be omitted without loss of continuity.

18 units of clothing and 10 units of food. (A consumption pattern for a household that contains quantities of two or more distinct goods is called a *bundle* or a *combination* of goods.) Now offer the household an alternative bundle of goods, say 13 units of clothing and 15 units of food. This alternative has 5 units fewer of clothing and 5 units more of food than the first one. Whether the household prefers this bundle depends on the relative valuation that it places on 5 units more of food and 5 units fewer of clothing. If it values the extra food more than the foregone clothing, it will prefer the new bundle to the original one. If it values the food less than the clothing, it will prefer the original bundle. There is a third alternative: If the household values the extra food the same as it values the foregone clothing, it would gain equal satisfaction from the two alternative bundles of food and clothing. In this case the household is said to be indifferent between the two bundles.

Assume that after much trial and error a number of bundles have been identified, each of which gives equal satisfaction. These are shown in Table 8–2.

There will of course be combinations of the

Figure 8–7 An indifference curve

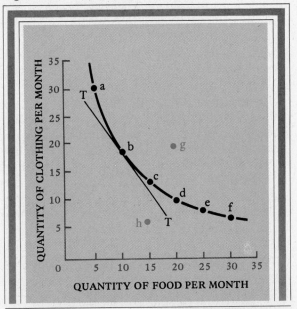

An indifference curve shows combinations of food and clothing that yield equal satisfaction and among which the household is indifferent. Points *a* to *f* are plotted from Table 8–2. The smooth curve through them is an indifference curve: each combination on it gives equal satisfaction to the household. Point *g* above the line is a preferred combination to any point on the line; point *h* below the line is an inferior combination to any point on the line. The slope of the line *T-T* gives the marginal rate of substitution at point *b*. Moving down the curve from *b* to *f* the slope flattens. This shows that the more food and the less clothing the household has, the less willing it will be to sacrifice further clothing to get more food.

Table 8–2 Alternative bundles available to a household

Bundle	Clothing	Food
a	30	5
b	18	10
c	13	15
d	10	20
e	8	25
f	7	30

By assumption, these bundles each give equal satisfaction to the household, which is thus "indifferent" among them. These bundles define a series of points which lie on a single indifference curve for the household.

two commodities other than those enumerated in the table that will give the same level of satisfaction to the household. All of these combinations are shown in Figure 8–7 by the smooth curve that passes through the points plotted from the table. This curve is an indifference curve. In general, an **indifference curve** shows all combinations of goods that yield the same satisfaction to the household. A household is *indifferent* between the combinations indicated by any two points on one indifference curve.

Any points above and to the right of the curve show combinations of food and clothing that the household would prefer to combinations indicated by points on the curve. Consider, for example, the combination of 20 food and 18 clothing, which is represented by point *g* in the figure. Although it might not be obvious that this bundle must be preferred to bundle *a* (which has more clothing but less food), it is obvious that it will be preferred to bundle *c,* because there is both less clothing and less food represented at *c* than at *g.* Inspection of the graph shows that *any* point above the curve will be obviously superior to *some* points on the curve in the sense that it will contain both more food and more clothing than those points on the curve.

But since all points on the curve are equal in the household's eyes, the point above the curve must thus be superior to *all* points on the curve. By a similar argument, points below and to the left of the curve represent bundles of goods that are inferior to bundles represented by points on the curve.

The hypothesis of a diminishing marginal rate of substitution

Now look closely at the shape of the indifference curve in Figure 8–7. The downward slope of this curve indicates that, if the household has its clothing purchases reduced, it must have its food purchases increased if its overall level of satisfaction is to remain constant. Not only is the indifference curve downward sloping, it is also convex viewed from the origin (i.e., the slope becomes flatter and flatter as one moves down and to the right). The slope of an indifference curve represents the **marginal rate of substitution** of one commodity for the other, in terms of satisfaction.

This convex shape represents the basic hypothesis of indifference theory. The hypothesis of a *diminishing marginal rate of substitution* is that the less of one good and the more of another that a household has, the less willing it will be to give up some of the first good to get further units of the second good. It plays the same role in indifference theory that the hypothesis of diminishing marginal utility plays in utility theory.

The hypothesis is illustrated in Table 8–3, which is based on the example of food and clothing shown in Table 8–2. The last column of the table shows the rate at which the household is prepared to sacrifice units of clothing per unit of food obtained. At first the household will sacrifice 2.4 units of clothing to get 1 unit more of food, but as its consumption of clothing diminishes and that of food increases, the household becomes less and less

Table 8–3 The marginal rate of substitution between clothing and food

Movement	(1) Change in clothing	(2) Change in food	(3) Marginal rate of substitution (1) ÷ (2)
From *a* to *b*	−12	5	−2.4
From *b* to *c*	− 5	5	−1.0
From *c* to *d*	− 3	5	− .6
From *d* to *e*	− 2	5	− .4
From *e* to *f*	− 1	5	− .2

The marginal rate of substitution of clothing for food declines as the quantity of clothing in the bundle declines and the quantity of food increases. This table is based on Table 8–2. When the household moves from *a* to *b*, it gives up 12 units of clothing and gains 5 units of food; it remains at the same level of overall satisfaction. The household at point *a* was prepared to sacrifice 12 clothing for 5 food (i.e., $\frac{12}{5}$ = 2.4 units of clothing per unit of food obtained). When the household moves from *b* to *c*, it sacrifices 5 clothing for 5 food (a rate of substitution of 1 unit of clothing for each unit of food).

willing to sacrifice further clothing for more food.[8]

The indifference map

So far we have constructed only a single indifference curve. There must, however, be a similar curve through other points in Figure 8–7. Starting at any point, such as *g,* there will be other combinations that will yield equal satisfaction to the household and, if the points indicating all of *these* combinations are connected, they will form another indifference curve. This exercise can be repeated as many times as we wish and as many indifference curves as we wish can be generated. The farther away any indifference curve is from the origin, the higher is the level of satisfaction given by any of the combinations of goods indicated by points on the curve.

A set of indifference curves is called an **indifference map,** an example of which is shown in Figure 8–8. It specifies the household's tastes by showing its rate of substitution between the two commodities for every level of current consumption of these commodities. When economists say that a household's tastes are *given,* they do not mean that the household's current consumption pattern is given; rather, they mean that the household's entire indifference map is given.

The equilibrium of the household

Indifference maps describe the preferences of households. Budget lines describe the possibilities open to the household. To predict what households will actually do, both of

[8] Movements between widely separated points on the indifference curve have been examined. In terms of a very small movement from any of the points on the curve, the rate at which the household will give up clothing to get food is shown by the slope of the tangent to the curve at that point. The slope of the line *T* which is a tangent to the curve at point *b* in Figure 8–7 may thus be thought of as the slope of the curve at that precise point. It tells us the rate at which the household will sacrifice clothing per unit of food obtained when it is currently consuming 18 clothing and 10 food (the coordinates of point *b*).

Figure 8–8 An indifference map

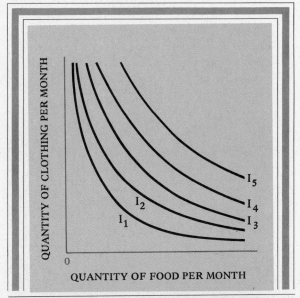

An indifference map consists of a set of indifference curves. All points on a particular curve indicate alternative combinations of food and clothing that give the household equal satisfaction. The further the curve from the origin, the higher the level of satisfaction it represents. Thus I_5 is a higher indifference curve than I_4 and represents a higher level of satisfaction.

these sets of information must be put together. This is done in Figure 8–9. The household's budget line is shown in the figure by the straight line, while its tastes are shown by its indifference map (a few of whose curves are shown in the figure). Any point on the budget line is attainable. But which point will actually be chosen by the household that is interested in maximizing its satisfactions?

Since the household wishes to maximize its satisfactions, it wishes to reach its highest attainable indifference curve. Inspection of the figure shows that if the household purchases any bundle on its budget line where an indif-

Figure 8–9   The equilibrium of a household

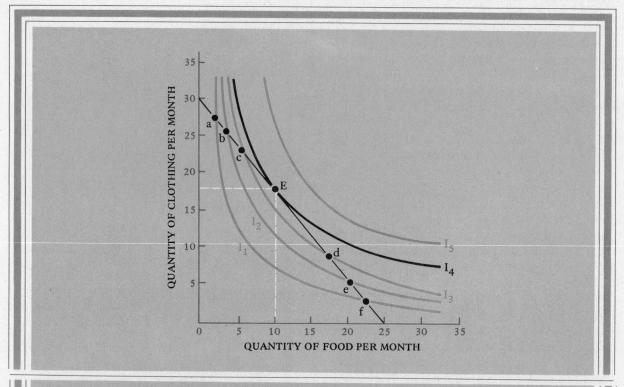

Equilibrium occurs at *E* where an indifference curve is tangent to the budget line.   The household has an income of $750 a month and faces prices of $25 a unit for clothing and $30 a unit for food. A combination of *C* and *F* indicated by point *a* is attainable, but by moving along the budget line higher indifference curves can be reached. The same is true at *b* and *c*. At *E*, however, where an indifference curve is tangent to the budget line, it is impossible to reach a higher curve by moving along the budget line. If the household did alter its consumption bundle by moving from *E* to *c* or *d*, for example, it would move to lower indifference cuves and thus to lower levels of satisfaction.

ference curve cuts the budget line, a higher indifference curve can be reached. Only when the bundle purchased is one where an indifference curve is tangent to the budget line is it impossible for the household to alter its purchases and reach a higher curve.

The household's satisfaction is maximized at the point at which an indifference curve is tangent to its budget line.

At such a tangency position, the slope of the

indifference curve (the marginal rate of substitution of the goods in the household's preferences) is the same as the slope of the budget line (the relative prices of the goods in the market). The common sense of this result is that if the household values goods at a different rate than the market does, there is room for profitable exchange. The household can give up some of the good it values relatively less than the market and take in return some more of the good it values relatively higher than the market does. When the household is prepared to swap goods at the same rate as they can be traded on the market, there is no further opportunity for it to raise its satisfaction by substituting one commodity for the other.

The household is presented with market information (prices) that it cannot itself change. It adjusts to these prices by choosing a bundle of goods such that, at the margin, its own subjective evaluation of the goods conforms with the evaluations given by market prices.

The reaction of the household to a change in income

We have seen that a change in income leads to parallel shifts of the budget line—inward toward the origin when income falls and outward away from the origin when income rises. For each level of income there will be an equilibrium position at which an indifference curve is tangent to the relevant budget line. Each such equilibrium position means that the household is doing as well as it possibly can for that level of income. If we move the budget line through all possible levels of income, and if we join up all the points of equilibrium, we will trace out what is called an **income-consumption line,** an example of which is shown in Figure 8–10. This line shows how consumption bundles change as income changes, with relative prices held constant.[9]

The reaction of a household to a change in price

We already know that a change in the relative price of the two goods changes the slope of the budget line. If the price of food is varied

[9] This income-consumption line can be used to derive the type of curve relating consumption of one commodity to income first introduced on page 78. To do this, take the quantity of either good consumed at the equilibrium position on a given budget line and plot it against the level of money income that determined the position of the particular budget line. By repeating this for each level of income, the required curve is produced.

Figure 8–10 The income-consumption line

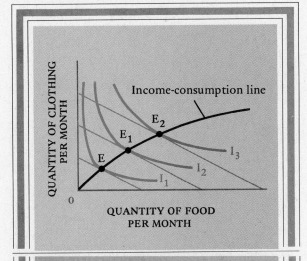

The income-consumption line shows how the household's purchases react to a change in income with relative prices held constant. Increases in income shift the budget line out parallel to itself, moving the equilibrium from E to E_1 to E_2. By joining up all the points of equilibrium, an income-consumption line is traced out.

continuously, there will be an equilibrium position for each price. Connecting these traces out a **price-consumption line.** See Figure 8–11. Notice that as the relative price of food and clothing changes, the relative quantities of food and clothing purchased also change. In particular, as the price of food falls the household buys more food.[10]

We are now very close to deriving a demand curve for food. Figure 8–11 shows how the quantity of food consumed varies as the price of food varies. This gives us the information needed to plot a demand curve. All we need to do is to transfer this information to a new diagram with the price of food on one

[10] There is a rarely encountered but theoretically possible exception to this rule, a Giffen good, which is described in the appendix to this chapter, which begins on page 865.

Figure 8–11   The price-consumption line

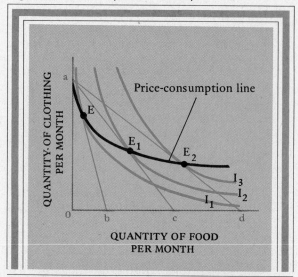

The price-consumption line shows how the household's purchases react to a decrease in one price with money income and other prices held constant. Decreases in the price of food (with money income and the price of clothing constant) pivot the budget line from *ab* to *ac* to *ad*. The equilibrium position moves from E to E_1 to E_2. By joining up all the points of equilibrium, a price-consumption line is traced out.

axis and the quantity of food consumed on the other.[11]

Summary

1. Marginal utility theory distinguishes between the total utility gained from the consumption of all units of some commodity and the marginal utility resulting from the consumption of one more unit of the commodity. The

---

[11] The derivation of demand curves from indifference curves is further explored in the second part of the appendix to this chapter, which can be found on page 875.

---

basic assumption about a household's tastes made in utility theory is that the utility the household derives from the consumption of successive units of a commodity per period of time will diminish as the consumption of that commodity increases.

2. The household maximizes its utility and thus reaches equilibrium when the utility derived from the last *dollar* spent on each commodity is equal. Another way of putting this is that the marginal utilities derived from the last *unit* of each commodity consumed should be proportional to their prices.

3. It is vital to distinguish between total and marginal utilities because most choices are related to marginal utilities and cannot be predicted from a knowledge of total utilities. The paradox of value involved a confusion between total and marginal utilities. Whether goods are ''necessities'' or ''luxuries,'' while perhaps determining the total utilities they produce, tells nothing about marginal utilities. But it is marginal utilities that are required for defining elasticity and understanding market behavior.

4. Indifference curves and indifference theory provide an alternative way of studying household consumption behavior. The basic constructs of indifference curve analysis are the budget line and the indifference map.

5. The budget line shows all of the combinations of two commodities that just use up the household's income. The budget line indicates the household's real income— the amount of purchasing power available to the household. The position of the budget line depends on the household's money income *and* money prices.

6. While the budget line describes what the household *can* purchase, indifference curves describe the household's tastes and, therefore, refer to what it would *like* to do. A single indifference curve joins combinations of commodities that give the household equal satisfaction and among which it is therefore indifferent.

7. The basic hypothesis about tastes is that of diminishing marginal rate of substitution. This hypothesis states that the less of one good and the more of another that the household has, the less willing it will be to give up some of the first good to get a further unit of the second. The geometrical expression of this hypothesis is that the indifference curve is convex viewed from the origin.

8. An indifference map is composed of a set of indifference curves. Each curve joins points of equal satisfaction. Curves further away from the origin represent higher levels of satisfaction than curves closer to the origin.

9. The household maximizes its satisfactions, given its budget line, at the point at which an indifference curve is tangent to its budget line.

10. The income-consumption line shows how quantity consumed changes as income changes. The price-consumption line shows how quantity consumed changes as price changes.

11. A change in relative prices changes the relative quantities of different commodities consumed, there being a tendency to consume relatively more of commodities whose relative price falls and relatively less of commodities whose relative price rises.

12. The appendix to this chapter carries further the discussion of two topics: the measurement of real income through index numbers and the derivation of downward-sloping demand curves using indifference theory. It can be found on page 869.

Concepts for review

Market demand and individual household demand curves
The hypothesis of diminishing marginal utility
Conditions for maximizing utility
The interpretation of $MU_x/MU_y = p_x/p_y$
The paradox of value
The budget line
Real income and money income
Indifference curves and indifference maps
The marginal rate of substitution
The tangency of the budget line and an indifference curve
The price-consumption and income-consumption lines

Discussion questions

1. Why is market demand the *horizontal* sum of individual demand curves? Is the vertical sum different? What would a vertical sum of individual demand curves show? Can you imagine any use of vertical summation of demand curves?

2. Which of the choices implied below involve a consideration of marginal utilities and which total utilities?
a. The State Legislature debates whether 17-year-olds should be given the vote.
b. A diet calls for precisely 1,200 calories per day.
c. My doctor says I must give up smoking and drinking or else accept an increased chance of heart attack.
d. In 1976 Armand Hammer decided to buy the Rembrandt

painting *Juno* for a record \$3.25 million and called it the "crown jewel of my collection."
e. I enjoyed my golf game today, but I was so tired that I decided to stop at the seventeenth hole.

3. Are the transactions described in the following quotations consistent with total utility? Interpret "worthless" and "priceless" as used here.
a. "Bob Koppang has made a business of selling jars of shredded U.S. currency. The money is worthless, and yet he's sold 53,000 jars already and has orders for 40,000 more—at \$5.00 a jar. Each jar contains about \$10,000 in shredded bills."
b. "Leonardo da Vinci's priceless painting *Genevra de' Benci* was sold to the National Gallery of Art for \$5 million."

4. *The New York Times* called it the great liver crisis. Chopped liver is a delicacy on the table, particularly the kosher table, but in 1976 it was a glut on the market. Prices had sunk to a 20-year low as supplies had risen to an all-time high due to a very high cattle slaughter. What do the following quotations from the *Times's* story tell you about the marginal and total utility of liver?
a. "Grade A-1 liver is being used for cats and dogs instead of people. It's unheard of, it's a waste," says the manager of Kosher King Meat Products. "Even Israel is drowning in chopped liver."
b. "They're falling all over their feet to sell to me," said the president of Mrs. Weinberg's Kosher Chopped Liver Co., which uses 3,500 pounds of liver daily. "I've been offered prices so low I can't believe them."
c. "The nature of people being what they are, even though they like a good bargain, they're not going to eat something that doesn't agree with their taste."

5. John Ehrlichman, after leaving government service but before serving a prison sentence, was quoted as saying: "When I get to be king of the world, everybody is going to have four or five hours every day just for themselves, and the world will be a better place." What does this tell you about Mr. Ehrlichman's utility schedule? Under what circumstances would the world be a better place if someone made it obligatory for everyone to have several hours "just for themselves"?

6. Is a household relatively better off if its money income is decreased by 10 percent or if the prices of all the goods it buys are increased by 10 percent? Does it matter in answering this question whether the household spends all of its income?

9

Demand theory in action

Much of what economists do to earn a living involves the use of demand measurements. Economists are asked by electric utility companies to draw up long-term investment plans based upon the demand for electric power over the next decade; the National Park Service asks economists to review its systems for selling grazing rights and timber stands to private firms. Whether—and to what extent—raising prices will help ease the deficit of the New York City subway system or the Panama Canal are questions that cannot be correctly answered without knowledge of price elasticity of demand. When the FAO (the United Nations Food and Agricultural Organization) or a producers co-op wants to make agricultural demand projections by crops and areas it needs to know income elasticities of demand. Many industries need to know the cross elasticities of demand for their products with oil and gas in order to estimate the effects on them of the sharply rising prices of oil and gas.

To deal effectively with many substantive issues, knowledge of relevant demand conditions is indispensable. Fortunately a great deal of the demand information the economist requires is available. In this chapter we first look at some of the wealth of empirical knowledge that has been accumulated over the last few decades.

Even where information is not already available, it is often possible to obtain it without great cost or difficulty. The methods for obtaining it have been carefully worked out. Solutions to two of the most troubling problems are discussed in the second part of the chapter.

Critics of demand theory do not quarrel with the *need* for demand information, or even with the usefulness of applied economics, but they have questioned whether the *theory* of demand is either wrong or empty in the sense that it tells us only that "anything can happen." In the final part of this chapter we consider these criticisms.

Measurement of demand

MODERN MEASURES OF DEMAND

Over the last few decades, the solution of the statistical problems associated with demand measurement has led to a large accumulation of data on demand elasticities. The value of these data to the applied economist is the ultimate proof of the usefulness of demand theory. In this chapter we can do no more than illustrate the great wealth of available data.

Price elasticities

Table 9–1 shows a few estimated price elasticities of demand, covering both agricultural and nonagricultural commodities. Much of the pioneering work on demand measurement concerned the price elasticity of demand of agricultural products. This attention was due in part to the large price variations (caused by fluctuating crops and competitive market conditions) in those commodities; such price variations provided the sort of empirical evidence needed to measure demand elasticities. It was due also to concern about the level of farm incomes and the relation of farmers' welfare to fluctuating crops. Professors Henry Schultz in the United States and Richard Stone in the United Kingdom were prominent in these efforts. Many agricultural research centers (such as the Giannini Foundation of the University of California) extended this work and even today devote efforts to the estimation of price elasticities of foodstuffs. These data mostly confirm the general belief in low price elasticities for individual crops and also for food products as a whole.

The policy payoff of this knowledge in terms of understanding the farm problem was enormous; it represents an early triumph of empirical work in economics. (See the discussion in Chapter 7.)

Although agricultural commodities often

Table 9–1 Estimated price elasticities of demand in the United States[a] (selected commodities)

Inelastic demand (less than unity)	
Potatoes	0.3
Sugar	0.3
Public transportation	0.4
All foods	0.4
Cigarettes	0.5
Gasoline	0.6
All clothing	0.6
Consumer durables	0.8
Demand of approximately unit elasticity[b]	
Beef	
Beer	
Marijuana	
Elastic demand (greater than unity)	
Furniture	1.2
Electricity	1.3
U.K. lamb and mutton (U.K.)	1.5
Automobiles	2.1
Millinery	3.0

[a] For the United States except where noted.
[b] Greater than 0.9 and less than 1.1.

The wide range of price elasticities is suggested by these selected measures. These elasticities, from various studies, are representative of literally hundreds of existing estimates. Explanations of some of the differences are discussed in the text. Can you advance a hypothesis as to why cigarettes and gasoline are inelastic, but electricity elastic? why furniture is more elastic than all consumer durable goods?

have inelastic demands, notice in Table 9–1 that some commodities, such as beef in the United States and domestically produced lamb and mutton in the United Kingdom, have been found to be elastic. The reason for this is that they have close substitutes. For example British households can choose between locally produced lamb and mutton and imported lamb and mutton (which typically has a somewhat lower quality and price than the domestic product). Similarly, American households can and do choose between beef, pork, and chicken on the basis of price. The broader the category of related products, the lower the observed price elasticity of demand.

Although the importance of the agricultural problem led early investigators to concentrate on the demand for foodstuffs, modern studies have expanded to include virtually the whole range of commodities on which the household spends its income. Particular interest has attached to the demand for consumers' durables such as cars, radios, refrigerators, television sets, and houses. Demands for these types of goods are particularly interesting because they constitute a large fraction of total demand and because such demands can be markedly variable from one year to the next. Because the commodity is durable, it can always be made to "make do" for another year; thus purchases can be postponed with greater ease than can purchases of nondurables such as food and services. If enough households decide simultaneously to postpone purchases of durables for even six months, this decision can have a major effect on the economy.

How then can we explain the relatively low (0.8) price elasticity for durables shown in Table 9–1? Again, the answer lies in the broadness of the category. When the price of TV sets rises, the alternative to many buyers may be to replace their lawnmower or their vacuum cleaner instead of buying that extra TV set. Durables as a whole are less elastic than individual kinds of durable goods. Another example of this same phenomenon: while automobiles have a relatively high price elasticity of demand, Ford Pinto automobiles surely have a much higher price elasticity than all automobiles.

Because most specific manufactured goods have close substitutes, studies show they tend to have price-elastic demand. Millinery, for example, has been estimated to have an elasticity of 3.0. In contrast, "all clothing" tends to be inelastic.

The accumulated data on price elasticity confirm this generalization:

Any one of a group of close substitutes will tend to

have an elastic demand, even though the demand for the group as a whole may be inelastic.

Income elasticities

Table 9–2 provides a sample of the vast amount of collected data on income elasticities. Because the demand over time for particular basic commodities is so greatly affected by income elasticities, the FAO has estimated income elasticities for dozens of products, country by country.

These data tend to show that the more basic or staple a commodity, the lower is its income elasticity: food as a whole has an income elasticity of 0.2, durables of 1.8. In the United States pork and such starchy roots as potatoes are inferior goods; their quantity consumed falls as income rises.

Does the distinction between luxuries and necessities explain differences in income elasticities? The table suggests that it does. The case of meals eaten away from home is one example; such meals are almost always more expensive, calorie for calorie, than meals prepared at home. It would thus be expected that at lower ranges of income restaurant meals would be regarded as an expensive luxury, the demand for which would, however, expand substantially as households became richer. This is in fact what happens. Does this mean that the market demand for the foodstuffs that appear on restaurant menus will also have high income elasticities? Generally the answer is no; when a household eats out rather than preparing meals at home, the main change is not in what is eaten but in who prepares it. The additional expenditure on "food" goes mainly to pay the wages of cooks and waiters and to yield a return on the restaurateur's capital. Thus, when a household expands its expenditure on restaurant food by 2.4 percent in response to a 1 percent rise in its income, most of this represents an increased demand for a service to replace the cook's unpaid work rather than an increased demand for food. Most of the extra expenditure on "food" goes to persons in the service industry; little, if any, finds its way into the pockets of farmers. We have here a striking example of the general tendency for households to spend a higher proportion of their income on services as their income rises.

The interesting relationship shown in the table between whole milk, cheese, and cream suggests that as incomes rise people tend to change the form of the milk products they consume—less whole milk, more cheese, and more cream. (Ice cream, not included in the FAO data, had a high income elasticity for American consumers in measurements of two decades ago. Today the income elasticity is lower. To an earlier generation ice cream was a special treat; at current American income levels and prices, ice cream has become a staple.)

Empirical studies tend to confirm the fact that, as income rises, household expenditures follow broadly similar paths in different countries. Summarizing recent studies, Robert Ferber wrote that they "tend to bear out earlier findings on income elasticity yielding low elasticities for food and housing, elasticities close to unity for clothing and education, and higher elasticities for various types of recreation, personal care, home operation and other services." Of course there are exceptions to across-country uniformity, as Table 9–2 shows. If a commodity plays a very different role in the consumption patterns of different groups it may be expected to have different demand characteristics even at comparable levels of income. Wine is a basic part of the French consumption bundle, and its consumption in France is little affected by changes in level of income. Wine in Canada and the United States is evidently a luxury good rather than a necessity at lower levels of income. The difference in income elasticity of demand for poultry in the United States and in Ceylon is a matter of the level of average income as well as of differences in taste.

The accumulated data on income elasticity confirm this generalization:

The more basic an item in the consumption pattern

Table 9–2 Estimated income elasticities of demand[a] (selected commodities)

Inferior goods (negative income elasticities)	
Whole milk	−0.5
Pig products	−0.2
Starchy roots	−0.2
Inelastic normal goods (0.0 to 1.0)	
Coffee	0.0
Wine (France)	0.1
All food	0.2
Poultry	0.3
Cheese	0.4
Beef	0.5
Housing	0.6
Cigarettes	0.8
Elastic normal goods (greater than 1.0)	
Gasoline	1.1
Wine	1.4
Cream (U.K.)	1.7
Wine (Canada)	1.8
Consumer durables	1.8
Poultry (Ceylon)	2.0
Restaurant meals (U.K.)	2.4

[a] For the United States except where noted.

Income elasticities vary widely across commodities and sometimes across countries. The basic source of food estimates by country is the FAO, but many individual studies have been made of which the results reported here are a tiny sample. Explanations of some of the differences are discussed in the text. Can you advance a hypothesis as to why gasoline is more income elastic than cigarettes or housing? why coffee is less income elastic than beef?

of households, the lower will be its income elasticity.

Cross elasticities of demand

Many of the most interesting studies of cross elasticity have been made in the course of attempts to determine whether specific products are substitutes as part of antitrust inquiries (see Chapter 18, page 297). Whether cellophane and Saran Wrap, or aluminum cable and copper cable, are or are not substitutes may determine questions of monopoly under the law. As we have seen, the sign and size of cross elasticities sheds light on whether or not goods are substitutes.

Other variables

Modern studies show that demand is often influenced by a wide variety of socioeconomic factors—family size, age, geographical location, type of employment, wealth, and income expectations—not included in the traditional theory of demand. Although significant, the total contribution of all of these factors to changes in demand tends to be small. Typically, less than 30 percent of the variations in demand are accounted for by these "novel" factors and a much higher proportion by the traditional variables of prices and current incomes.

PROBLEMS OF MEASUREMENT

We have presented here just the tip of the iceberg of accumulated knowledge about the determinants of demand and the quantitative magnitude of specific demand relationships. Any economist who wishes to make an applied study of a particular market is likely to have some established evidence on which to draw. As time goes by, further evidence accumulates at a rapid rate and we find ourselves far beyond merely wondering if demand curves slope downward. Not only do we now know the approximate shape of many demand curves, we also have information about how demand curves shift.

This relatively recent explosion of knowledge resulted when econometricians overcame major problems in measuring demand relationships. A discussion of these problems must be left to a course in econometrics, but one aspect of such measurements is sufficiently troubling to most students to make it worth mentioning: Since in a market economy all kinds of things are happening at once, how can they be sorted out into the neat theoretical categories we have created? When market demand changes over time, it is in-

variably the case that the influences that affect demand will all be changing. What, for example, is to be made of the observation that the quantity of butter consumed per capita rose by 10 percent over a period in which average household income rose by 5 percent, the price of butter fell by 3 percent, and the price of margarine rose by 4 percent?

A first set of questions concerns how much

The identification problem

The three-part diagram below illustrates the so-called identification problem. If, as in (i), the demand curve stays put while the supply curve moves up and down—perhaps because of crop variations in some agricultural commodity—then market observations in prices and quantities (shown by the black dots) trace out the demand curve. If, as in (ii), the supply curve stays put while the demand curve moves about—owing perhaps to changes in the number of consumers or their incomes—market observations trace out the supply curve.

So far so good. But what if both curves shift randomly back and forth between the four positions shown in (iii)? In such a situation a series of market observations will be obtained that will not trace out either the demand or the supply curves that generated them. A few such points are shown in the panel. Points E_1, E_2, E_3, and E_4—market observations of quantities and prices at different times—do not *identify* either the demand curve or the supply curve.

The identification problem is surmountable. The key to identifying the demand and supply curves separately is to bring in other variables than price and then to relate demand to one (or more) of them and

of the change is due to income elasticity of demand, how much to price elasticity, and how much to the cross elasticity between butter and margarine. If there is only this one observation, the question cannot be answered. If, however, there is a large number of observations showing, say, quantity demanded, income, price of butter, and price of margarine every month for four or five years, it is pos-

sible, as we saw in Chapter 3, to discover the separate influence of each of the variables. The most frequently used technique for estimating the separate effect of each of these variables on demand is called multiple-regression analysis, which can be used directly to estimate each of the elasticities mentioned.

A second set of questions concerns using data on quantity actually *consumed* to estimate

supply to *some other* variables. For example, supply of the commodity might be related not only to the price of the commodity but also to its costs of production, and demand might be related not only to the price of the commodity but also to consumers' incomes. Provided that both of these other factors, cost of production and income, vary sufficiently, it is possible to determine the relation between quantity supplied and price as well as the relation between quantity demanded and price.

Neglect of the identification problem can cause serious errors in interpreting economic data. Consider this analysis: "Last year the price of scotch whisky rose by 10 percent and scotch imports hardly fell at

all, so we know that the market for scotch in the United States must have a low elasticity of demand." Has the author really identified the demand curve? He may have if the rise in price reflects a shift of the supply curve. But if the rise in price was mainly due to a rise in demand for scotch, he may actually have discovered that the short-run supply curve of scotch is very inelastic (because scotch takes several years to manufacture). The general rule to keep in mind is that, unless there is additional information that provides clues to how much each curve shifted, nothing can be told about the shape of either the demand or the supply curve from price and quantity data alone.

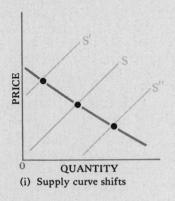

(i) Supply curve shifts

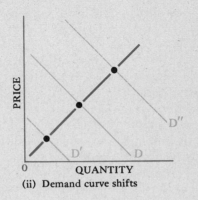

(ii) Demand curve shifts

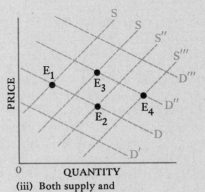

(iii) Both supply and demand curves shift

quantity *demanded*. The problem arises because both demand shifts and supply shifts can change the quantity actually consumed, and thus the shape of the demand curve may not be definitively established from data on prices and quantities alone. This **identification problem,** too, is amenable to statistical solution, as suggested in the box.

Criticisms of demand theory

Some critics have dismissed demand theory completely on the grounds that it is based on the ridiculous assumption that all households make decisions on the basis of careful marginal calculations about the effects of minor adjustments in expenditure patterns. They argue that this assumption might well describe the behavior of some middle-class, record-keeping groups but not that of most households.

Other critics maintain that demand theory has very little substantive content. According to them, the theory is a complex theoretical apparatus that in essence offers little more than the proposition that most demand curves slope downward most of the time. If this is all we get from the elaborate theory, then demand theory really is a lot of sound and fury signifying (almost) nothing. It is time to consider these criticisms.

DOES DEMAND THEORY MAKE UNREASONABLE ASSUMPTIONS ABOUT RATIONAL HOUSEHOLD DECISION MAKING?

In developing the theory of household behavior in Chapter 8, we deduced that if households wished to maximize their utility or satisfaction they would vary their consumption patterns in a way that makes relative marginal utilities exactly proportional to relative market prices (marginal utility theory) or marginal rates of substitution exactly equal to the relative market prices (indifference theory). It

is tempting to dismiss these theories out of hand, saying that it is unrealistic to pretend that households always act with the mechanical consistency apparently assumed by such theories. Critics of the theories will point to their own behavior and to that of households of their acquaintances to support their argument that people sometimes do things that are not calculated to maximize their utility, such as occasionally buying strawberries in spite of, or even because of, a rise in their price, or spending a whole week's pay on a binge or a frivolous purchase and regretting it for the rest of the week.

What can be made of these criticisms? The answer depends on what we want demand theory to accomplish. Consider an automobile firm wondering about the effect on its sales of an increase in price. Three possible uses of demand theory may be distinguished. The first use is to study the aggregate behavior of all households—as graphically illustrated, for example, by the market demand curve for a product. The second use is to make probabilistic statements about an individual household's actions under certain circumstances. The third use is to make statements about what each household will certainly do. Clearly the first is what interests the automobile firm: It cares not about what every last household does, nor (really) about what *you* do; it cares about whether in aggregate, and by how much, its sales will decrease if it raises its price.

This sort of aggregate use of the theory of demand is the most common one in economics. The predictions developed in Chapter 7, you will recall, depend on having some knowledge of the shape of the relevant market demand curves, yet they do not require the ability to predict the behavior of each individual household. The second use, though much less common than the first, is occasionally important; it is sometimes desirable to be able to say what a single household (or a subset of all households) will probably do. The third use is by far the least important, because it is rarely necessary, possible, or even interesting to try to make categorical statements about what each household will always do.

Fortunately, the criticisms cited apply only to the third use of demand theory. The observation that households sometimes behave in an inconsistent fashion would, if carefully documented, refute only the prediction that *all* households *always* behave as assumed by the theory. In order to predict the existence of a relatively stable downward-sloping market demand curve (the first use), or to predict what an individual household will probably do (the second use), we do not require that *all* households behave as is assumed by the theory all of the time. Consider two illustrations. First, some households may always behave in a manner not assumed by the theory. Households whose members are mental defectives or have serious emotional disturbances are obvious possibilities. The inconsistent or erratic behavior of such households will not cause market demand curves to depart from their downward slope, provided these households account for a minority of total purchasers of any product. Their erratic behavior will be swamped by the normal behavior of the majority of households. Second, an occasional irrationality or inconsistency on the part of every household will not upset the downward slope of the market demand curve so long as these isolated inconsistencies do not occur at the same time in all households. As long as such inconsistencies are unrelated across households, occurring now in one and now in another, their effect will be offset by the normal behavior of the majority of households.[1]

The downward slope of the demand curve requires only that at any moment of time most households

[1] See the discussion in Chapter 2, pages 20–21.

are behaving as assumed by the theory. This is quite compatible with inconsistent behavior on the part of some households all of the time and on the part of all households some of the time.

IS DEMAND THEORY ONLY AN ELABORATE WAY OF SAYING THAT ANYTHING CAN HAPPEN?

Demand theory predicts that the quantity of a good demanded varies with its own price, the prices of other goods, income, and tastes. Critics argue that because quantity demanded may rise, fall, or stay unchanged as any one of these influencing factors changes, the theory is merely an elaborate way of saying "anything can happen."

While it is true that anything can happen, this does not mean that every possible outcome is equally likely. If further theory or empirical work can tell us when one outcome is more likely than another, the theory will prove useful.

To discuss this issue, it is necessary to consider the relation between quantity demanded and each of the variables that is supposed to influence it. We shall ask in each case if the theory offers interesting or useful predictions about the behavior of demand and then if there is evidence confirming these predictions.

Quantity demanded and the commodity's own price

Early demand theory predicted that all demand curves must always slope downward. This prediction was known for a long time as the law of demand: The price of a product and the amount demanded vary inversely with each other. Criticisms of the law of demand have taken various forms, focusing on the Giffen good, the conspicuous consumption good, and (by far the most important) the good whose demand is perfectly inelastic.

The Giffen good. Great interest was attached to an apparent refutation of the law of demand by the Victorian economist Sir Robert Giffen. Giffen is reputed to have observed and documented that during the nineteenth century a rise in the price of imported wheat led to an increase in the price of bread, but that the consumption of bread by the British working class increased. If this observation is correct (i.e., if Giffen really made it—which now appears to be in doubt—and if his measurements were correct), it would refute the prediction that *all* demand curves *always* slope downward. It would not be inconsistent with the theory because this is precisely the sort of exception envisaged by modern theory and mentioned in the appendix to Chapter 8 (see page 869). This kind of exception is, in any case, extraordinarily limited in theory and is all but unknown in observations of actual markets.[2]

Conspicuous consumption goods. Thorstein Veblen in *The Theory of the Leisure Class* (1899) suggested that some commodities were consumed not for their intrinsic qualities but because they carried a snob appeal. The more expensive such a commodity became, the *greater* might be its ability to confer status on its purchaser.

This is, of course, possible. Elizabeth Taylor and Joe Namath may buy diamonds, not because they particularly like diamonds per se but because they wish to show off their wealth in an ostentatious but socially acceptable way. They are assumed to value diamonds precisely because they are expensive; thus a fall in price might lead them to stop

buying diamonds and to switch to a more satisfactory object of conspicuous consumption. If enough households acted similarly, this could lead to an upward-sloping rather than a downward-sloping market demand curve for diamonds.

Assertions of this sort of behavior are not uncommon. A *New York Times* business editor recently speculated that "a key factor in [Cadillac] Seville's success may well be pricing it *above* its lengthier brothers, eliminating any chance of besmirching Seville's reputation as a cheaper Cadillac."

To the best of our knowledge, however, no one has ever observed statistically an upward-sloping market demand curve for commodities such as diamonds or luxury cars that are used for ostentatious display. Indeed an FTC study of discount patterns by type of car showed that over 50 percent of new luxury cars sold at discounts of 10 percent or more and 80 percent sold at discounts of over 5 percent. Evidently even luxury car dealers find they can sell more cars by giving discounts—i.e., that demand slopes downward.

The reason for this, notwithstanding the undoubted snob appeal of certain goods, is not hard to discover. Consideration of the countless lower-income consumers who would be glad to buy diamonds or Cadillacs if only they were sufficiently inexpensive suggests that upward-sloping demand curves for a few individual wealthy households are much more likely than is an upward-sloping market demand curve for the same commodity. Recall the discussion (page 137) about the ability of the theory of the downward-sloping demand curve to accommodate odd behavior on the part of a small group of households (this time the "odd" group is the rich rather than the mentally defective or the emotionally disturbed).

Perfectly inelastic demand curves. Even if demand curves do not slope *upward to the right* as

[2] The commodity must be a good with a large negative income effect (an inferior good) *and* play so large a part in most households' budgets that an increase in its price leads to a large decrease in households' real incomes. An example might be bread in a very poor economy where it is the staple of the diet of many people. Suppose, in such an economy, that the price of bread rises sharply. This may be expected to lead to larger expenditures on bread, which will further impoverish many households to the point where they are forced to substitute bread (even though it is more expensive) for other more luxurious forms of nourishment.

the previous cases have suggested, the substantial insight provided by the law of demand would be diminished if there were many important commodities for which changes in price had virtually no effect on quantity demanded.

It is surprising how often this assumption of a vertical demand curve is implicit. A characteristic response of urban bus or subway systems to financial difficulties is to propose a percentage fare increase equal to the percentage their deficit is of their revenues. Even professors are not immune: At a recent meeting of the American Association of University Professors, a motion was introduced "to raise annual dues by 20 percent, in order to raise revenues by 20 percent," notwithstanding the empirical evidence that a previous increase in dues had led (as the theory would predict) to a significant drop in membership. It was once widely argued that the demand for gasoline was virtually perfectly inelastic—on the ground that people who had paid thousands of dollars for cars would never balk at a few pennies extra for gas. The events of recent years have proven how wrong that argument was: Higher gas prices have led to smaller cars, to more car pools, to more economical driving speeds, and to less pleasure motoring.

As we have seen, a mass of evidence has accumulated that suggests that most demand curves do in fact slope downward to an appreciable degree.[3]

For practical purposes, the hypothesis of the downward-sloping demand curve can be regarded as being in conformity with the evidence.

Most firms have an intuitive idea of the elasticities they face, although they seldom use the economist's language in referring to them. There also seems to be evidence that even sophisticated business executives sometimes underestimate price elasticities and thus overprice their commodities. When Columbia Records took a great gamble in 1938 and cut the price of its classical records in half, it turned them overnight from a high-priced luxury into a commodity available to the ordinary person. The response was enormous and, to the surprise of many other record producers, sales expanded so much that total consumers' expenditure on classical records increased greatly. Cases in which companies have raised prices and been surprised at the resulting drop in sales have also been documented (see page 279 for one example).

Quantity demanded and household income

Demand theories give no single prediction about how quantity demanded changes as income changes. They say that a rise in income may cause the quantity demanded to rise, to fall, or to remain unchanged. This states only that anything can happen; hence it makes no useful predictions about what could be expected to happen to demand when income changes. But this does not mean that the theory is empty; various kinds of empirical observations help to make it meaningful.

The approximate income elasticity of demand often tends to be identifiable from the technical data about commodities.[4] An inferior good is typically the cheaper and less satisfactory of a number of commodities, all of which satisfy more or less the same need. Consider transport. When people are very poor, they walk. At a slightly higher level of income, they can acquire a bicycle; cycling was the dominant form of transport for industrial workers in Europe as recently as the 1950s. At higher levels of income, bicycles

[3] This does not mean that such demand curves are necessarily elastic. (See Chapter 6 if you are unclear about the concept of price elasticity.) A downward-sloping demand curve can be inelastic, in which case an increase in price, while leading to a decrease in quantity sold, will lead to an increase in revenue to the seller.

[4] Income elasticity, it will be recalled, measures the ratio of the percentage change in quantity of a commodity demanded to the percentage change in income bringing it about. A positive income elasticity indicates a normal good, a negative income elasticity an inferior good. (See Chapter 6.)

can be dispensed with and motorized bicycles, motor scooters, and motorcycles acquired instead; Italy was once overrun with motor scooters and enormous numbers of these are still used by workers in Portugal. Finally, the level of income is reached, as it was in the more advanced industrial countries of western Europe during the 1950s and 1960s, at

"Affordable housing" and the theory of demand

By 1976 the residential home building industry was in the midst of what the press described as a revolutionary switch from big, expensive, fancy houses to smaller, cheaper, no-frills houses. While this might have reflected a change in taste for houses, the evidence strongly suggests it was an economic response to economic events. The theory of demand predicts that housing demand will be responsive to changes in household income, to changes in the price of housing relative to other goods households buy, and to the prices of substitute and complementary commodities.

The central fact is that by the end of 1975 the American house building industry was in a massive slump: between 1972 and 1975, housing starts fell from 2.4 to 1.2 million units. What were the causes? Because of the economic recession of 1973–1975, real disposable income was well below its usual growth rate. Instead of growing by 3 to 4 percent per year, it actually fell slightly. Demand theory predicts this would lead to a decrease in quantity of housing demanded. The price of new residential housing was up 37 percent between 1972 and the end of 1975, about 10 percentage points above the price rise for nonshelter items and about twice the rise in cost of renting. Demand theory predicts such changes in relative prices would lead to decreases in quantity demanded, as consumers spent more of their incomes on substitute (rental) housing and

on other goods. When buying a house one cannot avoid "buying" a complementary package of municipal services (whose "price" is property taxes); most home buyers also "buy" a mortgage (and pay interest). The "prices" of these complementary goods —property taxes and mortgage interest rates—rose sharply over the period. This too is predicted to lead to a decrease in quantity of housing demanded. Thus economists were not surprised by the slump, although its severity was not fully expected; even they had underestimated demand elasticity.

Builders must take some of the blame. As one of them said recently, "We just didn't pay much attention to costs; if something cost $500 more, we said, 'Fine. We'll just get an extra thou' for it.'" Not surprisingly, they sold fewer houses: The elasticity of demand turned out to be higher than the builders thought it was.

Home builders began to realize that perhaps they might do more than wait for the recession to end and interest rates to fall. Because their profits were already low, they could cut prices only if they cut costs. One way of doing so was described by Bill Levitt (who a generation ago had made Levittown a household word):

Panelization is a method of building standardized modules . . . that are already painted and have the wiring, plumbing, insulation and so forth installed in

which ordinary workers feel they can dispense with their two-wheeled conveyances and acquire an automobile. For each of these modes of transportation there is a range of in-

the factory. . . . The bulk of the work can be done by machinery and by people who work on assembly lines like automobile workers. You won't have to pay $15 an hour to construction workers—only what General Motors pays for its assembly line workers, $4 or $4.50 an hour.

The builders were doing what the theory of demand predicts. They were buying more of a relatively inexpensive substitute (factory workers' labor) in response to a rise in the price of construction workers' labor. Other ways of cutting costs included using plans that called for standard lengths of wood (saving carpenters' time), using standardized rather than custom-built plumbing and heating systems (saving plumbers' wages), and eliminating carpeting, fireplaces, and unneeded walls and partitions. Builders in many areas have brought back the basic $20,000–35,000 three-bedroom house in place of the $35,000–50,000 houses that were unaffordable by many potential home buyers. Buyers are responding in what builders hope will prove to be a flood.

Carla A. Hills, then Secretary of Housing and Urban Development in the Ford administration, described the response of the house builders as an example of "the genius of the free enterprise system." Whether or not it is that, it is surely evidence that markets work in the manner predicted by the theory of demand.

come over which the income elasticity of demand is high, and then a higher range over which the income elasticity falls and eventually becomes negative.

A similar example of variable income elasticities concerns the solar hot-water heaters seen on most roofs in Israel. The solar water heater is a simple device that, once purchased and installed (for about $300), provides a tankful of hot water every sunny day for many years. There are no operating costs: Gravity and the sun do all the work. When families are very poor, the expenditure of $300 seems too high for the luxury of hot water. When they become relatively rich, they prefer a larger supply and a more sure one than the solar heater can provide. One of the leading manufacturers of these heaters feels that in another decade Israel will have outgrown his product. He hopes by then that some African nations will be rich enough to afford them, but not so rich as to want a more reliable but more expensive source of hot water.

Another important set of empirical observations shows clearly that income elasticities change only gradually over time. Over the last 40 years, many service industries have encountered income elasticities that are well in excess of unity and rising over time. These elasticities are not expected to drop suddenly to very low levels, and thus it is possible to predict that, unless service industries achieve rates of productivity growth very much in excess of the national average, there will be a continuing pressure coming from the price system for more resources to move into the service industries. The fact that income elasticities are observed not to change rapidly or capriciously permits predictions about the near future on the basis of present knowledge.

A third set of observations reveals that with respect to broad categories of consumption expenditure, households in any one Western country behave in a fashion roughly similar to those in other Western countries. (Indeed, it is not even clear that the qualification *Western* is necessary if income levels are approximately the same.) At low levels of income, food tends to have a fairly high income elasticity of demand, but as the level of income rises, the income elasticity of demand for food tends to fall well below unity, so that only a small amount of any additional income gets spent on food. This phenomenon has been observed in every growing country that has approached the levels of income currently enjoyed by America and western Europe. Thus it can be predicted that as long as productivity growth continues in agriculture, the long-run drift from the land will continue in Western countries, and that when other countries of the world succeed in achieving sustained rates of growth, they will encounter within a predictable time period the problem of a declining agricultural sector.

Similarly, a significant phenomenon of the past two decades in the United States and the most highly developed countries of western Europe is that the income elasticity of demand for consumer durables has been declining, while that for many services has been rising. Other countries can look forward to similar pressures on the pattern of resource allocation within a generation.

The real incomes of most Western countries are doubling every 30 years or so. Thus, over such a period of time, changes in income exert a major influence on changes in demand.

A knowledge of what income elasticities are and are likely to be is one of the most potent tools at the economist's command for predicting the future needs of the economy in myriad different aspects.

Quantity demanded and the prices of other commodities

The theory of demand predicts that the quantity demanded of one commodity may be affected by the changing prices of other commodities: It will tend to increase as the price of a complementary good declines (because they are used jointly) and it will tend to decrease as the price of a substitute good declines (because its users shift to the now relatively cheaper substitute). Of course there are also many pairs of commodities which are sufficiently unrelated that a change in the price of one has no appreciable effect on the quantity demanded of the other. These three reactions—quantity demanded rising, falling, or remaining unchanged—cover all conceivable possibilities. The basic theory does not rule out any possibility, so by itself it is of no more use in predicting the reactions to changes in the prices of other goods than it is in predicting reactions to changes in income. Just as with income, however, this is not the end of the story. It is often possible to tell from the technical nature of the goods alone which will be substitutes and which complements. This is often easy to do not only with consumers' goods but with factors of production. Although the demand for factors will not be considered fully until Part Six, it is worth noting here just how often technical data tell where to expect complementarity and where substitutability. Steel plates, electric welders, and welder operators are complementary, so it can be predicted that a fall in the price of any one will lead to an increase in the demand for all three. Cranes and crane operators, steam shovels and trucks, trains and rails, roads and signs, any piece of equipment and its human operator—these are all examples of pairs of goods that are complements for each other. This list can be expanded more or less indefinitely. For each set of complementary goods, it can be expected that a fall in the price of one good will lead to a rise in demand for the others. A similar list could easily be drawn up for inputs that are substitutes, and it would include such things as wood, bricks, and concrete in construction; manure and artificial fertilizers; a roomful of statistical clerks with desk calculators and a

Figure 9–1 Alternative interpretations of two price-quantity observations

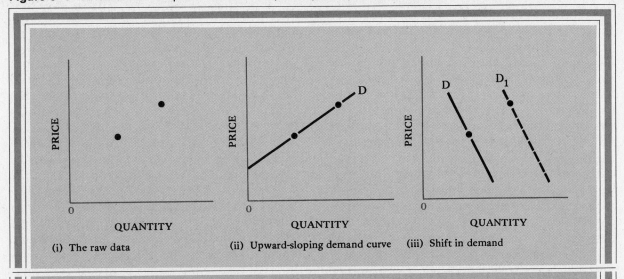

(i) The raw data (ii) Upward-sloping demand curve (iii) Shift in demand

Two observations are insufficient to permit choice between competing explanations. The two observations shown in (i) could be accounted for by either the upward-sloping demand curve drawn in (ii) or the shift in the downward-sloping curve drawn in (iii). It is impossible to be sure which explanation is correct.

small electronic digital computer. With these pairs of substitute goods, it can be expected that a fall in the price of one of them will lead to a fall in the demand for the other.

There are also many consumers' goods for which complementarity or substitutability can be predicted in advance. Complementarity exists, for example, between razors, razor blades, and shaving cream; golf clubs and golf balls; grass seed and lawn mowers; electric stoves and electricity; houses and mortgages; wedding rings and the services of obstetricians, marriage-guidance counselors, and divorce-court judges.[5] The list of substi-

tute goods would include such obvious examples as cabbage and spinach, beef and pork, private automobiles and public transport, gas stoves and electric stoves, vacations in Arizona and on the Italian Riviera, and skiing in Colorado and in Switzerland. It could be extended to cover many pages. If the technical data tell which goods are substitutes and which are complements, then the effect of a change in the price of one good on the demand for the other can be predicted. As the above examples show, this can be done in a very large number of cases.

Quantity demanded and tastes

Changes in demand that are due to changes in taste cannot be identified because taste changes cannot often be measured. This can cause trouble when the relation between demand and other factors is considered. Whenever something happens that does not agree with theory, it is always possible that a

[5] A reader of an earlier edition objected to this passage, and her objection clearly illustrates the difference between positive and normative economics. Whatever the ethics of divorce, if it is known that a fairly stable (or rising) fraction of marriages ends in divorce, it can be predicted with some confidence that an increase in marriages now will lead to an increase in the demand for the services of divorce lawyers and judges in the future.

change in tastes accounted for what was seen. Say, for example, incomes and other prices were known to be constant, while the price of some commodity rose and, at the same time, more was bought. This could mean an upward-sloping demand curve or a shift in the demand curve caused by a change in tastes. The two possibilities are illustrated in Figure 9–1. If there are only two observations, it will be impossible to distinguish between these two possibilities because there is no independent way of telling whether tastes changed. But if there are many such observations, it is possible to get some idea of where the balance of probabilities lies between these two situations. If, *after removing the effects estimated to be due to changes in income*

and other prices,[6] there are 26 observations (say, the price changed each week over a period of six months) that look like those illustrated in Figure 9–2, the point will have to be stretched a great deal to avoid the conclusion that the evidence conflicts with the hypothesis of a downward-sloping demand curve.[7]

Of course, this conflict can always be explained away by saying that tastes must have changed in favor of this commodity each time that its price rose and against the commodity each time that its price fell. This "alibi" can certainly be used with effect to explain away a single conflicting observation, but it would be uncomfortable to use the same alibi 26 times in six months, and one would suspect a fault in the hypothesis that quantity demanded and price vary inversely with each other in the case of this commodity.

This is now a problem in statistical testing. Economists will not usually abandon a theory after only one conflicting observation, but they are prepared to abandon it as soon as the probability becomes very low that the observations could have been wrong if the theory is correct. Thus, statistically, the theory is testable.

Figure 9–2 Twenty-six price-quantity observations

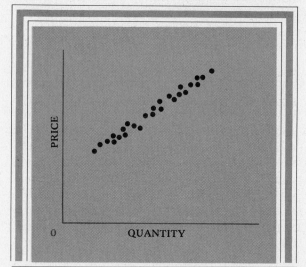

Many observations permit confident choice between competing explanations. Under the circumstances outlined in the text, the explanation that the demand curve slopes upward is very much more likely than the alternative explanation—that tastes have changed 26 times.

Summary

1. Knowledge of demand elasticities is of major importance in applied economics. Modern work on the mea-

[6] This can be done through multiple-regression analysis or other more sophisticated statistical techniques. (See Chapter 3.)

[7] This is easily confirmed by the following calculations. Assuming that changes in tastes are not related to changes in price, it is possible to calculate the odds on the observations in Figure 9–2 being consistent with a downward-sloping but continually shifting demand curve. If tastes changed each week, there is a 50–50 chance that they changed in favor of or against the commodity. Then there is a 50–50 chance that tastes changed in the direction to offset the price change. In the second week, there is also one chance in two. The chances that they changed the "right" way in both weeks are $\frac{1}{2} \times \frac{1}{2} = \frac{1}{4}$, and the chances that they changed the right way for 26 successive weeks are $(\frac{1}{2})^{26} = 1/67,108,864$.

surement of demand has provided a great deal of evidence on the size of the reaction of quantity demanded to prices, incomes, and other socioeconomic data.

2. The price elasticity of a commodity group tends to be higher the more narrowly it is defined and the more adequate are its substitutes. Any one of a group of close substitutes will tend to have an elastic demand even though the group as a whole has a highly inelastic demand.

3. Income elasticity tends to be lower the more basic, or staple, is the commodity. Thus luxuries tend to have higher income elasticities than necessities. The patterns of measured income elasticity are remarkably similar across countries.

4. Economists concerned with the measurement of demand have faced and surmounted a number of serious technical problems. Regression analysis has proved useful in dealing with situations where many things vary at once.

5. Demand theory does not, as some critics assert, assume that all households act with perfect rationality all of the time. The predictions of demand theory about the market demand function require only that at any one time most of the households in the market are behaving as assumed by the theory.

6. The fact that "anything is possible" in modern demand theory does not mean the theory is empty, if we can specify the conditions under which different outcomes are to be expected. The so-called law of demand leads to the prediction that the market demand curve for a commodity will slope downward and to the right except in very special circumstances. Possible exceptions to the general prediction of demand have been suggested but have received no empirical support. A great accumulation of empirical evidence supports the law of demand.

7. While demand theory makes no single prediction about the effect of a change in income on quantity demanded, useful predictions can be made about the relationship because (a) it is often possible to identify approximate income elasticities from technical data; (b) income elasticities change gradually rather than erratically from year to year; (c) income elasticities tend to be similar at similar levels of income in different countries, so that knowledge of what happened at a certain level of income in country A helps to predict what will happen when country B reaches that same level of income.

8. While demand theory makes no single prediction about the effect on the quantity demanded of a change in the price of another commodity, the theory is nevertheless useful because it is often possible to tell from technical data alone whether goods are complements or substitutes.

9. Changes in tastes are an ever-present possible alibi to explain away any observations that appear to conflict with the theory. If prices are cut and less is sold, one can always say that the price cut just happened to be accompanied by a change in tastes away from the commodity. If however, there is a large number of observations of changing prices and quantities, it is possible to calculate the probability that taste changes account for what was seen. If, to save a hypothesis, highly improbable circumstances are needed, it is preferable to reject the hypothesis.

Concepts for review

The role of statistical measurement of demand
The difference between price and income elasticities and what such elasticities show
The difference between an inferior good and a Giffen good
The difference between a luxury and a conspicuous consumption good
The difference between inelastic and perfectly inelastic demand curves

Discussion questions

1. When no-frills houses came on the market they were regarded as a response to high prices. But they have captured more of the market than expected. Some builders estimate they may ultimately constitute 80 percent of all houses sold. Suggest alternative explanations of this unexpected success. A leading builder says, "It's just like people driving smaller cars and drinking beer instead of Scotch." Is it also like students wearing long hair instead of short, or today's parents having fewer children than their parents did? Which of these things represent changes in taste, and which repre-

sent responses to changes in prices or incomes? If you don't know, what economic data would be useful in answering the question?

2. "A survey shows that most people prefer butter to margarine." What exactly might this mean? Supposing it to be true, can you account for the facts that many people buy some of both butter and margarine each month and that in total more pounds of margarine are sold than pounds of butter?

3. In the early empirical studies of demand theory, agricultural products were studied extensively. Can you think of a reason why these early studies were able to identify many demand curves without great difficulty?

4. A reliable newspaper reports that synthetic motor oil is gaining in sales despite its high price relative to natural oil. What can account for a synthetic oil's selling at $3.95 a quart when the best conventional oils were readily available at about $1.00?

5. Predict the effect on the demand for owner-occupied housing of (a) a rise in mortgage interest rates, (b) a decline in the price of rental housing. If over the period in which both (a) and (b) occurred the quantity of new housing sold increased, what would you conclude about the theory of demand?

6. It has been observed recently that obesity is a more frequent medical problem for the relatively poor than for the middle-income classes. Can you use the theory of demand to shed light on this observation?

7. At an auction in New Orleans, a Los Angeles oilman bid against the owner of Brennan's Restaurant and ended up paying $14,200 for a 1806 bottle of Chateau Lafite-Rothschild. Wine authorities say it may not even be drinkable. But the bottle may be the last of its kind and the buyer said he wanted it for his collection. Does this behavior suggest an upward-sloping demand curve for luxuries? If the wine is undrinkable, will the price paid for the bottle prove to have been unwisely high?

8. Suggest commodities that you think might have the following patterns of elasticity of demand.
a. High income elasticity, high price elasticity
b. High income elasticity, low price elasticity
c. Low income elasticity, low price elasticity
d. Low income elasticity, high price elasticity

PART FOUR

PRODUCTION AND COST

10

The firm, production, and cost

Ask your roommate and your neighbor to name ten American business firms, and the odds are overwhelming that their lists will include some of these firms: General Motors Corporation, U.S. Steel, General Electric, American Telephone & Telegraph, Dow Chemical, Standard Oil, Du Pont, the Bank of America, United Airlines, the Prudential Insurance Company, and the National Broadcasting Company. Drive around Ypsilanti, Michigan, and note at random ten firms that come into view. They will likely include an A & P supermarket, Richardson's Pharmacy, a Shell service station, Schaeffer's Hardware Store, Haabs, and the First National Bank of Ypsilanti. Drive through Iowa or Nebraska and look around you: Every farm is a business firm as well as a home.

Firms developed and survive because they proved to be efficient institutions for doing certain things, particularly organizing resources to produce goods and services that consumers wish to purchase and organizing their sale and distribution.

But if General Motors, Haabs, and the Iowa farm are all *firms,* what do they have in common? It is not hard to enumerate ways in which they are different. But there may also be insight to be gained in treating them all under a single heading, and this is just what economic theory does. Economists usually assume that their behavior can be understood in terms of a common motivation. Whether the firm is Ma and Pa's Bar and Grill or the Ford Motor Company and whether a particular decision is made by the board of directors, the third vice-president in charge of advertising, or the owner-manager is regarded as irrelevant to predicting what decisions are made.

Before studying how the firm is treated in economic theory, we shall examine more closely the firm in America today, to see from what we are abstracting. Criticisms that the theory neglects differences among firms will be considered in Chapter 19.

The organization of production

PROPRIETORSHIPS, PARTNERSHIPS, AND CORPORATIONS

There are three major forms of business organization: the single proprietorship, the partnership, and the corporation. In the **single proprietorship,** there is a single owner who makes all decisions and who is personally responsible for everything done by the business. In the **partnership,** there are two or more joint owners either of whom may make binding decisions and each of whom is personally responsible for everything done by the business. In the **corporation,** the firm is regarded in law as having an entity of its own, and the owners (the stockholders) are not each personally responsible for everything that is done by the business. Owners elect a board of directors who hire managers to run the firm subject to the board's supervision.

In the United States today, there are about seven million single proprietorships (not counting agriculture), one million partnerships, and nearly two million corporations. These figures may be misleading. Corporations account for more than two-thirds of the nation's privately produced income. In the important sectors of manufacturing, transportation, public utilities, and finance, corporations do virtually all of the business. In trade and in construction, they do about half of the total business. Only in agriculture and in services (e.g., medicine, law, barbering, accounting) is the corporation relatively unimportant, and even here its share of the business is steadily rising.

The proprietorship and the partnership: advantages and disadvantages

The major advantage of the single proprietorship is that the owner can readily maintain full control over the firm. The owner is the Boss. The disadvantages are, first, that the size of the firm is limited by the capital the owner can personally raise and, second, that the owner is personally responsible in law for all debts of the firm.

The ordinary (or general) partnership overcomes to some extent the first disadvantage of the proprietorship but not the second. Ten partners may be able to finance a much bigger enterprise than could one owner, but they are still subject to unlimited liability. Each partner is fully liable for all of the debts of the firm. This liability is independent of the amount of money a particular proprietor may have invested in the firm. Thus, if a tenth partner makes $1,000 available (or $100, or nothing, for that matter) when joining a firm that subsequently becomes bankrupt with debts of $100,000, this individual, and each of the other nine partners, is fully liable for the $100,000. If none of the other partners should have salable personal assets, while the tenth partner has a house, a car, furniture, and some investments, he or she, may lose all personal possessions so that the debts of the partnership can be cleared. Obviously, people with substantial personal assets will be unwilling to enter such a partnership unless they have complete trust in all the other partners and a full knowledge of all the obligations of the firm. This need for trust is compounded because each partner usually has full power to sign contracts that bind the firm in its ordinary lines of business. Thus one partner's fortune is at the mercy of any other partner's judgment. As a direct consequence of this authority and of the fact of unlimited liability, it is difficult to raise money through a partnership from persons who merely wish to invest. Investors may be willing to invest $1,000 but not be willing to jeopardize their entire fortune; if, however, a person joins a partnership in order to do the former, he or she may also do the latter.

A further disadvantage of an ordinary partnership is that any time a partner dies or resigns the partnership agreement must be redrawn. This may make it difficult to have as a partner someone who is not genuinely interested and involved in the business, but who is willing merely to invest in it, since such a partner may wish, at any time, to dissolve the partnership in order to liquidate his or her interest.

The **limited partnership** is designed to avoid some of these difficulties. General partners continue to have unlimited authority and unlimited liability, but a second type of partner is permitted. The limited partner's liability is restricted to the amount that he or she has invested in the firm. Such partners may not participate in the management of the firm or engage in agreements on behalf of the partnership. In effect, the limited partnership permits some division of the functions of decision making, provision of capital, and risk taking.

In most respects, this division of responsibility is more effectively achieved through the corporation. But there are certain professions in which the general partnership form is traditional. These include law, medicine, and (until very recently) brokerage. Part of the reason for the survival of partnerships in these fields is that each depends heavily on a relationship of trust with its clients, and the partners' unlimited liability for one another's actions is thought to enhance public confidence in the firm.

The corporation: advantages and disadvantages

The corporation is regarded in law as an entity separate from the individuals who own it. It can enter into contracts, it can sue and be sued, it can own property, it can contract debts, and it can generally incur obligations that are the legal obligations of the corporation *but not of its owners*. This means that the corporation can enter into contracts in its own right and that its liability to adhere to such contracts can be enforced only by suing the corporation, not by suing the owners. The right to be sued may not seem to be an advantage, but it is, because it makes it possible for others to enter into enforceable contracts with the corporation.

While some corporations are very small or are owned by a very small group of stockholders which also manages the business, the most important type of corporation is one that issues shares that are purchased by the general public. When a company sells its shares, it obtains the money paid for the shares and the shareholders become the company's owners. They are entitled to share in corporate profits. Profits, when paid out, are called **dividends.** **Undistributed profits** also notionally belong to the owners, but they are usually reinvested in the firm's operations. If the corporation is liquidated, shareholders split up assets that remain after all debts are paid.

Diffuse ownership of corporate shares usually means that the owners cannot all be managers. Stockholders, who are entitled to one vote for each share they own, elect a board of directors. The board defines general policy and hires senior managers who are supposed to translate these broad guidelines into detailed decisions.

Should the company go bankrupt, the personal liability of any one shareholder is limited to whatever that shareholder has actually invested in the firm, which is the money spent to purchase its shares. This is called **limited liability.**

The most important aspect of a corporation from the point of view of its owners is that they have limited liability.

The corporation's advantage is that it can raise capital from a very large number of individuals, each of whom shares in the firm's profits but has no liability for corporate action beyond risking the loss of the amount invested. Thus investors know their exact maximum risk and may sit back and collect dividends without needing to know anything about the policy or operation of the firm that they collectively own. Because of this, very large quantities of capital can be raised.

Because shares are readily transferable among individuals (a form of exchange that stock markets are organized to facilitate), a corporation can have a continuity of life that is unaffected by frequent changes in the identity of its owners.

From the individual owner's point of view, there are disadvantages in investing in a corporation. First, the owner may have little voice in the management of the firm. For example, if those who hold a majority of the shares decide that the corporation should not pay dividends, an individual investor cannot compel the payment of "his" share of the earnings. Second, the income of the corporation is taxed before dividends are paid and the investor is also taxed on his or her individual dividends. This "double taxation" of corporate income was once much discussed in the public finance literature. Some view it as clearly unfair and discriminatory; others view it as the price to be paid for the advantage of incorporation. Judging from the continuing importance of the corporation in the United States, despite a corporate income tax rate of about 50 percent, the price has not been prohibitive.

THE RISE OF THE MODERN CORPORATION

The corporate form of organization is employed today wherever very large enterprises are found. The principal reason for this is that it has decisive advantages over any other form in raising the vast sums of capital required for major enterprises. Historically, wherever and whenever large accumulations of capital in a single firm were required, the limited liability, joint-stock company developed. The corporate form is spreading now even to the service industries and agriculture as firms in these industries grow to the point where they need large quantities of capital to function effectively.

Although historians have found roots of the corporation in Roman law and in the medieval guild system, the direct predecessor of the modern corporation was the chartered company of the sixteenth century. The Muscovy Company, granted a charter in 1555, the East India Company, first chartered in 1600, and the Hudson's Bay Company, chartered in 1609 and still going strong in Canada two hundred and seventy years later, are famous early examples of joint-stock ventures with limited liability. These companies were granted charters by the Crown to make it possible for English merchants to trade with particular regions. The special needs of having large numbers of investors to finance a ship that would not return with the cargo for years—if it returned at all—made this *exceptional* form of organization seem desirable. In the next three centuries, the trading company's critical attributes (e.g., large capital requirements and need to diversify risk) were recognized to exist in other fields, and charters were increasingly granted in the fields of insurance, turnpikes and canals, and banking, as well as foreign trade. The Industrial Revolution, which made the large firm efficient, extended the needs for large amounts of capital committed over long periods of time to many more fields, and, during the nineteenth century, the demand for a general rather than a special privilege of incorporation became strong. General laws permitting incorporation with limited liability, *as a matter of right rather than special grant of privilege,* became common both in England and in the United States during the latter half of the nineteenth century.

Today, incorporation is relatively routine, although it is subject to a variety of state laws. Moderate fees are charged for the privilege of incorporation, and competition among the states for the incorporation fees has served greatly to liberalize the conditions for incorporation throughout the country. Delaware is an example of a small state that at one time had a highly disproportionate share of incorporations because of its permissiveness. In the insurance field, Connecticut took the lead;

most insurance companies founded before 1930 have Connecticut charters.

THE FIRM IN ECONOMIC THEORY

Clearly, General Motors and Alice's Restaurant make decisions in different ways. Indeed, within a single large corporation not all decisions are made by the same people or in the same way. Nor are decisions all equally important. To take an example, someone at General Motors decided to introduce a new model car in 1975. Someone else decided to call it the Chevette. Someone else decided how and where to produce it. Someone else decided its price. Someone else decided how to promote its sales. The common aspect of these decisions is that all were made in pursuit of the same goal—the manufacture and sale of successful automobiles and other products that earn profits for the owners of General Motors.

Economic theory assumes that the same principles underlie each decision made within a firm and that the decision is uninfluenced by who makes it. Thus the firm can be regarded as a decision-making unit that has objectives and that makes decisions designed to achieve these objectives.

Motivation: profit maximization

It is assumed that the firm makes decisions in such a way that its profits will be as large as possible. In technical language, it is assumed that the firm *maximizes its profits*. The concept of profits requires careful definition, and this will be done later in this chapter. For now we may treat it in the everyday sense of the difference between the value of the firm's sales and the costs to the firm of producing what is sold.

The assumption of profit maximization provides a principle by which a firm's decisions can be predicted.

Economists predict the firm's behavior in regard to the various choices open to it by studying the effect that making each of the choices would have on the firm's profits. They then predict that from these alternatives the firm will select the one that produces the largest profits.

At this point you may well ask if it is sensible to build an elaborate theory based on such a simple assumption about the motives of businessmen. It is well known that some businessmen are inspired by motives other than an overwhelming desire to make as much money as possible. Cases in which businessmen have sought political influence or been influenced by philanthropic motives are not difficult to document. This theory does not say, however, that profit is the only factor that influences the businessman. It says only that profits are an important enough consideration that a theory that assumes profit maximization to be the businessman's sole motive will produce predictions that are substantially correct. It follows from this that to point out that businessmen are sometimes motivated by considerations other than profits does not constitute a relevant criticism of the theory. It is always possible that profit-maximizing theory could be substantially wrong. If so, the way to demonstrate this is to show that the predictions that follow from the theory are inconsistent with the facts.

Why is this assumption made? First, it is necessary to make *some* assumption about what motivates decision makers if the theory is to predict how they will act. Second, a great many of the predictions of theories based upon this assumption have been confirmed by observation. Third, there is no general agreement that an alternative assumption has yet been shown to yield substantially better results. The assumption has, however, been criticized, and alternatives have been suggested. These are examined in Chapter 19.

Factors of production

The firm is in business to make profits. It does this by producing and selling some commod-

Different kinds of firms

In economic theory the firm is defined as the unit that makes decisions with respect to the production and sale of commodities. This single definition covers a variety of business organizations from the single proprietorship to the corporation, and a variety of business sizes from the unshaven inventor operating in his garage and financed by whatever he can extract from a reluctant bank manager to vast undertakings with tens of thousands of shareholders and creditors. We know that in large firms decisions are actually made by many different individuals. We can, nonetheless, regard the firm as a single consistent decision-making unit because of the assumption that all decisions are made in order to achieve the common goal of maximizing the firm's profits.

Whether a decision is made by a small independent proprietor, a plant manager, or a board of directors, that person or group is the firm for the purpose of that decision. This is a truly heroic assumption; it amounts to saying that for purposes of predicting those aspects of their behavior that interest us, we can treat a farm, a corner grocery, a department store, a small law partnership, General Motors, and a giant multinational corporation, all under the umbrella of a single theory of the behavior of the firm. If this turns out to be even partially correct it will prove enormously valuable in revealing some unity of behavior where to the casual observer there is only a bewildering diversity.

You should not be surprised, therefore, if at first encounter the theory appears rather abstract and out of touch with reality. In order to generalize over such a wide variety of behavior, the theory must ignore many features with which we are most familiar and which distinguish the farmer from the grocer and each of them from the Exxon Corporation. Any theory that generalizes over a wide variety of apparently diverse behavior necessarily has this characteristic because it ignores those factors that are most obvious to us and which create in our minds the appearance of diversity. If it were not possible to do this, it would be necessary to have dozens of different theories, one for each type of firm. The task of learning economics would then be much more complex than it now is!

ity. Production is something like a sausage machine. Certain things, such as raw materials and the services of capital and labor, are fed in at one end, and a product emerges at the other. The materials and factor services that are used in the process of production are called **inputs,** and the products that emerge are called **outputs.** One way of looking at the process is to regard the inputs as being combined to produce the output. Another equally useful way is to regard the inputs as being used up, or sacrificed, in order to gain the output.

Each distinct input into the production process can be regarded as a factor of production. There are literally hundreds of inputs entering into the output of a specific good. Among the inputs entering into automobile production are, to name only a few, sheet steel, rubber, spark plugs, electricity, night watchmen, cost accountants, fork-lift operators, managers, and painters. These inputs can

Technological versus economic efficiency: an example

Suppose, given the state of technology, there are only four known ways to produce 100 widgits per month:

	QUANTITY OF INPUTS REQUIRED	
	Capital	*Labor*
Method A	6	200
Method B	10	250
Method C	10	150
Method D	40	50

Method B is technologically inefficient because it uses more of both inputs than does method A. It thus wastes 4 units of capital and 50 units of labor. Among the other three methods, method A uses the least capital, but it is the most labor-using.★ Method D conserves labor but uses much more capital. Method C is intermediate between them. (If you are tempted to consider method D technologically most efficient because it uses only 90 units of all resources, think again.)

★ This is yet a third concept of efficiency, "engineering efficiency," in which least use of a particular factor is involved. When an engineer speaks of the efficiency of an engine, he may mean how much of the fuel it turns into power. Similarly, a maker of labor-saving machines might consider method D the most efficient because it uses the least amount of labor.

Methods A, C, and D are all technologically efficient because no one of them uses more of both resources than either of the others.

Which one is the least costly—that is, is economically efficient? We cannot tell without knowing the costs of capital and of labor. Economic efficiency depends on factor prices. Consider the three cases shown in the table below. As we move from Case I to II to III, a unit of labor becomes increasingly expensive *relative to* a unit of capital.

Method A is economically efficient when labor is cheap relative to capital. Method C becomes efficient when labor gets somewhat more expensive relative to capital. Finally, when labor gets very expensive relative to capital, Method D, which uses least labor per unit of capital, becomes economically efficient.

To test your understanding, answer these questions:

1. Can a technologically *inefficient* method ever be economically efficient?

2. Is there a set of factor prices for which *both* method C and method D will be economically efficient?

	FACTOR PRICES PER UNIT		TOTAL COST OF FACTORS		
	Capital	*Labor*	*Method A*	*Method C*	*Method D*
Case I	$50	$3	$ 900	$950	$2,150
Case II	20	5	1,120	950	1,050
Case III	15	5	1,090	900	850

be grouped into four broad classes: (1) those that are inputs to the automobile manufacturer but outputs to some other manufacturer, such as spark plugs, electricity, and sheet steel; (2) those that are provided directly by nature, such as land; (3) those that are provided directly by households, such as labor; and (4) those that are provided by the machines used for manufacturing automobiles.

The first class of inputs is made up of goods produced by other firms. These products appear as inputs only because the stages of production are broken up between different firms so that, at any one stage, a firm is using goods produced by other firms as inputs. If these products are traced back to the firms that provided them, it will be found that they were produced with the same four types of inputs. Eventually, however, if these products are traced back to their sources, it will be found that all production can be accounted for by the services of only three kinds of inputs, which are often called the basic factors of production: all the gifts of nature such as land and raw materials, to which the economist gives the term **land;** all physical and mental efforts provided by people, which are called **labor** services; and all machines and other products that are not themselves components of the final goods. This third type of input is called **capital** and is defined as man-made aids to further production.

Extensive use of this factor of production—the services of machines and other capital goods—is one of the distinguishing features of modern as opposed to primitive production. Instead of making all consumers' goods directly with only the aid of such simple tools as nature provides, productive effort goes into the manufacture of tools, machines, and other goods that are not desired in themselves but only as an aid to making further goods. The use of capital goods renders the production processes *roundabout.* Instead of making what is wanted directly, a roundabout process is used, making first the goods that will be used to help to make what is finally wanted.

Economic efficiency

Firms must decide not only what to produce and how much, but by what method their goods will be produced. In general, there is more than one way to produce a given product. Indeed, if this were not the case, there would be no need for firms to face the decision of *how* to produce. It is possible to produce agricultural commodities by farming a small quantity of land, combining a great deal of labor and capital with each acre of land, as is done in Belgium; it is also possible to produce the same commodities by farming a great deal of land, using only a small amount of labor and capital per acre of land, as is done in Australia.

What does it mean to ask which process is best? One meaning of "best" is that, if the output is the same, the best process is the one that uses the fewest inputs or, in other words, the one that is technically most efficient. **Technological efficiency** measures use of inputs in physical terms; **economic efficiency** measures use in terms of costs.

The economically most efficient method is the one that *costs* the least. Economic efficiency depends on factor prices *and* on technological efficiency.

Cost and profit to the firm

THE MEANING AND MEASUREMENT OF COST

Economic efficiency has been defined in terms of cost. But what is cost? **Cost,** to the producing firm, is the *value* of the factors of production used in producing its output.

Notice the use of the word "value" in the definition. A given output produced by a given technique, say 6,000 cars produced each week by American Motors with its present production methods, will have a given set of inputs associated with it—so many man-hours of various types of laborers, supervisors, managers, and technicians, so many tons of steel, glass, and aluminum, so much electric light and other services, and so many hours of the time of various machines. To know the cost of this diverse set of factor inputs, the value of each in money terms must be calculated. The sum of these separate costs is the total cost to American Motors of producing 6,000 cars per week. "Costing" may be very easy in some cases and very difficult in others.

Purpose in assigning costs

An interest in costs is a direct consequence of the notion that factor services are scarce and, as a result, valuable. Thus, in using them up to produce outputs, the firm uses valuable things. From the point of view of a profit-maximizing firm, the profit from production consists of the difference between the value of the outputs and the value of the inputs. Knowing costs, then, is a precondition to knowing profits, and knowing profits is necessary to understand behavior. An economist might discuss this behavior for a variety of reasons: (1) to *describe* actual behavior of a firm, (2) to *predict* how the firm's behavior will respond to specified changes in the conditions it faces, (3) to *help* the firm make the best decisions it can in achieving its goals, and (4) to *evaluate* how well firms use scarce resources.

The same measure of cost need not be correct for all of these purposes. For example, if the firm happens to be misinformed about the value of some resource, it will behave according to that misinformation. In describing or predicting the firm's behavior, economists should use the information the firm actually uses, even if the economist knows it is incorrect. But in helping the firm to achieve its goals, economists should substitute the correct information.

Economists use a well-established definition of costs in solving problems of the kind cited in items 3 and 4 of the list above. If businessmen use the same definition and have the same information, the economist's definition will be appropriate for problems of types 1 and 2 as well. This will be assumed for the moment.

Opportunity cost

Although the details of economic costing vary, they are governed by a common principle that is sometimes called user cost but is more commonly called **opportunity cost.**

The cost of using something in a particular venture is the benefit foregone (or opportunity lost) by not using it in its best alternative use.

An old Chinese merchants' proverb says: "Where there is no gain, the loss is obvious." The economic sense of this proverb is that the merchant who shows no gain has wasted time—time that could have been used in some other venture. The merchant has neglected the opportunity cost of his time.

What is given up *is* the cost of the indicated action. One of the problems in evaluating costs is that different people (or groups) may see or care about different alternatives. Jones views the alternative to watching television on a Saturday afternoon as playing golf; his wife regards the alternative as a family outing. In this chapter and the next, analysis will be limited to cost as seen by the firm. In Chapter 13, other points of view will be considered.

THE MEASUREMENT OF OPPORTUNITY COST BY THE FIRM

In principle, measuring opportunity cost is easy. The firm must assign to each factor of production it has used a monetary value equal to what it has sacrificed in order to have the use of the factor. Applying this principle to specific cases, however, reveals some tough problems.

Purchased and hired factors

Assigning costs is most straightforward for those factors that the firm buys on a competitive market where price is set by the forces of supply and demand and where, in addition, the firm uses up the entire quantity of the factor purchased during the period of production. Many raw material and intermediate-product purchases fall into this category. From the point of view of the firm purchasing in a competitive market, if it pays $9 per ton for coal delivered to its factory, it has sacrificed its claims to whatever else $9 can buy, and thus the purchase price is a reasonable measure of the opportunity cost of using one ton of coal. It does not matter whether the firm pays cash or charges its purchases. The purchases become inputs in the period when they are used.

For hired factors of production, where the rental price is the full price, the situation is identical. Borrowed money is paid for by payment of **interest.** An **interest rate** is the money price paid to use $1 for one year. Interest payments measure the opportunity cost of borrowed funds. Most labor services are hired, but typically the cost is more than the wages paid because employers usually must contribute to social security, to pension funds, and to various kinds of unemployment and disability insurance and other fringe benefits. The cost of these must be added to the direct wage in determining the opportunity cost of labor services used.

Imputed costs

The cost must also be assessed for factors of production that the firm uses but neither purchases nor hires for current use. Since no payment is made to anyone outside the firm, these costs are not so obvious. Such costs are called **imputed costs.** If the most profitable lines of production are to be discovered, the opportunity cost of these factors should be reckoned at values that reflect what the firm might earn from the factors if it shifted them to their next best use. Some important imputed costs arise because of the use of owners' money, the depreciation of capital equipment, the need to compensate risk taking, and the need to value any special advantages (such as franchises or patents) that the firm may possess.

The cost of money. Consider a firm that uses $100,000 of its own money that could have been loaned out to someone else at interest at a rate of 7 percent per year.

Thus $7,000 (at least) should be deducted from the firm's revenue as the cost of funds used in production. If, to continue the example, the firm makes only $6,000 over all other costs, then one should say not that the firm made a profit of $6,000 by producing but that it lost $1,000 for if it closed down completely and merely loaned out its money to someone else, it could have earned $7,000.

The cost of money may be higher than this if the best alternative use of the money could yield more than the market interest rate. Many firms cannot obtain nearly as much money as they would wish by borrowing. If a firm is rationed in the amount of funds it can borrow, it will place a high value on the funds that it does have. In these circumstances, the firm must look at the other ventures it might have undertaken in order to assign opportunity cost because its inability to raise all the capital it wants means that it will be unable to do all the things it wants. Many business firms operate with "cut-off rates of return" that approximate the opportunity cost of money to the firm. They are chosen to approximate the return on projects that the firm cannot undertake because it lacks sufficient funds.[1]

---

[1] Empirical studies of certain American manufacturing industries suggest that the opportunity cost of money is substantially in excess of the rate of interest on bonds and long-term loans. An accurate figure may well be as high as 25 percent. The fact that it is so high helps explain why many firms are anxious to retain a major portion of their profits and why many stockholders (who do not have similar personal investment opportunities) are willing to have corporations pay dividends that are substantially less than earnings and reinvest the remainder to earn their internal rate of return.

Opportunity cost more generally

Opportunity cost plays a vital role in economic analysis, but it is a fundamental principle that applies to a wide range of situations. It is one of the great insights of economics. Consider some examples:

■ Hard-Luck Harry loses $100 a week in a dice game. He knows the game is crooked but plays anyway because, as he says, "it's the only game in town." A reform mayor is elected and shuts down all gambling establishments. What is the opportunity cost to Harry?

■ George Bernard Shaw, on reaching his ninetieth birthday, was asked how he liked being ninety. He is reputed to have said, "It's fine, when you consider the alternative."

■ Llewelyn Formed likes to hear both Walter Cronkite and John Chancellor. If he finally settles on Chancellor, what is the opportunity cost of this decision?

■ M. C. Pigg, a 31-year-old bachelor, is thinking about marrying at last. But, although he thinks Grace is a lovely girl, he figures that if he marries her he will give up the chance of wedded bliss with another girl he may meet next year. So he decides to wait a while. What additional information do you require to determine the opportunity cost of the decision?

■ Serge Ginn, M.D., complains that now that he is earning large fees he can no longer afford to take the time for a vacation trip to Europe. In what way does it make sense to say that the opportunity cost of his vacation depends upon his fees?

■ Ms. Anne Thrope doesn't like bankers, so she keeps her life's savings of $10,000 hidden in her mattress. What does it cost her per year to dislike bankers? One answer might be that it is the loss of interest she would have earned if she had placed her money in a savings account at 5 percent ($500 per year) plus the added cost of the extra fire and theft insurance she carries on her house and belongings. This is the right answer if she regards the savings account as her best alternative. (She could dislike bankers and still earn money on her savings by investing in government bonds, real estate, or stocks. But perhaps Ms. Thrope dislikes governments, risk, and businessmen, too.)

■ Retired General William Russ, who is married to a very wealthy woman, has decided to contribute $5,000 to a political candidate he likes very much. His lawyer points out to him that since he is in the 50 percent tax bracket, and since political contributions are not deductible from his income, the real cost of his contribution is the same as giving an extra $10,000 to his favorite charity, the Gen. Russ Foundation. Is the opportunity cost of the political contribution $5,000 or $10,000?

■ Minnie the Moocher enters a local joint with 60¢ in her pocket, intending to buy a hamburger and a beer. She finds that a hamburger costs 50¢ and beer 35¢. After some thought, she buys the beer. What was her opportunity cost?

Depreciation. The costs of using assets the firm owns such as buildings, equipment, and machinery consist of the cost of the money tied up in them and a charge, called depreciation, for the loss in value of the asset because of its use in production. The economic theory of depreciation can be highly complex under certain circumstances (e.g., in periods of inflation) and is beyond the scope of this book. But since we are interested in opportunity costs, **depreciation** must be defined to include the loss in value due to physical wear and tear *and* to obsolescence.

The economic depreciation cost of using an asset for a year is the loss in value of the asset during the year.

Accountants use various conventional methods of depreciation based on the price originally paid for the asset. While such historical costs are often useful approximations, they may, in some cases, seriously differ from the depreciation required by the opportunity cost principle. Two examples of the possible error involved follow.

Example 1. A woman buys a $4,000 automobile that she intends to use for six years. She may think this will cost her $667 per year. But if after one year the value of her car on the used-car market is $3,000, it has cost her $1,000 to use the car during the first year. Why should she charge herself $1,000 depreciation during the first year? After all, *she* does not intend to sell the car for six years. The answer is that one of the purchaser's alternatives was to buy a one-year-old car and operate it for five years. Indeed, that is the very position she is in after the first year. Whether she likes it or not, she has paid $1,000 for the use of the car during the first year of its life. If the market had valued her car at $3,900 after one year (instead of $3,000), the depreciation would have been only $100.

Example 2. In the previous example an active used-asset market was considered. At the other extreme, consider an asset that has no alternative use. This is sometimes described as the case of "sunk" costs. Assume that a firm has a set of machines that it purchased some time ago for $100,000. These machines have an expected life of ten years, and the firm's accountant calculates the "depreciation cost" of these machines at $10,000 per year. Assume that the machines can be used to make one product and nothing else. Since they are installed in one part of the firm's plant, they cannot be leased to any other firm, and their scrap value is negligible. In other words, the machines have no value, except to this firm in its current operation. Assume that if the machines are used to produce this product, the cost of all other factors utilized will amount to $25,000, while the goods produced can be sold for $29,000.

Now, if the historically determined depreciation "costs" of running the machines are added in, the total cost of operation comes to $35,000; with revenues at $29,000, this makes an annual loss of $6,000 per year. It appears that the goods should not be made!

The fallacy in this argument lies in adding in a charge based on the historical cost of the machines as one of the costs of current operation. The machines have no alternative uses whatsoever. Clearly their opportunity cost is zero. The total costs of producing this line of goods is thus only $25,000 per year (assuming all other costs have been correctly assessed), and the line of production shows an annual profit of $4,000, not a loss of $6,000.

To see why the second calculation leads to the correct decision, notice that if the firm decides this line of production is unprofitable and does not continue it, it will have no money to pay out and no revenue received on this account. If the firm takes the economist's advice and pursues the line of production, it will pay out $25,000 and receive $29,000, thus making it $4,000 per year richer than if it had not done so. Clearly, production is worth undertaking. The amount the firm happened to have paid out for the machines in the past is of no relevance whatsoever in deciding the correct use of the machines once it has installed them on the premises.

"Bygones are bygones," and they should have no influence on deciding what is currently the most profitable thing to do.

The bygones-are-bygones principle extends well beyond economics and is often ignored in poker, in war, and perhaps in love. Because you have invested heavily in a poker hand, a battle, or a courtship does not mean you should stick with it if the prospects of winning become very small. At every moment of decision, you should be concerned with how benefits from this time forward compare with current and future costs.

Risk taking. One very difficult problem in imputing costs concerns the evaluation of the service of risk taking. Business enterprise is often a risky affair. Some enterprises are more risky than others, and someone must take the risk in each case. The risk is in fact borne by the owners of the firm who, if the enterprise fails, may lose the money they have invested in the firm. The owners will not take these risks unless they receive a remuneration in return. They expect to receive a return that exceeds what they could have obtained by investing their money in a virtually riskless manner, say, by buying a government bond. In the sense in which the term has been used, risk taking is a factor of production and thus has a cost. It is a service that must be provided if the firm is to carry on production, and it must be paid for by the firm. If a firm does not yield a return sufficient to compensate for the risks involved, the firm will not be able to persuade people to contribute money to it in return for a part ownership in the firm. Investors demand a higher return on a risky venture than on a certain one because, in addition to having their capital used, they run the

risk of never getting it back. The return they receive on a risky investment must be high enough to compensate for this risk. In order to earn the required return on the total investment—the successful and the unsuccessful —investors require a greater return on the successful investments. Suppose in investing $100,000 in a class of risky ventures, a businessman expects $10,000 to be lost. Suppose further that he requires a 20 percent return on his total investment. In order to earn $20,000 profit and recover the $10,000 expected loss, he needs to earn $30,000 profit on the $90,000 of successful investment. This is a rate of return of $33\frac{1}{3}$ percent. He charges 20 percent for the use of the capital, $13\frac{1}{3}$ percent for the risk he takes. Some forms of risk may be paid for directly—by purchasing insurance, for example. Others are paid for by high returns on successful ventures.

Special advantages. Suppose a firm owns a valuable patent or a highly desirable location, or produces a popular brand-name product such as Coca-Cola, Chevrolet, or Marlboro. Each of these involves an opportunity cost to the firm in production (even if it was acquired free) because if the firm does not choose to *use* the special advantage itself, it could sell or lease it to others. Typically, the value of these things will differ from their historical cost.

PROFITS: THEIR MEANING AND SIGNIFICANCE

Profits, defined loosely above, and in everyday usage, may be given a series of more precise definitions. **Economic profits** on goods sold are defined as the difference between revenues received from the sale and the opportunity cost of the resources used to make them. (If costs are greater than revenues, such "negative profits" are called *losses*.)

This definition includes in costs (and thus excludes from profits) the imputed returns to capital and to risk taking. This use of the words "profit" and "loss" gives specialized definitions to words that are in everyday use. They are, therefore, a potential source of confusion to the student who runs into other uses of the same words. Table 10–1 may help clarify the definition.

Some economists, while following substantially the same definitions, label as **normal profits** the imputed returns to capital and risk taking just necessary to prevent the owners from withdrawing from the industry. These normal profits are, of course, what has been defined as the opportunity costs of risk taking and capital. Whatever they are called, they are costs that have to be covered if the firm is to stay in operation in the long run.

Other definitions of profits

Businessmen define profits as the excess of revenues over the costs with which accountants provide them. We explore in the appendix to this chapter (see page 880) some of the differences between accountants' and economists' views of business transactions. Some of these differences affect the meaning of profits. Accountants do not include as costs charges for risk taking and use of owners' own capital, and thus these items are recorded by businessmen as part of their profits. When a businessman says he *needs* profits of such and such an amount in order to stay in business, he is making sense within his definition, for his "profits" must be large enough to pay for those factors of production that he uses but that the accounting profession does not include as costs.

The economist would express the same notion by saying that the businessman needs to cover *all* of his costs, including those not accepted by accounting conventions. If the firm is covering all its costs (in the sense that we have defined costs), then it follows that it could not do better by using its resources in any other line of activity than the one currently being followed. Indeed, it would probably do worse in most other lines of activity.

A situation in which revenues equal costs (economic profits of zero) is a satisfactory one—because all factors, hidden as well as visible, are being rewarded at least as well as in their *best* alternative uses.

With zero profits then, in the economist's sense of that concept, you can do no better, although you might do worse. To reverse the Chinese proverb cited earlier, "Where there is no loss compared to the best alternative use of every factor, the gain is obvious."

The income tax authorities have yet another definition of profits, which is implicit in the thousands of rules as to what may be (and what may not be) included as a deduction from revenue in arriving at taxable income. In

Table 10–1 The calculation of economic profits: an example

Gross revenue from sales	$1,000
Less: direct costs of goods sold (materials, labor, electricity, etc.)	650
"Gross profits" (or "contributions to overhead")	350
Less: indirect costs (depreciation, overhead, management salaries, etc.)	140
"Net profits" before income taxes	210
Less: imputed charges for own capital used and for risk taking } = "normal profits"	100
Economic profits before income taxes	110
Less: income taxes payable	100
Economic profits after income taxes	$ 10

The main difference between "economic profits" and the usual everyday definition of profits is the subtraction of imputed charges for use of capital owned by the firm and for risk taking. Income tax is levied on whatever definition of profits the taxing authorities choose, usually closely related to "net profits."

some cases, the taxing authorities allow more for cost than the accountant recommends; in other cases, they allow less.

It is important to be clear about different meanings of the term "profits," not only to avoid fruitless semantic arguments, but because a theory that predicts that certain behavior is a function of profits defined in one way will not necessarily predict behavior accurately, given some other definition. For example, if economists predict that new firms will seek to enter an industry whenever profits are earned, this prediction will frequently be wrong if the accountants' definition is used to determine profits. The definition of profits as an excess over all opportunity costs is for many purposes the most useful, but if you wish to apply it to business behavior or to tax policy, you must be prepared to make the appropriate adjustments. And if you wish to apply accounting or tax data to particular theories, you must be prepared to rectify the data.

Profits and resource allocation

When resources are valued by the opportunity cost principle, their costs show how much these resources would earn if used in their best alternative uses. If there is some industry in which all firms' revenues exceed opportunity costs, all the firms in that industry will be earning profits. This will mean that owners of factors of production will want to move resources into this industry because the earnings potentially available to them are greater there than in alternative uses of the resources. If in some other industry firms are incurring losses, some or all of this industry's resources are more highly valued in other uses, and owners of the resources will want to move them to those other uses.

Economic profits and losses play a crucial signaling role in the workings of a free-market system.

Profits in an industry are the signal that resources can profitably be moved into the industry. Losses are the signal that the resources can profitably be moved elsewhere. Only if there are zero economic profits is there no incentive for resources to move into or out of an industry.

Summary

1. The firm is the economic unit that produces and sells commodities. The economist's definition of the firm abstracts from real-life differences in size and form of organization of firms.

2. The single proprietorship, the partnership, and the corporation are the major forms of business organization in the United States today. The corporation is by far the most common business wherever large-scale production is required. The corporation is recognized as a legal entity; its owners, or shareholders, have a liability that is limited to the amount of money they have actually invested in the organization. Corporate ownership is readily transferred by sale of shares in organized securities markets.

3. Economic theory assumes that the same principles underlie each decision made within the firm and that the actual decision is uninfluenced by who makes it. The key behavioral assumption is that the firm seeks to maximize its profit.

4. Production consists of transforming inputs (or factors of production) into outputs (or goods and services). It is often convenient to divide factors of production into categories. One common classification is land, labor, and capital. Land includes all primary products, labor means all human services, and capital connotes all man-made aids to further production. An outstanding feature of modern production is the use of capital goods and roundabout methods of production.

5. Because there is more than one way to engage in production, the firm must decide *how* to produce. Efficiency is a measure of the relative amount of input necessary to produce a given output. Technological efficiency evaluates units of input in physical terms. Economic efficiency evaluates them in terms of costs.

6. The opportunity cost of using a resource is the value of that resource in its best alternative use. If the opportunity cost of using a resource in one way is less than or equal to the gain from using the resource in this way, there is no superior way of using it.

7. Measuring opportunity cost to the firm requires some difficult imputations in cases involving resources not purchased or hired for current use. Among these imputed costs are those for use of owners' money, depreciation, risk taking, and any special advantages that the firm may possess.

8. A firm maximizing profits, defined as the difference between revenue and opportunity cost, is making the best allocation of the resources under its control, according to the firm's evaluation of its alternatives.

9. Profits and losses provide important signals concerning the reallocation of resources. Profits earned in some enterprise provide a signal that more resources should move into similar enterprises. Losses show that some resources have better uses elsewhere and serve as a signal for them to move out of that enterprise.

10. The appendix to this chapter, which begins on page 880, introduces balance sheets and profit and loss statements and uses them to discuss some of the differences between the concepts of profits used by accountants and economists.

Concepts for review

The firm in theory and in the U.S. economy
The role of profit maximization
Single proprietorship, partnership, and corporation
Advantages of the corporation
Factors of production
Economic efficiency
Opportunity costs
Economic and other definitions of profits
Profits and resource allocation

Discussion questions

1. Many modern firms go through stages of being in turn a proprietorship, a partnership, and a corporation. Can you suggest why such an evolution might be sensible? Other firms started as corporations. Might this too be sensible? If you were to start a business, which form would you choose? Why?

2. Can the economic theory of the firm be of any help in analyzing the productive decisions of such nonprofit organizations as governments, churches, and colleges? What, if any, role does the notion of opportunity cost play for them?

3. In *The Engineers and the Price System* Thorstein Veblen argued that businessmen who made decisions about financing, pricing, and the like were largely superfluous to the operation of a business. In his view, knowledge of the technology would be sufficient to ensure efficient operation of firms. Discuss Veblen's contention.

4. "There is no such thing as a free lunch." Can anything be costless? Gas stations have traditionally provided many free services, including windshield cleaning, air pumps for tire inflation, and road maps. Now, many sell road maps and have discontinued free services. Indeed self-service stations are becoming increasingly popular with motorists who like the lower gas prices of those stations. Under what conditions will profit-maximizing behavior lead to the coexistence of full-service and self-service gas stations? What would determine the proportions in which each occurred?

5. What is the opportunity cost of:
a. a politician being fined $10,000 and sent to prison for one year
b. lending $500 to a friend
c. not permitting an $116 million electric power dam to be built because it would destroy the snail darter, a rare 3-inch long fish found only in that particular river
d. towing icebergs to Saudi Arabia to provide drinking water at the cost of 50¢ per cubic meter

6. Is straight-line depreciation an appropriate method of assessing the annual cost to the typical American household of using a passenger automobile? Some firms that use trucks allocate the cost on a per-mile basis. Might this method be more nearly appropriate for trucks than for automobiles owned by households?

7. Having bought a used car from Smiling Sam for $400, you drive it two days and it stops. You now find that it requires an extra $250 before it will run. Assuming that the car is not worth $650 fixed, should you make the repairs?

8. "The higher the opportunity cost, the poorer the investment." Do you agree with this statement? If you do not, how could you reformulate the maxim so that you did agree?

9. Which concept of profits is implied in the following quotations:

a. "Profits are necessary if firms are to stay in business."

b. "Profits are signals for firms to expand production and investment."

c. "Increased depreciation lowers profits and thus benefits the company's owners."

Production and cost in the short run

General Motors, Ford, Chrysler, and American Motors among them produced and sold 7.3 million new cars in the United States in 1974. GM's production was 3.6 million, Ford's 2.2 million, Chrysler's 1.1 million, and American Motors 0.4 million. The prices charged for comparable models were approximately the same, but the profits *per automobile* made and sold were very different for the companies not only in 1974 but on the average over many years. General Motors has consistently shown the highest profit per unit; Ford has been next most profitable, while Chrysler and American Motors each earned much lower profits per car than the other two. The reason lies in the *cost* of making and selling a car, which tends to be lower the more cars are produced. Over the past three decades a number of smaller producers, among them Packard, Crosley, Studebaker, and Kaiser-Frazer, had found costs higher than revenues, and after suffering heavy losses they left the industry. This example illustrates one aspect of the theory of cost of production: the variation of levels of cost with the level of output.

Another aspect of the theory of costs concerns factor prices. When in 1973 rising chicken feed prices reached the point where it cost more to feed chickens as they grew than they sold for when full-grown, chicken farmers were led to shut down temporarily. Similarly, when meat packers in March 1973 were caught in a squeeze between the maximum price at which they could sell and the rising cost of the livestock they bought, some of them too suspended production.

In order to understand firms' behavior, we need to know what determines their costs of production and how those costs vary as output varies. The principle of opportunity cost shows how to put a money value on the factor services that are used up in the process of production. These money values for all the factor services used to produce a certain output are added up to get the total cost of producing that output. But how are these costs related to output?

Real choices open to the firm

If the rate of a firm's sales has fallen off, should production be reduced correspondingly or should it be held at its old rate with the unsold amounts being stored up against an anticipated rise in sales in the future? If production is to be reduced, should one whole plant be closed down or should all the plants be operated on short time? If demand increases sharply and unexpectedly, how can more production be squeezed out of the existing facilities?

All of these matters concern how best to use the *existing* plant and equipment. They also concern time periods too short to build new plants or to install more equipment. The decisions made will be implemented quickly: A plant can be shut down on a week's notice, overtime can be increased tomorrow, and new workers can be added to production as soon as they can be hired and trained.

More weighty decisions must be made when the managers consider a longer time horizon. Should the firm adopt a highly automated process that will greatly reduce its wage bill, even though it will have to borrow large sums of money to buy the equipment? Or should it continue to build new plants that use the same kinds of techniques it is now using? Should it build new plants in an area where labor is plentiful but that is farther from its sources of raw materials? These matters concern what a firm should do when it is changing or replacing its plant and equipment. Decisions about these matters may take a long time to implement.

In the examples given above, managers make decisions from known possibilities. Large firms also have research and development staffs whose job it is to discover new methods of production. But the firm must de-

cide how much money to devote to this function and in what areas the payoff for new development will be largest. If, for example, a shortage of a particular labor skill or raw material is anticipated, the research staff can be told to try to find ways to economize on that input or even eliminate it from the production process.

TIME HORIZONS FOR DECISION MAKING

In order to reduce to manageable proportions the decisions firms are constantly making, economists organize them into three theoretical groups: (1) how best to employ existing plant and equipment (the "short run"); (2) what new plant and equipment and production processes to select, given the framework of known technical possibilities (the "long run"); and (3) what to do about encouraging the invention of new techniques (the "very long run"). In employing these periods economists abstract from the more complicated nature of real decisions and focus only on the key factors that restrict the range of choice in each set of decisions.

The short run

Short-run decisions are those made when the quantity of some inputs cannot be varied. The firm cannot get more of the **fixed factors** than it has on hand,[1] and it is committed to make any money payments that are associated with these fixed factors. Factors that can be varied in the short run are called **variable factors.**

In the short run, what matters is that at least one significant factor is fixed. The factor is

---

[1] Sometimes it is physically impossible to increase the quantity of a fixed factor in a short time. For example, there is no way to build a hydroelectric dam or a nuclear power plant in a few months. Other times it might be physically possible, but prohibitively expensive, to increase the quantity. For example, a suit-manufacturing firm could conceivably rent a building, buy and install new sewing machines, and hire a trained labor force in a few days if money were no consideration. Economists would regard prohibitive cost along with physical impossibility as a source of fixed factors.

fixed in the sense that while the firm may or may not use all that it has, it cannot get more for the duration of the short run. The fixed factor is usually an element of capital (such as plant and equipment), but it might be land, the services of management, or even the supply of skilled salaried labor.

The short run does not correspond to a fixed number of months or years. In some industries it may extend over many years; in others it may be only a matter of months or even weeks. Furthermore, it may last a different period of time for expansion of an industry than for contraction of it. In the electric power industry, for example, where it takes three or more years to acquire and install a steam-turbine generator, an unforeseen increase in demand will involve a long period during which the extra demand must be met as best as can be with the existing capital equipment. Once installed, this equipment has a very long life, and a decrease in demand leaves the firm committed, possibly for decades, to all the costs of this equipment that do not vary with output. By way of contrast, a machine shop can acquire new equipment or sell existing equipment in a matter of a few weeks, and thus the short run is correspondingly short. An increase in demand will have to be met with the existing stock of capital for only a short time, after which it will be possible to adjust the stock of equipment to the level made desirable by the higher demand.

The long run

Long-run decisions are those made when the inputs of all factors of production may be varied but when the basic technology of production is unchanged. Again, the long run does not correspond to a specific period of time.

The special importance of the long run in production theory is that it corresponds to the situation facing the firm when it is *planning* to go into business, to expand substantially the scale of its operations, to branch out into new products or new areas, or to modernize, replace, or reorganize its method of production.

The firm's *planning decisions* characteristically are made with fixed technical possibilities but with freedom to choose from a variety of production processes that will use factor inputs in different proportions.

The very long run

Unlike the short and the long run, the **very long run** concerns the opportunities arising from changing technology. A central characteristic of society, at least since the Industrial Revolution, has been the change in technology that leads to new and improved products and new and improved methods of production. Sometimes the firm adopts technological changes made by other firms; for instance, many industries were revolutionized by the development of the transistor. At other times these technological changes may be affected by what the firm itself does, particularly in its programs of research and development. In the latter case long-run decisions are made about how much to invest in such programs.

CONNECTING THE RUNS: THE PRODUCTION FUNCTION

Despite the fact that it is convenient to treat production decisions in several stages—or in separate compartments—they are thoroughly interrelated. The plant built today (a long-run decision) affects tomorrow's short-run decisions. Similarly, an alternative to coping with an inadequate-sized plant by running overtime shifts (a short-run expedient) is constructing a new wing (a long-run decision) or an entirely new plant (another long-run decision), or searching for a new technique of production (a very-long-run decision).

The various "runs" are simply different aspects of the same basic problem: getting output from inputs efficiently. They differ in terms of what the firm is able to change.

The relation between factor services used as

inputs into the production process and the quantity of output obtained is called the **production function.** A simplified production function in which there are two factors of production, labor and capital, will be considered here. This simplification is convenient for exposition. The conclusions apply equally when there are many factors. The variation of output and cost under the assumption that one of the two factors is fixed is examined in this chapter. (Capital is taken to be the fixed factor and labor the variable one.) The long-run situation in which both factors can be varied is studied in Chapter 12.

Table 11–1 The variation of output with capital fixed and labor variable

(1) Quantity of labor (L)	(2) Total product (TP)	(3) Average product (AP)	(4) Marginal product (MP)
0	0	—	
			15
1	15	15.0	
			19
2	34	17.0	
			14
3	48	16.0	
			12
4	60	15.0	
			2
5	62	12.4	

The relation of output to changes in the quantity of labor can be looked at in three different ways. Capital is assumed fixed at 4 units. As the quantity of labor increases, the rate of output (the total product) increases. Average product increases at first and then declines. The same is true of marginal product.

Marginal product is shown between the lines because it refers to the *change* in output from one level of labor input to another. When graphing the schedule, *MP*s of this kind should be plotted at the midpoint of the interval. Thus, graphically, the marginal product of 12 would be plotted to correspond to quantity of labor of 3.5.

Short-run choices

TOTAL, AVERAGE, AND MARGINAL PRODUCTS

Assume that a firm starts with a fixed amount of capital (say 4 units) and contemplates applying various amounts of labor to it. Table 11–1 shows three different ways of looking at how output varies with the quantity of the variable factor. As a preliminary step, some terms need to be defined.

1. **Total product** (*TP*) means just what it says: the total amount produced during some period of time by all the factors of production employed. If the inputs of all but one factor are held constant, total product will change as more or less of the variable factor is used. This variation is shown in columns (1) and (2) of Table 11–1, which gives a total product schedule.[2] Figure 11–1(i) shows such a schedule graphically. (The shape of the curve will be discussed shortly.)

2. **Average product** (*AP*) is merely the total product per unit of the variable factor, labor. The number of units of labor will be denoted by *L*.

$$AP = \frac{TP}{L}$$

It is shown in column (3) of Table 11–1. Notice that as more of the variable factor is used, average product first rises and then falls. The level of output (34 units in the example) where average product reaches a maximum is called the **point of diminishing average productivity.**

3. **Marginal product** (*MP*), sometimes called **incremental product,** is the change in total product resulting from the use of 1 unit

[2] In this table we use unrealistically small numbers in order that the underlying arithmetic will be simple. This will help in understanding the various product concepts and their relations to cost concepts, shown in Table 11–2.

Figure 11–1 Total, average, and marginal product curves

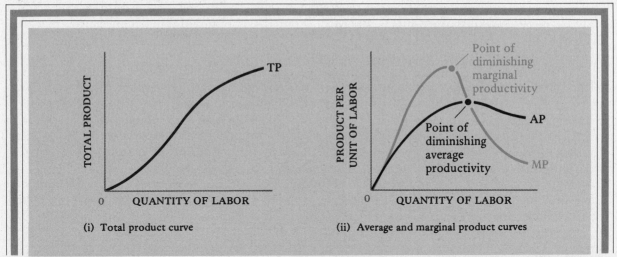

(i) Total product curve

(ii) Average and marginal product curves

TP, *AP*, and *MP* curves often have the shapes shown here. In this figure total product increases with the quantity of labor, first at an increasing rate and then at a decreasing rate. This implies that average and marginal product curves rise at first and then decline.

more of the variable factor[3] [7]

$$MP = \frac{\Delta TP}{\Delta L}$$

Computed values of marginal product are shown in column (4) of Table 11–1. The figures are placed between the lines of the table to stress the fact that the concept refers to the *change* in output caused by the *change* in quantity of the variable factor. For example, the increase in labor from 3 to 4 units ($\Delta L = 1$) raises output by 12 from 48 to 60 ($\Delta TP = 12$). Thus the *MP* equals 12, and is recorded between 3 and 4 units of labor. Note that the *MP* in the example rises and then falls. The level of output where marginal product reaches a maximum is called the **point of diminishing marginal productivity.**

[3] The Greek delta (Δ) is a standard symbol meaning "the change in." Thus ΔL is read "a change in the quantity of labor." For the definition of marginal product we want a 1-unit change in labor, that is, $\Delta L = 1$.

Figure 11–1 (ii) plots average product and marginal product curves. Although three different schedules are shown in Table 11–1 and three different curves are shown in Figure 11–1, there is only one relationship between output on the one hand and labor input on the other. Fully specifying the average product schedule, for example, would imply specific total product and marginal product schedules. Whichever of these measures proves most convenient may be used.

Finally, bear in mind that the schedules of Table 11–1 and the curves of Figure 11–1 all assume a specified quantity of the fixed factor. If the quantity of capital had been, say, 6 or 10 instead of the 4 units that were assumed, there would be a different set of total product, average product, and marginal product curves. The reason for this is that if any specified amount of labor has more capital to work with, it can produce more output—that is, its total product will be greater.

The hypothesis of diminishing returns

The variations in output that result from applying more or less of a variable factor to a given quantity of a fixed factor are the subject of a famous economic hypothesis. Usually it is called the **law of diminishing returns,** but it has also been given other names. Most accurately it is called the **hypothesis of eventually diminishing returns.**

The hypothesis states that if increasing amounts of a variable factor are applied to a given amount of a fixed factor, eventually a situation will be reached in which each additional unit of the variable factor adds less to total product than did the previous unit. The applications of this hypothesis are many. Winston Churchill during World War II noted the diminishing returns to dropping more and more bombs on German steel mills because many of the later bombs merely redistributed the rubble from earlier ones. A second or third seat belt on a car or plane passenger would add less to the safety of the passenger than the first one, and so on.

The foregoing examples were stated in terms of diminishing marginal productivity. But it is also necessary to know what happens to average product, and the hypothesis also states that eventually the output per unit of the variable factor will decline. [8]

The law of diminishing returns states that if increasing quantities of a variable factor are applied to a given quantity of fixed factors, the marginal product and the average product of the variable factor will eventually decrease.

Evidence in favor of the hypothesis of diminishing returns is strong. Were the hypothesis generally incorrect, there would be no reason to fear that the present population explosion will bring with it a food crisis. If the marginal product of additional workers applied to a fixed quantity of land were constant, then world food production could be expanded in proportion to the population merely by keeping a constant fraction of the population on farms. But with fixed techniques, the hypothesis of diminishing returns predicts an inexorable decline in the marginal product of each additional laborer because an expanding population has a fixed world supply of agricultural land. Thus, unless there is a continual improvement in the techniques of production, continuous population growth will bring with it, according to the hypothesis of diminishing returns, declining living standards over much of the world and will eventually result in widespread famine.

Diminishing returns may also be looked at in terms of varying factor proportions. Consider a 1,000-acre farm on which the amount of labor is increased in successive years from 1 to 100 to 1,000 to 10,000 man-years. This means that the proportions in which the two factors are being used is being varied, the amount of land per worker decreasing from 1,000 acres to 10 acres to 1 acre to 0.1 acre over the four years. The variation in the productivity of labor occurs because as labor is increased, with land held constant, each laborer has less and less land to work with. It may well be that marginal productivity rises at first because there is no way for 1 worker to farm 1,000 acres efficiently. But we should not be very surprised to learn that although the total output of the farm increased in the third and fourth years, the output per laborer declined. Because the hypothesis of diminishing returns relates to the results of varying the proportions in which factors of production are used it is sometimes referred to as the **law of variable proportions.**

THE SHAPE OF THE MARGINAL PRODUCT CURVE

The hypothesis of diminishing returns predicts only that sooner or later the *MP* curve will decline. It is conceivable that marginal and average returns might diminish from the outset, so that the first unit of labor contributes most to total production and each successive unit contributes less than the previous unit. It is also possible for the marginal product to rise at first and decline later. Consider further the bombing of a German steel mill. The very first bomb, even if a direct hit, could not knock out the factory; thus the "production of damage" would be expected to rise with further bombs. Eventually, when the operation of the steel plant was already crippled, later bombs, while adding to the problems of resuming production, would surely have less effect than earlier ones.

One way of looking at initially increasing and subsequently diminishing returns is with respect to the organization of production. Consider use of variable numbers of laborers in a manufacturing operation. It may be possible as the number of laborers increases to break the tasks done by labor into a large number of separate jobs with each laborer specializing in one job. This process is called the *division of labor.* Output per worker will rise over the range in which additional units of the variable factor permit more and more efficient divisions of labor to be adopted. According to the hypothesis of diminishing returns, the scope for such economies must eventually disappear and sooner or later the marginal and average products of additional workers must decline.

The relation between marginal and average curves

Notice that in Figure 11–1 (ii) the *MP* curve cuts the *AP* curve at the latter's maximum point. Although the relation between marginal and average curves is a mathematical one and not a matter of economics, it is very important to understand how these curves are related. [9]

The average product curve slopes upward as long as the marginal product curve is above it; it makes no difference whether the marginal curve is itself sloping upward or downward. The common sense of this relation is that if an additional worker—say in

this case that it is a man—is to raise the average product of all workers, his output must be greater than the average output of all other workers. It is immaterial whether his contribution to output is greater or less than the contribution of the worker hired immediately before him; all that matters is that his contribution to output exceeds the average output of *all* the workers hired before him. (The relation between marginal and average measures is further illustrated in the box.)

SHORT-RUN VARIATIONS IN COST

We now shift our attention from the firm's production function to its costs. We consider firms that are not in a position to influence the prices of the factors of production they employ. These firms must pay the going market price for all factors.[4] Given the prices paid for factors and the physical returns summarized by the product curves, the costs of different levels of output can quickly be computed.

Cost concepts defined

The following brief definitions of several cost concepts are closely related to the product concepts just introduced.

1. **Total cost** (*TC*) means just what it says: the total cost of producing any given level of output. Total cost is divided into two parts, total fixed costs (*TFC*) and total variable costs (*TVC*). **Fixed costs** are those costs that do not vary with output; they will be the same if output is 1 unit or 1 million units. These costs are also often referred to as "overhead costs" or "unavoidable costs." All of those costs that vary directly with output, rising as more is produced and falling as less is produced, are called **variable costs.** In the previous example, since labor was the variable factor of production, the wage bill would

---

[4] The important problems that arise when the firm is in a position to influence the prices it pays for its factors of production are considered in Chapter 21.

The batting average of Ted Williams: marginal and lifetime

The relationship between "marginal" and "average" concepts is a very general one. An illuminating example comes from the *Baseball Encyclopedia*. The table below gives the batting average (number of hits—output—divided by official times at bat—input) of Ted Williams over his illustrious career as a member of the Boston Red Sox. For each year, column (2) gives his batting average for his whole major league career before that year. It is his lifetime average on opening day. Column (3) gives his average during the current, or "marginal," year.

Whenever his current year average is above the lifetime-to-date average, the latter rises. See, for example, 1941, 1948, and 1957. Whenever his current year is below the lifetime the latter falls. See, for example, 1946, 1950, and 1959. Notice that this is true whether the marginal itself is rising or falling. For example, both 1950 and 1951 were below average years for Williams and lowered his average, even though 1951 was better than the previous year had been (marginal rising) and 1950 was worse than the previous year had been (marginal falling). *If the average is to fall,*

Year	(1) Games played	(2) Lifetime batting average on opening day	(3) Batting average during year
1939	149	.000	.327
1940	144	.327	.344
1941	143	.335	.406
1942	150	.359	.356
1943–45★	0	.358	—
1946	150	.358	.342
1947	156	.355	.343
1948	137	.353	.369
1949	155	.355	.343
1950	89	.354	.317
1951	148	.351	.318
1952–53★	43	.348	.406
1954	117	.350	.345
1955	98	.349	.356
1956	136	.350	.345
1957	132	.349	.388
1958	129	.352	.328
1959	103	.351	.254
1960	113	.346	.316
Lifetime	2292	.344	

★ Military service.

all that matters is that the marginal is below the average.

be a variable cost. Variable costs are often referred to as "direct costs."

2. **Average total cost** (*ATC*), also called **average cost** (*AC*), is the total cost of producing any given output divided by the number of units produced, or the cost per unit. *ATC* may be divided into **average fixed costs** (*AFC*) and **average variable costs** (*AVC*) in just the same way as total costs were divided.

Although average *variable* costs may rise or fall as production is increased (depending on whether output rises more rapidly or more slowly than total variable costs), it is clear that average fixed costs decline continuously as output increases. A doubling of output always leads to a halving of fixed costs per unit of output. This is a process popularly known as "spreading one's overhead."

3. **Marginal cost** (*MC*), sometimes called

incremental cost, is the increase in total cost resulting from raising the rate of production by 1 unit. Because fixed costs do not vary with output, marginal fixed costs are always zero. Therefore marginal costs are necessarily marginal variable costs, and a change in fixed costs will leave marginal costs unaffected. For example, the marginal cost of producing a few more potatoes by farming a given amount of land more intensively is the same, whatever the rent paid for the fixed amount of land. [10]

These three measures of cost are merely different ways of looking at a single phenomenon, and they are mathematically interrelated. Sometimes it is convenient to use one, and sometimes another.

Short-run cost curves

Take the production relationships in Table 11–1 and assume that the price of labor is $10 per unit and the price of capital is $25 per unit. The cost schedules computed for these values are shown in Table 11–2.[5] Figure 11–2 plots cost curves that are similar in shape to those arising from the data in Table 11–2. Notice that the marginal cost curve cuts the *ATC* and *AVC* curves at their lowest points. This is another example of the relation (discussed above) between a marginal and an average curve. The *ATC* curve, for example, slopes downward as long as the marginal cost curve is below it; it makes no difference whether the marginal cost curve is itself sloping upward or downward.

In Figure 11–2 the average variable cost curve reaches a minimum and then rises. With fixed factor prices, when average product per worker is a maximum, average variable cost

[5] If you do not see where any of the numbers come from, review Table 11–1 and the definitions of cost just given.

Table 11–2 The variation of costs with capital fixed and labor variable

		TOTAL COST ($)			AVERAGE COST ($ PER UNIT)			
Labor (L)	Output (q)	Fixed (TFC)	Variable (TVC)	Total (TC)	Fixed (AFC)	Variable (AVC)	Total (ATC)	Marginal cost (MC)
0	0	100	0	100	—	—	—	
								0.67
1	15	100	10	110	6.67	0.67	7.33	
								0.53
2	34	100	20	120	2.94	0.59	3.53	
								0.71
3	48	100	30	130	2.08	0.62	2.71	
								0.83
4	60	100	40	140	1.67	0.67	2.33	
								5.00
5	62	100	50	150	1.61	0.81	2.42	

The relation of cost to level of output can be looked at in several different ways. These cost curves are computed from the product curves of Table 11–1, given the price of capital of $25 per unit and the price of labor of $10 per unit. Notice that the average curves are cost per unit of output. Thus, for example, the ATC of $3.53 arises because 34 units of output cost a total of $120. The marginal cost of $.71 shown in the next line is the increase in total cost of $10 associated with hiring one more laborer *divided by* the increase in output of 14 caused by employing one more laborer (output rises from 34 to 48). For graphical purposes, marginal costs should be plotted midway in the interval over which they are computed. The *MC* of $.71 would be plotted at output 41.

Figure 11–2   Total, average, and marginal cost curves

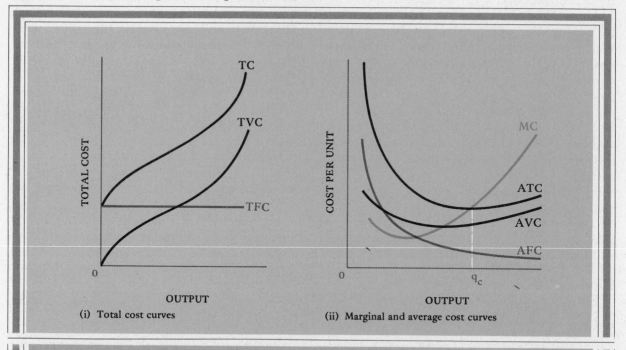

(i)   Total cost curves

(ii)   Marginal and average cost curves

TC, AC, and *MC* curves often have the shapes shown here. (i) Total fixed cost does not vary with output. Total variable cost and the total of all costs ($TC = TVC + TFC$) rise with output, first at a decreasing and then at an increasing rate. (ii) The total cost curves in (i) give rise to the average and marginal curves in (ii). *AFC* declines as output increases. *AVC* and *ATC* fall and then rise as output increases. *MC* does the same and intersects *ATC* and *AVC* at their minimum points. Capacity output is q_c, the minimum point on the *ATC* curve.

is a minimum. [11] The common sense of this proposition is that each additional worker adds the same amount to cost but a different amount to output, and when output per worker is rising, the cost per unit of output must be falling—and vice versa.

The hypothesis of eventually diminishing average productivity implies eventually increasing average variable costs.

Short-run *ATC* curves are often drawn U-shaped. This reflects the assumptions that (i) average productivity is increasing when output is low but (ii) at some level of output average productivity begins to fall fast enough to cause average total costs to increase.

The definition of capacity

The output that corresponds to the minimum short-run average total cost is often called the **capacity** of the firm. Capacity, in this sense, is not an upper limit on what can be produced. In the example of Figure 11–2 (ii) capacity output is q_c units, but higher outputs can be achieved, provided the firm is willing to accept the higher per-unit costs that accompany output "above capacity." A firm producing with **excess capacity** is producing at an output smaller than the point of minimum average total cost. These concepts give the word "capacity" a meaning different from its meaning in everyday speech, but the concepts will prove useful and need cause no confusion.

A family of short-run cost curves

A short-run cost curve shows how costs vary with output for a given quantity of the fixed factor—say a given size of plant.

There is a different short-run cost curve for each given quantity of the fixed factor.

A small plant for manufacturing nuts and bolts will have its own short–run cost curve. A medium–size and a very large–size plant will each have its own short–run cost curve. If a firm expands and replaces its small plant with a medium–size plant it will move from one short–run cost curve to another such curve. This change from one size of plant to another size of plant is a long-run change, and the study of how short–run cost curves of different size plants are related to each other is the subject of the next chapter.

Summary

1. The firm's production decisions can be classified into three groups: (a) how best to employ its existing plant and equipment (the short run); (b) what new plant and equipment and production processes to select, given the framework of known technical possibilities (the long run); and (c) what to do about encouraging, or merely adapting to, the invention of new techniques (the very long run).

2. The short run involves decisions in which one or more factors of production are fixed. The long run involves decisions in which all factors are variable, but in which technology is unchanged. In the very long run, technology can change.

3. The production function describes the ways in which different inputs may be combined to produce different quantities of output. Short-run and long-run situations can be interpreted as implying different kinds of constraints on the production function. In the short run, the firm is constrained to use no more than a given quantity of some fixed factor; in the long run, it is constrained only by the available techniques of production.

4. The theory of short-run cost behavior depends on the productivity of variable factors when applied to fixed factors. The concepts of total, average, and marginal product represent alternative ways of looking at the relation between output and the quantity of the variable factor of production.

5. The hypothesis, or "law," of eventually diminishing returns asserts that if increasing quantities of a variable factor are applied to a given quantity of fixed factors, the marginal and the average product of the variable factor will eventually decrease. This hypothesis leads directly to implications of rising marginal and average costs.

6. Given physical productivity schedules and the costs per unit of factors, it is a simple matter of arithmetic to develop the whole family of short-run cost curves.

7. Short-run average total cost curves are drawn as U-shaped to reflect the expectation that average productivity increases for small outputs but eventually declines sufficiently rapidly to offset advantages of spreading overheads. The output corresponding to the minimum point of a short-run average total cost curve is called the plant's capacity.

8. There is a whole family of short-run cost curves, one for each quantity of the fixed factor.

Concepts for review

Interrelations of short run, long run, and very long run
Marginal and average productivity
The hypothesis of diminishing returns
The relation between marginal and average curves
The relation between productivity and cost $ATC = AFC + AVC$
Marginal cost and average cost
Capacity and excess capacity

Discussion questions

1. Is the short run the same number of months for increasing output as for decreasing it? Must the short run in industry A be the same length for all firms in the industry? Under what circumstances might the short run actually involve a longer time span than even the very long run?

2. How would the following factors increase or reduce the relative importance of short-run decisions for management?

a. a guaranteed annual-employment contract of at least 48 40-hour weeks of work for all employees.

b. a major depression in economic activity during which there is substantial unemployment of labor and in which equipment is being used at well below capacity-levels of production

c. a speeding-up of delivery dates for new easy-to-install equipment

3. Indicate whether each of the following conforms to the hypothesis of diminishing returns; and, if so, whether it refers to marginal or average returns, or both.

a. "The bigger they are, the harder they fall."

b. As the fishing pressure in the Salmon River increased, the total number of fish caught increased, but the number of fish per fisherman decreased, the average hours fished for each fish caught increased, and the average size of the fish caught declined.

c. For the seventh year in a row, the average depth of drilling required to hit oil in Texas increased.

d. Five workers produce twice as much today as ten workers did forty years ago.

4. Consider the education of a human being as a process of production. Regard years of schooling as one variable factor of production. What are the other factors? What factors are fixed? At what point would you expect diminishing productivity to set in? Are you sure it would set in during his lifetime for an Einstein?

5. Suppose that each of the following news items is correct. Discuss each in terms of its effects on the level of average total cost.

a. The U.S. Office of Education reports that the increasing level of education of our youth has led both to higher productivity and to increases in the general level of wages.

b. During the winter of 1977 many factories were forced by fuel shortages to reduce production and to operate at levels of production far below capacity.

c. For the third year in a row, the Post Office's production exceeded its capacity.

d. NASA reports that the space program has led to development of electronic devices that have led to innovations in many industries.

6. "Because overhead costs are fixed, increasing production lowers costs. Thus, small business is sure to be inefficient. This is a dilemma of modern society which values both smallness *and* efficiency." Discuss.

12

Cost in the long run

The long run is defined as a situation in which all factors are free to be varied. Whereas in Chapter 11 we were concerned with the question of the firm's adjusting the input of a variable factor to its fixed factor in such a way as to achieve most cheaply a given level of output, we now ask instead: By which of the many possible methods will any given output be produced? Should the firm adopt a technique that uses a great deal of capital and only a small amount of labor, or should it adopt a technique that uses less capital and more labor? What implications will these decisions have for the firm's costs?

INPUT DECISIONS IN THE LONG RUN

Because there are several ways of achieving the same total output, it is necessary to choose among them. The hypothesis of profit maximization provides a simple rule for doing this: Any firm that is trying to maximize its profits should select the method that produces its output at the lowest possible cost. This implication of the hypothesis of profit maximization is called the implication of **cost minimization.**

From the alternatives open to it, the firm chooses the least costly ways of achieving any specific output.

If there is a stable, required output rate, and if the costs of factors are known, that is all there is to it. In other words, the firm selects the economically efficient way of producing any level of output. (If you have forgotten the distinction between economic and technological efficiency, see pages 154–155.)

These long-run planning decisions are important because today's variable factors are tomorrow's fixed ones. A firm deciding on a new plant, fully equipped, will have many alternatives to choose among, but once installed the new equipment is fixed for a long time. If the firm errs now, its very survival may be threatened; if it estimates shrewdly and its rivals don't, it may reward both its owners and its foresighted managers with large profits and bonuses.

These decisions are among the most difficult and most important the firm makes. They are difficult because the firm must anticipate what methods of production will be efficient not only today but in the years ahead when costs of labor and raw materials may have changed. The decisions are difficult, too, because the firm must estimate how much output it will want to be producing. Is the industry of which it is a member growing or declining? Is it going to increase or decrease its share of the market? Will new products emerge to render its buggy whips less useful than an extrapolation of past sales suggests?

Conditions for cost minimization

What should the firm do to make its costs as low as possible? In the most general terms it is simple enough to say this: Using the best judgment possible, the firm should choose the least costly alternative for producing whichever output it desires to produce. The firm does not have the least costly alternative if it would be possible to substitute one factor for another in such a way as to keep its output constant while reducing its total cost. This can be stated more formally in this way: The firm should substitute one factor (for example, capital) for another factor (for example, labor) as long as the marginal product of the one factor *per dollar expended on it* is greater than the marginal product of the other factor *per dollar expended on it*. The firm cannot have minimized its costs as long as these two magnitudes are unequal. This leads to the following important condition of cost minimization (using K to represent capital, L labor, and p the price to the firm of a unit of the factor).

$$\frac{MP_K}{p_K} = \frac{MP_L}{p_L} \qquad [1]$$

This condition is directly analogous to the condition for the utility-maximizing household, given on page 113, in which the household equated the marginal utility per dollar of two goods.[1] To see why this condition needs to be fulfilled if costs of production are really minimized, suppose the left-hand side was equal to 10, showing that the last dollar spent on capital produced 10 units of output, while the right-hand side was equal to 4, showing that the last dollar spent on labor added only 4 units to output. In such a case, the firm by using $2.50 less of labor would reduce output by approximately 10 units. But it could regain that lost output by spending approximately $1 more on capital.[2] Making such a substitution of capital for labor would leave output unchanged and reduce cost by $1.50. Thus the original position was not the cost-minimizing one! Anytime the two sides of [1] are not equal, there are factor substitutions that will reduce costs.

By rearranging the terms in [1] we can look at the cost-minimizing condition in a slightly different way.

$$\frac{MP_K}{MP_L} = \frac{p_K}{p_L} \qquad [2]$$

The ratio of the marginal products on the left-hand side compares the contribution to output of the last unit of capital and the last unit of labor. If the ratio is 4, this means 1 unit more of capital will add 4 times as much to output as one unit more of labor. The right-hand side shows how the cost of 1 unit more of capital compares to the cost of 1 unit more of labor. If it is also 4, it does not pay the firm to substitute capital for labor or vice versa. But suppose the right-hand side is 2. Capital, although twice as expensive, is 4 times as pro-

---

[1] Later in this chapter the condition is given a graphic analysis similar to that given household behavior in the second half of Chapter 8.

[2] The argument in the previous two sentences assumes that the marginal products do not change very much when expenditure is changed by a few dollars. If they did not change at all the "approximatelys" could be eliminated.

The significance of the principle of substitution to the economy as a whole

The relative prices of factors of production will tend to reflect their relative scarcities. One country has a great deal of land and a small population. Here the price of land will be low while, because labor is in short supply, the wage rate will be high. Producers of agricultural goods will tend to make lavish use of the cheap land while economizing on expensive labor; thus a production process will be adopted that utilizes a low ratio of labor to land. A second country is small in area and has a large population. Here the demand for land will be high relative to its supply and land will be relatively expensive while labor will be relatively cheap. Firms producing agricultural goods will tend to economize on land by using a great deal of labor per unit of land; thus a productive process will be adopted that uses a high ratio of labor to land. Similar decisions will be made with respect to the relative scarcities of any factors: If capital is scarce relative to other factors, it will be expensive and firms following their own self-interest will use it sparingly; if capital is plentiful relative to other factors, it will be cheap and firms will adopt production processes that make lavish use of capital.

Thus relative factor prices will reflect the relative scarcities (in relation to demand) of different factors of production: abundant factors will have prices that are low relative to the prices of factors that are scarce. Firms seeking their own private profit will be led to use large amounts of the factors with which the whole country is plentifully endowed and to economize on factors that are in scarce supply in the whole country.

Once again we see that the price system is an automatic control system. No single firm needs to be aware of national factor surpluses and scarcities. Prices determined on the competitive market tend to reflect these, and individual firms that never look beyond their own private profit are nonetheless led to economize on factors that are scarce to the nation as a whole. Thus the price system leads profit-maximizing firms to take account of the nation's relative factor scarcities when deciding which of the possible methods of production to adopt.

This discussion suggests why we should not be surprised to discover that methods of producing the same commodity differ among countries. In the United States, where labor is highly skilled and very expensive, a steel company may use very elaborate machinery to economize on labor. In China, where labor is abundant and capital very scarce, a much less mechanized method of production is appropriate. The Western engineer who believes that the Chinese are way behind Westerners because they are using methods long discarded in the West as inefficient may be missing the truth about economic efficiency in use of resources. The suggestion, often made, that to aid underdeveloped countries we need merely to export Western "know-how" is incomplete.

ductive, and it will pay the firm to switch to a method of production that uses more capital and less labor. If, however, the right-hand side is 6 (or *any* number more than 4), it will pay to substitute labor for capital.

This formulation shows how the firm can adjust the things over which it has control (the quantities of factors used, and thus the marginal products of the factors) to the things that are typically given to it by the market (the prices or opportunity costs of the factors). A precisely analogous adjustment process was involved (see page 114) in households' adjusting their consumption of goods to the market prices of those goods.

The principle of substitution

Suppose that a firm is producing where the cost-minimizing conditions shown in [1] or [2] are met but that the cost of labor increases while the cost of capital remains unchanged. As we have just seen, the least-cost method of producing any output will now use less labor and more capital than was required to produce that same output before the factor prices changed. The prediction called the **principle of substitution** follows from the assumption that firms try to minimize their costs.

Methods of production will change if the relative prices of factors change. Relatively more of the cheaper factor will be used and relatively less of the more expensive one.

This prediction plays a central role in the way the market system allocates resources because it relates to the way the individual firm will respond to changes in relative factor prices. Such changes in relative factor prices are caused by the changing relative scarcity of factors to the economy as a whole. The individual firm is thus motivated to use less of factors that have become scarcer to the economy.[3]

[3] A numerical example of the principle of substitution is shown on page 154. As labor became relatively more expensive, moving from Case I to Case III, the firm shifted from method A, using much labor, to method D, using less labor.

COST CURVES IN THE LONG RUN

There is a best (least-cost) method of producing each level of output when all factors are free to be varied. In general this method will not be the same for different levels of output. If factor prices are given, a minimum cost can be found for each possible level of output and, if this minimum achievable cost is expressed as an amount per unit of output, we can obtain the long-run average cost of producing each level of output. When this information is plotted on a graph, the result is called a **long-run average cost curve** (*LRAC*). Figure 12–1 shows such a curve.

This long-run average cost curve is determined by the technology of the industry (which is assumed to be fixed) and by the prices of the factors of production. It is a "boundary" in the sense that points below the curve are unattainable, points on the curve are attainable if sufficient time elapses for all factors to be adjusted, and points above the curve are also attainable. Indeed, points above the *LRAC* curve may represent the best that can be done in the short run when all factors are not freely variable.

The *LRAC* curve divides the cost levels that are attainable with known technology and given factor prices from those that are unattainable.

The shape of the long-run average cost curve

The long-run average cost curve in Figure 12–1 is shown as falling at first and then rising. This curve is often described as being U-shaped, although "saucer-shaped" might be more descriptive.

Decreasing costs. Over the range of output from zero to q_m the firm has falling long-run average costs. An expansion of output results in a reduction of costs per unit of output once enough time has elapsed to allow adjustments in the techniques of production. Since the prices of factors are assumed to be constant,

Figure 12–1 A long-run average cost curve

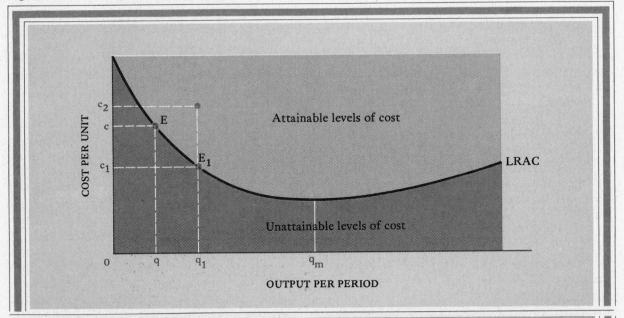

The long-run average cost curve provides a boundary between attainable and unattainable levels of cost. If the firm wishes to produce output q, the lowest attainable cost level is c per unit. Thus point E is on the *LRAC* curve. E_1 represents the least-cost method of producing q_1. Suppose a firm is producing at E and desires to increase output to q_1. In the short run it will not be able to vary all factors, and thus costs above c_1, say c_2, must be accepted. In the long run a plant optimal for output q_1 can be built and cost of c_1 can be attained. Output q_m is that at which the firm attains its lowest possible per unit cost of production for the given technology and factor prices.

the reason for the decline in costs per unit must be because output increases faster than inputs as the scale of the firm's production expands. Over this range of output the firm is often said to enjoy long-run **increasing returns.**[4] Increasing returns may arise as a result of increased opportunities for specialization of tasks made possible by the division of labor even with no substitution of one factor of

production for another. Or they may arise because of factor substitution. Even the most casual observation of the differences in production technique used in large-size and small-size plants shows the existence of the differences in factor proportions. These differences arise because large, specialized machinery and equipment is useful only when the volume of output that the firm can sell justifies its employment.

For example, the use of the assembly line technique, body-stamping machinery, and multiple-boring engine-block machines in automobile production are economically effi-

[4] Economists often shift back and forth between speaking in physical terms (i.e., increasing *returns* to production) and cost terms (i.e., decreasing *costs* of production). Thus the same firm may be spoken of as having decreasing costs or enjoying increasing returns.

cient only if individual operations are to be repeated thousands of times. The use of elaborate harvesting equipment (which combines many individual tasks that might be done by hand and by tractor) provides the least-cost method of production on a big farm but not on a few acres.

Typically, the substitution involved is of capital for labor and of complex machines for simpler ones. Automation is a contemporary example of this kind of substitution. Electronic devices can handle a very large volume of operations very quickly, but unless the level of production requires very large numbers of operations, it does not make sense to use these techniques.

Increasing costs. Over the range of outputs greater than q_m the firm encounters rising costs. An expansion in production, even after sufficient time has elapsed for all adjustments to be made, will be accompanied by a rise in average costs per unit of output. If costs per unit of input are constant, this rise in costs must be the result of an expansion in output less than in proportion to the expansion in inputs. Such a firm is said to suffer long-run **decreasing returns.**[5] Decreasing returns imply that the firm suffers some diseconomy of scale. As its scale of operations increases, diseconomies—of management or otherwise—are encountered that increase its per unit costs of production.

Lowest LRAC. At the output q_m in Figure 12–1 the firm has reached its lowest possible long-run costs per unit of output. If the firm were to produce at that output it could be said to be producing efficiently in the sense that

---

[5] Long-run decreasing returns differ from the short-run diminishing returns that we encountered earlier. In the short run at least one factor is fixed and the law of diminishing returns ensures that returns to the variable factor will eventually diminish. In the long run all factors are variable and it is possible that physically diminishing returns would never be encountered—at least as long as it was genuinely possible to increase inputs of all factors.

the costs of producing a unit of output would be as low as they possibly could be (for given technology and factor prices). We shall see in Chapter 14 that under certain conditions (called those of perfect competition) each firm will, in equilibrium, produce at the minimum point on its *LRAC.*

Constant returns. The firm's long-run average costs are shown in Figure 12–1 as falling to output q_m and rising thereafter. Another possibility should be noted: The firm's *LRAC* might have a flat portion over some range of output around q_m. If such a flat portion existed, the firm would be said to be encountering constant costs over the relevant range of output. This would mean that the firm's average costs per unit of output were not changing as its output changed. Since factor prices are assumed fixed, this must mean that the firm's output is increasing exactly as fast as its inputs are increasing. Such a firm would be said to be encountering **constant returns.**

THE RELATION BETWEEN LONG-RUN AND SHORT-RUN COSTS

The various short-run cost curves mentioned at the conclusion of Chapter 11 and the long-run curve studied in this chapter are all derived from the same production function, and each assumes given prices for all factor inputs. In the long run, all factors can be varied; in the short run, some must remain fixed. The long-run average cost curve (*LRAC*) shows the lowest cost of producing any output when all factors are variable. The short-run average cost curve (*SRAC*) shows the lowest cost of producing any output when one or more factors is not free to vary.

The short-run cost curve cannot fall below the long-run curve because the latter curve represents the *lowest* attainable costs for every output. It might be the same curve, but the law of variable proportions predicts that as output is changed, a different-sized plant

Jacob Viner's famous error

The student who finds the relationship between *SRAC* and *LRAC* hard to understand may take some comfort from the fact that when these relations were first being worked out by economists, one of the world's leading economic theorists, the late Jacob Viner of Princeton University, instructed his draftsman to draw the *LRAC* through the minimum points of the *SRAC* but "so as never to lie above" the *SRAC*. He reports of his draftsman, "He is a mathematician, however, not an economist, and he saw some mathematical objection to this procedure which I could not succeed in understanding. I could not persuade him to disregard his scruples as a craftsman and to follow my instructions, absurd though they might be."

Viner's article was published in 1931. Since that time generations of students have experienced great satisfaction when they finally figured it out. Professor Viner's article, justly a famous one despite the error, was often reprinted, but he always rejected suggestions that he correct the error because he did not wish to deprive other students of the pleasure of feeling one-up on him.

The economic sense of the fact that tangency is *not* at the minimum points of *SRAC* rests on the subtle distinction between the most efficient way to utilize a given plant and the most efficient way to produce the amount of output required. It is the second point that interests us as economists. If bigger plants can achieve lower costs per unit, there will be a gain in building a bigger plant and underutilizing it whenever the gains from using the bigger plant are enough to offset the costs of being inefficient in the use of the plant. If there are some gains from building bigger plants (if *LRAC* is declining), there is always some underutilization that is justified.

would be required to achieve the lowest attainable cost. This is illustrated in Figure 12–2. Note that the short-run cost curve is tangent to (touches) the long-run curve at the level of output for which the quantity of the fixed factor is optimal and lies above it for all other levels of output.

We saw at the end of Chapter 11 that a *SRAC* curve such as the one shown in Figure 12–2 is but one of many such curves. Each curve shows how costs vary as output is varied from a base output, holding some factors fixed at the quantities most appropriate to the base output. This is illustrated in Figure 12–3. The long-run curve is sometimes called an **envelope curve** that encloses the whole family of short-run curves.[6]

SHIFTS IN COST CURVES

The cost curves we have derived so far show how cost varies with output given constant factor prices and fixed technology. Changes

---

[6] Each short-run curve touches the long-run curve at one point and lies above it everywhere else. This leads to an important, though subtle, consequence. Two curves that are tangent at a point have the same slope at that point. If *LRAC* is decreasing where it is tangent to *SRAC*, then *SRAC* must also be decreasing. Thus, unless *LRAC* is horizontal at the point of tangency, it will not be tangent at the minimum point of *SRAC*.

Figure 12–2 Long-run and short-run average cost curves

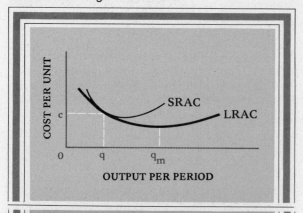

The short-run average cost curve is tangent to the long-run curve at the output for which the quantity of the fixed factors is optimal. If output is varied around q units with plant and equipment fixed at the optimal level for producing q, costs will follow the short-run cost curve. If some output other than q is to be sustained, costs can be reduced to the level of the long-run curve when sufficient time has elapsed to adjust all factor inputs. While $SRAC$ and $LRAC$ are at the same level for output q, since the fixed plant is optimal for that output, for all other outputs there is too little or too much of the fixed factor and $SRAC$ lies above $LRAC$.

in either technological knowledge or factor prices will cause the whole family of short- and long–run cost curves to shift. Loss of existing technological knowledge is a rare thing, so technological change normally works in one direction only, to shift cost curves downward. Improved ways of making existing commodities mean that lower cost methods of production become available. Factor prices can, however, exert an influence in either direction. If a firm has to pay more for any factor that it uses, the cost of producing each

level of output will rise; if the firm has to pay less, costs will fall.

A rise in factor prices shifts the whole family of short- and long-run cost curves upward. A fall in factor prices or a technological advance shifts the whole family of cost curves downward.

ISOQUANTS: AN ALTERNATIVE ANALYSIS OF THE FIRM'S INPUT DECISIONS[7]

The production function gives the relation between the factor inputs that the firm uses

[7] The remaining material in this chapter can be omitted without loss of continuity.

Table 12–1 Alternative ways of producing 6 units of output

K	L	ΔK	ΔL	Rate of substitution $\Delta K/\Delta L$
18	2			
		−6	1	−6.0
12	3			
		−3	1	−3.0
9	4			
		−3	2	−1.5
6	6			
		−2	3	−0.67
4	9			
		−1	3	−0.33
3	12			
		−1	6	−0.17
2	18			

An isoquant describes the firm's alternative methods for producing a given output. The table lists some of the methods indicated by a production function as being available to produce 6 units of output. The first combination uses a great deal of capital (K) and very little labor (L). Moving down the table, Labor is substituted for capital in such a way as to keep output constant. Finally, at the bottom of the table, most of the capital has been replaced by labor. The rate of substitution between the two factors is calculated in the last three columns of the table. Note that as we move down the table, the absolute value of the rate of substitution declines.

Figure 12–3 The envelope relation between the long-run average cost curve and all the short-run average cost curves

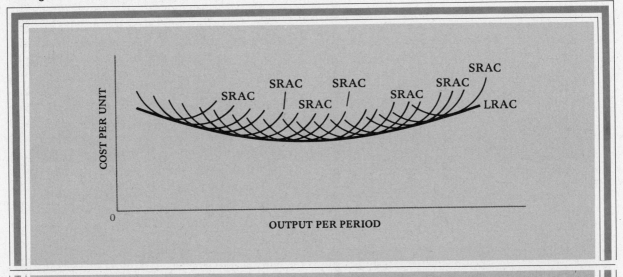

To every point on the long-run cost curve there is an associated short-run curve tangent at that point. Each short-run curve shows how costs vary if output varies, with the fixed factor held constant at the level that is optimal for the output at the point of tangency.

and the output that it obtains. In the long run the firm can choose among many different combinations of inputs that will yield it the same output. The production function and the choices open to the firm can be given a graphical representation using the concept of an isoquant.

A single isoquant

Table 12–1 gives a hypothetical illustration of those combinations of two inputs (labor and capital) that will each serve to produce a given quantity of output. The data from Table 12–1 are plotted in Figure 12–4. A smooth curve is drawn through the points to indicate that there are additional ways, not listed in the table, of producing 6 units.

This curve is called an **isoquant,** and it shows the whole set of technologically efficient possibilities for producing a given level

of output—6 units in this example.[8] It is analogous both to the contour line on a map that shows all points of equal altitude and to an indifference curve that shows all combinations of commodities that yield an equal utility.

As we move from one point on an isoquant to another we are *substituting one factor for another* while holding output constant. If we move from point *b* to point *c*, we are substituting 2 units of capital for 3 units of labor. The **marginal rate of substitution** measures the rate at which one factor is substituted for another with output held constant. Graphically the marginal rate of substitution is measured by the slope of the isoquant at a particular point. Table 12–1 shows the calculation of

---

[8] This is an example of graphing a three-variable function in two dimensions. See page 861 for another illustration.

Figure 12–4 An isoquant for output of six units

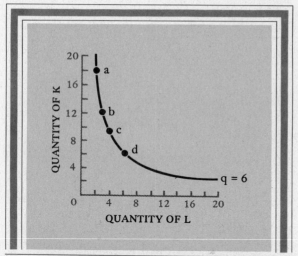

An isoquant shows all technologically efficient ways of producing a given level of output. This figure graphs the data from Table 12–1. (Points *a* to *d* refer to the first four rows of the table.) The convex shape of the isoquant reflects a diminishing marginal rate of substitution. Starting from point *a*, which uses relatively little labor and much capital, and moving to point *b*, 1 additional unit of labor can substitute for 6 units of capital (while holding production constant). But from *b* to *c*, 1 unit of labor substitutes for only 3 units of capital. To replace the next 3 units of capital (to move from *c* to *d*) requires adding 2 units of labor. Capital is becoming scarcer. In order to keep production constant, moving from *a* to *b* to *c* to *d*, larger and larger quantities of labor must be added to compensate for equal reductions in the quantity of capital. The geometrical expression of this is that moving along the isoquant to the right, the slope of the isoquant becomes flatter.

some rates of substitution between various points of the isoquant. [12]

The marginal rate of substitution is related to the marginal products of the factors of production. To see how, consider an example.

Assume that at the present level of inputs of labor and capital the marginal product of a unit of labor is 2 units of output while the marginal product of capital is 1 unit of output. If the firm reduces its use of capital and increases its use of labor so as to keep output constant, it needs to add only one-half unit of labor for one unit of capital given up. If, at another point on the isoquant with more labor and less capital, the marginal products are 2 for capital and 1 for labor, then the firm will have to add two units of labor for every unit of capital it gives up. The general proposition that this example illustrates is:

The marginal rate of substitution is equal to the ratios of the marginal products of the two factors of production.

Isoquants satisfy two important conditions: they are downward-sloping and they are convex viewed from the origin.[9] What is the economic meaning of each of these conditions?

The downward slope indicates that each of the factor inputs has a positive marginal product. If the input of one factor is reduced and that of the other is held constant, output will be reduced. Thus, if one input is decreased, production can only be held constant if the other factor input is increased. Thus the marginal rate of substitution has a negative value: Increases in one factor must be balanced by decreases in the other factor if output is to be held constant.

Now consider what happens as the firm moves along the isoquant of Figure 12–4 downward and to the right. This movement means that labor is being added and capital reduced so as to keep output constant. If labor is added in successive increments of exactly one unit, how much capital may be dispensed with each time? The key to the answer is that both factors are assumed to be subject to the law of diminishing returns. Thus the gain in

[9] The same two basic conditions are satisfied by the indifference curves of consumer theory.

output associated with each additional unit of labor added is *diminishing* while the loss of output associated with each additional unit of capital foregone is *increasing*. It therefore takes ever-smaller reductions in capital to compensate for equal increases in labor. This implies that the isoquant is convex viewed from the origin.

An isoquant map

The isoquant drawn in Figure 12–4 referred to 6 units of output. There is another isoquant for 7 units, for 7,000 units, and for every other rate of output. Each isoquant refers to a specific output and connects alternative combinations of factors that are technologically efficient methods of achieving that output. If we plot a representative set of these isoquants on a single graph, we obtain an **isoquant map.** Such a map is shown in Figure 12–5. The

Figure 12–6 Isocost lines

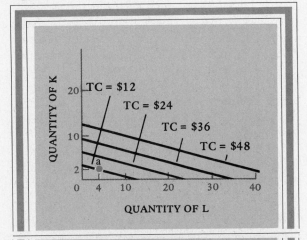

Each isocost line shows alternative factor combinations that can be purchased for a given outlay. The graph shows the four isocost lines that result when labor costs $1 a unit and capital $4 a unit and expenditure is held constant at $12, $24, $36, $48, respectively. The line labeled $TC = \$12$ represents all combinations of the two factors that the firm could buy for $12. Point *a* represents 2 units of K and 4 units of L.

Figure 12–5 An isoquant map

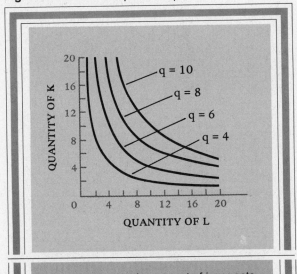

An isoquant map shows a set of isoquants, one for each level of output. The figure shows four isoquants drawn from the production function and corresponding to 4, 6, 8, and 10 units of production.

higher the level of output along a particular isoquant, the further away from the origin it will be.

Isoquants and the conditions for cost minimization

Finding the efficient way of producing any output requires finding the least-cost factor combination. To find this combination when both factors are variable, factor prices need to be known. Suppose, to continue the example, that capital is priced at $4 per unit and labor at $1. In Chapter 8, a budget line was used to show the alternative combinations of goods a household could buy; now an **isocost line** is used to show alternative combinations of factors a firm can buy for a given outlay. Four different isocost lines are shown in Figure 12–6. The slope of each of them reflects *relative* factor prices, just as the slope of the budget line in Chapter 8 represented relative product prices. For given factor prices a series of parallel isocost lines will reflect the alternative levels of expenditure on factor purchases that are open to the firm. The higher the level of expenditure, the farther from the origin is the isocost line.

In Figure 12–7 the isoquant and isocost maps are brought together. The economically most efficient method of production must be a point on an isoquant that just touches (i.e., is tangent to) an isocost line. If the isoquant cuts the isocost line, it is possible to move along the isoquant and reach a lower level of cost. Only at a point of tangency is a movement in either direction along the isoquant a movement to a higher cost level. The lowest attainable cost of producing 6 units is $24, and this cost level can be achieved only by operating at the point where the $24 isocost line is tangent to the 6 unit isoquant. The lowest average cost of producing 6 units is thus $24/6 = $4 per unit of output.

Figure 12–7 The determination of the least-cost method of output

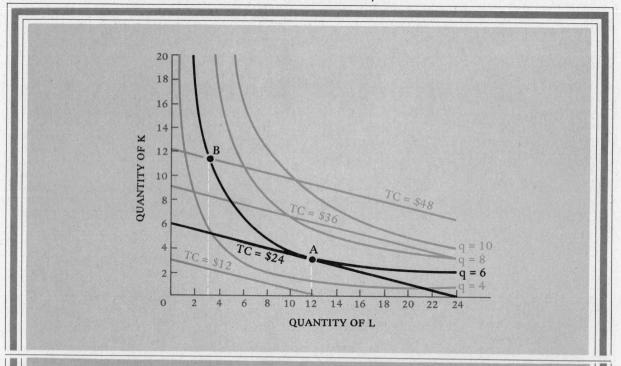

Least-cost methods are represented by points of tangency, such as *A*, between isoquant and isocost lines. The isoquant map of Figure 12–5 and the isocost map of Figure 12–6 are brought together. Consider point *A* in the figure. It is on the 6-unit isoquant and the $24 isocost line. Thus it is possible to achieve the output *q* = 6 for a total cost of $24. There are other ways to achieve this output, for example, at point B, where *TC* = $48. Moving along the isoquant from point *A* in either direction increases cost. Similarly, moving along the isocost from point *A* in either direction lowers output. Thus either move would raise cost per unit.

Figure 12–8   The effects of a change in factor prices on costs and factor proportions

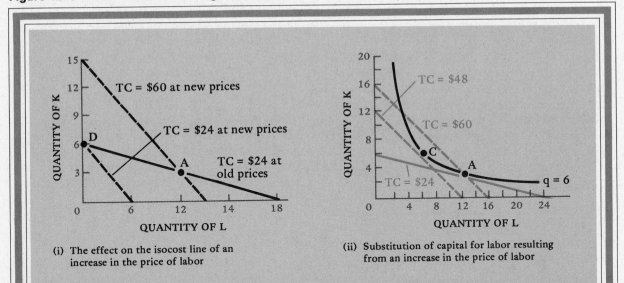

(i) The effect on the isocost line of an increase in the price of labor

(ii) Substitution of capital for labor resulting from an increase in the price of labor

An increase in the price of labor pivots the isocost line inward and thus increases the cost of producing any output. It also changes the slope of the isocost line and thus changes the least-cost method of producing. (i) The rise in price of *L* from $1 to $4 a unit (price of *K* constant at $4) pivots the *TC* line inward. Any output previously produced for $24 will cost more at the new prices, if it used any amount of labor. The new cost of producing at *A* rises from $24 to $60. (ii) The steeper isocost line is tangent to the isoquant at *C* not *A*. Costs at *C* are higher than they were before the price increase but not as high as if the factor substitution had not occurred.

The least-cost position is given graphically by the tangency point between the isoquant and the isocost lines.

Notice that point *A* in Figure 12–7 indicates not only the lowest level of cost for 6 units of output but also the highest level of output for $24 of cost.[10]

The slope of the isocost line is given by the ratio of the prices of the two factors of production. The slope of the isoquant is given by the ratio of their marginal products. When the firm reaches its least-cost position, it has equated the price ratio (which is given to it by the market prices) with the ratio of the marginal products (which it can adjust by varying the proportions in which it hires the factors). In symbols,

$$\frac{MP_K}{MP_L} = \frac{p_K}{p_L}$$

This is equation [2] on page 178. We have now derived this result by use of the isoquant analysis of the firm's decisions. [13]

Isoquants and the principle of substitution

Suppose now that with technology unchanged—that is, with the isoquant map fixed—the price of one factor changes. Suppose with the price of capital unchanged at $4

[10] Thus we find the same solution if we set out *either* to minimize the cost of producing 6 units of output *or* to maximize the output that can be obtained for $24. One problem is said to be the "dual" of the other.

per unit, the price of labor rises from $1 to $4 per unit. Originally, the efficient factor combination of producing 6 units was 12 units of labor and 3 units of capital. It cost $24. To produce that same output in the same way would now cost $60 at the new factor prices. Figure 12–8 shows why that is not efficient: The slope of the isocost line has now changed and this makes it efficient to substitute the now relatively cheaper capital for the relatively more expensive labor.

This result illustrates the principle of substitution.

Changes in relative factor prices will cause a partial replacement of factors that have become relatively more expensive by factors that have become relatively cheaper.

Of course, substitution of capital for labor cannot fully offset the effects of a rise in cost of labor, as Figure 12–8(i) shows. Consider the output attainable for $24. In the figure there are two isocost lines representing $24 of outlay—at the old and new price of labor. The new isocost line for $24 lies everywhere inside the old one (except where no labor is used). The isocost line must therefore be tangent to a lower isoquant. This means that if production is to be held constant, higher costs must be accepted—but because of substitution it is not necessary to accept costs as high as would accompany an unchanged factor proportion. In the example 6 units can be produced for $48 rather than the $60 that would have been required if no change in factor proportions had been made.

This leads to the predictions that:

A rise in the price of one factor with all other factor prices constant will (1) shift upward the cost curves of commodities that use that factor and (2) lead to a substitution of factors that are now relatively cheaper for the factor whose price has risen.

Both of these predictions were stated in the first part of this chapter; now they have been derived formally using the isoquant technique.

Summary

1. There are no fixed factors in the long run. The profit-maximizing firm chooses, from the alternatives open to it, the least costly way of achieving any specific output. A long-run cost curve represents the boundary between attainable and unattainable levels of cost for the given technology.

2. The principle of substitution says that efficient production will substitute cheaper factors for more expensive ones. The methods of production will tend to change if the relative prices of factors change; relatively more of cheaper factors and relatively less of more expensive ones will be used.

3. The slope of the long-run cost curve depends on the relationship of inputs to output as the whole scale of a firm's operations changes. When a firm increases its output, it may encounter increasing returns because of the division of labor and the opportunity to employ more and more specialized machinery. In this case the firm's *LRAC* curve will be declining. The firm may also encounter decreasing returns when it increases its output. In this case the *LRAC* curve will be rising. Constant returns, when the firm doubles all its inputs and doubles its output are also possible, in which case the *LRAC* curve will be horizontal.

4. The relation between long-run and short-run cost curves is shown in Figures 12–2 and 12–3. Every "long-run" cost corresponds to *some* quantity of each factor and thus is on some short-run cost curve. The short-run cost curve shows how costs vary when that particular quantity of a fixed factor is used to produce outputs greater than or less than those for which it is optimal.

5. Decreases in factor prices or technological advances that make it possible to produce the same amount of output with lower quantities of all inputs shift cost curves downward. Increases in factor prices shift the cost curves upward.

6. An isoquant is a "contour line" that shows all the combinations of factors that can be used to produce a given amount of output. The slope of the isoquant is the marginal rate of substitution between the two factors of production and is equal to the ratio of their marginal products.

7. An isoquant is downward-sloping because both factors have positive marginal products. If one is diminished the other must be increased if output is to be held constant. The isoquant is convex viewed from the origin because both factors have diminishing marginal productivity as a

result of which equal reductions in one factor (rising marginal productivity) must be compensated for by larger and larger increases in the other factor (falling marginal productivity).

8. An isoquant map is a series of isoquants, each one of which gives the combinations of two factors that will produce a given level of output.

9. The firm will be minimizing its costs of producing a given level of output if it produces where an isoquant is tangent to an isocost line. This implies that the ratio of the marginal products of the factors is equal to the ratio of their prices.

10. A change in factor prices will lead all firms to substitute the factor whose relative price falls for the factor whose relative price rises. Thus the cheaper is any one factor relative to other factors, the larger is the quantity of that factor firms will desire to use.

Concepts for review

The implication of cost minimization
The interpretation of $MP_K/MP_L = p_K/p_L$
The principle of substitution
The relationship of short-run and long-run cost curves
Reasons for the shape of *LRAC*
A single isoquant and an isoquant map
The marginal rate of substitution
The tangency of an isoquant and an isocost line as the least-cost position
Substitution along an isoquant as a result of a change in relative factor prices

Discussion questions

1. Why does the profit-maximizing firm choose the least costly way of producing any given output? Might a nonprofit-maximizing organization such as a university or a church or a government intentionally choose a method of production other than the least costly one? Might an ordinary business corporation do so intentionally?

2. In Dacca, Bangladesh, where gasoline costs $1.70 a gallon and labor is typically paid less than 10¢ an hour, Abdul Khan pedals a bicycle-ricksha (pedicab) for his living. It's exhausting work that is coming under increasing at-

tack by those who feel it is an inhuman practice. "We really want to get rid of them and move to motorized taxis, but I'm afraid it will take a long, long time," says the Bangladesh Information Officer. Ricksha drivers earn a dollar a day which is more than a skilled worker gets in Dacca. Explain the use of pedicabs in Dacca but not in New York or Tokyo. Comment on the Information Officer's statement.

3. Use the principle of substitution to predict the effect of each of the following:
a. During the 1960s salaries of professors rose very much more rapidly than stipends to teaching assistants. During the 1970s salaries of teaching assistants rose more rapidly than those of professors.
b. The cost of land in big cities increases more rapidly than the cost of high-rise construction.
c. Gold leaf is produced by pounding gold with a hammer. The thinner it is, the more valuable. The price of gold is set on a world market, but the price of labor varies among countries.
d. The formation of OPEC leads to a four-fold increase in the price of crude oil.
e. Wages of textile workers and shoe-machinery operators rise more rapidly in New England than in South Carolina.

4. The long-run average-cost curve can be thought of as consisting of points from each of a number of short-run average-cost curves. Explain in what sense any point on the long-run curve is also on some short-run curve. What is the meaning of a move from one point on a long-run cost curve to another point on the same curve? Contrast this with a movement along a short-run curve.

5. The director of federal energy programs urged the American people to make necessary "long-run adjustments to the energy shortage by reducing energy input per unit of output. How exactly might this be done? Is this use of "long-run" the economists' use of that concept.

6. Israel, a small country, imports the "insides" of its automobiles, but manufactures the bodies. If this makes economic sense, what does it tell us about cost conditions of automobile manufacture?

7. In each of the following situations, what is the shape of each isoquant, and how will the factor combination for a particular output be affected by changes in the relative prices of the factors?
a. the two factors of production are perfect substitutes (that is either can substitute for all of the other; for example, soybean oil and peanut oil in making shortening)
b. the two factors of production are perfect complements (that is they must be used in fixed proportions, for example taxis and taxi tires)

13

The very long run: progress and pollution

An old story tells of a stranger arriving at the entrance of a long, dark tunnel where he discovers an elderly man groping in the gravel for a lost watch. After helping him in his fruitless search, the stranger asks the old man if he is sure he lost his watch there. "Oh, no," he says, "I lost it in the tunnel; I'm looking here because the light is better."

The theory of cost that has been developed in Chapters 10 to 12 is one of the pillars of twentieth-century economic theory, but our development of it has neglected two really important aspects. In this chapter we remedy that neglect, even though this requires us to look where the light is not so good. We look first at the very important effect on cost of invention and innovation, then at some costs the private firm may not consider but that are real costs for society just the same.

Progress and productivity

There are three sets of changes in the very long run that tend to dominate the production function. First is the change in the techniques available for producing existing products. Over an average person's lifetime, these changes often can be dramatic. Sixty years ago roads and railways were built by gangs of workers using buckets, spades, and draft horses; today bulldozers, steam shovels, giant trucks, and other specialized equipment have completely banished the workhorse from construction sites and to a great extent have displaced the worker with his shovel. Indeed, the pace of general mechanization has been so fast that within the space of one lifetime, humanity's more than 4,000-year partnership with the horse in war and peace all but came to an end. About the same amount of coal is produced today as fifty years ago, but the number of coal miners is less than one-tenth of what it was then.

Second is the change in new goods and services that become available. Television, polio vaccine, panty hose, and many other consumer products of today did not exist two generations ago. Other products are so changed that their nominal connection with the "same" commodity produced in the past is meaningless. A 1979 Ford automobile is very different from a 1929 Ford or a 1954 Ford. The modern jets—such as the jumbo 747 and DC-10 and the supersonic Concorde—are each revolutionary compared with the DC-3, which itself barely resembled the *Spirit of St. Louis.* In their first year of operation, 100 Boeing 747s logged passenger miles that would have required a fleet of 23,000 DC-3s.

Third, the changes in standards of such things as health and education improve the quality of inputs, particularly labor services. Today's managers and workers are in better health and are better clothed and better housed than their counterparts in their grandfathers' generation. On the average they are better educated. Even unskilled workers tend to be literate and competent in arithmetic, and their managers are apt to be trained in modern scientific methods of business control.

Critics of the theory of cost argue that to neglect these long-term changes in methods and kinds of production and to focus instead on the variation of cost with output under fixed technology is to overlook the major determinants of cost and to give undue attention to the minor ones.

Economists have always recognized that long-term technological change is a vital feature of the history of industrialized countries. The important issue is not whether such forces exist but how they are to be explained.

Are they influenced by the production decisions of firms, or are they beyond the control of firms so that although they affect production decisions they are not caused by them?[1]

In discussing these issues, it is impossible simply to discuss the cost of a well-defined unit of a well-defined product. Measuring output and cost in a world of changing products is hard and involves a serious index-number problem.[2] Economists often utilize the notion of **productivity,** defined as a measure of output per unit of resource input, instead of simply the cost of a unit of output. This does not resolve the difficulties of measuring output, but it shifts the attention to society's ability to get more and better output out of the basic resources of the economy. A widely used measure is output per man-hour of labor. Labor is taken as representative of the economy's basic resources because we are a society of people and we value our leisure. There is enough year-to-year stability in the nature of products produced that rates of increase in productivity year by year provide useful measures of progress caused by technical change.

PRODUCTIVITY

"Better things for better living" is the slogan of a major American manufacturer, and it is a goal that most families share and that many have achieved. There is no doubt whatever that over the last 100, 50, or even 20 years, the material standard of living of the typical American family has increased enormously. Indeed, our great-grandparents would have regarded today's standard of living in most industrialized countries as unattainable (if not incomprehensible).

The apparently modest rate of increase of output per man-hour of labor of 2 percent per year leads to a doubling of output per man-

[1] In other words we ask whether technological changes are exogenous or endogenous. See page 24.

[2] See pages 869–879 for a discussion of the problems involved.

hour every 35 years. Productivity in the United States has increased at more than this rate over the last 100 years.

Since World War II, productivity growth in the United States has been closer to 3 percent per year (which doubles output every 23 years).

In other countries it has been even higher. In Japan, for example, it has increased at over 7 percent per year, a rate that doubles output per man–hour approximately every 10 years.

SOURCES OF INCREASING PRODUCTIVITY

Long-run increases in efficiency can be divided into several types. Mere population growth, other things being equal, will permit higher productivity if most products are subject to increasing returns to scale. This is very important for countries that are small enough that their present markets do not permit them to exploit fully known economies of scale. It is less important for large countries such as the United States. Substitution of more and more capital for labor will, as the level of production expands, lead to greater productivity if there are increasing returns to substitution of capital. Better raw materials, better trained or educated labor, or better machines will increase productivity even if no changes in factor quantities or proportions take place. Better organization of production can alone account for increases in productivity. New ideas can raise efficiency by being applied to new products. Imagination can design a better mousetrap, with no change in the quantity, quality, or proportions of factors.

In practice, these factors are intertwined. All but the scale effects are related to the processes of invention and innovation that are continuously improving raw materials and machines, improving ways to combine factors, and improving the products they make.

The importance of change is so basic that a few examples are worth considering. Energy to plow fields, to turn machines, to move goods, to provide heat, and to transform natural resources is a major determinant of the productive power of an economy. In 1900, more than half of all energy requirements were supplied by human beings, horses, mules, and oxen. By 1976, animal and human power provided less than 10 percent of all energy; it has been increasingly replaced by such inanimate sources of power as coal, oil, gas, and water power. The overall growth in inanimate fuels is shown in Figure 13–1. Total energy from these fuels increased fivefold over the first seven decades of this century—an increase more than twice as large as the increase in population.

While this is in itself a major substitution of factors of production, it conceals even greater ones. In 1900, almost nine-tenths of energy from inanimate fuels came from coal. Today, less than one-quarter comes from coal. (The rise in the use of petroleum and natural gas is also shown in the figure.) Today, 75 percent of our energy comes from these sources. A few decades from now, atomic energy or solar energy will probably be playing a dominant role as the process of energy substitution continues.

The uses of individual fuels have also changed. The primary use of coal at the beginning of the century was to produce steam to drive steam engines. As late as 1950, both railroads and home heating were important sources of demand for coal; today, neither uses coal in significant amounts. Coal now is used primarily to generate electric power. Electrical energy production has increased tenfold since 1920 and is still increasing. But coal producers are finding increasing competition from nuclear energy in supplying energy for electric power. In 1970, less than 1 percent of all electrical facilities used nuclear fuel; but 30 percent of new capacity on order was nuclear. Rising costs of nuclear construction and fears of a nuclear accident slowed the substitution of nuclear energy during the first half of the 1970s. But the

Figure 13–1 The production of inanimate energy, United States, 1900–1975

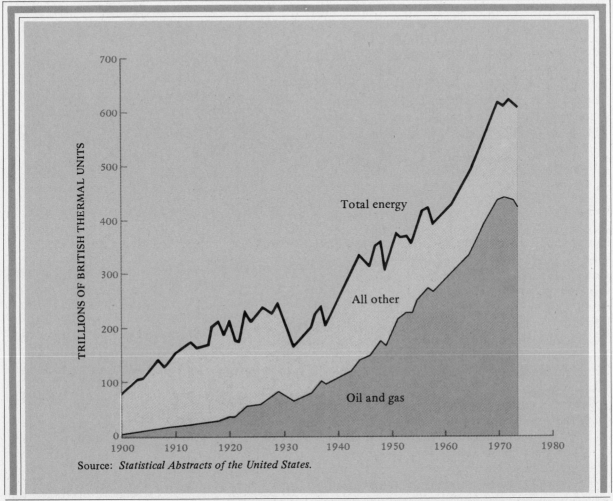

Source: *Statistical Abstracts of the United States.*

The production of inanimate energy has grown enormously in this century and increasingly has replaced animal and human power. The explosive growth in production of energy has occurred through use of oil and gas. Whether the rising costs of oil and gas will lead to a reversal of these trends is a major unknown of the next decades. Much of the answer depends on the development of technology with respect to nuclear and solar energy and the gasification of coal.

trend is again upward. The steadily rising cost of energy is leading to increased attention to yet other fuels, among them solar energy and geothermal energy (based on tapping the heat within the earth's interior).

Similar changes have occurred with respect to other inputs. If you review the statistics from the Census of Manufactures, you will see the declining relative importance of primary metals, lumber products, and textile-mill products and the corresponding increase in importance of transportation equipment, fabricated metal products, and machinery of all kinds. Within these categories are still further changes. For example the kind and quality of metals has changed: steel replaces iron and aluminum substitutes for steel in a process of change that makes a statistical category such as "primary metals" seem unsatisfactory and obsolete.

INVENTION AND INNOVATION

An **invention** is defined as the discovery of something new, such as a new production technique or a new product. An **innovation** is defined as the introduction of an invention into use. Invention is cumulative; a useful invention is used, a useless one is discarded. Except where whole societies disappear, knowledge is seldom lost, and the state of technical knowledge improves or stays the same. For this reason, the cumulative impact of many small inventions may be fully as large as or larger than that of the occasional dramatic invention such as the steam engine, the cotton gin, or the sewing machine. Indeed, none of these famous inventions burst into full bloom as a result of a single act of creative inspiration; each depended on the contributions of prior inventors.

The backlog of past inventions constitutes society's technical knowledge and, in turn, conditions innovation, for innovation can occur only when there has already been an invention. If there is a dramatic rise in labor costs, firms may wish to change to a labor-saving process, but they cannot do so if the process has not yet been invented.

Thus, to understand innovation, we must also understand what creates the pool of inventions from which innovation will occur.

Are invention and innovation exogenous to the firm?

There is substantial evidence that innovation is an endogenous process. New products and

The causes of invention

Folk wisdom—even the proverb—expresses hypotheses about what it is that leads inventors to try to build better mousetraps and even (like Walt Disney) to invent better mice. Historians of science and students of economic history, such as the late Harvard Professor Abbot Payton Usher, have spent years studying the history of inventions and the writings of inventors to determine what were their underlying motivations.[*] Among the hypotheses put forward are these:

Invention is a random process. Some people are by nature both curious and clever. Thousands of attempts will be made to invent better ways of doing things. Many fail, and those inventors remain nameless, but a few succeed. These are the Fultons, Edisons, Whitneys, and Fords. The successful inventions become a pool of potential innovations, and, when the climate is right, they are introduced into production.

Invention is a response to the institutional framework. Things such as the patent laws, the tax structure, or the organization of business enterprise stimulate or retard the process of invention. Invention, in this view, is not exogenous to society, but it does not respond primarily to economic variables, and it certainly is exogenous to the individual *firm*.

[*] Usher's *A History of Mechanical Inventions,* published in 1929, is the classic work.

Invention and innovation are the product of the inherent logic and momentum of science. Science has a logic and momentum of its own. There was a time for the discovery of the steam engine, the airplane, hybrid corn, the transistor, and the rocket. Particular people are the instruments, not the causes, of scientific discovery. Had Edison never been born, we would still have had, at about the same time, both the light bulb and the phonograph. According to this view, the present is the electronic age and automation is the result of introducing electronic devices into production.

Necessity is the mother of invention. Ignorance is only skin deep. With enough funds, human beings can do anything—split the atom, conquer cancer, fly to Mars, cultivate the desert, and even cure the common cold. The pace and rate of invention depend on how many resources are devoted to solving problems. When a firm finds a particular factor becoming scarce, it will discover ways to economize on using it or it will develop a more plentiful substitute for it. (For example, the scarcity of high-grade iron ore led to the development of ways of using low-grade ores.) In this view, automation is a response to expensive labor. The impetus for invention may thus come from within the firm, but it may also come from without. Governments may set priorities and sponsor the research that leads to major discoveries and innovations. Atomic energy, for example, is the result of the desire to develop superweapons during World War II. The space and missile programs are responsible for some current discoveries that have industrial applications as well.

Profits are the spur. The profit motive leads individuals and firms not only to seize the best-known methods but to develop new ways to meet both old and new needs and wants. Profit opportunities, however, are vitally connected to the economic climate and to economic circumstances.

Which of these hypotheses is correct? Very possibly all of them. They are not self-contradictory, and the evidence for one cannot be regarded as disproving the others. The fact that some firms spend millions of dollars on research and development to oversome specific problems or invent new products does not negate the fact that Charles Martin Hall discovered, in the chemistry laboratories of Oberlin College, the technique that made the wide industrial use of aluminum possible. The fact that many patentable discoveries are given free to the world does not prove that others are not motivated by the prospect of huge personal gain.

new methods are introduced when it appears profitable to introduce them. This tends to happen in periods of prosperity and rising incomes. Business investment in both product development and process improvement is known to lag in periods of depression and unemployment.

It is uncertain, however, whether the stock of technical knowledge that exists at any moment in time is itself to be explained in economic terms. Clearly, some invention is a response to activities of firms, as evidenced by the fact that American private firms now spend over $13 billion on research and development each year. At least some firms regard discovery as an important activity. But less is spent on such activities by American industry than is spent on advertising or packaging, and much basic research occurs in government and university laboratories rather than in industrial and commercial ones. Thus the extent to which invention is endogenous is currently in doubt.

Does it matter whether invention responds to economic signals? An example will serve to suggest that it does. Today the nation's reserves of petroleum appear inadequate in the long run. The price of oil has more than quadrupled in the last five years, and the principle of substitution suggests that other fuels will be substituted for it. Theory also predicts that the costs of producing all goods that depend on oil as a raw material will necessarily rise. Now, if invention is truly unaffected by this sort of signal, society will have to wait patiently until some inventor happens to find ways to produce these goods using much less oil or someone discovers a way to increase the supply of available oil. If the world's inventors are busy doing something else, the wait may be a long one. However, if invention is endogenous, one may expect the higher price of oil and the products that use it to have several effects that mitigate the shortage. One effect is to stimulate the search for new methods of finding oil. A second is to stimulate the search for economizing on oil

consumption by discovering oil-saving techniques. A third is to encourage the development of new sources of fuel that will substitute for oil.

The fact that all of these things are happening now suggests that invention and innovation are surely endogenous to some extent. The most publicized alternatives are nuclear and solar energy. But inventors also consider what others regard as fanciful. Two companies in the Southwest have already signed agreements to provide 1.2 billion cubic feet of "bio-gas" made from cow manure. Its proponents claim that it is in every way as good as natural gas and that it could supply up to 15 percent of total American energy requirements if we utilized all the available cow manure.

In any event, most students of the problem believe that the oil shortage, while real enough, does not portend the end of American industrial society because of the imminent exhaustion of our oil supplies. Put differently, because of rising prices and costs, the search for a solution to the oil shortage is being given high priority.

It is worth noticing that if innovation is even partly endogenous, these adaptations *will result from* the price rise. There are those who have urged the government to hold down the price of oil during this period of shortage for political reasons or to save individuals and firms from the hardships that a rising price of oil imposes on them. But such a policy, if it occurs, will inhibit the long-run process that promises to free us from excessive dependence on foreign oil.

PAST AND FUTURE PRODUCTIVITY GROWTH

Decreases in cost levels that are possible by choosing among known techniques and among alternative levels of output are limited in scope. We can, of course, never do better than a 100 percent utilization of what is currently known. Improvements by invention are potentially limitless. For this reason, the long-term struggle to get more from the world's limited resources is critically linked to discovery.

Economics used to be known as the dismal science because some of its predictions were dismal. The classical economists' basic prediction about the very long run was that the world's population would continue to expand and that the pressure of more and more persons on the world's limited resources would cause a decline in output per person.[3] Human history would be one of more and more people living less and less well, with the surplus of persons that could not be supported at all dying off in plague, famine, and pestilence. This prediction has been dramatically correct in some of the countries now called underdeveloped. It has, however, been wrong for the industrial countries for several reasons. First, because of voluntary restriction on population growth, the population did not expand as rapidly as was foreseen by economists writing before the wide availability of birth-control techniques. Second, pure knowledge and its applied techniques have expanded so rapidly during the last 150 years that our ability to squeeze more out of limited resources has expanded faster than the population has expanded.

Even in the industrial nations the race between consumption and production is a close one, and if the rate at which the frontiers of knowledge are being expanded should again fall below the rate of population increase, economics may once again become a dismal science.

Is progress what we want?

Progress has come to mean growth, and growth has long meant industrialization. Applied to the economy as a whole, industrialization and its accompanying changes in productivity clearly have vastly increased our material well-being and permitted more and more people to escape the ravages of hunger and the relentless struggle to subsist.

But nothing is without its cost, and in the case of growth this is increasingly being recognized. The gasoline engine, the steel mill, the jet airplane, DDT, plastics, and the skyscraper with its hundreds of thousands of electric lights are the artifacts of our progress over the last century. Have they lowered the quality of life more than they have raised it? Will they, as some fear, make the next century our last? We must turn to the question of social cost.

Social cost

The advancement of science that has brought growth in its wake has pushed back the frontiers of ignorance. Humanity has come to be remarkably confident about its ability to deal with new problems as they arise. But progress almost always creates new problems as it solves old ones, as the following vignette illustrates.

Since the nineteenth century, American growth has been heavily dependent on steel. Steel requires iron ore. The great steel boom led to the exhaustion of America's high-grade iron ore and threatened disaster to the economy of the upper Midwest. Invention and innovation resolved the crisis by discovering economically efficient ways to utilize abundant low-grade taconite ore to produce a handful of iron ore per ton of the taconite rock. Every year from 1956 to 1974 the Reserve Mining Company dumped more than 60,000 tons of noxious taconite tailings a day into Lake Superior from its plant in Silver Bay, Minnesota.

Electricity and paper are key products of an industrial society. Southern California Edison Company's Mohave power plant is designed to trap 97 percent of the fly ash that would otherwise become air pollution. However, the remaining 3 percent puts a ton of soot into

---

[3] This is an implication of the hypothesis of diminishing returns. See page 170.

the air every hour. The most prominent navigational beacons on Vancouver Island, British Columbia, are not on marine charts; they are plumes of evil-smelling smoke from the island's several paper mills.

These examples, and hundreds more, concern the production of goods and services by private firms. They also concern the use of society's basic resources such as timber, coal, labor, iron ore, water, and air. In each of these examples, the pollution connected with production is not an accidental event, as is the periodic breaking up of oil tankers off the world's beaches or the blowout of oil in the Santa Barbara channel. The pollution is the result of calculated decisions. How can this occur? Is pollution the inevitable cost of progress?

COST TO WHOM?

Cost, as we have defined it, concerns the value of resources used up in the process of production. According to the opportunity cost principle, value is the benefit the resources would produce in the best alternative use. But who decides what resources are used and what is their opportunity cost? When a timber company buys a forest, it perhaps regards the alternative to cutting the trees this year as cutting them next year, or five years hence. But citizens in the area may value the forest as a nature sanctuary or a recreation area. The firm values the forest for the trees; the local residents may value the trees for the forest. These differences in point of view lead to the important distinction between private cost and social cost.

Private cost measures the value of the best alternative uses of the resources available to the producer.

As was noted in Chapter 10, private cost is usually measured by the market price of the resources that the firm uses.

Social cost measures the value of the best alternative uses of resources that are available to the whole society.

For some resources, the best measure of the social cost may be exactly the same as the private cost: the price set by the market may well reflect the value of the resources in their best alternative use. For other resources, as already suggested by our examples, social cost may differ sharply from private cost. The policy problems caused by such differences between private and social costs will concern us in Chapter 24; here we are concerned to understand how they arise and whose point of view is "private" and whose represents "society."

POLLUTION

A major source of difference between private cost and social cost arises when firms use resources they do not regard as scarce. This is characteristic of most examples of pollution.

Water pollution

The reason the Reserve Mining Company dumped the taconite tailings—the waste that remains after the taconite rock has been crushed and the flakes of magnetic iron have been extracted from it—is that it had to dispose of its wastes and Lake Superior was right there and, from the company's point of view, was free. Lake Superior's Great Trough, a 900-foot-deep trench, is only five miles offshore, and it took the tailings without impeding navigation. The alternative for the company was to dump the tailings onto waste heaps many miles inland. Such a land disposal installation would cost the company about $400 million to build—plus the cost of shipping 180 freight cars of tailings each day.

Given the choice of methods of waste disposal, the firm chose to minimize *its* cost by using the free lake. How large the cost of land disposal would prove to be is in dispute. The Department of the Interior estimated the cost to be only about 3 percent of the value of output produced each year. The company claims the costs to be nearer 10 times as much. Obviously it matters greatly who is right.

But whatever the cost of alternative disposal, from society's point of view Lake Superior is clearly not a *free* resource: It is used for recreation, for fishing, and for drinking water and it is geologically and biologically a unique feature of the world. This one company added more sediment to the lake each month than all the tributary streams added in a year, and this sediment was particularly laden with lead and with asbestos fibers that found their way into the Duluth water supply.

Assigning measures of cost to these things is difficult, but impairment of the lake's ecology clearly is costly. Suppose, hypothetically, that an unimpaired ecology is valued at more than the costs of avoiding the pollution. If the mining company had to pay whatever cost it imposed upon society by use of this resource, it would not have neglected them. It would have discovered that shipping its wastes to land disposal areas was cheaper than dumping them in the lake. But as long as it can avoid paying for the use of Lake Superior, it will use it. This behavior confirms the prediction that we derived from the principle of substitution: Efficient production will substitute a cheaper factor for a more expensive one.

Private efficiency economizes use of the resources the producer pays for. Social efficiency economizes the use of all of society's resources.

Pollution characteristically involves use of air or water or other natural resources by people or firms who do not have to pay the full cost of their use. The indirect effects of this use may be as important as the direct effects.

Many people have found they can indeed get wash whiter by using detergents than by using soap, and it costs only a few cents more. But the cost to our lakes and rivers is not included. Lake Erie, once a beautiful and productive body of water, came close to death because of all sorts of man-discharged wastes —including detergents. The quip was that you don't drown in Lake Erie anymore—you decay. This near destruction of Lake Erie was not the work of one plant, or one city, but of the thousands of industrial, municipal, and individual users in both the United States and Canada who saw the lake as a free and apparently limitless sewer.

Oceans, too, are treated as a repository of sewage, oil, industrial wastes, bombs, and even deadly gases. Private firms and cities up and down every coast use the oceans as a depository for sewage and industrial wastes. New York City, for example, dumps one-quarter of its sewage "raw" into New York harbor, to run into the Atlantic on the ebbing tide. The city used to dump it all; in the last decade it has spent hundreds of millions of dollars in treatment plants, but water quality still is getting worse. The "sludge" from the treated sewage is dumped into the Atlantic 12 miles offshore. Such "careful" communities as New York dump their wastes only on the outgoing tide, so as not to foul their shorefront, but this assumes oceans (unlike the beaches) have limitless capacity to absorb wastes.

That assumption is proving dramatically false. DDT used as a pesticide and chemical wastes from Japan's industrial plants contaminated much of the western Pacific and led to poisoning of many of those who ate the fish caught by Japanese fishermen. Federal scientists surveying the Atlantic found vast stretches befouled by floating oil, tar, and plastics. The contaminated areas were over 50 percent of all areas surveyed and approached 90 percent in the Caribbean. This was not always so: sightings of oil and tar before 1967 (when the Suez Canal was closed) were almost unknown. The plastics are more than an eyesore; they appear to be ingested by fish with fatal results. Indeed PCB (polychlorinated biphenyl), thought to result from these plastics, may prove as deadly to marine organisms as DDT. Metals of all kinds are another major problem. Lead from automobile exhaust finds its way into the oceans, and in the Pacific has been found at 10 times its natural level. Cadmium, chromium, copper, iron, manganese, mercury, nickel, and zinc all are present in heavy doses in New York harbor. Mercury poisoning of swordfish was discovered in 1971 and reduced consumption from 28 million pounds in 1970 to 25 *thousand* pounds in 1975.

Rivers, no less than lakes and oceans, have been deteriorating steadily. While such dramatic episodes as Allied Chemical's dumping kepone into the James River of Virginia and General Electric's dumping PCBs into the Hudson River get worldwide publicity, they are not isolated events. A map of polluted rivers leaves no region untouched.

Water pollution is avoidable in principle: effluent control is expensive, but its technology is well understood. Notwithstanding much attention and many efforts at control in recent years, current reports suggest that water pollution is getting worse, not better.

Air pollution

Air pollution, too, occurs because producers use resources without paying for them. Approximately 150 million tons of pollutants are pumped into the air over America each year. Roughly 60 percent of it comes from automobiles, another 17 percent from industrial smokestacks, and 14 percent from electric power plants. While air pollution caused by particles can be effectively controlled by electrostatic precipitation, these particulates account for less than a tenth of the weight of air pollutants, and they are far less likely to be lethal than sulfur dioxide, carbon monoxide, and the nitrogen oxides—all pollutants which, to a very great extent, cannot be eliminated with available technology.

Avoiding pollutants is often not as easy as it might seem at first. People have not yet discovered a large pollution-free source of energy. Electricity, which seems so quiet and pollution free, is today mainly generated by burning coal. Some air pollution could be avoided by substituting nuclear-powered generating plants, but this threatens a serious problem of thermal pollution. Thus to replace the gasoline engine by an electric car would

change the nature of the pollution threat rather than avoid it.

While the problems are more severe in some places (most notably Los Angeles) than in others, many of the nation's airsheds are already well on the way to dangerous levels of pollution. A smog in Pittsburgh in November 1975 killed 14 people. Some cities have "air pollution alerts" during which citizens are urged to stay indoors with the windows closed. Some biologists fear that present levels of air pollution threaten more than the cleanliness of cities, the wear of paint on houses, and the health of citizens. While these things, as well as medical expenses and lost time at work, are part of the social cost imposed by air pollution, there may be bigger hidden costs. The oxygen supply of the earth may be threatened. North America is already an oxygen importer from the rest of the world: It consumes more oxygen than its plants and trees create. Air pollution both adds to the carbon dioxide levels in the atmosphere (thus creating the need for more trees to convert it to oxygen) and at the same time actually kills trees that convert carbon dioxide into oxygen. Automobile-generated smog, for example, has destroyed thousands of acres of ponderosa pine in the San Bernardino area of California.

EXTERNALITIES

When a paper mill produces pulp for the world's newspapers, more people are affected than its suppliers, employees, and customers. Its water-discharged effluent hurts the fishing boats which ply nearby waters, and its smog makes many resort areas less attractive than they would be, thereby reducing the tourist revenues that local motel operators and boat renters can expect. These effects are examples of what are called **externalities** or, sometimes, **third-party effects** because parties external to the basic bargain are affected. Externalities can be for good as well as for ill—when I paint my house, I enhance my neighbors' views and also the value of their property. Divergences between social and private costs arising from externalities are not limited to pollution problems. A few additional examples will illustrate the diversity of the problem.

"Where have all the herring gone?"

The world's oceans once teemed with fish, but today a worldwide fish shortage is upon us. Consider the herring crop. The year 1968 was a bad one for the world's herring catch: The crop was only 250,000 tons, down from the peak year of 1966 when the world's fishing fleets used a new technology of larger boats and small-mesh nets to take 1,700,000 tons of the silvery fish. Apparently the 1966 herring crop never got a chance to spawn! The year 1969 was regarded as a key year: Would the catch begin to rise and would nature replenish its herring crop? During the first nine months of 1969, the herring catch was only one-quarter as large as it had been in 1968, and the prognosis was grim. By 1973, the herring crop was increasing, and we appeared to have had a narrow escape. By 1976, however, the crop was still only a fraction of what it had been in the peak year. As a result, fishing boats are going into deeper water for cod, haddock, and yellowtail—which year by year are getting scarcer. There seems no doubt that overfishing was the culprit that nearly upset the whole food chain. How can this happen?

Fish are one example of what is called a **common-property resource.** No one owns the oceans' fish until they are caught. Thus a fisherman can sell them only when he has caught them. Even if he realizes that doubling the catch this year will hurt next year's catch, he cannot afford to hold back unless everyone else does the same. A similar problem in oil-field drilling has been solved by collective action. Under the simple *rule of capture,* oil belongs to the person who pumps it up. Thus I am motivated to drill wells near my property line and pump oil from under your land.

You do the same to me. But drilling too many holes and pumping too fast results in the loss of the natural pressure of the field and greatly reduces the ultimate total recovery from the field. By what are called prorationing agreements, U.S. oil fields are now subject to unified control in which production rates are not allowed to exceed those that provide for efficient recovery of the oil with all landowners allowed a proportional share of the field-wide production.

In oil, the loss of everyone's profits made cooperation an obvious solution. International competition in the fishing industry, particularly among Russian, Norwegian, British, Canadian, Icelandic, and American fishing fleets, has transcended the ability of individual governments to conserve these resources. Many countries, starting with Iceland and followed by Norway, the United States, and Canada, are claiming exclusive rights to fishing off their shores for 200 miles, and they are using gun boats to enforce this claim in what used to be regarded as international waters. English and Soviet fishing fleets fought hard to avoid being shut out of the world's best fishing waters, and the 1974 "cod war" between England and Iceland is surely not the end of conflicts of this kind.

Even if the effects of the decline in the fishing industry are regarded as purely a problem for that industry (which, of course, they are not: unemployed fishermen and unavailable fish impose costs on all of us), these effects represent an externality to the individual act of fish production. When one fisherman takes one too many unspawned fish, he affects every other fisherman's catch next year. Yet this effect—a cost to someone—does not play a role in the fisherman's private calculation of the cost of catching that fish. Thus there is a discrepancy between private and social cost.

"Come fly with me"

Suppose that the probability of a midair plane crash is roughly proportional to the number of planes in the air. Suppose too that I have the choice of flying from Phoenix to Tucson in my own plane or on a commercial airliner that has 100 of its 150 seats filled. In choosing to fly by myself, I decide that the extra "cost" to me of taking this risk can be compensated for by taking out some extra life insurance.

What I have neglected is part of the social cost of my action: the increased risk for every other person in the air over Arizona that results from one more plane in the air. Thus, if my private decision between flying my own plane or taking a commercial flight was close, the social decision may well have been wrong.

DDT: "the perfect pesticide"

DDT was invented in 1874, but its insecticidal properties were not discovered until 1939, and it was not until World War II moved to the malaria-ridden Pacific three years later that its full powers were revealed. This happened almost by accident. Small amounts of DDT in one part of a laboratory testing dozens of insecticides against mosquitoes killed all the insects in *all* parts of the laboratory and continued to do so day after day even after the entire laboratory was scrubbed clean. This lasting power was to prove the blessing and the curse of DDT. Hailed as the perfect pesticide, its use by the American army in Pacific war zones all but eliminated typhus and greatly limited malaria in regions where it was used, by attacking, respectively, the louse and the mosquito that carried these diseases. After the war it was found to be equally effective in controlling agricultural pests, particularly the cotton boll weevil. When in 1948 the Swiss chemist Paul Mueller won the Nobel prize for his discovery of its value as a pesticide, few doubted his contributions to the world's well-being. DDT use grew steadily in the United States and throughout the world, until the peak year, 1958, when 78 million pounds were used in the United States alone.

Gradually it was learned that DDT did more than kill unwanted insects. Once sprayed, the chemical did not break down for years; thus it entered the food chain and worked its way up from insects to birds and fish, to small mammals, and to larger and larger birds and mammals—including human beings. Arctic penguins, though thousands of miles from any sprayed areas, have measurable amounts of DDT in their bodies. DDT has thinned the egg shells of large birds to the point where breakage threatens many species, among them the peregrine falcon, the osprey, and the eagle.

Rachel Carson in 1962 began the public debate about DDT in her book *The Silent Spring,* in which she labeled DDT an "elixir of death." It was not until 1969 that formal attempts to ban the use of DDT began. By 1970 use in the United States had dropped to 14 million pounds; most of this was in connection with cotton production. By 1973 the ban in the United States was complete, but because DDT *is* long lasting the effects of past uses will be felt for decades to come.

Meanwhile use of DDT is growing abroad, and the World Health Organization (WHO) continues to use it because of fear of catastrophic food losses and epidemics. WHO distributes over 20 million pounds of DDT per year, largely among the underdeveloped countries. Switching to less persistent pesticides is hampered by the high cost of substitutes which cost two to six times as much. Private cost impels WHO to continue to use DDT despite its known external disadvantageous results.

WHO IS TO BLAME?

Much of the rhetoric of our new-found concern with ecology is directed against the heartless, profit-mad, giant corporation that perverts the environment for its own crass purposes. Our examples give some support to this view. The Reserve Mining Company is wholly owned by the Republic Steel Company and by Armco Steel Company. Allied Chemical Company and General Electric Company are well-known giants. But environmental problems transcend the capitalistic system. The Soviet Union mirrors the United States in its growing awareness of air and water pollution and the ravaging of the landscape by strip mining. It established in 1973 a national environmental protection service, and its spending on environmental control, now at the rate of $2 billion per year, is scheduled to rise to $4 billion by 1980. Nationalized industries pollute just as much as privately owned ones if they are operated in the same way.

It does not matter who the decision makers are; whenever they do not take account of the full social costs of their actions, the potential for a harmful externality exists. Consider the examples of the previous section. Overfishing has resulted from lack of total coordination and comes as much from international rivalry as from capitalistic motivation. The Soviets and the Norwegians no less than the North Americans have been responsible. Indeed, the (capitalistic) oil industry found a similar problem easy to solve. Crowding the airways because of private aviation occurs from *individual choice* as much as from profit orientation. Finally, the DDT story shows that public agencies such as the U.S. Army and Department of Agriculture can produce unfortunate externalities by neglecting to look into the future effects of their actions and that other *public* agencies (in this case, WHO) can knowingly impose social costs on people over all the planet.

Within the private free market, the consumer along with the producer must bear part of the responsibility. Is General Motors culpable for providing a 300-horsepower car when a 100-horsepower car would pollute much less? Many Americans have made it abundantly clear—most recently with the 1977 models—that they want big cars. When American Motors failed to make them and Ford and Chrysler did, AMC's losses mounted while its competitors earned profits. When General Motors put major emphasis on producing and selling compact Vegas and Chevettes, it found itself out of step with consumer preferences and suffered large losses on those models—models which pollute less, use less fuel, and in other ways seem more socially desirable than their bigger counterparts. They did not make the same mistake the next year.

The fact that consumers are partially responsible does not excuse the callous, often thoughtless, and sometimes deliberately deceptive practices of some private firms. The introduction of insufficiently tested drugs, the careless dumping of poisons into rivers, and the "rigging" of tests on emissions control by a leading auto manufacturer are recent cases in point.

THE SIGNIFICANCE OF DIVERGENCIES BETWEEN SOCIAL AND PRIVATE COSTS

The purpose of identifying discrepancies between social and private costs is to permit sensible decisions about the use of resources. Identification is a vital step, but it is only the first step, a fact that is sometimes overlooked in the indignation that accompanies a particularly shocking example of neglect of social costs.

A vital second step in coping with externalities is to balance the benefits and costs of activities that have externalities.

Two examples will serve to illustrate the problem. Using salt on snowy and icy highways has proven exceedingly effective and is known to save many lives in northern states each winter, but the brine runoff fouls some inland waters. Is the cost in water pollution worth bearing? Consider further the decision of the World Health Organization to continue using DDT in underdeveloped countries. Perhaps the eradication of insect-borne diseases justifies the use of the pesticide despite its adverse effects elsewhere. Caterpillar Tractor Company, in a recent advertising campaign, used the slogan, "There are no simple solutions. Only intelligent choices." It is, of course, the absence of simple solutions that makes the problems difficult.[4]

Possibly the hardest sort of evaluation concerns balancing of present benefits (or costs) against future costs (or benefits). Birth control pills still involve unknown risk to some users, yet they are proving a potent weapon in our struggle to cope with the population explosion. Many would argue that the use of pills was justified even before the full extent of the risks was known, for delay in coping with population growth involves high social costs. How long should the beneficial effects of a drug be withheld from those who need it in order to avoid the risks to others? Most people would probably agree that introduction of the Salk polio vaccine was justified even though it killed some people. At an opposite extreme, the drug Thalidomide was surely introduced prematurely and had disastrous effects on some unborn babies. Much depends on the size of the expected benefits and costs; the economist can sometimes be of major help in identifying and measuring the benefits and costs.

The third step (after identification of discrepancies and balancing of benefits and costs) is to decide what to do and how best to do it. Discussion of this (policy) aspect of the problem is deferred to Chapter 24.

---

[4] This is not an argument against those like Ralph Nader who view much of what goes on with highly articulate alarm. Indignation and the muckraker's techniques are among the legitimate weapons of our society. They are particularly effective in directing attention to the possibly dangerous neglect of side effects. Their efforts are better suited to identifying abuses than to the critical second step of balancing costs and benefits.

Summary

1. The importance of progress (in the very long run) is the vast increase in material well-being that it makes possible. The standard of living of all industrialized countries has increased enormously in the past century. The rise in productivity (output per unit of input) in America has averaged over 2 percent for the last century.

2. Long-run increases in productivity arise in many ways, including mere growth (owing to economies of scale), changes in factor proportions, improvements in the quality of inputs, and improvements in the techniques of production and the nature of products. Most of these are related to invention and innovation.

3. Whether innovation responds to economic signals is important for economic policy. If it does, it may quickly provide partial escape from limitations imposed by a fixed technology. Stimulating innovation may be as important, or more important, than using resources efficiently with known methods.

4. Gloomy predictions about the very long run made by the classical economists led economics to be known as the dismal science. These predictions have been proved unfounded in most Western countries. The classical economists did not foresee the voluntary restriction on population growth or the very rapid rate of invention and innovation that has occurred. But progress is not an unmixed blessing, as evidenced by the pollution of the environment that accompanies growth.

5. The potential conflict between private and public interest can be expressed in terms of private cost and social cost. Private cost measures the value of the best alternative use of the resources available to the producer; social cost measures the value of the best alternative use of the resources available to the whole society. If social costs are not the same as private ones, decisions made by reference to private costs will lead to socially inefficient allocations of resources.

6. Pollution is an example of an externality. An important source of pollution is producers' use of water and air that they do not regard as scarce. Since they do not pay the costs of misuse of these resources, they are not motivated to avoid the costs.

7. There are many kinds of externalities in addition to pollution. They are called externalities because parties not directly involved in a market bargain are affected by them.

Overfishing of the oceans and neglect of dangerous side effects of drugs or insecticides are important examples.

8. There is no single culprit or organization of society that produces externalities and pollution. It may be the capitalistic corporation that neglects social good for private profit. It may be the consumers who will not pay what it costs to dispose of their wastes without damage to their neighbors. It may be the government itself that acts "privately" in building a dam or running its army camps. Pollution and other externalities are problems today in all the world—in the USSR, Sweden, Greece, and Yugoslavia, no less than in the United States and the United Kingdom.

9. Identifying discrepancies between private and social costs is a vital first step in coping with them. A second step is balancing benefits against costs, and a third step is deciding what to do and how best to do it.

Concepts for review

The distinction between production and productivity
Sources of increasing productivity
Invention and innovation
Private and social cost
Pollution as an externality
The conflict between pollution and progress
Whose costs are "private"?

Discussion questions

1. Name five important modern products that were not available when you were in grade school. Make a list of major products that you think have increased their sales at least tenfold in the last thirty years. Check your judgment by consulting series in the *Statistical Abstract of the United States, Business Statistics* (biennial of the U.S. Department of Commerce), or similar sources. Consider to what extent the growth in each series may reflect product or process innovation.

2. By 1977 approximately 10,000 firms had switched from a 8-hour per day, 5-day week to a 4-day week, with each day 10 hours long. Output per week appears to have increased significantly. Is this an increase in productivity? Is it an inno-

vation? Would you predict that this success will lead to a general substitution of the 4-day week for the 5-day week wherever the latter is now standard?

3. What do you believe to have been the primary spur for each of the following inventions and innovations: color television, the cotton gin, nuclear power, penicillin, the assembly line, radar, the smashing of the atom, the nuclear bomb, the Frisbee, synthetic rubber, polio vaccine, the airplane, the motion pictures, and the wheel? Are any of these attributable to more than one source?

4. The Aswan Dam has been called Egypt's "wall against hunger," by virtue of its provision of both irrigation water and electric power to the Nile Valley. Among its less salutory side effects are:
a. The reduced flow of water and silt in the river have allowed the Nile Delta to be overrun by sea water, leaving harmful salts.
b. Lake Nasser, in back of the dam, has become a breeding place for malaria mosquitoes.
c. Homes of 122,000 Nubian villagers have been inundated, along with countless antiquities for 310 miles upstream from the dam.
   Should the dam have been built? Discuss the issues involved, using the concepts of private and social costs and of externalities.

5. Each of the following activities has known harmful effects: (a) cigarette smoking , (b) driving a car at 55 mph, (c) private ownership of guns, (d) drilling for offshore oil. In each case, identify whether there is a divergence between social and private costs.

6. During a Pittsburgh air pollution alert a newspaper reporter interviewed a 69-year-old, retired steelworker. He said: "I've got a heart condition myself, and I know that when I look out the window and see the air like it was this morning, I've got to stay inside. Yesterday, I tried to drive to the store, and I couldn't see 50 feet ahead of me, it was so thick, so I just came home. I remember that when I was young, we never thought about pollution. Everybody was working, and everybody had money, and the smoke stacks were smoking, and the air was dirty, and we were all happy. I think the best air we ever had in Pittsburgh was during the Depression. That's when nobody was working." Comment on this statement in terms of the issues discussed in this chapter.

7. When the Audubon Society, a private group, brought suit against the state of Wisconsin and the federal government to stop the building of a highway through a marshy area used by migrating waterfowl, were considerations of social versus

private cost involved? If so, who represented the private and who the social interest? If not, what was the dispute about? Might *each* of the following groups view the costs differently from the Audubon Society, and from each other: the American Automobile Association, the Rod and Gun Club of Wisconsin, the Committee to Stamp Out Poverty in Wisconsin?

8. Comment on each of the following recent news headlines in terms of the issues discussed in this chapter.
a. "Automation in the Printing Industry Promises Progress—and Problems"

b. "Today the Tennessee Valley Authority is Assailed as Threat to Environment"
c. "Pollution Crisis Feared in Baltic. Political Differences Hinder Coordinated Action"
d. "U.N. Panel Warns of the Hazards of Peaceful Nuclear Power"
e. "Pollution in Greek Harbor Cancels 450-year-old Epiphany 'Dive for Cross' ceremony"

PART FIVE

MARKETS AND PRICING

14

Pricing in competitive markets

Is Goodyear in competition with Goodrich? Does Macy's compete with Gimbels? Is the farmer from Wheatland, Iowa, in competition with a wheat farmer from North Platte, Nebraska? In the ordinary meaning of the noun "competition" and the verb "compete," the answers to the first two of these questions are plainly yes, and the answer to the third question is probably no. Goodyear and Goodrich both advertise extensively to persuade the same group of tire buyers to buy *their* product. Goodrich has even been trying to confuse the issue: "See that blimp up there? It's theirs, not ours. If you want Goodrich tires you'll just have to remember Goodrich." Everyone knows that Macy's and Gimbels watch each other like hawks and that swarms of comparison shoppers check their respective prices and qualities every day. But there is nothing that the Iowa farmer can do that will affect the sales or the profits of the Nebraska farmer. Indeed they do not even know each other, and if they ever do meet it will be as fellow members of a noble, if unappreciated, profession.

Firm behavior and market structure

To sort out the questions of who is competing with whom and in what sense do they compete, it is necessary to distinguish between the behavior of individual firms and the type of market in which the firms operate. Economists use the term *market structure* to refer to the latter concept. The concept of competitive behavior is quite distinct from the concept of competitive market structure. The degree of *competitive behavior* refers to the degree to which individual firms indulge in active competition with one another. The degree of *competitiveness of the market structure* refers to the degree to which individual firms have power over that market—power to influence the price or other terms on which their product is sold. In everyday use the term "competition" usually refers only to competitive behavior; economists, however, are interested both in the behavior of individual firms and in market structures.

Goodrich and Goodyear certainly engage in competitive (i.e., rivalrous) behavior. It is also true that both individually and together they have some power over the market. Either firm could raise its prices and still continue to sell tires; each has the power to decide—within limits set by buyers' tastes and the prices of competing tires—what price consumers will pay for its own product.

The Iowa and the Nebraska wheat farmers do not engage in active competitive behavior with each other. They operate, however, in a market over which they have no power. Neither one has significant power to change the market price for its wheat by altering its own behavior.

To get to one extreme of competitive market structures, economists use a theory in which no one firm has any market power. There are so many firms that each must accept the price set by the forces of market demand and supply. In this theory of the perfectly competitive market structure there is no need for individual firms to behave competitively with respect to one another since none has any power over the market and one firm's ability to sell its product is uninfluenced by the behavior of any other single firm. The apparent paradox that interfirm competition does not occur in perfectly competitive markets is resolved when we recognize the distinction between interfirm competitive *behavior* and the competitive *structure* of the market in which the firm operates.

The theory of the perfectly competitive market structure applies directly to a number of real-world markets. It also provides a benchmark for comparison with other market structures in which there are few enough firms that each one has some significant market power.

THE SIGNIFICANCE OF MARKET STRUCTURE

Although market demand curves and cost curves of individual firms are the basic elements of the theory of product pricing, they are not themselves sufficient to provide a theory of price. Hypotheses are needed that tell how these elements interact and finally come together in the market. At the outset we need to define two basic concepts, the market and the industry.

From the point of view of a household, the **market** consists of those firms from which it can buy a well-defined product; from the point of view of a firm, the market consists of those buyers to whom it can sell a well-defined product. A group of firms that sells a well-defined product, or closely related set of products, is said to constitute an **industry.** The market demand curve is the demand curve for an industry's product.

Consider a firm that produces a specific product for sale in a particular market and competes for customers with other firms in the same industry. If a profit-maximizing firm knows precisely the demand curve it faces, it knows the price it could charge for each rate of sales, and thus it knows its potential revenues. If it also knows its costs, it can readily discover the profits that would be associated with any rate of output, and it can choose the rate that maximizes its profits. But what if the firm knows its costs and only the *market* demand curve for its product? It does not know what its own sales would be. In other words, it does not know its *own* demand curve. In order to determine what fraction of the total market demand will be met by sellers other than itself, it needs to know how other firms will respond if it changes its price. If it reduces its price by 10 percent, will other sellers leave their prices unchanged or will they also reduce them? If they reduce their prices, will they do so by less than 10 percent, by exactly 10 percent, or by more than 10 percent? Obviously, each of the possible outcomes will have a different effect on the firm's sales and thus on its revenues and profits.

The answers to questions about the relation of a firm's demand curve to the market demand curve depend on such things as the number of sellers in the market and the similarity of their products. These are aspects of **market structure,** which is defined as the characteristics of market organization that are likely to affect a firm's behavior and performance.

For example, if there are only two large firms in an industry, each may be expected to meet most price cuts that the other makes; but if there are 5,000 small firms, a price cut by one may go unmatched. For another example, if two firms are producing identical products, they may be expected to behave differently with respect to each other than if they were producing similar but not identical products. These two aspects of market structure (number of sellers and similarity of product) suggest the central hypothesis of the branch of economics called industrial organization: Firm behavior will be affected by market structure.

There are many other aspects of market structure that may affect firm behavior. These include the ease of entering the industry, the nature and size of the purchasers of the firm's products, and the firm's ability to influence demand by advertising. To reduce these aspects to manageable proportions, economists have focused on a few theoretical market structures that are thought to represent a high proportion of the cases actually encountered in market societies. In this chapter and the next two, we shall look at four of these: perfect competition, monopoly, monopolistic competition, and oligopoly.

Before we consider any of these market structures we must deal with the rules of behavior that are common to all firms who seek to maximize their profits.

BEHAVIORAL RULES FOR THE PROFIT-MAXIMIZING FIRM[1]

Common sense tells us that a firm should produce only if it will do better than by not producing. The firm always has the option of producing nothing. If it produces nothing, it will have an operating loss equal to its fixed costs. If it decides to produce it will add its variable cost of production to its fixed costs and the receipts from the sale of its products to its revenue. If revenue exceeds variable cost it will pay the firm to produce; if revenue is less than variable cost the firm will actually lose less by not producing than it will by producing. This leads to the first rule for profit maximizing.

Rule 1. A firm should not produce at all if the average revenue from its product does not equal or exceed its average variable cost. [14]

If a firm decides that, according to rule 1, production is worth undertaking, it must decide how much to produce. Common sense dictates that on a unit-by-unit basis, if any unit of production adds more to revenue than it does to cost, that unit will increase profits; if it adds more to cost than to revenue, it will decrease profits. If the firm is in a position where a further unit of production will increase profits, it should expand output; if it is in a position where the last unit of production decreased profits, it should contract output. The notion of the change in cost brought about by an additional unit is, of course, marginal cost (*MC*). A parallel concept, **marginal revenue** (*MR*), may be defined as

---

[1] Formal proofs of the propositions discussed in the text are given in the Mathematical Notes.

the change in total revenue resulting from the sale of one additional unit.

A second common sense rule may now be stated formally.

Rule 2. Assuming that it pays the firm to produce at all, it will be profitable for the firm to expand output whenever marginal revenue is greater than marginal cost; expansion must thus continue until marginal revenue equals marginal cost. [15]

These two rules can be restated as three necessary conditions for a firm to be maximizing its profits. It must be producing an output where (a) price is at least as great as average variable cost, (b) marginal revenue equals marginal cost, and (c) the marginal cost curve cuts the marginal revenue curve from below.[2]

These rules apply to all profit-maximizing firms whatever the market structure in which they operate. The rules refer to the firm's costs and its revenues. Before we can apply the rules we need to consider particular market structures in order to provide links between the demand curve for an industry's product and the demand curves—and thus the revenue curves—facing individual firms.

The theory of perfect competition

In considering the theory of perfect competition, we study first the critical assumptions of perfect competition, then we derive the demand curve for a competitive firm, and finally, we examine the equilibrium of the competitive *industry* in both the short run and the long run.

THE ASSUMPTIONS OF PERFECT COMPETITION

The theory of **perfect competition** is built on two critical assumptions, one about the behavior of the individual firm and one about the nature of the industry in which it operates.

The *firm* is assumed to be a **price taker.** This means that the firm is assumed to act as if it can alter its rate of production and sales within any feasible range without its action's having any significant effect on the price of the product it sells. Thus the firm must passively accept whatever price happens to be ruling on the market.

The *industry* is characterized by **freedom of entry and exit.** This means that the industry is one in which any new firm is free to set up production if it so wishes and in which any existing firm is free to cease production and leave the industry if it so wishes. Existing firms cannot bar the entry of new firms and there are no legal prohibitions on entry or exit.

The ultimate test of the theory based on these assumptions will be the usefulness of its predictions, but because students are often bothered by the first assumption, it is worth examining whether it is in any way reasonable.[3] To see what is involved in the assumption of price taking, contrast the demands for the products of an automobile manufacturer and a wheat farmer.

---

[2] The third condition is designed to distinguish between profit-maximizing and profit-minimizing positions. Consider an output where $MC = MR$ and call it q_m. For this to be a profit-maximizing output, marginal cost should exceed marginal revenue for outputs greater than q_m (indicating that increasing output would decrease profit) while marginal cost should be less than marginal revenue for outputs less than q_m (indicating that decreasing output would also decrease profit). The graphical expression of this condition is that the MC curve must cut the MR curve from below. Consider the alternative in which MC cuts MR from above: For outputs just less than q_m marginal cost exceeds marginal revenue, which indicates that these units reduce profits and thus that profits could be increased by *reducing* output. For outputs just in excess of q_m marginal revenue exceeds marginal cost, which indicates that these units increase profits and thus that profits could be inceased by *increasing* output. In this case q_m is a point of *minimum* profits can be increased either by raising or by lowering output from q_m.

[3] The facts of the American economy will be considered in Chapter 16.

The "traditional" assumptions of perfect competition: a historical digression

Instead of assuming that firms are price takers, one might assume a set of conditions that (if they existed) would make price taking probable. This used to be standard practice, and it is still sometimes adopted by assuming that (1) there is a very large number of sellers, no one of whom commands a large share of the total market; (2) the products of different sellers are identical and buyers have no preference among sellers; (3) there are so many buyers that sellers and buyers do not establish personal relationships with one another; and (4) buyers are perfectly informed about the prices of different sellers.

This list, while *sufficient* to yield price-taking behavior, is not *necessary* to it, for there are many other sets of conditions that lead to price taking, and the listed points may be greatly modified without changing price-taking behavior.

Failure to appreciate this point has occasioned much fruitless debate. In the real world, for example, large numbers of buyers are never perfectly informed. Does this mean that perfect competition is never applicable? The answer is no, provided that substantially less than perfect knowledge is still conductive to sellers behaving as price takers. What matters is that firms should be price takers; the reasons why they should do so may differ among times and places.

An automobile manufacturer. General Motors is aware of the fact that it has some market power. If it substantially increases its prices, sales will fall off; if it lowers prices substantially, it will be able to sell more of its products. If GM contemplates a large increase in production that is not a response to some known or anticipated rise in demand, it knows that it will have to reduce prices in order to sell the extra output. The automobile manufacturing firm is *not* a price taker. The quantity that it is able to sell will depend on the price it charges, but it does not have to accept passively whatever price is set by the market. In other words, the firm manufacturing automobiles is faced with a downward-sloping demand curve for its product. It may select any price-quantity combination consistent with that demand curve.

A wheat farmer. In contrast, an individual firm producing wheat will be one of a very large number of firms all growing the same product; one firm's contribution to the total production of wheat will be a very small drop in an extremely large bucket. Ordinarily the firm will assume that it has no effect on price and will think of its own demand curve as being horizontal. Of course the firm can have *some* effect on price, but a straightforward calculation will demonstrate that the effect is small enough that the firm can justifiably neglect it.

The market elasticity of demand for wheat is approximately 0.25. This means that if the quantity of wheat supplied in the world increased by 1 percent, the price would have to fall by 4 percent to induce the world's wheat buyers to purchase the whole crop. Even a very large farmer produces a very small fraction of the total crop. In a recent year an extremely large Canadian wheat farm produced about 50,000 tons, only about 1/4,000 of the world production of 200 million tons. Suppose that a large wheat farm increased its production by 20,000 tons, say from 40,000 to 60,000 tons, a very large percentage increase in its own production but an increase of only 1/100 of 1 percent in world production. Table 14–1 shows that this increase would lead to a decrease in the world price of 4/100 of 1 percent (4¢ in $100) and give the firm an elasticity of demand of 1,000! This is a very high elasticity of demand; the farm would have to increase its output 1,000 percent to bring about a 1 percent decrease in the price of wheat. Because the farm's output cannot be varied this much, it is not surprising that the firm regards the price of wheat as being unaffected by any changes in output that it could conceivably make.

It is only a slight simplification of reality to say that the firm is unable to influence the world price of wheat and that it is able to sell all that it can produce at the going world price. In other words, the firm is faced with a perfectly elastic demand curve for its product—it is a price taker.

The difference between firms producing wheat and firms producing automobiles is one of degree of market power. The wheat firm, as an insignificant part of the whole market, has no power to influence the world price of wheat. But the automobile firm does have power to influence the price of automobiles because its own production represents a significant part of the total supply of automobiles.

Table 14–1 The calculation of a firm's elasticity of demand (η_F) from market elasticity of demand (η_M)

Given $\eta_M = 0.25$
World output = 200 million tons
Firm's output increases from 40,000 to 60,000 tons, a 40% increase over the average quantity of 50,000 tons

Step 1. Find the percentage change in world price

$$\eta_M = -\frac{\text{percentage change in world output}}{\text{percentage change in world price}}$$

$$\text{Percentage change in world price} = -\frac{\text{percentage change in world output}}{\eta_M}$$

$$= -\frac{\frac{1}{100} \text{ of } 1\%}{0.25}$$

$$= -\tfrac{4}{100} \text{ of } 1\%$$

Step 2. Compute the firm's elasticity of demand:

$$\eta_F = -\frac{\text{percentage change in firm's output}}{\text{percentage change in world price}}$$

$$= -\frac{+40\%}{-\tfrac{4}{100} \text{ of } 1\%} = +1,000$$

Because even a large change in output to the firm is a minute change in world wheat production the effect on world price is very small. Thus the firm's elasticity of demand is high. This table relies on the concept of elasticity of demand developed on page 73. Step 1 shows that a 40 percent increase in the firm's output leads to only a tiny decrease in the world's price. Thus, as step 2 shows, the firm's elasticity of demand is very high: 1,000.

The arithmetic is not important, but understanding why the wheat farm will be a price taker in these circumstances is vital.

DEMAND AND REVENUE CURVES FOR THE PERFECTLY COMPETITIVE FIRM

Students sometimes confuse the individual firm's demand curve under perfect competition with the market demand curve for the product. The market demand curve is downward sloping for the reasons discussed at length in Part Three. A consequence, as we saw, is that a rightward shift of the supply curve will lead to a fall in market price, other things being equal.

The demand curve facing a single firm in perfect competition is infinitely elastic because variations in its production *over the range that we need to consider for all practical purposes* will have such a small effect on price that the effect can safely be assumed to be zero. Of course, if the single firm increased its production by a vast amount, a thousandfold say, this would cause a significant increase in supply and the firm would be unable to sell all it produced at the going price. The perfectly elastic demand curve does not mean that the firm could actually sell an infinite amount at the going price; rather, that the variations in production *that it will normally be practicable for the firm to make* will leave price virtually unaffected. This is illustrated in Figure 14–1.

Total, average, and marginal revenue curves. The notions of total, average, and marginal revenue are the demand counterparts of the notions of total, average, and marginal cost that were considered in Chapter 11. We focus now on the receipts to a seller from the sale of a product.

Total revenue (TR) is the total amount received by the seller. If q units are sold at p dollars each, $TR = p \times q$.

Figure 14–1 Three demand curves of differing elasticity.

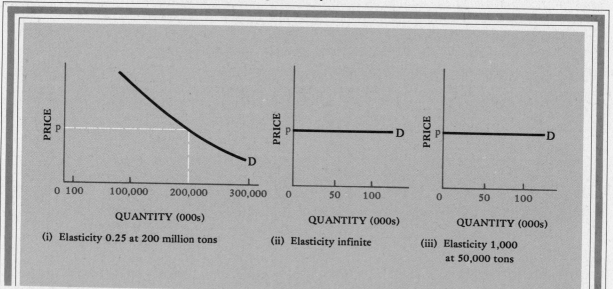

(i) Elasticity 0.25 at 200 million tons

(ii) Elasticity infinite

(iii) Elasticity 1,000 at 50,000 tons

For pratical purposes, the demand curves in (ii) and (iii) are indistinguishable from each other. The firm's demand curve in (iii) appears horizontal because of the change in the quantity scale compared to (i). If one stretched the quantity scale in (i) to 1,000 times its present size, that demand curve, too, would appear horizontal.

Table 14–2 Revenue concepts for a price-taking firm

Price p	Quantity sold (units) q	$TR = p \cdot q$	$AR = TR/q$	$MR = \Delta TR/\Delta q$
$3.00	10	$30.00	$3.00	
3.00	11	33.00	3.00	$3.00
3.00	12	36.00	3.00	3.00
3.00	13	39.00	3.00	3.00

When price is fixed, *AR = MR = p*. Marginal revenue is shown between the lines because it represents the change in total revenue (e.g., from $33 to $36) in response to a change in quantity (from 11 to 12 units),

$$MR = \frac{36-33}{12-11} = \$3 \text{ per unit.}$$

Average revenue (*AR*) is the amount of revenue *per unit* sold. This is the price of the product.

Marginal revenue (*MR*), sometimes called incremental revenue, has already been defined. It is the change in total revenue resulting from the sale of an additional unit of the commodity. [16]

Calculations of these revenue concepts for a price-taking firm are illustrated in Table 14–2. The table shows that as long as the firm's output does not affect the price of the product it sells, both average and marginal revenue will be equal to price at all levels of output. Thus, graphically (as shown in Figure 14–2), average revenue and marginal revenue are both horizontal lines at the level of market price. Since the firm can sell any quantity it wishes at this price the same horizontal line is also the *firm's* demand curve.

If the market price is unaffected by variations in the firm's output, then the firm's demand curve, the average revenue curve, and the marginal revenue curve coincide in the same horizontal line.

Total revenue, of course, does vary with output; since price is constant, it follows that total revenue rises in direct proportion to output.

Figure 14–2 Revenue curves for a price-taking firm

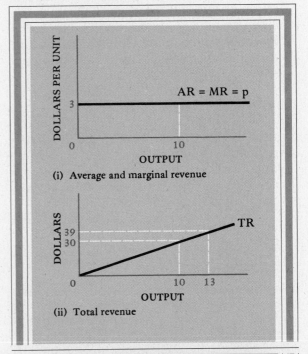

(i) Average and marginal revenue

(ii) Total revenue

This is a graphic representation of the revenue concepts of Table 14–2. Because price does not change, neither marginal nor average revenue varies with output. When price is constant, total revenue is a rising straight line from the origin.

Short-run equilibrium: firm and industry

EQUILIBRIUM OUTPUT OF A FIRM IN PERFECT COMPETITION

The firm in perfect competition (being a price taker) can adjust to differing market conditions only by changing the quantity it produces. In the short run it has fixed factors, and the only way it can vary its output is by using more or less of those factors that it can vary.

Thus the firm's short-run cost curves are relevant to its output decision.

We saw earlier that any profit-maximizing firm will seek to produce at a level of output where marginal cost equals marginal revenue. We saw in the immediately preceding section that a perfectly competitive firm's demand and marginal revenue curves coincide in the same horizontal line whose height represents the price of the product. Thus price equals marginal revenue, and it follows immediately that a perfectly competitive firm will equate its marginal cost of production to the market price of its product (as long as price exceeds average variable cost).

The market determines the price at which the firm can sell its product. The firm then picks the quantity of output that maximizes its profits. This is the output for which $p = MC$. When the firm is maximizing profits, it has no incentive to change its output. Therefore, unless prices or costs change, the firm will continue producing this output because it is doing as well as it can do, given the situation it faces. The firm is thus said to be in **short-run equilibrium.** This equilibrium is illustrated in Figure 14–3.

The competitive firm is a mere quantity adjuster. It pursues its goal of profit maximization by increasing or decreasing quantity until it equates its short-run marginal cost with the prevailing price of its product—a price that is given to it by the market.

The market price to which the perfectly competitive firm responds is itself set by the forces of demand and supply. The individual firm, by adjusting its quantity produced to whatever price is ruling on the market, helps to determine market supply. The link between the behavior of the firm and the behavior of the competitive market is provided by the market supply curve.

SHORT-RUN SUPPLY CURVES

The supply curve shows the relation between the quantity supplied and price. For any given price we need to ask what quantity will be supplied. This question may be answered by supposing that a price is specified and determining how much each firm will choose to supply. Then a different price is supposed and quantity supplied again determined—and so on, until all possible prices have been considered.

The supply curve of one firm

Figure 14–4(i) shows a firm's marginal cost curve with four alternative demand curves. The firm's marginal cost curve gives the marginal cost corresponding to each level of output. A supply curve is needed that gives

Figure 14–3 The equilibrium of a competitive firm

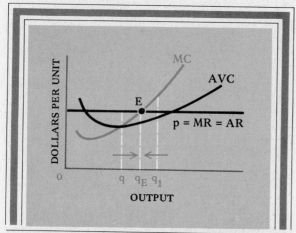

The firm chooses the output for which $p = MC$ above the level of AVC. When $p = MC$ as at q_E, the firm would decrease its profits if it either increased or decreased its output. At any point left of q_E, say q, price is greater than the marginal cost, and it pays to increase output. At any point to the right of q_E, say q_1, price is less than the marginal cost, and it pays to reduce output. The equilibrium output for the firm is q_E.

Figure 14–4 Deriving the supply curve for a price-taking firm

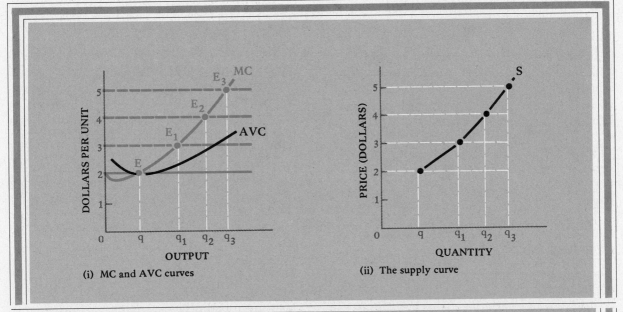

(i) MC and AVC curves

(ii) The supply curve

For a price-taking firm, the supply curve has the same shape as its *MC* curve above the level of *AVC*. As prices rise from 2 to 3 to 4 to 5, the firm wishes to increase its production from q to q_1 to q_2 to q_3. For prices below \$2, output would be zero because the firm is better off if it shuts down. The point *E*, where price equals *AVC*, is called the shutdown point. The firm's supply curve is shown in (ii).

the quantity the firm will supply at every price. For prices below *AVC*, the firm will supply zero units (rule 1). For prices above *AVC*, the firm will equate price and marginal cost (rule 2 modified by the proposition that $MR = p$ in perfect competition). From this it follows that:

In perfect competition the firm's marginal cost curve above *AVC* has the identical shape as the firm's supply curve.

This proposition is so obvious that it sometimes causes difficulty to the student who is looking for something difficult and profound. If you are not absolutely certain that you understand the proposition, construct the firm's supply curve for yourself. Given per-

fect competition, profit maximization, and the cost curves of Figure 14–4(i), you can discover the output of the firm corresponding to any given market price. You can then plot the firm's supply curve on a graph of your own by relating market price to quantity produced by the firm. Once you have done this, you will see that the supply curve you have constructed is identical in shape to the marginal cost curve above *AVC* (see Figure 14–4).

The supply curve of an industry

Figure 14–5 illustrates the derivation of an industry supply curve for an example of only two firms. The general result may be stated:

In perfect competition the industry supply curve is

the horizontal sum of the marginal cost curves (above the level of average variable cost) of all of the firms in the industry.

The reason for this is as follows: Each firm's marginal cost curve tells us how much that firm will supply at any given market price. The industry supply curve is the sum of what each firm will supply at each market price, and hence is the sum of the marginal cost curves of all of the firms in the industry.

This supply curve, based as it is on the short-run marginal cost curves of the firms in the industry, is the industry's **short-run supply curve.**

THE DETERMINATION OF SHORT-RUN EQUILIBRIUM PRICE

The short-run supply curve and the demand curve for the industry's product together determine the market price. (This happens in the manner analyzed in Chapter 5.) Although no one firm can influence market price significantly, the collective actions of all firms in the industry (as shown by the industry supply curve) and the collective actions of households (as shown by the industry's demand curve) together determine market price at the point where the demand and supply curves intersect.

At the equilibrium market price each firm is producing and selling a quantity for which its marginal cost equals the market price and no firm is motivated to change its output in the short run. Since total quantity demanded equals total quantity supplied there is no reason for market price to change in the short run; the market and all the firms in the industry are in short-run equilibrium.

SHORT-RUN PROFITABILITY OF THE FIRM

Although we know that when the industry is in short-run equilibrium, the competitive firm

Figure 14–5 The derivation of an industry supply curve

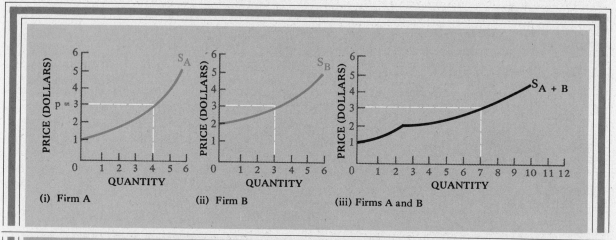

The industry supply curve is the horizontal sum of the supply curves of each of the firms in the industry. At a price of $3 firm A would supply 4 units and firm B would supply 3 units. Together, as shown in (iii), they would supply 7 units. If there are hundreds of firms, the process is the same: Each firm's supply curve (which is derived in the manner shown in Figure 14–4) shows what the firm will produce at any given price *p*. The industry supply curve relates the price to the sum of the quantities produced by each firm.

Figure 14–6 Alternative short-run equilibrium positions of a competitive firm

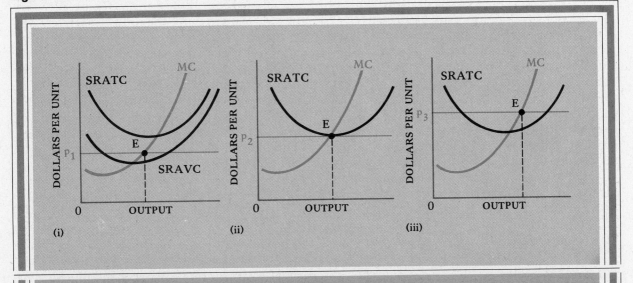

When it is in short-run equilibrium a competitive firm may be suffering losses, breaking even, or making profits. The diagrams show a firm with given costs faced with three alternative prices p_1, p_2, and p_3. In each part of the diagram E is the point at which $MC = MR$ = price. Since in all three cases price exceeds AVC the firm is in short-run equilibrium.

In (i) price is p_1 and the firm is suffering losses because price is below average total cost. Since price exceeds average variable cost, it pays the firm to keep producing, but it does *not* pay it to replace its capital equipment as the capital wears out.

In (ii) price is p_2 and the firm is just covering its total costs. It does pay the firm to replace its capital as it wears out since it is covering the full opportunity cost of its capital.

In (iii) price is p_3 and the firm is earning profits in excess of all its costs.

is maximizing its profits, we do not know *how large* these profits are. It is one thing to know that a firm is doing as well as it can in particular circumstances; it is another thing to know how well it is doing.

Figure 14–6 shows three possible positions for a firm in short-run equilibrium. In all cases, the firm is maximizing its profits by producing where $p = MC$, but in (i) the firm is making losses, in (ii) it is just covering all costs, and in (iii) it is making profits in excess of all costs. In (i) it might be better to say that the firm is minimizing its losses rather than maximizing its profits, but both statements mean the same thing. The firm is doing as well as it can do, given its costs and prices.

All three of these are possible short-run equilibrium positions for the profit-maximizing firm in perfect competition. But not all of them are possible equilibrium positions in the long run.

Long-run equilibrium

THE LONG RUN IN OUTLINE

The key to long-run equilibrium under perfect competition is entry and exit. We have seen that when firms are in *short-run* equilibrium they may be making profits or losses or they may be just breaking even. Since costs include the opportunity cost of capital, firms that are just breaking even are doing as well as they could if they invested their capital elsewhere. Thus there will be no incentive for existing firms to leave the industry; neither will there be an incentive for new firms to enter the industry because capital can earn the same return elsewhere in the economy. If, however, existing firms are earning profits over all costs, including the opportunity cost of capital, new capital will enter the industry to share in these profits. If existing firms are making losses, capital will leave the industry because a better return can be obtained elsewhere in the economy. Let us consider the process in a little more detail.

Figure 14–7 The effect of new entrants on the supply curve

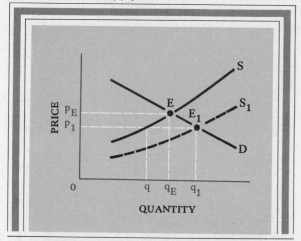

PRICE / QUANTITY

New entrants shift the supply curve to the right and lower the equilibrium price. The initial equilibrium is at E. If the supply curve shifts to S_1 by virtue of entry, the equilibrium price must fall to p_1 while output rises to q_1. At this price before entry, only q would have been produced. The extra output is supplied by the new productive capacity.

If all firms in the competitive industry are in the position of the firm in Figure 14–6(iii), new firms will enter the industry attracted by the profits being earned by the existing firms. Suppose that in response to high profits for 100 existing firms, 20 new firms enter. The market supply curve that formerly added up the outputs of 100 firms now must add up the outputs of 120 firms. At any price, more will be supplied because there are more suppliers. This shift in the short-run supply curve, with an unchanged market demand curve, means that the previous equilibrium price will no longer prevail. The shift in supply will cause the equilibrium price to fall, and both new and old firms will have to adjust their output to this new price. This is illustrated in Figure 14–7. Entry will proceed and price will continue to fall until all firms in the industry are just covering their total costs. Firms will then be in the position of the firm in Figure 14–6(ii), which is called a *zero-profit equilibrium.*

Profits in a competitive industry are a signal for the entry of new capital; the industry will expand, forcing price down until the profits fall to zero.

If the firms in the industry are in the position of the firm in Figure 14–6(i), they are suffering losses. They are covering their variable costs, but the return on their capital is less than the opportunity cost of this capital; the firms are not covering their total costs. This is a signal for exit of capital. As plant and equipment wears out it will not be replaced. As a result, the industry's short-run supply curve shifts left and market price rises. Capital continues to exit and price continues to rise until the remaining firms can cover their total costs—that is, until they are all in the zero-profit equilibrium illustrated in Figure 14–6(ii). Exit then ceases.

Losses in a competitive industry are a signal for the exit of capital; the industry will contract, driving price up until the remaining firms are covering their total costs.

In all of this we see profits fulfilling their function of allocating resources among the industries of the economy. For many purposes this is as far as we need to go with the analysis of the long run.

A MORE DETAILED ANALYSIS OF THE LONG RUN[4]

For some purposes it is important to understand some complications omitted from the foregoing broad treatment. The rest of this chapter is devoted to a more detailed examination of the long-run behavior of a perfectly competitive industry.

Consider the position of the firm and the industry when full long-run equilibrium obtains as illustrated in Figure 14–8.

1. *No firm will want to vary the output of its existing plants: short-run marginal cost (SRMC) must equal price.*

2. *Profits earned by existing plants must be zero.* (If they were positive there would be entry; if they were negative there would be exit; in neither case would the industry be in long-run equilibrium.) This implies that short-run *ATC* must equal price—that is, firms must be in the position of the firms in Figure 14–6(ii).

3. *No firm can earn profits by building a plant of a different size.* This implies that each existing firm must be producing at the lowest point on its long-run average cost curve.

Taken together these conditions mean that all firms in the industry should be in the position illustrated in Figure 14–8.[5]

We have already seen why the first two conditions must hold. Now let us look at the

---

[4] The remainder of this chapter may be omitted without loss of continuity.

[5] The text discussion implies that all existing firms and all new entrants face identical *LRATC* curves. This merely means that all firms face the same set of factor prices and have the same technology available to them. There are some apparent complications when different units of the same factor have different efficiencies; these complications are further discussed in the box on page 226–227.

Figure 14–8 The equilibrium of a firm when the industry is in long-run equilibrium

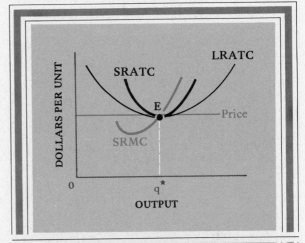

In long-run competitive equilibrium the firm is operating at the minimum point on its *LRATC* curve. In long-run equilibrium each firm must be: (i) maximizing short-run profits, $SRMC = p$; (ii) earning profits of zero on its existing plant, $SRATC = $ price; and (iii) unable to increase its profits by altering the size of plant. These three conditions can only be met when the firm is at the minimum point on its *LRATC* curve, *E*.

third condition. Figure 14–9 shows two firms that have $SRMC = SRATC = $ price. Each of these firms can, however, increase its profits by discarding its present plant when it wears out and building a plant of different size. The smaller firm should increase its plant size, thereby lowering its average total costs. The larger firm should build a smaller plant, thereby also lowering its *ATC*. Since each firm is a price taker each of these changes will increase the firm's profits.

The only way in which a price-taking firm can be in long-run equilibrium with respect to its size is by producing at the minimum point on its *LRATC* curve.

Figure 14–9 Short-run versus long-run equilibrium of a competitive firm

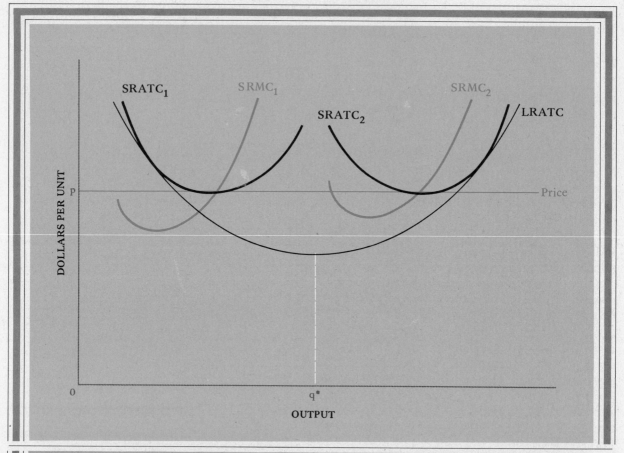

A competitive firm that is not at the minimum point on its *LRATC* curve cannot be in long-run equilibrium. Suppose two firms have identical *LRATC* curves but one firm has too small a plant, with
costs *SRATC*₁, while the other firm has too large a plant, with costs of *SRATC*₂. Both firms are in
short-run equilibrium at price $p = MC = ATC$ but neither is in long-run equilibrium. Firm 1 can
increase its profits by building a larger plant (thereby moving downward to the right along its
LRATC curve). Firm 2 can increase its profits by building a smaller plant (thereby moving
downward to the left along its *LRATC* curve).

The firm must be producing at the point labeled $q\star$ in Figures 14–8 and 14–9.

An industry is nothing more than a collection of firms; for an industry to be in long-run
equilibrium each firm must be in long-run
equilibrium. It follows that when a perfectly
competitive industry is in long-run equilibrium all firms in the industry will be selling at
a price equal to minimum *SRAC*—that is,
they must be in zero-profit equilibrium, as in
Figure 14–6(ii). It follows that the short-run
industry supply curve—which tells us how
much all existing firms will supply at each
market price—must intersect the market demand curve at that particular price.

The long-run response of a perfectly competitive industry to a change in demand

Now suppose that the demand for the product increases. Price will rise to equate demand with the industry's short-run supply. Each firm will expand output until its short-run marginal cost once again equals price. Each firm will earn profits as a result of the rise in price, and the profits will induce new firms to enter the industry. This shifts the short-run supply curve to the right and forces down the price. Entry continues until all firms are once again just covering average total costs. To recapitulate: The short-run effects of the rise in demand are a rise in price and output; the long-run effects are a further rise in output and a fall in price.

Now consider a fall in demand. The industry starts with firms in long-run equilibrium as shown in Figure 14–8 and the market demand curve shifts left and price falls. There are two possible consequences.

First, the decline in demand forces price below ATC but leaves it above AVC. Firms are then in the position shown in Figure 14–6(i). The firms can cover their variable costs and earn some return on their capital, so they remain in production for as long as their existing plant and equipment lasts. But it is not worth replacing capital as it wears out. Exit will occur as old capital wears out and is not replaced. As firms exit the short-run supply curve shifts left and market price rises. This continues until the remaining firms in the industry can cover their total costs. At this point it will pay to replace capital as it wears out, and the decline in the size of the industry will be brought to a halt. In this case the adjustment may take a very long time, for the industry shrinks in size only as existing plant and equipment wears out.

The second possibility occurs if the decline in demand is so large that price is forced below the level of AVC. In this case firms cannot even cover their variable costs and some will shut down immediately. Thus the reduction in capital devoted to production in the industry occurs rapidly because some existing capacity is scrapped or sold for other uses. Once sufficient capital has been withdrawn so that price rises to a level that allows the remaining firms to cover their AVCs, the rapid withdrawal of capital will cease. Further exit occurs more slowly, as described above.

Entry of new capital into a profitable industry occurs at the speed at which new plants can be built and new equipment installed. Exit of existing capital from an industry with losses may occur very quickly if price is less than average variable cost but only at the rate at which old plant and equipment wears out if price exceeds average variable cost.[6]

This adjustment process is examined in greater detail in the following section.

The long-run industry supply curve

Possible adjustments of the industry to the kinds of changes in demand just discussed are shown by the **long-run industry supply (LRS) curve.** This curve shows the relation between equilibrium price and the output firms will be willing to supply after all desired entry or exit has occurred.

The long-run supply curve connects positions of long-run equilibrium after all demand-induced changes have occurred.

When induced changes in factor prices are considered, it is possible for LRS to rise, fall, or to remain constant. The various cases are illustrated in Figures 14–10 to 14–12.

The long-run supply curve in Figure 14–10 is horizontal. This indicates that the industry will, given time, adjust its size to provide whatever quantity may be demanded at a constant price. Such conditions obtain if

---

[6] If the capital has no alternative use it may not be scrapped; instead it may be "mothballed" in case of future need. As far as its influence on current production and price is concerned, however, it has withdrawn from the industry.

Can there be differences among competitive firms?

Everyone knows that if there are two barbers in town one is both better and faster than the other, that two farmers may have different qualities of land, or that the Acme Company is better managed than its competitor, the Zenith Company. In the discussion in the text, an industry has been regarded as consisting of many firms. The question arises as to which firm we have been talking about and illustrating in such graphs as those of Figures 14–6 and 14–9. Alfred Marshall, whose *Principles of Economics* (first published in 1896) synthesized neoclassical economics, spoke of the "representative" firm, but we can be more precise by considering a simple example.

Suppose there are two artichoke farmers, Aaron and Zipf, each of whom owns his own farm. Aaron's farm is much more productive than Zipf's farm in the sense that the variable cost per bushel is lower. Indeed, suppose that Aaron's advantage is $3 per bushel, and suppose that for either farm the best output is 1,000 bushels per year. At this output, Zipf just covers his costs but Aaron seems to earn a profit of $3,000 over all of his costs. This $3,000, however, is due not to Aaron's skill in producing but to his having the good fortune to own prime artichoke land. If Aaron and Zipf traded farms, Zipf would earn the extra $3,000. The $3,000 is called, following David Ricardo, the *economic rent* of the land.★ It reflects the superior quality of a factor of production (in this case, land), and it can be appropriated by whoever owns the superior factor of production. If Aaron were tired of farming, he could surely lease ("rent" in everyday usage) his land to someone else like Zipf for an amount close to $3,000 per year more than anyone would pay for Zipf's land. According to the opportunity cost principle, this is a *cost of production* to Aaron. He gets it for owning the land, not for producing on it. To see this clearly, suppose you own the land and lease it to Aaron. When Aaron's lease comes up for renewal, how much rental will you charge him in excess of what Zipf pays? (You cannot get away with more than $3,000. Need you settle for much less?)

As long as there are many potential users, the owners of a scarce resource can cash in on its superior earning power. If the owner of the resource is a firm, it means only that the firm earns the rent. From the point of view of the total cost of *production,* such rents become fixed costs. Thus, although the variable costs of firms that are producing may differ, their total costs (including marketable special advantages) will not.

---

factor prices do not change as the output of the whole industry expands or contracts. An industry with a horizontal long-run supply curve is said to be a **constant-cost industry.** While conditions of constant *LRS* may exist, such conditions are not necessary. Other possibilities are considered below.

Changing factor prices and increasing long-run supply curves. When an industry expands its output it needs more inputs. The increase in demand for these inputs may bid up their prices. Such growth-induced changes in prices may be expected whenever rapid growth occurs. The reason for this is that a

Assuming total costs for all producing firms in a competitive industry are the same is a consequence of the opportunity cost principle. It does not deny the fact that there are differences among firms; it says only that these differences will be included in the total costs of production.

Consider a further example. Suppose the Acme Company's cost advantage is due to a superior manager. Competition for his services will drive his salary (or other remuneration) up to the point where he is getting paid for the special value of his talents. But suppose that Acme has this employee under long-term contract at a very modest wage. Surely the firm cannot sell this special advantage. But it can! It can sell the employee's contract to another firm (this happens regularly with baseball players under exclusive contract). Or it may lease his services (as movie studios lease their stars' services to other studios). Or the owners of the firm might sell the firm to others for a price that includes the value of the special contract. Special advantages inhere in factors of production, not in the process of production. Thus they become costs of production according to the opportunity cost principle.

* We shall have an extended discussion of the concept of economic rent in Chapter 20.

Figure 14–10 A long-run supply curve under conditions of constant cost

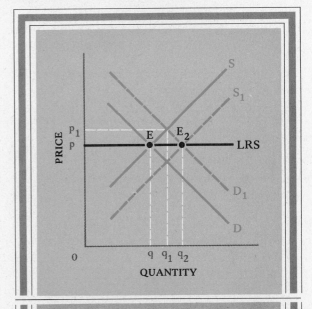

The long-run supply curve connects equilibrium points after the demand-induced shifts in the supply curve. The shift in demand from D to D_1 first raises the price to p_1 as industry output expands along the short-run supply curve. Firms will be earning profits and entry will thus occur. This induces a shift in the short-run supply curve from S to S_1. The long-run supply curve is LRS. In the case illustrated the increase in supply is just sufficient to keep the price at p. Thus output has been "at constant cost" in the long run.

large industry demands large quantities of certain key materials and certain kinds of skilled labor. As the industry grows larger and larger these become increasingly scarce. Thus growth of the steel industry increases the demand of steel producers for iron ore, for coking coal, and for blast furnace operators, none of which is in perfectly elastic supply. Increasing scarcity of these inputs will tend to raise their price, and this in turn will raise the cost of producing steel.

If costs rise with increasing levels of industry output, so too must the price at which the producers are willing to supply the market. The common sense of this result is that if firms were just covering their costs before the increase in demand, the price they receive will have to rise enough to cover any increases in factor prices they must pay.

To see more specifically why this result occurs, remember that an increase in the price of inputs will shift the marginal cost (and average cost) curves of all firms upward. This shift in the marginal cost curves of all firms shifts the industry short-run supply curve to the left.

The effect on supply of growth in industry output may be thought of for analytic purposes as occurring in two stages: an increase in the number of firms with no increase in

The economics of declining industries

At any moment in time some of an economy's industries will be expanding and some declining. Declining industries typically do not shut down completely; they continue to produce because their products are wanted by some consumers even though the total demand for their output is declining. Because demand is not sufficient to employ all of the industry's existing capital profitably, the industry must shrink in size.

Declining industries typically present a sorry sight to the observer. Revenues have fallen below long-run total costs, and as a result new equipment is not brought in to replace old equipment as it wears out. The average age of equipment in use thus rises steadily. The superficial observer seeing the industry's very real plight is likely to blame it on the antiquated equipment in use. The truth is that the antiquated equipment is the effect rather than the cause of the industry's decline. The economically correct response to a steadily declining demand is not to replace old equipment but to continue to operate with existing equipment as long as it can cover its variable costs of production. To modernize at high capital costs would make the plight worse because costs would rise in the face of declining demand and prices.

A striking example of the confusion of cause and effect in a declining industry occurred during the debate over the nationalization of the coal industry in Great Britain in the period between the two world wars.

The view that public control was needed to save an industry from the dead hand of third-rate, unenterprising private owners was commonly held about the British coal industry and was undoubtedly a factor leading to its nationalization in 1946. This view was held by the Commission which reported in 1926 on the state of the coal industry: "It would be possible to say without exaggeration of the miners' leaders that they were the stupidest men in England; if we had not had frequent occasion to meet the owners."

Sir Roy Harrod has taken the opposite view, arguing that the contrast between the rundown state of the coal industry in South Wales and Yorkshire and the advanced state of the pits in Nottinghamshire and Derbyshire represented the correct response of the owners to the signals of the market.

The mines of Derbyshire and Nottinghamshire were rich, and it was worth sinking capital in them. If similar amounts of capital were not sunk in other parts of the country, this . . . [was] because it was known that they were not worth these expenditures.

factor prices and an induced increase in factor prices. Figure 14–11 shows how these two stages lead to an upward-sloping *LRS* curve.

In reality the two stages occur simultaneously. In recent years the very rapid increase in the demand for electric power in the

Figure 14–11 A rising long-run supply curve

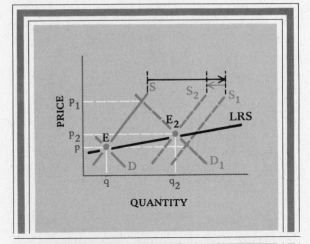

If growth in industry size increases factor prices, the *LRS* will be upward-sloping. Suppose an industry is in equilibrium at E. Then demand increases from D to D_1. In the short run price will rise to p_1. In the long run this increases the number of firms, thereby shifting the supply curve from S to S_1 (as shown by the black arrow). This is the supply curve that would pertain with expanded number of firms if input prices did not change. But the increase in industry production bids up the prices of factors used, thereby, shifting the supply curve leftward from S_1 to S_2 (as shown by the colored arrow). Equilibrium E_2 is at price p_2. Price has risen from p to p_2 because firms must recover the costs imposed by the higher input prices.

Economic efficiency does not consist in always introducing the most up-to-date equipment that an engineer can think of but rather in the correct adaptation of the amount of new capital sunk to the earning capacity of the old asset. In not introducing new equipment, the managements may have been wise, not only from the point of view of their own interest, but from that of national interest, which requires the most profitable application of available capital . . . it is right that as much should be extracted from the inferior mines as can be done by old-fashioned methods [i.e., with equipment already installed], and that they should gradually go out of action.*

The general point illustrated by this debate is extremely important: The "antiquated" methods used by a declining industry are the consequence and not the cause of decline. It is in the public and the private interest that these antiquated methods be employed in declining industries. Capital resources are scarce. To install new plant and equipment in a genuinely declining industry is to use the nation's scarce resources of new capital where they will not lead to the largest possible increases in the value of output.

* Roy Harrod, *The British Economy* (McGraw-Hill, 1963), page 54.

United States has led to a large increase in the number of electric generating plants. This in turn has led to sharp increases in the demand for inputs, and hence increases in their price. This development has been particularly marked with the prices of coal and oil, key fuels used in electricity generation. Indeed, one of the aspects of what is today called the "energy crisis" is that greatly increased demands for energy have bid up the prices of basic fuels. As one commentator said, "talk of the energy crisis is mood music for higher fuel prices." Higher fuel prices in turn will lead to higher prices of the things the fuel is used to make.

Rising *LRS*—**rising supply price** as it is sometimes called—is often a characteristic of sharp and rapid growth. A competitive industry with rising long-run supply prices is often called a **rising-cost industry.**

Can the long-run supply curve decline? So far we have suggested that the long-run supply curve may be constant or rising. Could it ever decline, thereby indicating that higher out-

puts were associated with lower prices in long-run equilibrium?

It is tempting to answer yes because of the opportunities of more efficient scales of operation using greater mechanization and more effective specialization of labor. But this answer would not be correct for perfectly competitive industries because each firm in long-run equilibrium must already be at the lowest point on its *LRATC* curve. If a firm could lower its costs by building a larger, more mechanized plant, it would be profitable to do so without waiting for an increase in demand. Since any single firm can sell all it wishes at the going market price, it will be profitable to expand the scale of its operations as long as its *LRATC* is falling.

There is a reason, however, why the long-run supply curve might slope downward: the expansion of an industry might lead to a fall in the prices of some of its inputs. If this occurs, the firms will find their cost curves shifting downward as they expand their outputs.

As an illustration of how the expansion of one industry could cause the prices of some of its inputs to fall, consider the early stages of the growth of the automobile industry. As the output of automobiles increased, the industry's demand for tires grew greatly. This, as suggested earlier, would have increased the demand for rubber and tended to raise its price, but it also provided the opportunity for Goodyear, Firestone, and other tire manufacturers to build large modern plants and reap the benefits of increasing returns in tire production. At first these economies were large enough to offset any factor price increases and tire prices charged to manufacturers of automobiles fell. Thus automobile costs fell because of lower prices of an important input.

To see the effect of a fall in input prices caused by the expansion of an industry, suppose that the demand for the industry's product increases. Price and profits will rise and new entry will occur as a result. But when expansion of the industry has gone far enough

Figure 14–12 A declining long-run supply curve

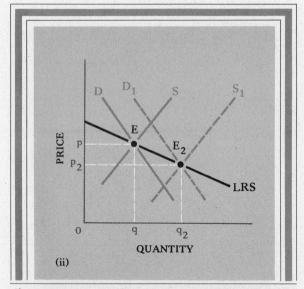

(ii)

If growth in industry size reduces factor prices, the LRS will be downward sloping. From an original equilibrium at E, an increase in demand to D_1 leads to an increase in supply to S_1 and a new equilibrium at E_2. Price p_2 is below the original price p because lower factor prices allow firms to cover their total costs at the lower price.

to bring price back to its initial level, cost curves will be lower than they were initially because of the fall in input prices. Firms will thus still be earning profits. A further expansion will then occur until price falls to the level of the minimum points on each firm's new, lower *LRATC* curve. (This case is illustrated in Figure 14–12.) An industry that has a declining long-run supply curve is often called a **falling-cost industry.**

The response of a perfectly competitive industry to a change in technology

Consider an industry in long-run equilibrium. Since the industry is in equilibrium, each firm must be in zero-profit equilibrium. Now assume that some technological development lowers the cost curves of newly built plants. Since price is just equal to the average total cost for the old plants, new plants will now be able to earn profits and they will be built immediately. But this expansion in capacity shifts the short-run supply curve to the right and drives price down. The expansion in capacity and the fall in price will continue until price is equal to the *ATC* of the *new* plants. At this price old plants will not be covering their long-run costs. As long as price exceeds their average variable cost, however, such plants will continue in production. As the outmoded plants wear out they will gradually disappear. Eventually a new long-run equilibrium will be established in which all plants use the new technology.

What happens in a competitive industry in which technological change occurs not as a single isolated event but more or less continuously? Plants built in any one year will tend to have lower costs than plants built in any previous year. Figure 14–13 illustrates such an industry. Real-world industries that are like this in having continual technological changes have a number of interesting characteristics.

One is that plants of different ages and different levels of efficiency will exist side by side. This characteristic is dramatically illustrated by the variety of vintages of steam turbine generators found in any long-established electric utility. Critics who observe the continued use of older, less efficient plants and urge that "something be done to eliminate these wasteful practices" miss the point of economic efficiency. If the plant is already there, the plant can be profitably operated as long as it can do anything more than cover its variable costs. As long as a plant can produce goods that are valued by consumers at an amount above the value of the resources currently used up for their production (variable costs), the value of society's total output is increased by producing these goods.

A second characteristic of such an industry is that price will be governed by the minimum *ATC* of the most efficient plants. Entry will continue until plants of the latest vintage are just expected to earn normal profits over their lifetimes. The benefits of the new technology are passed on to consumers because all units of the commodity, whether produced by new or old plants, are sold at a price that is related solely to the *ATC*s of the new plants. Owners of older plants find their returns over variable costs falling steadily as more and more efficient plants drive the price of the product down.

A third characteristic is that old plants will be discarded (or "mothballed") when the price falls below their *AVC*. This may occur well before the plants are physically worn out. In industries with continuous technical progress, capital is usually discarded because it is economically obsolete, not because it has physically worn out. This illustrates the economic meaning of obsolete: old capital is obsolete when its average variable cost exceeds the average total cost of new capital.

Does a long-run competitive equilibrium exist?

A necessary condition for a long-run competitive equilibrium to exist is that any economies of scale that are available to a firm should be exhausted at a level of output that is small relative to the whole industry's output.

Figure 14–13 Plants of different age in an industry with continuing technical progress

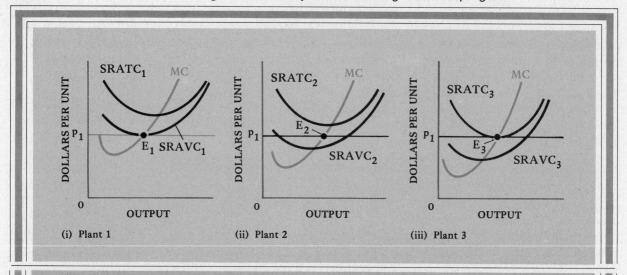

(i) Plant 1   (ii) Plant 2   (iii) Plant 3

Entry of progressively lower-cost firms forces price down but older plants with higher costs remain in the industry as long as price covers average variable cost. Plant 3 is the newest plant with the lowest costs. Price will be determined by the average total costs of plants of this type since entry will continue as long as the owners of the newest plants expect to earn profits from them. Plant 1 is the oldest plant in operation; it is just covering its *AVC* and if the price falls any further it will be closed down. Plant 2 is a plant of intermediate age. It is covering its variable costs and earning some return on its capital. The return will shrink over time as entry of new plants with lower and lower costs drives prices lower and lower.

We have seen that a competitive firm will never be in equilibrium on the falling part of its *LRATC*—if price is given and costs can be reduced by expanding scale, profits can also be increased by doing so. Thus firms will grow in size at least until all scale economies are exhausted. Provided the output that yields the minimum *LRATC* for each firm is small relative to the industry's total output, there will be a large number of firms in the industry and the industry will remain competitive. If, however, reaching the minimum *LRATC* makes firms so large that they have significant market power, they will cease to be price takers and perfect competition will cease to exist. Indeed if scale economies exist over such a large range that one firm's *LRATC* would still be falling if it served the entire market, a single firm may come to monopolize the market. This is what the classical economists called the case of *natural* monopoly; it is considered further in Chapter 18.

Only if the firm's *LRATC* curve is U-shaped will there be a determinate size of the firm in a competitive industry. To see why, assume instead that *LRATC* falls to a minimum at some level of output and then remains constant for all larger outputs. All firms would have to be at least the minimum size, but they could be just that size or much larger since price would equal *LRATC* for any output above the minimum efficient size. In other words, there would then be no unique size for the firm.

There are very good reasons why the *LRATC* curve for a single-plant firm may be expected to be U-shaped. There is a great deal in modern technology that results in lower average costs for large, automated factories compared with smaller factories in which a few workers use relatively unsophisticated capital equipment. As a single plant becomes too large, however, costs may rise because of the sheer difficulty of planning for, and controlling the behavior of, a vast integrated operation. Thus we have no problem accounting for a U-shaped cost curve for the *plant*.

What of the U-shaped cost curve for the *firm*? A declining portion will occur for the same reason that the *LRATC* for one plant declines when the firm is so small that it operates only one plant. Now, however, let the firm be operating one plant at the output where its *LRATC* is a minimum. (Call that output $q\star$.) What if the firm decides to double its output to $2q\star$? If it tries to build a vast plant with twice the output of the optimal size plant, the firm's average total cost of production may rise (because the vast plant has higher costs than a plant of the optimal size). But the firm has the option of *replicating* its first plant in a physically separate location. If the firm obtains a second parcel of land, builds an identical second plant, staffs it identically, and allows its production to be managed independently, there seems no reason why the second plant's minimum *LRATC* should be different from that of the first plant. *Because the firm can replicate plants and have them managed independently, there seems no reason why any firm faced with constant factor prices should not face constant LRATCs at least for multiples of the output for which one plant achieves the lowest plant LRATC.*

In the modern theory of perfect competition a U-shaped *firm* cost curve is merely *as-*

sumed. Without it—although a competitive equilibrium may exist for an arbitrary number of firms—there is nothing to determine the equilibrium size of the firm and hence the number of firms in the industry when price equals each firm's *LRATC* (and when therefore there is incentive for neither entry nor exit). The basic point is that for perfect competition to persist there must be something that stops firms, not just plants, from increasing in size indefinitely.

Summary

1. Competitive behavior is concerned with how individual firms compete against each other; competitive market structure is concerned with the degree of power that individual firms have to influence such market variables as the price of the product. Under perfect competition individual firms are powerless to influence market price. Therefore they do not have any incentive to indulge in competitive behavior against their fellow producers in the same industry.

2. A profit-maximizing firm will produce at an output where (a) price is at least as great as average variable cost, (b) marginal cost equals marginal revenue, and (c) the marginal cost curve cuts the marginal revenue curve from below.

3. The two critical assumptions of the theory of perfect competition are that firms are price takers and that the industry displays freedom of entry and exit. A firm that is a price taker will adjust to different market conditions by varying its output.

4. The perfectly competitive firm's short-run supply curve is the same shape as its MC curve above AVC. The perfectly competitive industry's short-run supply curve is the horizontal sum of its firms' supply curves (i.e., the horizontal sum of the firms' marginal cost curves).

5. When perfectly competitive firms are in short-run equilibrium they must, if they are producing at all, be covering their variable costs. But they may be making losses (price less than average total cost), making profits (price greater than average total cost), or just covering all costs (price equal to average total cost).

6. Because the long run concerns the time over which capital can enter or leave an industry, profits and losses are the key to long-run equilibrium. If existing firms are making losses, capital will leave; if they are making profits, new capital will enter. Only if they are just covering their full costs—no more and no less—can the industry be in long-run equilibrium.

7. In long-run equilibrium all firms are producing at the lowest point on their *LRATC* curves. This implies that profits cannot be increased by varying the output of the present plants, building more plants of the same size, or building plants with a different level of capacity.

8. A rise in demand in a competitive industry leads in the short run to a rise in price, output, and profits. In the long run it brings an entry of capital, a further increase in output, and the elimination of profits. A fall in demand leads in the short run to a reduction of price, output, and profits. In the long run it causes exit of capital, a further reduction in output, and elimination of losses.

9. The long-run supply curve of a competitive industry may be constant, upward sloping, or downward sloping, depending on whether factor costs remain constant, increase, or decrease as the industry expands.

Concepts for review

Competitive behavior and competitive market structure
Price taking and a horizontal demand curve
Behavioral rules for the profit-maximizing firm
Average revenue, marginal revenue, and price under perfect competition
Short-run and long-run equilibrium of firms and industries
Conditions for U-shaped cost curves for a plant and for a firm
The long-run industry supply curve

Discussion questions

1. Consider the suppliers of the following commodities. What are the elements of market structure that you might want to invoke to account for differences in their market behavior? Do you think any of these might be characterized as perfectly competitive industries?

a. television broadcasting
b. automobiles
c. sand and gravel
d. medical services
e. mortgage loans
f. retail fruits and vegetables
g. soybeans

Do you think any of these might be characterized as perfectly competitive industries?

2. Which of the following observed facts about an industry are inconsistent with its being a perfectly competitive industry?
a. Different firms use different methods of production.
b. There is extensive advertising of the industry's product by a trade association.
c. Individual firms devote 5 percent of sales receipts to advertising their own product brand.
d. There are 24 firms in the industry.
e. The largest firm in the industry makes 40 percent of the sales and the next largest firm sells 20 percent, but the products are identical and there are 61 other firms.
f. All firms made large profits in 1977.

3. In which of the following sectors of the American economy might you expect to find competitive behavior? In which might you expect to find industries that were classified as operating under perfectly competitive market structures?
a. manufacturing
b. agriculture
c. transportation and public utilities
d. wholesale and retail trade
e. criminal activity

4. In the 1930s the U.S. coal industry was characterized by easy entry and price taking. Because of large fixed costs in mine shafts and fixed equipment, however, exit was slow. With declining demand, many firms were barely covering their variable costs but not their total costs. As a result of a series of mine accidents, the federal government began to enforce mine-safety standards, which forced most firms to invest in new capital if they were to remain in production. What predictions would competitive theory make about market behavior and the quantity of coal produced? Would coal miners approve or disapprove of the new enforcement program?

5. Suppose entry into an industry is not artificially restricted but takes time because of the need to build plants, acquire know-how, and establish a marketing organization. Can such an industry be characterized as perfectly competitive? Does ease of entry imply ease of exit, and vice versa?

6. What, if anything, do each of the following tell you about ease of entry into an industry?
a. Profits have been very high for two decades.
b. No new firms have entered the industry for 20 years.
c. The average age of the firms in a 40-year-old industry is less than seven years.

7. In the early 1970s grain prices in the United States rose substantially. Explain how each of the following may have contributed to this result; then consider how a perfectly competitive grain industry might be expected to react in the long run.
a. Crop failures caused by bad weather around the world in 1971.
b. Rising demand for beef and chickens because of rising population and rising per capita income.

c. Great scarcities in fishmeal, a substitute for grain in animal diets, because of a mysterious decline in the anchovy harvest off Peru.
d. Increased Soviet purchases of grain from the United States.

8. As a result of the great grape boycott of the 1970s on behalf of striking agricultural workers, the demand for table grapes fell significantly. Assuming that grape growers are price takers, predict their response to this decline in demand in the short run. Under what conditions might it lead to an increase in price in the long run? Are there any conditions under which the boycott might lead to a decrease in the price of grapes in the long run?

15

Pricing in monopoly markets

Is AT&T a monopoly? How about IBM, U.S. Steel, the National Football League, and the Coca-Cola Company? Just as the word "competition" has both an everyday meaning and a somewhat more specialized technical one, so too does the word "monopoly." Monopoly, as economists use the concept, is a market structure that leads to certain predicted kinds of market behavior.

The word "monopoly" comes from the Greek words *monos polein,* which mean "alone to sell." It is convenient for the present discussion to think of **monopoly** as the situation in which the output of an entire industry is controlled by a single seller. This seller will be called the monopolist. Later in this chapter monopoly is defined in a less restrictive way.

A monopolist selling at a single price

Consider first an industry producing a single product in which a monopolist sets a price and supplies the entire quantity that buyers wish to purchase at that price. In contrast to the competitive firm, the monopolist is a price setter, not a price taker. The monopolist faces a downward-sloping demand curve and can pick any price-quantity combination on the demand curve.

THE MONOPOLIST'S REVENUE CURVES

Because the monopolistic firm is assumed to be the only producer of a particular product, its demand curve is identical with the demand curve for its product. The market demand curve, which shows the aggregate quantity that buyers will purchase at every price, also shows the quantity that the monopolist will be able to sell at any price that it sets. Given the market demand curve, the monopolist's average revenue and marginal revenue curves can be readily deduced.

Table 15–1 The relation of average revenue and marginal revenue: a numerical illustration

Price p = AR	Quantity q	TR = p · q	MR = ΔTR/Δq
$9.10	9	$81.90	
9.00	10	90.00	$8.10
8.90	11	97.90	7.90

Marginal revenue is less than price because price must be lowered to sell an extra unit. A monopolist can choose either the price or the quantity to be sold. But choosing one determines the other. To increase sales (in this example) from 10 to 11 units per period, it is necessary to reduce the price (on all units sold) from $9 to $8.90. The extra unit sold brings in $8.90, but the firm sacrifices 10¢ on each of the 10 units that it could have sold at $9 had it not wanted to increase sales. The net addition to revenue is the $8.90 minus 10¢ times 10 units, or $1, making $7.90 altogether. Thus the marginal revenue resulting from the increase in sales by 1 unit is $7.90, which is less than the price at which the units are sold.

Marginal revenue is shown displaced by half a line to emphasize that it represents the effect on revenue of the *change* in output.

When the seller charges a single price for all units sold, average revenue per unit is identical with price. Thus the market demand curve is also the average revenue curve for the monopolist. But marginal revenue is less than price because the monopolist has to lower the price that it charges on *all* units in order to sell an *extra* unit (Figure 15–1). This is an important difference from the case of perfect competition; it is explored numerically in Table 15–1 [17].

Figure 15–2 illustrates the average and marginal revenue curves for a monopolist, based on a downward-sloping straight-line demand curve.[1]

[1] It is helpful (for sketching revenue curves, etc.) to remember that if the demand curve is a downward-sloping straight line, the *MR* curve also slopes downward and is twice as steep. Its price intercept (where $q = 0$) is the same as that of the demand curve, and it cuts the quantity axis (where $p = 0$) at just half the output that the demand curve does. [18]

Marginal revenue, total revenue, and elasticity of demand

A demand curve represents a single relationship between quantity and price, but there are many different ways of looking at it.

Figure 15–3 shows how total revenue and elasticity of demand (η) are related to *AR* and *MR*. The changes in revenue are uniquely related to elasticity of demand. Consider first the part of the demand curve where elasticity is greater than unity. This means that total

Figure 15–1 The effect on revenue of an increase in quantity sold

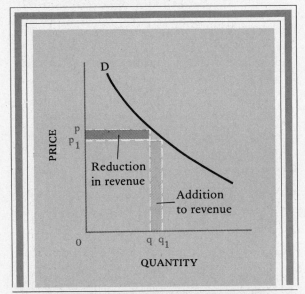

For a downward-sloping demand curve, marginal revenue is less than price. A reduction of price from p to p_1 increases sales by 1 unit from q to q_1 units. The revenue from the extra unit sold (i.e., its price) is shown as the lighter shaded area. But to sell this unit, it is necessary to reduce the price on each of the q units previously sold. This loss in revenue is shown as the darker shaded area. Marginal revenue of the extra unit is equal to the *difference* between these two areas.

revenue rises as quantity increases, and hence the total revenue curve is upward-sloping. Because total revenue is increasing as quantity is increasing, marginal revenue must be positive. Consider next the point at which elasticity of demand is exactly unity. Here total revenue remains constant as quantity sold increases. This implies that marginal revenue is zero. Consider finally the part of the demand curve where elasticity is less than unity. This means that total revenue falls as quantity increases, and hence the total revenue curve is now downward-sloping. This implies that marginal revenue is negative. Marginal revenue thus goes from positive to negative as the demand curve goes from elastic to inelastic,

Figure 15–2 Demand, average revenue, and marginal revenue curves for a monopolist

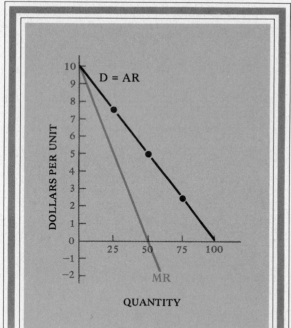

For the monopolist, *MR* does not equal price. The demand curve is the *AR* curve; the *MR* curve is below and steeper than the *AR* because the demand curve slopes downward.

Figure 15–3 The relation of total, average, and marginal revenue to elasticity of demand.

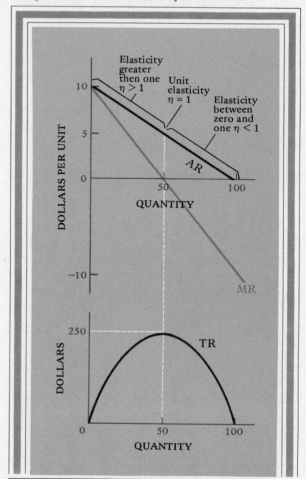

When *TR* is rising, *MR* is greater than zero and elasticity is greater than unity. In this example, for outputs from 0 to 50, marginal revenue is positive and elasticity is greater than unity and total revenue is rising. For outputs from 50 to 100, marginal revenue is negative and elasticity is less than unity and total revenue is falling.

or (what is the same thing) as the total revenue curve stops rising, reaches its maximum, and begins to fall. (The relation between elasticity and total revenue was discussed in more detail in Chapter 6.)

This relationship has an immediate but important implication. Since marginal cost is greater than zero, the profit-maximizing monopoly (which produces where MR equals MC) will produce where MR is positive, that is, where demand is elastic.

A profit-maximizing monopolist will never push its sales of commodity into the range over which the commodity's demand curve becomes inelastic.

The common sense of this is that if demand is inelastic, marginal revenue is negative. Thus the monopolist can both increase its revenue and reduce cost by reducing its sales.

PROFIT MAXIMIZATION IN A MONOPOLIZED MARKET

To describe the profit-maximizing position of a monopolist, we need only bring together information about the monopolist's revenues and its costs and apply the rules developed in Chapter 14.

The monopolist produces an output such that marginal revenue equals marginal cost, and charges whatever price its demand curve shows is necessary to sell that output. Because price is greater than marginal revenue, it is greater than marginal cost, which is in contrast to the situation in perfect competition. Moreover, in equilibrium the monopolist may be earning profits because entry of new firms does not push price down to the level of average total cost. Figure 15–4 illustrates the equilibrium of a monopolist. The conditions for

Figure 15–4 The profit maximizing position of a monopolist

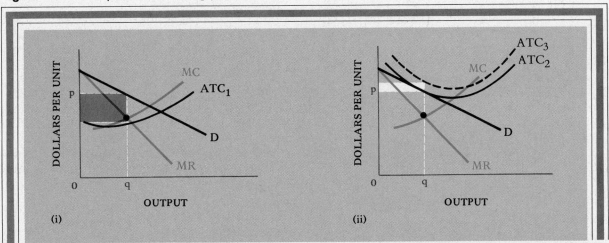

Profit maximizing output is q, where $MR = MC$; price is above MC. The rules for profit maximization require $MR = MC$ and $p > AVC$. (AVC is not shown in the diagram, but would be below ATC). This happens at output q. Whether there are profits or not depends upon the position of the ATC curve. In (i) where average total cost is ATC_1 there are profits, as shown by the shaded area. In (ii) where average total cost is ATC_2, profits are zero. If average total costs rose to ATC_3, the monopolist would suffer losses, as shown by the white area in (ii).

Figure 15–5 The range of profitable outputs open to the monopolist

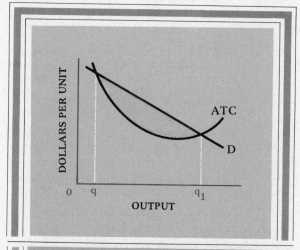

There may well be a range of outputs over which a monopolist earns some profits. In this example the output that maximizes profits for the firm is a specific point between q and q_1 (where $MR = MC$), but at any level of output between q and q_1 the firm earns some profit.

profit maximization are each met: Marginal cost equals marginal revenue, and price is greater than average variable cost. (Average variable cost is not shown in the diagram, but we assume it is far enough below ATC so that even for ATC_3 it is below p at output q.) The amount of profit or loss is represented by the shaded rectangle in 15–4(i) and by the white rectangle in 15–14(ii).

Two common misconceptions about monopoly profits should be avoided. First, nothing guarantees that a monopolist will make profits. If the ATC curve is shifted upward from the level in Figure 15–4(i), but all other curves are left unchanged, profits shrink as the curve moves up. When the ATC curve gets so high that it just touches the demand curve, as does ATC_2 in Figure 15–4(ii), the monopolist does better at that output than at other levels of output. The second common misconception about monopoly profits is that a monopolist who is not maximizing profits must be making losses. Figure 15–5 shows that this is not the case. The monopolistic firm can, if it chooses, not maximize profits and still earn some profits—a point of some importance to which we will return in Chapter 19.

A monopolist's supply curve? Notice that in describing the monopolist's profit-maximizing behavior we do not introduce the concept of a supply curve, as we did in the discussion of perfect competition.

A supply curve relates the quantity supplied to the price offered. In perfect competition, the industry short-run supply curve is known as soon as the marginal cost curves of the individual firms are known. This is because the profit-maximizing firms equate marginal cost to price. Given marginal costs, it is possible to know how much will be produced at each price.

In monopoly a unique relation between market price and quantity supplied does not exist.

Like all profit-maximizing firms, a monopolistic firm equates marginal cost to marginal revenue; but, unlike firms in perfect competition, for the monopolist marginal revenue does not equal price. Because the monopolist does *not* equate marginal cost to price, it is possible for different demand conditions to give rise to the same output but to differing prices.[2]

EQUILIBRIUM OF THE FIRM AND INDUSTRY

If a monopolist is the only producer in an industry, there is no need to have a separate

---

[2] In order to know the amount produced at any given price, it is necessary to know something about the shape and position of the marginal revenue curve in addition to knowing the marginal cost curve. This means that there is not a supply curve independent of the demand curve for the monopolist's product.

theory of the firm and the industry, as is necessary with perfect competition. The monopolist *is* the industry. Thus the profit-maximizing position of the firm illustrated in Figure 15–4 is the short-run equilibrium of the industry.

In a monopolized industry, as in a perfectly competitive one, profits provide an incentive for new firms to enter the industry. If such entry occurs, the equilibrium position will change and the firm will no longer be a monopolist. **Barriers to entry** are impediments to the entry of new firms into an industry.

If monopoly is to persist in the long run, there must be barriers to the entry of other firms into an industry.

Barriers may come about in a variety of ways. Patent laws, for instance, may create and perpetuate monopolies by conferring on the patent holder the sole right to produce a particular commodity. A firm may be granted a charter or a franchise that prohibits competition by law. Monopolies may also arise because of economies of scale. The established firm that is able to produce at a lower cost than any new, small competitor may well be able to retain a monopoly through a cost advantage.

A monopoly may also be perpetuated by force or by threat. Potential competitors can be intimidated by threats ranging from sabotage to a price war in which the established monopoly has sufficient financial resources to ensure victory.

It is the barriers to entry in one form or another that allow the profits of a monopolist to persist over time. In perfect competition, a short-run equilibrium in which firms earn profits cannot last because entry occurs and forces prices down to the level of cost. Because there need be no entry, the short-run profitable equilibrium of a monopolist can continue indefinitely.

The nature and extent of monopoly power

The *theory* of monopoly just developed assumes that the monopolist has no expectation whatever of any competition. Thus the monopolist's only problem is to select the price-quantity combination that maximizes its profits. The price selected by the monopolist becomes the industry's price, and its output is the industry's output. In other words, the firm's demand curve is the industry demand curve; no other seller, present or potential, threatens its position as sole supplier.

It is difficult to imagine a firm without any competition whatsoever. A firm may have a complete monopoly on a particular *product* at a given moment in time, but every product has some present or potential substitutes for the *services* it provides. Some products have fairly close substitutes, and even a single seller producing such a product will have close rivals for customers' expenditure. Other products may have no close substitute now, but new products may be developed that will compete with it. For these reasons it is useful to recognize monopoly power as a variable that can be relatively slight or nearly complete, rather than as an attribute which either exists or does not exist.

Monopoly power exists to the extent that a firm is insulated from loss of customers to other sellers.

How is the extent of monopoly power to be defined? The mere fact that a firm's demand curve slopes downward means that if the firm raises its price, it will lose some sales. But there may be limits on the firm's power over price other than the slope of the market demand curve. Any producer facing a downward-sloping demand curve could choose the price-quantity combination (where $MR = MC$) that appears to maximize its profits. *But this price might not turn out to be the long-run profit-maximizing price* because the choice of a particular price-quantity combination may itself lead to changes in the behavior of other firms that in turn *shift* the original firm's demand curve. If, for example, a firm raises its price and as a result its demand curve shifts to the left, its sales and its profits will be less than the firm would have expected on the basis of the original demand curve.

Consider an example. The Coca-Cola Company is the sole producer of Coca-Cola and faces a downward-sloping demand curve. But the Coca-Cola Company is not a complete monopolist. To see why, suppose that the demand curve for its product shows that if the price of Coca-Cola is cut by 20 percent *and if* all other soft drink suppliers keep their prices at their present levels, sales of Coke will increase by 50 percent. This would almost surely result in an increase in the company's profits. Since the Coca-Cola Company is unquestionably free to cut its price by 20 percent, why does it not do so? The answer is that if it did, other prices would not remain unchanged—and the company knows it. Its very action of reducing prices would almost surely cause sellers of other soft drinks to reduce *their* prices. If they did, Coca-Cola's sales would not increase as much as its *ceteris paribus* demand curve predicts. Sales would not increase by 50 percent; instead they might increase by (say) only 10 percent. In such an event the company's profits would decrease rather than increase. Thus the Coca-Cola Company, though having a monopoly of Coca-Cola sales, does not have a monopoly of soft drink sales, although it may well have some market power.

The larger are the *shifts* in a firm's demand curve that are induced by its own price changes, the less is its monopoly power. Such shifts have two main sources. The first (illustrated in the Coca-Cola example) is the reactions of sellers of those other products that substitute to some extent for the product of the seller. The second is the entry of new sellers who succeed in capturing part of the sales

that the seller included in "its" demand curve. Such shifts in the demand curve, from either cause, limit the market power of the firm and reduce its profits.

Since no firm is perfectly insulated from all other products or for all time, total monopoly power does not exist. But the extent of shifts in a seller's demand curve due to other producers' actions is a *quantitative* variable. In some cases, such shifts may be very minor; in others, they may be very large.

It is well to note at this point that a single seller is neither sufficient for, nor necessary to maximum monopoly power. The Coca-Cola example demonstrated that it is not sufficient. It is not necessary because two sellers (who are not faced by the threat of entry) could agree between themselves to set a common price and/or to share the market and act in exactly the same way as if they were a single-firm monopoly. Such behavior is known as **collusion.**

MEASURING MONOPOLY POWER

It is important to measure the extent of monopoly power in various markets for two major reasons. First, to use the theory that predicts that behavior in monopolistic markets will differ from behavior in perfectly competitive markets, one must be able to approximate the extent of monopoly power in various markets. Second, because it is a matter of public policy that uncontrolled monopoly power is undesirable, government agencies such as the Department of Justice and the Federal Trade Commission that are to enforce those policies must know where monopoly power exists if they are to control or eliminate it.

Measuring monopoly power is not easy. Ideally, one would like to compare the prices, outputs, and profits of firms in any industry with what prices, outputs, and profits would be if all firms were under unified (monopoly) control and were fully insulated from entry. But this hypothetical comparison does not lend itself to measurement.

Concentration ratios

In practice, two alternative measures are widely used. The first of these is the **concentration ratio,** which shows the fraction of total market sales controlled by the largest group of sellers. Common types of concentration ratios cite the share of total industry sales of the largest four or eight firms. How well concentration ratios measure effective monopoly power is a matter of some debate among economists. Clearly, market share is one measure of the *potential* power to control supply and set price.

The inclusion in concentration ratios of the market shares of several firms rests upon the possibility that large firms will collude and adopt a common price-output policy that is no different from the one they would adopt if they were in fact under unified management. Such common behavior may occur even without an actual agreement to collude. Lawyers speak of **conscious parallel action** and economists of **tacit collusion** to refer to such behavior. Concentration ratios measure the *actual* exercise of monopoly power only if overt or tacit collusion occurs. High concentration ratios may be necessary for the exercise of monopoly power, but they are not sufficient. It is, nevertheless, interesting to know where the *potential* for monopoly power does exist.

Profits as a measure of monopoly power

Many economists, following the lead of Professor Joe S. Bain, use profit rates as a measure of monopoly power. By "high" profits, the economist means returns sufficiently in excess of all opportunity costs that potential new entrants desire to enter the industry. If profits are and remain high, so goes the logic of this measure, it is indirect evidence that

neither rivalry among sellers nor entry of new firms prevents existing firms from pricing as if they were monopolists.

Using profits in this way requires care because, as we have seen (page 161), profits as reported in firms' income statements are not pure profits over opportunity cost. In particular, allowance must be made for differences in risk and in required payments for the use of the owners' capital.

While neither concentration ratios nor profit rates are ideal measures of the degree of market power that a firm, or group of firms, actually exercises, both are of some value and both are widely used. In fact, concentration ratios and high profit rates are themselves correlated. Because of this, alternative classifications of industries, according to their degree of monopoly power measured in these two ways, do not differ from one another very much. In spite of the difficult problems of measuring monopoly power, the theory of monopoly is widely used by both economists and policy makers.

Price discrimination

Raw milk is often sold at one price if it is to go into fluid milk, but at a lower price if it is to be used to make ice cream or cheese. Doctors usually charge rates for their services that vary according to the incomes of their clients. Movie theaters charge lower admission prices for children than for adults. Railroads charge different rates per ton mile for different kinds of products. Electric companies sell electricity more cheaply for industrial use than for home use. State universities charge out-of-state students higher tuition than residents.

Such price differences could never persist under perfect competition. Yet many of the examples we have cited have existed for decades. Persistent price differences clearly require the exercise of some monopoly power because the seller is exerting some influence over the price at which its product is sold. Why should a firm want to sell some units of output at a price well below the price that it gets for other units? Why, in other words, does it practice price discrimination?

Price discrimination occurs when a producer sells a specific commodity to different buyers at two or more different prices, for reasons not associated with differences in cost. Not all price differences represent price discrimination. Quantity discounts, differences between wholesale and retail prices, and prices that vary with the time of day or the season of the year are not generally considered price discrimination because the same physical product sold at a different time or place or in different quantities may have very different costs. If an electric power company has unused capacity at certain hours of the day, it may be cheaper to provide service at those hours than at peak demand hours. If the price differences reflect cost differences, they are nondiscriminatory. If, however, price differences rest merely on different buyers' valuations of the same product, they are discriminatory. It does not cost a movie theater operator less to fill a seat with a child than an adult, but it may pay to let the children in at a discriminatory low price if few of them would attend at the full adult fare.

WHY PRICE DISCRIMINATION PAYS

Persistent price discrimination occurs either because different buyers may be willing to pay different amounts for the same commodity or because one buyer may be willing to pay different amounts for different units of the same commodity.

Consider differences among buyers. Think of the demand curve for a market containing individual buyers, each of whom has indicated the price he or she is prepared to pay for a single unit. Suppose a single price is charged. Each unit sold is one for which

buyers were willing to pay *at least* the price indicated. If the seller can make every buyer pay the maximum he or she is willing to pay, the seller can increase its profits by capturing the amounts in excess of the single price that buyers were willing to pay.[3]

Another way of seeing the same point is to review the effect on revenue of increasing sales by one unit. Using a single price, it was necessary, as shown in Figure 15–1, to reduce price in order to increase the quantity sold by one unit. The reduction in price applies to all units sold, the first q units as well as the new unit. This reduction was not necessary to sell *them* (since they were already being sold at the higher price). If the firm had been able to sell the last unit at the lower price without reducing the price on the first q units (if, in other words, the firm had been able to discriminate), it would have profited thereby.

WHEN IS PRICE DISCRIMINATION POSSIBLE?

However much the local butcher would like to charge the banker's wife twice as much for hamburger as he charges the taxi driver, he cannot succeed in doing so. Madame Banker can always shop for her meat in the supermarket, where her husband's occupation is not known. Even if the butcher and the supermarket agreed to charge her twice as much, she could hire the taxi driver to do her shopping for her. The surgeon, however, may succeed in discriminating (if all reputable surgeons will do the same) because it will not do the banker's wife much good to hire the taxi driver to have her operations for her.

To succeed in price discrimination a seller must be able to control the supply of the product (in the sense of controlling what is offered to a particular buyer) and must be able to prevent the resale of the commodity from one buyer to another.

[3] These amounts are often referred to as "consumers' surplus." The discriminating monopolist extracts some of this consumers' surplus.

The first of the two conditions—control over supply—is the feature that makes price discrimination an aspect of the theory of monopoly. Monopoly power in some form is necessary to (but not sufficient for) price discrimination.

The second of the two conditions—ability to prevent resale—tends to be associated with the character of the product or the ability to classify buyers into readily identifiable groups. Services are less easily resold than goods; goods that require installation by the manufacturer (e.g., heavy equipment) are less easily resold than are movable goods (such as household appliances). An interesting example of nonresalability occurs in the case of plate glass. Small pieces sell much more cheaply per square foot than bigger pieces, but the person who needs glass for a $6' \times 10'$ picture window cannot use four pieces of glass, each of which is $3' \times 5'$.

Transportation costs, tariff barriers, and import quotas serve to separate classes of buyers geographically and may make discrimination possible. Price discrimination will thus be possible where the supplier(s) can control the amount and distribution of supply and where the buyers can be separated into classes among which resale is either impossible or very costly.

The examples just discussed relate directly to discrimination among classes of buyers. Discrimination among units of output follows similar rules. Thus the tenth unit purchased by a given buyer in a given month can be sold at a different price than the fifth unit only if the seller can keep track of who buys what. This can be done by the seller of electricity through meter readings or by the magazine publisher, who can distinguish between renewals and new subscriptions. The operator of a car wash and the manufacturer of aspirin find it more difficult, although by such devices as coupons and "one-cent" sales, they too can determine which unit is being purchased.

It is, of course, not enough to be able to separate buyers or units into separate classes. For price discrimination to be profitable, the different groups must have different degrees of willingness to pay. The hypothesis of diminishing marginal utility (see page 110) would lead to the prediction that different valuations are placed by an individual on different units, and differences in income and in tastes would lead to the prediction that different subgroups will have different elasticities of demand for a given commodity. Thus the potential for profitable price discrimination is often present. [19]

THE POSITIVE EFFECTS OF PRICE DISCRIMINATION

The positive consequences of price discrimination are summarized in two propositions.

1. For any given level of output the best system of discriminatory prices will provide higher total revenue to the firm (and thus also higher average revenue) than the best single price.

To see that this is reasonable, remember that a monopolist with the power to discriminate *could* produce exactly the same quantity as a single-price monopolist and charge everyone the same price. Therefore it need never get *less* revenue, but it can do better if it can raise the price on even one unit sold.

2. Output under monopolistic discrimination will generally be larger than under single-price monopoly.

To see that this is reasonable, remember that a single-price monopolist stops selling at an output where price is greater than *MC*. Suppose now the monopolist is able to sell additional units without reducing the price on units already salable. Since price is greater than *MC* on some units not yet sold, it will be profitable to lower the price a bit and sell some additional units. Thus if a firm can price its product unit by unit, it will pay it to produce more than if it is limited to a single price.

The common sense of this is that a monopolistic firm which must charge a single price produces less than the perfectly competitive industry because it is aware that by producing and selling more it drives down the price against itself. Price discrimination allows it to avoid this disincentive. To the extent that it can sell its output in separate blocks, it can sell another block without spoiling the market for the block already being sold. In the case of *perfect* price discrimination, where every unit of output is sold at a different price, the profit-maximizing firm will produce every unit for which the price charged will be greater than or equal to its marginal cost. It will, therefore, produce the same output as the firm in perfect competition. In each case, the price of the last unit sold will equal the marginal cost.

THE NORMATIVE ASPECTS OF PRICE DISCRIMINATION

The predicted combination of higher average revenue and higher output does not in itself have any *normative* significance. We cannot say that price discrimination is per se better or worse than any other scheme of pricing. It will often lead to a different distribution of output and typically lead to a different distribution of income. The particular patterns will depend on many facts, including ones we have introduced. Having specified the differences, people can debate their desirability. Economic analysis can describe the consequences of price discrimination, but it cannot finally evaluate them.

This remark may not satisfy the student who is aware that price discrimination has a bad reputation among economists and lawyers as well as among laymen. The very word "discrimination" has odious connotations. But was discrimination by airlines in giving students lower standby fares really bad? Whether an individual judges price discrimination as "evil" depends on the details of the case as well as on personal value judgments.

PRICE DISCRIMINATION: SYSTEMATIC AND UNSYSTEMATIC

The foregoing discussion has been concerned with systematic and persistent price discrimination. Systematic price discrimination most

Is price discrimination bad?

The consequences of price discrimination can differ in many ways from case to case, and no matter what any one individual's values are, he or she is almost bound to evaluate individual cases differently.

Secret rebates. A very large oil-refining firm agrees to ship its product to a market on a given railroad provided that the railroad gives the company a secret rebate on the transportation cost and does not give a similar concession to rival refiners. The railroad agrees and is thereby charging discriminatory prices. This rebate gives the large oil company a cost advantage that it uses to drive its rivals out of business or to force them into a merger on dictated terms. (John D. Rockefeller was accused of using such tactics in the early years of the Standard Oil Company.)

Use of product. When the Aluminum Company of America had a virtual monopoly on the production of aluminum ingots, it sold both the raw ingots and aluminum cable made from the ingots. At one time ALCOA sold cable at a price 20 percent *below* the price it charged for ingots. (Of course, the cable price was above ALCOA's cost of producing cable.) It did so because users of cable could substitute copper cable, but many users of ingot had no substitute for aluminum. In return for its "bargain

often consists of classifying buyers according to their age, location, industry, income, or the use they intend to make of the product, and in charging different prices for the different "classes" of buyers. It may also take other forms, such as charging an individual more

for the first unit bought than for subsequent units, or vice versa.

Another sort of price discrimination is frequently found. Any firm that occasionally gives a favorite customer a few cents off, or shaves its price to land a new account, is also

price" for cable, ALCOA made the purchasers of cable agree to use it only for transmission purposes. (Without such an agreement, any demander of aluminum might have bought cable and melted it down.)

Covering costs. A product that many people want to purchase has a demand and cost structure such that there is no single price at which a producing firm can cover total costs. However, if the firm is allowed to charge discriminatory prices, it will be willing to produce the product and it may make a profit. This is illustrated in the figure.

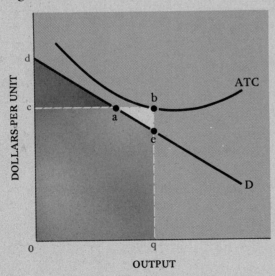

Because *ATC* is everywhere higher than the demand curve, no single price would lead to revenues equal to costs. A price-discriminating monopolist may be able to cover cost. The total cost of output q is the area $Ocbq$. The maximum revenue attainable at any output by perfect discrimination is the area under the demand curve. For output q that area, shown as shaded, exceeds total cost since the dark shaded triangle cda is greater than the white triangle abe.

Equitable fares. British Railways is not allowed to discriminate between passengers in different regions. To prevent discrimination, a fixed fare per passenger mile has been specified and must be charged on all lines, whatever their passenger traffic and whatever the elasticity of demand for the services of the particular line. In the interests of economy, branch lines that cannot cover costs are often closed down. This means that some lines close even though their users would prefer rail transport to any of the available alternatives and even though the strength of their preference is such that they would voluntarily pay a price sufficient for the line to yield a profit. Nonetheless, the lines are closed because it is thought inequitable to discriminate against the passengers of these lines.

engaged in price discrimination. If these practices are used irregularly, they are called unsystematic discrimination. Such discrimination is not really part of the price structure, and we have ignored it in this chapter. This does not mean that it is unimportant; on the contrary, unsystematic price discrimination plays a very real role in the dynamic process by which prices change in response to changed conditions of supply and demand.

The causes and consequences of systematic and unsystematic price discrimination are very different.

Legislation is, however, generally unable to distinguish between the two kinds of price discrimination and so hits at both. If legislation is motivated solely by a desire to attack systematic discrimination, it may have unforeseen and possibly undesired effects on unsystematic discrimination. If unsystematic price discrimination is important for the working of competition, prohibiting it may aid the maintenance of monopoly power.

Summary

1. The analysis of monopoly is begun with two simplifying assumptions: first, that an entire industry is supplied by a single seller, who is called a monopolist; second, that the monopolist sets a single price and supplies the entire quantity that buyers wish to purchase at that price.

2. Under these circumstances, the monopolist's *own demand curve* is identical with the *market demand curve* for the product. The market demand curve is the monopolist's average revenue curve. The marginal revenue resulting from the sale of another unit by a monopolist will always be less than the price obtained for that unit.

3. When the monopolist is maximizing profits (i.e., producing where $MR = MC$), marginal revenue will be positive, and thus elasticity of demand will be greater than unity. The amount of profits that a monopolist earns is not predicted by the theory. The amount may be large, small, zero, or negative in the short run depending upon the relation of demand and cost.

4. The presence of profits in a monopolized industry provides that same incentive to entry as it does in perfect competition. Therefore, for monopoly profits to persist in the long run, there must be effective barriers to entry. Such barriers include patent laws, charters, grants or franchises, economies of scale, and coercive tactics.

5. Every monopolist will find that some substitutes exist for its product. Monopoly power exists when a firm is to some extent insulated from loss of customers to other sellers; the degree of monopoly power may best be thought of as a quantitative variable. Monopoly power is limited both by the presence of existing substitute products and by the development of new products.

6. Two of the most widely used measures of the degree of monopoly power are the concentration ratio, which shows the fraction of the sales of an industry controlled by a group of the largest sellers, and the comparison of profits in one industry with those earned in other industries of similar risk and invested capital. In spite of some difficult measurement problems, monopoly power is usefully measured by either of these methods, which are themselves highly intercorrelated.

7. Price discrimination occurs when different units of the same commodity are sold for different prices, for reasons not associated with differences in costs. Different buyers may be charged different prices, or the same buyer may be charged different prices on different units of the commodity purchased.

8. The conditions under which a seller can succeed in charging discriminatory prices are, first, that it can control the supply of the product offered to particular buyers and, second, that it can prevent the resale of the commodity from one buyer to another.

9. Commodities that are highly susceptible to price discrimination include services, equipment requiring installation by the manufacturer, and commodities whose buyers can be isolated geographically by transport costs or international trade barriers.

10. Two predictions about price discrimination are (a) for any given level of output the best system of discriminatory prices will provide higher total revenue to the firm than the best single price, and (b) output will usually be larger than under a single-price monopoly.

11. The consequences of price discrimination can differ from case to case. Any individual is almost certain to evaluate individual cases differently, whatever his or her per-

sonal set of values. Further, there may be important differences in the effects of systematic and unsystematic price discrimination.

Concepts for review

The relationship of price and *MR* for a monopolist
The relationships among *MR*, *TR*, and elasticity
Measures of monopoly power
Price discrimination
Conditions that make price discrimination both possible
and profitable

Discussion questions

1. Imagine a monopoly firm with fixed costs but no variable or marginal costs—for example, a firm owning a spring of water that produces indefinitely, once certain pipes are installed, in an area where no other source of water is available. What would be the firm's profit-maximizing price? What elasticity of demand would you expect at that price? Would this seem to be an appropriate pricing policy if the water monopoly were municipally owned? Suppose now that entry becomes easy because of the discovery of many additional springs. What price behavior would you expect to occur? What price equilibrium would be predicted?

2. Suppose that only one professor teaches economics at your school. Would you say that this professor is a monopolist who can exact any "price" from students in the form of readings assigned, tests given, and material covered? Suppose that two additional professors are hired; has whatever monopoly power that existed been decreased?

3. Each of the following firms has some "monopoly power": Xerox Corporation, Pepsi-Cola Company, Mobil Oil, Eastern Airlines. In each case, what do you think is the basis of the monopoly power? Can you think of other bases of monopoly power not represented in this list? Give an example of each. How might you decide which of the companies above has the greatest degree of monopoly power?

4. Which of these industries—licorice candy, copper wire, outboard motors, coal, local newspapers—would you most like to monopolize? Why? Does your answer depend on several factors or just one or two? Which would you as a consumer least like to have monopolized by someone else? If your answers are different in the two cases, explain why.

5. A movie exhibitor, Aristotle Murphy, owns movie theaters in two Indiana towns of roughly the same size, 50 miles apart. In Monopolia he owns the only chain of theaters; in Competitia there is no theater chain, and he is but one of a number of independent operators. Would you expect movie prices to be higher in Monopolia than in Competitia in the short run? In the long run? If differences occurred in prices, would Mr. Murphy be discriminating in price?

6. Airline rates to Europe are higher in summer than in winter. Canadian railroads charge lower fares during the week than on weekends. Electricity companies charge consumers lower rates, the more electricity they use. Are these all examples of price discrimination? What additional information would you like to have before answering?

7. Discuss how sure you are that each of the following represents price discrimination. Which are (in your view) the most socially harmful?

a. standby fares on airlines that are a fraction of the full fare cost

b. standby fares, as above, but available only to bona fide students under 22 years of age

c. first class fares that are 50 percent greater than tourist fares, recognizing that two first class seats use the space of three tourist seats

d. negotiated discounts from the list price, where sales personnel are authorized to bargain hard and get as much in each transaction as the traffic will bear

e. higher tuition for out-of-state students at state-supported colleges and universities

f. higher tuition for law students than for history students

16

Industrial organization and theories of imperfect competition

Texaco, Shell, and Mobil are three of the "major" oil companies. They are not, singly or collectively, monopolists nor are they firms in perfect competition. Yet they are typical of many real firms in our economy. Similar comments apply to the Coca-Cola and Pepsi-Cola companies. Do the two basic theories of pricing behavior we have studied—perfect competition and monopoly—have any relevance to their behavior? The essential features of perfect competition are price taking and free entry; the essential features of monopoly are blockaded entry and a demand curve that is substantially the same for the firm and for the industry. Do the theories of perfect competition and monopoly provide a sufficient basis for predictions about price and market behavior in the real economy? Forty years ago most economists would have said yes; today most would say no, although the matter is still subject to debate.

This chapter first looks at some statistics to see how well the assumptions about monopoly and competition *describe* the American economy. This is not the whole of the matter, for it is the method of science to abstract from the full complexity of reality, and it might well be that descriptively unrealistic models were analytically adequate to make predictions that were confirmed by observations. If this were true, one would be able to predict the behavior of all American industries by classifying each as competitive or monopolistic *for purposes of predicting responses*. Many economists believe that although the models of monopoly and perfect competition are clearly useful there is a need for other models as well. This chapter suggests some of them.

Structure of the American economy

It is relatively easy to divide American industries into two broad groups—those with a large number of relatively small firms and those with a few relatively large firms.

Sectors with many small firms

Between 40 and 50 percent of the economy's national product comes from sectors of the economy that are predominantly characterized by a large number of small firms. This includes most agricultural production, most services (travel agents, lawyers, plumbers, television technicians), most retail trade (stores, gas stations), most wholesale trade, most construction, and industries whose major business is exchange (real estate agents, stockbrokers). At first glance each of these might seem to fall within the framework of a competitive model.

The competitive model does quite well in describing some industries whose major business is exchange rather than production. The New York Stock Exchange is a notable example, and commodity exchanges are similar. But other applications are less easily made. Agriculture seems to fit fairly well in most ways. The individual farmer is clearly a price taker, entry into farming is easy, and exit is possible though not in fact very rapid. But agricultural prices in the United States are not left to the workings of the competitive market alone; they are heavily influenced by government policies. In the retail trades and services, most firms think they have some influence over prices; the local grocery (or supermarket or discount house or department store) not only considers weekend specials (or sales) crucial to business success but also spends a good deal of money advertising them. In wholesaling, the sales representative is regarded as a key figure—which would not be true if the firm were a mere quantity adjuster.

Thus, all in all, the competitive model does not *describe* very much of the American economy. Whether it explains more behavior than it describes will be discussed later.

Industries characterized by a few large firms

About 50 percent of the national product is produced in sectors of the economy consisting of industries dominated by a few very large firms. The names of these firms are part of the average citizen's vocabulary. In this category fall most transportation firms (e.g., the Penn Central Railroad, the Santa Fe Railroad, United Airlines, American Airlines, Greyhound), communications (AT&T, NBC, CBS, Western Union), public utilities (American Electric Power, Consolidated Edison), and much of the largest sector of the American economy, the manufacturing sector. But while it is clear that this manufacturing sector is not described by the competitive model, neither can it easily be characterized as monopoly.

Examples of single-firm monopoly outside the regulated areas are few. The Aluminum Company of America was the sole producer of primary aluminum in the United States from 1893 until World War II. Even during this period, however, some aluminum was imported and some aluminum scrap was reprocessed, thereby giving ALCOA less than complete control over supply. Nevertheless ALCOA and a few other companies have been reasonably accurately described as monopolies. The United Shoe Machinery Company had a monopoly on certain types of shoe machinery until antitrust decrees limited its exercise of monopoly power. The National Cash Register Company, the International Nickel Company, the Climax Molybdenum Company, and International Business Machines all had control, at one time or another in the past, over more than 90 percent of the output of the industries in which they operated.

In transportation and public utilities it is much easier to find examples of monopolies, but these are precisely the kind of "natural monopolies" in which public regulation of price does occur. Telephone and telegraph rates are reviewed and approved by the Federal Communications Commission, railroad rates by the Interstate Commerce Commission, pipeline rates by the Federal Power Commission, and rates of electric power producers by various state and local regulatory commissions.

Table 16–1 Concentration ratios in selected manufacturing industries, 1972

Industry	Four-firm concentration ratio
Automotive	
Vehicles	93
Parts	61
Cigarettes	84
Office machines	60
Tires and tubes	73
Soaps and detergents	62
Aircraft	
Planes	66
Engines and parts	77
Aluminum	
Primary	79
Rolling and drawing mills	73
Radio and television	
Sets	49
Equipment	19
Steel mills and blast furnaces	45
Chemicals	
Organic industrial	43
Plastics	27
Pharmaceutical	26
Machinery	
Farm	47
Construction	43
Metal stamping	9
Nonferrous wire	41
Petroleum refining	31
Foods	
Cereals	90
Bread and cake	29
Fluid milk	18
Canned fruit and vegetables	20
Soft drinks	14
Forest products	
Paper mills	24
Pulp mills	59
Clothes	
Men's and boys' suits and coats	19
Women's and misses' dresses	9
Fur goods	7
Commercial printing, lithography	4

Source: U.S. Department of Commerce, *1972 Census of Manufactures,* 1975.

Concentration ratios vary greatly among manufacturing industries. These data, from the 1972 census of manufactures, show the share of the industries' shipments accounted for by the four largest firms.

PATTERNS OF CONCENTRATION IN MANUFACTURING

Table 16–1 shows current four-firm concentration ratios in selected major manufacturing industries that together account for about 40 percent of all manufacturing shipments. Notice that, descriptively, few of these industries fit either of the models studied so far. Among the high-concentration industries such as automobiles, aluminum, and cigarettes, the very high concentration is achieved by three or four firms in apparently vigorous rivalry with one another. That these firms have appreciable market power is undoubted; that they may be described by the monopoly model is questionable. The competitive model conceivably fits the two or three industries at the bottom of the list, but even here there are doubts.

Style considerations play a significant role in women's clothing, and many manufacturers believe they have some control over price. Metal stamping firms, print shops and soft drink bottlers, while very numerous nationally, operate in small regional and local markets in which there is a small number of sellers in direct rivalry with one another, who do not regard themselves as price takers.

The dominant market structure in manufacturing is called **oligopoly.** This is a market structure in which firms have enough market power that they may not be regarded as price takers (as in perfect competition) but are subject to enough rivalry that they cannot consider the market demand curve as their own. In most of these cases entry is neither perfectly easy nor wholly blockaded. In these industries, a small number of firms—between three and a dozen—tend to dominate the industry and newcomers find it hard to get established. While the American automobile industry is a somewhat extreme example of this, its experience is revealing. Today three large firms and one much smaller firm constitute the industry. No one has successfully entered the industry in the more than fifty years since the Dodge brothers split with Ford and started making their own cars. Henry Kaiser attempted to enter in 1946. His Kaiser-Frazer came on the market, but despite the postwar boom in car sales the company suffered staggering losses and quietly withdrew in 1953.

What makes the automobile industry unusual is the absence of a "competitive fringe." The cigarette industry is similar— only eight firms in the entire industry. In contrast there are 152 petroleum refiners, but the 102 smallest firms together account for only 5 percent of value of output. There are 136 tire and tube manufacturing companies, of which the smallest hundred supply in aggregate less than 2 percent of the market. Oligopoly is not inconsistent with a large number of small sellers if the "big few" dominate the decision making in the industry.

A second market structure, called **monopolistic competition,** deals with cases in which, despite relatively easy conditions of entry, product differences give the firms some ability to set prices rather than simply adjust to a market price.

The need for intermediate categories to describe the American economy is suggested by Table 16–2, which shows that in more than two-thirds of manufacturing industries, the four largest firms control between 20 and 80 percent of the value of shipments. This is too much to be described as competitive and too little to be described as a monopoly.

The inability of the theories of monopoly and perfect competition to describe the modern economy made economists of fifty years ago uncomfortable. And uncomfortable economists theorize. We now look at some of the alternative theories that were appealing in part because they were descriptively realistic. Part of this appeal was expressed by Professor R. L. Bishop when he said that with these alternative theories, economists were at last able to explain "why we are a race of eager sellers and coy buyers, with purchasing

Table 16–2 Manufacturing industries, classified by 1972 concentration ratios

Concentration ratio (percentage)	Number of industries listed by the census	Percentage of value of total shipments of all manufacturing industries
80–100	22	9
60–79	54	14
40–59	116	21
20–39	170	34
Less than 20	90	22
Total	452	100

Source: U.S. Department of Commerce, *1972 Census of Manufactures,* 1975.

Notice the importance measured both in numbers and in value of shipments of industries in the three middle groups. These data were computed from the 1972 census of manufactures. The concentration ratios are those for the four largest firms in each industry.

agents getting the Christmas presents from the salesmen rather than the other way around." There were, of course, reasons for the new theories other than their descriptive realism, as will be seen.

The theory of monopolistic competition

"There's a drugstore on every corner." The line from the play *Brother Rat* is only a slight exaggeration in many big cities, where there are more drugstores than are required to meet the needs of the population. Most of these stores could handle more business than they get. On the shelves of each drugstore are half a dozen or more brands of aspirin, each of which is chemically identical to all the others. Most cities and most highways have many more gas stations than are needed to provide all the cars on the highway with fast and effective service. Walk into almost any supermarket and count the number of different brands of paper napkins. Notice that, although price, packaging, and quantity differ every brand is selected by at least some customers.

These phenomena, as well as the large role played in American life by advertising and "salesmanship," have led to a theoretical model that predicts behavior in industries characterized by a large number of firms selling similar but differentiated products, with much effort devoted to nonprice competition. **Nonprice competition** means diverse kinds of activity to attract customers such as variations in the quality of products, in their packaging and labeling, in advertising, and in the employment of large sales staffs whose job it is to market the product.

THE THEORY

Consider an industry in which there is a large number of producers and free entry into, and

Figure 16–1 The short-run equilibrium of a firm in monopolistic competition

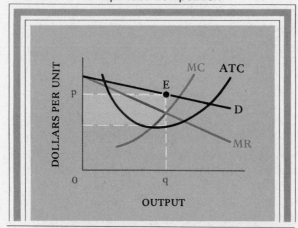

Short-run equilibrium of a monopolistically competitive firm is the same as for a monopolist. Short-run equilibrium occurs at output q where $MR = MC$. Profits may exist; in this example they are shown by the shaded area.

exit from, the industry, but in which each producer sells a product that is somewhat differentiated from that sold by its competitors. There is, for example, a large number of competing firms selling soft drinks. Each drink differs in physical composition; it has a different packaging; and (as advertisers say) it has a different "brand image" from its competitors. Industries of this kind are referred to as being monopolistically competitive. This term describes a situation similar to perfect competition—with the single important difference that each producer sells a somewhat differentiated product.

The fact of **product differentiation** between firms means that each firm does not face a perfectly elastic demand curve for its product because some people will prefer it to other products even though it is somewhat more expensive. If the firm raises its price slightly, it will lose some but not all of its business to its competitors. As its price is raised more and more above the prices of similar products, the firm can expect that fewer and fewer customers will persist in buying its brand. However, if its price is lowered below that charged by competitors, the firm can expect to attract customers—but not everyone will be attracted by a small price differential. Thus the firm will be faced with a downward-sloping demand curve for its product. Generally, the less differentiated the product is from its competitors, the more elastic this curve will be. (If there is no differentiation, the demand curve will be perfectly elastic because the smallest increase in price above those of competitors will lose *all* of the firm's customers, while the smallest decrease in price below those of competitors will attract *all* of the competitors' customers. We are then back at perfect competition.)

The demand and cost curves for a firm in monopolistic competition are shown in Figure 16–1. The demand curve is downward-sloping but relatively flat for reasons discussed above. The short-run equilibrium of the firm is like that of a monopolist. The firm is not a passive price taker; it may juggle price and quantity until profits are maximized where $MR = MC$.

Equilibrium of a monopolistically competitive industry

What about the long-run equilibrium of the industry? The firm shown in Figure 16–1 is earning profits above opportunity costs. Therefore, there will be an incentive for new firms to enter the industry. As more firms enter, the total demand for the product must be shared among this larger number of firms, so each can expect to have a smaller share of the market. At any given price, each firm can expect to sell less than it could before the influx of new firms. Thus the demand curve for the firm's product will shift to the left. This movement will continue as long as there are profits; profits provide an attraction for new firms to enter, and the industry will continue to expand.

As the firm's demand curve shifts leftward, the profits disappear and finally a position of equilibrium is reached where $MR = MC$ but profits are zero. This is shown in Figure 16–2.[1]

A zero-profit equilibrium is possible under conditions of monopolistic competition, in

Figure 16–2 The long-run equilibrium of a monopolistically competitive firm

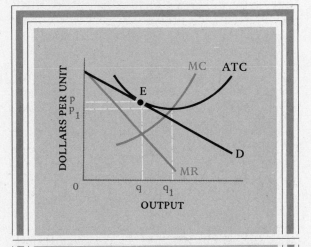

In the long run a monopolistically competitive industry has zero profits and excess capacity. Starting from the equilibrium shown in Figure 16–1 entry of new firms shifts the firm's demand curve to the left and eliminates profits. Point E, where demand is tangent to ATC, represents long-run equilibrium. Price is p and quantity is q. Price is greater and quantity is less than the purely competitive equilibrium price and quantity (p_1 and q_1). At equilibrium, the monopolistically competitive firm has excess capacity of qq_1.

[1] Notice that the demand curve at long-run equilibrium does *not* go through the point of minimum ATC. Suppose it did, as in the diagram below:

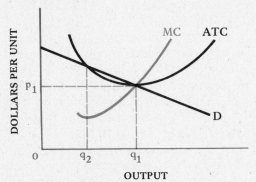

Output q_1 is not an equilibrium level because the firm could reduce output and make profits. Any output between q_1 and q_2 is profitable and such profits will invite further entry.

spite of the fact that the individual firm is faced with a downward-sloping demand curve. Each firm is forced into a position in which it has *excess capacity*. That is, it is producing a lower quantity than the capacity level. The firm in Figure 16–2 could expand its output and reduce average costs, but it does not make use of this productive capacity because to do so would be to reduce average revenue even more than average costs. The reason for this is that it would have to lower its price to sell the extra output, and the resulting loss of revenue would more than offset the lower cost of production.

PREDICTIONS

The theory of monopolistic competition leads to several major predictions that differ from those of the theory of perfect competition. The first of these predictions has already been developed.

The zero-profit equilibrium of a monopolistically competitive firm occurs at an output less than the one at which average total cost is a minimum.

This prediction is known as the **excess-capacity theorem.** It is an implication of the assumptions of downward-sloping demand curves and free entry. To recapitulate: Free entry pushes firms to the point at which the demand curve is tangent to the average total cost curve. The demand curve slopes downward because buyers are supposed to think in such terms as, "I *prefer* Del Monte peaches"; "I *trust* Mr. Green, even if he is a little more expensive"; and "Isn't that the brand Joe Dimaggio uses?" But if the demand curve slopes downward, it must be tangent to average total cost in its declining portion.[2]

Potentially, this is one of the most important insights in the whole theory of the firm. It says that profits will eventually be eliminated in spite of the downward-sloping demand curve because so many firms will enter the industry that individual firms will be unable to utilize all of the capacity at their command.

Two further predictions about prices are closely related to the excess-capacity theorem and are also illustrated in Figure 16–2.

Under monopolistic competition equilibrium price will be greater than marginal cost and greater than the level of minimum *ATC*. [20]

If the cost curves are the same under monopolistic and perfect competition, this means that equilibrium price will be greater than under

[2] Two curves that are tangent have the same slope at the point of tangency. But the demand curve slopes downward by assumption; therefore, average total cost must also slope downward.

perfect competition. To the extent that it is considered socially desirable to have price equal to marginal cost and as low as possible, the predicted results of monopolistic competition are less socially desirable than those of perfect competition.

How important is the theory of monopolistic competition?

A great debate exists between the devotees and the critics of the theory of monopolistic competition. The devotees call the theory a revolution of major importance; the critics, in general, say the theory does not help us to make a single statement about the economic events in the world we sought to analyze.

You may wonder why such a debate can persist. After all, the two theories make different predictions; surely one or the other must predict more accurately. Although it is a legitimate point, satisfactory tests between the competing theories are difficult to arrange. Part of the trouble is that it is difficult to get the two sides to agree on a fair test.

Consider a popular example of differentiated products: the market for soaps and detergents. Among the well-known brands currently on sale in the United States are Cheer, Dash, Dawn, Gain, Oxydol, Tide, Dreft, Ivory Snow, Ivory Liquid, Joy, Cascade, Camay, Lava, Safeguard, Zest, Mr. Clean, Top Job, Spic and Span, Comet, and Cinch. Surely this is impressive differentiation, and the fact that most of the names are familiar to most Americans is impressive evidence of the advertising of these products.

On first glance, the above list of products might appear to provide a perfect ex-

A further prediction of the theory is that firms in monopolistically competitive industries will offer consumers a wider variety of brands, styles, and perhaps qualities to choose among than will firms in perfect competition. This is the other side of the coin of product differentiation, and it is one whose importance is easily overlooked, for wider choice is itself a benefit. Whether the added cost of differentiated output (and production at less than capacity) is "worth it" to buyers is an open question.

ample of monopolistic competition. But *every one* of the products named above is manufactured by a single company, Procter & Gamble, which, with Lever Brothers, dominates American sales of soaps, cleansers, and detergents. Does Procter & Gamble really believe that if it lowers its prices, Lever Brothers will not lower theirs as well? Does the soap industry fail to earn revenues that exceed costs? Does it have free entry? The answer is no to all three questions.

The fact that the theory of monopolistic competition is consistent with nonprice competition does not mean that the presence of nonprice competition is due to monopolistically competitive behavior.

Thus it would be inappropriate to use the soap industry to test the predictions of the theory of monopolistic competition. But what industry should be used? If a proponent of monopolistic competition theory points to the many brands of aspirin as confirming the theory, an opponent might say that the plethora of aspirin compounds on the market reflects the fact of buyers' ignorance or misinformation, not the structure of the market. If a proponent points to the evident product differentiation in consumer products and the heavy expenditures on nonprice competition, the opponent can claim that much of it is done by manufacturers of automobiles, cigarettes, washing machines, and television sets, each of which has very few sellers and large profits over time. Because neither monopolistic nor perfect competition is designed to explain *all* market structures, neither theory can be refuted by demonstrating that it does not apply in a particular situation.

So meager has been the empirical testing of the predictions of these theories that the case for one as against the other cannot be said to be established. They may both be useful in different cases. They may indeed be in conflict on some issues; if they are, then they are in principle testable. But testing will require more effort than has so far been expended.

Some economists, feeling that this debate will never be resolved, combine the two theories into what may be called *atomistic competition*. This is a theory whose central assumptions are:

1. that sellers always perceive their demand curve to be much flatter than it really is (because they ignore parallel actions of other sellers)
2. that there is free entry and exit.

This theory embraces both perfect and monopolistic competition.

Monopolistic competition is predicted to produce a wider range of products but less cheaply than perfect competition.

Economists have often assumed that product differentiation is not worth it, that consumers would be better off with single brands and somewhat lower prices. But this is a decision for individuals to make for themselves, not for economists to make for them.

Yet another prediction of the theory is this:

It will usually pay the monopolistically competitive firm to engage in nonprice competition of a kind that it would not pay to use in perfect competition.

To see that this is an implication of the theory, recall that a firm in perfect competition can sell as much as it wants to at the going price and that it regards itself as a price taker. Therefore there is no need for the firm to spend money in order to increase the amount it can sell. But, in monopolistic competition, expenditures on product differentiation, product quality, and advertising *can* alter the firm's demand curve. Expenditures on advertising and other forms of nonprice competition may thus increase short-run profits.

These are real differences between the theories of perfect competition and monopolistic competition. If one is interested in making predictions about tendencies for capacity utilization, product variety, and nonprice competition, the theories need to be tested in order to establish which one of them provides the more nearly accurate predictions about the real world.

MONOPOLISTIC COMPETITION AFTER FORTY YEARS

How revolutionary was the theory of monopolistic competition? Perhaps surprisingly this is still a matter of current controversy. But there is little disagreement that at the very least it contributed two important things to the development of economics. At the time that it was first developed, perfect competi-

tion was under severe attack for the lack of realism of its assumptions. The theory of monopolistic competition recognized the facts of product differentiation—the ability of firms to influence prices, and advertising. By incorporating all of these new assumptions into a new theory, economists were encouraged to consider the question of their effects on the operation of the price system.

A second major contribution of the theory is that many economists have been profoundly influenced by it. It rekindled economists' interest in such important things as how and when firms took each other's reactions into account, about what made for easy or restricted entry, and about the significance to competition of different products that were roughly similar to one another.

Competition among the few: the theory of oligopoly

The word "oligopoly" comes from the Greek and means, roughly, "few sellers." Oligopoly is often described as "competition among the few."

In order to establish some points of comparison, consider the nature of "rivalry" in each of the three market structures considered so far. All firms are, in a sense, rivals in competing for consumers' limited expenditures. When a monopoly firm changes its price, however, there are no other sellers to react. Thus the firm's *ceteris paribus* demand curve is its actual demand curve. Firms in either perfect or monopolistic competition recognize that other sellers of the same or very similar products exist, but they do not engage in personal rivalry because there are so many firms that it is useless to try to forestall the actions of some of them. Competitors are treated as an impersonal mass that constitutes merely the "behavior of other producers." In oligopoly, however, the whole price-output problem of the firm takes on a new dimension: that of the possible reactions of the firm's few competitors.

In addition to being concerned with how *buyers* of its products will react to any change it makes in prices, quantities, or quality, the oligopolist must anticipate how each of a few identified rivals will react. The firm's policy now depends on how it *thinks* its competitors will react to its moves, and the outcome of the firm's policy depends on how they *do* in fact react. Here there is no simple set of rules for the equilibrium either of the firm or of the small group of firms that constitutes the industry. Neither is there a set of simple predictions about how the firms will react, either individually or collectively, to various changes in taxes, costs, and demand. Everything depends on the policy that the firm pursues, on the policies that its competitors pursue, on how each reacts to the other's changes, and on how each thinks the other will react.

It is often said that under these circumstances price and output are *indeterminate*. Such a statement is misleading, for price and output do somehow get determined. What it means is that, under oligopoly, price and output are not wholly determined by the same factors as in monopoly or in large-group cases. In small-group cases, an additional set of factors—competitors' real and imagined reactions to each other's behavior—helps determine price and output.

Because the problem is complex, there is no single well-developed theory of how oligopolistic markets function. The oligopoly problem has been approached in two quite different ways.

DEVELOPING THEORETICAL MODELS BY ASSUMING HOW FIRMS REACT

One approach has been to develop a series of models by assuming that individual firms will react in particular ways and then seeing

what follows from these assumptions. A. A. Cournot, in 1838, developed the first known theory of duopoly. He had each firm choose its profit-maximizing output on the assumption that the other firm would hold its own output constant. He then showed that if each firm in turn adjusted to the last move made by its competitor (on the assumption that the competitor would make no further moves), a stable equilibrium would be reached in which the market was divided between the two firms in a deterministic way. The assumption that each firm expects no reaction from its competitor—even though the competitor always does react—seems rather naive, and economists in the 135 years since Cournot have suggested many alternatives. They have sought to make oligopoly models more nearly relevant than Cournot's special, though path-breaking, effort.

The German economist H. von Stackelberg developed a theory in the 1930s that included Cournot's model as a special case and in which it was possible to handle the question of whether it would pay the firm to be a price leader or a price follower. A follower is one who lets the leader set any price and then passively adjusts to it; a leader sets its own price, confident that the follower will accept it.

Also in the 1930s, Columbia University's Harold Hotelling approached the oligopoly problem from a novel direction and developed a series of models in which there was a tendency for competition among a few oligopolists to produce a result that was, in a clearly definable way, less socially desirable than the result produced by a single monopolist.

Some recent developments in the theory of oligopolistic behavior have occurred in the theory of games. This theory, a study of rational strategies in small-group situations, has done a great deal to increase our knowledge of how to behave rationally—that is, how to choose actions that maximize the chance of obtaining our stated objectives—in such diverse fields as military strategy and poker. Some economists feel that the theory shows promise of providing an analytical structure suitable for the handling of oligopoly problems. *But an analytical technique is only as useful as the real-world information that it is used to analyze.* Even the most powerful new techniques will be empty without empirical knowledge of how firms actually behave in typical small-group situations.

Currently there is a major revival of interest in the theories of monopolistic competition and oligopoly. It is still too early to say what will result from this new bout of theorizing; so far, attempts to explain oligopolistic behavior by the development of general models have produced disappointingly few results. There are few clear predictions that are capable of being tested against evidence.

GENERALIZING FROM HYPOTHESES ABOUT OBSERVED BEHAVIOR

Many economists believe that what is required is much more empirical knowledge of how firms actually do react in small-group situations. They believe that, until such knowledge can be used to narrow drastically the range of cases shown to be possible by general theoretical models, there can be little hope of developing genuinely useful theories of oligopolistic behavior.

The second major approach to the problem of understanding oligopolistic behavior has been the attempt to build up a theory by developing testable hypotheses to explain actual aspects of observed behavior. The hope has been that these piecemeal explanations would eventually develop into a general theory that will be successful in explaining and predicting oligopolistic behavior.

The theory of oligopoly is in transition. Economists have rejected a number of very simple models and are fashioning the building blocks that perhaps will produce a more complex theory. Here we shall (1) describe a general hypothesis that serves as a framework for integrating many subsidiary hypotheses, (2) describe some of the subsidiary hypotheses in order to convey their flavor, and (3) discuss two or three hypotheses at greater length.

The hypothesis of qualified joint profit maximization

While explicit collusion is illegal in the United States, why cannot a small group of firms who recognize their independence simply act in a common manner? Such tacit collusion has been called "quasi-agreement" by Professor William Fellner. If all firms behave as if they were branches of a single firm, they can achieve the ends of a monopolist by adopting price and output policies that will maximize their *collective* (joint) *profits*. Every firm is interested, however, in *its own* profits, not the industry's profits, and it may pay one firm to depart from the joint profit-maximizing position if, by so doing, it can increase its share of the profits.

The hypothesis of qualified joint profit maximization thus rests on the notion that a firm in an oligopolistic industry is responsive to *two* sets of influences.

The oligopolistic firm wants to cooperate with its rivals to maximize profits; but it also wants to receive as large a share of the profits as possible.

The conflicting pressures on an oligopolistic firm may be illustrated with regard to price. If a group of firms recognize that they are *interdependent* and face a downward-sloping demand curve, their joint profits will depend on the price they all charge. Despite this, an aggressive seller may gain more than its rivals by being the first to cut price below the monopoly level. If a firm adopts such a price-cutting strategy in order to raise its share of the profits, it must balance what it expects to gain by securing a larger *share* against what it expects to lose because there will be a smaller total to go around among all firms as the rival firms subsequently lower their prices below the joint profit-maximizing level.

A hypothesis must consist of more than merely identifying two opposing tendencies. The hypothesis of qualified joint profit maximization is that the relative strength of the two tendencies (toward and away from joint profit maximization) varies from industry to industry in a systematic way that may be associated with observable characteristics of firms, markets, and products. As such, it becomes a framework for more specific hypotheses that will help to predict actual behavior.

Some specific hypotheses about oligopolistic behavior

Each of the following is an example of the kind of hypothesis that can be embedded in the framework of qualified joint profit maximization. It is not important to memorize them, but it is important to see that each is testable and that if it is confirmed, it will help to explain market behavior.

1. *The tendency toward joint maximization is greater for small numbers of sellers than for larger numbers.* The argument offered in support of this hypothesis concerns both ability and motivation. When there are a few firms, they are sure to be in direct rivalry with one another and will soon discover this fact of life. Thus there is no chance that any one can gain sales without inducing retaliation by its rivals. At the same time, a smaller number of firms can coordinate their policies with less difficulty than a larger number.

2. *The tendency toward joint maximization is greater for producers of very similar products than for producers of sharply differentiated products.* The argument here is that the more nearly identical the products of sellers, the closer will be the direct rivalry for customers and the less the ability of one firm to gain a decisive advantage over its rivals. Thus, other things being equal, such sellers will prefer joint efforts to achieve a larger pie to individual attempts to take customers away from each other.

3. *Stable joint-maximizing behavior tends to be easier in a growing rather than a contracting industry.* The argument here is that under expansionary circumstances firms tend to be able to utilize their capacity fully without resorting to attempts to "steal" their rival's customers. In contrast, when firms have excess capacity, their marginal costs are very low and they are tempted to give discounts or secret price concessions in order to pick up customers. Eventually their rivals retaliate and large price cuts may become general.

4. *Prices will tend to be more inflexible the more uncertain the firm is about what its rivals' responses will be.* Uncertainty can take many forms and have many consequences. One of these concerns the willingness to jeopardize a moderately satisfactory situation for one that might be much worse. In periods of industry-wide excess capacity, firms that are covering costs may be unwilling to rock the boat by a price change in either direction. One version of this hypothesis, the so-called kinked demand theory, is discussed at the end of this chapter.

5. *Prices will tend to be more inflexible, the more effective is tacit agreement.* Because price changes are costly, owing to the need to print new price books, advertise anew, and so on, a monopolist might well change prices infrequently. When this is the case a group of tacitly agreeing oligopolists would do the same. In contrast, oligopolists striving to increase their own shares might make more frequent price changes than a monopolist. This hypothesis is an alternative to hypothesis 4: It argues that price stability may be itself an object and a consequence of tacit agreement, not a result of uncertainty about how rivals will react.

6. *Nonprice competition will tend to be more vigorous, the greater the limitation on price competition.* Suppose firms agree tacitly to avoid price cutting in order to avoid expensive and potentially explosive price wars in which each of two or more sellers attempts to undersell the other. This hypothesis says that the basic

rivalry of the sellers for customers will find other outlets as firms seek to maintain or improve their market positions.

7. *Industry price will tend to be closer to the joint profit-maximizing price, the greater the barriers to entry of new firms.* This hypothesis rests on the possibility that the threat that new firms will enter an industry leads existing firms to adopt lower prices in order to discourage entry. The greater the barriers to entry, the less the need for such price reductions. This "limit-price" hypothesis is examined in more detail below.

8. *Nonprice competition will tend to be greater, the weaker the other barriers to entry of new firms.* The argument here is that advertising or product differentiation may give an established firm an advantage over potential entrants that is very possibly a crucial deterrent to entry. This motive for advertising is greater, the greater the threat of entry.

BARRIERS TO ENTRY

Barriers to entry of new firms into a profitable industry play an important role in many hypotheses about oligopoly behavior. Such barriers arise as a result of advantages of existing firms over potential entrants.

Absolute cost advantages

An absolute cost advantage means that existing sellers have average cost curves that are significantly lower over their entire range than those of potential new entrants. Among possible sources of such an advantage are control of crucial patents or resources, knowledge that comes only from "learning by doing" in the industry, and well-established credit ratings that permit advantageous purchasing and borrowing. Each of these may be regarded as only a temporary disadvantage of new firms, which, given time, might develop their own know-how, patents, and satisfactory credit ratings.

Existing firms can translate temporary disadvantages of new firms into the certainty of temporary losses for a new firm and thus discourage entry.

Call the lowest price at which a new firm can enter a market without incurring a loss the **limit price.** Existing firms, by charging a price just below the limit price, sacrifice some of their short-run profits in order to forestall entry of new firms. Such entry, if it occurred, would shift the demand curves of existing firms to the left and reduce their long-run profits.

It may or may not pay to use a limit price. One would have to estimate the level of demand for the individual firm's product before and after entry, as well as the length of time before entry occurred, before one could say whether the existing firms would be better off to charge the limit price or the price that maximized profits (ignoring entry). In general, the greater the barrier to entry, the closer the limit price is to the joint profit-maximizing price.

Scale advantages of existing sellers

Suppose existing firms have no absolute cost advantage but have established a loyal set of customers and have a large share of the existing market. Suppose the technology of the industry is such that there are economies of large-scale production. Under these circumstances, new firms, which inevitably begin with only a small share of the market, will have high costs. They will thus find it hard to compete with large established firms that have low costs because they are large enough to exploit existing economies of scale. This important point is illustrated in Figure 16–3. If a very large scale is required to achieve minimum average costs, and if it takes time for the firm to establish itself in the market and to have the demand for its product build up to a higher level, the firm must accept losses. These losses, if large, will provide a formidable barrier to entry.

The nature of this kind of barrier to entry depends on the shape of the cost curve and

Figure 16–3 Increasing returns as a barrier to entry

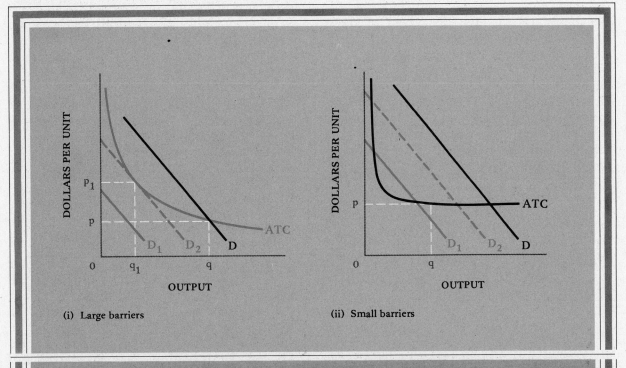

(i) **Large barriers**   (ii) **Small barriers**

The barrier to entry is larger the greater the minimum efficient scale of production. In each part of the figure D and ATC represent demand and cost curves for existing firms that can thus earn profits at prices above p. Suppose a new entrant with the same ATC curve as established firms can only expect to start with the share of the market represented by D_1. In (i) it cannot cover costs at any price. It will suffer losses, at least until its share of the market demand expands to give it demand D_2. Even then, it can break even only if it can charge a price of p_1. In (ii) the new entrant with demand D_1 suffers only small losses at p and can cover costs at prices slightly above it. By the time its demand grows to D_2, it is at no cost disadvantage relative to its larger rivals.

particularly on the size of what is called the **minimum efficient scale (MES)**. This term refers to the smallest size of plant that can reap all of the available economies of scale. Figure 16–3(i) illustrates a large *MES* and a large entry barrier; Figure 16–3(ii) a small *MES* and a correspondingly smaller entry barrier.

Created barriers to entry
Where an industry has a high *MES,* existing firms can forestall entry by lowering price.

Suppose existing firms in an industry have a small *MES*. Can they, nevertheless, forestall entry? Let us examine two possibilities.

Brand proliferation. If the product is one in which consumers switch brands frequently, then increasing the number of brands sold by existing firms will reduce the expected sales of a new entrant. Say that an industry contains three large firms each selling one brand of cigarettes, and say that 30 percent of all smokers choose brands in a random fashion each year. If a new firm enters the industry, it can expect to pick up 25 percent of these smokers (it has one brand out of a total of four available brands). This would give it 7.5 percent (25 percent of 30 percent) of the total market the first year merely as a result of picking up its share of the random switchers, and it would keep increasing its share year by year thereafter.[3] If, however, the existing three firms had five brands each, there would

---

[3] Because it is smaller than its rivals it will lose fewer customers to them by random switching than it will gain from them.

Figure 16–4   Advertising cost as a barrier to entry

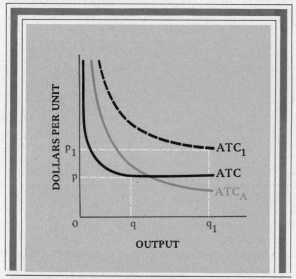

Large advertising costs can increase the *MES* of production and thereby increase entry barriers. The colored *ATC* curve is similar to the one in Figure 16–3(ii); it shows that the *MES* without advertising is at *q*. The black curve ATC_A shows that advertising cost per unit falls as output rises. Advertising increases total cost to ATC_1 and raises *MES* to q_1. Advertising has given a scale advantage to large sellers and has thus created a barrier to entry.

---

be fifteen brands already available and a new small firm selling one new brand could expect to pick up only one-sixteenth of the brand switchers, giving it less than 2 percent of the total market the first year, and its gains in subsequent years would also be less.

Advertising. A second defensive policy that may be adopted by an industry that faces potential entrants owing to a low *MES* is to attempt to shift the average total cost curve (of itself *and* of potential entrants) upward by techniques such as advertising ("He's got a Big Mac attack" or "have a flick of my Bic") and providing services ("free installation and maintenance"). If there is much brand-image advertising, a new firm will have to spend a great deal on advertising its product in order to bring it to the public's attention. If the firm's sales are small, advertising costs *per unit sold* will be very large. Only when sales are large, so that the advertising costs can be spread over a large number of units, will costs per unit be brought down to a level low enough that they will not confer a significant competitive disadvantage on the new firm.

Figure 16–4 illustrates how heavy advertising can shift the cost curves in an industry with low *MES* to make it one with a high *MES*. In essence, what happens is that a scale advantage of advertising is added to a low *MES* of production with the result that the overall *MES* is raised. Thus a new entrant who must both produce and advertise finds itself at a substantial cost disadvantage relative to its established rivals.

A firm with no natural barriers to entry may be able to create them by use of nonprice competition.

Advertising of course does things other than provide barriers to entry. Among them, advertising may perform the useful function of informing buyers about their alternatives thereby making markets work more smoothly. Indeed, a new firm may find advertising is essential (even if existing firms do not advertise at all) simply to call attention to its entry into an industry where it is unknown.

These hypotheses about nonprice competition creating barriers to entry help clarify two apparently paradoxical aspects of everyday industrial life: the fact that one firm may sell many different brands of the same product and the fact that each firm spends much money on advertising, competing not only against products produced by rival firms but against other products produced by the same firm. The soap and cigarette industries provide classic examples of this behavior. In both industries there is only a small number of firms, but there is a very large number of only slightly differentiated products. The explanation is that technological barriers to entry are weak in these industries—a small plant can produce at an average total cost just about as low as that of a large plant. Product differentiation and brand-image advertising create substantial barriers where technological ones are weak, and thus they allow existing firms to move in the direction of joint profit maximization without fear of a flood of new entrants attracted by the high profits.

PRICE INFLEXIBILITY: IS THERE A KINKED DEMAND CURVE?

During the 1930s it was observed that prices in manufacturing were relatively "sticky" —that is, they tended to change infrequently, even in the face of declining costs—and that firms in the manufacturing sector seemed to hold to prices and adjust quantities if necessary. At the same time, agricultural prices were quite flexible. (See the table on page 94.) Because manufacturing tended to be oligopolistic, economists began to hypothesize that relative price inflexibility was an attribute of oligopoly.

One ingenious hypothesis of this kind was put forward by Paul Sweezy. The **kinked demand curve** hypothesis is explained in Fig-

Figure 16-5 The kinked demand curve

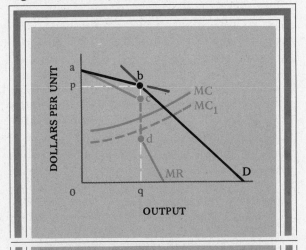

With a kinked demand curve prices tend to be inflexible despite changes in cost. At the market price *p*, the firm sells *q*. It believes that if it lowers price, everyone else will follow suit, and its sales will increase along the demand curve *bD*. But the firm believes that if it raises price, no one else will follow, and its sales will follow the demand curve *ba*. The black curve *abD* is the firm's perception of its own demand curve. The corresponding marginal revenue curve is the *discontinuous* curve *acdMR*. A shift in marginal cost from *MC* to *MC*$_1$ changes neither the price nor the output that maximizes profits.

ure 16–5, where the demand curve is drawn with a sharp kink at the prevailing price. It is as if the firm had two different demand curves: a steep one for price cuts and a flat one for price increases. This kink in the demand curve causes a discontinuity in the marginal revenue curve. [21]

With the kinked demand curve there is an interval in which the firm's price will be unchanged despite changing economic conditions.

We can quickly see that the kinked demand curve hypothesis is a theory about oligopoly rather than about the other market forms that have been studied. In perfect competition, the firm is a price taker and adjusts output to every change in marginal cost. The monopolistic competitor feels no one will follow it up *or* down and thus acts as if its demand curve is elastic in both directions. The monopolist does not have rivals who fail to follow it on price rises.

The kink reflects the psychological state of mind of oligopolistic firms. Sellers are supposed to fear poor results if they change price in either direction and thus are highly motivated to maintain the status quo.

The kinked demand curve has been much discussed and debated. It is certainly a possible explanation of a tendency toward price rigidity. But as we noted above, in contrasting hypotheses 4 and 5 on page 261, it is not the only possible explanation. Prices may be "sticky" simply because there are costs involved in changing them (new price lists must be printed and distributed to customers and sales staffs, for example) or because sellers do not want to upset customers with frequent price changes. Prices may also tend to be more inflexible than even a monopolist would want because they are collusively agreed and the participants do not wish to renegotiate them frequently. In this explanation it is negotiating costs, not fear of adverse response by one's rivals, that is the deterrent to frequent price changes and that accounts for price inflexibility.

Whether or not the kink (or an alternative such as administered prices) is an important element in the theory of oligopoly pricing is still under debate; the evidence seems to many economists to relegate the kink to the role of an interesting but infrequent special case. In any event, the kink does not offer a general theory of oligopoly price; it predicts a tendency for a price, once set, to be maintained, but it says nothing about how a price is set.

A FINAL WORD

Many hypotheses about oligopolistic behavior have been mentioned. Some of them have been tested; others have not. But all are subject to empirical testing. When testing has proceeded to a point where we can be reasonably sure which hypotheses are confirmed and which are rejected, it will be much easier to use those that are confirmed as the building blocks for a more comprehensive theory of oligopolistic behavior. There can be no doubt, however, that even in our introductory treatment of this subject we have come very close to one of the frontiers of modern economics.

Summary

1. A review of the structure of the American economy shows that while there are both large-firm and small-firm sectors, most of the industries involved do not conform descriptively to the picture of either perfect competition or monopoly.

2. One frequent pattern (oligopoly) exists when firms have enough market power that they may not be regarded as price takers, but are subject to enough rivalry that they cannot consider the market demand curve as their own. A second pattern (monopolistic competition) exists when, despite easy entry and numerous firms, product differentiation allows firms to have and to recognize some influence on price.

3. The theory of monopolistic competition is meant to apply to those markets that are characterized by a large number of firms selling similar but differentiated products, with much effort devoted to nonprice competition.

4. The theory is based on the following assumptions: Firms seek to maximize profits; they make price and output decisions on the basis of downward-sloping demand curves; they face these downward-sloping curves in spite of having numerous competitors because their products are somewhat differentiated from those of all other competitors; there is freedom of entry and exit.

5. One important implication of the theory of monopolistic competition is the excess-capacity theorem: the equilibrium of the firm occurs at an output less than the one at which average total cost is a minimum. Closely related to it are the implications that price will be higher in monopolistic competition than in perfect competition, that it will be above marginal cost, and that there will be a number of varieties, types, and possibly qualities of output available to customers of the industry. A further important implication is that it may pay the monopolistically competitive firm to engage in forms of nonprice competition that it would not pay a perfectly competitive firm to use.

6. The basic characteristic of oligopoly is that the firms in an industry recognize to some substantial extent that they are interdependent and that anything they do will probably lead to a reaction by rival sellers.

7. There is no simple set of predictions about the outcome of oligopolistic situations. Everything depends on the strategies adopted by the various rivals. Therefore, instead of a single theory, there are many possible patterns of behavior to understand, explain, and predict. A very general hypothesis that serves as a useful framework is the hypothesis of qualified joint profit maximization, which says that firms that recognize that they are rivals will be motivated by two sets of opposing forces, one set moving them toward joint profit maximization and the other moving them away from it.

8. To suggest the way in which observable variables such as size and number of sellers, nature of the product, and conditions of demand may influence these two sets of forces, eight specific hypotheses were suggested. This list is illustrative of a much larger list that might be provided.

9. Existing firms may have absolute cost advantages or scale advantages over potential entrants and may adopt policies that take cognizance of these barriers and serve to limit entry. Moreover, brand proliferation or advertising may be used to create barriers to entry even where no natural barriers exist.

Concepts for review

Concentration ratios
Why monopolistically competitive demand curves slope downward
The excess-capacity theorem
The alleged wastefulness of nonprice competition
Oligopoly
The hypothesis of qualified joint profit maximization
Minimum efficient scale
Determinants of barriers to entry

Discussion questions

1. Is the consumer benefited by lower prices, by higher quality, by more product variety, by advertising? If there are trade-offs necessary (more of one means less of another) how would you evaluate their relative importance with respect to the following products?
a. vitamin pills
b. beer
c. cement
d. bath soap
e. women's dresses
f. television programs
g. prescription drugs

2. White sidewall tires cost about $1 per tire more to manufacture than black sidewall tires, and they lower somewhat the durability of tires. At the retail level the extra cost of a white sidewall tire is at least $5 per tire. Yet 70 percent of all passenger car tires manufactured in the United States in 1977 were white sidewalls. What, if anything, do these facts tell you about the market structure of the manufacture, distribution, or marketing of automobile tires? If white sidewalls are found to be somewhat more likely to suffer blowouts, should their use be prohibited by law?

3. It is sometimes said that there are more drugstores and gasoline stations than are needed. In what sense might that be correct? Does the consumer gain anything from this plethora of retail outlets? How would you determine the optimal number of movie theaters or gasoline stations in a city of 100,000 people?

4. Are any of the following industries monopolistically competitive? Explain your answer.

a. textbook publishing (fact: there are over 50 elementary economics textbooks in use somewhere in the United States this year)
b. college education
c. cigarette manufacture
d. restaurant operation
e. automobile retailing

5. It has been estimated that if automobile companies did not change models for 10 years, the cost of production would be reduced by approximately 30 percent. In view of this fact, why are there annual model changes? Which, if any, of the reasons you have suggested depend upon the industry's being oligopolistic? Should frequent model changes be forbidden by law?

6. In December 1976 the OPEC nations could not agree on the appropriate size of an increase in the price of crude oil. Eleven nations increased their price by 10 percent, but two, including Saudi Arabia, the country with the largest reserves, raised their price by only 5 percent. Predict what the results were likely to be.

7. Some analysts of the beer industry believe that the big national companies are going to get bigger and the smaller companies will disappear relatively rapidly. Their reasoning is that big national brewers have decisive advantages over local and regional brewers. What are these analysts assuming about the cost conditions in the beer industry? Is this assumption consistent with the December 1972 report by *Fortune* indicating that a small regional brewery has higher labor productivity than the newest but larger plant of Anheuser Busch? Suppose that the efficient size of *plant* in the industry is small, might there be reasons to expect multiplant firms to predominate?

8. Many people in advertising have felt that economists, with their emphasis on efficiency in the allocation of resources, have not been duly appreciative of the role of advertising in influencing consumer preferences. What roles does economic analysis give to advertising? Which are regarded as improving resource allocation and which as worsening it?

9. Does the kinked demand curve rest on a state of mind of buyers, of sellers, or on actual market conditions? Would such a state of mind, or such conditions, be more likely in a period of great excess capacity or a period of shortages? Can prices ever change under the kinked demand theory?

17

Price theory
in action

Price theory helps us to understand and to make predictions about things that are reported in the newspapers every day: the effect of a grain shortage on the price of chicken feed, for example, and the increased use of car pools when gasoline became hard to find and its price rose. In this chapter we shall apply price theory to a few straightforward, real-world situations. In the first the effects of boycotts are examined. In the following examples the theories of monopoly and perfect competition are used to study how producers in competitive industries often try, through collective action, to obtain monopolistic profits. The last set of examples shows why one cannot analyze all practical problems with only the tools of competition and monopoly.

Boycotts and their effect on market price

A **boycott** is defined by the dictionary as the process of "engaging in a concerted refusal to have anything to do with something or someone." Consumers were urged to boycott grapes and lettuce by farm unions seeking to put pressure on the producers who were their employers; the meat boycott of 1973 was designed to bring down the price of meat; when producers of milk and cattle attempted to withhold their products from the market, they too were trying, by a concerted refusal to sell, to influence market results.

In economic terms, a boycott is an attempt to shift the demand or supply curve of a product to the left. A successful buyers' boycott shifts the demand curve; a sellers' boycott shifts the supply curve.

THE 1973 MEAT BOYCOTT

In 1973 a much-publicized boycott of supermarket meat counters was undertaken in an attempt to force an end to skyrocketing meat prices. The background was straightforward: A long-term rising trend in consumption of better cuts of meat resulted from the combination of rising levels of household income and the fact that meat has a high income elasticity of demand. Between 1955 and 1972 per capita consumption of beef, lamb, and pork had doubled, and this alone led to a steady rightward shift of the demand curve for meat. In addition, population was increasing in the United States, and this too increased the market demand for meat. Of course output was also increasing, but as it increased, costs of factors of production used in meat production rose. These rising costs led to rising prices. For a while all of this occurred relatively gradually, average meat prices rising by 2 to 5 percent per year. Then, in 1972, the pace of price changes suddenly accelerated. A worldwide grain shortage caused the price of cattle feed to shoot up suddenly, shifting up costs (and supply curves) of cattle and meat production.

Continuing rightward shifts in the demand curve, combined with a sharp leftward shift of the supply curve, are predicted to lead to sharply rising prices. This is precisely what happened. Prices of meat increased at a rate of 5 percent a *month* between December 1972 and the following March. They were a major contributing factor as food prices rose at a rate unprecedented in the memories of most Americans. In the weekly trip to the supermarket, families saw the costs of the things they were accustomed to buying rising so sharply that they had to make major changes in their purchases.

Consumers clamored for price ceilings or some other form of government intervention. At the start of 1973, President Nixon remained adamant in his refusal to impose ceiling prices on food. As meat prices rose sharply during the first quarter of 1973, a housewives' revolt was increasingly talked about in the press. By late March a formal meat boycott was organized and Americans were urged to refrain from buying meat starting the first week in April in order to force prices down. On March 30 President Nixon imposed price ceilings on meat at both the wholesale and the retail levels, a move that was widely characterized in the press and in Congress as "too limited and too late" to prevent further price increases. On April 2 the much-publicized boycott began. *The New York Times,* on April 3, applauded the action editorially:

Never underestimate the power of the embattled consumer. Outraged by President Nixon's belated decision to fix ceilings on meat prices only after they had soared to the highest levels in history, millions of Americans are seeking—almost spontaneously—to impose their own discipline on the marketplace by refusing to buy steak, chops or other cuts of meat at the present wildly inflated prices.

RESULTS OF THE BOYCOTT

Consider this boycott in terms of the competitive theory of supply and demand. Suppose first that housewives permanently reduced their purchases of meat and supply curves remained the same. The decrease in demand would lead to a leftward shift in the demand curve and a decrease in price. This is what the boycott leaders wanted. But suppose, once prices fell, consumers ended their boycott and resumed purchasing at the old rate. Demand would increase and prices would go back up. Thus, while a permanent boycott (perhaps based on "meatless Tuesdays") could permanently reduce the price of meat, a temporary boycott is predicted to bring only temporary relief, other things remaining unchanged. (See Figure 17–1 (i).)

In fact, during the spring of 1973 the expected short-run price reductions did *not* occur, even though meat purchases were greatly reduced. Ranchers responded to the boycott as you would expect them to if they

Figure 17–1 Boycotts

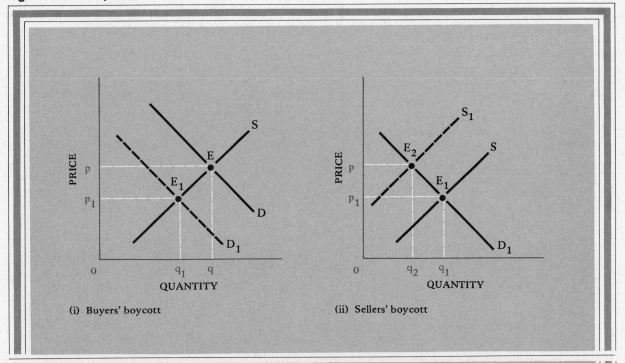

(i) **Buyers' boycott**

(ii) **Sellers' boycott**

A buyers' boycott shifts the demand curve leftward; a sellers' boycott shifts the supply curve leftward.
(i) With equilibrium at E, a buyers' boycott shifts demand to D_1 and price falls to p_1. When the boycott ends, unless people's tastes have changed, demand rises to D and price will again rise to p.
(ii) With equilibrium at E_1, because of the buyers' boycott, producers withhold supplies from the market and shift the supply curve from S to S_1. Price rises to p. As long as both boycotts are in effect, equilibriun is at E_2 and it is quantity that is greatly changed, not price.

expected it to be short-lived: they held cattle off the market in anticipation of the end of the boycott. They did not want to sell at a low price cattle that could be kept on the ranch for a few extra weeks and sold later at a higher price. Of course, if the boycott had been permanent they would have been forced to sell the cattle sooner or later; as it was, the temporary withholding of meat (which was in effect a reverse boycott by ranchers) had the effect of a compensating leftward shift of the supply curve for meat. The reduction in supply was

sufficient that by April 15 prices were at the pre-boycott ceiling levels. Thus, in the short run, the boycott and withholding led to a decrease in both demand and supply and no reduction in price. (See Figure 17–1 (ii).) Whatever the psychological benefits to either party, neither side had gained. Ranchers sold and households ate less meat than they had before the boycott.

In the longer run the organized boycott of consumers and the more or less spontaneous boycott of ranchers both petered out, but the market did not readily return to normal conditions. The longer-run effects were complicated by the March 30 price ceilings that remained in effect. Meat packers were caught in a squeeze between the (uncontrolled) prices of cattle at the feedlot, which were rising in response to continuing rises in the costs of feed, and the price-controlled wholesale prices of meat. By July many packers found themselves losing money on every steer butchered, and some of them shut down. By August the statistics showed U.S. cattle slaughter 50 percent less than it had been the previous year, despite the fact that beef prices were 60 percent higher than they had been a year before. Throughout August the situation worsened. More meat packers shut down, black markets in meat developed, and importing from Canada and Mexico increased.[1] In September the Administration gave up on direct price control and price ceilings were removed. Prices immediately rose sharply. By the end of August shipments of cattle to the market had risen, meat packing plants were reopening, and wholesale meat prices began to fall—but remained 25 to 30 percent above the levels of the previous year.

Besides confirming earlier predictions about the effects of price controls, this episode confirmed two important theoretical predictions:

1. A boycott to decrease prices by decreasing demand will not lead to a permanent decrease in price without a permanent decrease in demand.

2. A buyers' boycott can be offset by a sellers' boycott, which is likely to occur if sellers expect the buyers' boycott to be temporary. If both boycotts occur, a decrease in quantity sold rather than a decrease in price will result.

---

[1] Some U.S. ranchers sold cattle to Canadian slaughterhouses which sold the beef back to U.S. customers—largely restaurants—at prices far above the domestic ceiling prices. All of this was legal since imported beef had no ceiling price.

The attempt to monopolize perfectly competitive industries

In 1973 housewives were agitated by what they regarded as excessively high prices and looked to collective action to bring prices down. Sellers of goods and services, however, often seek collective action to raise what they consider excessively *low* prices. Cocoa producers in west Africa, wheat producers in the United States and Canada, the Organization of Petroleum Exporting Countries (OPEC), coffee growers in Brazil, taxi drivers in many cities, and labor unions throughout the world have all sought to obtain, through collective action, some of the benefits of departing from perfectly competitive situations. Basically they have sought to form organizations to sell the goods or services they supply.

The motivation behind this drive for monopoly power is easy to understand. The equilibrium position of a perfectly competitive industry is one in which a restriction of output and a consequent increase in price will always increase the profits of all producers. This is particularly obvious when (as is so often the case with agricultural goods) the demand for the product is inelastic at the equilibrium price; then marginal revenue is negative and marginal cost is positive. Thus a reduction in output will not only raise the total revenues of producers but also reduce total costs. It is equally true that the industry's profits can always be increased, even if demand is elastic at the competitive equilibrium price. At such an equilibrium, each firm is producing where marginal cost equals price. Because the market demand curve slopes downward, the industry's marginal revenue is less than price—and thus less than marginal cost. Therefore, in competitive equilibrium, the last unit sold necessarily contributes less to the industry's revenue than to its costs.

In a perfectly competitive industry it always pays the producers to enter into an effective agreement to restrict output.

When competitive firms attempt to restrict output, however, certain problems arise. These can be seen in the following case studies.

THE INSTABILITY OF PRODUCERS' CO-OPS

A **producers' cooperative** is a joint selling organization for a group of producers. Such a co-op (as it is often referred to) often acts as a **cartel** and attempts to reduce the output of a commodity by getting each producing firm to agree to restrict its output. While there is an incentive under perfect competition for all producers to enter into such an agreement, there is also an incentive for each producer to violate it. Obviously, if everyone responds to this second incentive, the gains from cooperative action will be lost. To see how this would happen, suppose that a producers' cooperative raises prices by cutting production. Suppose that every firm except one restricts its output. That one firm will be doubly well off in that it can sell its original output at the new, higher price received by all other firms that have restricted their production. But the same is true for *each* firm.

Thus, unless the co-op is very carefully policed and has the power to enforce its quota restrictions on everyone's output, there will be a tendency for members to begin to violate quotas once prices have been raised. Furthermore, the co-op must have power over all producers, not merely over its members; otherwise, a producer could avoid the quota restriction merely by leaving the co-op.

A co-op organized mainly to restrict output is subject to competing pressures. Each producer is surely better off if the co-op is formed and is effective; but each firm is even better off if every other firm plays ball while only it does not. Yet if everyone cheats (or stays out of the co-op), all will be worse off. These tendencies are illustrated in Figure 17–2. They may be summarized in two predictions:

1. Output-restricting producers' co-ops in competitive industries can raise producers' incomes provided they are able to enforce quotas on the outputs of all producers.

2. Such co-ops will tend to be unstable because of the incentives for individual producers to violate the quotas.

The history of schemes to raise farm incomes by limiting crops bears ample testimony to the accuracy of these predictions. Crop restriction agreements often break down, and prices fall as individuals exceed their quotas. The great bitterness and occasional violence that is sometimes exhibited by members of crop-restriction schemes against nonmembers and members who cheat is readily understandable.

MILK WITHHOLDING IN WISCONSIN

The previous discussion illustrated the need to be able to police the activities of members of any output-restricting scheme. Another case shows the problems that occur when the producers' organization covers substantially fewer than the total number of producers in the industry.

In 1967, when this episode occurred, there were 72,000 dairy farmers in Wisconsin, of whom about 4,300 were members of a militant farm organization known as the National Farmers Organization. The NFO members controlled about 6 percent of the milk produced in the state. Angry about low milk prices and recognizing the inelasticity of the market demand curve, the NFO proposed to withhold milk from the market. By dumping it in rivers, fields, and roads, they hoped to dramatize the plight of the dairy farmer and raise the price of milk by 20 percent. The elasticity of demand for milk is approximately 0.5. To achieve a 20 percent price increase would require a reduction in quantity sold of about 10 percent. Although the NFO urged all farmers, whether members or not, to join

Figure 17–2 The dilemma of producers' co-ops

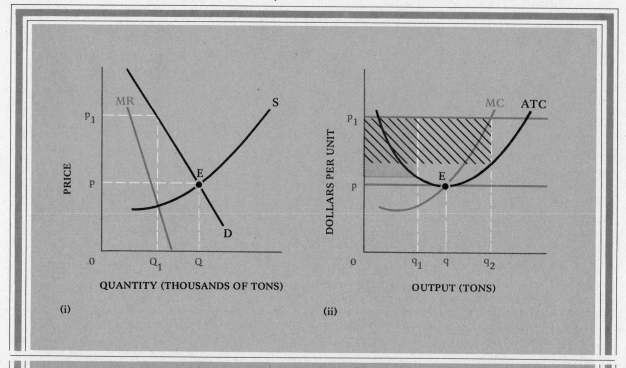

Producers all benefit if they restrict output; any one producer benefits if others reduce output but he does not. Market conditions are represented in (i); conditions for an individual farmer in (ii). (Note the change of scale.) Before the co-op is formed, the market is in competitive equilibrium at price p and output Q, and the individual farmer is producing output q and just covering costs. A co-op is formed and reduces industry output to Q_1 by persuading each farmer to produce only q_1. This output, where supply equals marginal revenue, maximizes joint profits with price p_1. The individual farmer earns profits shown by the shaded area.

Once price is raised to p_1, however, the individual farmer would like to increase output to q_2 and thus earn the profits shown in the diagonally striped area. But if all farmers try to increase their outputs, price will fall back toward p.

them, in fact only members withheld supplies, and they withheld *all* of their milk. During a three-week period, these member farmers removed about 40 million pounds of milk (enough for 18 million quarts), or about 6 percent of the total usually supplied during the three-week period. Even if this withholding action had had the full effect predicted by the theory of competition for the given demand elasticity, it would have raised prices by 12 percent and *benefited the farmers who were continuing to produce,* not those who were dumping their milk. The participants lost approximately $1.7 million, or an average of $400 each, in the action. The nonparticipants lost nothing, but neither did they gain anything, because the price of milk did not rise at all.

The action failed because the total response was too small and too unevenly shared. With elasticity of demand at 0.5, the participating producers could have produced at most a 12 percent price increase since they controlled only 6 percent of the output. Just as in the case of the boycott of meat, any such increase in price would have persisted only as long as reduction in flow continued. Withholding milk for a week or three weeks and then resuming full production would at most drive prices up only until supply increased and brought them down. A monopoly would seek to decrease the supply as a long-term policy. For a co-op to achieve the same results would require a long-term withholding, and this could benefit the withholders only if a great majority of producers shared both in the withholding and in the production of what was sent to market. When the NFO failed to enlist the general support of milk producers, its attempt to raise the incomes of its members was doomed to fail.[2]

Whether the NFO was foolish is perhaps another matter. If its purpose was to raise the income of its members by direct market action, it clearly (and predictably) failed. If, however, the primary purpose was to achieve a political solution, it may be that the dramatic (and expensive) action demonstrated the intensity of the members' feelings of grievance. Many of the NFO members, however, believed they would succeed because of the laws of supply and demand. Even a neophyte economist could have told them otherwise.

---

[2] Why did the prices not rise even temporarily? By an incredible blunder, the withholding action was timed to coincide with Easter vacations, and thus the school demand for about 5 percent of fluid-milk production was absent. Spring also is the time of year when cows produce the most milk. Normally, the spring surplus in the fluid-milk market is reflected in an increased diversion of milk to production of butter, cheese, and powdered milk. The withholding action did little more than absorb the surplus and had no effect on the fluid-milk market. During the third week cheese and butter production did drop, but because of inventory adjustments even their prices did not rise.

THE PRICE OF HAIRCUTS

Including all the producers in the industry and being able to police their actions is not enough for the success of a profit-increasing scheme. It is also necessary to prevent new producers, attracted by monopoly profits that have been obtained by output restriction, from entering the industry.

This example is typical of what happens in many cities. It concerns the efforts of the barbers in a particular city to avoid the rigors of competition. Assume that there are many barber shops and freedom of entry into barbering in the sense that anyone who qualifies can set up as a barber. Assume that the going price for haircuts is $3 and that at this price all barbers feel their income is too low. The barbers hold a meeting and decide to form a trade association. They reach agreement on the following points: First, all barbers in the city must join the association and abide by its rules; second, any new barbers who meet certain professional qualifications will be required to join the association before they are allowed to practice their trade; third, the association will recommend a price for haircuts that no barber shall undercut.

The barbers intend to raise the price of haircuts in order to raise their incomes. You are called in as a consulting economist to advise them as to the probable success of their plan. What do you predict?

The first thing you need to know is whether the organization is strong enough to enforce its minimum price on members and to prevent barbers from operating outside of the organization. If it is not this strong, you will predict that their plan will not succeed in raising the price above the market level. But suppose you are persuaded that the organization does have the requisite strength to enforce a price rise to, say, $4. What are your predictions about the consequences of the price increase?

You now need to distinguish between the short-run and the long-run effects of an increase in the price of haircuts. In the short run the number of barbers is fixed. Thus, in the short run, the answer is simple enough: It all depends on the elasticity of the demand for haircuts. If the demand elasticity is less than 1, total expenditure on haircuts will rise and so will the incomes of barbers; if demand elasticity exceeds 1, the barbers' revenues will fall. Thus you need some empirical knowledge about the elasticity of demand for haircuts. You might be lucky enough to be able to refer to a full-scale econometric study of the demand for haircuts. However, it is unlikely, in the case of haircuts, that such a study is available, and you will probably have to try to gain some idea of demand elasticity by studying the effects of changes in haircut prices either at other times or in other places.

When you propose making such a study, one of the leaders of the organization (who has taken a course in economics) tells you not to waste your time, because "except for the hippies who don't cut their hair at all, haircuts are a necessity, and therefore their demand is almost perfectly inelastic." You reject this argument for two reasons. You realize, first, that the time between haircuts is by no means fixed. An increase in the average period between haircuts from four weeks to six weeks would represent a 33 percent fall in quantity demanded. If such a change were occasioned by, say, a 25 percent rise in price, the elasticity of demand over this range would be 1.33. You realize also that people can have their hair cut elsewhere than in a barbershop. The sale of hair clippers for home use soared in America during the 1950s and 1960s as a direct response to sharp rises in the relative price of haircuts.

Let us suppose, however, that on the basis of the best available evidence you estimate the elasticity of demand over the relevant price range to be 0.45. You then predict that barbers will be successful in raising incomes in the short run. A 33 percent rise in price will be met by a 15 percent fall in business, so the total revenue of the typical barber will rise by about 13 percent.[3] In predicting the consequences, you will also want to estimate the length of the short run for this industry.

Now what about the long run? If barbers were just covering costs before the price change, they will now be earning profits. Barbering will become an attractive trade relative to others requiring equal skill and training, and there will be a flow of barbers into the industry. As the number of barbers rises, the same amount of business must be shared among more and more barbers, so the typical barber will find business—and thus profits—decreasing. Profits may also be squeezed from another direction. With fewer customers coming their way, barbers may compete against one another for the limited number of customers. The association does not allow them to compete through price cuts, but they can compete in service. They may spruce up their shops, offer their customers expensive magazines to read, and so forth. This kind of competition will raise operating costs.

These changes will continue until barbers are just covering their opportunity costs, at which time the attraction for new entrants will subside. The industry will settle down in a new position of long-run equilibrium in which individual barbers make incomes only as large as they did before the price rise. There will be more barbers than there were in the original situation, but each barber will be working for a smaller fraction of the day and will be idle for a larger fraction (the industry will have excess capacity). Barbers may prefer this situation; they have more leisure. Customers may or may not prefer it: They have shorter waits even at peak periods and they

---

[3] Suppose the quantity of haircuts originally was 1,000. At $3 this produced revenue of $3,000. A rise in price to $4 and a fall in quantity to 850 created revenue of $3,400, a 13 percent increase. More generally, let p and q be the price and quantity before the price increase. Total revenue after the increase is $TR = (1.33p)(.85q) = 1.13 \, pq$.

get to read a wide choice of magazines, but they pay more for haircuts.

But you were hired to report to the barbers with respect to the effect on their incomes, not their leisure. The report that you finally present will say: "You will succeed in the short run (because you have estimated demand to be inelastic), but your plan is bound to be self-defeating in the long run unless you are able to prevent the entry of new barbers."

The important lesson to be learned from this example is that:

Unless producers can control entry, they cannot succeed in keeping earnings above the competitive level in the long run.

If price competition is ruled out, then profits will be driven down by the entry of new firms and the resulting creation of excess capacity. Producers' associations that are successful in keeping earnings up are those that are successful in restricting entry.

THE DECLINE AND FALL OF A PATENT MONOPOLY

The case of the barbers suggested that monopoly profits cannot be maintained unless there are effective barriers to entry. Even if prices are not brought down by new entrants (because of effective group control over price), excess capacity will continue to develop until each firm's profits are reduced to zero. How easy is it to raise barriers to entry to protect monopoly profits? One might think that a patent that confers a legal monopoly to produce a product would be sufficient, but restriction is not that simple.

Profits are a challenge to those who want their share of them; they are the carrot of the free-enterprise system, and no producer is immune to potential competition from those who would compete for his or her share of the consumer's dollar. Consider the case of ball-point pens.

In 1945, Milton Reynolds acquired a patent on a new type of pen that used a ball bearing in place of a conventional point. He formed the Reynolds International Pen Company, capitalized at $26,000, and began production on October 6, 1945.

The Reynolds pen was introduced with a good deal of fanfare by Gimbels, who guaranteed that the pen would write for two years without refilling. The price was set at $12.50 (the maximum price allowed by the wartime Office of Price Administration). Gimbels sold 10,000 pens on October 29, 1945, the first day they were on sale. In the early stages of production, the cost of production was estimated to be around 80¢ per pen.

The Reynolds International Pen Company quickly expanded production. By early 1946 it employed more than 800 people in its factory and was producing 30,000 pens per day. By March 1946 it had $3 million in the bank.

Macy's, Gimbels' traditional rival, introduced an imported ball-point pen from South America. Its price was $19.98 (production costs unknown).

The heavy sales quickly elicited a response from other pen manufacturers. Eversharp introduced its first model in April, priced at $15. In July 1946 *Fortune* magazine reported that Sheaffer was planning to put out a pen at $15, and Eversharp announced its plans to produce a "retractable" model priced at $25. Reynolds introduced a new model but kept the price at $12.50. Costs were estimated at 60¢ per pen.

The first signs of trouble emerged. The Ball Point Pen Company of Hollywood (disregarding a patent-infringement suit) put a $9.95 model on the market, and a manufacturer named David Kahn announced plans to introduce a pen selling for less than $3. *Fortune* reported fear of an impending price war in view of the growing number of manufacturers and the low cost of production. In October, Reynolds introduced a new model, priced at $3.85, that cost about 30¢ to produce.

By Christmas 1946 approximately 100 manufacturers were in production, some of them selling pens for as little as $2.98. By February 1947 Gimbels was selling a ball-point pen made by the Continental Pen Company for 98¢. Reynolds introduced a new model priced to sell at $1.69, but Gimbels sold it for 88¢ in a price war with Macy's. Reynolds felt betrayed by Gimbels. Reynolds introduced a new model listed at 98¢. By this time, ball-point pens had become economy items rather than luxury items, but they still were highly profitable.

In mid 1948 ball-point pens were selling for as little as 39¢ and costing about 10¢ to produce. In 1951 prices of 25¢ were common. In 1977 there was a wide variety of models and prices, ranging from 19¢ upward, and the market appeared stable, orderly, and only moderately profitable. Ball-point pens were no passing fad, as everyone knows. Their introduction has fundamentally changed the writing-implement industry in America and in the world.

The ball-point pen example has interested observers in many fields. Lawyers have been concerned about the ease with which patent rights were circumvented. Psychologists have noted the enormous appeal of a new product even at prices that seemed very high. Advertising men have regarded it as a classic case of clever promotion.

From the point of view of economic theory, it illustrates several things:

1. A firm that innovates, taking the risks of introducing a new product, may gain a temporary monopoly. In the short run such a monopoly can charge prices not remotely equal to costs and earn enormous profits.

2. Entry of new firms (even in the face of obstacles) will often occur in response to high profits.

3. Entry will, in time, drive prices down to a level more nearly equal to the costs of production and distribution.

4. The lag between an original monopoly and its subsequent erosion by entry may nevertheless be long enough that the profits to the innovator, as well as to some of the imitators, may be very large.[4]

Different observers might stress different aspects of the evidence sketched in the ball-point pen example. Some would see it as an example of the power of competition in stimulating production of a desired commodity and ultimately making it available at low cost to the consumer. Others would see it as evidence of the ability of monopoly to exploit the public. Still others would see it as an example of the great incentive that capitalism provides to the successful innovator (or promoter) to find and introduce a new product. To a degree, all would be right.

The case of the ball-point pen is no isolated example; it is typical of what happens when a successful innovation brings a new product onto the market. A more recent example is the pocket calculator that has virtually ousted the slide rule as the applied scientist's constant companion. It is so easy to operate that it is carried and used regularly by many who would never have used a slide rule. When they were first introduced less than a decade ago pocket calculators were relatively expensive items, often costing over $100. They were also relatively crude in their capabilities. Nonetheless they proved popular; sales and profits rose and firms rushed to enter the lucrative new line of production. Competition led simultaneously to product improvement and price reduction. By the late 1970s models that perform the basic calculations could be bought for under $10, and sophisticated, scientific, and programmable pocket calculators could be bought for under $50.

---

[4] It is estimated that Reynolds earned profits as high as $500,000 *in a single month*—or about 20 times its original investment.

Is oligopoly theory necessary?

So far in this chapter, a combination of the theories of perfect competition and monopoly have been used quite successfully. You may wonder if this always proves to be the case. The answer is no. Sometimes there are instances in which another theoretical structure is needed. In the two following examples, for instance, there are only three firms in the industry, and the theories of neither monopoly nor perfect competition provide satisfactory explanations of what we know has taken place.

CIGARETTES

The American cigarette industry is one of the most highly concentrated of manufacturing industries. It has three dominant firms: the American Tobacco Company, R. J. Reynolds, and Liggett & Myers. If the industry were analyzed using the theory of monopoly, it could be predicted that the cigarette companies would avoid competing with one another either in buying tobacco or in setting the price of cigarettes. It would also be possible to predict substantial profits for many years. These things *have* happened. In an antitrust suit against the three companies, it was shown that they conspired to purchase tobacco in auctions without bidding against one another and that they followed a uniform high-price policy (high relative to cost) in the finished product. A dramatic (and monopolistic) episode occurred in June 1931, when, in the depths of the Depression and in the face of the lowest tobacco-leaf prices in a quarter of a century, the three big cigarette companies (which then controlled 90 percent of the market among them) all raised their prices.

But here the monopoly analogy begins to break down. The policy proved spectacularly unsuccessful. Smokers shifted in large numbers to cheaper brands made by other companies, and ultimately prices fell well below the May 1931 level as the big three tried to regain their market shares. (They have never again achieved as large a share as they held in May 1931.)

The profits of these cigarette companies were and remain well above the average for all manufacturing industries. In this respect, the theory of monopoly predicts well, as it does in predicting the lack of competition in the leaf market and the absence of serious price competition in the last thirty years.

But there are other characteristics of the industry that are readily observable and that are not predicted by the theory of monopoly. The most notable is the enormous expenditure on advertising by each of the companies. Such expenditure raises costs and lowers profits. It has two aspects. First, it represents intense nonprice competition among the existing sellers, who recognize that there is no profit in competing through price cutting; second, it represents an attempt to raise barriers against potential competitors.

The high cost of establishing a new brand name represents a substantial barrier to entry. The theory of oligopoly predicts that advertising will occur for these reasons. (See page 264.) Some kinds of advertising are consistent with monopoly theory. If a monopolistic firm, through advertising, can change consumers' preferences toward its product in such a way as to shift the demand curve to the right, or make it more inelastic, it may increase revenues by more than the cost of the advertising. But such advertising is product-oriented advertising (Smoke!), not brand-name advertising (Winston tastes good . . .). It certainly would not pay a monopolist to advertise two of its brands in competition with each other. Neither the kind nor the amount of cigarette advertising is of the sort predicted by the theory of monopoly.

STEAM-TURBINE GENERATORS

Three electrical manufacturers—General Electric, Westinghouse, and Allis-Chalmers—

produce more than 95 percent of all the steam-turbine generators in the United States. In 1960 these three firms were charged with having held a series of meetings beginning at least as early as June 1957 for the purpose of agreeing on prices and sharing the market among themselves. Subsequently each of the firms pleaded guilty. Is a theory of oligopoly needed to explain this behavior, or is the theory of monopoly sufficient? Certainly the behavior as charged in the indictments is fully consistent with the theory of monopoly. For the period from July 1957 to May 1958 the conspiracy apparently succeeded in producing something very close to joint profit-maximizing behavior, including extensive price discrimination.

Midway in 1958, however, the conspiracy came apart at the seams. The three sellers became involved in vigorous price competition among themselves, and prices fell drastically. The precise cause is unknown, but the threat by the TVA to ask for foreign bids on a turbine generator it required, a slackening of demand, and rumors of antitrust prosecution were causative factors. All attempts to stop the price cutting were in vain. Behavior had ceased to be monopolistic.

In analyzing the market behavior in this industry, the monopoly model would have led to accurate predictions for one period and to very poor predictions for another period. Simple models that predict with accuracy under some circumstances but not under others are useful if we know, or can define, the situations in which they will work and those in which they will not work.

Complex theories often take the form of defining the range of relevance of simpler theories. For example, if the theory of oligopoly were to tell us that the monopoly model will work well for steam-turbine generators in periods of strong demand but will not work when firms develop excess capacity, the theory would be useful in itself and would also increase the usefulness of monopoly theory.

MIXTURES OF MARKET STRUCTURES

The cases described in this chapter illustrate the relevance of price theory to familiar problems. While they were chosen to illustrate points one at a time, they are by no means the only cases where price theory is helpful. Think of the energy crisis, which plays a large role in the economic news these days. The true extent and full consequences may not yet have emerged, but it is clear that this too is grist for the mill of price theory. As an example of one energy problem consider petroleum.

When the Organization of Petroleum Exporting Countries (OPEC) was first formed in the early 1970s it initiated enormous increases in the price of crude oil. As a result the price of gasoline at filling stations in the United States nearly doubled within a very short space of time. Producers and distributors of small, fuel-saving cars such as American Motors and Volkswagen found demand for their product rising; other automobile manufacturers found large cars not selling. These producers stopped production and laid off workers while they strained to shift production into their relatively few plants suitable for producing small cars. Used-car dealers found their big cars overpriced but their small cars being snapped up at existing prices, so they changed the structure of their prices. A cold winter inspired a public clamor for relaxation of government restrictions on use of less clean energy sources such as coal, and long lines at gas stations led many to join the oil industry in a plea to permit renewed drilling for offshore oil.

Once the immediate gasoline shortage had passed and the public was used to higher prices the demand for large cars revived. The demand thus proved highly inelastic in the face of the increases in the cost of running cars. Just how inelastic it will continue to be if the price of gasoline doubles and doubles again remains to be seen. If such price rises should occur, the public's reaction to them will seriously affect the profits of the four U.S. car manufacturers. Those that successfully predict and/or adapt to market changes will fare better than those that lag behind or guess wrong. (In 1976, for example, the big three car producers made record profits while American Motors suffered losses because its too-compact cars were not in heavy demand.)

To analyze the various aspects of a single situation, neither competition alone nor monopoly alone would suffice. These reactions were in markets of all of the types we have studied. The OPEC countries first made joint decisions in textbook monopoly fashion. Then in 1976 they failed to reach a unanimous decision on a joint price increase. Saudi Arabia refused to raise its prices as much as did most of the other OPEC countries, and many observers wondered if the potential instability of producers' cartels was once again manifesting itself. The struggles of the automobile manufacturers occurred within the framework of an oligopolistic industry, as did the price and output behavior of the large American oil refiners. Used-car dealers and independent oil dealers attempted to sell products in the ways predicted by competitive theory.

It is too soon for a thorough case study of these and other aspects of the energy crisis, but the relevance of price theory for the unfolding consequences is apparent. Price theory, after all, is meant to explain tomorrow's headlines as well as yesterday's.

Summary

1. A boycott in which some purchasers refuse to purchase a product sold in a competitive market reduces demand and, as long as it lasts, exerts downward pressure on price. This effect can be offset by a sellers' response —organized or spontaneous—in which supplies are withheld from the market. In either case, when the boycott ends the effect on price is reversed. Unless a boycott leads to a permanent change in supply or demand it does not have a permanent effect on price.

2. Groups supplying goods or services under conditions that approximate those of competitive equilibrium have a strong incentive to organize to restrict output. The reason is that their collective profits will surely increase, since the last units being produced have marginal costs in excess of marginal revenues.

3. To achieve and retain the benefits of monopolization requires more than just agreeing to restrict output. To be effective, an output-restriction scheme must be able to police and enforce its output quotas since it is in any one producer's interest to violate its quota.

4. The NFO's milk-withholding program illustrates the difficulties that face a producers' organization that includes only a fraction of the total producers in the industry. Not only is it more difficult to achieve a substantial restriction in total output, but the benefits of any price increases that are achieved will accrue to those who continue to produce. For a minority to withhold *all* of their supply while a majority continue to supply the market can only hurt financially those who withhold, unless it is the means for a negotiated or a political settlement of their grievances.

5. Including all producers in the organization and being able to enforce agreements may be necessary, but it is not sufficient for effective monopoly, as the case of the barbers shows. If entry is not effectively limited, the gains in profit that will accrue to the industry will attract new entrants and will so divide the market that monopoly profits will be dissipated. Even though the new entrants are successfully brought into the association and abide by the higher price, excess capacity will develop and each firm's profits will disappear.

6. The strength of the drive to enter a highly profitable industry is illustrated in the case of ball-point pens where a legal barrier to entry (in the form of a patent) did not prevent other producers from competing for the consumer's dollar. A patent provided monopoly power, and extraordinary profits, for a time; as competition developed, however, price declined and profits were eroded.

7. While the theories of competition and monopoly alone and in combination take us a long way, they are not adequate to all cases. Oligopoly theory adds something to the understanding of the real world; one of its purposes is to suggest the characteristics of those situations in which one simpler theory or another may apply.

8. Many problems are complex and require simultaneous use of monopoly theory, competitive theory, and the theory of oligopoly.

Concepts for review

Purchasers' boycott and producers' boycott
Long-run effects of a temporary boycott
The motive for output restriction in a competitive industry
Sources of instability of cartel agreements to limit output
Effects of entry

Discussion questions

1. There is no law against consumer boycotts. When coffee prices soared in the mid 1970s, each of the following statements was made. Comment on them in terms of the theory of boycotts.

a. Elinor Guggenheimer (New York City Commissioner of Consumer Affairs): "We've heard all about the cold weather in Brazil and the damaged coffee trees. What we haven't heard is any valid explanation of why the consumer should be forced to bear the impact of this frost. We're going to ask supermarkets and restaurants to stress coffee alternatives, tea and soup. If enough people don't drink coffee, at some point prices will have to be turned around."

b. William Safire (columnist): "Let the boycott go forward, not only to cut the price, but to put the cartelniks of OPEC on notice: When challenged to economic war, even a little one, the American public is willing to make sacrifices. An effective coffee boycott would send a message to monopolists of oil."

c. Coffee importer: "The U.S. customer is not the prime factor in the coffee market. The 43 coffee-producing nations couldn't care less if Americans drink coffee, because other people will. Americans can spite themselves, and hurt *me,* but they won't touch Brazil."

2. The OPEC cartel was formed in 1973 with the explicit purpose of agreeing to raise petroleum prices. OPEC was to do this by having each member nation raise the tax it charged producers on each barrel. In 1973 the Persian Gulf members of OPEC increased the taxes charged from less than $2 to over $7 a barrel. International cartels are notorious for their instability. In what ways was OPEC potentially stronger than a cartel based upon agreements among individual firms in different countries? The following statements were subsequently made about the cartel; comment on each of them.

a. Japanese minister of trade and industry, Komoto: "An outrageous act that ignores economic principles and is therefore regrettable."

b. Milton Friedman (in 1976): "OPEC will break up within the next year because it will not be able to withstand the competitive pressure resulting from the vast sources of oil being discovered in many areas."

c. *Time:* "The decision of Saudi Arabia in 1976, to only raise prices 5 percent when other OPEC members raised prices 10 percent seems to have touched off a classic capitalist price war."

3. Technological advances of the 1950s dramatically boosted chicken and egg production in the United States. Petaluma, California, became the center of a booming industry. The Petaluma egg producers tried unsuccessfully and persistently to restrict supply by forming voluntary associations. Why do you think these associations did not succeed? In 1972 the California State Marketing Board did what the private associations failed to do: It compelled cutbacks in production. Why do you suppose it did so, and why was it more successful than the voluntary associations?

4. Profit-making blood banks account for about 10 percent of all blood used in transfusions in the United States. They buy blood from commercial donors and sell blood to hospitals. The Food and Drug Administration wants to put them out of business, but the Council on Wage and Price Stability—also a government agency—wants to encourage more commercial blood donation. Private provision under appropriate safeguards, COWPS suggests, may be the most appropriate way of assuring adequate supplies of quality blood at low prices. Discuss whether or not competition ought to be permitted in blood supply.

5. Use price theory in discussing the following news stories.

a. The analysis sent out by a leading stock brokerage firm: "Prices of digital watches are following the pattern of pocket calculators—down 25 percent a year. This is just what we expected; it is normal. Expect squeezed profit margins and some bankruptcies."

b. Donald Hollister, inventor of a new long-lasting light bulb that won't burn out for at least 10 years: "Even if this catches on, I expect to do well, but not to make a million dollars. The idea is too simple."

c. "Barbers are providing special inducements to long haired youths: free beard trims with every haircut."

d. Newspaper report from Greensville, South Carolina, about the growth of "gut row": "It's a bit mind boggling to see so many fast-food restaurants in one place. All the national chains are there—Burger King, McDonald's, Shakey's Pizza—and you have your choice of chicken, seafood, barbecue or even native favorites like sausage biscuits."

Monopoly versus competition

Monopoly has been regarded with suspicion for a very long time. Even today in some quarters it is given a major portion of the blame for inflation, for the energy shortage, for discrimination in employment, and for inequalities in income. It is widely believed that modern economic theory has *proved* that monopoly is a system whereby the powerful producer exploits the consumer, whereas the competitive system always works to the consumer's advantage. In *The Wealth of Nations* (1776), Adam Smith—the founder of classical economics—developed a ringing attack on monopolies and monopolists. Since that time, most economists have criticized monopoly and advocated freer competition.

Is the hostility toward monopoly justified? This chapter compares monopoly and competition in terms of their predicted effects and then looks at the principal policies for dealing with monopoly in the United States. Throughout the discussion, "monopoly" refers to monopoly power, not merely to the case of a single seller.

Comparisons between monopoly and competition

THE EFFECT OF CHANGES IN COST ON PRICE AND QUANTITY PRODUCED

Decreases in prices were considered by nineteenth-century economists to be the principal way in which the benefits of progress were passed on to consumers. They are still an important way. For this reason, economists are interested in the way in which prices respond to changes in cost.

Consider the case of an invention that lowers the marginal cost of production. In a competitive industry, the fact that each firm's marginal cost curve shifts downward means that the industry supply curve (which is the sum of the marginal cost curves) also shifts downward. As a result of the invention, any given output will be provided at a lower price than it was before while any given price will call forth a higher output. Thus the cost-saving invention lowers price and raises output. This is illustrated in Figure 18–1(i). The effect of an identical change in marginal cost on the price and output of the monopolist is shown in Figure 18–1(ii). The downward-shifting marginal cost curve intersects the marginal revenue curve at a higher level of output than it did previously. Because the demand curve is unchanged, it follows that the price must fall. Thus the benefit from any fall in costs will, to some extent, be passed on to consumers in terms of lower prices in the cases of both competition and monopoly.

But while prices will fall in both cases, they will not usually fall to the same degree.

Other things being equal, prices and quantities will change less in monopoly than in competition in response to a change in marginal costs.

Figure 18–1 The effect on price of a reduction in marginal cost

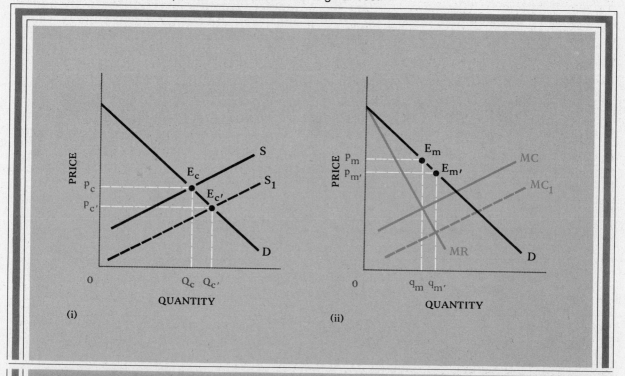

A reduction in marginal cost leads to a greater decrease in price and a greater increase in quantity in a competitive industry than in a monopolized one. The demand curve is the same in both parts of the diagram, and the competitive short-run supply curve (S) is the same as the monopolist's marginal cost curve (MC). When marginal cost decreases the curves shift downward to S_1 and MC_1. The new competitive output is where D and S_1 cross. The new monopolistic output is where MC_1 and MR cross. Because MR declines more steeply than D, the increase in output (and consequent decrease in price) is less under monopoly than under competition.

The reason for this is that the monopolist is guided by the marginal revenue curve, which is steeper than the demand curve. The same vertical fall in marginal costs leads to a lesser increase in quantity and thus a lesser fall in price.

THE MONOPOLIZATION OF A COMPETITIVE INDUSTRY

The classical case against monopoly is to a great extent based on this prediction:

If a perfectly competitive industry should be monopolized, and if the cost curves of all productive units are unaffected by this change, the price will rise and the quantity produced will fall.

Assume that a competitive industry is monopolized as a result of a single firm's buying out all the individual producers. Further assume that each plant's cost curve is unaffected by this change. This means that the marginal costs will be the same to the monopolist as to the competitive industry.

When the industry is monopolized, it becomes profitable to drive price up by restricting output for precisely the same reasons it pays a producers' co-op to do so (see page 272). As long as neither market demand nor costs change, it will always pay the monopolist to restrict output below, and to raise price above, the perfectly competitive level. This is illustrated in Figure 18–2.

DIFFERENCES IN EFFICIENCY OF COMPETITION AND MONOPOLY

Even if prices are higher and output lower under monopoly as compared with competition, are we justified in saying that one price-output situation is *in any sense* better, or more nearly optimal, than the other? The theoretical economists, in their case against monopoly, argue that perfect competition leads in equilibrium to a more efficient allocation of resources than monopoly. (Through-

Figure 18–2 The monopolization of a competitive industry

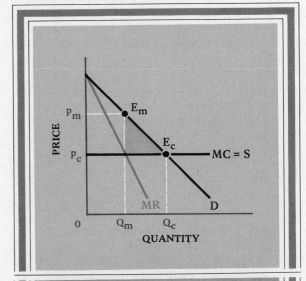

When a competitive industry is monopolized, output falls and price rises. This is illustrated for the case of constant costs. The competitive industry's supply curve and the monopolist's marginal cost curve are identical. The industry faces demand curve *D*. A competitive industry would produce Q_c at price p_c. The monopolist reduces output to Q_m because units between Q_m and Q_c add more to his cost than to his revenue. The shaded area shows that consumers were willing to pay more for each unit of lost output than its marginal cost of production.

out this discussion, remember that we are assuming that the costs of production are not affected by whether the producer is a monopolist or a perfect competitor.)

The essence of the argument rests upon two propositions: (1) In perfect competition, marginal cost equals price, and (2) at equilibrium, the level of cost is the lowest level attainable, given the technology of the society.

The significance of having outputs produced at their lowest possible costs is obvious. But what is the special significance of marginal cost equaling price under perfect competition but not under monopoly?

Marginal cost shows the opportunity cost of producing the last unit of the commodity actually produced. Price indicates what consumers are prepared to pay for the last unit of the commodity purchased; that is, it represents the marginal utility an extra unit would provide.[1] In competitive equilibrium price equals marginal cost. Consumers are paying for the last unit purchased exactly its opportunity cost (which represents the value of best alternative use of the resources). If price equals marginal cost everywhere in the economy, no change in what is produced can increase the value of output to consumers.

In monopoly, by way of contrast, price exceeds marginal cost. From this it follows that for the last unit they actually purchase, consumers pay an amount greater than its opportunity cost. Furthermore, consumers would be prepared to buy additional units for an amount greater than the cost of producing these units, as is shown in Figure 18–2 by the shaded area. (Consumers have no opportunity to purchase these extra units because the monopolist restricts output in order to maximize its profits.)

In an economy in which price equals marginal cost in some industries but is greater than marginal cost in a monopolized industry, a shift in resources to the monopolized industry will increase the value of output to consumers.

Consumers will be "better off" in a well-defined sense when marginal cost equals price in all industries than when it is less than price in some industries.

An economy in which $p = MC$ in all industries is said to exhibit **allocative efficiency**.

Is allocative efficiency a satisfactory goal?

An economy in which every market is perfectly competitive will have marginal cost everywhere equal to price and thus will be allocatively efficient. An economy in which some industries are perfectly competitive and others are monopolistic is not allocatively efficient. If resources are moved from uses where price equals marginal cost to uses where price exceeds marginal cost, it will be possible to make some households better off without making any household worse off.[2]

Whether $p = MC$ is a sufficient basis for saying competition is good and monopoly bad is more complicated.

1. Is perfect competition the alternative to monopoly? One reason the nineteenth-century economists so firmly rejected monopoly was that they viewed perfect competition as the realistic alternative. If it were, and if costs were unaffected by market structure, then monopoly would indeed lead to higher prices, smaller outputs, and allocative inefficiency.

Even if the result of perfect competition is accepted as being more desirable than that of monopoly, this does not in itself tell us about the real policy decisions that face us. The alternative of perfect competition was much easier to believe in a hundred years ago than it is today because large firms and highly specialized equipment had not yet become important except in a handful of industries. Today the effective choice is not between monopoly and perfect competition but between more or less oligopoly. (Look again at the tables on pages 252 and 253 to re-

---

[1] To see why this is so, consider a man who buys 100 units of a commodity at the market price of 20¢ per unit. Because he has a downward-sloping demand curve, he gets all but the last unit at a price less than he would be prepared to pay. But while he receives more satisfaction from his total purchase than the dollars he spends are worth to him, the price does measure what he is prepared to pay for the last unit he purchases. To obtain additional units, he is prepared only to pay an amount less than the market price (which is why, at present, he does not buy additional units).

[2] A situation in which it is impossible to make some households better off without simultaneously making others worse off is called a **Pareto-optimal** situation. An economy in which every industry is perfectly competitive is thus Pareto-optimal.

mind yourself of the actual structure of American manufacturing.) For this reason, the antimonopoly argument based on the allocative efficiency of perfect competition must be carefully treated.

2. Does p = MC always imply efficient use of resources? It is well known that there are several situations in which achieving the condition of competition, $p = MC$, does not necessarily lead to efficient allocation of resources.

The condition may not pertain simultaneously everywhere in the economy. In a world with some oligopolies, for example, there is no general presumption of what the effect will be of prices equaling marginal costs somewhere in the economy. Specifically, if there are many oligopolies and one is broken up and made into a competitive industry, there is no general presumption (even in a theoretical model) about the likelihood of this moving the society closer to or farther away from an optimum. This proposition illustrates what is known as the "theory of the second best": We may know how to identify the best of all possible worlds (from the limited point of view of the optimum we are discussing), but we may have little clear idea about how to order two states of the very imperfect world in which we live.

Private and social costs may diverge. Producing a good up to the point at which the price just equals the *firm's* marginal cost is efficient from society's point of view only if the firm's private costs reflect the opportunity costs to society of using the resources elsewhere. But as we saw in Chapter 13, this is often not the case, and if the competitive firm uses resources it does not pay for (such as the environment), it may produce too much from society's viewpoint; the smaller output of the monopolist may be more nearly socially optimal.

There may be advantages of large-scale production. If there are unexploited long-run advantages of large-scale production, of learning by doing, or of innovation or invention, then a shift from competition to another market structure may lower rather than raise prices. This important point will be demonstrated shortly.

3. Is efficiency the only economic goal? A competitive economy distributes output as well as produces it. A freely functioning competitive system reflects its past by giving effect to inequalities in the distribution of income and the ownership of assets. Executives and their children exert more influence on market allocations than do taxi drivers and their children. Society often chooses to change income distribution, even at the expense of allocative efficiency.

Of course, one might first achieve a desired income distribution and then seek an efficient allocation of resources. But such an ideal outcome may not be practicably attainable, and a choice between a desirable change in income distribution and a desirable increase in allocative efficiency may be required.

THE NONECONOMIC APPEAL OF COMPETITION

The fact that the conditions required for competition to produce efficient results can so easily be violated in the real world raises the question of why the theory of perfect competition has always held such appeal for economists. Part of the answer is that the notion of allocative efficiency, in which no one could be made better off without making someone else worse off, provides an attractive ideal, other things being equal.

More of the answer is the appeal of the perfectly competitive model to the liberal who is wary of the exercise of power by private organizations or by the state. For one who believes in the individual and dislikes and distrusts all power groups, the perfectly competitive model is almost too good to be true. In the perfectly competitive world, no single firm and no single consumer has any power over the market. Individual consumers and producers are passive quantity adjusters responding to market signals and always doing what is most desirable from the society's point of view. The impersonal force of the market produces an appropriate response to all changes. If tastes change, for example, prices will change, and the allocation of resources will change in the appropriate direction; yet throughout the whole process, no one will have any power over anyone else—dozens of firms react to the same price changes—and if one firm refuses to react, there will be countless other profit-maximizing firms eager to make the appropriate changes.

Figure 18–3   A case in which monopolization leads to lower prices

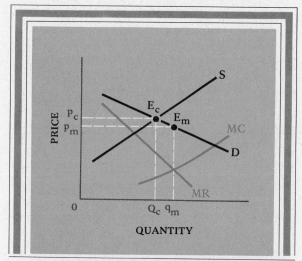

If monopolization lowers costs sufficiently, it may lead to greater output and lower price than competition. *D* and *S* are the demand and supply curves of a competitive industry that is in equilibrium at E_c with p_c and Q_c. If costs are unaffected by monopolization, *S* becomes the monopolist's marginal cost curve and the monopolist will restrict output and raise price. However, if monopolization reduces costs to *MC*, the equilibrium will be at E_m, with p_m less than p_c and q_m greater than Q_c.

Power may be feared not only generally but specifically. Big monopolies may bribe congressmen and corrupt presidents. Monopolists may engage their prejudices against minorities or women and they may encourage corrupt or illegal behavior by their employees. Competitive firms without market power may be unable or less able to do these things. If, for example, in competition one firm discriminates against women, there may be dozens of other firms that will recognize that profit maximization is not consistent with discrimination on the basis of sex. In these circumstances the discriminating firm will suffer losses as a result of its prejudices and will be forced from the industry if it persists in such uneconomic activities.[3]

THE EFFECT OF MARKET STRUCTURE ON COST

It is now necessary to drop the assumption that costs of production are unaffected by the kind of market structure that exists. Specifically, are costs unaffected when an industry is monopolized? If any savings occur from combining numerous competing groups into a single integrated operation, then the costs of producing any given level of output will be lower than they were previously. If this cost reduction does occur, it is possible for output to be increased and price to be lowered as a result of the monopolization of a perfectly competitive industry. Such a situation is illustrated in Figure 18–3.

There are other possibilities. A monopoly might reduce cost but still raise prices.[4] Or it might reduce the efficiency of production and so shift the marginal cost curve upward. In this case (compared to the competitive industry) monopolization will certainly raise price and lower output.

[3] This argument is discussed in more detail on page 363.

[4] This would be the case, for example, given the demand and supply curves shown in Figure 18–2, since *MR* is negative at the competitive price.

Either more theory or some empirical information about the effects of monopolization on an industry's cost structure is required in order to predict the effect of monopolization on price and output. If monopolization usually results in large cost savings, then it may be that monopolization usually results in a fall in price and an increase in output. If, however, monopolization usually either leaves costs more or less unchanged or increases them, then it will cause a rise in price and a fall in output.

THE INCENTIVE TO INNOVATE

As far as profits are concerned, both the monopolist and the perfect competitor have an incentive to innovate. There has been an extended debate over which market structure provides the greater incentive.[5]

Innovation under a monopoly

A monopolist can always increase its profits if it can reduce costs. And because it is able to prevent the entry of new firms into the industry, these additional profits will persist into the long run. Thus, from the standpoint of maximizing profits, the monopolist has both a short-run and a long-run incentive to reduce costs by innovation.

Innovation, however, takes research and development, and these take money. The monopolistic firm may have an advantage over the competitive firm in that funds for research and development are more readily available to it. In the first place, it may have profits to invest in such ventures even though credit is tight. In the second place, tax laws that permit the writing off of business expenses may make research and development a relatively cheap endeavor. Suppose that this year a monopolist expects to make $2 million profit on which it will have to pay taxes of

approximately $1 million. If it spends the $2 million on research and development, it will show no profits for tax purposes this year and the firm will save $1 million in taxes. In effect, it can get $2 million worth of research for only $1 million. Successful research will eventually lead to future profits and will strengthen the firm's position as a monopolist. Of course, in later years it will have to pay taxes on the profits it earns—unless they are again spent on research and development.

Innovation under competition

The firm in perfect competition has the same profit incentive to innovate as the monopolist in the short run—but not in the long run. In the short run, a reduction in costs will allow the firm that was just covering costs to earn profits. In the long run, other firms will be attracted into the industry by these profits. Existing firms will copy the cost-saving innovation, new firms will enter the industry using the new techniques, and the profits of the innovator will eventually disappear.

The effectiveness of profits as an incentive to reduce costs for a firm will depend on the magnitude of the extra profits and the length of time over which they persist.

If it takes only a few months for existing firms and new entrants to copy and install any new invention, then the innovating firm's profits will be above normal for only a short time and the extra profits actually earned may not be sufficient to compensate for the risks and the costs of developing the new innovation. In such cases the direct incentive to innovate would be absent from a competitive industry. Alternatively, if it takes several years for other firms to copy and install the cost-saving innovation, then the profits earned over these years by the innovating firm might be more than sufficient to compensate for all costs and risks and might yield a handsome profit as well. In this case the incentive to innovate is present in a competitive industry.

---

[5] At this time, we suggest you read again the discussion of invention and innovation on pages 196–199.

The greater incentive to innovate?

Might competition be *more* conducive to innovation than monopoly? Some think so. A monopolist who does not innovate may be missing larger profits, but it can still have some profits. But, the argument says, if the competitive firm does not innovate, some of its competitors are likely to do so and it will find itself in a position in which it cannot even keep up with its competitors, thus incurring losses and eventual bankruptcy.

A very different view was that of the distinguished Austrian (and later American) economist Joseph A. Schumpeter. In brief, his argument was that only the incentive of profits led entrepreneurs to take the great risks involved in innovation, and that monopoly power was much more important than competition in providing the climate under which innovation occurred. The profits of the monopolist provided the incentive for other people to try to get their share. This might involve imitating the monopolist's product (thereby eroding the monopoly market) or it might involve trying to come up with a wholly new product that would better serve the underlying wants that were making the monopolist rich. As a result no monopoly would last forever; it would not even last very long if it failed to innovate and anticipate its future competition. Schumpeter called the process of one monopoly being replaced by another the *process of creative destruction*. In *Capitalism, Socialism and Democracy* (1942) he said:

What we have got to accept is that it has come to be the most powerful engine of that progress and in particular of the long-run expansion of total output not only in spite of, but to a considerable extent through, this strategy which looks so restrictive when viewed in the individual case and from the individual point of time. In this respect, perfect competition is not only impossible but inferior, and has no title to being set up as a model of ideal efficiency. It is hence a mistake to base the theory of government regulation of industry on the principle that big business should be made to work as the respective industry would work in perfect competition.

Patents and the incentive to innovate

Economists who believe that competitive market structures best serve consumers by assuring them low prices, but who worry about the possible lack of incentives to innovate under competition, believe that other institutions, such as the patent laws, can provide the necessary incentives. Patent laws confer a temporary monopoly on the use of an invention. They represent an attempt to lengthen the short-run period during which whoever controls the invention can earn supernormal profits as a reward for inventing it. Once the patent expires, and sometimes even before, as we saw in the case of ball-point pens, other firms can copy the innovation and, if there are no other barriers to entry, production will expand until profits fall to normal. There is little doubt that were there no patent laws, many inventions would be copied sooner and the original innovators would not earn as much extra revenue to compensate them for the costs and risks of development.

Because patented items *can* be imitated the real advantage of patents to the competitive firm should not be exaggerated. Some have argued that patents may be of even greater advantage to a monopolistic than to a competitive firm. A monopolist, so goes the argument, has the resources to develop, patent, and "keep on the shelf" processes that might enable a potential competitor to challenge its position.

Public policy toward monopoly: antitrust

The theory of monopoly leads to two principal predictions. (1) Where monopoly power exists in an industry, it will lead to a restriction on the flow of resources into the industry and thus to the employment of fewer resources in the industry than would be used under competitive conditions. (2) Because of this, monopolists will be able to earn profits in excess of opportunity costs and will command a larger share of the national income than they would under conditions of competition. In short, monopoly power may alter the allocation of resources and the distribution of income.

While other theoretical arguments demonstrate that there is no necessary reason why cost conditions should be predicted to be the same for a monopolistic and a competitive industry, contemporary economic policy is, in fact, still much conditioned by the views of the nineteenth-century economists.

The belief that competition produced ideal results and monopoly worse ones led economists to the notion of prohibiting *by law* the practice of monopoly.

Antitrust laws, which were a major part of the classical down-with-monopolies policy, prohibit monopoly, attempts to monopolize, and conspiracies in restraint of trade. They give the courts the power to stop such practices as well as to dissolve a monopoly into a number of independent companies, if deemed necessary.

Before discussing these laws and their effectiveness, we should note two things:

1. Monopoly power, when exercised by those who are relatively poor rather than relatively rich, has frequently been supported rather than opposed by the government. For example, the efforts of farmers to increase farm income have not only been condoned but actively promoted by public policies of crop restriction, price supports, and exemption from antitrust laws of producers' cooperatives. Labor unions are also exempted from antitrust prosecutions, and the efforts of unions to achieve some degree of monopoly power over the supply of labor were also actively supported by those public policies that encouraged the growth of unions.

2. Noneconomic motives for dealing with the "monopoly problem" also exist. Principal among them is the distrust of power; many people fear the political influence of those with substantial economic power. The hypothesis that big business wields enormous political power and thus threatens the open society is often presented. Such studies may utilize statistics showing the size and share of *total* manufacturing assets held by the nation's largest 200 or 500 corporations. This "macro-concentration" does not concern monopoly power in any market; rather, it concerns bigness in the economy.

THE NATURE OF ANTITRUST POLICY

By and large, economists have regarded monopolistic restrictions on resource flows as adverse on the grounds that they hinder the efficient use of resources. Because those with monopoly power are usually relatively well off, any redistribution of income toward the monopolist also conflicts with the desire for greater equality in income distribution. When large firms have acquired sizable shares of the output of major industries, they have usually become objects of public concern, and the clamor for the government to "do something" about monopoly has been loud. Antitrust policy has been aimed at such firms.

Monopolistic power may be achieved or perpetuated in many ways:

1. by firms conspiring among themselves (colluding) to restrict output, raise prices, or otherwise failing to compete with one another

2. by firms adopting practices "in restraint of trade," such as contracts that bind a purchaser to buy all of its supplies from a single seller

3. by a firm employing "predatory" practices against rival sellers in an effort to force them into bankruptcy, "good behavior," or merger

4. by a merger of existing firms into a new dominant firm

5. by one firm acquiring control of other firms through purchasing their stock or acquiring their physical assets

6. by a firm finding monopoly "thrust upon it" (in the words of the distinguished American jurist Learned Hand) either by its natural efficiency as a single producer or by successful innovation.

Each of the first five of these ways has been the object of antitrust legislation. The basic tools of antitrust policy are the laws that seek to eliminate practices that lead to monopoly. Such practices may be either criminal or civil offenses. In criminal law, a firm found guilty may be fined and its officers may be fined and/or sentenced to jail. While criminal cases can be brought only by the government, civil cases can be brought either by the government or by private litigants. In civil cases the firm, if found in violation of the law, may be required by the court to abandon certain practices, or it may be forced to dissolve itself into a number of separate companies under procedures approved by the court. In the legal phrase, a firm found violating the law must "cleanse itself" of its violation in a manner prescribed by the court. In private cases, a firm may be obliged to pay injured parties an amount up to three times the amount of damages caused by the violation. "Treble damages," as they are called, were designed to provide a substantial incentive to private firms to root out violations of the law that might escape the notice of government prosecutors. While private antitrust actions are extremely numerous and a few have led to landmark decisions, the bulk of antitrust policy is made via the government antitrust suit.

WHO MAKES OUR ANTITRUST POLICIES?

Antitrust laws prohibit certain forms of activity. Since they are laws, they are enforced in the courts, and the enforcement in the main follows the usual legal procedures. There are both federal and state antitrust laws, the former being far the more important. Government cases originate either within the Antitrust Division of the Department of Justice or within procedures of the Federal Trade Commission (FTC). Many cases never go to trial because they are settled by agreement between the Department of Justice or the FTC and the companies. Justice Department and private cases go to trial before federal district courts. FTC cases are heard first by the Commission. In all cases appeal is to the appropriate Circuit Court of Appeals and then to the Supreme Court. Supreme Court decisions, here as elsewhere, stand until modified by other decisions of this highest court.

The overall effect of antitrust policy at any time rests on three things: the nature of the laws themselves, the courts' attitude toward the law and their interpretation of it, and the vigor with which prosecutions are brought by the Justice Department and the FTC. All three have changed over time, and therefore the overall antitrust climate has changed. Let us examine each briefly.

Principal laws promoting competition

The Sherman Antitrust Act (1890) was the first of the major pieces of legislation that arose in response to the great growth in the size of firms during the last half of the nineteenth century. Section 1 of the act declared illegal every contract, combination, or conspiracy in restraint of trade. Section 2 made it illegal to monopolize or to attempt to monopolize. It also prohibited conspiracies or combinations that resulted in monopolization. Although the language of the Sherman Act was strong, it was also vague, and it was to be some time before the courts were able to define the act's scope more specifically.

The Clayton Antitrust Act (1914), was an attempt to be more precise and to strengthen the powers of the antitrust prosecutors by al-

Principal antitrust provisions

Sherman Antitrust Act (26 Stat 209, 1890, as amended)

§1. Every contract, combination in the form of trust or otherwise, or conspiracy, in restraint of trade or commerce among the several States, or with foreign nations, is hereby declared to be illegal. . . . Every person who shall make any contract or engage in any combination or conspiracy shall be deemed guilty of a felony and on conviction thereof, shall be punished by a fine not exceeding one million dollars if a corporation, or, if any other person, one hundred thousand dollars, or by imprisonment not exceeding three years, or by both . . . in the discretion of the Court.

§2. Every person who shall monopolize, or attempt to monopolize, or combine or conspire with any other person or persons, to monopolize any part of the trade or commerce among the several States, or with foreign nations, shall be deemed guilty of a felony . . .

§8. That the word "person," or "persons," wherever used in this act shall be deemed to include corporations. . . .

Clayton Antitrust Act (38 Stat 730, 1914, as amended)

§2. (Including Robinson–Patman Amendments, 1938.)

(a) That it shall be unlawful for any person engaged in commerce, in the course of such commerce, either directly or indirectly, to discriminate in price between different purchasers of commodities of like grade and quality . . . where the effect of such discrimination may be substantially to lessen competition or tend to create a monopoly in any line of commerce. . . . *Provided,* That nothing herein contained shall prevent differentials which make only due allowance for differences in the cost . . . resulting from the differing methods or quantities in which such commodities are . . . sold or delivered. . . .

§3. That it shall be unlawful for any person engaged in commerce, in the course of such commerce, to lease or make a sale or contract . . . on the condition, agreement, or understanding that the lessee or purchaser thereof shall not use or deal in the . . . commodities of a competitor . . . where the effect of such . . . agreement . . . may be to substantially lessen competition or tend to create a monopoly in any line of commerce.

§7. (As amended by Celler–Kefauver Act of 1950.)

That no corporation engaged in commerce shall acquire . . . the whole or any part . . . of another corporation engaged also in commerce, where in any line of commerce in any section of the country, the effect of such acquisition may be substantially to lessen competition, or to tend to create a monopoly. . . .

§16. That any person, firm, corporation, or association shall be entitled to sue and have injunctive relief, in any court of the United States having jurisdiction over the parties, as against threatened loss or damage by a violation of the antitrust laws. . . .

Federal Trade Commission Act (38 Stat 717, 1914, as amended)

§5. (a)

(1) Unfair methods of competition . . . and unfair or deceptive acts or practices in or affecting commerce, are hereby declared unlawful.

(6) The Commission is hereby empowered and directed to prevent . . . using unfair methods . . . or deceptive acts or practices in commerce.

§5. (1)

Any person . . . who violates an order of the commission to cease and desist . . . shall pay a civil penalty of not more than $10,000 for each violation . . . each day of continuance . . . shall be deemed a separate offense.

lowing them to strike at potentially anticompetitive practices "in their incipiency." It also identified certain practices as illegal "where the effect may be substantially to lessen competition." Its most important provisions were Section 7, applying to acquisition of stock in a competing company; Section 2, limiting the practice of price discrimination; and Section 3, regulating exclusive dealing and tying contracts. (A tying contract requires a buyer to purchase other items in order to purchase the item it wants.) An important provision in the Clayton Act specifically exempted labor from the antitrust provisions.

Although the Clayton Act made it illegal to take over control of another firm by purchasing its stock when the adverse effect on competition was substantial, it neglected to prohibit taking over control by purchasing the firm's plant and equipment. Thus, although it dealt with the trust, or "loose-knit" combination of competitors, it neglected the merger, or "close-knit" combination. In 1950 this loophole was closed by passage of the Celler-Kefauver Act, which applied the same provisions to asset acquisitions as had previously applied only to acquisitions of stock.

The Federal Trade Commission Act (1914) created an independent commission to investigate industrial practices and to police unfair and predatory practices. Although initially the FTC had substantial powers to issue "cease and desist orders" without being subject to judicial review, the Supreme Court denied it this power in 1919. The FTC has not, in fact, played the vital fact-finding role its proposers envisaged, although it continues to perform a number of functions and to exercise some policy influence in the antitrust field. It does do a fair amount of policing of unfair trade practices, which are defined by Section 5 of the act. Further, by virtue of an unwritten agreement with the Antitrust Division, it exercises primary supervision in a number of industries.

The Hart-Scott-Rodino Antitrust Improvement Act (1976) amended both the Sherman and Clayton acts in ways that increased penalties and made mergers somewhat easier to attack.

Trends of judicial interpretation

The first important series of antitrust prosecutions occurred at the beginning of the twentieth century. Two decisions of major importance were issued in 1911 when, in forcing the Standard Oil Company and the American Tobacco Company to divest themselves of a large share of their holdings of other companies, the Supreme Court enunciated the "rule of reason." Not all trusts, but only *unreasonable* combinations in restraint of trade, merited conviction under the Sherman Act. The rule of reason received a narrow interpretation in the famous U.S. Steel case (1920), in which the Court found that the company had not violated the law, even though it found that the organizers of the company had *intended* to monopolize the industry, and even though the company had at an earlier time conspired to fix prices. The Court held that U.S. Steel had not succeeded in *achieving* a monopoly (indeed, its vain attempts at price fixing proved it!). The fact that it was a big company that controlled half the industry and had potential monopoly power was, the Court ruled, beside the point. The decision said in part, "The law does not make mere size an offense. It . . . requires overt acts."

The U.S. Steel decision and a series of related ones reached a climax in the International Harvester case (1927), in which the Court not only reiterated that mere size was not an offense but added that neither was the existence of unexerted monopoly power, no matter how impressive that power might be. These decisions reflected the business-oriented mood of the country during the 1920s, a mood shared by a highly conservative Supreme Court. Under this interpretation, which was to last until World War II, the antitrust laws were virtually unenforceable so far as attacks on the structure of heavily concentrated industries were concerned.

A sharp break in this situation occurred in a series of cases prosecuted in the late 1930s, which reached the Court both before and just after World War II. A landmark decision in *U.S.* v. *Socony-Vacuum Oil Co.* (1940) enunciated a strong rule against price fixing: "Under the Sherman Act a combination formed for the purpose and with the effect of raising, depressing, fixing, pegging or stabilizing the price of a commodity in interstate commerce is illegal *per se.*" Thus where price fixing was concerned no test of reasonableness or sound social purpose would be applied.

An even more basic attack on the rule of reason was enunciated in the Aluminum Company of America (ALCOA) case. Prosecution of the case was begun in 1937 (a date of some importance, as we shall see), but the decision was not handed down until 1945. The decision directly reversed the U.S. Steel and International Harvester decisions and found ALCOA to be an illegal monopoly even though it had engaged in no unreasonable behavior. The decision suggested that beyond some point mere size would in itself be an offense. This reversal was possible because the mood of the country—and the composition of its courts—had changed sharply. This case, and some others, led some people to speak of the "new Sherman Act." Although subsequent decisions somewhat modified the strongly anti-big-business aspects of the ALCOA case, there is no doubt that in the postwar period it became possible to use the antitrust laws against highly concentrated oligopolistic industries without having to expect the government's case to be thrown out of court.

The modification of Section 7 of the Clayton Act in 1950, together with the onset of the "Warren Court," ushered in a period of virtually unbroken triumphs for the government in its antitrust cases. Four members of that Court, Chief Justice Warren and Associate Justices Black, Brennan, and Douglas, formed a solid antitrust block and needed but one more vote to command a majority. They usually found it. In particular, in the merger field, every **horizontal merger** (i.e., between two companies selling the same or similar products) brought to the Supreme Court was found by it to constitute a substantial lessening of competition and thus to be illegal. In the Von's Grocery case (1965), a merger of two supermarkets was ruled illegal although the merged firms would have had only a 7.5 percent share of the local (Los Angeles) market.

In the **vertical merger** field (i.e., between a supplier and a customer), the merger of Brown Shoe Company with a chain of retail stores (Kinney) was found illegal even though Kinney sold less than 2 percent of the nation's shoes and Brown supplied only 8 percent of Kinney's needs.

Conglomerate mergers (i.e., between firms that are neither horizontally nor vertically related and are therefore not in the same market) had long been thought to be outside the reach of antitrust laws unless specific anticompetitive practices were involved. However, in a series of decisions since 1965, the Court has slightly opened the door to attacking them under Section 7 of the Clayton Act.

The Warren Court has been replaced by the Burger Court, four of its nine members having been appointed by President Nixon and one by President Ford. This Court's views on antitrust matters are not clearly defined, but in a few close decisions it has indicated that the pendulum has swung away from the position (as stated by Justice Stewart in a dissenting opinion) where "the government always wins."

Periods of vigorous prosecution by the Justice Department

Courts, whatever their predilections, decide only those cases that come before them.

Whether to prosecute and which cases are chosen is largely decided by the Antitrust Division, whose head is a presidential appointee.

When the Sherman Act was passed in 1890, it was adopted with little discussion and attracted remarkably little attention. It was not until Theodore Roosevelt succeeded William McKinley in the White House that "trust-busting" became an activity of any note. Roosevelt, the hero of San Juan Hill, tried to storm the hill of big business. It was he who, in 1903, set up the Antitrust Division in the Department of Justice, and it was his administration that initiated the series of major prosecutions that led to the Standard Oil, American Tobacco, and U.S. Steel decisions. The decisions of the Supreme Court on these and related cases, as well as a sharply conservative turn in the climate of economic opinion, took the steam out of antitrust, and few major antitrust prosecutions were commenced for twenty-five years, from 1912 to 1937.

Despite fears among businessmen about Franklin Roosevelt's radicalism, no administration before or since has given such encouragement to policies in restraint of trade! Roosevelt's first administration (1933–1937) was so concerned with stemming the Great Depression that under the National Recovery Administration it fostered industry councils that were encouraged to fix prices, limit outputs, and try to restore stability to demoralized markets.

The appointment of Thurman Arnold in 1937 to the leadership of the Antitrust Division marked the beginning of a most vigorous period of antitrust activity. The Department of Justice, no doubt partly because of a very marked change in the composition of the Supreme Court, attempted to bring cases that would reopen issues that had been foreclosed by the rule of reason. The fruits of this activity included the previously mentioned ALCOA and Socony-Vacuum decisions.

Antitrust policy was pushed to the sidelines by the overriding problems of World War II,

the postwar readjustment, and the Korean War and did not begin to reemerge until the 1950s. A relatively vigorous antitrust policy was pursued during the Eisenhower and Kennedy administrations. When President Johnson appointed Donald F. Turner as head of the Antitrust Division, many expected a sharp increase in antitrust activity. Turner, a professor at the Harvard Law School, had been an outspoken advocate of taking market structure as an indication of market power, regardless of market conduct. Thus a potential return to the vigor of the Thurman Arnold period of prosecution (with a very sympathetic Supreme Court) seemed to foreshadow a new era for the Antitrust Division. Partly because energies were once again diverted by more pressing problems—principally the war in Vietnam—this did not occur.

A potentially important feature of the Johnson period was the issuance in 1968 of merger guidelines that attempted to define the structural conditions that would lead the Justice Department to attack proposed mergers. Guidelines had long been advocated by Turner as a means of lessening uncertainty among businessmen and reducing the need to litigate. Because the actual guidelines were too vague, because the personnel in the Antitrust Division changed sharply after the election of Nixon, and because the great merger wave of 1966–1968 receded, the guidelines have been of only limited influence.

Richard McLaren, President Nixon's first antitrust chief, took a vigorous but different approach to merger prosecutions. He urged upon the courts new theories by which conglomerate mergers (which had become very important in the preceding few years) might be brought within the reach of Section 7. His efforts had limited success. Thomas Kauper shifted attention heavily toward price fixing activities and the activities of firms in regulated industries. Important recent cases have been filed against IBM and against AT&T. The Carter administration's antitrust stance has not yet been revealed.

THE SUCCESS OF ANTITRUST POLICY

Many students of the subject feel that antitrust laws have proven remarkably ineffective in counteracting bigness and the concentration of market power in the United States. However, although the Sherman Act is nearly ninety years old, the combination of reasonably permissive (from the government's point of view) interpretation by the courts and reasonably active governmental activity has been present only for the last thirty years. *Antitrust is, in this sense, in its early development.* Its potential impact is not known, for it has never been well tested. Economists are not in general agreement as to whether the structure of American industry has been influenced very much by antitrust legislation. American industry is highly concentrated (see Chapter 16), but empirical studies show no tendency for the concentration either to increase or to decrease drastically. Would the pattern be very different if there had been no antitrust laws, or if the laws we have had been vigorously enforced for half a century? We do not know for sure. Many economists and antitrust lawyers feel that our antitrust laws have been more nearly successful in inhibiting restrictive practices than in altering the basic structure of the economy.

ECONOMICS AND THE LAW

Economic concepts such as competition, monopoly, and markets lie at the very heart of antitrust policy, and economists are employed in the Justice Department, by the FTC, and by lawyers for private companies. Market definition, for example, plays a critical role in antitrust merger litigation: Section 7 of the Clayton Act requires evaluation of a merger by asking whether "in any line of commerce, in any section of the country the effect of such acquisition may be substantially to lessen competition or to tend to create a monopoly."

"Line of commerce" and "section of the country" involve product and geographic market definitions because competition occurs only within sensibly defined markets. A great many antitrust cases have turned on market definition. Here are a few of the questions the courts have asked and answered: Is cellophane in the same market as wax paper, Saran wrap, and other flexible wrapping materials? (Yes, said the Supreme Court in 1956.) Are glass jars and tin cans in the same market? (Yes, said the Supreme Court in 1964.) Are insulated aluminum and copper cable in the same market? (Yes, said the District Court; No, said the Supreme Court in 1964.) Are New York and Philadelphia banks in the same market and thus in competition with one another? (No, said the courts in 1963.) Do different grades of coal in Illinois constitute an economic market? (No, said the District Court in 1972, in part because it found the relevant market to be energy. The Supreme Court did not reverse the decision.) Even though courts decide these matters, the matters themselves involve economic questions, and economic studies or witnesses were introduced by both parties in each of these litigations.

But while antitrust policies use economic theory and economic expertise, our antitrust laws ignore certain distinctions that economists think are important. In particular, the role of big business, even monopoly, in promoting dynamic advances, as argued by Professor Schumpeter, has many adherents but is largely ignored by antitrust policies in America, as is the distinction between oligopoly and monopoly.

Economists themselves, in fact, are divided as to whether these distinctions are important. Some feel that public policy ought to be based on things such as size and market share, without regard for actual conduct or performance. Others offer their own "rule of reason," called "workable competition." They argue that the real choice is between more or less oligopoly and that the positive effects of a given market share, or merger, on prices,

Figure 18–4 The problem of natural monopoly

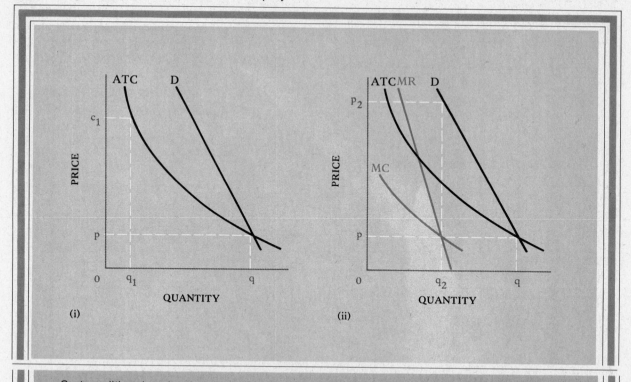

Cost conditions in a situation of natural monopoly are such that a single firm is required to achieve the economies of scale, but a monopolist finds it profitable to restrict output to maximize profits. The cost and revenue curves are identical in the two parts of the diagram. (i) Because ATC declines sharply, efficiency is served by having a single firm. Clearly, one firm producing at q would be more efficient than several firms producing q_1 each, at a cost of c_1 per unit. (ii) But an unregulated monopoly would restrict output to q_2 and charge price p_2, thus depriving consumers of the advantages of large-scale production.

on profits, and on costs should be determined in each individual case. This seems so reasonable you may wonder why some people object. They object because they feel that workable competition will lead to endless studies and no action. Because economists do not speak with a unified voice on this matter, it is perhaps not surprising that the basic nature of the antitrust program continues to be set by the lawyers.

Public policy toward monopoly: public utility regulation

NATURAL MONOPOLY

The public utility concept grew out of the recognition by economists that when there were great economies of large-scale production, competition would be impractical if not impossible. The cost advantage of having one railroad between two points rather than fifty railroads (or one water company in a city, or one telephone system in a country) is obvious. In such situations, sometimes characterized as those of **natural monopoly,** it would be inefficient to have a large number of firms each producing a small output at a high cost per unit. If such a situation existed, any firm that got bigger than its rivals would soon find itself in a position to cut price below its rivals' costs and monopolize the industry. While sensible public policy would not want to compel the maintenance of a large number of small, inefficient producers, neither would it want to give the monopolist the opportunity to restrict output, raise price, and appropriate as profits the gains available by virtue of large-scale production.

The dilemma of natural monopoly to which public utility regulation is a response is illustrated in Figure 18–4. To achieve low costs, a single large producer is necessary. But an unregulated profit-maximizing monopoly would restrict output, raise price, and fail to provide the large volume of output at a low price that the technology makes possible.

One possible response to this dilemma is to have government assume ownership of the single firm and instruct (or delegate to) the managers of the nationalized industry how to produce and price in the national interest. Many countries have done precisely that with telephone and railroad services, among others. The characteristic United States response since the late nineteenth century, when the modern regulatory commissions were first utilized, has been to allow private enterprise but to regulate its behavior.[6]

Public utility regulation gives to appropriate public authorities (usually specially constituted regulatory commissions such as the Interstate Commerce Commission and the Wisconsin Public Utilities Commission) control over the price and quantity of service provided by a natural monopoly, with the object of achieving the efficiency of a single seller without the output restriction of the monopolist.

In return for giving a company a franchise or license to be the sole producer, the public utility regulators reserve the right to regulate its behavior.

Regulation of roughly this kind is common in many forms of transportation (railroads, airlines, trucking, and pipelines) and in the provision of telephone service, electric power, water, and gas.

THE THEORY OF NATURAL MONOPOLY REGULATION[7]

What price should a regulatory commission permit? It might wish to set price equal to marginal cost (the way it would be in perfect competition), but such a price and quantity would surely lead to losses, since marginal cost is necessarily below average cost when average cost is falling (see pages 172–174). This is illustrated in Figure 18–5. Some means of continuing subsidization of these losses would be required. An alternative is to permit the company to charge a price that allows it to cover all its costs and earn a fair return on its investment.

Because average total cost has been defined to include such a fair return, this means that the regulatory objective attempts to set price equal to average total cost. In essence, this is the objective of most regulatory commissions with regard to pricing in natural monopoly

---

[6] Note however that in the United States the Post Office from the start was treated as a government monopoly and many municipalities today run their own water and electric companies.

[7] It is a mistake to think all or even most regulation is directed toward the control of natural monopoly. The Food and Drug Administration and the Securities and Exchange Commission are mainly concerned with consumer protection. Many of the activities of the Federal Communications Commission and the Federal Aviation Administration concern orderly use of airwaves and skyways. We limit our discussion to natural monopoly regulation.

Figure 18–5 Pricing strategy for a regulatory commission

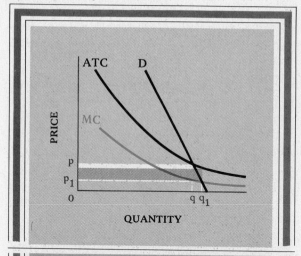

Average cost pricing is the goal of regulatory commissions, which seek the lowest prices possible without losses for natural monopolies. Although perfect competition leads to production where price equals marginal costs, here the price cannot be set at p_1, where demand equals marginal cost, because the firm would necessarily suffer losses (the shaded area). Price p covers all costs (including the opportunity cost of capital). The corresponding output q achieves most of the cost advantages of large-scale output.

situations. This theory is extraordinarily simple. The practical problems of putting theory into effect are very much more difficult.

PROBLEMS OF IMPLEMENTING THE THEORY

Because there are many different regulatory agencies, there is enormous variety in the details of regulation. Despite the variety of regulatory practice, there is enough similarity in both goals and certain general problems that arise again and again that the problems can be discussed generally.

A primary objective of regulation has been setting prices in such a way as to both cover costs and achieve the large outputs required to reap the economies of scale that characterize natural monopoly situations. Generally, having set prices, regulatory agencies permit price increases if profits fall below "fair" levels and require price reductions if profits exceed such levels. This leads to some practical difficulties.

The definition of costs

If a company is to be allowed to charge a price determined as "cost plus a fair profit" (as the regulators put it), and if its price is below the profit-maximizing one, it is clearly in its interest to exaggerate its reported costs, if it can. One major activity of regulatory commissions has been to define rules of allowable costing, as they affect both permissible rates of depreciation and reasonable expenses and expenditures. Freezing the rate of return removes the profit motive for keeping costs down. But although the firm does not care, the public presumably does, and thus cost supervision is an important activity of public utility regulation. Without it, the regulated industries' managers might have no incentive to be efficient and might simply let costs drift upward.

The rate base

Suppose it is agreed that a firm should be allowed to earn a rate of return of 8 percent on its capital. The **rate of return** is defined as the ratio of profits to invested capital. What is the value of the capital to which 8 percent is to be applied? The allowable amount is called the **rate base.** There has been no more controversial area than this in public utility regulation. Should the original cost or the reproduction cost of the firm's assets be used? It does not make much difference unless prices are changing, but in the inflationary situation of the last thirty years, reproduction cost is uniformly higher than original costs and thus leads to higher bases, higher permitted profits, and higher rates to users. Regulatory commissions (and the courts) have vacillated on this issue.[8]

The precise nature of regulatory rules is important because the rules affect the incentives of those regulated. Economists Harvey Averch and Leland Johnson have shown that a regulated utility has a lesser incentive to resist high capital costs than an unregulated one, and that in some circumstances it pays the unregulated utility to buy relatively unproductive equipment. This is true because if profits depend upon the rate base, it often pays the firm to increase its rate base. Thus the notion of "necessary and prudent investments" enters into regulatory rules. This tendency for one regulation to lead to a need for yet further regulation has been called the tar-baby effect, after a fictional creature made of tar which overcame an attacker by enmeshing it.

A fair return

The permitted rate of return that is implicit in the theory of public utility regulation is the opportunity cost of the owners' capital with allowances for risk. Regulatory commissions have paid some attention to overall earnings rates in the economy, and the level of permitted earnings has changed slightly over time. But equity and tradition have played a much larger role than considerations of opportunity cost. Most regulatory rates are in the neighborhood of 6 to 9 percent, and these nominal rates are often difficult to interpret.

It is common to speak of the regulatory rate of return as "guaranteed," but this is not strictly accurate. In principle, it is a maximum "target" rate of return. Actual earnings may be larger or smaller over the short run because of economic factors and regulatory lags. If actual earnings are larger, the regulatory commission will refuse to grant price increases and may even seek to lower prices and reduce future profits. If the actual earnings are lower, the regulatory commission will permit price increases.

It is possible for a utility to earn more than the nominal target rate if it is in an industry where its unregulated profits would be growing. For example, suppose the permitted rate of return is 6 percent, and a certain company earns 10 percent in one particular year. No one confiscates its "excess" return, and it will take the regulatory commission six months or more to force it to reduce rates to the point where its earnings are again 6 percent. If this situation tends to recur, the average profit over time will be in excess of 6 percent—possibly well in excess. Of course, in a declining industry or in a rapid inflation the reverse situation can occur, and a firm may find its profits falling short of the permitted rate. Even though its petition to raise rates is approved, it may take time and the end result is likely to be an average profit rate less than the official permitted rate.

The curtailment of service

Because profits are not guaranteed, a regulated utility in a declining industry may have a serious problem. If it is failing to make profits equal to the permitted rate, it may apply for permission to increase its prices, but if its demand is elastic, a rise in rates will lead to a reduction in its revenues and may reduce profits. Privately owned urban transit systems and passenger rail lines have proven unprofitable because of secularly declining demand as people shift to substitutes: private cars and airplanes. Given elastic demand curves, when transport companies raise fares (hoping to increase revenues) they find they only lose additional customers to other means of transport.

At this point a bus company, for example, may look to its costs to see how it can avoid

[8] One suggestion—to take the market value of a firm's assets—sounds reasonable but in fact is not because, as we shall see in Chapter 22, the market value of a firm's assets depends on the firm's earnings. *Any* amount of profits is consistent with an asset base capitalized to yield that amount of profits.

losses. Often it finds that some parts of its service (such as routes to outlying neighborhoods) no longer cover the variable costs of providing them, and it proposes to the regulatory authority that it drop this service. Often the regulators say no. The reason may be that there would be social costs to abandoning the bus service (such as increased congestion in the downtown area as even more people used their own cars) that loom large to the regulators but not to the bus company.

Of course, if a utility is losing money and if no adjustment of prices or service can save it, it will eventually discontinue service via bankruptcy or "sell out" to the public, to be run as a subsidized public enterprise.

EVALUATING PUBLIC UTILITY REGULATION

The moral of the public utility experience is that what looks like a simple and straightforward theory of regulating natural monopoly turns out to be highly complex in practice. In large part this is because regulated companies adapt their behavior to the rules that are imposed on them, and thus begins a chain of adaptation and change by regulators and regulated that produces a complex and cumbersome apparatus. Moreover the need for due process in decisions that affect property rights has made procedures and decisions legalistic and resource-using. Not only are there costs of running regulatory commissions, and costs imposed on the courts by the seemingly endless appeals, but there are regulatory costs imposed on businesses as they strive to comply with regulatory paperwork. Are the benefits worth the costs?

Some, including Chicago's George Stigler and Richard Posner, believe that the evidence shows that the levels of prices, quantities, and profits are about the same under regulation as they would have been without it; they even go so far as to suggest that unregulated monopoly would have performed better. Others, including the 1971 Ash Commission, feel that the deficiencies lie in the structure of regulation and that changing the way regulation is carried out will improve things. Still others think that the failures of regulation require nationalization or new legislation defining a novel approach to what regulators should do.

There is, however, a remarkable consensus that regulation has failed to achieve the benefits sought. Perhaps the most widely held view is that regulation, even if effective at first, becomes too rigid and unresponsive to change and as a result fails to recognize and to permit such competition as is possible. Given changing technology, yesterday's natural monopoly of a single railroad may become but one mode of transportation in a competitive transportation industry. Wire telephone communications are no longer unique, given radio and satellites. Even the Post Office is not the only way to send written messages and parcels from one place to another. Thus the scope of natural monopoly regulation keeps changing. But regulators tend to cling to, and in some cases are legally committed to, rules and assumptions that may no longer fit the real world.

Changes in regulation in some form or another seem likely to occur over the next decade in response to this growing consensus. The pressures for some deregulation have been increased by the allegation—taken seriously by some—that regulatory rules have contributed significantly to the stubborn persistence of inflationary forces in the U.S. economy both by encouraging a "cost plus" mentality in pricing and by limiting entry into regulated areas.

Which of many proposed directions for regulatory reform will be followed is unclear at this stage. The present regulatory commissions are not without political support in Congress and are generally staunchly defended by *the regulated industries themselves*. To some, this last point is the most telling criticism of all.

Summary

1. Most economists reject monopoly and advocate competition as the standard for market behavior. The case against monopoly rests in part on the predictions that prices will change less in response to cost changes in monopoly than in competition and that if costs, demand, and products are unchanged, the monopolization of a previously competitive industry will lead to a rise in price and a decline in output.

2. The traditional economic case for competition rests on two properties of competitive equilibrium: that price is equal to marginal cost and that the level of cost is the lowest attainable, given the technology of the society. Under rather strict conditions, this leads to an allocation of resources that is efficient in the sense that it is impossible to make some consumers better off without making others worse off.

3. The noneconomic case for competition lies in its impersonality and the total absence of groups in the society with market power. Firms and households respond to market signals that they take as given to achieve an optimal allocation of resources.

4. Several qualifications may be noted. Strictly, the existence and desirability of the allocative efficiency of competitive equilibrium require (a) that competitive conditions obtain everywhere in the economy; (b) that there be no substantial discrepancies between private and social costs and benefits; (c) that perfect competition involves no cost disadvantage to society, such as unexploited economies of large-scale production; and (d) that the particular distribution of income that accompanies a competitive equilibrium is not itself a matter of concern.

5. If costs are not independent of market structure, the prima facie case against monopoly is weakened. There are reasons why costs may differ as between monopoly and competition. If, as Schumpeter believed, the incentive to innovate is much greater under conditions of monopoly, costs and prices over time may be lower under monopoly than they would have been if perfect competition had prevailed.

6. The policy implications of the classical view of monopoly and competition led in two directions: public utility regulation to deal with natural monopoly and antitrust laws to deal with other kinds of monopoly.

7. The basic tool of antitrust policy is the series of laws that seeks to eliminate practices that lead to monopoly.

The overall effect of antitrust policy at any time rests on three things: the nature of the laws themselves, the attitude and interpretation of the courts, and the vigor with which prosecutions are brought by the Department of Justice. A conjunction of conditions favoring a vigorous and aggressive antitrust policy has been present only in the period since World War II.

8. Economists' opinions as to what antitrust law ought to be are divided between a view based largely on the mere existence of market power and a discretionary view that attempts to evaluate the workability of competition. Many believe that antitrust laws have been more nearly successful in inhibiting restrictive practices than in altering the basic structure of the economy.

9. The original philosophy of public utility regulation was to grant a monopoly where necessary to achieve the advantages of large-scale production but to prevent the monopolist from restricting output and raising price. The most common regulatory approach has been to regulate prices. This is done by watching profits: allowing price increases only if necessary to permit the regulated utility to earn a fair return on its capital and requiring price decreases if profits rise above the approved level.

10. Implementation of this straightforward theory encounters difficulties because any set of rules becomes a set of signals that induces patterns of response from those regulated. Thus it has been necessary for regulators to define carefully "proper" costs, how the costs should be measured, what the appropriate rate base is, what constitute "necessary and prudent" additions to capital equipment, and what constitutes a fair return. They have also been forced to determine when and whether utilities can discontinue providing services to those groups in the community from whom (private) revenues do not cover (private) variable costs. Whether overall public utility regulation has had much effect and, if so, whether the effects have been beneficial on net balance is a matter of current debate.

Concepts for review

Effects of monopolizing a competitive industry
Competition and allocative efficiency
The effect of market structure on costs
Purposes of antitrust legislation
Natural monopoly
Difficulties of public utility regulation

Discussion questions

1. "I think there are some people, in and out of government, who get a little confused and associate bigness with badness. Success alone is now evidence enough to warrant intensive scrutiny by the government to determine how the success can be remedied—as if it were some sort of disease. The age of Orwell's doublethink, prophesied for 1984, has come early. For now, to win is to lose. The real losers are the consumers. They lose the advantages of free competition; new and better products, lower prices and wider choices." Comment on these views of GM Chairman Murphy.

2. Economists Armen Alchian and Reuben Kessel have advanced the hypothesis that monopolists choose to satisfy more of their nonmonetary aims than do perfect competitors. Consider three aims.
a. exercising the prejudices of the monopolists against certain racial minorities
b. enjoying a good life with big expense accounts
c. promoting their political philosophies by advertising and broadcasting
What theoretical arguments could support the Alchian-Kessel hypothesis? How might you test this hypothesis?

3. Evaluate the wisdom of having the antitrust division use profits as a measure of monopoly power in deciding whether to prosecute a case. Would such a rule be expected to affect the behavior of firms with high profits? In what ways might any changes be socially beneficial and in what ways socially costly?

4. Price fixing agreements are (with some specific exemptions) violations of the antitrust laws. Consider the effects of the following. In what way, if at all, should they be viewed as being similar to price fixing agreements?
a. a manufacturer "recommending" minimum prices to its dealers
b. manufacturers selling their own output at retail through company-owned retail outlets at fixed prices
c. a trade association that publishes "average industry total costs of production" every month

5. The Department of Justice merger guidelines permit a "failing company" defense to an otherwise illegal acquisition but reject an "efficiency" defense. Thus a merger that keeps a failing and presumably inefficient firm in business is permitted, but one that achieves a more efficient level of production is not. Can you develop any arguments in support of this policy?

6. Under what circumstances might some aspect of market structure or market conduct be treated as illegal per se— that is, without considering the effect in the particular case?

7. The WREDD Brick Company, the second largest of five suppliers of bricks in the Zackville area, plans to merge with one of the following companies:
a. the Good Old Brick Company, Zackville's largest
b. the largest lumber company in town
c. the smallest brick supplier in town
d. the All Brick Construction Company
e. the Bank of Zackville
f. Sam's Used Car Lot
Classify each potential merger as horizontal, vertical, or conglomerate. How might each merger affect competition? Which would seem to you most objectionable? Least objectionable? Why?

8. One of the most controversial proposals before Congress asks for the "vertical distintegration" of the oil companies. "If you break up the oil companies, you'll pay through the hose," says an oil company ad. "Bringing down oil prices must start with the vertical separation of oil exploration, production, transmission, refining and retail sale," says a consumer advocate. What are the implicit assumptions underlying each of these views?

9. "In a competitive market the least-cost production techniques are revealed by entry and exit, while in public-utility regulation they are revealed by commission rate hearings. It is easier to fool the commission than the market: Therefore, wherever possible, competition should be permitted." Discuss.

10. It is often asserted that when a regulatory agency, such as a public utilities commission, is established it will ultimately become controlled by the people it was intended to regulate. This argument raises the question of who regulates the regulators. Can you identify why this might happen? How might the integrity of regulatory boards be protected?

11. There is a raging debate about whether or not to deregulate airline fares. Take as facts (1) that passenger traffic on most airlines is growing, (2) that major airlines show losses in each recent year, (3) that unregulated intrastate airlines charge lower fares than the regulated airlines are permitted to charge, and they earn profits. Are these facts mutually consistent? Evaluate the following assertions.
a. "Price regulation now serves to stifle competition, increase cost to travelers, makes the industry less efficient than it could be, and denies large segments of the American public access to lower cost air transportation."
b. "Price deregulation would not result in long-term fare reductions. At best, there would be a brief flurry of price cutting. Even if CAB was abolished and the present managements of all airlines eliminated, the main factors pushing up fares would continue to push them up."
c. "Deregulation of airfares will hurt the consumer."

19

Who runs the firm and for what ends?

Ralph Nader and John Kenneth Galbraith have made their names household words by excoriating the managers of large corporations for irresponsibility toward the welfare of consumers. Not long ago Henry Ford II personally invited 1,300 of America's largest companies to join him in supporting the Committee on Constructive Consumerism, with a budget of $7 million per year, in order to win back public confidence. "Catching the Conscience of the Corporation" and "The 'Bottom Line' [Profits] Is No Longer Where It's At" were headlines of recent articles in *The New York Times* about activities of corporations. How does this public consciousness square with the economic theory of profit-maximizing firms we have been studying?

In economic theory, the firm is a producer of goods and a seller of products. Assumptions are made about the firm's motives and its opportunities, and these are used to derive testable predictions about market behavior.

The assumptions of the standard theory suppress the notion of the firm as an organic collection of individuals and also suppress any conflict in motivation among the owners of a firm or between the owners and the managers.

Firms in standard theory are efficient, single-purpose organizations that seek to maximize their profits by responding to market demand curves and factor costs. Demand curves and factor costs are determined by forces that are mainly beyond the control of individual firms.

In making these assumptions, has the theory lost contact with the world it purports to explain? This question, a matter of lively current controversy, is examined in some detail in this chapter. Here we discuss some of the major criticisms directed at the assumptions just outlined, beginning with criticisms that strike at the very core of microeconomic theory—the theory that provides the foundations of our view of the overall working of the market economy.

Does the firm manipulate the market?

In conventional theory, demand curves depend decisively on consumers' tastes and incomes and are to a significant degree independent of the actions of firms. Firms are assumed to be in business to make money, which they do by producing and selling the goods and services that are desired by consumers. The successful firm is the one that best satisfies consumers' demands, while the firm that consistently fails to do this will eventually fail. The ultimate source of all profits is consumers' desires. (Even monopoly profits depend on consumers' willingness to buy the product that the monopolist controls.) The need for firms to respond to consumers' desires is an important part of any argument for the value of the free-enterprise system. If firms did not so respond, there would be little justification in allowing them to exert major influences on the allocation of the country's resources and on the choice of what to produce.

THE HYPOTHESIS THAT THE FIRM CONTROLS THE MARKET

A very different hypothesis is given its most prominent expression by Galbraith and Nader. In this view it is *not* consumers' real wants that create the market signals that in turn provide the profit opportunities that motivate business behavior. Instead, large corporations have great power to create and manipulate demand. Firms must plan, and invest, for an uncertain future, and the profitability of the enormous investments that they make is threatened by the unpredictability of events. Firms render the future less unpredictable in order to protect their investments by actively manipulating market demand and by co-opting government agencies that are supposed to control their activities. We shall now examine this hypothesis in some detail.

Manipulation of demand

The most important source of unpredictable events that may jeopardize corporate investments is unexpected shifts in market demand curves. To guard against the effects of unexpected declines in demand, corporations spend vast amounts on advertising that allows them to sell what they want to produce rather than what consumers want to buy. At the same time, corporations hold off the market products that consumers would like to buy. One way to do this is by buying up patents on new goods and then doing nothing with them. This reduces the risks inherent in investing in wholly new and untried products and avoids the possibility that those new products that are successful might spoil the market for an existing product.

According to this hypothesis, we consumers are the victims of the corporations; we are pushed around at their whim, persuaded to buy things we do not really want, and denied products we would like. In short we are brainwashed ciphers with artificially created wants and have no real autonomy with respect to our own consumption.

Corruption of public authorities

A second threat to the long-range plans and investments of corporations comes from uncontrollable and often unpredictable changes in the nature of government interference with the freedom of the corporation. This political threat is met by co-opting or corrupting the members of Congress who pass laws affecting corporations and the government agencies that are supposed to be regulating them. Corporation managers, according to the theory, indirectly subvert public institutions (from universities to regulatory agencies). Government, instead of regulating business and protecting the public interest, has become the servant of the corporation. It supplies the corporate sector with such essential inputs into its productive process as educated, trained, healthy, and socially secure workers. Government also serves the giant corporation through policies concerning tariffs, import quotas, tax rules, subsidies, and research and development. These policies protect and insulate the industrial establishment from competitive pressures and reinforce its dominance and its profitability.

Corruption of our value system

These tasks, and the requirements of production, create a class of managers—a technostructure—that exerts the dominant influence in the corporation. The managers have great power. The corporations they manage earn large profits that can be reinvested to further the achievement of the values of the ruling technostructure—values that emphasize industrial production, rapid growth, and highly materialistic aspirations at the expense of the better things of life (such as cultural and aesthetic values) and the quality of the environment.

More important, the industrial managerial group joins with the military in a military-industrial complex that utilizes, trains, and elevates the technicians to positions of power and prestige not only in industry but in the army, in the defense establishment, and in the highest positions of government. In so doing, the corporations and their managers threaten to dominate if not subvert our foreign policies as well as our domestic ones.

The New Industrial State

The foregoing is an outline of what Galbraith calls the New Industrial State.[1] If Galbraith's

[1] These views did not, however, originate with the publication in 1967 of Galbraith's book by that title or with the formation of "Nader's Raiders." Much earlier James Burnham wrote *The Managerial Revolution* and Robert Brady sounded an alarm in *Business as a System of Power.* Thorstein Veblen had predicted the technocratic takeover of society in *The Engineers and the Price System* in 1921, and Karl Marx predicted the subversion of the government bureaucrat by the businessman over a century ago.

theories of the behavior of modern corporations were substantially correct, we would have to make major revisions in our ideas of how free-market economies work.

According to the concept of the New Industrial State, the largest corporations (1) tend to dominate the economy, (2) largely control market demand rather than being controlled by it, (3) co-opt government processes instead of being constrained by them, and (4) utilize their substantial discretionary power in ways that go against the interests of society.

THE EVIDENCE FOR THE HYPOTHESIS

Superficially at least, many of the facts of the American economy lend support to all aspects of the Galbraith hypothesis. Corporations do account for approximately two-thirds of all business done in the United States today, and large corporations dominate the corporate sector. Of nearly 200,000 manufacturing corporations, roughly 1 percent of them have $10 million or more in assets. These large corporations hold approximately 85 percent of manufacturing assets. The 200 to 250 largest corporations—$\frac{1}{10}$ of 1 percent of all manufacturing corporations—control approximately 50 percent of the total assets of manufacturing.

The giant corporations are well known to all of us: General Motors, Exxon (Standard Oil), U.S. Steel, Sears Roebuck, General Electric, and so on. Many of them are highly profitable, and most are so widely owned that management, rather than stockholders, exercises effective control. If power comes with size, a "few" people—several thousand strategically placed executives of a few hundred leading corporations—have great power over economic affairs. Moreover, these people are primarily white, male, wealthy, and politically conservative. As for political influence, individual corporations and trade associations have lobbyists and exercise whatever persuasion they can. Executives of many of these corporations serve on public commissions and frequently take important government positions. Executives often make large contributions to political campaigns. Political influence is exercised at all levels of government; indeed there have been cases where entire city governments have been effectively in the pockets of local corporations.

The political activities of corporations are not confined to the United States. The Lockheed Corporation was recently implicated in scandals involving million-dollar bribes to secure foreign orders. The list of persons involved includes (among many others) a former Japanese prime minister, the husband of the ruling Queen of the Netherlands, and several former Italian Christian Democrat cabinet ministers. There is no longer any doubt that corporations have succeeded in corrupting governments at the highest levels (or at least in harnessing the corruption that was already there) and have achieved through political channels results that they might never have achieved in the marketplace.

The great corporations, along with many smaller firms, spend vast amounts on advertising—as the hypothesis predicts. In 1975 total advertising expenditure was $28 billion. This sum was 2.4 percent of the value of the contribution of the private sector to the GNP. These expenditures are obviously designed to influence consumers' demand, and there is little doubt that if firms such as Lever Brothers, Gulf Oil, Schlitz, and GM cut their advertising, they would lose sales to their competitors.

It is also true that much of the pollution of our environment is associated with industries that consist of well-known large firms. If automobiles, electric power, steel, oil, industrial chemicals, detergents, and paper are the primary sources of our pollution, surely Ford, Consolidated Edison, Bethlehem Steel, Texaco, Monsanto, Proctor & Gamble, and International Paper are significantly to blame.

Each of these is among the 100 largest nonfinancial corporations.

DOUBTS ABOUT THE HYPOTHESIS
Sensitivity to market pressures
Even the largest and most powerful industries are not immune to market pressures. Ford's Edsel was a classic example of market rejection of a product. The penetration of small foreign cars into the American market forced the automobile industry into first the compact car and then the still cheaper small cars of the Pinto generation. The decline of railroading as a mode of passenger travel is manifest in many ways, as the financial history of once great railroading corporations shows. The failure of Penn Central is one example. Another is reflected in the fact that the Pullman Company was the nation's tenth largest firm in 1909; today it is not even in the top 300. The rise of air and motor travel and the decline of railroading were accompanied by a rise in the use of oil and a decline in the use of coal. More recently, the surge in demand for electric power and the shortage of oil have revitalized the coal industry.

Changes in demand and in taste are sometimes sudden and dramatic, but in the main they are gradual and continuous and less noticeable month by month than decade by decade. On the average about two new firms enter the top 100 every year, and as a consequence two others leave. This means a significant change over a decade.

Turnover in the list of leading companies is continuous and revealing. Only two, U.S. Steel and Exxon (Standard Oil of New Jersey), were in the top 10 both in 1909 and a half-century later. Consider these giants of 1909, none of them among the largest 250 today: International Mercantile Marine (today United States Lines), United States Cotton Oil, American Hide and Leather, American Ice, Baldwin Locomotive, Cudahy, International Salt, and United Shoe Machinery. They have slipped or disappeared largely because of the relative decline in the demand for their products. Today's giants include automobile, oil, and airline companies and electric power producers—for the obvious reason that demand for these products is very strong.

Are these demand shifts explained by corporate manipulation of consumers' tastes through advertising or by more basic changes? Advertising has two major aspects: it seeks to inform consumers of the characteristics of the available products and it seeks to influence consumers by altering their demands. The first aspect, informative advertising, plays an important part in the efficient operation of any free-market system; the second aspect is one through which firms seek to control the market rather than being controlled by it.

Clearly, advertising does influence consumers' demand. We have observed that if GM stopped advertising, it would surely lose sales to Ford and Chrysler, but it is hard to believe that the automotive society was conjured up by Madison Avenue or that when you are persuaded to "fly the friendly skies of United" your real alternative is to use a Conestoga wagon, a bicycle, or even a Greyhound bus—more likely you are foregoing American, Eastern, or Northwest Airlines. Careful promotion can influence the success of one rock group over another, but could it sell the waltz to today's teenager? Advertising—taste making—unquestionably plays a role in shaping demand, but so too do more basic human attitudes, psychological needs, and technological opportunities.

Certainly advertising shifts demands among very similar products. It is hard to believe, however, that the American economy or the average American's system of values would be fundamentally changed if there were available one more or one less make of automobile or TV set or brand of shoes. A look at those products that have brought basic changes to the economy—and perhaps to our value systems—suggests that these products succeeded *because consumers wanted them,* not because Madison Avenue brainwashed people into buying them. Consider a few of the major examples.

The automobile transformed American society and is now in demand everywhere in the world, even in Communist countries where only informative advertising exists. The Hollywood movie had an enormous influence in shaping our world and in changing some of our values; it was—and still is—eagerly attended everywhere in the world whether or not it is accompanied by a bally-hoo of advertising. The airplane—and the jet in particular—has shrunk the size of the world: It has allowed major league sports to expand beyond the confines of the Northeastern and Midwestern United States (and those cities which could be reached by an overnight bus or rail journey); it has made the international conference a commonplace among professionals; and it has made European, Hawaiian, and Caribbean vacations a reality for the many rather than for the very few. For better or worse, the revolution in behavior caused by the birth control pill is still being worked out. TV has changed the activities of children (and adults) in fundamental ways and has brought to viewers a sense of immediacy about distant events that newspapers could never achieve. It also provided news coverage that both caused and partially compensated for the decline in the number of newspapers in many American cities.

Many factors, including advertising and salesmanship, affect consumers' purchasing patterns. However, the new products that have really influenced the allocation of resources and the pattern of society—such as those mentioned in the previous paragraph—have succeeded because consumers wanted them; most of those that failed did so because they were not wanted—at least not at prices that would cover their costs of production.

The evidence suggests that the allocation of resources in the American economy owes more to the tastes and values of consumers than it does to corporate advertising and related activities.

Thus the Galbraithian view that corporations are able to create the demand for their products seems less consistent with the evidence than the conventional view that consumers are a major force in determining the economy's allocation of resources.

Who controls the government?

Is government subservient to big business? Lobbying is a legal, large-scale activity employed by many groups. Big business has its influence, but so too do farmers, labor unions, and small business groups. American corporations have certainly exercised illegal and improper influence on both domestic and foreign governments. Whether they do so on a large scale within the United States is an important question that requires serious examination. Cases of corrupt behavior have been documented at all levels of government; it does not follow from this, however, that government is subservient to the corporations and that decision making by the former is *dominated* by the wishes of the latter. It is easy to assert that "everyone knows that the oil lobby dominates Congress," but such assertions do not resolve empirical questions. Lobbying and influence may well help to explain why for years the United States imposed quotas on foreign oil imports, but lobbying by the oil companies did not prevent a delay of the Alaska pipeline for many years, the reduction in special tax reliefs, or restrictions imposed on offshore oil drilling. Relaxation of many antipollution restrictions came because of the oil shortages of the 1970s, not political pressure. Government contracts bolster the aerospace industry, but Boeing and Lockheed are in deep financial trouble, partly as a result of government decisions. Tobacco companies have seen government agencies first publicize the hazards of their principal product and then restrict their advertising.

Thus, while business often succeeds in its attempts to protect its commercial interests through political activity, it does so within limits. Where the truth lies between the extremes of "no influence" and "no limits" a matter now being subjected to substantial research. It is a matter that will be clarified by further research, not by mere assertion. In the meantime we can safely say, first, "corporations have a lot of political influence" and, second, "there are some serious constraints on the ability of corporations to exert political influence over all levels of American government."

Neglect of the public interest?

One aspect of the Galbraithian critique has found a receptive public: the apparent disregard by large corporations of the adverse effect of productive activities on the environment. The problems of pollution, discussed in some detail in Chapter 13, arise from activities of both small and large corporations and from activities of government units and citizens as well. Do such polluting activities represent in a significant degree irresponsible behavior by corporations that can be countered by such things as Campaign GM,–"a campaign to make General Motors responsible"? Are they instead to be regarded as examples of a market failure due to an externality? (See page 202 if you have forgotten this concept.) If the latter, they require not an exhortation to responsible behavior but some form of government policy action of the kind discussed in Chapter 24.

What has come to be known as the "consumerist" view, or consumerism, is that corporations ought to be forced to serve the consumers' or the general public's interest, not merely the interests of their stockholders. Thus, for example, GM's directors must be made to recognize that automobiles both pollute and cause accidents and that GM's abundant resources should be invested in developing and installing both safety and antipollution devices. This, consumerists argue, is a good and proper use of GM's profits, even if GM's stockholders do not see it that way and even if automobile purchasers do not want to pay the cost of the extra safety and anti-pollution devices.

The main arguments *for* this view are that only the company can know the potentially adverse effect of its action and that by virtue of holding a corporate charter, the corporation assumes the responsibility to protect the general welfare while pursuing private profits.

The main argument *against* the consumerist view is that managers of companies have neither the knowledge nor the ability to represent the general public interest; they are largely selected, judged, and promoted according to their ability to run a profit-oriented enterprise, and the assumption that they are especially competent to decide broader *public* questions is unjustified. Moral (as distinct from economic) decisions—such as whether to make or use nerve gas, to make or use internal combustion engines, to manufacture or smoke cigarettes, and to manufacture or utilize DDT or aerosol sprays—cannot properly be delegated to individual corporations or their executives. Some of them are individual decisions; others require either the expertise or the authority of a public regulatory agency, and whoever makes decisions on behalf of the public must be politically responsible to the public.

Those who oppose the consumerist view hold that most required changes in corporate behavior should be accomplished not by exhorting business leaders to behave responsibly, nor by placing consumer representatives on the corporation's board of directors, but by regulations or incentives that force or induce the desired corporate behavior. Let corporations pursue their profits—subject to public laws. For example, Congress can require all cars to have seat belts or require auto manufacturers to install antipollution valves or to meet specific standards of emission levels. Another alternative is to open the way for law-suits against corporations that either enjoin certain behavior or force corporations to pay for the damages their products cause.

The controversy over policy alternatives is both current and important, and much of the credit for the dialogue is due to Galbraith and Nader. It is essential to recognize that the policy issues at stake—whether and how to change the behavior of corporations—can arise whether corporations are primarily responding to market signals or whether they are impervious to them. If society does not approve the results of corporate behavior, it will want to control the behavior, whatever the cause, provided the costs—including undesirable side effects—do not exceed the benefits.

Who controls the modern corporation?

Galbraith's is not the only modern line of criticism of the theory of firm behavior. Most of the other critics, however, accept (what Galbraith denies) that industries face market demand curves which the firms can influence only marginally. The critics then go on to suggest that firms will behave in ways different from those suggested by the theory with respect to given market demands.

Corporations play a dominant role in much of American industry, and large corporations have dominant market shares in many industries. But who or what *is* the corporation? In some corporations, a small group or family provided most of the original capital, and the firm grew with little or no sale of equities to the public. American examples are the Ford Motor Company, which until 1956 was wholly owned by the Ford family; the Great Atlantic and Pacific Tea Company (Hartford family); E. I. du Pont de Nemours and Company (du Pont family); and the Aluminum Company of America (Mellon family). At the other extreme, the giant American Telephone and Telegraph Company is owned by more than 3 million shareholders, no one of whom owns as much as 1 percent of the 550 million outstanding shares.

Between these extremes lie the majority of corporations. The characteristic pattern of corporate ownership is that tens of thousands or hundreds of thousands of shareholders own minute fractions of the total, while dominant groups (often including other corporations) hold from 3 percent to 20 percent of the voting stock.

In major areas of the business world the days of the single proprietor who is both owner and manager of a company are gone forever. Diversification of ownership is a major characteristic of the modern corporation. Does it matter? Three hypotheses have been advanced about the consequences for corporate control of widespread ownership of corporate stock.

THE HYPOTHESIS OF MINORITY CONTROL

It is quite possible for the owners of a minority of the stock to control a majority of the shares that are voted and thus to exercise effective control over the decisions of the corporation.

This possibility arises because not all shares are actually voted. Each share of common stock has one vote in a corporation. Shares must be voted at the annual meeting of stockholders, either in person or by assigning a **proxy** to someone who will be attending. Any individual or group controlling 51 percent of the stock clearly controls a majority of the votes. But suppose one group owns 30 percent of the stock, with the remaining 70 percent distributed so widely that few of the dispersed group even bother to vote; in this event, 30 percent may be the overwhelming majority of the shares *actually voted*. In general, a very small fraction (sometimes as small as 5 percent) of shares actively voted may ex-

ercise dominant influence at meetings of stockholders.

The hypothesis of minority control is that a well-organized minority often controls the destiny of the corporation against the wishes of the majority.

The possibilities of minority control are enhanced through the device of a **holding company,** a corporation organized to hold the stock of another corporation. Suppose that in a certain corporation, A, ownership of 20 percent of the stock would give control. Now a new corporation, B, is formed and purchases 20 percent of the stock in A. Corporation B can now control A. If 20 percent ownership of B is sufficient to control B's affairs, an amount of money equal only to 4 percent of the value of A's stock (20 percent of 20 percent) is required for a group to gain control of B and thus of A. Now suppose a new corporation, C, is formed to purchase 20 percent of Corporation B. Control of C, albeit by ownership of a minority of its stock, can give control indirectly of A. This pyramiding of control through holding companies has no limits in logic, but it is limited both in law and in practicality. (It should also be mentioned that holding companies serve many purposes other than the rather suspect one described here.)

Dispersed ownership and minority control are well established in the corporate sector of the U.S. economy. But the hypothesis requires more than that a minority control the voting shares; it also requires that stockholders be able to exert a significant influence on the firm's behavior *and* that the controlling minority have interests and motives different from the holders of the majority of the firm's stocks. If all stockholders are mainly interested in having the firm maximize its profits, then it does not matter, as far as market behavior is concerned, which set of stockholders actually influences the firm's policy. There is no accepted evidence to show that controlling groups of stockholders generally seek objectives different from those sought by the holders of the majority of the firm's stocks. Of course, disagreements between stockholder groups sometimes arise. A colorful but rare phenomenon in corporation history is the **proxy fight,** in which competing factions of stockholders (or management) attempt to collect the voting rights of the dispersed and generally disinterested stockholders.

THE HYPOTHESIS OF THE SEPARATION OF OWNERSHIP FROM CONTROL

A different possible consequence of diversified ownership was suggested in the 1930s by A. A. Berle and Gardiner Means. They hypothesized that, because of diversified ownership and the difficulty of assembling stockholders or gathering proxies, the managers rather than the stockholders exercise effective control over the decisions of the corporation.

The hypothesis of the separation of ownership from control says that managerial control is possible *and* that it leads to different behavior than would stockholder control.

The argument offered in support of the first part of the hypothesis is this: Stockholders elect directors, who appoint managers. Directors are supposed to represent stockholders' interests and to determine broad policies that the managers carry out. In order to conduct the complicated business of running a large firm, a full-time professional management group *must* be given broad powers of decision. Although managerial decisions can be reviewed from time to time, they cannot be supervised in detail. In fact, the links are typically weak enough that top management often does truly control the destiny of the corporation over long periods of time. As long as directors have confidence in the managerial group, they accept and ratify their proposals, and stockholders characteristically elect and reelect directors who are proposed to them. If

the managerial group behaves badly, it may later be removed and replaced—but this is a drastic action and a disruptive one, and it is infrequently employed. Within very wide limits, then, effective control of the corporation's activities does reside with the managers (who need not even be stockholders in the corporation). Although the managers are legally the employees of the stockholders, they are able to remain largely unaffected by them. Indeed, the management group characteristically asks for, and typically gets, the proxies of a large enough number of stockholders to elect directors who will reappoint it—and thus it perpetuates itself in office.

Professors Berle and Means made a pioneering study of the ownership of the 200 largest nonfinancial corporations in 1929. They showed that corporations in which no dominant ownership group could be identified as having as much as 10 percent of the stockholdings accounted for 60 percent of the total assets owned by all 200 corporations studied. The percentage of assets thus held is even higher today—above 80 percent—than it was in 1929. What is the significance of this fact?

The hypothesis of the separation of ownership from control requires not only that the managers be able to exert effective control over business decisions, but that they wish to act differently from the way the stockholders and directors wish to act. If the managers are motivated by a desire to maximize the firm's profits—either because it is in their own interests to do so or because they are legally compelled or voluntarily choose to reflect the stockholders' interest—then it does not matter that they have effective control over decisions. Only if the managers wish to pursue different goals than those of the owners will the behavior of the firm be different according to whether the managers or the owners exercise effective control. A theory that takes the separation of ownership and control as its starting point and then proceeds on the assumption that managers are motivated by desires other than to maximize the profits of the firm is considered later in this chapter.

THE HYPOTHESIS OF INTERCORPORATE CONTROL GROUPS

As early as the passage of the Clayton Act in 1914, Congress had recognized the possibility that an individual might exercise an anticompetitive influence on the behavior of corporations by holding directorships in two or more of them.[2] Congress feared that a small group of men, through the control of boards of directors, could come to control major competitors and alter their market behavior.

The hypothesis of intercorporate control groups says that otherwise independent companies are subject to common control through interlocking directorates.

The factual basis of this hypothesis is that many individuals are directors of many companies. These interlocking directorships have been widely studied; for example, the directorships of the 74 largest companies in 1965 included 182 individuals each of whom was a director of at least two companies in the group. If each member of a small group holds directorships in several companies, the group could control the boards of directors of many different companies without being so obvious as to have the identical set of persons on each and every board. By controlling the boards of directors, this group might be able to exert effective and relatively unostentatious control over the companies themselves in ways that they, rather than the stockholders, choose. For the hypothesis of intercorporate control groups to have implications for behavior requires more than interlocking directorates; it requires that boards of directors be able to control the policies of corporations in ways that would not be approved of by managers or by stockholders. Notice that this requirement places the hypothesis in conflict with the previous one, for one cannot hold simultaneously that managers make the effective decisions, ignoring the interests of shareholders and directors, and that directors make the effective decisions, ignoring the interests of managers and shareholders.

There is much evidence about interlocks, but there is no substantial evidence that the common directors exert any significant influence altering the firm's behavior from what it would be if no such interlocking existed. Why, then, do they occur? There may be good reasons for them even if they do not systematically alter firm behavior. Some individuals are wanted by many corporations for the prestige their names convey. Certain bank officers appear on many different boards of directors and represent their bank's interest in companies to which they have loaned money.

Criticism of the economist's concept of the firm

Many business people, business economists, students of large and complex organizations, and others have been highly critical of economic theory for regarding the large and complex modern corporation as "a simple profit-maximizing computer." In one sense their criticisms are interrelated because they all concern profit maximization. It is useful to consider them under three categories: the information available to the firm, the organization of the firm, and the motivation of the firm.

INFORMATION AND THE MODERN FIRM

A naive line of criticism says that the profit-maximizing theory will prove inadequate be-

---

[2] Section 8 forbids interlocking directorships among competing firms under certain conditions, but the provision is seldom applied.

cause business people, however hard they may try, *cannot* reach decisions the way the theory predicts. In particular they cannot set marginal revenue equal to marginal cost if they are not aware of these concepts. The economic theorist uses the mathematical concepts of marginal cost and marginal revenue to discover what will happen as long as, by one means or another—by guess, hunch, clairvoyance, luck, or good judgment—the person in business does approximately succeed in maximizing profits. The constructs of the theory of the firm are, in other words, merely tools employed by the economist to predict the consequences of certain behavior patterns. They are not meant to describe *how* the person in business reaches decisions. The predictions of the theory are independent of the thought process by which business decisions are actually reached.

A famous analogy concerns how one might analyze whether it is safe for a driver to pass a truck on a two-lane road. The analyst must consider a complex equation relating the automobile's speed, the truck's speed, the car's ability to accelerate, the possibility of an oncoming car and its speed and distance, weather conditions, and so on. But the driver (unlike the analyst) need not solve a mathematical equation to make his or her decision. Yet if the driver and the analyst are competent, both will reach the same decision.

A more sophisticated line of criticism is that the information available to producers is simply not adequate to permit them to reach the decisions that the economist predicts they will make. This argument generally takes one of three forms: that business executives are the victims of their accountants and base decisions on accounting concepts (which differ from economic concepts); that the lag between accumulating and processing data is such that important decisions must be made on fragmentary and partially out-of-date information; and that, because acquiring full economic information is costly, firms cannot

afford to acquire as much information as economists assume them to have. While the growing importance of business consultants and the establishment of research departments within large firms suggest that firms recognize the inadequacy of their information, they also suggest that firms do try to overcome these limitations.

The hypothesis of full-cost pricing

Out of these lines of criticism has come the hypothesis of **full-cost pricing.**

The full-cost pricer, instead of equating marginal revenue to marginal cost, sets price equal to average cost, as measured by accountants, plus a conventional markup.

The **markup** may be either so much per unit or a percentage of average costs. Price having thus been set, sales are determined by what the market will absorb at that price.

This hypothesis explicitly denies that firms will charge the price that will maximize their profits (except coincidentally). The full-cost hypothesis portrays business executives as rather conservative creatures, prisoners of habit and their accounting records, instead of the alert profit seeker of traditional theory.

There is little evidence to support the view that this hypothesis is superior in its predictive value to profit-maximizing theory. So far as the theory is made to rest on the inadequacy of accounting records, Professor James Earley has effectively refuted it by showing that modern accounting procedures do not limit firms to the use of average costs. But the belief that the theory is appropriate for *some* firms cannot be refuted either by showing that firms are not forced to be full costers by modern accounting methods or by showing that some firms do not choose to follow full-cost methods.

Many analysts who believe that firms follow full-cost pricing also believe that they treat average costs per unit as constant. If so, prices would not respond to shifts in demand.

A major difference between the theories then is that in the profit-maximizing theory shifts in either demand or cost exert an important influence on prices, whereas under full-cost pricing only cost considerations apply. Because prices do appear to respond to demand shifts, doubt is cast upon either full-cost pricing or the assumption of constant average total costs.

Many economists believe that the full-cost theorists discovered the rule of thumb by which day-to-day decisions are made within the firm but that the critical decision of what the markup should be is made periodically by high-level management with profit maximization as an important objective. The fact is that the size of markups varies very sharply in response to changing business conditions. Markups expand during prosperity and contract in periods of declining demand. This kind of evidence, too, tends to cast doubt on the full-cost hypothesis.

THE ORGANIZATION OF THE FIRM

A major attack on the predictive power of the profit-maximizing firm comes from a group of economists whose central concern is with what is called **organization theory.** In terms borrowed from social psychology, they argue that in big organizations decisions are made after much discussion by groups and committees and that the structure of the *process* affects the *substance* of the decisions.

The central prediction of organization theory is that different decisions will result from different kinds of organizations, even if all else is unchanged.

Although it has proved easier for organization theorists to express their central point of view than to formulate specific testable hypotheses, they have formulated a number of the latter. One is that a large and diffuse organization finds it necessary to develop standard operating procedures to help it in making decisions. These decision rules arise as compromises among competing points of view and, once adopted, are changed only reluctantly. One prediction following from this hypothesis is that the compromises will persist for long periods of time, despite changes in conditions affecting the firm. Even if the compromise was the profit-maximizing strategy in the first place, it will not remain so; thus profits will not be maximized. Another prediction is that decision by compromise will lead firms to adopt conservative policies and avoid large risks. Thus smaller firms not faced with the necessity of compromising competing views will take bigger risks than larger firms.

THE MOTIVATION OF THE FIRM

A more basic criticism of the "marginalist" theory of the firm (often made by organization theorists) is that firms do not seek to maximize profits at all. Of course, they must make *some* profits or they will go out of business. But once some minimum level of profits has been achieved (technically, once a profit constraint is satisfied), they pursue totally different goals. The actions necessary to achieve these other goals are substantially different from those necessary to achieve profit maximization. For this reason, the deductions based on the assumption of profit maximization will tend to be at variance with the facts.

This is stronger than saying that firms are prevented from achieving maximum profits by the lack of information available to their executives or by the organization's structure. This criticism states that the managers themselves do not *wish* to maximize profits.

What, if anything, do they maximize instead? There are several different hypotheses.

The satisficing hypothesis

Organization theorists have criticized the profit-maximizing model and suggested an alternative that they call **satisficing.** Professor Herbert Simon says, "We must expect the firm's goals to be not maximizing profits but attaining a certain level or rate of profit, holding a certain share of the market or a certain level of sales."

According to the satisficing hypothesis, firms will strive hard to achieve certain target levels of profits, but having achieved them they will not strive to improve their profit position further.

This means that the firm could produce any one of a range of outputs that yield at least the target level of output rather than the unique output that maximizes profits. This lack of uniqueness is illustrated in Figure 19–1.

The sales-maximization hypothesis

Another theory, first offered by Professor William Baumol, is that firms seek to maximize not their profits but their sales revenue. Firms, it is assumed, wish to be as large as possible and, faced with a choice between profits and sales, would choose to increase their sales rather than their profits.

This hypothesis starts from the separation of management and ownership. In the giant corporation, the managers need to make some minimum level of profits to keep the shareholders satisfied; after that they are free to seek growth unhampered by profit considerations. This is a sensible policy on the part of management, so the argument runs, because salary, power, and prestige all vary with the size of a firm as well as with its profits; generally, the manager of a large, normally profitable corporation will earn a salary considerably higher than that earned by the manager of a small but highly profitable corporation.

The sales-maximization hypothesis says that managers of firms seek to maximize their sales revenue, subject to a profit constraint.

Sales maximization subject to a profit constraint leads to the prediction that a sales-maximizing firm will sacrifice some profits by setting price below, and output above, their profit-maximizing levels. This is shown

Figure 19–1 Output of the firm under satisficing, profit maximizing, and sales maximizing

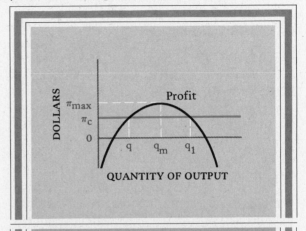

The "best" level of output depends on the motivation of the firm. The figure shows the level of profits associated with each level of output. A profit-maximizing firm produces output q_m. A satisficing firm, with a target level of profits of π_c, is willing to produce any output between q and q_1. A sales-maximizing firm, with a minimum profit constraint of π_c, produces the output q_1. Thus satisficing allows a range of outputs on either side of the profit-maximizing level while sales maximization predicts a higher output than does profit maximizing.

in Figure 19–1. Notice that, unlike satisficing, sales maximization predicts a specific output level.

Both sales-maximizing and satisficing behavior are constrained by outside forces. If the present management departs too far from profit-maximizing behavior, it leaves its firm vulnerable to a takeover bid by a new owner who does intend to maximize profits.

The long-run profit-maximization hypothesis

In order to take account of various criticisms of the assumption of profit maximization,

How far can corporations depart from profit-maximizing behavior?

Many of the criticisms of modern microeconomic theory assume that firms seek to do things other than maximize their profits. If the present management elects not to maximize its profits, this implies that some other management could make more money by operating the firm. A major restraint on existing managements is the threat of a stockholder revolt or a takeover bid. As we shall see in some detail in Chapter 22, the maximum amount one can afford to pay for any asset depends on how much it is expected to earn. If I can make an asset produce more than you, I can rationally outbid you for it.

A management that fails to come close to achieving the profit potential of the assets it controls becomes a natural target for acquisition by a firm that specializes in taking over inefficiently run firms. The management of the acquiring firm makes a **tender offer** (or **takeover bid** as it is sometimes called) to the stockholders of the target firm, offering them what amounts to a premium for their shares, a premium it can pay because it expects to increase the firm's profits. Managers who wish to avoid takeover bids cannot let the profits of their firm slip far from the profit-maximizing level—because their unrealized profits provide the incentives for takeovers. Some, though by no means all of the so-called conglomerate firms, have specialized in this kind of takeover. In the last decade the example par excellence of this has been International Telegraph and Telephone, which acquired (among other companies) Avis Car Rental, Continental Baking, Sheraton Hotels, Canteen Food Service, and Hartford Life Insurance. In each case it substantially increased the operating profits of the acquired company after the takeover. The pressure of the threat of takeovers must be regarded as limiting the discretion of corporate management to pursue goals other than profit maximization.

some economists modify profit maximization to mean long-run profit maximization. For example, sales maximization is interpreted as long-run profit maximization because sales are the key to growth and growth is the key to future profits. This eliminates any conflict between sales and profit maximization. In much the same way, the "long-run" approach can be used to account for other facts that appear to contradict predictions based on short-run profit maximization. For one example, consumer goodwill gained by not taking advantage of temporary shortages may be worthwhile in terms of long-run profits.

For another example, a firm may be right to avoid risky ventures, even if they promise large short-run profits, because the surest way to long-run profits is to survive in the short run. Long-run profitability requires survival, and survival requires caution.

It is, however, exceptionally difficult to give such a long-run theory any testable content. If we are not careful, we may find ourselves rationalizing, whenever we find a firm not maximizing profits, by saying merely that it was maximizing over *some time period other than* the one we were considering. Unless we include in our theory a means of identifying the long-run period over which profits are supposed to be maximized, our theory becomes consistent with absolutely any business behavior and as a result becomes totally uninteresting.

It is not unreasonable, however, to regard profit maximizing as occurring over a realistic time horizon, such as one or two years, rather than day by day. Nor is it unreasonable to construct a testable theory of a firm attempting to maximize the "present value" of future profits.[3] In either of these ways long-run maximization can be brought into a profit-maximizing model.

Economics is a continually developing subject; its theories are under constant scrutiny and even attack. Some of the major debates concerning the profit-maximizing theory of the firm have been reviewed in this chapter. On the one hand, the Galbraithian view that firms create their own market conditions seems difficult to maintain in the face of the evidence. On the other hand, it seems unlikely that simple profit-maximizing theory will be rich enough to capture all aspects of corporate behavior. Thus the theory may benefit by expansion to include elements of such theories as satisficing and sales maximization.

Profits are, however, unmistakably a potent force in the life—and death—of firms. The resilience of profit-maximizing theory and its ability to predict how the economy will react to major changes (such as the recent dramatic increases in energy prices) suggests that firms are at least strongly motivated by the pursuit of profits and that, other things being equal, they prefer more profits to less profits. Despite four decades of criticism, the profit-maximizing theory of the firm is alive, well, and still developing.

[3] The concept of present value is developed in Chapter 22. It is sufficient here to understand that the value to you *now* of $100 to be given to you five years from now is greater than zero but less than $100.

Summary

1. A sweeping attack on the traditional theory of the behavior of the firm is made by Galbraith (along with Nader and others). He argues that large corporations manipulate markets, tastes, and governments rather than respond to market and governmental pressures. While there is evidence about the undoubted size and influence of large corporations, there is also much evidence of market influence on corporate behavior.

2. In recent years, serious concern has developed over whether the corporation should represent the interests of its owners and managers or whether it should be responsible to a broader public interest. "Consumerists" argue for the latter point of view; others prefer to rely on markets and government control to protect the public interest.

3. The widespread ownership of the modern corporation leads to the question of who really controls the modern corporation. Three hypotheses are examined.

a. A minority group often controls the corporation against the wishes of the majority. The fact of minority control is widely accepted, but there is little evidence to suggest that the minority usually coerce the majority.

b. Because of the widespread ownership of the corporation, stockholders cannot exert effective control over the managers; thus the latter have the real control of the organization and operate it for their advantage rather than that of their stockholders. This hypothesis has some serious, but by no means universal, support.

c. A small group of people effectively control a large section of the economy through the mechanism of interlocking directorates. This hypothesis is not widely accepted (although the fact of interlocking directorships is not in dispute).

4. Is the behavior of the modern corporation sufficiently different from that predicted by the theory of the firm that the theory must be modified or replaced? Many critics have answered yes and have suggested alternative theories.

5. The hypothesis of full-cost pricing is based on the nature of the information that the business executive has or chooses to consult, which is alleged to lead business people to behave differently than conventional theory predicts. Organization theorists hypothesize that the structure of the decision-making process vitally affects the nature of that process.

6. Both satisficing and sales maximization can be stated as genuine alternatives to the theory of short-run profit maximization. The same is possible with long-run profit maximization, but only if the nature of the "long run" is made specific; otherwise, it is simply an alibi or rationalization for every shred of contradictory evidence.

Concepts for review

The New Industrial State
The long-run sensitivity of firms to market pressures
Consumerism
Ownership, management, and control of corporate decisions
Full-cost pricing
Sales maximizing, satisficing, and long-run profit maximizing as alternatives to the theory of short-run profit maximizing

Discussion questions

1. In 1976 the automobile manufacturers introduced their 1977 models. GM and American Motors (AMC) put major emphasis on smaller, more economical cars, and Ford and Chrysler stayed with their 1976 model sizes. Read the following news headlines (which appear in chronological order) and then discuss what light they shed on the hypothesis that firms control the market.
a. "GM's 1977 Line Runs Ahead of the Pack. The big question: Do people want small cars?"
b. "Ford, Chrysler beam; AMC in trouble on sales."
c. "GM's Fuel-Saving Chevette: Right Car at the Wrong Time."
d. "Price Cuts and Rebates Lift Sales of Small AMC and GM Cars."
e. "GM Confirms Plans to Drop the Subcompact Vega."

2. "Because automobile companies were interested only in profits, they would not produce the safer, less polluting, but more expensive cars that the public really wanted. Legislation was necessary, therefore, to force producers to meet consumer needs." Discuss.

3. Assume that each of the following assertions is factually correct. (The first is a matter of current controversy; the rest

are unquestioned.) Taken together, what would they tell you about the prediction that big business is increasing its control of the U.S. economy?
a. The share of total manufacturing assets owned by the 200 largest corporations has been rising steadily for the last 25 years.
b. The number of new firms begun every year has grown steadily for the last 25 years.
c. The share of manufacturing in total production has been decreasing for 40 years.
d. Profits as a percent of national income are no higher now than half a century ago.

4. "Our economy, like an engine, must have fuel to operate. And the fuel our economy runs on is profit. Profits keep it going—and growing. But there is strong evidence that the economy's fuel supply is running low. Profits of U.S. corporations today are about 5 percent on sales—less than the 1965 rate.

"We Americans have become accustomed to a quality of life that can survive only through profits. For profits not only create jobs and goods, they furnish essential tax revenues. Federal, state and local taxes finance the countless programs that our citizens demand—from paving the roads on which we drive to building our country's defense forces . . . to helping millions of Americans who need some form of assistance."

Comment on this excerpt from an Allied Chemical Corporation advertisement.

5. "The business of the businessman is to run his business so as to make profits. If he does so he will serve the public interest better than if he tries to decide what is good for society. He is neither elected or appointed to that task." Discuss.

6. "Our list prices are really set by our accounting department; they add a fixed markup to their best estimates of fully accounted cost and send these to the operating divisions. Managers of these divisions may not change those prices without permission of the Board of Directors, which is seldom given. Operating divisions may, however, provide special discounts if necessary to stay competitive." Does this testimony by the president of a leading manufacturing company support the full-cost pricing hypothesis?

7. The leading automobile tire manufacturers (Goodyear, Firestone, etc.) sell original equipment (OE) tires to automobile manufacturers at a price below the average total cost of all the tires it makes and sells. This happens year after year. Is this consistent with profit-maximizing behavior in the short run? In the long run? If it is not consistent, what does it show? Do OE tires compete with replacement tires?

PART SIX

FACTOR PRICING AND THE DISTRIBUTION OF INCOME

The distribution of national income

Are the poor getting poorer and the rich richer as Karl Marx thought they would? Are the rich getting relatively poorer and the poor relatively richer as Alfred Marshall hoped they would? Is inequality of income a social constant determined by forces possibly beyond human understanding and probably beyond human influence as Vilfredo Pareto thought?

Each year society produces a certain total output. This output gets divided—more or less unequally—among the individuals and groups in the society. The theory of income distribution is concerned with what determines the fraction of total income that goes to a particular individual or group.

The founders of classical economics, Adam Smith and David Ricardo, were concerned with the distribution of income among what were then the three great social classes: workers, capitalists, and landowners. To deal with this question they defined three basic factors of production: labor, capital, and land. The return to each of these factors was the income of each of the three classes in society. Smith and Ricardo were interested in two questions: (1) What determines the income of each group relative to the total income? and (2) How will a nation's economic growth affect this distribution of income? Their theory predicted that landlords would become relatively better off and that capitalists would become relatively worse off as society progressed. Karl Marx accepted this classical pair of questions but provided very different answers: He concluded that capitalists would become relatively better off and workers relatively worse off as growth occurred. These and other nineteenth-century debates focused on the distribution of income among the major factors of production. This is now referred to as the **functional distribution of income.** Table 20–1 shows data for the functional distribution of income in the United States in 1975.

Table 20–1 The functional distribution of national income in the United States, 1975

Type of income	Billions of dollars	Percentage of total
Employee compensation	$ 929	76.9
Corporate profits	92	7.6
Proprietors' income	90	7.5
Interest	75	6.2
Rental income	22	1.8
Total	$1208	100.0

Source: *Survey of Current Business,* October 1976.

Total income is classified here according to the nature of the factor service that earned the income. While these data show that employee compensation is more than three quarters of national income, they do not show that workers and their families receive only that fraction of national income. Many households will have income in more than one category listed in the table.

Table 20–2 Incomes of American families,[a] 1975

Income class (thousands of dollars)	Percentage of families
Less than 5.0	12.1
5.0 to 9.9	21.2
10.0 to 14.9	22.3
15.0 to 24.9	30.3
25.0 or more	14.1

[a] The census definition of a family is two or more persons related by blood, marriage, or adoption and residing together.

Source: *Current Population Reports,* Series P-60, No. 103.

Although median family income was about $13,700 in 1975, many received much less and some a great deal more.

Table 20–3 Inequality in family income distribution, 1975

Family income rank	Percentage share of aggregate income
Lowest fifth	5.4
Second fifth	11.8
Middle fifth	17.6
Fourth fifth	24.1
Highest fifth	41.1
	100.0
(Top 5 percent	15.5)

Source: *Current Population Reports,* Series P-60, No. 103.

While far from showing overall equality, income distribution is relatively equal for the middle 60 percent of the distribution. If the income distribution were perfectly equal, each fifth of the families would receive 20 percent of aggregate income. The present distribution is virtually unchanged from that of twenty years ago.

Around the beginning of the present century, the great Italian economist Pareto studied what is now called the **size distribution of income,** the distribution of income between different households without reference to the social class to which they belonged. He discovered that the inequality in income distribution was great in all countries and, more surprisingly, that it was quite similar in many countries. Pareto speculated that the degree of inequality of income was determined by basic economic and social forces and was little influenced by differing national institutions and policies.

The studies of Pareto (and many others) shifted some of the emphasis away from the functional distribution of income. After all, some capitalists—such as the owners of small retail stores—are in the lower portion of the income scale, while some wage earners—such as skilled athletes—are in the upper end of the income scale. Today the most frequent objective is to mitigate the most extreme inequal-

ities, no matter who is affected. Tables 20–2 and 20–3 show that even in America, in 1975, there were many families with very low incomes and that there was much inequality in the distribution of income.

Inequality in the distribution of income is shown graphically in Figure 20–1. The curve of income distribution in the figure, called a **Lorenz curve,** shows how much of total income is accounted for by given proportions of the nation's families. For example, in 1975 the bottom 20 percent of all U.S. families earned only 5.4 percent of all income earned.

In 1975 almost 26 million Americans (or 12 percent of the total population) were living below the official poverty level of about $5,500 for a nonfarm family of four. Who are these American poor? A disproportionate number are black. Whether you are black or white, your chances of being poor are greater if you live in the South, the lower the level of your educational attainment, if you work on a farm, and if you are frequently unemployed.

Why are there so many poor in a country as rich as America? Many of the causes of poverty are noneconomic. Discrimination is known to contribute heavily to black poverty. Age, poor health, and the breakup of marriages often limit the ability of the head of the household to enter into the labor force. But poverty is also often caused by the very low market prices of some kinds of labor. Why can some people be fully employed and yet earn so little as to be below the poverty line? This is not an isolated phenomenon; at the present time 40 percent of U.S. households who are below the poverty line have an employed head of household.

In explaining and dealing with the problem of the distribution of income among various groups in the society who make up the poor, we are dealing not with the traditional groups of landowners, laborers, and capitalists but instead with groups identified by characteristics of race, age, education, or region of residence.

We shall look more closely at the poverty problem in Chapter 23. In order to understand this and other problems concerning the distribution of income, we must first study how the income of households is determined and what forces cause it to change.

It is tempting to give superficial explanations of differences in income. People often say, "People are paid what they are worth." But the economist must ask, Worth what to whom? What gives a particular man his value? His wife, his mother-in-law, and his employer may all respond differently. Sometimes people say, "People earn according to their ability." But note that incomes are dis-

Figure 20–1   A Lorenz curve of family income in the United States

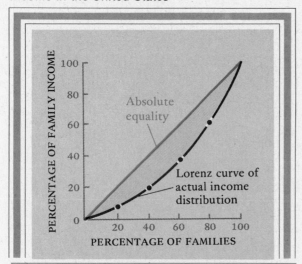

The size of the shaded area between the Lorenz curve and the diagonal is a measure of the inequality of income distribution. If there were complete income equality, the bottom 20 percent of income receivers would receive 20 percent of the income, etc., and the Lorenz curve would be the diagonal line. Because the lower 20 percent receive only 5 percent of the income, the actual curve lies below the diagonal. The lower curve shows actual American data. The extent to which it bends away from the straight line indicates the amount of inequality in the distribution of income.

tributed in a very much more unequal fashion than any *measured* index of ability, be it IQ, physical strength, or typing skill. In what sense is Jack Nicklaus five times as able a golfer as Homero Blancas? His average score is only 1 percent better, but he earns five times as much. In what sense is Barbara Walters ten times as able a reporter as Jane Pauley?

If answers couched in terms of worth and ability are easily refuted, so are answers such as, It's all a matter of luck or It's just the system. We are concerned now with discovering if the theories of economics provide explanations of the distribution of income that are more satisfactory than the ones mentioned above.

THE THEORY OF DISTRIBUTION

Every element of income has, in a purely arithmetical sense, two components: the quantity of the income-earning service that is provided and the price per unit paid for it. The amount a woman earns in wages depends on the number of hours she works and the hourly wage she receives. The amount a group of workers (say union members) earns depends on how many of them there are and how much each earns. The amount of dividends a stockholder receives depends on the number of shares of stock he or she owns and the dividends that each share pays.

Because factor prices are one of the two elements that determine factor incomes, a theory of factor prices is essential to a theory of distribution.[1]

A theory of factor prices is just a special case of the theory of supply and demand and involves little that is not already familiar.

---

[1] If the prices of all other factors of production, the prices of all goods, and the level of national income are held constant, then fluctuations in a factor's money income will cause fluctuations in its relative earnings (i.e., its earnings compared to those of other factors) and in its share of total national income.

Figure 20–2 The determination of factor price and income in a competitive market

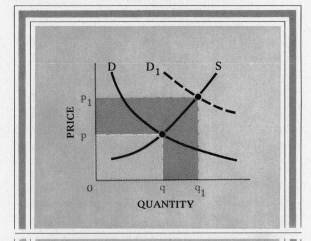

Demand and supply for factors determine prices and quantities of factors in competitive factor markets. With demand and supply curves D and S, the price of the factor will be p and the quantity employed q. The total income earned by the factor is the lighter shaded area. A shift in demand from D to D_1 raises equilibrium price and quantity to p_1 and q_1. The income earned by the factor rises by the darker shaded area.

Price theory states that the competitive market price of any commodity or factor is determined by demand and supply. The competitive market determination of the equilibrium price and quantity—and thus also the money income—of a factor of production is illustrated in Figure 20–2.

In order to elaborate on this theory of factor pricing, we develop a theory of the demand for factors, then a theory of their supply, and finally combine the theories into a theory of the determination of equilibrium prices and quantities. In this chapter we consider competitive markets. In Chapter 21 we go on to determine the effect of various departures from competitive conditions such as those brought about by employers' associations and unions.

The demand for factors

The demand for a factor of production is said to be a **derived demand** because a firm requires labor, raw materials, machines, and other factors of production, not for their own sake but in order to produce the goods and services that it sells.

The demand for any factor of production depends on the existence of a demand for the goods that it helps to make.

Examples of derived demand are easy to find. The demand for computer programmers and repairmen is growing as industry turns increasingly to electronic computers. The demand for college professors and textbooks decreases when the number of students going to college falls off. Anything that increases the demand for a commodity—population changes, changes in tastes, and so on—will increase the demand for the factors required to make it. Typically, one factor will be used in making many commodities, not just one. Steel is used in dozens of industries, as are the services of carpenters.

The total demand for a factor will be the sum of the derived demands for it in each productive activity.

WHAT DETERMINES THE DEMAND CURVE FOR A FACTOR?

The demand curve for a factor of production shows how the quantity demanded of that factor will vary as its price varies, the price of all other factors held constant. Let us ask what would happen to quantity demanded if there were a fall in the price of the factor. Because the demand is a derived demand, the effect must be traced through to the products that the factor is used to make.

A fall in the price of a factor is expected to increase the quantity demanded for two distinct reasons: The first is related to the effect of a change in the factor's price on the price of the product it helps to produce and consequently on the quantity demanded; the second is related to a substitution of one factor for another.

The relation between the demand for factors and the demand for commodities

A fall in the price of a factor reduces the overall costs of producing all commodities that use the factor. This fall in costs leads to a fall in the price of these commodities and to an increase in the quantities produced and sold. If more commodities are to be produced, more factors are needed. Thus there is an increase in the quantity demanded of all of the factors that make up the affected commodities.

Other things being equal, this effect will be larger (1) the more elastic the demand for the product that the factor helps to make and (2) the larger the proportion of total costs of producing the product represented by payments to this factor. To see point (1), notice that if the fall in price of the commodity causes a large rise in the quantity demanded (i.e., the demand for the commodity is very elastic), there will be a large increase in the quantity of the factor now needed. But if the fall in price of the commodity causes only a small rise in its quantity demanded (i.e., the demand for the commodity is inelastic), there will be only a small increase in the quantity of the factor now required.

To see point (2), suppose that unskilled labor accounts for 50 percent of the total costs of producing some commodity, whereas skilled labor accounts for 10 percent. A 10 percent decrease in the price of unskilled labor would lower the cost of producing the commodity by 5 percent (10 percent of 50 percent), but a 10 percent decrease in the price of skilled labor would lower the cost of the commodity by only 1 percent (10 percent of 10 percent). Thus, of the two, the same percentage decrease in unskilled labor's price would occasion a larger decrease in the price of the commodity and hence a larger increase in the quantity demanded of the commodity and of the factors that are used to make it.

Substitution of one factor for another

The second main reason it may be expected that more of a factor will be demanded when its price falls is that the cheaper factor will be used to replace partially other factors whose prices have not fallen. This is simply the operation of the principle of substitution first studied on pages 179–181.

How easy it is to substitute one factor for another depends on the substitutes available and the technical conditions of production. A contractor in Anaheim, California, may normally use Anaheim laborers. But should they raise their wage demands the contractor might well be able to bring workers from Azusa or Cucamonga at only the additional cost of the daily transportation fares. It is well known that a bushel of wheat can be produced by combining land either with a lot of labor and a little capital or with a little labor and a lot of capital, and that manufactured goods can be made either by capital-intensive or by labor-intensive techniques.

It is often possible to vary factor proportions in quite surprising ways. For example, in automobile manufacture and in building construction, glass and steel can be substituted for each other merely by varying the dimensions of the windows. But such easy substitutions are not the end of the story. A factory may have a particular technique embodied in its equipment; if so, its management cannot easily vary factor proportions in the short run in response to changes in relative factor prices. But plant and equipment are continually being replaced, and more or less capital-intensive methods can be adopted in new plants in response to changes in factor prices.

Elasticity of demand for a factor

The responsiveness of demand for a factor to a change in its price is measured by the elasticity of demand for the factor. We can summarize the discussion above in terms of elasticity.

The elasticity of demand for a factor will vary directly with:

1. the elasticity of demand of the final product it makes
2. the proportion of the total cost of production accounted for by the factor
3. the ease with which it may be substituted for other factors

THE DERIVATION OF DEMAND FOR FACTORS

Precisely how is the demand for the factor derived from the demand for the product? Let us examine the firm's situation when it is in equilibrium with respect to the factors it is hiring.

The conditions for maximizing profits in the short run were discussed in Chapter 14. When one factor is fixed while another is allowed to vary, the profit-maximizing firm increases its output to the level at which the last unit produced adds just as much to costs as to revenue, that is until marginal cost equals marginal revenue. Another way of stating this is to say that the firm will increase production up to the point at which the last unit of the variable factor employed adds just as much to revenue as it does to costs.

All profit-maximizing firms will hire units of the variable factor up to the point at which the marginal cost of the factor equals the marginal revenue produced by the factor.

This implication of profit-maximizing behavior is true of all profit-maximizing firms, whether they are selling under conditions of perfect competition, monopolistic competition, oligopoly, or monopoly.

Because we have already used the term "marginal revenue" to denote the change in revenue resulting when the rate of sales is increased by 1 unit, we shall use another term, **marginal revenue product (MRP),** to refer to the change in revenue caused by the sale of the product contributed by *an additional unit of the variable factor.* We may now state more formally the equilibrium condition stated in color above:

The marginal cost of the variable factor = the marginal revenue product of that factor [1]

If the firm is unable to influence the price of the variable factor by buying more or less of it (i.e., if the firm is a price taker when *buying* factors), then the marginal cost of the factor is merely its price. The cost, for example, of adding an extra unit of electric power is the price that must be paid per unit of electricity purchased. In these circumstances, we may state the condition of [1] above in this form:

$$w = MRP \qquad [2]$$

where w is the price of the factor.

This statement is sometimes called the **marginal productivity theory of distribution.** It is merely an implication of two assumptions: that the firm is a profit maximizer and that the firm *buys* its factors in markets in which it is a price taker. (Note that the second assumption says nothing about the firm's behavior in the market in which it *sells* its product. In the product market the firm can equally well be a monopolist or a perfect competitor.)

A profit maximizing firm that is a price taker in factor markets hires a factor up to the point at which its price equals its marginal revenue product.

Now consider a single firm with only one variable factor and one fixed factor. Assume that the marginal revenue product of the variable factor is known. From this *MRP,* we derive the firm's demand curve for the factor on the assumption that, presented with a price of the factor, the firm goes on hiring factors until marginal revenue product is equal to its price. This is shown in Figure 20–3.

The demand curve for a factor is derived from the downward-sloping part[2] of the marginal revenue product curve.

Is it reasonable to expect the *MRP* curve to slope downward? The presence of diminishing returns is sufficient to assure this result, as can be easily shown. Marginal revenue product depends on two things: (1) the physical increase in output that an additional unit of the variable factor makes possible, multiplied by (2) the increase in revenue derived from that extra output. The first of these is called the **marginal physical product (MPP);** the second is the by now familiar concept of marginal revenue.

In symbols:

$$MRP = MPP \times MR \qquad [3]$$

The hypothesis of diminishing marginal returns was introduced in Chapter 11. This hypothesis says that *MPP* has a declining section over some range of output. If marginal revenue is constant (as it is in perfect competition), *MRP* has the same shape as *MPP* and must also decline.

Marginal revenue, however, may not be constant. If *MR* declines as output increases

---

[2] The condition for maximum profits given in equation [1] is only one of the necessary and sufficient conditions for profit maximization. It is also necessary that *MRP* cut *MC* from above. In equation [2] this means that *MRP* must be declining for the intersection with the factor price to be a position of maximum profit. To see why this is so, examine Figure 20–3, where $6,000 is equal to *MRP* at the levels of employment of both 15 and 50. Using 15 workers leads to a point of *minimum* profit. Each of the first 15 workers contributes less to the value of the product than $6,000. Every additional worker between 15 and 50 adds more to the value of the product, but after 50 the workers would again contribute less than their wage. There is no point in employing a fifty-first worker, who would add only $5,900 to the value of the product but would add $6,000 (in wages) to costs. Why does not a similar argument apply to the fourteenth worker or the first? The reason is that you cannot have a fiftieth if you do not have a first or a fourteenth.

Figure 20-3 The derived demand for a factor in a competitive factor market

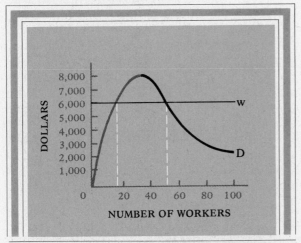

The demand curve for a factor is identical in shape to the downward-sloping portion of the *MRP* curve. The entire curve is the *MRP*. It shows the increase in revenue resulting from the sale of the additional output produced by one more unit of the variable factor. A profit-maximizing firm will go on hiring the factor until the last unit employed adds as much to revenue as to costs. If, for example, the price of the factor, *w*, were $6,000 per year, 50 units would be employed. The heavy curve is the derived demand curve.

(as it does in monopoly and in any other situation in which the firms demand curve declines), then *MRP* must decline even more sharply. The hypothesis of diminishing marginal productivity thus implies diminishing *MRP* and a downward-sloping demand curve for the factor. [22]

The supply of factors

If we continue to use natural gas at the rate we used it in 1976, we will have used up all the proved reserves of natural gas in the United States by 1988. There is enough coal in the United States to last for more than 500 years at present rates of consumption. Yet even in 1976 we continued to substitute gas for coal. Was this madness? When we use our natural resources are we depriving our grandchildren of their basis for a good life? Should we not conserve our resources by using as few of them as possible?

There are two important questions concerning supplies of factors: (1) What determines the total supply of a factor to the whole economy? and (2) What determines the supply available to a particular use?

THE TOTAL SUPPLY OF FACTORS

At first it might seem plausible to assume that the total supplies of factors available to the economy are fixed. After all, there is an absolute maximum to the world's land area; there is an upper limit to the number of workers; there is only so much coal, oil, copper, and iron ore in the earth. In none of these cases, however, are we near the upper limits. The *effective* supplies of land, labor, and natural resources are thus not fixed in any meaningful sense. What, then, causes variations in the supply of a factor of production available to the *whole economy?*

The total supply of labor

The total supply of labor means the total number of hours of work that the population is willing to supply. This quantity, which is often called the **supply of effort,** is a function of the size of the population, the proportion of the population willing to work, and the number of hours worked by each individual. These in turn are affected by many things.

Population. Populations vary in size, and these variations may be influenced to some extent by economic factors. There is some evidence that the birth rate is higher in good times than in bad. Much of the variation in population is, however, explained by sociological and biological factors rather than economic ones.

What is a person worth? The economics of superstar salaries

Joe Namath, an aging but flamboyant quarterback with injured knees, was paid $450,000 to play for the New York Jets in 1976, a season in which they won only three of their fourteen games (for the second year in a row). At the end of the dismal season, the Jets owners gladly accepted the resignation of the club's coach but wanted Broadway Joe to play again in 1977 at the same salary. Sportscasters and fans agreed that the team played better and had more chance of winning with their second-string quarterback, who was paid less than one-tenth of Namath's salary. Yet the Jets continued to want to play—and pay—Joe Namath. Can this be sound economics?

It can be and it is. The principal products the Jets sell are football tickets and television rights to their games. The Jets, despite their won-lost record, have been and are a major drawing card, not only in New York but throughout the country. Joe Namath was a main reason for this. He is still remembered as the David who in 1969 led the Jets of the scorned American Football League to victory over the mighty National Football League Champion Baltimore Colts, quarterbacked by John Unitas. Eight years later thousands of extra fans paid to see the Jets because of Namath. On the road during 1976, the Jets attracted roughly 10,000 more fans per game (in the same stadiums) than did the Buffalo Bills with

1976's reigning superstar, O. J. Simpson. For the season the Jets are estimated to have earned about $240,000 in their share of extra ticket sales for seven games away from home—just because of Namath. At home Namath is credited with attracting more than 10,000 extra fans per game, and this was worth at least another $350,000 in ticket sales to the football club. Add in the additional value in television rights, and Joe was plainly a bargain: his marginal revenue product was more than his wage.

When ABC lured Barbara Walters away from NBC with a five-year contract at a million dollars a year, it was economic calculation that was at work, not sympathy for the women's movement. ABC's share of the television news audience had slipped from 23 rating points in 1973 to 19 points in 1976. (Each "rating point" represents well over a million viewers.) Because more viewers make the 30- and 60-second spot announcements sold to advertisers more valuable, each additional rating point is estimated to yield the network $1.5 million per year in additional advertising revenue. Was Barbara worth her million? It will depend upon what her marginal product over the five years turns out to be: If she raises the rating of ABC by even one point, she will have paid her way.

Mark Fidrych, who started 1976 as a $16,500 per year rookie pitcher for the De-

Labor force participation. The number of people in the labor market, the **labor force,** varies considerably in response to economic and social conditions. Generally, a rise in the demand for labor and an accompanying rise in the earnings of labor will lead to an increase in the proportion of the population willing to work. Persistent unemployment may lead

troit Tigers, became an overnight sensation in 1976 by winning ball games *and* talking to the ball. As word of his zany antics spread, people came to the ballpark to watch. Whenever he was scheduled to pitch, an estimated 15,000 extra fans showed up to see The Bird. His salary will be over $50,000 in 1977, and it will continue to go up if he continues to draw additional fans. Arnold Palmer made golf prizes swell and earnings of professional golfers soar by a magnetic personality that made golf a major spectator sport and brought national television coverage. Chris Evert (assisted by Billie Jean King and MCP Bobby Riggs) did the same for women's tennis.

Notice that it is not the direct product produced that is responsible for high salaries. It is not yards gained or birdies scored that made Namath and Palmer rich, nor is it interviews conducted or hours on the air that led to Barbara Walter's high salary. It is tickets sold, or advertising sold, that converts the physical feats of these people into marginal revenue product. Will the extraordinary skills of Russian gymnasts or Japanese volleyball players one day make athletes in those sports worth their weight in gold? It will depend upon some entrepreneur's ability to generate a market for their product. Whatever happened to Mark Spitz?

unemployed workers to become discouraged and to withdraw from the labor force.

Social changes can cause major variations in participation rates. The women's liberation movement, for example, has sharply increased labor force participation in the United States. A lowering of retirement ages will decrease it.

Hours worked. Generally, a rise in real wages such as has occurred in most Western countries over the last two centuries leads people to consume more goods—and to consume more leisure. This means that over time, as wages rise, people are willing to work fewer hours per week, a fact that *ceteris paribus* will lead to a decline in the supply of labor.

Taxes, welfare benefits, and the supply of effort. Many believe that today's high income taxes tend to reduce the supply of effort by lowering the incentive for people to work. They protest that it is not worth their while to work because of the crushing tax burdens they have to shoulder. Such objective evidence as exists on this subject suggests, however, that high taxes do not always reduce the supply. To the extent that they do, the aggregate effect may be quite small. A good deal of research has shown that while some persons may reduce their work effort in response to rising taxes, others feel poorer and thus work longer to be able to maintain their after-tax incomes. The most recent research suggests at most a small net disincentive up to a level of marginal tax rates of 50 percent, such as exists today in the United States. However, at rates of 70 and 80 percent important distortions may occur. A "brain drain" from the United Kingdom resulted from high tax rates that discouraged "extra" earning as well as from relatively low salaries in many professional, scientific, and managerial occupations. Here it is not necessarily the absolute level of taxes, but the presence of an alternative where one can both work hard and keep more of one's income.

A similar question is whether welfare payments and other forms of aid to the poor make them less willing to accept employment. This question is receiving a good deal of current attention. Some significant disincentives have been found, but they do not appear massive. Many of those receiving payments are unable to work, and most of those who can work find it worthwhile to do so for their sense of participation in society as well as for the extra income. However, for a sizable—and much noticed—number, there is no doubt that welfare has become a substitute for work.

The total supply of land

In the traditional classification of factors of production, land is defined to include natural resources. Here it is convenient to consider arable land and natural resources separately.

Arable land. If the term "land" is used to refer to the total area of dry land, then the total supply of land in a country is almost completely fixed. It was nineteenth-century practice (following Ricardo) to define land as the *original and inexhaustible powers of the soil.* But dust bowls were a phenomenon unknown to Ricardo, who also did not know that the deserts of North Africa were once fertile plains. Clearly the supply of fertile land is not inexhaustible; considerable care and effort is required to sustain the productive power of land, and if the return to land is low, the fertility of the land may be destroyed within a short time. However, a high return to land may make it worthwhile to increase the supply of arable land by irrigation and other forms of reclamation.

Natural resources. People worry—usually when it is too late—about exhausting natural resources. The great iron ore deposits of the Mesabi Range were exhausted in 1965, and America's known supplies of oil and gas had shrunk by 1975 to less than a twelve-year supply.[3]

The problem of actual exhaustion of natural resources does not arise as often as one might think. There is frequently a large undiscovered or unexploited quantity of a given resource or of an adequate substitute. The exhaustion of high-grade iron ore reserves in the United States did not end steel production—partly as a result of the discovery of ways to use low-grade iron ores once thought worthless, and partly because new supplies in Labrador and the Caribbean have been developed.

Emerging shortages may lead to their own corrections. As long as oil remains sufficiently valuable, it will pay to find more of it. If the cost of finding oil becomes too high, the supplies that it is economically feasible to find will decrease—at those prices. Before that event, however, free-market prices would surely rise. A sufficient increase in the price of oil will make it economically worthwhile to process the vast quantities of heretofore unexploited shale oil. Consumers will feel the scarcity in terms of higher prices, and this will lead them to use less oil; this in turn will decrease the rate of exhaustion of known reserves.

One of the dangers of government regulation is that it may prevent these self-correcting responses. In the United States the Federal Power Commission kept the field price of natural gas artificially low. This encouraged consumption, discouraged exploration, and depleted reserves. During the exceptionally cold winter of 1977 a crisis developed, with schools, factories, and offices closing because there was not enough gas to maintain heat.

Ultimately, of course, there is an upper limit, and resources can be totally exhausted; worse, they can be polluted or otherwise despoiled so as to render them useless long before they have been consumed.

---

[3] It should not be inferred that supplies of oil and gas will be exhausted by 1988. The known supply was reported to be about twenty years in every year from 1920 to 1950; in other words, each year as much was discovered as was used. What *is* new in recent years is that discovery has lagged behind production.

The total supply of capital

Capital is a man-made factor of production and its supply is in no sense fixed. The supply of capital in a country consists of the stock of existing machines, plant, equipment, and so on. This capital is used up in the course of production, and the stock is thus diminished by the amount that wears out each year. However, the stock of capital is increased each year by the production of new capital goods. Taking the long view and ignoring cyclical fluctuations, there has been a fairly steady tendency in all developed countries for the stock to increase over time.

THE SUPPLY OF FACTORS TO PARTICULAR USES

The theory of the allocation of factors to particular uses is a general one which applies with only minor variations to all factors of production. Most factors have many uses; a given piece of land can be used to grow a variety of crops, and it can also be subdivided for a housing development. A machinist in Detroit can work in a variety of automobile plants, or in a dozen other industries, or even in the physics laboratories at Ann Arbor. A lathe can be used to make a great variety of products and requires no adaptation when it is turned from one use to another.

Factors must somehow be allocated among all the different uses to which they can possibly be put. If their owners are concerned only with making as much money as they can, they will move their factor to that use at which it earns the most money. Such a movement out of one use into another would continue until the earnings of each of the units of one kind of factor in all of its various possible uses were the same. Because owners of factors are known to take other things besides money into account—such as risk, convenience, and a good climate—it is not sufficient to consider only monetary incentives; we must consider the sum of both monetary and nonmonetary rewards.

The hypothesis of equal net advantage

The **hypothesis of equal net advantage** says that owners of factors will choose that use of their factors that produces the greatest net advantage to themselves. (Net advantage includes both monetary and nonmonetary rewards.)

This hypothesis plays the same role in the theory of distribution as the assumption that firms seek to maximize profits plays in the theory of production. It leads to the prediction that each of the units of one kind of factor of production will be allocated among various uses in such a way that their owners receive the same net return in every use.

The problem with this hypothesis is that it is difficult—if not impossible—to test it because we do not know how to measure non-monetary advantages.[4] The hypothesis can be made operational, however, if we assume (as is no doubt often the case) that the differences in nonmonetary advantages between two uses of a factor remain constant over time. We can then predict that variations in monetary advantages will widen or narrow the gap and that some resources will flow in response to the change.[5]

It is not necessary to make the strong assumption that nonmonetary advantages are constant; instead we need only assume that they change more slowly than monetary ones. If so, we can derive this prediction:

[4] An example will suggest why. It used to be said that faculty members at the University of Wisconsin paid $1,000 a year for the privilege of living on the shores of Lake Mendota. The story is still told, but with recent salary trends in mind the figure has been upped to $4,000. We know of no way to estimate the value of Lake Mendota to the residents of Madison; we can observe only that they appear to be willing to accept less pay to live there. But imputing a value to the lake by determining how much less pay they are willing to accept depends on the hypothesis being true—and thus gives no basis for testing it and no way of discovering if it is wrong.

[5] To return to Lake Mendota, if we assume that its value is stable, then a widening salary differential between the University of Wisconsin and other universities would lead to the predictions (1) that some people, formerly content, would now leave the university to take higher paying jobs elsewhere and (2) that the university would have more trouble recruiting new staff.

A change in the relative rate of pay of a factor between two uses will lead to a shift of some units of that factor to the use whose rate of pay has increased.

This prediction implies a rising supply curve for a factor in any particular use. When the price of a factor rises, more of it will be supplied. Such a supply curve (as all supply curves) can *shift* in response to changes in other variables. One of these variables that can shift the supply curve is the size of nonmonetary benefits.

Factor mobility

When considering the supply of a factor to a particular use, the most important concept is **factor mobility.** If a factor moves easily between uses in response to small changes in incentives, it is said to be highly mobile. In this case the factor will be in very elastic supply in any one of its uses because small increases in the price offered will attract a large flow of the factor from other uses. If the factor does not move easily from one use to another even in response to large changes in remuneration, it is said to be highly immobile. In this case the factor will be in very inelastic supply in any one of its uses because even a large increase in the price offered will attract only a small inflow from other uses.

Mobility of land. Land, which is physically the least mobile of all factors, is paradoxically one of the most mobile in an economic sense. Consider agricultural land. Within a year at most, one crop can be harvested and a totally different crop planted. A farm on the outskirts of a growing city can be sold for subdivision and development on very short notice. Once land is built upon, as urban land usually is, its mobility is much reduced. One can convert a site on which a hotel has been built into an office-building site, but it takes a very large differential in the value of land use to make it worthwhile because the hotel must be torn down.

Although land is highly mobile between alternative uses, it is completely immobile as far as location is concerned. There is only so much land within a given distance of the center of any city, and no increase in the price paid can induce further land to locate within that distance. This locational immobility has, as we shall see, important consequences.

Mobility of capital. Most capital equipment, once constructed, is comparatively immobile among uses. A great deal of machinery is utterly specific: once built, it must either be used for the purpose for which it was designed or else not used at all. (It is the immobility of much fixed capital equipment that makes the exit of firms from declining industries a slow and difficult process.) Of course many kinds of capital equipment are mobile—a shed may be used for a large number of purposes, and a lathe can be used to make a wide variety of products.

Over long periods of time the allocation of a country's capital stock among uses does change substantially. When capital goods wear out, firms may simply replace them with identical goods. But the firm has many other options: It may buy a newly designed machine to produce the same goods, it may buy machines to produce totally different goods, or it may spend its resources in other ways. Such decisions lead to changes in the long-run allocation of a country's stock of capital among various uses.

Labor mobility. Labor is unique as a factor of production in that the supply of the service implies the physical presence of the owner of the source of the service. Absentee landlords can obtain income from land located in remote parts of the world while continuing to live in the place of their choice. Investment can be shifted from iron mines in northern Minnesota to mines in Labrador while the owners of the capital commute between New York and the French Riviera. But when a worker employed by a firm in Pittsburgh decides to supply labor service to a firm in Chicago, the worker must physically travel to Chicago. This is all quite obvious, but it has an important consequence.

Because of the need for physical presence, non-monetary considerations are much more important in the allocation of labor than in the allocation of other factors of production.

People may be either satisfied with or frustrated by the kind of work they do, where they do it, the people they do it with, and the social status of their occupations. Since these factors influence their decisions about what they do with their labor services, they will not move every time they can earn a higher wage.

Nevertheless, according to the hypothesis of equal net advantage, occupational and job movement should occur if there are changes in the wage structure. The mobility that does occur depends upon many forces. For example, it is not difficult for a secretary to shift from one company to another or to take a job in New York City instead of in Jersey City, but it can be difficult for a secretary to become an editor or a fashion model in a short period of time. There are three considerations here: ability, training, and inclination. Lack of any one of these will stratify some people and make certain kinds of mobility difficult for them.

One important key to labor mobility is time. In the short term it is often difficult for people to change occupations; in the long term it is much easier.

Some barriers may seem insurmountable for a person once his or her training has been completed. It is not easy, and it may be impossible, for a farmer to become a surgeon or a truck driver to become a professional athlete, even if the relative wage rates change greatly. But the children of farmers, doctors, lawyers, and athletes, when they are deciding how much education or training to obtain, are not nearly as limited in their choices as their parents, who have completed their education and are settled in their occupations. For this reason the labor force is not static. At one end of the age distribution people enter the labor force from school; at the other end they leave it via retirement or death. The turnover due to these causes is about 3 or 4 percent per year. Over a period of twenty years, a totally different occupational distribution could appear by redirecting new entrants to jobs other than the ones left vacant by persons leaving the labor force, without a single individual ever changing jobs. The role of education in adapting people to needed jobs is very great. In a society in which education is provided to all, it is possible to achieve large increases in the supply of any desired labor skill within a decade or so.

The price of factors in competitive markets

We have now developed theories of both the demand for and the supply of factors of production. This is all that is needed for a theory of factor pricing in competitive markets. If factor prices are free to vary, prices and quantities employed will tend toward the point at which quantity supplied equals quantity demanded. Furthermore, shifts in either the demand for or the supply of factors will have the same effects on prices, quantities, and factor incomes as are predicted by standard price theory.

The theory of factor prices is an absolutely general one. If one is concerned with labor, one should interpret factor prices to mean wages; if one is thinking about land, factor prices should be interpreted to mean land rents, and so on.

FACTOR PRICE DIFFERENTIALS

Everyone knows that prices of factors such as labor or land vary. Consider the prices of a number of closely related factors such as different kinds of labor. If all of these factors were identical and if all benefits were monetary, then all their prices would tend toward the same level. Factors would tend to move from low-priced occupations to high-priced ones. The quantities supplied would diminish in occupations in which prices were low, and the resulting shortage would tend to force prices up; the quantities of factors supplied would increase in occupations in which prices were high, and the resulting surplus would force factor prices down. The movement would continue until there were no further incentives to transfer—that is, until factor prices were equalized. Factor prices, however, are not always equalized. Factor price differentials are regularly observed and may be divided into two distinct types.

Labor mobility and immobility

Labor mobility—between places, between jobs, between occupations, and even between social classes—has been studied extensively. The studies show, among other things, that:

1. Labor mobility of every kind increases as the time span increases.

2. Labor is more mobile between jobs in the same location than between different locations because movement of the family is a deterrent.

3. Labor is more mobile between jobs in the same occupation than between occupations because of the time required to acquire new skills.

4. Education is more important than family background in determining occupation. While it is still an advantage to have a successful parent (successful in the sense of the parent's having an occupation at the high end of the income scale), it is not nearly as important as it was fifty years ago. What is helpful in today's America is having the education that a successful parent helps one acquire.

5. While relative wages do matter, job opportunities are often even more important in influencing labor movement, both among places and among occupations.

While there are many "man-made" encouragements to labor mobility, such as education, training, and employment agencies, there are also barriers. Many organizations, private and public, adopt policies that affect personnel and impede their mobility as workers. When labor unions negotiate seniority rights for their members, they protect older employees from being laid off but they also make them reluctant to change jobs. When an employer provides employees with a pension plan, the employees may not want to forfeit this fringe benefit by changing jobs.

Unions may also limit entrance into an occupation. Licensing is required in dozens of trades and professions. Barbers, electricians, doctors, and, in some places, even peddlers must have licenses. There is, of course, a perfectly legitimate reason for requiring licenses in those cases in which the public must be protected against the incompetent or the quack or the nuisance. Licensing, however, can also have the effect of limiting supply. Discrimination based on racial prejudice and other similar attitudes further limit the mobility of labor.

Dynamic differentials

Some factor price differentials reflect a temporary state of disequilibrium. These are self-eliminating and are called **dynamic differentials.** They are brought about by such things as the growth of one industry and the decline of another. Such differentials themselves serve to cause reallocations of factor supplies, and these reallocations will in turn act to remove the differentials. Consider the effect on factor prices of a rise in the demand for air transport and a decline in the demand for railroading. The theory predicts an increase in the airline industry's (derived) demand for factors and a decrease in the railroad industry's demand for factors. Relative factor prices are thus predicted to go up in the airline industry and down in railroading. The differential in factor prices will itself foster a net movement of factors from the railroad industry to the airline industry, and this movement will cause the price differentials to lessen and eventually disappear. How long this process takes depends on how easily factors move from one industry to the other—that is, on the extent of factor mobility.

Equilibrium differentials

Some factor price differentials may persist in equilibrium without generating forces that eliminate them. These **equilibrium differentials** are related to differences in the factors themselves (e.g., land of different fertilities or labor of different abilities), to differences in the cost of acquiring skills, and to different nonmonetary advantages of different factor employments.

It is usual to pay people in academic and research jobs less than they would be able to earn in the world of commerce and industry because there are substantial nonmonetary advantages attached to the former. If labor were paid the same in both jobs, many people would try to move out of industry and into academic employment. Excess demand for labor in industry and excess supply in universities would then cause industrial wages to rise relative to academic ones until the movement of labor stopped.

Equilibrium differentials may also be caused by differences in skills. If there is a chronic shortage of skilled workers, the skilled worker will earn more than the unskilled worker. Although there will be some movement from unskilled to skilled jobs, it is not likely to be sufficient to eliminate this differential. People will not acquire scarce skills, even if they are able to do so, unless the differentials in pay remain large enough to pay for the costs and time spent in acquiring them.

It is important to realize that the high pay of the skilled relative to that of the unskilled merely reflects relative demand and supply conditions for the two types of labor. There is nothing in the nature of competitive markets that ensures that skilled workers always get high pay just because they are skilled. When, for example, the demand for expert harness makers declined, they were in excess supply and their wages came down; history is replete with examples of particular groups of highly skilled workers who lost their privileged position when there was a change in the supply of or the demand for their services. Many people feel that it is both unjust and incomprehensible that since World War II truck drivers have been earning more money than schoolteachers. Whatever the justice of the matter, it is certainly not incomprehensible; at the same wage there would be excess demand for truck drivers and excess supply of school teachers.

The two kinds of differentials are closely linked to factor mobility and the hypothesis of net advantage. Dynamic differentials lead to, and are eroded by, factor movements; equilibrium differentials are explained in part by different nonmonetary benefits.

Dynamic differentials tend to disappear over time; equilibrium differentials may persist indefinitely.

TRANSFER EARNINGS AND ECONOMIC RENT

The amount that a factor must earn in its present use to prevent it from transferring to another use is called its **transfer earnings;** any excess that it earns over this amount is called its **economic rent.** The distinction is critical in predicting what changes in earnings will cause factors of production to enter or leave a particular employment.

The concept of economic rent, a surplus over transfer earnings, is analogous to the notion of economic profit as a surplus over opportunity cost.

Origins of the concept of economic rent

The present concept of economic rent arose out of a policy controversy. In the early part of the nineteenth century, when classical economics was in full bloom, there was a controversy about the high price of wheat in England. The high price was causing great hardship because bread was a primary source of food. Some argued that "corn" (then the generic term for all grains) had a high price because landlords were charging very high rents to tenant farmers. In order to meet these land rents, the prices that farmers charged for their corn also had to be raised to a high level. In short, it was argued that the price of corn was high because the rents of agricultural land were high. Those who held this view advocated restricting the power of the landlords and somehow forcing them to behave more reasonably.

Others—including, notably, David Ricardo—held that the situation was exactly the reverse. The price of corn was high, they said, because there was a shortage of corn caused by the Napoleonic wars. Because corn had a high price it was profitable to produce it and there was keen competition among farmers to obtain land on which to grow corn. This competition in turn forced up the rents of corn land. If the price of corn were to fall so that corn growing became less profitable, then the demand for land would fall and the price paid for the use of land (i.e., its rent) would also fall. Those holding this view advocated removing the tariff so that imported corn could come into the country, thereby increasing the supply and bringing down both the price of corn and that of the land on which it was grown.

Stated formally, the essentials of Ricardo's argument were these: Land was regarded as having only one use, the growing of corn. The supply of land was regarded as given and unchangeable—that is, in perfectly inelastic supply. Nothing had to be paid to prevent land from transferring to a use other than growing corn because it had no other use and no self-respecting landowner would leave his land idle as long as he could obtain some return, no matter how small, by renting it out. Therefore, all of the payment to land—that is, rent—was a surplus over and above what was necessary to keep it in its present use. Given the fixed supply of land, the price depended on the demand for land, which was *derived* from the demand for corn. Rent, the term for the payment for the use of land, thus became the term for a surplus payment to a factor over and above what was necessary to keep it in its present use.

The modern view of economic rent

Subsequently two facts were realized. First, land itself often had many alternative uses, and from the point of view of any one use, part of the payment made to land would necessarily have to be paid to keep it in its present use. Second, factors of production other than land also often earn a surplus over and above what is necessary to keep them in their present use. Television stars and great athletes, for example, are in very short and fairly fixed supply and their potential earnings in other occupations are probably quite moderate. But because there is a huge demand for their services, as television stars or athletes, they may receive payments greatly in excess of what is needed to keep them from transferring to other occupations.

Thus it appears that all factors of production are pretty much the same; part of the payment made to them is a payment necessary to keep them from transferring to other uses, and part is a surplus over and above what is necessary to keep them in their present use. This surplus is now called economic rent whether the factor is land or labor or a piece of capital equipment.

The division of factor earnings between rents and transfer earnings

In most cases, the actual earnings of a factor of production will be a composite of transfer earnings and economic rent. It is possible, however, to imagine cases in which all earnings are *either* transfer earnings *or* economic rent. The possibilities are illustrated in Figure 20–4. If the supply curve is perfectly elastic (horizontal), the whole of the price paid is a transfer earning: if the purchasing industry does not pay this price, it will not obtain any quantity of the factor. If the supply curve is perfectly inelastic (vertical), the whole of the payment is an economic rent: even a price barely above zero would not lead suppliers to decrease the quantity supplied. After all, some price is better than none.

The more usual situation is that of a gradually rising supply curve. In this case, a rise in the price serves the allocative function of attracting more units of the factor into the employment, but the same rise in the factor's price presents an extra economic rent to all the units of the factor already employed. (The owners of these units were willing to supply them at the original price.)

This is quite a general result. If a factor becomes scarce in any or all of its uses, its price will rise and this will serve the allocative function of attracting additional units, but it will also give an economic rent to all those units of the factor already in that employment, whose transfer earnings were already being covered.

Figure 20–4   The division of factor payments between economic rent and transfer earnings

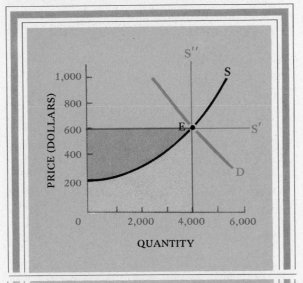

The division of total factor payments between economic rent and transfer earnings depends on the shape of the supply curve. A single demand curve is shown with three different supply curves. In each case the competitive equilibrium price is $600 and 4,000 workers are hired and the total payment to labor ($2,400,000) is represented by the entire shaded area.

(a) When the supply curve rises to the right (the black curve, S) part of the payment is rent, part transfer earnings. The 4,000th worker is just receiving his transfer earnings because if the wage fell below $600 a month he would not work. However, other workers would stay in the industry at a lower wage. If a separate bargain were made with each worker so that each was paid only his transfer earnings, the total payment would be the area under the black supply curve, shown as the lighter shaded area. Because the same wage must be paid to everyone, however, the total wage payment is larger, and the extra payment, shown as the darker shaded area, represents economic rent.

(b) When the supply curve is horizontal (the colored line S') the whole payment is transfer earnings because even a small decrease in price offered would lead all units of the factor to move elsewhere.

(c) When the supply curve is vertical (the colored line, S") the whole payment is rent because a decrease in price would not lead any of the units of the factor to move elsewhere.

POLICY IMPLICATIONS OF THE DISTINCTION BETWEEN RENTS AND TRANSFER EARNINGS

Using wage increases to increase the quantity of a factor supplied

If the U.S. government wants more physicists, should it subsidize physicists' salaries? As we have seen, such a policy may well have an effect on supply. It will persuade some students uncertain about whether to become engineers or physicists to become physicists. Whether it is an efficient use of the money will depend on the slope of the supply curve. Clearly, however, raising all physicists' salaries may mean that a great deal of money will have to be spent on extra payments to people who are already physicists. These payments will be economic rents, since existing physicists have demonstrated that they are prepared to be physicists at their old salaries. If these rents are a large part of the total subsidy, an alternative policy may produce more physicists per dollar. One such alternative is to subsidize scholarships and fellowships for students who will train to become physicists. The National Science Foundation and the Atomic Energy Commission did precisely this.

If the supply curve is quite inelastic, an increase in the quantity supplied may be

Henry George and the single-tax movement

Taxation of land value has had enormous appeal in the past. The **single-tax movement** of which Henry George (1839–1897), a printer by trade, was the guiding genius caught the imagination of hundreds of thousands of people. George ran for mayor of New York City in 1886 and very nearly won, campaigning on the issue of the single tax. His book *Progress and Poverty* (1880) is, as books on economic issues go, an all-time best seller. George's idea was to tax away the "unearned increment" that accrued to landowners and to finance all government undertakings thereby. What was its appeal?

The fixed supply of land, combined with a rapidly rising demand for it, means that the owners of land gain from the natural progress of society without having to contribute anything. Many people, including Henry George, have been incensed at this "unearned increment" and have proposed taxing away the huge fortunes accruing to landlords in a rapidly growing society. A further appeal of taxes on land values arises from the fact that economic rent can be taxed away without affecting the allocation of resources.

Two problems arise, however, in any attempt to tax this economic rent. First, the theoretical statement refers to economic rent, not to the payment actually made by tenants to landlords. Because what is called rent in the world is partly an economic rent and partly a return on capital invested by the landowner, the policy implications of taxing rents depend on being able to identify economic rent in practice. At best, this is a very difficult thing to do; at worst, it may be impossible.

The second problem is a normative one. If, in the interests of justice, it is hoped to treat all recipients of economic rent similarly, insurmountable difficulties will be encountered because economic rent accrues to factors other than land. It accrues to the owners of any factor that is fixed in supply and that faces a rising demand. Opera

achieved more easily and at less cost by policies designed to shift the supply curve to the right than by the policy of raising price. This is because, given a highly inelastic supply curve, much of the payment needed to bring forth additional quantity is a rent to previously employed people. See Figure 20-4.

Urban land values and land taxes

The high payments made for the services of urban land are largely economic rents. The land is scarce relative to the demand for it, and it commands a price very much above what it could earn in agricultural uses. The payment it receives is thus well in excess of what is necessary to prevent it from transferring from urban uses back to agricultural uses. A society with rising population and rising per capita real income tends also to have steadily rising urban land prices. This fact has created a special interest in taxes on land values.

Suppose there is a tax on the economic rent of land. If the same tax rate is applied to all uses of land, the relative profitability of different uses will be unaffected and a landlord will not be tempted to change the allocation of land among uses. Land will not be forced out of use because land that is very unprofitable will command little rent and so pay little tax. Thus there will be no change in the supply of goods that are produced with the aid of land, and because there is no change in supply, there will be no change in prices. Furthermore, the tax cannot be passed on to consumers. Farmers will be willing to pay just as much (and no more) as they would have offered previously for the use of land. Agricultural prices and rents will be unchanged, and the whole of the tax will be borne by the landlord. The net rents earned by landlords will fall by the full amount of the tax. Therefore a tax on land rents that are truly economic rents falls solely on landowners and is not passed on to the users of land or the consumers of the produce of land. This is the kind of argument that lay behind the popular appeal of the single-tax movement discussed in the box.

singers will gain in exactly the same way as landlords when the society becomes richer and the demand for opera increases without any corresponding increase in the supply of singers. No one has yet devised a scheme that will tax the economic rent but not the transfer earnings of such divergent factors as land, franchises, baseball players, and supreme court justices.

The appeal of the single tax has now receded, both because of the difficulties just described and because, with the great increase in the size of the government, even an effective tax on economic rent could hardly be expected to finance the majority, let alone the entirety, of government expenditures. The movement has left one curious anachronism in the tax policies of those cities that levy their real estate taxes at a higher rate on the assessed value of the land than on the assessed value of the buildings erected on the land.

Summary

1. The functional distribution of income refers to the shares of total national income going to each of the major factors of production. It focuses on sources of income. The size distribution of income refers to the shares of total national income going to various groups of households. It focuses only on the size of income, not its source.

2. The income of a factor of production can be broken into two elements: (a) the price paid per unit of the factor and (b) the quantity of the factor used. The determination of factor prices and quantities is an application of the

same price theory used to determine product prices and quantities. In competitive factor markets price is determined by the demand for and supply of the factor.

3. The demand for any factor is a derived demand, one derived from goods and services the factor is used to make. A fall in the price of a factor may lead to an increase in the quantity demanded of the factor in two ways: (a) It will decrease the cost of commodities the factor helps to make, thus increasing the output of those commodities and thereby increasing the quantity of the factor demanded. This effect will be larger the more elastic the demand for the goods that the factor helps to make and the more important the factor is in the total costs of producing the goods. (b) It will lead to the substitution of the now cheaper factor for factors whose prices have not fallen. This effect will be larger the easier it is to substitute one factor for another in production.

4. In equilibrium, a profit-maximizing firm will hire units of any variable factor until the last unit hired adds as much to costs as it does to revenue. The addition to revenue is called the marginal revenue product. If factors are bought in a competitive market, the addition to cost is the price of a unit of a factor. From this comes the important condition that in equilibrium the price of a factor will equal its marginal revenue product.

5. The total supplies of most factors of production are variable over time. The total supply of labor depends on the size of the population, the proportion of the population willing to work, and the number of hours each individual is willing to work. The total supply of arable land is subject to wide variations, upward by reclamation and downward by neglect of the principles of soil conservation. The total stock of capital can be easily varied.

6. The hypothesis of equal net advantage is a theory of the supply of factors to particular uses. Owners of factors will choose the use that produces the greatest net advantage, allowing both for monetary and nonmonetary advantages of a particular employment.

7. Factor mobility is important. Land is mobile between uses that do not depend on changing its geographical location, but it is totally immobile between uses that depend critically on location. Any piece of capital equipment has a limited life, but the fact that firms can decide to "replace" a discarded piece of capital with a totally different piece means that the composition of the nation's capital stock can be changed significantly from decade to decade. Labor mobility is greatly affected by nonmone-

tary advantages and disadvantages. The longer the period of time allowed to elapse, the more mobile is the labor force because of the importance of education and training to labor mobility.

8. In competitive factor markets, prices are determined by demand and supply, but factor price differentials occur. Dynamic differentials in factor earnings serve as signals of disequilibria and induce movements of factors that eventually remove the differentials. Equilibrium differentials reflect more permanent differences in the nature of factors and nonmonetary benefits and can persist more or less indefinitely.

9. Transfer earnings are what must be paid to a factor to prevent it from transferring to another use. Economic rent is the difference between a factor's transfer earnings and its actual earnings. If the supply of a factor is completely inelastic, all its earnings are rents; if the supply is completely elastic, all its earnings are transfer earnings; if the supply curve is upward-sloping, part of the factors' earnings are transfer earnings and part are rent.

10. The fact that not all of a factor's earnings are transfer earnings has potentially important policy implications. One is that increasing the factor's price may be a relatively expensive way to induce increases in the quantity of the factor supplied. Another is that taxes on economic rents, if they could be designed, would not affect the allocation of resources.

Concepts for review

Factor demand as a derived demand
Marginal revenue product
The marginal productivity of theory of distribution ($w = MRP$)
Factor mobility
The hypothesis of equal net advantage
Dynamic and equilibrium differentials in factor prices
Transfer earnings and economic rent

Discussion questions

1. Other things being equal, how would you expect each of the following to affect the size distribution of after-tax in-

come? Do any of them lead to clear predictions about the functional distribution of income?

a. an increase in unemployment

b. rapid increases in all prices and interest rates

c. an increase in food prices relative to other prices

d. an increase in social security benefits and taxes

e. a sharp increase in the tax on corporate profits

2. The demands listed below have been rapidly increasing in recent years. What derived demands would you predict have risen very sharply? Where will the extra factors of production demanded be drawn from?

a. the demand for electric power

b. the demand for medical services

c. the demand for international and interregional travel

3. Can the following factor prices be explained by the marginal productivity theory of distribution?

a. The actor Broderick Crawford is paid $25,000 for appearing in a ten-second commercial. The model who appears in the ad with him is paid $250.

b. First prizes in the British Tennis Championships at Wimbledon in 1976 were: men's singles $25,000, women's singles $20,000, men's doubles $12,000, and women's doubles $4,000.

c. The same jockey is paid 50 percent more money for winning a ¾ mile race with a $150,000 first prize than a 1½ mile race with a $100,000 prize—on the same horse.

d. The head football coach at Michigan State University is paid *not* to coach in the third year of a three-year contract.

4. Overall participation in the work force has remained at about the same proportion of the total population for the last 20 years, but its composition has changed substantially. Among the features of the labor force over this period are:

a. Virtually all married men between 25 and 45 years of age have participated in the work force in each year.

b. The percentage of women aged 40 and over has risen sharply.

c. The percentage of men over 55 has dropped.

d. The percentage of both men and women under 25 has declined.

Hypothesize about the social and economic changes that might explain these conditions. How do they relate to the theory of distribution?

5. What, if anything, do each of the following have to do with factor mobility?

a. A newspaper advertisement by the New Jersey Development Council: "Open your new plant in the Garden State.

Our sizable labor force of skilled and unskilled workers is a major benefit for any employer. New Jersey workers are experienced, easy to find, easy to train. And just as important for your profit picture, they like it in New Jersey and don't move away."

b. Trailways Bus Company offered one-way bus tickets to anywhere in the United States at half price to anyone in Detroit who had been unemployed for six months or more. Hundreds of people bought these "opportunity fare" tickets.

6. Contrast your expectations of the mobility and pay levels of members of the following occupations. Pay attention to how mobility affects factor pay and how education affects mobility.

a. a migrant farm worker

b. a high school football coach

c. a composer of classical music

d. a college president

7. A recent study showed that after taking full account of differences in education, age, hours worked per week, weeks worked per year, etc., professionally trained people earned approximately 15 percent less if they worked in universities than if they worked in government service. Can this be accounted for by the theory of distribution?

8. Distinguish between economic rent and transfer earnings in each of the following payments for factor services.

a. the $150 per month a landlord receives for the use of an apartment he leases

b. the salary of the president of the United States

c. the $1 million annual salary of Barbara Walters

d. the salary of a window cleaner who says, "Its dangerous, dirty work, but it beats driving a truck."

9. Which of the following are dynamic and which equilibrium differentials in factor prices?

a. the differences in earnings of football coaches and wrestling coaches

b. a "bonus for signing on" for a construction company seeking carpenters in a tight labor market

c. differences in monthly rentals charged for three-bedroom houses in different parts of the same metropolitan area

10. Charles O. Finley, the millionaire owner of the Oakland Athletics baseball team, sold his star player rather than pay the "astronomical, unjustified salary he is demanding." Another baseball owner bought the contract, paid the salary, and declared himself delighted. Was one of them necessarily wrong?

21

Collective bargaining, discrimination, and the determination of wages

Why do automobile workers get the same pay for the same work, no matter where they work in the United States? Why do carpenters get different wages in different locations? Why do coal miners, who work in a declining industry, get higher rates of pay than equally skilled workers in many expanding industries? How does a worker in a plant employing 5,000 people "ask for a raise?" How does a worker let her employer know that she would be glad to trade so many cents per hour in wages for a better medical insurance scheme? Why do strikes occur?

The competitive theory of factor price determination, the subject of the preceding chapter, yields many useful and confirmed predictions about factor prices, factor movements, and the distribution of income. Indeed, for the pricing of many nonhuman factors, there is little need to discard or to modify the competitive model. Much of what is observed about labor markets is also consistent with the theory. But not all of it is.

Labor is, in many ways, the exceptional factor of production. The factors that govern working conditions and pay are vitally important to workers and their families. When employees and employers negotiate the price to be paid to the factor of production called labor, they are negotiating about something that is vital to most households. It is not surprising that people are sometimes prepared to fight over such negotiations. Considerations other than material advantage enter the relationship between employer and employee, for it is a relationship between people who look for loyalty, fairness, appreciation, and justice along with paychecks and productivity and who if they feel these are denied them can often respond with aggression, malice, and hatred.

Labor unions, employers' associations, and the institutions and customs governing collective bargaining are features of the real world that have developed in response to the exceptional conditions governing the bargaining between free people about the terms on which one will work for another. If these institutions are important determinants of what happens, it must be because the nature of the institution influences the wages and working conditions that are finally agreed on.

Because labor markets are characteristically imperfectly competitive, and sometimes monopolistic, the theory of factor price determination must be extended somewhat before it can be applied to the full range of problems concerning the determination of wages.

Theoretical models of wage determination

The effect a labor union has on the wages earned by its members depends partly on the kind of market in which the union is operating. Two extreme but relevant cases are, first, the one in which there are so many employers that no one of them can influence the wage rate by varying its own demand for labor and, second, the one in which there is a single purchaser of labor, either a single firm or an association of several firms operating as a single unit in the labor market. In the former case, labor is said to be purchased under competitive conditions; in the latter case, under monopsonistic conditions. **Monopsony** means a single buyer; on the purchasing side, it is the equivalent of a monopoly (a single seller). What is the effect of introducing a union into each of these extreme situations? First we assume that the union sets a wage unilaterally and the employers decide how much labor to hire at that wage. Later in the chapter we consider other types of union-employer bargains.

A UNION IN A COMPETITIVE LABOR MARKET

Where there are many employers and many unorganized workers there is a competitive factor market of the kind analyzed in the previous chapter and illustrated in Figure 21–1. When a union enters such a market and sets a union wage, employers are presented with a supply of labor that is perfectly elastic up to the maximum number who would like to work at that wage. The union can set the wage above the competitive level and thereby increase the pay earned by those who remain in employment. But this has two other effects: (1) As a consequence of a downward-sloping demand curve, the quantity of labor demanded diminishes and (2) as a consequence of an upward-sloping supply curve, the quantity of labor supplied increases.

Figure 21–1 A wage-setting union in a competitive labor market

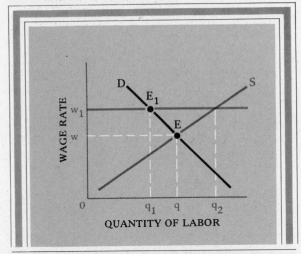

A union can raise the wages of those employed in a competitive labor market at the expense of the level of employment. The competitive equilibrium is at E; the wage is w and employment q. If a union enters this market and sets a wage of w_1, there will be q_2 workers who would like to work at that wage. The new equilibrium is at E_1 with a wage of w_1, employment of q_1, and unemployment of q_1q_2.

Figure 21–2 Monopsony in a labor market

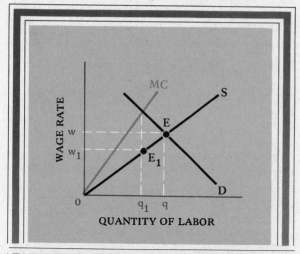

A monopsonist lowers both the wage rate and the level of employment below their competitive levels. *D* and *S* are the competitive demand and supply curves. In competition equilibrium is at *E*, the wage rate would be *w*, and the quantity of labor hired *q*. The marginal cost of labor (*MC*) to the monopsonist is above the average cost. The monopsonistic firm will maximize profits at E_1. It will hire q_1 labor where the marginal cost of the last worker is just equal to the value of that worker's marginal contribution to output as shown by the demand curve. The wage paid to get q_1 workers is only w_1.

When a union raises wages in a competitive industry, employment will fall and a pool of unemployed labor will be created.

Pressure to cut wages may develop from the unsuccessful job hunters, and the union must be able to resist this pressure if the higher wage is to be maintained.

A MONOPSONISTIC LABOR MARKET WITHOUT A UNION

Now consider a labor market in which there are many unorganized workers but only a small number of firms. For simplicity, consider a case in which the few purchasers cooperate with each other in order to act as a single unit so that there is a monopsony in the labor market. A situation in which the purchaser of labor is a monopsonist and there is no labor union is analyzed in Figure 21–2.

The employers' association realizes that facing a rising supply curve for labor, it can pick a wage rate and take the quantity of labor offered, or it can pick the quantity of labor to hire and pay the wage rate required to bring forth that quantity of labor. While the employers' association can offer any wage rate that it chooses—the laborers must either work at that rate or change occupation or location—the wage rate chosen will affect the profitability of its operations. For any given quantity that the monopsonist wishes to purchase, the labor supply curve shows the price per unit that it must offer; to the monopsonist, this is the average cost curve of the factor. In deciding how much labor to hire, however, the monopsonist will be interested in *marginal cost* because it is aware that it can bid up the wage against its own interest.

Whenever the supply curve of labor slopes upward, the marginal cost of employing extra units will exceed the average cost.[1] It exceeds the wage paid (the average cost) because the increased wage rate necessary to attract an extra worker must be paid to everyone already employed.[23] The profit-maximizing monopsonist will equate marginal cost of labor with its marginal revenue product (shown by the demand curve for labor). In other words, a monopsonist will go on hiring labor until the last unit increases total costs by as much as it increases total revenue.

---

[1] If, for example, 100 units of labor are employed at $2 per hour, then total cost is $200 per hour and average cost per hour is $2. If 101 units are employed, and the wage rate is driven up to $2.01, then total labor cost becomes $203.01 an hour. Although average cost is only $2.01, the total cost has been increased by $3.01 as a result of hiring one more laborer. Thus the marginal cost of this extra labor is $3.01.

Monopsonistic conditions in the factor market will result in a lower level of employment and a lower wage rate than would rule when the factor is purchased under competitive conditions.

This is because the monopsonistic purchaser is aware that by trying to purchase more of the factor it is driving up the price against itself. It will therefore stop short of the point that is reached when the factor is purchased by many different firms, no one of which can exert an influence on the wage rate.

A UNION IN A MONOPSONISTIC MARKET

Now let a wage-setting union enter a monopsonistic market. The result is shown in Figure 21–3. The union gains its effect by presenting the employer with a perfectly elastic supply up to the maximum number who wish to work at the going rate. There is no point in the employer's reducing the quantity demanded in the hope of driving down the rate; neither is there any point in holding off hiring for fear of driving the wage up. The employing firm is presented with perfectly elastic average cost and marginal cost curves of labor up to the maximum number who wish to work at the union wage, and it must do the best it can with it.

Because a wage-setting union has the effect of turning the employer into a price taker in the labor market, the union facing a monopsonist can duplicate the competitive results.

The union may choose to raise wages further. If it does, the argument is exactly the same as that surrounding Figure 21–1. If the wage is raised above the competitive level, the employer will no longer wish to hire all the labor offered at that wage. A pool of workers who want to work but cannot find employment will develop and the actual quantity of employment will fall. This is illustrated in Figure 21–3. It is important to notice, however, that the union can raise wages substantially above their competitive level before

employment falls to a level as low as it was in the preunion monopsonistic situation.

So far we have dealt with the simple case of a union that fixes a wage and allows employment to be determined by demand. Other methods of raising wages are available, and unions have goals other than high wages. Before we consider these further, we need to review some institutional and historical details about labor markets. In the process, we shall

Figure 21–3 A wage-setting union enters a monopsonistic labor market

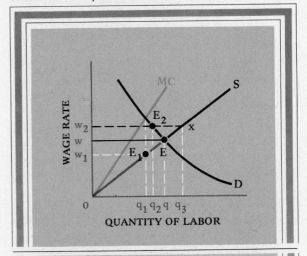

By presenting a monopsonistic employer with a fixed wage, the union can raise both wages and employment over the monopsonistic level. The monopsony position before the union enters is at E_1, with a wage rate of w_1 and q_1 workers hired. A union now enters and sets the wage at w. The supply curve of labor becomes wES and wages and employment rise to their competitive levels of w and q without creating a pool of unemployed workers. If the wage is raised further, say to w_2, the supply curve becomes w_2xS and the quantity of employment falls below the competitive level to q_2 while a pool of unsuccessful job applicants of q_2q_3 develops.

be able to use the theory already developed to understand some past events and some present institutions.

Labor market institutions

Potential monopsonists: employers' associations

The large firm has some degree of monopsony power just by virtue of its size and the number of employees with which it deals. It recognizes that its actions affect the wage rate, especially the rates received by those kinds of labor that are in some way limited to the industry in which the firm operates. This limitation will result when one large firm's need for this kind of labor represents a large fraction of the total demand for it. If steelworkers were not organized, the U.S. Steel Corporation would exercise substantial monopsony power in its dealings with them because U.S. Steel represents a large share of the demand for whatever special talents may be required for making iron and steel.

Employers' associations are groups of employers who band together for a number of purposes, one of which may be to agree on a common policy in labor negotiations. If all steel companies offer the same terms, they can exercise even more monopsony power than any one of them could on its own. The steelworker who did not wish to accept the common conditions would have no alternative but to seek work in another industry. Today formal employers' associations which appoint official bargaining representatives exist on a local level in many industries, including the hotel, restaurant, newspaper printing, and construction industries. There are regional or national associations in the garment manufacturing, hosiery, textile, coal mining, and furniture manufacturing industries, among others.

At least as important as formal associations are informal ones in which the several firms in an industry follow the lead set by a key firm. The industrywide pattern characterizes many manufacturing industries today. The automobile industry, for example, achieves nationwide agreement with its workers without the formal apparatus of an employers' association.

Potential monopolists: unions

No one bothers to define unions any more, perhaps because everyone knows what they are, or perhaps because a union is so many things: a social club, an educational instrument, a political club, one more source of withholding money from a worker's pay, a bargaining agent for an individual worker, and, to some, a way of life. For the purposes of our discussion of labor markets, a **union** (or **trade union** or **labor union**) is an association of individual workers that speaks for them in negotiations with their employers.

Unions today have two different principles of organization: the craft (or trade) union and the industrial union. In the **craft union,** workers with a common set of skills are joined in a common association, no matter where or for whom they work. The craft principle of organization was and is the hallmark of the American Federation of Labor (AFL). The **industrial union** is organized along industry lines: All workers in a given plant or industry are collected into a single union. This is the pattern developed by the member unions of the Congress of Industrial Organizations (CIO). Among the prominent industrial unions are the United Automobile Workers and the United Steelworkers.

The two principles of unionism conflict. Should a carpenter employed in the steel industry be represented by the carpenters' union or the steelworkers' union? Disputes over which union shall have the right to *organize* (i.e., bring into their union) a particular group of workers are known as **jurisdictional disputes.** They have led to prolonged, bitter, and bloody battles of union against union, and they have played an important role in American labor history. In the United States, since the merger of the AFL and CIO in 1955, jurisdictional disputes have become somewhat less common.

Jurisdictional disputes may involve more than mere power struggles between rival unions over who shall represent a particular group of workers. If the jurisdictional dispute concerns which occupation should do a certain job, the outcome of the dispute will affect the employment level of the workers of the two occupations—increasing the demand for the services of the winning group and decreasing it for the losing group. (While workers of the losing group may be able to shift unions, they will sacrifice whatever seniority they have in their union. Thus, if there is excess supply, they will bear the brunt of the unemployment that is caused by a wage above the competitive level.)

Many jurisdictional disputes involve the different philosophies of different unions—for example, in the trade-off between higher wages (for those who keep their jobs) and lower total employment. In the past, AFL unions tended to go for high wages for the skilled craftsmen in a plant, whereas the CIO wanted to organize the whole plant to provide employment and income to more workers, even to the disadvantage of some strategic crafts.

American unions, whether craft or industrial, operate at the local level, at the national (or international)[2] level, and also as a federation of unions.

The important level for most of the economic functions of the union is the national level. The national officers do the bargaining, set the policies, and set the tone. Individual workers, however, belong to a local to which

they pay dues (a part of which goes to the national). There are about 200 national unions, which have over 75,000 locals. The local for a craft union is geographical—the Chicago chapter of the carpenters, say. The local for an industrial union is a plant or a company—the Ford local of the United Automobile Workers, for example.

The **federation** is a loose organization of national unions. Before 1955, the AFL and CIO were two separate organizations, but today there is one federation, the AFL–CIO. The federation has little real power but serves an important role as spokesman for organized labor. Its function in recent years has been largely a public relations and political one; it has thrown its support behind certain candidates, its representatives have testified before Congress, and so on. For example, George Meany, long time president of the AFL–CIO, took the lead in keeping normally Democratic labor officially neutral in the 1972 presidential election and then was prominent among labor leaders at first in opposing Jimmy Carter for the 1976 Democratic nomination and then in supporting him in the election campaign against Gerald Ford. In this way Meany attempts to speak for labor even though a group as large as organized labor does not have a single view on many issues. In this respect the federation is not unlike a political party.

Kinds of bargaining arrangements: open, closed, and union shops

In an **open shop** a union represents its members but does not have exclusive bargaining jurisdiction for all the workers in the shop. Membership in the union is not a condition of getting or keeping a job.

Unions vehemently oppose such an arrangement, and economic theory explains why. If, on the one hand, the employer accedes to union demands and raises industry wages, the nonmembers achieve the benefits of the union without paying dues or sharing the

[2] In the early history of U.S. unionism, "going international" was a matter of great psychological importance to small unions. Most American unions are international because most have at least one Canadian local. Canadian locals today account for approximately one million members of American unions.

risks or responsibilities. If, on the other hand, the firm chooses to fight the union, it can run its plants with the nonunion members, thereby weakening the power of the union members in the fight.

If the union does succeed in raising wages above their competitive level, there will be an excess supply of labor (see Figure 21–1). With an open shop, there is nothing to prevent unemployed nonunion workers from accepting a wage below the union one, thereby undermining the union's power to maintain high wages.

If it is necessary for all members of an occupation to join the union in order to get a job, then the union can prevent its members from accepting less than the union wage and so have the power to maintain high wages in spite of the existence of excess supply. This arrangement is called a closed shop. In a **closed shop** only union members may be employed and the union controls its membership as it sees fit. Employers traditionally regard this as an unwarranted limitation of their right to choose their employees. Since passage of the Taft-Hartley Act in 1948, its use has been virtually prohibited in the United States.

The **union shop** is intermediate to a closed and open shop. In a union shop a firm may hire anyone it chooses at the union wage, but every employee must join the union within a specified period. This leaves employers free to hire those individuals they wish to hire but gives the union the power to enforce its union wages because other workers are prevented from accepting employment at lower wages.

Weapons of conflict: strikes, picket lines, boycotts, strikebreakers, lockouts, blacklists

The **strike,** the union's ultimate weapon, is the concerted refusal to work by the members of the union. It is the strike or the threat of a strike that backs up the union's demands in the bargaining process. Workers on strike are, of course, off the payroll, so many unions set

aside a portion of the dues collected to have a fund for paying striking workers. **Picket lines** are made up of striking workers who parade before the entrance to their plant or firm. One of their objectives is to get public opinion on their side; another is to force a total shutdown in the plant's operation. Other union members will not, by time-honored convention, "cross" a picket line. Thus, if bricklayers strike against a construction firm, carpenters will not work on the project, although they themselves may have no grievance against the firm, nor will any teamster deliver supplies to a picketed site. Pickets represent an enormous increase in the bargaining power of a small union. (Much of the bitterness against jurisdictional disputes arises from the fact that an employer may be unable to settle with either union without facing a picket line from the other union.) A **labor boycott** is an organized attempt to persuade customers to refrain from purchasing the goods or services of a firm or industry whose employees are on strike. The long (four and a half years) and ultimately successful grape boycott organized by Cesar Chavez's United Farm Workers Organizing Committee that ended in 1970 is a prominent example.

The **lockout** is the employer's equivalent of the strike. By closing the plant the employer locks out the workers until such time as the dispute is settled. **Strikebreakers (scabs)** are workers brought in by management to operate the plant while the union is on strike. A **blacklist** is an employers' list of workers who have been fired for playing a role in union affairs that was regarded by the employer as undesirable. Other employers are not supposed to give jobs to blacklisted workers.

Collective bargaining

The process by which unions and employers (or their representatives) arrive at and enforce their agreements is known as **collective bargaining.** This process has an important difference from the theoretical models with which we began this chapter. There we assumed that the union set the wage and the employer decided how much labor to hire. In collective bargaining the wage is negotiated. In terms of Figure 21–3, it may be that the employer wants the wage to be w_1, but the union wants w_2. Depending on each side's market power and their bargaining strength, the final agreed wage may be anywhere in between. Thus, in collective bargaining, there is always a substantial range over which an agreement can be reached, and in particular cases the actual range will depend on the goals and strengths of the two bargaining parties and on the skill of their negotiators.

The evolution of the modern union

When representatives of the United Automobile Workers sat down with representatives of the Ford Motor Company in 1976 to discuss wages, contributions to pension funds, number and length of holidays, and other issues, they were engaged in what has been termed "mature collective bargaining." At the end of the negotiations, the newspapers showed the smiling representatives shaking hands, and each of the approximately 200,000 workers in the Ford plants then knew the conditions under which he or she would work for the next three years. Should an employee have a grievance at any time, he or she reports it to the union representative (called a **shop steward**), and a carefully designed procedure is set in motion to settle the dispute.

Unionism today is both stable and accepted. It was not always so. Within the lifetime of many of today's members, unions were fighting for their lives and union organizers and members were risking theirs. In the 1930s the labor movement evoked the loyalties and passions of people as a great liberal cause, in ways that seem quite extraordinary today. Indeed unions today often appear as conservative or even reactionary groups of hard hats. Why the change and how did it come about?

The urge to organize

Trade unionism had its origin in the pitifully low standard of living of the average nineteenth-century worker and his family. Much of the explanation for the low standard of living throughout the world lay in the small size of the national output relative to the population. Even in the wealthiest countries, an equal division of national wealth among all families in 1850 would have left them all in poverty by our present standards.

Poverty had existed for centuries. It was accentuated, however, by the twin processes of urbanization and industrialization. The farmer who was moderately content working the land usually became restive and discontented when the family moved into a grimy, smoky nineteenth-century city, lived in a crowded, unsanitary tenement, and took employment in a sweatshop or a factory. The focus of resentment was usually the employer.

The employer set the wages, and the wages were low. The boss was often arbitrary and seldom sympathetic. And the boss himself was usually conspicuously better off than his employees. Unhappy workers had, of course, the right of all free people to quit their job—and starve. If they grumbled or protested, they could be fired—and worse still, blacklisted, which meant no one else would hire them.

Out of these conditions and other grievances of working men and women came the full range of radical political movements. Out of the same conditions also came a pragmatic American form of collective action called **bread-and-butter unionism,** whose goals were higher wages and better working conditions rather than social and political reform.

The industrial worker perceived that ten or a hundred employees acting together had more influence than one acting alone and dreamed of the day when all would stand solid against the employer. (The word "solidarity" occurs often in the literature and songs of the labor movement.) The union was the organization that would provide a basis for confronting the monopsony power of employers with the collective power of the workers. But it was easier for a worker to see this as a solution than it was to achieve it. Organizations of workers would hurt the employer, and employers did not sit by idly; they too knew that in union there was

strength. "Agitators" who tried to organize other workers were fired and blacklisted, and in some cases they were beaten and killed.

REQUIREMENTS OF A SUCCESSFUL UNION

In order to realize the ambition of creating some effective power over the labor market, it was necessary to gain control of the supply of labor and to have the financial resources necessary to outlast the employer in a struggle for strength. There was no right to organize, and the union had to force a usually hostile employer to negotiate with it. Unions started small among the highly skilled and spread slowly.

There are good theoretical reasons that help

Poverty, United States, 1903

Stories of the workers' very real suffering during the Industrial Revolution and the years that followed could fill many volumes, but an example will at least illustrate some of the horrors that lay behind the drive for change and reform. (The quotation comes from *Poverty*, by Robert Hunter, published in 1904.)

In the worst days of cotton-milling in England the conditions were hardly worse than those now existing in the South. Children—the tiniest and frailest—of five and six years of age rise in the morning and, like old men and women, go to the mills to do their day's labor; and when they return home, they wearily fling themselves on their beds, too tired to take off their clothes. Many children work all night—"in the maddening racket of the machinery, in an atmosphere insanitary and clouded with humidity and lint." It will be long before I forget the face of a little boy of six years, with his hands stretched forward to rearrange a bit of machinery, his

pallid face and spare form showing already the physical effects of labor. This child, six years of age, was working twelve hours a day in a country which has established in many industries an eight-hour day for men. The twelve-hour day is almost universal in the South, and about twenty-five thousand children are now employed on twelve-hour shifts in the mills of the various Southern states. The wages of one of these children, however large, could not compensate the child for the injury this monstrous and unnatural labor does him; but the pay which the child receives is not enough, in many instances, even to feed him properly. If the children fall ill, they are docked for loss of time. . . . The mill-hands confess that they hate the mills, and no one will wonder at it. A vagrant who had worked in a textile mill for sixteen years once said to a friend of mine: "I done that [and he made a motion with his hand] for sixteen years. At last I was sick in bed for two or three days with a fever, and when I crawled out, I made up my mind that I would rather go to hell than go back to that mill."

explain why the union movement showed its first real power in the sectors of small groups of relatively skilled workers. First, it was easier to control the supply of skilled workers than unskilled ones. Organize the unskilled and the employer could find replacements for them. But the skilled workers—the coopers, the bootmakers, the shipwrights—were another matter. There were few of them, and by controlling the conditions of apprenticeship they controlled the access to their trade. The original craft unions were, in effect, closed shops: One had to belong to the union to hold a job in the craft, and the union set the rules of admission.

Second, a union of a small number of highly skilled specialists could attack the employers where they were vulnerable. Because a particular skilled occupation may be difficult to dispense with in an industrial process, other factors cannot easily be substituted for it. Because labor in a particular skilled occupation is likely to account for a relatively low proportion of total costs, the effect on the employer's overall costs of giving in to a small group's demand for a wage increase is much less than the effect of giving in to an equivalent demand from the numerous unskilled workers. In other words, the difficulty of substituting other factors and a relatively small contribution to total costs combined to create an inelastic demand for skilled factors (see page 326). This inelastic demand for their services gave the unions of skilled workers an advantage in fighting the employer not enjoyed by other groups of workers. In the early days, unions needed every advantage that they could get since antiunionism was for some, a matter of principle, a crusade, and a way of life.

Even where unions gained a foothold in a strategic trade they had their ups and downs. When employment was full and business booming, the cost of being fired for joining a union was not so great because there were other jobs. However, during periods of de-pression and unemployment the risks were greater. An individual worker knew that if he or she caused trouble, unemployed members of the trade would be there to take the job. Solidarity could yield to hunger. Membership in trade unions showed a clear cyclical pattern, rising in good times and falling in bad.

THE HISTORICAL DEVELOPMENT OF AMERICAN UNIONS

The beginnings: before 1933. The American Federation of Labor, founded in 1886 by Samuel Gompers, an immigrant from England, and a cigar maker, was totally committed to organizing the skilled trades, to pursuing bread-and-butter issues, and to restricting labor supply. It is no coincidence that Gompers, although himself an immigrant, led the AFL in vigorous opposition to further immigration; restriction of supply was the key to preserving union power.

Because it was impossible to control supply, the prospects for unionization were bleak for the unskilled. Their hope lay in political reform, in socialism, in cooperatives, or in revolution. The Knights of Labor, organized in 1869, sought one big union for all workers and at its peak in 1886 had 700,000 members. But the political climate was hostile, and the Knights collapsed in 1887 as a result of many causes, including some unsuccessful strikes of unskilled workers. The depression of 1887 finished this ambitious venture in political rather than bread-and-butter unionism.

The AFL avoided noble causes and continued its steady growth among the skilled until the end of World War I. In 1900 it had 2 percent of the labor force (just over half a million members) and by 1920 it had 5 million members, 10 percent of the labor force. By 1922, in the face of depression and the strong antilabor attitude of government and business alike, union membership had declined to 8 percent, and by 1933, after a decade of gradual decline, to about 6 percent of the labor force.

The New Deal: 1933–1945. The dramatic effect of the New Deal on union membership is illustrated in Figure 21–4. What happened? First, the monstrousness of the Great Depression created a climate of public opinion openly hostile to big business. Second, the Wagner Act (1935) guaranteed the *right* of workers to organize and to elect, by secret ballot, an exclusive bargaining agent by majority vote of the employees. And, third, the unskilled were organized in industrial

Figure 21–4 Union membership as a percentage of the labor force in the United States, 1900–1975

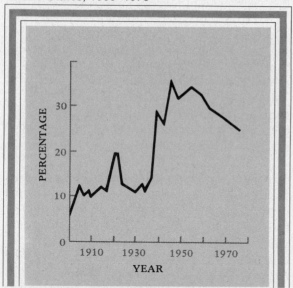

The great spurt in union membership occurred after passage of the Wagner Act (1935) and before the end of World War II. As a result of the great expansion in the labor force since 1960, the *number* of union members has increased slightly but union membership as a percentage of the labor force has steadily declined. The percentages are of total nonagricultural employment.

unions. The Wagner Act provided the means to control the supply of even unskilled labor. The great industrial unions in steel and in automobiles, following the leadership of John L. Lewis of the United Mine Workers, organized, split from the conservative AFL, formed the CIO, and struck for recognition. Using bold tactics such as the sit-down strike, where employees sat down in the plants and thus prevented employers from operating with strikebreakers, the CIO won recognition and members. It doubtless benefited from an atmosphere of public opinion in which there was no disposition on the part of the government or the courts to try to stop them. The Supreme Court decision upholding the legality of the Wagner Act ratified their victory. Thus the unions won—by force, by violence, and finally by law—the recognition that was required to convert monopsony into a situation in which unions could articulate their grievances and bargain to assuage them.

After World War II. The New Deal period and its legislation were frankly and avowedly prolabor. The country as a whole recognized that labor had been the underdog and sought to redress the balance. By the end of World War II the attitude had changed—for several reasons, including an increasing number and the changing character of strikes. The long series of strikes during the organizing period, undertaken to compel employers to recognize and deal with unions, were received with a good deal of public sympathy. But the jurisdictional strikes between rival AFL and CIO unions were less comprehensible to public and employer alike. And the aggressive tactics of some unions, most notably the United Mine Workers, particularly in the immediate prewar and wartime periods, added to the alienation. Immediately after the war, work stoppages soared in number, as Figure 21–5 makes clear.[3]

[3] Even at their peak in 1946, however, the days lost in strikes were less than 1.5 percent of the total days worked. But a major strike is headline news, and the 1 percent of negotiations that break down get widespread attention.

Figure 21–5   Worker days lost by strikes in the United States, 1935–1975

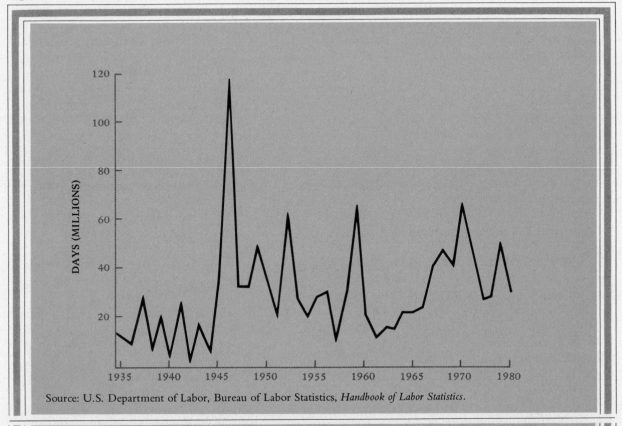

Source: U.S. Department of Labor, Bureau of Labor Statistics, *Handbook of Labor Statistics*.

There is great variability in strike activity from year to year, but even at its peak (in 1946) strike days lost were only about 2 days per year per employed worker.   These data are published monthly in the BLS *Monthly Labor Review*. Sometimes a single strike creates a bulge—for example, the strike of the UAW against General Motors in 1970. Other times, as in 1946, a wave of strikes seems to spread across the land. The 1946 wave is generally regarded as having led to the Taft-Hartley Act of 1948.

The Taft-Hartley Act (1948) corrected some of the excesses encouraged by New Deal legislation. Among its many provisions, unfair labor practices on the part of unions as well as management were defined and prohibited, use of the closed shop was limited, and strikes that "imperiled the national health and safety" were subject to an 80-day cooling off period. The most controversial feature of the act was the encouragement it gave to states to pass **right-to-work laws.** These laws permit the open shop—the right to work without belonging to a union. In virtually every recent Congress, supporters of organized labor have attempted to repeal this provision, so far without success.

Since 1950 union membership has continued to grow in absolute numbers to over 20 million, but in spite of that growth the percentage of the labor force in unions has declined steadily. Part of the reason is continued employer opposition; part is the absence of employment growth in traditionally unionized industries and in industries with large concentrations of employees. The biggest growth in recent unionization has been among government employees as a result of new, permissive legislation. The biggest question mark is the future of unionism among employees in white-collar, professional, and service fields. Some observers believe that if inflation continues for very long it will accelerate a trend toward unionization in these traditionally unorganized occupations.

The dominant development in the nature of unionization over the last three decades has been the stabilizing of union-management relations in industry after industry. Strikes still occur, and always will, for they are a key part of the poker game of collective bargaining. But strikes are now overwhelmingly directed toward specific issues and negotiations rather than recognition or jurisdiction, and the violence and passions of a generation ago are largely gone. Labor unions are now part of the establishment.

Methods and objectives of the modern union

Union constitutions are extremely democratic documents. All members have one vote, officers are elected by the vote of the membership, the rights of individual workers are fully protected, and so on. In practice, however, the relation between the members of a union and its national officers is closer to that of the relationship between stockholders and managers of a giant corporation than to that of the American people and their government. Although there is an occasional major fight for union office, such as the contested race for the presidency of the Steelworkers in 1977, contested elections occur less than 15 percent of the time and close contests are rare indeed. Unions, though democratic, tend

toward one-party democracy in the vast majority of cases. Union leaders are highly paid professionals whose business is to run the union, while the main business of the union member is to earn his or her living on the job. The union members' indifference is understandable; they are paying dues that permit the union to pay generous salaries to union leaders to look out for the rank and file's interests—and as long as the leadership "delivers," all goes well. But delivers what and to whom?

Unions are naturally interested in the wages obtained by their members. But they have other objectives, and they have methods of obtaining their objectives other than bargaining for wage increases.

RESTRICTING SUPPLY TO INCREASE WAGES

At the beginning of this chapter we saw that if a union raises the wage above the competitive level, it will create a pool of people eager to work at the going wage rate but unable to find employment. An alternative is to determine the quantity of labor supplied and let the wage be determined on the open market. This is illustrated in Figure 21–6. The union can restrict entry into the occupation by methods such as lengthening apprenticeship periods and restricting openings for trainees. Such tactics make it more difficult and more expensive to enter the occupation. Under these conditions, the quantity supplied is reduced at any given wage rate and the supply curve of labor shifts to the left. This has the effect of raising wages without anyone's ever having to negotiate a rate above what would naturally emerge from the free operation of the competitive market. Furthermore, there is no pool of unemployed wanting to work at the new higher wage but unable to find employment. Thus there is no wage-reducing pressure from unemployed persons who are trained for the occupation but are unable to find jobs.

The choice unions may face between the tactics of wage setting and supply restriction will be affected by the relative ease of enforcing one or the other kind of arrangement and the public acceptability of its tactics. In this respect unions are no different than professional groups, who may treat unions with utter disdain. Consider the professions of medicine and law. Since professional standards may be regarded as necessary to protect the public from incompetent practitioners, doctors and lawyers may find it publicly acceptable to limit supply by controlling entry into their profession.

Doctors are in short supply—and doctors' incomes are the highest of any profession—because of the difficulties of getting into an approved medical school, long and hungry years of internship and residency, and various rules concerning certification. (Interestingly, even though doctors oppose unions, there is an active unionization movement among interns and residents who want to reduce the very barriers that keep doctors scarce.) Whatever the need for high standards of entry into medical practice, there is no doubt that doctors' earnings are high *because* the barriers to entry into the profession prevent increases in the proportion of the population admitted to medical practice. Most investigators have concluded that restrictions on entry into medicine are much greater than they need be to protect the public and that earnings are substantially higher as a result.

Lawyers, by contrast, have been less successful in limiting entry into their profession. The major law schools admit only a small fraction of the qualified applicants, and they have not expanded sufficiently to keep pace with the sharply increased demand for admission. But new law schools, often of lower quality than existing ones, have sprung up to serve the growing excess demand. These new schools have proved financially beneficial to the institutions or individuals who organized them. Their graduates have, for the most part,

Figure 21–6 Raising wages by restricting entry

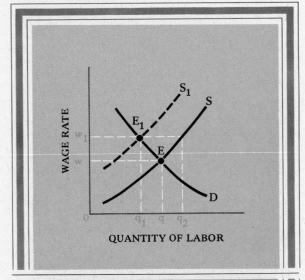

By restricting entry into an occupation, a union can shift the supply curve and raise wages. A competitive industry would be in equilibrium at E. When the supply curve shifts to S_1, the wage rises to w_1 and employment falls to q_1. Compare this to the strategy of simply imposing the wage w_1. In each case q_1 workers obtain employment at q_1. By shifting the supply curve no pool of unsuccessful job applicants is created (as it was when a wage of w_1 was imposed).

gained access to the profession, often with the aid of "cram schools" that prepare them for the bar exams.

Lawyers, faced with an inability to limit competition by limiting entry into the profession, have turned to "wage setting"—having their state bar associations prescribe and enforce minimum fees for activities such as drawing a will, probating an estate, and representing a client in court. As the theory predicts, many lawyers are underemployed in the sense that they have fewer clients than they could comfortably handle.[4] In contrast, doctors are typically overworked.

Restriction of supply will tend to raise wages. Raising wages without restricting supply will lead to unemployment or underemployment.

While it is clear that unions and professional associations can raise wages in particular industries, it is not clear how often this is their effect or their objective. Professor Albert Rees, one of the leading students of the influence of unionism on wages, concluded that perhaps a third of the trade unions have raised the wages of their members by 15 to 20 percent above what they might be in a nonunion situation, another third by 5 to 10 percent, and the remaining third not at all. This may be a matter of the objectives of particular unions as well as of their market power.

COMPETING GOALS

Wages versus employment

A union that sets wages above the competitive level is making a choice of higher wages for some and unemployment for others. Should the union strive to maximize the earnings of the group that remains employed? If it does, some of its members will lose their jobs and the union's membership will decline. Should it instead maximize the welfare of its present members? Or should it seek to expand employment opportunities (perhaps by a low-wage policy) so that the union membership grows?

Different unions decide these questions differently. The United Mine Workers Union has employed a high-wage, shrinking-employment strategy for decades, and both employment and union membership have fallen. John L. Lewis, leader of the mine workers for half a century, is reputed to have said that he would take care of the miners but that their

sons should find work in the cities. The longshoremen's union has achieved high wages but chooses to ration the available jobs among its members rather than reduce its membership. It thus spreads the underemployment around. In the garment trades, the demand for labor is relatively elastic and the major unions have traditionally accepted lower wages than they could have attained in order to protect the employment of their members. The key construction unions in New York City in 1976 accepted a 25 percent cut in their wage rate on rehabilitation construction because of a very high (30 percent) unemployment rate among their members.[5]

Wages versus employment poses a long-run as well as a short-run problem. In the auto industry, for example, the high-wage policy of the United Automobile Workers has led the major manufacturers to install more and more labor-saving equipment. Thus, even when the auto industry operates at or near capacity, there is substantial and increasing unemployment among UAW members. There are about a hundred thousand fewer jobs today than there were ten years ago. One response to this loss of job opportunities is to spread the work around by bargaining for shorter working hours, in the form of both a shorter work week and more days of paid holidays. The four-day, 32-hour work week is a major target of several American unions for the end of the decade.

Wages versus job security

People who were in their teens and twenties during the Great Depression are now in the age group that dominates the leadership of unions. Not surprisingly, they have a strong

---

[4] See the discussion of barbers in Chapter 17.

[5] This "wage discrimination" is similar to price discrimination (see Chapter 15). So-called rehabilitation construction is often financed by hard-pressed municipal governments that would postpone this sort of construction if they had to pay full-scale union wages. Thus the unions, while maintaining their full-scale rate on new construction, hope to expand the use of their members' services.

defensive attitude toward their jobs. They lived through a period when unemployment was above 20 percent of the total labor force and nearer 50 percent in many of the hardest hit areas. They saw people grow up, marry, and raise children on relief or part-time work.

In a period of heavy unemployment, technological change is likely to mean unemployment for those whose jobs are lost by the change. The installation of a labor-saving machine in a factory might condemn someone to an indefinite future on relief. It is little wonder that new machines were opposed bitterly and that job-saving restrictive practices were adhered to with tenacity.

The heritage of this fear survived in featherbedding practices such as the standby musician at the radio studio and the meticulous division of tasks in the building trades. Because much of the period from 1942 to 1970 was a time of full employment and a time when new jobs were available to replace old ones destroyed by technological change, the survival of these attitudes and practices was less clearly in labor's interest than it had been before the war. Furthermore, under the impact of a rate of growth of real income of between 2 and 3 percent per capita per year, such practices are doomed to failure, for growth necessarily means change, both in the techniques of production and in the pattern of demand. In the post-World War II period the attitude of many unions slowly changed from one of resisting technological change to one of collaborating with it and trying to reduce some of its costs to individuals who are adversely affected. The return of higher unemployment rates in recent years has, however, led again to increased resistance to rapid innovation.

Wages versus fringe benefits

Newspapers usually report the settlement of a contract negotiation in such terms as "The package settlement of $1.20 per hour was approved late yesterday. Of this, 72¢ was in wages, 24¢ in increased contributions to the union's welfare and pension fund, and the remainder in other fringe benefits, including increased holidays and sick leave." In the automobile industry in 1976, one-third of the total labor cost of the average worker was paid not in direct wages but in fringe benefits. Why do unions and employers not simply agree to a wage and let it go at that? Why should the average employed automobile worker have earned $13,400 in wages in 1976 but cost the company $20,000?

From the employees' point of view, fringe benefits have some appeal. Many benefits are not taxable as current income. Pension funds and the like allow employees to provide for their future and that of their families more cheaply than by purchasing private insurance, and their benefits may protect them even if they lose their jobs.

There may also be advantages to employers in giving indirect, or fringe, benefits. One advantage is that the real cost of fringe benefits per hour is often difficult to estimate. Although the union may claim it has gotten 80¢ in benefits, the employer may believe it will in fact come to less. A second advantage is that some forms of fringe benefits (such as pension funds) tend to bind the worker more closely to the company, thereby decreasing the turnover rate among employees. If employees lose part of their benefits by changing jobs, their mobility is decreased.

Also important to both union and employer is that fringe benefits provide scope for bargaining. A union official may have promised the rank and file not to take less than $1.50, and the employer's representatives may have assured their directors that they would stand firm at $1.00. In negotiation they may agree on 90¢ in wage increases and 70¢ in fringe benefits. Both negotiators may claim success, whereas either would feel reluctant to accept a straight $1.25 wage increase.

The face-saving aspects should not be taken lightly. Fringe benefits began to be important during World War II when the War Labor

Board was bent on a policy of wage stabilization. Having forbade direct wage increases, the board used fringe benefits to "save" its popular, though unenforceable, policy. Today fringe benefits have become so important that they are estimated to be between one-fourth and one-third of the value of basic pay for all industrial workers.

Discrimination and wages

In 1973 the American Telephone and Telegraph Company settled an antidiscrimination suit against it and paid $15 million in back pay and an additional $23 million a year in raises to women and minority males against whom it had allegedly discriminated in job assignments, pay, and promotions. In 1976 United Airlines paid more than $1 million to settle similar complaints. These settlements, and others, focus on what many had long suspected—that discrimination by race and by sex has an economic aspect.

The problems of racial discrimination and sex discrimination are different from one another, and so is the nature of the policies required to eliminate them. With respect to the economics of discrimination there are differences but also similarities.

BLACK-WHITE DIFFERENTIALS IN LABOR MARKETS

The readily measurable differences between blacks and whites in their rewards from participation in labor are dramatic. By the mid 1970s, a decade of vigorous equal employment activity notwithstanding, the median black family had earnings of less than 60 percent of those of the median white family. This reflected fewer jobs, lower paying jobs, longer periods of unemployment, and more frequent recourse to part-time employment. Unemployment among blacks runs at about twice the level for whites—roughly 12 percent to 6 percent in relatively good times; in sharp recessions the ratio increases. Blacks tend to have less seniority than whites of similar ages, often because of past discrimination. The seniority they do have tends to be in the less skilled, lower paid job categories. Blacks tend to have poorer health and shorter working lives.

All of these things contribute to lower economic status, but not all of them represent racial discrimination; many of them remain even when there is equal pay for equal work. Whites and blacks have, on average, different educational backgrounds and different sorts of professional or vocational training. Since these things affect employment opportunities and also actual pay rates within occupations, is it not possible that they, rather than discrimination, account for the differentials?

To answer this question it is necessary to note that discrimination might be present not only directly (refusing to hire blacks because they are black) but also indirectly (refusing to hire blacks because they are not well trained, when training has been denied them because they are black).

A black man and a white man with identical health, education, and training fare differently in a world where, when other things are equal, white is the preferred color—and where it may be preferred even if other things are not equal. Satchel Paige was surely among the ten best pitchers in the history of baseball—many consider him the best—yet he earned less from baseball than many white ballplayers of only average ability of his generation. Direct employment discrimination against black athletes has ended in the last 25 years, but it remains in many occupations.

Indirect discrimination is both harder to measure and more difficult to deal with. It is well known that education, training, and aspiration each play an important role in labor market success, and individuals differ in these respects for reasons other than race or sex.

White male farm workers earn much less per hour and per lifetime than white male doctors for reasons not related to discrimination. To see how discrimination is related to such possibly nondiscriminatory characteristics as age, occupation, and education, one need only recognize that if racial and sexual prejudice and discrimination vanished from the world today, their effects would be felt for generations. The black man whose grandfather and father were illiterate farm workers because they were denied a decent education even after they were freed from slavery is unlikely to have had the opportunity or motivation to get much education himself. For one thing, he will have been needed on the farm to help feed the family. More important, he may have been raised in a culture that failed to see in education either the path to economic opportunity or a desirable end in itself.

While education is important, and could be changed in a generation, aspiration is more complex. The sociology of aspiration is beyond the scope of this book, but it is well known that cultural patterns develop and persist. The drive for upward mobility depends on both the chances of success and the attitudes of those left behind. Absence of actual opportunities in the past often fosters a culture that does not highly value the occasional successes. Immigrants to a land of great opportunity tended to expect a son to do better than his father (although they were less likely to hold a similar view about a daughter). Minorities, unlike immigrants, often regard any outstanding achievement as a potential betrayal of those left behind. This attitude is now thought to be spreading among the black community, possibly as an unexpected result of a growing feeling of black solidarity. The greatest stigma among blacks has long been attached to those who attempted to "pass" as whites. Today one can pass without a light skin—by achieving a white education, entering a white occupation, and living in a white world. A few make it,

but the studies show it is a very small fraction of the black population. Those who do are often scorned, not honored, by the rest. If the attitude continues to develop that success in "the white man's world" is treason to one's race, the attributes of poverty may long outlast the discrimination originally responsible for it. If the young black is put under cultural pressure not to do too well in at least some of the ways newly opened, it will take longer to eliminate the racial elements of differences in economic status.

FEMALE-MALE DIFFERENTIALS IN LABOR MARKETS

Whereas difficulty in getting and keeping jobs is a critical part of the black worker's problem, the problems of women in the labor force result more from lower wages than from higher unemployment rates. In 1976 the unemployment rate for adult men was 5.9 percent. For women it was 7.4 percent—higher but not much higher. The unemployment rate of adult white females is only slightly above that of adult white males.

Women's employment in the labor market has been rising steadily and dramatically. In 1940 women constituted only 25 percent of total employment; by 1950 the number was 30 percent; by the mid 1960s it had reached 35 percent; and it passed 40 percent in 1976.

But getting jobs is not the whole story. It has long been clear that women and men make and are offered different occupational choices, that proportionately fewer women than men reach higher paying jobs in the occupations in which both work, and that the average earned income of females in the labor force is well below that of males of similar ages. A number of careful studies have established that in the early 1970s, labor market earnings were at least 25 percent lower for employed women than for employed men of the same age and race.

To what extent are these differences discriminatory and to what extent are they the result of such circumstances as women often having very different lifetime patterns of participation in the labor force? On average, women have experienced significant periods of withdrawal from the labor force (or only part-time continuation in it) in order to have and raise children, and women have tended to have fewer years of education and training than men.

Direct discrimination in some occupations is relatively easy to identify by taking groups with similar characteristics and comparing their employment and pay status. For example, comparing starting salaries in college teaching of new Ph.D.s from the same graduate schools in a given subject and a given class of institutional employment, Professors Frank Stafford and George Johnson found the average pay of females was about 6 percent below that of males (with allowance for differences in age and prior experience). They attributed this part of a larger male-female pay differential to direct discrimination.

Women have also suffered indirect discrimination. They have been refused admission or discouraged from seeking entry into certain occupations; for example, they have traditionally been pushed into nursing rather than medicine, social work rather than law, and secretarial rather than managerial training programs. Girls raised in a culture in which their education seems less important than that of their brothers, or where they are raised to think of themselves as potential homemakers and are urged to prepare themselves to attract and serve a husband, are less likely to acquire the skills or the opportunities for many high-paying forms of employment that are wholly within their capabilities.

Discrimination against women may be eliminated more quickly than discrimination against blacks and other racial minorities; the effect of Women's Liberation on attitudes—male as well as female—has been very great in a very short time. Between 1971 and 1975 the fraction of earned doctorates awarded to women rose from 14 to 21 percent. By 1975 nearly half of the first-year graduate enrollments were women, so this upward trend is likely to continue. In 1975, 12.5 percent of first professional degrees (law, medicine, etc.) were awarded to women—compared to 6.5 percent four years earlier. Current enrollments in these fields were more than 25 percent women. These trends reflect affirmative action on the part of schools, changed attitudes on the part of women, and brighter employment prospects for women than even five years before.

ECONOMIC DISCRIMINATION

In the face of evident differentials in occupations, in employment, and in earnings between blacks and whites and between males and females, it may seem virtually beyond debate that direct economic discrimination can and does occur. Yet the occurrence of such discrimination under competitive conditions has been challenged by some economists and, to the extent it occurs, has been considered to be a by-product of monopoly. Their argument merits a close look. We are concerned here with discrimination between two sets of workers who are in every sense equally qualified. Our discussion is phrased in terms of black versus white, but it applies equally to female versus male, alien versus citizen, Catholic versus Protestant, or any other prejudicial basis for dividing workers that may exist in the minds of people.

A model of the effect of discrimination

It is helpful to build a simplified picture of a world without discrimination and then introduce discrimination. While this reverses the contemporary problem (predicting the effect of removing discrimination), it provides insight into the effects of discrimination.

Suppose there are two groups of equal size

Figure 21–7 Pure economic discrimination

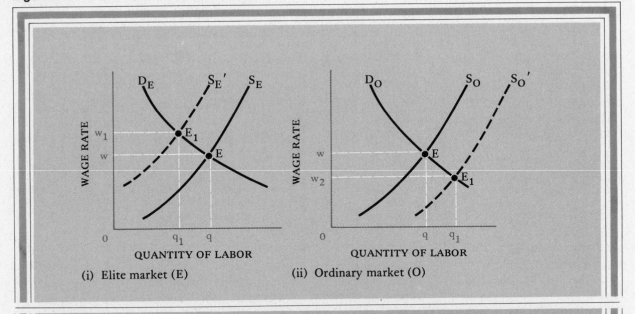

(i) Elite market (E) (ii) Ordinary market (O)

If market E discriminates against one group and market O does not, the supply curve shifts upward in E and downward in O, and wages rise in E and fall in O. Market E requires above-average skills, while market O requires only ordinary skills. When there is no discrimination, demands and supplies are D_E and S_E in market E, and D_O and S_O in market O. Initially, the wage rate is w and employment is q in each market. When all blacks are barred from E occupations the supply curve shifts to S_E' and the wage earned by the remaining workers, all of whom are white, rises to w_1. Blacks put out of work in the E occupation now seek work in the O occupation. The resulting shift in the supply curve to S_O' brings down the wage to w_2 in O occupations. Since all blacks are in O occupations they have a lower wage rate than many whites. The average white wage is higher than the average black wage.

in a society: One is white; the other is black. Except for color, the groups are the same—each has the same proportion who are educated to various levels, each has identical distributions of talent, and so on. Suppose also that there are two occupations: Occupation E (for elite) requires people of above-average education and skills, and occupation O (ordinary) can use anyone, but if the wages are the same, employers in occupation O will prefer to hire the above-average worker. There is no racial discrimination; everyone is color blind. The nonmonetary advantages of the two occupations are equal.

The competitive theory of distribution suggests that the wages in E occupations will be bid up slightly above those in O occupations (in order to be sure to get the workers of above-average skills) and that the whites and blacks of above-average skill will flock to E jobs while the others, white and black alike, will have no choice but to seek O jobs. Because skills are equally distributed, each occupation will have half whites and half blacks.

Now we introduce discrimination in its most extreme form: All E occupations are hereafter open only to whites; all O occupations are open to either whites or blacks. The immediate effect is to reduce by 50 percent the supply of job applicants for E occupations (you must be both white and above average) and to increase by 50 percent the supply of applicants for O jobs (you may be either black or a below-average white). Wages rise sharply in E occupations and fall in O occupations. This is illustrated in Figure 21–7. The take-home pay of those in O occupations falls, and although the group includes white and black, it has now become approximately two-thirds black.

Discrimination, by changing supply, can decrease the wages and incomes of a group that is discriminated against.

In the longer run, further changes may occur. Notice that total employment in E industries falls. Employers may find ways to utilize slightly below-average labor and thus lure the best qualified white workers out of O occupations. This will raise O wages slightly, but it will also make them increasingly black occupations. Another long-run effect may be that black children will see that it no longer pays to acquire above-average skills—that is, they will find it does not pay to invest in human capital. They will become locked into O occupations (even if the discrimination policy is reversed) and will teach their children that education is for whites only.

IS ECONOMIC DISCRIMINATION POSSIBLE IN COMPETITION?

It has been argued that the simple model suggested above is impossible in a world of competition. The argument says that E employers would not be so foolish as to refuse to hire qualified black workers whose marginal product exceeded their wage. Any firm that violated the taboo and hired blacks would make profits and take business from any prejudiced competitor. This argument says that (in the absence of government policy requiring discrimination, as is found in South Africa) economic discrimination might exist as a result of monopolies and other market imperfections but that it could not exist in a

perfectly competitive world. A monopolistic firm is in a sheltered position; it can afford to invest some of its owners' monopoly profits in indulging their prejudices by hiring only white employees even if a black could do a given job better than a white. In a truly competitive situation, however, a firm could not afford to discriminate. The fierce winds of competitive lead to the survival of only the fittest and thus force firms that want to survive to make choices based solely on considerations of profit. Thus, the argument concludes, if only we could make the economy more competitive and less monopolistic we would eliminate economic (as contrasted to social or political) discrimination. It is an intriguing idea; is it correct?

If only one employing firm were color prejudiced in a world of otherwise unprejudiced individuals, that employer would suffer by giving in to its prejudices. To maximize profits it needs both to minimize cost—which means hiring the most productive workers available at the going wage rate regardless of color—and to equate marginal cost with marginal revenue without distinguishing between "white marginal revenue" and "black marginal revenue." To distinguish between labor inputs or potential customers on the basis of color would not be profit-maximizing behavior, and the firm that did so discriminate could be driven to bankruptcy by its more efficient competitors.

But consider the other extreme. Assume that there is a single unprejudiced employer in a society of otherwise prejudiced persons. Will it pay the unprejudiced firm to ignore the prejudices of others? If it violated the society's prejudices, the firm's white customers might be so incensed that many would cease to buy from the firm—after all, they have lots of other suppliers to turn to. They may value their prejudices even if it costs them a few cents on the dollar. Similarly, if the employer hired those workers whose productivity was highest regardless of color, it might find that indignant (and prejudiced) white workers responded with slowdowns and strikes. In that event, production would fall off and expenses per unit would rise. In such a world, competition forces the unprejudiced firm to discriminate!

Finally, consider the more realistic case where some people are strongly prejudiced, some are slightly prejudiced, and some have no prejudice at all. A world of perfectly competitive profit maximizers would not eliminate discrimination as long as enough consumers were prejudiced. Most people do not care whether their automobiles are produced with white or black labor; nor do they seem to care about the color of the hands that shine their shoes. But enough people have prejudices about the color of the hands that cut their hair to reduce greatly the demand for black barbers in white areas and and to punish severely any integrated barbershop proprietor who hires black barbers. In a society in which consumers are free to buy what they want, "consumer sovereignty" means firms will respond to the "king's" prejudices as well as to his desires. Similarly, discrimination will not be eliminated if a sufficient number of white workers with a choice of where and how to work have racial prejudice about who should be their co-workers.

Economic discrimination is not only possible, it may be profitable if there are prejudiced people in the society.

Summary

1. A wage-setting union entering a competitive market can raise wages, but only at the cost of reducing employment and creating a pool of unsatisfied workers who would like to work at the going wage but are unable to gain employment.

2. A wage-setting union entering a monopsonistic market may increase both employment and wages over some range. If, however, it sets the wage above the competitive level, it too will create a pool of unsatisfied workers who are unable to get the jobs they want at the going wage.

3. An employers' association is a group of employers who band together for the purpose of adopting a common policy in labor negotiations. A union is an association of workers that speaks for the workers in negotiations with their employers. Unions are subdivided into craft unions and industrial unions. In general, individual union members belong to a local union to which they pay dues (part of which goes to the national union). The local union belongs to a national or international union. A federation is a loose organization of national unions.

4. Three kinds of bargaining arrangements are (a) the open shop, where, though a union represents its members, union membership is not a condition of getting or keeping a job; (b) the closed shop, where only workers who are already union members may be employed; and (c) the union shop, where the employer is free to hire whom he chooses, but where all new employees must join the recognized union within a specified period.

5. American unionism developed first in the skilled trades, along craft lines, where it was possible to control supply and prevent nonunion members from undercutting union wages. Widespread organization of the unskilled did not occur until after the legal right to organize was established by the Wagner Act in 1935. The emergence of mature collective bargaining is a relatively recent development in the stormy and sometimes bloody history of American labor unions.

6. Unions must decide on their goals. There is a basic conflict between the goals of raising wages by restricting supply, thereby reducing the union's employed membership, and preserving employment opportunities for its members and potential members. Other trade-offs concern wages and hours of leisure, wages and job security, and wages and fringe benefits.

7. Discrimination by race and by sex has played a role in labor markets, as in other aspects of American life. Precisely how much of the wage and employment differentials between whites and blacks and males and females is due to discrimination is a matter of continuing research. Indirect discrimination has had an effect through limiting the opportunities for education and training available to those subject to discrimination and through lowering people's aspirations in their choices of training and of careers. Direct discrimination can affect wages and employment opportunities by limiting the supply in the best-paying occupations and increasing it in less attractive occupations.

Concepts for review

Monopsony power
Union power
Collective bargaining
Goals of unions
Economic discrimination

Discussion questions

1. A union that has bargaining rights in two plants of the same company in different states almost always insists on "equal pay for equal work" in the two plants. It does not always insist on equal pay for men and women in the same jobs. Can you see any economic reasons for such a distinction?

2. Predict the effect of each of the following on the wages of employees in the affected industries. What, if anything, can you say about total earnings of all employees in each case?
a. an increase in the production of coal due to the increasing shortage of other fossil fuels
b. passage of a law permitting public employees to bargain collectively and to strike
c. reducing the apprenticeship period for entry into a skilled trade from five years to two years
d. making a Ph.D. degree compulsory for all junior college teachers

3. "The labor of a human being is not a commodity or article of commerce," the Clayton Act states. The context of this statement was a provision that gave labor unions some measure of exemption from antitrust action. Why should wage fixing not be in violation of the antitrust laws when price fixing is?

4. Today, more than 40 years after the Wagner Act, many government units still refuse to allow public employees the right to strike. What, if anything, distinguishes a policeman or a secretary in the state government of Nebraska from a nightwatchman or a secretary for an insurance company in Omaha?

5. Why were craft unions more successful than industrial unions in the late nineteenth century in the United States?

Why was this not true in the late 1930s? American unions have traditionally supported laws restricting immigration and raising minimum wages. Do these provisions make economic sense to organized labor generally?

6. A labor union that has a union shop contract with a particular employer is in some ways in the same position as a firm that has a monopoly of key raw materials used by the firm. Do you see any differences? Contrast the considerations that enter into the question of the best price (or wage) to charge. Who do you think is in a stronger position to bargain with General Motors, the United Auto Workers, or the Goodyear Tire and Rubber Company?

7. Interpret the following statements or practices in terms of the theory of distribution.
a. news headline: "Law, fastest growing profession, may find prosperity precarious: number of lawyers seen as key factor"
b. a requirement that every passenger train carry a fireman even though there may be nothing for him to do
c. a requirement that one must pass an English language proficiency test to be a carpenter in New York City
d. "The great increase in the number of women entering the labor force for the first time means that relatively more women than men earn beginning salaries. It is therefore not evidence of discrimination that the average wage earned by females is less than that earned by males."

8. Suppose it is accepted that, on average, unions have raised the wages of their members. How can this be reconciled with the low and declining percentage of employees who are union members?

9. "On a proportional basis, there are 'too many' blacks and 'too few' Jews among professional athletes. This shows that while sports has finally overcome racial prejudice, it has not overcome religious prejudice." Comment.

10. "Of nearly 40 million working women, 40 percent are in traditionally female occupations—secretaries, nurses, cashiers, waitresses, elementary school teachers, beauticians, maids, and sales clerks, for example. While this may result from past sex stereotyping, the notion that only a woman can do these jobs may also benefit women by preserving employment opportunities for them, given the high unemployment rates among black males and teenage males." Discuss this argument.

Interest and the return on capital

The capitalist is prominent in the folklore of both classical and Marxist economics—in the first as a hero; in the second, a villain. Do capitalists' earnings come mainly from the exploitation of labor, or are they necessary payments to factor owners for use of productive resources?

What gives rise to interest rates, and what functions do they perform? Is the charging of interest robbery, as some early churchmen thought, or were early economists right in believing that it fulfills an essential function in the economy? Why does the rate of interest vary with the purpose for which the money is borrowed? How do firms and households decide how much to borrow? What is the difference between interest and profits, and do they both exist in socialist as well as in capitalist economies? These are some of the questions on which the theory of capital and interest sheds light.

The productivity of capital

Capital goods are man-made aids to further production. They include, among other things, tools of all kinds, machines, and factories. The important thing about capital goods is that production that makes use of them is usually more efficient than production that does not. Of course, you can make more with a tool than by using only your bare hands; but for production using capital to be efficient, it is necessary to allow for the resources used to make the tools. A comparison of two alternative situations will illustrate this. In the first, given amounts of labor and raw materials are applied directly to the production of consumption goods without any capital equipment to help. They produce output at a rate of so much per year. In the second, the same amounts of labor and raw materials are used, but in a different way. At first the available resources are used to construct capital goods. After the equipment has been produced, enough labor and raw materials are set aside to maintain the equipment and to replace it as it wears out, while the remaining resources are set to work making consumption goods with the help of the newly made capital equipment. If the use of capital is warranted, production of consumption goods will be higher in the second situation than in the first. The difference between the two flows of output is a measure of the **productivity of capital.**

The extra output is not achieved without cost. While resources were being used to construct the capital equipment in the second situation, the output of goods available for consumption would be lower than in the situation in which no capital creation occurred.

A decision to produce capital goods generally entails a current sacrifice and a future gain.

The current sacrifice occurs because resources are diverted from producing for consumption to producing for capital, and the future gain occurs because production with the new capital is higher than without it (even after allowing for the maintenance and replacement of worn-out capital).

THE RETURN ON CAPITAL

Take the receipts from the production and sale of goods by a firm and subtract all relevant costs of production including the appropriate costs for purchased goods and materials, for labor, for depreciation, and for the manager's own contributed talents. Subtract from this an allowance for taxes the firm will have to pay, and what is left may be called the **return to capital.** This amount is available to the firm to pay interest on borrowed capital, to pay dividends to its owners, and to provide undistributed profits for reinvestment.

The economist finds it convenient to divide the gross return to capital into three parts: (1) the **pure return on capital,** which is the amount that capital could earn in a riskless in-vestment; (2) a **risk premium,** which compensates the owners for the actual risks of the enterprise; and (3) the economic profits. Risk taking and economic profits were discussed in detail in Chapter 10. Owners must be compensated for the risks they take in order to induce them to commit their capital to risky ventures; risk taking is thus to be regarded as input into the production process and payment for it is a real (though imputed) cost. Economic profits from the sale of a good are defined as the excess of revenues over the opportunity cost of *all* the resources required to produce the good. They provide a signal that additional resources could be efficiently employed in the production of the good.

The first element—the pure return to capital—is an element of cost that requires more extensive discussion. What determines its size? Why is it high in some time periods and low in others? What causes it to change?

In discussing such questions, it is usual to deal with a rate of return *per dollar* of capital. This concept requires placing a money value on a unit of capital (the "price of capital goods") and a money value on the stream of earnings resulting from the productivity of capital. If we let X stand for the annual value of the productivity of a unit of capital, and P for the price of a unit of capital, the ratio X/P may be defined as the **rate of return on capital.** As a preliminary to understanding the determinants of the rate of return on capital, we must define two key concepts: marginal efficiency of capital and present value.

The marginal efficiency of capital

It is convenient to think of society as having a quantity of capital that can be measured in physical units. The term **capital stock** refers to this total quantity of capital.[1] As with any

---

[1] The idea of stock of capital being measured by a single number is a simplification. Society's stock of capital goods is made up of a diverse bundle of factories, machines, bridges, roads, and other man-made aids to further production. For expository purposes, it is useful to assume that all of these can be reduced to some common unit and summed to obtain a measure of the society's *physical* stock of capital.

Human capital

While capital goods usually are discussed in terms of tangible assets such as buildings or machines, the notion of a capital asset as something that produces an increase in the stream of future output suggests another sort of capital good. Consider a high school graduate who has enough schooling to get and keep a job. Instead of taking a job, however, she elects to go to college, and possibly to graduate or professional school. During her college career, her contribution to society's current output is small (only a summer job perhaps), but because of her education, her lifetime contribution to production may be substantially larger than it would have been had she taken a job after high school.

The choice of whether to take a job now or to continue one's education has all the basic elements of an investment decision, and it is useful to regard the student as making an investment to acquire capital. Because the capital is embodied in a person—in terms of greater skills, knowledge, and the like—rather than in a machine, this is known as acquiring **human capital.** Major elements of human capital are health and education of all sorts. An ex-

tended education program requires, for example, that resources be withdrawn from the production of goods for current consumption; the resources include materials in the school, the services of the teachers, and the time and talents of the pupils. The education is productive if the difference between the value of the lifetime output of the untrained worker and the lifetime output of the trained one exceeds the value of the resources—teachers, buildings, and so on—used up in training her. If so, education increases the value of total production of the economy.

The payoff to education as an investment in human capital has been extensively studied, and many investigators have concluded that investment in higher education pays, in the sense just defined. Of course, education also has other payoffs: it may be valued for cultural or social reasons, and it may bestow benefits or costs on individuals other than those who are educated. But the fact that it may be more than a capital investment does not prevent it from being an investment. The same is true of a painting by Rembrandt.

other factor of production we can measure the average and the marginal productivity of capital. The marginal productivity of capital is the contribution to output of the last unit of capital added to a fixed quantity of other factors. This output is valued at market prices and expressed as a return per dollar's worth of capital.

The rate of return on the *last* dollar of capital employed is called the **marginal effi-**

ciency of capital (MEC).[2] A schedule that relates the rate of return on each additional dollar of capital stock to the size of the capital stock is called the **marginal efficiency of capital schedule.** The *MEC* schedule is constructed on the assumptions that the society's

[2] Like the other *marginal* concepts that we have repeatedly encountered, the *MEC* is the ratio of two changes. In this case, it is the change in the return to capital divided by the change in the capital stock that brought it about.

population is fixed and that technology is un-changing. These assumptions are made in order to focus on changes in the quantity of capital, other things remaining equal. As more and more capital is accumulated with given technical knowledge and a constant population, the ratio of capital to labor increases. This increase is called **capital deepening.** To see why it occurs, consider the difference between a single firm and the whole economy.

When a single firm wants to expand its output it can buy another piece of land, build a factory identical to the one it now has, and hire new labor to operate it. In this way, the firm is able to replicate what it already has.

Figure 22–1 The marginal efficiency of capital

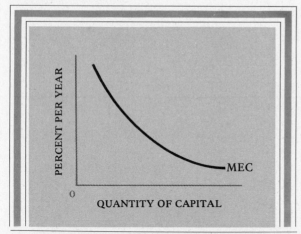

The *MEC* schedule shows the relation between the size of the capital stock and the rate of return on the marginal unit of capital. The *MEC* schedule slopes downward because of the law of diminishing returns applied to capital. Each successive unit of capital adds less to production than each previous unit. Thus the schedule, which shows the value of additional output per each additional dollar's worth of capital added to the capital stock, is downward-sloping.

Each worker in the new factory can have the same amount of capital as each worker in the old factory, and output per worker and per unit of capital can remain unchanged. Increasing the quantity of capital without changing the proportions of factors used is called **capital widening.** For the economy as a whole, this is possible only as long as there are unemployed quantities of labor and of all other factors of production. The additional workers, for example, must be drawn from somewhere; and in a fully employed economy, what one small firm can do the whole economy cannot do. If the size of the capital stock is to increase while the total labor force remains constant, the amount of capital per worker must increase. This means that capital deepening must occur.

What is the effect of capital deepening on the marginal efficiency of capital? Capital is assumed to be subject to diminishing returns, just as are all other factors of production. As the capital stock grows and capital deepening occurs, the amount of output per unit of capital will fall. This is because each unit of capital has, as it were, fewer units of labor to work with than it had previously. As more and more capital deepening occurs, the marginal return to capital declines. Thus the *MEC* schedule when plotted graphically is downward-sloping. Such an *MEC* schedule is illustrated in Figure 22–1.

The present value of future income

The productivity of capital takes the form of producing a stream of output extending into the future that, as it is sold, yields a stream of income to the firm. How is the price of capital related to the productivity of capital? To know what price a firm would be willing to pay for a piece of capital, we must be able to put a present value on the stream of income that the capital will yield to the firm.

The value of a single future payment. How much would you be prepared to pay *now* to acquire the right to receive $100 in cash in one year's time? Say the interest rate on savings accounts is 5 percent. How much would you have to deposit in a savings bank now in order to have $100 a year from now? It would surely not be profitable for you to pay more than this amount. Alternatively, what is the most you could borrow today in return for your promise to repay $100 in one year if the interest rate is 5 percent? Both approaches can be reduced to the question of how much money *now* is equivalent to $100 next year if the interest rate is 5 percent. Letting X stand for this unknown amount, we can write $X(1.05) =$ $100. Thus $X = \$100/1.05 = \$95.24$ which tells us that the value today of $100 next year is $95.24 if the interest rate is 5 percent. That sum is said to be the present value of $100 next year. In general, the term **present value (PV)** refers to the value now of a payment, or payments, to be made in the future.

The particular numerical value depends on the interest rate used to "discount" (i.e., reduce to its present value) the $100 to be received one year hence. If the interest rate is 7 percent, the present value of the $100 receivable next year is $100/1.07 = $93.45. In general, the present value of X dollars one year hence at an interest rate of i percent per year is

$$PV = \frac{X}{(1 + i)}$$

One hundred dollars two years hence has a present value (at 5 percent) of

$$\frac{\$100.00}{(1.05)(1.05)} = \$90.70$$

because $90.70 put in a savings bank now would be worth $100 in two years. In general, we may write, for the present value of X dollars after t years at i percent,

$$PV = \frac{X}{(1 + i)^t}$$

The present value of a given sum will be smaller the further away the payment date and the higher the rate of interest.

The value of an infinite stream of payments. So much for a single sum payable in the future; now consider the present value of a stream of income that continues indefinitely. At first that might seem very high since as time passes the total received grows without reaching any limit. Consideration of the previous section suggests, however, that one will not value highly the far distant payments. To find the present value of $100 a year, payable forever, we need only to ask how much money would have to be invested now at an interest rate of i percent per year to obtain $100 each year. This is simply $i \times X = \$100$, where i is the interest rate and X the sum required. This tells us that the present value of the stream of $100 (or the "present value of an annuity of $100") is

$$PV = \frac{\$100}{i}$$

If the interest rate were 10 percent, the present value would be $1,000, which merely says that $1,000 invested at 10 percent would yield $100 per year, forever. Notice that PV here, as above, is *inversely* related to the rate of interest. The higher the interest rate, the less is the present value of any stream of payments that goes on forever.

If one can buy an asset at its present value, the investment will yield neither gain nor loss. For example, if one can buy the right to receive $100 a year forever for $1,000, and borrow the capital at an interest rate of 10 percent, annual receipts ($100) and interest payments ($100) will be exactly offsetting.

THE VALUE OF AN ASSET

Many assets are valued only because of the streams of income they are expected to produce.[3] For any such asset, its value will tend to be equal to the present value of the income

---

[3] Assets can yield utilities in forms other than income streams. A painting, a house, and valuable jewelry are cases in point, but they may be regarded as yielding a stream of utilities each of which could be given a monetary value.

stream produced. Thus this present value is often called the **capitalized value** of the asset producing the income stream.

Every expected income stream can be reduced to a present value. In the previous section we considered finding the present values of amounts at specific future dates and of infinite streams of income. All actual streams of income can be treated as the sum or difference of such streams and amounts; thus the present value of *any* stream of future payments can be computed.[4] As a result, the capitalized value of an asset can always be computed.

The relation between interest and the return on capital

Given the concepts just discussed we can develop a simple theory that relates the *MEC* to the rate of interest. It is helpful to begin with the behavior of an individual firm.

THE DEMAND FOR ADDITIONAL CAPITAL BY A FIRM

Suppose that for $8,000 a firm can purchase a machine that yields $1,000 a year net of all costs into the indefinite future. Also suppose that the firm can borrow (and lend) money at an interest rate of 10 percent. The present value of the stream of income produced by the machine is $1,000/0.10 = $10,000; the present value of $8,000 now is (of course) $8,000. Clearly the firm can make money by purchasing the machine. Another way to see this is to suppose that the only uses a firm has for its money are to buy the machine and to lend out its $8,000 at 10 percent interest. It

will pay to buy the machine since the firm can do so and earn $1,000 a year net, while if it lends the $8,000 to someone else at 10 percent it will earn only $800 per year.

Let us now restate the argument in more general terms. If X is the annual stream of net income produced by the machine, if P is its purchase price, and if i is the interest rate that correctly states the opportunity cost of capital to the firm, then the capital good should be purchased if

$$\frac{X}{i} > P$$

The term X/i is the present value of the stream of income produced by the capital good or, in other words, the capitalized value of the asset.

It pays to purchase a capital good whenever the present value of its future stream of net income exceeds the purchase price of the capital good.

This relationship can be looked at in another way by rearranging terms in the algebraic inequality above:

$$\frac{X}{P} > i$$

The expression X/P shows the annual net income produced by the capital good as a fraction of the price of the good. Earlier we defined this as the rate of return on the capital and called it the *MEC*. In the above form the condition is restated to say:

It pays to purchase a capital good whenever its *MEC* exceeds the interest rate that could be earned on the money invested in it.[5]

The firm will go on investing in new capital equipment as long as its rate of return, the *MEC,* exceeds the opportunity cost of cap-

---

[4] For example, receiving $100 per year for three years might be considered either as the present value of $100 next year plus the *PV* of $100 two years hence plus the *PV* of $100 three years hence, or as the *difference* between the *PV* of $100 received each year from now to infinity and the *PV* of $100 received from year four to infinity.

[5] In this chapter we assume that the rate of interest reflects the opportunity cost of capital to the firm. We saw on page 157 that this may not always be the case. When the market rate of interest and the firm's own opportunity cost of capital diverge the *MEC* must be equated to the latter, not the former.

ital, *i*. The *MEC* declines as the firm's capital stock rises, and the firm will reach equilibrium with respect to its capital stock when *MEC* is equal to *i*.

THE ECONOMY AS A WHOLE

Assume for the moment that the interest rate is free to vary and that the only demand to borrow money is from firms wishing to obtain funds to invest in new capital equipment. The whole economy has an *MEC* schedule showing how the return on the marginal unit of new capital declines as the capital stock grows.

Consider what would happen if the rate of interest were substantially below the *MEC*. All firms would wish to borrow money to invest in new capital; there would be an excess demand to borrow funds and the rate of interest would be bid up toward the *MEC*. Now consider what would happen if the interest rate were above the *MEC*. No firms would wish to borrow funds for new investment; there would be an excess supply of funds for lending and the rate of interest would fall toward the *MEC*.

Competition among borrowers and lenders of funds for new investment will cause the rate of interest to move toward the *MEC*.

The important general conclusion that follows from this section is that the equilibrium rate of interest is related to the marginal productivity of capital. In an economy with a large capital stock and a low *MEC,* the rate of interest will tend to be low. In an economy with a small capital stock and a high *MEC,* the rate of interest will tend to be high. This relation is illustrated in Figure 22–2.

Other influences on the rate of interest

If the desire to invest in new capital were the only reason to borrow money and if the interest rate were completely free to vary, there would be no more to the story than has been told above. In fact, however, there are other forces that influence the interest rate, and these can cause the rate of interest to diverge from the *MEC*.

Other demands for money to borrow. Households borrow money to buy goods on time and to buy houses and such financial assets as stocks and bonds. State and local governments borrow to build highways and schools. The federal government borrows to finance part of its expenditures. Each of these is a major component of the aggregate demand for funds to borrow.

Government control of interest rates. Not only is the government a demander of money to borrow, it also affects the supply of funds

Figure 22–2 The equilibrium rate of interest for a fixed capital stock

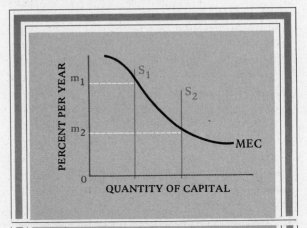

The rate of interest tends toward the *MEC*. Suppose S_1 and S_2 represent the capital stocks of two different economies. Economy 1 has a small stock of capital, S_1, and its rate of interest will tend toward its high *MEC* of m_1. Economy 2 has a large stock of capital, S_2, and its rate of interest will tend toward its low *MEC* of m_2.

available for lending. (We shall see how it does this when we study monetary policy in Chapter 35.) Governments commonly use their influence to affect the rate of interest for purposes of public policy.

Bank administration of interest rates. The rate of interest does not fluctuate in response to every minor fluctuation in demand and supply. As a result, the interest rate is not always determined in such a way as to equate i with MEC. Banks, for example, consider many factors when they fix the rate of interest that they charge on loans. They are reluctant to change these rates every time changes occur in the demand for money to borrow. If there is an excess demand for loanable funds (perhaps because the MEC is much greater than the interest rate) banks, rather than raise the rate of interest, often ration the available supply of funds among their customers. In doing this they use such criteria as the borrower's credit rating, how long the banker has known the borrower, and the amount of business the borrower does. This behavior is called **credit rationing** and it is commonly found in lending institutions in most Western countries. When the market rate of interest is below the pure return on capital, money will appear "tight"—hard to borrow—to the typical businessman.

Expectations about business conditions. In discussing the willingness of firms to borrow money and invest it in capital goods, we have stressed the relation between the rate of interest and the marginal efficiency of capital. Even though capital is physically productive in the sense that more can be produced with it than without it, no one will wish to invest in new equipment if there is no demand for the products produced by the capital goods. In times of severe business depression, the demand to borrow and invest money may fall to very low levels as a result of a declining demand by households for consumption goods.

Market expectations can be incorporated in the marginal efficiency framework by recognizing that the productivity of capital is measured in terms of the *values* (not the quantities) of goods it produces and that these values depend on people's willingness to buy the goods. The MEC is probably very elastic in a fully employed economy so that a small reduction in the rate of interest will lead to a

Inflation and interest rates

An inflation means that the purchasing power of money is falling. When this occurs it becomes very important to distinguish between the real rate and the money rate of interest. The **money rate of interest** is measured simply in dollars paid. If you pay me $8 interest for a $100 loan for one year, the money rate is 8 percent.

Consider further my $100 loan to you at 8 percent. The real rate that I earn depends on what happens to the overall level of prices in the economy. If the price level remains constant over the year, then the real rate that I earn is also 8 percent. This is because I can buy 8 percent more real goods and services with the $108 that you repay me than with $100 that I lent you. If, however, the price level were to rise by 8 percent, the real rate would be zero because the $108 you repay me will buy the same quantity of real goods as did the $100 I gave up. If I were unlucky enough to have lent money at 8 percent in a year in which prices rose by 10 percent, the real rate would be minus 2 percent. The real rate of interest concerns the ratio of the purchasing power of the money returned to the purchasing power of the money borrowed, and it may be different from the large increase in investment in new capital. When a depression develops, however, and the output of existing capital cannot be sold, it might not be worth borrowing money for new investment even at a zero rate of interest.

The significance of multiple influences

Because the rate of interest is influenced by many factors other than the demand to borrow money for new investment, the rate of interest can diverge from the *MEC*. If it is well below the *MEC,* there will be a heavy desire to borrow and invest in new capital; the stock of capital will grow and the *MEC* will begin to fall toward the rate of interest. If, however, the rate is held above the *MEC,* there will be little or no desire to borrow to invest in new capital. Capital may not even

money rate. The **real rate of interest** is the *difference* between the money rate and the rate of change of the price level.

If lenders and borrowers are concerned with the real costs measured in terms of purchasing power, the money rate of interest will be set at the real rate they require plus an amount to cover any expected rate of inflation. Consider a one-year loan that is meant to earn a real return to the lender of 5 percent. If the expected rate of inflation is zero, the money rate set for the loan will also be 5 percent. If, however, a 10 percent inflation is expected, the money rate will have to be set at 15 percent.

To provide a given expected real rate of interest the money rate will have to be set at the desired real rate of interest plus the expected annual rate of inflation.

This point is often overlooked, and as a result people are surprised at the high money rates of interest that exist during periods of rapid inflation. For example, from 1973 to 1974, when prices rose by about 10 percent, many financial commentators expressed shock at the fact that money interest rates to prime borrowers rose to an unprecedented 12 percent. Yet the implied real rate of interest of 2 percent was actually a decrease from the previous year.

If an inflation is fully expected, the money rate can be set to give any desired real rate of interest. Problems arise, however, when the inflation rate changes unexpectedly. Consider, for example, a loan contract that the parties wish to carry a 3 percent real rate of interest. If a 7 percent inflation rate is expected, the money rate will be set at 10 percent. But what if the inflationary expectations turn out to be wrong? If the inflation rate is only 4 percent, the real rate of interest will be 6 percent. If, on the other hand, the inflation rate is 12 percent, the real rate of interest will be −2 percent; the lender, even after paying the interest on the loan, will give back less purchasing power at the end of the period than he or she borrowed at the beginning.

Unexpected changes in the rate of inflation cause the real rate of interest on contracts already drawn up to vary in unexpected ways. An unexpected fall in the inflation rate is beneficial to lenders; an unexpected rise is beneficial to borrowers.

Figure 22–3 The effect of a divergence between the *MEC* and the rate of interest

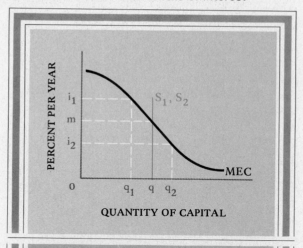

The relation between the *MEC* and the rate of interest will influence how the quantity of capital changes over time. Two economies have the same capital stock, *q*, and the same *MEC* of *m*. In one economy the interest rate, i_1, exceeds *m*. In the second economy the interest rate, i_2, is less than *m*. In both economies the rate of interest will tend toward *m* if it is free to vary. As long, however, as the rates remain at i_1 and i_2, there will be $q - q_1$ too much capital in economy 1 and $q_2 - q$ too little in economy 2. Thus there will be little demand to borrow money and invest in new capital in economy 1 and a great demand to do so in economy 2.

be replaced as it wears out. As the capital stock shrinks, the *MEC* will rise toward the rate of interest. These forces are illustrated in Figure 22–3.

In general there is a tendency for the interest rate and the marginal efficiency of capital to be drawn toward each other. Since the stock of capital (and thus the *MEC*) can change only slowly, most of the short-term adjustment is done by the interest rate. If, however, the interest rate were fixed, the

MEC would change to adjust to it. One way or the other, there is a tendency for these two rates to come together.

A COMPLICATION: MANY RATES OF INTEREST

In the real world there are many different rates of interest, not just a single one. Speaking in terms of a single rate can, however, be a valid simplification for many purposes because the whole set of rates does *tend* to move upward or downward together. Concentrating on one "typical" rate as "the" rate of interest in such cases is quite acceptable. For some purposes, however, it is important to take into account the multiplicity of interest rates.

At any moment of time, there are many different market rates of interest. At the time that you receive an interest rate of 6 or 7 percent on deposits at a savings and loan association, you may have to pay 11 or 12 percent to borrow from the same savings and loan association to buy a house. Interest rates on consumer installment credit of 16 percent and 20 percent are common. A small firm pays a higher interest rate on funds it borrows from banks than does a giant corporation. Different government bonds pay different rates of interest, depending on the length of the period for which the bond runs. Corporation bonds tend to pay interest at a higher rate than government bonds, and there is much variation among bonds of different companies. Considering the extreme mobility of money, why do such great differences exist? Why do funds not flow between different uses to diminish these differences? The answer is that quoted interest rates are composites of many things.

Differences in risk. Corporation bonds generally have higher interest rates than U.S. government bonds because they have a greater degree of risk. At one point in 1970, bonds of

Ling-Temco-Vought (LTV) were selling at a price that made their "interest rate" more than 50 percent per year at the same time that some U.S. government bonds were yielding only 8 percent. Why? Investors were sure of the ability of the U.S. government to pay both the interest and the principal on their bonds, but they were less sure about LTV, which was having financial difficulties in 1970. Much of the high interest rate on the LTV bonds was a risk premium. By 1976 the effective rate of interest on these LTV bonds had declined to about 12 percent. Clearly investors had become much happier with LTV's financial position and were no longer demanding the enormous risk premium that they required in 1970.

Secured loans, where the borrower pledges an asset as collateral, tend to have lower interest rates than unsecured loans, other things being equal. Loans secured by houses (mortgages) tend to have lower interest rates than loans secured by automobiles, in part because it is harder to run away with a house than with a car.

Differences in duration. The *term* (duration) of a loan may likewise affect its price. The same bank will usually pay a higher rate of interest on a certificate of deposit that cannot be redeemed at the bank (without penalty) for at least one year than on a straight savings account, which can be withdrawn in a matter of minutes. Yet many savers prefer savings accounts because they want to be able to withdraw their money on short notice. Except when interest rates are thought to be temporarily abnormally high, borrowers are usually willing to pay more for long-term loans than for short-term loans because they are certain of having use of the money for a longer period. Lenders usually require a higher rate of interest the longer is the time before the borrower must repay. Thus, other things being equal, the shorter the term of a loan, the lower are the interest rates.

Differences in costs of administering credit. There is great variation in the cost of different kinds of credit transactions. It is almost as cheap (in actual numbers of dollars) for a bank to lend United Airlines $1 million that the airline agrees to pay back with interest after one year as it is for the same bank to lend you $2,500 to buy a new car on an installment loan that you agree to pay back over two years in 24 equal installments.

The loan to you requires many more bookkeeping entries than the loan to the airline. In addition, it is easier—and thus less costly—to check United Airlines' credit rating than it is to check yours. The difference in the cost *per dollar* of each loan is considerable. The bank may very well make less profit per dollar on a $2,500 loan at 20 percent per year than on a $1 million loan at 10 percent per year. In general, the bigger the loan and the fewer the payments, the less the cost per dollar of servicing the loan. Why, then, do banks and finance companies usually insist that you repay the loan in frequent installments? They worry that, if you do not pay regularly, you will not have the money when the loan comes due.

In the market for borrowed funds there will be a *structure of interest rates* for credit transactions of different kinds. Such rates will be set to take account of such factors as risk premiums, duration of loan, and costs of administration. Nevertheless, it is useful to talk about movements of interest rate structures up and down as changes in "the" interest rate.

Sources of funds for investment

So far in this chapter we have considered the financing of investment by borrowed money. In fact, loans are only one of several sources of finance for new investment available to firms. Most firms use several sources simultaneously; a profit-maximizing firm that is free to do so will obtain funds from each source

Actual versus nominal interest rates

Things are not always as simple as they may seem in computing interest rates.

Suppose that you wish to borrow $1,200 for one year, and you have heard that the interest rate is 6 percent per year. You go to your bank and say, "Give me $1,200 now and I will pay back $1,272 one year from today." The banker looks troubled and says he would be glad to lend you the money, but would you mind paying $106 a month instead? You are good at arithmetic, so you know that $106 × 12 = $1,272. You agree to his plan. You find out later that you have agreed to pay interest at a rate of about 12 percent per year instead of 6 percent!

The key difference is that in your proposal you had the use of the full $1,200 for the whole year, whereas, in his proposal, you had it *all* for only one month. After the first monthly payment of $106 (of which $6 was the correct interest charge for 1 month at 6 percent per year), you had the use of only $1,100 for the second month. (If you pay $6 to use $1,100 for one month you will be paying at the rate of over 6.5 percent per year.) Jump to the last month, when now you owe only $100. If you pay $6 to use $100 for one month you are paying interest at the rate of 6 percent *a month* or 72 percent a year. The banker's proposal involves your having an average loan of $600 for 12 months, and the $72 interest you pay is 12 percent of this amount.

Another popular scheme is to deduct the interest in advance. Instead of lending you $1,200 the bank gives you $1,128 ($1,200 less the 6 percent interest for 1 year), and you pay back $100 per month for 12 months. You will end up paying a little more than $12\frac{3}{4}$ percent. (It is higher than it was in the previous case because, although you paid $72 interest in both cases, you only had the use of $1,128 in this case instead of $1,200.)

Finally, in response to your desire for $1,200, the bank might ask you for the $72 interest, plus a "carrying charge" of $28. It will give you $1,100 to be paid back in 12 monthly installments of $100 each. You will be paying interest at the rate of over 19 percent per year.

In no area in American commerce are there so many misinformed buyers as in the retail market for money. The practices described above are indulged in not only by loan sharks but by reputable banks and finance companies. The Truth-in-Lending Act passed in 1968 has greatly discouraged such practices by requiring that borrowers be informed of the rate of interest they are actually paying.

---

until the marginal cost of the last dollar obtained from each is the same.[6] (Otherwise the

firm could reduce its costs by shifting from higher-cost sources of funds to lower-cost sources.) The analysis of the first part of the chapter can now be generalized. When the *MEC* exceeds the cost of obtaining funds for new investment, firms will try to raise funds not only by borrowing but by tapping their

[6] If one firm could obtain all the funds it wished from each source at constant marginal costs, it would use only the cheapest source. But firms usually face rising marginal costs of funds from each source, and thus firms typically obtain their funds from many sources.

other main sources of funds. When the *MEC* is less than the opportunity cost of capital, the demand for new investment funds from all sources will be low or nonexistent.

FINANCING THE MODERN CORPORATION

The most important ways in which firms can obtain funds for new investment are (1) selling shares, stocks, or equities (as they are variously called) either by private or public sale; (2) borrowing by the sale of bonds; (3) borrowing from banks; and (4) reinvesting the firm's profits.

The money that a firm raises for carrying on its business is sometimes called its **money capital** as distinct from its **real capital,** the physical assets that constitute its plant, equipment, and inventories. Money capital may be broken down into **equity capital,** provided by the owners, and **debt,** which consists of the funds borrowed from persons who are not owners of the firm. The use of the term "capital" to refer to both an amount of money and a quantity of goods can be confusing, but it is usually clear from the context whether a sum of money or a stock of equipment is being referred to. The two uses are, of course, not independent of each other, since much of the money capital raised by a firm will be used to purchase the capital goods that the firm requires for production.

STOCK AND STOCKHOLDERS

The owners of the firm are its **stockholders** —persons who have put up money to purchase shares in the firm. They make their money available to the firm and risk losing it in return for a share in the firm's profits. Stocks in a firm often proliferate into a bewildering number of types. Basically, however, there is common stock and preferred stock. **Common stock** usually carries voting rights and has a residual claim on profits. After all other claims have been met, the remaining profits, if any, belong to the common stock holders. There is no legal limit to the profits that may be earned by the company and therefore no limit to potential dividends that may be paid out to common stock holders. Firms are not obliged by law to pay out any fixed portion of their profits as dividends, and in fact the practice among corporations as to the payout ratio varies enormously. Some firms pay out a large fraction and hold back only enough to meet various contingencies, others choose to pay small or no dividends for years in order to reinvest retained funds in the enterprise.

The basic difference between **preferred stock** and common stock is that preferred stock carries with it a right to a preference over common stock to any profits that may be available after other obligations have been met. If profits are earned, the corporation is obliged to pay a dividend to preferred stock holders, but there is a stated maximum to the rate of dividends that will be paid per dollar originally invested.

BONDS AND BONDHOLDERS

The **bondholders** are creditors, not owners, of the firm. They have loaned money to the firm in return for a **bond,** which is a promise to pay a stated sum of money each year by way of interest on the loan and to repay the loan at some stated time in the future (say 10, 20, or 30 years hence). This promise to pay is a legal obligation on the firm's part whether or not profits have been made. If these payments cannot be met, the bondholders can force the firm into bankruptcy. Should this happen, the bondholders have a claim on the firm's assets prior to that of any of the stockholders. Only when the bondholders and all other creditors have been repaid in full can the stockholders attempt to recover anything for themselves.

The disadvantage to the corporation of raising capital through the sale of bonds is that interest payments must be met whether or not there are profits. Many a firm that would have survived a temporary crisis had all its capital been share capital has been forced into bankruptcy because it could not meet its contractual obligations to pay interest to its bondholders.

LOANS FROM FINANCIAL INSTITUTIONS

Much of a firm's short-term and some of its long-term monetary needs are met through bank loans. This is true of giant corporations as well as of small businesses. Indeed, making commercial and industrial loans is one of the major activities of the banking system (which we shall discuss in Chapter 33). Banks, however, limit the amounts they are willing to lend companies, typically to specified fractions of the companies' total financial needs.

Many small businesses that are not well established cannot sell stocks to the public, nor can they raise all the funds they require from banks. Such companies often seek funds from other financial institutions such as insurance companies and small loan companies, usually at higher rates of interest. Several government agencies have been established to help them get access to funds at "reasonable" rates. The Small Business Administration is one of these. Little needs to be said about such loans at this stage, except to note that term (i.e., short-term) borrowing tends to be expensive to firms and that they prefer to raise money capital in other ways for long-term purposes.

REINVESTED PROFITS

An additional source of funds, very important for the established firm as distinct from the new one, is through the reinvesting, or plowing back, of the firm's own profits. One of the easiest ways for the controllers of the firm to raise money is to retain some of the firm's own profits rather than pay them out as dividends to shareholders. This has become an extremely important source of funds in modern times, and about $30 billion per year is obtained for investment in the United States in this fashion. If the shareholder does not wish his or her profits to be reinvested, there is very little that can be done about it except to sell the stock to someone else and invest in a company with a different dividend policy.

SECURITIES MARKETS (STOCK MARKETS)

If a household buys shares newly issued by a company, it hands over money to the company and becomes one of its owners. Once this has been done, the household cannot get its money back from the company except in the unlikely event that the company is liquidated. If the household wishes to get its money back, the only thing it can do is to persuade someone else to buy its shares in the company.

Similarly, when a household buys a bond from a company it cannot get its money back from the company until the expiration of a stated period of time. If, for example, I buy a 1998 bond in 1978, the bond will be redeemed by the company (i.e., the loan will be paid back) only in 1998. If I wish to get my money back at an earlier date, the only thing I can do is to persuade someone else to buy the bond from me.

An organized market where stocks and bonds are bought and sold is a **stock market** or a **securities market.** Such markets include not only the well-known New York Stock Exchange and the American Stock Exchange but also the whole network of "over-the-counter" markets that are handled by brokers and specialists. The selling of existing shares on the stock market indicates that the company's existing ownership is being transferred; it does not indicate that the company is raising new money from the public.

Securities markets are important because by providing for the ready transfer of corporate securities they make it possible for individuals to invest without committing themselves for long periods.

Because of the existence of securities markets, people are willing to put their savings in securities that are not themselves directly or quickly redeemable. For example, if I want to invest in a particular stock or bond that pays an attractive yield, I may do so even though I know now that I want to withdraw my money after only a year. Given a securities market, I can be confident that I can sell the stock or bond a year hence.

But while securities markets provide for the quick sale of stocks and bonds, they do not guarantee that the seller will get the price at which the securities were bought. The price at any time is the one that will equate the demand and supply for a particular security, and fluctuations in stock prices are common.

Prices on the stock market

Figure 22–4 shows the fluctuations in a widely quoted index of stock market prices. In January 1973 the Dow Jones index showed the average price of leading U.S. industrial stocks to be well above the figure for mid 1970. People who bought a representative selection of industrial stocks in 1970 and held them to January 1973 saw the average value of their holdings rise by a third (and, of course, they earned dividends as well). Prices fell after that until by December 1974 the index was only 58 percent of what it had been in January 1973. People who bought stocks in 1970 and held them until the end of 1974 first saw the paper value of their stocks rise by a third and then saw these gains quickly disappear until the stocks were worth at the end of 1974 only about 85 percent of what they paid for them in 1970. Even worse, those who bought stocks near the top of the market saw the value of their purchases cut nearly in half within 24 months.

What causes such rapid gains and losses, and what do they have to do with the kind of investment we have been talking about so far in this chapter? In one sense, it is correct to say simply that the prices reflect supply and

Figure 22–4 Fluctuations in an index of stock prices, 1960–1976

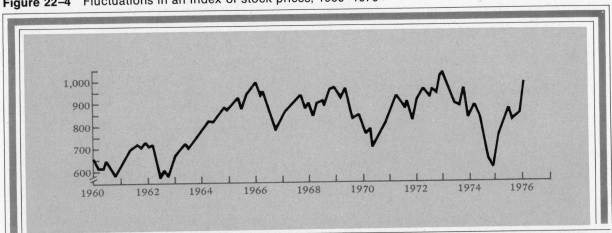

Stock market fluctuations are sharp and irregular. The chart shows monthly variations in the Dow Jones Industrials Index of thirty leading stocks.

demand. But we are now in a position to say a good deal about what affects supply and demand.

Investors who put their money in a savings bank earn a fixed return on their investment and also have their investments insured by a government agency. Those who invest in stocks and bonds buy the right to an income stream (in the form of dividends or interest) and also the possibility of capital gains (if the prices of the securities rise) or capital losses (if the prices fall). Because of this second possibility, expectations play a large role in security pricing and make stock market analysis as much an exercise in psychology as in economics and accounting.

THE RELATION BETWEEN PRICES AND EARNINGS

We have already seen that the value of an asset is related to its yield. One important element in stock market prices is the fact that the asset (stock or bond) gives the owner a claim to a stream of payments from the firm. How yields affect stock and bond prices can be studied first when the claim is a certain one and then when there is some uncertainty attached to the claim.

A riskless bond

Consider a bond that pays an amount of interest every year forever. Such a bond is called a **perpetuity.** Suppose a perpetuity is issued by the U.S. government that promises to pay $100 per year forever, and suppose you are absolutely certain that each and every payment will be made.

If, in addition, it is known with certainty that interest rates will not change, then the value of this perpetuity will simply be the present value of the income stream. The market price of the perpetuity will be $P = X/i$, for it would surely pay to bid the price up that high, and no one would be willing to pay more.

Thus, to take a specific example, if the rate of interest on a riskless asset is as low as 3 percent (as it was a mere 15 years ago), and you are sure that this rate will continue, the bond will be worth $3,333.33 because such a sum invested at 3 percent will yield $100 a year. If the perpetuity is offered for sale at any price above $3,333.33, no one will purchase it because the yield would be less than the 3 percent available on similar investments. If the perpetuity is offered at a price less than $3,333.33, many will rush to buy it because the yield on the investment will exceed the 3 percent generally available.

Now let us drop the assumption that interest rates are known not to change, but retain the assumption that the bond is riskless in the sense that there is no chance of default on its interest payments. Even though the $100 per year forever is absolutely safe, this would not be a riskless investment. Of course, if all the investor cared about was receiving $100 per year, it would (by assumption) be riskless. But the possibility of selling the bond and getting one's investment back must also be taken into account. Consider what happens if the interest rate rises, as it did during the first half of the 1970s. If the rate of interest rises from 3 percent to 5 percent, the present value of the perpetuity shrinks to $2,000, because that sum invested at 5 percent will yield the $100 a year that the perpetuity yields. If an investor bought the asset for $3,333.33 when the interest rate was 3 percent, he or she could sell it for only $2,000 after the rate had risen to 5 percent. If the change occurred within a year, the investor would have $2,100 at the end of the year (the present value of the bond plus one year's interest earned), having parted a year ago with $3,333.33!

This inverse relationship between changes in interest rates and changes in the value of assets is very important.[7]

---

[7] The relation is further discussed in the box on page 644, which could well be read at this time.

A rise in the rate of interest lowers the capitalized value of any asset that yields a fixed money income and confers a capital loss on owners of such assets.

A fall in the rate of interest raises the capitalized value of any asset that yields a fixed money income and confers a capital gain on owners of such assets.

If investors anticipate a future increase in interest rates, they will be willing to pay only a fraction of the present value of the asset calculated at the present rate of interest. At the beginning of 1976, for example, corporate bonds were yielding around 8 percent. People who thought interest rates were going to fall wanted to buy bonds immediately in the expectation of a rise in their price. People who thought interest rates would rise above 8 percent wanted to sell bonds whose current price reflected the current interest rate because they expected prices would fall further. Whether the price of a "riskless" bond (in the sense of a certain income stream) is at any moment selling above or below its present value depends on the number of people who want to buy or sell, and this in turn is related to expectations about the future course of interest rates.

A risky bond
Suppose the perpetuity we discussed above had been issued by a Brazilian tin mining company. If you worried that the company might fail, or that the government of Brazil might seize the company and repudiate foreign claims to its funds, you would presumably pay much less for this bond than for the perpetuity of the U.S. government. When New York City's financial crisis became widely publicized in 1975, the price of the city's bonds fell drastically. The new, higher interest rate represented by the lower market price of these bonds was a risk premium to cover the risk of delayed interest payments or even default.

Corporation and municipal bonds are given quality ratings by Moody's and Dun and Bradstreet. The ratings attempt to evaluate two kinds of risks: the risk of interest not being paid and the risk of the bond not being redeemed for its full value. These risks are, of course, additional to the risks of a capital loss resulting from a rise in the general interest rate.

The prices of common stock
We have already seen that the stockholders are the owners of the company and that they share in its profits. Because stocks, unlike bonds, carry no promise or legal obligation to pay anything, they contain added elements of uncertainty.

Earnings. A firm's earnings may rise or fall because of business conditions, the skill of its management, or for other reasons. The value of a stock derives in good part from the income stream that it is expected to confer on its owner. This might be measured by the stream of dividends the firm is expected to pay or by the firm's expected earnings. Most firms pay out only a fraction of their earnings as dividends, choosing to reinvest the undistributed profits. While these reinvested profits do not provide income directly to the stockholders, they do lead to future earnings, and by increasing the value of the company they tend to lead to increases in stock prices. It is generally believed that earnings are a better guide than dividends to understanding the prices of common stocks.

Thus one element in stock prices is the company's earnings rate. Assume that it was certain that a company would earn $12 per share per year indefinitely and that the rate of interest on a riskless loan was expected to remain at 5 percent. The company's stock would tend to a value of $240 a share because the present value of $12 per year at 5 percent is $240.

Risk and uncertainty. Present earnings are not, of course, guaranteed to go on indefinitely. The greater one's doubt about the ability of the company to maintain its earnings, the lower is the amount one would be willing to pay for a share of the stock. In the example above, perhaps investors demand an overall rate of return of 10 percent, half of which is a pure return and half a premium based on the risk of a sharp decline in future earnings. In those circumstances, a $12 per share rate of current earnings would tend to lead the company's shares to sell at $120 per share.

Two companies with identical earnings per share may find their stock selling at very different prices. The ratio of price to earnings—called the price earnings or **PE ratio,** or **P/E**—varies among companies because buyers have very different expectations of future earnings per dollar of present earnings. For example, in 1971 RCA stock was selling at 28 times earnings (PE ratio = 28), Teledyne was at 14.7 times earnings, and Gulf & Western at 7.8 times earnings. Had the earnings continued as in 1971, the rate of return on RCA stock would work out to be less than 4 percent, on Teledyne about 7 percent, and on Gulf & Western nearly 13 percent. Why did not investors rush to sell RCA stock and buy the better yielding Gulf & Western instead? One possible answer is that they expected future earnings of RCA and Teledyne to grow relative to Gulf & Western.

PE ratios can change dramatically over time as investors reevaluate the trend of probable earnings of a company. Teledyne, for a dramatic example, had a PE ratio of about 25 in 1966; it rose to 41.6 in 1967 and then began to fall until in 1971 it reached the 14.7 cited above. What had happened? In 1966 and 1967 Teledyne was one of the so-called glamour stocks, and the market projected great future growth in its earnings. Thus in 1967 people were willing to buy Teledyne stock for a price that yielded a rate of return of only 2.4 per-

cent. Many of them even borrowed money from banks or brokers at a rate of interest of 8 or 9 percent to do so. They would have been proven right *if* earnings had grown greatly; when earnings did not grow, expectations changed and investors reevaluated their views of Teledyne's earnings—and the price of its shares fell accordingly.

The dynamics of price changes. Assume as before that a share of stock is earning $12 per year. Assume that because of risk the actual price of the share of stock is $120, reflecting a yield (including risk premium) of 10 percent. Suppose now that the fortunes of the company change and its earnings rise to $24 per share per year. If 10 percent remained the appropriate discount rate, the market value of the stock would rise to $240. This is the familiar pattern.

Now suppose that before this change in earnings is announced you get a hot tip about it. Clearly you are in luck. You can rush out and buy all the shares you can afford at $120 a share, wait for the price to rise to $240, and then sell out. You will have made a 100 percent capital gain on an investment that lasted for possibly no more than a few months.

But perhaps you are not the only person to foresee this change. Careful study of the company's fortunes may have made it clear to many investors that earnings should double fairly soon. Everyone who foresees this will try to buy in at $120, hoping to sell out at $240. A few people who are lucky enough to get there first may succeed in doing almost this. But if many people foresee the change, the rush of anticipatory buying will push up the current price of the stock and its PE ratio will rise. How far will it go? It depends on how many people try to buy in. If it were not for errors and overreactions, the stock would rise to a level that reflected perfectly the anticipated increase in earnings. In a year's time, when the shares are *actually* earning $24, the price will be $240. But anyone who buys the stock now will only get $12 in earnings this year.

The price should begin to rise at once but not immediately all the way to $240. Say it rises to $229 at once. The purchaser at that price could anticipate $12 in earnings and $11 in capital gains by the end of the year—and he or she would be earning approximately 10 percent on the investment, the same rate as before. In a perfectly orderly stock market, where all changes in earnings were perfectly anticipated, one might expect the price to rise quickly to $229 and then gradually to $240 over the course of the year.

Now suppose that all of these expectations are mistaken—that the company's earnings do not rise above $12 per share. Suppose, on the basis of earlier expectations, the stock is rising toward $240 when it is learned that the expectations of higher earnings per share are mistaken. The price will plunge as people seek to sell out the stock that is now recognized to be very much overpriced. A few may sell quickly enough to realize capital gains. Those who bought towards the peak of the market and do not sell out quickly will suffer capital losses. Thus there is a speculative dimension to stock market prices that adds to the fascination with the market and has consequences of its own.

Speculative swings

Expectations about future stock prices are important. These can be based on such factors as present earnings, careful estimates of future earnings, or the vague feeling that stock prices will be rising or falling.

In major stock market booms, people begin to expect rising stock prices and hurry to buy while stocks are cheap. This action bids up the prices of shares and creates the capital gains that justify the original expectations. This is often called the phenomenon of self-realizing expectations. Everyone gets rich on paper in the sense that the market value of their holdings rises. Money making now looks easy to

others and they also rush in to buy, and further purchases push up prices still further. At this stage, attention to current earnings all but ceases and the PE ratios may rise without any fall in the interest rate or any rise in expected earnings. If a stock can yield, say, a 50 percent capital gain in one year, it does not matter much if the current earnings represent only a small percentage yield on the purchase price of the stocks. Everyone is "making money" and more people become attracted by the get-rich-quick opportunities. Their attempts to buy in bid up prices still further, and current earnings represent an ever-diminishing percentage yield on the current price of the stocks.

Capital gains are so attractive that investors may buy stocks on margin—that is, borrow money to buy them, using the stocks themselves as the security for the loans. In doing this, many investors may be borrowing money at a rate of interest considerably in excess of the rate of yield on current dividends. If $50,000 is borrowed at 10 percent (interest, $5,000 per year) to buy stocks yielding a current dividend return of only 4 percent (dividend, $2,000 per year), never mind, says the investor's logic, the stocks can be sold in a year or so for a handsome capital gain that will more than repay the $3,000 of interest not covered by dividends. Some people have the luck or good judgment to sell out near the top of the market, and they actually do make money. But others wait eagerly for ever greater capital gains, and in the meantime they get richer and richer—on paper.

Eventually something breaks the period of unrestrained optimism. Some investors may begin to worry about the very high prices of stocks in relation not only to current yields but to possible future ones even when generous allowances for growth are made. Or it may be that the prices of stocks become depressed slightly when a sufficiently large number of persons try to sell out to realize their capital gains. As they offer their securities on the market they cannot find purchasers without some fall in prices. Even a modest price fall may be sufficient to persuade other people that it is time to sell out. But every share that is sold must be bought by somebody. A wave of sellers may not find new buyers at existing prices, and prices will come down. Panic selling may now occur. A household that borrowed $50,000 to buy stocks near the top of the market may find the paper value of its holdings sliding below $50,000. How will it repay its loan? Even if it does not worry about the loan, its broker will. The household may sell now before it loses too much, or its broker may "sell his customer out" to liquidate the loan before it is too late. All of this brings prices tumbling down and provides another example of self-realizing expectations. If enough people think prices are going to come down, their attempt to sell out at the present high prices will itself create the fall in prices the expectation of which caused selling.

This, of course, is a very simple and stylized description of a typical speculative cycle. But, although simple, it describes the basic elements of market booms and busts that have recurred throughout stock market history.[8] It happened in the Jay Cooke panic of 1873 and in the Cleveland panic of 1893. What was possibly the biggest boom of all began in the mid 1920s and ended on Black Tuesday, October 29, 1929. The collapse was dramatic: The average price of 50 leading stocks in November 1929 was about 50 percent below the September peak. Nor did it

stop there. For three long years, stock prices continued to decline until the average value of stock sold on the New York Stock Exchange had fallen from its 1929 high of $89.10 a share to $17.35 a share by late 1933.

Are these booms and busts now only ghosts from a lurid and reckless past? Until 1969, many would have said, The modern investor is too sophisticated. It can never happen again. But look again at Figure 22–4. The Dow Jones index of the prices of leading industrial stocks tumbled by 30 percent between December 1968 and April 1970—in just over a year. The market then recovered, and by January 1973 prices had reached an all-time high. This "boom" was followed by an even bigger "bust": In a two-year period prices fell to less than 60 percent of their January 1973 values.

Stock markets: investment marketplaces or gambling casinos?

Stock markets fulfill many important functions. It is doubtful that the great aggregations of capital needed to finance modern firms could be raised under a private-ownership system without them. There is no doubt, however, that they also provide an unfortunate attraction for many naive investors whose get-rich-quick dreams are more often than not destroyed by the fall in prices that follows the occasional booms they help to create. To some extent, public policy has sought to curb the excesses of stock market speculation through supervision of security issues. This is handled by the Securities and Exchange Commission, which was set up in 1934 in an attempt to curb some of the excesses of the sort that accompanied the 1929 boom. The SEC seeks, among other things, to prevent both fradulent or misleading information and trading by "insiders" (those in a company with confidential information). Moreover, the government can limit the ability of speculators to trade on margin (see pages 662–663).

[8] Readers who want to try their hand in the market should note one particular simplification in our discussion. The downturn from a real speculative boom is usually more drawn out and ragged than the one we have described. Typically, there will be two or three breaks in prices, each followed by recoveries that occur when investors start buying to take advantage of the "bargains" when prices fall from their former heights. Possibly these recoveries take prices to new records; the recoveries may, however, shorten in duration and strength as more and more investors lose confidence in the belief that small falls in prices present them with bargain prices. Finally, a break occurs that is not followed by a recovery, and the full downslide commences.

All in all, the stock market is both a real marketplace and a place to gamble. As in all gambling situations, those who are less well informed and less clever than the average tend to be losers in the long term.

Summary

1. Capital is all man-made aids to production; it includes machines, buildings, trucks, and human capital. When production with capital is more efficient than production without it (even when full allowance is made for the resources needed to produce and maintain the capital goods), capital is said to be productive.

2. The amount of revenue available to the owners of the firm's capital is the excess of a firm's revenue over the amount payable to factors of production other than capital, and after allowance for taxes and depreciation. This can be divided into a pure return on capital, a risk premium, and economic profits.

3. The marginal efficiency of capital schedule is downward-sloping if there are diminishing returns as more capital is added to fixed quantities of other resources with constant technical knowledge.

4. A piece of capital equipment is valued because it promises an expected stream of future income to its owners. The value of this capital equipment is the present value of the stream of net income it is expected to produce. A single payment of X after t years has a present value of $X/(1 + i)^t$. A stream of income of X dollars per year in perpetuity has a present value of X/i.

5. A profit-maximizing firm will invest in a machine whenever the present value of the future stream of expected income—the capitalized value of the machine—exceeds the purchase price of the machine or (what is the same thing) whenever the rate of return on the capital exceeds the rate of interest that correctly reflects the opportunity cost of capital to the firm. At equilibrium, the firm will purchase capital equipment until the marginal rate of return is equal to the rate of interest.

6. The society as a whole will tend to acquire capital stock as long as the *MEC* is greater than the opportunity cost of money invested in capital, *i*. If there is competition among borrowers and lenders of money, the rate of interest will tend toward the *MEC*.

7. There are important influences on the market rate of interest other than those connected with the productivity of capital and the characteristics of loans. Among these are (a) expectations about price level changes, (b) expectations about the future state of the economy, (c) demands for funds to borrow for purposes other than investment in capital goods, (d) government control of interest rates as a tool of monetary policy, (e) bank administration of interest rates.

8. The amount of investment that firms wish to undertake will depend on the relation between the market rate of interest and the *MEC*.

9. At any moment in time there is a whole structure of interest rates. Individual rates depend on the riskiness, duration, and liquidity of a loan and also on the cost to the lender of processing the loan and collecting payments of interest and principal.

10. Corporations can raise money in four main ways: by selling shares in the firm; by selling bonds, which are evidences of debt; by borrowing from banks or other financial institutions; and by reinvesting (or plowing back) their own profits.

11. Securities (stock) markets allow firms to raise new capital from the sale of newly issued securities and allow the holders of existing securities to sell their securities to other investors.

12. Prices on the stock market tend to reflect the public's expectations both of firms' future earnings and of future changes in prices (for whatever reason). This necessarily puts a strong speculative dimension into security prices and large speculative swings do occur. Such swings are accentuated by the phenomenon of self-realizing expectations.

Concepts for review

The productivity of capital
The marginal efficiency of capital and the *MEC* schedule
The pure return on capital
The present value of future income and the capitalized value of assets
The inverse relationship between interest rates and the prices of assets
Reasons for the multiplicity of market interest rates
Equity capital and debt
Functions of securities markets
Self-realizing expectations

Discussion questions

1. The Atlas Company has calculated that it has the following opportunities to invest.

a. $20,000 to make a critical replacement of an inadequate machine, with an estimated rate of return of 200 percent

b. $100,000 in an additional machine with an estimated return of 10 percent

c. $50,000 for plant expansion with a return of 25 percent
How much would the company probably be willing to invest at an interest rate of 20 percent? of 10 percent? What assumptions are you making about risk in your answers?

2. Each of the following is sometimes described as an "investment" in everyday usage. Which represent investments in capital in the economist's sense?

a. building of the Aswan Dam by the government of Egypt

b. acquisition of a law degree at Harvard

c. purchase of a newly discovered Picasso painting. (Does it matter to your answer if the purchaser is the Metropolitan Museum or a private collector?)

d. purchase by one company of the stock or assets of another company

3. The future profits of Skeeter, Inc., a going concern, are estimated at $100,000 annually for the indefinite future. What is the present value of the business at interest rates of 5 percent, 10 percent, and 25 percent? What factors will determine the appropriate rate of capitalization to use for a prospective buyer of Skeeter, Inc.?

4. Irving Fisher, a distinguished Yale economist, argued that the durability of both capital goods and consumer goods was affected by the rate of interest. Assume that the more durable a house is, the higher is its present cost of construction. Would you expect rising interest rates to lead to more or less durable houses being built? Would you expect rising interest rates to foster or discourage sales of mobile homes?

5. How might each of the following affect the pure rate of return on capital? How might they affect the market rate of interest?

a. a major innovation in a specific industry

b. an increase in the rate of inflation

c. a wave of corporate bankruptcies

d. a substantial increase in economic activity due to renewed confidence in the business outlook

6. Suppose you are offered, free of charge, one of each of the following pairs of assets. What considerations would determine your choice?

a. a perpetuity that pays $20,000 a year forever; an annuity that pays $100,000 a year for only 5 years

b. owning an oil drilling company that earned $100,000 after corporate taxes last year; owning a bond that paid $100,000 interest last year

c. owning a municipal bond that provides for a tax-free interest payment of $1,000 per year; owning a U.S. government bond that provides a taxable interest payment of $1,500 per year

7. Many stores, including the large mail-order chains, sell for cash or credit at the same prices. If you do not pay your bill completely within 30 days (and you are encouraged to make partial payments) a service charge of 1.5 percent per month of the unpaid balance is added to the bill. What circumstances make it desirable

a. to pay cash

b. to pay the bill within the next month

c. to pay in "easy monthly installments"
Explain whether unpaid bills by customers represents a capital investment by the firm. Is the 1.5 percent per month paid by customers on their unpaid bills a pure return on the money that the firm has tied up?

8. In 1974 interest rates on industrial bonds hit the highest levels in 45 years. In 1975 they fell sharply and then gradually crept upward during 1976. Suppose you had accurately predicted all this in late 1973. How might you have "cashed in" on your foresight by buying or selling bonds? Would you expect all bonds to respond in a similar way to these changes in interest rates? Would the person who owned a bond purchased in 1972, whose due date was 1986, be affected by these changes in interest rates?

9. Update Figure 22–4 on the Dow Jones Industrial Index. Looking at data in the *Economic Report of the President* (or the *Survey of Current Business*), can you "explain" the changes that have occurred in the years since 1976? What data did you look at in attempting to explain what happened? What other data, not in the President's report, might have been useful?

National income divided by the total population is the average income for all Americans. Some individuals and groups get much more than the average and others get much less. Distribution theory is concerned, among other things, with explaining why this happens.

Possibly the most discussed aspect of distribution theory concerns the proportion of national income going to the very poor. Poverty and attempts to alleviate it have played a large part in the political debates of the 1960s and 1970s, and the intensity of the debate shows no sign of waning. It is to the problem of poverty that we first turn our attention in this chapter.

Poverty, inequality, and mobility

The distribution of income between rich and poor: the problem of poverty

The theory of distribution offers a number of reasons for variations in what different individuals and households can earn. People differ in the talents they possess and the factors they own; consequently both the quantity of factor services they can sell and the price they can receive will vary. There will always be 10 percent of the population who are poorer than the other 90 percent. In this sense, if poverty is regarded as a matter of low relative income, it is necessarily here to stay, for we inescapably have the (relatively) poor among us.

Clearly poverty means more than relative income. Some standard of the minimum amount of income needed by a family is required to define the **poverty level** below which a family is said to be poor. Such a standard specifies a number of dollars based on some experts' estimates of need and cost of living. In 1975 the poverty level was defined as $5,469 per annum for a nonfarm family of four.

The extent of poverty may be measured either by the number and percentage of persons in households having incomes below this level or by measuring the **poverty gap:** the number of dollars required to raise everyone's income to this level. In 1975 roughly 25.9 million persons (12 percent of the population) were classified as poor, and the poverty gap was approximately $16 billion.

But the poverty level also reflects the expectations and aspirations of the society. The American poverty level of approximately $1,367 per year per person will seem low to most of the readers of this book, but it is above the per capita income of three-quarters of the world's population. This should not lead you to minimize the poverty problems; the black American living in Harlem and working as a porter at Grand Central Station needs more clothes, transportation, and other things than an Indonesian peasant. Visit the slums of any American city and you will not lightly dismiss poverty as a problem.

Both the number and the percentage of the poor change. In 1933, President Franklin D. Roosevelt could speak of a third of a nation as

Figure 23–1 Percentage of Americans below the poverty level

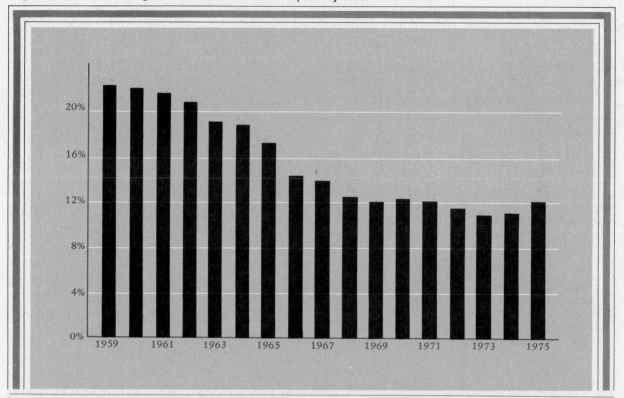

Poverty declined steadily in the 1960s, but a declining trend is not evident in the early 1970s. The officially defined cutoff points for poverty levels of income are reestimated annually by the government. For 1975, a single person with an income of $2,717 or less and a family of four with an income of $5,469 were considered poor.

being in poverty. By 1959, the official definitions had 22 percent of the nation below the
poverty line. Figure 23–1 charts the course of
poverty in America since that date. The
steady downward trend from 22 to just over
12 percent in the decade from 1959 to 1969 is
impressive. Since that time poverty has fluctuated substantially, rising particularly in
periods of heavy unemployment. In 1975, a
period of heavy recession, there were more
people below the poverty line than in any
year since 1967.

While the failure to achieve a downward
trend in the percentage of Americans in
poverty during the 1970s is disappointing for
those who would like to eradicate poverty, the
long-term trend over the last century is impressive.

Historically, the greatest source of relief of poverty
has come through economic growth.

Less than one hundred years ago poverty
was a general condition of the urban masses
everywhere in the world. Total output was so
low that all but a privileged minority was
inevitably condemned to poverty. Today, in
most advanced industrial countries, output
has risen until the *typical* industrial worker
enjoys a high material standard of living.
While he or she has many unmet wants, the
provision of minimum requirements of food,
clothing, and shelter is not a major problem
for the average worker. Nevertheless poverty
still exists and is an especially serious problem
for many minority groups.

If growth in productivity continues to
average even 2 percent per year, average living standards will double again in the next 35
years. This will surely further reduce the
number of people living in poverty. But it is a
mistake to expect too much from growth.
Today, after a century of rapid growth, the
poor—like death and taxes—are still with us.
It is safe to predict that if we rely merely on
growth of average income, they will be with
us a century hence. For the poverty problem
is no longer rooted in low *average* productivity but in the fact that particular groups have
been left behind in the general rise of living
standards. It is no consolation—indeed it adds
to the gall—that theirs is poverty in an increasingly affluent society. Starvation, hunger,
and malnutrition are suffered by millions of
individual Americans, and some Americans
born in 1978 will starve to death.

WHO ARE THE POOR?

There are poor among people of all ages,
races, and educational levels, among the
working as well as the unemployed and the
retired. But some groups have very much
higher incidences of poverty than do others.
Table 23–1 shows that poverty is particularly
high among members of minority groups,
those under 18 years of age (particularly if
they are black), those unemployed or not in
the labor force, and those with limited educational attainments. The rise in poverty in 1975
was mainly accounted for by groups not
usually heavily represented in the poverty
data—white households with a male head of
employable age. Almost half of the people
who first entered the ranks of poverty in 1975
became poor because they had been unemployed so long that they had exhausted their
unemployment benefits. This suggests that
much of the rise in poverty was due to the
severe recession that beset the country in the
middle of the decade and thus did not represent a reversal of the secular trend for poverty
to decline decade by decade.

Table 23–2 considers the problem somewhat differently. Instead of focusing on the
prevalence of poverty among certain subgroups in the population, it looks at those
who are poor and describes some of their
characteristics. Most interestingly, a great
many of the poor are employed, many are
aged, and many did not complete high school.
Moreover, many are members of small families. These data may help dispose of two

Table 23–1 The incidence of poverty among American persons and families, 1975

Characteristic	Percentage of population who fall below the poverty line
All persons	12
All families	11
Race	
White	10
Black	30
Spanish origin	27
Youth and race	
Children under 18 years of age and living in families	16
White	13
Black and other	41
Employment status of family head	
Employed (including armed forces)	5
Unemployed	21
Not in the labor force	22
Education of family heads over 24 years of age	
Elementary school only	18
1–3 years high school	14
4 years high school	6
Some college	3

Source: U.S. Department of Commerce, Bureau of the Census, *Current Population Reports,* Series P-60, No. 103.

Race, employment status, education, and age all affect the likelihood of poverty. The percentages show the fraction of persons in the designated class whose incomes fall below the poverty level. Thus, while only five percent of family heads with some college education were below the poverty level, 41 percent of nonwhite children living in families were so classified.

superficial caricatures: One is the slothful father feigning a disability because he is too lazy to go out and do an honest day's work; the other is the family with so many children that an ordinarily decent wage is spread so thin that the whole household is reduced to poverty. Of course, individual households that come close to these extremes can be found, but most poor households do not.

WHY ARE THERE POOR?

To answer the question we need to recognize that the poor come from many groups and that the causes of their poverty are various. The fact that many of the poor are over age 65 reflects the fact that age and illness force peo-

Table 23–2 Selected characteristics of American families below poverty line, 1975

Characteristic	White (percentage)	Black (percentage)
Employment status of family head		
Employed (including armed services)	43	31
Unemployed	9	9
Not in labor force	48	60
	100	100
Age of head		
Under 25 years	15	17
25–44 years	44	48
45–64 years	27	22
65 years and over	14	13
	100	100
Education of family heads (who are over 24 years of age)		
Elementary school	42	43
1–3 years high school	22	31
4 years high school	24	22
College	12	4
	100	100
Size of family		
2 or 3 persons	57	43
4 or 5 persons	28	29
6 or more	15	28
	100	100

Source: U.S. Department of Commerce, Bureau of the Census, *Current Population Reports,* Series P-60, No. 103.

Employment status, age, education, and size of family all affect the likelihood of poverty. Nearly half the whites and one-third of the blacks who are in poverty are in families whose head is employed, and well over one-half of both blacks and whites are in families whose heads did not finish high school.

ple out of the labor market; the fact that so many of those who are poor are under age 18 reflects both the plight of the children in families without a working head (often families with a father who died or deserted) and the high school dropout's difficulties in finding employment. Other important groups include the rural poor, who strive in vain to earn a decent living from marginal or submarginal farmlands; the urban working poor, who simply lack the skills to command a wage high enough to support themselves and their families above the poverty level; the immobile poor who are trapped by age and obsolescing skills in areas and occupations where the demand for their services is declining faster than their number; and, most important, the minority poor—blacks, Indians, Puerto Ricans, Chicanos, Chinese—who constitute only one-eighth of the population but almost one-third of the poor, and who often suffer the additional barriers of discrimination.

Thus there can be no simple answer to the question, What causes poverty in the midst of plenty? It is partly a result of mental and physical handicaps, partly of low motivation, and partly of the raw deal that fate gives to some—such as the children of the young father who dies unexpectedly, having been meaning to take out that life insurance policy almost any day. Partly it is a result of current and past prejudice. Partly it is a result of unwillingness or inability to invest in the kind of human capital that does pay off in the long run. Partly it is a result of the market's valuing the particular abilities that one does have at such a low price that, even in good health and with full-time employment, the income that can be earned leaves one below the poverty line. Partly, too, it is a result of fluctuations in the level of economic activity. For example, the decline in economic activity between 1973 and 1975 was accompanied by an increase of 3.8 million in the number of poor.

An individual may be poor for a combination of reasons. There are blacks among Southern farmers and among urban school dropouts. If you are black, under age 18, and in the labor force, your chances of being unemployed are about 10 times what they would be if you were a white male between ages 20 and 40.

As Table 23–1 shows, poverty among nonwhites is particularly acute.

As recently as 1963, more than half of the nation's blacks lived in poverty, and in 1975 the number was 30 percent.

Let us take a closer look at poverty among black Americans.

BLACK POVERTY

Black may be beautiful, but it certainly is poor. In spite of some genuinely high incomes, the average black is poor. This is the result of two related circumstances. The first is that blacks have many of those characteristics that are associated with poverty: A disproportionate number of them are less well educated than the average; working blacks are heavily concentrated in industries with declining demands for labor; their health has often been seriously impaired by malnutrition or untreated diseases; a disproportionate number of black households do not have a male head. The second factor is discrimination.

Whatever the combination of reasons, and despite attempts to deal with them as a matter of public policy, the gap in incomes remains and does not show signs of diminishing. (See Table 23–3.) There is one hopeful sign in the recent data: the large and highly significant difference in educational levels is being reduced.

In 1960 only 42 percent of blacks between the ages of 20 and 24 had completed 4 years of high school; in 1974, 72 percent of the same age group had completed high school. While

Table 23–3 The income gap between whites and other races in the United States, 1964–1975

YEAR	MEDIAN FAMILY INCOME		INCOMES OF BLACKS AND OTHER RACES AS PERCENTAGE OF WHITE INCOME
	Whites	*Blacks and other races*	
1964	$ 6,858	$3,839	56
1965	7,251	3,994	55
1966	7,792	4,691	60
1967	8,234	5,094	62
1968	8,937	5,590	63
1969	9,794	6,191	63
1970	10,236	6,516	64
1971	10,672	6,714	63
1972	11,549	7,106	62
1973	12,595	7,596	60
1974	13,356	8,265	62
1975	14,268	9,321	65

Source: U.S. Department of Commerce, Bureau of the Census, *Current Population Reports,* Series P-60, Nos. 101 and 103.

The income gap between black and white families remains large and is no longer shrinking. These comparisons suggest that the progress made during the mid 1960s in closing the income gap between whites and nonwhites has stopped.

in these respects blacks were still below whites in level of participation, the gap has narrowed. Higher educational attainments do not translate into higher incomes at once; incomes earned as a result of education arise only after the newly educated group finish their education and find better paying jobs. Of course, education alone is not enough. If more and better employment opportunities are not opened to blacks, the increase in income that should follow an increase in educational attainments will not come about in full measure.

"WAGING WAR" ON POVERTY

Eliminating poverty is easier than solving problems such as air pollution and cancer, for which cures are as yet unknown. For an amount estimated at about $16 billion per year, every family now below the poverty level could be given a sufficient income sup-

plement to bring it to that level. Congress could, in other words, close the poverty gap. Although $16 billion is a lot of money, it is less than 13 percent of the national defense budget, and it represents only about 1 percent of the total income earned in the nation.

Poverty, once an ineradicable scourge of mankind along with pestilence and plague, is now within the realm of control in America. Traditionally, and currently, energies have been divided between attacking the causes of poverty and attempting to help some of the poor through payments of money to alleviate their poverty.

Partly as a moral matter, partly as a practical one, the basic presumption has been that able-bodied heads of households should provide for their families' needs by working. Thus a three-pronged strategy developed: (1) provide job opportunities for all who are able to work; (2) provide social insurance, related to work, for temporary periods of unemployment and for the permanent period of retirement; and (3) provide monetary assistance to those categories of poor who are unable to work for reasons of age, health, or family status.

Providing employment opportunities

Families with an employed member have very much less chance of being below the poverty level than those without one. One aspect of fighting poverty is to encourage economic growth and avoid general unemployment. (These macroeconomic policies are discussed in Part Eleven.) Another aspect is to fight the forms of discrimination that deny employment opportunities to the members of minority groups among whom poverty is many times more prevalent than among whites. But more than 40 percent of all the poor families have a full-time working head; for these, the working poor, the problem is the lack of skills that command a high wage, not an absence of demand for the skills they do have. Programs of education, training, and retraining are designed to alleviate these causes of poverty. So far these programs have proved both expensive and limited in the number of people they can reach. Educational opportunities for the children of the poor may free them from inheriting poverty, but such progress is measured from generation to generation, not from year to year.

Social insurance

The second prong of traditional antipoverty legislation is social insurance. The Social Security Act, first passed in 1935, pays Old Age and Survivors Insurance (OASI) to millions of Americans who are "old" and to the widows and orphans of eligible workers. In excess of $60 billion a year is now paid in such benefits (including medical payments), and this amount keeps countless millions off the poverty roles. Indeed, a significant proportion of this amount goes to people who are nevertheless *below* the poverty level, and this

amount, though insufficient to eliminate their poverty, clearly reduces the size of the poverty gap.

Medicare and Medicaid tend to avoid or lessen the poverty of the aged who incur major medical expenses. Another $12 billion annually is paid in unemployment insurance—much of which prevents or mitigates poverty.

Successive increases in eligibility for coverage and in the size of benefits, including increases to match rises in the cost of living, promise to make social insurance an increasingly effective antidote to poverty for the majority of Americans. Some of the poor, however, do not meet the conditions for eligibility for social security.

Categorical assistance

The poorest of the poor are those who have never worked or for whom employment is not the answer. So-called categorical assistance programs are designed to identify categories of the poor who cannot use labor market participation to avoid poverty, either directly by way of earnings or indirectly by way of employment-related social insurance. Among the important categories are Old Age Assistance (OAA) for needy aged not eligible for OASI, aid to the blind and disabled, and aid to families with dependent children (AFDC). Approximately 10 million Americans receive aid under one or more of these programs. All of the programs have certain common characteristics. They are administered by the states, which share the costs with the federal government. States individually determine both eligibility and levels of payment. Eligibility is limited to demonstrated cases of need; and maximum payments under each of these programs are reduced dollar for dollar if the family has other income.

In addition to these long-standing programs, a series of special programs were instituted as part of a so-called War on Poverty on the part of the Kennedy and Johnson administrations. Grants for food stamps, rent supplements, disadvantaged youth, and alleviating rural poverty are examples of special programs initiated during the Kennedy-Johnson years. Only a few survived in the Nixon and Ford administrations. It is not yet apparent whether the Carter administration's new programs will prove significant.

SCOPE AND ADEQUACY OF PRESENT PROGRAMS

After a decade of steady increases in government spending for the poor, the programs leveled out in the first half of the 1970s. By 1975 they were not quite $40 billion per year. Other things being equal, the poverty gap would be much larger without these programs.

Forty billion dollars a year is a lot of dollars but a hard figure to relate to. To gain some perspective it may be thought of as roughly 4 percent of total personal consumption expenditures; about 12 percent of government purchases of goods and services (less than half as much as is included in the defense budget); or as about $200 for every person in every family above the poverty level. Whether in these terms we are spending a lot or a little depends on an individual's values.

Despite the scope of these programs, and despite the fact that without them the plight of the poor would be more desperate than it now is, many believe that the programs could be made more effective and that a new approach is required. The Nixon and Ford administrations halted the trend of increasing expenditures directed at the removal of poverty. Supporters of this change often spoke of halting the runaway rise in welfare expenditures. Opponents spoke less charitably of the administration's having decided "to live in peace with poverty."

A time to intensify the attack on poverty?

Those who advocate a return to a more ac-

tive and increasingly expensive attack on the problems of poverty have tended to put primary emphasis on two points: first they believe that relief of poverty should become almost entirely a federal program, rather than placing heavy reliance on state and local governments, and, second, they believe that assistance to the poor should be based on their level of income rather than on *categories* of eligibility. Thus it would no longer matter why someone is poor, only that he or she is poor.

The emphasis on federal funding stems in part from the fact that state and local governments face a far greater fiscal crisis than does the federal government (for reasons discussed in Chapter 25) and in part from the vast differences in treatment of the poor from city to city and state to state. The poor are not distributed evenly throughout the United States—half live in the South, many of the rest in northern urban slums. Much of the state and local tax base is generated in political jurisdictions in which poverty is not a major problem. Thus the tax burden of fighting poverty locally falls very unevenly. Differences in ability and willingness to pay lead to great differences in programs. For one example, a woman with no income and three dependent children in Newark, New Jersey, who is eligible for aid could receive $4,272 per year; in Biloxi, Mississippi, she would get at most $720. While each amount is below the poverty line, the difference in the realized levels of poverty are enormous—and they are not explained by differences in the cost of living.

The emphasis on general rather than categorical assistance arises because of the gaps in the poverty program that otherwise occur. Put differently, general assistance attempts to erase any implicit distinctions between deserving and undeserving poor. Some discussion of a proposed new policy, the so-called negative income tax, will be found in Chapter 25.

A time to cut back the attack on poverty?

Those who oppose further increases in expenditure on poverty programs tend to emphasize both the tax burden on the average citizen resulting from further increases in the costs of these programs and the alleged adverse effects on incentives generated by the programs themselves. These critics argue that welfare expenditures are already at cripplingly high levels, and in support they point to state and local as well as to federal expenditures. Many cities are saddled with high proportions of their total budgets going to welfare expenditures.

Advocates of the view that expenditures are already large enough to cause concern also argue that, although there are larger items in the combined budget for all levels of government, there are few other items over which so much discretion may be exercised. On the one hand, less could no doubt be spent on such items as defense and schools. Many people feel, however, that significant cuts in these items are both impractical and undesirable. On the other hand, a genuine option does exist with welfare expenditures. One of the few realistic hopes of keeping government expenditure under control, so goes this view, lies in holding a tight rein on the expansion of welfare costs and in particular eliminating payments to the dishonest and lazy people who are receiving payments without being in real need.

The alleged disincentive effects concern the supply of effort and were discussed briefly in Chapter 20. One such disincentive effect relates to citizens who pay the extra taxes that must be levied if welfare expenditure is to be increased. A second such effect is on the beneficiaries of government welfare payments: Children who grow up knowing they have a welfare safety net under them may not develop the attitudes or gain the skills needed to climb above the level of the net. This effect may be particularly noticeable in those who, because of the limitations of their abilities, could never in any case hope to climb far above the level provided by the welfare safety net. Not only may this be a long-term general worry, but welfare schemes themselves have often had unnecessarily strong disincentive effects built into them. Any scheme that reduces welfare payments by one dollar for every dollar that the recipient earns provides a 100 percent tax rate on earnings and surely provides a short-term disincentive to work. (One of the virtues of the so-called negative income tax is that it reduces this particular type of disincentive effect.)

More or less welfare expenditure?

There is disagreement about the desirable direction of change regarding levels of welfare expenditure. Some advocates suggest holding welfare payments at their present levels. Some suggest mounting a final attack designed to remove significant poverty forever from the American scene. Others would proceed cautiously along some middle course, advancing slowly and always being ready to halt or to pull back if serious undesirable side effects appear.

Choosing among the possible moves depends in part on value judgments of what is good and right and worth doing, and in part on positive factual assessments of what can be done and what will be the effects of doing it or not doing it. Positive economic research can help us to narrow the range of our uncertainties, even if it cannot tell us what we should finally decide to do. Today a great deal of research effort is being put into studying the effects of welfare expenditure on incentives—both of the recipients and of the taxpayers who must ultimately foot the bill. Hopefully this research will help us in evaluating the costs and benefits of such policies as "holding the line against any further disastrous increases in welfare expenditure" and "rushing forward quickly for a final assault on the now-pregnable bastions of poverty."

Is distribution theory relevant?

Does distribution theory help us to understand how factor earnings are determined and why they vary? Does it help us to understand —and thus to predict—the movement of labor and other factors of production among occupations, industries, and regions? Does the growth of powerful unions, giant corporations operating in oligopolistic markets, and international cartels mean that distribution theory, based mainly on the theory of competitive markets, is now outmoded? Is it possible that distribution in the modern world is explained more by the politics of bargaining and the political marketplace than by the forces of competitive markets?

The theory of distribution focuses attention on the allocation of resources among alternative uses. This allocation helps to determine both the quantities of the various goods and services that are produced and the methods by which they are produced. Factor pricing, and hence the distribution of income, is seen as a by-product of this market-allocation system.

Does the theory satisfactorily explain the allocation process in our economy? If this question is to be answered yes, it is necessary to give affirmative answers to two more basic questions. First, do market conditions of demand and supply play important roles in determining factor earnings? Second, do factors move in response to changes in factor earnings? Each is discussed in the following sections.

DO MARKET CONDITIONS DETERMINE FACTOR EARNINGS?

Factors other than labor

Many, if not all, nonhuman factors are sold on competitive markets. The theory predicts that changes in the earnings of these factors will be associated with changes in market conditions. The overwhelming preponderance of evidence supports this prediction of the theory, as the examples that follow illustrate.

The competitive market theory of factor pricing provides a good explanation of raw-material prices and hence of the incomes earned by their producers. The prices of plywood, tin, rubber, and hundreds of other materials fluctuate daily in response to changes in their demand and supply. The responses of factor markets to the many shortages that seemed to characterize the American economy in the 1970s provide dramatic confirmation. When the price of agricultural commodities shot up following a grain shortage, incomes of farmers soared. When oil became scarce, prices rose and oil producers and owners of oil properties found their profits and incomes rising rapidly. Not only did the relative prices of oil products rise, so also did the relative prices of commodities (such as chemical fertilizers and air travel) that make use of petroleum products.

Land in the heart of growing cities provides another example. Such land is clearly fixed in supply, and values rise steadily in response to increasing demand for it.[1] Very high land values even make it worthwhile to destroy durable buildings in order to convert the land to more productive uses. Many of New York's old and once-favorite hotels have been pulled down in response to the intense demand for high-rise office buildings. The skyscraper is a monument to the high value of urban land. In many smaller cities, the change from shopping downtown to shopping in outlying shopping centers has lessened the demand for land downtown and influenced relative land prices. The increase in the price of land on the periphery of every growing city is a visible example of the workings of the market. And recent increases in the world demand for American agricultural products has led to an

---

[1] A friend is fond of saying, "Nobody buys land anymore: its price is much too high because everybody wants it."

increased demand for agricultural land and a bidding up of its market value.

Similar examples can be found in almost every issue of such publications as the *New York Times* and the *Wall Street Journal,* but the point should now be clear.

The prices and earnings of nonhuman factors are successfully predicted by the theory of factor pricing in competitive markets.

Labor

When we apply the theory to labor, we encounter two important sets of complications. First, labor being the human factor of production, nonmonetary considerations loom large in its incentive patterns, and thus market fluctuations may have less effect. Second, labor markets are a mixture of competitive and noncompetitive elements, the proportions of the mixture differing from market to market. These complications make the question, "Do market conditions determine factor earnings?" harder to answer. Monopolistic elements and nonmonetary rewards, both difficult to measure, require careful specification if the theory that labor earnings respond to market forces is to be testable. Nevertheless, there is a mass of evidence to go on.

Market fluctuations in demand and supply. Do earnings respond to normal fluctuations of demand and supply as the theory predicts? Here the evidence is that they often do. The competitive theory predicts that a decline in the demand for a product will cause a decline in the derived demand for the factors that make the product and thus a decline in their owners' incomes. A rise in the demand for a product will have the opposite effect. Cases come easily to mind.

With the advent of the automobile, many skilled carriage makers found the demand for their services declining rapidly. Earnings fell, and many in the older age brackets found that they had been earning substantial economic rents for their scarce but highly specific skills. These people were forced to suffer large income cuts when they moved to other industries. Persons who acquired skills wanted in the newly expanding automotive industry found the demands for their services and their incomes rising rapidly.

More recently there has been a large increase in the earnings of first class hockey players. This was brought about in part by an increase in demand for hockey players consequent on the formation of the World Hockey League and in part by the introduction of competitive bidding for players, which reduced the ability of employers to hold down wages by acting as monopsonists. Doctors are another group who have gained from an increased demand for their services. With the rise in real incomes in the twentieth century the typical household has spent an increasing proportion of its income on medical services. The resulting rise in demand has greatly increased the incomes of doctors relative to the incomes of many other groups in the society.

College professors are an example of a group that gained as a result of changes in labor markets during the 1960s and then lost out in the 1970s. The relative earnings of a college professor were much higher by 1970 than they had been twenty years previously. This was particularly so at the starting end of the scale, where intense competition for the scarce supply of good students who had just obtained Ph.D.s forced up their price all through the 1960s to levels that would have seemed princely only fifteen years before. In response to these high incomes, many more college graduates went on to get advanced degrees, and a rising proportion stayed on to teach and do research in universities. The supply of new Ph.D.s began to arrive on the market in 1969–1970, and for the first time in ten years starting salaries of Ph.D.s hired for the fall of 1970 were not significantly higher than salaries for those hired the previous year. By 1973 the average percentage increase in academic salaries was not only below the average percentage increase in all American incomes but was insufficient even to keep pace with the increase in the cost of living. The relative downward pressure on college professors' salaries has continued into the mid 1970s.

Another group that has been suffering the chill winds of the consequences of factor price determination on competitive markets is college graduates. During the early 1970s the earnings of college graduates fell relative to other workers, and employment opportunities dropped sharply, especially for new graduates. The downturn is explained by slackening demand due to changes in industrial structure (e.g., substituting sophisticated computers for college-trained persons) and continued growth of supply.

These examples suggest the more general proposition:

Earnings of labor no less than of nonlabor factors

respond to significant changes in the conditions of demand and supply.

Price changes induced by market conditions have little to do with abstract notions of justice or merit. If you have some literary talent, why can you make a lot of money writing copy for an advertising agency on Madison Avenue but very little money writing poems? It is not because an economic dictator or group of philosophers has decided that advertising is more valuable than poetry. It is because in the American economy there is a large demand for advertising and only a tiny demand for poetry.

Effects of monopoly elements in labor markets. A strong union—one able to bargain effectively and to restrict entry of labor into the field—can cause wages to rise well above the competitive level. Highly skilled plasterers, plumbers, and electricians have all managed to restrict entry into their trades and as a re-

Table 23–4 Employment and hourly wages indexes: railways and coal, selected years

	CLASS I RAILROADS		BITUMINOUS COAL	
	Employment index (1947 = 100)	*Hourly wages index [a]*	*Employment index (1947 = 100)*	*Hourly wages index [a]*
1947	100	98	100	130
1950	90	109	86	135
1955	78	105	51	133
1960	58	116	40	139
1965	47	115	31	134
1970	41	116	33	137
1975	36	126	47	150

Source: U.S. Department of Labor, Bureau of Labor Statistics.
[a] All U.S. manufacturing industries = 100.

In spite of a large decline in demand for labor services in the 1950s and 1960s, powerful unions have succeeded in holding the wages of miners and railroad workers well above the average wage for all manufacturing industries. These data show that working in declining industries need not mean receiving declining relative wages. In railroading, wages of remaining employees increased relative to the average wage rate in U.S. manufacturing. In coal mining, relative wages did not decline despite a drastic decrease in employment opportunities up to the late 1960s. In each case strong unions were responsible.

sult maintain wages well above their transfer earnings. Many similar cases have been documented. Unions can and do succeed in raising wages and incomes when they operate in small sections of the whole economy; the high earnings do attract others to enter the occupation or industry, and the privileged position can be maintained only if entry can be effectively restricted.

Not only can monopoly elements raise incomes above their competitive levels, they can also prevent incomes from falling in response to decreases in demand. Of course, if the demand disappears more or less overnight, there is nothing any union can do to maintain incomes. But the story may be different when, as is more usually the case, demand shrinks steadily over a few decades. Railroads and coal mining, which were once thriving industries, faded through the 1950s and 1960s to pale shadows of their former selves. Year by year the levels of employment in these industries shrank in response both to declining demand and to the increased use of labor-saving techniques.

Competitive theory predicts low incomes for labor in these two industries, exit of the most mobile factors under this forceful disincentive, and hard times for those who decide to stick it out.

As Table 23–4 shows, this has not been the pattern in either railroading or coal. The wages of coal miners and railroad employees have remained some of the highest in the entire industrial field. However, the predicted departure has occurred. Employment in coal mining fell from above 400,000 in 1947 to 112,000 in 1969, and employment on the railroads fell from more than 1.3 million to 572,000 in the same period. What happened in each case was that powerful unions were able to prevent wages from falling, but the decline of job opportunities discouraged the young from entering these industries.[2] As workers

left the industries because of retirement, ill health, or death, they were not replaced. Some people argue that the "restrictive behavior" of unions in these cases has led to a more orderly, humane, and civilized phasing out than would have occurred had the adjustment been left to a free market. In the latter case, those who remained in the industry, and who were needed by it, would have suffered depressed conditions in order that the disincentive could operate on those who did leave and on those who might otherwise have entered.

Taken together, the competitive theory of factor markets and a bit of monopoly theory appear to explain a good deal of the variation in relative earnings of different groups in the labor force.

DO FACTORS MOVE IN RESPONSE TO CHANGES IN EARNINGS?

Factors other than labor

In the previous section we saw that earnings tend to change in response to demand and supply conditions. Changes in earnings are signals that have the effect of attracting resources into lines of production in which they are more needed and out of lines in which they are less needed.

Land is transferred from one crop to another in response to changes in the relative profitabilities of the crops. Land on the edge of town is transferred from rural to urban uses as soon as it can earn substantially more as a building site than as a cornfield. Materials and capital goods move from use to use in response to changes in earnings in these uses. The most casual observation will show the allocative system working pretty much as described by the theory.

---

[2] Coming into the 1970s, the railroad industry continued to decline while the coal industry enjoyed a renaissance as the demand for coal-powered electricity generating stations grew by leaps and bounds. As Table 23–4 shows, employment in coal grew by 42 percent (the employment index rose from 33 to 47). At the same time, hourly wages that had been high but fairly stable relative to other wages throughout the 1950s and 1960s rose relatively by almost 10 percent (from 137 to 150).

In the case of nonhuman factors, there is strong evidence that the theory is able to predict events with reasonable accuracy.

Labor

Labor mobility can occur in many dimensions. Labor can move among occupations, industries, skill categories, and regions. These categories are not exclusive; to change occupation from a farm laborer to a steelworker, for example, a person will also have to change industries and probably towns.

The mobility of labor is as well documented as it is impressive. When wages on the West Coast soared during World War II, workers flocked to the coast to take lucrative jobs in the rapidly expanding aircraft and shipbuilding industries. When new oil fields were discovered in Alaska and northern Canada, high wages attracted welders, riveters, and the many other types of labor that the oil fields required. Table 23–5 shows one way of looking at the very substantial reallocations of the labor force that have actually occurred in the American economy.

Unions, pension funds, and other institutions can and do inhibit labor mobility substantially and, by influencing supplies of labor in various markets, exert a substantial influence on labor earnings. It is easier to move from one occupation to another within one industry when there exists a single industrial union than it is when each occupation in the industry is organized in its own craft union. It is easier to move between two industries in the same occupation when both are organized by craft unions than it is when each has its own industrial union.

Although various barriers to the entry of labor exist in particular markets, few seem able to withstand for long the pressures of severe excess demand. Prejudice against females, for example, did not long withstand the excess demand for labor during World War II. Once millions of men had been absorbed into the armed forces, occupations traditionally closed to women suddenly opened up. Employers, with their profits at stake, quickly decided they would rather have Rosie for a riveter than have no riveter at all. This occurred without social pressures arising out of concern for discrimination against women. Once the excess demand disappeared after the war, however, many of the old prejudices reasserted themselves—and barriers were not again lowered until they were directly assaulted by the Women's Liberation movement. Similarly, no matter how strong an industrial union, it cannot long prevent entry of new labor when the derived demand for labor increases greatly as a result of a large rise in the demand for the industry's product.

Table 23–5 Percentage allocation of the nonagricultural labor force

	Manufacturing	Mining	Construction	Transportation & public utilities	Wholesale & retail	Finance, insurance, real estate & services	All levels of government
1930	34.1	3.4	4.8	12.5	19.5	15.7	10.0
1950	33.7	2.0	5.2	8.9	20.8	16.1	13.3
1970	27.3	0.9	5.0	6.4	21.2	21.6	17.7
1975	23.8	1.0	4.5	5.8	22.0	23.7	19.2

Source: *Economic Report of The President*, 1977.

Significant reallocations of labor occur over the long term. The proportions of the labor force in manufacturing and in transportation and public utilities has declined significantly over the years, while the porportions in various service industries and in government have risen.

In all of these cases, however, a mixture of the theories of competitive and monopolistic factor markets can go a long way in explaining what we see and in predicting many of the consequences of changes in market conditions on labor mobility.

Regional mobility of labor presents a more mixed picture. Substantial regional movement does occur but often at a rate not rapid enough to prevent major regional inequalities in earnings from occurring and persisting. On the one hand, the regional distribution of population has been shifting toward the sun belt and other centers of rapid economic growth in the United States; on the other hand, depressed Appalachian areas have remained regions of excess labor supply for over twenty years since coal mines in Pennsylvania and West Virginia began to shut down.

Although it is relatively easy to get some out-migration, it is difficult to get large-scale transfers in a short period of time. When demand falls rapidly, pockets of poverty tend to develop. In Appalachia, labor has been leaving but poverty has increased. The reason for this is that the rate of exit has been slower than the rate of decline of the economic opportunities in the area. Indeed, the exit itself causes further decline: when a family migrates, both the supply of labor and the demand for labor decline. This is because all the locally provided goods and services that the family consumed before they migrated now suffer a reduction in demand.

In the last half of the 1960s non-market-oriented policies increased in popularity with the U.S. authorities, apparently in the belief that no set of changes in market signals would suffice to secure the necessary movement of labor within an acceptable time period. The federal government gave retraining a prominent role in its distressed-area programs. But such strides as have been made are minute relative to the need, and only a tiny fraction of the unemployed have completed retraining at this time.

Interregional labor movement occurs, but it does not always occur rapidly enough to avoid regional pockets of extreme unemployment and poverty.

General criticisms of distribution theory[3]

The theory of distribution is much criticized, particularly its marginal productivity element. Indeed, in some quarters "marginal productivity" is almost a dirty word (for reasons that will emerge later). Yet for better or worse we have been using this theory throughout this chapter. We have done this every time we used the concept of a firm's or an industry's demand for a factor of production arising out of the profit-maximizing decisions of firms. A brief summary of the theory of distribution will help to put some of the criticisms into perspective.

THE THEORY RESTATED

The standard theory of distribution is easily summarized. One half—the so-called marginal productivity theory of distribution—explains the demand for factors of production. The other half—the hypothesis of equal net advantage—concerns the supply of factors of production to particular uses.

These two halves can in turn be explained in terms of a very few basic propositions. The demand for a factor is a derived demand, depending on the marginal physical productivity of a factor and the demand conditions for the commodities made by the factor. The addition to revenue caused by employing another unit of some variable factor depends on the addition to physical output contributed by that factor and the change in total revenue

[3] This section may be omitted without loss of continuity.

when the rate of sales is increased by this amount.

The curve that displays this information is called the marginal revenue product curve of the factor. As long as the *factor* is purchased under competitive conditions, and as long as firms are maximizing short-run profits, each type of factor will be paid a remuneration equal to its marginal revenue product. This is true regardless of whether the *product* is sold under conditions of perfect competition, imperfect competition, or monopoly, and it is merely an implication of profit maximization. This marginal productivity theory stands or falls with the theory of profit maximization. A firm that is not equating the marginal revenue products of each of its factors with that factor's price is not maximizing its profits. A firm that is maximizing its profits is necessarily equating each factor's price to its marginal revenue product.

The theory of factor supply asserts that factors will move between occupations in search of the highest net advantage. Factors will move among uses, industries, and places, taking both pecuniary and nonpecuniary rewards into account. Factors will move in such a way as to equalize the net advantages to the owners of factors. Because there are impediments to the mobility of factors, there may be lags in the response of factors to changes in relative prices. Thus the elasticity of supply will depend on what factor is being discussed and what time horizon is being considered.

None of the above reads like grist for a mill of intense political or economic debate. We may thus wonder what it is about so prosaic a theory that arouses rather intense hostility among some of its critics. Part of the hostility is related to misconceptions about what the theory does and does not say and some is related to extreme claims made for the theory by some of its early supporters. Two points are common enough to warrant specific comment.

TWO IMPORTANT MISCONCEPTIONS

Is marginal productivity theory inhumane?

It is sometimes argued that marginal productivity theory fails to account for the differences between human services and other services. The theory is thus thought to be inhumane because it treats human labor in the same way it treats a ton of coal or a wagonload of fertilizer. One must be careful to distinguish one's emotional reaction to a procedure that treats human and nonhuman factors alike from one's evaluation of it in terms of economics. Anyone who accepts this criticism must explain carefully why separate theories of the pricing of human and nonhuman factors are needed in order to make predictions about behavior. The marginal productivity theory is only a theory of the *demand* for a factor. It predicts only what profit-maximizing employers would like to buy. It predicts that desired purchases of a factor depend on the price of the factor, the technical conditions of production, and the demand for the product made by the factor. *Supply* conditions undoubtedly differ between human and nonhuman factors, but these differences are accommodated within the theory. No evidence has yet been gathered to indicate that it is necessary to have separate theories of the demand for human and nonhuman factors of production.

Does the theory define a just distribution of income?

In a world of perfectly competitive factor markets, the theory predicts that in equilibrium all factors receive payment equal to the values of their marginal products. Some eminent economists in the past spoke as if this led to a just distribution because factors were rewarded according to the value of their own contributions to the national product. "From each according to his ability; to each according to his own contribution" might have been the slogan for this group. One of its most famous exponents was the American economist John Bates Clark (1847–1938). Many critics of the low levels of wages that then prevailed reacted passionately to a theory that was claimed to justify them.

It is not necessary here to enter into normative questions of what constitutes a just distribution of income. It is, however, worth getting the facts straight. According to the marginal productivity theory, each worker does not receive the value of what he or she personally contributes to production. The worker receives, instead, the value of what one more worker would add to production if that worker were taken on while all other factors were held constant. If one million similar workers are employed, then each of the one million receives a wage equal to the extra product that would have been contributed by the millionth laborer if he or she had been hired while capital and all other factors remained unchanged. Whether such a distribution of the national product is just or not, one cannot say that each unit of a factor receives as income the value of its own contribution to production. Indeed, where many factors cooperate in production, it is generally impossible to divide total production into the amounts contributed by each unit of each factor of production.

Whether payment according to marginal product is more or less just than payment according to some other criterion has not been generally agreed. It is, however, possible both to hold that marginal productivity does tend to determine how people get paid and to believe that government policies that change the distribution of income are desirable. Many economists hold both positions.

DOES THE THEORY EXPLAIN THE FUNCTIONAL DISTRIBUTION OF INCOME?

Now reconsider the questions first asked on page 322, at the beginning of our discussion of distribution. The functional distribution of income concerns how income is distributed among such broad aggregates as wages, rent, interest, and profits. Careful studies show that the functional distribution of income does change over time, often in puzzling ways.

Theories explaining the functional distribution of income among what were then the three great classes of society—laborers, landlords, and capitalists—figured prominently in the writings of classical economists such as Ricardo, Malthus, and Marx. With the development of marginal analysis in the last half of the nineteenth century, emphasis shifted to the determination of factor prices and quantities in millions of individual markets. Such a theory about individual markets offers few general predictions about the functional distribution of income. It holds that to discover the effect of some change, say a tax or a new union, on the functional distribution between wages, profits, and rent, we would need to be able to discover not only what would happen in each individual market of the economy but also to aggregate to find the overall result.[4] Clearly, we are a long way from being able to do all this with our present state of knowledge.

It may well be, therefore, that general predictions about the effects of events, such as the rise of unions, on overall distribution cannot be easily derived. Many economists would argue that economic theory has little to say about great issues on the level of labor and capital's overall shares of the total national product. They could also argue that the ability of marginal productivity theory to deal with

---

[4] To do this accurately we would, among other things, need to know the degree of monopoly and monopsony in each market, we would need to be able to predict the effect on oligopolists' prices and outputs of changes in their costs, and we would need to have a theory of the outcome of collective bargaining in all market situations. We would also need to know how much factor substitution would occur in response to any resulting change in relative factor prices. Finally, we would need a general equilibrium theory linking all of these markets together.

detailed questions of distribution is nonetheless a remarkable triumph.

One reason that questions concerning the overall functional distribution are practically unanswerable is that it only makes sense to talk about laws governing distribution into three main factor shares if labor, capital, and land are each relatively homogeneous and each subject to a common set of influences not operating on the other two factors. In fact, however, there may well be as much difference between two different types of labor as between one kind of labor and one kind of machine. Thus there is no more reason to expect that there should be simple laws governing the overall functional distribution of income between land, labor, and capital than to expect that there should be simple laws governing the overall distribution of income between blondes and brunettes or catholics and protestants.

Summary

1. The concept of poverty involves both relative and absolute levels of income. Today roughly one-eighth of all Americans are classified as living in poverty. Since the aggregate poverty gap is small relative to national income, the possibility exists of eradicating poverty in the United States.

2. Economic growth, though it has led to a reduction of poverty, will by itself never eradicate it, for many of those most in need do not share directly in the fruits of growth. Thus public programs are thought to be required.

3. Poverty is particularly acute among such minority groups as blacks. This reflects in part the minority group's lower average stock of human capital—especially education and training—and in part discrimination that has prevented utilizing more fully the skills and talents that the group's members have. Recent years have seen no significant decrease in the relative income disadvantage of blacks to whites.

4. Methods currently used to reduce poverty include antidiscrimination laws that seek to expand employment opportunities for blacks and other minority groups; retraining programs intended to match people with available jobs; social insurance that helps the able-bodied to meet risks of such problems as unemployment and retirement; and categorical assistance designed to serve those ineligible for other programs.

5. Poverty programs are a matter of lively current debate. Some people feel that it is possible and desirable to make further major reductions in poverty now. They place particular importance on an income supplement to the poor regardless of why they are poor. Others feel that further expensive attacks on poverty are undesirable both because of the additional burden it would place on the average taxpayer and because of disincentive effects generated by welfare programs.

6. Market conditions exercise a powerful influence on factor earnings. This is most evident for nonhuman factors such as raw materials and land. For labor, the influence of nonmonetary factors is greater because the owners of labor must accompany their labor services to work. Nevertheless, market forces exert powerful influences on earnings of labor.

7. There is much evidence of movement of factors in response to changes in earnings. Factor mobility is again typically greater for nonhuman factors than for labor.

8. An important misconception is that marginal productivity theory is inhumane because it fails to make necessary distinctions between labor and other factors. But the derived *demand* for factors is not different for labor and for other factors. The important differences between human and other factors occur on the supply side.

9. A second misconception is that distribution according to marginal productivity satisfies the canons of justice because everyone gets from the pool of total output what he or she contributes to it. This argument is factually inaccurate.

10. Marginal productivity theory of distribution successfully predicts changes in factor earnings that occur for particular groups in response to changes in the market conditions that affect them. It has little to say, however, about changes in the broad functional distribution of income among labor, land, and capital.

Concepts for review

Poverty and the poverty gap
Correlates of poverty
Categorical assistance and social insurance
The marginal productivity theory of distribution (demand for factors)
The hypothesis of equal net advantage (supply of factors)
Functional and size distributions of income

Discussion questions

1. In what ways are the problems of poverty in the United States likely to be different from the problems of poverty in an underdeveloped poor country, such as Bangladesh? In what ways are they easier to solve in one place than in the other?

2. The official poverty level used in the United States is based only on money income. It does not take into account food stamps, subsidized housing, or special tax treatment of those at the low end of the income scale. Do these omissions lead to an exaggerated view of the poverty problem? Should the poverty line rise if average income of the American people rises, with no increase in the prices of individual items of consumption?

3. Suppose that your objectives are (first) to eradicate poverty and (second) to reduce unemployment. Evaluate the probable effectiveness of each of the following in meeting each objective.
a. increasing welfare payments
b. increased labor union membership
c. creating a program of public works to hire the poor
d. ending employment discrimination against blacks

4. A proposed program of rental allowances to the poor has been attacked in Congress as giving money to slumlords instead of to the poor and thereby worsening the distribution of income. Evaluate this position. Argue the case for and against assistance that is tied to a particular kind of expenditure rather than giving the money to the poor to spend as they think best.

5. Egalitarian U has the policy of paying all faculty members of the same rank and years of experience the same salary regardless of field. Further, it grants promotion strictly on the basis of years of service at EU. Elitist Tech has a nominal salary scale but meets offers made from outside to members of the faculty whom it especially wants to keep. Where would you rather be a student? Where would you rather teach? Does it matter in answering these questions whether your field is medieval history or chemical engineering?

6. Is the Empire State Building immobile? Is the Empire State Building more mobile among uses than the use of the land it sits on? How about the uses of the pyramids of Egypt? What resources can you think of that are immobile over a time span as long as 25 years? In general, are a factor's earnings likely to be greater or smaller if its mobility is relatively low?

7. The supply of regular New York taxicabs is rigidly controlled by a licensing system that keeps the number of cabs well below what it would be in a free-market situation. A "medallion" issued for a nominal fee by the city confers the right to operate a cab. The medallion, however, is freely salable: in 1977 its price was about $40,000. Evaluate the effect on the price of the medallion of
a. an increase in average incomes of New Yorkers
b. increased operation of "gypsy cabs" (cabs without medallions)
c. increases in parking-lot fees and parking violation fines in New York
Suppose that you had been on the margin about whether to buy a medallion and become a licensed cab operator in 1977. A 50 percent increase in taxi fares was then authorized. How, if at all, would this affect your decision? Toronto uses a similar scheme, but the price of a medallion there is only about one-half as much as it is in New York. What might account for this difference?

8. Which of the following are valid predictions of the theory of distribution? Are any of them based on misconceptions about the theory?
a. An increase in the demand for a product will lead, *ceteris paribus,* to an increase in the wage rate of labor used to produce it.
b. A labor-saving technological change will tend to lead to increasing wages if the quantity of output does not change.
c. The value of a person's labor to the employer is the maximum amount the person can expect to be paid, but the wage paid may well be less than this amount.
d. A firm selling its product in a competitive market will pay lower wages to carpenters than a monopolistic seller, if they both hire carpenters in the same labor market.

PART SEVEN

THE MARKET ECONOMY: PROBLEMS AND POLICIES

24

The price system: market success and market failure

There are two caricatures of the American economy. In one, America is pictured as the last stronghold of free enterprise with millions of Americans racing in a mad and brutal chase for the almighty dollar. In the other, American business people, workers, and farmers are pictured as slowly strangling in a web of red tape spun by a spider called government regulation. Neither is realistic. It is true that many aspects of economic life, perhaps more than in most other countries, are determined by the operation of a free-market system. In the United States, private preferences, expressed through private markets and impinging on private profit-seeking enterprises, determine much of what is produced, how it is produced, and the incomes of productive factors. But even casual observation makes it clear that public policies and public decisions also play a large role. Not only do laws restrict what people and firms may do, but taxes and subsidies influence their choices. Large amounts of public expenditure are not market determined, and these lead to a distribution of national product very different from what would exist in a system that relied entirely on private markets. The United States is in fact a mixed economy.

The reason this (and every other) economy is a mixed economy relates to what an unkind critic called the economist's two great insights: markets work and markets fail. In this chapter we look, first, at when and how markets work; second, at when and how they fail; and, finally, at strategies for coping with market failure.

The interdependent economy

As their incomes rose in the period after World War II, American families increasingly chose to consume beef instead of cheaper and less satisfying foods, with the result that in two decades consumption of beef per capita nearly doubled. Where did the extra beef come from? How was it produced? What happened to the earnings of stockyard workers in Chicago as a result of the increased demand?

These questions should sound familiar, for they (or ones like them) have been discussed throughout this book. But heretofore individual markets have been treated as if they were functioning more or less in isolation. This was a very great simplification, as can be seen by noting that the theory of factor pricing would have led (other things being equal) to the prediction of an increase in the demand for stockyard workers and a rise in their pay. But the dramatic fact is that today the once-famous slaughterhouses of Chicago are all gone! The derived demand for services of Chicago stockyard workers and meatpackers disappeared despite the increase in demand for the product they helped to produce. To understand this apparent paradox, it is necessary only to recognize that the market for Chicago stockyard workers is part of an interlocking system in which other things do not remain equal.

What happened was this: As theory predicts, a rising demand for beef increased the demand for corn for feed and led to a rise in the price of corn as cattle feeders vied with other users for the corn crop. Cattle feed became increasingly expensive, and major efforts were devoted to increasing its supply. Scientists sought a cheaper substitute for corn and developed a new feed grain, milo, which could grow abundantly in the semiarid western plains of Kansas, Nebraska, Oklahoma, and Texas, where corn could not survive because of excessive heat and insufficient rain. Milo caught on, and a series of improvements in its productivity have made it an abundant source of cattle feed. The replacement of corn by milo destroyed the profitability of shipping cattle east for fattening and butchering. Transportation costs could be minimized by both feeding and butchering the cattle in the West and shipping butchered cuts to eastern

and midwestern markets. With modern refrigeration equipment this proved economical. Furthermore, the waste and bone are left behind and no longer need to be transported along with usable meat as far as Chicago. As feed lots were established in the plains, the meatpacking industry began to close its aging and increasingly obsolete plants in terminal markets such as Chicago and to build new, modern, streamlined facilities farther west where the cattle are. The derived demand for stockyard workers and meatpackers declined in Chicago, and while some new labor was required in the western plants, it tended to be of a different kind. Despite the surging demand for beef, meatpackers and stockyard workers found their jobs disappearing.

How markets can coordinate

Changes of the kind that occurred in the meatpacking industry, or changes that result from crop failures, international incidents, strikes, or changes in tastes, show the nature of unplanned responses to impacts on the economy. Whether the event that created the initial impact was planned (as in the case of a strike) or unplanned (as in the case of changes in demand), further changes are caused by the responses of individuals and firms to such signals as changes in prices, wages, and profits. For example, when shortages develop, prices and profits rise and profit-seeking entrepreneurs are led to produce more of the goods in short supply. The price system produces a series of automatic signals, and a large number of different decision-making units (firms and households) do in fact coordinate their efforts.

With a price system it is not necessary to foresee and to coordinate all necessary changes. Such changes occur automatically as a result of the separate decisions made by a large number of individuals, each seeking a private profit and all responding to changes in demands and prices.

It is important to recognize that "unplanned" and "uncoordinated" are very different conditions. It was the great discovery of the early economists that in a competitive price system, which is *unplanned,* private decision makers, by seeking private gains and responding to such signals as prices, costs, and profit rates, could produce *coordinated* reactions to changes in demand and supply.

From the undoubted fact that the price system coordinates responses, it does not follow that the price system has been proved to be the best system for regulating everything in the economy. There is a difference between the word "automatic," which we have used, and the phrase "perfectly functioning," which we have not used.

Are markets necessary?

While markets can be used to allocate resources, other allocative devices are also possible.

Consider for a moment operating without a market mechanism. Instead of a series of automatic adjustments, suppose that a series of planning boards makes all decisions. Suppose that the Board in Control of Women's Clothing hears that pantsuits and high-style blue denim clothing are becoming the fad in neighboring countries and orders a certain proportion of all women's clothing factories to make these items for the next season. (It might do so by trying to guess the proportions women will want of different kinds of clothing, or it might do so on the basis of its own members' preferences as to what women ought to wear.) Suppose it also gives every woman a number of coupons, each of which may be exchanged for an article of clothing. Conceivably the quantities of each kind of clothing produced would be just right, given the preferences of the population. But what if the board misguessed, greatly overproducing blue denim and underproducing pantsuits? Long lines would appear at the pantsuit counter while mountains of blue denim piled up in store inventories and factories. One may argue whether this is a satisfactory distribu-

tion system or an efficient one, but there is no doubt that it could work. Once the board saw the lines for pantsuits, it could order a change in quantities produced. Meanwhile it could store the extra blue denim for another season—or ship them to a country with different tastes.

To say that markets may not be necessary does not mean that it does not matter whether allocation is done by markets or by central planning. Many consumers may be greatly inconvenienced if the board (in the example above) is slow to correct its initial mistake; yet the members of the board may have no very great incentive to admit and rectify a mistake quickly. In a market system, where similar errors of judgment can and do occur, things might be different. In the first place decision making is decentralized; not all manufacturers would misjudge, and those that were producing pantsuits could earn large profits both by raising prices and by running extra shifts to increase pantsuit production. Furthermore, producers of blue denim might be motivated both to shift their production quickly to a more popular commodity and to make blue denim more attractive to consumers by cutting their price. Unlike the members of the planning board, the producers under a market system would be motivated to correct their initial mistakes as quickly as possible. Those who were slowest to adjust would lose the most money and might even be driven out of business.

In this example planning is less satisfactory than some use of markets for at least two reasons. First, centralized planning requires inputs such as administrators and computer services—which means real costs in terms of productive resources used. Second, centralized planning is not automatically self-correcting.[1] Many other decisions, such as

[1] As we shall see in Chapter 45, for these reasons even economies of the Soviet type, which are committed to planning as a matter of principle, are increasingly using a price system to get the market mechanism to decide many detailed questions of production, distribution, and resource allocation.

how to reduce current consumption and how to raise investment to foster a more rapid rate of growth, may also be made either by planning or by the market.

WHEN MARKETS WORK WELL

In Chapter 13 we encountered the distinction between private costs and social costs (and the related notion of externalities). A similar distinction can be made between private benefits from production and social benefits. Both consumers and firms benefit from production—the consumers in the form of utility derived from the goods acquired, the firms in the form of revenues and profits from the sale of goods produced. Private benefits are those that accrue to the parties directly involved in a private transaction—the purchaser of a good in terms of the utility it gives him or her and the producer in terms of the revenues from the sale. But there may be others (third parties) who are benefited by the transaction, and the benefits to them must be added to the private benefits to find the full social benefits. For example, when one person buys and refurbishes the only run-down house on the block, everyone on the block benefits from the removal of the eyesore.

Net social benefit may be defined as the difference between social benefits and social costs; **net private benefit** is the difference between private benefits and private costs.

Private producers seek to maximize net private benefits (by equating marginal private benefits with marginal private costs).

If marginal net social benefits are exactly the same as marginal net private benefits, then private producers will be motivated to allocate resources in just the ways that are socially beneficial, and the market system can be said to have been efficient and to have worked in the social interest.

If, however, marginal net private benefits and marginal net social benefits are different, then private producers, responding to private benefits and costs, will fail to achieve the re-

sults that are optimal by social valuations —and the market system is said to have failed. The term "failure" which is commonly used in this context may convey the wrong impression. It does *not* mean that nothing good has happened, only that the *best* outcome has not been achieved. Social benefits will usually be produced, but they will not be as high as they could have been if marginal social benefits and costs had been equated. Divergences between social and private valuations and other sources of market failure will be illustrated later in the chapter.

A second virtue of competitive market allocation, in addition to its potential for efficiency, is that it is impersonal and does not give one individual—either planner or shopkeeper—a great deal of power over others. For example, if the market is determining prices, the service station operator will sell gasoline to anyone who enters the station. But if the price of gasoline is kept well below its equilibrium value, the operator will be unable to satisfy everyone who comes into the station and will be forced to decide whom to satisfy and whom to leave unsatisfied. The seller acquires a degree of market power and the discretion to serve whomever he or she wishes (regular customers, perhaps). Many regard avoidance of this kind of discretion as a major advantage of an impersonal system. More generally, the absence of power that inheres in a thoroughly decentralized system is highly attractive to all who fear the exercise of centralized power.

These are familiar arguments representing the core of classical liberalism. As we shall see, the facts that markets are often efficient and usually impersonal do not compel (as some nineteenth-century liberals supposed they did), adherence to a policy of **laissez faire,** a policy that implies the absence of any governmental interference with private decisions. But they do explain the willingness to use markets where markets do the job reasonably well.

Two crucial questions of social policy are

factual ones. Where do differences between marginal net private and net social benefits exist, and how large are they? If there is a consensus that in certain aspects of production such differences exist and are large (as appears to be the case in the United States in pollution control, elementary education, conservation, and some aspects of recreation), governmental actions to replace or interfere with private-market solutions are likely to occur.

The reason most economies are mixed is that markets are thought to do certain things well and other things badly. Different societies judge these matters differently, as we shall see in Chapter 45. But at any moment in history, in any economy, the arguments are likely to be about situations where there is no consensus on the assessment of how well the market works.

HOW THE PRICE SYSTEM WORKS: THE NOTION OF GENERAL EQUILIBRIUM

In this chapter (and in Chapter 4) we have given an overview of how markets allocate resources in response to changes in supply and demand. In other chapters we have looked in detail at what happens in individual markets, but we have largely neglected the fact that various markets are interdependent, that changes in one market must be accommodated by changes in other markets.

Clearly there is a difference between what is possible in one market and what is possible in the whole economy. If you suddenly decide that you want a new small car, it is a simple matter (provided you have the money) to go out and buy it. But everybody cannot do what anybody can do, even if each individual is equally able. If 5 million people simultaneously decide they want new small cars immediately, most of them will be disappointed. First they will find that all the sales personnel are busy. Then they will find that the price has risen—dealers will be offering lower trade-ins or lower discounts. Some potential

buyers will be told that they will have to wait weeks, months, or even years for delivery. After World War II, for example, demand for new cars was so high relative to available supplies that waits of 10 to 18 months for delivery were common. All of this is only one part of the story. Although in the short run the main market response to changes in demand may be rising prices and the rationing of available goods, in the longer run more small cars will be produced.

But if more resources are used to produce cars, less of something else must be produced (unless more resources can be obtained). Thus there must be changes in other sectors. How do these come about? Whose decisions contribute to them? Does the final result provide an allocation of resources that is in some sense satisfactory? If so, does the adjustment occur in a quick and orderly way? The study of general equilibrium analysis is necessary to answer these questions.

It is often useful to think of changes in the economy as occurring in three stages: (1) the *impact* effect on some sector of the economy of some initial change, (2) the *spillout* effects of this change onto other sectors of the economy, and (3) the *feedback* of changes into the sector where the impact originally occurred. Where the second and third stages are large, looking only at the initial sector of the economy will prove inadequate.

Sometimes the only *important* changes occur in the sector of initial impact. While spillout and feedback occur, they are so diffused that it is not necessary to trace them. Throw a pebble in a pond and, while the ripples spread to the far shores and eventually return, they can probably be ignored for most purposes. When this is so, **partial equilibrium analysis,** which neglects spillout and feedback effects in other sectors, is sufficient. In other situations these effects are too important to neglect. Drop a bomb in the pond, and the waves will rush over the banks, wreak damage on shore, and then return to the pond

Partial versus general equilibrium

An economy is an interlocking and inter-reacting system. An impact on any sector has effects there, but those effects will spill out and become impacts to other sectors. These in turn may feed back onto the original sector.

Virtually every change in the economy produces all three effects: impact, spillout, and feedback; but not all are always large. The basic assumption of partial equilibrium analysis is that the spillouts and feedbacks in a sector are small enough that they may be ignored for the question being discussed.

All partial equilibrium analyses are based on the assumption of *ceteris paribus*. This assumption is always violated to some extent because anything that happens in one sector must cause changes in some other sectors. What matters is that the changes induced throughout the rest of the economy are sufficiently small and diffuse that the feedbacks they in turn have on the originating sector can safely be ignored.

Partial equilibrium analysis is useful because economists have found that for many kinds of decisions the effects on the rest of the economy are relatively small and the feedbacks are negligible. The smaller the sector under consideration, the more likely it is that feedbacks will prove to be negligible.

In many instances spillouts and feedbacks are large, and to ignore them by doing partial analysis causes serious error; this is the province of general equilibrium analysis. If, for example, the steel industry raises its prices, the costs in most U.S. manufacturing industries will rise and the chain of repercussions may very well feed back in a sizable way on the demand for steel.

There is no simple rule for determining whether partial or general analysis is better. The test is whether the predictions of a partial theory are refuted by the facts and whether the aspects of the problem neglected are of major interest.

---

laden with debris. Where spillouts and feedbacks are large, **general equilibrium analysis** is important. It is concerned crucially with interactions among sectors of the economy.

The GM strike of 1970: a case study of interactions

On September 14, 1970, the United Automobile Workers (UAW) and General Motors (GM) broke off negotiations over a new contract and a strike began that was not to be settled until November 12. In September all U.S. production of GM cars ceased and was

not effectively resumed for more than three months.

Impact. At the time of the strike, GM had about 780,000 employees around the world, sold over 7 million cars per year, and had sales revenues of about $2 billion per month. The UAW represented 1.4 million auto workers and had a strike fund of $120 million. At the level of benefits paid, the fund was exhausted in the seventh week of the strike. The central issue in dispute was wages. At the time the strike began the average auto worker was paid $4.05 per hour. General Motors was offering an increase of 38¢ per hour, and the UAW was demanding 61¢. (Eight weeks later they were to agree on 51¢.)

The direct impact of the strike was on the automobile industry, particularly on the 400,000 striking GM workers. Instead of earning about $160 per week, each received a maximum of $40 in strike benefits from the union. They and their families restricted their consumption and dug into their savings.

General Motors, of course, suffered a loss of sales (of roughly $5 billion) and of profits, which had been $740 million during the last six months of 1969. During the last six months of 1970, GM lost $212 million, a swing of nearly $1 billion, mostly, though not entirely, because of the strike.

Every week of nonproduction meant the nonpayment of approximately $70 million in GM payrolls and about $200 million for steel, tires, and other supplies. The direct tax loss to federal, state, and local governments was estimated at about $100 million per week.

Spillout. Not surprisingly, a strike on this scale had wide impact on the American economy, and its effects were soon felt in many other industries. General Motors, the nation's largest steel and tire buyer, makes sizable purchases from many other industries as well. It purchases 15 percent of the nation's lead (for automobile batteries), 6 percent of its aluminum, and 2 percent of its copper. It is a major shipper by both truck and rail, and the credit used by automobile buyers to finance their purchases is an appreciable part of the total of consumer credit. All of these suppliers and *their* suppliers and employees quickly felt the pinch of the strike.

Some of the immediate spillout effects were readily predictable. On October 3, three suppliers announced layoffs—4,000 workers at Jones and Laughlin Steel, 1,100 at Uniroyal Tires, and 2,500 at the A. O. Smith Company in Milwaukee (makers of auto frames).

Other effects were less readily predictable but no less easy to understand. Among these was the layoff of city employees, including police and firemen in Pontiac, Michigan, as that automotive city struggled with a budget crisis caused by loss of tax revenues. Flint, Michigan (home of Buick and Chevrolet assembly plants), reported a surprising *boom* in the sale of lumber because many striking auto workers used their increased free time to make needed home repairs and extensions.

As time went on, the effects of lost income spread widely. By November, nationwide retail store sales had declined by 1 percent as many families in and out of the industries directly affected curtailed their expenditures, some in anticipation of possible layoffs if the strike continued. Overall it was estimated that the eight-week strike led to a loss of nearly $15 billion in the value of goods and services produced—only one-fifth of it in lost automobile production. Not all of this loss was permanent; with the end of the strike and the resumption of production in January, some backlog demand for new cars made itself felt. But much of the loss in production and sales was gone forever, as was the income of those who had lost weeks of work.

Feedback and more impacts. Both the losses in family income and the 7 percent increase in automobile prices—attributed by GM to the strike and the cost of the new contract—had a feedback effect in the automobile industry: Automobile sales, which are sensitive to both price and income changes, declined.

Many of the strike's longer-run effects had not worked their way through the economy six months after the strike had ended. Even the minor ripples from the GM strike became significant impacts in other industries and other markets. The state of Michigan budget, already in trouble, was pushed $10 million further into deficit as a result of the lost tax collections; consequent layoffs of state employees, reductions in state programs, and tuition increases at the state's universities produced effects that were to be felt for years to come.

In contrast to this experience, a one-week strike by the UAW against Chrysler in September 1973 caused hardly a ripple in the economy. Whatever impacts were felt were largely absorbed within the industry. The 1976 contracts were finalized only after a four-week strike against the Ford Motor Company. Although this strike was more serious in its effects than the Chrysler strike, there were fewer people involved, for much less time, than in the earlier GM strike. Although its impacts were not negligible, they were substantially smaller and less generally felt than those of the GM strike.

Market failure

If attitudes can be judged by behavior, it is clear that a majority of Americans believe that an unrestricted, unmodified private enterprise system is not the best of all possible worlds. What led free and rational people to reach this judgment? What has led them to lessen their reliance on unrestricted workings of the free market and, in a significant number of cases, to impose rules regulating markets or to substitute some collective action for individual action?

SOURCES OF MARKET FAILURE

Differences between private and social valuations

We have seen that differences between marginal private and social benefits may lead to market failure. Consider some further examples. The increasing recognition that automobile exhaust is a major source of air pollution has led to demands that manufacturers and users attach emission control devices to existing cars, even though the evidence is clear that neither manufacturers nor individual users want to pay the extra costs of such devices.

Many times the two parties to a transaction neglect other (third party) interests. If Mr. Smith and Ms. Jones both want to make a certain exchange, is it their business and theirs alone? It depends on the exchange. If Smith owns a building lot in a residential area (on which he intends to build a house in five years) and decides to "get some money out of it" in the meantime by leasing it to a farmer to pasture goats, or to a carnival operator to run sideshows, the neighbors may well object. A person with a contagious disease who is unwilling to purchase medical care jeopardizes the health of others; in this case the person's unwillingness to make the transaction causes the externality.

Sometimes the adverse third party effects are less obvious and more controversial, resting on moral values rather than clear and present dangers. Marijuana and hardcore pornography are valuable in the private market, but their sale is often prohibited.

Sometimes *how* a service is provided may affect the valuation of the service. It is possible to imagine alternatives to the system of free public schools; if it were abolished, a private-school system would be established and the poor could be subsidized to make sure that education was available to everyone. Public schools may be better or worse than private schools, but they are likely to be different, particularly because persons other than parents, teachers, and owners influence their policies. Much of the case for public education rests on the advantages to you of having other people's children educated in a particular kind of environment.

Market imperfections

A free-market economy functions by responding to *signals* provided by prices, costs, and profits. These signals call attention to relative scarcities and surpluses and induce firms and the owners of factors of production to move resources from areas in which demand is low relative to supply to areas in which supply is low relative to demand. Extraneous things that seriously change these signals or prevent a speedy response to them are market imperfections that may lead to the market's failure to perform efficiently.

One kind of market imperfection is factor immobility. If increases in a factor's pay do not lead quickly to increases in supply, the market will fail to reallocate resources promptly in response to changing demands. Monopoly power creates market imperfections by preventing enough resources from moving in response to market signals. In this case, barriers to entry rather than factor immobility frustrate the flow of resources. Another kind of market imperfection is ignorance; signals can work only if they are received.

Collective consumption goods

Certain goods or services, if they provide benefits to anyone, necessarily provide them to a large group of people. Such goods are called **collective consumption goods.** National defense is the prime example of a collective consumption good. An adequate defense establishment protects everyone in the country whether they want it or not, and there is no market where you can buy more of it and your neighbor less. The quantity of national defense provided must be decided collectively. Other examples of collective consumption goods include the beautification of a city, a levee to protect a city from a flood, and a hurricane-warning system. In general, market systems cannot compel payment for a collective good since there is no way to prevent a person from receiving the services of the good if he or she refuses to pay for it. Governments, through their power to tax, can compel payments by all.

While many collective consumption goods are provided by governments, private groups can be formed to provide them as well. A neighborhood association can acquire land in common to provide open space, even if the city will not acquire it to provide a park; or it may agree to restrictions on how property owners will allow their property to be used, even if it cannot get a zoning ordinance to do the job. A variety of privately financed medical research organizations such as the American Cancer Society seek to find a cure for a disease that, if found, will benefit contributors and noncontributors alike.

The ability to collect revenue

A good that is not a collective consumption good may still not be suitable for private production if the cost of collecting revenue for individual consumers is prohibitive. Here it is not the nature of the good but the absence of an efficient private mechanism to collect revenue that leads to private-market failure. City freeway systems with many access points and many short-journey travelers are unsuitable for private ventures because the cost of collecting tolls is too high. It is no accident that virtually all toll roads are intercity roads, where relatively few access points are needed and where the average journey is a long one.

The large role government plays in multipurpose water-resource projects is explained by the fact that it alone has a mechanism for financing such projects. Suppose the privately owned Skunk Power and Light Company decides to build a dam across the Muskrat River in order to produce hydroelectric power to sell on the market. Its engineers and economists determine that the company's profits will be maximized if the height of the dam is 80 feet. When the tentative plans are announced, someone realizes that if SP&L builds a 100-foot dam instead of an 80-foot dam, it will create a beautiful lake in back of the dam, provide an emergency water supply for nearby communities, and provide flood control for 200 miles downstream. Suppose the beneficiaries of these extras would be willing to pay for them once they exist. SP&L realizes, however, that it has no effective means of charging for them.

Consider the lake. The higher dam will flood certain lands but create valuable shoreline property. The owners of this property will gain if their property fronts on the lake. Suppose SP&L says to these people, "After we create this lake you should pay us $X per year because we will have increased the value of your property." We guess the typical owner would answer, "Look, you're flooding my south forty and you want *me* to pay you? I'll sue." Because SP&L cannot capture these benefits as revenues, it decides to build the smaller dam.

If benefits are not marketable, it is likely that private producers will not be motivated to provide them. The government, however, can raise revenues by taxation. If it chooses, it can force the *beneficiaries* to pay by such means as raising the assessed value of the land whose value has been increased.

The neglect of nonmarket goals

Exclusive reliance on markets, even if they perform efficiently with respect to allocation of resources among competing uses, may lead to neglect of other goals that seem important to members of society. Consider three.

The protection of the individual. Disregard for the special needs of the feeble-minded, the ill, and the young is often regarded as a kind of market failure. In an unhindered free market, the adult members of a household would make decisions about how much education to buy and thereby exert a profound effect on the lives of their children. Selfish parents might buy no education while egalitarian ones might buy the same quantity for all their children regardless of their abilities. Society may interfere in these choices, both to protect the child of the selfish parent and to ensure that some of the scarce educational resources are distributed according to intelligence rather

than wealth. All households are forced to provide a minimum of education for their children, and strong inducements are offered —through public universities, scholarships, and other means—for gifted children to consume more education than either they or their parents might voluntarily choose if they had to pay the entire cost themselves.

In the case of education society interferes to protect children from possibly deleterious decisions taken on their behalf by others. In other cases the state seeks to protect individuals against themselves. Laws prohibiting opium and other hard drugs and laws prescribing the installation of seat belts protect individuals against their own ignorance or shortsightedness. Arguments for and against such policies go well beyond economics. Advocates of such laws say, for example, that this is one way of educating people about what is in their own best interests. Opponents often argue that it is a basic tenet of a free society that the individual must be assumed to be the best judge of his or her own interests and that the individual's right to do what he or she thinks best, even to take what may seem to others to be reckless risks of life and limb, should only be interfered with if the behavior has serious adverse effects on others.[2]

The existence of "social obligations." In a market system you can pay someone to do things for you. If you can persuade someone else to clean your house in return for $25, presumably both parties to the transaction are better off: You would prefer to part with $25 rather than clean the house yourself, and your household help prefers $25 to not cleaning your house.

---

[2] There are many other arguments. Advocates of seat belts and other compulsory safety regulations claim that disabled survivors of "unnecessary" auto accidents may become public charges and that this gives the state a right to prevent such injuries from occurring. Opponents reply that this slim possibility is not enough to justify governmental interference with individual freedom.

Normally society does not interfere with people's ability to negotiate mutually advantageous contracts if there are no external effects. Such freedom is not, however, allowed where an activity is regarded as a social obligation. Prime examples are military service in wartime and jury duty, in which if one is selected, he or she is not permitted to hire a substitute.[3]

Compassion. A free-market system rewards certain groups and penalizes others. The workings of the market may be stern, even cruel; consequently society often chooses to intervene. Should heads of households be forced to bear the full burden of their misfortune if, through no fault of their own, they lose their jobs? Even if they lose their jobs through their own fault, should they and their families have to bear the whole burden, which may include starvation? Should the ill and aged be thrown on the mercy of their families? What if they have no families? Both private charities and a great many government policies are concerned with modifying the distribution of income that results from such things as where one starts, how able one is, how lucky one is, and how one fares in the free-market world.

COPING WITH MARKET FAILURE

While private collective action can sometimes remedy the failures of private individual action, by far the most common antidote to private market failure is reliance on some form of government intervention. The central authorities have five major means for influencing the kinds of goods and services produced, how they are produced, and their distribution among the population:

1. rule making

2. giving private parties legal rights to intervene in other private parties' activities

3. use of taxes, subsidies, or penalties to change private incentives

4. making gifts and grants to households and firms with or without strings attached

5. public provision of goods and services.

Discussion of each of these five forms of government microeconomic policy occurs in this chapter and the next one.

Rule making as a tool of microeconomic policy

Rules in a multitude of forms require or prohibit certain activities. Rules require people to send their children to school and to have them inoculated against smallpox and diphtheria. Laws that prohibit abortion and pornography represent an attempt to enforce a particular moral code on the whole society. In Chapter 18, two important forms of policy-by-rules—antitrust policy and regulation of public utilities—were discussed. There are many other examples: Working conditions are regulated. Children cannot be served alcoholic drinks. Prostitution is prohibited in most places, even between a willing "buyer" and a willing "seller." Many business practices are illegal. In most states you are forced to purchase insurance for the damage you might do with your private motor car. A person who offers goods for sale, including his or her own house, cannot refuse to sell them just because of dislike for the customer's color or dress. There are rules against fraudulent advertising and the sale of substandard, adulterated, or poisonous foods.

Rule making often seems the simplest and most direct way of compelling desirable behavior in the face of market failure, but the simplicity is deceptive. Consider the requirement of the installation of a particular antipollution device to reduce automobile emissions. Such legislation may be the outcome of congressional debate on pollution control; having

---

[3] This has not always been the case; during the Civil War a man could avoid the draft by hiring a substitute to serve in his place.

passed the bill, Congress may feel it can turn to other things. But problems remain to be solved before the rule can achieve its purposes: The device may not work well unless it is kept in working order by individual drivers, yet it may not be feasible to inspect vehicles to be sure that the device is working. Even if inspection is technically feasible, the resource cost of inspection and enforcement may be prohibitive and may well have been left unconsidered in the rush to require the device. And even a well-designed rule may work only until those regulated figure out a way to evade its intent while obeying its letter.

Since regulations requiring legislative action cannot be quickly enacted or easily modified, one means to introduce flexibility into rule making is to create commissions or other agencies with substantial discretionary powers. The vast array of federal, state, and local agencies—for example, the Federal Trade Commission, the Food and Drug Administration, the Federal Communications Commission, the Civil Aeronautics Board, the Securities and Exchange Commission, the Environmental Protection Agency, state utility commissions, and local zoning boards —all reflect the faith that we have placed in delegated rule making. Whether this faith is justified is a subject of current major debate. Some, such as Professor George Stigler, believe that regulation has proven at best ineffective and at worst perverse; others, while not uncritical of some regulatory failures, see successes as well and regard regulatory agencies as a crucial means of coping with some forms of market failure.

Structuring incentives to persuade rather than to compel desired behavior

Market incentives can, in principle, always be corrected to overcome sources of market failure. Market imperfections such as ignorance can be offset by the government's providing or requiring others to provide market information. Subsidies, fellowships, and retraining can all be used to increase labor mobility.

Because the existence of externalities is a major source of market failure, much attention has been given to means of inducing decision makers to take them into account. Charging a producing firm for the pollution it causes may motivate the firm to alter its production in a way that is socially desirable. How such a charge would cope with the problem is illustrated in Figure 24–1. It reflects a situation in which a producer imposes costs on some outsiders.

Imagine a factory that spews forth fumes and smoke that adversely affect residents of the neighborhood. Suppose (to simplify our task) that we can find out from the outsiders how much compensation they require to put up with the pollution. We call this amount a measure of the external cost imposed.

As long as the firm is unaffected by these costs it will neglect them and produce too much output, for the firm is motivated to produce any unit for which the net *private* benefit is positive, even if the net social benefit is negative. If, however, a procedure is found that compels the firm to pay the full external costs, then its net benefit after paying them is the same as the social net benefit, and it is no longer motivated to produce where that is negative. Procedures that make firms bear the external costs they impose are said to involve **internalization** of the external effects of production.

There is a variety of ways to internalize external costs. If the amount of the external cost imposed per unit of output is known, it is possible to impose an **effluent charge,** or pollution tax, that compels the producer to pay a tax on every unit of polluting production. Such a charge might lead the producer to find a way to produce without polluting or else to clean up the pollution. That is a wholly acceptable alternative; presumably the producer will choose the most economical

Figure 24–1 The consequence and correction of externalities

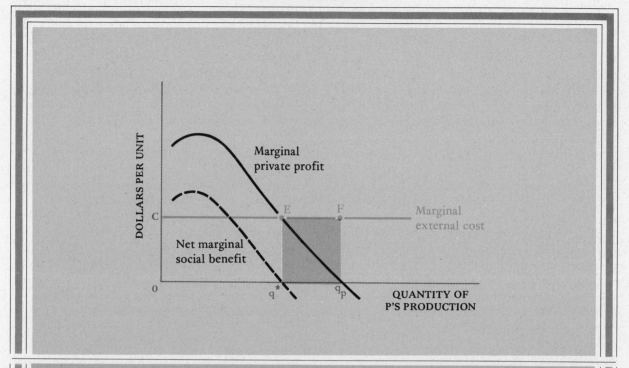

Internalizing an externality can motivate optimal behavior. The profit or loss on each unit of production (marginal private revenue *minus* marginal private cost) earned by a private firm, *P,* is shown by the solid black curve. The firm is motivated to produce all units that make a positive contribution to its profits. Its equilibrium output is q_p where marginal profit is zero. This production imposes an external cost of *$C per unit* on outsiders (call them *S*), as shown by the colored line. Subtracting this additional social cost from the private marginal profit curve yields the net marginal social benefit curve shown by the dashed black line. The socially optimal output is $q\star$ where marginal social benefit equals zero. At this output, marginal private profit is just equal to marginal external cost. (Note that the only way to avoid all the external costs is for *P* to produce nothing.) At $q\star$ the outsiders, *S*, are still having costs inflicted on them by *P*, but *S*'s costs *plus P*'s private costs are just equal at the margin to *P*'s profit from production.

Suppose the firm is required to pay an "effluent tax" of *$C per unit*. Its marginal profit curve now becomes the dashed black line. The externality has been *internalized* and the profit-maximizing firm reduces its output from q_p to $q\star$. It does this because any units produced beyond $q\star$ would now subtract from total profits: given the tax, marginal profits are negative beyond $q\star$.

response. Another way to internalize external costs is to give legal standing to private citizens to sue for damages against polluters or to seek court injunctions against polluting activities. The legal action makes it costly for polluters; there will be damage payments if they

lose and legal payments win or lose. Finally, producers may be subsidized to overcome the external damage they do and thus be motivated to avoid the pollution in order to earn the subsidy.

Unfortunately, the practical difficulties sur-

Avoiding undesirable externalities and the Coase theorem

Look again at Figure 24–1. Note that profit-maximizing producer, P, will produce q_p instead of the socially optimal output, $q^\star$. How might socially optimal output be achieved?

I. Direct determination of quantity produced

1. The government might nationalize the industry and direct it to produce $q^\star$.

2. The government might determine $q^\star$ and then try to impose that output on the private producer. This could be attempted either (a) by fining the firm heavily if its output exceeds $q^\star$ or (b) by giving the firm a subsidy if its output does not exceed $q^\star$. To be effective the fine or subsidy must exceed the profits resulting from producing beyond $q^\star$.

II. Government intervention to internalize the externality

3. The government can place an effluent tax on P of $\$C$ per unit. This forces P to take the full social costs into account and, as we saw in Figure 24–1, P is then motivated to produce at $q^\star$.

4. P can be made legally liable to compensate S. Firm P could then be forced to pay $\$C$ per unit (to S) in addition to its private costs of production. P is then motivated to produce at $q^\star$.

III. A private agreement between P and S

5. Even if P has no liability to compensate S, and even if the government does not levy a tax on P, the socially optimal result can still occur. This is because it will pay S to bribe P to produce at $q^\star$. Since every unit P produces imposes a cost of $\$C$ on S, it is worthwhile for S to bribe P any amount up to $\$C$ for every unit by which P will reduce production. Each unit produced between $q^\star$ and q_p adds less than $\$C$ to P's profits and thus P should be prepared to stop producing each of these in

return for a bribe equal to or greater than its marginal profit. Thus S can bribe P to reduce output from q_p to $q^\star$. Below $q^\star$, however, the marginal private profit to P is greater than the cost that P's production imposes on S. Thus S cannot persuade P to produce less than $q^\star$ since at outputs less than $q^\star$ the minimum bribe P would accept is more than $\$C$.

Each scheme will produce the same socially optimal output $q^\star$. Each, however, yields a different distribution of costs and benefits. We leave it as an exercise for the reader to discover how P and S would rank.

Each scheme will have a different cost of enforcement and a different probability of evasion. Each will also have a different degree of flexibility in the face of changing conditions. But, in spite of their differences, each scheme can ensure that there is an optimal quantity of resources allocated to the production of the commodity.

Professor Ronald H. Coase of the University of Chicago once put these propositions in a most startling way. He assumed that there were no transaction costs. Then, he pointed out, it does not matter which party, P or S, is fined or made legally liable for preventing an undesirable result. Since it is in their combined interest to avoid production beyond $q^\star$, it will pay them jointly to avoid the result. Therefore laws and court proceedings fixing legal liability for a vast range of events such as pollution damage, defective products, and so on may be irrelevant to efficient allocation of resources.

Critics of Coase have been quick to point out that in many cases transaction costs are not negligible, considerations of equity or income distribution are paramount, or one party is so much better able to identify and control adverse effects that the party should be made responsible on the grounds of efficiency. In these cases, laws still affect the allocation of resources as well as to the distribution of gains and losses.

rounding the use of any of these devices are substantial. Estimating appropriate per unit charges, monitoring the actual performance, and proving violations are never costless and are sometimes all but impossible. Effluent charges on industrial water pollution have been successfully used (for example, by the West German government on the Rhine). Pollution discharged into water is easily charged for because both the volume and the chemical content of a factory's discharges are easily measured. But consider the air pollution caused by the automobiles made by, say, the Chrysler Corporation. No matter how the cars are equipped, the actual discharge will depend on the way they are driven, how often they are driven, how the control devices are maintained, and the kind of fuel used. The damage done by the same chemical discharge into the air will be very different in a smog-prone area such as Los Angeles than in the Mohave Desert.

Despite the difficulties, each of these devices for internalizing externalities may be useful some of the time.

The optimal correction of market failure

The spirit of our times has led many to treat all problems of market failure, such as pollution, as a national scandal and perhaps an imminent crisis of survival. The problems of externalities in fact run the entire range from threats to our survival to minor nuisances. Virtually all activity leaves some waste product behind it; to say that all pollution must be removed whatever the cost is to try for the impossible and to ensure a vast commitment of society's scarce resources to many projects that will yield a low social value.

Control of pollution and other externalities is costly; it makes sense only where the benefits have a higher value than the costs.

Pollution control may have great benefits at first and then encounter diminishing returns.

Thus in the example of Figure 24–1 the optimal level of output was not zero even though those who bore the external cost would have liked that solution. Some instances of need for external control of undesirable externalities (e.g., control of nuclear wastes) are obvious and dramatic; others are more nearly marginal. Which activities to prohibit, which to modify, which to clean up after, and which to tolerate are important choices. In making them the economist can help by carefully designating costs and benefits. Moreover, these choices may vary among communities and over time. Poor communities may welcome new industries for the employment and tax revenues they bring, while richer ones may seek to block industries from establishing plants near them in order to avoid the unpleasant externalities they bring.

POLLUTION CONTROL

It is convenient to pull together our discussion of the problems of externalities and their control with reference to a current major issue: How and to what extent should we deal with pollution? The problem is complex for two reasons: first, pollution is not one problem but a variety of different problems of varying origin and varying severity; second, pollution is the unfortunate by-product of valuable productive activities.

Pollution did not arise in a single way, nor will it be controlled in a single way. Some pollution problems, like litter and sewage, have been long recognized and can be readily kept in control when enough resources are devoted to their remedy. Other problems, such as sulfur dioxide in the air, threaten to become serious but seem remediable in time. Others, such as the threat of DDT to the survival of the peregrine falcon, were not even suspected until a remedy was perhaps no longer available. Still others, like fluorocarbons (the propellant used in many aerosol containers), have effects that are still subject to debate, that may be hard to reverse, and that could be disastrous. It is alleged that these gases may reduce the ozone layer that protects the earth from the most harmful of the sun's ultraviolet radiations. The lag between releasing the gases and their reaching the ozone layer is more than ten years. This means that *if* the more pessimistic estimates of the destructive effects on ozone are correct, we are already committed to a long period of serious consequences that include an increase in the incidence of skin cancer—even if all fluorocarbons are never used again.

Costs of pollution

If pollution is allowed to occur, its cost is the damage that it does. If pollution is prevented, its cost is the value of what must be given up to prevent the pollution. When Chicago's sewage sludge was dumped into Lake Michigan, the costs were the damage to the lake. Later it was apparently decided that the costs of alternative disposal were less, for dumping was prohibited. At first the sludge was burned at a cost of $55 per ton (plus an unknown amount of air pollution). More recently the sludge has been shipped by train to central Illinois to enrich the soil of land reclaimed by strip miners. The cost of this form of sludge disposal is $52 per ton (minus whatever value is added to the land it fertilizes).

Aggregate costs of pollution damage are hard to estimate, but they are substantial. In 1970 the pollution damage done by sulfur dioxide alone was estimated at $8 billion. Even where pollution is easily avoided, the cost is often high. A government study released in 1973 estimated out-of-pocket air and water pollution control costs for the next decade would be roughly $25 billion per year and would result in price rises of up to 20 percent in the chief polluting industries. Clearly the

resources used for pollution control are not available for other uses.

There may be other costs as well. Armco Steel, faced with antipollution ordinances, closed eight open-hearth furnaces in Houston, Texas, because it was economically unprofitable to invest more funds in old plants. The immediate cost was the elimination of many jobs in an area where unemployment was already a problem. Allegations that jobs will be lost if tough antipollution standards are enforced are often heard, but their truth is not always easy to assess. For example, the New York State Commissioner of Commerce claimed in 1976 that New York would lose $32 million in business from the GE plant that he asserted would close if tough anti-water pollution laws were enforced; the New York State Environmental Conservation Commissioner responded, however, that "it's just a nineteenth-century fiction to say that GE will move out of the state if forced to clean up the river or restrict its discharges."

In some cases, even when there is no doubt about the outcome, loss of jobs may be accepted as a necessary price of preventing the still greater economic harm that would ensue if the pollution persisted. In other cases the very risk of losing a major employer will be regarded as too high a price to pay. For example, after a six-year campaign that brandished such slogans as "We want jobs, not fish," a coalition of business people, government officials, labor leaders, and clergy finally persuaded the federal government that proposed controls for emissions into the Mahoning River would have destroyed Youngstown, Ohio's steel industry (the town's major source of employment). Although similar water pollution practices are being prohibited elsewhere, the government finally decided to allow the Youngstown steel firms to persist in their emissions rather than risk the closing of the mills.

An important aspect of pollution control

concerns the extent to which we are willing to sacrifice economic growth and material gain for the sake of our environment. It is one thing to compel small changes in the way we allow Commonwealth Edison to produce electricity or General Motors to produce cars—even if these changes add 10 to 25 percent to the costs of products we buy. It is another thing to urge, as some have, that we should start preparing for a no-growth, constant-living-standard economy. Would the avoidance of pollution be worth the cost? It depends, of course, on the alternative, and here people disagree about the facts.

Strategies of control

In some circumstances the cheapest response to pollution is to put up with it; the cost of control is greater than the damage imposed. In other circumstances it pays to allow the pollution and then to clean up after it. It certainly is cheaper, for example, to provide trash collection services on beaches and highways than to prohibit their use. It is usually cheaper for strip coal miners to restore the land they ravage than to abandon the coal reserves.

Occasionally prohibition does seem the cheapest way out. Cleaning up after offshore oil leaks proved sufficiently costly that offshore oil drilling was suspended. When the price of oil rose sharply in 1974, a new alternative became economic: installing expensive safeguards against blowouts, which previously had not been worthwhile. Even these safeguards are not absolute guarantees against major blowouts—as the North Sea oil spill of 1977 showed.

Means of control

Virtually every type of microeconomic policy tool has been tried. Rule making in the form of requiring devices in automobiles and smokestacks and in specifying tough allow-able limits for future emissions have been used. Such rules had the effect, by 1973, of virtually prohibiting the use of high sulfur coal for electricity generation (incidentally adding to the energy crisis). Fines such as the $1 million assessed Chevron Oil for an oil blowout, the $7 million charged the Ford Motor Company for rigging its 1972–1973 pollution tests, and the $4.2 million imposed on American Motors for unlawfully selling cars in 1975 that exceeded California's strict automotive pollution control standards may be presumed to have been noticed by other firms. Lawsuits seeking damages by private parties, by conservation groups, and by lawyers on behalf of classes of affected persons are under way in every section of the country. The potential damage payments run into billions of dollars.

Many of the problems of pollution have required collective action rather than simple restructuring of private incentives. Interstate compacts to control pollution in the Great Lakes appear to have arrested the growing pollution there and even to have achieved some improvement in water quality. A convention to control dumping of poisonous wastes in the world's oceans was signed by 91 nations in November 1972, but its effects were small because enforcement was left to the individual countries. The convention, for all its pathbreaking success, stopped far short of a general antidumping policy; it covers only discharges outside the territorial limits of individual countries. In February 1976 twelve countries signed a convention to fight pollution in the Mediterranean Sea. Results cannot be assessed yet, but some control will have to come soon if the rapidly deteriorating Mediterranean is not to go the way of Lake Erie.

Although they may be major polluters themselves, governments have often taken the lead in pollution control. Government subsidies for research on pollution and grants-in-aid to private researchers represent another form of government expenditure in pollution control. Governments already provide a large fraction of all municipal sewage disposal facilities, and demands are growing for government provision of production if private producers prove unable to provide goods and services on terms that meet public standards.

ACHIEVEMENTS OF AMERICAN ENVIRONMENTAL POLICY

Protection of the American environment is under the control of the Environmental Protection Agency (EPA). This enormous agency directs among other things the nation's largest public works program: the $18 billion program of federal grants to communities to improve sewage disposal. It also administers the two most important federal antipollution laws. Under the Clean Air Act of 1970, all states have had to formulate detailed, federally approved programs for meeting federal air quality standards. Under the 1972 Water Pollution Control Act, fluid wastes can be discharged only under a state permit that either certifies compliance with federal standards or promises completion of a cleanup program by a specific date.

In spite of significant pressure during the recession of the mid 1970s to cut back on environmental spending, both to save the expenditures themselves and to assist business, the antipollution line generally seems to have been held. A recent survey concluded that "rhetoric about cutting back on environmental protection appears more prevalent than action." In January 1976, for example, machinery went into operation at U.S. Steel Corporation's vast South Works in Chicago to recycle the more than 36,000 pounds of wastes that had been flowing daily into a river that drains into Lake Michigan.

In its report published in 1976 the EPA reviewed the first five years of its operations. It noted the banning of DDT and several other pesticides that are believed to have carci-

nogenic or other harmful effects on human beings and animals. In its pollution control program it initiated some 10,000 enforcement actions—5,000 on water, 1,000 on air, and 4,000 on pesticides—and assessed more than $10 million in penalties. In turn the EPA has been sued almost daily; of 1,000 cases of litigation in which it has been involved, some 500 are still pending.

Pollution control continues to be a controversial matter. One of the most significant victories won by environmentalists in recent years occurred in April 1976 when a consortium of electric companies announced the cancellation of the projected $3.5 billion Kaiparowits power plant. The plant was to have been built in the midst of a spectacular area of southern Utah that abounds in natural wonders and contains several national parks. It was to have been the largest coal-fired electricity plant in the nation and to have supplied electricity to Arizona and southern California. The decision to abandon the scheme—attributed by the developers to the high cost of fighting the conservationists and meeting EPA regulations—represented a major victory for conservationists and could also be characterized as a significant setback for the national energy development program.

Chasing a moving target

Because population and production keep growing year after year, even the stepped-up antipollution activities of recent years have proven inadequate. In 1976 the National Wildlife Federation reported that its most recent survey had shown that the overall quality of the nation's environment had declined somewhat in the previous year. The survey covered seven aspects of environment and reported improvements in only one (air pollution), zero change in a second (timber resources), and deteriorations in the other five: water pollution, mineral reserves, wildlife, soil, and open space. Perhaps it is a major accomplishment merely to have slowed the pace of environmental deterioration. The difference between control of our environment today and control in the past is that today we increasingly recognize the problem. Recognition does not guarantee solution, but it surely must precede it.

Summary

1. The various markets in the economy are coordinated by the price system. Changes in prices often result from emerging scarcities and surpluses, leading decision makers in far-flung markets to make adaptations in response to a change in one market of the economy. But such adaptations, which are affected by prices, also help to determine the prices. It is this general interrelation that is the great insight of general equilibrium analysis.

2. The case for the free market is that it provides an efficient and impersonal way of making the almost infinite number of decisions that an economic system must make about what to produce and how to distribute the fruits of production. Markets work well to serve society's needs when marginal social and private valuations are nearly the same, for then private producers pursuing private goals serve public goals as well. This is often, though not always, the case.

3. A market economy consists of thousands of interrelated markets. Anything important that happens in one market will have major spillout effects on some other markets and could conceivably have repercussions in every other market of the economy. These effects may then feed back onto the original market.

4. Market failure may occur for a variety of reasons: (a) differences between private and social valuation, (b) market imperfections, (c) the existence of collective consumption goods, (d) the inability or high cost of private producers collecting revenue from private users, and (e) the neglect by private producers of nonmarket goals.

5. Microeconomic policy concerns activities of the central authorities that alter the unrestricted workings of the free-market system in order to affect either the allocation of resources among uses or the distribution of income among people.

6. Major tools of microeconomic policy include (a) rule making, (b) legal arming of private parties to intervene in other parties' activities, (c) structuring of private incentives by taxes, subsidies, or penalties, (d) making of gifts or grants, and (e) public provision of goods and services. None is without its uses or its limitations.

7. Externalities lead to market failure and invite correction. But externalities are worth correcting only if adverse effects exceed benefits. A balancing can be achieved if external costs and benefits can be included along with internal ones in the determination of optimal outputs. Thus devices such as effluent charges that internalize external costs may lead private producers to avoid market failure.

Concepts for review

The difference between central planning and market coordination
How the price system coordinates
Differences between private and social valuations
Impact, spillout, and feedback
Partial and general equilibrium analysis
Causes of market failure
Externalities
Internalizing externalities
The optimal amount of pollution

Discussion questions

1. For each of the following events indicate some sectors that would feel impacts, some subsequent spillouts to other sectors, and any potentially important feedback that might require general equilibrium analysis.
a. The quadrupling of coffee prices by Brazil.
b. The decision of an automobile manufacturer to build a large assembly plant employing 5,000 workers near a town with only 11,000 total population, situated 40 miles from the nearest city.
c. Promulgation of rules requiring, and taxes encouraging, much greater gasoline economy of motor cars.

2. The president of Goodyear Tire and Rubber Company complained that government regulation had imposed $30 million of "unproductive costs" on his company per year. These costs of compliance were broken down:

environmental regulation	$17
occupation safety and health	7
motor vehicle safety	3
personnel and administration	3

Discuss how to determine whether these costs were "productive" or "unproductive."

3. Develop the case for (or against) government interference in the areas of education, medicine, airport construction and location, egg production, logging, electricity generation, and the location of a privately financed toll highway. Which of these do you think least suitable for government action?

4. Can you think of any grievance that a large group of the population might have that would not warrant government action? How does economic analysis help decide policy questions of this sort?

5. Consider each of the following. What portion of the cost ought the beneficiaries to bear? In each case give the basis for any subsidy.
a. urban mass transit fares
b. abortions on demand
c. plastic surgery for victims of fires
d. garbage collection
e. postal service to newspapers and magazines
f. police protection for political candidates
g. fire protection for churches

6. Suppose the facts asserted below are true; should they trigger government intervention? If so, what policy alternatives are available?
a. The Concorde jet is twice as fast, twice as noisy on take-off and landing, and carries half the passengers of jumbo jets.
b. Hospital costs have been rising at about four times the rate of increase of personal income, and proper treatment of a serious illness has become extraordinarily expensive.
c. The cost of the average one-family house in Washington, D.C., is now over $70,000, out of the reach of most government employees.

d. Cigarette smoking tends to reduce life expectancy by eight years.
e. Saccharin in large doses has been found to cause cancer in Canadian mice.

7. While public goods and private goods are sometimes treated as alternatives, they are often complementary. Providing roads, for example, provides a key input to private production of truck and bus services. Provide a few more examples. Can you give some examples where private and public goods are really substitutes for one another?

8. Consider the possible beneficial and adverse effects of each of the following forms of government interference.
a. Charging motorists a tax for driving in the downtown areas of large cities—and using the revenues to provide peripheral parking and shuttle buses.
b. Prohibiting doctors from purchasing malpractice insurance.
c. Mandating no-fault auto insurance, in which the car owner's insurance company is responsible for damage to his or her vehicle no matter who causes the accident.
d. Requiring automobile manufacturers to warrantee the tires on cars they sell, instead of (as at present) having the tire manufacturer be the warrantor.

9. Consider the problem of motorcycle noise pollution. What is the "optimal level of permissible noise"? How might it be determined? A given level of noise permitted might be achieved in a variety of ways; name several, including at least one that does not regulate the motorcyclist in any way. Which is the fairest way? Which is the most effective way?

10. Consider the following (alleged) facts about pollution control and indicate what, if any, influence they might have on policy determination.
a. In 1976 the cost of meeting federal pollution requirements were $47 per person.
b. More than a third of the world's known oil supplies lie under the ocean floor, and there is no known blow-out proof method of recovery.
c. Sulfur removal requirements and strip mining regulations have led to the tripling of the cost of a ton of coal used in electrical generation.
d. Every million dollars spent on pollution control creates 67 new jobs in the economy.

Public finance and public expenditure

Microeconomic policy is those activities of the central authorities that alter the unrestricted workings of the free-market system in an effort to affect either the allocation of resources among uses or the distribution of income among people. Such an abstract definition may sound like nothing on earth and certainly like nothing on the floor of the U.S. Congress. Yet a review of preceding chapters provides examples of many specific microeconomic policy issues: the discussions of price controls and agriculture in Chapter 7, of public policy toward monopoly and the regulated industries in Chapter 18, of policies toward alleviating poverty in Chapter 23, and of policies with respect to pollution and other external effects in Chapter 24. Two primary policy tools are the power to tax and the power to spend. These are treated in this chapter.

Public finance and taxation

The main purpose of taxes is to raise the money needed to finance government expenditures. But taxes necessarily have other effects. By changing relative prices of goods, taxes affect what is produced and how. By taking more income from some groups than others, taxes can change the distribution of income. Policy makers, aware of these effects, often use tax structure as a policy tool to affect the allocation of resources or to redistribute income. There is a bewildering array of taxes in the economy, some highly visible (such as sales taxes and income taxes) and others all but invisible to the consumer because they were imposed on raw materials producers or manufacturers at an early stage. People are taxed on what they earn, on what they spend, and on what they own. The variety and importance of various kinds of taxes are illustrated in Table 25–1.

Table 25–1 Federal, state, and local tax receipts, by source

Kind of tax	FEDERAL		STATE		LOCAL		ALL GOVERNMENT	
	Billions of dollars	*Per-centage*	*Billions of dollars*	*Per-centage*	*Billions of dollars*	*Per-centage*	*Billions of dollars*	*Per-centage*
Personal income	122.4	40	18.8	16	2.6	3	143.8	28
Corporate income and related	40.6	13	6.6	6		0	47.3	9
Social Security and related	80.5	27	17.9	15	2.2	2	100.6	19
Subtotal (income related)	243.5	80	43.3	37	4.8	5	291.7	56
Excise and sales	21.1	7	43.3	37	6.5	7	70.9	14
Property	0.0	0	1.5	1	50.0	51	51.5	10
All others	38.0	13	28.7	25	36.5	37	103.1	20
Total	302.6	100	116.8	100	97.8	100	517.2	100

Source: *Facts and Figures on Government Finance,* 19th Biennial Edition (New York: Tax Foundation), 1977.

The federal government places major reliance on income taxes; state governments on excise and sales taxes; and local governments on property taxes. Different levels of government rely on different kinds of taxes. The most important are highlighted by the percentages printed in color. The data are for fiscal year 1975.

TAX POLICY AND THE DISTRIBUTION OF INCOME

The capacity to influence the distribution of income by tax policy can be readily seen in a few statistics. The federal government collected more than $300 billion in taxes in 1975 roughly half of that from individuals. The states and municipalities collected another $200 billion. Altogether an amount equal to roughly one-third of the total national income is taxed each year. Clearly a government that chooses to tax the rich and exempt the poor can have an effect on the distribution of income. An important economic question is the extent to which it does; this involves both the effect on income distribution of particular taxes and of the tax system as a whole.

The concept of progressivity

Rhetoric about income distribution and tax policy often invokes the important but hard to define concepts of "equity" and "equal-ity." Equity—fairness—is a normative concept; what one group thinks is fair may seem outrageous to another. But equality is a straightforward concept—or is it? To tax people equally might mean several things. It might mean that each person should pay the same tax, which would be very hard on the unemployed worker and very easy on Walter Cronkite. It might mean that each should pay the same proportion of his or her income, say a flat 25 percent, whether rich or poor, living alone or supporting eight children, healthy or suffering from a disease that requires heavy use of expensive drugs. It might mean that each should pay an amount of tax such that everybody's income after taxes is the same—which would remove any incentive to earn above average income. Or it might mean none of these. Instead of dealing in "equal-ity," which is vague, the distributional effects of taxes are usually discussed using the concept of **progressivity of taxation.**

A tax is *proportional* if it takes amounts of

money from people in direct proportion to their income.

A tax is *regressive* if it takes a larger percentage of income from people, the lower their income.

A tax is *progressive* if it takes a larger percentage of income from people, the larger their income.

A tax system is said to be progressive if it tends to decrease the inequality of income distribution and to be regressive if it increases it.

It is easier to assess the progressivity or regressivity of particular taxes than of the tax system as a whole.

The regressivity of sales and excise taxes

If two families each spend the same proportion of their income on a certain commodity that is subject to a sales or an excise tax, the tax will be proportional in its effects on them. If the tax is on a commodity (such as food) that takes a larger proportion of the income of the lower-income families, it will be regressive; if it is on one (such as jewelry) where the rich spend a larger proportion of their income than the poor, it will be progressive.

Commodities with inelastic demands provide easy sources of revenue, and in many countries commodities such as tobacco, alcohol, and gasoline are singled out for very heavy rates of taxation. But these commodities usually account for a much higher proportion of the expenditure of lower-income than higher-income groups, and taxes on them are thus regressive.

While a set of excise taxes might be either regressive or progressive, many studies leave no doubt that the sales and excise taxes of the kind in use in the United States today are as a whole regressive.

The regressivity of property taxes

The progressivity of the property tax has also been studied extensively. It is well known that the rich live in more expensive houses than the poor, but all that this establishes is that the rich tend to pay more dollars in property tax than do the poor. Because the rich tend to live in different communities than do the poor and thus pay taxes at different rates, and because they tend to spend a different proportion of their income for housing, the question of the progressivity or regressivity of the property tax is difficult and controversial. Most studies have shown that the proportion of income spent for housing tends to decrease with income. Many but not all public finance experts believe that the property tax tends to be regressive in its overall effect.

The progressivity of personal income taxes

The personal tax rate is itself a function of taxable income, and it is useful to distinguish between two different rates. The **average tax rate** paid by an individual or by a couple is their income tax divided by total income. The **marginal tax rate** is the amount of tax the taxpayer would pay on an additional dollar of income.

Table 25–2 shows the applicable rates on federal income tax in 1976, and Figure 25–1 shows the fraction of taxable income paid in taxes.

In structure, the federal personal income tax is highly progressive because the average rate rises steadily with income. However, because of the special definitions given to net income by the tax laws, the overall effect of the federal income tax is actually less progressive than Table 25–2 suggests. To arrive at taxable income, total income is modified by certain exemptions from income, by capital gains provisions, and by a variety of permitted deductions from gross income. Moreover, income earned by personal services, as distinct from property, is subject to a maximum marginal tax rate of 50 percent, instead of the 70 percent shown in the table.

Despite modifications, the federal income tax is progressive in effect as well as in structure.

The unknown progressivity of corporate income tax

The federal corporate income tax is, for practical purposes, a flat-rate tax of 48 percent of profits as defined by the taxing authorities. It is difficult to determine its effects on income

Table 25–2 The rate structure of the federal income tax, 1976

(1) Taxable income after deductions and exemptions	(2) Personal income tax	(3) Average tax rate, percentage (2) ÷ (1)	(4) Marginal tax rate, percentage (tax on extra dollar)[a]
$ 1,000	$ 140	14.0	15
2,000	290	14.5	16
3,000	450	15.0	17
4,000	620	15.5	19
8,000	1,380	17.2	22
16,000	3,260	20.4	28
32,000	8,660	27.1	42
44,000	14,060	32.0	50
52,000	18,060	34.7	53[b]
88,000[b]	31,020[b]	35.3[b]	60
100,000	45,180	45.2	62
200,000	110,980	55.5	70
500,000	320,980	66.0	70
1,000,000	670,980	67.1	70
10,000,000	6,970,980	69.7	70

[a] The marginal tax rate on personal service income is limited to a maximum of 50 percent.
[b] For incomes above $52,000, actual taxes and tax rates will be less than the amounts shown if part of the income is earned by personal services.

Both marginal and average tax rates rise with income; thus the tax is progressive in structure. These data give the amount of federal tax to be paid at different income levels by a married couple in 1976. The marginal tax rate rises with income and reaches 50 percent at $44,000. However, these rates are based on taxable income, not total income, received. Because of a variety of deductions and exemptions, the effective average tax rates on income received are much lower than those shown in column (3).

Figure 25–1 Federal income tax, married couple filing joint return, 1976

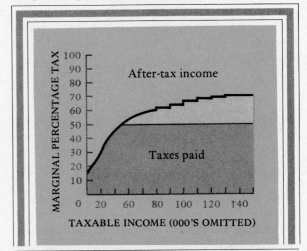

MARGINAL PERCENTAGE TAX

After-tax income

Taxes paid

TAXABLE INCOME (000'S OMITTED)

The marginal rate of tax rises sharply for the first $50,000 of taxable income, and more slowly thereafter to a maximum of 70 percent. For any level of taxable income, the maximum amount of taxes paid is the shaded area under the heavy black curve. If all income is personal service income, the tax is only the darker shaded area. The progressivity of the income tax decreases sharply after an income level of $88,000 is reached.

distribution, for there is great controversy over the extent to which it is "shifted" to consumers.[1] So far as the tax falls on stockholders, they as a group tend to be wealthier than individuals who do not own stock, and there is thus a tendency toward progressivity. But within the stockholder group, lower-income stockholders bear a disproportionate share of the tax relative to wealthy stockholders. If a dollar were paid out in dividends instead of taxes, the rich stockholders would keep a much smaller share than the poorer

[1] The question of tax incidence—that is, who really pays a tax imposed on one group—is discussed later in this chapter.

stockholders because of their high marginal personal tax rates. Thus rich stockholders sacrifice less after-tax income when the corporation tax is imposed—they bear a tax that is a lower fraction of their income than do lower-income stockholders.

The progressivity of the tax system

To assess the way in which the whole tax system, as distinct from any one tax, affects income distribution is more difficult. One aspect concerns the mix of taxes of different kinds. Federal taxes (chiefly income taxes) tend to be in aggregate somewhat progressive. State and local authorities rely heavily on property and sales taxes and thus have tax systems that are regressive. In Florida and Connecticut, which have no state income tax, the overall tax burden is less progressive than it is in Wisconsin and New York, each of which has a large state income tax.

But the matter of assessing progressivity is even more complex. An example will suggest why. Single people often complain about tax exemptions given to married couples for children. They may say, "Why should I pay part of the cost of children that are, in any case, only contributing to the world's disastrous population explosion?" Whatever one thinks about the population explosion, one can ask whether the single person is correct in believing that the tax system discriminates in favor of married couples with children. Certainly a household with children pays less income tax than a household with the same income but no children, and less than a single person with the same income. But this is not the whole story. A sales tax on food, for example, tends to fall more heavily on a large family than on a small one. Any tax on expenditures falls less heavily on one who saves some income (and thus the burden depends on ability or willingness to save). Whether the tax system as a whole favors married couples is a matter of empirical study, and the answers are not yet known.

The difficulty of determining progressivity is increased by the fact that income from different sources is taxed at different rates. For example, in the federal individual tax, income from royalties on oil wells is taxed more lightly than income from royalties on books; profits from sales of assets (called capital gains) are taxed more lightly than wages and salaries; and some bond interest is tax exempt while most interest income is taxed. To evaluate progressivity, one needs to know the way in which different levels of income correlate with different sources of income.

The combined effect of all U.S. taxes, federal, state, and local, is virtually proportional today for families with incomes between $5,000 and $50,000 and progressive only above $50,000. For very low-income families, the tax structure is regressive. If the purpose of the tax structure has been to be neutral with respect to the overall income distribution, it has been a success. If its purpose has been to be an instrument of general redistribution from rich to poor, it has not achieved its objective.

The negative income tax proposal

There are many versions of **negative income tax (NIT)** proposals; the one described here will illustrate the basic idea. The underlying belief is that a family of four should be entitled to a minimum annual income—say, $3,200. The aim is to guarantee this income level without eliminating the incentive to become self-supporting. This is done by combining a grant with a tax. Below some level of income the family is paid by the government (i.e., pays a "negative tax"). At some higher level it breaks even (it neither receives money from the government nor pays any tax), and above this break-even level it pays a positive tax. An example, based upon a marginal negative tax rate of 50 percent, is illustrated in Table 25–3.

The supporters of the negative income tax stress these principal advantages:

1. A minimum level of income becomes a matter of right, not of charity.

2. It promises to wipe out the most pressing aspects of the problem of poverty.

3. As a potential replacement for many other relief programs, it promises to aid the poor with much less administrative cost, without the indignity that often accompanies relief, and without the myriad exceptions that are involved in most programs.

4. It does not remove the incentive to find work. Most existing relief programs reduce the benefits of recipients dollar for dollar if they earn income. The NIT makes it worthwhile financially to find work and to raise one's income so that a positive tax is paid.

5. It removes whatever incentive people might have to migrate to states with better welfare programs, but it does not discourage migration to places where work may be available.

The net cost of such a scheme would depend on which other programs of aid to the needy were curtailed and on the effect on the incentives of those covered. Current estimates of the cost of the plan described here are about $8 billion a year. Obviously this program does not guarantee the elimination of poverty at a stroke. To institute the same type of program with a basic income of $5,000 for a family of four (just below the poverty level) would cost much more: approximately $30 billion per year as currently estimated.

The overall progressivity of government policies

Looking at *tax* progressivity alone may be misleading. A regressive tax (say a sales tax) may be used to provide funds for increasing welfare payments to the needy and thus end up redistributing income to the poor. But this is not the whole story; government expenditures include more than welfare payments. Expenditures for schools, highways, defense,

Table 25–3 One version of the negative income tax with 50 percent marginal tax rate

(1) Family income	(2) Tax	(3) Family income after tax (1) − (2)
$ 0	$−3,200	$3,200
800	−2,800	3,600
1,600	−2,400	4,000
2,400	−2,000	4,400
3,200	−1,600	4,800
4,000	−1,200	5,200
4,800	− 800	5,600
5,600	− 400	6,000
6,400	0	6,400

Instead of having a zero income tax up to some level and a positive tax thereafter, there is a continuous variation of tax with income. Under this plan a family with no income is entitled to $3,200. For every dollar the family earns between $0 and $6,400, its receipts from the government are reduced by 50 cents. Column (2) shows the "tax" at different levels of income. Column (3) shows the total income available for spending. The "break-even" income is $6,400, at which the family neither receives a grant nor pays a tax. On incomes above $6,400, taxes are paid.

and the space program and pay for civil servants are large parts of total expenditures, and they increase the demand for scientists, technicians, carpenters, and others already relatively well off. Such expenditures probably have the effect of redistributing income from the poor to the middle- and upper-middle-income recipients.

The overall effect of all government policies on the distribution of income is currently unknown, but it is being studied. Economists now recognize it as a more interesting question than simply assessing the progressivity of the tax structure. This is illustrated by the fact that two leading policy alternatives being discussed for alleviating poverty are, first, raising government welfare expenditures and, second, utilizing a negative income tax. The same effect on income distribution can be accompanied by very different effects on progressivity of the *tax* system.

TAX STRUCTURE AND THE ALLOCATION OF RESOURCES

The American tax system influences the allocation of resources by changing the *relative* prices of different goods and factors and the relative profitability of different industries and different uses of factors of production. These, in turn, affect resource movements.

How much do taxes affect prices, and are all taxes the same in this respect? What is the effect, for example, of the taxes now imposed on producers of luggage, or automobiles, or gin? Do such taxes leave prices unchanged, or do they cause prices to rise? Does the producer pay the tax or pass it along to the consumer through higher prices? Issues of this kind are discussed in detail in public finance courses; in this chapter we introduce the question by looking at the problem of **tax incidence;** that is, who really pays the taxes that are levied? The incidence of the tax system is the aggregate of the incidence of the taxes individually. We shall examine a few representative taxes.

The incidence of an excise tax in a competitive industry

An **excise tax** is one that is placed on the sale of a specific commodity. A common form is for the producer to be charged so many dollars on each unit produced. This is called a per unit or a **specific tax.**[2] Examples include

[2] Another common form is for the tax to be a fixed percentage of the value of the commodity—an **ad valorem tax.** There is, for example, a 10 percent federal tax on wagers and an 8 percent tax on airfare on domestic flights.

Do landlords or tenants pay the property tax?

Landlords characteristically protest that the crushing burden of property taxes makes it impossible for them to earn a reasonable living from renting buildings to tenants who abuse the property. Tenants typically reply that landlords shirk their responsibilities for building maintenance and that the whole burden of the tax is passed on to the tenants in the form of higher rents. Both sides cannot be right in alleging that they each bear the whole burden of the tax! They are arguing, of course, about the incidence of the property tax.

To examine the incidence, suppose that the city imposes a property tax and each of the thousands of landlords in the city decides to raise rents by the full amount of the tax. The theory of demand predicts that there will be a decline in the quantity of rental accommodation demanded as a result of the price increase. Higher rents will induce some city dwellers to move outside the city limits (where rents for equivalent accommodations are now relatively lower) and will also induce some of those who stay to economize on space now that it has become more expensive. The decline in the quantity demanded without any change in the quantity supplied will cause a surplus of rental accommodations at the higher prices. Landlords will find it difficult to re-

federal taxes of $4.00 per thousand on cigarettes, 7 cents per gallon on jet fuel, and $10.50 per gallon of 100 proof spirits.

The effect of excise taxes can be shown using a simple supply and demand analysis.

place tenants who move out, and the typical unit will remain empty longer between tenancies. Prospective tenants will find many alternative sites from which to choose and will become very particular in what they expect from landlords.

Some prospective tenants, seeing vacant apartments, will offer to pay rents below the asking price. Some landlords will accept the offer rather than earn nothing from vacant premises. Once some landlords cut their rentals, others will have to follow suit or leave their properties unrented for long periods of time. As the rent received by landlords falls, there will be a supply reaction. There will be a movement down the supply curve when, for example, some homeowners become less willing to rent out parts of their homes. More important, there will be a shift of the supply curve. When apartment buildings are replaced (as they are continuously in a big city), it will not pay to build them quite as high as before. This shift in supply prevents the price from falling to its pretax level.

Eventually rentals will reach a new equilibrium at which the quantity demanded equals the quantity supplied. This equilibrium will be higher than the original pretax rent but lower than the rent that passes the whole tax on to the tenants. Thus the burden of the tax is shared by landlords and tenants.

Notice that this result does not depend on who writes the check to pay the tax bill. In many European countries, the tenant rather than the landlord is sent the tax bill and pays the tax directly to the city; even in this case, however, the landlord bears part of the burden. As long as the existence of the tax reduces the quantity of rented accommodations demanded below what it otherwise would be, the tax will depress the amount received by landlords, and in this way landlords will bear part of its burden.

Notice also that this result emerges even though neither landlords nor tenants realize it. Because rents are changing for all sorts of other reasons, neither of them is likely to have much idea of what equilibrium rentals would be in the absence of the tax. It does not do much good just to look at what happens immediately after tax rates are changed, because, as we have already seen, landlords may begin by raising rents by the full amount of this tax. Although they think they have passed it on, this creates a disequilibrium, and in the final position prices will have risen by less than the tax.

The supply schedule of a competitive industry shows the relation between the price that producers get for their product and the total amount that all suppliers are willing to produce and sell. If no tax is levied, sellers receive the whole market price for which the commodity is sold. If a specific tax is levied, on each unit sold, however, sellers will receive the market price of the commodity *minus* the amount of the tax. If the producers are to receive the same amount per unit as they were receiving before the tax, the market price will have to rise by the full amount of the tax.

Assuming that the willingness of sellers to supply the commodity is unchanged, then, after a tax has been levied, every quantity supplied will be associated with a market price higher by the full amount of the tax than the one previously required. This is illustrated in Figure 25–2. Graphically, the effect of a tax on a commodity is to shift every point on the supply curve vertically upward by the amount of the tax.

What happens to price depends on demand as well as supply. As long as the demand curve slopes downward and the supply curve upward, the imposition of a tax will raise the

Figure 25–2 The incidence of a specific tax

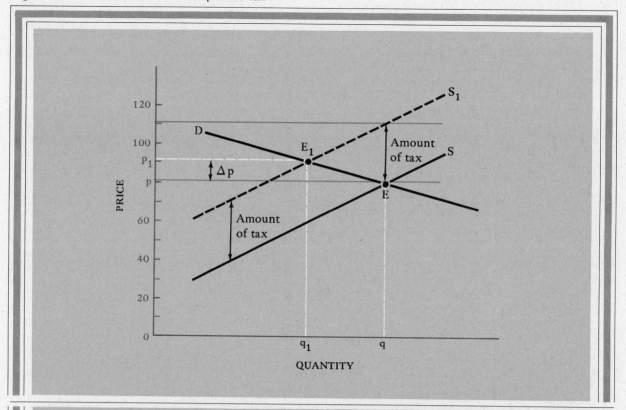

When equilibrium price rises by less than the amount of the tax, part of the tax burden is borne by producers. The supply schedule S reflects producers' willingness to supply goods. For example, at $p = \$80$, they will supply q units. Now a tax of $30 per unit is imposed on producers. In order to keep $80, the firm must charge $110. The supply curve shifts by the full amount of the tax up to S_1. Equilibrium shifts from E to E_1 and the equilibrium price rises from p to p_1. This increase, from $80 to $90, is less than the full amount of the tax. If the price had risen to $110, there would have been an excess of quantity supplied over quantity demanded.

price paid by the consumers and lower the price received by producers, in both cases by less than the amount of the tax.

The incidence of an excise tax falls partly on producers and partly on consumers.

The shapes of the demand and supply curves affect the proportions in which the tax incidence falls on producers and customers. At the extremes, if the demand curve is vertical, all of the tax can be passed on; if it is horizontal, none of it can be. For a given demand curve, the more steeply the supply curve rises, the less the equilibrium price will rise as a result of a tax, and thus the more will the incidence fall on a producer. (We suggest that you draw a series of diagrams to satisfy yourself that these assertions are correct.)

The incidence of license fees and other lump-sum taxes

In many cities and states you must purchase an annual license to drive a truck, operate a liquor store, or do dry cleaning. What effect do such taxes have? A moment's thought will show that such taxes increase the *fixed* costs of the firm but do not increase *marginal* costs.

The effect of such a tax is different under conditions of perfect competition and of monopoly. Because the tax increases fixed costs (by the amount of the tax) but not marginal costs or marginal revenues, the short-run profit-maximizing level of output cannot be affected in either competition or monopoly. Hence a modest lump-sum tax leaves price and output unchanged in the short run. Initially the full incidence of this tax is on the producer. (Of course a lump sum might be so high that it causes the producers to abandon the business at once.)

In the long run the tax also has no effect on a monopolist's price and output. Assuming that the monopolist was previously making profits, the tax merely reduces the level of these profits. Because the monopolist was making as much money as possible before the

tax, there is nothing that it can do to shift any of the tax burden onto its customers. If the monopolist raises prices in an attempt to pass the tax on to its customers, this will have the effect of reducing profits still further because it will move the firm away from the profit-maximizing level of output.

In the case of perfect competition the tax *is* expected to affect price and output in the long run. If the industry was in equilibrium with zero profits before the tax was instituted, then the tax would lead to losses. Although nothing would happen to price and output in the short run, equipment would not be replaced as it wore out. Thus, in the long run, the industry would contract, the supply curve would shift up, and price would rise until the firms remaining in the industry were again covering costs. At this point the whole tax burden had been passed on to consumers.

Notice that the long-run incidence falls wholly on consumers and is exactly opposite to the short-run incidence, which falls wholly on producers! This is the sort of thing that makes figuring out tax incidence in the real world so difficult.

The incidence of the corporation income tax

Evaluating the incidence of the corporation income tax is difficult because the definition of profits for tax purposes is not the same as that of the economist's pure profits. (See page 161 if you have forgotten this distinction.)

A tax on pure profits. Economic theory predicts that a general percentage tax on pure profits will have no effect on price or output, and thus the full incidence of such a tax will fall on producers. To see this quickly, suppose that one price-quantity combination gives the firm higher profits (without considering taxes) than any other. If the government imposes a 20 percent profits tax, the firm will have only 80 percent as much profits after tax as it had before; *this will be true for each possible level of output.* The firm may grumble, but it will not pay it to alter its price or output. Furthermore, such a tax can never force a firm to shut down because there is no tax liability unless the firm is earning profits. If profits are zero, so are taxes, and the firm is covering all its opportunity costs.

Notice that the argument of the previous paragraph is independent of the tax rate. [24] It applies equally if the tax rate is 10 percent or 75 percent.

A tax on corporation income. American corporate income taxes are taxes on profits as defined by the tax laws. The definitions make them a tax on a combination of pure profits plus some of the return to capital and risk taking.

Because such a profits tax will have the effect of reducing the returns to these important factors of production, it can have significant effects on the allocation of resources and on the prices and output of goods. The taxing authorities define profits in such a way that risk premiums are excluded from cost and included in profits. Suppose a risky industry requires, say, a 10 percent return on its capital to make owners willing to take the risk involved in investing in the industry. Suppose that the industry is earning 15 percent on its investment before taxes. A 50 percent corporate income tax will reduce the return to $7\frac{1}{2}$ percent, below the point that makes investment attractive, and resources will leave the industry. Obviously price and output changes will occur. As firms leave the industry, and as supply decreases, prices will rise until the remaining firms can earn a sufficient level of after-tax profits so that they are once again compensated for the risks involved. Thus customers must bear part of the burden of the tax through a price increase.

The theory predicts that a tax on pure profits will have no effect on the price and output policy of firms and thus will be borne by producers. But a tax on profits, as they are defined by the taxing authorities, will have a definite effect on prices and outputs and thus will be shared by the consumer.

The incidence of personal income taxes

Personal income taxes are the largest source of tax revenue in the United States today, and virtually every wage earner is aware of the withholding of this tax from his or her paycheck. Surely, one would think, the tax on personal income is born directly by the taxpayer. Not necessarily!

The theory of distribution predicts that labor will move between industries and occupations until net advantages, including both monetary and nonmonetary gains, are equalized. Income taxes affect the relative wages of occupations with different proportions of untaxed benefits (such as long vacations, use of expense accounts, ample fringe benefits, and pleasant working conditions). By so doing they will lead to changes both in the labor supply in different industries and in the relative prices of different goods and services that use different factors in different proportions.

Consider, for example, the case in which occupation A (e.g., garbage collection) pays $250 a week but has no nonmonetary advantages while occupation B (e.g., milk delivering) pays $200 a week but offers nonmonetary advantages valued at $50 a week. Without an income tax, the two occupations are equally attractive to new entrants to the labor force. Now suppose a tax of 20 percent is imposed on money income. Garbage collecting yields $200 a week take-home pay and $200 total advantages. Milk delivering yields $160 a week take-home pay and $210 total advantages. Relative total advantages have changed, and some people who would have become garbage collectors will now try to become milk deliverers, thereby causing a decrease in supply and a rise in wages in garbage collection and an increase in supply and a fall in wages in milk delivering.

Thus part of the burden of the income tax is shifted from the workers remaining in garbage collection to those who were originally milk deliverers. Ultimately, as a result of the change in relative wages, there will be a fall in the price of milk relative to the price of garbage collection, and this will trigger other changes in behavior.

The overall allocative effect of the tax structure

How different is the bill of goods produced as a result of tax policies? This is another question that economists are studying but have not yet succeeded in answering definitely.

The tax structure is often deliberately used to change incentives and thus to affect resource allocation. At the same time it may have effects that are quite unintended. One way in which tax structure affects resource allocation is by allowing deduction of some expenditures from income before computing the amount of taxes payable. Every $100 spent by a wealthy family in the 70 percent marginal tax bracket on an item that is tax deductible costs only $30 in after-tax income. Every $100 they spend on items that are not tax deductible costs the full $100 in after-tax income. Interest payments for a mortgage are, in the U.S. tax code, tax deductible, while payments for rental housing are not deductible. This encourages home ownership by lowering the cost of buying a house relative to the cost of renting one. The incentive to home owning was probably intended, but an incidental result is that the incentive effect is much less for a poor person than for a rich one. The value of the deduction for interest is much greater to someone in the 70 percent marginal tax bracket than to someone in the 20 percent bracket. If a bank charges each of them 7 percent interest, the richer person really pays only 2.1 percent interest; the poorer one pays 5.6 percent interest. Thus the relative advantage given to owning over renting rises as income rises—or, put the

other way around, the lower one's income, the less the incentive given to obtain a property stake in the society. This is surely an unintended effect.

Public expenditure as a tool of micro policy

In recent years, expenditures by federal, state, and local government units in the United States—i.e., in the public sector—have amounted to about 30 percent of the nation's expenditures. Defense, international relations, education, and social security are the largest items; collectively they amount to about half the total. Public welfare, highways, and interest on the public debt, although frequently mentioned, add up to only another 15 percent of the total. The remainder covers everything else, from police protection and sanitation to general administration of government and space research. About two-thirds of the expenditure is made by the federal government, 20 percent by local governments, and the rest by states.

TYPES OF GOVERNMENT EXPENDITURE

Table 25–4 shows the size and changing importance of different types of federal government expenditures. Until 1974 the largest category of federal expenditures (and still the dominant type for state and local government expenditures) was for provision of goods and services that the market fails to provide or is not allowed to provide. Foremost among these (in volume of expenditure) are the defense and defense-related activities of the federal government, but expenditures on police services, education, roads, conservation, and urban redevelopment are similar in character. In these activities the government acts like a firm, using factors of production to produce outputs. It is producing them rather than

Table 25–4 The changing form of federal expenditure

	PERCENTAGE OF TOTAL			AMOUNT (BILLIONS OF 1972 DOLLARS)[a]			
	(1)	(2)	(3)	(4)	(5)	(6)	(7)
							Increase
Type of expenditure	1955	1965	1975	1955	1965	1975	1955–1975
Purchases of goods and services	65.3	54.4	34.5	89.5	102.0	95.8	6.3
Transfer payments to domestic persons	18.2	24.4	40.9	24.9	45.9	113.7	88.8
Grants-in-aid to state and local governments	4.6	9.0	15.2	6.2	16.8	42.2	36.0
Net interest paid	6.8	6.8	6.6	9.3	12.7	18.3	9.0
All other[b]	5.1	5.4	2.8	7.1	10.2	7.7	0.6
Total	100.0	100.0	100.0	137.0	187.6	277.7	140.7

Source: *Economic Report of the President, 1977.*

[a] Using implicit price deflators for government purchases of goods and services.
[b] Includes transfer payments to foreigners and net subsidies of government enterprises.

Transfer payments to persons and grants-in-aid to state and local governments have been steadily growing in importance. Federal government expenditure has more than doubled (in constant dollars) since 1955, and virtually all of the increase has been in transfer payments and grants-in-aid, as column (7) shows.

leaving them to the free market because the people acting through their state legislatures, Congress, and city councils, have decided that it should. They are responding to the various sources of market failure discussed in Chapter 24. By and large these outputs are of collective consumption goods, of goods with strong externalities, or of services whose benefits are not marketable.

Although such purchases of goods and services are large, as the table shows, they have remained roughly constant in real terms in the last twenty years and have been overtaken by transfer payments as the largest form of government expenditure. Transfer payments and grants-in-aid have been steadily increasing in importance, and together they account for virtually all of the growth in real government expenditure in recent decades. They each require a closer look. What are they, and why have they been growing so rapidly?

Federal transfer payments to individuals

Transfer payments generally are defined as payments to private persons or institutions that do not arise out of current productive activity. (They do not include intergovernment transfers.) Welfare payments are transfers; so, too, are social security payments, pensions, veterans' benefits, fellowships, unemployment insurance, and Medicare payments. Some federal transfers are made to foreigners as part of aid programs. Some transfer payments are private, such as private pensions and charitable contributions by individuals and corporations. Many are made by state and local governments, often using funds they have received as federal grants-in-aid. The greatest part, which we consider here, are paid by the federal government to individuals.

The bulk of these transfer payments are part of public income-maintenance programs:

in 1976 roughly $150 billion was spent for such programs. Of this, over $70 billion was in the form of old-age, survivors, disability, or health payments to 33 million beneficiaries under the social security system. Other large amounts were payments of railroad and public employee retirement pensions (over $25 billion) and veteran's compensation ($12 billion). Federally paid public assistance payments amounted to over $16 billion. Unemployment benefits (under state supervision, but using federal funds) were over $17 billion in 1975.

The growth of these payments reflects several things. First, the coverage and level of social security (including Medicaid and Medicare) is steadily increasing. Second, the attention to reducing poverty, discussed in Chapter 23, has been responsible for much of the increase. Third, the heavy unemployment of the early 1970s has greatly increased unemployment compensation payments. Unemployment benefits were $17.4 billion in 1975 compared with $2.3 billion in 1969.

The percentage of all family income received in the form of government transfer payments has increased sharply, from under 5 percent in 1955 to 7 percent in 1965 and to more than 13 percent in 1975. Not all of this is the giveaway that critics of the "welfare state" sometimes charge; much of it reflects past payments of social security taxes and pension contributions by persons who are the beneficiaries. But much of the increase is a response to efforts to alleviate poverty and reduce income inequality.

Because of the commitments of the Carter administration and the Democratic Congress, it seems likely that the upward trend in the size of transfer payments will continue over the next several years.

Grants-in-aid and the crisis of the cities

In addition to the federal government there are 50 state governments, 3,000 county governments, 8,000 municipalities, and 17,000 townships. Further, there are about 20,000 districts for schools and another 20,000 for miscellaneous purposes such as sewage. Each of the more than 80,000 governmental units spends public money, and each must get the money to spend. Not all units have equal access to revenue, and this fact necessitates both division of responsibilities and intergovernmental grants-in-aid.

Grants-in-aid are of two general types: categorical and general. At present, 85 percent of all federal grants are **categorical grants-in-aid,** that is, for specific categories of assistance such as highways, education, and welfare payments. Not only are such grants restricted as to use, but they usually require some degree of state or local matching. General grants-in-aid without restriction or matching requirements are now called **revenue sharing.** They were negligible until 1972. The initial program ran from January 1972 to December 1976 and distributed $30 billion. Revenue sharing is as yet only a small part of the total of grants-in-aid, but most experts expect that revenue sharing will increase and categorical assistance decrease in relative importance in the next decade.

Grants-in-aid from federal to state and local governments have been among the most rapidly increasing forms of public expenditures. Between 1955 and 1965 such grants increased (in real terms) by 170 percent, and between 1965 and 1975 they increased by another 150 percent. Overall they were nearly seven times as large, in constant dollars, in 1975 as they had been twenty years earlier. (Over the same period *total* federal expenditure approximately doubled.) This growth is a response to a growing inability of state and local communities to manage their finances. It is important to understand why. Since the problem is most acute at the local level, we shall focus on the problem of the cities, but similar considerations apply (to a lesser degree) to states.

Despite a trend to more prosperity in the country generally, the growing fiscal crisis of local governments may be viewed as the product of three forces: (1) the fact that tax revenues of local governments are relatively unresponsive to growth in average income, (2) the rapidly rising quantities of local government services required, and (3) the rising cost per unit of providing these services. Together they contribute to local governments' steadily worsening financial situation and their demand for federal assistance.

Tax revenues. Income taxes tend to provide revenues that increase somewhat faster than average income. The larger the percentage of

Should higher education be subsidized?

Governments often provide goods and services that they produce at a price that is well below total costs. The case against the practice of providing free or subsidized goods and services is that the public is encouraged to consume the good or service to the point where the utility from the last unit consumed is low—indeed, in the case of a good provided free, it is zero. This means that resources are being used whose marginal utility is less than the value of other goods that could have been produced instead.

The case for free or subsidized provision was previously suggested. Some public goods are difficult or impossible to sell on a market. Thus, if they are to be provided at all, they must be provided free. In other cases, important third-party effects make it desirable to encourage a level of consumption beyond what the individual household would voluntarily choose if it had to pay the full cost itself. While there are some relatively uncontroversial cases such as providing free milk in schools attended by poor children, or general free elementary education, the case for subsidizing college and professional education is controversial.

The facts are clear—higher education, both private and public, is heavily subsidized. Relatively few institutions, public or private, recover as much as 60 percent of their costs from student fees. Most private institutions and all public ones receive major amounts of public support in addition to private endowments.

The question does not concern the need for scholarship and loan funds for poor but deserving students, but instead asks how much subsidy, independent of need, should be provided.

Supporters of heavy subsidization argue that the whole society gains from the widest possible spread of education and that it is in the general interest to encourage more education than people would voluntarily choose on the basis of their own self-interest. The economic payoff to society of investments in human capital has been studied extensively. These studies show that education is productive in the sense of producing enough extra output later to compensate for the sacrifice of current output required to provide the education.

Critics of the present system accept the evidence but ask why the general public (a majority of whom are not college graduates) should subsidize others to obtain an investment in human capital that is a good investment from their own selfish points of

income raised by income taxes, the stronger is the fiscal position of the government unit as income rises. While 81 percent of federal tax receipts and 37 percent of state tax receipts today come from income taxes, only 5 percent of local taxes are so raised.

Local governments cannot readily increase their reliance on income taxes. As the percentage of personal income taken by the federal government has grown, the resistance of taxpayers to higher taxes of any kind has grown—and this is especially true of further taxes on income. Many state and local governments have tried to impose (or increase) income taxes; however, the electoral defeats of officials who advocated these taxes, and the interstate and intercity competition to attract people and industries by having lower taxes than neighboring jurisdictions, have severely limited the amount of additional revenue that state and local governments have been able to raise in this way.

State and local governments thus rely heavily on property, sales, and excise taxes. Revenues from these taxes rise more slowly than income in the short run, and in the long run they rise only at the same rate as the income levels *of the population in their jurisdictions*. In many of the largest cities average income is actually falling because of the movement of many higher-income families to the suburbs and the higher unemployment rates in the cities. As a result many local governments' revenue yields are decreasing on a per capita basis. This worsening revenue position is accentuated as an increasing proportion of urban property is devoted to public service functions and thus taken off the tax rolls.

view. After all, say the critics, those who get the education will earn the higher incomes their education permits. Let them borrow the money if necessary.

Education is, of course, more than an investment in future production, and this can cut either way: a stay at a university may be valued by the student because of cultural or social reasons or because it saves the student the necessity of deciding what to do next; each of these reasons argues against subsidy. But education may also provide the nation with a generation that is better trained and better able to cope with pressing social problems than the previous one, and this might justify a subsidy.

There is no general rule as to the appropriate degree of subsidy; the case for and against providing a commodity at less than cost varies greatly with the nature of the commodity and the externalities conferred by having more of it than the market would provide. It also depends on other uses of the money. Thus today, as most states face tough budgetary decisions, they are tending to raise the proportion of the cost borne by the students—that is, to decrease the subsidy—by rapidly raising tuition levels.

The rising demand for government services. State and local government expenditures have been rising more rapidly than their residents' incomes. One reason for this is the high income elasticity of demand for city services. As societies become wealthier, their residents want more parks, more police protection, more and better schools and colleges, and more generous treatment of their less fortunate neighbors. This alone, combined with the limited tax sources available, would create budgetary problems for local governments in a period of rising incomes and rising expectations—a fact that many mayors have learned the hard way. Taxpayers increasingly want the social services that governments provide, but they do not want to accept the taxes required to pay for them. Elected officials arouse the people's wrath if they fail to provide wanted programs, but they also do so if they provide the services and then raise taxes.

A second and more important rise in the quantity of local government services required has to do with the changing character of central-city populations and the increased demands for local government expenditures associated with these changes. The outward migration from the cities to the suburbs has been highly selective: It has consisted predominantly of the wealthier members of the community and has led to ever-increasing proportions of low-income groups in the central cities. This in turn has led to more poverty, more crime, and more demand for the public services to cope with them.

The rising relative cost of local government services. Government services tend to use much labor of a kind whose productivity (output per man-hour) has increased much less rapidly than its cost. Thus cost per unit of output has risen. While the national average of output per man-hour in manufacturing has risen over 50 percent in the last decade, the size of the beat covered by a police officer, the number of students taught by each schoolteacher, and the number of families that can be effectively handled by a social worker have not risen in proportion. Because wage levels tend to rise with national average productivity, the costs of services in the low-productivity sectors have soared.

Rising costs per unit and rising quantities of local government services have combined to lead to an increase in local government expenditures that is much more rapid than the rise in tax revenues.

Overall it is estimated that, on average, state and local expenditures have risen at 1.67 times the rate of increase of national income. Much of the rising level of federal contributions to

state and local government is a response to this problem. That it has not been solved was made clear by New York City's fiscal crisis of 1975, by the sharply worsening plights of Philadelphia, Chicago, Detroit, and other cities, and by the urgency with which the nation's mayors have pressed the Carter administration for vastly increased federal programs.

COPING WITH THE URBAN CRISIS

How does a problem become a crisis? When it does, can the crisis be resolved? Not all cities have the same problems; some have had ample reserve sources of taxable income and wealth on which to fall back, other cities have not had such reserves. What causes the problems in the first place?

The economics of urban decay

The selective flight to the suburbs (and beyond) that has triggered the urban crisis is a function of many things—among them, different preferences of different groups in the population, rising incomes, and sometimes prejudice. If one seeks to understand why it is that more and more families choose to trade the traditional advantages of the big city for cleaner neighborhoods, safer streets, and whiter schools, it is helpful to explore the dynamics of suburban migration. Much of this can be understood in economic terms. The scenario that follows suggests some causes of the urban crisis.

The flight of the wealthy. As the relatively wealthier residents of a densely populated city find their incomes rising, they choose increasingly to spend some of their extra income on bigger houses, more spacious lots, and tree-lined streets. Very high real estate prices in the central cities make extra space a luxury, but low-cost land just outside the central cities beckons. The savings on this land more than compensate for costs involved in commuting to work or coming to town to shop or to be entertained. Thus suburban communities begin to be formed. As more of the upper-income residents move out, the concentration of lower-income residents in the city increases.

The disenchantment of the middle classes. The services required by the poor are of a different type from those sought by the middle class. More money goes to welfare, social work, and police, and less goes to civic symphonies, schools, parks, and amenities. At the same time, the average income per capita that is subject to taxation declines as the relatively wealthy move beyond the reach of city tax authorities. Remaining middle-class residents discover that they are paying more taxes but receiving fewer services of the kind they value. They find the museums closed, the park toilets unclean, and the civic swimming pools keeping shorter hours. Their schools curtail the "frills" in the curriculum, such as interscholastic athletics, foreign languages, and music and art. Their children's teachers are increasingly burdened with larger classes and with more disciplinary problems. Life in the city costs more but offers less.

Meanwhile the housing vacated by the migration from the top of the income distribution tends to be converted to cheaper housing as three or four families move in where one used to live. It also becomes run down because it does not pay landlords to maintain it at its former standard. If the poor are black or Chicano, their increasing presence in the schools, the streets, and the parks does not go unnoticed by the whites.

Upper-middle-class residents who remain will see their tax burdens rising, their neighborhoods becoming more crowded, the older sections of "their" city deteriorating, the racial composition of their schools changing, and the crime rate increasing. Some will move into more expensive neighborhoods or send their children to private schools, but

more and more will discover that they too can flee to the suburbs. People find that it is not too expensive to move into communities that are made up of people like themselves, who share their tastes in how to spend money, in what to demand from the schools, and in the pride of having painted houses and manicured lawns. To such people (who of course would deny they had a shred of racial prejudice) the cost of commuting does not seem too high to pay for all of that!

Shifting employment opportunities. Many discover that they do not even have to commute, for jobs move out to the suburbs, too. Stores and banks follow their customers, first by establishing branches in suburban shopping centers, later by actually closing the central-city branches. Clerical, custodial, and unskilled jobs are thus available outside the city. Industry, too, has moved outward, partly because of an available labor force, partly because the federally supported interstate highway system and a burgeoning trucking industry give suburban plants the ready access to their suppliers and markets that formerly only the inner-city rail centers provided. Industry also moves to avoid rising taxes. (In the 1960s, three-fourths of all new industrial expansion in the United States occurred in the suburbs.)

The inner city becomes a ghetto. While the jobs go, not all the workers follow. Many inner-city residents, held together by the bonds of race, language, or poverty as well as by lack of cars and lack of middle-class aspirations, stay put. Unemployment increases, more families need welfare, housing deteriorates further, clean streets seem less important—and, of course, the tax base continues to shrink.

A reform mayor raises the sales tax or proposes a city income tax and finds that these measures only hasten the exodus. At this stage the city may actually be underpopu-

Ford to City: drop dead*

New York City did not die during its fiscal crisis of 1975, despite the reluctance of the Ford administration to provide federal aid, but it came close to bankruptcy. (President Ford, for his part, lost an election in 1976 that he would have won had he carried New York State.) Many of New York's problems arose from the scenario described in the text, and in this way the city was not unlike many others in the world.

But New York had—indeed has—problems that made it particularly vulnerable. Some of these were not its fault. (1) New York City has long been the point of entry and settlement of immigrants to America. In recent decades the "huddled masses" from Europe have been replaced as in-migrants by Southern blacks and Puerto Ricans. It is not New York City policy but U.S. policy that encouraged over a million Puerto Ricans to come to New York and caused dramatic changes in the city's population. Between 1970 and 1975 the white population *decreased* by 600,000 while the nonwhite *increased* by over 100,000. Because the new New Yorkers were characteristically poor, undereducated, and often non-English speaking, they added extraordinary costs to the city's welfare, school, and other programs. (2) The widespread unemployment—well over 25 percent among the New York nonwhite population—that led to burgeoning welfare rolls (over a million

residents on welfare during 1975) reflects failures of *national* policy. (3) OPEC's price rises for oil hit the East Coast cities harder than most cities because they are more heavily dependent on imported oil. (4) More of New York City's real estate belongs to the state and federal governments or to religious and educational institutions than is true of most other cities. This property is tax-exempt by *federal* law that deprives the *city* of nearly a billion dollars of vitally needed tax revenue a year.

New York City also contributed a lot to its own problems. Its budgetary deficits reflect a generosity—some would say extravagance—that more than matched its pocketbook. Its levels of welfare benefits were among the nation's highest. Its per capita cost for higher education (three times the national average) was due to a university system (CUNY) featuring open admission and free tuition for 190,000 students. CUNY's large faculty received compensation at the very top level of university salaries in the country. The city's 400,000 municipal employees received an average of $16,000 a year in base pay and cost the city an additional $11,000 in fringe benefits. This $27,000 average cost per employee is well above the levels for similar employees in most other cities. Public hospitals, public housing, and public transit were generously funded although these are regarded as discretionary functions for a city government. Not only were the budgets for such functions high; during the early 1970s they were rising at over 10 percent per

---

* Page one headline, *New York Daily News,* October 30, 1975.

year, twice the average of 27 other large cities. The growing budgets, unmatched by revenue increases, led to persistent and growing deficits. The 1975 deficit was a staggering $800 million.

Cities, unlike the federal government, cannot spend more than they raise in taxes, receive as gifts, or borrow, for they cannot print money. Cities borrow for three reasons, two of them responsible: (1) to finance long-term capital investment projects such as schools or hospitals, (2) to smooth out seasonal fluctuations in the patterns of expenditures and receipts, and (3) to cover current account deficits. The third is irresponsible and unacceptable to bondholders because the revenue to repay the bonds is nowhere provided for. Yet this is precisely what New York did, by a series of fiscal tricks and strategems, from 1960 on. By 1975 it had $12 billion in bonds outstanding, of which at least a quarter represented a hidden accumulation of current account deficits. As these bonds came due, money was needed to repay the bondholders, but there was no current surplus available. The obvious solution: borrow even more. Rumors of trouble led to the downgrading of city bonds and made investors unwilling to buy new issues to replace the old. Default seemed imminent.

The city, in desperation, looked to state and federal governments for loans to meet the crisis and borrowed from its employees' pension funds. President Ford's no to the city's appeal for help was soon modified and both state and federal loans were made. These averted default, but only after the city had agreed to budget cuts and increased taxes. These "prudent" budgetary measures did not solve the long-run problems. Expenditure cuts and layoffs increase unemployment and therefore increase welfare costs. Cuts in police services, in schoolteachers, and in garbage pickup only add to the exodus of middle-class people caused by the decline in quality of life; promises of tax increases lead ever more of the wealthier individuals and business firms to leave the city.

While the city's past forms of fiscal irresponsibility and budgetary largesse have been brought under control, the basic problem remains unchanged: out-migration continues, the city becomes less rich, less clean, and less safe every month. Both wealthier former residents and potential visitors spend their money elsewhere. As these things happen the city becomes ever less able to balance its own budget. Without a long-run solution another crisis is inevitable.

Is there a long-run solution? Many believe that only a recognition that welfare and unemployment are *national* problems to be solved or paid for nationally offers cities like New York any hope. In November 1976 New York City bonds rose sharply in price and outstanding unsold issues were snapped up. This reflected investors' expectations that the new Carter administration would assume federal responsibility for these problems. We shall see.

lated. Existing residents abandon the worst neighborhoods as they deteriorate—and move on to and begin the cheapening of more expensive housing. The worst slums may become homes for new immigrants from rural areas, the South, or Puerto Rico, or they may be abandoned and begin to crumble. Rats, disease, crime, and decay spread.

The cry for help. The city has passed the point of self-help—only a massive dosage of money will help, but those who are left cannot pay. The city may be able to borrow if its taxpayers approve the taxes needed to pay bond interest or if the banks will lend it money. But the smaller tax base limits the amount it is possible to borrow. The city recognizes that it can recover its tax base if it can annex suburban areas, but those who have escaped the city's problems reject the overtures for annexation, and their political influence in the state governments is sufficient to prevent forced annexation. The city itself, hopeless, now tries to persuade the state or federal government to channel funds to it. Substantial funds are required simply to maintain the status quo, and programs for urban reconstitution or reconstruction must contend with other demands on public budgets. The cities get some help, but it is too little and too late.

However bleak this story may seem, it comes close to representing the plight of many American cities today.

Policy alternatives

One might attack urban decay by channeling efforts and funds into rebuilding the city itself. Alternatively, one might attack the problems of poverty, unemployment, and prejudice that contribute so heavily to urban deterioration. Present programs are of both kinds. Welfare payments, although channeled through state and local governments, are payments to the poor who happen to live in the cities. Grants for slum clearance, roads, and school construction are for the cities themselves.

The potential conflict of interest is perhaps most clearly seen in urban renewal slum-clearance projects, which have proved more effective in forcing slum dwellers out of sight than in providing better housing for the poor. In Chicago, for example, urban renewal has destroyed three housing units for every one created. While it has much improved the lot of the upper-class white residents of Hyde Park, it has worsened life in the black ghetto.

Currently half a dozen plans for meeting the crisis are under discussion. A great expansion in unconditional revenue sharing would give revenues to state and local governments on a per capita basis, in effect making residents of wealthy states and rich suburbs pay part of the costs of areas densely populated by the poor. How much revenue sharing money has reached the hardest hit areas is not clear, for much of it was channeled through state governments that see other needs to be as important as those of the cities. An alternative approach favored by many is increasingly to federalize aid to the poor wherever they reside by guaranteeing a minimum family income sufficient to permit escape from slum conditions. Others hope to provide this minimum income not by grants to individuals, categorical or otherwise, but by manipulation of the tax structure—specifically by introducing a negative income tax.

It is one thing to prevent the utter collapse of major cities; it is another to *solve* their problems. However it is to be done, it will require both money in massive amounts and a degree of ingenuity in spending the money effectively. What is *not* clear is whether the search for a solution is very high on the list of national priorities.

EVALUATING GOVERNMENT EXPENDITURES

The existence of collective consumption goods (and all the other reasons given in Chapter 24 that may motivate public provision of goods) along with the presence of seemingly intractable problems of urban decay make it apparent that certain problems will not be solved without government expenditure. But will government expenditures do the job? Part of the public's current disenchantment with proliferating government programs is that many of them, while goodhearted, seem ineffective and wasteful. Even if the objectives can be achieved, there remains the basic question of whether a particular activity ought to be provided at all—and if it should, how much money should be devoted to it. In a world of scarcity, many things must be left undone. The question of whether a program of public expenditure, whose potential effectiveness is not in doubt, should be approved involves several more specific questions.

Absolute merit: do benefits exceed costs?

As a purely formal matter, the appropriate test for a given project is, first, that the value of its total benefits exceed its total costs and, second, that the project be expanded to the point where the marginal benefit equals the marginal cost. There is a clear analogy to the maximizing rules for the private firm that should undertake an activity if total revenues exceed total costs and increase the activity until $MR = MC$.

Beyond this formal solution is the question, often a very difficult one, of deciding what *are* the benefits, what are the costs, and how to measure them. At its peak in 1966, the federal government's space program was spending $6 billion per year. Ten years later space expenditure was a minor budgetary item. How should one estimate what the benefits of space research are, and whether they were worth $6 billion in 1966? The federal government had developed techniques of evaluation, called Program Planning Budgeting Systems (PPBS), designed to provide estimates of benefits and costs in order at least to see whether the former exceed the latter. But the example of space research suggests why benefit measurement fundamentally in-

volves issues of concept rather than accounting: it concerns not whether we put men on the moon but whether that feat was worth the billions it cost.

Relative merit of public and private expenditures

How do we know if the country has the right balance between the public and private sectors? It is possible that there should be more schools and fewer cars—or more cars and fewer schools.

Because automobiles and houses are sold on the market, consumer demand has a significant influence on the relative prices of these commodities, and through prices on the quantities produced and thence on the allocation of the nation's resources. This is true for all goods produced and sold on the market. But there is no market that provides relative prices for automobiles versus public schools; thus the choice between allowing money to be spent in the private sector versus spending it for public goods is a matter for direct decision by Congress and other legislative bodies.

John Kenneth Galbraith is the best known and most articulate exponent of the view that we systematically starve the public sector. His best-seller *The Affluent Society* (1958) proclaimed the message that a correct assignment of marginal utilities would show them to be higher for an extra dollar's worth of expenditure on parks, clean water, and education than for an extra dollar's worth of expenditure on the television sets, deodorants, and blenders that we buy in such large quantities only because of advertiser-created wants. It is such things that would have to be sacrificed to obtain the additional output in the public sector. In this view, the political process often fails to translate preferences for public goods into effective action; thus more resources are devoted to the private sector and fewer to the public sector than would be if the political mechanism were as effective as the market.

The opposite view has its supporters. James Buchanan and Roland McKean, for example, argue that society has already passed the point where the value of the marginal dollar spent by the government is greater than the value of that dollar left in the hands of households or firms that would have spent it had it not been taxed away. They argue that decision makers in the public sector habitually use much lower expected rates of return in evaluating possible lines of expenditures than do businesses. If firms, for example, are so short of capital that they have unexploited investment opportunities yielding, say, 20 percent while the public sector only expects a 7 percent return on its investments, it follows that the market value of goods sacrificed in the private sector exceeds the market value of the corresponding goods produced in the public sector. The opportunity cost of public expenditures thus exceeds the benefits.

This debate is not readily settled on a scientific basis because of the difficulty of measuring benefits when the things produced (e.g., clean air or the preservation of the Everglades) are not readily marketable.

The appropriate size of government

The debate over whether the marginal public project has a higher value (as Galbraith believes) or a lower value (as Buchanan believes) than the resources could produce in the private sector has obvious consequences for the size of government. Those holding the first view want a bigger role for government than those holding the second.

A different, though closely related, issue concerns the size of the government as such, quite independent of particular projects done or left undone. Some think it should be kept down, believing that its rise portends a slide toward socialism or serfdom. Others think it clearly too low because, left to themselves, consumers are too crass and materialistic and will choose to consume in the private sector too many of society's resources—resources that might better be devoted to the public welfare or saved for future generations. Gov-

ernments, they feel, can protect people from their greed and ignorance.

Many of the views are neither finely reasoned nor scientifically determined, but they may be very real. A Gallup poll in 1976 revealed that Big Government ranked just behind Unemployment and Inflation as the answer to the question, What's wrong in America today? Thirty-nine percent gave that response. In another survey, 56 percent believed *more* rather than less government expenditure for regulation of economic activities was required.

A first point to recognize in evaluating such apparently inconsistent views is that the aggregate budget of the public is spent on a variety of items, some of which seem unnecessary to each person, but different people or groups have different lists of items.

The budget for the public sector is built up by approving particular projects. Piecemeal decisions are made on social security increases, federal aid to housing, national defense, the space program, national parks, and the budget of a state university. It does not help practical policy to say simply, the size of the government sector must be reduced (or increased) by 20 percent; it is necessary to decide which 20 percent must go or be added. Often the proponents of a program are more articulate, better informed, or better organized than the opponents.

Much of the debate about the size of the government rests on different views of how decisions are made. There is often an implicit theoretical structure that leads to the prediction that the way in which politicians will change the size of government will itself affect living standards, welfare, or some other economic goal.

The conservative view. Budgetary conservatives feel that the whole political process tends to be wildly wrong in judging the absolute efficiency with which it can do any job. They argue that benefit-cost comparisons may be a satisfactory method for choosing among public expenditure projects but not for comparing them to private alternatives. Government economists and legislators, in this view, do a good job on the question *which* but not on the question *whether*. They point to the fact that there are many legislators who want to economize on public expenditures until they come to a project that will be built in their own state or district. Logrolling is the name given to trading votes in order to assure a majority in support of *your* project.[3] This kind of bias, they believe, explains why there are nearly three million federal employees and almost twelve million more in state and local governments. They urge cutting overall budgets first and only then considering what items to cut.

The liberal view. A very different position is held by many budgetary liberals. They will concede that there may be waste and even corruption in government expenditure, but they argue that there is much merit, too. They have a low opinion of the budgetary process; they believe Congress does a *poor* job in comparing, say, education (undervalued) with defense (overvalued), space exploration (glorified) with poverty (tolerated), and subsidies to farmers (wasteful) with expenditures on medical research (needed). They believe that if Congress cuts the budget, it will not find the waste, nor will it curtail expenditures on defense, space, or agriculture, but will further starve health, education, and welfare. Because they distrust the budgetary process, they oppose all general cuts in the budget and usually support increases; they are willing to have legislators spend many billions for defense if that is the price needed to persuade enough of them to spend some billions for human needs.

[3] A classic illustration of logrolling was the 1964 Water Resources Research Bill, which provided federal support in establishing 50 Water Resource Research Centers, one in each state, regardless of the size of the state or the urgency of its water-resource problems.

An overview of microeconomic policy

We have been looking at the role of the government in the market economy throughout the microeconomic part of this book. Now, at the end, let us pause for perspective. One of the most difficult problems for the student of the U.S. economic system is to maintain his or her perspective about the scope of government activity in the market economy. There are literally tens of thousands of laws, regulations, and policies that affect firms and households. Many feel that a significant amount of deregulation could be accomplished and would be beneficial.

But private decision makers still have an enormous amount of discretion about what they do and how they do it. One pitfall is to become so impressed (or obsessed) with the number of ways in which government activity impinges on the individual that one fails to see these as only small changes in the market signals and constraints under which decision makers operate within a system that basically leaves them free to make their own decisions. In the private sector of the economy, most individuals choose their occupations, earn their livings, spend their incomes, and live their lives. In this sector, the firm, too, is formed, chooses its products, and lives, grows, and sometimes dies.

A different pitfall is to fail to see that many, and perhaps most, of the highly significant amounts paid by the private sector to the government as taxes also buy goods and services that add to the welfare of the individual and the society. By and large the public sector complements the private sector, doing things the private sector would leave undone or do very differently. To recognize this is not to deny that there is often waste, and sometimes worse, in public expenditure policy. Nor does it imply that whatever is, is just what people want. Social policies and social judgments evolve and change.

Yet another pitfall is to fail to recognize that the public and private sectors compete in the sense that both make claims on the resources of the economy. Thus government activities are not without opportunity costs, except in those rare circumstances in which they use resources that have no alternative use.

The policies in operation at any time are not the result of a single master plan that specifies precisely where and how the public sector shall seek to complement, help along, or interfere with the workings of the market mechanism. Rather, as individual problems arise, governments attempt to meet them by passing ameliorative legislation. These laws stay on the books, and some of them become obsolete and unenforceable. This is true of systems of law in general. As a result, it is always possible and often easy to find outrageous examples of inconsistencies and absurdities in any system. A distinguished professorship at Harvard gives its incumbent the right to graze a cow in Harvard Yard. Laws still exist that permit the burning of witches. Neither is enforceable. Many anomalies exist in our economic policies; for example, laws designed to support the incomes of small farmers have created some agricultural millionaires, and commissions created to assure competitive results may be instead protecting monopolistic ones. Neither individual policies nor whole programs are above criticism.

In a society that elects its policy makers at regular intervals, however, the majority view on the amount and type of government interference that is desirable will have some considerable influence on the interference that actually occurs. Fundamentally, a free-market system is retained because it is valued for its lack of coercion and its ability to do much of the job of allocating society's resources. But we are not mesmerized by it; we feel free to intervene in pursuit of a better world in which to live.

Summary

1. Two of the most powerful tools of microeconomic policy are taxation and public expenditure.

2. While the main purpose of taxes is to raise revenue, they represent a means both to change incentives and to redistribute income. Tax policy is potentially a powerful device for income redistribution because the progressivity or regressivity of different kinds of taxes varies greatly. Federal taxes are, overall, progressive because of their heavy reliance on income taxation; state and local taxes are, on balance, regressive, particularly because of their heavy reliance on property and sales taxes.

3. The total American tax structure is roughly proportional except for very low-income groups (for whom it is regressive) and very high-income groups (for whom it is progressive). Considering both government expenditures and taxes, the public sector is thought to be progressive in its overall effect on income distribution.

4. Evaluating the effects of taxes on resource allocation requires first determining tax incidence—that is, determining who really pays the taxes. For most taxes, the incidence is shared. Excise taxes, for example, affect prices and are thus partially passed on, but part is absorbed by producers. The actual incidence is complex and depends on such economic considerations as demand and supply elasticities.

5. Tax policy can affect the allocation of resources by changing the relative attractiveness of different kinds of expenditure. It can do this by changing the relative prices of goods through a system of sales or excise taxes, and it can do it by allowing certain deductions or exemptions from income as it is defined for tax purposes.

6. A large part of government expenditure is for the direct provision of goods and services which are provided free or at nominal cost. Defense, education, and highways are important examples. This is a response to the various sources of private-market failure discussed in Chapter 24.

7. Transfer payments to persons are a large and growing part of total government expenditure. They play a major role in modifying the distribution of income and serve greatly to mitigate the problems of income inequality and poverty in the country.

8. Grants-in-aid from federal to state and local governments reflect the capacity of different government units to

raise revenue relative to their expenditure needs. State and local governments find that their revenue sources grow no more rapidly than average income, but the cost of the services they must provide increases much faster. To avoid deficits they require access to the funds raised by federal income taxes.

9. The urban crisis is in large part a result of the selective migration of residents to the suburbs and out of reach of the urban taxing authorities. Such migration develops a dynamic that feeds itself, and increasingly central cities have become havens for the poor, with rising needs and a shrinking tax base.

10. Currently there are two types of legislation for aid to the cities: (a) aid to the cities themselves, in the form of grants-in-aid for specific purposes or general revenue sharing and (b) aid to the poor, who account for so much of the urban population.

11. Evaluating public expenditures involves reaching decisions about absolute merit (do benefits exceed costs?), about the relative merit of public and private expenditures, and about the desirable size of government.

12. The U.S. economy is a mixed economy and a changing one. Each generation faces anew the choice of which activities to leave to the unfettered market and which it will use public expenditures or taxes to encourage or repress.

Concepts for review

Progressivity and regressivity of individual taxes and of the tax system
Negative income tax
Tax incidence
The need for grants-in-aid to state and local governments
Sources of the urban crisis
Choosing between private and public expenditures

Discussion questions

1. The American taxpayer is assaulted by dozens of different taxes with different incidence, different progressivity, and different methods of collection. Discuss the case for or against using at most two different kinds of taxes. Discuss the case for a single taxing authority that would share the revenue with all levels of government.

2. Under federal tax law, municipal bond interest is tax exempt. Who benefits from this provision? What are its effects on the distribution of income and the allocation of resources?

3. "A tax on energy consumption is bound to be regressive; the advocacy of such a tax by the Carter administration shows that it has forsaken its pledge to be the protector of the consumer against the monied interests." Evaluate this statement. Who would benefit and who lose if instead of a 25 percent tax on energy use, producers raised prices by 25 percent?

4. Classify each of the following programs as "transfer payment," "grant-in-aid," "purchase of goods and services," or "none of the above."
a. payments of wages and family living allowances to soldiers serving overseas
b. unemployment insurance payments to unemployed workers
c. payments to states for support of highway construction
d. a negative income tax
e. pensions of retired Supreme Court justices
f. the corporate income tax
g. moving allowances paid to foreign service personnel

5. "Taxes on tobacco and alcohol are nearly perfect taxes. They raise lots of revenue and discourage smoking and drinking." In this statement, to what extent are the two effects inconsistent? How is the incidence of an excise tax related to the extent to which it discourages use of the product?

6. How might each of the following affect the incidence of a real estate property tax imposed on central city rental property?
a. The residents of the community are largely blacks who face racial discrimination in neighboring areas.
b. The city installs a good, cheap rapid-transit system that makes commuting to the suburbs less expensive and more comfortable.
c. The income tax laws are changed to eliminate the deductibility of property taxes from taxable income for those who itemize deductions.

7. Under the federal tax laws, all state and local income taxes can be deducted from income in computing the federal tax liability. Suppose two local communities each impose a 10 percent tax on personal incomes. Richville is

composed of families who earn $100,000 per year or more. Uniontown consists mainly of workers' families earning about $10,000 per year. Who really pays the taxes in each case? What, if anything, prevents Richville from raising its taxes?

8. What issues are involved in deciding whether federal grants-in-aid to state and local governments should be categorical grants or general revenue sharing with no strings attached? How—if at all—does this issue differ from that raised in Chapter 23, question 4?

9. Comment on each of the following with respect to New York's urban crisis.
a. Ron Nessen, then President Gerald Ford's press secretary: "New York's financial problem is not a natural disaster or an act of God. It is a self-inflicted act by the people who have been running New York City."
b. Governor Hugh Carey of New York: "We need only recognition by the Federal Government that we are part of this country, and that we are suffering because of the economic distress in this country."
c. John Portman, Atlanta developer: "There really is no investor interest in New York, and that's basically the problem."
d. George McGovern: "If the U.S. can give economic aid to our former enemies in Vietnam, why should it deny it to our troubled cities?"

10. If governments tend to step in when markets fail, why are not similar functions performed similarly in different countries? Medical care, sport fishing rights, steel production, broadcasting, telephone service, and garbage collection are provided publicly in some Western countries and privately in others. What accounts for the diversity?

11. Evaluate each of the following statements about the role of government in the economy.
a. "Big government, not big business, is this country's problem. We are convinced that government should not try to perform economic functions that the market-place performs more efficiently and more equitably. In our view, the proper and most productive role of government lies in balancing off various national needs, formulating policies, setting objectives, establishing appropriate incentives to the private sector to achieve those objectives, monitoring progress toward objectives, and, perhaps most important, providing leadership."
b. "Social spending threatens our way of life. If social spending continues at the same rate as it has over the last 20 years, by the year 2000 half the people of this nation will be living off the other half."
c. "It is private spending that has gone unchecked in an orgy of mindless consumption. That and so-called defense expenditures swallow our national income and make ours an overfed, overentertained, polluted, and impoverished society."

PART EIGHT

NATIONAL INCOME AND FISCAL POLICY

National income

Between 1929 and 1976 the number of persons employed in the American economy rose from 48 to 86 million and the average amount produced by each employed person more than doubled. The economy's productive capacity grew both because more people were put to work and because each person worked more productively. As a result, the total output of goods and services was almost four times as large at the end of the period as it had been at the beginning. Inflation accompanied this rise in output. Because of the increase in the price of almost everything, average prices in 1976 were over four times as high as in 1929. The *market value* of the nation's output was roughly sixteen times that of 1929.

In the years since World War II, population in the United States has increased from 140 million to 215 million and the number of employed persons from 57 million to 86 million. Today's American is much richer than was the American of 1946: on average he or she had $5,000 to spend or save in 1976 against $1,100 in 1946. Of course most things cost more: the same goods that cost $1,100 in 1946 would have cost $3,124 in 1976. Even so, after inflation, and after taxes, the average American had 75 percent more purchasing power in 1976 than he or she had thirty years earlier—and more leisure too.

Statements such as those above abound in newspaper and magazine articles concerning the performance of the American economy. Where do these figures come from? Precisely what do they measure? How can they help and how can they mislead when we attempt to assess the performance of the economy?

Many of these measures are provided by statisticians (called national income statisticians or accountants) employed by the U.S. Department of Commerce. Notice first that these are measures of broad *aggregates* and *averages* such as the total value of goods produced, the total employment, and the average of all market prices. They are not detailed statistics, such as the outputs of wheat and coal, or the prices of those commodities, or the number of wheat farmers and coal miners actually at work. Study of broad indicators of performance is a part of macroeconomics, while study of the close-up pictures of individual markets belongs to microeconomics.[1]

The concept of national income

National income refers to the total market value of all goods and services produced in the economy during a year and to the total of all incomes earned over the same period of time. It is the basic concept in macroeconomics. **National income accounting** is the set of rules and techniques for measuring the total flow of output (goods and services) produced and the total flow of inputs (factors of production) used by the economy. To see exactly what national income includes, how it is measured, and what it can tell us, we shall study it in some detail. We start with the national income of a very simple economy and then introduce, one by one, the complications needed to make it applicable to real-world economies.[2]

THE SPENDTHRIFT ECONOMY

In the Spendthrift economy there are two groups of decision makers—households and firms. We assume (for the moment) that firms

earn all of their incomes by selling goods and services to households, and that households earn all of their incomes by selling factor services to firms.[3] Each group spends all of its incomes buying goods or services from the other group. In this simple economy, households receive incomes in the form of wages and salaries as suppliers of labor services and in the form of profits paid to them as owners of firms. Households spend all of their incomes by purchasing goods and services produced by firms. Firms sell all of their outputs to households and receive money in return. All of the money received by firms is in turn paid out to households as wages and profits. In short, neither households, nor firms save anything in the Spendthrift economy; everything that one group receives goes to buy goods and services from the other group. Expenditure is the rule of the day!

The Spendthrift economy is illustrated in Figure 26–1 (which is similar to Figure 4–1). Payments are shown flowing from households to firms in return for goods and services purchased and from firms to households in return for factor services purchased.

Now suppose we wish to calculate the total value of the economy's annual output. We can do this by making calculations based on either side of the circular-flow diagram shown in Figure 26–1. The output-expenditure approach uses calculations based on the flows on the right-hand side of the figure, while the factor-payments approach uses calculations based on the flows on the left-hand side of the figure.

The output-expenditure approach to national income

When we use the output-expenditure approach to measure the total value of output, we calculate the total expenditure needed to purchase the nation's output. In the simple Spendthrift economy all output is sold to

---

[1] The distinction between these two branches of economics was discussed in detail in Chapter 4, and those who have not come to the present chapter directly from Chapter 4 should review it at this time. Macro and micro derive from the Greek words *makros* and *mikros,* which mean, respectively, long or large and short or small.

[2] This method of argument is common in economics and is based on the idea that it is easier to study things one at a time rather than all at once. Indeed, early economists made this explicit when they spoke of abstractions from reality followed by a build-up to realism through a series of "successive approximations." This is a useful method of discussion provided one remembers that the second step is as essential as the first.

[3] We shall deal with sales between firms very soon.

Figure 26–1 The circular flow of income in the Spendthrift economy

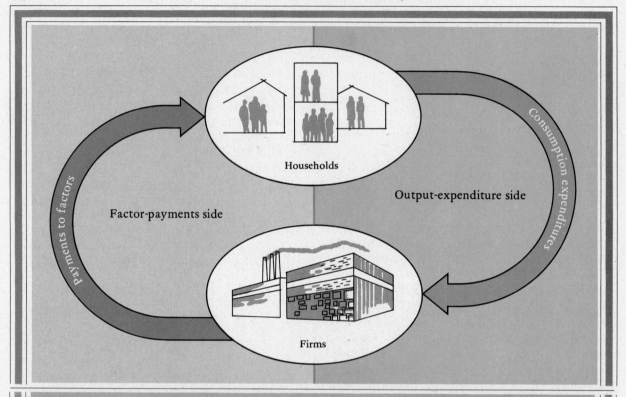

Payments to factors

Factor-payments side

Households

Output-expenditure side

Consumption expenditures

Firms

National income may be viewed either as the expenditure required to purchase total output or as the factor payments generated by the production of total output. In the Spendthrift economy the value of goods produced by firms is equal to the value of goods purchased by households. This is equal by definition to the value of factor earnings arising from the production of goods and services.

households, and we can get the total we require by measuring the actual expenditure of households on currently produced goods and services. In more complex economies many groups other than households purchase a part of the economy's output, while another part is not sold at all (it is held by the firms that produce it for sale in the future). In such economies it is often simpler to calculate the sales value of the economy's total output directly rather than to calculate the expenditure on that output by those who purchase it, but both approaches will yield the same total

since they merely measure opposite sides of the same transactions. (When the bookstore sells you a book for $14.95, its sale and your purchase are both $14.95.)

As soon as we allow for the fact that many sales of one firm are actually made to other firms, it becomes clear that we cannot calculate the total output of the economy by simply adding up the output of all firms. For the total sales of all firms is greater than the total available to be purchased by all households in this more complicated version of the Spendthrift economy. Suppose, for example, that

Value added through stages of production

Because the output of one firm often becomes the input of other firms, the total value of goods sold by all firms greatly exceeds the value of the output of final goods. This general principle is illustrated by a simple example in which firm R starts from scratch and produces goods (raw materials) valued at $100; the firm's value added is $100. Firm I purchases raw materials valued at $100 and produces semimanufactured goods that it sells for $130. Its value added is $30 because the value of the goods is increased by $30 as a result of the firm's activities. Firm F purchases the semimanufactured goods for $130 and works them into a finished state, selling them for $180. Firm F's value added is $50. The value of final goods, $180, is found either by counting only the sales of firm F or by taking the sum of the values added by each firm. This value is much smaller than the $410 that we would obtain if we merely added up the market value of the commodities sold by each firm.

	TRANSACTIONS BETWEEN FIRMS AT THREE DIFFERENT STAGES OF PRODUCTION			
	Firm R	*Firm I*	*Firm F*	*All firms*
A. Purchases from other firms	$ 0	$100	$130	$230 = Total interfirm sales
B. Purchase of factors of production (wages, rent, interest, profits)	100	30	50	180 = Value added
Total A + B = value of product	$100	$130	$180 = Value of final goods and services	$410 = Total value of all sales

we took the value of all farmers' sales of wheat and added to it all flour mills' sales of flour, plus the sales of bakeries, plus the sales of bread by all retail stores. The resulting total would be much larger than the value of the final product (bread) produced by the economy; we would have counted the value of the wheat four times, of the flour three times, of the bread produced by the bakery twice, and of the services of the retail store once.

To avoid this problem of *double counting,* national income accountants use the important concept of the value added. Each firm's **value added** is the value of its output *minus* the value of the inputs that it purchases from other firms. Thus a flour mill's value added is the value of its output of flour *minus* the value of the grain it buys from the farmer and minus the values of any other inputs such as electricity and fuel oil that it buys from other firms.

In macroeconomics a firm's output is defined to be its value added; the sum of all values added is the value of all goods and services produced by the economy.

The idea of value added suggests an important distinction between intermediate and final products. **Intermediate products** are all goods and services used as inputs into a further stage of production. **Final products** are the output of the economy after eliminating all double counting. In the previous example, grain, flour, electricity, and fuel oil were all intermediate products used at various stages in the process that led to the production of the final product, bread. The earlier statement that all output in the Spendthrift economy is sold to households must refer to final products. Intermediate products can, of course, be sold by one firm to another.

The factor-payments (factor-income) approach

The second approach is usually referred to simply as the factor-payments approach, although it is sometimes called the factor-income approach.

It is usual in macroeconomics to distinguish four main components of factor incomes: **rent,** which is the payment for the services of **land; wages and salaries** (often referred to simply as wages), which are the payment for the services of **labor;** and interest and profits, both of which are payments for the services of **capital.** In order to obtain its capital goods a firm requires money. This is made available by those who lend money to the firm and by those who put up their own money and risk its loss in order to become the firm's owners. **Interest** is earned by those who lend money

to the firm, and **profits** are earned by those who own the firm.[4]

In the Spendthrift economy the only components are wages and profits. The profits, moreover, are all paid out to the owners of firms as **dividends.** Thus the whole of the value added is assumed to be either wages or dividends, and the total of factor payments must equal the total national income measured by the output-expenditure approach. An example of the calculation of national income in the Spendthrift economy is given in Table 26–1.

The Spendthrift economy, though a good place to begin our study, leaves out too much of the important complexity of the real economy. We shall now introduce some necessary complications one at a time, concentrating on the output-expenditure approach. On page 471 we shall return to the factor-payments approach and see how it is reconciled with the output-expenditure approach to assure that both approaches yield the same measured level of national income.

THE FRUGAL ECONOMY

The Spendthrift economy is an economy of

[4] The concepts of rent, wages, interest, and profits used in macroeconomics do not correspond exactly to the microeconomic concepts that go under the same names. The details of the differences need not detain us in an introductory treatment, but the reader should be warned that differences exist.

Table 26–1 National income in the Spendthrift economy (millions of dollars)

Factor payments		Value of output	
Wages	$ 900	Final goods and services sold to households	$1,000
Dividends	100		
National income (GNP)	$1,000	National income (GNP)	$1,000

Both sides add up to the same total because the whole value of final output is paid out as wages or as dividends. In the Spendthrift economy goods and services produced and sold to households account for the total value of all production. Factor incomes earned by households consist of wages and dividends.

the here and now; all income is spent on goods and services for current consumption and all current output is consumed. In the Frugal economy households and firms look to the future, and as a result both saving and investment occur.

Saving

Saving is income not spent on goods and services for current consumption. Both households and firms can save. Households save when they elect not to spend part of their current income on goods and services for consumption. Firms save both when they deduct from their gross revenues depreciation allowances which can be used to keep their capital stock intact and when they elect not to pay out to their owners some of the profits that they have earned. While all profits belong legally to the owners, typically only some are actually paid out as dividends while the rest are withheld by firms to finance part of their investment. **Undistributed profits** are profits held back by firms for their own uses. They constitute saving made on behalf of the owners of firms since they are incomes of the owners not spent on current consumption.

Investment

We may define **investment** as the production of goods not for present consumption. Such goods are called **investment goods.** They are produced by firms and they may be bought either by firms or by households. Most investment is done by firms, and in this simple Frugal economy we shall concentrate solely on such investment. Firms can invest either in capital goods, such as plant and equipment, or in inventories.

Investment in inventories. Virtually all firms hold stocks of their inputs and their own outputs. Such stocks are called **inventories.** Inventories of inputs allow production to continue at the desired pace in spite of short-term fluctuations in the deliveries of inputs bought from other firms. Inventories

of outputs allow firms to meet orders in spite of temporary, unexpected fluctuations in the rate of output or sales.

Inventories are an inevitable part of the productive process, and they require an investment of the firm's money since the firm has paid for them but has not yet sold them. An accumulation of inventories counts as current investment because it represents goods produced but not used for current consumption; a drawing down—often called a decumulation—counts as *dis*investment because it is a reduction in the stock of goods produced in the past.

Investment in capital goods. All production uses capital goods: man-made aids to production such as hand tools, machines, and factory buildings. The total amount of capital goods in the country is called the **capital stock.** The act of creating new capital goods is an act of investment.

Gross and net investment. The total investment that occurs in the economy is called **gross investment.** Gross investment may be thought of as divided into two parts, replacement investment and net investment. The amount of replacement investment required to maintain the existing capital stock intact is called the **capital consumption allowance** or simply **depreciation. Net investment** is gross investment minus the capital consumption allowance. It is net investment that increases the economy's total stock of capital, while the replacement investment keeps the existing stock intact by replacing what has been worn out or otherwise used up.

The output-expenditure approach in the Frugal economy

The current production of final commodities in the Frugal economy can be divided into two sorts of output. First, there are consumption goods and services actually sold to households. Second, there are investment goods that consist of capital goods plus inventories of semifinished and finished commodities still in the hands of firms. *C* stands for currently produced consumption goods and *I* for currently produced investment goods. The value of national output or national income in the Frugal economy can be expressed as *C* + *I*.

In an economy that uses capital goods, as does the Frugal economy, it is helpful to distinguish between "gross" and "net" concepts of national income (or national product). **Gross national income** (or **gross national product, GNP**) is the sum of all values added in the economy; it is the sum of the values of all final goods produced for consumption and investment. **Net national income** (or **net national product, NNP**) is GNP minus the capital consumption allowance. NNP is thus a measure of the net output of the economy after deducting from gross output an amount necessary to maintain the existing stock of capital intact.

An example of the calculation of national income in the Frugal economy is given in Table 26–2.

The equality of expenditure and the value of final output in the Frugal economy

In the Spendthrift economy the value of final output was equal to the value of expenditure on that output by assumption: all final goods were sold to households. In the Frugal economy, while some final output is sold to households, some—such as plant and equipment—is sold to other firms and some—such as newly produced inventories of a firm's own output—is not sold at all. How then is total *expenditure* on final goods kept equal to the total value of final output produced? The answer is that the national income accountant defines "expenditure" to be the amount required to purchase final output, not the amount actually spent on it. The national income accountant includes production of goods for inventories as part of total expenditure since the firm certainly spends money on the factor services necessary to produce goods for its own inventories. The accountant calculates the economy's total expenditure as the value of actual purchases of final goods and services sold *plus* the market value of final commodities currently produced and added to inventories. This definition makes total expenditure the same thing as the value of all final commodities produced.

Table 26–2 National income in the Frugal economy (millions of dollars)

Value of output	
Consumption goods and services (*C*)	$1,000
Investment goods (*I*)	
Capital goods	175
Inventory accumulation	25
Gross national product (GNP)	$1,200
Capital consumption allowance	105
Net national product (NNP)	$1,095

In the Frugal economy GNP is *C* + *I*. GNP and NNP differ by the amount of the capital consumption allowance. The value of output means the value of final commodities produced. In the Frugal economy this is the value of consumption goods and services and investment goods, which include capital goods and inventory accumulation.

THE GOVERNED ECONOMY

We now give our economy a government. The Governed economy contains central authorities—usually called simply "the government"—who levy taxes on firms and households and who engage in numerous activities such as defending the country, making and enforcing the laws, building roads, running schools, and predicting the weather. Governments affect national income both by their expenditures and by their taxes.

Government expenditures

When the government produces goods and services that households desire, such as roads and air traffic control, it is engaged in useful activity. It is obviously adding to the sum total of valuable output in the same way as private firms producing the trucks and airplanes that use the roads and air lanes. With other government activities the case may not seem so clear. Should expenditures by the federal government to send a rocket to the moon or to pay a civil servant to file and refile papers from a now defunct department be regarded as contributions to GNP? Should payments by governments to the aged be part of national income? If so, what is the "product" produced? Everyone knows some people who feel that many (or even most) of the activities "up in Washington" or "down at City Hall" are wasteful if not downright harmful, and everyone knows others who feel that it is governments (not private firms) that are producing the really important things of life, such as pollution control.

The national income statistician avoids entering into such speculation as to which government expenditures are—or are not—worthwhile and instead counts everything that produces goods or services and uses factors of production. Just as the national product includes, without distinction, the output of both gin and Bibles, it includes all the bombers and all the upkeep of parks, along with the services of internal revenue agents, CIA agents, and even members of Congress. Government expenditure that is included is given the symbol G; GNP in the Governed economy can therefore be expressed as GNP = $C + I + G$.

Transfer payments

There is an important exception to the rule that all government expenditure is included in the GNP. When a government agency makes welfare payments to a mother of five children whose husband has deserted her, income is transferred to the welfare recipient but the government does not receive, nor does it expect to receive, any productive services from the deserted mother in return for the welfare payments. The expenditure itself adds neither to employment of factors nor to total output. This is true whether the government raises the welfare money by taxes, by borrowing, or by creating new money. Payments made to households by the government that are not made in return for the services of factors of production are called government transfer

Table 26–3 National income in the Governed economy (millions of dollars)

Value of output		
Consumption goods and services (C)		$1,000
Investment (I)		
Capital goods		175
Inventory accumulation		25
Government		
Total government expenditure	320	
Less transfer payments	40	
Government contribution to GNP (G)		280
GNP		$1,480
Capital consumption allowance		105
NNP		$1,375

In the Governed economy, GNP = C + I + G. All government expenditures except transfer payments are a part of GNP. This economy differs from the Frugal economy in the addition of government expenditure for goods and services. Transfer payments, unlike all other government expenditures, are not made in return for factor services used for the output of goods or services and are therefore excluded.

payments, or more simply **transfer payments.** Such payments do not lead directly to any increase in output and for this reason they are not included in the nation's GNP.

The government expenditure included in the GNP is net of any transfer payments.

Table 26–3 shows a simplified set of national income accounts for the Governed economy using the output-expenditure approach.

THE OPEN ECONOMY

None of the three economies considered so far engaged in trade with foreign countries. Such economies are often referred to as **closed economies.** In contrast, **open economies** engage in significant amounts of foreign trade: Some of the goods produced at home are sold abroad while some of the goods sold at home are produced abroad.

The GNP of any economy, open or closed, is the total value of final goods and services produced *in that economy.* Some care is required, however, when the expenditure approach is used to measure the GNP of an Open economy. It is necessary to allow for the facts that part of the expenditure on the domestic economy's GNP comes from foreign firms, households, and governments and that part of the expenditure of domestic firms, households, and governments goes to the GNP of foreign countries. Thus we must look beyond the nationality of the purchaser. A Volkswagen purchased by an American adds to German GNP, while the expenditure of the Russians for American grain adds to American GNP.

To allow for these facts, the GNP of the Open economy may be thought of as being calculated in three steps. First, the total expenditure by domestic firms, governments, and households on all final goods wherever they are produced is calculated (this is $C + I + G$). Second, the value of all im-

Components of income in the output-expenditure approach

Personal consumption. The expenditures included under personal consumption in the output-expenditure approach represent almost all purchases by households of currently produced goods and services *except* purchases of houses. Why are house purchases excluded from personal consumption? Purchase of old housing should be excluded from any category of the GNP because it is a mere transfer of assets, the assignment among persons of property rights in already produced goods. Expenditure on new housing construction, however, is part of the GNP, but it is included under investment.

Housing of course is an important element of the expenditure of all households; therefore the national income accountants include under personal consumption both rent paid (by households that do not own their housing) and an estimated imputed value for owner-occupied housing that is the equivalent of rent.

The difference between the treatment of houses and that of household purchases of other durable goods such as automobiles and washing machines is arbitrary. An automobile might be viewed as an investment that produced a stream of services over several years; a tennis racket lasts more than one year, too. But the line has to be drawn somewhere and the accountants draw it at housing.

Gross private domestic investment. The primary components of investment are residential housing, plant and equipment, and the net change in business inventories. Remember that "gross" means that these are total amounts spent for construction and producers' durables, whether (1) as replacement of outmoded or worn-out machines and buildings, or (2) as net additions to the capital stock.

In dealing with inventories, only net changes are included because only in this way is double counting avoided. Remember that GNP aims to measure the value of goods produced but is largely computed by measuring the *sales* by firms. An accounting identity

$$\text{sales} \equiv \begin{array}{l}\text{opening}\\\text{inventory}\\\text{of goods}\\\text{on hand}\end{array} + \begin{array}{l}\text{production}\\\text{for the}\\\text{year}\end{array} - \begin{array}{l}\text{closing}\\\text{inventory}\\\text{of goods}\\\text{on hand}\end{array}$$

can be transformed into

$$\text{production} \equiv \text{sales} + (\text{closing inventory} - \text{opening inventory})$$

The term in parentheses measures the net change in inventories and it must be added to sales to obtain the value of all of production.

Net exports. Net exports means the difference between exports and imports of goods and services. The reason the national income accountants include only the excess over imports is explained on page 468.

Exports as shown include not only merchandise exports but also military sales to foreign governments, income on foreign investments, and sales of other services. Imports include not only merchandise but also American military expenditures overseas, tourist expenditures, purchase of such foreign services as shipping and insurance, income paid on foreign investments in the United States, and pensions paid to Americans living abroad.

Government purchases of goods and services. There are, in principle, many ways in which one might account for government activity. Governments might, for example, be viewed as giant firms that hire factors of production and produce products that are "sold" to consumers for taxes. In fact, the national income statisticians reject this notion, and also the notion that government expenditures should be divided between consumption and investment. Instead, they simply set up a separate category called "government purchases of goods and services." Almost all government expenditures for goods and services are thus included. (We say "almost all" instead of "all" because certain government enterprises, such as the post office, which sell output to households and firms, are treated as business firms.) *Transfer payments* such as social security payments, unemployment insurance, relief payments, and veterans' pensions are excluded. An important additional exclusion is interest on the national debt. This exclusion implicitly (and arbitrarily) assumes that such payments are transfer payments that do not reflect use of a factor of production—in contrast to interest paid to households by firms who have borrowed the money.

ported commodities, *M,* is deducted. This gives the total purchases of domestic spending units on all domestically produced goods and services. Third, the value of all exports, *X*, which indicates domestic production sold abroad, is added. The resulting figure is the nation's GNP.

In symbols the GNP for the Open economy is $GNP = C + I + G + (X - M)$.

The value $X - M$ is called **net exports.** This value is usually small in relation to the total value of either X or M. Thus the correction to GNP when we move from a closed economy, where $GNP = C + I + G$, to an open economy, where $GNP = C + I + G + (X - M)$, will not usually be large. However, a change in either X or $M,$ not matched by a change in the other, will cause the GNP to change in the same way as would a change in *C, I,* or *G.*

THE U.S. ECONOMY

Our model is now complete. A real economy is a frugal, governed, and open economy. Table 26–4 shows the GNP and NNP of the American economy classified into the categories of the output-expenditure approach. (The box on page 466 provides some detail about how the components are defined.)

Table 26–4   The output-expenditure approach to GNP and NNP, 1976 (billions of dollars)

Personal consumption expenditures (*C*)		$1078.6
Durable goods	$156.3	
Nondurable goods	440.3	
Housing	165.8	
Other services	316.2	
Gross private investment (*I*)		241.2
Plant	55.4	
Equipment	106.1	
Residential housing	66.2	
Changes in business inventories	13.5	
Net exports of goods and services (*X − M*)		6.8
Exports	161.9	
Imports	155.1	
Government purchases of goods and services (*G*)		365.8
Federal	133.4	
State and local	232.3	
Total: GNP		$1692.4
Less: Capital consumption allowance		179.7
NNP		$1512.7

Source: *Survey of Current Business, January 1977*

American GNP can be broken down into the headings used for the earlier model economies: *C, I, G,* and *(X − M).* Consumption is by far the largest element of aggregate expenditure followed by government and private investment. Net exports are minute in comparison.

Table 26–5 The factor-payments approach to GNP, 1976 (billions of dollars)

Wages and other compensation of employees			1028.4
Profits			150.6
Corporation, after taxes		53.9	
Dividends	35.1		
Undistributed	18.8		
Proprietors		96.7	
Business and professional	73.8		
Farm	22.8		
Rental income of persons			23.5
Net interest			82.1
Business taxes			214.4
Indirect		149.7	
Corporate profits		64.7	
Capital consumption allowance			179.7
Miscellaneous adjustments			13.7
Total GNP			1692.4

Source: *Survey of Current Business, January 1977*

The GNP can be classified according to types of factor payments. The major components of GNP in this division are wages, profits, interests, and rents, all of which are incomes to households. In addition the table must include capital consumption allowances, business taxes, and a series of miscellaneous adjustments.

The factor-payments approach

Table 26–5 shows the same GNP as shown in Table 26–4, now classified according to the factor-payments approach. Clearly it is a good deal more complex than the left-hand side of Table 26–1, where the only elements of factor payments were wages and dividends. Let us examine the sources of most important additional "payments."[5] First consider complications encountered in the Frugal economy due to saving and investment. Because households saved in the past they may well earn interest on those savings in the current period. Because households invested in residential housing in the past they may receive current income in the form of rent or rental value of owner-occupied housing. Because firms have capital goods that are being used up, some part of their sales revenue is held back to provide a depreciation allowance. Because firms do not pay out all of their profits as dividends, there are undistributed profits.

Next consider complications that arise from government activity. Some part of the value of final goods produced by firms is neither paid to households nor invested, nor saved, but is paid to governments in any of a large variety of taxes. All of these taxes must be included in the payments approach. Social security contributions of both employer and employee, income taxes withheld, and corporate income tax payments, as well as sales and excise taxes paid to the government by manufacturers and retailers, are all part of the market value of final output. While some of these taxes, such as social security contributions, may be regarded as indirect factor incomes, others, such as excise taxes, are not in any sense factor incomes, nor are they payments to households. Yet they must be included along with actual factor payments in "factor payments" in order to make value of "payments" equal to value of output. (The box on page 470 provides additional detail about the components of income in the factor-payments approach and how they are defined.)

[5] We put "payments" in quotation marks to emphasize that the payments are notional, not actual. For example, undistributed profits or income taxes payable are not really payments to anyone just yet.

Components of income: factor-payments approach

Wages and other compensation of employees. In this category are all payments to and on behalf of employees, including take-home pay, income taxes withheld, social security contributions, and contributions to pension funds. Obviously, only some of these payments go to households; some go to governments, some to trust funds, some to unions, and so on; but in total they represent the "labor cost" of production.

Corporate profits. All corporate profits before income taxes are treated as factor payments. Dividends become actual payments to owners for the use of their capital and for risk taking. Undistributed profits are treated as notional payments to owners for the same purposes, and corporate income taxes are regarded as payments to governments that must be included.

The income of proprietors. Unincorporated enterprises such as small businesses, professions, partnerships, and farms generate income flows to their owners, and these incomes, before taxes, are included. Approximately one-quarter of the total is farm income.

Rental income. Rental income includes rents paid to persons, plus the estimated imputed rent for owner-occupied housing that was added to consumption in the expenditures approach. "Rents" also include royalties from patents and copyrights.

Net interest. Net interest is defined arbitrarily as interest earned by persons in the United States, *less* interest paid by the U.S. government and less consumer interest payments.

Indirect business taxes. All taxes paid by businesses must be included. We have in earlier categories included social security and withholding and income taxes paid by corporations and unincorporated enterprises. We now add all the sales and excise taxes paid by businesses.

Many people find it baffling that such taxes are treated as part of national income. In a purely double-entry bookkeeping sense they must be included. The value of a final good is, by *definition,* equal to profits + taxes + all other costs. Therefore, taxes must be included to make the factor-payments approach yield the value of final output.

Capital-consumption allowance. This item reflects an estimate of the depreciation of the nation's capital stock. It is a "payment" imputed out of the value of production, and its purpose is to recognize the contribution made by the nation's capital stock to current production of goods and services.

Miscellaneous adjustments. A number of small additional items are required to make the accounts balance. These include government subsidies to business (subtracted); surpluses of government enterprises (added; they are like business profits); business transfer payments (added because they use part of business sales dollars); inventory valuation adjustments (added or subtracted depending on the nature of the adjustment). Finally, even after all of the above, there is usually a small "statistical discrepancy" that is required to make the accounts balance.

The reconciliation of expenditure and payments approach[6]

In the real economy there is no need for expenditures actually made on goods and services in a given year to equal payments actually made to households and governments in the same year, for many reasons. Consider three:

1. Some of the goods produced during the year are not sold during the year, either because as of the end of the accounting period they are still unfinished or because they are in

transit or in inventories awaiting purchase. Some elements of their cost have already been paid out to households (as wages, for example), whereas others, such as profits, have not been earned, much less distributed.

2. Income is not always paid out to households at the time that it is earned. Salaries, for example, are usually paid one month in arrears, while distributed profits may not be paid out for as much as six months or a year after they are earned. Thus *payments* of factor incomes may be out of step with *earnings* of factor incomes.

3. In an expanding economy when produc-

[6] This section can be omitted without loss of continuity.

Table 26–6 "Payments" and "expenditure" approaches to the income statement of a single firm

ORDINARY ACCOUNTING		NATIONAL INCOME ACCOUNTING	
Revenues		*Expenditure approach*	
Value of goods produced and sold	$100 →	Value of output	100
		Interfirm purchases	−20
		Value added: to GNP expenditure approach	$80
Use of revenues		*Payments approach*	
Purchases from firms	20		
Wages, including taxes withheld	25 →	Wages	28
Social security contributions	3 →		
Interest paid or payable to persons	5 →	Interest	5
Rent paid or payable to persons	5 →	Rental income	5
Excise taxes	7 →	Indirect business taxes	7
Depreciation allowance	10 →	Capital consumption allowance	10
Total cost of goods sold	75		
Gross profits	25		
Allowance for income taxes	12 →	Corporate profits taxes	12
Net profits	13		
Dividends payable	5 →	Dividends	5
Retained earnings	8 →	Undistributed profits	8
Uses of profits	$13	Total payments: to GNP payments approach	$80

The full sales value of output *and* every dollar of "payments" from that value appear once each in the national income accounts, thereby assuring that the accounts measure the same total by either approach. The value of output minus interfirm purchases is this firm's value added and is an entry in the output-expenditure approach to GNP. This $80 of value added is all payments to factors, depreciation allowance, taxes, or profits and thus appears in the factor payments categories. The arrows run from every item on the left (except totals and subtotals) to the appropriate "payments" category in the national income accounts.

The significance of arbitrary decisions

National income accounting is replete with arbitrary decisions. Goods that are finished and held in inventories are valued at market value, thus anticipating their sale even though the actual sales price may not be known. In the case of a Ford in a dealer's showroom, this practice may be justified because the *value* of this Ford is perhaps virtually the same as that of an identical Ford that has just been sold to a customer. But what is the correct market value of a half-finished house or an unfinished novel? Accountants arbitrarily treat goods in process at cost (rather than at market value) if the goods are being made by business firms; they ignore completely the value of the novel-in-process. While these decisions are arbitrary, so would any others be.

Clearly, practical men must arrive at some compromise between consistent definitions and measurable magnitudes. The imputation of a market value to an owner-occupied house, but not to the services of the housewife, who certainly occupies and often owns the house, probably is justified only by such a compromise.

The definition of final goods provides further examples. Business investment expenditures are treated as final products, as are all government purchases. Intermediate goods purchased by business for further processing are not treated as final products. Thus, when a firm buys a machine or a truck, the purchase is treated as a

final good; when it buys a ton of steel, however, the steel is treated not as a final product, but as a raw material that will be used as an input into the firm's production process. (But if the steel sits in an inventory, it is regarded as a business investment and thus *is* a final good.)

Such arbitrary decisions surely affect the size of measured GNP. Does it matter? The surprising answer, for many purposes is No. In any case, it is an error to believe that just because a statistical measure falls short of perfection (as all statistical measures do) it is useless. Very crude measures will often give estimates to the right order of magnitude, whereas substantial improvements in sophistication may make only second-order improvements in these estimates. In the third century B.C., for example, the Alexandrian astronomer Eratosthenes measured the angle of the sun at Alexandria at the moment it was directly overhead 500 miles south at Aswan, and he used this angle to calculate the circumference of the earth to within 15 percent of the distance as measured today by the most advanced measuring devices. For the purpose of the controversy in which he was engaged—the approximate size of the earth—his measurement was decisive. For the purpose of launching a modern earth satellite it would have been disastrously inadequate.

Absolute figures mean something in general terms, although they cannot be

---

tion is increasing, purchases of factor services—and hence payments by firms to households—will be running ahead of the sales of finished output and therefore ahead of payments by households to firms.

National income accountants have thus had to utilize a conceptual double-entry scheme that forces a numerical equivalence of the two approaches. This is accomplished by substituting *notional* expenditures and payments for

taken seriously to the last dollar. In 1976 GNP was measured as $1,692 billion. It is certain that the market value of all production in the United States in that year was not $100 billion, nor was it $10,000 billion. It was not $500 billion, but it might well have been $1,800 or $1,500 billion had different measures been defined with different arbitrary decisions built into them. International and intertemporal comparisons, though tricky, may be meaningful when they are based on measures all of which contain roughly the same arbitrary decisions. American per capita GNP is roughly three times the Spanish and 60 percent higher than the Japanese. Other measures might differ, but it is unlikely that any measure would reveal that either the Spanish or the Japanese per capita production was higher than the per capita production in the United States. But the statistics also show that GNP per capita was 4 percent higher in Switzerland than in Sweden, a difference too small to have much meaning. American output has been growing at 2.8 percent per year since World War II; it is unlikely that another measure of output would have indicated a 6 percent increase. Further, the Japanese output has been growing at about 9 percent per year, and it is inconceivable that another measure would change the conclusion that Japanese national output rose faster than American national output over recent decades.

actual expenditures and payments. How they do this may most easily be seen by starting with the sort of income statement of the firm that would be prepared by ordinary accountants.

Ordinary accountants begin with sales and end "on the bottom line" with net profit. They then account for the use of that profit. This is illustrated in the left-hand side of Table 26–6. "Net profit" all goes somewhere and thus ends up equal to "uses of profit" to the last penny.

For national income accountants "value added" must exactly equal "total payments" for each firm. The way in which they assure this is shown on the right-hand side of Table 26–6. While this table looks only at the accounting for a single firm's contribution to GNP, the same sort of double-entry bookkeeping would guarantee that every dollar's worth of output produced (which shows up in the GNP measured by the expenditure approach) is matched by exactly one dollar's worth of "payments" (which shows up in the GNP measured by the payments approach). This inevitably requires some arbitrary assumptions and classifications, but it captures in numbers the spirit of the two sides of the circular flow illustrated in Figure 26–1.

RELATED MEASURES OF NATIONAL INCOME

GNP is but one of several widely used measures of national income. NNP, previously defined, is the national product produced after making allowance for the using up of the nation's capital stock. Two other important measures are personal income (PI) and disposable income (DI). The interrelations among these four measures are shown in Table 26–7.

Personal income. **Personal income** is income earned by or paid to individuals, before allowance for personal income taxes. Some personal income goes for taxes, some for saving, and the rest for consumption. A number of adjustments to NNP are required to arrive at personal income. The most important ones are: (1) the subtraction from NNP of business earnings retained by cor-

Table 26–7   Various national income measures, 1975 (billions of dollars)

A.	Gross national product (GNP)	1692.4
	Less: Capital consumption allowance	179.7
B.	Net national product (NNP)	1512.7
	Less	
	Retained earnings	83.6
	Business taxes (including social security)	272.5
	Misc. adjustments	6.4
	Plus	
	Transfer payments to individuals	225.2
C.	Personal income (PI)	1375.4
	Less: Personal tax payments	193.6
D.	Disposable income (DI)	1181.8

Source: *Economic Report of the President, 1977*

Each of the four related national income measures focuses on a different aspect of the national output. GNP measures the market value of total output. NNP measures the net value of output after an allowance for replacing worn-out capital stock. Personal income measures income earned or received by persons, before personal income taxes. Disposable income is a measure of after-tax income of persons, which they have available to spend or to save.

porations, (2) the subtraction from NNP of taxes paid by business, and (3) the addition of government transfer payments and payment of government interest to persons. The first two represent parts of the value of output not paid to persons; the third represents payments to households that households have available to spend or to save, although they are not part of GNP.

For most purposes PI is less useful than disposable income. Because disposable income measures are published only every three months, forecasters who need monthly data may use PI instead.

Disposable income. **Disposable income** is a measure of the amount of current income that households have to spend or to save. It is calculated as personal income minus personal taxes.

The important relation between GNP and DI may be summarized:

Disposable income is GNP *minus* any part of it that is not actually paid over to households, *minus* the personal income taxes paid by households, *plus* transfer payments received by households.

Interpreting national income measures

The information provided by measures of national income can be extremely useful for many purposes, but unless carefully interpreted it can also be seriously misleading. Furthermore, each of the specialized measures—GNP, NNP, DI, and others that we shall consider shortly—gives us slightly different information, so that each may be the best statistic for studying a certain range of problems.

MONEY VALUES VERSUS REAL VALUES

The GNP measures the total *money* value of final goods produced during a year. Thus it has a price and a quantity component, and a particular change in the GNP can be caused by many different combinations of price and quantity changes. A 10 percent rise in GNP might, for example, have been caused by a 10 percent rise in prices, all quantities remaining unchanged; a 10 percent rise in output, all prices remaining unchanged; or smaller increases in both prices and quantities. For some purposes the money value of national income is just the measure required. Sometimes, however, we wish to know what is happening to the *quantity* (rather than the *value*) of output. To do this we need to separate changes in the GNP that were caused by changes in market prices from changes that were caused by variations in the quantities of output. Changes of the latter kind are defined as "real" changes to distinguish them from mere "money" changes.

Over any long period of time, changes in the GNP reflect both real quantity changes and money price changes. In 1929 American GNP was $103 billion; in 1975 it was $1,499 billion. How much of this increase results from a change in the volume of goods and services produced and how much from a general rise in prices?

To answer this question, the GNP series has to be "deflated," which means adjusting it for the change in the level of prices. This is done by an index number[7] developed for that purpose and called the **GNP deflator.** The deflation for selected years is shown in Table 26–8. This explains the kinds of calculations behind the statements in the second paragraph of this chapter.

When the GNP is measured in terms of the prices prevailing at the time of measurement, it is said to be measured in current dollars.

[7] See the appendix to Chapter 8, page 869, for a general discussion of index numbers.

Table 26–8 GNP in current and constant dollars

Year	(1) GNP in billions of current dollars	(2) Index of prices 1972 = 100	(3) GNP in billions of 1972 dollars
1935	72	27.6	261
1945	212	38.0	559
1955	399	61.0	655
1965	688	74.3	926
1972	1171	100.0	1171
1975	1516	127.2	1192

Source: *Economic Report of the President, 1977*

Current-dollar GNP tells us about the money value of output; constant-dollar GNP tells us about changes in physical output. The dollar figure in column (1) is divided by the index in column (2). The resulting ratio multiplied by 100 gives the "constant-dollar" figures of column (3). The index used is the Implicit Price Deflator for GNP, prepared by the Office of Business Economics, Department of Commerce. Because the price index used is 100 in 1972, we say the constant-dollar GNP is measured in 1972 dollars. In 1955 actual GNP (in 1955 dollars) was $399 billion. But prices in 1955 were well below prices in 1972. The value of 1955 GNP at 1972 prices is estimated to be $655 billion.

When it is deflated to give a real series, it is said to be measured in **constant dollars.** A constant-dollar series for the GNP is meant to measure the value of the nation's output over a series of years at the prices ruling at some particular year, called the **base year.** The choice of a base year is arbitrary. What matters is that changes in the GNP measured in constant dollars give an estimate of changes in real output. Figure 26–2 graphs the GNP in both constant and current dollars.

TOTAL OUTPUT VERSUS PER CAPITA OUTPUT

The rise in real GNP over this century has had two main causes: first, an increase in the amounts of land, labor, and capital used in production; second, an increase in output per unit of input. In other words, more inputs

Figure 26–2 GNP, 1929–1976, in current and constant dollars

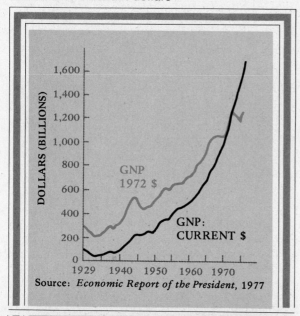

Source: *Economic Report of the President,* 1977

The money value of the GNP has grown much faster than real output. Although much of the growth in GNP over the last four decades has been caused by price rises, it is clear that the real production of goods and services has also grown substantially, as shown by the constant-dollar curve. Since the mid sixties, however, increases in the money value of current-dollar GNP have been much greater than increases in constant-dollar GNP.

is called **per capita GNP.** GNP divided by the number of persons employed tells us the average output per employed worker. GNP divided by the total number of hours worked measures output per hour of labor input. A widely used measure of the purchasing power of the average person is disposable income per capita, in constant dollars. This measure is shown in Figure 26–3.

OMISSIONS FROM MEASURED NATIONAL INCOME

Finally, we come to a series of omissions from the GNP, and thus also from the NNP, DI,

Figure 26–3 Disposable income per capita in constant 1972 dollars

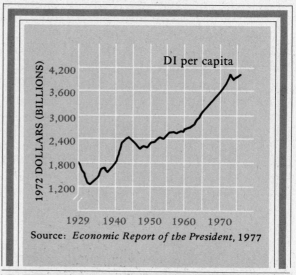

Source: *Economic Report of the President,* 1977

Disposable income per capita in constant dollars provides a measure of the real purchasing power available to the average American household. Disposable income per capita fell during the late 1920s and during World War II, but it has risen decade by decade since the thirties. It is perhaps the best measure of material standards of living that is regularly prepared, but it is deficient for that purpose in that it leaves out the contribution of government expenditure to living standards.

have been used, and each input has become more productive. For many purposes we want the measure of total output: for example, if we wish to assess a country's potential military strength or to know the total size of its market. For other purposes, however, we prefer per capita measures, which are obtained by dividing a total measure such as GNP by the number of persons in some group.

There are many useful per capita measures. GNP divided by the total population gives us a measure of how much GNP there is on average for each person in the economy; this

and other measures based mainly on parts of the GNP. The importance of these omissions can be assessed only when we know the purpose for which the income data is to be used.

Illegal activities

The GNP does not measure illegal activities even though many of these are ordinary business activities in that they produce goods and services that are sold on the market and generate factor incomes. The liquor industry during Prohibition was an important example because it accounted for a significant part of the nation's total economic activity. Today the same is true of many forms of gambling, prostitution, and the illicit production and distribution of soft and hard drugs. If we wish a measure of the total demand for factors of production in the economy or of the total marketable output—whether or not we as individuals approve of particular products—we should include these activities. Probably the main reason for leaving them out is that, because of their illicit nature, it would be hard to find out enough about them to include them even if we wanted to.[8]

Nonmarketed economic activities

When a bank teller hires a carpenter to build a bookshelf in her house, the value of the bookshelf enters into the GNP; if the teller or her husband builds the bookshelf, the value of the bookshelf is omitted from the GNP. In general, any labor service that does not pass through a market is not counted in the GNP. Such omissions include, for example, the services of housewives, any do-it-yourself activity, and voluntary work such as canvassing

[8] Some of them do get included since people often report their earnings from illicit activities as part of their earnings from legal activities in order to avoid the fate of Al Capone. He having avoided conviction on many counts was finally caught for income tax evasion. Don Corleone, the Godfather in Puzo's famous novel about the Mafia, undoubtedly reported part of his illegal earnings as belonging to his legal business. Thus total GNP would come closer to reflecting all income earned in the nation, but it would overstate the contribution of olive oil importing and understate the contribution of gambling and similar enterprises.

for a political party, participating in the operation of a day-care center, or leading a Boy Scout troop.

Does the omission of nonmarketed economic activities matter? Once again, it all depends. If we wish to measure the flow of goods and services through the market sector of the economy, or to account for changes in the opportunities for employment for those households who sell their labor services in the market, this omission is desirable. If, however, we wish to measure the overall flow of goods and services available to satisfy people's wants, whatever the source of the goods and services, then the omissions are undesirable and potentially serious. In most advanced industrial economies the nonmarket sector is relatively small, and it can be ignored even if GNP is used for purposes for which it would be appropriate to include nonmarketed goods and services. The omissions become serious, however, when one is using GNP or DI figures to compare living standards in very different economies. Generally, the nonmarket sector of the economy is larger in rural than in urban settings and in underdeveloped than in developed economies. Be a little cautious, therefore, in interpreting data from a country with a very different climate and culture. When one hears that the per capita GNP of Nigeria is $150 per year, one should not imagine living in Washington, D.C., on that income. Certainly the average Nigerian is at a low level of real income compared to an urban American, but the measured GNP figure does not allow for the fact that many of the things that are very costly to an American—such as fruit and a warm house—are provided free to the Nigerian by wild fruit trees and a warm climate, and by a host of nonmarketed goods and services.

Factors affecting human welfare but not included in the value of output

Many things that contribute to human welfare are not included in the GNP. Leisure is an example. In fact, although a shorter work week may make people happier, it will tend to reduce measured GNP.

GNP does not allow for the capacity of different goods to provide different satisfactions. A million dollars spent on a bomber or a missile makes the same addition to GNP as a million dollars spent on a school, a stadium, or candy bars, expenditures that may produce very different levels of consumer satisfaction.

GNP does not measure the quality of life. To the extent that material output is purchased at the expense of overcrowded cities

MEW: a measure of economic welfare

The philosophy of the national income statistician might be expressed in the observation "Man does not live by bread alone, but it is nonetheless important to know how much bread he has." GNP and related measures do not measure human welfare, nor were they intended to do so. But they are often so interpreted—for example in the implicit assumption that high levels or fast growth rates of GNP per capita make for a better life.

A pioneering attempt to develop a better measure of welfare has been made by Professors William Nordhaus and James Tobin. They call their measure MEW (for Measure of Economic Welfare).

The basic philosophy behind MEW is that the end product of economic activity is household welfare, which in turn depends more on consumption than on production. GNP is a measure of production, while MEW is an attempt to measure all "consumption" that contributes to human welfare. Nordhaus and Tobin start with consumption as defined by the national income accountant, deduct items that they believe do not contribute to welfare, and add items that they believe contribute to welfare but are not included in consumption as measured in the national income accounts.

Their two most important deductions are estimates of (1) expenditures that do not directly contribute to a better life, such as the cost of commuting to work and public expenditures for road maintenance, sanitation services, police protection, and national defense; (2) allowances for losses in welfare from the "negative externalities" connected with urbanization, pollution, and congestion.

The two most important additions are estimates of (1) the value of output that does not pass through the market and (2) the value of leisure.

Leisure is a *most* important and most difficult part of the calculation. Nordhaus and Tobin try three different methods of valuing leisure, and the importance of this calculation is illustrated by the fact that in 1965 the index of MEW for the United States (with 1929 = 100) has three widely different values depending on which measure of valuing leisure is chosen. The values are 119, 143, and 226! The first indicates a virtual standstill, the last a major increase in MEW.

One difficulty in estimating the value of leisure is the need to distinguish between voluntary leisure (more time to enjoy the fruits of life) and involuntary leisure (unemployment). On two of the three ways used to value leisure MEW was higher in 1935 than in 1929 in spite of the fact that in 1935 America was in the midst of the worst

and highways, polluted environments, defaced countrysides, maimed accident victims, longer waits for public services, and a more complex life that entails a frenetic struggle to be happy, GNP measures only part of the total of human well-being.

---

depression in recorded history, during which millions suffered the indignity of prolonged periods of involuntary unemployment.

Even for voluntary leisure, it is not at all obvious what value to put on an hour's leisure. One way is to measure its value by what is given up in order to obtain it (i.e., its opportunity cost). Since the real wage rate—the goods and services that can be bought with the income earned from an hour's work—has been rising steadily over the years, the value of leisure measured by this approach has also been rising steadily over the years.

An alternative approach seeks to measure the value of leisure according to the enjoyment that it actually provides. Although it may be difficult to measure such intrinsic values, the approach does open up the possibility that an hour's leisure might have an unchanging value over time, because an hour with "a book of verses underneath a bough, a loaf of bread, a jug of wine and thou" yielded as much utility in 1899 as it does in 1979. Indeed, this approach is at least consistent with the heretical thought that 80 years ago, when people knew how to use their leisure, an hour's leisure might have yielded more utility than it does in the hectic present when we have lost the gentle art of doing nothing.

WHICH MEASURE IS BEST?

To ask which is *the* best national income measure is something like asking which is *the* best carpenter's tool. The answer is "It all depends on the job to be done."

There are many related national income measures. There is no true, or best, measure for all purposes. The advantages and disadvantages of each can be assessed only in relation to the particular problem for which it might be used.

The use of several measures of national income rather than one is common because they provide answers to different questions. GNP provides the best answer to the question "What was the market value of goods and services produced for final demand?" NNP answers the question "By how much did the economy's production exceed the amount necessary to replace capital equipment used up?" Disposable income answers the question "How much income do consumers have to allocate between spending and saving?" Additionally, real (constant-dollar) measures eliminate purely monetary changes and allow comparisons of purchasing power over time; per capita measures shift the focus from the nation to the average person.

For yet other purposes, such as providing an overall measure of economic welfare, we may wish to supplement or modify conventional measures of national income. We can do this along the lines suggested by Professors Nordhaus and Tobin (see box) or in other ways. Even if we do, we are unlikely to discard GNP (and its progeny) entirely in favor of such a measure. Economists and politicians interested in the ebb and flow of economic activity that passes through the market and in the rise and fall in employment opportunities for factors of production whose services are sold on the market will continue to use GNP as a measure that comes closest to telling them what they need to know.

Summary

1. National income refers to the total market value of goods and services produced in the economy during a year and to the total of all incomes earned over the same period of time. Gross national product (GNP) is one of a series of widely used measures of national income.

2. GNP may be calculated either by the output-expenditure approach or by the factor-payments approach. Both approaches yield the same value for GNP. Total expenditure is made equal to total output by counting as expenditure not only all output that is sold but also output that is added to inventories. Factor payments are equal to total output because the definitions used assign the whole value of final output to one or another payment category.

3. The value of the output of final goods and services can be found by taking the sum of the *values added* in the economy. Value added is the market value of the firm's output minus the cost of purchases from other firms.

4. Using the output-expenditure approach, GNP = C + I + G + (X − M). C represents consumption expenditures of households and I represents investment in capital goods such as plant equipment, residential construction, and inventory accumulation. Gross investment can be split into replacement investment (necessary to keep the stock of capital intact) and net investment (net additions to the stock of capital). G represents government expenditures except transfer payments. (X − M) represents the excess of exports over imports; it will be negative if imports exceed exports.

5. The factor-payments approach to GNP divides the same total GNP according to who notionally receives the fruits of the production and sale of goods. Wages, interest, rents, profits, taxes, and depreciation allowances are the major categories.

6. Several related but different national income measures are used. Net national product (NNP) measures total output after deducting an allowance for output needed to keep the capital stock intact. Disposable income (DI) gives the amount of income that actually is available to households to spend or save. Each one measures a different thing and each is best suited to answering some particular set of questions.

7. For many purposes it is useful to *deflate* money measures such as GNP to get "real" or "constant-dollar" measures. GNP measured in constant dollars expresses the value of output measured in the prices ruling in some particular year and thus provides a measure of real income. For other purposes total measures such as GNP are usefully converted to a per capita or a per worker basis.

8. GNP and related measures of national income must be interpreted with regard for their limitations. GNP does not measure all production. It excludes production resulting from illegal activities, and it excludes most output that does not pass through markets (such as that produced by do-it-yourself activities). Moreover, GNP does not measure human welfare.

9. Notwithstanding its limitations, GNP remains the best measure available for estimating the total economic activity that passes through the markets of our economy and for accounting for changes in the employment opportunities that face households who sell their labor services on the open market. Related measures usefully help to answer other important questions.

10. Measuring national income involves a series of practical difficulties because production, sales, purchases, and payments are imperfectly coordinated in particular accounting periods and because not all goods are marketed. National income accountants resolve these difficulties by a series of workable but nonetheless arbitrary definitions and conventions.

Concepts for review

National income, GNP, NNP, DI
Output-expenditure and factor-payments approaches to measuring national income
Final goods and value added
GNP = C + I + G + (X − M)
Major characteristics of the GNP
Limitations of GNP as a measure of welfare

Discussion questions

1. If Canada and the United States were to join together as a single country, what would be the effect on their total GNP (assuming that output in each country is unaffected)? Would any of the components in their GNP's change significantly?

2. "Everytime you rent a U-haul, brick in a patio, grow a vegetable, fix your own car, photocopy an article, join a food co-op, develop film, sew a dress, avoid purchasing a convenience food, stew fruit, or raise a child, you are committing a productive act, even though these activities are not reflected in the gross national product." To what extent are each of these things "productive acts"? Are any of them included in GNP?

3. What would be the effect on the measured value of America's *real* GNP of (a) the destruction of a thousand homes by flood water; (b) a Supreme Court ruling that abortion was illegal under any circumstances; (c) a complete cessation of all imports from Rhodesia and South Africa; and (d) the outbreak of a new Arab-Israeli war in which American troops became as heavily involved as they were in Vietnam. Speculate on the effects of each of these events on the true well-being of the American people.

4. A Social Security Administration study, using 1972 data, found the "average American housewife's value" to be $4,705. It arrived at this total by adding up the hours she spent cooking, multiplied by a cook's wage, the hours spent with her children, multiplied by a babysitter's wage, and so on. Should the time a parent spends taking children to a concert be included? Are dollar amounts assigned to such activities a satisfactory proxy for market value of production? For what, if any, purposes should such values be excluded from national income?

5. Use the end papers at the back of this book to calculate the percentage increase over the most recent two decades of each of the following magnitudes: (a) GNP in current dollars; (b) GNP in constant dollars; (c) disposable income in constant dollars; and (d) disposable income per capita in constant dollars. Can you account for the relative size of these changes?

6. Consider the effect on measured GNP *and* on economic well being of each of the following: (a) a reduction in the standard work week from 40 hours to 30 hours; (b) hiring all welfare recipients as government employees; (c) an increase in oil prices that leads to a general inflation: and (d) an increase in the salaries of priests and ministers, as a result of increased contributions of church goers.

What determines national income?

Reliable data for American national income stretch back for 50 years, revealing a pattern of long-term progress interspersed with relatively minor, but not unimportant, short-term fluctuations, causing alternating bouts of unemployment and inflation.

The most visible pattern in historical statistics of American national income is the relentless upward movement of any measure of real national income, including total income, income per employed worker, and income per capita. Consider an American man who entered the labor force in 1929 and retired in 1975. At the time he started work, GNP per employed person was $6,411 (in 1972 dollars); when he retired it was $12,811 (in 1972 dollars). Disposable income per person rose over the same period from $1,886 to $4,012, both measured in 1972 dollars. Obviously the material living standards of the average American are very much higher today than they were in 1929.

If a long-term trend of onward and upward is the major theme in the GNP story, a strong secondary theme is short-term fluctuations. Between 1929 and 1933, to take the most extreme example of short-term fluctuations, real GNP fell by just over 30 percent and unemployment rose from 3.2 percent of the labor force to 25 percent. Although nothing in quite these dramatic terms has occurred since, short-term fluctuations in the GNP occur more or less continuously.

In this chapter we begin to study how and why national income changes. This is important not only for theory but for policy: short-term fluctuations bring hardship and suffering to many Americans. While a week or two of unemployment can often be almost a holiday, a month or more tends to become grave. When many months are involved, unemployment can mean financial disaster, particularly in a society where so much is bought on the installment plan. It can also be demoralizing, especially if unemployment tends to be blamed on the individual failings of the unemployed.

In periods of heavy unemployment the unemployed as a whole are quite powerless to create employment by their own efforts. Although it is always possible that by searching long and hard enough one individual may find employment, it is not possible for every individual to do so; if the number of jobs available is substantially less than the number who would like to work, then the iron law is that there must be unemployment at least equal to the excess of would-be workers over available jobs.

Inflation, too, is a matter of major concern. In one way or another it affects everyone, but its harmful effects are greatest on those who live on fixed money incomes whose purchasing power is eroded by increases in prices. Bouts of inflation have in the past occurred mainly under conditions of full employment and rising consumption, investment, and government expenditure.

Background to the theory of national income

Why does national income behave in the way it does? Can governments do anything to influence the course of national income, employment, and prices? In particular, can they do anything to prevent lapses from full employment and to restrain the inflations that appear to accompany periods of relatively full employment?

To deal with these and many related questions, we need to develop a theory of national income. We begin with preliminary definitions and assumptions; then, because it is easier to study complex things one at a time rather than all at once, we shall proceed in a series of small steps. In this chapter we shall build a theory of what determines the level of national income. In the next two chapters we shall use this theory to explain why it changes. After that we shall investigate what the government can do to influence either the short-term fluctuations or the long-term growth of the GNP.

PRELIMINARY DEFINITIONS AND ASSUMPTIONS

Potential GNP

When we look at GNP data, the long-term upward trend tends to dominate what we see and to obscure the shorter-term fluctuations. To separate the long-term and short-term movements the President's Council of Economic Advisers in 1962 introduced a series called the **potential GNP.** This was the GNP that could have been produced if the economy had been kept at full employment, which was until 1976 defined as existing when 4 percent of the labor force is unemployed.[1] It has recently been revised to incorporate a higher rate of unemployment, approximately 5 percent. (The apparent paradox of saying that there is full employment when there is in fact 4 or 5 percent unemployment is discussed in the box.) In Figure 27–1 the long-term upward trend can be seen from the potential GNP series, while the fluctuations can be seen by the varying gaps between potential and actual GNP. The accumulated gap for period 1974–1976 was about $280 billion, a dramatic measure of the lost output due to short-term fluctuations of the economy. The periodic bouts of unemployment and inflation that have accompanied the short-term fluctuations in unemployment are shown in Figure 27–2.

Potential GNP is also often called **full-employment GNP.** Both terms mean exactly the same thing: the GNP that could be produced if the labor force were fully employed. In their theories, economists usually use the generic concept of national income, Y,

[1] The concept of potential GNP was significantly modified in 1977. See the *Economic Report of the President, 1977,* pp. 48–58 for a full discussion. The revised measure of potential GNP is based upon a higher level of "full-employment" unemployment, nearer to 5 percent for recent years. The reasons why a higher unemployment rate may be appropriate are discussed in Part Eleven. Figure 27–1 is based on the revised concept.

Figure 27-1 Actual and potential GNP, 1952–1976.

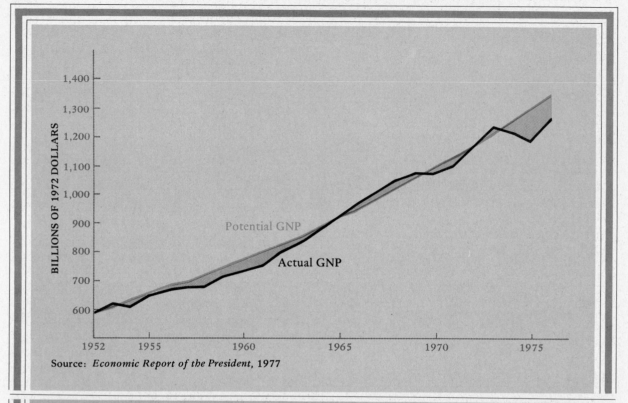

Source: *Economic Report of the President, 1977*

While potential GNP grows steadily, actual GNP shows year-to-year fluctuations. Potential GNP is what the economy could produce with "full employment." Potential GNP rises over time due to increases in the size of the labor force and increases in the average productivity (output per worker) of those employed. The economy has occasionally exceeded its potential GNP, which merely means that unemployment fell below its full-employment level of 4 or 5 percent. For most of the last twenty years actual GNP has fluctuated below potential GNP. The shaded area below the blue line represents the real GNP lost due to the failure to achieve full employment.

rather than such specific concepts as GNP or NNP. Usually, however, Y may be thought of as being interchangeable with GNP.[2] It is common to use the symbol Y_F to denote full-employment income.

[2] Some economists prefer to use NNP rather than GNP. As noted in the last chapter, one's purpose should govern. If we wish to explain employment and inflation, GNP rather than NNP is the relevant concept since both jobs and pressure on the nation's productive capacity depend on the economy's total output, whether the output is being used to produce capital to replace what has worn out or for any other purpose.

Equilibrium income

Equilibrium is a state of rest usually brought about by a balance between opposing forces. National income is said to be in equilibrium when there is no tendency for it either to increase or to decrease. The national income achieved at that point is referred to as the **equilibrium national income.** In this chapter we study the forces that determine the size of the equilibrium national income, and in the next chapter we shall study the effects

The meaning of full employment

The labor force is defined to include both those at work (the employed) and those looking for work (the unemployed). In 1975 in the United States of 154 million persons 16 years of age or more, 2.2 million were in the armed forces and 93.1 million were in the civilian labor force. These two groups of the labor force accounted for 62 percent of the noninstitutional population age 16 or older. The remaining 38 percent consisted of those in school, housewives, the retired, and others not able or not wishing to work. Approximately 7.8 million of those in the labor force were unemployed but looking for work in the week in which the survey was taken. This represented 8.5 percent of the civilian labor force and was regarded as a high level of unemployment. But what of the situation two years earlier, when the percentage was 4.9 percent? Is 4.9 percent a little or a lot? It is much less than the 25 percent unemployed in 1933 and much more than the 1.2 percent unemployed in 1944. The yardstick used to answer that question is the concept of *full employment*.

Does full employment mean the same thing as zero unemployment? The answer to this question is an emphatic no. Various causes of unemployment can be distinguished. Some of them follow unavoidably from the functioning of a market system, and they give rise to what is often called frictional unemployment. A primary source of *frictional unemployment* is labor turnover. People leave jobs for many different reasons. Some quit and some are fired, but almost all of them find new jobs, though it may take time. Because at every moment of time there will be a group of individuals moving from one job to another, there will always be some proportion of the labor force out of work.

The unemployment that is consistent with normal functioning of the economy is thought to be between 4 and 5 percent, and this figure may be used as one definition of full employment. The number itself changes as the composition of the labor force changes: the increasing proportion of married women and youths in the labor force is widely thought to have raised the minimum level.

Another concept of full employment defines it as occurring at the level of unemployment that is compatible with a low and stable rate of inflation. It is a difficult value to estimate this level, but most measures place it at not less than five percent unemployment. These matters are discussed in detail in Part Eleven.

Because unemployment and inflation are often political issues, the terms "full employment" and "price stability" tend to acquire a purely political dimension, with the "in's" proclaiming them at higher levels of unemployment and price increases than do the "out's."

---

on national income of a change in any one of these forces.

Some simplifying assumptions

We start with some simplifying assumptions (noting again that it is easier to study things one at a time rather than all at once). These assumptions are designed to isolate the main forces that determine actual national income.

Figure 27–2 Fluctuations in unemployment and prices 1948–1976

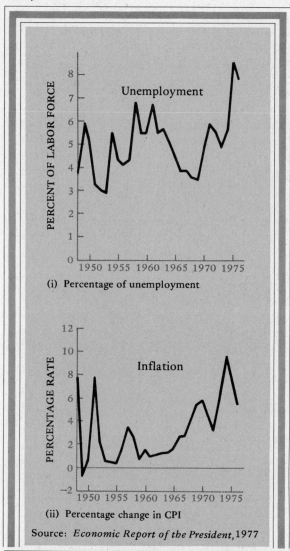

(i) Percentage of unemployment

(ii) Percentage change in CPI

Source: *Economic Report of the President,* 1977

The unemployment rate has fluctuated between a low of 2.9 percent (1953) and a high of 8.5 percent (1975), while the annual rate of change in consumer prices has fluctuated between −0.9 percent (1949) and 11 percent (1974). Until very recently in the United States these two indicators tended to move in opposite directions. When actual GNP is well below potential GNP, unemployment tends to be high and inflationary pressures low; when actual GNP is near (or even above) potential GNP, unemployment tends to be low and inflationary pressures high.

1. *Potential national income is constant.* This assumption allows us to isolate the forces that strongly influence national income over short periods of time. When Y_F is constant, real (constant-dollar) national income changes only because of changes in the amount of employment of factors of production.

Because an economy's productive capacity changes but slowly from year to year, potential national income also changes only slowly. Thus, although the cumulative effects of small annual changes in Y_F can be dramatic over several decades, the effects are relatively minor over a period of a year or two. As a result, assuming Y_F to be constant is not greatly unrealistic for short periods of time.

2. *There are unemployed supplies of all factors of production.* This assumption implies that output can be increased by employing land, labor, and capital that is currently unemployed. Figures 27–1 and 27–2 suggest that this assumption has been factually correct for most, if not all, of the last 28 years. In subsequent chapters we shall study the behavior of national income when unemployment has reached such a low level that it is difficult, if not impossible, to increase output by putting to work factors of production that are currently unemployed.

3. *The level of prices is constant.* The reason for making this assumption now is that it allows us to isolate the causes of changes in real national income. When prices are fixed, any change in national income must reflect a change in real quantities produced; whereas if prices increase, a change in national income may reflect a mixture of price and quantity changes. Later, when we come to study the causes of inflation, we will drop this assumption.

NATIONAL INCOME IN THE SPENDTHRIFT ECONOMY

Our point of departure will be the Spendthrift economy introduced in the last chapter, an economy so unrealistic that its national income never changes.

Recall the three essential features of this simplified economy. First, there are only two groups of decision makers: firms and households. Second, households spend all of their incomes buying consumption goods and services produced by firms. Third, firms pay all of their earnings out to households in the form of wages and distributed profits; there are no deductions for taxes (since there is no government) or for business saving (since there is no investment in new capital).

The circular flow of income in this economy is a genuinely closed circuit: whatever is received by households is passed on to firms, and whatever is received by firms is passed on to households. No existing expenditure is ever withdrawn from the flow and no new expenditure is ever injected into it from outside.

If we start national income at any level in this economy, that level will persist indefinitely. If firms produce $1,000 worth of goods per month, they will pay out $1,000 in wages and dividends and households will spend $1,000 on buying the output of firms. Households will be just able to spend all their income at current market prices and firms will be just able to sell all of their output at these same prices. Thus there is no reason for anyone to alter his or her behavior. The same would be true if we started production out at $10,000 per month, at $1 million per month, or at any other figure (as long as resources were available to produce the output).

Any level of national income once set going will persist forever since there is no reason for it to change. Since Y can be in equilibrium at any level, there is nothing—except accident— to explain why it is at one level rather than another. Thus we do not yet have a theory of what determines the *level* of income.

Unreal though this economy is, using it as a model allows us to isolate the forces that do determine the level of national income in more complicated economies such as the Frugal economy, to which we now turn.

National income in the Frugal economy

The simplest version of the Frugal economy differs from the Spendthrift economy in two essentials. First, households spend only part of their incomes on consumption, and they save the rest. Second, firms devote only part of their efforts to producing consumption goods for sale to households, and the remainder goes to producing investment goods. The firms that purchase the new capital goods are said to be *investing*. To simplify matters at the outset, we assume that all saving is done by households and all investing is done by firms. Under these circumstances disposable income is equal to GNP.

Note that, given these assumptions, saving and investment decisions are made by different groups: Saving decisions are made by households and investment decisions are made by firms.[3] Thus there is no reason why a change in the desire of households to save or of firms to invest should automatically be matched by a similar change in the desire of the other group.

INVESTMENT DECISIONS

Firms make plans about how much to invest in new capital equipment. In this chapter it is convenient to study how the level of national income adjusts to a fixed level of investment. So we assume that firms plan to make a constant amount of investment in plant and equipment each year and that they plan to hold their inventories constant. In Chapter 28 we shall drop these assumptions and study the important effects on national income caused by changes in the level of investment.

CONSUMPTION-SAVING DECISIONS

Each household makes plans about how much to spend on consumption and how much to

[3] Even after we allow for business saving and household investment, it remains true that the group of decision makers making saving decisions is not identical with the one making the investment decisions.

save. These are not, however, independent decisions. Since saving is income not spent on consumption, it follows that households have to decide on a single division of their income between saving and consumption.

In macroeconomics we are not concerned with the individual household but with the aggregate of all households, and since each household divides its income between saving and consumption, it follows that total household income (which in the Frugal economy is total national income) must be so divided. Letting C stand for total household consumption and S for total household saving, we can express this as $Y \equiv C + S,$ which says that, by definition, consumption and saving together account for all of household income. But we must go beyond this definition and ask what determines the division between consumption and saving. The term **consumption function** is used to describe the relationship between consumption expenditure and all the factors that determine it. The consumption function is one of the most important relations in macroeconomics.[4] Consumption is the largest single component of aggregate expenditure, and if we are to predict the effects of changes in the level of investment or government expenditure on income and employment, we must know how consumption varies in response to changes in income. This is true not only for the Frugal economy but for more complex economies as well.

THE CONSUMPTION FUNCTION

How households actually divide their income between C and S is, of course, an empirical question. Really there are at least two related questions: (1) how do households divide their incomes over the long term, and (2) how do they respond to short-term fluctuations in income? In order to discuss this concisely, economists use some technical vocabulary.

[4] The concept of a functional relationship is discussed on page 24.

Average and marginal propensities to consume

A numerical example of a schedule relating national income to desired consumption expenditure is presented in the first two columns of Table 27–1.

The **average propensity to consume (APC)** is total consumption expenditure divided by total income. The calculation of APC for the consumption schedule illustrated in Table 27–1 is found in the third column of the table.

The **marginal propensity to consume (MPC)** relates the *change* in consumption to the *change* in income that brought it about. It is the change in income divided into the resulting change in consumption: $MPC = \Delta C/\Delta Y$ (where the Greek letter Δ means "a change in"). Table 27–1 shows the calculations of the MPC in the last column. [25]

The shape of the consumption function

Economists have studied in substantial detail the relation between consumption expenditure and income in both the long and short run.[5] Not surprisingly behavior is different in the two cases.

The long-run consumption function. Some studies have used 10-year averages of consumption expenditure and income. Thus the time-series data used consisted of decade-by-decade averages of consumption and income. When plotted on a graph, one point would relate average consumption in, say, 1900–1909 to average income in that period; another point would relate average consump-

[5] Most studies of the consumption function have related consumption to disposable income. In the simple Frugal economy Y and Y_d are the same. In more complicated economies they will differ. For our theory of income determination it is convenient to have consumption as a function of total national income (Y), not disposable income (Y_d). But this causes no problems as long as Y_d and Y are systematically related to one another. [26] If for example, disposable income is always 60 percent of national income, then whatever the relation between consumption, C, and disposable income, Y_d, we can always substitute $0.6Y$ for Y_d. If, to carry the example further, consumption were always 90 percent of Y_d, then C would always be 54 percent (60 percent of 90 percent) of Y.

Table 27–1   The calculation of the average propensity to consume (*APC*) and the marginal propensity to consume (*MPC*) (millions of dollars)

National income (Y)	Desired consumption (C)	APC = C/Y	ΔY (Change in Y)	ΔC (Change in C)	MPC = ΔC/ΔY
$ 0	$ 100	—			
			$ 100	$ 80	0.80
100	180	1.800			
			300	240	0.80
400	420	1.050			
			100	80	0.80
500	500	1.000			
			500	400	0.80
1,000	900	0.900			
			1,000	800	0.80
2,000	1,700	0.850			
			1,000	800	0.80
3,000	2,500	0.833			
			1,000	800	0.80
4,000	3,300	0.825			

The *APC* measures the proportion of total income consumed and the *MPC* measures the proportion of any increment to income that is consumed. These data are hypothetical. The *APC* calculated in the third column exceeds unity below the breakeven level of income since consumption exceeds income. Above the breakeven level the *APC* is less than unity. The last three columns are set between the lines of the first three columns to indicate that they refer to changes in the levels of income and consumption.

In this example, the *MPC* calculated in the last column is constant at 0.80 at all levels of *Y*. This indicates that 80¢ of every additional $1 of income is spent on consumption and 20¢ is used to increase saving (or decrease dissaving).

tion in 1910–1919 to average national income in that period; and so on. The characteristic of such data is that they average out the effects of cyclical fluctuations in national income and focus attention on the long-run reaction of consumption to long-run trend changes in national income.

Such studies suggest that there is a highly stable long-run division of national income between consumption and saving—in other words, that consumption tends to be a stable fraction of national income. In technical terms the *APC* tends to be constant over time; so too does the *MPC*. Further, *MPC* tends to be approximately equal to *APC* in

these long-run studies [27] Figure 27–3 shows a long-run consumption function that exhibits these properties. The figure also shows a construction called the **45° line** that joins all those points at which the values measured on the two axes are equal, that is, where expenditure (*E*) equals income (*Y*).[6]

The 45° line proves handy as a reference line. For example, in Figure 27–4 it helps locate the breakeven level of income at which

[6] Provided that we use the same scales on the two axes, the line has a slope of +1 or, what is the same thing, it makes a 45° angle with both axes. To remind us of what it shows, the line in the figure is labeled *E* = *Y*, and to remind us of its position, one of the 45° angles is shown.

Figure 27–3 The shape of a long-run consumption function

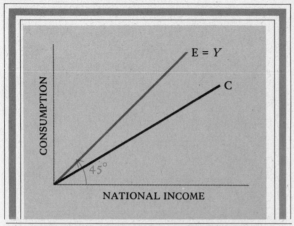

Empirical evidence suggests that a constant proportion of national income is spent for consumption in the long run. The long-run consumption function is concerned with decade-to-decade changes in consumption. The evidence suggests that both *APC* and *MPC* are constant, which implies a consumption function that is a straight line through the origin. The 45° line joins all points where expenditure equals income. Since not all income is spent, the long-run *C* function is below the 45° line. Since not all increments to income are spent, the *C* function is flatter than the 45° line.

consumption expenditure equals total income. Graphically, this is where the consumption line cuts the 45° line.

The short-run consumption function. Empirical studies of year-to-year changes in income and consumption (i.e., when each observation consists of income and consumption expenditure over the same year) for a period of ten years or so have found a close relation between the two. In general, years with higher-than-average levels of income tend to be years with higher-than-average levels of

consumption, and vice versa. Figure 27–4 illustrates two different shapes of short-run consumption functions. The essential features of these functions are:

1. There is a breakeven level of income that is the level of income at which households just consume all of their income.

2. Below the breakeven level, households consume in excess of their current income. They do this by borrowing or by using up past savings, which is known as **dissaving.**[7]

3. Above the breakeven level of income, households consume only part of their income and save the rest.

4. Any increase in household income causes consumption expenditure to rise but by less than the rise in income. For example, every increase in household income of $1 might cause households to raise their consumption expenditure by 80¢.[8]

Using the concepts of the average and marginal propensities to consume we can restate the four assumptions as two summary propositions:

1. There is a breakeven level of income at which *APC* = 1. Below this level, *APC* is greater than unity and above it *APC* is less than unity.

2. The *MPC* is greater than zero but less than unity for all levels of income.

Both consumption functions of Figure

[7] Clearly this cannot go on forever, which is one reason why assumption 2 does not describe long-term behavior; but it can go on for some time, and it does appear to describe short-term behavior.

[8] This fourth assumption was described by John Maynard Keynes (widely regarded as the first to stress the consumption function) in his classic *The General Theory of Employment, Interest, and Money:* "The fundamental psychological law, upon which we are entitled to depend with great confidence both *a priori* from our knowledge of human nature and from the detailed facts of experience, is that men are disposed, as a rule and on the average, to increase their consumption as their income increases, but not by as much as the increase in their income."

Figure 27–4 Two short-run consumption functions

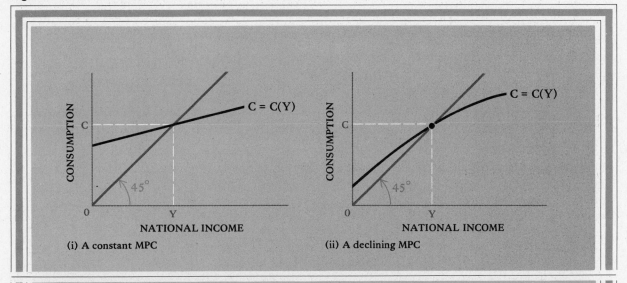

(i) A constant MPC

(ii) A declining MPC

Each of these consumption functions has a declining *APC* and an *MPC* of less than unity. Each of these short-run consumption functions differs from the long-run function of Figure 27–3 in the fact that it crosses the 45° line at a breakeven level of income and has a declining average propensity to consume. Each is consistent with the hypotheses listed in the text. The straight line function in (i) has a constant *MPC*, while the curve in (ii) has a declining *MPC*.

27–4 are consistent with these hypotheses. While the hypotheses greatly restrict the nature of the relationship between consumption and income, it is well to notice that they only predict an *MPC* between 0 and 1 and are thus consistent with an *MPC* very near to unity (say 0.99) or very near to zero (say 0.01).

They are also consistent with an *MPC* that remains constant as income rises, as shown in the left part of Figure 27–4, or with an *MPC* that declines as income rises, as shown in the right part of the same figure. Empirical studies of year-to-year changes in income and consumption have tended to find the *MPC* to be constant rather than diminishing as income increases; they are therefore consistent with the straight-line consumption function drawn in Figure 27–4(i).

THE SAVING FUNCTION

Because households have only one decision to make on how to divide their income between consumption and saving, it follows that if we know the dependence of consumption on income we also know the dependence of saving on income. Table 27–2 illustrates this.

We may define two saving concepts that are exactly parallel to the consumption concepts of *APC* and *MPC* already defined. The **average propensity to save (*APS*)** is the proportion of total income devoted to savings. It is total saving divided by total income: $APS = S/Y$. The **marginal propensity to save (*MPS*)** relates the change in total saving to the change in total income that brought it about: $MPS = \Delta S/\Delta Y$. Calculations from Table 27–2 will allow you to confirm for yourself that, in the example given, the *MPS* is constant at 0.2 at all levels of income, while the *APS* rises with income. (For example *APS* is zero at $Y = \$500$ and 0.175 at $Y = \$4,000$.) [28] Figure 27–5 graphs the consumption and saving schedules given in Table 27–2.

THE AGGREGATE DEMAND FUNCTION

There are only two kinds of goods and services produced in the Frugal economy: consumption goods and investment goods. Thus total desired expenditure on final goods must

Table 27–2 Consumption and saving schedules (millions of dollars)

National income	Desired consumption expenditure	Desired saving
$ 0	$ 100	−$100
100	180	− 80
400	420	− 20
500	500	0
1,000	900	+ 100
2,000	1,700	+ 300
3,000	2,500	+ 500
4,000	3,300	+ 700
5,000	4,100	+ 900

In the Frugal economy all income is either spent on consumption or is saved. These schedules show desired consumption and desired saving at each level of income. Consumption and saving each increase steadily as income rises. In this sample the breakeven level of income is $500 million. At an income of $100 million, $180 million is spent on consumption. Since this must involve new borrowing or the consumption of past saving, households in aggregate are dissaving. As income rises, dissaving decreases for income levels up to $500 million and saving increases above $500 million.

Figure 27–5 The consumption and saving functions

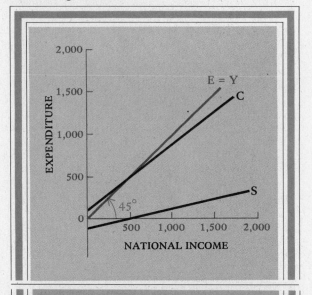

Both consumption and saving rise as income rises. This diagram plots the data from Table 27–2. The *C* and *S* lines relate desired expenditures on consumption and on saving to national income. At the breakeven level of income the consumption line cuts the 45° line and the saving line cuts the horizontal axis. Since saving is all income not spent on consumption ($S = Y − C$), the vertical sum of the *S* and the *C* lines must by definition coincide with the 45° line (i.e., at each level of income, total income must be accounted for by the amount saved plus the amount consumed).

be the sum of desired consumption expenditure and desired investment expenditure. We may now ask how *changes* in national income affect the total expenditure that households and firms desire to make. To answer this question we require a function that relates the level of *desired* expenditure to the level of income. Such a function is sometimes called an **aggregate demand (AD) function.** (Table 27–3 illustrates how such a function can be

Table 27–3 The equilibrium of national income in the Frugal
economy: the income-expenditure approach (millions of dollars)

National income (Y)	Desired consumption (C)	Desired investment (I)	Aggregate demand (AD = C + I)	
$ 0	$ 100	$300	$ 400	|
100	180	300	480	Pressure on income to
400	420	300	720	increase
500	500	300	800	
1,000	900	300	1,200	↓
2,000	1,700	300	2,000	Equilibrium income
3,000	2,500	300	2,800	↑
4,000	3,300	300	3,600	Pressure on income to
5,000	4,100	300	4,400	decrease

**National income is in equilibrium where aggregate desired expenditure equals national
income.** In the Frugal economy aggregate demand is the sum of desired expenditures
on consumption and investment. When national income is below its equilibrium level,
aggregate demand exceeds the value of current output. This creates an incentive for
firms to increase output and hence for national income to rise. When national income
is above its equilibrium level, aggregate demand is less than the value of current output. This creates an incentive for firms to reduce output and hence for national income
to fall. Only at the equilibrium level of national income is aggregate demand exactly
equal to the value of the current output.

calculated, given the consumption function
and the level of desired investment at each
level of income.) The AD function tells how
much firms and households would like to
spend on purchasing final output at each level
of income. Since the aggregate demand function shows the total amount that everyone
wishes to spend on the economy's output, it is
sometimes called an **aggregate expenditure
function.**

The aggregate demand function relates desired
expenditure to national income.[9]

EQUILIBRIUM INCOME

Conditions that must be fulfilled if something
is to be in equilibrium are called **equilibrium
conditions.** We now wish to see how the
equilibrium level of national income is deter-

mined in the Frugal economy. This can be
studied in two ways: through the income-
expenditure and the saving-investment approaches. While both give the same answer—
and can be used interchangeably—each offers
different insights, so it pays to study both.

These two approaches to studying equilibrium conditions must not be confused with
the two approaches to measuring national income discussed in the previous chapter: the
output-expenditure and the factor-payments
approaches. It is a matter of *definition* that the
measured value of the nation's output is the
same under either of those two measurement
approaches—they are merely different ways
of looking at a single magnitude: the value of
total final output produced. There is no
reason, however, why the amount that households and firms *desire* to spend on purchasing
total output should be equal to the value of
total output. If these two magnitudes are not
equal, then (as we shall see) national income
will change.

[9] It thus differs from the demand curve of microeconomics,
which relates the quantity people wish to purchase of some
commodity to its market price.

The income-expenditure approach to equilibrium

Look again at Table 27–3 and recall that in the simple Frugal economy all factor incomes generated by production are actually paid out to households so that household disposable income is the same as the value of output. Assume to begin with that firms are producing final output of $1,000—and thus national income is $1,000. According to Table 27–3, total desired expenditure on consumption and investment is $1,200 at that level of income. If firms persist in producing a current output of only $1,000 in the face of aggregate demand of $1,200, one of two things must happen.[10]

One possibility is that households and firms will be unable to spend the extra $200 that they wish to spend, so shortages and lines of unsatisfied customers will appear. These provide a signal to firms that they can increase their sales if they increase their production. When they do so national income rises.

The second possibility is that households and firms will succeed in meeting their desired expenditures by purchasing goods produced in the past. Indeed, the only way that plans to purchase more than is currently being produced can be fulfilled is by purchasing inventories of goods produced in the past. In the present case, if plans to buy $1,200 worth of commodities were fulfilled in the face of current output of only $1,000, then inventories would have to be reduced by $200. As long as inventories lasted, this situation could persist with more goods being sold than were currently being produced. Sooner or later, however, inventories would run out. But long before this happened, firms would take steps to increase their output. This would allow their extra sales to be made without a further decumulation of inventories. Thus in this case, as well as in the first case, the final response to an excess of aggregate demand over current output is a rise in national income.

At any level of national income at which aggregate demand exceeds total output there will be a strong tendency for national income to rise.[11]

Now consider the $4,000 level of national income in Table 27–3. At this level of income households and firms wish to spend only $3,600 on consumption and investment goods. If firms persist in producing a total output of $4,000 worth of goods, $400 worth must remain unsold. Therefore inventories must rise. Firms will, however, be unwilling to allow inventories of unsold goods to rise indefinitely; sooner or later they will cut back on the level of output to make it equal to the level of sales. When they do, national income will fall.

At any level of income for which aggregate demand falls short of total output, there will be a strong tendency for national income to fall.

Now look at the national income of $2,000 in the table. At this level, and only at this level, the desired expenditure of households and firms is exactly equal to national income. Households are able to buy just what they wish to buy without causing inventories to be depleted, and firms are just able to sell all of their current output so that their inventories are neither rising nor falling. There is no incentive for firms to change their total output. Thus national income will tend to remain steady; it is in equilibrium.

The equilibrium level of national income occurs where aggregate demand is exactly equal to total output.

The results just obtained are quite general and do not depend on the numbers chosen for this specific illustration. A glance at Table 27–3 will show that there is *always* a tendency

---

[10] Remember that for the moment we have ruled out the possibility of increases in prices—which is another possible reaction to a shortage.

[11] The sort of increase in prices mentioned in the previous footnote would also increase the (money) value of national income.

Figure 27–6   The circular flow of income in the simple Frugal economy

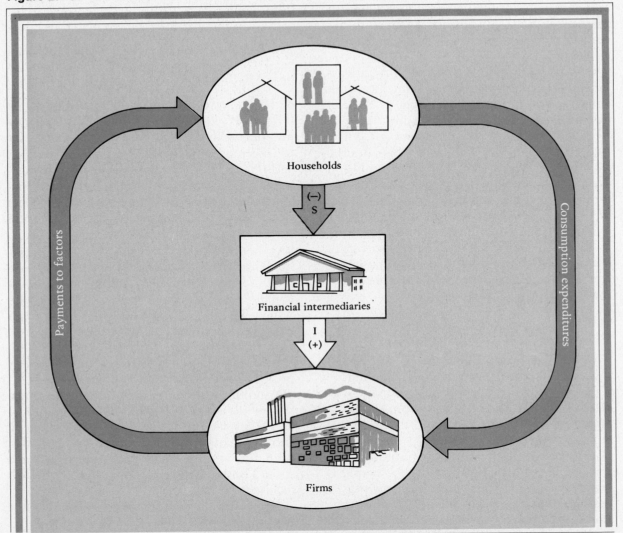

Saving is a withdrawal from and investment is an injection into the circular flow of income between households and firms.   In the simplest version of the Frugal economy, all saving is done by households and all investment is done by firms. Saving withdraws funds from the circular flow and thus exerts a contractionary force, while investment injects funds into the circular flow and thus exerts an expansionary force on the circular flow. The flow of national income is in equilibrium when these two forces balance each other—i.e., when firms desire to invest the same amount as households desire to save.

for national income to be pushed in the direction of its equilibrium value.[12] Only when aggregate desired expenditure is equal to income is there no tendency for national income to change.

It is important to notice that equilibrium income is not the same thing as full-employment income. The latter is the national income that would be produced if there were a 4 percent unemployment rate. The former is the level of income at which desired expenditure equals total income. Nothing in our model guarantees that they will be the same, and equilibrium income may be above or below full-employment income. The amount of unemployment in the economy will depend on the relation between the two; the further below full-employment income is equilibrium income, the more unemployment there will be at equilibrium.

The saving-investment approach to equilibrium

The circular flow of income in the Frugal economy is shown schematically in Figure 27–6. Unlike the Spendthrift economy, the circular flow in the Frugal economy is not a closed circuit because saving is a withdrawal and investment is an injection.[13] The circular flow itself is the flow of expenditure from households to firms and back again. Saving is income received by households and *not* passed back to firms through household consumption expenditure. Saving thus represents a withdrawal from the circular flow. Investment creates income for the firms that make the investment goods, and this income arises from the spending of those firms that buy the

capital goods, not from the spending of households. Investment thus represents an injection of income into the circular flow.

Saving exerts a contractionary force on national income. Investment exerts an expansionary force on national income.

There are, of course, many channels by which the funds saved by households find their way into the hands of firms who wish to invest. By far the most important are financial markets and financial intermediaries. In financial markets firms that wish to raise funds to invest, sell stocks and bonds. Savers who wish to become part owners of firms, buy shares in firms and savers who wish to lend their savings to firms, buy bonds issued by firms. Financial intermediaries are such institutions as banks, savings and loan associations, and insurance companies. They take in savings as deposits on which they pay interest and then make loans on which they charge a higher rate of interest than they pay to their depositors. Thus both financial markets and financial intermediaries provide links between the withdrawal of saving and the injection of investment. But, since saving decisions are made by one group of decision makers and investment decisions by another group, there is no automatic reason why the amount that savers wish to save should be equal to the amount investors wish to invest.

Given the above discussion, you should not be very surprised to find that the circular flow is in equilibrium—with national income neither rising nor falling—when the volume of withdrawals through saving is equal to the volume of injections through investment. Let us see how this comes about.

Look now at Table 27–4. We have already discovered through the income-expenditure approach that in this example the equilibrium level of income is $2,000. But consider what would happen if the value of output were held at $1,000. At this level of income, households wish to save only $100, while firms wish to

---

[12] This requires only that aggregate demand is less than income when national income is above its equilibrium value, and greater than income when national income is below its equilibrium value—conditions that are assured by the assumed shape of the consumption function. [29]

[13] The concepts of withdrawals and injections were first introduced and defined in Chapter 4. They are discussed in greater detail later in this chapter.

Table 27–4 The equilibrium of national income in the Frugal economy: the saving-investment approach (millions of dollars)

National income (Y)	Desired saving (S)	Desired investment (I)	
$ 0	−$100	$300	
100	− 80	300	
400	− 20	300	Pressure on income
500	0	300	to increase
1,000	100	300	↓
2,000	300	300	Equilibrium income
3,000	500	300	↑
4,000	700	300	Pressure on income
5,000	900	300	to decrease

In the simple Frugal economy national income is in equilibrium when firms desire to invest the same amount as households desire to save. Below the equilibrium level of income, desired investment injects more spending into the circular flow than desired saving withdraws from it. This imbalance between the expansionary forces of investment and the contractionary forces of saving tends to cause national income to rise. Above the equilibrium level of national income, desired investment is less than desired saving and the opposite imbalance between expansionary and contractionary forces tends to cause national income to fall. Equilibrium occurs at the level of income of $2000.

invest $300. We have seen that one of two things must happen if output is held at this level. Either firms and households are unable to buy all that they wish because the production is not available or they succeed in buying what they wish but inventories are drawn down because the value of sales exceeds the value of current output.

In the first case, the people who are unable to buy all that they wish are forced to save money that they really wish to spend. Lines of unsatisfied customers develop, and firms see that they could sell more if only they were producing more. In the second case, firms who find their inventories being depleted make less than the $300 total investment that they desire to make because the disinvestment in inventories must be offset against the $300 spent on

capital equipment. Since firms do not wish to deplete their inventories, they increase their production in order to end this unintended inventory depletion. In either case there is a tendency for output and income to rise in response to a situation in which households wish to withdraw less from the circular flow by saving than firms wish to add to it by investing.

Now consider a level of income above the equilibrium, say $4,000. At this income, desired saving exceeds desired investment. If firms insist on producing the quantity of output valued at $4,000, they will be unable to sell all of it and inventories will rise. There will be undesired investment and firms will cut back on their output to eliminate the unwanted increase in inventories; this reduces national

Figure 27-7 The determination of equilibrium national income

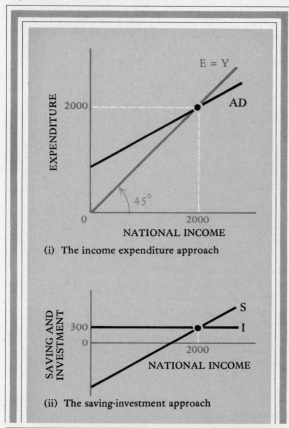

(i) The income expenditure approach

(ii) The saving-investment approach

Equilibrium national income is the level of income at which the aggregate demand curve intersects the 45° line and at which the saving and investment lines cross. Below the equilibrium level of income in (i) the AD curve lies above the 45° line, showing that desired expenditure exceeds income. Above equilibrium income the AD curve lies below the 45° line, showing that desired expenditure is less than income. Below the equilibrium level of income in (ii) the investment curve lies above the saving curve, indicating that desired investment exceeds desired saving. Above equilibrium the saving curve lies above the investment curve, indicating that desired saving exceeds desired investment.

Parts (i) and (ii) necessarily give the same equilibrium level of national income.

income. National income falls in response to a situation in which households wish to withdraw more from the circular flow by saving than firms wish to add to it by investing.

Only when the level of national income is $2,000 will firms and households all be able to save and invest just what they wish to save and invest at an unchanging level of income. Thus in the Frugal economy (but only in that economy) national income is necessarily in equilibrium when saving is equal to investment.

A graphical illustration of equilibrium

Figure 27-7 shows the equilibrium level of national income first using the aggregate demand function and then using the saving and investment functions.

Aggregate demand cuts the 45° line. Where aggregate demand (AD), which is desired expenditure, cuts the 45° line, desired expenditure equals the value of final output and equilibrium is achieved.

We have now developed a simple but very powerful way of describing the determination of equilibrium national income, a general result that holds for this and all more complex models. As we have seen, national income is in equilibrium where aggregate demand (aggregate desired expenditure) is equal to total output (national income).

Graphically, equilibrium occurs at the level of income at which the aggregate demand line intersects the 45° line.

Saving equals investment. As the figure shows, the saving and investment curves intersect at the level of national income where the AD curve cuts the 45° line. This is no coincidence. Desired saving—the difference between income and desired consumption—is the vertical distance between the 45° line and the consumption line. Desired investment—the difference between aggregate demand and desired consumption—is the vertical distance between AD and the consumption line. Where AD and the 45° line cross, these distances are necessarily the same (i.e., desired saving equals desired investment). [30]

This result, which applies only in the case of the Frugal economy, is that national income is in equilibrium when desired saving is equal to desired investment; or, graphically, where the saving line intersects the investment line.

A LINK BETWEEN SAVING AND INVESTMENT?

Earlier in this chapter we stressed that saving and investment decisions were made by different groups and that there was, for example, no necessary reason why households should decide to save the same amount as firms decide to invest. We have just concluded, however, that in the Frugal economy national income is in equilibrium when saving is equal to investment. Does this not mean that we have found a mechanism that ensures that households end up desiring to save an amount equal to what firms desire to invest? The answer is yes. Is there not then a conflict between what we said at first and what we have now concluded? The answer is no.

The explanation of the apparent conflict provides the key to the theory of the determination of national income in the Frugal economy. There is no reason why the amount that households wish to save at a randomly selected level of national income should be equal to the amount that firms wish to invest at that same level of income. This is the meaning of the statement made at the outset. But when desired saving is not equal to desired investment, there are forces at work in the economy that cause national income to change until the two do become equal. This is the meaning of the later statement.

The graphic expression of this argument is that the saving line does not everywhere coincide with the investment line. Where it does

not, desired saving does not equal desired investment at the indicated level of income. But the two lines do intersect somewhere, and the equilibrium level of income, in the Frugal economy, occurs at that intersection point.

A generalization of the theory of equilibrium national income

In the Spendthrift economy there were neither withdrawals from nor injections into the circular flow of income. Consumption was the only use of income and the circular flow remained constant at whatever its present level happened to be. The Frugal economy had one withdrawal (saving) and one injection (investment). The general case has several withdrawals and injections, but the equilibrium conditions for the Frugal economy can be readily generalized to cover all circular-flow models.

THE WITHDRAWALS-INJECTIONS APPROACH IN THE GENERAL CASE

In the Frugal economy one way of describing the equilibrium condition for national income was to say that saving must equal investment. This equilibrium condition requires a slight but important reinterpretation before it can be extended to all circular-flow models. Saving, in the Frugal economy, is only an example of what is called a *withdrawal* from the circular flow of income. A withdrawal is any income received by households not passed on through spending to firms and any income received by firms not passed on through income payments to households. Withdrawals exert a contractionary force on the circular flow. Investment, in the Frugal economy, is only an example of what is called an *injection* into the circular flow. An injection is income received by either a firm or a household that does not arise out of spending of the other group. Injections exert an expansionary force on the circular flow of income.

The general statement of this equilibrium condition for all circular-flow models is that withdrawals equal injections.

In the Frugal economy saving is the only withdrawal and investment is the only injection. Thus it makes no difference if we say that national income is in equilibrium when saving equals investment or when withdrawals equal injections. In more complex models, however, there are many withdrawals and many injections. In such economies national income will be in equilibrium when the aggregate contractionary force of all withdrawals is equal to the aggregate expansionary force of all injections.

All that is required to apply the general case to any particular model is to identify the withdrawals and injections in the model and to make assumptions about how each is related to national income.

Kinds of injections

In the Frugal economy investment was the only injection. We have seen that investment is an injection because it is income received by firms that does not arise out of the spending of households.

Whatever the source of funds, investment injects expenditure into the circular flow.

A second injection is government expenditure for goods and services.[14] Such expenditure creates income for firms that does not arise from the spending of firms. If, for example, the government spends money to buy missiles from private firms, the incomes of these firms will rise, as will the incomes of those households who supply factor services to the firms.

[14] Remember that the government expenditure included in GNP is total government spending *less* transfer payments. See **Part 8, pages 465-466.**

Whatever the source of the funds, government expenditure on goods and services injects expenditure into the circular flow.

A third injection is exports. When foreign firms and households buy American goods or services, they are creating income for American firms that does not arise from the spending of American households; such exports are thus an injection into the circular flow.

Whatever the source of the funds, exports inject expenditure into the domestic circular flow.

Using the symbols J for injections, I for investment, G for government expenditure, and X for exports, we summarize total injections into the circular flow as: $J = I + G + X$.

Kinds of withdrawals

In the Frugal economy saving was the only withdrawal. Saving is a withdrawal because it is income received by households or firms that is not passed on to other households or firms. Of course, saving may subsequently find its way back into the circular flow if savers spend or invest their savings. When they do, they generate consumption or investment expenditure.

Whatever subsequently happens to the money, the act of saving withdraws expenditure from the circular flow.

A second withdrawal from the circular flow is the amount of taxes levied by governments. When the government taxes firms, some of what firms earn is not available to be passed on to households. When the government taxes households, some of what households earn is not available to be passed on to firms. Of course, some of the tax revenue will find its way back into the circular flow when the government subsequently spends it on commodities purchased from firms or factor services purchased from households. If the government does not spend part of the money, however, but merely lets it accumulate as a reserve against some future expected expenditure, that part will remain outside of the flow.

Whatever subsequently happens to the money raised, taxes withdraw expenditure from the circular flow.

A third withdrawal from the circular flow is imports. When households spend their incomes on imported goods instead of domestic ones, incomes are created for foreign firms and foreign households instead of for domestic firms and domestic households. Similarly, purchases of foreign-made machinery by American firms may seem to the purchasers to be just like other investment expenditures, but such expenditures do not enter the American circular flow. Likewise some American government expenditures, such as food and supplies purchased abroad to support American troops or diplomats abroad, are subtractions from the circular flow.

Imports take many forms. When the members of an American family buy a Datsun, or when they take a vacation in Europe, they are purchasing—importing— foreign-made goods and services. They are also importing when they buy an American-made good whose manufacturer purchased some of the raw materials from foreigners. The wool in an American-made lamb's wool sweater, for instance, may have been imported from a sheep ranch in Australia. Each of these expenditures is an import because each creates income for foreign firms.

Whatever subsequently happens to the money spent, imports withdraw expenditures from the circular flow.

Letting W stand for withdrawals, S for saving, T for taxes, and M for imports, we may summarize withdrawals from the circular flow as: $W = S + T + M$.

Figure 27–8 shows the model of the circular flow of income in the economy, with saving, taxes, and imports shown as withdrawals and investment, government expenditure, and exports shown as injections.

Equilibrium in terms of withdrawals and injections

Let us start by assuming that all injections, I, G, and X, are constant. This allows us to study how national income adjusts to a fixed level of investment, government expenditure, and exports. Later we shall study the response of national income to a change in these injections.

Withdrawals, however, cannot be assumed to be constant. We have already seen that the theory of the consumption function predicts that saving will rise as national income rises. The government's tax revenue can also be expected to rise as national income rises: If all tax rates are held constant, tax yields will rise with income. Sales taxes and taxes on personal and business incomes will all produce more money as the value of total output produced and total incomes earned increases. Imports may be expected to exhibit similar behavior. They will tend to rise as national income rises, both because domestic households spend a fraction of their consumption expenditure on foreign rather than on domestically produced commodities and because almost all domestic output has some import content of raw materials and semimanufactured goods. Iron ore, oil, paper, and lumber are only a few of the many examples. Thus we expect all withdrawals—S, T, and M—to rise as income rises.

If withdrawals are less than injections there will be a net expansionary force in the economy. Income will rise. Tax receipts, saving, and imports will all rise along with income, and the expansion will come to a halt when total withdrawals have risen to the level of total injections. If withdrawals exceed injections, there will be a net contractionary force in the economy. Income will fall. Tax receipts, saving, and imports will all fall along

Figure 27–8 The circular flow of income in the general case

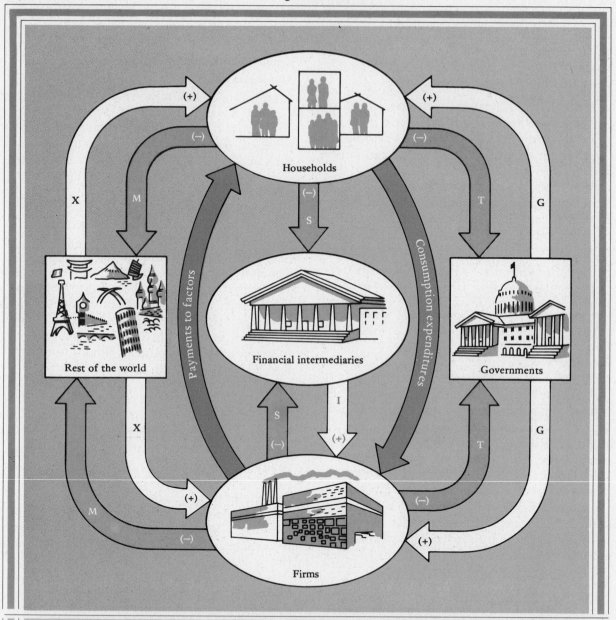

There are many withdrawals from and injections into the circular flow. The basic circular flow of the spendthrift economy (shown in color) is augmented by a series of injections shown as (+) arrows. These are government purchases (G), investment (I), and exports (X). The circular flow is diminished by a series of withdrawals shown as (−) arrows. These are saving (S), taxes (T), and imports (M).

with income, and the contraction will come to a halt when total withdrawals have fallen to the level of total injections. When (but only when) $W = J$, national income will be in equilibrium.

THE INCOME-EXPENDITURE APPROACH IN THE GENERAL CASE

Utilizing the income-expenditure approach in the Frugal economy, we saw that national income will be in equilibrium when (but only when) aggregate demand is exactly equal to total output. This holds without any modification at all. All that needs to be done in moving from one circular-flow model to another is to identify any new components of aggregate demand and to determine (or assume) how each new component is related to national income.

To find total desired expenditure (i.e., aggregate demand) for the output of the domestic (i.e., national) economy, we must take consumption, plus investment, plus government expenditure, plus exports, *minus* imports. We are thus first taking all of the expenditures for final goods and then subtracting that portion that is for foreign-made goods and foreign-provided services. What is left is the aggregate demand for domestic output. This may be expressed as:

$$AD = C + I + G + (X - M).$$

National income as we have seen will be in equilibrium where aggregate demand (aggregate desired expenditure) is equal to national income because in that case desired purchases will exactly total production.

EQUILIBRIUM NATIONAL INCOME: A GENERAL GRAPHICAL APPROACH

Figure 27–9 shows the equilibrium level of national income in terms of both the income-expenditure and the withdrawal-injection approaches. The analysis is essentially the same whether aggregate expenditure is merely $C + I$, as in the Frugal economy, or

Figure 27–9 Equilibrium of the circular flow

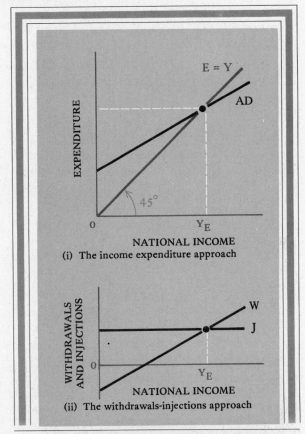

(i) The income expenditure approach

(ii) The withdrawals-injections approach

In the general case the equilibrium level of national income occurs where the aggregate demand line crosses the 45° line, and equivalently where the withdrawal and injection lines cross. (i) Different models of the circular flow include different elements of aggregate demand, but whatever the model, the equilibrium condition using the income expenditure approach is that aggregate demand equals national income. This is at income Y_E.

(ii) Different models of the circular flow include different elements of withdrawals and injections, but whatever the model, the equilibrium condition is that total desired withdrawals equal total desired injections. This occurs at income Y_E.

$C + I + G + (X - M)$, as in the general case. The analysis is the same when there is one injection and one withdrawal, as in the Frugal economy, or several of each, as in the general case.

Equilibrium income always occurs where the withdrawals line cuts the injections line, which is also where the aggregate demand line crosses the 45° line.

When the aggregate demand line lies above the 45° line, national income tends to increase; when the aggregate demand line lies below the 45° line, national income tends to decrease.

Summary

1. Short-term fluctuations in national income are readily observed in the data for the United States and other economies. This chapter presents a simple theory of what determines the level of national income.

2. The simple theory of the determination of national income is based on three simplifying assumptions: (a) potential national income is constant; (b) there are unemployed supplies of all factors of production; (c) the price level is constant.

3. In the Spendthrift economy, households spend all of their income and firms distribute all of their receipts as factor incomes. There are neither withdrawals from nor injections into the circular flow, and whatever national income we begin with will continue forever.

4. In the Frugal economy, households save and firms invest. We first study how national income is affected by the desire to save. The consumption function shows how households desire to divide their income between consumption and saving at different levels of income.

5. Over long periods, the fraction of income spent on consumption tends to be roughly constant, giving the consumption function the shape shown in Figure 27–3. In response to year-to-year changes in income, consumption is thought to behave as shown in Figure 27–4. At low levels of income the average propensity to consume (APC) exceeds unity (there is dissaving); at some break-even level of income APC equals unity; at all higher levels APC is less than unity (there is positive saving). The marginal propensity to consume (MPC) is assumed to be positive but less than unity for all levels of income.

6. The aggregate demand function relates total desired expenditure to total national income. In the Frugal economy aggregate demand includes desired consumption and desired investment. AD is assumed to rise with income. Stated in terms of the income-expenditure approach, national income is in equilibrium when aggregate demand equals national income; graphically, this is where the aggregate demand line cuts the 45° line.

7. Saving is a withdrawal that exerts a contractionary force on the circular flow of income. Investment is an injection that exerts an expansionary force on the circular flow of income. National income in the Frugal economy is in equilibrium when desired saving is equal to desired investment; graphically, this is where the saving and investment lines intersect.

8. There is no reason why firms should desire to invest the same amount as households desire to save out of any given level of national income. When these two magnitudes are not equal, however, income will change (rising when desired investment exceeds desired saving and falling when desired saving exceeds desired investment) until the equilibrium level of income, at which desired saving and investment are equal, is reached.

9. In the general case there are more elements of aggregate demand and more categories of injections withdrawals, but the basic principles of income determination are not changed. Aggregate demand is $C + I + G + (X - M)$ and national income is in equilibrium when AD equals national income; graphically this is at the level of income where AD cuts the 45° line.

10. Injections include investment, government expenditure on goods and services, and exports (symbolically, $J = I + G + X$). Withdrawals include saving, taxes, and imports (symbolically, $W = S + T + M$). Equilibrium income occurs where desired injections equal desired withdrawals, that is, where $J = W$; graphically this is where the injections and withdrawal lines cross.

Concepts for review

Potential national income, full-employment national income, and equilibrium national income

The meaning of full employment

The consumption function

Average and marginal propensities to consume and save

The aggregate expenditure function

The income-expenditure and the withdrawal-injection approaches to determining equilibrium national income

The saving-investment approach as a special case of the withdrawal-injection approach

Discussion questions

1. Under what circumstances might potential GNP and actual GNP move in opposite directions? What might happen to future potential GNP if, as often occurs during a major war, a country devotes as many resources as possible to producing arms and cuts down on the resources used to produce and maintain capital equipment?

2. "The concept of an equilibrium level of national income is useless because the economy is never in equilibrium. If it ever got there, no economist would recognize it anyway." Discuss.

3. Interpret each of the following statements either in terms of the *shape* of a consumption function or the *values* of *MPC* and/or *APC*.

a. *"Tom Green has lost his job and his family is existing on its past savings."*

b. "The Grimsby household is so rich that they used all the extra income they earned this year to invest in a wildcat oil drilling venture."

c. "The widow Harris can barely make ends meet by clipping coupons on the bonds left to her by dear Henry, but she would never dip into her capital."

d. "We always thought Hammerstein was a miser, but when his wife left him he took to wine, women, and song."

4. Can you think of any reasons why an individual's marginal propensity to consume might be higher in the long run than in the short run? Why it might be lower? Is it possible for an individual's average propensity to consume to be greater than unity in the short run? In the long run? Can a country's average propensity to consume be greater than unity in the short run? In the long run?

5. Is it possible that two countries, in each of which withdrawals equal injections at $50 billion, can each be in equilibrium but at different levels of income? Is it possible that two countries with the same levels of consumption and investment but with different levels of withdrawals can be in equilibrium with the same level of income?

6. Along the 45° line on the basic diagram, what relationship holds between total expenditures and total income? In determining equilibrium graphically, are we restricted to choosing identical vertical and horizontal scales?

7. When aggregate desired expenditure equals total output in the Frugal economy, explain why it must also be true that desired savings equals desired investment. Explain why this is not necessarily so in the Governed economy. In the Frugal economy must saving equal investment?

28

Changes in national income

In Chapter 27 we investigated the conditions for national income to be in equilibrium. Recall that when equilibrium is obtained, there is no tendency for national income either to rise or to fall. National income does not, however, remain in a position of unchanging equilibrium; in fact, it changes continuously.

Why national income changes

Must we conclude that the theory of equilibrium national income is so in conflict with observation as to be useless? The answer is no. The theory can be used to explain changes in national income that are observed, to predict some of the circumstances that would cause future changes in national income, and to suggest ways in which the government can alter the course of national income.

In this chapter we take a step toward showing how all this can be done by using the theory of the determination of equilibrium national income to study why income changes. Isolating the main forces that can cause equilibrium income to change in our model allows us to develop possible explanations of why actual national income changes in reality.

As a preliminary to this study, we emphasize an important distinction between movements along curves and shifts of curves.

MOVEMENTS ALONG CURVES VERSUS SHIFTS OF CURVES

If desired consumption expenditure rises, it makes a great deal of difference whether the rise is in response to a change in national income or to an increased desire to consume *at each level of national income* including the present one. The former change is represented

Figure 28-1   Movements along and shifts of curves

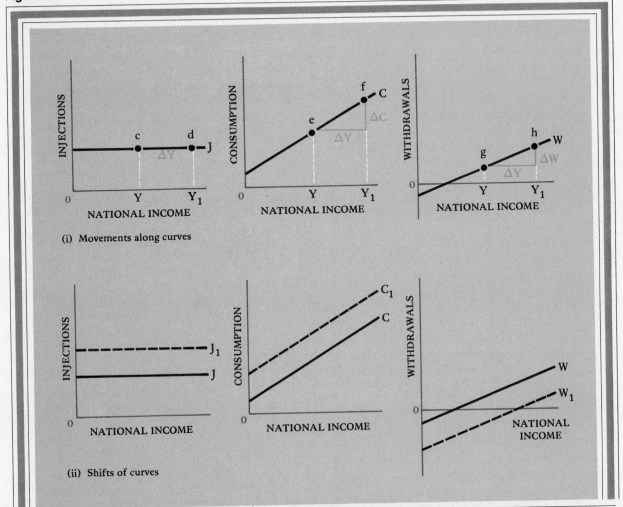

(i) Movements along curves

(ii) Shifts of curves

A movement along a curve occurs in response to a change in income; a shift of a curve indicates a different level of injections, withdrawals, or consumption at each level of income.   In part (i), in response to an increase in income from Y to Y_1, we must *move along* the J, C, and W curves to determine the new flows of injections, consumption, and withdrawals, respectively. The change in income ΔY leads to an increase in withdrawals of ΔW and in consumption of ΔC. Injections do not change—i.e., ΔJ equals zero and is not shown. The slopes of the curves show the ratios of the changes in the variables to the changes in income and are known as marginal propensities.

In each panel of part (ii), the curve *shifts* to the dashed line. The change is not a consequence of a change in income but a change in the whole relationship with income. The indicated shifts represent a rise in the injection schedule, a rise in the consumption schedule, and a fall in the withdrawal schedule.

by a movement along the aggregate consumption schedule; it is the response of consumption to a change in income. The latter change is represented by a shift in the consumption schedule that occurs in response to a change in the proportion of income that households desire to consume. This type of change that can itself disturb an existing equilibrium and cause national income to move from one equilibrium level to another.

Figure 28–1 illustrates this important distinction. The lines in the figure conform to our assumptions about how consumption, injections, and withdrawals are related to national income. The components of injections—*I*, *G*, and *X*—have all been assumed constant. Thus the sum of the three is shown as a constant amount that does not vary with national income. Consumption expenditure, however, is assumed to rise as income rises, and the consumption line thus slopes upward. The three withdrawals—*S*, *T*, and *M*—are all assumed to rise as national income rises. Their sum—total withdrawals—is thus also assumed to rise as income rises, as shown by the upward-sloping *W* schedule in the figure.

The response of injections, consumption, and withdrawals to a change in income is indicated by a movement along the injection, consumption, and withdrawal schedules and is shown graphically by the *slope* of the relevant curve.

The response of any flow, such as consumption, to a change in income is called a **marginal propensity.** In Chapter 27 we defined the marginal propensities to save and to consume as the changes in saving and in consumption that were brought about by a change in income; that is, $\Delta S/\Delta Y$ and $\Delta C/\Delta Y$. The marginal propensities that relate to the curves in Figure 28–1 are the marginal propensities to consume that we have encountered already and the two aggregate propensities that relate changes in total injections ($I + G + X$) and changes in total withdrawals ($S + T + M$) to changes in national income. In the order in which they

appear in the figure, these are (1) marginal propensity to inject expenditure = $\Delta J/\Delta Y$; (2) marginal propensity to consume = $\Delta C/\Delta Y$; (3) marginal propensity to withdraw expenditure = $\Delta W/\Delta Y$. Graphically, these marginal propensities are shown by the *slopes* of the relevant injection, consumption, and withdrawal curves in Figure 28–1(i).

Marginal propensities relate to movements along curves and tell us how much a particular flow responds to a change in income.

Flows of expenditures or withdrawals can change for a second reason: the curves *themselves* may shift, indicating a new level of the relevant flow for *each* level of national income. Such shifts are illustrated in Figure 28–1(ii).[1]

A SHIFT IN THE INJECTION SCHEDULE

What will happen to national income if there is a change in the investment expenditure of private firms, in government expenditure, or in exports? What will happen if, say, the Ford Motor Company invests $25 million in a new plant to build more small cars, if the U.S. government embarks on an extensive rat-extermination program, or if U.S. exports of prefabricated housing soar? Fortunately, the same analysis can be used to study all three changes because each involves an upward shift in the injection schedule.[2]

Figure 28–2 shows that this upward shift

[1] While the figure shows three such shifts, the shift in consumption and the shift in withdrawals are necessarily interrelated. Consider again the Frugal economy in which households save whatever part of their income that is not spent on consumption. An upward shift in the consumption schedule, for example, indicates an increase in the desired consumption expenditure that is associated with each level of income. In this case, desired household saving must fall at each level of income, since *S* is all disposable income not spent on consumption. Therefore, since saving is one component of aggregate withdrawals, a rise in the consumption schedule implies a fall in the withdrawal schedule.

[2] It is extremely important to remember that we are dealing with continuous flows measured as so much per period of time. An upward shift in the injection curve means that *in each period* injections are more than they were previously.

will raise the equilibrium level of national income. After the shift, at the original level of income, injections exceed withdrawals, and this causes income to rise. As income rises, withdrawals rise in response to the change in income. The rise in income continues until withdrawals are once again made equal to the (now higher level of) injections. In other words, the upward shift of the injection curve has induced a movement along the withdrawal curve until the flow of injections is again equal to the flow of withdrawals.

What will happen to national income if there is a fall in investment, exports, or government spending—if, for example, an anticipated fall in automobile sales causes the General Motors Corporation to postpone some major investment projects, if exports of refrigerators to Mexico fall because of increases in Mexican tariffs, or if the government severely reduces its expenditure on urban renewal? Each of these changes involves a downward shift in the injection schedule. The reduction in injection expenditure in each case causes income to fall. Withdrawals fall in response to the fall in income, which continues until withdrawals reach the new, lower level of injections. This, too, is illustrated in Figure 28–2.

We have now derived two important predictions of the theory of national income.

1. A rise in investment expenditure, exports, or government expenditure will raise the level of national income, other things being equal.

2. A fall in investment expenditure, exports, or government expenditure will lower the level of national income, other things being equal.

A SHIFT IN THE WITHDRAWAL SCHEDULE

What will happen to national income if domestic households suddenly go on a spending spree and decrease their savings? Suppose that the spending spree is caused in part by a great improvement in new model American cars, so that households not only save less but

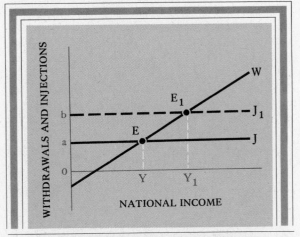

Figure 28–2 The effect on national income of a change in injections

An upward shift in the injection curve—because investment, government expenditure, or exports have increased—increases equilibrium national income. With injection curve J, equilibrium is at E, where income is Y and withdrawals and injections are both a. When the injection curve shifts upward to J_1, income must rise to Y_1 to restore equilibrium. Income rises until withdrawals rise to b to equal the new level of injections. A decrease in injections can be represented by a shift from J_1 to J. Equilibrium income falls from Y_1 to Y.

switch their expenditure from imported to domestically produced automobiles. Suppose, also, that the spending spree is enhanced by a reduction in income tax rates with no corresponding cuts in government expenditure.

Each of these changes causes a downward shift in the withdrawal function, indicating that at each level of income the flow of withdrawals will be lower than it was previously. A fall in the withdrawal schedule is shown in Figure 28–3. The decrease in withdrawals at the initial equilibrium level of income means that injections now exceed withdrawals at that level of income. This causes income to rise until withdrawals increase (in response to

Figure 28–3   The effect on national
income of a change in withdrawals

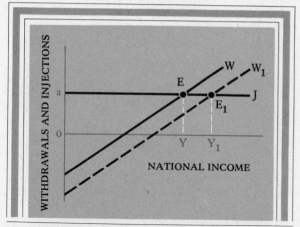

A downward shift in the withdrawal schedule—because saving, tax rates, or imports
have decreased—increases national income.   With the withdrawal schedule W,
equilibrium occurs at E where injections
and withdrawals are both a. If the withdrawal curve shifts downward to W_1,
withdrawals are less than injections at Y.
This causes income to rise to Y_1 where
withdrawals are once again equal to injections. An increase in withdrawals can be
shown by letting the withdrawal schedule
rise from W_1 to W. This reduces equilibrium national income from Y_1 to Y.

ample, to national income if many households
decide to postpone purchases of air condi-
tioners and color television sets for a year,
putting the income into their savings accounts
instead; if tariffs on oriental rugs are lifted and
rug buyers shift from domestic to imported
rugs; or if Congress approves an increase in
the rates of personal income tax that it is not
expected to reverse in the foreseeable future.
These three examples involve a rise in S, in
M, and in T, and in each of these cases the
withdrawal schedule will shift upward. This
is the reverse of the previous case, and equilibrium income will decrease, as shown in
Figure 28–3.

We have now derived two further important predictions from our theory.

3. A fall in tax rates, the saving schedule, or the import schedule will raise the level of national income, other things being equal.

4. A rise in tax rates, the saving schedule, or the import schedule will lower the level of national income, other things being equal.

The four predictions just derived have all
concerned changes in the level of national income. Given the three simplifying assumptions on pages 485–486, the predictions
imply associated changes in the levels of employment and unemployment. With potential
income constant, with unemployed supplies
of all factors of production, and with constant
prices, any increase in national income brings
with it an increase in total employment and a
decrease in unemployment. A decrease in national income brings with it a decrease in total
employment and an increase in unemployment.

The paradox of thrift

These predictions have one important and
rather surprising application. It is frequently
assumed by analogy with an individual
household that for the whole economy thrift
is always good and prodigality always bad;
that the former leads to increased wealth and
prosperity and the latter to eventual bank-

the rise in income) enough to equal injections
once again.

This important mechanism is worth re-
stating. Initially, the withdrawal schedule
shifts downward so that at the original equilibrium level of income withdrawals now are
less than injections. This causes income to
rise. As income rises withdrawals rise in
response. Provided that injections remain
constant, income must go on increasing until
withdrawals return to their initial level so as
to make them once again equal to the unchanged level of injections.

Now consider an upward shift in the withdrawal schedule. What would happen, for ex-

ruptcy. But is a penny saved really as good as a penny earned?

Prediction 4 (above) tells us what we should expect to happen if all households try simultaneously to increase the amount that they save. *The increase in thriftiness will decrease the equilibrium level of national income!* The upward shift in the withdrawal schedule causes withdrawals to exceed injections at the initial equilibrium level of income. National income falls and this induces a decline in withdrawals. The decline in income must continue until withdrawals have been reduced to their original level so that they are once again equal to the unchanged level of injections.[3]

The contrary case, a general decrease in household thriftiness and an increase in consumption, causes a downward shift in the withdrawal function. The attempt on the part of households to reduce saving causes withdrawals to be less than injections. This causes an increase in national income, and the increase continues until the actual volume of withdrawals has been restored to its original level but at a new, higher level of national income.

We have now derived the predictions of the so-called paradox of thrift.

Other things being equal, the more frugal and thrifty are spending units, the lower will be the level of national income and total employment. The more prodigal and spendthrift are spending units, the higher will be the level of national income and employment.

The prediction is not actually a paradox. It is in fact a straightforward, and very important, corollary of prediction 4 that in turn follows logically from the theory of the determination of national income. It seems paradoxical to those who expect the way in which a single household should act if it wishes to raise its wealth and its future ability to consume ("save, save, and save some more") to be directly applicable to the economy as a whole.

The paradox of thrift applies to governments as well as to households. If governments decide to save more they must raise taxes or cut expenditure. The first alternative shifts the withdrawal schedule upward and the second shifts the injection schedule downward. Either policy causes national income to fall until withdrawals are once again equal to injections. If governments decide to save less (i.e., to become more spendthrift), they lower taxes and/or raise spending. This shifts the withdrawal schedule downward and/or the injection schedule upward. Either policy raises equilibrium national income.

The policy implication of this prediction is that substantial unemployment is correctly combated by encouraging governments, firms, and households to *spend* more, not by encouraging them to save more. In times of unemployment and depression, frugality and parsimony will only make things worse. This prediction goes directly against the idea that we should tighten our belts when times are tough. The idea that it is possible to spend one's way out of a depression touches a very sensitive point in the consciences of people raised in the belief that success is based on hard work and frugality and not on prodigality; as a result, the idea very often arouses great emotional hostility.

The implications of the paradox of thrift were not generally understood during the Great Depression of the 1930s. Country after country adopted policies that were, in the light of today's knowledge, disastrously misguided. President Franklin D. Roosevelt, in his first inaugural address (1933), urged:

Our greatest primary task is to put people to work . . . [this task] can be helped by insistence that the Federal, State, and local governments act forthwith

[3] This result, that increased thrift decreases equilibrium income, may seem more intuitively plausible if you remember that an increase in saving out of household income is equivalent to a decrease in household consumption expenditure. Other things remaining the same, this will shift the aggregate demand function downward, and it will cross the 45° line at a lower level of income than it did before.

on the demand that their costs be drastically reduced. . . . There must be a strict supervision of all banking and credits and investment.

Across the Atlantic, King George V told the House of Commons in 1931 that, "The present condition of the national finances, in the opinion of His Majesty's Ministers, calls for the imposition of additional taxation, and for the effecting of economies in public expenditure." At the time, unemployment in America stood at 23 percent of the labor force and that in Britain at 21 percent!

You should not read on until you are sure that you know what national income theory predicts to be the outcome of the policies recommended in the 1930s. The suffering and misery of that unhappy decade would have been greatly reduced if those in authority had known even as much economics as is contained in this chapter.

Assumptions underlying the paradox of thrift

The striking prediction of the paradox of thrift depends critically on two of the basic assumptions on which the elementary theory of national income is based.

1. There is a significant amount of unemployment of all resources, so the level of output depends on total spending and anything that reduces spending reduces output and employment.

2. Injections are assumed to be completely independent of withdrawals; in particular, the volume of investment is independent of the volume of saving. There is no reason, according to the theory, why the amount that firms wish to spend on investment at any level of income should bear any particular relation to the amount that households wish to save. If the Smiths and the Greens save more, so the theory implies, there is no reason why the Johnsons or Acme, Inc., should decide to increase their investment expenditure to make up for their neighbors' saving.

If the economy is at full employment, then the first assumption will not be correct. In such circumstances a decrease in household saving and an increase in consumption expenditure will not cause an increase in real output and employment since full employment already exists. In such circumstances the effect of an increase in spending will probably be to cause an inflation. An increase in saving, however, with its accompanying decrease in spending, will tend to reduce output and employment.

If the second assumption is incorrect, none of the predictions of the paradox of thrift need hold. If, for example, the withdrawal and injection functions are linked together because changes in household saving cause changes in investment, there would be offsetting shifts in *both* the withdrawal and injection functions whenever the desire to save changed. An increase in the desire to save, for example, would shift upward the withdrawal function but, by permitting more investment, would also shift up the injection function, and no downward pressure on national income might emerge.

The predictions of the paradox of thrift, and most of the other predictions of the elementary theory of national income, depend critically, therefore, on the assumption that saving and investment decisions are taken to a great extent by different groups in society and that there is no mechanism whereby a change in the amount that is desired to be saved at a particular level of income will cause a change in the amount that is desired to be invested at the same level of income.

COMPENSATING SHIFTS IN INJECTIONS AND WITHDRAWALS

We have seen that national income is in equilibrium when total desired withdrawals equal total desired injections. The condition for income to be in equilibrium may be written as $W = J$. There is, however, no need for any particular withdrawal to equal any particular injection. The equality of overall W and J in equilibrium does not necessarily imply that saving equals investment $(S = I)$, that government expenditure equals tax revenue $(T = G)$, or that imports equal exports $(M = X)$. Governments can spend more than they raise in taxes, in which case we say there is a **budget deficit.** The deficit may be covered by borrowing, which increases the national debt. Governments may also spend less than they raise in taxes, in which case we say there is a **budget surplus.** The surplus will be used to repay past borrowing, thereby reducing the national debt. Similarly, households can save more than firms wish to borrow for voluntary investment, and the surplus can pile up as idle funds deposited with banks and other financial institutions; at other times firms can invest more than households voluntarily wish to save, and the extra funds for investment can be borrowed from banks or other financial institutions. Finally, imports can be more or less than exports, and the deficit or surplus on foreign trading can be covered by international borrowing and lending.

It follows from all this that it is possible to have compensating changes in various withdrawals and injections.

If any injection changes, an equal and opposite change in another injection would leave total injections, and hence equilibrium national income, unchanged. Also, an equal change in some withdrawal, in the same direction as the change in injections, would leave equilibrium national income unchanged.

Consider an equilibrium situation $(W = J)$ in which both the government budget and international payments are in balance. This means that $G = T$ and $M = X$. Because, in equilibrium, total withdrawals must equal total injections, it follows that $S = I$. Now assume that fear of a recession leads to a decrease in the desire to invest on the part of private firms, causing a downward shift in the

injection function. The theory predicts that, *ceteris paribus,* this will lead to a fall in income and employment. *But other things do not have to remain equal.*

Although there may be no automatic tendency for a compensating change, the government can choose policies designed to be offsetting. Indeed, if it wishes to compensate exactly for the decrease in private investment, the government has two possible courses of action. First, it can increase government spending by exactly the same amount that investment has decreased, leaving *total* injections $(G + I + X)$ unchanged. Equilibrium national income will thus remain at its original level. While total injections remain equal to total withdrawals, G will now be greater than T (there is a budget deficit) and I less than S. Second, if the government does not wish to increase spending, it may cut taxes sufficiently to compensate for the fall in investment expenditure. In this case, there is a fall in withdrawals to compensate for the initial fall in injections. Again, income will not change, but the government will end up with a budget deficit, this time because its tax revenue will fall while its expenditure remains unchanged. As in the first case, I will be less than S.

Making compensating changes in injections and withdrawals is a basic part of government policy designed to stabilize national income in the face of shifts in flows of private spending.

These changes will be considered in detail in Chapter 30.

AN ALTERNATIVE METHOD OF DERIVING THE BASIC PREDICTIONS

We saw in Chapter 27 that the equilibrium level of national income can be determined using either the withdrawals-injections approach or the income-expenditure approach. You should not be surprised to learn, therefore, that the four predictions derived on pages

Figure 28–4   Shifts in aggregate demand and changes in equilibrium income

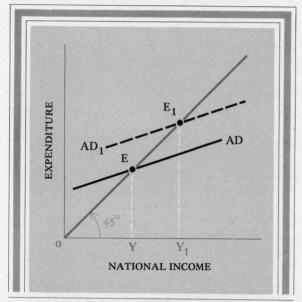

Upward shifts in aggregate demand increase equilibrium income; downward shifts in aggregate demand decrease equilibrium income. Suppose aggregate demand is AD. Equilibrium is at E, with income Y. Anything that increases aggregate demand—an increase in C, I, G, X, or a decrease in M—will shift aggregate demand upward, say to AD_1. It will therefore cut the 45° line at a higher level of income, shift the equilibrium point to E_1 at the level of income Y_1. A downward shift in aggregate demand can be shown by a shift from AD_1 to AD, and a decrease in equilibrium income from Y_1 to Y.

that shifts it downward will decrease income.

As we saw, the components of aggregate demand are:

$$AD = C + I + G + X - M$$

It is immediately clear that a rise in I, G, or X will raise AD and thus increase equilibrium income (prediction 1); a fall in I, G, or X will lower AD and thus decrease equilibrium income (prediction 2).

Changes in withdrawals are a bit more complicated. A fall in imports raises AD directly; a downward shift in the saving schedule means an upward shift in the consumption schedule and thus an increase in AD. A fall in taxes leaves households and firms with more money, some of which they will spend for consumption and investment, thereby increasing aggregate demand. All of these decreases in withdrawals lead to an increase in AD—and therefore to an increase in equilibrium income (prediction 3). By parallel but reverse arguments, a rise in imports, saving, or tax schedules leads to a fall in AD—and therefore to a decrease in equilibrium income (prediction 4).

The multiplier: a measure of the magnitude of changes in income

The direction of the effect on national income of various changes in injections has been considered, but what about the *magnitude* of these changes? If the annual flow of injections changes by some amount (ΔJ), by *how much* will income change? The economist must know the answer to this question in order to determine the effects of changes in expenditures in both the private and the public sectors. Between 1973 and 1975 gross private investment in the United States fell by over $35 billion. How much of a drop in income would have resulted had nothing been done by the government? Clearly, it matters

508–510 using the withdrawals-injections approach can also be derived using the income-expenditure approach. Without repeating the entire analysis in detail, the essence of the argument can be illustrated by referring to Figure 28–4.

Anything that shifts the AD curve upward will increase equilibrium income; anything

whether the drop would have been $35 billion or $140 billion. Another example: President Ford in 1976 proposed a tax cut that would reduce the government's annual tax yield by $28 billion. To predict the effect of this policy on employment, one had to know how much national income would increase as a result. If government measures taken to stimulate the economy in times of depression have a larger effect than estimated, demand may rise too rapidly and full employment may be achieved with demand still rising. This will have an inflationary effect because no further increase in output can occur to meet further increases in demand. If, on the other hand, the government greatly overestimates the effect of its measures, much time will have been wasted. There is also a danger that the policy will be discredited as ineffective, even though the correct diagnosis is merely that too little of the right thing was done.

THE DEFINITION OF THE MULTIPLIER

A central prediction of national income theory is that an increase in expenditure, whatever its source, will cause an increase in national income that is greater than the initial increase in expenditure. The **multiplier** is defined as the ratio of the change in national income to the initial change in expenditure that brings it about. The change in expenditure might come, for example, from an increase in private investment, from new government spending, or from additional household consumption expenditure accompanied by a decline in household saving.

The importance of the multiplier in national income theory makes it worthwhile using more than one approach to develop it and to show why its value exceeds unity.

THE MULTIPLIER:
AN INTUITIVE STATEMENT

What would you expect to happen to national income if there were a rise in government expenditure on road building of $1 billion per year with no corresponding rise in taxes? Would national income rise by only $1 billion? Anyone who has mastered the theory developed so far should not have much trouble in replying, "No, national income will rise by more than $1 billion." This can be argued in either of two ways, remembering that we are dealing with flows and that a rise of $1 billion means that much extra spent on roads each year. First, we can say that a permanent increase in government expenditure of $1 billion per annum will cause further induced increases in consumption expenditure. The impact of the initial rise will be felt by the construction industry and by all those industries that supply it. Income and the employment of factors will rise by $1 billion as a result. But these newly employed factors will spend much of their income buying food, clothing, shelter, holidays, cars, refrigerators, and a host of other products. This is the induced rise in consumption expenditure, and when output expands to meet this extra demand, employment will rise in all of the affected industries. When the owners of factors that are newly employed spend their incomes, output and employment will rise further; more income will then be created and more expenditure induced. Indeed, at this stage we might begin to wonder if the increase in income will ever come to an end. This question is more easily answered if we look at the second way in which the process of income expansion might be described.

The initial rise in government expenditure is a rise in injections. This will increase income, but as income rises the volume of withdrawals (tax receipts, imports, and saving) will rise. Income will continue to rise until additional withdrawals of $1 billion have been generated. At this point, withdrawals will have risen by as much as the original (permanent) rise in injections and, assuming we began from a position of equilibrium, we will be back in equilibrium. For example, if 40 percent of all income is withdrawn through

The multiplier: a numerical approach

Suppose that the economy behaves in this simple way: Every time people receive some additional income they promptly spend 60 percent of it on domestically produced goods and services and withdraw 40 percent for taxes, saving, and purchases of foreign goods and services. This economy's marginal propensity to spend is 0.60 and to withdraw is 0.40.

Now suppose that injections increase in the form of the government's spending $1 billion a year on new roads. National income rises by $1 billion. But that is not the end of it; there is a second round of spending. The factors involved directly and indirectly in road building withdraw $400 million for saving, taxes, and imports but they spend an extra $600 million each year on domestically produced goods and services. The recipients of this $600 million in turn spend an extra $360 million a year (60

percent of $600 million), which is a third round of additions to aggregate expenditure. And so it continues, with each successive recipient of new income spending 60 percent of it on domestically produced goods. Each additional round of expenditure creates new income and yet an additional round of expenditure.

The table below carries the process through ten rounds. The student with sufficient patience (and no faith in mathematics) may compute as many rounds in the process as he or she wishes and notice that the sum of the rounds of expenditures approaches $2.5 billion, which is two and a half times the initial injection of $1 billion. This argument then leads to the same result as did the intuitive argument in the text. The multiplier is 2.5, given these numerical assumptions about spending and withdrawals.

	Increases in expenditures	Increases in withdrawals
	(millions of dollars)	
Assumed increase in government expenditure per period	$1,000.00	
2nd round (increase in expenditures and withdrawals)	600.00	$ 400.00
3rd round ,, ,, ,, ,, ,,	360.00	240.00
4th round ,, ,, ,, ,, ,,	216.00	144.00
5th round ,, ,, ,, ,, ,,	129.60	86.40
6th round ,, ,, ,, ,, ,,	77.76	51.84
7th round ,, ,, ,, ,, ,,	46.66	31.10
8th round ,, ,, ,, ,, ,,	28.00	18.66
9th round ,, ,, ,, ,, ,,	16.80	11.20
10th round ,, ,, ,, ,, ,,	10.08	6.72
Sum of 1st 10 rounds	2,484.90	989.92
All other rounds	15.10	10.08
Total [31]	$2,500.00	$1,000.00

taxes, saving, and imports, then the rise in income will come to a halt when income has risen $2.5 billion. At this higher level of income, an extra $1 billion in withdrawals will have been generated, and since the rise in withdrawals equals the initial rise in injections, income will no longer be rising.

Thus the increase in income does come to a halt. In this example, the multiplier is 2.5 because a rise in government expenditure of $1 billion causes a rise in national income of $2.5 billion. The actual numerical value of the multiplier depends critically on the fraction of national income withdrawn and the fraction spent. As we shall see, the size of the multiplier is the reciprocal of the fraction of income withdrawn—in this example, 1/.4 = 2.5.

THE MULTIPLIER: A GRAPHIC REPRESENTATION

Figure 28–5 illustrates the multiplier. With injections equal to withdrawals at $300 billion each, national income is shown in equilibrium at $1,200 billion. Now suppose injections rise by $1 billion, perhaps due to a new government road building program. A new equilibrium level of income will occur where withdrawals are equal to the now higher level of injections. In this case, the new level of income is $1,202.5 billion. The ratio of the increase in income (ΔY) to the increase in injections that brought it about (ΔJ) is the multiplier. Let K be the multiplier; then, in this example,

$$K = \frac{\Delta Y}{\Delta J} = \frac{2.5}{1} = 2.5$$

This much is simply definition; it repeats in symbols the definition given on page 515 In order to understand what determines the size of the multiplier, remember that, by the time the new equilibrium is reached, withdrawals must have increased until they are again equal to injections. Income must increase enough to induce people to increase

Figure 28–5 The multiplier

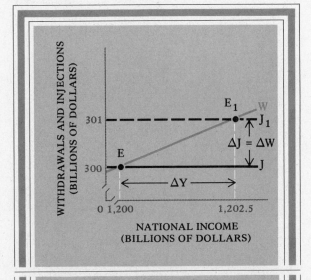

Graphically, the multiplier is the reciprocal of the slope of the withdrawal curve. The shift in injections by $1 billion from J to J_1 increases equilibrium income from $1,200 billion to $1,202.5 billion. This increase, ΔY, is larger than the increase in injections, ΔJ, that brought it about. The multiplier is defined as $K = \Delta Y/\Delta J$. It is 2.5 in this case. In order to restore equilibrium, withdrawals must change by the same amount as injections so that $\Delta J = \Delta W$. Thus when at equilibrium $\Delta Y/\Delta J = \Delta Y/\Delta W$. The latter is the reciprocal of the slope of the withdrawal curve.

their withdrawals by the required amount. Comparing the new equilibrium level of income brought about by the increase in injections, to the old one, $\Delta J = \Delta W$. (If the change in withdrawals were not equal to the change in injections, W could not equal J at both levels of income.) Thus we can substitute ΔW for ΔJ in the equation above: $K = \Delta Y/\Delta W$. But $\Delta Y/\Delta W$ is merely the reciprocal of the slope of the withdrawal

Figure 28–6   The effect on the multiplier of the slope of the withdrawal curve

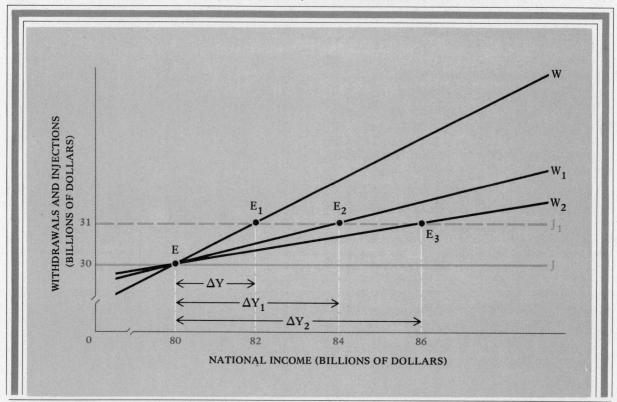

The steeper the withdrawal curve, the smaller is the value of the multiplier.   A shift in injections by $1 billion from J to J_1 produces different effects depending on the slope of the withdrawal curve. W, W_1, and W_2 represent three different withdrawal schedules. In response to $\Delta J = \$1$ billion, the respective changes necessary to restore equilibrium are $\Delta Y = \$2$ billion, $\Delta Y_1 = \$4$ billion, and $\Delta Y_2 = \$6$ billion. The multipliers are 2, 4, and 6, respectively. The flatter the withdrawal curve, the larger must be the increase in income before withdrawals rise to the new level of injections; thus the larger is the value of the multiplier.

function. Letting $w = \Delta W/\Delta Y$ represent the slope of the withdrawal function, called the "marginal propensity to withdraw expenditure" on page 508, it is clear that $K = 1/w$.

Given that consumption rises with income, the prediction that the multiplier, K, is greater than unity can easily be derived. If some part of any rise in income is spent on consumption, the increase in withdrawals must be less than the increase in income; that is, w must be less than 1. But because $K = 1/w$, K must be greater than 1. Two important predictions about the multiplier have now been derived. The first is:

The value of the multiplier is equal to the reciprocal of the fraction of national income withdrawn, $K = 1/w$.

The second, which follows from the theory of the consumption function, is:

Because *w* is less than 1, *K* must be greater than 1. The smaller is *w*, the larger is *K*.

This is illustrated in Figure 28–6. The result that the multiplier decreases as *w* increases has a strong common sense explanation. In the example with which we began the discussion, the government spends an additional $1 billion per year on road building without raising tax rates. Because the households that gain the extra income generated by this government expenditure will raise their own expenditure, this will increase national income and thereby induce further spending. The greater is the increase in expenditure (the smaller the increase in withdrawals) caused by each increment to income, the greater will be the final increase in national income.

If, at one extreme, the marginal propensity to withdraw were zero, then income would go on increasing without limit because each new increment in income would cause an equal increment in new expenditure that would cause a further equal increment in income. In this case the multiplier would be infinite. If, at the other extreme, the marginal propensity to withdraw were unity, then the initial recipients of the $1 billion of income generated by the government's road-building program would spend none of it and would thus induce no further expenditure. The rise in income would be only the initial rise of $1 billion directly caused by the government's road-building expenditure. In this case the multiplier would be unity.

HOW LARGE IS THE MULTIPLIER IN THE UNITED STATES TODAY?

The predictions and the policy implications of a multiplier of 1.5 or 2 are very different from those of a multiplier of 5 or 10. Will $10 billion of new investment expenditure increase national income by $15 billion or by $50 billion? Clearly this is an important question.

If the marginal propensity to withdraw in-come is known or can be estimated, the magnitude of the effect on income of a change in any injection or of any shift in consumption can be estimated.

Many studies of the American economy have been made and they suggest that as a rough order of magnitude the GNP multiplier is about 2. This may not sound very precise. But only about three decades ago economists thought the multiplier might be as high as 5 or 8. Today we are confident that an increase in injections of $10 billion will lead to an increase in GNP of roughly $20 billion—maybe only $18 billion or maybe as much as $25 billion—but we are certain that (other things remaining approximately equal) it will not increase GNP by so much as $50 billion or so little as only $11 billion. For practical purposes this acquired knowledge makes an enormous difference in our ability to control the economy.

Inflationary and deflationary gaps

So far we have stuck to the assumptions that there are some unemployed resources and that prices are constant. In these circumstances, every change in aggregate expenditure causes a change in real national income, output, and employment. What would happen if a rise in desired aggregate expenditure brought the economy into the range of full employment of all resources? Once this occurred, further sharp rises in aggregate expenditure could not be met by increases in real output. It would be likely that prices would rise instead.

Situations of unemployment are referred to as deflationary, and situations in which there is full employment and excess aggregate demand are referred to as inflationary. In *deflationary situations* prices often tend to be fairly steady and real output tends to vary as ag-

Figure 28–7 The L-shaped relation

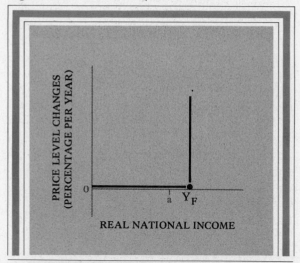

PRICE LEVEL CHANGES
(PERCENTAGE PER YEAR)

0

a Y_F

REAL NATIONAL INCOME

According to the L-shaped relation inflation will never occur unless the economy
is at the full-employment income. The
L-shaped relation between the level of real
national income and changes in the price
level reflects the following assumptions:
(1) To the left of full-employment output,
Y_F, fluctuations in aggregate demand
cause variations in output and employment, with a constant price level; (2) once
the economy's real income reaches Y_F,
further increases in aggregate demand
cause rising prices but leave output and
employment unchanged.

situations, and we may now see one way in
which this can be done.

The L-shaped relation

In elementary treatments, a sharp distinction
is drawn between two situations. The first is
characterized by unemployed supplies of all
factors of production, and in this situation all
changes in aggregate demand are met by
changes in output and employment while
prices remain unchanged.[5] This is the situation that we have dealt with until now. The
second situation is characterized by full employment of all factors of production, and in
it all increases in aggregate demand are met
by increases in prices—that is, by an inflation.

The assumptions described here are shown
in Figure 28–7 by a so-called **L-shaped relation** between the level of output and changes
in prices.[6]

In an economy to which the L-shaped relation applies, real national income and employment vary with the level of aggregate
expenditure as long as national income is
below the full-employment point. Once national income reaches the full-employment
point, however, further increases in real output and employment are impossible. To see
the effect of further increases in aggregate
expenditure in such situations, suppose that
the economy has been at equilibrium at the

gregate expenditure varies.[4] In *inflationary situations* output tends to be fairly steady at its
full-employment level but prices tend to rise.

So far our macro models have all been applied to deflationary situations. We will
shortly need to extend them to inflationary

[4] This is unfortunate terminology because the word "deflation" commonly refers to decreases in the price level, and thus
in this context it suggests that prices will be falling. The assumption in the present theory is that prices are constant at less
than full employment. A better term might be "contractionary." But, for better or worse, the term "deflationary" has
come to be attached to situations of less than full employment.

[5] It is a matter of common observation that the price level tends
to be very sticky in a downward direction. There has not been a
year since World War II in which the American price level has
declined significantly, in spite of unemployment rates of up to
8.5 percent of the labor force. Even in the 1930s, in the face of
massive unemployment, only very modest reductions in the
price level were observed and then only in a very few years.
Thus the assumption that the price level does not fall in times
of unemployment is very close to the mark.

[6] You may wonder how a ⌐-shaped relation came to be
described as L-shaped. The reasons are to be found in the history of early post-Keynesian economics, and we need not
spend time on them here. Perhaps it would be simpler to accept
the alternative explanation that since it was an English economist who first conferred the name and since English economists commonly begin their works with quotations from
Lewis Carroll, this particular economist was making an
obscure allusion to *Alice Through the Looking-Glass* when he
called a ⌐-shaped relation L-shaped.

Figure 28–8 Deflationary and inflationary gaps

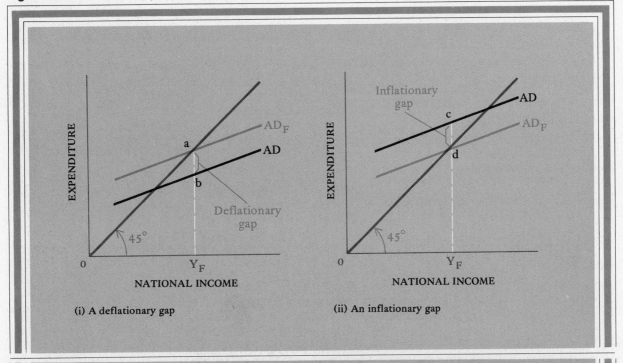

(i) A deflationary gap   (ii) An inflationary gap

The deflationary gap measures the amount by which aggregate demand would fall short of national income at full-employment income. The inflationary gap measures the amount by which aggregate demand would exceed national income at full-employment income. AD_F is the level of aggregate demand that would lead to equilibrium a the full-employment level of income Y_F. (This is the level of income in Figure 28–7 where the corner occurs in the L-shaped relation.) AD is the actual level of aggregate demand. (i) AD is too low to achieve equilibrium at Y_F. The deflationary gap is measured by the vertical distance between AD and the 45° line at the full-employment level of income—the distance *ab*. Note that it is a *vertical* distance showing the shortfall in expenditure, not the loss of income due to insufficient aggregate demand. (ii) AD shows that there is excess aggregate demand at the full-employment level. The inflationary gap is the distance *cd*, the vertical distance between AD and the 45° line at the full-employment level of income.

full-employment level of national income and that the aggregate expenditure schedule then shifts upward. Real output cannot increase no matter how great expenditure may be. If total desired expenditure exceeds the value of full-employment output, all that will happen is that prices will rise. Instead of national income rising because more output is produced at constant prices, national income will rise

because the full-employment level of real output will be sold at higher and higher money prices.

THE "GAPS" DEFINED

If national income is in equilibrium at less than full employment, a sufficiently large upward shift in the aggregate demand function would raise national income to its full-employment level.

The extent to which the aggregate demand schedule would have to shift upward to produce the full-employment level of national income is called the **deflationary gap.**

The deflationary gap is represented graphically in Figure 28–8(i).

Figure 28–9 Inflationary and deflationary gaps in terms of injections and withdrawals

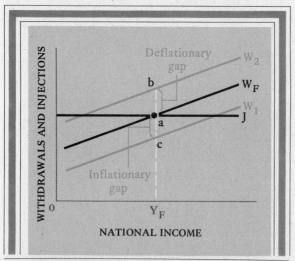

The inflationary and deflationary gaps may also be expressed in terms of desired withdrawals and injections at full-employment national income. For the given level of injections, W_F is the level of withdrawals that leads to an equilibrium level of income Y_F with full employment and no inflation. The higher level of withdrawals, W_2, leads to a lower level of income. The distance *ab* is the deflationary gap. The lower level of withdrawals, W_1, would have injections in excess of withdrawals by the amount *ac* when Y_F was reached. This amount is the inflationary gap—the amount by which injections would have to be decreased, or withdrawals increased, to yield full-employment income without further expansionary pressures.

If aggregate demand exceeds output at the full-employment level of income there is inflationary pressure—enough output to satisfy demand at current prices cannot be produced.

The extent to which the aggregate demand schedule would have to shift downward to produce the full-employment level of national income without inflation is called the **inflationary gap.**

The inflationary gap is represented in Figure 28–8(ii). An alternative illustration of both gaps is given in Figure 28–9.[7]

USING THE CONCEPTS OF THE "GAPS"

The modern theory of income determination is an elaboration of the original model put forward by John Maynard Keynes in *The General Theory of Employment, Interest and Money,* first published in 1936. In the original Keynesian model, the emphasis was on deflationary rather than inflationary conditions. This was not surprising since Keynes was concerned to find cures for the Great Depression, which had had disastrous consequences for the tens of millions of workers who made up the massive armies of unemployed in Western industrial nations. Indeed, the Depression was helping to undermine the very social fabric of Western democracies; finding a cure for it was then the most pressing social problem.

The extension of the theory to cover problems of full employment and inflation did not come until World War II, when those problems replaced the nightmare of persistent, massive unemployment in the minds and consciences of people. The concept of the inflationary gap proved the vehicle for extending the theory beyond the conditions that it was originally designed to explain.

The concepts of both inflationary and de-

[7] Both gaps can be expressed in terms of a single difference: aggregate desired expenditure at full-employment income *minus* full-employment income. If this difference is negative we speak of a deflationary gap; if it is positive we speak of an inflationary gap.

flationary gaps prove useful in discussing policy questions of how to achieve stability in the economy. That discussion can be foreshadowed by noting that one way to combat unemployment is to estimate the size of the deflationary gap and attempt to eliminate it by policies that shift the aggregate expenditure curve upward. Similarly, one way to combat inflation is to estimate the size of the inflationary gap and attempt to eliminate it by policies that shift the aggregate expenditure curve downward. Such policies are discussed in detail in Chapters 30 and 31.

A word of warning

The sharp distinction between deflationary and inflationary gaps illustrated in Figures 28–8 and 28–9 represents a severe simplification of reality that can aid us greatly in our study of some problems. Later on we will drop this simplification and study the very important case in which the economy is in the border region between the two situations. In this region there is enough unemployment so that output can be increased but some resources are close enough to being fully employed that there is also some inflationary pressure in the economy. In such circumstances a rise in aggregate expenditure will lead both to a rise in real output and to a rise in prices. Such situations are dealt with in Chapter 42. Meanwhile, we can make good use of the simplified model in which national income is *either* less than full-employment income and prices are constant *or* at its full-employment level and prices are constant if there is no inflationary gap or rising if there is one.

Summary

1. The slopes of injection, consumption, and withdrawal schedules are designated as the marginal propensities to inject, consume, and withdraw, respectively. The sizes of these determine the effect on income of movements along the schedules. Shifts of the schedules indicate a different level of injections, consumption, or withdrawals associated with each level of income.

2. National income will be increased by a rise in consumption, exports, government expenditure, or investment and by a fall in imports, taxes, or saving. National income will be decreased by the opposite changes.

3. These predictions have an important counterintuitive application: the paradox of thrift. What is true for the individual is not true for the nation. If everyone reduces consumption and increases saving, national income will fall. Leading governments demonstrated ignorance of this by their economic policies during the Great Depression when they tried to fight the Depression by cutting their expenditures because their tax revenues had fallen.

4. A decrease in one injection need not lead to a fall in income if it is offset by a rise in another injection or a fall in a withdrawal. The possibility of compensating shifts gives policy makers the opportunity to offset changes in the private sector by changes in government expenditure or taxation.

5. The magnitude of the effect on national income of shifts in the injections schedule is given by the multiplier. This is defined as $K = \Delta Y / \Delta J = 1/w$, where w is the marginal propensity to withdraw.

6. It is a basic prediction of national income theory that the multiplier will be greater than unity. Its actual size is a most important magnitude. As a rough order of magnitude for the United States today, the GNP multiplier is taken to be about 2. (An increase in injections of \$$X$ billion will tend to lead to an increase in GNP of about \$$2X$ billion.)

7. The notions of inflationary and deflationary gaps are ways to characterize the levels of aggregate demand relative to the level required to achieve full employment. An inflationary gap means that aggregate demand is more than sufficient to produce full-employment national income at constant prices. A deflationary gap means that it is not sufficient.

Concepts for review

Shifts of and movements along the $W, J, C,$ and AD schedules

The effect on national income of changes in $I, G, X, S, T,$ and M

The paradox of thrift

Compensating shifts in withdrawals and injections

The multiplier

The relation between the size of the multiplier and the slope of the withdrawal schedule

The L-shaped relation

Inflationary and deflationary gaps

Discussion questions

1. In what direction would each of the following change national income, *ceteris paribus*? Which withdrawal or injection would be affected first? Would other elements of withdrawals and injections also change? Be sure to distinguish between movements along schedules and shifts of schedules.

a. the production and sale of fighter planes to Israel

b. a decrease in personal income tax withholding for low-income taxpayers

c. the institution of a new federal program of $2 billion of payments to the elderly

d. a spurt in consumer spending for CB radios accompanied by a reduction in savings

e. a decision to end the space-shuttle program

2. The fallacy of composition is defined as a fallacy in which what is true of a part is inaccurately assumed to be true also of the whole. Can the "paradox" in the paradox of thrift be explained by applying this point of logic? Explain.

3. Predict whether each of the following events will, *ceteris paribus,* increase, decrease, or leave unchanged the size of the multiplier:

a. a shift from foreign travel to holidays at home

b. an expansion of federal expenditures on the interstate highway program.

c. decisions by corporations to pay out a smaller percentage of their earnings in dividends and increase their bank balances whenever national income falls.

d. widespread adoption by cities of a city income tax.

4. If you were running a country's economic stabilization program, would you prefer the country to have a large or a small multiplier?

5. The president of the Chamber of Commerce of Southeastern Connecticut commented on the effects in his area of a 22-week strike at a shipyard where the lost payroll was $2 million per week: "You don't just figure $2 million a week times 22 weeks, you have to multiply that by four or five. That shipyard is the prime source of money in this region. Money comes into the region from Washington and then the shipyard worker's wife takes it to the grocery, and the grocery clerk takes it to the gas station, and so on until it leaves the area in taxes or some other way." Interpret his statement in terms of the analysis of this chapter.

6. Homer Hardcrust, chairman of the Council of Economics Advisers, proposes that because of the economic situation the government should prepare an austerity program and cut down government expenditures to set an example for private households. Under what economic conditions might Hardcrust's advice make sense? Under what conditions would it worsen the situation?

7. "We now have approximately 70 percent of our industrial capacity being used; which means that 30 percent or so is not being used. With eight million people unemployed, that's another tremendous untapped reservoir of workers and capacity that can be tapped before you have pressures of an inflationary type." Does the speaker (President Carter, at a 1977 news conference) express views consistent with the L-shaped relation?

Cycles and fluctuations in national income

Changing, always changing; this is the dominant characteristic of the GNP for as far back as records exist. Long-term growth and short-term fluctuations are the two major components of the GNP changes that we observe. Long-term growth is seen in the steady upward trend in the potential GNP—the GNP that can be produced when the economy is at full employment. Long-term growth will be studied in Chapters 43 and 44. Shorter-term fluctuations are seen in oscillations of actual GNP around the level set by potential GNP. Such oscillations are related to changes in what is actually produced, and these changes cause variations in the amount of productive resources left unemployed. Short-term fluctuations in GNP are the subject of the present chapter.

THE HISTORICAL RECORD

Figure 29–1 shows the year-to-year changes in real GNP. What produces such changes? If, on the one hand, any of the components of aggregate demand—consumption, investment, government expenditure, or net exports—should fall without a compensating change in any of the other components, total demand will fall. Total output will soon be reduced in response, and employment and actual GNP will fall. If, on the other hand, any of the components of aggregate demand rise without a compensating change in any of the other components, total demand will rise. This will cause a rise in real output, and employment and real GNP will rise—at least until all available factors of production become fully employed.

Fluctuations in aggregate demand have always been the major reason for short-term fluctuations in the GNP. Events of the mid 1970s, however, have made the citizens of advanced industrial countries acutely aware of other possible causes. If supplies of such critical raw materials as oil or iron ore are drastically reduced, output will fall and unemploy-

Figure 29–1 Annual changes in real GNP

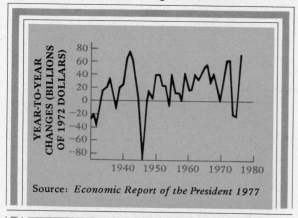

Source: *Economic Report of the President 1977*

Real national income changes continually from one year to the next. Despite a strong upward trend shown by the fact that most changes are increases, real national income does not rise steadily year after year. Generally, two or three years of very rapid increase tend to be followed by two or three years of slow increase, or even decline, in GNP.

ment will rise even though there is enough demand to buy the whole of the economy's potential GNP. If goods cannot be produced, they cannot be sold.

In Chapter 28 we developed a theory of how national income changes in response to changes in the various components of aggregate demand. If there were merely occasional sharp shifts in these components, we would expect national income to show occasional sharp changes followed by long periods of little or no change. This is not, however, the picture suggested by Figure 29–1; instead, the short-term situation is one of continual change but at a varying rate. This general picture is confirmed for a much longer period by the data in Figure 29–2. Evidently there are factors at work causing the economy to dis-

play continual short-term fluctuations around its long-term rising growth trend.

The short-term behavior of the economy cannot be fully caught by a single statistic. Figure 29–3 shows three important economic series; each of these series, as well as each of a dozen other widely used series, tells us something about the general variability of the economy. It is obvious that some series vary more than others and that they do not all move together.

Traditionally fluctuations such as those illustrated in Figure 29–2 have been called **business cycles.** In recent years the use of the term "cycle" has been criticized because modern analysts do not wish to imply a mechanical regularity in short-term fluctuations. But "business cycle" has proven to be a very durable term, and economists use it interchangeably with "business fluctuation" with no intention of implying any such mechanical regularity.

There is a fairly general consensus among students of economic fluctuations that:

1. There is a common pattern of variation that more or less pervades all economic series.
2. There is substantial difference from cycle to cycle in duration and in amplitude.
3. There are differences among economic series in their particular patterns of fluctuation.

IS THERE A PRINCIPAL CAUSE OF CYCLES?

Professor Alvin Hansen, one of the most distinguished American students of business cycles, once reported that between 1795 and 1937 there were 17 cycles of an average duration of 8.35 years. A shorter "inventory cycle" of 40 months' duration was also found, as well as longer cycles associated with building booms (15 to 20 years) and major innovations (40 to 50 years).

Classifying and describing business fluctuations does not account for them. The theory of the business cycle was once treated as a thing apart from the main body of economics; dozens of theories were spawned to explain each kind of real or imagined cyclical regularity. Many of the greatest economists of the 1930s—Gottfried Haberler, Wesley Mitchell, Alvin Hansen, Joseph Schumpeter—wrote books with titles such as *Business Cycles* and *Prosperity and Depression,* and the topic was considered a special branch of economic analysis. Today, business fluctuations are treated as part of, not separate from, macroeconomic theory. They are the dynamic aspects of the theory of income determination. While housing expenditures, inventory investment, and investments in new processes may all be cyclical phenomena, they are also forms of expenditure that affect aggregate demand. So, too, is consumption.

Why does the U.S. economy undergo business fluctuations? It seems apparent from the behavior of the economy that some elements of aggregate demand must be continuously changing. Such a situation would cause the equilibrium level of national income to be changing continuously and would cause the actual level of national income to be moving in pursuit of this equilibrium income.

What are the possible sources of these continuous disturbances? The theory of income determination suggests four main candidates—shifts in each of the four main components of aggregate demand: consumption, investment, government expenditure, and net exports.

Net exports can be eliminated immediately because they are too small a proportion of American national income to cause major fluctuations of the sort actually observed.[1]

What about government expenditure, which is today a large component of aggregate demand? It is clear from Figure 29–2 that every war in this century has been accompanied by a rapid expansion of economic activity. Wars result in an enormous increase in federal government expenditures as people and materials are shifted from civilian to military uses. This shift is usually reversed in the postwar period. For example, federal government purchases of goods and services (measured in constant dollars at 1972 prices) rose from $26 billion in 1940 to $268 billion in 1944 and then fell to $36 billion by 1947. Changes in government purchases of goods and services during 1941–1946 were the principal cause of changes in GNP during that period.

Empirical research suggests that, aside from periods of major wars, American government expenditures have not been destabilizing. For peacetime periods before 1940, government expenditures were both small and relatively stable. Since World War II they have been large, but the research of Professor Bert Hickman and others shows that, partly by design and partly by luck, government expenditures in the United States have not tended to contribute to fluctuations in national income. Instead they have tended to stabilize income by rising when the other elements of aggregate demand were falling and falling when the other elements were rising.

If changes in foreign trade or government expenditure do not account for observed cyclical behavior, we must look to consumption and investment, the remaining components of aggregate demand, to find the major culprit.

Shifts in consumption

Consumption is an important enough part of national income for shifts in it to cause major

---

[1] They can, of course, be the source of minor disturbances to the economy as a whole, and they can cause major disturbances to small sectors of the economy—those sectors concerned with exporting and importing.

Figure 29–2   American business activity since 1870

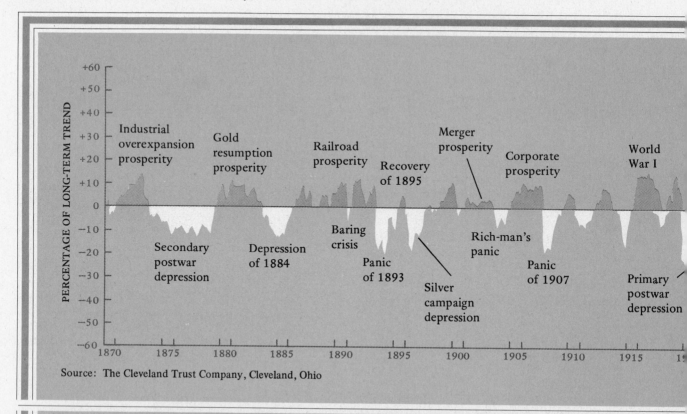

Source: The Cleveland Trust Company, Cleveland, Ohio

Cyclical ups and downs have dominated the short-term behavior of the U.S. economy at least since 1870. This chart is constructed by taking some single index of general economic activity, fitting a trend line to it, and plotting deviations of the index from its trend value. It shows well the tendency

fluctuations in income and employment. About two-thirds of total expenditure in the United States is made up of consumption expenditures. If households were to reduce their consumption expenditure by 3 percent, this would amount to a reduction of 2 percent in total expenditure. Combined with a multiplier of 2, this would cause the GNP to decline by 4 percent. Perhaps this does not sound like very much, but if employment were to change merely in proportion to in-

come, this could change a situation of 4 percent unemployment (the level often considered to be full employment) to one of 8 percent, which is near the highest level of the post-World War II period. Clearly, even relatively small percentage fluctuations can have important effects on the economy. Such fluctuations have occurred in the past.

In discussing the effects of shifts in the consumption function on GNP, it is useful to distinguish between factors that change the func-

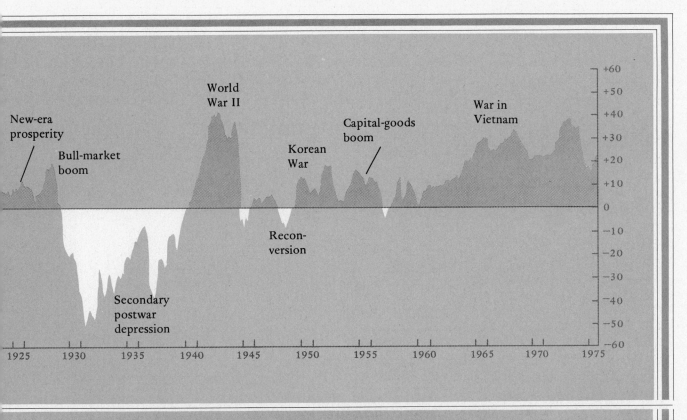

New-era
prosperity

Bull-market
boom

World
War II

Korean
War

Capital-goods
boom

War in
Vietnam

Recon-
version

Secondary
postwar
depression

+60
+50
+40
+30
+20
+10
0
−10
−20
−30
−40
−50
−60

1925   1930   1935   1940   1945   1950   1955   1960   1965   1970   1975

for an economy to fluctuate. There is no great significance to being above or below zero because the zero line is based on an arbitrary trend. But major booms and depressions are unmistakable.

tion relating household consumption to household disposable income, and factors changing the relation between disposable income and GNP. (We first encountered the distinction on page 488, footnote 5.)

SHIFTS IN THE RELATIONSHIP BETWEEN CONSUMPTION AND DISPOSABLE INCOME

From time to time tastes change; when they do, consumption levels and patterns may change. A large number of households may decide that they no longer like this year's car models and elect to save the money they were going to spend on a new car this year. If they do, the consumption function will shift downward this year. Incomes earned in Detroit (and many other places) will fall, and unemployment will rise. The unemployed auto workers will cut their spending on other products, and a multiplier process will be set up that will magnify and spread the original

Figure 29–3   Three indicators of economic activity 1950–1976

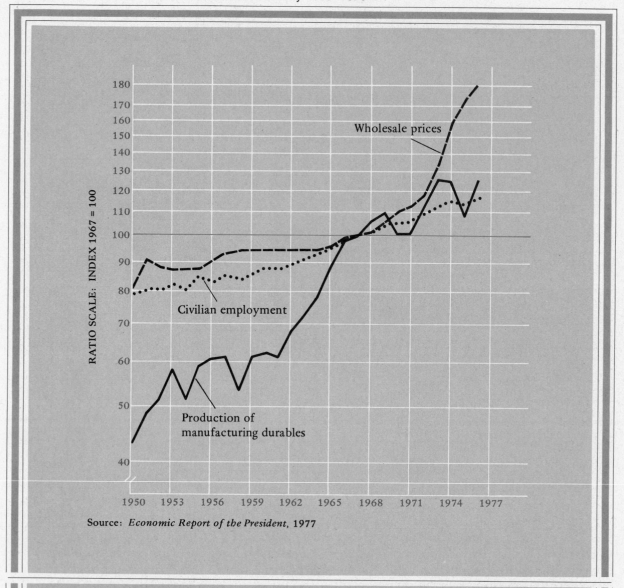

Source: *Economic Report of the President,* 1977

Short-term variability and a long-term upward trend characterize many indices of American economic activity, including these three.   All three series are index numbers with 1967 = 100, so all pass through 100 at 1967. All series exhibit short-term variability, although in varying degree. Wholesale prices were much more stable than production of durables in 1950–1970 but have been more volatile during the early 1970s. Civilian employment appears quite stable because even large changes in un-employment, say from 4 percent to 8 percent of the labor force, make a relatively small percentage change in employment: from 96 percent to 92 percent.

cut in spending on new automobiles into a general fall in income and employment.

While the demand for an individual commodity (such as cars) often shifts sharply from year to year due to more or less inexplicable fads or changes in taste, the aggregate proportion of consumer income going to current expenditure tends to be relatively more stable. The division between consumption and saving does sometimes shift, and we must look at some of the reasons for this.

Demand for durable goods

Because consumers' expenditures on such nondurable goods as food and clothing and on services such as automobile repairs cannot be long postponed, such forms of consumer expenditure are relatively stable. Quite a different pattern applies to purchases of durable goods from television sets to automobiles; they are easily postponable. If many consumers are led to postpone such purchases—which on average account for about 15 percent of all consumer expenditures—this will lead to sharp shifts in the consumption function.

What are the factors that can cause consumers to go on buying spurts in some periods and hang back in others?

Price expectations. If households expect an inflation to occur, they may purchase now durable goods they would otherwise purchase at some time in the future. In such circumstances purchases at today's prices may be an attractive use of accumulated savings. However, if households expect a deflation they may postpone purchases of durables in order to purchase them later at a lower price.

Existing stocks of durable goods. During periods of crises purchases of durables are often postponed. This may be due to scarcity in times of war or to uncertainty about the future during periods of strikes or exceptional unemploy-

ment. When such postponements occur, the age of the existing stock of durables grows. Once the end of the period of crisis comes there is likely to be a sudden outburst of expenditures out of accumulated savings. The consumption function may shift sharply upward for a year or two and then shift down as the backlog of demand is exhausted.

Terms of credit. Most durable consumer goods are purchased on credit, which may range from a few months to pay for a stereo to up to five years to pay for an automobile. If credit becomes more difficult or more costly to obtain, many households may postpone their planned, credit-financed purchases. If the typical down payment rises, or if monthly carrying charges rise, some consumers will postpone replacing a television set or do without the recreational vehicle they had planned to buy. Instead they may add the purchase price to their savings deposit at the bank (which is probably advertising new, higher rates of interest).

Notice here that government policy makers can, by controlling the cost and availability of credit, attempt to shift the consumption function and thereby affect aggregate demand.

Changes in income distribution

Because the consumption function relates *aggregate* consumption expenditures of the nation's households to their aggregate disposable income, the consumption function can change without the habits of any individual changing. For example, if income is transferred from a rich family which saves 40 percent of its marginal income to a poor family which spends every dollar it gets, the consumption function would shift up, indicating more consumption and less saving at the same level of aggregate disposable income.

More generally, since different households have different marginal propensities to consume, aggregate consumption depends not only on aggregate income but also on the distribution of this income among households. Thus a change in the distribution of income will cause a change in the aggregate *level* of consumption expenditure that is associated with any given *level* of national income. In other words there will be a shift in the consumption function.

SHIFTS IN THE RELATIONSHIP BETWEEN DISPOSABLE INCOME AND NATIONAL INCOME

The transition from a relation between *consumption and disposable income* to one between *consumption and national income* is easily accomplished because disposable income and national income are themselves related to each other. Assume (1) that associated with each level of national income there is a particular level of disposable income and (2) that associated with each level of disposable income there is a particular level of consumption. It follows that each level of national income also has a particular level of consumption associated with it. For example, if households consume 90 percent of their disposable income and if disposable income is 70 percent of GNP, then consumption is 63 percent of GNP.

Even if the relationship between disposable income and consumption does not change, a change in the relationship of DI to GNP will shift the consumption function relating consumption to GNP.

Suppose to continue the example, that with no change in the 90 percent propensity to consume out of DI, personal income tax reductions increase disposable income from 70 to 80 percent of GNP. Consumption is thereby increased from 63 to 72 percent of GNP.

The policy consequence is apparent: although policy makers may find it difficult to change the propensity to consume out of

disposable income, they can very easily change the relation between national income and disposable income by altering tax rates. Thus, according to the theory that consumption depends on disposable income, government policy makers can shift the aggregate consumption function *and hence the aggregate demand function* by changing personal tax rates.

An increase in tax rates lowers the aggregate demand function by lowering the ratio of disposable income to national income. A decrease in tax rates has the opposite effect.

SHIFTS IN THE CONSUMPTION FUNCTION AND BUSINESS FLUCTUATIONS

There is no doubt that the consumption function does sometimes shift, both in response to consumer expectations and in response to government policies that change consumers' expenditure for any level of income. Empirical findings in the postwar period show however that such shifts are relatively infrequent and that the consumption function has remained remarkably stable over most of the years, too stable at least for consumption to be declared the major culprit in initiating *continual* fluctuations in business activity. Of course, occasional shifts when they do occur can cause serious disturbances to national income.

Investment and its determinants

The final candidate for principal source of disturbance is investment expenditure. Consider the period 1929–1932. In 1929 total investment expenditure of firms and households in the American economy was $16.2 billion, almost double the amount of expenditure needed to replace the capital goods that were used up that year in the process of producing a GNP of $103 billion. The American economy in 1929, then, was adding rapidly to its stock of capital equipment. Three years later, in 1932, total investment expenditure was $1 billion. This was less than one-sixth of the amount needed merely to keep the stock of capital intact. The American economy in 1932, with its GNP reduced to $58 billion, was rapidly reducing its stock of capital equipment.

Figure 29–4 shows the annual change in real (constant-dollar) private investment expenditures since 1930. Although investment expenditures are typically only 15 percent

Figure 29–4 Year-to-year changes in real gross private investment and GNP 1930–1976

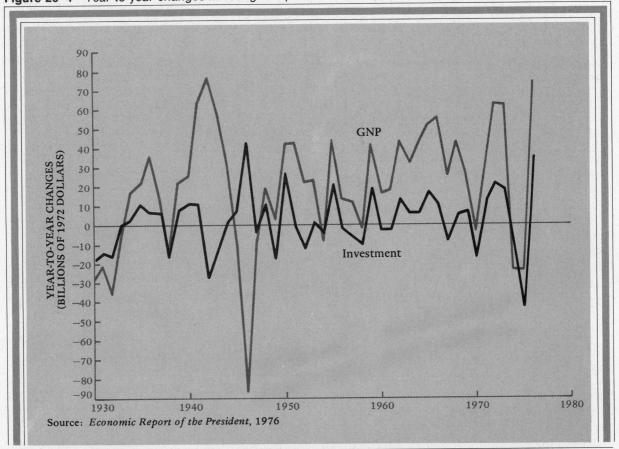

Source: *Economic Report of the President,* 1976

The fluctuations in gross private investment are sharp and closely related to changes in national income. The screened line repeats the curve of real GNP from Figure 29–1. The heavy line shows changes in investment. Except during World War II and its aftermath (when government expenditures dominated all other sources of aggregate demand), changes in private investment are very closely related to changes in national income.

of GNP, they are absolutely large enough ($188 billion in 1972) to cause major shifts in aggregate demand. More important, they are volatile. Investment (in 1972 dollars) rose to $207 billion in 1973 and then fell sharply for two years to under $140 billion in 1975 and rose to over $170 billion in 1976.

Figure 29–4 also suggests that changes in real investment are closely correlated with changes in real GNP—as indeed our theory of income determination predicts should be the case.

For modern students of macroeconomics, investment expenditures play a key role in any theory of cyclical fluctuations.

WHY DOES INVESTMENT CHANGE?

To find that investment is one of the prime causes of short-term fluctuations certainly tells us something; but we do not have the whole story unless we know why investment fluctuates. In discussing the theory of income determination in Chapters 27 and 28 we talked simply of shifts in investment, not of the underlying causes of such shifts. It would be quite possible for two economists to accept all that has been said so far in this chapter and yet advocate totally different theories of cyclical fluctuations.

One theory might be that investment depends mainly on business firms' anticipations of the future state of their markets. When there is confidence in the future, investment will be high; when there is pessimism, investment will be low. To go further in understanding fluctuations we would have to appeal to psychology to explain variations in business attitudes. The economist alone could not go beyond studying the consequences of exogenous, unexplained shifts in the investment function.

A second theory might be that monetary factors provide the major explanation of fluctuations in investment.[2] When credit is easily obtainable, interest rates are low and banks and other financial institutions are eager to lend money to investors; when credit is tight, interest rates are high and loans are hard to obtain. The first theory is close to that advocated by Keynes; the second is close to the one advocated by many monetarists.

The important point is that we can accept fluctuations in investment as the major cause of short-term fluctuations (with occasional assists from government and household expenditures) without committing ourselves to a particular theory of what causes fluctuations in investment—and hence in aggregate expenditure. As we have noted, between 1973 and 1975 real investment in the United States fell by over $60 billion. This is more than enough to account for the decline in GNP from 1973 to 1975.

While each dollar of investment is an injection into the circular flow and has the same consequences for aggregate demand, different types of investment respond to different sets of causes. Thus it is useful to discuss separately the determinants of investment in plant and equipment, changes in inventories, and residential construction. Table 29–1 shows these components for 1976 and Figure 29–5 shows how they behaved from 1929 through 1976.

INVESTMENT IN INVENTORIES

Inventory changes are the smallest of the three components of investment shown in Figure 29–5, but their size is not an adequate measure of their importance; they are one of the more volatile elements of total investment and therefore contribute importantly to shifts in the investment schedule.

Firms characteristically hold substantial inventories of raw materials, goods in process, and goods already produced but unsold. It is almost impossible to imagine a manu-

---

[2] The monetary sector is studied in detail in Part Nine.

facturing firm doing business successfully without some minimum holdings of inventories. In fact, most firms choose to hold inventories well above the necessary minimum level. They do this for many reasons; for one, it is usually cheaper to hold production constant in the face of daily, weekly, or even monthly fluctuations in sales than to adjust levels of production frequently. Although many things can influence the desired size of a firm's inventory holdings, the two most important factors are the size of a firm's sales and the rate of interest.

Table 29–1 Components of gross private investment, 1976

	Billions of dollars	*Percentage of total*
Plant and equipment	160.0	66.3
Residential structures	67.8	28.1
Changes in business inventories	13.4	5.6
Total	241.2	100.0

Source: *Survey of Current Business, 1977.*

Figure 29–5 Components of real gross private domestic investment 1929–1976

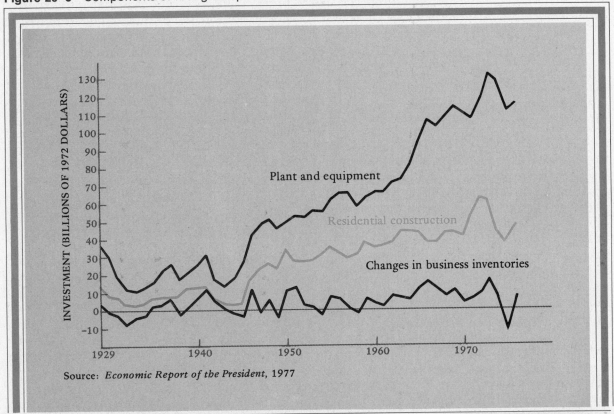

Source: *Economic Report of the President,* 1977

Each of the components shows enough variation to be a significant source of business fluctuations. Each component shows its own pattern of year-to-year fluctuations. Sometimes one, sometimes another, and sometimes all together account for the sharp changes in total investment shown in Figure 29–4.

Empirical studies show that the stock of inventories held tends to rise as a firm's rate of production and sales rises. But while the size of inventories is related to level of sales, the *change* in inventories (which is a form of investment) is related to the *change* in level of sales.

A firm may wish to hold inventories of 10 percent of its sales: If sales are $100,000, it will wish to hold inventories of $10,000; if its sales increase to $110,000, it will want to hold inventories of $11,000. When a firm with $10,000 in inventories wishes to increase its inventories by 10 percent it will require an additional $1,000 in inventories. *Over the period during which the stock is being increased,* there will be a total of $1,000 new inventory investment.

The higher the level of production and sales, the larger is the desired stock of inventories. Changes in the rate of production and sales cause temporary bouts of investment (or disinvestment) in inventories.

A firm holding inventories has money tied up—money that cannot be doing something else. The rate of interest represents the cost of borrowing this money, and obviously the higher the rate of interest the higher the cost of holding an inventory of a given size. Suppose a firm holds the level of inventories it desires, given its level of sales and the cost of holding inventories. Now suppose the rate of interest rises. As it does, the cost of holding inventories rises and, *ceteris paribus,* firms would be expected to hold smaller inventories. They can do this by letting their rate of output fall temporarily below their rate of sales. Alternatively, a fall in interest rates makes it less costly to have funds invested in inventories, and firms are expected to let inventories expand somewhat.

By causing firms to change the level of inventories that they desire to hold, a change in the rate of interest can lead to a flurry of investment or disinvestment as firms adjust their inventory levels to the new levels they plan to hold.

The higher the rate of interest, the lower the desired stock of inventories. Thus changes in the rate of interest cause temporary bouts of investment (or disinvestment) in inventories.

Unintended inventory investment

So far we have discussed the size of inventories that the firm *wishes* to keep. Such inventories provide a buffer between the rate of production on the one hand and the rates of purchase of inputs and sales of output on the other. Thus we would expect that unexpected fluctuations in any of these would lead first to unintended changes in inventories. If, for example, the firm's sales fall unexpectedly, inventories of unsold goods will pile up. The firm may take some time to assess whether this situation is temporary or permanent before adjusting its production. Meanwhile, the firm is making an unintended investment in inventories—unintended because the firm did not anticipate the fall in sales or the consequent build-up in inventories.

INVESTMENT IN RESIDENTIAL CONSTRUCTION

In recent years the value of expenditures on residential structures has varied between one-fifth and one-third of all gross private investment in the United States and has accounted for 4 to 5 percent of GNP. Figure 29–5 shows the course of residential construction in the United States since 1929. Notice the substantial fluctuations from year to year. Because expenditures for housing construction are both large and variable they exert a major impact on the economy.

To what does residential construction respond? Many of the influences on residential construction are noneconomic, dependent on demographic or cultural considerations such as new family formation. A rapidly expanding population will require more new construction than will a static population. Changes in marriage age also affect the demand for housing: If marriages are postponed, as during World War II, so too is family formation—and the demand for new housing units declines. But while demographic and cultural considerations affect people's hopes for housing, households must not only want to buy houses, they must be able to do so. Thus periods of high employment and high average family earnings tend to lead to increases in house building, and unemployment and falling earnings to decreases in such building.

The vast majority of houses are purchased with money borrowed on mortgages that run 20, 30, or even 40 years. Interest on the borrowed money typically accounts for about one-half of the purchaser's annual mortgage payments (the other half being repayment of principal). A rise in the rate of interest from 8 percent to 10 percent will lead to an increase of more than 15 percent in the monthly payment necessary to buy a given house. It is for this reason that variations in interest rates exert a substantial effect on the demand for housing.

Expenditures for residential construction tend to vary directly with changes in average income and inversely with interest rates.

INVESTMENT IN PLANT AND EQUIPMENT

Investment in plant and equipment is currently the largest and most rapidly growing component of domestic investment. Why does a business firm decide to build a new factory? Why does a firm decide to engage in major modernization programs this year rather than next?

Successful firms invest in plant and equipment not only because they like being surrounded by impressive pieces of hardware, but because they want to sell at a profit the goods that the equipment can produce. But profitability—and thus the level of investment in plant and equipment—depends on a variety of economic variables. We shall name several and then focus on one that plays a major role in discussions of business fluctuations: the rate of change of national income.

Innovation

Some effects of invention and innovation are discussed in Chapters 13 and 43. The relevance here is that innovations usually require new plant or equipment. In some instances (e.g., the basic changes that followed the introduction of railroads) innovation brings basic changes in the nature of the capital stock and leads to vast amounts of new investment. Because of the multiplier process, the effects of these investments spread widely throughout the entire economy.

Expectations

The decision to invest now is to a great extent an act of faith in the future. If businesses guess wrong, the penalties can be great. Business managers do their best to predict the extent of their firms' markets, but many things can influence those markets other than the tastes of households. A new Congress may adopt different taxing and spending policies that affect a business profoundly. An Arab oil embargo can shift the demand for large and small cars, for coal, for skis, for stay-at-home recreational activities, and for a host of other goods and services.

By and large, most firms make reasonably accurate decisions about investment most of the time. Occasionally, however, mob psychology dominates and a feeling of pessimism about the future can snowball into a general cut in investment expenditure. Or a feeling of optimism can generate an investment boom

The cost of buying a house on time

Few people who buy a house can pay cash, and most purchases are financed by borrowing money on a *mortgage*. A mortgage is a loan to the house purchaser (sometimes of as much as 85 or 90 percent of the purchase price, but 60 to 75 percent is common). In return, the borrower promises to make fixed monthly payments that cover interest on the money borrowed and repays the amount borrowed over some agreed period, commonly 20 years. (The monthly payments often include an amount to cover insurance and taxes, but this is ignored in what follows.) The house itself acts as security for the loan. Loans of this type are said to be *amortized,* which means that fixed payments cover the interest on the principal outstanding *and* repay the principal over a stated period.

Because the loan stretches over a long period, a great deal of the total amount paid by the borrower is interest on the outstanding loan. For example, on a 20-year mortgage for $10,000 at a nominal annual rate of 8 percent per year (a monthly rate of $\frac{8}{12}$ of 1 percent) interest, a total of $20,075 would be paid in 240 monthly installments of $83.65 each, making $10,000 to repay the principal of the loan and $10,075 as interest. At a 12 percent nominal annual rate (a monthly rate of 1 percent) the total payments would be $26,426 making $16,426 total interest as well as $10,000 to repay the principal.

Because interest is such a large part of the total payments on a mortgage, small changes in the rate of interest cause relatively large changes in the annual payments. For instance, a rise in the rate of interest from 8 percent to 10 percent increases the monthly payments on a 20-year mortgage by nearly 15.4 percent (from $8.37 to $9.66 per thousand dollars borrowed).

The interest on a mortgage is calculated on the amount of the loan still outstanding. After each payment the amount outstanding is reduced so that, with fixed annual payments, most of the total amount paid goes to paying interest in the early years and to repaying principal in later years. It follows that the purchaser's equity in the house builds up slowly at first and then more and more rapidly as the terminal date approaches.

Note in the table that when half the life of the mortgage has passed, only about a quarter of the principal has been repaid. In the first year of the mortgage, $993 goes as interest and only $165 to reduce the principal on the loan. In the last year, only $60 is interest and $1,098 goes to repay principal.

BREAKDOWN OF PAYMENTS MADE IN SELECTED YEARS ON A 20-YEAR MORTGAGE FOR $10,000 AT 10 PERCENT (ALL FIGURES TO THE NEAREST DOLLAR)

Year	Payments made over the year	Interest paid over the year	Principal (amount of loan) repaid over the year	Equity (amount of loan repaid over all previous years)
1	1,158	993	165	165
2	1,158	975	183	349
5	1,158	912	246	1,020
10	1,158	753	405	2,698
15	1,158	491	667	5,458
19	1,158	164	994	8,902
20	1,158	60	1,098	10,000

based on expectations that later turn out to be false.

Particularly in the short run, expectations can have a decisive influence on business investments. When, in 1930 and 1931, President Hoover kept saying "Prosperity is just around the corner" he was trying (in vain) to reverse a grim set of business expectations. When a few years later President Roosevelt spoke of "priming the pump" he, too, hoped to induce a change in these expectations.

The level of profits

Some economists, and many business analysts, lay great stress on the effect of profits on investment. It is assumed that business firms are not able (or do not wish) to borrow all the funds they require, but that they may use their own funds to finance their investment projects. Such funds can be obtained by not distributing profits to shareholders.

Profits thus become a key explanatory factor in investment because retained profits provide an important source of investable funds.

The rate of interest

Much investment in plant and equipment is made with borrowed money. It pays a firm to borrow money to finance its investment projects as long as the return on the investment (including an allowance for the riskiness of the project) exceeds the rate of interest. Thus a particular investment in a new machine becomes more attractive (other things being equal) the lower the rate of interest. To go from this conclusion to a prediction about how actual aggregate investment in plant and equipment responds to changes in the interest rate may be more complicated, because desired investment and actual investment may be different. It is important to see why this may be so.

The aggregate quantity of a society's capital goods is called its capital stock. Changes in the potential profitability of plant and equipment will lead to desired changes in capital stock, but capital goods cannot be produced (or worn out) overnight. Investment concerns actual expenditures for investment goods, not the desired level of the stock of capital. A desired increase in capital goods generates investment when the capital goods are actually produced. Suppose, for example, that in response to a fall in interest rates there is an increase of $10 billion in the desired capital stock. If the capital stock is raised by $10 billion within a year, net investment will rise to $10 billion for a year and then fall to zero. In this case a fall in the interest rate will lead only to a one-year increase in the amount of investment.

But the timing of investment will depend on how fast the stock of capital can be built up to its new desired level. The actual volume of investment in plant and equipment that takes place each year is limited by the capacities of the capital-goods and the construction industries.

Assume that in response to a fall in interest rates the firms in the economy decide that they want a total of 30,000 newly built and equipped factories in operation next year, but that factories can only be built and equipped at the rate of 10,000 a year. It will take three years before the desired addition to the capital stock is achieved. If, at the end of the first year, a rise in the rate of interest decreases the desired overall addition to the capital stock from 30,000 to 20,000 factories, this new change will have no effect on investment in year 2 because the capital-goods industries would still have to work to capacity to fill back orders.

Substantial variations in the interest rate can have a major effect on the length of the backlog rather than on the level of investment in a particular year.

Variations of this kind will affect the duration of an investment boom generated by changes in desired capital stock but may have only a minor (or even a zero) effect on the amount of investment occurring in one year during that boom.

Changes in national income[3]

The need for plant and equipment is obviously influenced by the demand for the goods the plant and equipment are designed to produce. If there is a rise in demand that is expected to persist and that cannot be met by increasing production with existing industrial capacity, then new plant and equipment will be needed. The production of such plant and equipment is investment. Once the new plants have been built and put into operation, however, the rate of new investment will fall off. This further illustrates an important characteristic of investment already encountered in the case of inventories: if the desired stock of capital goods increases there will be an investment boom while the new capital is being produced. But if nothing else changes, and even though business conditions continue to look rosy enough to justify the increased stock of capital, investment in new plant and equipment will cease once the larger capital stock is achieved. This aspect of investment leads to the accelerator theory of investment, which requires a closer look.

THE ACCELERATOR THEORY OF INVESTMENT

Because changes in the desired stock of capital goods lead to spurts in investment activity, the pattern of investment from year to year may prove quite changeable. According to the accelerator theory (usually called the

accelerator) investment is related to the rate of change of national income. When income is increasing, it is necessary to invest in order to increase the capacity to produce consumption goods; when income is falling, it may not even be necessary to replace old capital as it wears out, let alone to invest in new capital.

The main insight which the accelerator theory provides is the emphasis on the role of net investment as a *disequilibrium* phenomenon—something that occurs when the stock of capital goods differs from what firms and households would like it to be. Net investment would not occur when the desired quantities of inventories, buildings, or equipment had been achieved. Anything that changes those desired quantities can generate investment. The accelerator focuses on one such source of change, changing national income. This gives the accelerator its particular importance in connection with *fluctuations* in national income. As we shall see, it can itself contribute to those fluctuations.

How the accelerator works:
a numerical example

To see how the theory works, it is convenient to make the simplifying assumption that there is a particular capital stock needed to produce a given level of an industry's output. (The ratio of the value of capital to the annual value of output is called the **capital-output ratio.**) Given this assumption, suppose that the industry is producing at capacity and the demand for its product increases. If the industry is to produce the higher level of output, its capital stock must increase. This necessitates new investment.

Table 29–2 provides a simple numerical example of the accelerator that worked through step by step leads to three conclusions:

1. Rising rather than high levels of sales are needed to call forth net investment.

2. For net investment to remain constant, sales must rise by a constant amount per year.

[3] It is not the *level* of national income but the year-to-year change in income that is discussed here. A big increase in income can occur at either a high or a low level of income. The level of income too plays a role in determining the level of investment—through the effect of the level of income on expectations and on profits.[32]

Table 29–2 An illustration of the accelerator theory of investment

(1) Year	(2) Annual sales	(3) Change in sales	(4) Required stock of capital, assuming a capital-output ratio of 5/1	(5) Net investment: increase in required capital stock
1	$10	$0	$ 50	$ 0
2	10	0	50	0
3	11	1	55	5
4	13	2	65	10
5	16	3	80	15
6	19	3	95	15
7	22	3	110	15
8	24	2	120	10
9	25	1	125	5
10	25	0	125	0

With a fixed capital-output ratio, net investment occurs only when it is necessary to increase the stock of capital in order to change output. Assume that it takes $5 of capital to produce $1 of output per year. In years 1 and 2, there is no need for investment. In year 3, a rise in sales of $1 requires investment of $5 to provide the needed capital stock. In year 4, a further rise of $2 in sales requires an additional investment of $10 to provide the needed capital stock. As columns (3) and (5) show, the amount of net investment is proportional to the *change* in sales. When the increase in sales tapers off in years 7–9, investment declines. When, in year 10, sales no longer increase, net investment falls to zero because the capital stock of year 9 is adequate to provide output for year 10's sales.

3. The amount of net investment will be a multiple of the increase in sales because the capital-output ratio is greater than one.[4]

The data in Table 29–2 are for a single industry, but if many industries behave in this way, one would expect aggregate net investment to bear a similar relation to changes in national income. This is what the accelerator theory predicts. [33]

The accelerator theory says nothing directly about replacement investment, but it does have implications for such investment. When sales are constant (no net investment

required) replacement investment will be required to maintain the capital stock at the desired level. When sales are increasing from a position of full capacity both net investment and replacement investment will be required. When sales are falling so that the desired capital stock is below the actual capital stock, not only will net investment be zero but there will be a tendency to postpone replacement investment as well until the capital stock falls to the desired levels.

Limitations of the accelerator

Taken literally the accelerator posits a mechanical and rigid response of investment to changes in sales (and thus, aggregatively, to changes in national income). It does this by assuming a proportional relationship between changes in income and the size of the desired capital stock, and by assuming a fixed capital-

[4] In the example in the table the capital-output ratio is 5. Why should anyone spend $5 on capital stock to get $1 of output? It is not unreasonable to spend $5 to purchase a machine that produces only $1 of output *per year,* provided that the machine will last enough years to repay the $5 plus a reasonable return on this investment.

Figure 29–6 A stylized business cycle

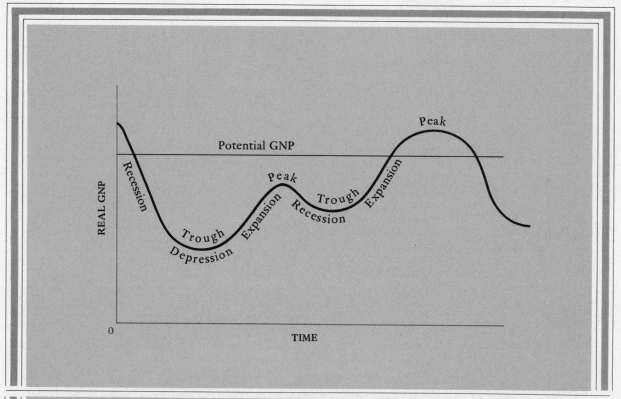

While the phases of business fluctuations are described by a series of commonly used terms, no two cycles are the same. Starting from a lower turning point, or trough, a cycle goes through a phase of expansion, reaches an upper turning point, or peak, and then enters a period of recession. Cycles differ from one another in the severity of their troughs and peaks and in the speed with which one phase follows another. Severe troughs are called depressions. Peaks are called inflations if a rapidly rising price level is a dominant symptom.

output ratio. Each assumption is invalid to some degree.

Changes in sales that are thought to be temporary in their effect on demand will not necessarily lead to new investment. It is usually possible to increase the level of output for a given capital stock by working overtime or extra shifts. While this would be more expensive per unit of output in the long run, it will usually be preferable to making investments in new plant and equipment that would lie idle after a temporary spurt of demand had subsided. Thus expectations about what is the required capital stock may lead to a much less mechanistic response of investment to income than the accelerator suggests.

A further limitation of the accelerator theory is that it takes a very limited view of what constitutes investment. The fixed capital-output ratio emphasizes investment in what economists call **capital widening,** the investment in additional capacity that uses the same ratio of capital to labor as existing capacity. It does not explain **capital deepening,** which is the kind of increase in the amount of capital per unit of labor expected in response to a fall in the rate of interest. Neither does the theory say anything about investments brought about as a result of new processes or new products. Furthermore, it does not allow for the fact that investment in any period is likely to be limited by the capacity of the capital-goods industry.

For these and other reasons, the accelerator does not by itself give anything like a complete explanation of variations in investment in plant and equipment, and it should not be surprising that a simple accelerator theory provides a relatively poor overall explanation of changes in investment. Sophisticated tests have found evidence of an accelerator-like relationship, but it is one complicated by other factors.

Elements of a theory of fluctuations

We have seen that the components of aggregate demand such as consumption and investment may be influenced by factors such as expectations, interest rates, and innovations. If any of these factors change, investment or consumption may be changed, and if investment or consumption change, national income will change as well. This might be the end of the story if we were trying to explain occasional erratic changes in national income. Most economic time series, however, display more or less continuous upswings and downswings. The evidence suggests that, whatever the initiating cause of a disturbance, the movements of the economy, up or down, tend to acquire a momentum of their own. After a while such cumulative movements appear to run their course and generate the seeds of their own reversal. Not all cycles are alike in duration or intensity, but each appears to have tendencies toward cumulative movements that eventually reverse themselves.

THE TERMINOLOGY OF BUSINESS FLUCTUATIONS

Although recurrent fluctuations in economic activity are neither smooth nor regular, a vocabulary has developed to denote their different stages. Figure 29–6 shows a stylized cycle that will serve to illustrate some terms.[5]

Trough. The trough is, simply, the bottom. If the trough is sufficiently severe it may be called a **depression.** A trough is characterized by unemployment of labor and a level of consumer demand that is low in relation to the capacity of industry to produce goods for consumption. There is thus a substantial amount of unused industrial capacity. Business profits will be low and in many individual cases they will be negative. Confidence in the future will be lacking and, as a result, firms will be unwilling to take risks in making new investments. Banks and other financial institutions will have surplus cash that no one whom they consider to be a reasonable credit risk wishes to borrow.

Expansion or recovery. When something sets off a recovery, the lower turning point of the cycle has been reached. The symptoms of an expansion are many: worn-out machinery will be replaced; employment, income, and consumer spending all begin to rise; expectations become more favorable as a result of increases in production, sales, and profits. Investments that once seemed risky may now be undertaken as the climate of business

[5] This vocabulary has tended to change in the last two decades, partly in response to increasing understanding of cyclical phenomena and partly because of changes in the nature of business fluctuations themselves. Once it was fashionable to speak of panic and crisis, of boom and bust, of prosperity and depression; today it is common to use less dramatic words such as expansion and contraction, recovery and recession, peak and trough.

opinion begins to change from pessimism to optimism. As demand expands, production will be expanded with relative ease merely by reemploying the existing unused capacity and unemployed labor.

Peak. The peak is the **upper turning point.** At the peak there is a high degree of utilization of existing capacity, labor shortages begin to occur, particularly in certain key skill categories, and shortages of certain key raw materials develop. Bottlenecks appear with increasing frequency. It now becomes difficult to increase output because the supply of unused resources is rapidly disappearing; output can be raised further only by means of investment that increases capacity. Because of such investment expenditure, investment funds will be in short supply. Because such investment takes time, further rises in demand are now met more by increases in prices than by increases in production. As shortages develop in more and more markets, a situation of general excess demand for factors develops. Costs rise but prices rise also, and business remains generally very profitable. When price increases become quite general and rapid, the peak is said to have become an **inflation.**

Losses are infrequent because a money profit can be earned merely by holding on to goods whose prices are rising and selling them later at higher prices. Expectations of the future are favorable and more investment may be made than is justified on the basis of current levels of prices and sales alone.

Recession. Beyond the upper turning point, the economy turns downward; if the contraction is sustained it is called a **recession.** Suppose that for some reason demand falls off and as a result production and employment fall. As employment falls, so do households' incomes; falling income causes demand to fall further and more and more firms get into difficulties. Prices and profits fall. New investments that looked profitable on the expecta-

tion of continuously rising demand and prices suddenly appear unprofitable; investment is reduced to a low level and it may not even be worth replacing capital goods as they wear out because unused capacity is increasing steadily.

CUMULATIVE MOVEMENTS AND TURNING POINTS

Many events occur in the economy at once, and all may contribute to rises and falls in national income. Our purpose at the moment is not to show the full complexity of a cyclical economy but to suggest that cumulative self-reinforcing and self-reversing movements can occur. This may be done concisely by putting together two now-familiar concepts —the multiplier and the accelerator. A simple theory emerges that, while not a complete theory of cyclical fluctuations, emphasizes many important interactions.

The interaction of the multiplier and the accelerator

The combination of the multiplier and the accelerator can cause upward or downward movements in the economy to be cumulative. Imagine that the economy is settled into a depression with heavy unemployment and that there then occurs a revival of investment demand. Orders are placed for new plant and equipment, and this creates new employment in the capital-goods industries. The newly employed workers spend most of their earnings; this creates new demand for the consumer goods that they buy. A multiplier process is now set up with new employment and incomes created in the consumer goods industries.

The spending of these newly created incomes in turn causes further increases in demand. At some stage this increased demand for consumer goods will create, through the accelerator process, an increased demand for capital goods. Once existing equipment is fully employed in any industry, extra output will require new capital equipment—and the accelerator theory takes over as the major determinant of investment expenditure. Such investment will increase or at least maintain demand in the capital-goods sector of the economy. So the process goes on, with the multiplier-accelerator mechanism continuing to produce a rapid rate of expansion in the economy.

The upper turning point

A very rapid expansion can continue for some time, but it cannot go on forever because eventually the economy will run into bottlenecks (or ceilings) in terms of some resources. For example, investment funds may become scarce, and as a result interest rates will rise. Firms now find new investments more expensive than anticipated and thus some are unprofitable to make. Or suppose that what limits the expansion is exhaustion of the reservoir of unemployed labor. Once this has happened, further expansion of the economy requires growth of the labor force or growth of labor productivity. The full-employment ceiling guarantees that any sustained rapid growth rate of real income and employment will eventually be slowed. At this point the accelerator again comes into play. A slowing down in the rate of increase in demand leads to a decrease in the rate of increase of production—and thus to a decrease in investment in new plant and equipment. This causes a fall in employment in the capital-goods industries and, through the multiplier, a fall in consumer demand. Once consumer demand begins to fall, investment in plant and equipment will be reduced to a low level because firms will already have more productive capacity than they can use. Unemployment begins to mount and the upper turning point has been passed.

The lower turning point

A rapid contraction, too, is eventually brought to an end. Consider the worst sort of depression you can imagine, one in which every postponable expenditure of households, firms, or governments is postponed. Even then aggregate demand will not fall to zero. First there is a minimum level of consumption expenditure that households will be obliged to make to sustain life. Thus, even if aggregate demand consisted only of consumption, it would not fall to zero because households can and will use up savings, or go into debt, to buy the necessities of life. Moreover transfer payments to households in the form of unemployment compensation and welfare payments will increase and will provide the funds to support consumption expenditures.

But of course consumption is not the only element of aggregate demand. Government expenditure will not fall to zero. Civil service salaries and national defense expenditures will continue. Moreover the political pressure for governments to increase their expenditures will surely grow and may be effective. Even business investment, in many ways the most easily postponed component of aggregate demand, will not fall to zero. In our most severe depression, between 1930 and 1932, investment fell drastically, but at the depth of the Depression it was still nearly $1 billion. In the industries providing food, basic clothing, and shelter, demand may remain fairly high in spite of quite large reductions in national income. These industries will certainly be carrying out some investment to replace equipment as it wears out, and they may even undertake some net investment.

Taken together, these minimum levels of consumption, investment, and government expenditure will assure a minimum equilibrium level of national income that, although well below the full-employment level, will not be zero. There is a floor! (This may be small comfort, however; it is possible for the economy to settle into a period of heavy unemployment for a long time, and if it does, many will suffer great hardship.)

Sooner or later, though, an upturn will begin. If nothing else causes an expansion of business activity, there will eventually be a revival of replacement investment because as existing capital wears out the capital stock will eventually fall below the level required to produce current output. At this stage new machines will be bought to replace ones that are worn out.

This rise in the level of activity in the capital goods industries will cause by way of the multiplier, a further rise in income. The economy has turned the corner. An expansion, once started, will trigger the sort of cumulative upward movement discussed earlier.

This kind of theory suggests why an economy that is subjected to periodic external shocks will tend to generate a continuously changing pattern of fluctuations, as first cumulative and then self-reversing forces come into play.

THE VARIETY IN CYCLICAL FLUCTUATIONS

No two cycles are the same. In some the recession phase is short; in others a full-scale period of stagnation sets in. In some cycles the peak phase develops into a severe inflation; in others the pressure of excess demand is hardly felt and a new recession sets in before the economy has fully recovered from the last trough. Some cycles are of long duration, some are very short.

Our discussion of cumulative movements, floors and ceilings, and turning points only hints at what happens in actual cyclical movements; this is as far as the theory can be carried without the use of complex dynamic models. But this type of theory can fit either a very modest fluctuation such as the recession of 1957–1958, a bigger fluctuation such as that of 1973–1975, or the massive disaster that was the 1930s. Cycles differ from one another in terms of the origin and the magnitude of the initiating shock. Sometimes, but not

always, economists can identify the initiating causes. (The causes of the Great Depression remain shrouded in controversy despite nearly four decades of study.) Inventories are believed by many economists, and housing by some, to lead to their own special patterns of fluctuation.

Inventory cycles

There are, as we have seen, good reasons to suppose that the required size of inventories is related to the level of firms' sales, and these are related to the level of national income. If firms maintain anything like a rigid inventory-to-sales ratio this will cause an accelerator-like linkage between investment in inventories and *changes* in national income.

Look back at the fluctuating investment in business inventories shown in Figure 29–5. Many observers believe these sharp and somewhat periodic fluctuations lead to an "inventory cycle" of roughly 40 months average duration.

A building cycle?

Economists have noted some long-run, wave-like movements in the statistics for expenditures on residential construction. These are sometimes referred to as "building cycles." Some economists suggest an acceleratorlike explanation that runs from external events to demographic changes, to changes in the demand for housing and other buildings, and thence to changes in construction activity.

Wars, by taking males away from home, and major depressions, by making people poor, tend to retard family formation and thereby tend to depress the demand for private housing. During such periods the construction industry may not even be replacing all of the housing that wears out, so the stock of housing is actually declining. But after the conclusion of the war (or depression) there is typically a great increase in marriages. The burst of household formation following on the new marriages leads to a large increase in the demand for housing and a boom in the construction industry as it strives to increase the stock of housing units. Inevitably, too, there are the postponed babies and an increase in the birth rate. (These things affect more than housing: As the extra children grow up, there is demand for all sorts of goods and services from diapers to football helmets and places in schools. Each of these may generate new and increased demands for buildings and factories.)

Depending on the capacity of the building industry, the boom may last many years before the desired increases in the stock of buildings of various kinds are achieved, but eventually the demand will taper off and the construction boom will have ended. Then, approximately 20 years after the end of the war or depression that triggered the boom, there is likely to be a further rise in the number of marriages and births as the new generation starts its process of family formation. This second boom, sometimes called an "echo effect," will be more spread out than the first one because people get married at various ages, but it may well be sufficiently concentrated to be felt as an upsurge in demand.

The evidence concerning construction expenditures over the past century is thought by many economists to provide support for the theory just outlined, a theory very much like the accelerator, though with changes in demographic factors (rather than changes in income) providing the impetus.

FLUCTUATIONS: A CONSENSUS VIEW?

Economists once argued long and bitterly about which was the best explanation of the recurrent cyclical behavior of the economy. Today, most agree that there need not be one cause or one class of causes for business cycles. In an economy that has tendencies for both cumulative and self-reversing behavior, any sort of large shock, whether from without or within the system, can initiate a cyclical swing. Wars are important; so, too, are major technological inventions. A major automobile strike could curtail production and bring on a recession. Monetary factors such as a sharp increase in interest rates and a general tightening of credit can be important by causing a sharp decrease in investment. Expectations can be changed by a political campaign or a development in another part of the world. The list of possible initial impulses, endogenous or exogenous, is long. It is probably true that the characteristic cyclical pattern includes many outside shocks that initiate, sometimes reinforce, and sometimes dampen the cumulative tendencies that exist within the economy.

Cycles differ also in terms of their internal structure. In some, full employment of labor may be the bottleneck that determines the ceiling. In others, high interest rates and shortages of funds for business expansion may nip an expansion and turn it into a recession while unemployment of labor is still an acute problem. These and other differences occupy the attention of economists concerned with understanding the cyclical economy.

An important part of controlling cycles is to anticipate correctly when a turning point is near. Control requires more than understanding; it requires countercyclical policies. Into this picture we must now bring the central authorities, who seek to influence the pattern of business fluctuations. The federal government tries both to prevent extremes of expansion and contraction from developing and to mitigate the most undesirable effects of those peaks and troughs that do occur.

Summary

1. Short-term fluctuations in GNP are usually, although not always, the result of variations in aggregate demand. Overall, these fluctuations show a fairly clear pattern that

is sometimes described as cyclical. In spite of the overall pattern, the evidence is that the cycles are irregular in amplitude, in timing, in duration, and in the way they affect particular industries and sectors of the economy.

2. One potentially important source of fluctuations is shifts in the consumption function due to changes in income distribution, availability of credit, stocks of durable goods, and price expectations.

3. Even if the relation of consumption to disposable income does not change, the government can shift the consumption function related to GNP by changing personal tax rates. An increase in personal taxes lowers disposable income relative to GNP and can decrease the level of consumption at every level of GNP.

4. Investment is large enough and volatile enough to cause fluctuations in aggregate demand. Most economists regard shifts in investment as a major cause of business fluctuations. Saying that does not, however, commit one to a particular theory of *why* aggregate demand and investment fluctuate. The three principal components of private investment are changes in business inventories, residential construction, and investment in plant and equipment. Each responds to somewhat different influences.

5. Changes in business inventories are the smallest of the three major components of investment expenditure but often account for an important fraction of the year-to-year changes in the level of investment. They are thought to respond both to changes in the level of production and sales and to the rate of interest.

6. Residential construction is a major component of investment, and one that shows a wavelike motion of its own. House building responds to economic (as well as noneconomic) influences, varying directly with the level of national income and inversely with the rate of interest. The rate of interest is important because interest payments are a large fraction of the mortgage payments that greatly affect a household's ability to purchase a house.

7. Investment in plant and equipment depends on a number of variables—among them innovation, changes in the level of national income, expectations about the future, the level of profits, and the rate of interest.

8. The accelerator theory relates net investment to changes in the level of national income on the assumption of a fixed capital-output ratio. Its central prediction is that rising income is required to maintain a positive level

of investment. Its central insight is that net investment is a disequilibrium phenomenon that occurs when the capital stock is different from the desired capital stock.

9. The accelerator does not provide a complete theory of investment. It neglects capital deepening and the influence of variables other than the rate of change of national income. Moreover, the actual world is not one with a fixed capital-output ratio. Nevertheless, an accelerator-like mechanism may help explain some of the fluctuations in total investment, in inventory changes, and in construction activity.

10. Economists break down a stylized cycle into four phases—trough, expansion, peak, and recession—which have certain characteristic features, although no two real-world cycles are exactly the same.

11. The elements of a theory of fluctuations are summarized in terms of a set of tendencies for *cumulative movements* and a set of ceilings or floors that lead to *turning points.* A theory that predicts cumulative but eventually reversing movements is a theory of fluctuations. Such a theory explains some characteristics of all cycles, but it fails to explain the great variety among cycles, which differ from one another in the nature of the initiating shock and in their internal structure and, as a consequence, in their duration and amplitude.

Concepts for review

"Business cycles" and "business fluctuations"
Causes of shifts in the consumption function
Consumption as a function of disposable income and of
  GNP
Components of investment
Intended and unintended inventory investment
The accelerator
Phases of the cycle
Cumulative upward and downward movements in economic activity
The interaction of the multiplier and the accelerator

Discussion questions

1. "In most years changes in government expenditure are larger than changes in inventories, and consumption is

larger than investment both in plant and equipment and housing combined. Therefore, the theorists who say that investment is the main culprit in causing cycles are neglecting the facts of our economy." Reply to this charge.

2. How and in what direction might each of the following shift the function relating consumption expenditure to *DI*:

a. introduction of free medical care

b. a change in attitudes so that we become a nation of conspicuous conservers rather than conspicuous consumers, taking pride in how little we eat or spend for housing, clothing, and so on

c. increases in income taxes

d. news that due to medical science everyone can count on more years of retirement than ever before

e. a spreading belief that all-out nuclear war is likely within the next ten years

f. sharp decreases in the down payments required on durable goods

3. Suppose the government wished to reduce private investment in order to reduce an inflationary gap. What policies might it adopt? If it wished to do so in such a way as to have a major effect on residential housing and a minor effect on plant and equipment expenditures, which measures might it use?

4. What effect on total investment—and on which category of investment—would you predict as a result of the following:

a. widespread endorsement of ZPG (zero population growth) by young couples

b. a sharp increase in the frequency and duration of strikes in the transportation industries

c. forecasts of record levels of real national income over the next five years

d. tax reform that eliminated the deductibility of interest expense from income to be taxed

5. Recently, when interest rates rose sharply, home construction fell dramatically but sales of mobile homes increased. How does the rise in the sale of mobile homes relate to the notion that investment responds to the rate of interest?

6. Empirical studies show that as the volume of a firm's sales increases, the size of its inventories of raw materials tends to increase in proportion. It is common for business firms to speak of such inventories in terms of "a 20-day supply of coal" rather than "52,000 tons of coal" or "$280,000 worth of coal." Why should relative size be more important than absolute quantity or dollar value?

7. Which "cause" of business investment is being relied on in each of the following quotes:

a. an aluminum industry spokesman, justifying a 50¢ a pound increase in aluminum prices: "We must have it to build the new capacity we need."

b. Economist Alan Greenspan in 1976: "Unless business panics about the election, the recovery will continue."

c. Bethlehem Steel, in a newspaper ad: "We need lower taxes not cheaper money or government deficits to help lower barriers to capital formation."

8. Since different series behave differently, does it make sense to talk about *a* business cycle? Predict the comparative behavior of the following pairs of series in relation to fluctuating changes in GNP:

a. purchases of food, purchases of consumer durables

b. tax receipts, bankruptcies

c. unemployment, birth rates

d. employment in New York, employment in Michigan

Check your predictions against the facts for the last two decades.

Theories and tools of fiscal policy

There is no doubt that the government can exert a major influence on the circular flow of income. Prime examples occur during major wars when governments engage in massive military spending and throw fiscal caution to the winds. As more and more money is spent, both GNP and employment tend to rise to unprecedented heights. U.S. federal government expenditure (measured in 1972 dollars) rose from $26 billion or 7.7 percent of GNP, in 1940, to $268 billion, or 47.3 percent of GNP, in 1944. At the same time the unemployment rate fell from 14.6 to 1.2 percent. Economists agree that the increase in the government's aggregate expenditure caused the rise in the GNP and the fall in unemployment. Similar experiences occurred during the rearmament of most European countries before, or just following, the outbreak of World War II in 1939.

Thus it is clear that governments can, through their spending and taxing policies, have major impacts on GNP and on employment. The use of these policies *in order to* influence employment and national income is called **fiscal policy.** This chapter deals with the theory of fiscal policy and the next deals with actual experience.

There is little doubt that, when appropriately used, fiscal policy can be an important tool for influencing the economy. In the heyday of fiscal policy in the 1940s, 1950s, and 1960s, many economists thought that the economy could be adequately regulated solely by varying the size of the government's deficit or surplus. That day is now past, although a few "pure fiscalists" are still to be found. Today most economists are aware of the limitations of fiscal policy, and there is much discussion of other tools of stabilization that can complement fiscal policy or possibly even replace it.

In this chapter we ask what might be expected from fiscal policy under the most favorable circumstances. The limitations of fiscal policy and the choices among alternative policies are studied in later chapters.

The theory of fiscal policy

FISCAL IMPACT ON THE ECONOMY

Not so many years ago it was generally accepted, and indeed many people still fervently believe, that a prudent government should always balance its budget. The argument is based on an analogy with what seems prudent behavior for the individual. It is a foolish individual whose current expenditure consistently exceeds his current revenue so that he gets steadily further into debt. It is then argued that what is good for the individual must be good for the nation.

The paradox of thrift, discussed in Chapter 28, suggests however that the analogy between the government and the household may be misleading. When the government follows a balanced budget policy, as most governments tried to do even during the Great Depression of the 1930s, it must restrict its expenditure during a recession because its tax revenue will necessarily be falling at that time. During a recovery, when its revenue is high and rising, it increases its spending. In other words, it rolls with the economy, raising and lowering its expenditure in step with everyone else.

By the end of the 1930s, many economists had come to the conclusion that the government, by going along with the crowd, was not making the most of its potential to control the economy in a beneficial manner. Why, they asked, should the government not try to stabilize the economy by doing just the opposite of what everyone else was doing—by increasing its demand when private demand was falling and lowering its demand when private demand was rising? After all, they might have added, even a prudent household will go into debt when it knows its income is unusually low and save to repay its debt when its income is unusually high. This idea seemed particularly important because government expenditures were such a large part of the aggregate demands of most Western countries (see Table 30–1).

When Milton Friedman said, "We are all Keynesians now," he was referring (among other things) to the general acceptance of the view that the government's budget is much more than just the revenue and expenditure statement of a very large organization. Whether we like it or not, the very size of the government's budget inevitably makes it a powerful tool for influencing the size of the GNP and the total amount of employment in the economy.

Precisely how do the government's fiscal actions influence national income? What objectives might the government reasonably hope to attain through its fiscal policy? What specific tools of fiscal policy are available to the government? These three questions are

Table 30–1 Government expenditure in selected countries

Country	Government expenditure on goods and services as a percentage of GNP, 1974
Israel	53
United Kingdom	36
Netherlands	27
Italy	26
Australia	25
Norway	24
France	21
United States	19
Canada	17
West Germany	14
Japan	11
Switzerland	9

Source: *International Financial Statistics,* March 1976.

Government expenditure is an important part of aggregate demand in most countries. The figures show government expenditure on currently produced goods and services as a percentage of GNP. The figures thus give the government's direct contribution to aggregate demand. Total government expenditure, which includes transfer payments, and which must be matched by taxes if the government's overall budget is to be balanced, is a still higher proportion of GNP than that indicated by the figures in the table.

the subjects of the three main parts of this chapter.

THE EFFECTS OF TAXES AND GOVERNMENT SPENDING

A household earns income over the year from the sale of the factor services that it controls, and it spends its income on purchasing goods and services. Its deficit or surplus on the year's transactions can be calculated by comparing its total income with its total expenditure. Similarly, governments raise current revenue by levying taxes, and they spend on all the projects they undertake. If current revenue is exactly equal to current expenditure, the government has a **balanced budget.** If revenues exceed expenditures, there is a budget surplus; if revenues fall short of expenditures, there is a budget deficit.

If the government raises its spending without raising its taxes, its extra expenditure may be said to be *deficit financed*. If the extra spending is accompanied by an equal increase in tax revenue, we speak of a *balanced budget change in spending*.

Financial implications of budget deficits and surpluses

If the government spends more than it raises, where does the money come from? If the government raises more than it spends, where does the money go? The difference between expenditure and tax revenue is reflected in changes in the level of the government's debt. If expenditures exceed revenues, the balance must be borrowed from someone; if revenues exceed expenditures, the balance pays off some of the loans that were made in the past.

A deficit requires an increase in borrowing, for which there are two main sources: the central bank[1] and the private sector of the economy—banks and other financial institutions, firms, and households. The government borrows money from these sources by selling treasury bills or bonds to them. A **treasury bill** is a promise to repay a stated amount in the near future (usually 30, 60, or 90 days), and it is sold in return for a smaller amount paid to the government now—the difference between the two sums representing the interest on the loan. A government bond is also a promise to pay a stated sum of money in the future but in the more distant future than a bill—possibly as much as 25 years from now.

A surplus allows the government to reduce its outstanding debt. Treasury bills and bonds may be redeemed from tax revenue when they fall due rather than from money raised by selling new bills and bonds.

When the government makes new loans from or repays old loans to the private sector, this action merely shifts funds between the two sectors. When the government "borrows" from the central bank, however, the central bank creates new money. Since the central bank can create as much money as it wishes while the private sector cannot, there is no limit to what the government can "borrow" from the central bank while there is a limit to what it can borrow from the private sector.

The effect of government expenditure on aggregate demand

Consider an increase in government expenditure made to purchase currently produced goods and services that is not matched by any change in tax rates. Such expenditure may provide a net addition to aggregate demand, in which case it will have a major impact on GNP and total employment. Alternatively, it may merely be an expenditure that would have been made in any event, but by other spending units (firms and households) and for other purposes. In this case the government spending will serve to reallocate expenditure among the sectors of the economy, but it will

[1] In the United States the central bank is the Federal Reserve System, which will be described and discussed in Chapter 33. The central bank controls the money supply and can create as much new money as is needed to finance any amount of government deficits.

have little effect on the overall level of aggregate demand, GNP, and total employment—the increase in government expenditure will have been matched by an equivalent decrease in private expenditure. Any reduction of *private expenditure* by firms and households that occurs as a result of an increase in *government expenditure,* is called the **crowding-out effect.**

In this chapter we discuss the important extreme case in which all government expenditure represents a net addition to aggregate demand: the crowding-out effect is zero. This may be called the Keynesian case since it was the case mainly assumed in the textbooks written in the wake of Keynes's *General Theory*. The opposite extreme case would occur if government expenditure merely replaced an equivalent amount of private expenditure; the crowding-out effect would then be 100 percent. Intermediate cases are also possible. If every extra $1 of government expenditure crowded out 60¢ worth of private expenditure, the crowding-out effect would be 60 percent and net additions to injections would be only 40¢. In this case, to get a desired net increase of $1 in new injections, the government would have to spend $2.50.

Probably the great majority of economists believe that intermediate cases, in which the crowding-out effect exceeds zero but is less than 100 percent, are more common than either extreme. The analysis of the present chapter will nevertheless help in understanding the general consequences of fiscal policy. The results obtained carry over in general terms (even if not in every specific detail) to all cases in which an increase in government expenditure causes some net increase in injections—that is, to all cases in which the crowding-out effect is less than 100 percent.[2]

---

[2] The crowding-out effect will be studied in more detail in Chapter 41 after the effects of money and interest rates have been allowed for. In the meantime we may notice that one way in which the crowding-out effect can work is for an increase in government expenditure to lead to a rise in the interest rate and for private expenditure to fall as a result.

The effect of taxes and expenditure on national income

How do the government's fiscal actions affect national income?

The key proposition in the theory of fiscal policy is that government taxes and expenditures can be used to remove inflationary and deflationary gaps.

The basic analysis needed to establish the above proposition was developed in Chapter 28. We will briefly summarize here the aspects of the analysis that are relevant to the removal

Figure 30–1 Increasing expenditure or lowering taxes to eliminate a deflationary gap

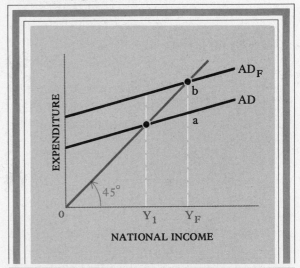

Policies that shift the aggregate demand curve upward can be used to eliminate a deflationary gap. Aggregate demand is AD and national income is in equilibrium at Y_1. Full-employment income is Y_F and the deflationary gap is *ab*. The government can remove this gap by increasing its expenditures by *ab*, holding tax rates constant, or by reducing tax rates sufficiently to cause the aggregate demand curve to shift upward by *ab*.

of inflationary and deflationary gaps by fiscal policy.

Figure 30–1 uses the income-expenditure approach to analyze the policy required for removing a deflationary gap. The appropriate policy is for the government to raise expenditure or to lower taxes[3] until the aggregate demand curve shifts upward enough to remove the gap. Figure 30–2 uses the same approach to analyze the policy required for removing an inflationary gap. The appropriate policy is for the government to lower expenditure or to raise taxes until the aggregate demand function shifts downward enough to remove the gap.

The same analysis can also be made using the withdrawals and injections approach. When there is a deflationary gap, a rise in government expenditure raises injections and a fall in tax rates lowers the withdrawals associated with each level of income. Each of the changes increases equilibrium national income. When there is an inflationary gap, a cut in government expenditure lowers injections and a rise in tax rates raises withdrawals. Each of these changes reduces the inflationary gap.

The size of deficits and surpluses

If the same job can be done by changing either tax rates or expenditure, does it make any difference which policy is chosen? To see that it does, look first at the amount of extra expenditure needed to remove a deflationary gap. If expenditure is raised by $1 billion per year, $1 billion worth of new expenditure is injected into the economy. Suppose the

marginal propensity to withdraw out of GNP is 0.5; the multiplier is then 2, and the final rise in national income will be $2 billion. Second, consider tax cuts. If the government cuts personal tax rates sufficiently to reduce its revenues by $1 billion, households will have an extra $1 billion of disposable income. Consumption expenditures, however, will rise *by less than* $1 billion because only part of the extra disposable income will be spent (the rest will be saved or otherwise withdrawn from the circular flow). If only 75¢ of every new dollar of household disposable income gets spent on domestically produced goods, then a cut in tax revenue of $1 billion will raise household expenditure by only $0.75 billion and, combined with a multiplier of 2, will raise GNP by $1.5 billion.

What must the government do if it wishes to generate $2 billion of extra GNP by a tax cut? Given a multiplier of 2, it will have to generate initial new expenditure of $1 billion. This will require (in this example) an initial cut in *tax revenue* of approximately $1.33 billion. With a marginal propensity to spend out of disposable income of 0.75, this will cause an initial increase in expenditure of $1 billion—the same that was obtained when the government raised its expenditure by $1 billion. A given increase in aggregate demand will require a larger budget deficit if tax cuts rather than expenditure increases are used.

The increase in government expenditure necessary to remove a given deflationary gap is less than the decrease in tax revenue necessary to do the same job.

The same analysis can be applied to an inflationary gap to arrive at a corresponding conclusion.

The decrease in government expenditure necessary to remove a given inflationary gap is less than the increase in tax revenue necessary to do the same job.

---

[3] A change in government revenue shifts the AD curve parallel to itself since there is the same rise in G at all levels of Y. A change in tax rates, however, is likely to change the slope of the AD function because tax revenues vary with national income. We illustrate both expenditure and tax rate policies by parallel shifts in the AD curve in the figures. This is for ease of illustration only. There is in any case no problem since there is always some change in tax rates that will remove any inflationary or deflationary gap.

This second conclusion follows from the fact that the initial effect of a decrease in government expenditure of $1 is a decrease in aggregate expenditure of $1, while the initial effect of an increase in tax revenue of $1 is a decrease in consumption expenditure (and hence in aggregate expenditure) of less than $1 because part of the $1 of tax revenue would have been withdrawn from the domestic circular flow and only the remainder would have been spent on consumption.

The initial and the final size of a deficit used to remove a deflationary gap. With tax rates held constant, total tax revenue rises and falls with national income. Thus, if government expenditure is held constant, deficits will decrease (or surpluses will increase) when income rises, and deficits will increase (or surpluses decrease) when income falls. This proposition has a number of important applications. We shall consider one of these now and others later.

We have seen that the government can eliminate a deflationary gap by increasing its spending by the amount of the gap while holding tax rates constant. The initial deficit is thus equal to the extra government expenditure. But income will now rise and so will tax receipts.

Can we say anything about the relative size of the deficit for which the government must initially budget and the deficit that will remain once the full-employment level of GNP has been established? Suppose, for example, that the deflationary gap is $10 billion and the government raises expenditure by $10 billion, creating an initial government deficit of that amount. National income now begins to rise under the impact of the extra injection of government expenditure and, with constant tax rates, the government's tax revenue rises. When national income reaches its new equilibrium level, the budget deficit will have been decreased substantially. If, for example,

Figure 30–2 Reducing expenditure or increasing taxes to eliminate an inflationary gap

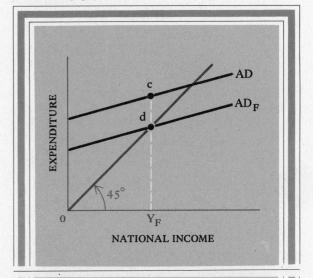

Policies that shift the aggregate demand curve downward can be used to eliminate an inflationary gap. Initially aggregate demand is AD, and with full-employment income at Y_F, the inflationary gap is *cd*. The government can remove this gap by reducing its expenditure by *cd*, holding tax rates constant, or by increasing its tax rates sufficiently to cause the aggregate demand curve to shift downward by *cd*.

the multiplier is 2 and taxes take 30 percent of all national income,[4] then in response to the new government expenditure of $10 billion, national income will rise by $20 billion and tax revenue will rise by $6 billion. Thus the initial budget deficit of $10 billion will, in this example, shrink to $4 billion when national income reaches its new equilibrium level.

[4] All of the important points in this chapter can be demonstrated using the simple assumption that taxes always take a constant proportion of national income. This makes the marginal and average propensities to tax the same (they are 0.3 in the present example).

Figure 30–3　Full-employment balance

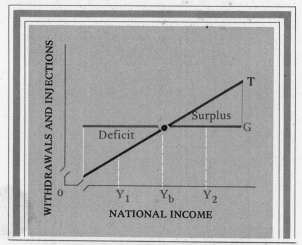

The balance between G and T at the full-employment level of income is called the full-employment balance. For given tax rates, total tax payments vary with the level of income, as shown by the line T. Government expenditure is assumed not to vary with income and is shown by the horizontal line G. The distance between the T and G line shows the deficit or surplus corresponding to each level of income. Y_b is the level of income for which the budget is balanced. If full-employment income is less than Y_b, say Y_1, there is a full-employment deficit; if full-employment income is greater than Y_b, say Y_2, there is a full-employment surplus. Only if the full-employment level of income is Y_b will there be a balanced budget at full employment.

Could the rise in income ever be large enough to eliminate the deficit completely? The answer is no. [34] The extra government expenditure is a new injection and income will rise until a matching flow of withdrawals has been generated. Since taxes are only one of several withdrawals, it follows that the rise in taxes must be less than the rise in government expenditure.

The full-employment deficit or surplus. It is now clear that we can talk not only about the *actual* (or "current") budget deficit or surplus at the present level of national income, but also about the *potential* budget deficit or surplus at any other level of national income, given current rates of taxes and expenditures. The potential deficit or surplus to which the President's Council of Economic Advisers has paid most attention is the one that would occur if the economy were at full employment; it is called the **full-employment balance.**[5] This concept is elaborated in Figure 30–3. Notice that the current deficit will be larger than the full-employment deficit for any economy whose current income is less than full-employment income; the reason is that as income rises the yield from a given set of tax rates rises and hence the deficit falls.

The balanced budget multiplier

So far the effects of changing either revenues or expenditures have been considered. What would happen if, during a time of unemployment, the government raised *both* its expenditures and its taxes, seeking to keep the budget balanced at all times? Although it is sometimes thought that such action would produce no net effect on the level of income, this need not be so. It has already been seen that $1 billion of extra G may have a different effect than a $1 billion reduction of T. If the government raises an extra $1 billion a year in new tax revenue at the same time that it spends an extra $1 billion a year, the circular flow will be unaffected *only* if the whole of the $1 billion of tax revenue would have been spent by the taxpayers on domestic goods. In such a case, the effect of the government's policy would be to reduce private expenditure

[5] The standard terminology can be confusing. The budget balance is the difference between revenue and expenditure. The balance may be positive (a surplus), negative (a deficit), or zero. If revenues are equal to expenditures so that the budget balance is zero, it is common to speak of a balanced budget. Thus the *budget balance* is $T - G$ while a *balanced budget* means that $T = G$.

by $1 billion and to raise its own expenditure by $1 billion; total expenditure, and hence national income and employment, would be unchanged. Usually, however, a rise in taxes causes not only a fall in consumption but a fall in imports and saving. Thus, if an extra $1 billion in taxes is taken away from households, they will reduce their spending on domestically produced goods by less than $1 billion. They might, for example, reduce domestic consumption expenditure by only $750 million, reducing imports and saving by $250 million. If the government spends the entire $1 billion on domestically produced goods, there will be an increase of $250 million in total demand. In this case the balanced budget increase in public expenditure will have an expansionary effect.

A balanced budget increase in government expenditure will have an expansionary effect on national income, and a balanced budget decrease will have a contractionary effect.

The **balanced budget multiplier** measures these changes. It is defined as the change in income divided by the balanced budget change in government expenditure that brought it about. Thus, if an extra $2 billion of government spending financed by an extra $2 billion of taxes causes national income to rise by $1 billion, then the balanced budget multiplier is 0.5; if income rises by $2 billion it is 1.

Pump priming

Three basic methods of dealing with deflationary or inflationary gaps have been discussed: changes in G, changes in T, and balanced changes in both G and T. A fourth method, called **pump priming,** was popularized by the Roosevelt administration in the 1930s and has supporters even today.

The theory of pump priming holds that less than the whole of a deflationary gap needs to be filled by government expenditure because the filling of only a small part of such a gap

will create such favorable expectations that private investment expenditure will rise to fill the remainder. There is nothing self-contradictory about the theory; it describes a world that could exist. Whether it works in the real world depends, first, on how quickly and by how much business expectations respond to a fairly small rise in income occurring during a slump. (During the Great Depression this response did not occur.) If business expectations do respond as hoped, a second response is then required. Private demand must rise sufficiently to justify the favorable business expectations. This latter condition is unlikely to be fulfilled if high marginal tax rates cause much of the new income to be siphoned off in taxes. If this happens, private demand may not expand fast enough to persuade firms to continue their expanded investment programs—which are the basic cause of the recovery.

COMPARATIVE EFFECTS OF ALTERNATIVE FISCAL POLICIES

Consider the effects on national income of three alternative fiscal policies: a deficit-financed increase in government expenditure of $1 billion, a $1 billion reduction in personal tax revenues, and a balanced budget increase of $1 billion in government expenditure and taxes. The effect of the first policy is to increase aggregate expenditure by $1 billion. The effect of the second policy is to increase aggregate expenditure by the fraction of the $1 billion that is spent on domestically produced output by those who find their disposable income increased. If personal income taxes are reduced, as much as 75 percent of the extra household disposable income may be so spent, thereby raising aggregate expenditure by as much as $750 million. In the third case, the government spends $1 billion that it raises in taxes from the private sector. The net effect on aggregate expenditure depends on the proportion of the tax money that would not have

The size of the balanced budget multiplier

For many purposes it is enough to know that the balanced budget multiplier is positive. The following analysis is presented for those who wish to study further the factors that determine its size.

Suppose that the government raises an extra $X in tax revenue and immediately spends it. The immediate (or impact) *increase* in aggregate expenditure is only the fraction of this revenue that would not have been spent if the money had remained in private hands. Let us call this fraction z. Then the immediate increase in aggregate expenditure is the amount zX. This amount is a net injection, and it will set up a multiplier process; the final rise in national income will be the initial increase times the multiplier. We saw on page 518 that the multiplier is the reciprocal of the marginal propensity to withdraw funds from the circular flow, that is, $1/w$. The change in income (ΔY) is thus

$$\Delta Y = \frac{z}{w} X$$

and the balanced budget multiplier is

$$K_B = \frac{z}{w}$$

Thus the balanced budget multiplier is the ratio of z, the fraction of tax revenue that would not have been spent on domestic consumption had it remained in private hands, and w, the marginal propensity to withdraw funds from the circular flow.

The size of the balanced budget multiplier depends critically on the form the extra taxes take—that is, whether they are income taxes, say, or excise taxes—for this determines the size of z. Consider two possibilities.

Example 1. Assume that the taxes are levied exclusively on personal incomes. The value of z then is the sum of the marginal propensities to save and to import out of disposable income. This value is approximately 0.25. This means that, of every dollar raised in new income taxes, 75¢ would have been spent in the domestic circular flow in any case and 25¢ would have been withdrawn for savings and imports. This means that the impact effect of the increased government expenditure will be to raise aggregate demand by $0.25X$. This addition to the circular flow will then be subject to all the withdrawals, including corporate taxes, savings, and personal income taxes. If $w = 0.5$, then $K_B = 0.25/0.5 = 0.5$. An increase of $1 billion of expenditure financed by $1 billion raised from personal income taxes will raise national income by approximately $500 million.

Example 2. Assume that taxes are increased "across the board": some on corporations, some on persons, some on excise items. In this case z is difficult to calculate and w may be taken as a good approximation to it. In other words, because money is being extracted from various places in the circular flow, it may be assumed that the fraction of it that would not have been spent on domestic production is the fraction of GNP that is generally withdrawn. If this guess proves correct, z will equal w and the balanced budget multiplier will be $K_B = w/w = 1$.

been spent on domestically produced output if the tax revenues had been left in private hands. For example, this proportion might be around 25 percent if the new revenue is raised by personal income taxes. The government, however, spends the whole $1 billion, and this represents $750 million that households would have spent anyway and $250 million that households would have saved and otherwise withdrawn from the circular flow. Aggregate expenditure will thus rise by $250 million.

The resulting increase in national income is found by applying the multiplier to these initial net increases in aggregate expenditure. Since the multiplier is the same whatever the source of the new expenditures, the effects on income of the three policies can be compared by determining the initial increase in aggregate expenditure caused by each.

Consider an increase in government expenditures of $X, a tax cut of $X, and a balanced budget increase in expenditure of $X as alternative policies. Government expenditure will yield the largest increase in national income, a tax cut the next largest, and a balanced budget expenditure the smallest increase.

It follows from this that if the government wishes to achieve a given increase in national income, the required increase in expenditure under a pure expenditure policy is less than the required reduction in taxes under a pure tax cut and that both of these are less than the change in expenditure and taxes required under a balanced budget change in expenditure.

The theory of pump priming is a little different from these three policies because it seeks to alter expectations and by so doing to *shift* the aggregate demand function. If this could be accomplished, a very small increase in G or decrease in T might be sufficient to effect a large rise in national income. Unfortunately, the shifts in expectations required by the pump priming theory have not occurred quickly in practice. At least during the initial stages of an attempt to achieve a desired level of national income, it thus seems necessary to fall back on the idea of removing the whole of a deflationary gap through increases in G and/or decreases in T. Later, when a recovery is in full swing and business confidence—and with it private investment expenditure—have recovered, G can be reduced or T increased.

Objectives of fiscal policy

We have seen that fiscal policy can be used to remove inflationary and deflationary gaps. We must now consider the second principal question of this chapter: What can the government reasonably expect to achieve by using fiscal policy?

Fiscal policy might be altered more or less continually in an effort to stabilize the economy completely, or it might be altered less frequently as a reaction to only those gaps that appear large in size and fairly persistent in duration.

FINE TUNING

In the heyday of Keynesian fiscal policy in the 1950s and 1960s many economists throughout the world advocated the use of fiscal policy to remove even minor fluctuations in national income around its full-employment level. These economists felt that G and T could be changed frequently and by relatively small amounts to hold national income almost exactly at its full-employment level. When this is attempted, fiscal policy is said to be used to "fine tune" the economy.

Fine tuning was never really a starter in the United States because of the length of the so-called **decision lag**—the lag between perceiving a problem and getting a decision to initiate the desired reaction to it. Many things contribute to the length of this lag. Experts must study the economy and agree among themselves on what fiscal changes are most desirable. They must then persuade the President to call for the action they endorse. The President must then temper their advice with what he believes to be politically possible as well as desirable. Then Congress must be persuaded to enact the necessary legislation. A majority of the legislators must be convinced to vote for the measure, either because it is in the country's interests or because it is politically advantageous for them to do so. The time required for this process can be very long, both for tax cuts and for expenditure increases.

While the American form of government makes the decision lag rather long, both the British system—used in the rest of the English-speaking world—and the systems used in most European countries make the decision lag very short. In these countries the decision lag is only the time taken for the cabinet (the executive branch) to become informed and reach a decision. Such decisions are subject to legislative approval, and the government falls if, as rarely happens, it is defeated on a major piece of legislation. In English-speaking countries an election follows, while in European countries a new government may be formed from the existing legislature. In either case, the government can usually count on effecting tax and expenditure changes once the cabinet has agreed on them.

In those countries where political institutions keep the decision lag short, fine tuning has often been attempted. Careful assessment of the results where such policies were followed shows that their successes, if any, fell far short of what was claimed for them.

Why was this? The basic reason lies in the very complexity of any economy. While economists and policy makers can identify broad and persistent trends, it is not possible for them to have detailed knowledge of what is going on at any moment of time, of all the forces that are operating to cause changes in the immediate future, and of all the short-term effects of small changes in the various components in G and T. Because of these imperfections in detailed knowledge, efforts at fine tuning often did as much to encourage minor fluctuations in the economy as to remove them. As a result of these experiences, fine tuning is rather out of favor at the present time. (One consequence of this is that the pressure that built up in the 1960s to change American political institutions in order to make some fine tuning politically feasible is now declining.)

THE REMOVAL OF PERSISTENT GAPS

In addition to the more or less continuous fluctuations that beset it, the economy occasionally develops fairly severe and persistent inflationary or deflationary gaps. One such inflationary gap developed in the late 1960s as arms expenditures associated with the Vietnam War accelerated. One such deflationary gap developed after 1973 when America, along with many other countries of the Western world, experienced the deepest and longest-lasting depression since the 1930s. Gaps of which these two are examples persist long enough for their major causes to be studied and understood and for possible fiscal remedies to be carefully planned and executed.

Many economists who do not believe in the viability of fine tuning believe that fiscal policy can be used to aid in removing persistent gaps.

Tools of fiscal policy

What are the major tools that governments can use to give effect to their fiscal policies? These tools can be classified in many ways; one important classification is based on the division between automatic and discretionary tools.

A declaration against fine tuning but in favor of removing persistent gaps

It is hard to say just when faith in fine tuning gave way to the more modest objective of alleviating only large and persistent inflationary and deflationary gaps. The change is clearly evident in this passage from the *Economic Report of the President,* published early in 1976.

There is a lesson to be drawn from past policy mistakes. The history of monetary and fiscal policies demonstrates that we have a great deal to learn about implementing discretionary policy changes. Our ability to forecast is at best imperfect, especially in an increasingly complex and interdependent world, and the difficulties in forecasting grow larger as we extend the period of which the forecast is made. This is a significant problem because of the time lags involved in altering the pace of economic activity through discretionary monetary and fiscal actions. There is a perception lag in diagnosing the problem, a reaction lag in selecting the appropriate response, and an implementation lag in having the policy prescription accepted and put into effect through our political and administrative processes.

We also lack reliable estimates of how long it takes before the economy responds to policies once they are undertaken and how large the response will be. This is especially true now because the high rates of inflation in recent years have made price expectations a much more important determinant of consumer and business behavior than they formerly were, but there has not been sufficient experience to pin down how inflationary processes affect key relationships within the economy. With respect to fiscal policy there is the additional complication that countercyclical increases in Government expenditures are difficult to check during later upswings. Because countercyclical policy changes may be slow to take hold and then hard to reverse, their effects may extend well past the time when they are most needed. Consequently a significant danger exists that, instead of smoothing economic fluctuations, discretionary changes in policy aimed at demand management may themselves become a source of economic instability.

The proper conclusion is not that we should forswear the use of discretionary policy. Some external shocks to the economic system can and should be offset. Furthermore, provided the growth in Federal outlays becomes more moderate than in the years just past, occasional discretionary adjustments of the income tax schedules are called for in order to prevent excessive growth in Federal taxes. In fact these changes may have to be more frequent if the rate of inflation continues at a somewhat higher average level than at comparable levels of economic activity in the past. Thus, discretionary policies do have an important function in our economic system. But we must be mindful of the great difficulties in successfully executing countercyclical policies.

In this passage the President's Council of Economic Advisers is clearly rejecting fine tuning but at the same time accepting the use of fiscal policy to remove large and persistent inflationary or deflationary gaps.

AUTOMATIC TOOLS OF FISCAL POLICY: BUILT-IN STABILIZERS

As a result of factors discussed in Chapter 29, the level of aggregate demand is continually fluctuating. A stabilization policy for fine tuning the economy would thus require a policy that was itself ever changing. If such a conscious fine tuning policy is impossible, must we then throw up our hands and say that nothing can be done through fiscal policy except in the face of major and long-lived inflationary or deflationary gaps?

Fortunately this is not the case. Much of the

Figure 30–4 Automatic stabilizing effects of taxes on national income

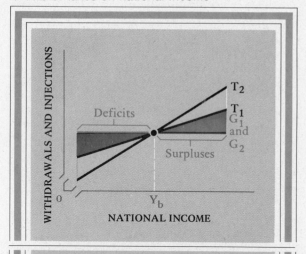

The more tax revenues change as income changes, the less national income fluctuates as a result of fluctuations in investment and other private expenditure. The subscripts 1 and 2 refer to different economies. Both have the same government expenditure function, but different tax functions. Economy 2 has a higher degree of built-in stability than economy 1. As income rises above Y_b, the budget surplus rises faster in 2 than in 1. And as income falls below Y_b, the budget deficit increases faster in 2 than in 1. Thus variations in the government deficit or surplus tend to mitigate both booms and slumps more in 2 than in 1.

Tax revenues tend to adjust automatically to changes in income in such a way as to stabilize. As incomes rise during a period of prosperity, tax revenues increase and, being a withdrawal, exercise a contractionary effect on national income. As tax revenues fall during a recession, the decrease in withdrawals has an expansionary effect. Figure 30–4 illustrates the stabilizing effect of taxes that rise as national income rises. The greater the tendency of tax receipts to vary as income varies, the greater the degree of built-in stability.

So far in this book we have taken government expenditures to be a constant. In fact, many government expenditures tend to vary in a systematic way with national income. Government expenditures are automatically stabilizing to the extent that they rise during periods of recession and depression and decline during periods of prosperity and boom. This follows directly from the facts that a rise in G has a stimulating effect on the economy similar to a fall in T while a fall in G has a contractionary effect similar to a rise in T.

A large degree of built-in stability is a good thing if the economy is tending to oscillate around a high level of income and employment. The same degree of built-in stability can, however, be very undesirable if the economy is in a serious slump. Consider an economy that is reviving from a severe depression under the impetus of new private investment or new government expenditure. The more rapidly tax yields rise as national income rises, the more rapidly withdrawals will rise. Thus the large rise in taxes will tend to bring an expansion quickly to a halt by reestablishing the equality between injections and withdrawals after only a small rise in income. The larger the marginal propensity to tax, the smaller will be the multiplier—and thus the smaller the expansion in income resulting from a given rise in injections.

Undesirable built-in stability that inhibits recovery from a period of low demand and

job of adjusting fiscal policy to an ever-changing economic environment is done automatically by what are called built-in stabilizers. A **built-in stabilizer** is anything that tends to cause injections to increase or withdrawals to decrease as national income falls and injections to decrease or withdrawals to increase as national income rises without the government's having to make policy decisions to bring about these changes.

high unemployment can be a very serious matter indeed.

Built-in stability is desirable when the level of income and employment being stabilized is close to full employment, but it is undesirable when the level being stabilized is well below full employment.

Some built-in stabilizers

Taxes. Most taxes tend to yield more the higher is national income. Sales and excise tax yields rise as total purchases and sales rise (and this happens as income rises). The same is true of taxes on payrolls such as social security taxes. Thus, with rates constant, the total tax yield and hence the total of withdrawals from the circular flow of income rises and falls as national income rises and falls.

The effect is even more marked with taxes that are progressive rather than proportional. Steeply progressive tax rates ensure that, as income rises, tax receipts rise more than in proportion. Whatever else is happening, these extra withdrawals exert a contractionary force on the economy. Conversely, if income falls, tax receipts fall sharply, withdrawals are reduced, and the contractionary pressures on the economy are to some extent alleviated.

Social insurance and welfare services. All welfare payments tend to rise in times of falling national income with its accompanying unemployment and hardship. Many welfare schemes are financed by taxes based on payrolls or earnings, and these taxes tend to yield less when income is low. Thus welfare schemes tend to be net injectors into the circular flow in times of slumps. They also tend to be net withdrawers in times of boom and full employment, when payments are low and revenues high. These net deficits and surpluses on welfare expenditures tend to stabilize the economy in just the same way as if the money were used to build dams or bridges.

The Old-Age Survivors' Insurance Program (popularly called social security) is financed by taxes (called social security premiums) which are paid by both employers and employees. Unemployment insurance is financed by a payroll tax on employers. During periods of depression, these tax collections decrease while payments to individuals under these programs rise. Thus both the Old-Age Survivors' Insurance Program and unemployment insurance serve as built-in stabilizers.

Agricultural-support policies. When there is a slump in the economy there is a general decline in the demand for all goods, including agricultural produce. The free-market price of agricultural goods tends to fall, and government agricultural supports come into play. (These are analyzed in Chapter 7.) This ensures that government expenditures on this form of activity will rise as the level of national income falls.

The origin of built-in stabilizers

Most of these built-in stabilizers are fairly new phenomena in this country. Fifty years ago farm-stabilization policies, steeply progressive income taxes, and large unemployment and other social security payments were unknown in the United States. Each of these built-in stabilizers is the unforeseen by-product of policies originally adopted for other reasons. The progressive income tax arose out of a concern to make the distribution of income less unequal. The growth of the government sector has been the result of many factors other than a desire for cyclical stability. Social insurance and agricultural-support programs were adopted more because of a concern with the welfare of the individuals and groups involved than with preserving the health of the economy. But, unforeseen or not, they work. (Even governments can be lucky.)

The Council of Economic Advisers has estimated that with the present tax system and schedules of unemployment compensation benefits, a decline in GNP automatically produces a reduction in government receipts and an increase in transfer payments that limits the decline in after-tax income to about 65¢ for each $1 of reduction of GNP. Thus, about a third of any decline is automatically offset.

The partial nature of the job done by built-in stabilizers

No matter how lucky governments have been in finding built-in stabilizers, these cannot reduce fluctuations to zero. Stabilizers work by influencing income in such a way as to produce stabilizing reactions to changes in income. But until the income change occurs, the stabilizer is not even brought into play.

The evidence of the behavior of the U.S. economy reviewed in the previous chapter suggests two important conclusions. First, fluctuations have been less extreme since 1945 than they were in earlier periods. This is due in part to the operation of powerful built-in stabilizers absent from the scene before World War II. Second, the magnitude of the post-1945 fluctuations has nonetheless been sufficient to cause policy makers serious concern.

DISCRETIONARY FISCAL POLICY

Short-term, minor fluctuations that are not removed by automatic built-in stabilizers cannot, with present knowledge and techniques, be removed by consciously fine tuning the economy. We have already noted, however, that larger and more persistent gaps sometimes appear. In these cases there is time for the government to operate a **discretionary fiscal policy,** which means to institute changes in taxes and expenditures that are designed to offset gaps. To do this effectively the Administration needs to make periodic conscious decisions to alter fiscal policy. The Council of Economic Advisers must study current economic trends and predict the probable course of the economy. If the predicted course is unsatisfactory, Congress must be persuaded to enact the necessary legislation.

In considering discretionary fiscal policy we will deal with two main questions. First, does it matter whether it is government expenditure or government tax revenue that is varied to achieve the desired budget deficit or surplus? Second, does it matter whether households and firms regard the government's fiscal changes as being temporary or as being long-lived?

The choice between changes in tax rates and government expenditures

There is often sharp debate on whether taxes or expenditures or both should be used to achieve those stabilizing changes that are generally agreed to be desirable. What issues are involved in these debates? What factors affect the choice between changes in G and changes in T?

Location of effects. The multiplier effects of an increase in aggregate demand tend to spread over the whole economy, causing a rising demand for virtually every commodity. If a slump is a general one with widespread unemployment, this will be an advantage. If, however, a slump has severely localized characteristics, with a major depression in a particular industry (such as automobiles) or area (such as Appalachia), then it may be desirable to achieve a disproportionate effect in the seriously depressed industry or area. In this case, raising expenditure has a distinct advantage over cutting taxes. The tax cut will have its initial impact on the entire economy, but by careful choice of projects much of the initial effect of extra expenditure can be channeled into the depressed industry or area. Thus, if specific impact effects are important, G has an advantage over T.

The size of the deficit and the size of the government sector. Different fiscal policies can have the same effects on GNP. Because they act in different ways they have different side effects on the size of government deficits and the size of the government sector.

A balanced budget increase in G and T requires no increase in the deficit, but it does require a larger increase in the volume of government spending than either of the other two policies. The policy of only increasing government expenditure produces a smaller increase in the size of G than does the balanced budget approach, but it does increase the deficit. A tax cut requires the largest deficit of the three policies, but the extra aggregate demand occurs in the private rather than in the government sector; thus the government sector need not expand at all.

Clearly, then, someone who wishes to remove some existing unemployment but dislikes both deficits and the rising importance of the government sector faces a conflict if fiscal policy is to be used.

To minimize the budget deficit a balanced increase in G and T is needed, but this policy will maximize the increase in the size of the government sector. To minimize the increase in the government sector a tax cut is called for, but this will maximize the increase in the deficit.

The problem is easier for someone who is concerned only with the size of the government sector (and not with the size of budget deficits). Such people fear a strong central government and feel that everything should be done to keep the fraction of GNP that is accounted for by the government as low as possible. They will favor tax cuts as a method of reducing a deflationary gap because a tax cut will prevent an increase in the importance of the government as a spending agent. Other people, however, feel that the public sector is systematically starved. They believe that far fewer publicly produced goods and services are provided than would be purchased if they could be purchased on the open market. When there is a deflationary gap, these people will advocate increases in government spending with or without tax increases. They do this in the hope that some of the increased expenditure will survive the cutback when the next inflationary gap develops.

Time lags. We have already discussed the decision lags of discretionary fiscal policy. Although these lags are long under the American political system there is no reason why they should be of significantly different lengths for changes in government expenditure and in tax rates.

There is, however, a second type of lag, and this lag may differ for changes in taxes and changes in expenditure. Once a fiscal change has been authorized, there will necessarily be some lag before it actually goes into effect. This lag is called an **execution lag.** Once Congress has passed appropriations for a new road-building program, for example, it will be some time before substantial income payments are made to private firms and households. Routes must be surveyed; land must be acquired, often by condemnatory procedures; public protests must often be heard; bids must be called for; and contracts must be let. All of this can take considerable time. However, the execution lag can be very short for welfare expenditures and for tax cuts. Once legislation for tax reduction has been passed by Congress, rates of withholding can be reduced quickly. Thus, only a matter of weeks after the tax cut is passed, wage earners may find themselves with more take-home pay because their employers are withholding tax payments at a lower rate than they were previously.

The choice between "temporary" and long-lasting fiscal changes

Consider the attempt to remove a persistent inflationary or deflationary gap through changes in tax rates. Such a gap, though persistent, is unlikely to be regarded as a permanent feature of the economy. The tax changes might therefore be advocated only for "the duration"—that is, for as long as the Administration thinks the gap would persist without the tax changes. It might have seemed reasonable at the time, for example, to expect the inflationary gap of the late 1960s to persist only as long as the Vietnam War. A discretionary fiscal policy designed to remove that gap could take the form, say, of a surcharge on income taxes for a two-year period. For another example, the recession that began in 1974 was fought by "temporary" tax rebates which had to be renewed by Congress every 6 months—with the clear implication that taxes would return to their "normal" levels when recovery was well under way.

Such tax changes cause changes in household disposable income and, according to the Keynesian theory of the consumption function, would cause changes in consumption. Consumption expenditure would increase as tax rebates rose in times of deflationary gaps and would decrease as tax surcharges rose in times of inflationary gaps. This theory of the effects of short-term tax changes relies on the theory that household consumption depends on current disposable income.

Permanent-income theories. Many of the recent theories of the consumption function have emphasized what is called a household's expected *lifetime income* or *permanent income* as the major determinant of consumption. According to such theories, households have expectations about their lifetime incomes and they adjust their consumption to these expectations. When temporary fluctuations in income occur, households maintain their long-term consumption plans and use their stocks of wealth as a buffer to absorb income fluctuations. Thus when there is a purely temporary rise in income, households will save all the extra income; when there is a purely temporary fall in income, households maintain their long-term consumption plans by using up part of their wealth accumulated through past savings. The two most important theories of this type are the *life-cycle* and the *permanent-income* hypotheses. The first is associated principally with Franco Modigliani and the second with Milton Friedman.[6]

[6] Professor Friedman was awarded the 1976 Nobel Prize in Economics for his work on the theories of money and stabilization policy.

To the extent that this kind of influence is at work it may have serious consequences for short-lived tax changes. A temporary rebate raises a household's disposable income but households, recognizing this as temporary, might not revise their expenditure plans and might save the money instead. Thus the hoped-for increase in aggregate expenditure would not materialize. Seen from the withdrawals-injections approach, the effect is that the decline in one withdrawal, government taxes, is balanced by an equal increase in another withdrawal, household saving. Overall withdrawals are unchanged and so is national income. Similarly, a temporary rise in taxes reduces disposable income, but that may merely cause a fall in saving. Thus total expenditure and total withdrawals are again unchanged, and a temporary surcharge fails to reduce the inflationary gap.

If households' consumption is more closely related to lifetime rather than to current income, then tax changes that are known to be of short duration may have only small effects on current consumption.

A word of warning. The permanent-income theory is not as immediately applicable to fiscal policy as it may seem at first sight. This is because what fiscal policy seeks to affect is *expenditure* (on consumption and investment goods) while the permanent-income type of theory seeks to explain the consumption of goods and services—which in the case of durables is spread over the whole life of the durable. This important but rather complex matter is discussed further in the appendix to this chapter, which begins on page 885.

Economic theory and political realism

So far we have discussed fiscal policy in relation to economic advantages and disadvantages. In the American government, however, the views of key elected representatives are critical. Thus the choice of which form of a contractionary fiscal policy to use in reducing an inflationary gap, or which form of an expansionary fiscal policy to use in removing a deflationary gap, is likely to be determined by what is politically possible rather than by a fine calculation about the trade-off between the size of the deficit and the size of the government. If the Ways and Means Committee says no tax change this year, then some other method of achieving the desired fiscal effects has to be found.

The ability of the economist to design alternative economic policies to achieve economic objectives is particularly important in such circumstances. Ideally, in a given situation at least one of the economist's policies will be both economically effective and politically acceptable.

Summary

1. Fiscal policy is the use of government expenditure and government taxes in an effort to remove inflationary and deflationary gaps. Such policy is more effective the smaller is the crowding-out effect, but it can work as long as the crowding-out effect is less than 100 percent.

2. The government can deal with a deflationary gap by increasing government expenditures, by decreasing taxes, or by a balanced budget increase in both G and T. An opposite set of policies is available for dealing with an inflationary gap.

3. When the government uses deficits or surpluses to affect the level of income, some but not all of the initial deficit or surplus will be offset by changes in tax revenues as the economy responds to the fiscal policy. It is helpful to calculate the *full-employment deficit or surplus* that would occur at existing rates of taxation and government expenditure if the full-employment level of national income were to be achieved.

4. Pump priming, unlike the other methods of fiscal policy, depends on a small initial government expenditure to induce a private response that will lead to the elimination of a deflationary gap. Although logically possible, the evidence does not suggest that this works as a policy in a severe depression.

5. The theory of fine tuning held that discretionary changes in government expenditure and tax rates could be used to remove short-term fluctuations in the economy and hold actual national income more or less continuously at its full-employment level. This theory has now been discredited. Short-term fiscal stabilization policy is thus left to be accomplished by automatic tools.

6. Automatic fiscal policy tools are often called built-in stabilizers, and they tend to increase government spending and decrease taxes during slumps and to increase taxes and decrease spending during booms without the government's having to take policy decisions to bring about these changes in each case.

7. Examples of built-in stabilizers are most taxes, particularly progressive income taxes, social security and unemployment insurance, and agricultural-support policies. If built-in stabilizers tend to stabilize income at or near its full-employment level, their effect is desirable. If they operate to stop an expansion well before full employment is reached, their effect is undesirable.

8. Discretionary fiscal policy refers to tax changes and/or expenditure changes that are consciously made. This policy is used in an attempt to remove fairly large and persistent inflationary and deflationary gaps that occur from time to time.

9. The choice among alternative fiscal policies may be influenced by the desire to have specific locational effects, by the policy makers' views of the desirability of increasing (or decreasing) the relative size of the government sector, by the nature of the time lags that may be expected, and by practical political considerations.

10. The effect of changes in fiscal policy may depend on whether households regard the changes in their disposable income as permanent or temporary and on how they vary their spending in response to changes that they regard as temporary.

11. The life-cycle and permanent-income hypotheses and the implications that they have for fiscal policy are further discussed in the appendix to this chapter, which begins on page 885.

Concepts for review

Fiscal policy
Budget deficits and surpluses
The effect of budget deficits and surpluses on aggregate demand
The crowding-out effect
Actual deficit and full-employment deficit
Fine tuning
The balanced budget multiplier
Built-in stabilizers
Discretionary fiscal policy
Decision lags and execution lags

Discussion questions

1. On presidential economics:
a. President Carter, in 1977, said, "There will be no new programs implemented under my administration unless we can be sure that the cost of those programs is compatible with my goal of having a *balanced budget* before the end of that term." Does this mean the President rejects fiscal policy? What might it mean?
b. President Ford in 1975 maintained that his proposed package of a $28 billion cut in federal expenditure and a $28 billion tax cut "as a short-term measure would not affect the economy in any significant way." Does this mean that President Ford believed the balanced budget multiplier was zero? If so, why then might he have proposed the package? If not, what might he have meant?

2. Arrange in order the following in terms of the expected size of their effect on aggregate demand and employment:
a. government subsidies to farmers of $10 billion, financed by an increase in income taxes of $10 billion
b. government deficit expenditure of $10 billion during a recession

c. government deficit expenditure of $10 billion near the end of a recovery
d. a general tax cut, costing $10 billion in lost revenue to the treasury

3. What is the crowding-out effect? Relate the size of the balanced budget multiplier to the size of the crowding-out effect.

4. J. K. Galbraith said, about coping with a deflationary gap by means of a tax rebate; "Those who advocate a tax cut do so in deeply conditioned disregard of its economic ineffectiveness, its demonstrated political disutility, and its patently reactionary social effects." What might Professor Galbraith have had in mind by his statement?

5. When the Carter tax proposal for a $50 rebate to every taxpayer with family income under $30,000 was made, two leading government figures disagreed about it: Secretary of the Treasury Blumenthal hailed it as a device to "provide a quick injection of spending" into a sagging economy. Federal Reserve Board Chairman Burns objected: "As far as I can judge, the economy is improving on its own." Two months later, Secretary Blumenthal had changed his mind and the proposal was withdrawn. Discuss these views in terms of the concepts of temporary and permanent changes, lags, and the efficacy of fine tuning.

6. Which of the following would be built-in stabilizers?
a food stamps for the needy
b. cost-of-living escalators on government contracts and pensions
c. income taxes
d. free college tuition for unemployed workers after six months of unemployment, provided that they are under 30 years old and have had five or more years of full time work experience since high school

7. When the government subsidizes particular industries or regions rather than industry generally, is this a sure sign of "playing politics" with fiscal policy?

31

Fiscal policy
in action

Governments inevitably have a major impact on GNP through their fiscal behavior. The very size of a government's budget guarantees that. The conscious use of the budget to influence GNP that constitutes fiscal policy is, however, by no means inevitable. Fiscal impact is unavoidable, but fiscal policy is a matter of choice.

In the late 1940s many advanced industrial countries accepted fiscal policy as an important tool of full-employment policy. National income theory together with the wartime experience of full employment generated by enormous government expenditures convinced their policy makers of the power of fiscal tools. These countries have used fiscal policy more or less continuously ever since without serious debate over the potency of the tools. (There has been serious debate, however, over whether or not the results produced were beneficial or harmful.) In the United States the acceptance of fiscal policy was less complete; it was not until the Kennedy-Johnson years of the 1960s that the "new economics" of fiscal policy gained widespread public acceptance. Then, within a very few years of the apparent victory of the new economics, the supporters of fiscal policy found themselves engaged in a major debate with monetarists, who maintained that the general potency of fiscal tools had been greatly overestimated by so-called Keynesian economists.

In the present chapter we shall consider American fiscal policy in the past, present, and future and then discuss the specific problem of the national debt that arises whenever fiscal policy is used. The controversy between the "Keynesians" and the "monetarists" will be postponed to Chapter 41.

Fiscal policy at work in the United States

BEFORE 1946

In 1932 Franklin Roosevelt was elected to the U.S. presidency on a platform of fighting the Great Depression with vigorous government policies. Not until America entered World War II, nearly a decade later, was massive unemployment ended. Did the experience of the 1930s prove the failure of fiscal policy? There is a widespread misconception that Roosevelt believed in deficit financing and that massive fiscal policy was tried during the 1930s and failed. Professor E. Cary Brown, after a careful study, concludes, however: "Fiscal policy seems to have been an unsuccessful recovery device in the 'thirties—not because it did not work, but because it was not tried."[1] The size of the *aggregate* government deficit for the entire decade of the 1930s was about $25 billion. This represents less than half the deficit for the single year 1942 or 1943, and it is clearly a drop in the bucket considering that GNP fell from $103 billion in 1929 to $56 billion in 1933. In 1933, at the depth of the Depression, the federal government was spending $2 billion for purchases of goods and services, only slightly more than the $1.3 billion spent in 1929. In 1933 state and local governments were spending an additional $6 billion but were collecting $5.9 billion in taxes.

The outcry at the time against reckless government spending was occasioned by the nature rather than the amount of the expenditures, many of which were earmarked for direct public works and for employment of out-of-work artists and others on various make-work projects. The word "boondoggle" was used to refer to such "unsound" expenditures. But the critics of that day did not understand the countercyclical aspects of public expenditures and public deficits. They did not appreciate that projects so financed would create income and employment quickly. Professor Brown concludes that the impact on aggregate demand of public expenditures was about what would be expected today, but that it was too small to do much good. Expenditures were wastefully small, not wastefully large. This was largely because President Roosevelt and his advisors were committed to the notion of pump priming (see page 8—101). They hoped that a small injection of government expenditure would generate a flow of new private investment that would eliminate the need for further public stimulus. It did not work, and today it seems hopelessly naive to have expected that it would. Indeed, at the same time that the government was running its small deficits in an effort to prime the pump, it was enacting sharp rises in the tax rates that would nip off any recovery before it got very far. The Revenue Act of 1932 virtually doubled full-employment tax yields, creating a very large full-employment surplus. When the partial recovery of 1936–1937 was barely under way, tax yields increased enough to balance the budget, although 14 percent of the labor force (7.7 million people) were still unemployed. Clearly the economy was operating under the crushing burden of too much built-in stability at too low a level of income.

The "daring" experiments in deficit financing of the 1930s were by modern standards too little and too late.

Given the deficits that were achieved, it would have taken a multiplier of 25 for the American economy to have come within striking distance of full employment; in fact, the multiplier in the 1930s was approximately 2.

Once the massive, war-geared expenditure of the 1940s began, income responded sharply and unemployment all but evaporated. Be-

[1] E. Cary Brown, "Fiscal Policy in the Thirties: A Reappraisal," *American Economic Review* (December 1956), pages 865–866.

tween 1940 and 1945, the federal government ran an aggregate deficit in excess of $200 billion. Government expenditures on goods and services, which had been running at under 15 percent of GNP during the 1930s, jumped to 46 percent by 1943, and unemployment reached the incredible low in 1944 of 1.2 percent of the civilian labor force.

The increase in aggregate demand changed a deflationary gap into an inflationary one, but the government was in no position to curtail its expenditures. It urged citizens to be patriotic and buy War Bonds instead of goods. It resorted to price controls, rationing, and a series of priorities for defense materials to mask the inflationary pressures. These substantially restrained the inflationary forces, although prices did rise by almost one-third during 1940–1945.

The performance of the American economy from 1930 to 1945 is quite well explained by modern income theory. It is clear that the central authorities did not effectively use fiscal measures to stabilize the economy. War cured the depression because war demands made acceptable a level of government expenditure sufficient to remove the deflationary gap. Had the first Roosevelt administration been able to run deficits of $40 billion per year instead of $2 to $4 billion per year, it might have ended the waste of the depression five years sooner. It is because we know this now that another Great Depression is unlikely.

AFTER WORLD WAR II

The most pressing economic problem of 1946 was the inflationary gap. People rushed to spend their wartime savings on new cars and houses that had been unavailable during the war and on new products such as television sets that had been developed during the war. The large volume of accumulated purchasing power combined with the time lag required to convert the economy from wartime to peacetime production led to the gap between

supply of and demand for these goods. Wartime price controls and rationing were removed. Between 1946 and 1948, prices rose more than they had in the entire wartime period.

From a longer-run point of view, the major economic development of 1946 was the passage of the Employment Act of 1946, which created the Council of Economic Advisers, a body charged with advising the President on the state of the economy and on how the goal of full employment could best be achieved.

Although a moderate inflation characterized the postwar years, so also did growth in real GNP. This growth continued into the decade of the 1950s, but it became increasingly sluggish, and unemployment began an upward creep from 2.9 percent in 1953 to 6.7 percent in 1961. Many worried that the combination of general prosperity, rising prices, and rising unemployment represented a new set of structural problems that could not easily be solved by the tools of macroeconomic policy.

The New Economic Policy of the 1960s

President Kennedy and his Council held a different view, and in the 1960s they undertook the first deliberate and calculated exercise in expansionary fiscal policy to be attempted in the United States. By late 1962 there was an existing budget deficit in excess of $4 billion but a large full-employment surplus (that is, if the economy had been able to reach full employment the government's budget would have been in surplus). President Kennedy asked Congress to enact a tax cut of approximately $10 billion. The Council regarded the tax cut as essential to reduce the full-employment surplus, which served to nip off booms before full employment was reached. The inability of the economy to attain anything like full employment during the late 1950s and early 1960s was consistent with this belief.

The idea behind this tax cut was neither

fine tuning nor overcoming some particularly persistent recession. The idea was rather to remedy the situation that had developed through the 1950s because government revenues grew faster than government expenditure as economic growth raised the value of full-employment, real national income. The full-employment surplus that had developed over the period would nip off any expansion before full employment was reached—as had happened previously in 1936. Those who supported the policy were accepting the power of the budget to influence national income without necessarily accepting the theory that the budget could be adjusted continually to fine tune the economy and thus mitigate the effects of short-term fluctuations in the private sector's aggregate expenditure.

To describe the objectives of this policy the Council of Economic Advisers developed a concept called **fiscal drag.** This concept denotes the increase in the full-employment surplus cause by economic growth. Economic growth increases the level of full-employment national income: the amount that can be produced when resources are fully employed rises as productivity rises.

With constant tax rates the amount of tax revenue that will be raised at full employment rises as full-employment income itself rises. If government expenditure remains constant, economic growth will produce a growing full-employment surplus.

To prevent an ever-stronger depressing effect from being exerted on national income by a growing full-employment surplus it is necessary to reduce the surplus periodically, either by increasing government spending or by reducing tax rates. The full significance of this long-term problem of fiscal policy in a growing economy was not appreciated until the 1960s.

In the previous chapter we noted that decision lags made it difficult ever to try to fine tune the American economy through discretionary fiscal policy. Certainly the possibility of effective fine tuning was made to look un-

likely by the decision lag on the tax cut that was finally enacted in 1964 after fully *two years* of heated congressional debate.

As well as changing the full-employment balance, the 1964 tax cut couldn't help but affect the current one. A reduction in taxes is predicted to increase national income, and both GNP and employment did rise. Although no *single* experiment can ever be decisive in the real world (because so many things are changing at once) the rise in GNP and employment was in line with the predictions based on macroeconomic theory and made by the President's Council of Economic Advisers. The full effect came rather late, and by that time the large increases in military expenditure due to escalation of the war in Vietnam as well as the expenditure-creating effects of the tax cut were exerting a substantial expansionary effect on the economy. A growing inflationary gap had replaced the deflationary gap of the late 1950s and early 1960s. The large 1967 deficit (owing to increased defense expenditures on top of a heavy domestic budget), coming with GNP already at the full-employment level, caused serious inflationary pressures in 1968.

The tax increase of June 1968 and the accompanying budget cut were delayed responses to danger signals clearly evident in the data much earlier. Once again decision lags had proved to be long: Presidential advisers had foreseen the developing inflationary gap two years earlier, and President Johnson made his first request to Congress a full 18 months before the tax increase was finally enacted.

The larger budget surplus of 1969 was meant to have a restraining effect on inflation. This effect was smaller in magnitude and slower in coming than had been expected.

The apparent failure of the contractionary budgetary policy of 1969—a tax surcharge and a curtailment of some expenditures combined to give a relatively large budget surplus—caused much debate among economists. Some saw it as a general failure of fiscal policy, others saw it as a demonstration that *temporary* tax surcharges and rebates were relatively ineffective in influencing aggregate demand, and still others felt that the contractionary budgetary stance was too short-lived to have any significant effect on the strong inflationary expectations that had by then become built into the system. Whatever the final outcome of that debate, there is no doubt that the period of accelerating inflation since 1966 coincided with a period of high and rising budget deficits in which the surplus of 1969 appears as merely a temporary, if large, deviation from trend.

In concluding this section we might ask what was new about the New Economic Policy. There were no major changes in basic macroeconomic theory during the 1960s, but it is common to regard 1961 as a major turning point in U.S. fiscal policy. The main reason is that the Kennedy administration (and the Council of Economic Advisers, then led by Walter Heller) for the first time in American history gave official notice to the existing theories of the macroeconomists. Moreover, the Council introduced the public to new concepts such as full-employment surplus, full-employment deficit, fiscal drag, and GNP gap (the difference between actual and potential GNP).

Fiscal policy in the 1970s

Figure 27–1 on page 484 is worth studying at this time. It shows that the American economy underwent a series of swings during the 1970s. The inflationary gap of the late 1960s gave way to a mild deflationary gap in 1970–1971. The trough was quickly passed and a period of sustained recovery followed. By 1973–1974 an inflationary gap had developed with national income just exceeding its full-employment level and prices rising at an accelerating rate that took inflation to two-digit figures by 1974. The turning point came early in that year, after which the American economy underwent (along with the economies of other Western countries) the most

severe recession since the 1930s. The trough was reached by early 1975 and a slow recovery was then begun that continued through 1977.

Fiscal policy has reflected these swings in the economy and has tried to some extent to offset them. Table 31–1 shows the actual and the full-employment balance for the federal government since 1969. The full-employment surplus of 1969 became a slight deficit in 1970 and a larger one in 1971. At the same time the actual deficit grew to be the largest in over twenty years. This indicated an attempt to exert an expansionary fiscal effect on the economy as the mild recession of 1970–1971 developed. In 1972, when the economy was already in the midst of a strong upswing, the budget became even more expansionary than it had been in the previous year, with a full-employment deficit of $21.5 billion and an actual realized deficit of $17.3 billion. As the recovery turned into an inflationary gap, fiscal

Table 31–1 Actual and full-employment budget balances for the federal government [billions of dollars; (−) indicates a deficit]

Year	Actual budget balance	Full-employment budget balance
1969	8.5	3.0
1970	−12.1	−2.6
1971	−22.0	−9.2
1972	−17.3	−21.5
1973	−6.7	−7.9
1974	−11.5	14.1
1975	−71.2	−12.5
1976	−58.3	−10.3

Actual budget deficits have been the rule throughout the 1970s. Because the economy has been operating at less than full employment throughout most of the 1970s, the actual budget deficits have exceeded the full-employment deficits in most years. But even the full-employment balance has shown a deficit in all but one year since 1970.

policy was reversed and full-employment surplus once again developed in 1974.

The contractionary fiscal policy of 1974 was largely unplanned and it reveals a major problem with fiscal policy during periods of rapid inflation. During an inflation prices and money incomes rise rapidly. Progressive income tax rates then yield more and more revenue even though there is no change in the structure of tax rates.

Fiscal drag develops when full-employment national income measured in current dollars rises due to an inflation just as it develops when full-employment national income measured in constant dollars rises due to economic growth.

The inflation continued well after the economic downturn in 1974 and the fiscal drag due to inflation more than offset the expansionary effects of the built-in stabilizers that tend to reduce taxes and raise government expenditures when output and employment begin to fall. As a result discretionary changes in fiscal policy were required in 1975 to try to offset the severe downturn that developed. In March 1975 Congress passed the Tax Reduction Act. This act gave rebates of $8 billion on 1974 taxes that had already been paid, reduced the rates of current withholding taxes (taxes deducted at source from wages and salaries) at a rate of $12 billion per year, and cut corporate tax liabilities by $4.5 billion. In all, the act cut 1975 federal tax receipts by about $42 billion. Much of this, however, was the result of once-only tax rebates and remissions. The tax cuts that remained in effect at the end of 1975 had the effect of reducing overall federal tax receipts by about $15 billion, or 5 percent of their 1974 level. (By comparison the tax cuts of 1964–1965 lowered federal tax receipts by about 10 percent.)

The persistence of the strong inflationary pressures that developed in the 1972–1973 boom posed a major problem. Inflation continued at a high rate well after the downturn

in economic activity of 1974. From 1974 to 1975 the consumer price index rose by more than 10 percent, and it was not until the latter part of 1975 that inflationary pressures seemed to be subsiding. Policy makers were thus faced with the coexistence of high unemployment and a high inflation rate—a combination that came to be called *stagflation*. They were reluctant to introduce too much fiscal stimulation into the economy lest they strengthen the fires of inflation. At the beginning of 1976 the Council of Economic Advisers opted for a slow recovery of the economy with a keen eye on the inflation rate. The Administration's policy was to encourage a gradual recovery from the recession as long as the rate of inflation did not rise but to cut back on any stimulus to recovery if inflationary pressures seemed to be building up.

In fact, the recovery accelerated through the end of 1975 and into early 1976, reaching a 9 percent annual rate during the first quarter of 1976. It then decelerated and achieved only a 4 percent annual rate over the last three quarters of 1976. The recovery was further slowed by the extraordinarily cold winter of 1976–1977, which caused local fuel shortages, forced many factories to close temporarily, and caused heavy unemployment in many areas. Nevertheless, the economy was clearly on a recovery track throughout 1976 as shown by the fact that real GNP rose by 6.2 percent over the year, employment increased by almost 3 million persons and the unemployment rate fell by nearly one percentage point.

Fiscal policy was somewhat less expansionary in 1976 than it had been in 1975. Although still at high levels, the actual budget deficit fell substantially and the full employment deficit fell slightly from its 1975 level. Part of this change was due to government expenditure being about $3 billion less than expected during the year. This was attributable, according to the Council of Economic Advisers, "to a combination of lower-than-expected rates of inflation, unemployment, and interest, as well as to delays in making new obligations and outlays, and to an apparent bias towards overestimation of expenditures in the budget.''

In his last months in office, President Ford called for new cuts in personal and corporate taxes to stimulate further recovery. In his turn, President Carter was variously advised to throw fiscal caution to the winds to stimulate a rapid recovery; to renew the fight against inflation, giving stimulation of recovery and reduction of unemployment a low priority; and to tread a middle road by fighting inflation and stimulating a further expansion of output! Early in 1977 the new administration's policies and priorities were not yet clear.

FISCAL POLICY IN THE FUTURE: SECULAR STAGNATION OR BOOM?

Two possible extreme situations are considered here. Although most observers do not regard either as a clear or present danger, it is instructive to see how fiscal policy could cope with them if they should arise.

Secular stagnation

Assume that with imports equal to exports and tax revenues equal to government expenditure there is a chronic tendency for saving to exceed investment at the full-employment level of national income. If the government insisted on following a balanced budget policy, there would be a continual tendency for the economy to settle into equilibrium at less than full employment. Of course, occasional spurts of investment might sometimes raise the economy to full employment, but if the average level of investment were too low, the economy would tend to display a chronic tendency toward unemployment. This would be called a situation of secular stagnation. There is nothing logically contradictory in such a situation; it requires

merely a public that desires to save more than firms wish to invest when the economy is at full employment.[2]

Suppose that chronic unemployment did become a serious problem. What remedy could the government then adopt? If the government adopted a policy of *continuing full-employment budget deficits,* national income could be held at its full-employment level. In this case resources will not be lying continuously idle; instead they will be in use, creating such public goods as schools, roads, opera houses, universities, and weapons. Clearly the policy of continuing budget deficits creates a higher level of employment and a higher level of real income than does the balanced budget policy. Yet the national debt will be increasing year after year. Surely *this* must matter.

The question of the national debt is examined later in this chapter. Notice, for now, that what the government is doing is merely borrowing that amount of full-employment savings that private firms will not spend. The total amount of spending is the same as it would have been if full employment had come about because the volume of private investment was higher than it actually was. All that has happened is that some of the money saved by the private sector is being channeled into the public sector. The amount that is being so channeled is the amount the private sector is unwilling to utilize for its own purposes. If this does not happen national income will fall until private savings are reduced to the amount that the private sector is willing to invest.

The belief that secular stagnation was in the offing for most advanced industrial countries was widely held during the 1930s. This belief was bolstered by the Keynesian theory that

[2] It also requires that the gap between full-employment saving and full-employment investment cannot be removed by driving down the interest rate to a very low level and thereby increasing the desire to invest.

Can America afford to cut defense spending?

Karl Marx predicted that the collapse of capitalist economies would be signaled by a series of larger and larger depressions, and the Great Depression of the 1930s seemed to many observers to be a confirmation of Marx's prediction. When the economies of the United States and other Western countries became persistently buoyant after World War II, many Marxists argued that it was military expenditures alone that were bolstering them. They argued that without such expenditures collapse would be sure and swift.

Macroeconomic theory suggests that Marx was not necessarily correct. With a GNP in the United States of nearly $1,200 billion in 1975 (at 1972 prices), it is clear that if defense expenditures fell from their 1975 level of $87 billion to, say, $8.5 billion (the level in 1940 in terms of 1972 prices), there would be problems. The magnitude of the problems would depend on what else happened and on how suddenly the change occurred.

If the government maintained its tax rates, reduced its expenditures by $80 billion overnight, and allowed the excess tax receipts to pile up in idle balances, theory predicts that the results would be disastrous. With a multiplier of 2, the reduction in national income would be approximately 15 percent and unemployment might rise dramatically, perhaps as high as 20 or 25 percent of the labor force.

Suppose, instead, that the government reduced both taxes and expenditures equally by $80 billion. The theory of the balanced budget multiplier predicts some adverse impact on the economy. If the balanced budget multiplier were 0.5, national income would fall by approximately $40 billion, or nearly 3.5 percent, with a corresponding rise in unemployment. Further tax cuts might be required.

The policy just described is one of cutting taxes and hoping that private spending will take the place of defense spending. In the short run there is a danger in returning too much money to the private sector because the capacity to produce civilian goods cannot expand overnight. The evidence suggests that there should be no insurmountable problems because, in the long run, if consumers' disposable income increased by 10 percent, the effect would be a rise in expenditure by 10 percent. The extra consumer spending will give rise to new opportunities for investment.

Of course the government has other policy options. Nonmilitary government expenditures could, for example, be substituted for defense expenditures, dollar for dollar if necessary. The massive expenditures advocated by many to deal with such

the long-run consumption function was such that saving would account for a larger and larger proportion of income as income increased owing to economic growth.[3] If this

happened, investment would have to become an ever-increasing fraction of national income if full employment were to be maintained with imports equal to exports and the government's budget in balance.

It was possible to develop a strongly persuasive intuitive argument for this hypothe-

[3] Alternative shapes of the consumption function are discussed in more detail in Chapter 27, See pages 488–491.

problems as urban renewal, retraining and reemployment of the longterm unemployed, the reequipping of all schools and hospitals to modern standards, pollution control, or the development of rapid transit systems could absorb funds as rapidly as do major defense programs and with a more positive effect on the standard of living.

Defense spending is unlikely to be reduced drastically and suddenly. A gradual relaxation of international tensions and a gradual reduction in required defense expenditure would create less critical transitional problems. The American economy has often had experience with expenditure changes of $10 to $20 billion per year, and there seems little doubt that increased public nondefense expenditures combined with tax reductions could accommodate a gradual shrinkage in the size of military spending with a gain rather than a loss in standards of living.

This discussion suggests that major reductions in defense spending need pose no insurmountable problems for economists. But the advice of economists is not always listened to. If the Administration or the Congress tried to run a budget surplus in order to reduce the national debt or even to cut both expenditures and taxes too rapidly, they could produce a depression of really serious proportions.

sized shape of the consumption function. But, as always, it is fact, not intuition, that must be the final arbiter. Fortunately, the long-run estimates of the consumption function suggest that this particular nightmare is factually unfounded—at least so far. These estimates suggest that over the long run the proportion of national income devoted by households to current consumption and the proportion saved tend to remain fairly constant. This means that private investment expenditure need expand only as fast as income is expanding in order to take up the desired savings of households and firms. Furthermore, there is evidence that to date new investment opportunities develop more or less as fast as old ones are utilized.

Secular boom

The hypothesis of secular stagnation engaged economists' attention because in the past some thought such a situation was imminent. It is possible to imagine, however, a reverse situation of secular boom in which, with imports equal to exports and a full-employment balanced budget there is a chronic tendency for full-employment savings to be less than full-employment investment. In this case the economy would display chronic boom and inflationary conditions. A remedial fiscal policy now would be to run a long-term budgetary surplus, thereby keeping the inflationary gap small or nonexistent so that full employment and growth could continue without chronic inflation.

The opportunity cost of government activity

In Chapter 1 it was seen that the cost of doing something can be measured in terms of the things that might have been done instead. The opportunity cost of government activity is measured in terms of foregone alternatives. The opportunity cost of a particular government expenditure depends on what factors of production the government project will use and from whence they are drawn. In times of heavy unemployment, most of the factors of production might otherwise have remained unemployed. In this case there is no opportunity cost in employing them in the government activity because there is no alternative current production sacrificed by so doing. In contrast, if, in a fully employed economy, the government builds dams, roads, schools, and nuclear submarines, the opportunity cost of these goods are the consumer goods and the capital goods that would have been produced instead.

In the language of Chapter 30 the opportunity cost of government expenditure depends on the crowding-out effect. If the crowding-out effect is zero (for which it is necessary that there are substantial unemployed resources), then there is no opportunity cost. If the crowding-out effect is 100 percent (for which it is sufficient that there be *no* possibility to expand aggregate output), then the opportunity cost of every $1 of government expenditure on goods and services is $1 less output of something else in the economy.

The opportunity cost of government activity depends on the source of the factors of production used by the government. If the factors had been unemployed there is no opportunity cost; if they had been employed, the opportunity cost is what they would have produced otherwise.

Supposing there is an opportunity cost, who bears it? If the factors of production used by the government are drawn away from the production of consumer goods and services, the opportunity cost is necessarily borne by the present generation; if they are drawn away from the production of capital goods, the opportunity cost will be spread out over the future because the current generation is giving up capital rather than consumption goods.

In the case in which factors are drawn away from private investment, government spending reduces investment and thus leads to a smaller stock of private capital; this lowers the economy's capacity to produce consumption goods in the future. If, to take the extreme case, the resources used by the government are drawn entirely from the production of capital goods, once the government activity ceases, the production of capital goods can be resumed. In the interim, however, a large supply of capital goods will have gone unproduced, and the consequences of this will be felt in the future. The stock of capital will for a long time be smaller than it would have been had the government activity not occurred. Because it is the stock of capital that provides the means of producing consumption goods, it follows that the output of such goods will be less than it otherwise would have been for as long as the stock of capital (*not* the current output of capital goods) is smaller than it would have been. Thus the opportunity cost in terms of a reduced output of goods for current consumption will be spread over a long period of time after the government activity ceases.

EFFECTS OF ALTERNATIVE MEANS OF FINANCING GOVERNMENT ACTIVITIES

There are three main ways in which a government can finance an expenditure.

1. It can raise the money by increasing taxes, thereby transferring purchasing power from taxpayers to itself.

2. It can borrow the money from willing lenders, thereby transferring current purchasing power from them to itself in return for the promise of future purchasing power.

3. It can create enough new money to permit itself to bid away the resources it needs.

The major effect of the method of financing government expenditures is on *who* bears the costs, not on how much they are.

The distribution of the costs

Consider an economy that is at full-employment national income, so that the government will necessarily incur real opportunity costs when it has goods and services produced.

Costs while the program is in operation. First, assume that the necessary revenue is raised by taxation. If the cost of a new government program is met by increases in taxes, then the current taxpayers bear the cost by having their purchasing power reduced by taxes. Their purchases of goods and services will be decreased, and resources will be transferred to the production of the government's goods. In this case the costs are distributed among the public by the government's decision on whom to tax.[4]

Second, assume that the revenue is raised by borrowing. If the government expenditure is financed by borrowing from households and firms, the reduction in purchasing power for current consumption is suffered by those who lend their money to the government instead of spending it on currently produced goods and services. People who do not buy government bonds do not postpone current consumption and thus do not bear any of the real current cost of the government activity. In this case the costs are accepted voluntarily by those who decide to save and buy government bonds.

Third, assume that the activity is financed by creating new money. (How this can be done will be studied in Chapter 33; here we are concerned with the consequences.) Because the economy is already in a state of full employment, this method of finance will cause inflation. Aggregate demand, already high enough to purchase all the output the economy is producing, becomes excessive as the government enters the market with its own new demand. The rise in prices will mean that households and firms with fixed budgets will be able to buy less than they would otherwise have bought, and the government will be able to obtain resources for its own activities. Thus fewer resources will

be available for private consumption and private capital formation.

In the aggregate the result of inflationary finance is the same as if the government had reduced private expenditure by taxation. The costs, however, are borne by those who are least able to protect themselves against the government-induced inflation rather than by those selected to pay increased taxes. Inflationary finance is usually regarded as a less just method of taxation than income and corporate taxes because it places much of the burden on the economically weak, the unfortunate, and the uneducated and places least burden on those best able to adjust to rising prices—often the richest and most powerful groups.

The government, in choosing whether to finance its expenditures by current taxation, by borrowing, or by creating new money, can exert a considerable influence on the distribution of the burden of the loss of real consumption opportunities its purchases make necessary.

Costs after the program is completed. Now consider what happens once the government project is finished. To the extent that it was financed by current taxes (or by inflationary creation of new money) the matter is finished once the government expenditure has been made. Resources can then be transferred back to the production of goods and services, and households' disposable income can be allowed to rise by reducing taxes. But to the extent that the government activity was financed by borrowing from the private sector, the debt remains after the activity has been completed. It is necessary to pay interest each year to the bondholders and eventually to repay the bonds as they reach maturity. To the extent that interest payments and eventual redemption of the bonds are made from tax revenue, taxpayers now suffer a reduction in their consumption below what it would otherwise have been. The transfer is thus re-

---

[4] This is so at least in the first instance. As is seen in Chapter 25 however, the burden of taxes can be shifted and with it the opportunity cost of the government's activity.

versed. In return for bearing the original reduction in consumption, bondholders (or their heirs) now enjoy a rise in consumption, and taxpayers who are not bondholders suffer a reduction. For a community, the cost in terms of foregone output was borne during the original activity. Once the activity is finished, total production of goods and services for the private sector of the economy goes back to normal. The opportunity cost could not be postponed, but individuals who did not buy bonds must now pay for their share of the cost of the activity by transferring some claims on current production to individuals who did buy bonds.

Are there real burdens resulting from the method of finance?

It has been seen that the current cost of government expenditure is the current production foregone and that the method of finance can influence the distribution of the cost within the society.

The method of finance can also affect the extent to which current generations can shift the real opportunity cost of government activity to future generations.

If, for example, new taxes are placed on consumption goods, most of the cutbacks in private production may be expected to fall on consumer goods. If, however, funds for the government activity are raised by a special tax on all business investment, it is likely that the production of capital goods rather than of consumption goods will be reduced.

Is there a systematic difference between taxing and borrowing with respect to the possible transfer of the burden to future generations? This is a matter of substantial debate. Some economists believe that the existence of government bonds, by making households feel wealthier than they otherwise would, may make them consume more and save less. This in turn may reduce private capital formation and thus transfer much of the cost of

government activity to the future via the reduction in capital stock.

It is possible that the method of finance can impose burdens on the community in addition to the opportunity costs already discussed. These additional burdens are those associated with the existence of a large national debt held within the private sector of the economy. The bonds will continue to exist after the activity is finished, and interest will have to be paid to those households, firms, and financial institutions that hold them. Extra money must be raised in taxes and paid out to bondholders. This is a transfer payment that does not of itself represent a net burden to the society. All we are doing is taxing Peter to pay Paul. There is a burden involved, however, because resources, in terms of tax collectors and inspectors and accountants and clerks to look after bond issues, will be used to raise taxes and pay bondholders. These resources could otherwise have been employed to make goods and services for current consumption. Such real costs are but a tiny fraction of the interest payments on the national debt. Because such interest payments are themselves just over 1 percent of GNP, the real collection and disbursement costs are minute.[5]

Foreign borrowing: a special case. There is one way in which, from the narrow point of view of a single country, the whole cost of the activity can be transferred to future generations. If the government activity is totally financed by foreign borrowing, then there is no need to cut down on current consumption at home. In this event the sacrifice in current consumption is borne by the citizens of the lending country.

[5] Another real effect occurs if the taxes required to raise the money to pay interest on the debt change market prices and thereby influence the allocation of resources. Since taxes required to service the national debt are a very small part of total taxes raised, these effects of the tax system will occur whether or not it is necessary to raise money to pay interest on the national debt. This cost too is minute.

Once the project has been completed, however, interest must be paid on this foreign debt, and usually the debt will have to be repaid. The paying of interest on this debt (and the repaying of the principal) gives foreigners a claim on the country's current production, and when they exercise this claim there will be less current production available for the citizens of the debtor country. In this way the burden of a current activity can be avoided by the current generation and can be passed on to a future one. But notice that this can be done only if the people of some other country can be persuaded to accept the current opportunity cost. From the *world's* point of view, the sacrifice of alternative outputs is necessarily incurred during the time of the activity. For one country, as for any one group, however, the current cost can be avoided by borrowing, provided some other group can be found that is willing to lend the money to finance the activity. The lending group shoulders the burden in terms of a current reduction in its consumption.

THE NATIONAL DEBT

There are at least three reasons why only the federal government has a fiscal policy:

1. Employment and price level policies are the legal responsibilities of the federal government.

2. Even if some state or local government wanted to get into the act it could not by itself have a large effect on national income. Budget deficits that would spell long-term disaster for even a large state government would be only a drop in the bucket of national aggregate demand.

3. Of the three methods of financing federal expenditure mentioned on page 578, only the first two are available to state and local governments.

The federal government gains a great deal of freedom in operating its fiscal policy because it can create the money it needs to spend. This ability is fraught with inflationary dangers, but it is there and it allows the federal government to settle on spending programs that are not necessarily geared to the funds it raises from taxes and borrowing from the private sector.

Because fiscal policy is in the exclusive domain of the federal government we concentrate our discussion on the federal government's debt—the national debt. In 1975 just over 70 percent of all government debt in the United States was federal debt.[6]

Fiscal policy may require substantial public borrowing to cover budget deficits. In recent decades the trend of the debt has been upward. (See Figure 31–1.) Does an increasing debt matter? Would an ever-increasing debt lead to an ultimate collapse of the free-enterprise economy? Does the debt represent a burden we are passing on to our heirs? It is to these and related questions that we now turn.

The national debt represents money that the federal government has borrowed by selling bonds to households, firms, and financial institutions. In this sense, the national debt is owed by all of us to some of us.

All government debt arises because the government has chosen to finance certain of its expenditures not by taxes but by borrowing. In discussing the significance of the debt, it is important to keep distinct the real costs of the government expenditure and the costs of the method of financing the expenditure. Both are important, but only the second is a cost of the debt.

The size of the debt

The national debt in December 1975 was $544 billion, more than $2,547 for every man,

---

[4] We saw in Chapter 25 that some local governments have recently gotten into serious debt difficulties. It is important to remember that the discussion that follows is directed only at federal government finance.

Who pays for wars?

When America entered World War II in 1941, there were substantial supplies of unemployed resources, and for a while it was possible to increase the output of both war goods and goods for current civilian consumption. Unemployment of all resources dropped rapidly. By mid 1942, full employment was reached and further increases in war production required substantial cutbacks in production of goods for current consumption by civilians. This cost was necessarily borne by the wartime generations. For example, no private cars were produced at all in America between 1942 and 1946.

Some of the war expenditures were financed by taxes. Net receipts per year of the federal government rose from $9 billion in 1940 to more than $42 billion in 1945. Because wartime taxes were heavy, households were forced to reduce their current expenditures and so release resources for war production. Some of the expenditures were financed by the creation of new money, and this created strong inflationary pressures. Heavy wartime controls slowed down the price rise during the war, but once the controls were removed the full effect was felt in terms of the postwar inflation. Some of the expenditures were financed by the sale of bonds to the private sector. In this case the bond purchasers voluntarily reduced their current consumption, thereby shouldering some of the burden of the current opportunity cost. (It is unlikely that bond purchasers anticipated the degree of inflation that was actually to occur. Thus they bore more of the cost than they intended because the real value of their savings was significantly reduced.)

There was also a considerable amount of capital consumption. The main object of wartime economic policy was to maximize current production so as to get the required output of military goods as quickly as possible. Preserving the potential of the economy to produce goods 10 years hence was of little military importance. To achieve these goals, long-term maintenance of capital equipment was often slighted. Providing that the capital would last "for the duration," maintenance could be foregone and resources normally used for maintenance could be freed for current production. Railway roadbeds were neglected, only the most urgent repairs to factories were undertaken, new residential construction was virtually impossible, and the average age of all capital equipment was allowed to rise. Thus when the war was over the postwar generation bore the cost of inheriting a capital stock that was older, more obsolete, and smaller than it would have been if the war had not occurred. In order to restore the capital stock to a reasonable level, both in quantity and quality, the postwar generation had to devote extra resources to the production of capital goods—and the cost was felt in a reduced supply of consumer goods and services.

woman, and child in the country. Just over 40 percent of the debt was held by the government itself and by Federal Reserve banks.[7] Interest payments on this part of the debt are only bookkeeping transactions. The debt actually held by the private sector is about $312 billion, or more than $1,460 per person.

[7] Federal Reserve banks buy government bonds in the course of operating monetary policy (see Chapter 33). Government departments can acquire government bonds when they have funds that they do not require for short, or even long, periods of time.

These "per person" figures are often quoted in an attempt to shock the reader, but they require interpretation. For a government, as for a household, the significance of debt depends on what it represents and on whether the income is available to pay the interest. No one would be shocked, for example, to find that an average American family of four had a mortgage of $18,000 on a $30,000 home.

Debt in relation to income. Consider the actual

Figure 31-1 Trends in the national debt

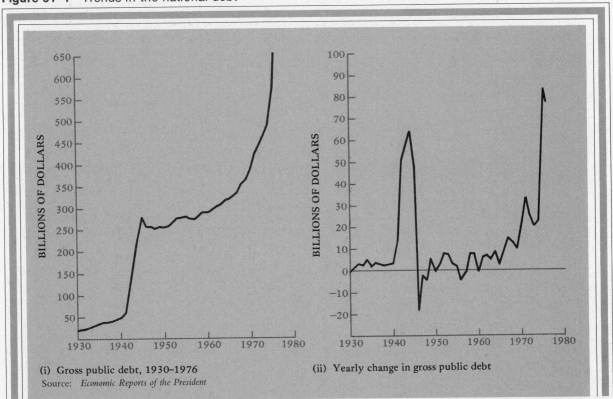

(i) **Gross public debt, 1930-1976**
Source: *Economic Reports of the President*

(ii) **Yearly change in gross public debt**

The trend in the national debt has been upward at least since 1930. The national debt has risen in most years since 1930. The rise has been relatively gradual except during World War II, and since 1972. The rise in 1975 was the largest increase ever in current dollar debt. However, measured in constant dollars the 1975 rise, while dramatic, was not as large as that which occurred during the peak borrowing years of World War II.

Figure 31-2 The relative significance of the national debt

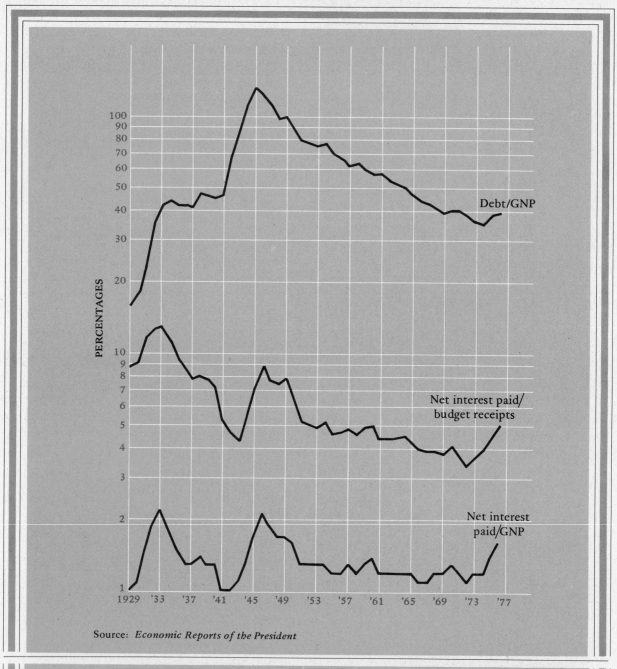

Source: *Economic Reports of the President*

The national debt itself and interest payments on it have not risen in proportion to the GNP since the end of World War II. Three significant ratios are plotted here on a ratio scale. The national debt, after rising sharply through the Great Depression and World War II, has been a declining fraction of GNP since 1945. Interest payments reached 2 percent of GNP in 1946, but for the last 20 years they have remained steady at under 1.5 percent. Such interest payments required the use of over 20 percent of all federal tax receipts during the early 1930s but now require only about 7 percent. Clearly the picture of a spendthrift government adding recklessly to the burden of the national debt is wrong.

size of the public debt. Figure 31–1(i) shows the growth of national debt in the United States. It leaves no doubt that the trend of the debt has been steadily upward. But as national income grows, the scale of government activity can be expected to grow. If the public sector is merely to maintain its relative share of the GNP, government expenditures would have to expand at the same rate as the GNP. If a constant proportion of government expenditures were financed by borrowing, government debt would be growing at the same rate as the GNP. This suggests that debt statistics should be looked at in the perspective of national income data.

How large is the debt as a fraction of the total value of the economy's annual production? How large are interest payments as a fraction of GNP? What proportion of the tax load is incurred because interest has to be paid on the national debt? Figure 31–2 shows these data.

Is there any limit to the size of the debt? In 1968 there was a "permanent" legal limit of $285 billion to the U.S. debt, but there was also a temporary limit of $365 billion. In 1971 the "permanent" limit was $400 billion and there was a "temporary" limit of $420 billion. The temporary limit was scheduled to expire June 30, 1972; instead it was extended and increased so that by mid 1973 it was $465 billion. In April 1974 a new permanent limit was set at $505 billion. By 1976 the limit was over $600 billion. Such permanent and temporary limits are pure window dressing; they are raised by Congress as the need to borrow more arises. Concern here is not with statutory limits but with economic ones.

To the extent that the money raised by borrowing is spent on items that add to national income, the borrowing creates the extra income out of which extra taxes can be raised to pay the interest. To the extent that the money is spent on items that do not add to national income, it will be necessary to increase existing taxes in order to provide funds to meet

the interest payments. Up to a point, this will not cause any serious problems because the process of paying interest on the debt involves only a transfer from some citizens (taxpayers) to other citizens (holders of government bonds).

If, however, the national debt grew so fast that the interest payments on the debt took up an ever-larger proportion of national income, there would be an ever-increasing tax burden to finance the interest payments.

Clearly, then, there is some small grain of truth in the worry over the size of the interest payments on the national debt. But this worry applies only to those expenditures that do not themselves help to create the extra income out of which interest payments can be met. And the worry only becomes significant if such new non-income-creating debt is a large fraction of current national income. Such a situation existed in the country during the crisis periods of World Wars I and II. Both of these periods were, by historical standards, very short. At no other time has the United States remotely approached a situation in which this class of debt was increasing at a rate anything like the rate at which national income was increasing. In fact, total debt has been declining as a percentage of national income.

A very good measure of whether the size of the debt is approaching dangerous levels is the willingness of borrowers to hold government bonds at various rates of interest.

Well before a government reached an absolute debt limit (in terms of its ability to raise the money to pay the interest on its bonds) the public would lose confidence in its debt. The price of bonds would fall and interest rates would rise as borrowers asked a premium for risk.[8] The fact that U.S. government bonds are

[8] New York City's recent financial troubles have led investors to worry about the security of loans to that city. As a result the interest rates on New York City bonds have risen well above the rates earned on bonds of cities who are not in similar financial straits. Indeed for a while there were no buyers at all; the issues were simply withdrawn from the market.

regarded as the least risky type of investment available provides compelling evidence that the financial community is not concerned about the size of the debt.

Summary

1. Conscious use of the government's spending and taxing powers to control the economy is relatively recent. The evidence of the 1930s is that fiscal policy did not end the Depression because it was not really used. The Roosevelt administration tried pump priming, and it failed. The size of government deficits and expenditures were far too small to overcome the massive deflationary gap, and the nature of the tax laws exerted such built-in stability at too low an income that when recovery did start it was nipped in the bud.

2. World War II generated the conditions that made people willing to accept government expenditures large enough to overcome the Depression's deflationary gap. Indeed, these expenditures created an inflationary gap as war needs grew more urgent and more demanding.

3. The Employment Act of 1946 created the Council of Economic Advisers and charged it with determining the state of the economy and advising on how full employment could best be achieved. This open invitation to deliberate use of fiscal policy as a stabilizing device was not to be fully implemented until the Kennedy administration took office in 1961. The tax cut of 1964 is widely regarded as providing confirmation of the ability of economic theory to predict the effect of governmental fiscal policies.

4. A major target of the 1964 tax cut was to overcome the fiscal drag imposed on a growing economy by a progressive tax structure and a fixed set of tax rates. A growing full-employment surplus tended to become a chronic depressant to the economy.

5. What was new in the 1960s was not the theory but the willingness of a President and a Congress to use the tools of fiscal policy. That willingness continues into the changed economic conditions of the 1970s. A major problem of the 1970s has been the control of inflation whether or not at full employment. Fiscal policy was used in 1975–1976 in an attempt to bring about only a slow recovery from the recession in order to keep the inflation rate from rising once more.

6. Who pays for government spending? If the government spends money to produce goods and services, the opportunity cost is what would have been produced instead. In an economy with unemployed resources, this opportunity cost may be zero; in an economy with fully employed resources, this cost must be positive.

7. The *distribution* of the burden of government expenditure is affected by the method of financing. Different groups bear the current cost if the funds are raised by taxes, by inflationary financing, by borrowing from willing lenders, or by borrowing from abroad.

8. The national debt represents money owed by all of us to some of us. In discussing the significance of the debt, which arises from expenditures in excess of taxes, it is important to keep distinct the costs of government expenditures and the costs of the method of financing these expenditures.

9. The size of the debt can be considered in relation to the size of national income. While the debt has been growing, its relative size has been declining, as has the size of interest payments as a fraction of GNP.

10. The size of the national debt could become a serious problem. This could happen if new debt were increasing so fast that interest payments were an ever-increasing proportion of national income. The evidence shows that this is nowhere near the case in the United States today.

Concepts for review

The "new economics"
Countercyclical fiscal policy
Fiscal drag
The opportunity cost of government activity
Possible burdens of the national debt

Discussion questions

1. In his first inaugural address, President Franklin D. Roosevelt expounded the doctrine of "sound finance"—that the government's budget should always be balanced. Government spending, however, rose faster than taxes could be increased, and deficits resulted. Would the effect of the New Deal on employment have been more or less favorable if

Roosevelt had been successful in keeping the budget balanced throughout his first term?

2. The Employment Act of 1946 makes no explicit mention of price stability as an objective of national income policy. Why do you suppose this is so? Can fiscal policy affect the price level as well as the level of employment?

3. How does growth in full-employment income produce fiscal drag? How may inflation produce fiscal drag? Is not fiscal drag just another name for a built-in stabilizer?

4. "Secular stagnation was the specter of the 1930s, but secular boom seems to be the problem of the 1970s." To what extent is this an accurate characterization? Which situation would you rather see if you had to choose one or the other? Why? Do you think various groups in the society might disagree on which alternative was desirable?

5. A study by the Public Interest Research Group in Michigan (PIRGIM) found that every $1 billion in new federal expenditure produced 55,000 jobs, but $1 billion in state and local expenditure created 100,000 jobs. If the study is correct, would a sound fiscal policy (other considerations aside) dictate more and more grants to state and local governments and less and less federal expenditure? Why or why not?

6. Consider the typical annual expenditures and revenues of the organizations listed below. Comment on the appropriate debt policy for each, taking into account their respective goals, life spans, and resources.
a. family household
b. private corporation (differentiate between a rapidly growing and a mature firm)
c. a village of 5,000 inhabitants
d. New York City
e. New York State
f. The U.S. Government
g. The United Nations

7. The national debt is essentially the net result of past and present fiscal policy; that is, the net debt increases when the government runs a budget deficit. Does increasing the national debt make a nation poorer? What effect, if any, does the national debt have on the distribution of income?

8. If Congress passed a law limiting government borrowing from the public in each year to X percent of the national income in that year, would this tend to stabilize or destabilize the economy? Does it matter how large X is? Would such a law be either necessary or sufficient to assure that the government debt did not become excessive?

PART NINE

MONEY, BANKING, AND MONETARY POLICY

Just about everyone understands the importance of money to his or her own welfare and believes that money is one of the most important things in life and that there is never enough of it. Money gives an individual command over goods, but increasing the world's money supply would not change the quantity of goods available. What, then, is the significance of money to the economy as a whole, and why are economists concerned about it? Indeed, what is money, and how did it come to play its present role?

The nature and history of money

The importance of money

THE "REAL" AND MONEY PARTS OF THE ECONOMY

Very early in the history of economics changes in the quantity of money were seen to be associated with changes in the price level. Eighteenth- and nineteenth-century economists developed the first comprehensive theories of the functioning of the economy, and money played a very special part in those theories. The economy was thought of as being conceptually divisible into a "real part" and a "monetary part."

The allocation of resources was determined in the real part of the economy by the forces of demand and supply. This allocation depended on the structure of *relative* prices. Whether a lot of beef was produced relative to pork depended on the relation between the prices of the two commodities. If the price of beef were higher than the price of pork and both commodites cost about the same to produce, the incentive would be to produce beef rather than pork. This argument depends on the relationship between the prices of the two commodities, not on the money price of each. At 50¢ a pound for pork and $1.50 for beef, the *relative* incentive will be the same as it would be at $1 for pork and $3 for beef. As with beef and pork, so with all other commodities: the allocation of resources between different lines of production depends on relative prices.

According to the early economists, the price *level* was determined in the monetary part of the economy. An increase in the money supply led to an increase in the money prices of all transactions. In the example above, an increase in the total money available might raise the price of pork from 50¢ to $1 a pound and the price of beef from $1.50 to $3, but in equilibrium it would leave relative prices unchanged

Figure 32–1 An index of wholesale prices in the U.S. 1785–1976 (1967 = 100)

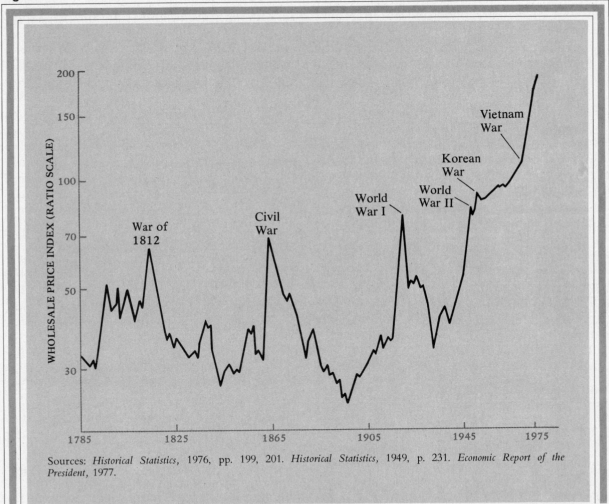

Sources: *Historical Statistics,* 1976, pp. 199, 201. *Historical Statistics,* 1949, p. 231. *Economic Report of the President,* 1977.

Persistent peacetime inflation has only recently become a problem in America. Although the price level has fluctuated throughout American history, no long-term trend was visible throughout the period from the Revolutionary War to 1930. Every major war produced an inflation that was subsequently reversed. The data are plotted on a ratio scale in which equal vertical distances represent equal percentage changes.

and hence have no effect on the real part of the economy, that is, on the amount of resources allocated to beef and to pork production (and to everything else). If the quantity of money were doubled, the prices of everything bought would double, but money income would also double, and everyone earning income would be made no better or worse off by the change. Thus, in equilibrium, the real and the monetary part of the economy have no effect on each other.

Because early economists believed that the most important questions—How much does the economy produce? What share of it does each group in the society get?—were answered in the real sector, they spoke of money as a "veil" behind which occurred the real events that affected material well-being. The doctrine that the quantity of money influences the level of money prices but has no effect on the real part of the economy is referred to as the doctrine of the **neutrality of money.**

Modern economists still accept the insights of the early economists that relative prices are a major determinant of the real allocation of resources and that the quantity of money has a lot to do with determining the absolute level of prices. In this chapter we first look at the experience of price level changes—one aspect of the importance of money—and then at the nature of money itself.

THE EXPERIENCE OF PRICE LEVEL CHANGES

Figure 32–1 shows the course of American wholesale prices from 1785 through 1975. Considerable year-to-year fluctuations are apparent. Major wars have been associated with sharp inflations and, up until World War II, they were all followed by sharp deflations. In spite of the large fluctuations that occurred during the nineteenth century, the price trend during the whole period was neither upward nor downward. World War II was the first war in American history that was not followed by a major deflation. The price level rose rapidly

from 1946 until the end of the Korean War in 1952. It then became relatively stable for a while, rising by only 13 percent between 1952 and 1967, an average of less than 1 percent per year. During the last decade we have experienced a significant new round of inflation. It started gradually but quickly accelerated, and wholesale prices rose 75 percent between 1967 and 1975.

Although admittedly a long time, a century and a half may still not be long enough to gain a clear perspective about long-term price fluctuations. Indeed, the nineteenth century was not a typical period in the history of price levels. The experience of the period since 1946 looks much more dramatic and unusual when compared only with the nineteenth century than when considered in the context of a longer perspective. An indication of the course of price levels in England over a longer period of time is given in Figure 32–2. A glance at the figure shows that there was an overall inflationary trend but that it was by no means evenly spread over the centuries.

Some further idea of the variability of price level experience can be obtained from Table 32–1, which looks at the price level over various subperiods within the seven centuries.

The period since World War II has been one of fairly general inflationary tendencies throughout the world. Table 32–2 shows the average rate of change in the price level of 21 countries over 15 years. Notice the great range and variability of experience from country to country; notice too that the rate of inflation increased in most countries after 1970.

WHY INFLATIONS AND DEFLATIONS MATTER[1]

Economists have devoted much effort in recent times to identifying and measuring the consequences of inflation. Even the early economists, with their strict division between the economy's real and monetary sectors, were

---

[1] We shall discuss inflations because they are the important phenomenon these days, but comparable arguments apply to deflations.

Figure 32–2   A price index of consumables in southern England, 1275–1959

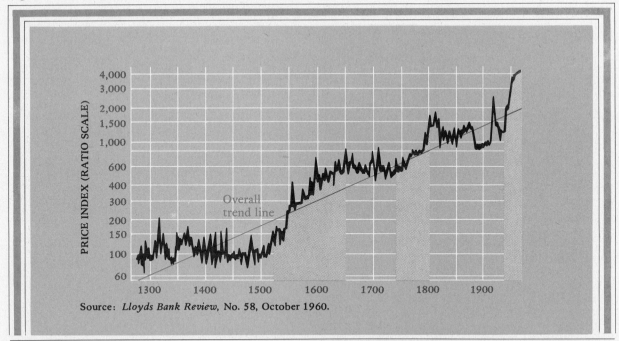

Source: *Lloyds Bank Review*, No. 58, October 1960.

Over the last seven centuries long periods of stable prices have alternated with long periods of rising prices.   This remarkable price series shows an index of the prices of food, clothing, and fuel in southern England from 1275 through 1959. The trend line shows that the average change in prices over the whole period was 0.5 percent per year. The shaded areas indicate periods of unreversed inflation. The series also shows that even the perspective of a century can be misleading because long periods of stable or gently falling prices tended to alternate with long periods of rising prices.

strongly opposed to rapid inflations or deflations because of the harm that could be done during the transition from one price level to another. Indeed, it may take years to move from one equilibrium price level to another, and in the course of the movement many people may get hurt. The consequences of an inflation depend significantly on whether or not it is anticipated.

The effects of unanticipated inflations

Unanticipated inflations cause more upset than do anticipated inflations. Contracts freely entered into when the price level was expected to remain constant yield hardships for some and unexpected gains for others once the unanticipated inflation begins.

A first effect of a continuing inflation is to influence the allocation of resources by changing *relative* prices (including *relative* wages), often in haphazard fashion. In a market economy changes in relative prices are supposed to signal resource shifts in response to changing patterns of demand and supply. In an inflationary period other influences may play a major (and potentially distorting) role. For example, members of strong unions will be able to keep their wages rising as fast as prices; they may even be able to do better

Table 32–1   Seven centuries of English prices

Period	Number of years in period	Percentage change in price level over whole period	Average annual percentage change over the period
1275–1525	250	+ 29	+ 0.12
1526–1650	125	+550	+ 4.40
1651–1744	94	− 38	− 0.40
1745–1813	69	+263	+ 3.81
1814–1893	80	− 51	− 0.64
1894–1920	27	+183	+ 6.78
1921–1932	12	− 59	− 4.92
1933–1960	28	+322	+11.50

Source: *Lloyds Bank Review*, No. 58, October 1960.

Long periods of relatively stable prices have alternated with long periods of continuous inflation. The table shows percentage changes in the price level over selected time periods. (These data come from the series graphed in Figure 32–2.) Notice, first, the very long periods during which the change in the price level averaged less than 1 percent per year. Most of the unreversed rises in the price level before 1960 occurred in three periods: 1526–1650, when Spanish gold and silver flowed into Europe 1750–1800, when banking spread from London into the English provincial cities, greatly increasing the supply of bank money; and 1939–1950, when there was massive deficit financing of World War II and its aftermath. The recent period of inflation (since 1960) is not included in these data.

than they would have done if prices had never risen. In other occupations, wages and salaries may be very slow to adjust and people in these occupations may lose substantially because of the inflation. Schoolteachers often find themselves in this group. Not only do these individuals suffer, but the change in relative wages will affect the allocation of resources. Suppose, for example, that the fall in the real income of teachers relative to that of plumbers reduces the supply of new entrants into the teaching profession below what it would have been in the absence of inflation. This is a real effect, and an adverse

one, unless there is a surplus of teachers and a shortage of plumbers.

A second effect of unanticipated inflations is to redistribute wealth from lenders to bor-

Table 32–2   Inflation rates of selected countries 1960–1970 and 1970–1975

Country	AVERAGE ANNUAL RATE OF INCREASE OF CONSUMER PRICES	
	1960–1970	*1970–1975*
Argentina	19.2	49.7
Canada	2.7	7.1
Chile	24.1	112.3
China (Nationalist)	3.3	11.5
Denmark	5.7	8.9
Ecuador	4.2	12.6
France	4.0	8.4
India	6.2	11.0
Iran	1.7	9.0
Italy	3.9	10.7
Japan	5.7	10.8
Mexico	2.7	11.4
Netherlands	4.0	8.3
Norway	4.4	8.0
South Korea	12.3	14.1
Switzerland	3.3	7.4
Syria	1.9	10.6
United Kingdom	4.0	12.2
United States	2.7	6.5
West Germany	2.6	6.0
Yugoslavia	11.7	17.6

Source: Computed from price indexes in IMF, *International Financial Statistics*, 1976.

Although rates of inflation vary greatly among countries, worldwide inflation clearly accelerated during the early 1970s. Annual rates of increase in prices, of the size shown in the table, cause substantial changes in price levels over 5 or 10 years. In Chile the price level was 11 times as high in 1970 as in 1960, and it was more than doubling every year thereafter. In Iran the price level increased only 18 percent over the decade of the 1960s. Despite these large differences among countries in rates of inflation, the economies of all were able to adjust to them without hyperinflation. By worldwide standards the rates of inflation in the United States and Canada were relatively modest over this period.

rowers, whereas unanticipated deflations do the opposite. To see why this is true, suppose that Mr. Jones lends Mr. Smith $100 at 5 percent interest for one year. If the price level rises by 10 percent over the year, Jones has actually earned a negative rate of interest on the loan. The $105 Jones gets back from Smith can buy fewer goods than the $100 Jones originally parted with. As well as doing without the money for a year, Jones is worse off in terms of purchasing power at the end of the year than at the beginning. Jones's loss, however, is Smith's gain. Smith did not even have to use the $100 in any productive business enterprise to show a gain. All he needed to do was to buy and hold goods whose prices rose merely by the average rate of inflation. At the end of the year Smith can sell these goods for $110, pay back the $100 he borrowed plus $5 interest, and show a gain of $5 for having done nothing more than hold goods instead of money. This sort of redistribution occurs not just on borrowing and lending contracts but on any form of contract that is stated in terms of monetary units.

A third effect of inflation, whether anticipated or unanticipated, is to reduce the living standards of those on fixed incomes. Consider the case of Mr. and Mrs. Prudent, who invested their personal savings in an annuity designed to provide them with a fixed annual dollar income after retirement. The Prudents saved enough throughout their working lives to provide themselves with an income of $10,000 a year on retirement; they figured that with the children no longer at home and with their durable goods already purchased, $10,000 would provide them with a good standard of living for their retirement years. If the price level doubles just before the Prudents retire, however, the purchasing power of their money income will be halved. They will still get $10,000 a year, but it will now buy only half as many goods as they had expected it to buy. Furthermore, if after the Prudents' retirement the price level continues to

rise slowly at, say, 3 percent per year, they will have to cut their real purchases of goods and services by a steady 3 percent each year. If they should live for 23 years after retirement, their living standard will have been halved once again. By that time they will be able to buy only as many goods per year as if the price level had never changed and they had saved only enough to provide themselves an income of $2,500 a year. Instead of realizing their expectations of a modest but satisfactory living standard, the Prudents will have been made progressively worse off, until finally they will have been reduced to poverty.

This may sound extreme, but it is not far from the experience of those Americans who saved during the 1920s and 1930s and found themselves living on fixed money incomes through the rapid inflation of the 1940s, the creeping inflations of the 1950s and 1960s, and the rapid inflation of recent years.

This reduction in the purchasing power of money savings is one of the most dramatic and most obvious effects of an inflation, and it helps to explain the hostility to inflation felt by anyone who has suffered seriously from it.

The effects of anticipated inflations

To the extent that inflations are anticipated some of these haphazard effects can be avoided by drawing up contracts in real terms or with "escalator clauses" that build changes in average price levels into specific wage and price contracts. Such contracts are not uncommon in labor agreements, in long-term raw material contracts, and in many government procurement agreements. Even without a formal contract in real terms it is possible to allow for the effects of an inflation if the inflation is foreseen. Wage and price contracts are major examples: if, say, a 10 percent inflation is expected over the next year, a money wage that rises by 10 percent over that period may represent the minimum demand of a union intent on preserving or increasing the purchasing power of its members. A banker will demand 9 percent interest for the use of money if 3 percent is the real rate of interest and 6 percent is the anticipated rate of inflation. While some people, such as old age pensioners, may not be able to avoid the ef-

fects of inflation even if they see it coming, most people can, most of the time.

Even a fully foreseen inflation has some real effects. This is because many practices—such as business accounting conventions, defini-

Hyperinflation

Can a sharp inflation go on year after year without triggering an explosive inflation that wholly destroys the value of a currency? The answer appears to be yes—at least some of the time. Inflation rates of 50, 100, and even 200 percent a year have occurred year after year and proven quite manageable as people adjust their contracts to real terms. While there are strains and side effects, the evidence shows such situations to be possible without hyperinflation.

Does this mean there is nothing to fear from rapid inflation? The historical record is not entirely reassuring. There have been a number of so-called hyperinflations in which at some point prices began to rise at an ever-accelerating rate until the nation's money ceased to be a satisfactory store of value even for the short period between receipt and expenditure. Look at the index of wholesale prices in Germany during and after World War I:

Date	Wholesale price index (1913 = 1)
Jan 1913	1
Jan 1920	13
Jan 1921	14
Jan 1922	37
July 1922	101
Jan 1923	2,785
July 1923	74,800
Aug 1923	944,000
Sept 1923	23,900,000
Oct 1923	7,096,000,000
15 Nov 1923	750,000,000,000

The index shows that a good purchased with one 100-mark note in July 1923 would have required *ten million* 100-mark notes for its purchase only four months later!

While Germany had experienced substantial inflation during World War I, averaging over 30 percent per year, the immediate postwar years of 1920 and 1921 gave no sign of an explosive inflation. Indeed, during 1920 price stability was experienced. But in 1922 and 1923 the price level exploded. On November 15, 1923, the mark was officially repudiated, its value already wholly destroyed. How could this happen?

When an inflation becomes so rapid that people lose confidence in the purchasing power of their currency, they rush to spend it. But people who have goods become increasingly reluctant to accept the rapidly depreciating money in exchange. The rush to spend money accelerates the increase in prices until people finally become unwilling to accept money on any terms. What once was money then ceases to be money.

The price system can be restored only by official repudiation of the old monetary unit and its replacement by a new unit. This destroys the value not only of money savings but also of all contracts specified in terms of the old monetary unit.

tions of allowable expenses given in tax laws, and many private pension schemes—make use of money definitions that cannot be altered even in the face of an inflation that is fully foreseen. In addition, not everyone has

There are approximately a dozen documented hyperinflations in world history, among them the collapse of the *continental* during the American revolution, the *ruble* during the Russian revolution, the *drachma* during and after the German occupation of Greece in World War II, the *pengo* in Hungary during 1945 and 1946, and the Chinese national currency during 1946–1948. Every one of these hyperinflations was accompanied by great increases in the money supply; new money was printed to give governments purchasing power they could not or would not obtain by taxation. And every one of them occurred in the midst of a major political upheaval in which grave doubts existed about the stability and future of the government itself.

Is hyperinflation likely in the absence of civil war, revolution, or collapse of the government? Most economists think not. What is very clear indeed is that inflation rates of 5 or 10 or 20 percent per year—which many Americans find so upsetting—do not mean the inevitable or likely onset of a disastrous hyperinflation, however serious their distributive and social effects may be.

the ability to find a way to adjust to an anticipated inflation without incurring substantial transactions costs—for example, paying commissions for buying and selling property. These transactions costs may be particularly high for those with relatively small amounts to protect.

Does everyone lose by inflations?

Contrary to popular opinion, inflation does not generally make everyone or even the vast majority of people worse off. This is because inflation does not normally have major effects on the economy's total output. For this reason, the popular concept of the average person being slowly impoverished as money prices rise steadily faster than his or her money income is mistaken. This is in sharp contrast to the overall effects of a serious recession. A recession typically will lower average living standards because many of the country's resources—its labor, its factories, and its raw materials—lie idle.

The main undesirable domestic effects of inflation, whether foreseen or unforeseen, are distributive: contracts stated in money terms do not have the effects in terms of real purchasing power that was expected of them. Since contracts are two-sided, one person's losses are another's gains.

Thus, *typical* households and firms are wrong when they say that inflation is pricing everything out of their reach.[2] When income-earning households and firms say that inflation is ruining them, what they are probably thinking is how much better off they would be if they had this year's money income to

---

[2] Some things may go nearly out of reach if their *relative* prices rise. For example, the rise in the relative price of prime cuts of beef over the last twenty years (because of rapidly rising demand as real income has risen) certainly has been dramatic, but this has not been due, as is often alleged, to inflation, but rather to a change in relative prices. Even if the overall price level had remained constant in America, prime cuts of beef would have risen in price, and households would have found it just as expensive to buy a steak *relative to their overall budget* as they do in today's inflationary world.

spend at the prices ruling several years ago. But this is impossible, since that much output is not available. Few would prefer the prices of, say, ten years ago and their money incomes of the same period because real income has been rising, inflation notwithstanding. Of course, some groups are seriously hurt by inflation, but the *average* household and the *average* firm are not, since in most years money income rises faster than money prices.

There is a danger that, in saying that the main effects of inflation are redistributional, we may be thought to be saying that inflation is unimportant. Redistributions of income can be very important matters. After all, the causes of the distribution of income among the various social classes was *the* major problem faced by the classical economists, and the call for a major redistribution from capitalists to workers was, and still is, an important part of Marxian economics. Redistributions are important, and rapid inflations often cause major, arbitrary, and socially destructive redistributions. People who have spent their whole life trying to save enough for a comfortable old age can find the purchasing power of their savings wiped out by inflation in a very few years. The continual erosion of the purchasing power of fixed money incomes is little short of tragic to those who suffer it, and such erosion is only one of the many serious redistributive effects of inflation.

Inflation has other effects, and these too may be serious. For example, there are social and personal tensions that arise from the race to keep up with the rise in prices and from the knowledge that some gain from inflation at the expense of others who lose.

The nature of money

Inflation is a monetary phenomenon in the sense that a rise in the general level of prices is the same thing as a decrease in the purchasing power of money. But what exactly *is* money? There is probably more folklore and general nonsense believed about money than about any other aspect of the economy. In the remainder of this chapter the functions of money will be described and the history of money will be outlined. One purpose of this account is to remove some of the misconceptions.

WHAT IS MONEY?

Traditionally in economics **money** has been defined as any generally accepted medium of exchange—anything that will be accepted by virtually everyone in exchange for goods and services.

Money has several different functions: to act as a medium of exchange, as a store of value, and as a unit of account.

Different kinds of money vary in the degree of efficiency with which they fulfill these functions, and different definitions of money may be required for different purposes.

A medium of exchange

An important function of money is to facilitate exchange. Without money the economic system, which is based on specialization and the division of labor, would be impossible, and we would have to return to a very primitive form of production and exchange. It is not without justification that money has been called one of the great inventions contributing to human freedom.

If there were no money, goods would have to be exchanged by barter, one good being swapped directly for another. This cumbersome system was first discussed in Chapter 4. The major difficulty with barter is that each transaction requires a double coincidence of wants: For an exchange to occur between A and B, not only must A have what B wants, but B must have what A wants. If all exchange were restricted to barter, anyone who was specialized in the production of one commodity would have to spend a great deal of time searching for satisfactory transactions. The use of money as a generally accepted **medium of exchange** removes these problems. People can sell their output for money and subsequently use the money to buy what they wish from others. The double coincidence of wants is not necessary when money is used as a medium of exchange. Efficient production demands a specialization of tasks, and this requires that people satisfy most of their desires by consuming goods produced by others. In any complex economy, such exchanges necessitate the use of some kind of money.

The difficulties of barter force people to become more or less self-sufficient. With money as a medium of exchange, everyone is free to specialize; with specialization in the direction of one's natural talents and abilities, the production of all commodities can be increased.

To serve as an efficient medium of exchange, money must have a number of characteristics: It must be readily acceptable; it must have a high value for its weight, otherwise it would be a nuisance to carry around; it must be divisible because money that comes only in large denominations is useless for transactions having only a small value; and it must not be readily counterfeitable because if money can be easily duplicated by individuals, it will lose its value.

Many radical social reformers have seen money as the root of society's evils and have dreamed of the day when the institution of money would be eradicated. Whenever this hope has been combined with a "back-to-the-land" social program and the simple, self-sufficient life for everyone, the goals are at least consistent. For the self-sufficient community that is small enough to base all transactions on barter can dispense with money. Sometimes the dream of abandoning money is combined with the ideas of a modern industrial socialist state that enjoys a high standard of living without private ownership. Here the goals are self-contradictory: efficient production demands a specialization of tasks, and this requires that people satisfy most of their desires by consuming goods produced by others. In any complex economy, such exchanges necessitate the use of some kind of money.

Of course, the nature of what serves as a medium of exchange can and does change over time. Recently there has been considerable discussion about a checkless society. In this type of society, one's salary is fed into the memory of a giant computer, and purchases are paid for by inserting an identity card into the seller's recording device, which immediately tells the central computer to reduce the credit in the buyer's account and increase the credit in the seller's account. Such a society would dispense with cash and checks but not with money. Credit in the computer constitutes each individual's medium of exchange. Call it by another name if you want, but for all practical purposes it is money.

A store of value

Money is a handy way to store purchasing power. With barter, some other good must be taken in exchange; with money, goods may be sold today and money stored until it is needed. This provides a claim on someone else's goods that can be exercised at some future date. The two sides of the barter transaction can be separated in time with the obvious increase in freedom that this confers. To be a satisfactory store of value, however, money must have a relatively stable value. If prices are stable, it is possible to know exactly how much command over real goods and services has been stored up when a certain sum of money has been accumulated. If prices change rapidly, there is no way of knowing how many goods can be bought when previously accumulated money is spent, and this reduces the usefulness of money as a store of value.

Although money can serve as a perfectly satisfactory store of accumulated purchasing power for a single individual, it cannot do so for the society as a whole. If a single individual stores up money, he or she will, when the time comes to spend it, be able to command the current output of some other individual. The whole society cannot do this. If, for example, all individuals saved their money and all simultaneously retired to live on their savings, there would be no current production to purchase and consume. The society's ability to satisfy wants depends on goods and services being available; if some of this want-satisfying capacity is to be stored up for the whole society, goods that are currently produced must be left unconsumed and carried over to future periods.

A unit of account

Money may also be used purely for accounting purposes without having any real physical existence of its own. For instance, a government store in a truly communist society might say that everyone had so many "dollars" to use each month. Goods could then be given prices and each consumer's purchases recorded, the consumer being allowed to buy until the allocated supply of dollars was exhausted. These dollars need have no existence other than as entries in the store's books, but they would serve as a perfectly satisfactory unit of account. Whether they could also serve as a medium of exchange between individuals depends on whether the store would agree to transfer dollar credits from one customer to another at the customer's request. Banks will transfer dollars credited to demand deposits in this way, and thus a bank deposit can serve both as a unit of account and a medium of exchange. Notice that the use of *dollars* in this context suggests a further sense in which money is a unit of account. People think about values in terms of the monetary unit with which they are familiar.

A further but related function of money is sometimes distinguished: that of a "standard of deferred payments." Payments that are to be made in the future, on account of debts and so on, are reckoned in money. Money is used as a unit of account with the added dimension of time because the account is not settled until the future.

THE ORIGINS AND GROWTH OF METALLIC MONEY

The origins of money are lost in antiquity; most primitive tribes known today make some use of it. The ability of money to free people from the cumbersome necessity of barter must have led to its early use as soon as some generally acceptable commodity appeared. All sorts of commodities have been used as money at one time or another, but precious metals proved to have great advantages. They were in constant demand by the rich for ornament and decoration, and they were in continuous supply (because they do not easily wear out). Thus they tended to have a high and stable price. They were easily recognized and generally known to be commodities that, because of their stable price, would be accepted by most people. They were also divisible into extremely small units (gold, to a single grain).

Precious metals thus came to circulate as money and to be used in many transactions. Before the invention of coins it was necessary to carry precious metals around in bulk. When a purchase was to be made, the requisite quantity of the metal would have to be weighed carefully on a scale. A sack of gold and a highly sensitive set of scales were the common equipment of the merchant and trader.

Such a system, although better than barter, was still rather cumbersome. Coins eliminated the necessity of weighing the metal at each transaction. The prince or ruler weighed the metal and made a coin out of it to which he affixed his own seal to guarantee the amount of precious metal it contained. Thus a certain coin was stated to contain exactly $\frac{1}{16}$ of an ounce of gold. If a commodity was priced at $\frac{1}{8}$ of an ounce of gold, two coins could be given over without weighing the gold. This was clearly a great convenience as long as traders knew that they could accept the coin at its "face value." The face value itself was nothing more than a guarantee that a certain weight of metal was contained therein.

The prince's subjects, however, could not let a good thing pass. Someone soon had the idea of clipping a thin slice off the edge of the coin. If he collected a coin stamped as containing half an ounce of gold, he could clip a slice off the edge and pass the coin off as still containing half an ounce of gold. ("Doesn't the stamp prove it?" he would argue.) If he were successful, he would have made a profit equal to the market value of the clipped metal. Whenever this practice became common, even the most myopic of traders would notice that things were not what they seemed in the coinage world. Mistrust would grow, and it would become necessary to weigh each coin before accepting it at its face value; out came the scales again, and most of the usefulness of the coins was lost. To get around this problem, the idea arose of minting the coins with a rough edge. The absence of the rough edge would immediately be apparent and would indicate that the coin had been clipped. This practice still survives on many coins today as an interesting anachronism to remind us that there were days when the market value of the metal in the coin (if it were melted down) was equal to the face value of the coin.

The subjects, presented with an opportunity to get something for nothing, were ingenious enough to surmount even the obstacle of the rough edge. They invented the practice of *sweating*. Sweating involved placing a large number of coins in a bag and shaking the bag vigorously. The dust that flaked off the coins was the reward. This practice seems never to have been as disruptive to the money system as that of clipping, possibly because it was difficult to remove very much metal without defacing the coin, and possibly because the disruptive effects were eclipsed by the upset caused by the prince's periodic debasement of coinage.

Not to be outdone by the cunning of his subjects, the prince was himself quick to seize the chance of getting something for nothing. Because he was empowered to mint the coins, he was in a very good position to work a *really* profitable fraud. When he found himself with bills that he could not pay and that it was inexpedient to repudiate, he merely used some suitable occasion—a marriage, an anniversary, an alliance—to remint the coinage. The subjects would be ordered to bring their coins into the mint to be melted down and coined afresh with a new stamp. The subjects could then go away the proud possessors of one new coin for every old coin that they had brought in. Between the melting down and the recoining, however, the prince had only to toss some inexpensive base metal into the works to earn himself a handsome profit. If the coinage was debased by adding, say, one pound of new base metal to every four pounds of old coins, five coins would be made for every four turned in. For every four coins brought in, the prince could return four and have one left over for himself as profit. With these coins he could pay his bills.

The result was inflation. The subjects had the same number of coins as before and hence could demand the same quantity of goods. Once the prince paid his bills, however, the recipients of the extra coins could be expected to spend some or all of them, and this would represent a net increase in demand. The extra demand would bid up prices. Debasing of coinage thus led to a rise in prices. It was the experience of such inflations that led early economists to propound the *quantity theory of money and prices*. They argued that there was a relation between the average level of prices and the quantity of money in circulation, such that a change in the quantity of money would lead to a change in the price level in the same direction. We shall have more to say about this theory in Chapter 34.

The early experience of currency debasement led to a famous economic "law" that has stood the test of time. The hypothesis is that "bad money drives out good," and it has come to be known as **Gresham's Law** after the Elizabethan financial expert Sir Thomas Gresham, who first explained the workings of the law to Queen Elizabeth.

To see why the law works, assume there are two kinds of gold coins, Royals and Sovereigns. Royals have not been debased—the gold in the coin is actually worth its face value. Sovereigns have been debased to the point that the gold in the coin is worth only 80 percent of its face value. If you possessed one of each type of coin, each with the same face value, and had a bill to pay, what would you do? Clearly, you would pay the bill with the debased Sovereign and keep the undebased Royal. You part with less gold that way. If you wanted to obtain a certain amount of gold bullion by melting down the gold coins (as was frequently done), which coins would you use? Clearly, you would use Royals because you would part with less "face value" that way—according to face value, five Sovereigns are equal to five Royals, but if you melt them down it only takes four Royals to get the same amount of gold as contained in five Sovereigns. The debased coins would remain in circulation and the undebased coins would disappear. Every time people got hold of an undebased coin they would hold on to it, and melt it down if necessary, while every time they got a debased one they would pass it on.

THE EVOLUTION OF PAPER MONEY

Another important step in the history of money was the evolution of paper currency. Artisans who worked with gold were called goldsmiths, and they naturally kept very se-cure safes in which to store their gold.[3] Among the public the practice grew up of storing gold with the goldsmith for safekeeping. In return, the goldsmith would give the depositor a receipt promising to hand over the gold on demand. If the depositor wished to make a large purchase, he or she could go to the goldsmith, reclaim the gold, and hand it over to the seller of the goods. Chances were that the seller would not require the gold but would carry it back to the goldsmith for safekeeping. Clearly, if people knew the goldsmith to be reliable, there was no need to go through the cumbersome and risky business of physically transferring the gold. The buyer need only transfer the goldsmith's receipt to the seller, who would accept it, secure in the knowledge that the goldsmith would pay over the gold whenever it was needed. If the seller wished to buy a good from a third party who also knew the goldsmith to be reliable, this transaction too could be effected by passing the goldsmith's receipt from the buyer to the seller. The convenience of using pieces of paper instead of gold is obvious. Thus, when it first came into being, paper money was a promise to pay on demand so much gold, the promise being made first by goldsmiths and later by banks. As long as these institutions were known to be reliable, such pieces of paper would be "as good as gold." Such paper money was *backed* by precious metal and was *convertible* on demand into this metal. When a country's money is convertible into gold, the country is said to be on a *gold standard.*

In nineteenth-century America, private banks operating under either federal or state charters commonly issued paper money nominally convertible into gold. **Bank notes** represented banks' promises to pay. In areas such as the American West, where banks were

---

[3] All the basic ideas about paper money can be explained by concentrating on the goldsmiths, although there were earlier sources of paper money in various negotiable evidences of debt.

small and often proved unreliable in meeting demands for payment in gold, bank notes had a shady reputation. The gold bag and scales persisted in America well into the second half of the nineteenth century.

Fractionally backed paper money

For most transactions, individuals were content to use paper currency; it was soon discovered, therefore, that it was not necessary to keep an ounce of gold in the vaults for every claim to an ounce circulating as paper money. It was necessary to keep some gold on hand because, for some transactions, paper would not do. If a man wished to make a purchase from a distant place where his local bank was not known, he might have to convert his paper into gold and ship the gold. Further, if he was going to save up money for use in the distant future, he might not have perfect confidence in the bank's ability to honor its pledge to redeem the notes in gold at that time. His alternative was to exchange his notes for gold and store the gold until he needed it. For these and other reasons, some holders of notes demanded gold in return for their notes. However, some of the bank's customers received gold in various transactions and stored this gold in the bank for safekeeping. They accepted promises to pay (i.e., bank notes) in return. At any one time, therefore, some of the bank's customers would be withdrawing gold, others would be depositing it, and the great majority would be trading in the bank's paper notes without any need or desire to convert them into gold. Thus the bank was able to issue more money redeemable in gold than it actually had gold in its vaults. This was a sensible thing to do because the money could be used to make profitable investments such as purchasing securities that yielded a return and granting interest-earning loans to households and firms.

This discovery was made by the early goldsmiths; from that time down to the present day, banks have had many more claims to pay outstanding against them than they actually had in reserves available to pay those claims. In such a situation we say that the currency is fractionally backed by the reserves.

The major problem of a fractionally backed, convertible currency is that of maintaining its convertibility into the precious metal by which it is backed. In the past, the imprudent bank that issued too much paper money found itself unable to redeem its currency in gold when the demand for gold was even slightly higher than usual. This bank would then have to suspend payments, and all holders of its notes would suddenly find them worthless. The prudent bank, which kept a reasonable relation between its note issue and its gold reserve, found that it could meet the normal everyday demand for gold without any trouble. It was always the case with fractionally backed currency, however, that if all noteholders demanded gold at once, they could not be satisfied. Thus, if ever the public lost confidence and en masse demanded redemption of their currency, the banks would be unable to honor their pledges and the holders of their notes would lose everything. The history of nineteenth- and early twentieth-century banking on both sides of the Atlantic is replete with examples of banks ruined by "panics," by sudden runs on their gold reserves. When this happened, the bank's depositors and the holders of its notes would find themselves holding worthless pieces of paper.

The so-called central bank was a natural outcome of this sort of banking system. For where were the commercial banks to keep *their* cash reserves? Their own vaults, although safer than those of their customers, were not safe against a really determined attempt at robbery. Where were the commercial banks to turn if they had good investments but were in temporary need of cash? If they provided loans for the public against reasonable security why should not some other institution provide loans to them against the same sort of security? Central banks evolved in response to these and other needs. At first they were private profit-making institutions providing services to ordinary banks, but their potential to influence the behavior of commercial banks and through them that of the whole economy led them to develop close ties with central governments. In Europe these ties eventually became formalized as central banks were taken over by governments. In the United States, the Federal Reserve System was created by Congress in 1914 to perform central banking functions.

The development of fiat currencies

As time went on, note issue by private banks became less common and central banks took control of the currency. In time *only* central banks were permitted to issue notes. Originally the central banks issued currency that was fully convertible into gold. In those days, gold would be brought to the central bank, which would issue currency in the form of "gold certificates" that asserted the gold was there on demand. The gold supply thus set an upper limit on the amount of currency. But, as has been seen, banks discovered they could issue (as bank notes) more currency than they had gold because not all of the currency was presented for payment at any one time. Thus even under a gold standard central banks had substantial discretionary control over the quantity of currency outstanding.

During the period between World Wars I and II, virtually all the countries of the world abandoned the gold standard. The reasons for this need not be gone into here. (They will be mentioned briefly in Chapter 39.) The result of abandoning the gold standard was that currency was no longer convertible into gold—or anything else. Money that is not convertible by law into anything valuable depends upon its acceptability for its value. Money that is declared by government order (or fiat) to be legal tender for settlement of all debts is called a **fiat money.**

Today virtually all currency is fiat money. Look at any bill in your wallet—it is not convertible into anything. Until recently much American currency bore the statement: "The United States of America Will Pay to the Bearer on Demand Twenty Dollars" (or whatever the currency was worth). The notes were signed by both the Secretary of the Treasury and the Treasurer. If you took this seriously and demanded $20, you could have handed over a $20 bill and received in return a different but identical $20 bill! Today's Federal Reserve notes simply say "The United States of America," "Twenty dollars," and "This note is legal tender for all debts public and private." It is, in other words, fiat money, pure and simple.

The meaning of the phrase **legal tender** is that if you are offered something that is legal tender in payment for a debt and you refuse to accept it, the debt is no longer legally collectible.

Not only is our paper money fiat money, so too is our coinage. Modern coins, unlike their historical ancestors, rarely contain a value of metal equal to their face value; indeed, the value of the metal is characteristically a minute fraction of the value of the coin. In 1966, faced with a shortage of silver for commercial purposes, the United States Treasury removed the silver from the 25¢ piece. Quarters, however, continued to be traded four to the dollar. Modern coins, like modern paper money, are merely tokens.

Why is fiat money valuable?

In the early days of the gold standard, paper money was valuable because everyone believed it was convertible into gold on demand. The experience of the people during periods of panic, of bank failures, and of so-called suspensions of specie payments served to demonstrate that the mere promise of convertibility was not sufficient to make money valuable. Gradually the realization grew that convertibility was not necessary, that paper money was valuable if it would be accepted in payment for goods and for debts and was not valuable when it would not be accepted. Today our paper money and our coinage is valuable because it is generally accepted. Because everyone accepts it as valuable, it *is*

valuable; the fact that it can no longer be converted into anything has no effect on its functioning as a medium of exchange.

Ordinary people are often disturbed to learn that present-day paper money is neither backed by, nor convertible into, anything more valuable—that it is thus nothing but

Where has all the coinage gone?

American tourists traveling in Chile or another country with rapid inflation often wonder aloud why paper currency is used even for transactions as small as the purchase of a newspaper or a pack of matches. Metallic currency in such places is often very scarce and sometimes nonexistent. Similarly the old-fashioned silver dollar, half-dollar, quarter, and dime have disappeared from the American scene. The reason for these things is a nice example of Gresham's Law.

Consider a country that has three different "tokens," each of them legal tender in the amount of 25 cents. One is a silver quarter with ten cents worth of recoverable silver in it; a second is made of cheaper metals with five cents worth of recoverable metal in it; the third is a 25-cent bill, a brightly colored piece of paper money that says plainly on its face "legal tender for all debts public and private."

If prices are stable and the government produces all three forms of money there is no reason why they should not all circulate freely and interchangeably. Each is legal tender and each is worth more as money than as anything else.

However, suppose an inflation starts and prices—including proportionally the prices of silver and other metals—begin to rise

sharply. By the time prices have tripled, the silver quarters will have disappeared because the silver in each one is now worth 30 cents, and people will hoard them or melt them down rather than spend them to buy goods priced at only 25 cents. While not everyone will do this, coins passing from hand to hand will eventually reach someone who withdraws them from circulation.

What about the coins made of cheaper metal? Since prices have tripled, they now contain metal worth 15 cents, still less than their face value. Will they too disappear? They will if there is a further inflation of, say, 100 percent. They may even disappear without such a further inflation if people begin to expect one. Suppose people believe there is a reasonable chance that metal prices will soon double again. It will be worth holding on to these coins and using paper money instead. Why spend coins which may in the foreseeable future be more valuable than their face value when you can spend paper that isn't worth anything at all *except* as money?

Thus inflation—and even the expectation of inflation—may make some money "good" and some "bad" in Gresham's sense. If it does, the bad will displace the good.

pieces of paper whose value derives from common acceptance and from confidence that it will continue to be accepted in the future. People feel their money should be more substantial than that; after all, what of "dollar diplomacy" and the "bed-rock solidity" of the Swiss franc. Whatever the man or woman in the street might wish to be the case, money is in fact only pieces of paper. There is no point in pretending otherwise.

The point is worth an example. Suppose that in 1978 some latter-day Goldfinger turned miser secretly tunneled into the gold vaults of a mythical country that maintained 100 percent gold backing for its currency and carried off 80 percent of the gold to a secret cave in the South Pacific, there to gaze lovingly upon his treasure. Suppose that the theft went undiscovered until 1987. Would a working man's wages in 1979 or 1983 be less valuable because of the theft? Would the car, the clothes, or the college education of his daughter, which he bought with his income and his savings, be less valuable? Would anyone at all be worse off? If in 1987 the theft were discovered and kept secret, would the situation change? The answer to all these questions is no. What matters is the acceptability of the currency, and that in turn depends on people's confidence in it. If the gold alone creates confidence, then knowledge of the theft might destroy the value of the currency. If confidence in it as a medium of exchange, as a store of wealth, or as a unit of account is unaffected, so too is its value.

If paper money is acceptable, it is a medium of exchange; if its purchasing power remains stable, it is a satisfactory store of wealth; and if both of these things are true, it will also serve as a satisfactory unit of account.

DEPOSIT MONEY

Even though private banks lost the ability to issue money by issuing bank notes, they did not lose the power to create money in the

Limits on the issue of currency by the Central Bank

As we have seen, the gold standard imposed an upper limit on the quantity of convertible currency that could be issued. When the United States abandoned the gold standard in 1934 many in Congress feared that the Federal Reserve Bank would issue too much currency, so Congress imposed the requirement that the Fed hold a certain fraction of gold backing (called the "gold cover") for currency.[*] If the gold backing had been taken seriously, gold would have placed an upper limit on the quantity of currency. Below that limit the central bank would have had discretionary power. Until this provision was repealed in 1968, the gold supply thus put an apparent upper limit on the quantity of currency that the Fed might issue. But at the time our gold holdings were vastly in excess of the amount required to back all of the currency the public wanted to hold. Thus in practice the theoretical limit placed on currency by gold never became binding. Indeed the removal of the gold cover occurred in 1968 when a shortage of gold for international

[*] The gold itself is in government vaults, much of it at Fort Knox, Kentucky. The central bank merely held gold certificates that asserted that the gold was there.

form of deposit money. Just *how* this is done is discussed in Chapter 33; we now ask what is "deposit money"?

Banks' customers frequently deposit paper money with the banks for safekeeping, just as in former times they deposited gold. Such a deposit is recorded as an entry on the custom-

payments led to the possibility that the requirement for gold backing might become binding. Like the ceiling on the national debt, the gold cover was designed to make people feel better, not to affect policy.

Does it matter that the central bank is not limited in its ability to issue currency? Consider the gold standard again. Gold derived its value because it was scarce relative to the demand for it (the demand being derived from both its monetary and its nonmonetary uses). Tying a currency to gold meant that the quantity of money in a country was determined by such chance occurrences as the discovery of new gold supplies. This was not without advantages, the most important being that it provided a check on governments' ability to cause inflation. Gold cannot be manufactured at will; paper currency can. There is little doubt that in the past, if the money supply had been purely paper, many governments would have attempted to pay their bills by printing new money rather than by raising taxes. Such increases in the money supply, in periods of full employment, would lead to inflation in just the same way as did the debasement of metallic currency. Thus the gold standard provided some check on in-flation by making it difficult for the government to change the money supply. Periods of major gold discoveries, however, brought about inflations of their own. In the 1500s, for example, Spanish gold and silver flowed into Europe from the New World, bringing inflation in its wake.

A major problem caused by a reliance on gold is that it is usually desirable to increase the money supply when real national income is increasing. This cannot be done on a gold standard, unless, by pure chance, gold is discovered at the same time. The gold standard took discretionary powers over the money supply out of the hands of the central authorities. Whether one thinks that this is a good thing depends on how one thinks the central authorities would use this discretion. In general, a gold standard is probably better than having the currency managed by an ignorant or irresponsible government, but it is worse than having the currency supply adjusted by a well-informed and intelligent one. "Better" and "worse" in this context are judged by the criterion of having a money supply that varies adequately with the needs of the economy but does not vary so as to cause violent inflations or deflations.

er's account. If the customer wishes to pay a bill, he or she may come to the bank and claim the money in dollars; he or she may then pay the money over to another person, and this person may redeposit the money in a bank. Just as with the gold transfers, this is a tedious procedure, particularly for large payments. It is more convenient simply to have the bank transfer by check claims to this money on deposit. As soon as such transfers became easy and inexpensive, and the checks became widely accepted in payment for commodities and debts, the deposits became a form of money called **deposit money.** When individual A deposits $100 in a bank, his account is credited with $100. This is the bank's promise to pay $100 cash on demand. If A pays B $100 by giving her a check that B then deposits in the same bank, the bank merely reduces A's account by $100 and increases B's by the same amount. Thus the bank still promises to pay out on demand the $100 originally deposited, but it now promises to pay it out to B rather than to A. What makes all of this so convenient is that B can actually deposit A's check in any bank, and the banks will arrange the transfer of credits.

Checks are in some ways the modern equivalent of old-time bank notes issued by commercial banks. The passing of a bank note from hand to hand transferred ownership of a claim against the bank. A check on a deposit account is similarly an order to the bank to pay the designated recipient, rather than oneself, money credited to the account. Checks, unlike bank notes, do not circulate freely from hand to hand; thus checks themselves are not currency. The balance in the demand deposit *is* money; the check transfers the money from one person to another. Because checks are easily drawn and deposited, and because they are relatively safe from theft, they are widely used. In a typical year in the United States approximately 25 billion checks are drawn.

Thus, when commercial banks lost the right to issue notes of their own, the form of bank money changed but the substance did not. Today banks have money in their vaults (or on deposit with the central banks) just as they always did. Once it was gold, today it is the legal tender of the times—paper money. It is true today, just as it was in the past, that most of the bank's customers are content to pay their bills by passing among themselves the bank's promises to pay money on demand; only a small proportion of the transactions made by the bank's customers is made in cash.

Today, just as in the past, banks can create money by issuing more promises to pay (deposits) than they have money available to pay out.

Demand deposits and time deposits

Demand deposits. If a customer has a deposit in a bank, it can be kept in one of two basic forms: a demand deposit or a time deposit. A **demand deposit** means that the customer can withdraw the money on demand (i.e., without giving any notice of intention to withdraw). Demand deposits are transferable by check. Such a check instructs the bank to pay without delay a stated sum of money to the person to whom the check is made payable. Banks in most countries do not pay any interest to customers who have money deposited on demand; in the United States banks are actually prohibited from paying interest on demand deposits.

Time deposits. A **time deposit** is an interest-bearing deposit that is legally withdrawable only after a certain amount of notice, such as 30 or 60 days. Although banks, savings and loan associations, and other savings institutions do not usually enforce this delay, they could legally do so if proposed withdrawals threatened their reserves. Until quite recently it was impossible to pay a bill by writing a check on a time deposit. Depositors wishing to use a time deposit to pay a bill had first to withdraw their money from savings accounts and then either pay the bill in cash or deposit the funds in a demand deposit and write a check on the latter.

This distinction between demand and time deposits has begun to erode with the authorization of the **negotiable order of withdrawal (NOW),** a checklike instruction to the savings institution to transfer funds from the depositor's time deposit to the recipient of the NOW. Use of NOW accounts began in Massachusetts and New Hampshire in 1973 and 1974 and shows signs of spreading widely.[4] If it becomes widespread, the distinction between time deposits and demand deposits as a medium of exchange will greatly decline, if not disappear. Precisely how close a substitute for demand deposits NOW accounts may become will depend on the legal restrictions on their use.

NEAR MONEY AND MONEY SUBSTITUTES

Over the past two centuries what has been accepted by the public as money has expanded from gold and silver coins to include, first, bank notes and then bank deposits subject to transfer by check. Until recently, most economists would have agreed that money stopped at that point. No such agreement exists today, and an important debate centers around the definition of money appropriate to the present world.

If we concentrate only on the medium-of-exchange function of money, there is little doubt about what is money in America today. Money consists of notes, coins, and deposits subject to transfer by check or checklike instruments. No other asset constitutes a generally accepted medium of exchange; indeed, even notes and checks are not universally accepted—as you will discover if you try to buy a pack of cigarettes with a $1,000 bill (or even a $100 bill in a corner grocery store) or if you try to walk out of a store on a Saturday afternoon with a mink coat after having offered your personal check in exchange. But these exceptions are unimportant. The problem of deciding what is money stems from the fact that anything that can fulfill the medium-of-exchange function can also fulfill the store-of-value one, but many things that can fulfill the second do not fulfill the first.

[4] In 1976 authority for NOW accounts was extended to the other four New England states and proposed legislation is pending in many others. NOW accounts are regarded as highly experimental by the Federal Reserve Board, and it is not possible at this time to be sure whether they will spread nationwide or be severely limited.

Near money

Assets which adequately fulfill the store-of-value function and are readily converted into a medium of exchange but are not themselves a medium of exchange are sometimes called **near money.**

As long as all sales and purchases do not occur at the same moment, everyone needs a temporary store of value between the act of selling and the act of buying. Whatever serves the function of a medium of exchange can be held and thus can also serve the function of a temporary store of value. But other assets can also be used for this store-of-value function. If, for example, you have a time deposit at a bank or a savings and loan association, you know exactly how much purchasing power you hold (at today's prices) and, given modern banking practices, you can turn your deposit into a medium of exchange—cash or a checking deposit—at a moment's notice. Additionally, your time deposit will earn some interest during the period that you hold it. Why then does not everybody keep their money in time deposits instead of in demand deposits or currency? The answer is that the inconvenience of continually shifting money back and forth may outweigh the interest that can be earned. One week's interest on $100 (at 5 percent per year) is only about 10¢, not enough to cover carfare to the bank or the cost of mailing a letter. For money that will be needed soon, it would hardly pay to shift it to a time deposit.

In general, whether it pays to convert cash or demand deposits into interest-earning savings deposits for a given period depends on the inconvenience and other transaction costs of shifting funds in and out and on the amount of interest that can be earned.

There is a wide spectrum of assets in the economy that yield an interest return and also serve as reasonably satisfactory temporary stores of value. The difference between these other assets and savings deposits is that their capital values are not quite as certain as are those of savings deposits. If I elect to store my purchasing power in the form of a government bond that matures in 30 days, its price on the market may change between the time I buy it and the time I want to sell it—say 10 days later. If the price changes, I will suffer or enjoy a change in the purchasing power available to me. But because of the short horizon to maturity, the price will not change very much. (After all, the government will pay its face value in a few weeks.) Such a security is, thus, a reasonably satisfactory short-run store of purchasing power. Indeed, any readily salable capital asset whose value does not fluctuate significantly with the rate of interest will satisfactorily fulfill this short-term, store-of-value function.

Money substitutes

Things that serve as a temporary medium of exchange, but are not a store of value, are sometimes called **money substitutes.** Credit cards are a prime example. With a credit card many transactions can be made without either cash or a check. But the evidence of credit, in terms of the credit slip you sign and hand over to the store, is not money because it cannot be used to effect further transactions. Furthermore, when your credit card company sends you a bill you have to use money in (delayed) payment for the original transaction. The credit card serves the short-run function of a medium of exchange by allowing you to make purchases even though you have no cash or bank deposit currently in your possession. But this is only temporary; money remains the final medium of exchange for these transactions when the credit account is settled.

CHANGING CONCEPTS OF WHAT IS MONEY

What is an acceptable medium of exchange has changed and will continue to change over time. The NOW account promises to broaden the spectrum if it catches on and is permitted by the banking authorities. New monetary assets (such as certificates of deposit) are continuously being developed to serve some, if not all, of the functions of money, and these are more or less readily convertible into money. There is thus no single, timeless definition of what is money and what is only near money or a money substitute.

Summary

1. Early economic theory regarded the economy as being divided into a real part and a money part. The real part was concerned with production, the allocation of resources, and the distribution of income. These were importantly influenced by relative prices. The monetary part determined the absolute level of prices at which the real transactions took place. This was determined by the quantity of money. Double the quantity of money and in the new equilibrium all money prices would double but relative prices and the entire real sector would be left unaffected.

2. Inflation has been a common but by no means constant state of affairs in world history. Although inflation is widespread in the world today, the rate of inflation varies greatly from country to country.

3. Three of the major effects of unanticipated inflations are (1) to influence the allocation of resources and the distribution of income by haphazardly changing relative prices and wages, (2) to influence the real outcome of borrowing and lending agreements and other contracts expressed in money terms, and (3) to reduce living standards of people living on fixed money incomes. Some but not all of these adverse effects may be avoided if the rate of inflation is accurately anticipated.

4. Traditionally in economics, money has referred to any generally accepted medium of exchange. A number of functions of money may, however, be distinguished—the major ones are a medium of exchange, a store of value, and a unit of account.

5. Money arose because of the inconvenience of barter and developed in stages from precious metal, to metal coinage, to paper money convertible to precious metal, to token coinage and paper money fractionally backed by precious metals, to fiat money, and to deposit money. Societies have shown great sophistication in developing monetary instruments to meet their needs.

6. Today there is debate about what constitutes money. Concentrating on the medium-of-exchange function, money is restricted to notes, coins, and deposits subject to transfer by check. It is difficult, however, to separate the medium-of-exchange function from the function of providing a temporary store of purchasing power between the selling and the buying of goods. Any readily salable asset that has a secure capital value can be a satisfactory store of purchasing power. If the asset also earns an interest return, it has an advantage over cash and demand deposits (as long as the interest earned exceeds the costs and trouble of transferring into and out of the asset). Time deposits are an example of such a near money.

7. The question of what is money is further complicated by the existence of money substitutes. For example, credit cards allow purchases and sales to be made without the use of currency or checks. While credit cards substitute for money at the time of purchase, the accounts must eventually be settled using money.

Concepts for review

Real and monetary parts of the economy
Effects of anticipated and unanticipated inflations
Functions of money
Gresham's Law
The gold standard and convertible money
Fully backed, fractionally backed, and fiat money
Legal tender
Deposit money and the use of checks
Demand and time deposits
Near money and money substitutes

Discussion questions

1. "For the love of money is the root of all evil" (I Timothy 6:10). If a nation were to become a theocracy and money were made illegal, would you expect the level of national income to be affected? How about the productivity of labor? Might classical economists have answered this question differently than modern ones?

2. Which of the following groups, if any, might be expected to *benefit* from a rapid unforseen inflation: (a) landlords, (b) storekeepers with large inventories, (c) printers of price lists, (d) homeowners with mortgages, (e) old-age pensioners, (f) tenants, (g) a government whose tax revenue comes mostly from a progressive income tax, (h) bond holders.

3. Consider each of the following with respect to its potential use as a medium of exchange, a store of value, and a unit of account. Which would you think might be regarded as money? (a) a $100 Federal Reserve note, (b) an American Express credit card, (c) a painting by Picasso, (d) a NOW account, (e) a U.S. Treasury certificate of indebtedness payable in three months, (f) a savings account at a savings and loan association in Las Vegas, Nevada, (g) one share of American Telephone & Telegraph Company stock, (h) a lifetime pass to Green Bay Packer football games.

4. We often read that money serves three purposes: (a) as a medium of exchange, (b) a unit of account, and (c) a store of value. Does something that serves as a country's medium of exchange necessarily serve as the unit of account? Is any one of the three absolutely essential?

5. When in 1976 the Austrian government minted a new 1,000 schilling gold coin—worth $59 face value—the one-inch diameter coin came into great demand among jewelers and coin collectors. By law, the number of such coins to be minted each year is limited. Lines of people eager to get the coins formed outside the Government mint and local banks.

"There is exceptional interest in the new coin," said a Viennese banker. "It's a numismatic hit and a financial success." It has disappeared from circulation, however. Explain why.

6. In Canada, American and Canadian coins often circulate side by side, exchanging at their face values, even though notes often are of unequal value. Someone who receives a U.S. coin has the option of spending it at face value or taking it to the bank and converting it to Canadian money at the going rate of exchange. When the rate of exchange was near "par," so that $1 Canadian was within plus or minus 3¢ of $1 U.S., the two monies circulated side by side. When the Canadian dollar fell to $0.925 U.S., predict which money disappeared from circulation according to Gresham's law. Why did a 2¢ differential not produce this result?

7. Some years ago a strike closed all banks in Ireland for several months. What do you think happened to money, near money, and money substitutes during the period?

8. During hyperinflations in several foreign countries after World War II, American cigarettes were sometimes used in place of money. What made them suitable?

The banking system and the supply of money

The total stock of money in the economy at any moment is called the **money supply** or the **supply of money.** This total may be defined in different ways. Economists and financial analysts today tend to use three different definitions, each of which is regularly reported in the *Federal Reserve Bulletin.* M_1, the narrowest definition, defines money as currency plus demand deposits; M_2 defines money as M_1 plus time deposits at commercial banks; M_3 defines money as M_2 plus deposits at nonbank thrift institutions such as savings and loan associations, credit unions, and mutual savings banks.[1]

The first definition concentrates on the medium-of-exchange function. The second and third definitions add in savings deposits, which serve the temporary store-of-value function and are in practice quickly convertible into a medium of exchange at a known and completely secure price ($1 on deposit in a savings account is always convertible into a $1 demand deposit or $1 in cash). Table 33–1 shows the principal elements in the money supply.

In our economy the quantity of money is affected both by the private commercial banking system and by the actions of the central bank. The commercial banks affect the money supply as an incidental, but very important, feature of the conduct of their own business affairs. In so doing, of course, they respond to what is happening in the economy—to the level of business activity, to interest rates, and to the demands of their customers for cash and for loans. The central bank, which in the United States is the Federal Reserve System, affects the money sup-

[1] NOW accounts (discussed on page 608) may eventually cut across these categories. They are currently treated as if they were ordinary savings accounts. To the extent that they become completely acceptable as a medium of exchange there is little doubt they will belong in M_1. During 1976 the Fed reported two additional concepts of money, M_4 and M_5. These add large negotiable certificates of deposit to M_2 and M_3 respectively. We may expect the official definitions to continue to change as the forms in which liquid assets are held change.

ply as a matter of deliberate monetary policy. Just how each of these influences operates is the subject matter of this chapter.

The commercial banks

Modern commercial banking systems are of two main types. In one system, there is a small number of banks, each with a very large number of branch offices; in the other system, there is a very large number of independent banks. The banking systems of Britain and Canada are of the first type, with only a few banks accounting for the overwhelming bulk of the business. The American system is of the second type. There are approximately 15,000 independent banks, some, such as the Bank of America, with hundreds of branches and others with only a single office. Branch banking in the United States is governed by state law. Interstate branching is not allowed. In some states such as New York and California, banks are permitted to branch statewide. Illinois and Missouri, among others, are "unit-bank" states and permit no branching. Other states such as Pennsylvania permit limited branching into areas near the home office. The basic functioning of the banking system is, however, the same in all of these systems.

The basic unit of the American banking system is the ordinary commercial bank which is a privately owned, profit-seeking institution. Commercial banks differ from one another in many ways. Some are very large (in 1977 the Bank of America had deposits in excess of $60 billion) and others are very small; some are located in big cities, others in small towns; some hold charters from the federal government (national banks), others from state governments (state banks).

All **commercial banks** have certain common attributes: They hold deposits for their customers, permit certain deposits to be transferred by check from an individual account to other accounts held in any bank in the country, make loans to households and firms, and invest in government securities.

It is these common features—particularly the holding of demand deposits—that distinguish commercial banks from other financial institutions, each of which may perform some but not all of these functions. Many other institutions such as credit unions, savings and loan associations, and mutual savings banks accept time deposits and grant loans for specific purposes. Finance companies make loans to households for practically any purpose—sometimes at very high effective interest rates. The Post Office and Western Union will transfer money, American Express will

Table 33–1 The stock of money in the United States on 30 November 1976 (billions of dollars)

Currency	80.3	
Demand deposits at commercial banks	229.5	
subtotal: M_1		309.8
Time deposits at commercial banks[a]	422.2	
subtotal: M_2		732.0
Deposits at nonbank thrift institutions	491.4	
total M_3		1223.4

[a] Excluding negotiable time certificates of deposit issued in denominations of $100,000 or more. On this date these amounted to $62.1 billion. Because their day-to-day price fluctuates on the market they are more like bonds than time deposits.

Source: *Federal Reserve Bulletin,* February 1977

The money supply can be defined in a variety of ways; M_1, M_2, and M_3 are the most commonly used. Deposit money and near money of one kind or another constitute a large part of the money supply. M_1 is the narrowest definition of money in widespread use, and it concentrates on items that directly serve as media of exchange. M_2 and M_3 add in near moneys that serve the store of value function and can be readily converted into demand deposits or cash on a dollar-for-dollar basis.

issue travelers' checks. Credit card companies will extend credit with which a wide range of purchases can be made on a buy-now, pay-later basis.

Nearly 40 percent of all commercial banks, including most of the larger ones, are members of the Federal Reserve System—often called "the Fed."[2] All national banks are obliged to be members, and any state bank may choose to join the system by agreeing to abide by its regulations. The administrative and regulatory authority of the Fed applies directly only to the member banks, which account for nearly 75 percent of all commercial bank deposits in the United States. Nonmember banks are, however, indirectly tied into the system since they are invariably *correspondents* of larger member banks. The nonmember banks keep their reserves on deposit with member banks, depend on them for loans if they are pressed for cash, and rely on them for a variety of other services that the Federal Reserve System provides for its members. In practice, therefore, all commercial banks, members and nonmembers alike, come under the effective regulatory influence of the Fed. This is one reason why it is common to speak of the banking *system,* as distinct from (and in addition to) the commercial banking industry.

INTERBANK ACTIVITIES

A second reason for speaking of a banking system is that commercial banks have a number of interbank cooperative relationships that would be quite illegal under the antitrust laws applicable to an ordinary industry but that are actually encouraged by the special laws relating to banking because they facilitate the smooth functioning of money and credit markets.

Check clearing and collection

Bank deposits are an effective medium of ex-

[2] We shall examine the functioning of the Federal Reserve System later in this chapter.

change only because banks accept each other's checks. If you live in Columbus, Ohio, and receive a check from someone drawn on a Chicago bank, you are likely either to cash it or to deposit it in a Columbus bank. If the rules of the banking business were different, so that you actually had to go to Chicago and present it to the bank on which it was drawn, you would be so inconvenienced that you would be unwilling to accept checks for most transactions. Fortunately, banks do accept one another's checks. But the problem of presenting the checks for payment remains. If a depositor in bank A writes a check to someone who deposits it in bank B, bank A now owes money to bank B.

There are, of course, millions of such transactions in the course of a day, resulting in an enormous sorting and bookkeeping job. Multibank systems make use of a **clearing house** where interbank debts are settled. At the end of the day, all the checks drawn by bank A's customers and deposited in bank B are totaled and set against the total of all the checks drawn by bank B's customers and deposited in bank A. It is necessary only to settle the difference between these two sums. The actual checks are passed through the clearing house back to the bank on which they are drawn. The bank is then able to adjust each individual's account by a set of book entries; a flow of cash between banks is necessary only if there is a net transfer of cash from the customers of one bank to those of another. For member banks in the United States, much of this clearing function is performed by the Federal Reserve System.

The sharing of loans

Large though the resources of a single bank may seem to an individual, they often are not large enough to permit that bank to meet all the credit needs of a large industrial customer such as Sears, Roebuck or General Motors who may wish to borrow as much as $50 or $100 million at one time. For such enormous loans, a group of banks may join together and offer a pool loan, agreeing on common terms and dividing the loan up into manageable segments.

On a different scale, it is not uncommon for a smaller bank to be approached by one of its customers for a loan larger than it can comfortably or safely make. A bank in, say, Peoria, Illinois, will then ask a larger bank (probably in St. Louis or Chicago) to participate in the loan at some agreed percentage. Such "participating loans" represent, in effect, interbank lending and along with pool loans serve to make available to a customer anywhere the resources of the entire banking system.

Bank credit cards

A relatively new form of interbank cooperation is the bank credit card. BankAmericard and Master Charge are the two most commonly used credit cards in America, and they are both run by large groups of banks. The card permits the holder to charge purchases of goods and services. The participating banks promptly pay the merchants and bill the credit card holder, who has the option of paying at once or paying later at the cost of a prespecified rate of interest. Banks find this highly profitable because it provides "instant" loans with a small amount of paperwork and a high rate of interest—typically $1\frac{1}{2}$ or 2 percent per month—18 to 24 percent per year.

COMMERCIAL BANKS AS PROFIT-SEEKING INSTITUTIONS

Banks are private firms that start with invested capital and seek to "make money" in the same sense as do firms making neckties or bicycles. Banks do not set out to "make money" in the literal sense, but nonetheless they do so as an incidental by-product of their attempt to make profits for their owners.

A commercial bank provides a variety of services to its customers. It provides them with a relatively safe place to store their money, it provides the convenience of demand deposits that can be transferred by personal check, it provides a safe and convenient place to earn a modest but guaranteed return on savings, and it often provides financial advice and estate-management services. The bank earns revenue by charging for these services through a variety of fees and charges, but these amounts are a small part of the bank's earnings. The largest part (typically about five-sixths) of a bank's earnings is derived from the bank's ability to invest profitably the funds placed with it.

Principal assets and liabilities

Table 33–2 is the combined balance sheet of the commercial banks in the United States. The bulk of a bank's liabilities are deposits that are owed to its depositors. The principal assets of a bank are the *securities* it buys (including government bonds), which pay it interest or dividends, and the *loans* it makes to individuals to buy houses, cars, television sets, and securities and to businesses to build factories, buy machines, and finance the purchase of goods and raw materials. A bank loan is a liability to the borrower (who must pay it back) and an asset to the bank because the bank expects not only to have the loan repaid but to receive interest on it that more than compensates it for the paperwork involved and for the risk of nonpayment.

Most of the money deposited with banks is "at work," having been invested in loans or securities. The way banks earn money is to lend and invest the money left with them in such a way as to earn more than it costs them to attract the deposits. Deposits are the lifeblood of a commercial bank. Without them, the bank has nothing to lend or to invest except the small amount of its own capital. Most of the services a bank offers are designed to attract or keep deposits. In the case of time deposits, it pays the depositor an interest rate (from 5 to $7\frac{1}{2}$ percent in 1976, depending on the term of the deposit) in the expectation that it can earn more than that by

Table 33–2 The consolidated balance sheet of U.S. commercial banks, January 26, 1977 (billions of dollars)

Assets		Liabilities	
Reserves (cash assets including deposits with Federal Reserve banks)	117.9	Deposits	
		Demand	$296.5
		Time	495.6
Loans	563.7	Other liabilities	115.8
U.S. government securities	99.8	Capital accounts	75.5
Other securities	148.0		
Other assets	54.0		
	$983.4		$983.4

Source: *Federal Reserve Bulletin,* February 1977

Reserves are only a small fraction of deposit liabilities. If all of the banks' customers who held demand deposits tried to withdraw them in clash, the banks could not meet this demand without liquidating $178.6 billion of other assets. This would be quite impossible without assistance from the Fed.

reinvesting the money. In the case of demand deposits, banks are not permitted to pay interest to their depositors but they can and do provide such services as free checking, monthly statements, and postage-paid deposit-by-mail envelopes. When the amount banks could earn by investing money deposited with them was small they charged depositors for these services; as the amount banks can earn has risen with rising interest rates, the service charges have decreased or disappeared.

Competition for deposits

Competition for deposits is active both among banks and between banks and other financial institutions. Savings and loan associations (S & Ls) and mutual savings banks are important competitors to commercial banks for time deposits.

These nonbank savings institutions specialize primarily in mortgage lending secured by residential real estate; their rapid postwar growth has reflected the high and growing demand for home financing. Competitive bidding for funds by commercial banks has

been inhibited, particularly during the 1950s, by the regulation of the maximum rates they are permitted to pay on time deposits. However, the competitive position of banks improved in the early 1960s as a result of increases in permitted interest rates and the introduction of a new type of time deposit known as a certificate of deposit. **Certificates of deposit (CD)** are savings deposits the evidence for which is a slip of paper, or certificate, rather than an entry in the saver's passbook. CDs have proliferated into many forms, but one of the most important is the large denomination, negotiable CD which is designed to attract funds from large businesses. These pay a higher rate of interest than do ordinary savings deposits.

Competition among banks for demand deposits takes the form of advertising, personal solicitation of accounts, and new and improved services. Large commercial banks often organize payroll- and pension-accounting schemes for industrial customers, and in some cases they actually undertake payrolling functions. The "lock box" is another kind of service: Banks establish locked post office boxes to which retail customers of large companies send their payments. Most gasoline companies have credit card customers remit to a lock box. The bank opens the remittances, deposits them to the company's account, and forwards notices of payment to the company. Among other features, this speeds the receipt of funds to the company and decreases their need to borrow money for working capital. All of these services are costly to the bank and represent inducements offered to customers in order to gain deposits.

RESERVES

The need for reserves

All bankers would as a matter of convenience and prudence keep *some* cash on hand against their deposits in order to be able to meet depositors' day-to-day requirements for cash. But the reserves required for these needs are far less than 100 percent. Just as the goldsmiths of old discovered that only a fraction of the gold they held was ever withdrawn, and just as banks discovered that only a fraction of convertible bank notes was actually converted, so, too, banks have discovered that only a fraction of their deposits will be withdrawn in cash at any one time. Most of the deposits of any individual bank stay on deposit with it; thus an individual bank need only keep fractional reserves against its deposits.

Many of the funds withdrawn by a depositor from one bank do not leave the banking system, even though they leave the bank. Even if Ms. Jones withdraws $4,000 from her bank to buy a new car, the chances are great that the car dealer will deposit the check received from Jones in its account. Thus the banking system as a whole will have merely transferred its deposit liabilities from one depositor to another and from one bank to another. For this reason, the banking system as a whole may operate with fewer reserves than would any one bank standing alone.

While one bank may be losing reserves others may be gaining them, and the bank experiencing a shortage can borrow from those banks with excess reserves.[3]

The reserves needed to assure that depositors can withdraw their deposits on demand will be quite small in normal times. But reserves must also be large enough to meet extraordinary demands for cash.

The psychological effect of a bank's refusing to give a depositor cash can be devastating. Until relatively recent times, such an event—or even the rumor of it—could lead to a "run" on the bank as all the bank's depositors sought to withdraw their money. Faced with such a panic, the bank would have to close its doors until it had borrowed funds or liquidated enough assets to meet the demand or until the demand subsided. But the closing of even one bank often led to demands for cash by nervous depositors elsewhere. Bankers were unable to collect their debts from people whose own money was in the closed banks. Thus, once many banks closed, a wave of foreclosures, bankruptcies, and further bank failures would ensue. Moreover, as many banks tried to sell their securities at the same time, the prices of those securities tended to fall disastrously, and the resulting decline in the value of the banks' assets added to the risk of their insolvency.

The need of the commercial banking system for reserves against this kind of depositors' panic has been diminished by governmental policies. In the first place the central bank can provide commercial banks with cash they need either by lending them money or by buying the securities they want to sell. In the second place, the government has provided federal deposit insurance which guarantees that depositors will get their money back even if the bank fails completely. Such insur-

---

[3] There is an active market, the federal funds market, in which excess reserves are loaned among banks on a short-term basis. In the first week of 1977, for example, $25 billion of transactions occurred in this market.

ance decreases the likelihood of a widespread panic because one bank's failure is much less likely to lead to a run on other banks. Most depositors will not withdraw their money as long as they are *sure* they can get it when they need it.

Actual and required reserves

Look again at Table 33–2 and observe that the banking system's cash reserves are but a fraction of its deposits. If the holders of even 40 percent of its demand deposits had demanded cash sometime in January 1977, the commercial banking system would have been unable (without outside help) to meet the demand, for its total cash assets were less than $118 billion.

The American banking system is a **fractional reserve system,** with banks holding reserves of much less than 100 percent of their deposits. The size of the reserves shown in Table 33–2 does not reflect only judgments of bankers; it reflects as well the legal requirements imposed on the banks by the Fed.

A bank's **reserve ratio** is the fraction of its deposits that it holds as reserves either as cash in its vaults or as deposits with the central bank. Those reserves that the Federal Reserve System requires the bank to hold are called **required reserves.** Any reserves that it holds over and above required reserves are called **excess reserves.** Reserves are required by the Fed both to assure the stability of the banking system and as part of its policy arsenal in attempting to control the money supply, as we shall discuss at the end of this chapter.

The creation and destruction of deposit money by the commercial banks

The kind of fractional reserve system described above creates the leverage by which commercial banks can create new money. If banks can increase their reserves, they can increase their deposits even more, and since

deposits are money, they can thus increase the money supply. We must now examine this process in detail.

Some simplifying assumptions

In order to focus on the essential aspects of how banks create money, we assume that banks can invest in only one kind of asset, loans, and that there is only one kind of deposit, a demand deposit.

The three other assumptions listed below are made provisionally. Later, when the basic ideas concerning the bank's creation of money have been developed, these assumptions will be relaxed.

Fixed required reserve ratio. It is assumed initially that all banks have the same required reserve ratio and that this ratio does not change. In our numerical illustration we shall assume that the required reserve ratio is 20 percent—i.e., that banks must have at least $1 of reserves for every $5 of deposits.

No excess reserves. It is assumed that all banks want to invest any reserves they have in excess of the legally required amount. This implies that they always believe there are safe investments they can make when they have excess reserves.

No cash drain from the banking system. The public is assumed to have a fixed amount of currency that it wishes to hold in circulation, an amount that will not change with changes in the total money supply. Thus changes in the money supply will take the form of changes in deposit money. If extra money is created, the money will be deposited in a bank; if money is destroyed, bank deposits will be decreased.

Armed with these assumptions we shall now examine money creation starting with the simplest possible situation and progressing to two more complex but more realistic ones. The three situations are: (1) a single new deposit in a system that has only one bank, (2) a single new deposit in a system with many banks, and (3) many new deposits in a many-bank system. Surprisingly, perhaps, the results are exactly the same in all three cases.

A MONOPOLY BANK, A SINGLE NEW DEPOSIT

Initially, suppose that the whole country is served by a single multibranch bank, called a *monopoly bank* because it has no competitors. The balance sheet of this monopoly bank is shown in Table 33–3.

The monopoly bank's assets consist of $200 of reserves, held partly as cash on hand and partly as deposits with the central bank, and $900 of loans outstanding to its customers. Its liabilities are $100 to those who initially contributed capital to get the bank started and $1,000 to current depositors. The bank's ratio of reserves to deposits is 200/1,000 = 0.20, exactly equal to its minimum requirement.

An immigrant now arrives in the country and opens an account by depositing $100 with the monopoly bank. This is a wholly new deposit for the bank, and its revised balance sheet is shown in Table 33–4.

As a result of the immigrant's new deposit, both cash assets and deposit liabilities have risen by $100. More important, however, the reserve ratio has also increased from 0.20 to 300/1,100 = 0.27. The monopoly bank now has excess reserves—with $300 in reserves it could support $1,500 in deposits.

The monopoly bank knows that any new deposit it creates will remain in the system. It is thus in a position to say to the next business executive who comes in for a loan, "We will lend your firm $400 at the going rate of interest." The bank does so by adding that amount to the firm's deposit account. The bank does not care how the businessman spends the money, for whoever receives the firm's checks will deposit them in the same bank (since there is no other).

Table 33–5 shows what happened when the

Table 33–3 The monopoly bank's initial balance sheet

Assets		Liabilities	
Cash and reserves	$ 200	Deposits	$1,000
Loans	900	Capital	100
	$1,100		$1,100

The monopoly bank has a reserve of 20 percent of its deposit liabilities. The commercial bank earns its money by finding profitable investments for much of the money deposited with it. In this balance sheet its loans are the earning assets of the bank.

Table 33–4 The monopoly bank's balance sheet after an immigrant deposits $100

Assets		Liabilities	
Cash and reserves	$ 300	Deposits	$1,100
Loans	900	Capital	100
	$1,200		$1,200

The immigrant's deposit raises deposit liabilities and cash assets by the same amount. Since both cash and deposits rise by $100 the cash reserve ratio that was formerly 0.20 now increases to 0.27. The bank has more cash than it needs to provide a 20 percent reserve against its deposit liabilities.

Table 33–5 The monopoly bank's balance sheet after making a $400 loan

Assets		Liabilities	
Cash and reserves	$ 300	Deposits	$1,500
Loans	1,300	Capital	100
	$1,600		$1,600

The loan restores the reserve ratio of 0.20. By increasing its loans by a multiple of its new cash deposit, the bank restores its reserve ratio of 0.20.

Table 33–6   The monopoly bank's balance sheet after a $50 cash withdrawal

Assets		Liabilities	
Cash and reserves	$ 250	Deposits	$1,450
Loans	1,300	Capital	100
	$1,550		$1,550

A cash withdrawal lowers the bank's reserve ratio. The cash withdrawal reduces both cash assets and deposit liabilities by the same amount. The reserve ratio, which was 0.20 before the withdrawal, is now only 0.17.

Table 33–7   The monopoly bank's balance sheet after the reserve ratio has been restored

Assets		Liabilities	
Cash and reserves	$ 250	Deposits	$1,250
Loans	1,100	Capital	100
	$1,350		$1,350

A multiple contraction of loans is necessary to restore the reserve ratio after a cash withdrawal. A withdrawal of $50 in cash reduces deposits by $50. A further contraction of $200 in loans and deposits is necessary to cause deposits to fall by five times the fall in cash. This restores the reserve ratio of 0.20.

Table 33–8   The initial balance sheet of the Immigrants Bank and Trust Company (IB&T Co.)

Assets		Liabilities	
Cash and reserves	$ 200	Deposits	$1,000
Loans	900	Capital	100
	$1,100		$1,100

The initial position is the same as that of the monopoly bank in Table 33–3. Although the balance sheet of the IB&T Co. is initially the same as that of the monopoly bank, the crucial difference is that the IB&T Co. is one of many banks in a multibank system, while the monopoly bank was itself the whole banking system.

new deposits were created. The new immigrant's deposit initially raised cash assets and deposit liabilities by $100. The new loans created an additional $400 of deposit liabilities. This restores the reserve ratio to its legal minimum (300/1,500 = 0.20), and no further expansion of deposit money is possible. As the bank's customers do business with each other, settling their accounts by checks, the ownership of these deposits will be continually changing. But what matters to the bank is that its total will remain constant.

The extent to which the bank can increase its loans *and thus its deposits* and thus the money supply depends on the reserve ratio. Because in this case the ratio is 1/5 (= 0.20), the bank is able to expand deposits to five times the original new acquisition of money. In general, if the reserve ratio is r, a monopoly bank can increase its deposits by $1/r$ times any new reserves. (This general relationship proves true of a banking system whether or not there is a monopoly bank.) [35]

The "multiple expansion of deposits" that has just been worked through applies in reverse to a withdrawal of funds. Suppose a depositor in a monopoly bank withdraws $50 (in the form of a $50 bill) and spends it in a new shop, whose owners decide to frame the bill and display it on their wall. The bank has lost both cash and a deposit. Its revised balance sheet is shown in Table 33–6. As a result of the loss of $50 cash and $50 deposits, the bank's reserve ratio has fallen to 250/1,450 = 0.17. This is below the legal minimum and the bank will have to take steps to restore the required ratio.

Say that the bank calls for repayment of some loans made to its customers and repayable at short notice, hoping thereby to raise its cash position to restore the required ratio. What happens, however, is that the loans are not repaid by cash but by the customers' drawing checks on their accounts in favor of the bank. This means that deposit liabilities are reduced by the repayment of the loan, but cash is unchanged. To restore the correct reserve ratio it will be necessary to reduce deposits—by calling in loans and not making new ones until deposits are once again only five times reserves.

The revised balance sheet when this has been achieved is shown in Table 33–7. The bank lost $50 in cash from the initial withdrawal of funds. To maintain a reserve ratio it was necessary to have deposits fall by $250. The initial withdrawal cut deposits by $50, but the remaining $200 had to be effected by reducing loans outstanding. The new position restores the deposit ratio to $250/$1,250 = 0.20. As a result of the withdrawal of $50, the quantity of deposit money shrinks by $250 and the volume of loans available to the bank's customers shrinks by $200.

MANY BANKS, A SINGLE NEW DEPOSIT

Deposit creation is somewhat more complicated in a multibank system than in a single-bank system, but *the end result is exactly the same.* It is more complicated because, when a bank makes a loan, the recipient of the loan may pay the money to someone who deposits it not in the original bank but in another bank. How this works is most easily seen under the extreme assumption that every new borrower immediately withdraws the borrowed funds from the lending bank and pays someone who deposits the money in another bank or banks.

Suppose that the Immigrants Bank and Trust Company is initially in the position of the monopoly bank (shown in Table 33–3), which is repeated in Table 33–8. Now suppose that, as before, an immigrant makes a wholly new deposit of $100. The bank's position after the deposit is shown in Table 33–9. This is exactly the same position as shown in Table 33–4 when the monopoly bank received the immigrant's deposit. The reserve ratio is once again 300/1,100 = 0.27, but here the similarity to the monopoly bank ends.

Table 33–9   The balance sheet of the IB&T Co. after a $100 cash deposit

Assets		Liabilities	
Cash and reserves	$ 300	Deposits	$1,100
Loans	900	Capital	100
	$1,200		$1,200

The immigrant's deposit raises deposit liabilities and cash assets by the same amount. Since both cash and deposits rise by $100, the cash reserve ratio, which was formerly 0.20, now increases to 0.27. The bank has more cash than it needs to provide a 20 percent reserve against its deposit liabilities.

Table 33–10   The IB&T Co. balance sheet after a new loan and cash drain of $80

Assets		Liabilities	
Cash and reserves	$ 220	Deposits	$1,100
Loans	980	Capital	100
	$1,200		$1,200

The bank lends its surplus cash and suffers a cash drain. The bank keeps $20 as a reserve against the new deposit of $100. It lends $80 to a customer, who writes a check to someone who deals with another bank. When the check is cleared, IB&T Co. has suffered an $80 cash drain, has increased its loans by $80, and has restored its reserve ratio to 0.20.

The Immigrants Bank cannot use its excess reserves to support $400 of new loans. When the bank makes new loans to its customers, they will make payments to other persons who will deposit the checks in their own banks. Because of this, the Immigrants Bank will suffer a cash drain—that is, the checks drawn against it will not be offset by deposits of checks drawn against other banks, and it will lose cash to other banks. But even though it cannot expand loans and deposits by as

Table 33–11 Changes in the balance sheets of second-generation banks

Assets		Liabilities	
Cash and reserves	+$16	Deposits	+$80
Loans	+ 64		
	+$80		+$80

Second-generation banks receive cash deposits and expand loans. The second-generation banks gain new deposits of $80 as a result of the loan granted by the IB&T Co., which is used to make payments to customers of the second-generation banks. These banks keep 20 percent of the cash that they acquire as their reserve against the new deposit and can make new loans using the other 80 percent. When the customers who borrowed the money make payments to the customers of third-generation banks, a cash drain occurs.

much as the monopoly bank, it can do something. It has more reserves than it requires, and even on the extreme assumption that every dollar that it lends will be withdrawn and deposited in another bank, there is an opportunity to make some profitable loans with the excess reserves on hand.

With its present level of deposits at $1,100, the bank needs only $220 of reserves (0.20 × $1,100 = $220) so that it can lend the $80 excess that it has on hand. Table 33–10 shows the position after this has been done and after the new deposit has been withdrawn to be deposited to the account of a customer of another bank. The Immigrants Bank once again has a 20 percent reserve ratio.

So far deposits in the IB&T Co. have increased by only the initial $100 of new immigrant's money with which we started, as was shown in Table 33–9. (Of this, $20 is held as cash reserve against the deposit and $80 has been lent out to a customer.) But other banks have received new deposits of $80 as the persons receiving payment from the initial borrower deposited these payments in their own banks. The receiving banks (sometimes described as "second-generation banks")

receive new deposits of $80, and when the checks clear, they have new reserves of $80. Because they require an addition to their reserves of only $16 to support the new deposit, they have $64 of excess reserves. They now increase their loans by $64. After this money is spent by the borrowers and has been deposited in other, third-generation banks, the balance sheets of the second-generation banks will have changed as shown in Table 33–11.

But the third-generation banks will now find themselves with $64 of new deposits. Against these they need only hold $12.80 in cash, so they have excess reserves of $51.20 that they can immediately lend out. Thus there begins a long sequence of new deposits, new loans, new deposits, and new loans. The stages are shown in Table 33–12. The series in the table should look familiar, for it is the same converging series we met before when dealing with the multiplier.

The banking system has created new deposits and thus new money, although each banker can honestly say, "All I did was invest my excess reserves. I can do no more than manage wisely the money I receive."

If r is the reserve ratio, the ultimate effect on the deposits of the banking system of a new deposit will be $1/r$ times the new deposit. [36] This is exactly the same result reached in the monopoly bank case.[4]

MANY BANKS, MANY DEPOSITS

The two cases discussed above, a monopoly bank and a single new deposit in a many-bank situation, serve this purpose: They show that under either set of opposite extreme assumptions the result is the same. So it is, too, in intermediate situations where banks suffer

---

[4] Indeed, the process might have been the same. Look again at Table 33–4. If the monopoly bank had merely loaned its excess reserves of $80, it would have soon received a new deposit of $80 in one of its branches. This in turn would give it excess reserves of $64, which it could loan—and so on.

Table 33-12   Many banks, a single new deposit

Bank	New deposits	New loans	Addition to reserves
Immigrants Bank	$100.00	$ 80.00	$ 20.00
Second-generation bank	80.00	64.00	16.00
Third-generation bank	64.00	51.20	12.80
Fourth-generation bank	51.20	40.96	10.24
Fifth-generation bank	40.96	32.77	8.19
Sixth-generation bank	32.77	26.22	6.55
Seventh-generation bank	26.22	20.98	5.24
Eighth-generation bank	20.98	16.78	4.20
Ninth-generation bank	16.78	13.42	3.36
Tenth-generation bank	13.42	10.74	2.68
Total first 10 generations	446.33	357.07	89.26
All remaining generations	53.67	42.93	10.74
Total for banking systems	$500.00	$400.00	$100.00

The banking system as a whole can create deposit money whenever it receives new reserves.   The table shows the process of the creation of deposit money on the assumptions that all of the loans made by one set of banks end up as deposits in another set of banks (called the "next-generation banks"), that the required reserve ratio (r) is 0.20, and that there are no excess reserves. Although each bank suffers a cash drain whenever it grants a new loan, the system as a whole does not, and the system ends up doing in a series of steps what a monopoly bank would do all at once; that is, it increases deposit money by $1/r$, which in this example is five times the amount of any increase in reserves that it obtains.

some, but less than total, cash drain to other banks. A far more realistic picture of the process of deposit creation is one in which new deposits (or new withdrawals) tend to accrue simultaneously to all banks, perhaps because of changes in the monetary policy of the government. Say, for example, that the community contains 10 banks of equal size and that each receives new deposits of $100 in cash. Now each bank is in the position shown in Tables 33–4 and 33–9, and each can begin to expand deposits based on the $100 of excess reserves (each bank does this by granting loans to customers).

Because each bank does one-tenth of the total banking business, an average of 90 percent of any newly created deposit will find its way into other banks as the customer pays by check to other people in the community. This will represent a cash drain from the lending bank to these other banks. However, 10 percent of each new deposit created by each other bank should find its way into this bank. All banks receive new cash and all start creating deposits simultaneously; no bank should suffer a significant cash drain to any other bank. Thus all banks can go on expanding deposits without losing cash to each other; they need only worry about keeping enough cash to satisfy those depositors who occasionally require cash. The expansion can go on with each bank watching its own ratio of cash reserves to deposits, expanding deposits as long as the ratio exceeds 1/5 and ceasing when it reaches that figure. The process will come to a halt when each bank has created $400 in additional deposits, so that for each initial $100 cash deposit, there is now $500 in deposits backed by $100 in cash. Now *each* of the banks will have entries in its books similar to those shown in Table 33–5.

The general rule, if there is no cash drain, is that a banking system with a reserve ratio of r can increase its deposits by 1/r times any new reserves.

The opposite case, corresponding to a general decrease in deposits, is left for you to do as an exercise.

EXCESS RESERVES AND CASH DRAINS

Two of the simplifying assumptions made earlier can now be relaxed.

Excess reserves. If banks do not choose to invest excess reserves, the multiple expansion discussed will not occur. Turn back to Table 33–4. If the monopoly bank had been content to hold 27 percent reserves, it might well have done nothing more. Other things being equal, banks will choose to invest excess reserves because of the profit motive. But there may be times when they feel the risk is too great. It is one thing to be offered 8 percent or even 16 percent interest on a loan, but if the borrower is going to default on the payment of interest and principal, the bank will be the loser. Similarly, if the bank expects interest rates to rise in the future, it may hold off making loans now so that it will have reserves available to make more profitable loans after the interest rate has risen.

There is nothing automatic about credit expansion. It rests on decisions of bankers. If banks do not choose to use excess reserves to expand their investments, there will not be an expansion of deposits.

Banks tend to hold larger excess reserves in times of business recession when there is a low demand for loans and sagging interest rates than they do in periods of boom when

Table 33–13 The monopoly bank's balance sheet after a credit expansion and an accompanying cash drain

Assets		Liabilities	
Cash and			
reserves	$ 280	Deposits	$1,480
Loans	1,300	Capital	100
	$1,580		$1,580

The maximum deposit expansion possible is reduced by a cash drain. This example differs from that shown in Table 33–5 because, after a new deposit of $100 land a new loan of $400, 5 percent of the newly created money is withdrawn as cash to be held by the public. Cash and deposits each fall by $20 and the reserve ratio falls below 20 percent.

the demand for loans is great and when interest rates are high.

The significance of relaxing this assumption about excess reserves is that it cuts the automatic link between creation of excess reserves and money creation. Excess reserves make it *possible* for the banks to expand the money supply, but only if they want to do so.

The money supply is thus at least partially determined by the commercial banks in response to such things as changes in national income and interest rates. The upper limit of deposits is, however, determined by the required reserve ratio and by the reserves available to the banks, both of which are under the control of the central bank.

Cash drain. Suppose firms and households find it convenient to keep a fixed *fraction* of their money holding in cash (say 5 percent) instead of a fixed *amount* of dollars. Then an extra $100 in money supply will not all stay in the banking system; only $95 of it remains on deposit while the rest is added to money in circulation. In such a situation any multiple expansion of bank deposits will be accompanied by a cash drain to the public that will reduce the maximum expansion below what it was when the public was content to hold all its new money as bank deposits. Table 33–13 shows the position of a monopoly bank after a credit expansion of $400 and a cash drain of $20.

The story of deposit creation when there is a cash drain to the public might be told as follows. Each bank starts creating deposits and suffers no significant cash drain to other banks. But because approximately 5 percent of any newly created deposits is withdrawn to be held as cash, each bank does suffer a cash drain to the public. The expansion goes on, each bank watching its own ratio of cash reserves to deposits, expanding deposits as long as the ratio exceeds 1/5, and ceasing when it reaches that figure. Because the expansion is accompanied by a cash drain, it will come to a halt with a smaller deposit expansion than in the no-cash-drain case.[5]

Central banks

All advanced, free-market economies have, in addition to commercial banks, a central bank that is responsible for control of the money supply and that exerts a strong influence over major financial markets. The central bank is an instrument of the government, whether it is in fact publicly owned or not. The Bank of England—the "Old Lady of Threadneedle Street"—is the oldest and most famous of the central banks; it began to operate as the central bank of England in the seventeenth century. In the United States the central bank is called the Federal Reserve System, and it was organized in 1914.

[5] It can be shown algebraically that the percentage of cash drain must be added to the reserve ratio to determine the maximum possible expansion of deposits. [37] Thus if r is the reserve ratio and v the cash drain, the commercial banking system can increase its deposits by $1/(r + v)$ times any new money received by it, instead of by the $1/r$ derived in math note [35] page 907. If $r = 0.20$ and $v = .05$ the expansion will be limited to 4 (= 1/.25) instead of 5 (= 1/.20) times the new reserves.

All central banks perform the same functions, but they have different forms of organization. The similarities of central banks in the functions they perform and in the tools they use are much more important than their differences. Although attention here is directed to the operations of the Federal Reserve System, the basic situation is not different for the Bank of England, the Bank of Greece, or the Bank of Canada.

BASIC FUNCTIONS OF A CENTRAL BANK

A **central bank** has four main functions: to serve as banker for commercial banks, as a bank for the government, as the controller of the nation's supply of money, and as a supporter of financial markets.

The first three of these functions are revealed by a study of the balance sheet of a central bank. Table 33–14 is such a balance sheet.

Commercial banks are organized for the purpose of earning profits; central banks are not. However, because the central bank holds many of its assets in the form of government interest-paying securities it is in a position to earn profits. Though central banks can hardly avoid making profits, they do so incidentally and simply turn them over to the central government.

Banker to commercial banks

The central bank accepts deposits from commercial banks and will, on order, transfer these to the account of another bank. In this way, the central bank provides each commercial bank with the equivalent of a checking account and with a means for settling debts to other banks. The deposits of the commercial banks with the central bank appear in Table 33–14. Notice that the reserves of the commercial banks deposited with the central bank are *liabilities* of the central bank (because it promises to pay them on demand), just as the money reserves of an individual or corporation deposited with a commercial bank are the liabilities of the commercial bank.

Table 33–14   Federal Reserve banks, Consolidated balance sheet, January 26, 1977 (billions of dollars)

Assets		Liabilities	
Gold certificates and other cash	$ 13.3	Federal Reserve Notes outstanding	$ 81.2
U.S. government securities	94.1	Deposits of U.S. Treasury	11.4
Loans to commercial banks	0.0[a]	Deposits of member-bank reserves	23.6
Other assets	16.8	Other liabilities	5.5
	$124.2	Capital	2.5
			124.2

Source: *Federal Reserve Bulletin,* February 1977.

[a] The actual amount was 0.046; it has been rounded off to 0.0.

The balance sheet of the Fed shows that it serves as banker to the commercial banks and the U.S. Treasury and as issuer of our currency; it also suggests the Fed's role as regulator of money markets and the money supply. The principal liabilities of the Fed are the basis of the money supply. Federal Reserve notes are currency and the deposits of member banks give commercial banks the reserves they use to create deposit money. The Fed's holdings of U.S. government securities arise both from its open market operations designed to regulate the money supply and financial markets, and from direct purchases from the Treasury.

Historically, one of the earliest services to be provided by central banks was that of "lender of last resort" to the commercial banking system; central banks would lend money to commercial banks that had sound investments (such as government securities and safe loans to individuals) but were in urgent need of immediate cash. If such banks could not obtain ready cash they might be forced into insolvency because they could not meet the demands of their depositors in spite of being in a basically sound position. Today's central banks continue to fulfill the lender-of-last-resort function. In a year such as 1976 when the banking system had ample reserves, such loans to commercial banks do not occur in significant amounts. In some recent years, however, borrowings by commercial banks from the Fed have amounted to as much as 3 or 4 percent of total reserves. In the United States the rate of interest the Fed charges on loans to its member banks is called the **discount rate.** While commercial banks thus may borrow from the central bank when they wish to build up their reserves, they frequently sell government securities or borrow on the federal funds market instead.

Banker to the government

Governments, too, need to hold their funds in an account into which they can make deposits and on which they can write checks. The U.S. Treasury keeps its checking deposits at the Federal Reserve banks, replenishing them from much larger tax and loan accounts kept at commercial banks. When the government requires more money, it too needs to borrow, and it does so by selling securities. Most of these are sold directly to the public, but when the central bank buys a government bond on the open market it is indirectly lending to the government. As of January 1977, the Federal

Reserve System held nearly $100 billion in U.S. government securities. There are a great variety of government securities, including Treasury bills, Treasury notes, and many series of bonds. We shall speak of them all generically and interchangeably as "bonds" or as "securities." These securities play an important role in the monetary system.

Regulator of the money supply

One of the most important functions of a central bank is to control the money supply. Notice in Table 33–14 that the overwhelming proportion of a central bank's liabilities (its promises to pay) are either Federal Reserve notes (money) or the deposits of commercial banks, which provide reserves for demand deposits (money) owned by households and firms.

The central bank can affect the levels of its assets and liabilities in a variety of ways, and as its liabilities rise and fall so does the money supply. Consider a single example. Suppose that the central bank buys $100 million worth of newly printed bonds from the Treasury. The bank's assets (government bonds) rise by

Currency control as a means of controlling the money supply

Controlling the quantity of currency it issues might seem to be the most obvious way for the government to control the money supply. After all the amount of coinage is directly controlled by the Treasury, and the rest of the currency in circulation is in the form of central bank notes. Look at the next piece of paper money you see; the odds are very great (if you live in the United States) that it will have the words "Federal Reserve Note" on it. Close to 90 percent of the currency in circulation is in the form of Federal Reserve notes.

The Treasury and the Fed would thus appear to be able to control the amount of currency in circulation by issuing more of it or by withdrawing some of it from circulation. In fact they are unwilling to try to tell the public how much of its money to hold in cash. They are not able to make the public hold more cash than it wants as long as banks will accept deposits. They could not make the public hold less cash than it wanted without serious risk to the stability of the monetary system. Suppose that with a given money supply the public decided it wished to hold a higher proportion in currency and a lower proportion in deposits (as it does, for example, every Christmas season). If the Fed wished to prevent this, it would have to take steps to reduce the cash available to the commercial banks so that they could not, or would not, turn their customers' deposits into cash. Because commercial banks have a legal obligation to pay cash whenever it is demanded by their customers, failure to do so would mean widespread bank insolvency and a consequent financial panic. (Even that would not work for very long; Federal Deposit Insurance payments would give depositors the cash they were legally entitled to receive.)

The Fed can and does influence the *total* money supply (currency plus demand deposits). It does not seek to influence how the total is divided between currency and deposits, and the proportion does change as habits and customs with respect to paying bills change.

$100 million and so do its liabilities (Treasury deposits). The government has an extra $100 million of purchasing power which it now spends. "As easy as printing money," you may say, and indeed it is the same thing.

Regulator of money markets

The central bank frequently enters money markets for reasons other than controlling the money supply. It may, as an arm of the government, attempt to keep interest rates low in periods when the government is increasing its debt, so as to reduce the government's cost of financing a given size deficit.

Central banks also assume a major responsibility to support the country's financial system and to prevent its serious disruption by widescale panic and resulting bank failures. Various institutions are in the business of borrowing on a short-term and lending on a long-term basis. An example is savings and loan associations, which take in short-term deposits from the public and lend on long-term mortgages. Large, unanticipated increases in interest rates tend to squeeze these institutions. The average rate that they earn on their investments rises only slowly as old contracts mature and new ones are made, but they must either pay higher rates to hold on to their deposits or they must accept wide-scale withdrawals that could easily bring about their insolvency. To prevent such financial disasters, central banks often use their open-market operations either to slow down the rate of change of interest rates or to narrow the range over which these rates fluctuate.

THE FEDERAL RESERVE SYSTEM

The most important thing to understand about the Federal Reserve system is this:

In its role as the central bank of the United States, the Federal Reserve System is the arm of the U.S. government responsible for its monetary policy.

This is stressed because things are not always as they seem, and the organizational structure of the system appears, at first glance, to consist of a number of banks that are privately owned and over which commercial banks rather than the government have control.

The basic elements in the Federal Reserve System are (1) the board of governors, (2) the Federal Advisory Council, which has no real powers, but whose 12 members advise the board of the views of commercial bankers, (3) the 12 Federal Reserve banks, (4) the Federal Open Market Committee, and (5) the more than 5,700 member commercial banks.

The board of governors. The board consists of seven members appointed by the President and confirmed by the Senate. Appointment is for 14 years. The length of term is of some importance because each member of the board serves beyond the term of the President who makes the appointment. The board members are top-level public servants who often, but not inevitably, come from the world of business or banking. In 1977 two of the members of the board, Chairman Arthur Burns and board member Henry Wallich, were professional economists. The board is responsible to Congress, but it works in close association with the Department of the Treasury. The board supervises the entire Federal Reserve System and exercises general policy control over the twelve Reserve banks.

The chairman of the board, currently Arthur Burns, is in a powerful position to influence the country's monetary policies.

The reserve banks. Twelve Federal Reserve banks serve the 12 districts into which the country is divided. The Federal Reserve banks are located in Boston, New York, Philadelphia, Cleveland, Richmond, Atlanta, Chicago, St. Louis, Minneapolis, Kansas City, Dallas, and San Francisco. Each of these banks is nominally owned by the member banks in its district. Each commercial bank that is a member of the system is required to purchase Reserve bank stock to an amount equal to 3 percent of the member bank's own capital. The commercial banks receive a flat 6 percent dividend on this investment. Each Federal Reserve bank has nine directors: three bankers elected by the member banks; three representatives of business, agriculture, or industry; and three public members appointed by the board of governors.

Although they are technically privately owned and operated, the Federal Reserve banks are actually operated under guidelines set down by the board of governors in what it deems to be the public interest.

The Federal Reserve banks have a strong tradition of service to the banking community within the policy lines laid down by the board of governors. Revenues they earn in excess of expenses and of fixed minimum profits are turned over to the U.S. Treasury. Most of the Reserve banks, along with the office of the board of governors, engage in research and publish many bulletins of interest to the financial communities they serve.

The open market committee. The Open Market Committee consists of 12 members, five of whom are presidents of Reserve banks, the other seven being members of the board of governors. This committee determines the open-market policy of the system, which deals principally with the question of how many government securities the Reserve banks should buy or sell on the open market.

Central banks and the money supply

Deposit money is a large part of the money supply, no matter how the supply of money is defined. Demand deposits of commercial banks account for roughly 75 percent of M_1,

the narrowest definition of money, and roughly 20 percent of M_3, the broadest measure in widespread use (see Table 33–1). The ability of commercial banks to create deposit money depends upon their reserves, as we have seen. The ability of the central bank to affect the money supply is critically related to its ability to affect the size and adequacy of these reserves of commercial banks. Three means of doing so are discussed in the remainder of this chapter.

CHANGING THE REQUIRED RESERVE RATIOS

One means of controlling the money supply is by way of required reserve ratios. We now relax our earlier assumption that required reserves were constant. Suppose the banking system is loaned-up (that is, it has no excess reserves). If the Fed now gradually increases the required reserve ratio (say from 20 percent to 25 percent), the dollar amount of reserves held by the commercial banks will no longer be adequate to support their outstanding deposits. Commercial banks will be forced to reduce their deposits until they achieve the new, higher required reserve ratio.[6] This decrease in demand deposits is a decrease in the money supply. The process is illustrated in Table 33–15.

The effect of a reduction in required reserve ratios is also illustrated in the table. Of course if banks do not choose to increase their loans, they need not respond in any way to a decrease in required reserves. A decrease in the required reserve ratio while creating excess reserves is only permissive, but in normal times the profit motive will lead most banks to respond by increasing loans and deposits —and thus will lead to an increase in the money supply.

Increases in required reserve ratios force banks

[6] They will do this by gradually decreasing their loans and/or selling some of their securities. In the short term they may borrow from the Fed to give them time to meet the increased reserve requirements without disrupting financial markets.

Table 33–15(a)   Balance sheet for a loaned-up banking system with a 20 percent reserve ratio

Table 33–15(b)   Balance sheet for a loaned-up banking system after a change in reserve ratio to 25 percent

Assets		Liabilities		Assets		Liabilities	
Reserves	$1,000	Deposits	$5,000	Reserves	$1,000	Deposits	$4,000
Loans	4,100	Capital	100	Loans	3,100	Capital	100
	$5,100		$5,100		$4,100		$4,100

Increasing the required reserve ratio forces a loaned-up bank to reduce its deposits—and thus decreases the supply of deposit money. The banking system in part (a) of the table has a ratio of reserves to deposits of .20. If the Fed now raises the required reserve ratio to .25, the reserves of $1,000 will only support deposits of $4,000. As shown in (b), the banking system can reduce its deposits by reducing its loans. A reduction in reserve requirements from .25 to .20 would permit a banking system in the position of (b) to expand its loans and deposits to those of (a) with no increase in its dollar reserves.

with no excess reserves to decrease deposits and thereby reduce the money supply. Decreases in required reserve ratios permit banks to expand deposits and thus may increase the money supply.

CHANGES IN THE DISCOUNT RATE

The central bank can use the terms on which it will lend funds to the commercial banks to affect the money supply. Such borrowing by member banks is said to take place at the Fed's discount window. Increases in the discount rate discourage such borrowing and cause banks that desire or need extra reserves to get them instead by selling bonds or liquidating loans. These latter activities, as we shall see, have a contractionary effect on the money supply. Decreases in the discount rate make borrowing from the Fed cheaper and (other things being equal) encourage credit expansion and increases in the money supply.

OPEN MARKET OPERATIONS

The most important tool that the central bank has for influencing the supply of money is the purchase or sale of government securities on the open market. At the end of 1976 the Federal Reserve held about $100 billion in gov-

ernment securities. In December 1960 it held only $25 billion. At the end of 1972 it held about $70 billion. In a typical year, the Fed buys and sells $15 to $25 billion worth of government securities. What is the effect of such purchases and sales?[7]

Purchases and sales by the central bank of government securities in financial markets are known as **open market operations.** There are active and well-organized markets for government securities, just as there is a stock market, and you or I, or General Foods, or the Bank of America, or the Federal Reserve Bank of New York can enter this market and buy or sell negotiable government securities at whatever price supply and demand establishes. If the Fed buys securities, it does not know from whom it buys them. And if it sells securities, it knows not to whom it sells them. Moreover, it does not care because the effects on the money supply of the purchase or sale are the same no matter who is at the other end of the transaction.

[7] It is necessary for some purposes to distinguish between the Federal Reserve banks' occasional purchase of government securities directly from the Treasury and their purchase or sale of such securities on the open market. The two are different kinds of transactions and have different effects. We are now talking about the latter.

Purchases on the open market

If a Federal Reserve bank buys a bond from a household or firm, it pays for it with a check drawn on the central bank and payable to the seller. The seller will deposit this check in its own bank. The commercial bank will present the check to the Fed for payment, and the central bank will make a book entry increasing the deposit of the commercial bank at the central bank. At the end of these transactions, the central bank will have acquired a new asset in the form of a bond and a new liability in the form of a deposit by the private bank. The seller will have reduced its bond holdings and increased its deposits. The commercial bank will have a new deposit equal to the amount paid for the bond by the central bank. The commercial bank will find its reserves and its deposit liabilities increased by an equal amount.

If the central bank buys securities in the open market, this increases the reserves of the commercial banks and permits them to expand deposits, thereby increasing the money supply.

Table 33–16 shows the changes to the balance sheets of the several parties in response to a Federal Reserve bank purchase of $100 worth of government securities from a household. After these transactions, the commercial banks have excess reserves and are in a position to expand their loans and deposits. The household that sold the bond to the Fed receives a check from the Fed in payment. When the household deposits this check in its own commercial bank account, its bank is placed in the same position as was the bank in Table 33–4 which received the new deposit from the immigrant.

Suppose the seller of the security had been a commercial bank instead of a private house-

Table 33–16 Balance-sheet changes caused by an open market purchase from a household

PRIVATE HOUSEHOLD			
Assets		*Liabilities*	
Bonds	−$100	No change	
Deposits	+ 100		
COMMERCIAL BANKS			
Assets		*Liabilities*	
Reserves (deposits with central bank)	+$100	Demand deposits	+$100
CENTRAL BANK			
Assets		*Liabilities*	
Bond	+$100	Deposits of commercial banks	+$100

The money supply is increased when the Fed makes an open market purchase from a household. When the Fed buys a $100 bond from a household, the household gains money and gives up a bond, and the commercial banks gain a new deposit of $100—and thus new reserves of $100. Commercial banks can now engage in a multiple expansion of deposit money of the sort analyzed earlier in this chapter.

Table 33–17 Balance-sheet changes caused by an open-market purchase from a commercial bank

COMMERCIAL BANKS		
Assets		*Liabilities*
Reserves	+$100	No change
Bonds	– 100	

CENTRAL BANK		
Assets		*Liabilities*
Bonds	+$100	Deposits of commercial banks +$100

The money supply is increased when the Fed makes an open market purchase from a commercial bank. When the Fed buys a $100 bond directly from a commercial bank, there is no change in the assets or liabilities of households, but commercial banks gain an increase in their deposits with the Fed of $100; these are direct additions to their reserves. Commercial banks can now engage in a multiple expansion of deposit money of the sort analyzed earlier in this chapter.

hold or firm. It would have traded one asset (a security) for another asset (an increased deposit with the central bank). The latter, but not the former, is part of its reserves. Table 33–17 summarizes the changes that would have taken place. The commercial banks again find themselves with excess reserves and are in a position to expand the money supply by expanding loans and deposits or by purchasing securities.

If the central bank buys a large volume of securities in the open market, the whole banking system gains new reserves. Whether the seller is a household, a firm, or a bank, the purchase by the Federal Reserve of securities on the open market sets in motion a number of book transactions that increase the banking system's reserves and thus make possible a multiple expansion of credit.

Sales on the open market

If the central bank sells a security to a household or firm, it receives in return the buyer's check drawn against its own deposit in a commercial bank. The central bank presents the check to the private bank for payment. Payment is made merely by a book entry reducing the private bank's deposit at the central bank.

Now the central bank has reduced its assets by the value of the security it sold and reduced its liabilities in the form of the deposits of commercial banks. The household or firm has increased its holding of securities and reduced its cash on deposit with a commercial bank. The commercial bank has reduced its deposit liability to the household or firm and reduced its reserves (on deposit with the central bank) by the same amount. Each of the asset changes is balanced by a liability change. Indeed, everything balances! But the commercial bank finds that by suffering an equal change in its reserves and its deposit liabilities, its ratio of reserves to deposits falls. If this ratio was previously at the minimum acceptable level, the commercial bank will have to take immediate steps to restore its reserve ratio. The necessary reduction in deposits can be effected by not making new investments when old ones are redeemed (e.g., by not granting a new loan when old ones are repaid) or by selling (liquidating) existing investments.

To understand this, set up the balance sheet changes that correspond to the verbal description of this case and work through what would have happened if the central bank had sold the security directly to a commercial bank. In this case there should be a reduction in the commercial bank's reserves by the value of the securities sold by the central bank and (if reserves are pushed below acceptable levels) pressure to contract the volume of demand deposits in order to reestablish an acceptable reserve ratio.

If the central bank sells securities on the open market it decreases the reserves of the commercial banks and forces them to contract deposits, thereby decreasing the money supply.

The question now arises, What if the public doesn't want to play ball? How can the central bank force the public to buy securities? The answer, of course, is that there is always a price at which the public will buy, and the central bank in its open market operations must be prepared to have the price of the securities fall if it insists on suddenly selling a large volume of them. As we shall see, a fall in the price of securities is the same thing as a rise in interest rates, so if the Fed wishes to curtail the money supply by selling bonds it may well drive up interest rates.

Notice in Table 33–14 that the Fed's holdings of government securities are large relative to the reserves of commercial banks. Thus by selling securities it can contract those reserves very sharply if it chooses. Similarly, by buying securities it can expand them. In its open market operations the central bank clearly has a potent weapon for affecting the size of member bank reserves—and thus for affecting the money supply.

Summary

1. The banking system in the United States consists of two main elements: commercial banks and the Federal Reserve System, which is the central bank. Each of these has an important effect on the money supply.

2. The money supply is the stock of money in the country at some moment. It is defined in various ways: M_1 is currency plus demand deposits; M_2 adds to this time deposits of commercial banks; M_3 adds time deposits of savings and loan associations and similar thrift institutions.

3. American commercial banks are profit-seeking institutions that allow their customers to transfer demand deposits from one bank to another by means of checks. They create and destroy money as a by-product of their commercial operations—by making or liquidating loans and various other kinds of investments.

4. Because most customers are content to pay their accounts by check rather than by cash, the banks need not keep anything like a 100 percent reserve against their deposit liabilities. Because of this, banks can create deposit money. If the banking system receives a new cash deposit, it can create new deposits to some multiple of this amount. The amount of new deposits created depends on the legal minimum reserves the Federal Reserve enforces on the banks, the amount of cash drain to the public, and whether the banks are motivated to hold any excess reserves.

5. There is nothing automatic about expansion of the money supply when reserves of commercial banks increase. If bankers do not choose to use excess reserves to expand their investments there will be no expansion. In normal times it is profitable for bankers to keep excess reserves small, but in times of severe depression they may not find the investment risks worth taking.

6. All advanced free-market economies have a central bank that serves as banker for commercial banks, banker for the government, controller and regulator of the money supply, and regulator and supporter of money markets.

7. The central bank of the United States is the set of Federal Reserve banks and its board of governors. Although nominally privately owned and operated, the Reserve banks are in fact parts of a system that functions as a central bank, and the effective power is exercised by the board of governors whose seven members are appointed by the President of the United States for 14-year terms.

8. The Fed can affect the money supply in a variety of ways, each of which affects the reserves of the commercial banking system. Among these are changing required reserves, changing the rate of interest at which it will lend to commercial banks, and open market operations.

9. The major tool of control, or policy instrument, used by the Fed is open market operations. Purchases of bonds on the open market are expansionary because they create new deposits that permit (but do not force) a multiple expansion of bank credit. Sales on the open market reduce bank reserves and force a multiple contraction of bank credit on the part of all banks that do not have excess reserves.

Concepts for review

The banking system
Assets and liabilities of a commercial bank
The creation and destruction of deposit money
Reserve ratio, required reserves, and excess reserves
Functions of a central bank
The discount rate
Open market operations

Discussion questions

1. How would you expect the following to change the *relative size* of M_1, M_2, and M_3: (a) allowing interest payments on demand deposits, (b) rules setting the same maximum interest rate on time deposits in savings and loan associations as in commercial banks, (savings and loans are now higher), (c) printing of twice as much currency as is now printed annually.

2. Commercial banks in the United States are no longer allowed to issue their own bank notes. How do they now create money? (Explain the process carefully.) How do they make profits? Is it possible for them to create money without being aware of it?

3. The *Wall Street Journal* (in 1972) asked: "Why do we have reserve requirements anyway? . . . Even if there were no reserve requirements, a prudent banker would hold reserves, but the amount each would hold would be a function of his personal assessment of risk." What are your thoughts on these points raised by the *Wall Street Journal?* Might reserves be lower without regulation? Is regulation of reserve requirements just one more example of a spreading government bureaucracy that interferes with the efficient working of the market?

4. If all depositors tried to turn their deposits into cash at once, they would find that there are not sufficient reserves in the system to allow them all to do this at the same time. Why then do we not still have panicky runs on the banks? Would a 100 percent reserve requirement be safer? What effect would such a reserve requirement have on the banking system's ability to create money? Would it preclude any possibility of a panic?

5. The reciprocal of the required-reserve ratio indicates the maximum multiple expansion of demand deposits that can take place with an increase in member-bank reserves. Why is the actual expansion likely to be less than the maximum?

6. What would be the effect on the money supply of each of the following:
a. a decline in the public's confidence in the banks
b. a desire on the part of banks to increase their levels of excess reserves
c. the monopolizing of the banking system into a single super bank
d. the increased use of credit cards
e. the repeal of regulations preventing banks from paying interest on demand deposits

7. "Federal Reserve notes are money, right? 'Good as gold', they tell you. *Don't you believe it!* The Federal Reserve banks know better. They list their gold certificates as *assets*, but they list their Federal Reserve notes as *liabilities*." Is there a sensible explanation for this confusing state of affairs?

34

The importance of money

Economists still accept the insight of the early economists that relative prices are a major determinant of the real allocation of resources and that the quantity of money has a lot to do with determining the absolute level of prices. They also stress, however, that money may exert a strong influence on the real sector of the economy.

In this chapter we shall study the famous "quantity theory" of money, which can be used to link money to the price level. Then we shall study contemporary theory of the relation between money and the rest of the economy, and we shall see why most economists now hold that money does exert a significant effect on the behavior of important real magnitudes as well as on the level of money prices.

The classical link between the money supply and the price level: the quantity theory

The oldest theory of the relation between money and the price level is the **quantity theory of money** that predicts a proportional relation between the two. This theory, in modernized form, is still with us today.

As a first step in showing the links between the supply of money and the price level, it is necessary to understand why firms and households choose to hold money balances (that is, cash and demand deposits). There is a cost in holding any money balance because the money held could have been used to purchase bonds instead and would then have earned interest as a return. It could, for example, be deposited with a savings and loan association or used to buy a 30-day treasury bill.

The opportunity cost of holding each dollar of money balances is the rate of interest that could have been earned if the money had been used to purchase bonds.

Clearly, then, money will be held only if it provides services to the holders that are at least as valuable as the opportunity cost of holding it.

The total amount of money balances that everyone wishes to hold for all purposes is called the **demand for money.**[1]

THE TRANSACTIONS DEMAND FOR MONEY

The reason for wanting to hold money originally stressed in the quantity theory is the so-called transactions motive. It is still thought to be important, although it is no longer believed to be the only major motive for holding money.

Virtually all transactions in an economy require money. Money is passed from households to firms to pay for the goods and services produced by firms; and money is passed from firms to households to pay for the factor services supplied by households to firms. These transactions force both firms and households to hold money balances called **transactions balances.**[2]

Consider the balances held because of wage payments. Assume, for purposes of illustration, that firms pay wages every Friday and that households spend all their wages on the purchase of goods and services, with the expenditure being spread out evenly over the week. Thus on Friday morning firms must hold balances equal to the weekly wage bill; on Friday afternoon households will hold these balances. Over the week, households' balances will be drawn down as a result of pur-

chasing goods and services. Over the same period, the balances held by firms will build up as a result of selling goods and services until, on the following Friday morning, firms will again have amassed balances equal to the wage bill that must be met on that day. On the average over the week, firms will hold balances equal to half the wage bill and so will households; thus total money balances held will be equal to the total weekly wage bill.

The size of these transactions balances depends, therefore, on the size of the wage bill. If the wage bill doubles, either because twice as many people are employed at the same rate or because the same number is employed at twice the wage rate, the balances held must double. The argument has been conducted in terms of the wage bill, but a similar analysis holds for payments for all factor services.

Because the size of the wage bill and other payments tend to vary directly with the level of national income, the transactions demand tends to vary directly with the level of national income.

Transactions balances must be held because payments and receipts are not perfectly synchronized. The more often that wages are paid, the more nearly synchronized payments and receipts will be and the smaller will the balance held need to be. Changes in social institutions such as the pattern of paying bills will thus affect the transaction balances required. Assume—an extreme example—that wages are paid daily instead of weekly. On the average, the total balances required will be equal to the total *daily* wage bill, which is of course only a fraction of the weekly wage bill, and thus a change to a shorter pay period should lead to a lower transactions demand for money.

A change in the pay period is only one example of an institutional change that can alter the transactions demand for money. A current example is the growth of short-term money substitutes such as credit cards. With short-term consumer credit you can come

---

[1] Notice that the quantity of money is a stock and that the demand for it is a demand for a stock: People wish to hold so many dollars in cash or deposits. This makes the demand for money different from the demand for goods, which is (usually) a flow demand. When we say, for example, that the demand for carrots is 7 million tons, we must say over what time period this is measured. If we specify "per month," then the demand is to purchase a flow of carrots of 7 million tons each month.

[2] The phrase "transactions balances" is a shorthand way of saying "*transactions* motive for holding money *balances*." The money itself is not earmarked for a particular purpose.

much closer to synchronizing your payments with your receipts. If, for example, you can charge all of your purchases and then pay the charge accounts on payday, you do not need transactions balances except during the small interval between receipt of your pay and paying your bills.

In most societies perfect synchronization of payments and receipts is not possible and transactions balances must be held. For given social institutions these balances will tend to vary directly with national income.

ASSUMPTIONS OF THE QUANTITY THEORY

The demand for money. The quantity theory assumes that the demand for money changes directly and in strict proportion to the level of national income—an assumption that is not unreasonable if the transactions demand is the only source of the desire to hold money balances.

To express this assumption in symbolic terms, let M_d stand for the demand for money, let Y stand for real national income, and let P stand for the average price at which goods and services are sold in the markets of the economy.[3] Then we can write the assumed relationship as

$$M_d = kPY$$

where k is a constant showing desired money balances as a fraction of the value of annual national income. If firms and households hold money balances equal to the value of two weeks' sales and purchases, k would be $\frac{1}{26}$ and the demand for money could be expressed as $M_d = 0.038PY$.

The supply of money. For the moment we shall assume that the overall quantity of money, which we designate by M, can be set at any amount desired by the Federal Reserve System operating in its capacity as the nation's central bank. Within broad limits, as we have seen, the privately owned commercial banks can exercise considerable control over the money supply. The limits themselves are determined by the central bank, which has the ultimate power to control major changes in the supply of money.

The demand for money and aggregate demand. The link between money and aggregate demand for commodities is provided in the classical quantity theory by the assumption that when firms and households do not hold the amount of money that they would like to hold, they try to alter their money holdings by altering their expenditures on commodities. If they have more money than they wish to hold, they raise their expenditures above their receipts so as to spend their unwanted money balances. This raises aggregate demand. If they have less money than they wish to hold, they cut their spending below their receipts so as to increase their holdings. This lowers aggregate demand.[4]

EFFECTS OF CHANGES IN THE MONEY SUPPLY: FULL EMPLOYMENT

Armed with these three assumptions, let us examine how changes in the money supply affect the economy. This is most conveniently studied first in the two extreme cases of full employment and heavy unemployment and then more generally.

Assume for the moment, as did most

---

[3] Up to now we have let Y stand for national income without distinguishing money and real income, since we had assumed constant prices. We now relax that assumption and need a more complex notation in which Y is real (constant-dollar) national income and PY is money national income.

[4] One important difference between the classical quantity theory and what may be called the modern quantity theory is this link between money and aggregate demand. Modern quantity theorists, along with other modern economists, recognize that the link will usually be indirect—from money to interest rates to expenditure—rather than from money directly to expenditure.

economists of 70 years ago, that full employment is the natural state of the economy, that any lapses from this state will be temporary and self-correcting, and that the full-employment income, Y_F, changes only slowly. Total output will thus usually be the full-employment output. In such a situation, changes in aggregate demand cannot cause changes in total output. If quantity produced is constant at the full-employment level, variations in aggregate demand can cause variations only in prices. If there is excess aggregate demand, prices must rise until the money value of aggregate output is made equal to aggregate demand measured in money terms. If aggregate demand is not sufficient to purchase full-employment output valued at existing prices, then the price level will fall until once again the value of total output is equal to the value of aggregate demand.

Now assume that in this sort of situation there is an increase in the supply of money. Firms and households do not wish to hold this additional money, so they spend it. This adds to aggregate demand at full employment and bids up prices. As prices rise, more money is required for transactions purposes. Eventually the price rise will be sufficient so that all of the extra money will be absorbed into transaction balances. When this happens, aggregate desired expenditure will no longer exceed income and the pressure for further price rises will be gone.

Now assume a drastic fall in the money supply. According to the quantity theory, firms and households will try to cut their spending in order to build up their holdings of cash. This reduces aggregate demand below income and in turn causes prices to fall (assuming output remains at the full-employment level). As prices fall, smaller transactions balances are required. Eventually prices will fall sufficiently so that the existing supply of money will be enough to satisfy everyone's transactions needs. People will

then no longer be trying to hold their spending below their income in order to add to their cash balances and the downward pressure on prices will cease.

EFFECTS OF CHANGES IN THE MONEY SUPPLY: UNEMPLOYMENT

When originally developed, the quantity theory was part of the classical model in which the equilibrium level of national income was always at full employment. But times change, and with them the assumptions that it seems interesting to use in one's theory. Just as Keynesian theory, originally developed to handle situations of deflationary gaps, can be adapted to analyze inflationary gaps, so the quantity theory can be adapted to handle situations of persistent unemployment.

This is easily done by considering situations in which the price level is fixed and there is unemployment in the economy. Now changes in aggregate demand brought about by changes in the supply of money will cause real income and employment to change in just the way that they change when aggregate demand changes for any other reason (see Chapter 28). In these circumstances the quantity theory becomes a theory of variations in real national income in response to monetary changes in the economy.

THE MODIFIED QUANTITY THEORY

The two extreme cases can be combined into a general case by using the L-shaped relation first encountered on page 520. In a situation where the L-shaped relation applies, increases in aggregate demand affect output, not prices, until full employment is reached. After that they affect prices, not output. Similarly, decreases in aggregate demand can reduce inflationary pressures to zero, but thereafter they are met by decreases in output and employment, not decreases in prices. In this modified

A formal statement of the quantity theory

The basic equations of the theory are given in the table. Equation [1] says that the demand for money depends on the value of transactions. Equation [2] says that the supply of money is a constant, M (set by the central bank at whatever level it desires). Equation [3] states the equilibrium condition that the demand for money must equal its supply. Substitution produces the basic relation among P, M, and Y as shown in Equations [4], [4a], and [4b].

Simple quantity theory. The original form of the quantity theory assumes that k is a constant given by the transaction demand for money and that Y is constant because of full employment. Thus M and P move proportionally; see Equation [4a]. Increases or decreases in the money supply lead to proportional increases or decreases in prices.

Modified quantity theory. The L-shaped relation modifies the simple quantity theory. It embodies two distinct assumptions: first, that the price level never falls, and second, that different variables are fixed in different situations.

THE EQUATIONS OF THE QUANTITY THEORY		
Demand for money	$M_d = kPY$	[1]
Supply of money	$M_s \equiv M$	[2]
Equilibrium condition	$M_d = M_s$	[3]
Equations [1], [2], and [3] give	$kPY = M$	[4]
Equation [4] may be rewritten as		
	$P = \left(\dfrac{1}{kY}\right) M$	[4a]
	$Y = \left(\dfrac{1}{kP}\right) M$	[4b]

For increases in M in full-employment situations, [4a] applies. The real level of national income, Y, is a constant, thus making the entire expression $1/kY$ a constant. In these circumstances the price level, P, rises in direct proportion to increases in M.

For changes in M in less than full-employment situations, and for decreases in M when at full employment with stable prices, [4b] applies. The price level, P, is constant, thus making the entire expression $1/kP$ a constant. In such circumstances, real national income, Y, varies in direct proportion to M.

quantity theory, the link between money and the level of aggregate demand is retained, but the consequences of changes in aggregate demand vary depending on whether there is full employment or unemployment.

The modified quantity theory makes the following predictions:

1. In situations of unemployment, changes in the quantity of money lead to changes in the levels of output and employment, with the price level unchanged.

2. In situations of full employment, increases in the quantity of money lead to increases in the price level, with output and employment unchanged.

3. In situations of full employment, decreases in the quantity of money first relieve any inflationary pressures and then lead to decreases in the level of employment and output once prices are stabilized.

In this theory the central bank by virtue of its control over the money supply has in its hands a powerful weapon for controlling prices and incomes. In some economic situations a change in the money supply will have its major effect on prices; in other situations the major effects will be on output and employment. (See the box on page 639 for a formal demonstration of these propositions.)

A modern view of the role of money

Modern theories of the role of money do not use the direct link between money and ag-gregate expenditure that the classical quantity theory employs. This is true both of modern monetarists and of neo-Keynesians. Since the indirect linkage is of critical importance to Keynesian theory, we shall discuss it in that context.

Keynesian theories emphasize the function of money as a store of wealth. They assume that if households have more of their wealth in the form of money than they wish, they do not immediately spend the extra money; instead they try to spend their surplus money on interest-earning assets, thereby merely transferring their wealth from one form, money, to another form, interest-earning assets. But this sort of transfer has an

---

The velocity of circulation and money balances

Often the quantity theory is presented using the concept of the velocity of circulation, V, instead of the proportion of the money income that people wish to hold in cash, k. The **velocity of circulation** is defined as national income divided by the quantity of money (Y/M). It may be interpreted as showing the average amount of "work" done by a unit of money while acting as a medium of exchange for the transactions that produce the country's national income. Thus, if the annual national income is $1,200 billion and the stock of money is $300 billion, then each dollar's worth of money is used 4 times on average to effect the exchanges required in producing national income.

Fortunately, there is a simple relation between k and V: One is the reciprocal of the other, as shown in the table. Thus it makes no difference whether we choose to work with k or V. An example may help to illustrate the interpretation of each. As-sume that the stock of money people wish to hold is equal to one-fifth of the value of the transactions. Thus k is 0.2 and V, the reciprocal of k, is 5. This indicates that if the money supply is to be one-fifth of the value of annual transactions, the average unit of money must account for $5 worth of transactions—that is, each dollar must be used on average 5 times in order to bring about an aggregate value of national income 5 times as large as the stock of money.

FROM K TO V

If the demand for money, kPY, equals the supply, M, we have, from the box on page 639.

$$kPY = M \qquad [4]$$

Rewriting [4] gives

$$PY = M\frac{1}{k} \qquad [5]$$

Letting V stand for $1/k$ gives

$$PY = MV \qquad [6]$$

effect on interest rates, through interest rates on investment and consumption, and finally on national income. The study of this sequence of events begins with the Keynesian view of the demand for money.

THE DEMAND FOR MONEY

Transactions demand, once again

The transactions demand for money, which played a key role in the argument of the quantity theorists, is one element (among several) in contemporary theories. Keynesians expect, as did the quantity theorists, that the transactions demand will take the form of currency and demand deposits and will rise and fall directly with the level of national income.

The transactions demand for money is also expected to be related to the rate of interest because wealth held as money is not earning interest for its owners. Thus, other things being equal, people are motivated to reduce their balances of idle cash to a minimum. One way this can be done is to make frequent switches between money and other assets. Consider a man who is paid monthly. He can hold all his unspent income in a demand deposit at his bank, in which case he will have an average transaction balance equal to half his monthly salary. But he could, dividing the month into four quarters, keep only a quarter of his salary in cash at payday and invest the other three-quarters in interest-yielding assets. Then, at the start of the second quarter, he would cash in a third of his assets and obtain enough cash to finance the second quarter's expenditure. He would do the same at the start of the third quarter and at the start of the fourth quarter when he would cash in the last of his assets. In this way he reduces his average transactions holding to one-eighth of a month's income (at the start of each quarter-month he has one-fourth of a month's income as a balance and by the end of the quarter he is down to nothing) and corre-

spondingly increases his average holding of interest-earning assets.

A similar line of argument could be used to show that if the same man made *daily* transfers of funds he could reduce his transactions balances yet further. But obviously the sensible arrangement will depend on how much interest can be earned and how costly (in terms of such things as trips to the bank, inconvenience, and brokerage fees) it is to switch assets. Since these transactions costs are certainly not negligible, balances held to meet transaction demands will not be negligible.

The higher the rate of return on interest-earning assets, the greater is the inducement to invest available funds rather than to hold money to bridge the gaps between receipts and payments. Put differently, in order to hold a smaller quantity of transactions balances, an individual must make more frequent switches between money and other assets and incur higher costs. The modern theory of transactions balances predicts that these costs will be less of an inhibition the higher is the rate of interest, and thus that the amount of money held for transactions purposes will be lower the higher is the rate of interest.

The precautionary motive

Uncertainty plays no role in the need for transactions balances. If there is uncertainty about the exact timing of receipts and payments, people will tend to hold extra money balances. Many goods and services are sold on credit, and the seller can never be quite certain when these goods will be paid for, whereas the buyer can never be quite certain of the day of delivery and thus of the day on which payment will fall due. In order to be able to continue in business without a recurring series of cash crises during times in which receipts are abnormally low and/or disbursements are abnormally high, firms carry money balances for precautionary motives. These are called **precautionary balances.** The larger such balances, the greater is the degree of insurance against being unable to pay bills because of some temporary fluctuation in either receipts or disbursements. If the firm is pressed for cash or has other very profitable uses for its funds, it may run down these balances and take the risk of being caught by some temporary fluctuations in receipts and disbursements. How serious this risk is depends on the penalties of being caught without sufficient reserves by some temporary fluctuation. A firm is unlikely to be pushed into insolvency, but it may have to incur considerable costs if it is forced to borrow money at high interest rates for short periods in order to meet such temporary crises.

The protection provided by a given quantity of precautionary balances depends on the volume of payments and receipts. A $100 precautionary balance provides a large cushion (50 percent) for a person whose volume of payments per month is $200, and a very small cushion (1 percent) for a firm whose monthly volume is $10,000. Haphazard fluctuations of the sort that give rise to precautionary balances may be expected to vary directly with dollar volume. To provide the same degree of protection as the volume of business rises, more money is necessary. Thus the firm's precautionary demand for money is expected to rise as the value of its sales rises. Aggregating over all firms and households, the total precautionary demand for money will rise as national income rises.

Firms can also be expected to hold more funds for precautionary purposes the lower the opportunity cost of holding such funds. If the market rate of interest provides a measure of how expensive it is to hold funds, then the precautionary demand for money can be expected to vary inversely with the rate of interest as well as directly with the level of income.[5]

[5] Institutional arrangements affect the precautionary demand just as they affect the transactions demand. In the past, for example, a traveler would have had to carry a substantial precautionary balance in cash, but today a credit card covers most unforeseen expenses that may arise while traveling.

THE SPECULATIVE MOTIVE

Whereas the transactions and precautionary motives emphasize money's role as a medium of exchange, the speculative motive emphasizes its role as a store of wealth. A household or firm can hold its wealth in money or in such interest-earning assets as bonds.[6] If there were perfect certainty that the price of bonds would never change there would be no speculative reason to hold any wealth in the form of money since bonds yield an interest payment while money does not.

But bond prices *do* change, and people form expectations about the direction of change. If the price of bonds is very high in relation to what people think is the normal price, people may wish to sell bonds now and postpone intended purchases of bonds until prices have come down. In such a situation, large quantities of money may be held in anticipation of a more favorable chance to purchase bonds in the future. If, however, the price of bonds is very low in relation to what is thought to be the normal price, the desire will be to buy bonds now and to postpone sales until a more favorable price can be obtained. In this case the tendency will be to hold as little money as possible and to hold bonds instead.

Balances held in anticipation of a fall in the price of assets are called **speculative balances**.[7] Use of the word speculative should not connote a frivolous desire to gamble. Instead it reflects the need to make decisions in a world in which prices fluctuate. The future is never certain, so any transaction that takes place over time is necessarily somewhat speculative. This applies to anything that is bought and sold, including stocks and bonds.

[6] For simplicity, attention is here confined to bonds and the bond market, but similar statements apply to stocks and the stock market.

[7] Once again this is a shorthand term for "*speculative* motive for holding money *balances.*" We have now introduced three motives for holding money balances—transactions, precautionary, speculative. The money is of course a single balance that may be used for each or all of these purposes.

If a household or a firm is holding reserves in the form of bonds, it is taking a risk that the bonds may fall in value. If the household or firm becomes convinced that prices will fall, the prudent act is to sell the bonds now and hold money instead. If this happens, speculative balances of money will be increased. Once bond prices are regarded as low and likely to rise, the prudent thing to do is to convert excess money into bonds.[8] If this happens, speculative balances of money will be decreased.

The influence of interest rates on the demand for money

We have seen that economists today identify several motives for holding money. *The interest rate affects each one.* The market rate of interest reflects the opportunity cost of money holdings (the money could be lent out and earn the market rate). Thus, the higher the rate of interest, the higher is the cost of holding money and the less money will be held for transactions and precautionary purposes. The rate of interest also influences decisions as to whether to hold money for speculative purposes. This occurs because of the inverse relationship between prices of bonds and interest rates. (This relationship is important; it is discussed in the box on page 644.) If the interest rate that can be earned on a bond seems low relative to long-term expectations, bond prices will seem high and bonds will be relatively unattractive to investors. People will tend to want to reduce their stock of bonds and build up their speculative balances. If interest rates seem high, bonds will seem low priced and will be attractive to investors; as investors buy bonds, speculative balances will be drawn down. Thus an inverse

[8] People who are *certain* about the direction in which they expect the price of bonds to move will tend to hold all their wealth in bonds (price of bonds expected to rise) or all their wealth in money (price of bonds expected to fall). When holders of wealth are uncertain about what will happen to bond prices in the future, many of them will want to hedge their bets by holding both bonds and money.

Figure 34-1 Two liquidity preference schedules

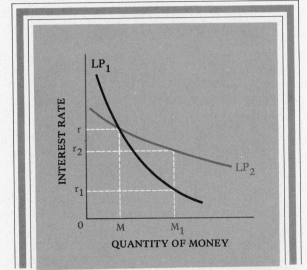

The *LP* schedule is downward sloping because a decrease in interest rates leads people to desire to hold larger money balances. The steeper the *LP* curve the greater the change in interest rates required to induce a given change in money holdings. LP_1 and LP_2 are alternative liquidity preference schedules. Suppose the money supply is *M* and the rate of interest is *r*. With either *LP* schedule people are holding the quantity of money they desire to hold. In order to persuade them to hold the extra money balances, MM_1, it is necessary for interest rates to fall—thereby lowering the opportunity cost of money balances and inducing the holding of speculative balances. If the *LP* curve is flat, as in LP_2, a relatively small reduction in *r* to r_2 suffices. If the *LP* curve is steep, as in LP_1, a large fall in interest rates to r_1 is required. LP_1 is said to be interest inelastic relative to LP_2.

relation between interest rates and the demand for money is predicted for speculative as well as for transaction and precautionary motives.

The inverse relation between bond prices and interest rates

A bond is a promise by the issuer to pay a stated sum of money as interest each year and to repay the face value of the bond at some future date, often 30 or more years distant. Some bonds, called perpetuities, simply pay interest forever and never repay the principal. For any bond, the price of the bond reflects the value of the stream of future payments its owner will receive.

The relationship between interest rates and bond prices is most easily seen in the case of a perpetuity. Assume that such a bond will pay $100 per year to its holder. The *present value* of this bond depends upon how much $100 per year is worth, and this in turn depends upon the rate of interest. (The discussion of the concept of present value in Chapter 22, pages 370–372, may profitably be read at this time.) A bond that will produce a stream of income of $100 a year forever is worth $1,000 at 10 percent interest because $1,000 invested at 10 percent per annum will yield $100 interest per year forever. But the same asset is worth $2,000 if the interest rate is 5 percent

per year because it takes $2,000 invested at 5 percent per annum to yield $100 interest per year. The lower the rate of interest obtainable on the market, the more valuable is a bond paying a fixed amount of interest. What is true of the perpetuity is equally true of any asset whose value arises from the stream of future income it produces, although the calculation of present value may be more complex if payments are irregularly spaced in the future and include a lump sum repayment of principal at maturity.

In general, the present value of an asset is inversely related to the interest rate.

Two important corollaries of this proposition are:

1. If the rate of interest falls, the value of an asset producing a given income stream rises.

2. If the market price of an asset producing a fixed income is forced up, this is equivalent to a decrease in the rate of interest earned by the asset.

When households and firms decide how much of their monetary assets they will hold as money rather than as bonds (and other interest-earning assets), they are said to be exercising their preference for liquidity. **Liquidity preference** thus refers to the demand to hold assets in the form of money rather than as interest-earning wealth. The schedule relating the demand for money to the interest rate is called the **liquidity preference schedule.** Two *LP* schedules are illustrated in Figure 34–1.

A recapitulation of the demand for money

The demand for money is defined as the total amount of money balances that everyone in the economy wishes to hold.

The previous discussion about the motives for holding money can be summarized by listing two hypotheses about the demand for money to hold.

1. The demand for money varies directly with the level of income.

2. The demand for money varies inversely with the rate of interest.

Both transaction and precautionary motives lead to the first hypothesis, and they are joined by the speculative motive in leading to the second hypothesis.

These hypotheses are critical to the modern Keynesian view of the role of money. But they are accepted by virtually all economists including the modern successors to the quantity theorists. Where contemporary economists disagree is on the relative importance of the two influences and on the shape of the liquidity preference schedule.

INTEREST RATES AND AGGREGATE DEMAND

The first link in the chain relating monetary changes to changes in the real sector is from money supply to interest rates. The second link is from interest rates to aggregate demand. We saw in Chapter 29 that expenditures on consumer durables, on inventory accumulation, on residential construction, and (possibly) on plant and equipment are all expected to respond to changes in the rate of interest. Other things being equal, a decrease in the rate of interest makes borrowing cheaper and also makes it less costly to have funds tied up in such non-interest-yielding assets as machines, houses, and consumer durables. Thus a decrease in interest rates is predicted to touch off bouts of new expenditure.[9]

The marginal efficiency of investment schedule

Modern economists hypothesize that overall there will be an inverse relation between the rate of interest and the quantity of invest-

Figure 34–2 Two marginal efficiency of investment schedules

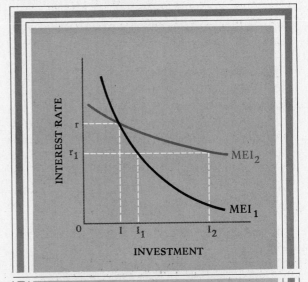

The *MEI* curve is downward sloping because a fall in the rate of interest increases the amount of investment. The steeper the *MEI* curve, the smaller the investment response to a given fall in interest rates. MEI_1 and MEI_2 are alternative marginal efficiency of investment schedules. Suppose the interest rate is r and the quantity of investment per period is I. With either *MEI* schedule people are investing the amount they wish. If the interest rate falls from r to r_1, each schedule predicts an increase in the level of investment. If MEI_1 applies, the increase in investment is relatively small, from I to I_1. If MEI_2 applies, a larger increase in investment occurs, from I to I_2. MEI_1 is said to be interest inelastic relative to MEI_2.

ment.[10] A schedule that summarizes the relation between investment and the rate of interest is often called the **marginal efficiency of**

---

[9] If this is not clear to you, review pages 531–540. While both consumption and investment may be expected to respond to changes in interest rates, Keynesian theory puts major emphasis on investment. We shall follow that emphasis here.

[10] As we saw on pages 537–540 (Chapter 29) the timing of investment in response to changes in interest rates may be complex; low interest rates may induce a temporary bout of new investment rather than a permanent increase.

investment (*MEI*) schedule; when graphed it plots the amount of investment per year on the horizontal axis and the rate of interest on the vertical axis. It relates the flow of investment per year to the rate of interest. Figure 34–2 shows two different *MEI* schedules.[11] Much of the debate about the effect of the interest rate on the volume of investment concerns how steep the *MEI* schedule is. The steeper it is, the smaller will be the change in investment in response to a given change in interest rates.

HOW MONEY SUPPLY AFFECTS NATIONAL INCOME

Using the concepts of *MEI* and liquidity preference, we can trace the effects of a change in money supply on aggregate demand—and thus on national income. This effect occurs through asset substitutions. The key assumption about behavior is that when people have excess money balances they seek to buy financial assets and when they have deficient money balances they seek to replenish their balances by selling financial assets. Let us look at the process in greater detail.

An increase in the money supply

Assume that the central bank and the banking system increase the supply of money until there is a 10 percent increase in the amount of money held by firms and households. Assume that firms and households attempt to use this extra money by buying bonds. The sudden rise in demand forces up the price of existing bonds and thereby causes the interest rate to fall until it reaches the point where people are willing to hold the additional supply of money because of both the speculative motive ("Hmm, bonds are getting pretty

expensive") and the precautionary motive (there has been a fall in the opportunity cost of holding money in reserve for all sorts of unexpected events). Thus the effect of an increase in the money supply is to lower the rate of interest.

The fall in interest rates will in turn affect spending if investment and consumption are at all sensitive to interest rates. This causes an upward shift of the aggregate demand function, which leads in turn, via the familiar multiplier, to an increase in national income. The process is illustrated in Figure 34–3.[12]

A decrease in the money supply

Now assume that the central bank decreases the money supply. Firms and households find that they do not have, and cannot so easily borrow, all the money they would like to hold at the going rate of interest. They try to convert some bond holdings into money. This rush to sell bonds forces bond prices down, which means a rise in interest rates; this in turn causes a reduction in investment and interest-sensitive consumption. Aggregate demand shifts downward. The multiplier process is now thrown into reverse, and national income falls by some multiple of the decline in investment spending.

Because a change in the money supply changes interest rates—and thereby investment and national income—the influence of money is spread throughout the whole economic system. The money supply is linked to aggregate demand by the interest rate. For this reason, money is not neutral in modern macroeconomics.

---

[11] It is important to distinguish the *MEI* schedule from the *MEC* schedule encountered in Chapter 22. *MEC* relates interest rates to the size of the capital *stock,* not to the flow of investment per year. Of course, to increase the capital stock it is necessary to invest until the new capital is created.

[12] In order to deal with these effects in as simple a manner as possible, this and subsequent figures abstract from the transactions demand for money. Only the influence of variations in the money supply on interest rates is allowed for. A complete analysis that allows for all effects—but does not change any of the conclusions in the text—is given in the appendix to this chapter.

Figure 34–3   The effect on national income of a change in the quantity of money

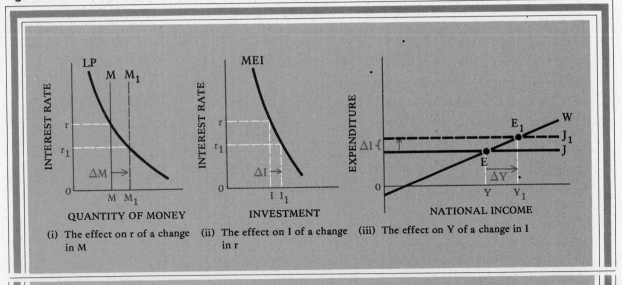

(i) The effect on r of a change in M

(ii) The effect on I of a change in r

(iii) The effect on Y of a change in I

An increase in the quantity of money drives down the rate of interest by raising the price of bonds; this increases investment and thus increases national income. (i) Initially the interest rate is at the level r and a quantity of money, M, is being held for precautionary and speculative reasons. The supply of money available for these purposes is increased by ΔM. At the ruling rate of interest, no one wishes to hold this extra money and everyone attempts to buy bonds with it. This forces the price of bonds up and the rate of interest down until at the interest rate r_1 all the additional money is absorbed into speculative and precautionary balances.
(ii) A fall in the rate of interest from r to r_1 increases the quantity of investment expenditure by ΔI.
(iii) The original equilibrium level of national income is Y. The rise in investment of ΔI is a rise in injections from J to J_1. Equilibrium national income rises by ΔY.

THE IMPACT OF MONETARY POLICY

The predictions developed so far concern the direction of the change in aggregate demand and income; the magnitude of the predicted effect depends on the shapes of the schedules for liquidity preference and marginal efficiency of investment. The influences of the shapes of these two schedules may be summarized:

1. A change in the money supply will have a larger effect on interest rates the steeper (less interest elastic[13]) the *LP* schedule.

2. A change in the rate of interest will have a larger effect on investment, and hence on national income, the flatter (more interest elastic[14]) the *MEI* schedule.

The combination of schedules that gives the largest effect on national income for a given change in the money supply is a steep *LP* schedule and a flat *MEI* schedule. The combination that leads to the smallest effect is a flat *LP* schedule and a steep *MEI* schedule.

[13] The elasticity of this schedule is defined as the percentage change in the quantity of money demanded, divided by the percentage change in the rate of interest.

[14] The elasticity of this schedule is defined as the percentage change in investment, divided by the percentage change in the rate of interest.

Figure 34-4 The quantitative effectiveness of monetary policy

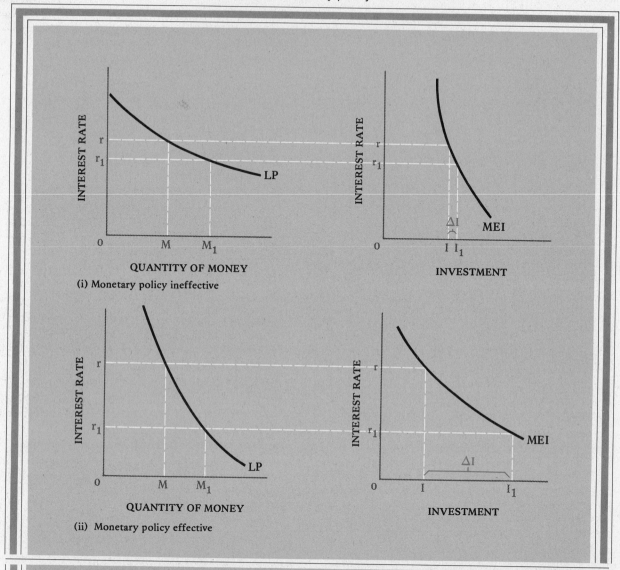

(i) Monetary policy ineffective

(ii) Monetary policy effective

Monetary policy is most effective when the *LP* curve is very inelastic and the *MEI* curve is very elastic. In both parts (i) and (ii) the same increase in the money supply from *M* to M_1 brings the rate of interest down from *r* to r_1. This fall in *r* leads to an increase in investment from *I* to I_1 (= ΔI). This new investment is an injection into the circular flow. The shapes of the curves in (i) cause monetary policy to have a small effect, while the shapes of the curves in (ii) cause monetary policy to have a large effect on investment—and thus on national income.

The implications of these shapes for deciding whether changing the money supply is an effective instrument for changing national income should be apparent. Not surprisingly, much of the controversy about the effectiveness of the money supply as a means for influencing national income—and thus monetary policy—has centered around the shapes of these two schedules. The more responsive investment is to changes in interest rates and the more responsive interest rates are to the change in the money supply, the more effective will be a given change in the money supply. This is illustrated in Figure 34–4 and will be elaborated on in Chapter 41.

Summary

1. The quantity theory of money provided early economists with the link between the money supply and the price level. They assumed that the transactions motive was the sole source of the demand for money—and that the demand for money was directly proportional to the level of national income.

2. Other assumptions of the quantity theory were that the supply of money was determined by the central bank and that when households and firms have more (or less) money than they wish, they increase (or decrease) their expenditures on goods and services to restore the desired money balances. An increase in the money supply leads to an increase in aggregate demand; a decrease in the money supply to a decrease in aggregate demand.

3. Given full employment (which the classical economists assumed to be the natural state of affairs), changes in the money supply lead to proportional changes in the price level with no changes in real output. Formally, since $P = \left(\frac{1}{kY}\right)M$ and the expression in brackets is assumed constant, M and P necessarily vary in direct proportion.

4. The quantity theory can be adapted to situations of unemployment. Given substantial unemployment, changes in the money supply lead to changes in the level of aggregate demand, which lead to changes in the price level until full employment is restored. Formally, since $Y = \left(\frac{1}{kP}\right)M$ and the expression in brackets is assumed constant, M and Y vary in direct proportion.

5. The modified quantity theory combines the two extreme cases summarized in points 3 and 4. It predicts that starting from a position of equilibrium, changes in the supply of money will lead to changes in aggregate demand. The effects of such changes will be mainly on prices if full employment exists or mainly on real income and employment if there is unemployment with rigid prices.

6. The modern view of the role of money begins by recognizing additional motives for holding money: the precautionary motive and the speculative motive. These motives have the effect of making the demand for money depend on the rate of interest as well as on national income. They create a link between the monetary and the real sectors of the economy via the rate of interest.

7. In this theory, a rise in the quantity of money leads to an attempt to purchase bonds, thereby pushing up the price of bonds and lowering the rate of interest. This leads to a rise in such interest-sensitive expenditures as investment and thus to a rise in income and employment (if there is unemployment) or in the price level (if there is full employment). A fall in the quantity of money has the opposite effects.

8. A given change in the money supply will have larger effects on national income (a) the more inelastic is the liquidity preference schedule and (b) the more elastic is the marginal efficiency of investment schedule. A highly elastic *LP* schedule together with a highly inelastic *MEI* schedule means that large changes in the quantity of money will bring about small changes in national income. An inelastic *LP* schedule together with an elastic *MEI* schedule will bring about large changes in national income. Thus these shapes affect the effectiveness of monetary policy.

9. A formal model of national income determination that links expenditure effects (discussed in Part Eight) and monetary effects (discussed in this part) is usually left to a more advanced course. The components of such an integrated model have all been specified; they are put together in the appendix to this chapter, which begins on page 890.

Concepts for review

Transactions, precautionary, and speculative motives for
holding money
The classical quantity theory of money
The modified quantity theory
The liquidity preference (*LP*) function
The marginal efficiency of investment (*MEI*) function
The shape of *LP* and *MEI* and the effect on national income of changes in the money supply.

Discussion questions

1. Describing a possible future "cashless society," a public report recently said: "In the cashless society of the future, a customer could insert a plastic card into a machine at a store and the amount of the purchase would be deducted from his 'bank account' in the computer automatically and transferred to the store's account. No cash or checks would ever change hands." What would such an institutional change do to the various motives for holding money balances? What functions would remain for commercial banks and for the central bank if money as we now know it disappeared in this fashion? What benefits and disadvantages can you see in such a scheme?

2. What motives do you think explain the following holdings?

a. the currency and coins in the cash register of the local supermarket at the start of each working day
b. the payroll account of Ford Motor Company in the local bank
c. cash holdings by a mutual investment trust fund that believes stock prices are going to fall
d. certificates of deposit that mature after one's retirement
e. the holdings of government bonds by private individuals

3. What would be the effects on the economy if Congress were to vote a once-and-for-all universal social dividend of $5,000 paid to every American over the age of 17 to be financed by the creation of new money? Would modern economists differ from classical quantity theorists in their analysis of its effects?

4. What sort of situation might lead a society to have a very flat liquidity preference schedule and a very steep marginal efficiency of investment schedule? Is this a good combination for those who wish to affect the level of income by changing the money supply?

5. One relationship encountered in this chapter and elsewhere is the inverse one between bond prices and interest rates. Be sure that you can explain just why this occurs. Is this a special feature of bonds, or does it apply to the value of other earning assets as well?

6. Suppose you are sure that the Fed is going to engage in policies that decrease the money supply sharply starting next month. How could you make speculative profits by purchases or sales of bonds now?

Monetary policy

We have seen that the central bank can affect the quantity of money and that the quantity of money can affect national income. This chapter looks at the use of monetary policy in the United States.

Objectives and instruments of monetary policy

Policy variables

Monetary policy is employed with certain ultimate objectives of policy in view. The variables that the authorities are interested in controlling—the objects of their policy—are called **policy variables.** The major policy variable that we shall consider in this chapter is national income. The Fed can seek to remove inflationary and deflationary gaps by its monetary policy and thus seek to keep national income at its full-employment level.

A second major policy variable that is sometimes important is the rate of interest. There are a number of reasons why the Fed may be concerned about the rate of interest quite separately from any effects that the rate may have on national income. First, the higher the rate of interest the higher is the cost of servicing the national debt. The government thus has an obvious concern to keep the interest rate it pays as low as possible, and the Fed may sometimes wish to assist the government in holding the rate down. Second, the Fed may be concerned to prevent interest rates from changing too rapidly and thereby causing severe financial strain on those who are vulnerable to rapid changes in interest rates. (The reasons why this may be a matter of serious concern are discussed on page 628.) Third, the Fed may be concerned with the American balance of payments. If American interest rates are high relative to those in the rest of the world, there may be an influx of foreign capital to take advantage of the high U.S. rates. If American rates are low relative to those in the rest of the world there may be a large outflow of capital from the United States to foreign financial centers. Rapid movements of international funds can be upsetting to the economy (as we shall see in Chapter 39). The Fed may thus desire to influence U.S. interest rates in order to influence these international capital flows.

Instrumental variables

Having selected its policy variables and formulated targets for their behavior, the Fed must decide how to achieve these targets. How can the policy variables be made to perform in the way that the Fed wishes? When the interest rate is the policy variable, the Fed can control it directly through its open market operations. The Fed cannot, however, directly control the level of national income. To influence a policy variable, such as national income, that it cannot control directly, the Fed seeks to influence those variables that it can control and that in turn have an influence on its policy variables. The variables that the Fed can control directly for the purpose of influencing other policy variables indirectly are called its **instrumental variables.** The Fed's two major instrumental variables are the rate of interest and the money supply. Both of these can be manipulated by the Fed and these manipulations can be used to exert ultimate influence on national income.

The level of national income is a policy variable. The money supply is an instrumental variable. The rate of interest may be either a policy variable— when the Fed has definite objectives for interest rates—or an instrumental variable—when the Fed causes changes in interest rates with a view to affecting national income.

CONTROLLING THE INTEREST RATE THROUGH MONETARY POLICY

If the Fed wishes to take the interest rate as its policy variable, control is relatively straight-forward. The Fed can influence interest rates by its open market operations. If the Fed buys bonds on the open market it is supplying money to the market. This will push up the price of bonds or—what is the same thing— push down interest rates. If the Fed sells bonds this takes money out of the market. The price of bonds will fall and interest rates will rise.

CONTROLLING NATIONAL INCOME THROUGH MONETARY POLICY

If the Fed wishes to make national income its main policy variable, its task is not as easy as when the rate of interest is its policy variable. The Fed must work through such instrumental variables as the money supply and the rate of interest. The theory of how changes in the money supply influence the level of income was described in Chapter 33. Let us now consider in more detail how this process operates for attempts both to contract and to expand the economy.

Contractionary monetary policy

Assume that the Fed believes there is too much inflationary pressure in the economy and that it wishes to reduce the level of aggregate demand or at least to slow down the rate at which demand is increasing. The Fed enters the open market and sells bonds. This pushes down the price of bonds and raises interest rates. When people pay for the bonds, they reduce their deposits. Banks thus lose reserves and are forced to restrict loans. The reduction in expenditure, brought about both by a rise in rates of interest and by bank credit rationing occasioned by their need to restore their reserve ratios, reduces aggregate demand. Households cut their borrowing for the purchase of housing and consumer durable goods; firms cut their borrowing for investment in capital goods and inventories; and state and local governments cut their borrowing because of the rising cost and short supply of credit. If firms, households, and governments all borrow less and spend less than they did previously because of a contractionary monetary policy, the level of aggregate demand will decrease. This in turn will lead to a magnified decrease in national income because of the multiplier process.

Expansionary monetary policy

Now assume that the Fed wishes to increase the level of aggregate demand or to slow down the rate at which it is contracting. The Fed enters the open market and buys bonds. This pushes up the price of bonds and lowers interest rates. When people sell their bonds, their deposits with commercial banks increase. Banks thus gain new deposits and new reserves and are able to indulge in multiple credit expansion that increases the money supply. The increase in expenditure brought about both by a fall in interest rates and by bank credit expansion increases aggregate demand. If firms, households, and local governments all increase their borrowing and spend more than they did previously because of the expansionary effect of monetary policy, the level of total expenditure will increase and there will be a magnified effect on national income because of the multiplier process.

Some problems of an expansionary policy. There are some situations in which an expansionary monetary policy can fail to have the intended effects. It has already been shown (page 643) that if the liquidity preference schedule is very flat, the purchase of bonds will have very little effect on the rate of interest. Assume that the price of bonds is already quite high and that the public feels that it cannot long remain so high. People will be inclined to hold demand or savings deposits instead of bonds both because they expect to be able to buy bonds later at a more favorable price and because they fear capital losses if they buy the bonds now.

If the Fed enters this market and offers to buy bonds, only a small increase in price will be needed to persuade the public to sell their bonds, which they already believe to be unusually high in price. When bond prices rise still further, the public becomes even more convinced that they should sell bonds now and hold money, hoping to buy back the bonds for a large gain when prices fall. In these circumstances the Fed's open market operations will succeed in increasing the money supply, but it need not drive the interest rate down much.

A second unfavorable situation occurs if the marginal efficiency of investment schedule is very interest inelastic. For example, the existence of substantial excess capacity in existing plant and equipment combined with unfavorable expectations about future sales would make businessmen very reluctant to engage in new investment on any terms. In such circumstances the amount of investment they are prepared to make would not be likely to change much in response to variations in interest rates.

In a severe depression a highly inelastic marginal efficiency of investment schedule is likely to occur and both unfavorable circumstances may occur simultaneously. In such circumstances even quite large increases in the money supply will have little effect in increasing aggregate demand.

A CONFLICT BETWEEN NATIONAL INCOME AND THE RATE OF INTEREST AS POLICY VARIABLES

The Fed cannot set policies with respect to both national income and the interest rate and expect to achieve them both by its open market operations. Assume, for example, that the Fed picks a rate of interest that it wishes to maintain. The Fed must now enter the open market and buy or sell whatever quantity of bonds is necessary to stabilize the interest rate at its desired level. If the Fed has to buy bonds to stop the rate of interest from rising above its target level, it will be expanding the money supply. If the Fed has to sell bonds to stop the rate of interest from falling below its target level, it will be contracting the money supply. In either case the Fed's policy with respect to the interest rate *determines* what it must do to the money supply. By choosing the rate of interest as the target variable the Fed loses control over the money supply—the money supply will rise or fall depending on whether the Fed is acting to prevent the interest rate from falling below or rising above its target value.

What are the consequences of a Fed policy to stabilize, or at least to reduce the fluctuations in, the rate of interest? Normally in the upswing of a business cycle interest rates rise as funds for investment become scarce. The rise in interest rates causes a reduction in all interest-sensitive expenditure, and this helps to restrain the boom. If, however, the Fed is committed to a policy of holding the rate of interest constant, it must supply all the funds that are demanded at the fixed rate of interest but not supplied by the private sector. The Fed's policy will cause the money supply to expand and will prevent interest rates from rising to restrain investment demand. This will cause the boom to be stronger than it otherwise would have been.

An analogous result occurs in the downswing of a cycle. Normally in a recession the falloff in the demand to borrow money leads to a fall in the rate of interest, and this helps to increase all interest-sensitive expenditure and thereby reduce the severity of the recession. If, however, the Fed is committed to holding the rate of interest constant, it will have to enter the market and sell bonds to keep their price from rising. This reduces the money supply and prevents interest rates from falling. The policy of stabilizing the rate of interest thus tends to make the downswing more severe than it otherwise would have been.

When the rate of interest is the target variable the money supply varies with the business cycle. Cyclical swings are larger than they would be if the Fed left interest rates free to vary.

A CONFLICT BETWEEN THE MONEY SUPPLY AND INTEREST RATES AS INSTRUMENTAL VARIABLES

Now suppose that the Fed takes the level of national income as its policy variable and is interested in controlling the interest rate and the money supply only as instrumental variables which are linked to national income. The Fed chooses either the rate of interest or the money supply as its instrumental variable. Since these two possible instrumental variables are not independent of each other it might not seem to matter which the Fed selects. If, for example, the Fed wishes to remove an inflationary gap by forcing interest rates up, it will sell securities and thus drive their prices down. These open market sales will also contract the money supply through the mechanism described earlier. Thus it is largely immaterial whether the Fed seeks to force interest rates up or to contract the money supply since doing one will accomplish the other. Similarly, driving interest rates down by open market purchases of government securities will tend to expand the money supply as the public gains money in return for the securities it sells to the Fed.

In spite of the interrelation between these two possible instrumental variables, many economists have argued that it is important that the Fed should use the money supply rather than interest rates as its main instrumental variable. Their argument is that it is much easier to assess the trends of the economy and to assess the current thrust of the Fed's policy if the money supply is used as the instrumental variable and targets are set for its behavior than if the rate of interest is used. The argument proceeds in three steps.

1. In times of business expansion, both interest rates and the money supply will be rising. Interest rates rise because of a heavy

demand to borrow money and because of an increasing shortage of loanable funds. The money supply expands because banks let their excess reserves run down to very low levels in order to meet the pressing demands for loans from firms and households that are their customers.

2. A restrictive monetary policy requires that the Fed increase the rate of interest and reduce (or slow down the rate of expansion of) the money supply. Thus, if the Fed seeks to restrain a business expansion that is threatening to get out of hand and produce a serious inflationary gap, it will wish to *accentuate* the rising trend in interest rates but to *reverse* the rising trend in the money supply. By selling bonds in the open market it does both.

3. It is easier, however, to discover if the Fed's current policy is contractionary, expansionary, or neutral if it is working through the money supply rather than interest rates. If a typical rate of interest rises to 9 percent during an expansion, we may be uncertain how much of this is due to the Fed's tightening of monetary policy and how much of it would have happened anyway. Indeed, the more rapid the expansion the more rapidly will interest rates tend to be rising without any assistance from the Fed. But if the annual rate of increase in the money supply is, say, 20 percent, this is unambiguously expansionary and it clearly shows that a much more restrictive policy is required to restrain the business expansion.

In the past the Fed has taken interest rates as its main instrumental variable. It would appear that this has sometimes led to uncertainty even within the Fed about how restrictive or expansionary was the current stance of its monetary policy.

In recent years there has been a shift from interest rates to the money supply as the major instrumental variable.

Of course, the Fed still seeks to influence a range of variables including both the money supply and interest rates. It is argued, however, that the use of the money supply, rather than interest rates, as a major instrumental variable gives a clearer indication of the actual stance of monetary policy and of how it should be changed.

Monetary policy in action

Having studied the objectives and instruments of monetary policy, we may now consider how monetary policy has actually worked in the period since World War II. Monetary policy is formulated by the Federal Open Market Committee (FOMC), which was described on page 629. The FOMC generally meets about every four weeks; its decisions are embodied in a directive issued to the Federal Reserve Bank of New York. Open market operations are conducted in the New York Fed by the manager of the system's Open Market Account.

THE "ACCORD"

The use of monetary policy as a tool of stabilization policy in the postwar period began in 1951 with the famous Treasury-Federal Reserve Accord. Under this agreement the Federal Reserve discontinued the practice, which had been carried on throughout World War II, of supporting the prices of Treasury securities to facilitate financing of the war effort. This practice had meant that the Fed held the interest rate down—thereby keeping the cost of servicing the debt low[1]—and that it supplied new money to buy any part of a government debt issue that the public would not buy at the fixed rate of interest. The effect

---

[1] During World War II this was a dominant objective of the Fed. Between 1941 and 1945 the federal government debt rose from about $50 billion to about $250 billion. This enormous debt offering was kept inexpensive to the Treasury by the Fed's keeping the interest rate on 3-month Treasury bills at $\frac{3}{8}$ of 1 percent and on 3-to-5-year bonds at under $1\frac{1}{2}$ percent.

Policy formulation by the Open Market Committee

The directives issued by the FOMC are made public after a lag of about one month in a "Record of Policy Actions" which also includes the background of economic conditions on which the decisions were based. The following excerpts from the record of the meeting held on December 16, 1975, indicates some of the factors the FOMC considers relevant to its deliberations.

The information reviewed at this meeting suggested that output of goods and services—which has increased at an annual rate of 13 per cent in the third quarter—was expanding more moderately in the current quarter and that prices were continuing to rise at a relatively fast pace. Staff projections suggested that growth would remain moderate in the first half of 1976 and that the rate of increase in prices would slow somewhat.

In November the rise in industrial production slowed further, in part because of declines in output of automobiles and of energy; increases were widespread among other products, but in general they were smaller than in the preceding 5 months. Recovery in nonfarm payroll employment also slowed further. However, the dollar volume of retail sales expanded significantly for the second consecutive month. Residential construction activity rose further, reflecting the uptrend in private housing starts in recent months. The unemployment rate—which had risen 0.3 percentage point to 8.6 per cent in October—fell back to 8.3 per cent in November.

Staff projections of real output in the first half of 1976 were similar to those of 4 weeks earlier. They suggested that consumption expenditures would expand at a moderate pace, that residential construction and business fixed investment would continue to recover, and that State and local government purchases of goods and services would pick up some-

what from the reduced pace in the second half of 1975. It was also anticipated that business inventory accumulation would be at a moderate rate. However, exports were projected to rise less than imports.

At its October meeting, the Committee had agreed that growth in the monetary aggregates on the average over the period from the third quarter of 1975 to the third quarter of 1976 at rates within the following ranges appeared to be consistent with its broad economic aims: M_1, 5 to $7\frac{1}{2}$ per cent; M_2, $7\frac{1}{2}$ to $10\frac{1}{2}$ per cent; and M_3, 9 to 12 per cent. . . . It was understood that the longer-term ranges, as well as the particular list of aggregates for which such ranges were specified, would be subject to review and modification at subsequent meetings. It also was understood that, as a result of short-run factors, growth rates from month to month might well fall outside the ranges contemplated for annual periods.

During the discussion some Committee members expressed confidence in the economic outlook for the quarters immediately ahead, while other members expressed doubt concerning the strength of the recovery. In view of the uncertainties regarding the behavior of the monetary aggregates in the December–January period, many members advocated giving greater weight than usual to money market conditions in conducting open market operations in the period until the next meeting. However, a number of members preferred to continue to base operating decisions primarily on the behavior of the monetary aggregates. There was some sentiment for a slightly more stimulative policy, but most members favored no essential change in policy.

At the conclusion of the discussion the Committee decided that operations in the period immediately ahead should be directed toward maintaining the bank reserve and money market conditions now prevailing, provided that monetary aggregates appeared to be growing at about the rates currently expected. The members concluded that growth in M_1 and M_2 over the December–January period at annual rates within ranges of tolerance of 4 to 7 per cent and 7 to 10 per cent, respectively, would be acceptable.

Source: *Federal Reserve Bulletin,* February 1976.

of this policy was that the Fed had no control over the money supply—which expanded rapidly, with serious inflationary consequences, whenever the government demand to borrow was too heavy to be met by private lending at the going rate of interest.

THE SHIFT FROM INTEREST RATES TO THE MONEY SUPPLY AS THE MAIN TARGET VARIABLE

The basic concern of monetary policy since the Accord has been the achievement of objectives such as full employment and price stability. To make them operational, however, the FOMC must translate these broader economic goals into targets concerning the monetary and credit variables over which the Fed has a direct influence.

Prior to 1970, the operating instructions of the FOMC were generally couched in terms of money market conditions, that is, short-term interest rates, member bank borrowings from the Federal Reserve, and the net excess reserve position of member banks.[2] Some references were made to monetary aggregates, but these were generally confined to statements concerning the desired behavior of bank credit.

In the 1970s monetary aggregates came to play a more prominent role, and the emphasis shifted from targets specified in terms of money market conditions to target rates of growth of the money supply. The measure used for this purpose has generally been the narrowly defined money supply (M_1), but broader definitions have also been taken into account. The shift to greater emphasis on controlling the money supply on the part of the Federal Reserve reflected the growing influence of the monetarist view that took place in the economics profession generally.

THE USE OF MONETARY POLICY SINCE THE ACCORD

Figure 35–1 shows the behavior of M_1, the narrowly defined money supply, and relates it to unemployment and the rate of inflation for the period since the accord. Two things stand out. First, monetary policy has shown sharp, short-period changes—from being quite expansive to being highly restrictive. Second, there has been a steady upward trend in the rate of monetary expansion.

The variability of monetary policy

From 1952 to 1967 the inflation rate was relatively low—under 3 percent—but unemployment frequently rose well above 4 percent. The Fed took national income as one of its main target variables with a view to influencing unemployment. The sharp variations in the rate of monetary expansion resulted to a great extent from the Fed's attempt to use monetary policy to fine tune the economy.

The 1954 recession led to an expansionary monetary policy; by 1956 unemployment had been reduced to a low level but an inflationary gap had also been opened up. In response, the Fed tightened monetary policy, and in 1957 the quantity of money was actually decreased.[3] From 1960 to 1964 unemployment, which rose sharply in 1957 and 1958, stayed above the 5 percent level, and this led the monetary authorities to progressively more expansionary policies (with only the exception of 1962), until by the middle of the decade the annual rate of monetary expansion exceeded $4\frac{1}{2}$ percent.

In 1966, with unemployment falling sharply in response to the strong recovery of the economy, the Fed applied the monetary brakes. This so-called credit crunch of 1966 cut the rate of monetary expansion in half. But the

[2] Net excess reserves are defined as total reserves *minus* legally required reserves *minus* borrowing from the Fed. These are sometimes also called free reserves.

[3] M_1 normally is increased over time in order to finance the growing level of full employment national income without putting deflationary pressures on the economy. Thus any rate of increase of less than 2 or 3 percent is plainly deflationary.

Figure 35-1   Changes in the money supply[a] related to inflation[b] and unemployment[c]

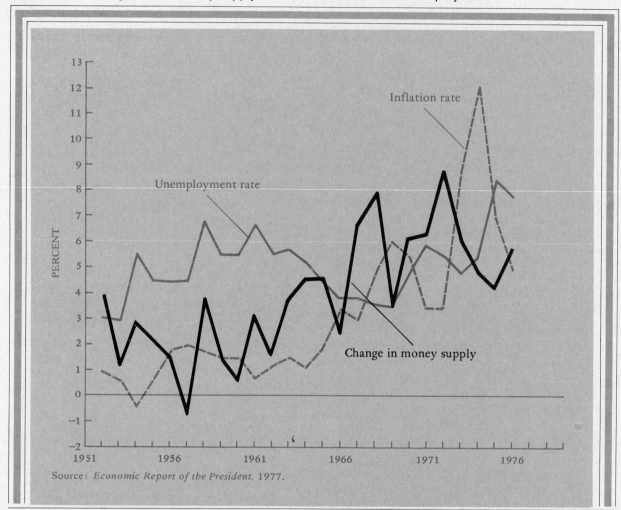

Source: *Economic Report of the President*, 1977.

The rate of monetary expansion has shown substantial short-term variability combined with a strong long-term upward trend. Rapid increases in the money supply tend to *cause* increases in national income as measured in current dollars. This may cause a reduction in unemployment when there is a deflationary gap and a rise in prices when there is an inflationary gap. Changes in the money supply are also partly the *effect* of changes in unemployment and prices if the Fed slows down the rate of monetary expansion in reaction to an inflation or speeds it up in reaction to heavy unemployment.

[a] annual percentage change in M_1
[b] annual percentage change in consumer price index
[c] percentage of the civilian labor force unemployed

policy was quickly reversed, and by 1968, in response to the government's need for cheap financing of the escalating war in Vietnam, monetary expansion was at the level of nearly 8 percent, which was unprecedented in the years since the accord.

The sharp inflationary gap that developed led to another abrupt reversal, and monetary expansion fell to 3.5 percent in 1969. But the restrictive policy was short lived, and a very expansionary policy followed over the next three years. From the peak rate of monetary growth of 9 percent, the Fed, in 1972, responding to the high rate of inflation that had built up during the early 1970's, once again reversed direction and steadily reduced the rate of monetary expansion until it reached just over 4 percent in 1975. In 1976, however, the rate rose again to nearly 6 percent, which was higher than the rate during any of the years of relatively low inflation from 1952–1966.

What was the effect of these frequent and abrupt shifts between expansionary and contractionary monetary policy stances? Many economists believe that such attempts at fine tuning actually destabilized the economy. They argue that slower, more gradual changes in the rate of monetary expansion would enable the Fed to respond to changing conditions in the economy without inducing severe short-term fluctuations. No doubt partly in response to these criticisms, the FOMC began in 1975 a practice of focusing explicitly on a longer-term horizon in formulating policy in response to a joint resolution of Congress. Target ranges of *annual* growth rates of monetary aggregates are now specified and the M_1 target in particular provides a focus for public discussion of policy.

The rising trend of monetary expansion

As the solid black line in Figure 35–1 shows, the fluctuations in monetary expansion have occurred around a sharply rising trend. This has been accompanied by a similar, rising trend in prices, and leads to an unmistakable correlation between the rate of monetary expansion and the rate of inflation. Correlation does not by itself prove causation, and there is some debate about the causes of the American inflation in recent years. But both the theory we have studied and the evidence suggest that the accelerating rate of monetary expansion is sufficient to account for the upward trend of inflation. Many economists feel there is virtually no chance of rolling inflation back to the relatively modest levels of the 1950s and 1960s until the rate of monetary expansion is brought back to the more modest annual amounts of those years.

Table 35–1   Required reserve ratios, January 31, 1977, of deposits of Federal Reserve members

Net demand deposits[a] (millions of dollars)	DEMAND DEPOSITS			TIME DEPOSITS		
	Present	STATUTORY		Present	STATUTORY	
		Minimum	Maximum		Minimum	Maximum
$ 0–2	7.0	7	14			
2–10	9.5	7	14			
10–100	11.75	7	14	3	3	10
100–400	12.75	7	14			
Over 400	16.25	10	22			

[a]Each deposit interval applies to that part of the deposits of *each* bank.

The required reserve ratios give the amount of reserves—cash and deposits with a Federal Reserve bank—that commercial banks must hold against various types of deposits. Savings deposits carry a very low legal reserve requirement, while demand deposits have a legal reserve requirement that increases with the size of the bank. Thus a bank with less than $2 million in deposits is required to have only 7 percent reserves against all of its deposits while a bank with over $400 million must hold 16.25 percent reserves against all its deposits in excess of $400 million.

USE OF TOOLS OTHER THAN OPEN MARKET OPERATIONS

The major method used by the Fed to control both interest rates and the money supply is its open market operations. The Fed does, however, have a number of other tools at its disposal.

Reserve requirements

Chapter 33 illustrated the importance of the reserve ratio in the expansion and contraction of credit. In 1934, the Federal Reserve Board was given authority by Congress to set (within limits) required reserve ratios for both demand and time deposits; Congress can (and has) changed the statutory limits from time to time. Table 35–1 summarizes the present reserve requirements.

The original logic of having lower reserves for small banks, as shown in the table, was that large banks held deposits of small banks that were their correspondents. It was believed that large banks thus needed more reserves to withstand a potential run on the banks by depositors, but such protection is no longer needed because they are protected by a variety of other means such as Federal Deposit Insurance.

It has often been noted that bankers feel their reserve requirements are set higher than is required for safe operation. It is clear why. It is unthinkable that the central bank would set reserve ratios below safe standards and thereby encourage reckless lending; but it is quite reasonable for it to set reserves "too high" (by safety standards) in order to give it freedom to maneuver in *both* directions if it wants to use variations in reserve requirements as a tool of control.

The use of reserve ratio changes. During the 1960s and early 1970s, changes in reserve requirements were used infrequently, as Table 35–2 shows. But during much of the period in which the board of governors has had authority to change reserve requirements, it

Table 35–2 Changes in reserve requirements, 1933–1976, for demand deposits of large banks (percentage of deposits)

Year	Month	Reserve city banks
In effect 1933		10
1936	August	15
1937	March	17.5
1937	May	20
1938	April	17.5
1941	November	20
1948	September	22
1949	May	21
	June–July	20
	August 1–11	19.5
	August 16–18	19
	August 25	18.5
	September 1	18
1951	January 11–16	19
	January 25–February 1	20
1953	July	19
1954	July 28–August 1	18
1958	February 27–March 1	17.5
	March 20–April 1	17
	April 24	16.5
1960	November	16.5
1966	July	16.5
1968	January	17
1969	April	17.5
1973	July	18
1974	December	17.5
1975	February	16.5
1976	January	16.25

Source: *Federal Reserve Bulletin.*

The decline in the required reserve ratios in 1974 and 1975 indicated a slight easing of monetary policy. Required reserve ratios vary somewhat by size of bank as shown in Table 35–1. The figures shown in this table are the large deposit rate—currently deposits in excess of $400 billion.

has made substantial changes in them. Changing reserve requirements, currently out of fashion with the present board of governors, may well come into use again.

The chief argument against manipulating the reserve ratio is that it is a ponderous weapon for changing excess reserves, whereas open market policy can be applied flexibly to achieve the same effects. The chief arguments for using reserve-ratio changes are that they cause less disruption in the market for government securities than open market operations and that even small changes serve effectively to "announce" the board's views about the desirable changes in the credit position of member banks.

The discount rate

The discount rate is the rate at which the Fed will lend funds to member banks who need to replenish their reserves. As a matter of policy, the Fed discourages any long-term borrowing from it by commercial banks, and the reserve banks tend to accommodate requests at their "discount window" only on a short-term basis. This suggests a relatively minor role for the discount rate as a policy weapon. Indeed, the volume of Fed discounts outstanding averaged only $145 million during the 12 months from mid 1975 to mid 1976—approximately 0.4 percent of member bank reserves. The highest single monthly figure during that period was only 1.1 percent.

Discounts rarely reach 5 percent of reserves, which makes them *quantitatively* a minor influence compared to open market policy. The importance of the discount rate is in the signal it gives about the trend of interest rates in general and the ease or tightness of credit.

Table 35–3 Average interest rates, selected years

Year	Discount rate (Federal Reserve Bank of New York)	Prime rate (4–6 months)	Three-month Treasury bills[a]	Corporate bonds
1929	5.16	5.85	—	4.73
1931	2.12	2.64	1.40	4.58
1935	1.50	0.75	0.14	3.60
1939	1.00	0.59	0.02	3.01
1942	1.00[b]	0.66	0.33	2.83
1945	1.00[b]	0.75	0.38	2.62
1948	1.34	1.44	1.04	2.82
1951	1.75	2.16	1.55	2.86
1955	1.89	2.18	1.75	3.06
1958	2.15	2.46	1.84	3.79
1961	3.00	2.97	2.38	4.35
1964	3.55	3.97	3.55	4.40
1967	4.19	5.10	4.32	5.51
1970	5.95	7.72	6.46	8.04
1972	4.50	4.69	4.07	7.21
1974	7.83	9.87	7.89	8.57
1976	5.50	5.35	4.99	8.43

Source: *Economic Report of the President,* 1972 and 1977.

[a] First issued in December 1929, these issues were tax exempt before March 1, 1941.
[b] From October 30, 1942, to April 24, 1946, a preferential rate of 0.5 percent was in effect for advances secured by government securities maturing in one year or less. The purpose was to encourage banks to buy government securities for financing the war.

Interest rates show considerable variation over the years. Although interest rates do vary substantially over the years the various rates all tend to move together. Notice the low of 0.02 percent on three-month Treasury bills in 1939, which seems almost incredible in light of the 1974 rate of almost 8 percent.

When the discount rate changes, so (with a very short lag) do the rates banks charge their customers. In response to rises in the discount rate, the stock market often plunges because investors feel it signals tight money and reduced investments by firms in the period ahead.

Use of discount rate changes. Table 35–3 shows the average discount rate for selected years since 1929. It shows that the discount rate has varied substantially and that it moves in a rough way with other rates of interest.[4] The table does not indicate whether the discount rate follows or leads changes in other interest rates, but, in one sense at least, the Fed's discount rate follows other developments. Open market operations that apply the monetary brakes by selling bonds tend to push up interest rates. Then, to discourage banks from turning to their discount windows, the Fed must raise the discount rate. But sharp changes in the discount rate often lead other rates in the economy by creating expectations about the relative abundance or scarcity of funds. During World War II and the postwar period, the discount rate was little used because the Fed was cooperating with the Treasury in an attempt to keep down the interest cost on the federal debt. During the 1950s and 1960s, discount policy reemerged as a major weapon, as Table 35–4 indicates.

Selective credit controls

Each of the major tools of monetary policy— open market operations, required reserve ratio changes, and discount rate policy— can be used to affect the general availability

---

[4] Considerations of risk, duration, and tax status, of course, affect different rates differently. For example, the interest rate on corporate bonds during the Great Depression was high because they were considered risky. Today they are considered safer. Because Treasury bills were considered virtually riskless, and were tax exempt, they could be sold at very low interest rates during the Depression when banks had large excess reserves that they were reluctant to lend to private firms because of the risk of nonrepayment.

of credit. But such changes exert an uneven impact on the economy. A tightening of credit conditions, for example, has its principal effect on those parts of the economy particularly dependent on credit—such as residential housing, consumer durables, and new, expanding firms that are usually in cash difficulties and particularly vulnerable to a tightening of credit.

The uneven impact of monetary policy on the economy is a potential disadvantage. This disadvantage may be offset, however, by the fact that the major weapons of monetary policy can be put into effect with very short decision lags. The board of governors can decide on open market operations, changes in reserve requirements, or discount rate changes one day and announce them as effective the next day.

When the uneven impact of monetary policy seems undesirable but its speed seems desirable, it is possible to supplement general monetary policy with **selective credit controls.** Among the selective controls that have been used at some time during the postwar period are margin requirements, installment-credit control, mortgage control, and maximum interest rates.

Margin requirements. Stock market speculation can be controlled by the Federal Reserve through its power to limit the fraction of the price of a stock that people can borrow through established financial channels. Since January 3, 1974, **margin requirements** have been set at 50 percent, meaning that a purchaser of a listed security has to put up 50 percent of the amount of the purchase using his own money. The balance may be borrowed from the brokerage firm through whom he buys the security. Since 1960 the margin requirement has varied between 50 percent and 90 percent. Such variations can have a substantial selective effect on stock market activity that is independent of the general credit picture. Thus, if the Federal Reserve wishes to impose moderate credit restraint generally but is particularly apprehensive about stock market speculation, it may combine a moderate amount of open market selling with a sharp increase in margin requirements.

Installment credit. The Fed was given temporary authority during World War II to specify requirements on minimum down payments and the duration of installment loans. Despite the effectiveness of Regulation W, as it was called, or perhaps because of it, Congress did not renew the Fed's authority for this sort of control when it expired after the Korean War. In other countries, notably Great Britain, installment-credit controls are an important tool of stabilization policy. When a central bank has control over the terms of consumer credit, it can affect the allocation of credit between consumer credit and other uses by an appropriate combination of policies. Suppose, for instance, that the central bank wishes to increase the funds available to business firms for investment without encouraging increased installment buying. It can buy bonds on the open market (thereby making credit generally easier) and also increase required down payments (thereby making consumer installment purchases more difficult).

Mortgage control. Housing sales are particularly sensitive to required down payments and lengths of repayment. Indeed, most home buyers are more interested in their monthly payments than in the price of the house or the rate of interest. Until 1953, the Federal Reserve had power to specify minimum down payments and maximum repayment periods. By lowering minimum down payments and lengthening the payoff period (under what was called Regulation X), it could stimulate home purchases and home construction; by tightening them it proved it could sharply curtail residential purchases and construction.

Although the Federal Reserve Board's authority over mortgages has lapsed, a variety

Table 35–4 Changes in the discount rate, 1960–1976, Federal Reserve Bank of New York

Date		Rate
1960	In effect January 1	4
1960	June	3.5
	August	3
1963	July	3.5
1964	November	4
1965	December	4.5
1967	April	4
	November	4.5
1968	March	5
	April	5.5
	August	5.25
	December	5.5
1969	April	6
1970	November	5.75
	December	5.5
1971	January	5.25
		5
	February	4.75
	July	5
1971	November	4.75
	December	4.5
1973	January	5
	February	5.5
	May	5.75
	May	6.00
1974	April	8.00
	December	7.75
1975	January	7.25
	February	6.75
	March	6.25
	May	6.00
1976	January	5.50
	November	5.25

Source: *Federal Reserve Bulletin.*

The discount rate is changed frequently. During 1974 the discount rate rose to a post-World War II record of 8 percent. A slight easing of monetary policy is evident through 1975 and 1976.

of other federal housing agencies that lend money for mortgages, or guarantee them, have substantial discretion in easing or restricting housing credit.

Maximum interest rates. The Fed has the

authority to set maximum interest rates that member banks may pay on time deposits. In 1976 the maximum amount payable on savings deposits was 5 percent while other time deposits were subject to ceilings of from 5 to 7.75 percent depending on the term of the deposit. Maximum interest-rate regulation affects the distribution of funds among such alternative near moneys as time deposits, savings and loan deposits, and short-term government bonds rather than their total quantity.

Moral suasion

If the commercial banking system is prepared to cooperate, the Federal Reserve banks can operate a tight-money policy merely by asking banks to be conservative in granting loans; when the need for restriction is over, the commercial bankers can then be told that it is all right to go ahead granting loans and extending deposits up to the legal maximum. The use of "moral suasion" does not depend on mere jawboning. Member banks do depend on the Federal Reserve banks for loans, and in the long run noncooperation with the Fed's "suggestions" can prove costly to a bank.

In countries such as Canada and Great Britain where there are only a few banks, control by moral suasion is presumably easier than in the United States where there are thousands of independent banks. After all, an official of the Bank of England could have a long telephone conversation with a senior official of every important British bank in the course of a morning. Such quick personal contact with the whole system would be quite impossible in the American banking system, but to talk to twenty leading bankers could accomplish a good deal.

MONETARY POLICY: SOME INTERIM CONCLUSIONS

There is general agreement among economists that rapid changes in the money supply have major effects on the economy, particularly on the price level. Thus most economists agree that control of the money supply is a necessary condition for avoiding rapid inflations.

There is also general agreement that changes in the money supply could be used, if we knew enough, to help in the government's efforts to stabilize the economy by avoiding the extremes of large inflationary and deflationary gaps.

There is disagreement on a number of important issues.

1. Is control of the money supply a sufficient means of controlling inflation? Some economists answer yes, but others think not and look to causes of inflation in addition to excessive monetary expansion.

2. How important is monetary policy as a potential tool of stabilization policy? Most economists give some potential role to monetary policy, but opinions vary greatly on how important its role should be. At one extreme some economists give it a relatively minor role as a supplement to fiscal policy; at the other extreme some economists give it the exclusive role, arguing that "fiscal policy" is effective only insofar as it causes changes in the money supply.

3. Should monetary policy be used as a stabilization device? Although many economists would answer "of course," surprisingly, some of those who believe that monetary policy is potentially very powerful argue against its use. They believe that we know so little about the precise timing of the important effects of monetary policy that we are likely to do—and in the past have done—more harm than good by using such policies. They argue for a constant rate of monetary expansion directed at a zero trend in the price level in the face of a positive trend rate of growth in real output. They would not however vary the rate of monetary expansion in an attempt to remove short-term inflationary or deflationary gaps.

This chapter has mainly emphasized the

areas of general agreement on the workings of monetary policy. The major areas of disagreement outlined just above will be studied in more detail in Chapter 41.

Summary

1. The ultimate objectives of the Fed's monetary policy are called its policy variables. Both national income and the interest rate may be policy variables.

2. Where the Fed cannot influence its policy variables directly it must work through instrumental variables that it can control and that will in turn influence its policy variables. The money supply is an instrumental variable. The rate of interest is also an instrumental variable when the Fed manipulates it with a view to influencing national income (but it may also be a policy variable when the Fed seeks to control interest rates for their own sake).

3. When the interest rate is a policy variable it is easily controlled through open market operations. National income as the policy variable can also be influenced by open market operations but less directly than can the interest rate. To reduce national income the Fed sells bonds on the open market, driving up the rate of interest and reducing the quantity of money. To increase national income the Fed buys bonds on the open market, driving down the rate of interest and increasing the quantity of money.

4. The Fed cannot have wholly separate monetary policies with respect to national income and the interest rate since the two are related. For example, a policy of stabilizing interest rates accentuates fluctuations in national income.

5. There is a debate as to whether the Fed should use the money supply or interest rates as its main instrumental variable when it seeks to influence national income as its main policy variable. Since changing either the money supply or the interest rate necessarily changes the other it might seem unimportant which variable is chosen. It is argued, however, that the expansionary or contractionary stance of monetary policy is much easier to assess when the money supply rather than the rate of interest is used.

6. The modern use of monetary policy in the United States dates from the 1951 "Accord" between the Treasury and the Fed under which the Fed ceased to have as its major objective minimizing the cost of financing the government's debt by control of interest rates.

7. In the 1950s and 1960s the rate of interest was the main instrumental variable through which the Fed sought to influence national income. In the 1970s emphasis has shifted to the money supply. The Fed has sometimes been criticized for alternating its policy stance between expansionary and contractionary pressures on national income too quickly and thereby contributing to cyclical swings in the economy.

8. In addition to control of the money supply and interest rates through open market operations the Fed has several other important tools of control: It can vary reserve requirements or the discount rate, and it can use a number of selective controls on credit. It can also use moral suasion.

9. It is generally agreed that rapid changes in the money supply and interest rates can have large effects on the economy. There is disagreement, however, on how much monetary policy can and should be used as a device for stabilizing the economy or coping with temporary bouts of inflation.

Concepts for review

Policy and instrumental variables
Conflicts between the rate of interest and national income
   as policy variables
Conflicts between the rate of interest and the money
   supply as instrumental variables
Alternative instruments of monetary policy

Discussion questions

1. In the study of banking history we often see the term "elastic currency." For example, to provide an elastic currency was a purpose behind the creation of the Federal Reserve System. What do you think this term might mean, and why might it be emphasized?

2. Early in 1977 *The New York Times* reported, "A year ago, it was widely believed that interest rates would bottom out early in 1976 and head higher. Instead, they have declined with few interruptions all year long and have dropped to their lowest levels in three years or more. The man Wall Street

credits for this achievement is Arthur F. Burns, 72-year-old chairman of the Federal Reserve Board." How might Dr. Burns have been responsible for this result? What does it imply about the money supply?

3. The Federal Reserve Board runs a facility in Culpeper, Virginia, which costs $1.8 million per year to maintain and to guard against robbery according to Senator Proxmire of Wisconsin. Inside this "Culpeper switch," a dugout in the side of a mountain, the government has hidden $4 billion in new currency for the purpose, it says, of "providing a hedge against any nuclear attack that would wipe out the nation's money supply." Comment on the sense of this policy.

4. Describe the chief weapons of monetary policy available to the Federal Reserve and indicate whether, and if so how, they might be used for the following purposes:
a. to create a mild tightening of bank credit
b. to signal that the Board of Governors favors a sharp curtailment of bank lending
c. to permit an expansion of bank credit with existing reserves
d. to supply banks and the public with a temporary increase of currency for Christmas shopping

5. It is often said that an expansionary monetary policy is like "pushing on a string." What is meant by such a statement? How does this contrast with a contractionary monetary policy?

6. Under what circumstances will changes in reserve requirements be ineffective in changing the money supply?

7. During the Christmas and the summer holiday season, the level of household spending rises and so does the amount of cash held by the public. Do you think the rise in the amount of cash causes the rise in spending or vice versa? Predict some of the effects of a law passed by Congress in October prohibiting the public from withdrawing extra cash from the banks until after the Christmas season.

8. In what situations might the following pairs of objectives come into conflict:
a. keeping the cost of government finance low *and* using monetary policy to change aggregate demand
b. signaling a tighter monetary policy by raising interest rates *and* accommodating the public's desire for money
c. maintaining stable interest rates *and* controlling inflation

PART TEN

INTERNATIONAL TRADE AND FINANCE

36

The balance of payments and exchange rates

Americans buy Volkswagons, Germans take holidays in Italy, Italians buy spice from Tanzania, Africans import oil from Kuwait, Arabs buy Japanese cameras, and the Japanese depend heavily on American soybeans as a source of food. *International trade* refers to all such exchanges of goods and services that take place across international boundaries. This trade gives rise to a number of characteristic problems. The complications that arise because different countries use different currencies are considered in this chapter. Chapter 37 is devoted to a more fundamental question: Is there anything to be gained from trade among nations? Chapter 38 deals with the pros and cons of interfering with the flow of international trade. Finally, Chapter 39 is devoted to a brief study of the international monetary systems under which the international exchange of goods and movements of capital have functioned in the twentieth century.

The nature of exchange rates

One of the major complications that distinguishes international trade from interregional trade (trade within one country) is that while different regions of the same country use the same money, different nations do not. The currency of one country is generally acceptable within the bounds of that country, but it will not usually be accepted by households and firms in another country.

When American producers sell their products they require payment in dollars. They must meet their wage bills, pay for their raw materials, and reinvest or distribute their profits. If they sell their goods to American purchasers, there is no problem; they will pay dollars for their purchases. If, however, producers sell their goods to Indian importers, either the Indians must exchange their rupees for dollars to pay for the goods or the U.S.

producers must accept rupees. They will accept rupees only if they know that they can exchange the rupees for the dollars that they require. The same holds true for producers in all countries; they must eventually receive payment in terms of the currency of their own country for the goods that they sell.

In general, trade between nations can occur only if it is possible to exchange the currency of one nation for that of another.

International payments that require the exchange of one national currency for another can be made in a bewildering variety of ways, but in essence they involve the exchange of currencies between people who have one currency and require another. Suppose that an American firm wishes to purchase a British sports car to sell in the United States. The British firm that made the car requires payment in its own currency (which is called "pounds sterling" and is indicated by the symbol £). If the car is priced at £3,000, the American firm can go to its bank and purchase a check for £3,000 and send this to the British seller. The exchange rate determines the price that is paid for this check.

These rates change over time. In the examples of this chapter we use the rate $1.67 to £1, which is toward the lower end of the rates that prevailed in 1976.[1] Thus the American importing firm would write a check on its own account for $5,000 in payment for a £3,000 sterling check or "draft." The British firm would deposit the check in its own bank. When all this was done, the banking system would have exchanged obligations to American firms for obligations to British firms. The deposits of the American firm, which are liabilities of its bank, would be reduced by $5,000 and the deposits of the British firm, which are liabilities of the British bank, would be increased by £3,000. Banks make a profit

[1] The actual rate used is $1.66 ⅔ = £1.00, or what is the same thing, £0.60 = $1.00. The quoted rate is rounded in the text to $1.67 = £1.00.

by charging a small commission for effecting these transactions.

Now assume that a British wholesale firm wishes to purchase ten American refrigerators to sell in Britain. If the refrigerators are priced at $500 each, the American seller will require a total payment of $5,000. To effect this payment, the British importing firm goes to its bank and writes a check on its account for £3,000 and receives a check drawn on a U.S. bank for $5,000. This reduces the deposit liabilities of the British bank by £3,000. When the American firm deposits this check, its deposits, which are the liabilities of the U.S. banking system, are increased by $5,000. Thus the banking system as a whole has merely switched liabilities, this time from British to American banks.

These two transactions cancel each other out, and there is no net change in international liabilities. The balance sheets of the British and the U.S. banks reflect these changes. (They are shown in Table 36–1). No money passes between British and American banks to effect these transactions; each bank merely increases the deposits of one domestic customer and lowers the deposits of another. Indeed, as long as the flow of payments between the two countries is equal, so that Americans are paying as much to British citizens as British citizens are paying to Americans, all payments can be managed as in the above example and there is no need for a net payment from British banks to American ones. When the flow of payments is not the same in both directions, problems arise, as will be seen shortly.

Foreign exchange refers to the actual foreign currency or various claims on it such as bank deposits or promises to pay that are traded for each other. The **exchange rate** is the price at which purchases and sales of foreign currency or claims on it take place: It is the amount of one currency that must be paid in order to obtain one unit of another currency. When the exchange rate between British pounds and U.S. dollars was £1 =

Table 36–1 Changes in the balance sheets of two banks as a result of international trade

U.K. BANK			U.S. BANK		
Assets	*Liabilities*		*Assets*	*Liabilities*	
No change	Deposits of car exporter	+£3,000	No change	Deposits of car importer	−$5,000
	Deposits of refrigerator importer	−£3,000		Deposits of refrigerator exporter	+$5,000

International payments are effected by a transfer of deposit liabilities among banks. When banks handle an international transaction, they transfer deposit liabilities from one country to another. The American's import of a car reduces deposit liabilities to U.S. citizens and increases deposit liabilities to British citizens. The Britisher's import of a refrigerator does the opposite. When a series of transactions are equal in value, there is only a transfer of deposit liabilities among individuals within a country.

$1.67, then £1 exchanged for $1.67 and $1 exchanged for £0.60. If a holder of sterling gave up £1, he received approximately $1.67 either in cash or as a claim in the form of a check or draft; if a holder of dollars gave up $1, he would get £0.60 in return. There are similar exchange rates between the U.S. dollar and every other nation's currency. In April 1977, $1 was worth approximately 887 Italian lire, 2.4 German marks, 69 Spanish pesetas, and 278 Japanese yen.

Arbitrage operations consist in buying currencies in markets where they are cheap and selling them where they are dear so as to make a profit on the transaction. Once the rates between the U.S. dollar and any two foreign currencies are determined, there is only one rate between the two foreign currencies that will *not* allow buyers and sellers of foreign exchange to engage in profitable arbitrage. Consider an example. Suppose that on a particular day the dollar is worth £0.60 and 800 lire. Given these two rates, the only rate between lire and sterling that rules out profitable arbitrage operations is £0.60 = 800 lire, which is the equivalent of £1 = 1,333 lire. Table 36–2 gives an example in which the rate between the pound and the lira is out of line with the other two. Arbitrage provides a

mechanism such that when rates of exchange are set on free markets, "disorderly cross-rates" such as those illustrated in the table will be quickly eliminated. When the disorderly cross-rates shown in Table 36–2 persist, arbitragers will be buying lire with dollars and selling lire against pounds. If rates are free to vary, this will tend to bid the rates toward a consistent level where it is no longer possible to make profits by arbitrage.

The balance of payments

THE BALANCE OF ACTUAL PAYMENTS

In order to know what is happening to the course of international trade, governments keep track of the actual *transactions* among countries. The record of such transactions is made in the **balance-of-payments accounts.** In order to study the behavior of the foreign exchange market, it would be better to determine the actual *payments* between nations and why they were made. In practice, this cannot be done. What is done instead is to record each transaction, such as the shipment of exports and the arrival of imported goods, and to classify each transaction according to the payments or receipts that would typically arise from it.

Any item that typically gives rise to a purchase of foreign exchange is recorded as a debit item on the accounts, and any item that typically gives rise to a sale of foreign exchange is recorded as a credit item.

If, for example, a British importer buys an American washing machine to sell in the United Kingdom, this appears as a credit in the U.S. balance of payments because when the machine is paid for, sterling will be sold (and dollars purchased). The United States thus gains foreign exchange on the deal. However, if an American shipping firm insures with Lloyds of London a cargo destined for Alexandria, Egypt, this represents a debit in the U.S. balance of payments because when the insurance premium is paid, the shipping firm will have to pay Lloyds in sterling. Because it will purchase sterling (by selling dollars), the United States stands to lose foreign exchange on the deal. Of course, what is a credit item to one country is a debit item to the other and vice versa. Thus the washing-machine transaction is a debit in the British balance of payments because it depletes foreign exchange, and the insurance transaction is a credit in the British balance of payments because it earns foreign exchange.

In order to use international movements of goods and services instead of actual payments to reflect the behavior of the foreign exchange market, it is necessary to make a number of assumptions, some of them quite arbitrary. How, for example, should gifts of goods to foreigners be recorded? If the goods had been sold, they would have given rise to earnings of foreign exchange, but when they are given away, they do not. To take another example, what is done about an export to a foreign firm that subsequently defaults on the debt it in-

Table 36–2   An example of rates of exchange giving the possibility of profitable arbitrage operations

One unit of this currency	EXCHANGES FOR THE STATED NUMBER OF UNITS OF THIS CURRENCY		
	Dollar	Lira	Pound
Dollar	1	800	0.60
Lira	0.00125	1	0.000909
Pound	1.67	1,100	1

Disorderly cross-rates mean that a profit can be made merely by buying and selling currencies at existing rates in different markets. In this example, a trader can start with $2 and purchase 1,600 lire. He can then use the lire to purchase £1.45, which can be exchanged for $2.42. The profit is $.42 on an investment of $2, or 21 percent. Because the transactions can be effected very quickly and with large amounts of money, very large profits can be earned. Because of this, however, such rates will not long persist.

curred when it bought the good on credit? These, and many related problems, are important both to the statistician who is attempting to measure the balance of payments and to the careful observer who is attempting to account for detailed movements in the flows of trade and payments. For more general purposes, it can be assumed that the balance of payments measures the actual flow of payments between nations.[2]

The first thing to notice about the record of international transactions is that *the balance of payments always balances.* Although it is quite possible for holders of sterling to want to pur-

[2] The procedures adopted for handling the two problems cited in this paragraph are as follows. The export of a gift is recorded as a credit item just as if the good had been sold, but a compensating debit item is recorded under "unilateral capital transfers." Thus it is assumed that the *money* is given away and that the money is then used to *buy* our goods. The export that is not paid for because the buyer defaults will appear as a normal credit item, and an offsetting debit will probably be recorded under "residual errors."

chase more dollars in exchange for pounds than holders of dollars want to sell in exchange for pounds, it is not possible for sterling holders actually to buy more dollars than dollar holders sell. Every dollar that is bought must be sold by someone, and every dollar that is sold must be bought by someone. Because the dollars actually bought must be equal to the dollars actually sold, the payments actually made between countries must be in balance, even though desired payments may not be.

In the balance-of-payments accounts, an attempt is made to record the reasons for the payments. These accounts show what volume of payment is (or will be) made by foreigners to Americans for such purposes as the purchase of American goods; the use of American services (shipping insurance, etc.); the lending of money to American households, firms, or governments; and the investment of money in America. The accounts also should show what volume of payments is (or will be) made by Americans to foreigners for the purchase of foreign goods; the use of foreign services; the lending of money to foreign households, firms, or governments; and the investment of money abroad.

Although the total number of dollars bought on the foreign exchange market must equal the total number sold, this is not true of purchases and sales for a particular purpose. It is quite possible, for example, that more dollars are sold for the purpose of obtaining foreign currency to import foreign cars than are bought for the purpose of buying American cars for export to other countries. In such a case, the United States has a balance-of-payments deficit on the "car account": the value of U.S. imports of cars exceeds the value of its exports of cars. For most general purposes, economists are not interested in the balance of payments for single commodities but only for larger classes of transactions.

Current account and capital account

The most important division in the balance-of-payments accounts is between the current account and the capital account. The balance of payments on *current account* includes all payments made because of current purchases of goods and services. There is no automatic reason why current account payments should balance (any more than the automobile account should). It is quite possible for more dollars to be sold in order to purchase imports than were bought in order to allow foreigners to purchase our exports. If so, the dollars must have come from somewhere, and the excess of sales over purchases on current account must be exactly matched by an excess of purchases over sales on the capital account.

The *capital account* records transactions for everything other than what is recorded in the current account. The main items are capital transfers and sales from (or purchases of) stocks of gold and foreign exchange. Consider an American citizen who wishes to invest abroad by lending money to a British industry. He is exporting capital from the United States to the United Kingdom. Suppose that he wishes to buy newly issued bonds being sold in London by an expanding British firm. In order to do this, he needs to obtain pounds. He is a demander of foreign exchange and a supplier of dollars. His transaction is, therefore, a debit item in the American balance-of-payments account.

It sometimes seems confusing to beginners that the export of capital is a debit item and the export of a good is a credit item. The apparent contradiction can be removed by looking at the transactions in this way: The capital transaction involves the purchase, and hence the *import,* of a British bond, and this has the same effect on the balance of payments as the purchase, and hence the import, of a British good. Both items use foreign exchange and are thus debit items in the American balance of payments.

Now assume that, in a given year, the value of American imports exceeds the value of American exports, considering all current account transactions. The foreign currency necessary to finance the imports that were in excess of exports had to come from somewhere. It must have been lent by someone or provided out of the government's reserves of gold and foreign exchange. If foreigners are investing funds in the United States, they will be selling foreign currency and buying U.S. currency in order to be able to buy American stocks and bonds. Such foreign lending can provide the foreign exchange necessary to allow the United States to have an excess of imports over exports. The other possibility is that foreign central authorities have increased their holdings of U.S. dollars by buying some from persons wishing to purchase their goods and supplying their currency in return.

A deficit on U.S. current account must be matched by a surplus on capital account, which means either borrowing or gifts from abroad or increasing the reserves held by the foreign central authorities.

What about a surplus on current account, a situation in which the value of exports exceeds the value of imports? This means that foreigners will not be able to obtain all the U.S. dollars they need to buy American goods from U.S. sources wishing to supply dollars in return for foreign currency in order to buy foreign goods. The excess of exports over imports could only have been paid for if foreigners obtained dollars from other sources. There are several possibilities. First, U.S. dollars may be provided by American investors eager to obtain foreign currency so that they can buy foreign stocks and bonds. In this case, the excess of exports over imports is balanced by U.S. loans and investments abroad. Second, the U.S. government, rather than its firms or citizens, may have lent money to foreign governments to finance their purchases of American-produced goods

or services. Third, the U.S. government may have given money away as aid, particularly to underdeveloped countries. Such gifts allow these countries to purchase more from the United States than they sell to us. Fourth, foreign governments may have reduced their holdings of U.S. dollars or gold by selling them to persons who wish to buy U.S. goods and accepting their own domestic currency in exchange.

A surplus on U.S. current account must be matched by a deficit on capital account, which means either loans and gifts to foreigners or the reduction of reserves of dollars held by the foreign central authorities.

The makeup of the current account. The current account is usually subdivided into the trade in visibles and invisibles. **Visibles** are goods— all those things such as cars, pulpwood, aluminum, coffee, and iron ore that can be seen and touched when they cross international borders. The balance of payments on visible accounts is usually referred to as the **balance of trade. Invisibles** are services—all those things that cannot be seen or touched, such as insurance and freight haulage and tourist expenditures. When a U.S. firm buys insurance from Lloyds of London for a shipment of goods consigned to Egypt, the firm consumes a British export just as surely as if it purchased and used a British-made automobile or sent its president on a vacation to Scotland. Payment for the insurance services and for the automobile and the vacation must be made in pounds, and thus each is a U.S. import and a British export. These items use foreign exchange and thus are entered as debit items on the invisible account. Another invisible item is the recept of interest and dividends on U.S. loans and investments in foreign countries. An American who holds shares in a British aircraft company will receive dividend payments in pounds. If the American wishes to spend these at home, he or she will need to exchange the pounds for dollars. Interest and dividends on foreign loans and investments thus provide foreign exchange and are entered as credit items on the invisible account.

The makeup of the capital account. Capital movements can be divided into movements of long-term capital, of short-term capital, and changes in the government's official reserve position. Why do international capital movements occur? Allowing for risk and other such factors, investors will seek to invest where the return is highest. Just as capital moves from industry to industry within one country in search of its most productive uses, so capital tends to move from country to country in search of the highest rates of return. Such capital movements mean that the households and firms of one country are making investments in another country.

Short-term capital is held for many reasons. The mere fact of international trade forces traders to hold money balances. Traders' receipts and expenditures are not perfectly synchronized, and they necessarily hold transaction and precautionary balances because they must be able to pay their bills when these fall due. It usually does not matter where such funds are held. The funds can easily be moved from one currency to another in response to small changes in incentives or because of real or imaginary fears of all sorts. When short-term capital is transferred from one country to another, purchases and sales of foreign exchange tend to occur and are entered in the balance-of-payments account.

The algebraic sum of all transactions on current account and on short- and long-term capital account is the official reserve transactions balance. If official monetary agencies did not intervene into foreign exchange markets, this balance would necessarily be zero. In fact, such intervention does occur, and as a result the remaining transactions show a nonzero balance.

The final section in the capital account represents transactions in the official reserves held by the central authorities. It shows how the balance on the remainder of the accounts was financed. Here there are two main items: changes in liquid liabilities to foreign official agencies and changes in official reserve assets. The first represents the change in liquid claims on official reserves held by foreign central banks. When the United States has a deficit on the rest of the accounts, foreign monetary authorities accumulate these claims. They may then hold on to them or they may demand payment in official reserve assets. To the extent that they do the former, they are lending to finance the U.S.'s deficit on the rest of the accounts. To the extent that they do the latter there is a loss of official reserve assets which include gold and foreign exchange (claims on other convertible currencies) and a number of other more recently developed media of official international payments (such as SDRs) that will be studied in more detail in Chapter 39.

Balance-of-payment deficits and surpluses

It has already been noted that when all the uses to which foreign currency is put and all the sources from which it came are added up, these two amounts are necessarily equal, and thus the overall accounts of all international payments necessarily balance.

It is common, however, to speak of a country as having a balance-of-payments deficit or surplus. What does this mean? These terms refer to the balance of the account, usually *excluding* changes in reserves held by the central authorities (and changes in claims on these reserves held by foreign central authorities). A **balance-of-payments surplus** means that the authorities are reducing their liquid liabilities to foreign central authorities or else adding to their holdings of official reserves in such forms as gold and foreign exchange. A **balance-of-payments**

Table 36-3 U.S. balance of payments, 1975 (billions of dollars)

No.	Item	Credits	Debits	Net credits (+) Net debits (−)	
	I. CURRENT ACCOUNT				
	Visibles				
1.	(Private) merchandise trade balance	$107.1	$98.1	$+ 9.0	
	Invisibles				
2.	Travel and transportation	11.7	14.2	− 2.5	
3.	Investment income	18.2	12.2	+ 6.0	
4.	Other services (net)			+ 4.7	
5.	Balance on private goods and services				$+17.0
6.	Military transactions	6.1	− 7.0	− 0.9	− 0.9
7.	Remittances, pensions, and other transfers (net)			− 1.7	
8.	U.S. government grants (excluding military)			− 2.9	
9.	Unilateral transfers (excluding military)				− 4.6
10.	Balance on current account				$+11.7
	II. CAPITAL ACCOUNT				
	Long-term loans (−) or borrowing (+)				
11.	Private			$−10.3	
12.	Government			− 1.7	
13.	Net long-term foreign investment				$−12.1
14.	Basic balance on current account and long-term capital				$− 0.4
15.	Non-liquid short-term private capital flows (net)			− 3.0	
16.	Allocation of new special drawing rights			—	
17.	Errors and omissions (net)			+ 4.6	
18.	Short-term capital movements				+ 1.6
19.	Net liquidity balance				$+ 1.2
20.	Liquid private capital flows				− 5.8
21.	Official reserves transactions balance				$− 4.6
	III. NET GOLD AND RESERVE ASSET MOVEMENTS				
22.	Liabilities to foreign official agencies incurred			$+ 5.2	
23.	U.S. official reserve assets (net)			− 0.6	
24.	Total				$+ 4.6
25.	Formal over-all net total				0

Source: *Survey of Current Business*, March 1977.

The overall U.S. payments deficit of $4.6 billion was financed mainly by U.S. liabilities accumulated by foreign official monetary authorities. The U.S. current account showed a surplus of $11.7 billion, but this was more than balanced by a deficit on the capital account (due to capital exports) of $16.1 billion, giving an overall deficit of $4.6 billion.

deficit means that the authorities are adding to their liquid liabilities to foreign central authorities or else reducing their stocks of official reserves. When one reads therefore that America had a balance-of-payments deficit of $4.6 billion in 1975, this means that the U.S. official reserves (net of claims that foreign central authorities held against these reserves) fell by $4.6 billion because all other transactions were in deficit by that amount.

A balance-of-payments deficit means that the reserves of the central authorities are being run down by the amount of the deficit; a surplus means that reserves are rising.

Table 36–3 shows the U.S. balance of payments for 1975. The deficit on the balance of payment was $4.6 billion. This was more than balanced by an accumulation of claims against U.S. official reserves held by foreign monetary authorities; as a result, U.S. official reserve assets rose by $0.6 billion.

When all of the items in the whole account are added up, they must show an overall balance of zero. This merely says that all foreign exchange purchased (debit items) must have come from somewhere (credit items).

THE BALANCE OF DESIRED PAYMENTS

In order to study exchange rates in a simplified setting, we shall consider trade between only two countries, Britain and the United States. Everything said, however, applies equally to trade among several countries or a hundred countries.

The British firm importing American goods requires dollars in order to purchase these goods from the American manufacturer. When it buys these dollars, it will offer pounds sterling in exchange. Thus the British firm is a demander of dollars and a supplier of pounds. An American firm importing goods from Britain requires pounds to buy goods from the British manufacturer. When the American firm buys pounds, it offers dollars in exchange. It is therefore a demander of

pounds and a supplier of dollars. This gives us all the conditions we need to determine a price: Some people are trying to trade pounds for dollars, and others are trying to trade dollars for pounds.

If, at the current rate of exchange, the demand for dollars exceeds the supply, it follows that holders of sterling are trying to make more payments in dollars than holders of dollars wish to make in sterling. In other words, *desired* payments between the two countries are not in balance. If the total volume of payments that holders of sterling wish to make to America is equal to the total volume of payments that holders of dollars wish to make to Britain, the demand for dollars will equal the supply and the demand for sterling will equal its supply. Desired payments between the two countries will be equal. Finally, if the amount that holders of dollars wish to pay to Britain exceeds the amount that holders of sterling wish to pay to America, the demand for sterling will exceed the supply and the demand for dollars will be less than the supply. Again, desired payments between the two countries will not be in balance.

Disequilibrium in the foreign exchange market (i.e., the demand for foreign currency does not equal the supply) means that the desired payments between the two countries are not equal.

Of course, as we have seen, *actual* payments must always be in balance because foreign exchange bought must equal foreign exchange sold. But there is no reason why, at the existing rate of exchange, *desired* payments should be in balance; people may wish to buy more foreign exchange than others wish to sell.

The determination of exchange rates

The theory that will be developed here applies to all exchange rates, but to make the argument easier to understand, we shall continue to deal with the example of trade between America and Britain and with the determination of the rate of exchange between their two currencies, dollars and pounds sterling. Because one currency is traded for another on the foreign exchange market, it follows that to demand dollars implies a willingness to supply pounds, whereas an offer (supply) of dollars implies a need (demand) for pounds. If, at an exchange rate of £1 = $1.667, a British importer demands $3.33, he must be offering £2; if an American importer offers $3.33, he must be demanding £2. For this reason, the theory can deal either with the demand for and the supply of dollars, or with the demand for and the supply of pounds sterling; both do not need to be considered. We shall conduct the argument in terms of dollars.

PRICE CHANGES CAUSED BY EXCHANGE RATE CHANGES

A British manufacturer wants to receive a certain payment for his goods in pounds sterling. It follows that the dollar price at which these goods must be sold in America depends on the exchange rate between pounds and dollars. If the manufacturer wishes to obtain £1 each for his goods, the goods must sell in America (ignoring the cost of transport) for $4 when the exchange rate is £1 = $4 and for $2 when the rate is £1 = $2. An American manufacturer wishes to receive a certain number of dollars when he sells his goods. It follows that the pound price for which these goods must be sold in Britain depends on the rate of exchange between sterling and dollars. If, for example, the rate of exchange goes from £1 = $2 to £1 = $1.50, the dollar price of British exports to America must fall and the sterling price of American exports to Britain must rise. In general, a rise in the value of the pound vis-à-vis the dollar raises the dollar price of British exports to America and lowers the sterling price of British imports from America. A fall in the value of the

pound has the reverse effect. When between January and August of 1976 the dollar price of the British pound fell from $2.03 to $1.71, the prices of those British goods that were exported to America at an unchanged sterling price fell in terms of dollars by 16 percent, while the sterling price of American goods exported to Britain at an unchanged dollar price rose by 16 percent.

The demand and supply curves for dollars

If a cut in the price of British goods causes a rise in the amounts Americans will spend for those goods, the American demand for them is said to be elastic. Similarly, if a cut in the price of American goods causes a rise in the amounts the British will spend for them, British demand for American goods is elastic.[3] Assuming both of these demands to be elastic is the simplest and most empirically relevant case to analyze.

Figure 36–1 plots the price of dollars (measured in pounds) on the vertical axis and the quantity of dollars on the horizontal one. Moving down the vertical scale, the dollar is becoming cheaper (i.e., it is worth fewer pounds); its value is depreciating on the foreign exchange market. Moving up the scale, the dollar is becoming more expensive; it is appreciating on the market.

What is the shape of the demand curve for dollars? If the dollar is depreciated in value, the sterling price of American exports falls. The British will buy more of the cheaper U.S. goods and will require more dollars for this purpose. The quantity of dollars demanded will rise. Now consider the opposite case, in which the dollar rises in value and hence the

---

[3] Elasticity is discussed in detail in Chapter 6. For those who have not read that chapter, elasticity of demand is defined as the percentage change in the quantity demanded divided by the percentage change in price that brought it about. If this number is greater than unity the demand is said to be *elastic,* and a fall in price leads to an increase in the total amount spent on the commodity. If the number is less than unity the demand is said to be *inelastic,* and a fall in price leads to a decrease in the total amount spent on the commodity.

price of American exports rises in terms of foreign currency. The British will buy fewer U.S. goods and will thus demand fewer U.S. dollars.

The demand curve for dollars on the foreign exchange market is downward-sloping when plotted against the sterling price of dollars.

What about the supply curve of dollars? When the dollar is depreciated, the price of British exports to the United States rises. Americans will buy fewer of the now more expensive British goods and will spend fewer

dollars on them. The amount of dollars being offered in exchange for pounds sterling in order to pay for these imports thus falls. Now consider the opposite case, in which the dollar is appreciated. British exports to the United States become cheaper, more will be sold, and more dollars will be spent on them. Thus more dollars will be offered in exchange for pounds in order to obtain the foreign exchange needed to pay for the extra imports.

The supply curve of dollars on the foreign exchange market is upward-sloping when plotted against the sterling price of dollars.

Figure 36–1   An exchange rate determined on a competitive market

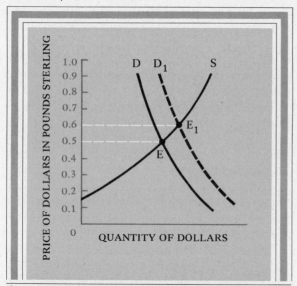

The equilibrium exchange rate equates the demand and supply on the foreign exchange market. The quantity of dollars demanded is originally equal to the quantity supplied at a price of £0.50 per dollar (or £1 = $2.00). If the demand of dollars rises to D_1, the equilibrium exchange rate changes to £0.60 per dollar—that is, the dollar appreciates in value and the pound depreciates.

WHAT DETERMINES THE EQUILIBRIUM EXCHANGE RATE?

Consider first a rate of exchange that is set on a freely competitive market. This rate, like any perfectly competitive price, fluctuates freely according to the conditions of demand and supply. To start the analysis, assume that the current price of dollars is so low (say £0.40 in Figure 36–1) that the quantity of dollars demanded exceeds the quantity supplied; that is, desired payments are not in balance because desired payments to the United States by holders of sterling exceed desired payments to Britain by holders of dollars. Dollars will be in scarce supply, some people who require dollars to make payments to America will be unable to obtain them, and the price of dollars will be bid up. The value of the dollar vis-à-vis the pound will appreciate, or the value of the pound vis-à-vis the dollar will depreciate, which is the same thing. As the price of dollars rises, the sterling price of U.S. exports to Britain rises and the quantity of U.S. dollars demanded to buy these goods falls off. However, as the dollar price of British exports to America falls, a larger quantity will be sold and the quantity of U.S. dollars supplied will rise. Thus a rise in the price of the dollar reduces the quantity demanded and increases the quantity supplied. Where the two curves intersect, quantity demanded equals quantity supplied—and the exchange rate is in equilibrium.

What happens if the price of dollars is too high? The quantity of dollars demanded will be less than the quantity supplied. With the dollar in excess supply, some people who wish to convert dollars into pounds will be unable to do so. The price of dollars will fall, fewer dollars will be supplied, more will be demanded, and an equilibrium will be reestablished. A competitive foreign exchange market is like other competitive markets in that the forces of demand and supply tend to lead to an equilibrium price in which quantity demanded equals quantity supplied.

Let us consider the effect on the exchange rate of various changes in the conditions that affect it.

A change in tastes

What will be the effect of a change in tastes whereby the British preference for American goods increases? At each sterling price charged in the British market, more U.S. goods will be demanded than were demanded previously. Thus, at each exchange rate, more U.S. dollars will be demanded (in order to pay for these goods). The demand curve for dollars shifts to the right. This extra demand for dollars raises the equilibrium price of dollars. Thus an increased preference on the part of British consumers for American goods will lead to an appreciation in the value of the dollar (a depreciation in the value of the pound).

The effects of a decreased preference of British for American goods or a changed preference of American consumers for British goods are left to the reader as exercises.

A fall in the domestic supply price of exports

Assume that the dollar price of U.S. export goods falls. This means that, at any given ex-change rate, the sterling price of U.S. exports will fall. What will this do to the exchange rate? If the dollar price of U.S. exports falls by X percent, then at each exchange rate the sterling price of these goods will also fall by X percent. As long as the British demand for U.S. goods is elastic, the quantity demanded will increase by more than X percent and the British will spend more dollars on imports from the United States. Thus a fall in the dollar price of U.S. exports will shift the demand for dollars to the right, and the sterling price of dollars will rise: The dollar appreciates and the pound depreciates.

A change in the price level of one country

What will happen if there is inflation in the United States with the price level stable in Britain? The dollar price of U.S. goods will rise, and American goods will become more expensive in Britain. This will cause the quantity of imports, and the quantity of dollars demanded by British importers in order to pay for the imports, to diminish.

At the same time, British exports to America will have an unchanged dollar price while the price of American goods sold at home will have been increased by the inflation. Thus British goods will be more attractive compared to American goods (because they have become *relatively* cheaper), and more British goods will be bought in America. This means that at any exchange rate the quantity of pounds demanded, and hence the quantity of dollars offered in exchange, will be increased.

An American inflation causes both curves to shift: The demand curve for dollars shifts to the left and the supply curve shifts to the right. As a result the equilibrium price of dollars must fall. Therefore, an American inflation leads to a depreciation in the value of the dollar and an appreciation in the value of the pound. (Remember that in this discussion the pound was chosen for illustrative purposes. American inflations have similar effects with respect to the mark, the yen, and all other foreign currencies.)

An equal percentage change in the price level in both countries

What if there is a 10 percent inflation in both the United States and Britain? In this case, the sterling prices of British goods and the dollar prices of U.S. goods both rise by 10 percent. At any given exchange rate, therefore, the dollar prices of British goods and the sterling prices of American goods will also rise by 10 percent. Thus the relative prices of imports and domestically produced goods will be unchanged in both countries. There is now no reason to expect any change in either country's demand for imports at the original exchange rate, so the inflations in the two countries leave the equilibrium exchange rate unchanged. The argument of this and the previous section can easily be combined to establish an important prediction:

If the price level of one country is rising relative to that of another country, the equilibrium value of its currency will be falling relative to that of the second country.

The effect of capital movements

What will happen if American investors wish to lend money in Britain? Perhaps they wish to make short-term loans by buying British treasury bills that have only a few weeks to run to maturity, or perhaps they wish to make long-term loans by buying ten-year bonds newly issued by an expanding British firm. In either case the American investors will require pounds sterling to pay for their purchases of securities. American investors will thus be supplying dollars and demanding pounds on the foreign exchange market. This will tend to appreciate the value of the pound and depreciate the value of the dollar.

A movement of investment funds has the effect of depreciating the exchange rate of the lending country and appreciating the exchange rate of the borrowing country.

International traders hold transactions balances just as do domestic traders. These balances are often lent out on short-term loan rather than being left idle. Naturally enough holders of these balances will tend to lend them, other things being equal, in those markets where interest rates are highest. Thus if one major country's short-term rate of interest rises above the rates in most other countries, there will tend to be a large inflow of short-term capital to take advantage of the high rate.

A restrictive domestic monetary policy will tend to cause high domestic interest rates; this will lead to inflow of foreign capital and an appreciation of the country's exchange rate. An expansionary monetary policy will tend to have the opposite effects.

FIXED EXCHANGE RATES

So far, the analysis has been concerned with the effects of various changes on the equilibrium rate of exchange. If exchange rates are left free to be determined by the forces of demand and supply, the theory just developed provides predictions about what happens to actual exchange rates. Such an exchange rate is called a **floating exchange rate.**

From the end of World War II until the early 1970s the rates of exchange between most currencies were set, or pegged, within very narrow limits by each country's domestic central bank. Such pegged rates are commonly spoken of as **fixed exchange rates.** When rates are fixed, fluctuations in the demand for and supply of dollars vis-à-vis other currencies cannot affect, except within very narrow limits, the actual exchange rate. They do change the magnitude of the excess demand for or supply of foreign exchange.

A change in a flexible rate is referred to as an **appreciation of the exchange rate** if the value of the currency in question rises and a

depreciation of the exchange rate if the value falls. A change in the rate at which a currency is fixed by its government is referred to as a **revaluation of the exchange rate** if the currency is increased in value and a **devaluation of the exchange rate** if the currency is reduced in value.

Managing fixed exchange rates

In our simple example, where only the United States and Britain are trading with each other, there are only *two* currencies and only *one* exchange rate between them. Thus the U.S. and British governments cannot make independent decisions on fixing exchange rates between their two currencies. In practice, it was foreign governments (in this example, the British government) that fixed the prices of their currencies in terms of U.S. dollars.

Having picked a fixed exchange rate for sterling against the dollar, the British authorities must then manage matters so that the rate can actually be maintained. The management of a fixed rate is illustrated in Figure 36–2. The first condition for successful management is that if the rate is not near the free-market equilibrium rate, *controls* of various sorts must be introduced to shift the demand curve for foreign exchange so that it intersects the supply curve at a rate very near the controlled one. This is usually done by restricting imports of goods and services or the export of capital.

The second condition is that short-run fluctuations in demand and supply must be canceled out by government sales and purchases of foreign exchange. In the face of unavoidable and uncontrollable short-term fluctuations in demand and supply, the central authorities can hold a fixed exchange rate only by entering the market and buying and selling as required to stabilize the price.

As long as the central authorities are trying to maintain an exchange rate *that equates demand and supply on average,* the policy can be

Figure 36–2   A fixed exchange rate

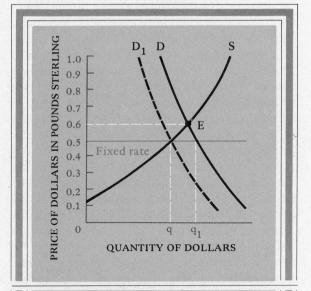

An exchange rate that overvalues the domestic currency leads to a balance-of-payments deficit unless restrictions are used to close the payments gap. Suppose demand and supply curves of dollars in the absence of government controls are D and S; equilibrium is at E with a price of £0.60 per dollar. If the exchange rate is fixed at £0.50 per dollar, the pound is worth $2.00, but at the free-market equilibrium it is worth only $1.67. There is an excess of dollars demanded over dollars supplied of qq_1, and this is the potential British balance-of-payments deficit. To maintain the fixed rate without a payments deficit, it is necessary to shift either (or both) the demand or the supply curve so that the two intersect at the fixed rate. If the curves are not shifted, and the payments deficit occurs, the fixed rate would have to be supported by reducing reserves of foreign exchange or gold by qq_1 per period.

successful. Sometimes the authorities will be buying and at other times they will be selling, and although their reserves will fluctuate, they will maintain a constant average level. If, however, there is a permanent shift in one of the curves, it will be very difficult to maintain the fixed rate. If for example, there is a major inflation in Britain, the equilibrium value of British currency will fall. The inflation increases the British demand for dollars in order to import now cheaper American goods, and it decreases the supply of dollars (because the British can now sell fewer of their more expensive goods to America). The equilibrium value of the pound falls, which is the same thing as saying that the equilibrium value of the dollar rises. If the Bank of England persists in trying to maintain the original rate, it will have to meet the excess demand for dollars by selling reserves of foreign exchange. This policy cannot persist indefinitely because sooner or later reserves become exhausted and the exchange rate will have to be changed to come closer to its free-market equilibrium value.

FIXED VERSUS FLUCTUATING EXCHANGE RATES

Until the early 1970s most governments did maintain fixed exchange rates for their currency.

Throughout the 1950s and 1960s a long debate had raged among economists and bankers about the relative merits of fixed versus fluctuating exchange rates. The whole debate was more notable (with a few major exceptions) for the passions involved than for the objectivity used in assessing empirical evidence. The supporters of fixed rates held that the stability of such rates is conducive to trade and that free-market rates might fluctuate so erratically as to disturb the free flow of international trade and to impair seriously long-run industrial planning based on a reasonable

assessment of a country's ability to sell goods abroad. In the final event, exchange rates were freed in the early 1970s and none of these drastic consequences ensued. Exchange rates have fluctuated but their movements have mainly followed long-run trends due to such factors as relative international rates of inflation. Short-term fluctuations have also occurred, but these do not seem to have been of sufficient magnitude to upset seriously the rising flows of worldwide international trade.

Summary

1. International trade can occur only if it is possible to exchange the currency of one country for that of another. The exchange rate between two currencies is the amount of one currency that must be paid in order to obtain one unit of another currency. Where more than two currencies are involved, there will be an exchange rate between each pair of currencies.

2. Arbitrage is the simultaneous buying and selling of anything, with a view to making a profit by buying where a given item is cheap and selling where it is dear. The possibility of arbitrage operations in foreign exchange markets ensures that "disorderly cross-rates" among several currencies cannot long persist.

3. Actual transactions among the firms, households, and governments of various countries are kept track of and reported in the balance-of-payments accounts. In these accounts, any transaction that uses foreign exchange is recorded as a debit item and any transaction that produces foreign exchange is recorded as a credit item. Transactions are divided into current account items—the import and export of goods and services—and capital account items, which include all remaining transactions. If all transactions are recorded, the sum of all credit items necessarily equals the sum of all debit items since the foreign exchange that is bought must also have been sold.

4. Although actual payments are necessarily in balance, desired payments need not be. If holders of dollars wish on all counts to purchase more foreign currency than holders of foreign currency wish to sell (in order to acquire dollars), desired payments are not in balance.

5. Exchange rates in a free market are determined by demand and supply. The supply of dollars (the demand for foreign exchange) arises from U.S. imports and U.S. capital exports; the demand for dollars (the supply of foreign exchange) arises from U.S. exports and U.S. capital imports.

6. A depreciation of the dollar lowers the foreign price of American exports and increases the quantity of dollars demanded; at the same time, it raises the dollar price of imports from abroad and thus lowers the quantity of dollars supplied to buy foreign exchange to be used to purchase foreign goods. Thus the demand curve for dollars is downward-sloping and the supply curve of dollars is upward-sloping when the quantities demanded and supplied are plotted against the price of dollars measured in terms of a foreign currency.

7. The dollar will tend to appreciate on the foreign exchange market if (among other things) there is a change in tastes in foreign countries in favor of American goods, there is a fall in the supply of American goods, or there is an inflation in foreign countries. Equal rates of inflation in all countries tend to leave exchange rates unaffected.

8. A movement of short- or long-term investment funds tends to appreciate the exchange rate of the borrowing country and depreciate the exchange rate of the lending country.

9. From the end of World War II to the early 1970s most countries maintained fixed exchange rates. Fixed rates pose two main problems: (a) If there are long-term shifts in demand and supply in the foreign exchange market, either the fixed rate must be changed periodically to accommodate such shifts or controls must be used to prevent the disequilibrium in demand and supply from occurring; (b) Short-term fluctuations must be ironed out by the central authority's sales and purchases of foreign exchange; these sales and purchases require that a reserve of gold and foreign exchange be held. The world is now on a system where many exchange rates are left to be determined by the forces of demand and supply on a relatively free market.

Concepts for review

Foreign exchange and exchange rates
Major components of the balance-of-payments accounts
Appreciation, depreciation, revaluation, and devaluation
   of exchange rates

The determination of equilibrium exchange rates
Balance-of-payments deficits and surpluses
Effects of inflations on exchange rates
Effects of capital movements on exchange rates
Fixed versus flexible exchange rates

Discussion questions

1. Indicate whether each of the following transactions increases the demand for dollars or the supply of dollars (or neither) on foreign exchange markets:
a. IBM moves $10 million from bank accounts in the United States to banks in Paris to expand operations there
b. the U.S. government extends a grant of $3 million to the government of Peru, which Peru uses to buy farm machinery from a Chicago firm
c. Canadian investors, responding to higher profits of U.S. rather than Canadian corporations, buy stocks through the New York Stock Exchange
d. U.S. oil companies build a pipeline across Canada to transport Alaskan oil to the United States
e. lower interest rates in New York than in London encourage British firms to borrow in the New York money market, converting the proceeds into pounds sterling for use at home
   Do these transactions affect the balance of payments, exchange rates, or both?

2. "The necessity of the government to balance the balance of payments through the settlement account is a relic of the past. It was a by-product of the adherence to a policy of fixed exchange rates." Do you agree?

3. What is the probable effect of each of the following on the exchange rate of a country, *ceteris paribus*?
a. the quantity of oil imports is greatly reduced, but the value of imported oil is higher due to price increases
b. the country's inflation rate falls well below that of its trading partners
c. rising labor costs of the country's manufactures lead to a worsening ability to compete in world markets
d. the government greatly expands its gifts of food and machinery to undeveloped countries
e. a major recession occurs with rising unemployment
f. the central bank raises interest rates sharply

4. Can speculation occur in foreign exchange markets if exchange rates are fixed? If they are free to fluctuate? Under

what circumstances will speculation help stabilize fluctuations in exchange rates?

5. The President of the Federal Reserve Bank of New York said recently, "Inflation is the enemy in maintaining international trade." What might he have had in mind? Compare the behavior of fixed versus fluctuating exchange rates in a world:
a. with no inflation, but short-run fluctuations in prices
b. with a substantial but similar degree of inflation everywhere in the world
c. with sharply varying degrees of inflation

6. Suppose in the foreign exchange market that £1 = $2.00, 1 French franc = $.20, and £1 = 12 French francs. How could an arbitrager make a profit? Assuming flexibility in exchange rates, how would such arbitrage eliminate this profit possibility? What would happen if exchange rates were fixed at these levels?

7. In recent years money wages have risen substantially faster in Canada than in the United States. Many Canadians have expressed the fear that their rapidly rising costs will price them out of U.S. markets. Did this fear make sense when the Canadian exchange rate was fixed relative to the American dollar? Does it make sense today when exchange rates are free to vary on the open market?

The gains from trade

The foundations of modern economics were laid by men intimately concerned with the problems of foreign trade. The great eighteenth-century British philosopher and economist David Hume, one of the first to work out the modern theory of the price system as a control mechanism, developed his theory mainly in terms of prices in foreign trade. Adam Smith and David Ricardo, the two British economists who developed to its full height the classical theory of the functioning of the economy, were greatly concerned with problems of trade. Smith, writing in 1776, attacked government intervention in foreign trade and was personally responsible for many reforms in the control of trade. Ricardo, writing in 1817, developed the basic theory of the gains from trade that is studied in this chapter. The repeal of the Corn Laws and the transformation of Britain in the mid nineteenth century from a country of high tariffs to one of complete free trade were to a significant extent the result of agitation by the economists whose theories of the gains from trade led naturally to a condemnation of all tariffs. The question of just how valuable is foreign trade continues to be debated today.

This chapter is devoted to two fundamental questions: (1) Is there any advantage in trade between nations? (2) If so, what principles determine which products a country should produce and export and which products it should import rather than produce?

INTERPERSONAL, INTERREGIONAL, AND INTERNATIONAL TRADE

Economists early recognized that the principles governing the gains from trade applied equally well to foreign trade and domestic trade. While governments tended to regard the two aspects of trade in very different lights, economists argued that the causes and consequences of international trade were merely an extension of the principles governing domestic trade. Thus economists—then and now—recognize that they are asking the same question when they ask what is the advantage of trade between two individuals, between two groups, between two regions, or between two countries. The advantages that may be realized as a result of trade are usually referred to more concisely as the **gains from trade**. The source of such gains is most easily studied by considering the differences between a world with trade and one without it.

First, consider trade among individuals. If there were no such trade, each person would have to be self-sufficient; he or she would have to produce all the food, clothing, shelter, medical services, entertainment, and luxuries of life that were required. Although a world of individual self-sufficiency is wildly unreal, it does not take much imagination to realize that living standards would be very low in such a world. Trade between individuals allows people to specialize in things they can do well and to buy from others the things they cannot easily produce. One who is a bad carpenter but a good doctor can specialize in medicine, providing a physician's services not only for his or her own family but also for a person who is an excellent carpenter yet has neither the training nor the ability to practice medicine. Thus trade and specialization are intimately connected. Without trade everyone must be self-sufficient; with trade everyone can specialize in what they do well and satisfy other needs by trading.

The same principles apply to regions. Without interregional trade, each region would have to be self-sufficient. With such trade, plains regions can specialize in growing grain, mountain regions in mining and lumbering, and regions with abundant power sources in manufacturing. Cool regions can produce wheat and other crops that thrive in such conditions, and tropical regions can produce bananas and coconuts. One would suspect—and soon we shall demonstrate—that the living standards of the inhabitants of all regions can be made higher if the inhabitants of each region specialize in producing the commodities in the production of which they have some natural or acquired advantage, and obtain other products by trade, than when each region is self-sufficient.

Identical remarks apply to nations. Whatever the divisions represented by national boundaries, they tend to be arbitrary with respect to the advantages of regional specialization and trade. There is no reason to expect that a national boundary will define an area that could be fully self-sufficient at little cost to itself. Thus nations, like regions or persons, can gain from specialization and the international trade that must accompany it.

SOURCES OF THE GAINS FROM TRADE

This preliminary discussion suggests one important possible gain from trade:

With trade, each individual, region, or nation is able to concentrate on producing things in which it has an advantage while trading to obtain things that it could not produce efficiently itself.

In order to concentrate on the sources of gains from trade one at a time, we begin by ruling out any gains in *productivity* that result from specialization. Assume that each region can produce goods at certain levels of productivity and that these levels are independent of the degree to which it specializes in the production of any good. What, in these circumstances, is the gain from regional specialization?

A special case—reciprocal absolute advantage

The gains from specialization are clear if there is a simple situation involving reciprocal absolute advantage. **Absolute advantage** relates to the quantities of a single product that can be produced with the same quantity of resources in two different regions. One region is said to have an absolute advantage over another region in the production of commodity X if an equal quantity of resources can produce more X in the first region than in the second.

Suppose region A has an absolute advantage over B in one commodity, while B has an absolute advantage over A in another. We refer to this as a case of reciprocal absolute advantage: Each country has an absolute advantage in some commodity. In such a situation total production of both can be increased (relative to a situation of self-sufficiency) if each region specializes in the commodity in which

it has the absolute advantage. Table 37–1 provides a simple example on the assumption that, with a given quantity of resources, America can produce 10 bushels of wheat or 6 yards of cloth, while England (with the same quantity of resources) can produce 5 bushels of wheat or 10 yards of cloth. Suppose at first that America and England are both self-sufficient, each producing wheat and cloth for its home markets. Now assume that trade is opened between the two countries and America moves resources out of cloth into wheat while England moves resources out of

Table 37–1 Gains from specialization with reciprocal absolute advantage

	ONE UNIT OF RESOURCES CAN PRODUCE	
	Wheat (bushels)	Cloth (yards)
America	10	6
England	5	10

CHANGES RESULTING FROM THE TRANSFER OF 1 UNIT OF AMERICAN RESOURCES INTO WHEAT PRODUCTION AND 1 UNIT OF BRITISH RESOURCES INTO CLOTH PRODUCTION

	Wheat (bushels)	Cloth (yards)
America	+10	− 6
England	− 5	+10
World	+ 5	+ 4

When there is reciprocal absolute advantage, specialization makes it possible to produce more of both commodities. The top half of the table shows the production of wheat and cloth that can be achieved in each country by using 1 unit of resources. The lower half shows the changes in production caused by the movement of 1 unit of resources out of cloth and into wheat production in America and in the opposite direction in England. There is an increase in world production of 5 bushels of wheat and 4 yards of cloth: worldwide, there are gains from specialization.

Table 37–2 Gains from specialization with comparative advantage

	ONE UNIT OF RESOURCES CAN PRODUCE	
	Wheat (bushels)	Cloth (yards)
America	100	60
England	5	10

CHANGES RESULTING FROM THE TRANSFER OF $\frac{1}{10}$ OF 1 UNIT OF AMERICAN RESOURCES INTO WHEAT PRODUCTION AND 1 UNIT OF BRITISH RESOURCES INTO CLOTH PRODUCTION

	Wheat (bushels)	Cloth (yards)
America	+ 10	− 6
England	− 5	+10
World	+ 5	+ 4

When there is comparative advantage, specialization makes it possible to produce more of both commodities. The productivity of English resources is left unchanged from Table 37–1; that of American resources is increased tenfold. England no longer has an absolute advantage in producing either commodity. Total production of both commodities can nonetheless be increased by specialization. The movement of $\frac{1}{10}$ of 1 unit of American resources out of cloth and into wheat and the opposite movement in England of 1 unit of resources causes world production of wheat to rise by 5 bushels and cloth by 4 yards. Reciprocal absolute advantage is not necessary for gains from trade.

wheat into cloth. The gains and losses in each country are summarized in the table. The total world production of both wheat and cloth increases when this reallocation of production takes place—as is shown by the fact that there is both more wheat and more cloth for the same use of resources.

These potential gains from *specialization* make possible gains from *trade*. England is producing more cloth and America more wheat than they did when they were self-sufficient. America is probably producing more wheat and less cloth than American consumers wish to buy, and England is producing more cloth and less wheat than English consumers wish to buy. If consumers in both countries are to get cloth and wheat in the proportions in which they desire them, it will be necessary for America to export wheat to England and to import cloth from that country.

International trade is necessary to achieve the gains that international specialization makes possible.

Because specialization and trade go hand in hand—no one would be motivated to achieve the gains from specialization without being able to trade the goods produced for goods desired—it is usual to use the term *gains from trade* to embrace them both.

A first general statement: comparative advantage

When each country has an absolute advantage over the other in one commodity the gains from trade are obvious: If each produces the commodity in the production of which it is more efficient than the other, world production will be higher than if each tries to be self-sufficient. But what if America can produce both wheat and cloth more efficiently than England? In essence, this was the question David Ricardo posed over 150 years ago, and his answer forms the basis of the theory of comparative advantage that is still accepted

by economists as a valid statement of the potential gains from trade.

Assume that American efficiency increases above the levels recorded in the previous example, so that a unit of American resources can produce either 100 bushels of wheat or 60 yards of cloth, while English efficiency remains unchanged, so that a unit of English resources can produce either 5 bushels of wheat or 10 yards of cloth. Now surely, America, which is better at producing both wheat and cloth than is England, has nothing to gain by trading with this inefficient foreign country! It *does* have something to gain, however, and it is important to see how this comes about.

The gain from specialization in this case is illustrated in Table 37–2. The new figures make America 10 times as efficient as she was in the situation of Table 37–1. Now if only one-tenth as many American resources are moved as in the earlier example, this duplicates exactly the changes in Table 37–1 and shows that it is still possible to increase world production of both wheat and cloth by having America produce more wheat and less cloth and England produce more cloth and less wheat.

There is a gain from specialization because although America has an absolute advantage over England in the production of both wheat and cloth, its margin of advantage differs in the two commodities. America can produce 20 times as much wheat as can England using the same quantity of resources, but only 6 times as much cloth. America is said to have a **comparative advantage** in the production of wheat and a comparative disadvantage in the production of cloth. England has a comparative disadvantage in the production of wheat and a comparative advantage in the production of cloth.

The most important proposition in the theory of international trade is:

The gains from specialization and trade depend on the pattern of comparative, not absolute, advantage.

A comparison of Tables 37–1 and 37–2 shows that the absolute *levels* of efficiency of two areas do not affect the gains from specialization. What matters is that the margin of advantage that one area has over the other must differ between commodities. As long as this is true, total world production can be increased if each area specializes in the production of the commodity in which it has a comparative advantage.

Comparative advantage is not only sufficient for gains from trade, it is also necessary. This is illustrated by the example in Table 37–3, in which America has an absolute advantage in both commodities but neither country enjoys a comparative advantage over the other in the production of either commodity. America is 10 times as efficient as Britain in the production of wheat and also in the production of cloth. Now, try as you may, there is no way to increase the production of both wheat and cloth by reallocating resources within America and within England. The lower half of the table provides one example of this. You should try others. It is possible to reallocate resources so as to get more of one commodity and less of the other, but this is also possible within either country. Absolute advantage without comparative advantage does not lead to gains from trade.

A second general statement: opportunity costs

Much of the previous argument has made use of the concept of a unit of resources and has also assumed that units of resources can be equated across countries, so that such statements as "America can produce 10 times as much wheat with the same quantity of resources as Britain" are meaningful. Measurement of the real-resources cost of producing commodities poses many difficulties. If, for example, Britain uses land, labor, and capital in proportions different from those used in the United States, it may not be clear which country gets more output "per unit of

Table 37–3 Absence of gains from specialization where there is no comparative advantage

	ONE UNIT OF RESOURCES CAN PRODUCE	
	Wheat (bushels)	*Cloth* (yards)
America	100	60
England	10	6

CHANGES RESULTING FROM THE TRANSFER OF 1 UNIT OF AMERICAN RESOURCES INTO WHEAT PRODUCTION AND 10 UNITS OF BRITISH RESOURCES INTO CLOTH PRODUCTION

	Wheat (bushels)	*Cloth* (yards)
America	+100	−60
England	−100	+60
World	0	0

Where there is no comparative advantage, there is no reallocation of resources within each country that will increase the production of both commodities. In this example America has the same absolute advantage over England in each commodity (tenfold). There is no comparative advantage, and world production cannot be increased by reallocating resources in both countries. Therefore specialization does not increase total output.

resource input." Fortunately, the proposition about the gains from trade can be restated without any reference to absolute efficiencies and in a way that should make even clearer the sources of gain in the previous examples.

To do this, return to the examples of Tables 37–1 and 37–2 and calculate the opportunity cost of wheat and cloth in the two countries. If resources are assumed to be fully employed, the only way to produce more of one commodity is to reallocate resources and thus produce less of the other commodity. Table 37–1 shows that a unit of resources in America can produce 10 bushels of wheat *or* 6 yards of cloth, from which it follows that the opportunity cost of producing a unit of wheat is 0.6 units of cloth while the opportunity cost of producing a unit of cloth is 1.67 units of wheat. These data are summarized in Table 37–4. The table also shows that in England the opportunity cost of 1 unit of wheat is 2 units of cloth forgone, whereas the opportunity cost of a unit of cloth is 0.50 units of wheat. Table 37–2 also gives rise to the opportunity costs in Table 37–4.

The sacrifice of cloth involved in producing wheat is much lower in America than it is in England, and world production can be increased if America rather than England produces wheat. Looking at cloth rather than wheat production, one can see that the loss of wheat involved in producing 1 unit of cloth is lower in England than in America. England is a lower (opportunity) cost producer of cloth than is America, and world production can be increased if England rather than America produces cloth. This situation is shown in Table 37–5.

The gains from trade arise from differing opportunity costs in the two countries.

The conclusions about the gains from trade in the hypothetical example of two countries and two commodities may be generalized:

Table 37–4 The opportunity cost of 1 unit of wheat and 1 unit of cloth in America and England

	Wheat	Cloth
America	0.6 yards cloth	1.67 bushels wheat
England	2.0 yards cloth	0.50 bushels wheat

Comparative advantages can always be expressed in terms of opportunity costs that differ between countries. These opportunity costs can be obtained either from Table 37–1 or Table 37–2. The English opportunity cost of 1 unit of wheat is obtained by dividing the cloth output of 1 unit of English resources by the wheat output. The resulting figure of 2.0 shows that 2 yards of cloth must be sacrificed for every extra unit of wheat produced by transferring English resources out of cloth production into wheat. The other three cost figures are obtained in a similar manner.

1. One country has a comparative advantage over a second country in producing a commodity if the opportunity cost (in terms of some other commodity) of production in the first country is lower. This implies however that it has a comparative disadvantage in the other commodity.

2. Opportunity costs depend on relative costs of producing two commodities, not on absolute costs. (To check this, notice that the data in both Tables 37–1 and 37–2 give rise to the opportunity cost in Table 37–4.)

3. If opportunity costs are the same in all countries, there is no comparative advantage and no possibility of gains from specialization and trade. (You can illustrate this for yourself by calculating the opportunity costs implied by the data in Table 37–3.)

4. If opportunity costs differ in any two countries, and both countries are producing both commodities, it is always possible to increase production of both commodities by a suitable reallocation of resources within each

Table 37–5 Gains from specialization when opportunity costs differ

CHANGES RESULTING FROM EACH COUNTRY'S PRODUCING ONE MORE UNIT OF COMMODITY IN WHICH IT HAS THE LOWER OPPORTUNITY COST		
	Wheat (bushels)	Cloth (yards)
America	+1.0	−0.6
England	−0.5	+1.0
World	+0.5	+0.4

Whenever opportunity costs differ between countries, specialization can increase the production of both commodities. These calculations show that there are gains from specialization given the opportunity costs of Table 37–4. To produce one more bushel of wheat, America must sacrifice 0.6 yards of cloth. To produce one more yard of cloth, England must sacrifice 0.5 bushels of wheat. Making both changes raises world production of both wheat and cloth.

country. (This proposition is illustrated in Table 37–5.)

If, but only if, opportunity costs differ among countries, specialization of each country in producing those commodities in which it has comparative advantages will make it possible to achieve gains from trade.

ADDITIONAL SOURCES OF THE GAINS FROM TRADE: LEARNING BY DOING AND ECONOMIES OF SCALE

So far it has been assumed that costs are constant. It has been shown that even then there are gains from specialization and trade as long as there are interregional differences in opportunity costs. If costs are not constant, additional sources of gain are possible. The early economists placed great importance on a factor that is now called learning by doing. They felt that as regions specialized in particular tasks, the workers and managers would become more efficient in performing them. As people acquire expertise, or know-how, costs tend to fall. A substantial body of modern empirical work suggests that this really does happen. If this is the case, then output of cloth per worker may rise in England as England becomes more specialized in that commodity, while the same may happen to output of wheat per worker in America. This is, of course, an additional gain to that which occurs if costs are constant.

A further reason why costs might fall as regions specialize concerns economies of larger-scale production.[1] If costs fall as output increases, world output can be greater when there is one large cloth industry in England and one large wheat industry in America, rather than two half-size cloth industries and two half-size wheat industries, one in each country.

---

[1] Readers who do not find it intuitively apparent that in some situations a larger level of output can lead to a lower cost per unit may wish to read (or reread) pages 180–182.

TERMS OF TRADE

So far it has been shown that world production can be increased if America and England specialize in the production of the commodity in which they have a comparative advantage and that specialization requires trade. How will these gains from specialization and trade be shared between the two countries? The division of the gain depends on the terms at which trade takes place. The **terms of trade** are defined as the quantity of domestic goods that must be given up to get a unit of imported goods. Thus the terms of trade are nothing more than the opportunity cost of obtaining goods through international trade rather than producing them directly.

In the example of Table 37–4, the American domestic opportunity cost of 1 unit of cloth is 1.67 bushels of wheat. If Americans can obtain cloth by international trade at terms of trade more favorable to them than 1.67 bushels of wheat, they will gain by doing so. Suppose that international prices are such that 1 yard of cloth exchanges for (i.e., is equal in value to) 1 bushel of wheat. At those prices, Americans can obtain cloth at a lower wheat opportunity cost by trade than by domestic production. Therefore the terms of trade favor selling wheat and buying cloth on international markets.

By a similar argument, English consumers in the example of Table 37–4 gain if they can obtain wheat abroad at any terms of trade more favorable than 2 yards of cloth per bushel of wheat, which is the English domestic opportunity cost. If the terms of trade are 1 bushel of wheat for 1 yard of cloth, the terms of trade favor English traders' buying wheat and selling cloth on international markets. Both England and America in this example gain from trade: Each can obtain the commodity in which it has a comparative disadvantage at a lower opportunity cost through international trade than through domestic production.

A graphic representation of the gains from trade

Suppose America has a comparative advantage in wheat and England a comparative advantage in cloth and that initially each country is self-sufficient. Each country will be operating at a point (such as *E* and *e* in the diagram below) on its own production—and consumption—possibility curve (shown as the heavy black line). The production possibility curves are straight lines because the opportunity cost of one commodity in terms of the other is assumed to be the same, no matter what are the current levels of output of each commodity. America's curve (*AB*) is steeper because the opportunity cost of producing cloth instead of wheat is high. America

has a comparative *advantage* in wheat and a comparative *disadvantage* in cloth.

Suppose America were offered the chance of obtaining cloth by trade at the English opportunity cost. It would pay America to produce nothing but wheat and then acquire cloth at the English opportunity cost. This would allow America to attain some point on *AC'*, which is drawn through *A* (America's fully specialized output of wheat) parallel to *CD*. Clearly consumption opportunities have increased: America could now reach a point such as E_1, which was unobtainable without trade. In such circumstances America would gain by trade and England would break even.

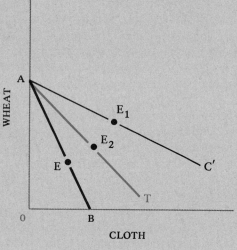

America's consumption possibilities

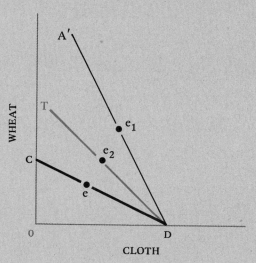

England's consumption possibilities

Suppose England were offered the chance of obtaining wheat at the American opportunity cost in terms of cloth sacrificed. It would pay England to produce nothing but cloth and to trade along DA' (drawn parallel to AB) to reach a higher point, say e_1, than was obtainable when wheat had to be obtained at the English opportunity cost. In such circumstances England would gain by trade and America would break even.

But this means there is a range of "prices" of cloth in terms of wheat—lower than America's high opportunity cost and higher than England's low opportunity cost—at which each country gains. Represent one such relative price by the slope of the colored line AT ($= DT$). If America produces only wheat and England only cloth, and they were willing to trade at this relative price, their consumption possibilities with trade are shown by the colored lines AT and DT. America can go to some point such as E_2, which gives it more wheat and more cloth than the self-sufficiency point E, while England can go to some point such as e_2, which gives it more wheat and more cloth than at its self-sufficiency point e. Thus the central generalization of the theory of the gains from trade is graphically illustrated: Trade allows each country to have more of each commodity than it could have if each country were self-sufficient.

Summary

1. The principles governing trade between any two groups are the same, be they individuals, regions, or nations.

2. One country (or region or individual) has an absolute advantage over another country (or region or individual) in the production of some commodity if, with the same input of resources in each country, it can produce more of the commodity than can the other.

3. In a situation of reciprocal absolute advantage it is easy to see that total production of both commodities can be raised if each country moves resources into the production of the commodity in which it has the absolute advantage. The gains from trade do not however require absolute advantage on the part of each country, only comparative advantage.

4. Comparative advantage refers to the relative advantage one country enjoys over another in various commodities. If, for example, America is 10 times as efficient as is England in producing commodity X and 12 times as efficient in producing commodity Y, America has a comparative advantage over England in Y (her margin of advantage over England is larger in Y than it is in X). Three other ways of saying the same thing are: (a) America has a comparative disadvantage in X; (b) England has a comparative advantage in X; (c) England has a comparative disadvantage in Y.

5. World production of all commodities can be increased if each country transfers resources into the production of the commodities in which it has a comparative advantage.

6. The gains from trade result from different opportunity costs in different countries, which in turn lead to differences in comparative advantage.

7. The theory of the gains from trade may be stated in this way: Trade allows all countries to obtain the goods in which they do not have a comparative advantage at a lower opportunity cost (in terms of units sacrificed of the commodities in which they do have a comparative advantage) than they would have to accept if they were to pro-

duce all commodities for themselves. This allows all countries to have more of all commodities than they could have if they made themselves self-sufficient.

8. As well as gaining the advantage of specialization according to comparative advantage, trade and specialization may allow a nation to realize the benefits of increasing returns to scale and learning by doing.

9. The terms of trade refer to the quantity of imported goods that can be obtained per unit of goods exported. They therefore measure the opportunity cost of obtaining goods by trade.

Concepts for review

Interpersonal, interregional, and international specialization

Absolute advantage, reciprocal absolute advantage, and comparative advantage

Gains from specialization and gains from trade

Opportunity cost and comparative advantage

Terms of trade

Discussion questions

1. Adam Smith saw a close connection between the wealth of a nation and its willingness "freely to engage" in foreign trade. What is the connection?

2. Suppose that the following situation exists. Assume no tariffs, no intervention by the government, and that labor is the only factor of production.

| Country | LABOR COST OF PRODUCTION OF ONE UNIT OF | |
	Artichokes	Bikinis
Inland	$20	$40
Outland	$20	$ X

Let X take different values—say $10, $20, $40, and $60. In each case, will there be trade? If so, in which direction?

3. It is probable that the United States with its advanced technology has an absolute advantage in the production of many manufactured products. Suppose it had such an advantage in all manufactured products. Should it then ever import any manufactured products?

4. Suppose, after 1865, the United States had become two separate countries with no trade between them. What predictions would you make about the standard of living compared to what it is today? Does the fact that Canada, the United States, and Mexico are separate countries lead to a lower standard of living in the three countries than if they were united into a new country called Northica?

5. Uruguay, formerly a significant exporter of raw beef and mutton, found it needed more exports to pay for its greatly increased imports of oil. Because the market for raw meat was limited, it decided to take advantage of its low wage rate by processing its beef, hides, and wool and then exporting these processed goods. Its exports doubled within a year with no change in exchange rates. What does this indicate about Uruguay's comparative advantages?

6. If the European Common Market led to such a rise in efficiency that the price of every good manufactured in Germany, France, and Italy fell below the price of the same good manufactured in the United States, what do you think would happen? Would Americans as a whole gain or lose because of this? Might some Americans be benefited and some hurt?

7. Studies of U.S. trade patterns have shown that very high wage sectors of industry are among the largest and fastest growing export sectors. Does this contradict the principle of comparative advantage?

8. The government of Brazil, by restricting exports of coffee, has greatly improved its balance of payments and raised its national income. Is it possible that Brazil is an exception to the proposition that there are gains from trade?

Tariffs

The nature and purpose of tariffs

A **tariff** is a tax applied on imports, often on an *ad valorem* (percentage of value) basis. Such a tax has the effect of raising the price of the taxed commodity. Tariffs can be used for two different and opposite purposes, for revenue and for protection. In the United States, customs revenues are about $4 billion per year. Although this amount is not negligible, it represents only 2 percent of federal tax revenue. The second and more common use is to raise the price of imported goods in order to discourage imports by offsetting (to some extent, at least) a cost advantage that foreign producers have over domestic producers of a particular product. The protective function of a tariff is opposed to the revenue function because the tariff will not yield much revenue if it is effective in cutting imports. This chapter concentrates on the protective feature of tariffs.

What determines the amount people are willing to pay for an imported good? Their tastes for the product naturally play a role, but beyond this the important limit is provided by the cost of purchasing the good domestically. If coal can be bought for $9 per ton at home, there will be no demand for identical foreign coal unless it can be provided for $9 per ton or less. When Americans find it cheaper to produce bituminous coal than to import it, there is no demand to import it at prevailing prices. However, it would cost in excess of $15 per pound to grow coffee in the United States. Because other countries can produce coffee at a fraction of this cost, the demand to purchase coffee at less than $15 per pound becomes a demand for imported coffee. Considered generally, there is a potential demand for those imports that can be delivered to a country at a cost lower than that at which they can be produced at home. At any time there is a whole array of potentially importable commodities, some with large cost savings, some with moderate ones, and some with no advantage at all.

A world of **free trade** would be one with no tariffs and no restrictions of any kind on importing or exporting. In such a world, a country would import all those commodities that it could buy from abroad at a delivered price lower than the cost of producing them at home.

Now suppose that a country imposes a 20 percent tariff on all imports. This does not prohibit trade, but by making all imported goods more expensive, it affects what it is profitable to import. Any foreign good that enjoys a cost advantage of less than 20 percent is now effectively prohibited. A 20 percent tariff thus provides protection to domestic industries that produce at a cost disadvantage of up to 20 percent. Imported goods that enjoy cost advantages in excess of 20 percent will still be in demand, but they will not be as big a bargain as they previously were. Because their price will be higher, a smaller quantity will be demanded than if there were no tariff.

If a country desires to prohibit trade in any specific commodity, it might do so by setting a tariff that is larger than the cost advantage of the lowest-cost foreign producer. If a country desires to prohibit all trade, it might do so by setting very high tariffs "across the board" or by setting a tariff on each item high enough to price that import completely out of the market.

In today's world two facts about international trade stand out. First, there is a great deal of it. Second, virtually every government interferes to some extent with free trade.

The reasons behind these facts need to be examined.

THE CASE FOR FREE TRADE

In Chapter 37 it was demonstrated that, where opportunity costs differ among countries, some degree of specialization with some consequent amount of trade will raise world standards of living. Free trade allows all countries to specialize in the production of commodities in which they have comparative advantages and thereby to produce (and thus to consume) more of all commodities than would be available if this kind of specialization had not taken place. In brief, free trade makes it possible to maximize world production and makes it *possible* for every household in the world to consume more goods than it could if free trade did not exist. There is abundant evidence to show that real differences in comparative costs do exist and that there are potential gains from trade because of these differences. There is, of course, also ample evidence that trade does occur, that no nation tries to be self-sufficient or refuses to sell to foreigners the things it produces cheaply and well.

This case for free trade is a powerful one that can be briefly stated. What needs to be explained is not the extent of trade but the fact that trade is not wholly free—the fact that tariffs and quotas exist 200 years after Adam Smith stated the case for free trade. Do these interferences exist merely because policy makers are ignorant of the principles of comparative advantage, or are there reasons (not included in the case for free trade) that make it sensible for a nation to levy some tariffs? Is there any valid case for interfering with trade? If there is, how does one find the balance between the advantages of more or less trade?

THE CASE FOR PROTECTIONISM

Protectionism refers to the protection of domestic industries from foreign competition. Such protection may be achieved either by tariffs that raise the price of foreign goods or by such nontariff barriers as quotas that make importing difficult or impossible. Two kinds of arguments for protection are common. The first concerns objectives other than maximizing output, and the second concerns the difference between the welfare of a single nation and that of the world.

Objectives other than maximizing output

It is quite possible for someone to accept the prediction that production is higher with free trade and yet rationally oppose free trade because of a concern with policy objectives other than production and consumption. There are, after all, policy goals other than maximizing national income.

For example, comparative costs might dictate that a country should specialize in the production of a single commodity, say bananas. The government might decide, however, that there are distinct social advantages to having a more diverse economy— one that would give citizens a wider range of occupations in which to develop their talents. The authorities might decide that the social and psychological gains from having a diverse economy more than compensate for a reduction in living standards by, say, 5 percent below what they could be with complete specialization of production.

Specializing in the production of one or two commodities, although dictated by comparative advantage, may involve risks that a country will wish to avoid. One such risk is a technological advance that renders its basic product obsolete. The quartz crystal seems to be threatening the Swiss watch industry in just this way. A different sort of risk is cyclical fluctuations in the prices of basic commodities, which may face depressed prices for years at a time, then periods of very high prices. For a country specializing in the production of such commodities, this means that the incomes of the producers will be subject to wide fluctuations. Even though the average level of income over a long period might be higher by specializing in production of such commodities, the serious social problems associated with a widely fluctuating national income may lead the government to decide to sacrifice some income in order to reduce fluctuations. Such a government policy might encourage the expansion of several stable industries that are protected by tariffs.

Yet another reason for protectionism may be the desire to maintain national traditions. For example, many Canadians are passionately concerned with maintaining a separate nation with traditions that differ from those of the United States. Many of these Canadians believe that the tariff helps them to do this, and they are prepared to accept a 5 or 10 percent cut in living standards in order to maintain this independence.[1]

The most frequently cited noneconomic defense of tariffs concerns national defense. It has traditionally been argued, for example, that the United States requires an experienced merchant marine in case of war and that this industry should be fostered by protectionist policies, even though it is less efficient than the foreign competition.

There is nothing irrational in a country's decision makers being willing to accept substantial costs in order to attain objectives other than the maximizing of living standards. Although most people would agree that, *ceteris paribus,* they prefer more income to less, economists cannot pronounce as irrational a nation that chooses to sacrifice some income in order to achieve other goals.

Tariffs as a means to higher national living standards

If a country produces a significant portion of the world output of some commodity, it may be able to exploit its monopoly position by interfering with the free flow of trade. By selling less of its commodity abroad and, of course, by buying less of other commodities the country can affect world prices and may be able to appropriate for itself a larger share of total world production than it would obtain if all prices were set on competitive markets. If other countries follow a fairly passive policy, one country may be able to reap

[1]How big a cut is really involved and whether the tariff really preserves independence are matters of current debate in Canada.

quite substantial monopoly gains. If, however, several countries all try to do the same thing, a battle of move and countermove will ensue until, at the end, everyone may be worse off than they were under free trade.

Probably the most important argument under this heading is the one relating to economies of scale, which is usually referred to as the **infant-industry argument for tariffs.** If an industry has large economies of scale, costs and prices must be high when the industry is small, but they will fall as the industry grows. In such an industry, the country first in the field has a tremendous advantage over latecomers. A newly developing country may find that its industries are unable to compete in the early stages of their development with established foreign rivals. A tariff may protect these industries from foreign competition while they grow up. Once they are large enough, they will be able to produce as cheaply as can foreign rivals and thus be able to stand on their own feet without tariff support.

A similar argument in favor of tariffs concerns learning by doing: If giving a domestic industry protection from foreign competition enables it to learn to be efficient, it may pay the government to protect the industry while it learns.

TRADE VERSUS TARIFFS

It appears from what has already been said that there is a very strong case for allowing trade in order to realize the gains from trade but that there may also be reasons for departing from completely free trade.

It is not necessary to choose between free trade on the one hand and complete protectionism on the other; a country can have some trade and some protectionism too.

Free trade versus no trade

It would undoubtedly be possible, by using greenhouses, to grow oranges, cotton, and other now-imported raw materials and food-stuffs in Norway and to grow coffee in the United States. But the cost in terms of other commodities foregone would be prodigious because these artificial means of production require lavish inputs of factors of production. It would likewise be possible for a tropical country currently producing foodstuffs to set up industries to produce all the types of manufactured products that it consumes. The cost in terms of resources used, for a small country without natural advantages in industrial production, could be very large. It thus appears that there is a large gain to all countries in having specialization and trade. The real output and consumption of all countries would be very much lower if each had to produce domestically all the goods that it consumed.

If it were necessary to make an all-or-nothing choice, virtually all countries would choose free trade over no trade.

Some trade versus no trade

Table 38–1 shows the level of tariffs on selected commodities in force today. It is clear that these tariffs are not sufficient to offset widely differing cost conditions in certain countries, the most dramatic being those associated with climate. Even the most casual observation reveals such major cost differences among countries that no one could doubt that there are significant gains from trading for commodities in which a country has a large comparative disadvantage. Careful empirical measurement might put an actual numerical value on the amount of gains, but it is inconceivable that it could refute the general hypothesis that production and consumption in the world, and in each major trading country, are higher with trade than they would be with no trade.

A little more trade versus a little less trade

At the level of tariffs existing today we have trade between nations, but it is not perfectly free. Would we be better off if all of today's

tariffs were reduced or increased a little bit? It is quite a jump from the proposition that "Some trade is better than no trade" to the proposition that "A little more trade than we have at present is better than a little less trade." Yet most arguments about commercial policy involve the latter sort of proposition, not the former. Most actual policy disagreements concern the relative merits of free trade versus controlled trade with tariffs on the order of, say, 5, 10, or 15 percent. Such tariffs would not cut out imports of bananas, coffee, diamonds, bauxite, or any of the commodities in whose production America would be really inefficient. (Yet these are just the commodities that defenders of free trade sometimes use as examples when the hypothesis of the gains from trade is challenged.) If one accepts the hypothesis that some trade is better than no trade, one is not necessarily committed to accepting the hypothesis that free trade is better than controlled trade with, say, 15 percent tariffs; nor is one committed to saying that 9 percent tariffs would be better than 10 percent tariffs.

As a simplified version of the sort of argument that really does take place over commercial policy, compare the effects of a 20 percent uniform *ad valorem* tariff with those of free trade. As a rule, tariffs are seldom advocated to protect industries that are extremely inefficient compared to foreign industries; they are usually advocated to protect industries that can very nearly compete, but not quite. How much would be gained by removing 20 percent tariffs or how much lost by imposing 20 percent tariffs in a situation of free trade? Tariffs of 20 percent will protect industries up to 20 percent less efficient than foreign competitors. If the costs of the different tariff-protected industries were spread out evenly, some would be 20 percent less efficient than their foreign competitors, but others would be only 1 percent less efficient, and their average inefficiency would be about half the tariff rate. In other words, they would be on average about 10 percent less efficient

Table 38–1 Tariffs on selected commodity groups (ad valorem rates)

Commodity	United States	EEC	Japan
Weighted average of all dutiable manufactures	9.0	9.6	10.7
Paper and paperboard	0.9	9.5	9.2
Plastics	8.6	10.0	12.1
Clothing and clothing accessories	25.5	16.5	18.1
Iron and steel, manufactured goods	7.9	8.0	8.7
Coal, petroleum, natural gas (crude)	3.2	0.4	10.6
Coffee	0.0	21.0	35.0
Rubber, manufactured articles	5.0	8.6	10.1

Source: GATT, Basic Documentation for Tariff Study, 1973 Summary Table No. 3 and *Commerce America,* April 12, 1976.

By contrast with Japan and the countries of western Europe, America is a relatively low-tariff country. The figures are based on rates that came into existence during 1972 after the completion of all tariff reduction in the Kennedy Round. The current (Tokyo Round) of multinational tariff negotiations is attempting to get agreement on further reductions by the start of 1978. The rates in the table are the rates generally available to any importer. Since 1970 several industrial countries have given lower ("preferential") rates for underdeveloped countries. The United States began offering such preferential rates in 1976.

than their foreign competitors. Suppose that as a result of tariffs, approximately 10 percent of a country's resources are allocated to industries different from the ones to which they would be allocated to if there were no tariffs. This means that about 10 percent of a country's resources would be working in certain industries only because of a tariff protection. If the average protected industry is 10 percent less efficient than its foreign rival, we have a situation in which approximately 10 percent of a country's resources are producing about 10 percent less efficiently than they would be if there were no tariffs. This causes a reduction in national income of something on the order of 1 percent as a result of tariff protection.

This rather rough-and-ready calculation is meant to do no more than illustrate why the gains from removing modest tariffs may be small. The conclusion has been established by three careful studies of the effect of tariffs in Great Britain and Europe. Professor P. J. Verdoorn estimated that the gain to the six European Common Market countries from eliminating tariffs on trade among themselves to be about 0.05 percent of their national incomes. Professor Harry Johnson estimated that the maximum cost to Britain of staying out of the Common Market would have been equal to approximately 1 percent of her national income. And Professor W. Welmesfelder estimated that the gain to Germany from major tariff reductions in 1956 and 1957 would have been less than 1 percent of German national income.

The net gains from somewhat freer trade than there is today are not so large as to make it certain that the removal of all remaining tariffs is desirable.

Even moderate costs associated with removing tariffs would offset the small predicted advantage. Whether this is in fact so is properly an empirical matter, not a logical one.

The main concern in this section has been not to argue for or against free trade but to investigate what can be said about trade and tariffs on the basis of economic analysis. There are benefits to be achieved by international trade, and there are benefits of a different sort to be achieved by imposing certain tariffs. Whether free trade is better than a policy of moderate tariffs depends on the policy goals that one is trying to attain and the magnitude of the benefits and costs of the actions. There is thus a highly important area for study and debate about trade and tariffs. There is also, however, a lot of assertion that does not advance the debate; fallacious arguments are

heard on both sides. Because these arguments have been around so long it is worthwhile discussing them.

Fallacious anti-tariff arguments

Free trade always benefits all countries. This is not necessarily so. The potential gains from trade may be offset by the costs of trade, such as unemployment or economic instability, or the interference with policy objectives other than maximizing income, and these may render some tariff interference desirable.[2]

Infant industries never grow up. It is often argued that to grant tariffs on an infant-industry basis is a mistake in practice because infant industries seldom admit to growing up and will cling to their tariff protection even when they are full-grown adults. Even if this alleged fact were true, it would not be a sufficient reason for avoiding such tariffs. If the economies of scale are realized, the real costs of production are reduced and resources are freed for other uses. Whether or not the tariff remains, a cost saving has been effected by the scale economies.

Fallacious pro-tariff arguments

The exploitation doctrine. According to this view, one trading partner *must* always reap a gain at the other's expense. Since the principle of comparative advantage shows that it is possible for both parties to gain from trade, even if one of them is more efficient than the other in all lines of production, it thus refutes the exploitation doctrine of trade. If opportunity cost ratios differ in two countries, specialization and the accompanying trade make it possible to produce more of all commodities

---

[2]To see how sensitive the gains from trade are to other considerations, suppose that totally free trade led to an allocation of resources that was 1 percent more efficient than one resulting from 20 percent tariffs, but led simultaneously to an average level of unemployment 1.2 percent higher. In this case, free trade would bring losses rather than gains.

and thus make it possible for both parties to get more goods as a result of trade than they could get in its absence. The answer to the question, Is it *possible* for trade to be mutually advantageous? is an emphatic yes.

If I buy a foreign good, I have the good and the foreigner has the money, whereas if I buy the same good locally, I have the good and our country has the money, too. This argument (sometimes attributed to Abraham Lincoln) is often voiced in a slogan such as "Buy American." The argument assumes that domestic money actually goes abroad physically when imports are purchased and that trade flows in only one direction. When American importers purchase Italian-made goods, they do not send dollars abroad. They (or some financial agent activated by their decision) buy Italian lire (or claims on them) and use these to pay the Italian manufacturer. They purchase the lire on the foreign exchange market by giving up dollars to someone who wishes to use them for expenditure in the United States. Even if the money did go abroad physically—that is, if an Italian firm accepted a shipload of dollars—it would be because that firm (or someone to whom it could sell the dollars) wanted them to spend in the only country where they are legal tender, the United States. Dollars ultimately do no one any good except as purchasing power. It would be miraculous indeed if green pieces of paper could be exported in return for a quantity of real goods. After all, the central bank has the power to create as much new money as it wishes. It is only because the green paper can buy American commodities that others want it.

We must protect our workers against low-wage foreign labor. "Surely," the argument goes, "the products of Oriental sweatshops will drive our products from the market, and the high U.S. standard of living will be dragged down to that of the impoverished Orient." Arguments of this sort have, through the years, swayed many voters. As a prelude to considering them, stop and think what the argument would imply if taken out of the international level and put into a local one, where the same principles govern the gains from trade. Is it really impossible for a rich person to gain from trading with a poor one? Would the local millionaire be better off if he did all his own typing, gardening, and cooking? No one believes that a rich person cannot gain from trading with those who are less rich. Why then must a rich group of people lose from trading with a poor group? "Well," you say, "the poor group will price their goods too cheaply." Does anyone believe that consumers lose from buying in a discount house or a supermarket, just because they sell at a lower price than the old-fashioned corner store? Consumers gain if they can buy the same goods at a lower price. If the Koreans pay low wages and sell their goods cheaply, then *their labor may suffer,* but we gain because we obtain their goods at a low cost in terms of the goods that we must export in return. The cheaper our imports are, the better off we are in terms of the goods and services available for domestic consumption.

Stated in more formal terms, the gains from trade depend on comparative, not absolute, advantages. World production is higher when any two areas, say the United States and Japan, specialize in the production of the goods for which they have a comparative advantage than when they both try to be self-sufficient.

Might it not be possible, however, that Japan will undersell the United States in all lines of production and thus appropriate all, or more than all, of the gains for herself, leaving the United States no better off, or even worse off, than if it had remained self-sufficient? The answer is No, and the clue to why this is not so is found in Chapter 36.

Assume that trade exists between the United States and Japan and that, at the present rate of exchange between dollars and yen, the Japanese can undersell the United States in all commodities. Everyone will want to buy Japanese goods, and thus everyone will need yen. No one will want to buy U.S. goods, and thus no one will need dollars. On the foreign exchange market there will be a big demand for yen and no yen for dollars. In a free market, the dollar will depreciate in value and the yen will appreciate. As this happens, the prices of U.S. exports will fall, whereas the prices of Japanese exports will rise. This will continue until some U.S. goods become cheaper than their Japanese equivalents. When this happens, the United States will begin to buy fewer goods from Japan and the Japanese will buy some goods from the United States. The dollar will continue to depreciate until demand and supply for dollars are equated, that is, until—ignoring capital movements—the demand for exports equals the demand for imports. Equality of demand and supply on the foreign exchange market ensures that trade flows in both directions.

Imports can be obtained only by spending the currency of the country that makes the imports. Claims to this currency can be obtained only by exporting goods and services or by borrowing. Thus, lending and borrowing aside, imports must equal exports. All trade must be in two directions. We can buy only if we can also sell. In the long run, trade cannot hurt a country by causing it to import without exporting. Trade, then, always provides scope for international specialization, with each country producing and exporting those goods for which it has a comparative advantage.

Exports are desirable because they raise national income; imports are undesirable because they lower it. In the theory of the circular flow, exports are injections that, *ceteris paribus,* raise national income, and imports are withdrawals that, *ceteris paribus,* lower national income. "Surely," this argument goes, "it is desirable to encourage exports and discourage imports."

Saying that exports raise national income means that they add to the value of output, but they do not add to the value of domestic consumption. In fact, exports are goods produced at home and consumed abroad, while imports are goods produced abroad and consumed at home. The standard of living in a country depends on the goods and services available for *consumption,* not on what is produced.

If exports were really good and imports really bad, then a fully employed economy that managed to increase its exports without any corresponding increase in its imports ought to be made better off thereby. Such a change, however, would result in a reduction in current standards of living because when more goods are sent abroad and no more are brought in from abroad, the total goods available for domestic consumption must fall.

What happens if a country does achieve a surplus of exports over imports for a considerable period of time? It will be accumulating claims to foreign exchange for which there are three possible uses: (1) to add to foreign exchange reserves, (2) to buy foreign goods, and (3) to make investments abroad. Consider each of these.

Foreign exchange reserves are required for the smooth functioning of a system of fixed exchange rates. Accumulation of reserves over and above those required to cope with fluctuations in private payments serves no purpose. Permanent excess reserves represent claims on foreign output that are never made effective.

British pounds or Indian rupees cannot be eaten, smoked, drunk, or worn. But they can be spent to buy British and Indian goods that can be eaten, smoked, drunk, or worn. When such goods are imported and consumed, they add to U.S. living standards. Indeed, the main purpose of foreign trade is to take advantage of international specialization; trade allows more consumption than would be possible if all goods were produced at home. From this point of view, the purpose of exporting is to allow the importation of goods that can be produced more cheaply abroad than at home.

An excess of exports over imports may be used to acquire foreign exchange needed to purchase foreign assets, but such foreign investments add to living standards only when the interest and profits earned on them are used to buy imports that do not have to be matched by currently produced exports—that is, when, in the future, they produce an excess of imports over exports. From this point of view, the purpose of exporting more than one is importing in order to make foreign investments is eventually to be able to import more than one is exporting.

In summary, the living standards of a country depend on the goods and services consumed in that country. The importance of exports is that they permit imports to be made. This two-way international exchange is valuable because more goods can be imported than could be obtained if the same goods were produced at home.

Tariffs reduce domestic unemployment. It is sometimes thought that an economy with substantial amounts of unemployment, such as the U.S. economy in the 1930s or the early 1970s, provides an exception to the case for freer trade. Assume there is a rise in exports without a corresponding rise in imports, perhaps because the government has put a subsidy on exports and increased the rates of tariffs charged on imports. According to the theory of the multiplier, this rise in exports will increase income and employment. Surely, in a time of unemployment, this is to be regarded as a "good thing."

Two points need to be made about such a policy. In the first place, the goods being produced by the newly employed workers in the export sector are not available for domestic consumption and so do not directly raise domestic standards of living. Would it not be

better if, instead of subsidizing exports, the central authorities subsidized the production of goods for the home market so that all the goods produced—instead of only those produced in response to the increased incomes—would contribute to a rise in domestic living standards? Or, if one objects to the government subsidization of private firms, the government could create new employment by building more roads, schools, and research laboratories. As a result, income and employment would go up but there would be something more tangible to show for it in the first instance than the smoke of ships disappearing over the horizon bearing the subsidized exports to foreign markets.

The second point to be made concerns the foreign effects of such a policy of fostering exports and discouraging imports in a situation of general world unemployment. Although the policy raises domestic employment, it will have the reverse effect abroad where it creates unemployment. Such a policy is referred to as "exporting one's unemployment." The foreign countries will suffer a rise in their unemployment because their exports will fall and their imports rise. This will set up a multiplier process that reduces their levels of income and employment. They will soon be forced to take steps to remove these effects. If they do this by restricting imports, the original country will lose the stimulus that it originally obtained by encouraging exports. If all countries try such a policy of expanding exports and discouraging imports, the net effect is likely to be a large fall in the volume of international trade without much change in the level of employment in any country.

Arguments about tariffs: a final word

Although one can think of many cases in which a tariff policy has been pursued after a rational assessment of the approximate cost, it is hard to avoid the conclusion that, more often than not, high tariff policies are pursued for rather flimsy objectives of national prestige with very little idea of the actual costs involved or because the central authorities believe one or another of the fallacious protariff arguments. The very high tariffs in the United States over the decades of the 1920s and 1930s are a conspicuous example.

Trade and tariffs in the world today

TARIFFS IN THE UNITED STATES

Figure 38–1 shows how tariffs have been used in U.S. history. The government of the United States has often been less sensitive to

Figure 38–1 Tariffs in the United States, 1828–1975

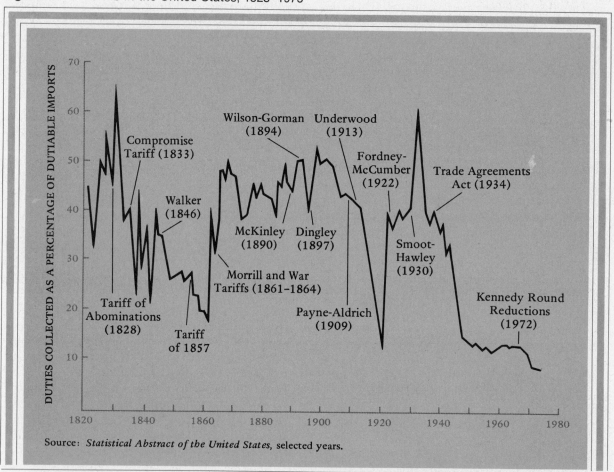

Source: *Statistical Abstract of the United States,* selected years.

U.S. tariffs have been lower in the post-World War II period than for any other period of comparable length in American history. Throughout its history the United States has alternated from being a high-tariff country to being a modest-tariff one. The average rate of tariff has been lower since World War II than ever before. The rate fell below 10 percent in 1971. It may be expected to fall below the current 8 percent level when the ongoing Tokyo Round of negotiations is completed.

arguments for freer trade than to the protests of producers who would be hurt by tariff reductions. Part of the reason was the relative unimportance of trade to the American economy—even today only about 7 or 8 percent of the economy's output is exported.[3] By contrast, trade is extremely important to the economies of many countries. Expressing exports as a percentage of GNP, the figures are 29 percent for Sweden, 25 percent for Great Britain, and 24 percent for Canada. The loss to these countries of their foreign trade would have a serious effect on their standards of living. Similarly, in the eighteenth and nineteenth centuries the rapidly developing industrial economies of Europe owed a great deal to trade, both for the imports of raw materials and foodstuffs and for the export of goods manufactured at home.

However, given a few years in which to develop domestic sources or invent synthetic substitutes for a few key imported raw materials, much of the existing foreign trade could be eliminated without too much effect on the standards of living of U.S. citizens.

Although foreign trade is not a large fraction of American national income, such trade is very important to particular industries. Large quantities of certain materials—petroleum, bauxite, coffee, iron ore, lumber, and newsprint—are imported. The loss of these supplies would cause serious difficulties to some industries, and substitute products would have to be developed, possibly at a very high cost. The existence of certain domestic industries—such as those producing bicycles, watches, TV sets, radios, clothing, and even automobiles—has been threatened from time to time by foreign competition, indicating that even if the existence of foreign trade is not critically important to the country as a whole, it does affect particular sectors of it in important ways. Representatives of these sectors are likely to lobby vigorously for protection.

While imports are not critically important to the U.S. economy, these imports are the exports of other countries and, in some cases, they are very important to those other countries. In Canada, for example, nearly two thirds of the trade is with the United States. Exports to the United States account for about one-sixth of Canadian GNP. A change in U.S. commercial policy that caused only a small ripple in the U.S. economy could cause a tidal wave in Canada.

Other countries are critical of and sensitive to changes in U.S. policy if those changes will have a vital effect on them. They fear that because it does not have such a vital effect on the United States, a policy change may sometimes be made without due consideration of its effects on others. It is unpleasant to be in the position of having your own welfare affected by decisions that do not matter much one way or the other to the person making them. Americans learned this lesson when OPEC embargoed oil shipments to the United States. Table 38–2 shows the importance of trade with the United States to the economies of some other countries.

There is no doubt that foreign trade contributes substantially to the standards of living of many countries and that even the United States with its low dependence on trade would have its living standard noticeably lowered if it were to refuse to participate in any of the gains from trade between nations. It is, as shown in Table 38–1, a relatively low-tariff country today.

INTERNATIONAL AGREEMENTS CONCERNING TRADE AND TARIFFS

In the past any one country could impose any desired set of tariffs on its imports. But when one country increases its tariffs, the action may trigger retaliatory changes by its trading partners. Just as an arms race can escalate, so

---

[3]Trade is much more important in the United States today than it was half a century ago, in the heyday of prohibitive tariffs.

Table 38–2   Percentages of trade
with the United States, 1974

Country	Percentage of exports to United States	Percentage of imports from United States
Canada	64	65
Mexico	62	66
Venezuela	49	46
Philippines	42	24
Nigeria	33	12
Japan	23	20
Brazil	22	25
New Zealand	14	13
Ghana	13	10
Iran	12	25
United Kingdom	11	10
Portugal	10	9
Australia	9	21
Thailand	8	13
Italy	8	8
Germany	8	8
Denmark	6	6
France	5	8
Sweden	5	7
Netherlands	4	9
Austria	3	3
USSR	1	3

Source: *Direction of Trade Annual 1970–74; Commerce America,* February 1976.

For many countries trade with the United States is a very large part of their total exports, imports, or both. Not surprisingly, the United States is the major trading partner of Canada and Mexico. But the United States as a market for exports or a source of imports is also vitally important to such distant countries as Venezuela, Brazil, Japan, Nigeria, Australia, and Iran.

can a tariff war; precisely this happened in the world during the 1920s and early 1930s.

Bilateral agreements

International attempts to roll back tariffs from the high levels of the late 1920s began with the passage of the 1934 Trade Agreements Act in the United States. This act authorized the President to enter into bilateral trade agreements with other countries providing for *reciprocal* decreases in any tariff of up to 50 percent. The act also provided for unconditional most-favored-nation treatment in any such agreement. This meant that if we agreed on a tariff with country X for some commodity today, it would be automatically lowered if tomorrow we agreed to a lower tariff on that commodity with country Y. Cordell Hull, President Franklin Roosevelt's Secretary of State from 1933 to 1944, made lowering of tariffs by reciprocal trade agreements a major activity of his years in office, and the effect on tariff levels is apparent in Figure 38–1.

There were serious drawbacks to bilateral negotiation. Because of the most-favored-nation clauses, one country was reluctant to make large reductions in tariffs on an important import except in return for a reciprocal reduction in the tariff it paid on an important export. But much trade is multinational; A imports from B, which imports from C, which imports from A. In these circumstances *bilateral* negotiations between A and B, B and C, and C and A might each fail to agree to tariff reductions. The solution, obviously, was for multinational negotiations, but these did not occur on a large scale until after World War II.

The General Agreement on Tariffs and Trade (GATT)

One of the most notable achievements of the post-World War II world in moving back from the high-water mark of protectionism achieved in the 1930s was the General Agreement on Tariffs and Trade (GATT). Under this agreement, GATT countries meet periodically to negotiate bilaterally on mutually advantageous cuts in tariffs. They agree in advance that any tariff cuts negotiated in this way will be extended to all member countries. Some significant tariff reductions have been effected by the member countries, but the total results have fallen far short of the hopes of the founders. Although tariffs are not as low as free traders might wish, it is probable that without GATT's imaginative attempt at post-World War II cooperation, tariffs would be significantly higher than they are now.

The most recent in the series of completed GATT agreements was the so-called Kennedy Round begun in November 1964 and completed in May 1967. It owes its name to President John F. Kennedy, who was instrumental in setting up formal negotiations and who obtained permission from Congress to negotiate reductions of up to 50 percent in existing U.S. tariff rates. The reductions finally negotiated averaged about one-third of existing world rates. They were phased over five years with the last installment in 1972. These are the most significant tariff cuts achieved since World War II.

To some extent, however, the tariffs were replaced by a series of **nontariff barriers to trade.** These are defined as anything other than tariffs that impedes the free flow of international trade; they include production and export subsidies, standards purporting to maintain the quality of imports, quotas on imports, complex administrative procedures, variable indirect taxation, and minimum allowed import prices. For this reason, it is hard to assess the overall quantitative effect of the Kennedy Round, but there can be little doubt that even when all qualifications are allowed, it represented a significant step in the direction of freer international trade.

In 1975 the so-called Tokyo Round of negotiations began, with 90 countries participating. This round is scheduled to be completed by the end of 1977.

The European Economic Community (EEC)

In 1945, Europe seemed on the verge of famine and collapse. Each of the war-devastated countries set out almost immediately to deal with its own crises of insufficient food, shelter, and fuel. In 1947, America came forward with the Marshall Plan, which gave U.S. aid and encouragement to the devastated continent. The Marshall Plan provided substantial impetus to the movement for common rather than disjointed action in dealing with the continent-wide crises, a movement that began with an attempt to reject the national rivalries that had caused two world wars within twenty-five years. A decade after the first tentative steps to cooperative recovery, the nations of western Europe were no longer in need of economic aid. Indeed, many were achieving rates of economic growth well above that of the United States and were moving toward an economic union that some hoped might be the first step toward an eventual political union.

In 1957, the Treaty of Rome created the European Economic Community (EEC), which is known popularly as the European Common Market or the Community. The six original members were France, Germany, Italy, Holland, Belgium, and Luxembourg. The EEC is dedicated to bringing about free trade, complete mobility of factors of production, and eventual harmonization of fiscal and monetary policies among the member countries. Tariff reductions were made according to a time schedule that eliminated all tariffs on manufactured goods within the Community before 1970. If the development continues, western Europe will be, before the end of the century, a single economic community with a free movement of goods, labor, and capital among the member countries.

On January 1, 1973, despite strong divisions within each country, Great Britain, the Republic of Ireland, and Denmark joined the Community, the first two after close votes in their parliaments and the latter after a plebiscite. At the same time, Norway voted in a plebiscite to remain outside.

Summary

1. Tariffs are taxes placed on imported goods; they can be used as a source of revenue or as a tool of protection to restrict or to prevent the importation of certain goods.

2. The case for free trade is that world output of all commodities can be higher under free trade than when protectionism restricts regional specialization.

3. Protection can be urged as a means to ends other than maximizing world living standards. Examples of such other ends are to produce a diversified economy, to reduce fluctuations in national income, to retain distinctive national traditions, and to improve national defense.

4. Protection can also be urged on grounds that it may lead to higher living standards for the protectionist country than would a policy of free trade. Such a result might come about through exploiting a monopoly position or by allowing inexperienced or uneconomically small industries to become sufficiently efficient that they can subsequently compete with foreign industries.

5. Virtually everyone would agree that free trade should be chosen if the only choice were between free trade and *no* trade. Most real choices facing nations today are not, however, about free trade versus no trade; rather they are about a *little more* trade (caused by a slight lowering of tariffs) versus a *little less* trade (caused by a slight raising of tariffs). Here the choice is not so obvious as the one between free trade and no trade. The potential gains from small reductions in tariffs must be balanced against other objectives and other effects.

6. Some fallacious antitariff arguments are that (a) because it is possible for free trade to be beneficial, free trade will in fact always be beneficial; and (b) because infant industries seldom admit to growing up and thus try to retain their tariff protection indefinitely, the whole country necessarily loses by protecting its infant industries.

7. Some fallacious protariff arguments are that (a) mutually advantageous trade is impossible because one trader's gain must always be the other's loss; (b) our high-paid workers must be protected by tariffs against the competition from low-paid foreign workers; (c) imports are to be discouraged because they are withdrawls from the circular flow that lower national income and cause unemployment; and (d) buying abroad sends our money abroad, whereas buying at home keeps our money at home.

8. Trade is very important in the national incomes of many countries, but it is relatively unimportant to the United States. Nonetheless, trade is of great importance to particular American industries, and few economists doubt that American living standards would be lowered significantly if America tried to make itself fully self-sufficient.

9. International negotiations have succeeded in lowering tariff barriers. In 1934 the United States took the lead in negotiating reciprocal trade treaties containing most-favored-nation clauses. After World War II the GATT began a series of multinational rounds of tariff reduction that have greatly lowered tariffs. However, many nations have substituted nontariff barriers to some extent. The EEC has eliminated tariff and nontariff barriers among its original members.

Concepts for review

Free trade and protectionism
The case for some protectionism
The case for free trade versus no trade
Fallacious protariff and antitariff arguments
Tariff and nontariff barriers to trade
Most-favored-nation treatment
Bilateral and multilateral agreements

Discussion questions

1. Suppose America had imposed prohibitive tariffs on all imported cars over the last three decades. How do you think this would have affected (a) the U.S. automobile industry, (b) the American public, (c) the kinds of cars produced by U.S. manufacturers?

2. George Washington, in his Farewell Address, argued that the United States should foster free trade, but at the same time avoid any complex political arrangements with foreign countries. Are free trade and absence of foreign entanglements compatible goals in time of peace? In a world where there is a threat of war?

3. Lobbyists for many industries argue that their products are essential to national defense and therefore require tariff protection. Suppose that supplies of a certain commodity are indeed essential in wartime. How does restricting im-

ports solve the problem? Are there any alternatives to import restrictions, and, if so, how might the alternatives be evaluated?

4. Import quotas are often used instead of tariffs. What real difference (if any) is there between quotas and tariffs? Explain why lobbyists for some American industries (cheese, sugar, shoes) support import quotas, while lobbyists for others (pizza manufacturers, soft drink manufacturers, retail stores) oppose them. Would you expect labor unions to support or oppose quotas?

5. Listed below are some recent average duties paid in the United States, by commodity classes.

Coffee	0%	Raw wool	23%
Sugar	7	Clothing	26
Whisky	19	Television sets	12
Iron ore		Crude petroleum	3
and scrap	0	Chemicals	16
Natural rubber	0	Newsprint	0

What economic and political reasons can you see for duties on some commodities being above the average rate (9 percent) of duty charged and for others being below it?

6. "The only pro-tariff argument that is likely to be valid for the whole world taken as an economic unit (rather than for a particular nation at a particular time) is the infant-industry argument." Explain why you agree or disagree with this statement.

7. The United States has greatly reduced tariffs since Congress passed trade legislation authorizing the President to negotiate tariff concessions with foreign countries. Why might Congress find it desirable to give the President this authority, rather than reserving the authority to itself?

8. When France increased tariff restrictions on foreign poultry, seriously hurting American chicken exporters, the United States reversed tariff reductions that had been made on brandy. Does this kind of "trade war" make any sense at all?

39

Twentieth-century international monetary systems

The gold standard, the dollar problem, the Bretton Woods system, the International Monetary Fund, the Smithsonian agreements, the European snake—all of these terms are part of the vocabulary of the international monetary system.

The monetary system under which the world has operated has changed several times in this century. Each change has followed a period of recurring crises and major upsets to world trade. Between the periods of crises there have been relatively long periods of stability. The system that started off the century was one of fixed exchange rates under the gold standard. A ten-year period of recurring crises began with World War I and ended with the onset of the Great Depression of the 1930s. The gold standard broke down and was abandoned by one country after another during this period. The 1930s saw a period of experimentation with flexible, market-determined exchange rates. This phase was ended by World War II, when governments fixed exchange rates and managed international payments with the successful waging of war as their main policy objective. In 1944 an era of fixed exchange rates in peacetime was once again instituted. This lasted for over a quarter of a century, until its shortcomings and periods of crises seemed to prevail over its advantages and periods of stability. After several attempts to patch up the system it finally broke down and was abandoned as countries once again went over piecemeal to the system of market-determined flexible exchange rates under which we now operate.

Do the issues involved in the workings and possible reform of the monetary system affect the welfare of ordinary citizens, or do they merely affect a small group of international traders, bankers, and financiers? Are there problems and issues that can be solved, or must we merely learn to live with them as best we can? Do economists agree on solutions—or on how to accommodate ourselves as best we can, if there are no permanent solutions? To answer these questions we shall consider the development of international institutions from the time of the gold standard to the present.

Before World War II

THE GOLD STANDARD

Although the detailed workings of the gold standard are now only of historical interest, a few of its features provide important insights into the present system.[1] The gold standard was not *designed*. Like the price system, it just happened. It arose out of the general acceptance of gold as the commodity to be used as money. In most countries, paper currency was freely convertible into gold at a fixed rate.

The gold standard is an example of a fixed exchange rate system. Rates of exchange between the standard units of currency of various countries were fixed by their values in terms of the standard unit, gold. In 1914, the U.S. dollar was convertible into 0.053 standard ounces of gold, while the British pound sterling was convertible into 0.257 standard ounces. This meant that the pound was worth 4.86 times as much as the dollar in terms of gold, thus making one pound worth U.S. $4.86.[2]

As long as all countries were on the gold standard, a person in any one country could be sure of being able to make payments to a person in any other country. If one were unable to buy or sell claims to the foreign currencies on the foreign exchange market, one could always convert one's currency into gold and then ship the gold.

The gold flow, price level mechanism

How was the gold standard supposed to work to maintain a balance of international payments? Consider a country that was in payments deficit because the value of what its citizens were importing (i.e., buying) from other countries exceeded the value of what they were exporting (i.e., selling) to other countries. The demand for foreign exchange would exceed its supply on this country's foreign exchange market. Some people who wished to make foreign payments would be unable to obtain foreign exchange. No matter—they would merely convert their domestic currency into gold and ship the gold. Therefore, some people in a surplus country would secure gold in payment for exports. They would deposit this to their credit and accept claims on gold—in terms of convertible paper money or bank deposits—in return. Thus deficit countries would be losing gold while surplus countries would be gaining it.

Under the gold standard, the whole money supply was linked to the supply of gold (see pp. 602–604). The international movements of gold would therefore lead to a fall in the money supply in the deficit country and a rise in the surplus one.[3] According to the quantity theory of money, changes in the domestic money supply cause changes in domestic price levels. Deficit countries would thus have falling price levels while surplus countries would have rising price levels. The exports of deficit countries would become relatively cheaper, while those of surplus countries would become relatively more expensive. The resulting changes in quantities

---

[1] The gold standard is in fact of more than mere historical interest since a few countries—most notably France—and a few economists—most notably Columbia's Robert A. Mundell—have seriously advocated returning to it.

[2] In practice, the exchange rate did fluctuate within narrow limits set by the cost of shipping gold. If it cost 2¢ to ship $4.86 worth of gold from New York to London, it would be worth buying pounds in New York as long as their price did not rise above $4.88. The values at which it paid to ship gold were known as *gold points*.

[3] When the person who received gold deposited it in a bank, this would put the bank in the position of the IB&T Co. in Table 33–9, page 621, and a multiple expansion of deposit money would ensue.

bought and sold would move the balance of payments toward an equilibrium position.

ACTUAL EXPERIENCE OF THE GOLD STANDARD

The half-century before World War I was the heyday of the gold standard; during this relatively trouble-free period, the automatic mechanism seemed to work well. Subsequent research has suggested, however, that the gold standard succeeded during the period mainly because it was not called on to do much work. Trade flowed between nations in large and rapidly expanding volume, and it is probable that existing price levels were never far from the equilibrium ones. No major trading country found itself with a serious and persistent balance-of-payments deficit, and so no major country was called upon to restore equilibrium through a large change in its domestic price level.

Inevitably there were short-run fluctuations, but these were ironed out either by movements of short-run capital in response to changes in interest rates or by changes in national income and employment.

In the 1920s, the gold standard was called on to do a major job. It failed utterly, and it was abandoned. How did this come about? During World War I, most belligerent countries had suspended convertibility of currency (i.e., they went off the gold standard). Most countries suffered major inflations, but the degree of inflation differed from country to country. After the war, countries returned to the gold standard (i.e., they restored convertibility of their currencies into gold). For reasons of prestige, some insisted on returning at the prewar rates. This meant that some countries' goods were overpriced and others' underpriced. Large deficits and surpluses in the balance of payments inevitably appeared, and the adjustment mechanism required that price levels should change in each of the countries in order to restore equilib-

rium. Price levels changed very slowly and, by the onset of the Great Depression, equilibrium price levels had not yet been attained. By this time, it was too late to achieve equilibrium, and the financial chaos brought on by the Depression destroyed the existing payments system.

THE 1930s: A PERIOD OF EXPERIMENTATION

After the abandonment of the gold standard, various experiments were tried with both fixed and fluctuating rates. Often a rate would be allowed to fluctuate on the free market until it had reached what looked like equilibrium, and it would then be fixed at that level. Sometimes, as with the British pound, the rate was left to be determined by a free market throughout the whole period. Sometimes rates would be changed in an attempt to secure domestic full employment without any consideration of the state of the balance of payments.

The period of experimentation coincided with the Great Depression of the 1930s. Trade everywhere was being reduced because of both rising unemployment and increasing uncertainty about the future of international markets. This was a terrible period of mass unemployment, and governments began to cast around for any measure, no matter how extreme, that might alleviate their domestic unemployment problem. One superficially plausible way of doing this was to cut back on imports and to produce those goods domestically. If one country managed to reduce its imports, then its unemployment might be reduced because people would be put to work producing goods at home to replace goods formerly imported. Other countries would, however, find their exports falling and unemployment rising as a consequence. Because such policies attempt to solve one country's problems by inflicting them on others, they are called **beggar-my-neighbor policies**.

If the policies worked, there would at least

be selfish arguments in their favor. But they only work as long as other countries do not try to protect themselves. When one country reduces imports to raise its domestic employment and other countries in turn find their exports falling and unemployment rising, these other countries may then retaliate by reducing their own imports and trying to lower their unemployment by producing the goods at home, and the first country will find its exports falling and unemployment rising as a result. The simultaneous attempts of all countries to cut imports without suffering a comparable cut in exports is bound to be self-defeating. The net effect of such measures is to decrease the volume of trade and thereby sacrifice the gains from trade without raising worldwide employment.

When unemployment is due to insufficient world aggregate demand, it cannot be cured by measures designed to redistribute, among nations, the fixed and inadequate total of demand.

In the 1930s the policy of discouraging imports and encouraging exports was attempted, using such instruments of commercial policy as import duties, export subsidies, quotas, prohibitions, and, particularly, exchange rate depreciation. If a country with a large portion of its labor force unemployed devalues its exchange rate, two effects can be expected: exports will rise and domestic consumers will buy fewer imports and more domestically produced goods. Both of these changes will have the effect of lowering the amount of unemployment in the country. If other countries do nothing, the policy succeeds. But again, the volume of unemployment in other countries will have increased because exports to the devaluing country will have been reduced. If other countries try to restore their positions, they may devalue their currencies as well. If all countries devalue their currencies in the same proportion, they will all be right back where they started, with no change in the relative prices of goods from

any country and, hence, no change in relative prices from the original situation. A situation in which all countries devalue their currencies in an attempt to gain a competitive advantage over one another is called a situation of **competitive devaluations.**[4]

The rise and fall of the Bretton Woods system, 1944–1972

The one lesson that everyone thought had been learned from the 1930s was that either a system of freely fluctuating exchange rates or a system of fixed rates with easily accomplished devaluations was the road to disaster in international affairs. In order to achieve a system of orderly exchange rates that would be conducive to the free flow of trade following World War II, representatives of most countries that had participated in the alliance against Germany, Italy, and Japan met at Bretton Woods, New Hampshire, in 1944 to agree on a system of international payments for the postwar world. The international monetary system that developed out of the agreements reached at Bretton Woods consisted of a large body of rules and understandings for the regulation of international transactions and payments imbalances.

It was the first and so far the only international payments system that was consciously designed and then implemented through international governmental cooperation. In the words of MIT's Charles P. Kindleberger, the Bretton Woods meeting was "the biggest constitution-writing exercise ever to occur in

---

[4] Under a paper-currency system, a simultaneous devaluation of all currencies would have no effect, beneficial or harmful. In a gold standard world, however, each country devalues by lowering the gold content of its currency. Thus a full round of competitive devaluations of X percent leaves relative exchange rates unchanged, but it raises the price of gold (measured in all currencies) by X percent. The effect of this is to enrich those producing gold and those holding stocks of it and thus to increase their claims on the world's output.

international monetary relations''. The system lasted until the early 1970s, when it broke down and was replaced by the piecemeal adoption of a system of flexible free-market exchange rates.[5]

The object of the Bretton Woods system was to create a set of rules that would maintain fixed exchange rates in the face of short-term fluctuations; to guarantee that changes in exchange rates would occur only in the face of long-term, persistent deficits or surpluses in the balance of payments; and to ensure that when such changes did occur they would not spark a series of competitive devaluations.

The basic characteristic of the Bretton Woods system was that U.S. dollars held by foreign monetary authorities were made directly convertible into gold at a fixed price (of approximately $35 an ounce) by the U.S. government while foreign governments fixed the prices at which their currencies were convertible into U.S. dollars. It was this characteristic that made the system a **gold exchange standard**: Gold was the ultimate reserve, but the currencies were held as reserves because directly or indirectly they could be *exchanged* for gold.

The rate at which each country's currency was convertible into dollars was fixed, or pegged. The pegged rate could be changed from time to time in the face of a "fundamental disequilibrium" in the balance of payments. A system with these two characteristics, a rate that is pegged against short-term fluctuations but that can be adjusted from time to time, is referred to as an **adjustable peg system**.

In order to maintain convertibility of their currencies at fixed exchange rates, the mone-

tary authorities of each country had to be ready to buy and sell their currency in the foreign exchange markets.[6]

In order to be able to support the exchange market by buying domestic currency, the monetary authorities had to have stocks of acceptable foreign exchange to offer in return. In the Bretton Woods system, the authorities held reserves of gold and claims on key currencies—mainly the American dollar and the British pound sterling. When a country's currency was in excess supply, their authorities would sell dollars, sterling, or gold. When a country's currency was in excess demand, their authorities would buy dollars or sterling. If they then wished to increase their gold reserves they would use the dollars to purchase gold from the Fed, thus depleting the U.S. gold stock. The problem for the United States was to have enough gold to maintain fixed-price convertibility of the dollar into gold as demanded by foreign monetary authorities. The problem for all other countries was to maintain convertibility (on a restricted or unrestricted basis, depending on the country in question) between their currency and the U.S. dollar at a fixed rate of exchange.

The Bretton Woods international payments system was an adjustable peg, gold exchange standard where the ultimate international money was gold. Countries held much of their exchange reserves in the form of U.S. dollars, which they could convert into gold, and British pounds sterling, which they could convert into dollars.

THE INTERNATIONAL MONETARY FUND

The most important institution created by the Bretton Woods system was the International

---

[5] Like the gold standard, the Bretton Woods system is of more than historical interest. Many people would like to return to a system of fixed exchange rates, but any such system would face problems similar to those that beset the Bretton Woods system. The design of any new system of fixed rates would inevitably be heavily influenced by the experience of the last thirty-five years.

[6] The exchange rates were not quite fixed. They were permitted to vary by one percent on either side of their par values. The central bank had to intervene to prevent the rate from going outside of the narrow bands of permitted fluctuations. Later the bands of permitted fluctuation were widened to 2.25 percent on either side of par.

Monetary Fund (also called the IMF and the Fund). The Fund had several tasks. First, it tried to ensure that countries held their exchange rates pegged in the short run. Second, it made loans—out of funds subscribed by member nations—to governments that needed them to support their exchange rates in the face of temporary payments deficits. Third, the Fund was supposed to consult with countries wishing to alter their exchange rates to ensure that the rate was really being changed to remove a persistent payments disequilibrium and that one devaluation did not set off a self-cancelling round of competitive devaluations. The importance of the Fund is attested by the fact that it has outlived the system that created it and is as active an instrument of international monetary cooperation today as it was under the Bretton Woods system.

PROBLEMS OF AN ADJUSTABLE PEG SYSTEM

Three major problems of the Bretton Woods system were (1) providing sufficient reserves to iron out short-term fluctuations in international receipts and payments while keeping exchange rates fixed; (2) making adjustments to long-term trends in receipts and payments, and (3) handling speculative crises. These problems would be present in any adjustable peg system that might be designed in the future.

Reserves to accommodate short-term fluctuations

The problem. Reserves are needed to accommodate short-term balance-of-payments fluctuations arising from both the current and the capital accounts. On current account, normal trade is subject to many short-term variations, some systematic and some random. This means that even if the value of imports

does equal the value of exports, taken on average over several years, there may be considerable imbalances in these over shorter periods of time.

On a free market, fluctuations in current and capital account payments would cause the exchange rate to fluctuate. To prevent such fluctuations when rates are fixed, the monetary authorities buy and sell foreign exchange as required to keep the exchange rate pegged. These operations require that the authorities hold reserves of foreign exchange.

The amount of reserves that the authorities need to hold depends on their estimate of the maximum amount of foreign exchange they might have to sell to stabilize the exchange rate in the face of a particularly unfavorable period of excess demand. If the authorities run out of reserves, they cannot maintain the pegged rate, so they will want to hold some safety margin over the maximum they expect to use. It is generally felt that the absolute size of any gap they may have to fill with their own foreign exchange sales increases as the volume of international payments increases.

Since there was a strong upward trend in the volume of overall international payments, there was also a strong upward trend in the demand for foreign exchange reserves.

The ultimate reserve in the Bretton Woods gold exchange standard was gold. The use of gold as a reserve caused two serious problems. First, the world's supply of monetary gold did not grow fast enough to provide adequate total reserves for an expanding volume of trade. During the early 1960s, as a result of a fixed price of gold, rising costs of production, and rising commercial uses, the world's stock of monetary gold was rising at less than 2 percent per year while trade was growing at nearly 10 percent per year. During the latter half of the decade the stock of monetary gold actually diminished, and by 1970 it was less than it had been in 1960. Gold, which had been 66 percent of the total monetary reserves in 1959, was only 40 percent in 1970 and had fallen to 30 percent by 1972; over this period, reserve holdings of dollars and sterling rose sharply. Clearly, the gold backing needed to maintain convertibility of these currencies was becoming increasingly inadequate. Second, the country whose currency is convertible into gold must maintain sufficient reserves to ensure convertibility. During the 1960s the United States lost substantial gold reserves to other countries that had acquired dollar claims through their balance-of-payments surpluses with the United States. By the late 1960s the loss of U.S. reserves had been sufficiently large to undermine confidence in America's continued ability to maintain dollar convertibility.

By 1970 there was an inadequate world supply of gold for monetary uses, and the United States had too small a proportion of the supply that did exist.

Under the Bretton Woods system the supply of gold was augmented by reserves of key currencies, the U.S. dollar and the British pound sterling. Because the need for reserves expanded much more rapidly than the gold stock in the period since World War II, the system required nations to hold an increasing fraction of their reserves in dollars and sterling. Of course they would do this only as long as they had confidence in the convertibility of these currencies, and maintaining confidence was made difficult by a continually declining percentage of gold backing for the dollar.

A major disadvantage of using a national currency as a supplementary reserve is the potential inability to maintain convertibility of that currency into gold. Another major disadvantage occurs if the country whose currency is used for reserves wishes to devalue because of severe balance-of-payments problems. If it does devalue, all countries holding that currency find the value of these reserves slashed.

If it tries to avoid devaluation, fear that it may be unable to do so impairs the usefulness of the currency as a reserve because other countries become reluctant to hold it.

SDRs, a new type of reserve. The desire to provide a supplementary reserve not tied to the currency of a particular country led to the development in 1969 of **Special Drawing Rights** (SDRs) at the IMF. SDRs were designed to provide a supplement to existing reserve assets by setting up a Special Drawing Account kept separate from all other operations of the Fund. Each member country of the Fund was assigned an SDR quota that was guaranteed in terms of a fixed gold value and that it could use to acquire an equivalent amount of convertible currencies from other participants. SDRs could be used without prior consultation with the Fund, but only to cope with balance-of-payments difficulties.

SDRs might have gone a long way toward alleviating the system's difficulties if the system had not been overwhelmed by much more fundamental problems in the early 1970s. In any case SDRs outlasted the Bretton Woods system that they were first designed to assist. At the beginning of 1975, SDRs constituted 5 percent of world reserves while gold accounted for 20 percent and the U.S. dollar for 35 percent. By 1978 the proportion of reserves accounted for by SDRs was much higher than in 1975 and still rising.

Adjusting to long-term disequilibria

The problem. With fixed exchange rates, long-term disequilibria (what the IMF used to call *fundamental disequilibria*) can be expected to develop because of secular shifts in the demands for and supplies of foreign exchange. There are two important reasons for these long-term shifts in demands and supplies in the foreign exchange market. First, different trading countries have different rates of inflation. Chapter 37 discussed how these cause changes in the equilibrium rates of exchange and, if the rate is fixed, caused excess supply or excess demand to develop in each country's foreign exchange market. Second, changes in the demands for and supplies of imports and exports are associated with long-term economic growth. Because different countries grow at different rates, their demands for imports and their supplies of exports would be expected to be shifting at different rates.

These long-term shifts in demand and supply imply that, even starting from a current account equilibrium with imports equal to exports at a given rate of exchange, there is no reason to believe that equilibrium will exist at the same rate of exchange 10- or 20 years later (any more than equilibrium relative prices would be expected to remain unchanged over 20 years within any one country).

The rate of exchange that will lead to a balance-of-payments equilibrium will tend to change over time; over a decade the change can be substantial.

Possible remedies. Governments may react to long-term disequilibria in at least three ways.

1. The exchange rate can be changed whenever it is clear that a balance-of-payments deficit or surplus is a result of a long-term shift in the demands and supplies in the foreign exchange market, rather than the result of some transient factor. This was the solution envisaged by the framers of the IMF when they allowed member countries, after consultation with the IMF, to change their exchange rates in the face of a "fundamental disequilibrium." During the period of the Bretton Woods system, there were two major rounds of exchange rate adjustments, each sparked by a devaluation of the second of the world's two reserve currencies, the British pound sterling. A further round sparked by the devaluation of the dollar began in December 1971.

2. Domestic price levels can be allowed to change in an attempt to establish an equilibrium set of international prices. Changes in domestic price levels have all sorts of domestic repercussions (e.g., reductions in aggregate demand intended to lower the price level are more likely to raise unemployment than to lower prices), and one might have expected governments to be more willing to change exchange rates—which can be done by a stroke of a pen—than to try to change the price level. A deflation is difficult to accomplish, while an inflation is thought to be accompanied by undesirable side effects.

3. Restrictions can be imposed on trade and foreign payments. Imports and foreign spending by tourists and governments can be restricted, and the export of capital can be slowed or even stopped. Surplus countries were often quick to criticize such restrictions on international trade and payments. As long as exchange rates were fixed and price levels proved difficult to manipulate, the deficit countries had little option but to restrict the quantity of foreign exchange their residents were permitted to obtain so as to equate it to the quantity available.

Handling speculative crises

The problem. When enough people begin to doubt the ability of the central authorities to maintain the current rate, speculative crises develop. The most important reason for such crises is that equilibrium exchange rates change, and over time they tend to get further and further away from any given set of fixed rates. When the disequilibrium becomes obvious to everyone, traders and speculators come to believe that a realignment of rates cannot long be delayed. At such a time, there is a rush to buy currencies expected to be revalued and a rush to sell currencies expected to be devalued. Even if the authorities take dramatic steps to remove the payments deficit, there may be doubt as to whether these measures will work before the exchange reserves are exhausted. Speculative flows of funds can reach very large proportions, and it may be impossible to avoid changing the exchange rate under such pressure.

Possible remedies. Speculative crises were, and will always be, one of the most intractable problems of any adjustable peg system. The impact of such crises might be reduced if governments had more adequate reserves. If a speculative crisis precedes an exchange rate adjustment, however, more adequate reserves may just mean that speculators will make larger profits since more of them will be able to sell the currency about to be devalued and to buy the currency about to be revalued before the monetary authorities are forced to act.

Governments tended to resist changing their exchange rates until they had no alternative. This made the situation so obvious that speculators could hardly lose, and their actions set off the final crises that forced exchange rate readjustments. More frequent and surprise changes made before they had become inevitable might have diminished the occurrence of speculative crises. They would, however, have removed the day-to-day certainty associated with the system of fixed exchange rates that was its chief advantage. Moreover, surprise changes might lead to suspicion that a devaluation was made to gain a competitive advantage for their exports rather than to remove a fundamental disequilibrium. After all, governments were not supposed to devalue until it was clear that they were faced with a fundamental disequilibrium, and if this was clear to them it was also clear to ordinary traders and speculators.

COLLAPSE OF THE BRETTON WOODS SYSTEM

The Bretton Woods system worked reasonably well for nearly twenty years. Then it was beset by a series of crises of ever-increasing severity that reflected the system's underlying weaknesses.

Speculation against the British pound

Throughout the 1950s and 1960s the British economy was more inflation prone than the U.S. economy and the British balance of payments was generally in a less satisfactory state. Holders of the system's second key currency, sterling, thus had reason to worry that the British government might not be able to maintain its pledge to keep sterling convertible into dollars at a fixed rate. When these fears grew strong there would be speculative rushes to sell sterling before it was devalued. The crises through the 1960s were of this kind. By the mid 1960s it was clear to everyone that the pound was seriously overvalued. Finally in 1967 it was devalued in the midst of a serious speculative crisis. Many other countries with balances of payments deficits followed, bringing about the first major round of adjustments in the pegged rates since 1949.

Speculation against the American dollar

The U.S. dollar was not devalued in 1967. The lower prices of those currencies that were devalued in 1967 plus increasing Vietnam War expenditures combined to produce a growing deficit in the American balance of payments. This deficit led to the belief that the dollar itself was becoming seriously overvalued. People rushed to buy gold because a devaluation of the U.S dollar would take the form of raising its gold price.

The first break in the Bretton Woods system came when the major trading countries were forced to stop pegging the free-market price of gold. Speculative pressure to buy gold could not be resisted, and the market price was allowed to go free in 1968. From that point there were two prices of gold: one was the official price at which monetary authorities could settle their debts with each other by transferring gold; the other was the free-market price, determined by the forces of private demand and supply independent of any intervention by central banks. The free-market price quickly rose far above the official U.S. price of $35 an ounce.

Once the free-market price of gold was allowed to be determined independently of the official price, speculation against the dollar shifted to those currencies that were clearly undervalued relative to the dollar.[7] The German mark and the Japanese yen were particularly popular targets, and billions and billions of dollars flowed into speculative holdings of these currencies. The ability of central banks to maintain pegged exchange rates in the face of such vast flights of funds was in question; on several occasions all exchange markets had to be closed for periods of up to a week.

The dollar, once the scarcest, most valuable currency in the world's foreign exchange markets, was weakening. During periods of crisis it was sometimes shunned by exchange dealers who did not want to buy it at today's price if devaluation would make it much cheaper tomorrow. At such times U.S. tourists in Europe would be shocked to find that their dollars were hard to exchange at any price. (Of course, dollars could always be exchanged at major banks when they were open, but a hotel keeper in Milan might be unwilling to accept dollars on Saturday when he feared that their price would be much lower when the exchange markets reopened on Monday.)

Devaluation of the dollar

Basic problems. By 1971 the American authorities had come to the conclusion that the dollar would have to be devalued. This uncovered a problem, inherent in the Bretton Woods system, that had so far gone virtually unnoted. Because the system required that each foreign country fix its exchange rate against the dollar, the American authorities could not independently fix their exchange rate against other currencies.[8] This system worked reasonably well while the American price level was relatively stable. Countries that were inflating a bit too fast could occasionally devalue their exchange rates, and countries that were inflating even more slowly than the United States could occasionally revalue their exchange rates in an upward direction. Occasional upward and downward readjustments relative to the dollar served to keep the system near equilibrium.

But if the United States began to inflate rapidly (or to do anything else that put it in a serious payments deficit with most other countries), it became necessary to devalue the U.S. dollar relative to most (or even conceivably all) other currencies. Any other country in this situation would merely unilaterally devalue its currency relative to the U.S. dollar. But the only way that the required U.S. devaluation could be brought about was for all other countries to agree to revalue their currencies upward relative to the dollar.

Under the Bretton Woods system any country other than the United States could devalue its currency by a unilateral decision; a U.S. devaluation, however, required the cooperation of all other countries against whose currency the dollar was to be devalued.

---

[7] Under a Bretton Woods type of system the dollar is devalued by raising the official price at which the Fed will allow foreign central banks to convert dollars into gold. When the free-market price was held the same as the official price, a devaluation of the dollar entailed a rise in the free-market price—and hence profit for all holders of gold. Once the free-market price was left to be determined by the forces of private demand and supply independent of any central bank intervention, there was no reason to believe that a rise in the official price of gold would affect the (much higher) free-market price. Speculators against the dollar then had to hold other currencies whose price was sure to rise against the dollar in the event of the dollar's being devalued.

[8] If, for example, the British authorities pegged the pound sterling at $2.40 as they did in 1967, then the dollar was pegged at £0.417 and the Fed could not independently decide on another rate. Similar considerations applied to all other currencies.

The new economic policy. Prompted by continuing speculation against the dollar, by an announced second quarter balance-of-payments deficit of $5.8 billion, and by a failure of traditional policies to solve unemployment and inflation at home, President Nixon in August 1971 announced his New Economic Policy. ("New" it was for America but, with the exception of the measure dropping gold convertibility, it was almost exactly the same policy package that the British government had used several times in the 1950s and 1960s in a vain attempt to solve the problems that put sterling, the world's second reserve currency, under periodic speculative attacks.)

Three of the main features of this policy were the suspension of the gold convertibility of the dollar, a 10 percent tariff surcharge on all imports of manufactured goods, and an announced intention to achieve a de facto devaluation of the dollar by persuading those nations whose balances of payments were in surplus to allow their rates to float upward against the dollar.

By ending the gold convertibility of the dollar the New Economic Policy brought the gold exchange standard aspect of the Bretton Woods system officially to an end.

The fixed exchange rate aspect of the system lasted a little longer.

The immediate response to the announced intention of devaluing the dollar was a completely predictable speculative run against that currency. The crisis was so severe that for the second time in the year foreign exchange markets were closed throughout Europe. When the markets reopened after a week, several countries allowed their rates to float, joining Germany and Holland who had done so earlier in the year. The Japanese, however, announced their intention of retaining their existing rate. In spite of their severe controls, $4 billion of speculative funds managed to

find their way into yen in the last two weeks of August, and the Japanese were forced to abandon their fixed rate policy by allowing the yen to float upward.

The Smithsonian agreements. After some very hard bargaining, an agreement between the major trading nations was signed at the Smithsonian Institution in Washington, D.C., in December 1971. The main element of the agreement was that the U.S. import surcharge was to be removed in return for other countries' agreeing to a 7.9 percent devaluation of the dollar against all other currencies. (The mechanism by which this was accomplished was that the United States would raise the official price of gold from $35 to $38 while other countries kept the "gold value" of their currencies constant—which required that the value of their currencies be appreciated 7.9 percent against the dollar.) At the same time, the currencies of some countries that had persistent balance-of-payments surpluses were to be revalued upward. In particular, the Dutch guilder, the Belgian franc, the German mark, the Swiss franc, and the Japanese yen were increased in value by amounts ranging up to 17 percent. Although a great deal of pressure was put on her, Canada held out successfully to maintain her policy of a floating exchange rate.

Thus the third major realignment of exchange rates since World War II was accomplished, and a regime of fixed exchange rates with nominal gold backing of currencies was reestablished. But the rise in the official price of gold to $38 could not by itself restore gold to its pre-1968 position. Since the free-market price of gold remained substantially above the official price, central banks were unlikely to want to use gold to settle debts. As long as gold was worth anything over $40 on the free market (it has varied between $100 and $200 an ounce since that time), it would not be sensible to use it to settle debts at a price of only $38; dollar credits were used instead.[9]

The de facto dollar standard

After the Smithsonian agreements, the world was on a de facto **dollar standard.** Foreign monetary authorities hold their reserves in the form of dollars and settle their international debts with dollars. But the dollar is not convertible into gold or anything else. The ultimate value of the dollar is given not by gold but by the American goods and services that dollars can be used to purchase. (Look again at the U.S. balance of payments in Table 36–3, page 675, and notice that the U.S. payments deficit was not settled by giving gold to foreign monetary authorities but by their accumulating dollar credits, which are short-term U.S. liabilities.) One major problem with such a dollar system is that the kind of American inflation that upset the Bretton Woods system is no less upsetting to a dollar standard because the real, purchasing-power value of the world's dollar reserves is eroded by such an inflation.

Breakdown of the system of fixed exchange rates

We have seen that the Smithsonian agreements brought about the third major realignment of exchange rates since they were fixed by the Bretton Woods agreements in 1944. The two earlier rounds were followed by several years of relatively settled conditions on the world's foreign exchange markets. Not so the Smithsonian round!

The U.S. inflation continued unchecked and the U.S. balance of payments never returned to the relatively satisfactory position that had been maintained all through the 1960s. Within a year of the agreements, spec-

[9] This is a splendid example of Gresham's Law, which states (see page 602) that bad money drives good money out of circulation.

ulators began to believe that a further realignment of rates was necessary. In January 1973 heavy speculative movements of capital once again began to occur.

Then on February 12 came a bombshell. The United States announced that it intended to propose a further 10 percent devaluation of the dollar, to be accomplished by raising the official price of gold to $42.22. Needless to say, intense speculative activity followed this extraordinary announcement. During the first week of March the major foreign exchange markets closed while governments decided how to react. When foreign exchange trading resumed on March 19, five of the member countries of the EEC decided to stabilize their currencies against each other but to let them float against the dollar. This joint EEC float is called the **snake.** Norway and Sweden later became associated with this arrangement. The other EEC countries (Ireland, Italy, and the U.K.) and Japan announced their intention to allow their currencies to float in value.

Fluctuations in exchange rates were severe. By early July the currencies of the five EEC countries involved in the joint float had appreciated about 30 percent against the dollar, but by the end of the year they had returned nearly to their February values.

The dollar devaluation, whose prior announcement had caused such uproar, was formally put into effect on October 18, after Congressional approval of the administration's proposal to raise the dollar price of gold to $42.22. Most industrialized countries maintained the nominal values of their currencies in terms of gold and SDRs, thereby appreciating in terms of the U.S. dollar by 11 percent.

The present system

The Bretton Woods system was abandoned in several stages. The two most important were the ending of gold convertibility of the U.S.

dollar in 1972 and the abandoning of the system of pegged exchange rates, completed by the end of 1973. By 1974, the foreign exchange situation could be summarized: Many industrial countries—Austria, Canada, Italy, Japan, Switzerland, the United Kingdom, and the United States—were not maintaining rates for exchange transactions within announced margins, while other industrial countries—Belgium, Denmark, France, Germany, Luxembourg, the Netherlands, Norway, and Sweden—maintained fixed bands for exchange transactions among their currencies but not against the dollar. A large proportion of the remaining countries maintained stable rates of exchange for their currencies in terms of one of the three major currencies—the U.S. dollar, pound sterling, or the French franc. This implied that their rates fluctuated against the major currencies to which their national currency was not tied.

Although exchange rates are determined on the free market, there is nevertheless substantial intervention in these markets by central banks. Central banks try to reduce short-term fluctuations in rates and sometimes try to resist longer-term trends. The difference between the present system and the previous one is that central banks no longer have announced values for their exchange rates (values that they are committed in advance to defend even at heavy cost). Central banks do not need to say what their targets are; they may change them with complete flexibility as circumstances change. Sometimes they leave the rate completely free from their own intervention while at other times quite heavy intervention occurs with the object of altering the exchange rate from what its value would be on the free market. Such a system is called a **managed float** or a **dirty float.** The rate floats because it is not pegged at any publicly announced par value. The floating rate, however, is managed (or dirty) because the central bank does intervene in the foreign exchange market to influence the rate.

In the period following the Smithsonian agreements governments held many meetings in an attempt to halt the drift toward a system of flexible rates. The Committee of Twenty was set up to study and make recommendations on reform of the payments system. Although agreement has been reached on many minor items, it seems safe to say that the steam has gone out of the drive to return to fixed exchange rates. As a result the world is very probably in for an extended period of a system of managed floating rates.

To manage exchange rates, central banks still hold reserves in the form of gold, foreign exchange, and SDRs. Since the dollar is no longer de facto convertible into gold the world remains on a de facto dollar standard. The growing importance of SDRs suggests that in the future the ultimate real reserve may become the SDR, which is a genuine international paper money. If this happens, the system will have become an "international paper money standard."

The present international monetary system is a dollar standard with managed exchange rate flexibility.

The late Professor Harry Johnson, formerly of the Universities of Chicago and Geneva, Switzerland, made a prediction in 1973 about the future of the international payments system.

There is a . . . hope that if the central bankers keep on acting as they have been acting, we shall never have a fundamental reform of the international monetary system. This will be all to the good because what is described in the platform oratory as fundamental reform is some sort of restoration of the fixed exchange system. So long as European and American central bankers and their allies remain stalemated . . . dirty floating will continue—and the world will eventually become used to floating exchange rates, the system that the majority of academics . . . have always recommended.

Four years later it seems that Professor Johnson had quite accurately foreseen the course of events.

The experiences of the period of managed intervention have been mixed. On the one hand, short-term movements in exchange rates have been more volatile than advocates of flexible rates would perhaps have hoped; on the other, exchange rates have been managed without any overt clashes of national interest and have been allowed to change to compensate for substantial national differences in inflation rates.

CURRENT AND FUTURE PROBLEMS

Management of exchange rates

The managed aspect of managed floating rates poses several potential problems for the international monetary system. These include the possibilities of mutually inconsistent exchange rate stabilization policies, competitive exchange rate depreciation, and instability of exchange rates in the face of speculative pressures. To help avoid these problems the IMF issued guidelines for exchange rate management in June 1974. The guidelines emphasized the point that exchange rate policy is a matter for international consultation and surveillance by the IMF and that intervention practices by individual central banks should be based on three principles: (1) exchange authorities should prevent sudden and disproportionate short-term movements in exchange rates and ensure an orderly adjustment of exchange rates to longer-term pressures; (2) in consultation with the IMF, countries should establish a target zone for the medium-term values of their exchange rates and keep the actual rate within that target zone; (3) countries should recognize that exchange rate management involves joint responsibilities.

The experiences of 1972 and 1973 underlined one of the most important problems faced by any exchange rate system in current circumstances: coping with the massive volume of short-term funds which can be switched very rapidly between financial centers. Short-term capital flows forced the abandonment of exchange rates that were agreed on in 1971 and have caused fluctuations in floating rates. Various attempts have been made to limit such flows. Italy has adopted a "two-tier" foreign exchange market where there is one price for foreign exchange to finance current account transactions and another price (and another set of controls) for foreign exchange to finance capital movements. Germany has used direct controls on overseas borrowing. There has also been a considerable extension of arrangements under which central banks in surplus countries lend the funds they are accumulating back to central banks in deficit countries, thereby greatly enhancing the ability of banks to maintain stable exchange rates in the face of short-term speculative flights of capital.

The rise in the price of oil

The most serious event affecting the future payments system—and indeed the whole of international economic relations—was the raising of the price of oil following the formation of the OPEC cartel. The price rises have generated an unprecedented imbalance in the international economic system in the form of a massive payments surplus for the oil producers and a corresponding deficit for the oil-importing countries. The producing countries cannot spend their oil revenues on goods and services fast enough,[10] nor can the consuming countries produce these goods and services at the necessary rate for all the oil revenues to be spent without creating enormous inflationary pressures.[11] As a result, the OPEC countries are piling up massive capital

[10] There is a limit to the speed with which any country can absorb foreign goods, and many oil-producing countries are at that limit. Ships wait months to unload for want of dock capacity, unloaded goods sit in wharfside stockpiles for months—even years—for want of transportation capacity, and so on.

[11] Production of the goods would produce factor incomes and thus add to domestic demand, but their export removes them from domestic markets and thus reduces domestic supplies.

balances, some in the form of very short-term loans.

It is estimated that by 1980 the cumulative payments surplus of the OPEC countries might reach as much as $300 billion (measured in 1974 dollars)! This vast sum is more than twice the value of all the world's total reserves of gold, foreign exchange, and SDRs.

It is generally agreed that the OPEC countries have no serious alternative to investing their surplus revenues in the advanced industrialized nations, thereby returning on capital account the purchasing power extracted from the current accounts of the oil-importing nations. This situation raises many serious problems. One of the most important arises from the potential havoc which would be brought to foreign exchange markets if surplus oil funds were invested in liquid assets and switched between currencies in response to changes in interest rates and expected capital gains arising from possible exchange rate alterations. Clearly some means must be found of placing the funds in less liquid investments and/or creating sufficient central bank cooperation to allow the funds to be moved without upsetting foreign exchange markets completely.

In March 1974, the IMF put forward proposals for medium-term loans from the oil-exporting countries and those industrialized countries in a relatively strong payments position, the proceeds to be lent to the countries most severely affected by rising oil prices. The first of these arrangements, called oil facilities, raised $2.8 billion and was drawn upon by forty countries before it expired in December 1975. A second oil facility, for 1976, raised approximately $12 billion and was also used heavily. In addition to arrangements conducted through the IMF, the OECD countries in March 1975 created a $20 billion "safety net" fund to finance their respective oil deficits.

Although the industrial countries have managed to arrange balance-of-payments finance without too much difficulty, major problems still face the less developed countries despite a rising total of OPEC disbursements to the third world.

New international reserves

Governments operating dirty floats need reserves just as do governments operating adjustable pegs. The search for an adequate supply of reserves has gone on unabated since the demise of the Bretton Woods system. In January 1976, agreement was reached for a 30 percent average increase in the quotas of funds that member countries must provide to the IMF and from which the IMF can make loans to countries wishing to support their exchange rates.

At the same time, several longer-term measures relating to the role of gold and the permissible types of future exchange rate regimes were agreed upon. Countries need no longer supply 25 percent of their IMF quotas in gold, nor are they obliged to use gold in other transactions they may undertake with the IMF. The IMF was also to sell one-sixth of its gold stock on the free market over a period of four years and use the proceeds to establish a trust fund that would provide balance-of-payments assistance on concessionary terms to the poorer countries. A further one-sixth of the IMF gold stock is to be transferred to IMF members at the official price.

The way has been paved to eliminate gold from the international monetary system and to establish the SDR as the principal reserve asset in place of the dollar.

SURVIVAL OF THE IMF IN A WORLD OF FLOATING EXCHANGE RATES

The IMF has proved to be a very resilient institution. Although it bitterly resisted the drift toward floating exchange rates, it has now accommodated itself to them and promises to be as effective a means of securing international financial cooperation under a system of managed floating rates as it was under fixed rates.

The changing position of the IMF is illustrated by the amendments to Article 4 of its charter that were under discussion in 1976. The main points were:

1. A general return to stable but adjustable par values for exchange rates can take place with the support of an 85 percent majority in the IMF.

2. Par values may not be expressed in terms of gold or other currencies but can be expressed in terms of SDRs.

3. The margins of fluctuation around par values remain at plus or minus 2.25 percent.

4. With the concurrence of the IMF, any country may abandon its par value and adopt a floating exchange rate.

5. The exchange rate management of a floating currency must be subject to IMF surveillance and must not be conducted so as to disadvantage other countries.

6. The agreed practices with respect to floating rates will operate until such time as a general return to par values is attained.

When these changes are adopted, the IMF will, while allowing for the return to fixed rates at some possible future date, have legalized floating rates within the framework of the IMF system and without any diminution of the powers of the IMF.

A FINAL WORD

One of the most impressive aspects of international payments history in the last thirty years has been the steady rise of more and more effective degrees of international cooperation. When the gold standard broke down and the Great Depression overwhelmed the countries of the world, "every man for himself" was the rule of the day. Rising tariffs, competitive exchange rate devaluations, and all forms of beggar-my-neighbor policies abounded.

After World War II the countries of the world cooperated in bringing the Bretton Woods system and the IMF into being. The system itself was far from perfect, and it finally broke down as a result of its own internal contradictions. But as the system came under growing strain during the late 1960s, international cooperation became increasingly sophisticated. Central banks, through joint cooperative actions, were able in 1970 to weather speculative crises that would have forced them to devalue their currencies in 1955. Furthermore, the international cooperation that was necessary to set the system up survived the collapse of the system itself.

This high degree of international cooperation prevented the collapse of Bretton Woods from plunging the world into the same chaotic period of beggar-my-neighbor policies that followed the breakdown of the gold standard. It also allowed the world to cope better than it otherwise could have with the terrible strains caused by the sharp rise in oil prices in the 1970s. The world still faces enormous oil-related problems: How can the real price of imported oil be covered without massive foreign borrowing? What will be the implications of large long-term foreign investments by OPEC countries? How can the payments system be stabilized against flows of short-term funds held by OPEC countries?

Whatever may be the problems of the future, it seems clear that there is more chance of coping with them—or even of just learning to live with them—when the countries of the world cooperate through the IMF and other international organizations than when it is a case of every man for himself and let the Devil take the hindmost.

Summary

1. Under the gold standard, the central authorities of each country kept their paper currency convertible into gold at a fixed rate, and the "gold content" of each currency established fixed rates of exchange between all the currencies. Because all currencies were freely convertible into gold, they were also freely convertible into each other.

2. The gold standard was supposed to work through changes in national price levels and from them to changes in the prices of imported and exported commodities. A deficit country would lose gold, its money supply would shrink, its price level would fall; thus imports would become relatively more expensive while exports became relatively cheaper, and both of these changes would tend to reduce the deficit. A surplus country would gain gold, expand its money supply, experience an inflation that would make its imports relatively cheap and its exports relatively expensive, and thus find its surplus being reduced.

3. Before 1914 this system was not required to remove major disequilibria in the balance of payments. In the 1920s the gold standard was required to do so and failed, both because price level adjustments could not take place fast enough and because governments were unwilling to allow their price levels to change solely because of the balance of payments.

4. The gold standard was abandoned and many experiments were tried throughout the 1930s. The use of exchange rate changes to increase local employment in the face of inadequate aggregate world demand was correctly discredited as a means of dealing with a worldwide unemployment problem.

5. The international payments system existing between 1944 and the early 1970s was called the Bretton Woods system. It put the world on an adjustable peg, gold exchange standard. To fix their rates of exchange vis-à-vis the dollar, foreign monetary authorities held reserves of gold and of the two reserve currencies, the British pound sterling and the U.S. dollar. Exchange rates were only to be changed in the face of a fundamental disequilibrium in the balance of payments.

6. The International Monetary Fund (IMF) was the major institution of the Bretton Woods system. It tried to ensure that countries pegged their exchange rates and changed them only in the face of fundamental disequilibrium. To this end it made loans of foreign exchange to countries trying to weather temporary balance-of-payments deficits.

7. Three major problems with any adjustable peg system are (1) to provide sufficient international reserves, (2) to adjust to long-term trends in receipts and payments, and (3) to handle periodic speculative crises. The SDR is a relatively new international paper money meant to provide adequate international reserves not linked to gold or the U.S. dollar.

8. The Bretton Woods system broke down under a series of speculative crises that stemmed from the failure of the system to provide sufficient international reserves and to accommodate devaluations of the U.S. dollar, which was the currency to which all other countries pegged their exchange rates.

9. The two major events in the transition from the Bretton Woods system to the present one were the abandonment of gold convertibility of dollars held by foreign central banks in 1971 and the drift toward managed flexibility of exchange rates that occurred mainly during 1972 and 1973.

10. The present system is a dollar standard with managed flexibility of exchange rates. The system is under very heavy strains because of the current account deficits of so many of the oil-importing countries and because of the enormous supplies of short-term foreign investment held by the oil exporters. International cooperation through the IMF is helping the world to deal with the major payments problems of the 1970s.

Concepts for review

The gold standard
The Bretton Woods system
A dollar standard
Kinds of foreign exchange reserves
Pegged exchange rates and adjustable pegs
Freely floating exchange rates
Dirty or managed floats

Discussion questions

1. What role in international payments does or did gold play under (a) the gold standard, (b) the adjustable-peg Bretton Woods system? (c) the present system? In 1974 *Barron's* had an editorial that was headed "Monetary Reform and Gold: You Can't Have One Without the Other." Is it likely that

this headline could appear in a respected financial magazine today?

2. "The price of gold soared as much as $5 an ounce on European bullion markets today. Dealers attributed it to fears that the President's economic policy might touch off more worldwide inflation. The dollar and the pound both declined sharply against the mark and the franc in busy trading on foreign exchange markets."

This quotation from *The New York Times* was made during the administration of one of the following Presidents. Guess which, and explain your answer.

William H. Taft	1909–1913
Franklin D. Roosevelt	1933–1945
Harry S. Truman	1945–1953
John F. Kennedy	1961–1963
Jimmy Carter	1977–

3. Might a person who regards inflation as the number one economic danger favor a return to the pre-1914 gold standard? Would you predict noninflationary results if in order to restore the gold standard, the price of gold had to be increased to $140 per ounce, either all at once or gradually?

4. The dollar is no longer convertible into gold because of a change in U.S. policy. Does this lack of conversion make the dollar any less useful as an international medium of exchange?

5. Are Americans benefited or hurt when the dollar is the standard form of international reserves?

6. "Under a flexible exchange rate system no country need suffer unemployment, for if its prices are low enough there will be more than enough demand to keep its factories and farms fully occupied." The evidence suggests that flexible rates have not generally eliminated unemployment. Can you explain why? Can changing exchange rates ever cure unemployment?

7. The OPEC oil price increase has caused grave problems in international payments and increased the need for IMF loans. Why has not market adjustment of exchange rates solved the problem?

8. A deficit in the U.S. balance of payments was generally welcomed in the early 1950s, but viewed with alarm in the late 1960s. Can you explain why? In 1975 the United States had an $11 billion surplus that was a source of concern both in Washington and among our trading partners. Should a country seek a perpetual balance in its exports and imports?

PART ELEVEN

MACROECONOMIC POLICY IN ACTION: THE CONTROL OF INFLATION AND UNEMPLOYMENT

40

The nature of unemployment and inflation

The President, the Cabinet, the Council of Economic Advisers, the Open Market Committee of the Federal Reserve System, and many others have a hand in setting macroeconomic policy in America. Whoever they are and whatever country they are operating in, macroeconomic policy makers who work in a basically free-market society set themselves some heroic tasks. They would like to bring the economy as close as possible to the full-employment level of national income, while at the same time ensuring both a high growth rate in national income and a low growth rate —zero if possible—in the price level. As we shall see in Chapter 42 these policy objectives can come into conflict with each other, and when they do, some painful choices may have to be made.

THE GOALS OF MACROECONOMIC POLICY

From time to time the emphasis given to particular goals of macroeconomic policy changes. Four major goals that have been prominent at one time or another over the last half-century are (a) maintaining a stable price level, (b) maintaining full employment, (c) maintaining a satisfactory balance of international payments, and (d) achieving a high rate of economic growth. Today's major issues in macroeconomic policy center around the first two of these goals. Before we consider them in detail, we should make some mention of the other two.

Concern about the balance of payments has been important in the recent past. It arises as a result of a prior policy decision to support a fixed exchange rate rather than to allow the rate to be determined on the free market. From the end of World War II to the early 1970s the world operated on a system of fixed exchange rates, called the Bretton Woods system (see Chapter 39). Under this system any country whose balance of payments was in deficit had to make the achievement of a satisfactory payments position a major goal—sometimes the overriding goal—of policy. Throughout the 1970s most major industrial countries have allowed their exchange rates to fluctuate on the free market. As a result, obtaining a satisfactory balance of payments in order to defend the existing exchange rate has ceased to be a dominant policy consideration. The adoption of floating exchange rates has allowed macroeconomic policy makers to turn their attention to domestic rates of inflation, unemployment, and growth while leaving the balance of payments more or less to take care of itself. The free-market exchange rate fluctuates (in the manner analyzed in Chapter 36) ensuring that international payments are in balance.

Governments, through their central banks, still intervene in foreign exchange markets, but they do so only with a view to smoothing out short-term fluctuations in exchange rates. This intervention can be important in some circumstances, but it is trivial compared with the overriding attention that must be given to the balance of payments when exchange rates are fixed.

Another objective of policy makers is the rate of growth of full-employment income. Economic growth is discussed more fully in Chapter 43; suffice it to say here that policy makers are concerned with both the benefits and the costs of economic growth. The major benefit of growth is the enormous increase in material living standards that occurs as the result of even small rates of growth, providing they are sustained over decades. The modest rate of growth, for example, of 3 percent per year doubles real output every 23 years; at this rate material living standards can rise eightfold during a single lifetime of 69 years. Economists and policy makers have recently become much more aware of the costs of growth than they were in the past. These costs exist in terms of too rapid change, social upheaval, serious harm to the environment, and more rapid exhaustion of scarce natural resources.

A certain amount is known about the causes of economic growth, but these causes are not sufficiently understood that policy makers can manipulate the economy's growth rate in the way that they are able to manipulate the amount of employment or even the amount of inflation.

In this part we concentrate on the twin policy objectives of full employment and price stability. This chapter considers unemployment and the inflation rate separately, asking why each is a cause for concern, why it changes, and how it can be controlled by the central authorities. The discussion will bring together much material that has been introduced in widely separated parts of this book. The following chapter deals with some debates over how these policy objectives may be achieved. Chapter 42 considers the problem of what happens when conflicts develop between price stability and full employment—in particular, what happens when a desirable reduction can be made in unemployment only at the cost of an undesirable increase in inflation.

Unemployment

Keynes distinguished between voluntary and involuntary unemployment. Voluntary unemployment occurs when there is a job available but the unemployed person is not willing to accept it at the going wage rate for persons now employed. Involuntary unemployment occurs when a person is willing to accept a job at the going wage rate but no such job can be found. Clearly when we are concerned about the undesirable social effects of unemployment in terms of lost output and human suffering, it is involuntary unemployment that concerns us. When we use the word unemployment hereafter we mean involuntary unemployment.

WHY POLICY MAKERS ARE CONCERNED

The social and political importance of the figure that expresses the unemployment rate is enormous. It is widely reported in newspapers; the government is blamed when it is high and takes credit when it is low; it is often a hot issue in elections; and few macroeconomic policies are formed without some consideration of their effect on it. No summary statistic, with the possible exception of the consumer price index, carries such weight as both a formal and an informal objective of policy as does the percentage of the civilian labor force unemployed.

There are two main reasons for worrying about unemployment: it produces economic waste and it causes human suffering. The economic waste is fairly obvious. Factor services are the least durable of economic commodities. If a fully employed economy with a constant labor force has 100 million labor years available to it in 1978, these must either be used in 1978 or wasted. If only 90 million are used because 10 percent of the labor force is unemployed, the potential output of the 10 million labor years is lost forever. In an economy characterized by scarcity, where there is not nearly enough output to meet everyone's needs, this waste of potential output seems undesirable to most people.

In addition to economic waste there is the human cost of unemployment. The severe hardship and misery that can be caused by prolonged periods of unemployment were discussed earlier; there is little doubt that these can be heavy costs. But it is wrong to think that if the number of unemployed rises by, say, 100,000, this means that 100,000 workers join the ranks of the permanently unemployed. Modern research has shown that short-term variations in the unemployment rate at or near the full-employment level are to a great extent caused by changes in the duration of short-term unemployment.

However, when a deep recession is followed by a long trough and only a slow recovery, as was the case in the mid 1970s, long-term unemployment increases.[1] People

begin to exhaust their unemployment insurance and are forced to fall back on savings, welfare, or charity. When this happens the human suffering caused by unemployment increases. Nearly half of the large number of persons who fell below the poverty level for the first time in 1976 did so because they had run out of unemployment insurance and were still unable to find a job because of the economy's persistently high level of unemployment.

Before a value judgment can be made about how high are the human costs of a rise in unemployment, we need to know how the increase is distributed between long-term and short-term unemployment. Unnecessary unemployment always imposes costs in terms of lost output, but the costs in terms of human suffering will usually be much higher for long-term than for short-term unemployment.

CAUSES OF UNEMPLOYMENT

To discuss the causes of unemployment it is helpful to distinguish among a number of kinds of unemployment.

Frictional unemployment

The amount of unemployment that is associated with normal turnover of labor is called **frictional unemployment.** People leave jobs for all sorts of reasons and they take time to find new jobs; old persons leave the labor force and young persons enter it, but often new workers do not fill the jobs vacated by those who leave. Inevitably all of this movement takes time and gives rise to a pool of persons who are frictionally unemployed while in the course of finding new jobs.

Frictional unemployment is inevitable in any free society; it may run as high as 3 or 4 percent of the American labor force.

National income theory seeks to explain causes of, and cures for, unemployment in excess of unavoidable frictional unemployment.

---

[1] See pages 543–544 for the terminology of business cycles.

Structural unemployment

Structural changes in the economy can be a cause of unemployment. As economic growth proceeds, the mix of required inputs changes, as do the proportions in which final goods are demanded. These changes require considerable readjustments in the economy. **Structural unemployment** occurs when the adjustments do not occur fast enough, so that severe pockets of unemployment occur in areas, industries, and occupations in which the demand for factors of production is falling faster than is the supply. In the United States today, for example, structural unemployment exists in Appalachia and in the aircraft industry.

Structural unemployment may be said to exist when there is a mismatching between the unemployed and the available jobs in terms of regional location, required skills, or any other relevant dimension.

As with many distinctions, the one between structural and frictional unemployment becomes blurred at the margin. In a sense structural unemployment is really long-term frictional unemployment. For illustration, consider a change that requires a reallocation of labor. If the reallocation occurs quickly we call the unemployment frictional while it lasts; if the reallocation occurs slowly—possibly only after the person who has lost a job dies or retires from the labor force and has been replaced by a new person with different and more marketable skills—we call the unemployment structural.

One useful measure of the total of frictional *plus* structural unemployment is the percentage of the labor force unemployed when the number of unfilled job vacancies is equal to the number of persons seeking jobs. When these two magnitudes are equal there is some kind of job opening to match every person seeking a job and the unemployment that occurs must be either frictional (people moving between jobs) or structural (a mismatching between the kinds of jobs available and the qualifications of the persons seeking employment).

Deficient-demand unemployment

Unemployment that occurs because there is insufficient aggregate demand to purchase full-employment output is called **deficient-demand unemployment.** One useful measure of this kind of unemployment is the difference between the number of persons seeking jobs and the number of unfilled job vacancies (i.e., total unemployment *minus* frictional and structural unemployment) expressed as a percentage of the labor force.

Deficient-demand unemployment may be measured by the number of unemployed who are not matched by any vacant job, whether suitable or unsuitable.

At a time of heavy unemployment, frictional, structural, and deficient-demand causes may all be operative. It will not usually be possible to say that one particular worker is unemployed because of deficient demand and another for structural reasons, nor will it be possible to say what proportion of the total of unemployment is accounted for by each cause. Nonetheless, all three causes can operate and can contribute to the total volume of unemployment.

Search unemployment

We have already seen that national income theory is concerned with causes and cures for the unemployment that is in excess of unavoidable frictional and structural unemployment. Unfortunately it is not all that easy in practice to draw dividing lines among the several types of involuntary unemployment we have discussed or between those who are unemployed involuntarily and those who are voluntarily not working. What do we say, for example, about an unemployed woman who refuses to accept a job at a lower skill category than the one for which she feels she is qualified? And what if she turns down a job for which she is trained because she feels that she may get a higher wage offer for the same job from another firm? People who could find work of the type for which they are fitted but who remain unemployed in order to search for a better offer than they have so far received are said to be in **search unemployment.** In one sense they can be said to be voluntarily unemployed because they could find some job; in another sense they can be said to be involuntarily unemployed because they have not yet succeeded in finding a job for which they are suited at a rate of pay that they believe exists somewhere in the economy. Those in search unemployment can be said to have been frictionally unemployed if they find an acceptable job in a reasonable period of time; they may be judged to be in structural unemployment if a long period of search reveals that there are no longer enough jobs to employ everyone with their particular training and experience.

Search unemployment is thus in a gray area between voluntary and involuntary, and between frictional and structural unemployment.

The basic cause of search unemployment is that workers do not have perfect knowledge of all available jobs and rates of pay and they may only be able to find information by searching the market.

In the face of this uncertainty it may be quite sensible to refuse the first job offer that one comes across since it may well prove to be a very poor offer when further market information has been collected. How long it pays to remain in search unemployment depends on the economic costs of being unemployed.

Two recent developments are believed to have increased the amount of search unemployment in many Western economies. First, there has been a large increase in the number of households with more than one income earner. If both husband and wife work, it is possible for one to support them both while the other looks for "a really good job" rather than accept the first job offered. Second, unemployment insurance reduces the income loss caused by being unemployed and may enable a person to prolong the search for the "right job."

Sufficient search unemployment to allow unemployed people time to find an available job that best uses their talents and training is socially desirable. Too much search—for example, holding off, to be supported by others, in the hope of stumbling into a job better than the one for which one is really suited—is clearly undesirable and an economic waste. Here again search unemployment is a gray area: some of it is useful and some of it is wasteful.

Measured and nonmeasured unemployment

The number of persons unemployed is estimated from the Current Population Survey, a sample survey conducted each month by the Bureau of the Census. Persons who are currently without a job but who say they have actively searched for one during the sample period are recorded as unemployed. The total number of persons estimated to be unemployed is then expressed as a percentage of the civilian labor force (employed plus unemployed) to obtain the figure for percentage unemployment.

There are reasons why this measured figure for unemployment may not reflect the number of people who are truly unemployed *in the sense that they would accept the offer of a job for which they are qualified if one were forthcoming.* On the one hand, the measured figure may overstate unemployment by including people who are not truly unemployed in the sense we have just defined. Many people who intend to remain unemployed for as long as their unemployment benefits last will tell the enumerator that they were looking for a job. They do this because they fear that they may lose their benefits if they answer honestly. Unemployment compensation provides needed protection against genuine hardships, but it also induces some people to stay out of work and collect their unemployment benefits for as long as these last. Such people have in fact voluntarily withdrawn from the labor force, but they will usually show up in the statistics as being in the ranks of the unemployed. On the other hand, the measured figure may understate involuntary unemployment by omitting people who would accept a job if one were available. If a slump lasts long enough so that jobs cannot be found even after unemployment benefits are exhausted, some people will become discouraged and stop seeking work. These people have voluntarily withdrawn from the labor force and will not be recorded as unemployed; they are, however, truly unemployed in the sense defined at the beginning of this paragraph.

These are but two of the many reasons why measured unemployment may be very different from some well-defined concept of true unemployment. In view of the enormous importance placed on the unemployment rate, the development of more reliable data for overall unemployment and for various subcategories must be one of the most socially important research projects now going on in economics.

TOOLS FOR CONTROL OF UNEMPLOYMENT

Frictional unemployment is inevitable in any changing economy, and thus a certain minimum amount of unemployment must be accepted as being "in the nature of things." Any policy measure that makes it easier or quicker to move between jobs can, however, reduce the volume of frictional unemployment somewhat.

Structural unemployment may be attacked by policies for retraining and relocating labor. These can be used as part of a general effort to increase the speed with which the supplies of various types of labor adjust to the changing pattern of demands.

Unemployment that is due to deficient aggregate demand can be attacked by increasing aggregate demand. This may be done by any of the expansionary fiscal and monetary policies discussed in Parts Eight and Nine of this book.

Genuine search unemployment may be reduced, first, by making it easier for individuals to locate job vacancies and, second, by increasing the chance that individuals will accept an offer received early in their search period. The first can be done, for example, by the provision of market information on job availability; the second requires increasing the cost of search to the unemployed individual. A reduction in unemployment benefits, for example, increases the income loss associated with continued search and makes it more likely that individuals will reduce the time they spend in search unemployment. This may not always be desirable; as we have observed, a certain amount of search unemployment is useful in ensuring that people find a job for which they are well suited. Phony (no intention of accepting a job) and unreasonable (looking for too good a job) search unemployment might be reduced by more careful screening of persons before they are allowed to collect unemployment benefits.

EXPERIENCE OF UNEMPLOYMENT

Figure 27–2 (on page 486) shows the behavior of the unemployment rate since the end of World War II. Throughout the period until 1970, the unemployment rate fluctuated cyclically but showed no clear rising or falling trend. During the 1950s the average rate was 4.5 percent and during the 1960s it was 4.8 percent—hardly a significant difference. During the 1970s, however, the cyclical fluctuations appeared to be superimposed on a rising trend. From 1970 to 1976 the *low* figure for unemployment was 4.9 percent, well above the *average* for the two decades of the 1950s and 1960s of 4.7 percent.[2] This low of 4.9 percent was achieved during the boom of 1972–

[2] Figures in this section are based on annual averages of unemployment.

1974, while the subsequent recession carried the rate to a high of 8.5 percent in 1975, the highest unemployment figure recorded since the Great Depression of the 1930s. Only time will tell if the high unemployment of the 1970s will prove to be a transitory phenomenon or the beginning of a major trend toward higher average levels of measured unemployment at all stages of the business cycle.

Inflation

WHY POLICY MAKERS ARE CONCERNED[3]

By and large, governments do not have policies about the price level per se. No one feels that the price level ruling in America in 1776 was intrinsically better or worse than the one ruling in 1976. Standards of living depend on the purchasing power of money income, and if all money incomes and all prices were doubled overnight, living standards of income earners would be left unchanged. What does matter, however, is what happens while the price level is changing—that is, the process of inflation or deflation. Whatever the present level of prices, there will be many economic consequences if it rises or falls sharply over the course of the next few years. Since sustained deflations have not occurred in the twentieth century, we confine our attention to increases in the price level, that is, to periods of *inflation*.

Contrary to popular belief, there is no strong evidence that inflation lowers full-employment real national income. Inflation does not seem permanently to raise the gap between actual and full-employment national income,[4] nor does it seem to lower the growth rate of full-employment income. Many economists

[3] This matter is discussed at greater length in Chapter 32, pages 592–598.

[4] But it can do so temporarily, as we shall see in some detail in Chapter 42.

have studied the effects of inflation, but no one has yet succeeded in establishing a definite relation between higher rates of inflation and lower rates of growth of full-employment income.

Since inflation seems neither to affect the rate of growth of full-employment national income nor to raise the average gap between actual and full-employment income, it follows that inflation does not reduce *average* living standards. A main consequence of inflation is to *redistribute* income among people, benefiting some and hurting others. The redistributions are often large and haphazard and productive of serious social tensions. This itself is one major reason for avoiding inflations.

CAUSES OF INFLATION

Most economists today agree that there are at least two senses in which inflation is a monetary phenomenon. The first is that the very rapid inflations in many countries, particularly those of South America, have been caused by rapid expansions of the money supply. Such expansions have been due to large and persistent government budget deficits that were often incurred to finance development projects that could not be paid for out of tax receipts. The second is that inflation, whatever its causes, cannot continue for a sustained period without increases in the money supply.

Beyond this agreement, there is serious controversy over the proximate causes of the mild inflations that the countries of North America and Western Europe underwent in the 1950s and 1960s and of the somewhat more rapid inflations that they have suffered so far in the 1970s. Several competing diagnoses—demand-pull, cost-push, price-push, structural rigidity, and expectational—have been advanced as explanations.

Demand-pull inflation

The theory of changes in the price level most widely accepted by economists is the one that links price level changes to inflationary and deflationary gaps.

In essence, the **demand-pull** theory of inflation says that changes in price levels are to be accounted for by changes in aggregate demand. A rise in aggregate demand in a situation of more or less full employment will create excess demand in many individual markets, and prices will be bid upward. The rise in demand for goods and services will cause a rise in demand for factors, and their prices will be bid upward as well. Thus inflation in the prices both of consumer goods and of factors of production is caused by a rise in aggregate demand.

Virtually all economists agree that excess aggregate demand can be, and often has been, a major cause of inflation.

Cost-push inflation

The **cost-push** theory of inflation says that rises in costs not themselves associated with excess demand—particularly wage costs—are the initiating cause of inflation. Powerful unions are seen as demanding increases in wages even when there is no excess demand for labor. Employers, the theory says, generally accede to these demands and pass the increased wage costs on to the consumer through higher prices. Thus the root cause of the inflation is union power, the original upward push to prices being generated from the cost side rather than from the demand side.

Price-push inflation

The **price-push,** or administered-price, theory of inflation is similar to the cost-push theory. The price-push theory predicts the same sequence of events as does the cost-push theory, but firms rather than unions are the main culprits. The theory says that sellers have monopoly power and would like to raise prices but are restrained from doing so by fear of antitrust action, adverse public opinion, or regulatory review of their prices. Under these circumstances cost increases can provide the necessary excuse for price increases. During wage negotiations, for example, sellers grant wage increases and then use them as an excuse to raise prices by more than is required to offset the rise in wage costs.

Structural rigidity inflation

The **structural rigidity** theory of inflation assumes that resources do not move quickly from one use to another and that it is easy to increase wages and prices but hard to decrease them.[5] Given these conditions, when patterns of demand and costs change, real adjustments occur only very slowly. Shortages appear in potentially expanding sectors, and prices rise because the slow movement of resources prevents the sector from expanding rapidly enough. Contracting sectors keep factors of production on part-time employment or even in full unemployment because mobility is low in the economy. Because their prices are rigid, there is no deflation in these potentially contracting sectors. Thus the mere process of adjustment in an economy with structural rigidities causes inflation to occur. Prices in expanding sectors rise, and prices in contracting sectors stay the same; on average, therefore, prices rise.

Expectational inflation

The **expectational** theory of inflation depends on a general set of expectations of price and wage increases. Suppose, for example, that both unions and firms expect that a 10 percent inflation will occur next year. Unions will tend to start negotiations from a *base* of a 10 percent increase in money wages (which would hold their real wages constant). They will argue that firms will be able to meet the extra 10 percent on the wage bill out of the extra revenues that will arise because product prices will go up by 10 percent. *Starting from this base,* unions will then negotiate over how much of an increase in real wages they can ob-

---

[5] This theory was developed in the 1960s by Charles Schultze, who in 1977 was appointed by President Carter to be Chairman of the President's Council of Economic Advisers.

tain. Firms will also be inclined to begin bargaining by conceding at least a 10 percent increase in money wages, since they expect that the prices at which they sell their own products will rise by 10 percent. The real substance of the debate between unions and employers will thus center around how much money wages can rise in excess of 10 percent, and here such factors as profits, productivity, and bargaining power will be crucial.

Thus if both labor and management expect an inflation of 10 percent (or any other figure), their behavior in wage and price setting will tend to bring that rate of inflation about, whatever the state of monetary and fiscal policy. This is yet another example of the common phenomenon of self-realizing expectations that we have met at several points in this book.

It is unlikely that an expectational inflation will break out all by itself because expectations of continuing inflation do not arise out of thin air. They are more likely to be a projection from actual rates of inflation in the recent past. If the economy has been experiencing inflation rates on the order of 3 or 4 percent in the recent past, it is unlikely that a spontaneous change in inflationary expectations will suddenly produce a 10 percent inflation.

What *is* likely, however, is that an expectational inflation may take over from a demand-pull inflation once the excess demand is reduced or eliminated. Say, for example, that the government has been generating a demand-pull inflation of 10 percent per year for two or three years as a result of spending well in excess of its tax revenue and creating new money to finance its budget deficit. Firms and unions may now expect this rate to continue; if so, they will grant 10 percent wage and price increases at a minimum. Next suppose that the government eliminates its budget deficit and stabilizes the money supply but that the expectations of 10 percent inflation persist. Wage and price increases of at least 10 percent will occur in the *expectation* of continuing inflation. At this point what was a demand-pull inflation becomes an expectational inflation.

The danger of expectational inflation is that it may cause a demand-pull inflation (or any other kind) that has gone on for several years to persist long after the original causes of the inflation have been removed.

Once inflationary expectations become established it may not be an easy matter to force decision makers to revise these expectations downward notwithstanding changed governmental fiscal and monetary policies.

A dominant cause?

Today few economists would rule out all structural influences, but almost none believe structural rigidity to be the major cause of inflations. Many economists believe that all significant inflations have their initiating causes in excess aggregate demand. Others believe that some of the mild inflations of the 1950s, 1960s, and early 1970s were initiated on the cost side. Most economists would agree that demand-pull inflations have occurred in the past and would accept that mild cost-push or price-push inflations are at least possible. Moreover, they believe that inflations once started often generate inflationary expectations that can cause the inflation to persist for some time after the initiating causes have been removed.

Debate continues on the balance between demand-pull and cost-push as forces causing inflation in the contemporary inflationary climate. The debate is important because the policy implications of different causes of inflation are different. Until the causes of inflation are fully understood, there will be debate about appropriate anti-inflationary policies. By the same token, however, the success or failure of particular policies may shed additional light on causes.

Of course there does not have to be only

one cause of inflation, and certainly the weight of different causes can vary from time to time and place to place. For this reason people who look for a single dominant cause of inflations may be obscuring the real issue of the balance between various causes at different times and places.

THE CONTROL OF INFLATION: VALIDATED AND UNVALIDATED INFLATION

When a cost-push, price-push, or expectational inflation is allowed to persist because the government permits the money supply to expand at the same rate as the inflation, economists speak of the inflation as being *validated* by increases in the money supply.

One of the most important propositions in the whole theory of inflation is that inflations cannot long persist, *whatever their initiating causes,* unless the inflations are validated by increases in the money supply.

Consider what would happen if an inflation were not validated by the monetary authorities. Suppose prices and wages rise (for whatever reason—cost-push, price-push, or expectations) while the amount of money is held constant. Even if the GNP measured in constant dollars remains unchanged for awhile, the GNP measured in current dollars rises. The money value of all transactions rises, and firms and households will need larger amounts of money to finance these transactions. Thus the amount of money demanded for transactions balances rises. But more money is not available. Bonds will be offered for sale in an attempt to build up transactions balances. This forces down the price of bonds and—what is the same thing—forces up the rate of interest. Investment and other interest-sensitive expenditure will fall as a result. This is a fall in aggregate demand.[6] Thus the net result of any inflation

[6] This analysis relies on the theory that is spelled out in much more detail on pages 643–646.

that is *not* validated by an increase in the money supply is a rise in interest rates, a fall in aggregate demand, a fall in real national income, and a rise in unemployment. [38]

A continuing inflation that is not validated by a continuing increase in the money supply must sooner or later produce ever-falling levels of output and ever-rising levels of unemployment.

Sooner or later the falling output and rising unemployment will bring the inflation to a halt. If the inflation is cost-push, unions may begin to worry more about jobs and less about wages as unemployment rises and firms may become less willing to pass on wage increases through higher prices now that their sales are steadily shrinking. If the inflation is an expectational one, rising unemployment and falling sales will sooner or later cause unions and firms to abandon their expectations that inflation will continue at a rapid rate.

This discussion reveals an important distinction. Demand-pull inflations caused by increases in the money supply (e.g., the government's financing a budget deficit by creating new money) can go on indefinitely because they bring their own monetary validation with them; all other kinds of inflation will be brought to a halt sooner or later by falling output and rising unemployment unless they are validated by increases in the money supply. But the consequence of bringing a cost-push, price-push, or expectational inflation to a halt by refusing to increase the money supply will be at least a temporary fall in output and rise in unemployment. If the push or expectations factors prove stubborn, the inflation may persist for some time in the face of falling output and rising unemployment.

When this occurs policy makers are faced with a serious dilemma: Should they let the recession persist, knowing that if it is deep and long-lasting enough it will break the inflationary spiral, or should they validate the inflation by increasing the money supply, thereby removing the disincentives (provided by the recession) to further increases in wages and prices? This dilemma will be discussed in its many and varied aspects in Chapter 42.

EXPERIENCE OF INFLATION

Figure 27–2 (on page 486) shows the inflation rate for each year since World War II. Like the unemployment figures, inflation rates showed no tendency for a rising trend until the late 1960s. The average rate of inflation in the 1950s was 2.2 percent, and from 1960 to 1967 it was 1.8 percent. The dramatic rise in the inflation rate began with the acceleration of expenditures for the Vietnam war. This drove the inflation rate to 4.7 percent in 1968 and to over 6 percent in 1969. The inflation rate subsided somewhat in the early 1970s, but its low of 3.4 in 1971 and 1972 still exceeded the average rate of each of the previous two decades. Then the inflation rate jumped to 8.8 percent in 1973 and 12.2 percent in 1974. The latter was a truly exceptional rate for a peacetime year.

In the course of 1974 the economy encountered an upper turning point and passed from boom to recession. As the slump developed in late 1974 and in 1975, the inflation rate fell. It was 7 percent in 1975 and 4.7 percent in 1976. Even in the depths of the most serious trough in business activity since the Great Depression of the 1930s, however, the inflation rate remained stubbornly above the rate achieved in the previous trough and well above the average rate for all the years in the previous two decades. Only time will tell if this represents a new trend toward a generally more inflationary economy or if, given a little more time, inflation rates will be reduced to the averages achieved in the earlier decades—which in retrospect have come to appear almost incredibly low.

The coexistence of high unemployment and high inflation rates represented a new and unpleasant policy challenge for the 1970s.

Summary

1. At one time or another four major goals of macroeconomic policy have been important: a satisfactory balance-of-payments position, a rapid rate of growth, and low levels of unemployment and inflation. Maintaining a satisfactory balance of payments was more important under the Bretton Woods system, when exchange rates were fixed, than at present, when exchange rates are flexible.

2. Unemployment may be voluntary or involuntary. Involuntary unemployment is a serious social concern both because it causes economic waste measured in terms of lost output and because it is a source of human suffering.

3. There are several kinds of unemployment: frictional unemployment, due to the time taken in moving from job to job as a result of normal labor turnover; structural unemployment, caused by the need to reallocate resources between occupations, regions, and industries as the structure of demands and supplies changes; and deficient-demand unemployment, caused by there being too low a level of aggregate demand.

4. Search unemployment occurs when persons remain unemployed to search for a job better than the first one they can find. Search unemployment will tend to increase as the costs of search decrease. It is thought to be higher now than in the past because of more generous and more widespread unemployment insurance and because of the increased prevalence of multi-worker households.

5. Unemployment can be reduced by raising aggregate demand, by making it easier to move between jobs, and by raising the cost of staying unemployed.

6. Control of inflation is a major goal of macroeconomic policy. Inflation redistributes income in haphazard ways, and this is sufficient to make it a matter of serious concern. There is no strong evidence that mild inflations change the average living standard of the population.

7. Inflation has many alleged causes. Demand-pull inflation occurs when there is an inflationary gap. Cost-push and price-push inflations occur when unions and price-setting firms raise wages and prices independently of the state of aggregate demand. Expectational inflation occurs when wages and prices rise (thereby causing an inflation) in the expectation that an inflation is going to occur.

8. A validated inflation, one in which the money supply increases in step with the rise in prices, can go on indefi-

nitely with no necessary fall in output. An unvalidated inflation will be accompanied by rising rates of interest and falling levels of output. Sooner or later unemployment will rise to the point at which the unvalidated inflation comes to a halt.

9. In the mid 1970s the American economy suffered from both a higher rate of unemployment and a higher rate of inflation than it has experienced in the two preceding decades. The goals of macroeconomic policy—full employment and relatively stable prices—were not being achieved.

Concepts for review

Frictional, structural, deficient-demand, and search unemployment
Definitions and problems in the measurement of unemployment
Demand-pull, cost-push, price-push, structural rigidity, and expectational inflation
Validated and unvalidated inflation

Discussion questions

1. How would *you* rank the following three economic goals in importance, and why: a stable price level, rapid economic growth, and high employment? Are there any other goals with which macroeconomics is or should be concerned?

2. The director of the National Urban League recently suggested that he believed the true unemployment figure for the United States was "at least double" the officially reported figure. What are possible sources of "hidden unemployment"? On the other side, are there possible reasons for expecting some exaggeration of the number of people reported as unemployed? Would you expect the relative strength of these opposing forces to change over the course of the business cycle? What would you expect if a short recession turned into a long and deep depression?

3. What source or sources of unemployment are the following writers focussing their attention on:
a. "We can reduce unemployment without increasing inflation by targeting unemployment programs toward those groups and to those geographical areas where unemployment is especially high."
b. "We have never had full-employment in this country and never will have. Even during World War II the unemployment rate was nearly 2 percent."
c. "If people on unemployment compensation were required to take a job when it is offered to them, the unemployment rate would drop 30 percent within three months."
d. "The cure for unemployment is spending. Public spending or private spending, foolish spending or shrewd spending, it doesn't really matter. Spend, spend, spend. Employ, employ, employ."

4. Maintaining a stable price level is a major goal of macro policy. One means to reach this goal was suggested in the "Letters" section of *Time:* "Sir/You did a commendable job of discussing inflation, but you failed to pinpoint the simple solution to the problem: return to the gold standard." Discuss this solution.

5. What source or sources of inflation are the following writers focusing their attention on?
a. "The one basic cause of inflation is government spending more than it takes in. The cure is a balanced budget."
b. "The breaking out of major labor negotiations in steel, auto's, and other basic industries will lead to double-digit wage increases and a serious inflationary effect."
c. "Wage settlements are high. The widespread publicity they are receiving will make it difficult to wind down inflation."
d. "While the CPI rose by 0.7 percent last month, most of the increase was in a very few sectors where bottlenecks are developing."

6. "Inflations cannot long persist whatever their initiating causes unless the inflations are validated by increases in the money supply". Why is this so? Does it not imply that control of inflation is simple: do not allow increases in the money supply to rise faster than the rate of increase of real national income?

41

Conflicts among policies: monetarists versus neo-Keynesians

Economists still debate the causes of the Great Depression, just as historians still debate the causes of World War I. But the overwhelming majority of economists agree that another episode like the Great Depression of the 1930s need never happen again. Indeed they believe that it would have been possible to bring the economy fairly rapidly out of the major recession that beset it in the mid 1970s. Monetarists and Keynesians would have differed in the emphasis placed on expansionary monetary and fiscal policies, but there is little doubt that, between the two kinds of policies, the economy could have been stimulated to a more rapid recovery than actually ensued. In spite of this impressive area of agreement, there is still a great deal of debate about the appropriate tools of macroeconomic policy and their effectiveness.

Views of macroeconomic policy

TWO EXTREME VIEWS[1]

There is current controversy over many aspects of macroeconomic policy, and in this controversy two extreme views can be discerned. In the first view, the free-market economy has strong self-regulating tendencies: If a satisfactory general climate is maintained, the economy will naturally tend toward full employment and a relatively stable price level. At the same time, the exercise of private inventiveness, spurred on by the profit motive, will result in a satisfactory growth rate of real national income. In this view, the government has only to maintain the conditions under which the free-market economy can function effectively. Monetary or fiscal mismanage-

---

[1] "Extreme" implies only the descriptive statement that the view lies at one end or the other of a spectrum of views. It does not imply a judgmental statement that the view is wrong, subversive, or otherwise undesirable. The history of ideas is full of examples where extreme views prove correct and moderate views wrong (and vice versa).

ment can disturb the economy's natural self-regulation and contribute to severe depressions and inflations, so the government's main problem is to manage its budget and the money supply correctly. Indeed, economic fluctuations may actually be the result of misguided attempts of government stabilization policies to assist the self-regulatory powers of the free-market economy. In this view, while government stabilization activities may have a strong influence on the economy, they are likely to be perverse except in periods of major depressions.

According to the second extreme view, the free-enterprise economy has weak self-regulatory powers and may readily settle into prolonged periods of heavy unemployment. Also, as a result of the restrictive practices of monopolies and a general tendency of large corporations to shun risks and adopt safe policies, the growth rate of income will tend to be sluggish. Furthermore, the enormous power of unions and large corporations may cause inflations that cannot be blamed on monetary mismanagement. In this view, active government intervention is vital. Without such major governmental efforts the economy will sometimes tend to undergo wide cyclical fluctuation and at other times to stagnate in stable positions of heavy unemployment. To prevent these situations from arising, the government must use its instruments of fiscal policy supplemented by monetary policy.

MONETARIST AND NEO-KEYNESIAN VIEWS OF STABILIZATION POLICY

The elements of these two extreme views can be combined into many different packages. We can, however, identify two groups of economists who accept two characteristic packages. One group holds that the economy tends to be relatively self-regulating and that monetary policy is much more potent than fiscal policy. Because of the importance they place on monetary factors, these economists

are called **monetarists.** The best known and undoubtedly the most influential member of this group is Professor Milton Friedman of the University of Chicago.

The second group holds the view that the economy cannot be relied on to produce full employment if left to itself; they also believe that although fiscal and monetary policy are both useful instruments, fiscal policy is generally the more potent of the two. The economists in this group are called **neo-Keynesians** (and sometimes just Keynesians) since they accept the macro model of the economy developed by the followers of Keynes out of the basic ideas in his *General Theory*. Three of the most influential members of this group are Professors James Tobin of Yale University, Paul Samuelson of MIT, and Walter Heller of the University of Minnesota and formerly chairman of the Council of Economic Advisers.

Stabilization policy concerns attempts to stabilize the level of national income by ensuring that serious inflationary or deflationary gaps do not persist, so that something close to full employment without rapid inflation can be achieved. Many of today's debates concerning stabilization policy involve the issues that divide the monetarists and the neo-Keynesians. We shall study these in terms of the disagreements over diagnoses, over the efficiency of alternative policy instruments, and over the cures prescribed.

The nature of the problem (diagnoses)

Why does the economy show the sort of short-run cyclical fluctuations in real income that we studied in Chapter 29? What accounts for inflation, and why does it proceed sometimes at a slow pace and sometimes at a rapid one? Many of the major disagreements between monetarists and neo-Keynesians occur over the first step that any economic doctor must take: diagnosis of the basic problem.

CYCLICAL FLUCTUATIONS

Monetarist views

Monetarists hold that monetary causes are the major source of serious fluctuations in national income.[2] The modern interpretation of American business cycles as having mainly monetary causes relies heavily on the evidence advanced by Milton Friedman and Anna Schwartz in their monumental *A Monetary History of the United States, 1867–1960.* They establish that there is a strong correlation between changes in the money supply and changes in the level of business activity. Major recessions are found to be associated with absolute declines in the money supply, and minor recessions with the slowing down of the rate of increase in the money supply below its long-term trend.

The correlation between changes in the money supply and changes in the level of business activity is now accepted by virtually all economists. But there is controversy over how it is to be interpreted: Do changes in the money supply cause changes in the level of business activity, or vice versa?

Friedman and Schwartz argue that changes in the money supply cause changes in business activity—for example, that the severity of the Great Depression of the 1930s was due to a major contraction in the money supply. Their analysis runs along these lines: The stock market crash of 1929, and other factors associated with a moderate downswing in business activity during the late 1920s, led to a reduction in the public's desire to hold de-

mand deposits and an increase in its desire for cash. The banking system could not meet this increased demand for liquidity without help from the Federal Reserve System.[3] The Fed had been set up to provide just such emergency assistance to banks that were in a basically sound position but unable to meet sudden demands for cash on the part of their depositors.[4] It refused, however, to extend the necessary help, and successive waves of bank failures followed as a direct result. During each wave, literally hundreds of banks failed, ruining many of their depositors and thereby making the already severe depression even worse. During the last half of 1931, for example, almost 2,000 American banks were forced to suspend operations! One consequence was a sharp drop in the money supply—by 1933 the money supply was 35 percent below the level of 1929.

For monetarists, fluctuations in the money supply cause fluctuations in national income.

Neo-Keynesian views

Neo-Keynesians emphasize variations in investment as a cause of business cycles and stress nonmonetary causes of these variations. Many pre-Keynesian economists had also taken this view.[5] There was an important difference, however; the theories developed by earlier economists were theories of alternating bouts of prosperity and depression. Economists who accepted such theories might or might not have believed that government policy could significantly shorten a period of

---

[2] The view that fluctuations often have monetary causes is not new. The English economist R. G. Hawtrey, the Austrian Nobel laureate F. A. von Hayek, and the Swedish economist Knut Wicksell are prominent among those who earlier gave monetary factors an important role in their explanations of the turning points in cycles and/or the tendency for expansions and contractions, once begun, to become cumulative and self-reinforcing. Modern monetarists carry on this tradition.

[3] As we saw in Chapter 33 banks are never able to meet from their own reserves a sudden demand to withdraw currency on the part of a large fraction of their depositors. Their reserves are *always* inadequate for such a task.

[4] This is the lender-of-last-resort function of a central bank discussed in Chapter 33.

[5] Like the monetarists, the neo-Keynesians are modern advocates of some views that have a long history. The great Austrian (and later American) economist Joseph Schumpeter stressed such explanations early in the present century. The Swedish economist Wicksell and the German Speithoff both stressed this aspect of economic fluctuations before the emergence of the Keynesian school of thought.

depression, but they would almost certainly have believed that in the absence of government intervention, the recovery and boom would almost inevitably follow the period of depression.

Underemployment equilibrium. What was new in Keynes's *General Theory* was the theory of **underemployment equilibrium:** The economy could come to rest with substantial unemployment and without any significant forces operating to push the economy back to full employment. This was more than a theory of cyclical alternations of prosperity and depression; it was a theory of the possibility of permanent (or at least very long-lived) depression.

A great deal of controversy did (and still does) go on about the sense in which we can speak of underemployment *equilibrium*. One of the simplest interpretations is given in the three paragraphs that follow.

The short-term equilibrium of the economy is at the level of income where withdrawals equal injections (or, as Keynes would have put it, where saving equals investment, since he worked with a one-withdrawal and one-injection model). In the face of any change in withdrawals or injections, the economy will move fairly quickly to a new equilibrium level of national income. Once there, however, national income will remain constant if withdrawals and injections do not change. This may well be at a level of income below the full-employment level.

If the economy comes to rest in a state of underemployment equilibrium, there will in fact be forces at work tending to move it back to full employment, but in practice these forces will be so weak and so slow-acting that they can be ignored for all practical purposes.[6]

[6] In Keynes's theory these forces would have been set in motion by a fall in the real wage rate, as prices fell more than wages. This would induce employers to hire more labor. As we saw in Chapter 29, other forces too might lead to a lower turning point—for example, the wearing out of capital goods needed to produce essentials.

Since forces tending to move the economy back to full employment probably do exist, it might be more accurate to describe a state of underemployment as a state of *underemployment disequilibrium* that is slowly moving toward a full-employment equilibrium. But since these forces act very slowly, they are of little interest in the context of coping with a major depression and its accompanying massive unemployment. For all practical purposes we may regard a situation where $W = J$ at less than full-employment income as a short-run equilibrium which can be changed only by a further shift of either withdrawals or injections. As Keynes said to those who, in the 1930s, were content to wait for long-run forces to produce full employment without government intervention, "In the long run we are all dead." Modern Keynesians might add that the Great Depression of the 1930s came to an abrupt end only after World War II forced the adoption of Keynesian remedies in the form of massive, deficit-financed government expenditures. They might well go on to conjecture that without these Keynesian remedies it might have taken another decade for full employment to have been produced by the economy's natural forces. Keynes did not, of course, hold that the economy would always settle in a position of underemployment equilibrium, only that it *could* settle there.

Modern neo-Keynesians use elaborations of the basic model of the circular flow of income developed by Keynes. They also accept the Keynesian views of the importance of such nonmonetary factors as new inventions and business confidence in explaining variations in investment. Although the idea of underemployment equilibrium has been muted somewhat, neo-Keynesians mostly accept the view that government action is necessary when the economy shows signs of suffering from a persistent deflationary gap.

The role of money as a cause of fluctuations in national income. Neo-Keynesians reject what they regard as the extreme monetarist view that only money matters in explaining cyclical fluctuations.[7] They believe that both monetary and nonmonetary factors are important in explaining the behavior of the economy. Although they accept that serious monetary mismanagement is one potential source of economic fluctuations, they do not believe that it is the only, or even the major, source of such fluctuations. Thus they must deny the monetary interpretation of business cycle history given by Friedman and Schwartz. Let us see how the neo-Keynesians argue to this conclusion.

Neo-Keynesians accept the correlation between changes in the money supply and changes in the level of economic activity, but their explanation reverses the causality suggested by the monetarists. The neo-Keynesians argue that changes in the level of economic activity tend to cause changes in the money supply rather than vice versa. They offer two main lines of argument.

First, they argue that since monetary authorities tend to stabilize interest rates as the target variable of monetary policy, they will tend to increase the money supply in times of expansion and decrease it in times of contraction. This creates the positive correlation. The Fed follows this monetary policy when an expansion gets under way because the demand for money will tend to increase and, if there is no increase in the money supply, interest rates will rise. The Fed can prevent this rise in interest rates (by buying bonds offered for sale at current prices), but in so doing it will, as

we saw in Chapter 33, increase banks' reserves and thereby inject new money into the economy. Similarly, in a contraction interest rates will tend to fall unless the Fed steps in and sells bonds to keep interest rates up. But this will decrease the money supply (see pages 630–633).

Second, neo-Keynesians argue that if the commercial banks always operated with reserves exactly equal to the legally required ratios, the money supply would be under the complete control of the Fed. The money supply would rise or fall only when the Fed (e.g., through its open-market operations) increased or decreased the reserves available to commercial banks. They point out that this, however, is not the case. Commercial banks do hold excess reserves and do vary the amount of such reserves that they hold. Banks tend, so goes the argument, to carry high excess reserves during recessions, both because they are afraid of cash drains to the public and because of the scarcity of profitable but relatively secure investments.

Then, as a recovery gets under way, confidence returns and demand for loans increases. Banks do not need to worry so much about a cash drain caused by a lack of confidence and are thus free to expand their loans, using up their excess reserves, in order to meet the increased demand from their customers. By the time the peak of the cycle is reached, banks may be down to their legal reserve ratios with no further excess reserves and thus no further ability to expand the money supply (unless the Fed makes more reserves available to them). Then, during a recession, banks recall loans and do not make new ones; instead they pile up excess reserves as insurance against a cash drain to the public and because profitable and relatively safe investments are once again difficult to find.

For both these reasons the money supply tends to be positively correlated with the cycle, but the direction of causation is the opposite from that given in the monetarist explanation.

[7] A few, such as Professor Nicholas Kaldor of Cambridge University in England, hold the opposite extreme view that money does not matter at all. Economists of Professor Kaldor's persuasion hold that the money supply is expanded and contracted by the commercial banking system more or less at will and that if the central bank tried seriously to control the economy by holding the money supply below what was needed, money substitutes would be quickly invented—as they have been in the past. To these ultra-Keynesians (more "Keynesian" than Keynes himself), money really does not matter at all, and the whole explanation of fluctuations is to be found in nonmonetary factors.

For neo-Keynesians, fluctuations in national income cause fluctuations in the money supply.

This argument applies to relatively mild cyclical swings; neo-Keynesians accept that major changes in the money supply can be the cause of changes in national income.

INFLATIONS

The monetarist view

Monetarists blame persistent inflationary gaps on excessive increases in the money supply. In doing this, they are the modern advocates of a very old tradition in economics, represented by the proponents of the quantity theory of money and prices.

Few economists would disagree with these two propositions: periods of rapid and sustained monetary expansion will cause inflation, and inflation cannot persist indefinitely unless the money supply is expanded. There is disagreement, however, over the question of whether *all* inflations, even the relatively mild ones experienced by Western countries in the 1950s and 1960s, are *caused by* excessive rates of monetary expansion. Might not some inflations be caused by nonmonetary factors?

Monetarists believe that virtually all inflations are caused by increases in the money supply. The inflation in the late 1960s, for example, was associated not only with an acceleration of government arms expenditure but also with a rapid expansion of the money supply. The slight slowdown in 1969 and the subsequent renewed outburst of inflation were all due, the monetarists argue, to the lagged effects of variations in the rate at which the Fed was permitting monetary expansion.

The neo-Keynesian view

Whereas extreme monetarists hold that inflation is *always* a monetary phenomenon, neo-Keynesians hold that nonmonetary factors can cause substantial inflations such as those experienced in the 1960s and early 1970s in North American and western European countries. A prime example would be an investment boom caused by the opening up of major new investment opportunities. Neo-Keynesians agree that such inflations cannot go on indefinitely unless "validated" by monetary expansions, but they are inclined to stress two further points. First, such inflations may go on for quite a long time even if there is no monetary expansion. Second, the necessary monetary expansion may occur for quite a while *as a response* of the commercial banking system to the heavy investment demand.

Instruments of policy (the potency of various medicines)

Monetarists and neo-Keynesians tend to disagree on the relative potency of fiscal and monetary policy. Monetarists believe that monetary policy exerts a major influence on the economy and that fiscal policy is relatively powerless except where it is really a disguised way of making changes in the money supply. Neo-Keynesians give a place to both fiscal and monetary policy, although they are usually inclined to place more emphasis on the former than on the latter. These views are critically affected by different views of the influence of interest rates.

THE INFLUENCE OF INTEREST RATES

The divergent views of monetarists and neo-Keynesians on the relative potency of fiscal and monetary policy follow directly from their assessment of the shapes of three critical economic relations. The first concerns the relation between the rate of interest and the demand for money as summarized in the liquidity preference schedule. The second concerns the relation between the rate of interest and aggregate demand, an important part of which is summarized by the marginal efficiency of investment schedule that relates investment expenditure to the interest rate.[8] The third relation concerns the extent to which the money supply varies with the interest rate.

The monetarist view

Monetarists hold that both the demand and supply of money are *interest inelastic* (i.e., relatively insensitive to changes in the rate of interest) while the aggregate demand function is highly *interest elastic* (i.e., relatively sensitive to changes in the rate of interest).[9] They argue as follows.

The most important motive determining the demand for money is the transactions motive, which depends mainly on income and is relatively interest inelastic. The speculative motive is interest elastic but except in times of severe depression it will not, according to the monetarists, be a major motive for holding money. Thus monetarists see the demand for

money in normal times as relatively sensitive to changes in national income but relatively interest inelastic.

Monetarists believe that the money supply is also relatively interest inelastic in normal times. They believe that, except in periods of major crises, banks tend to lend out as much as they can, keeping a minimum of excess reserves.[10] If this is so, commercial banks will not vary the money supply as the demand for loans and the interest rate vary; they will only expand and contract the money supply when the Fed takes some policy action that affects their reserves.

While monetarists thus hold that the demand and supply of money is relatively insensitive to interest rates, they take the opposite view with respect to desired expenditure, which they believe to be highly interest elastic. They believe that firms' investment decisions, as summarized in the marginal efficiency of investment schedule, respond significantly to quite small changes in the cost of borrowing money. They also point to certain household expenditures (such as that for new housing and consumer durables) that are known to be highly sensitive to the cost and availability of credit. Taking into account the response of business investment, residential housing, and consumers' durables, monetarists hold that aggregate demand is highly responsive to changes in interest rates.

The views on these three empirical relations are summarized in Figure 41–1(i). The significance of these particular shapes will quickly become apparent when we study the effects of monetary and fiscal policy.[11]

---

[8] The *MEI* and *LP* schedules were discussed in some detail in Chapter 34. The discussion on pages 642–646 may be usefully reviewed at this time.

[9] The interest elasticities of the demand for money, the supply of money, and aggregate demand are defined as follows:

$$\text{interest elasticity of the demand for money} = -\frac{\text{percentage change in the quantity of money demanded}}{\text{percentage change in the interest rate}}$$

$$\text{interest elasticity of the supply of money} = +\frac{\text{percentage change in the quantity of money supplied}}{\text{percentage change in the interest rate}}$$

$$\text{interest elasticity of aggregate demand} = -\frac{\text{percentage change in the aggregate amount of desired expenditure}}{\text{percentage change in the interest rate}}$$

The plus and minus signs are there to assure that each of the three terms is defined as a positive number. The greater the elasticity, the more responsive the function to a change in interest rates. When the elasticity so measured is greater than unity the function is said to be *interest elastic;* when less than unity, it is said to be *interest inelastic.*

[10] During crisis periods, with their accompanying fears of cash drains to the public, banks will want to hold substantial excess reserves.

[11] When we first encountered the aggregate demand function, in Chapter 27, it was plotted against the level of income. Implicitly the rate of interest was held constant. (See Figure 27–7 on page 498.) Now we are looking at the variation in aggregate demand (for a given level of national income) with changes in the rate of interest. This is standard mathematical procedure for a function of several explanatory variables: all but one is held constant, and the pattern of variation with respect to the re-

Figure 41–1 Monetarist and neo-Keynesian views on interest elasticities

(i) The monetarist view

(ii) The neo-Keynesian view

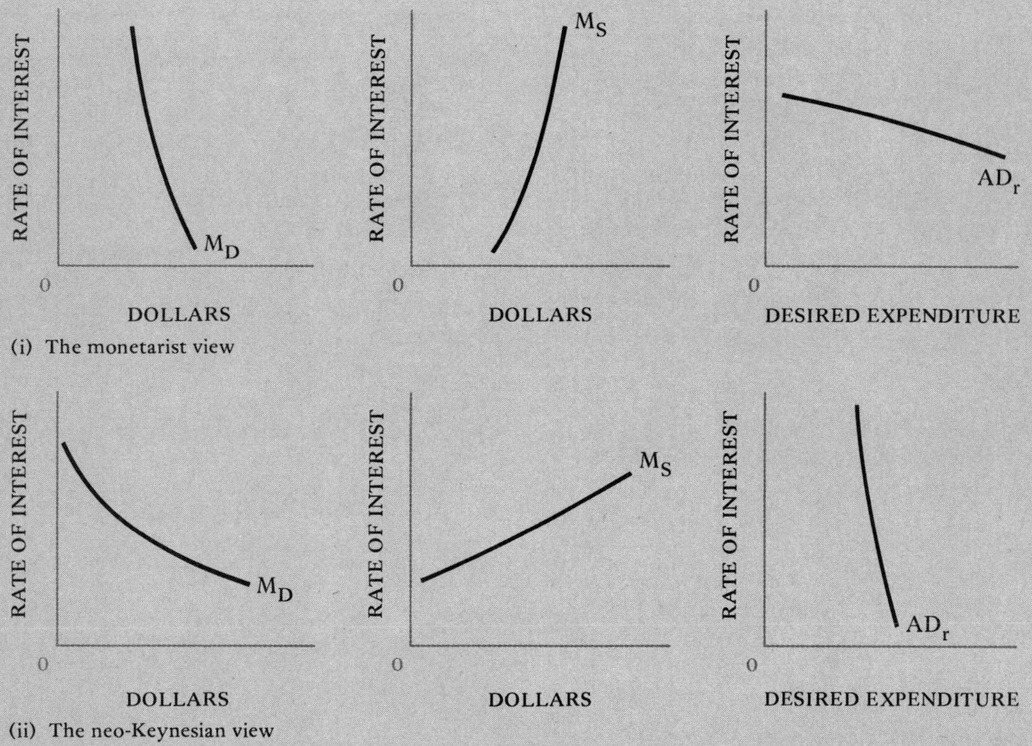

Monetarists and neo-Keynesians disagree over the interest elasticities of the demand for money, the supply of money, and the aggregate demand function. M_D stands for the demand for money, M_S for the supply of money, and AD for aggregate demand. We write AD_r for the function relating AD to the rate of interest to avoid confusion with the AD function of Chapter 27 that related AD to the level of national income. Monetarists hold that the demand and supply of money do not respond much to changes in the rate of interest, while aggregate demand is very sensitive to such changes. Neo-Keynesians hold that the demand for and the supply of money are very sensitive to changes in interest rate, while aggregate demand is insensitive to such changes.

---

maining variable is studied. [39] (We have followed this procedure in other places. See, for example, the variation of demand first with respect to price and then with respect to income in Chapters 5 and 6.) To make certain that the aggregate demand plotted in Figure 41–1 is not confused with that in Figure 27–1, it is labeled AD_r meaning aggregate demand with respect to the rate of interest.

The neo-Keynesian view

Neo-Keynesians take a sharply different view from the monetarists on the three critical empirical relations linking the rate of interest to the demand for money, the supply of money, and aggregate expenditure. They believe that both the demand and the supply of money are highly sensitive to interest rates, while aggregate expenditure is not. They argue as follows.

The speculative motive for holding money is very important because large switches in assets—between money and bonds, for example—occur whenever the public expects a change in interest rates. They stress the very close degree of substitution between money on the one hand and highly liquid interest-earning assets on the other hand; even small changes in interest rates can induce big switches. As a result the demand for money is itself highly sensitive to changes in the rate of interest.

Neo-Keynesians believe that modern evidence on bank behavior shows that commercial banks do vary the money supply substantially in response to variations in the demand for loans and in interest rates. They believe that banks typically hold substantial excess reserves, that these are high in periods of slump (when interest rates and the demand for loans are low), and that they fall to very low levels in periods of boom (when interest rates and the demand for loans are near their peak). This bank behavior makes the supply of money highly interest elastic. So too does the behavior of the Fed when it chooses to use the rate of interest as the target variable.

In contrast to the interest-elastic demand and supply of money, neo-Keynesians believe that aggregate expenditure is interest inelastic. The most important interest-sensitive component of aggregate expenditure is private investment by firms, and neo-Keynesians believe that such investment is relatively unresponsive to changes in interest rates. They hold, on the one hand, that when business conditions are poor it is not even possible to sell all of the potential output of existing capital, and firms will not then be moved to create more capital just because the interest cost of borrowing money falls a few percentage points. On the other hand, in booms, when

rates of profit are extremely high and the business outlook is rosy, firms will not be deterred from their investment plans by increases of a few percentage points in the cost of borrowing money. Although they concede the interest sensitivity of private residential construction and purchases of some consumer durables, neo-Keynesians feel that given the interest inelasticity of the marginal efficiency of investment schedule, the overall aggregate expenditure schedule is relatively interest inelastic.

The views on these three empirical relations are summarized in Figure 41–1(ii). The particular shapes assumed lead to an opposite view of the relative effectiveness of fiscal and monetary policy from that assumed by the monetarists.

MONETARY POLICY

The monetarist view

Given the monetarist view of the interest elasticities summarized in Figure 41–1(i), monetary policy becomes extremely effective. The monetarists' scenario for an expansionary monetary policy is illustrated in Figure 41–2(i), and it runs somewhat as follows.

The Fed buys bonds on the open market, thereby expanding the reserves of the commercial banks and at the same time raising the price of bonds. This both increases the money supply and lowers the rate of interest. Because the demand for money is relatively interest inelastic, a large fall in interest rates (i.e., a large rise in the price of bonds) occurs before the public is induced to sell its bonds to the Fed and accept money in exchange. Aggregate expenditure, however, responds sharply to this fall in the interest rate. Households and firms wish to borrow more for expenditure on such items as plant and equipment, residential housing, and consumers' durables, and banks are willing and able to lend more. Thus a large expansion in aggregate expenditure—and hence in national income—is induced.

Figure 41–2 Monetarist and neo-Keynesian views on monetary policy

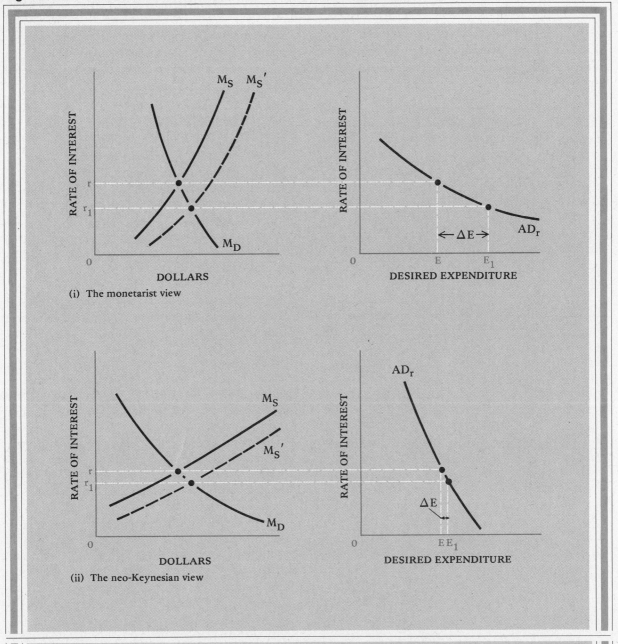

(i) The monetarist view

(ii) The neo-Keynesian view

Monetarist assumptions make monetary policy very effective; neo-Keynesian assumptions make it relatively ineffective. Initially the economy is in equilibrium with an interest rate of r and expenditure of E. In both parts of the diagram an expansionary monetary policy by the Fed shifts the money supply to M_s'. The rate of interest falls to r_1, and this causes an increase in expenditure of ΔE (from E to E_1).

(i) In the monetarist world ΔE is large. Monetary policy is effective.

(ii) In the neo-Keynesian world ΔE is small. Monetary policy is ineffective.

By a parallel but reverse argument, a contraction of the money supply raises interest rates and decreases aggregate expenditure sharply.

In the monetarist view, changes in the money supply lead to large changes in interest rates, and these in turn lead to major changes in aggregate expenditure.

The neo-Keynesian view

The Keynesian view of the interest elasticities summarized in Figure 41–1(ii) makes monetary policy relatively ineffective. A neo-Keynesian scenario for an expansive monetary policy is illustrated in Figure 41–2(ii), and it runs somewhat as follows.

The Fed expands the reserves of the commercial banks by buying bonds. Because the demand for money is highly interest elastic, only a small fall in the interest rate is necessary to induce the public to part with bonds and hold more money. This small fall in the interest rate has only a small effect on aggregate expenditure, which is interest inelastic. Thus the expansive monetary policy does not increase national income substantially.

By a parallel but reverse argument, contraction of the money supply tends to raise interest rates, but only a small increase is required to induce households to reduce their money holdings, and this small increase in interest rates does not do very much to discourage expenditure.

The basic problem with monetary policy, according to the neo-Keynesians, is that the highly interest-sensitive demand for money means that the Fed can induce only small changes in interest rates with its open market operations. The relatively interest-inelastic aggregate expenditure schedule then guarantees that whatever changes in interest rates the Fed is able to engineer will have only a very small effect on aggregate desired expenditure and hence on the level of economic activity.

In the neo-Keynesian view, changes in the money supply lead to small changes in interest rates, and these lead only to small changes in aggregate expenditure.

FISCAL POLICY

The monetarist view

The combination of interest elasticities assumed by the monetarists tends to make fiscal policy relatively ineffective, as illustrated in Figure 41–3(i).

Assume that a large increase in government expenditure starts off an expansion in the economy. As national income increases, more money is needed for transactions purposes and the demand for money increases. Households and firms try to meet their needs by borrowing money from financial institutions and by selling some of their existing bond holdings. Both of these moves tend to raise interest rates, the first by increasing the demand for loans and the second by forcing down the price of bonds. Because banks have few excess cash reserves, they cannot expand loans significantly in response to both the extra demand and the rise in interest rates. People economize on cash balances until the quantity of money demanded equals the available supply. Because the demand for money is relatively interest inelastic, a large rise in interest rates is required before this is accomplished. But the rise in interest rates tends to lead to a large reduction in the amount of aggregate expenditure, since aggregate expenditure is highly sensitive to changes in interest rates. The fall in *private* expenditure occasioned by the rise in interest rates largely offsets the initial increase in government expenditure, so the net effect in increasing aggregate expenditure is relatively small. The main effect of the increase in government expenditure is to crowd out private expenditure. (This is the crowding-out effect first mentioned on page 553).

Figure 41–3 Monetarist and neo-Keynesian views on fiscal policy

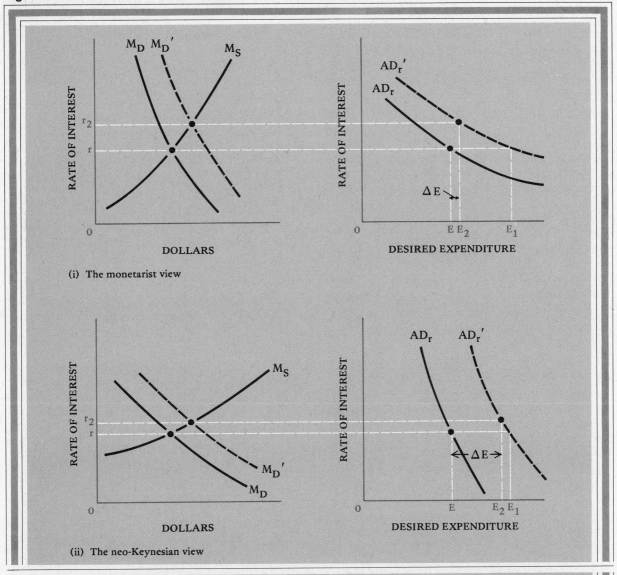

(i) The monetarist view

(ii) The neo-Keynesian view

Neo-Keynesian assumptions make fiscal policy very effective; monetarist assumptions make it relatively ineffective. Initially the economy is in equilibrium with an interest rate of r and expenditure of E. In both parts of the diagram we suppose an expansionary fiscal policy shifts the AD_r curve to AD'_r. This would lead to an increase in desired expenditure from E to E_1, *if the interest rate remained at r.* But when expenditure rises, the transactions' demand for money rises. This shifts M_D to M_D' and this leads to an increase in the rate of interest to r_2. This rise in interest rates leads to a reduction in desired expenditure from E_1 to E_2 (the crowding-out effect). The final effect on expenditure, ΔE, is smaller than the initial effect, EE_1, due to the crowding-out effect.

(i) In the monetarist world the crowding-out effect is large and ΔE small. Fiscal policy is ineffective.

(ii) In the neo-Keynesian world the crowding-out effect is small and ΔE large. Fiscal policy is effective.

Because they believe the crowding-out effect is close to 100 percent, monetarists believe that increases in government expenditure are largely offset by decreases in private expenditure.

By a parallel but reverse argument, a decrease in government expenditure will tend to lead to a sharp fall in interest rates that will induce a large rise in private expenditure. This in turn mostly offsets the fall in government expenditure.

In the monetarist view, because the crowding-out effect is large, fiscal policy is relatively ineffective in changing national income.

The neo-Keynesian view

The combination of interest elasticities assumed by the neo-Keynesians tends to make fiscal policy relatively effective, as illustrated in Figure 41–3(ii).

Assume that the government increases its expenditure in order to raise national income from a period of depression. As national income increases, more money is needed for transactions purposes and the demand for money will thus exceed the existing supply. The public will attempt to obtain the extra money that it requires both by borrowing from the banks and by selling bonds on the open market. Both of these actions tend to raise interest rates, but a relatively small rise in interest rates, along with a rise in the demand for loans, causes commercial banks to reduce excess reserves, thereby increasing the money supply. Also, because of the rise in interest rates (fall in the price of bonds), there is a large fall in the amount of money held for speculative purposes ("Bonds look cheap, so why hold wealth in the form of money?"). Thus the rate of interest needs to rise by only a small amount in order to equate the demand and supply of money once again. This small increase in interest rates has only a negligible effect in reducing the relatively interest-insensitive aggregate expenditure.

The crowding-out effect in this scenario is small: Most of the new government expenditure makes a net addition to aggregate expenditure and only a small amount is offset by a fall in investment and consumption expenditure; the expansion will continue until the full multiplier effect of the increase in government expenditure is worked out.

By a similar but reverse argument, a decrease in government expenditure has only a small effect on interest rates and induces only a small increase in private expenditure. Thus most of the decrease in government expenditure becomes a decrease in aggregate demand, and with the effect of the multiplier it leads to a magnified decrease in national income.

In the neo-Keynesian view, because the crowding-out effect is small, fiscal policy is relatively effective in changing national income.

Recommended policies (prescriptions)

From what has been said so far, one might expect that monetarists would be pushing for an active stabilization policy working through monetary policy and neo-Keynesians for an active stabilization policy with the accent on fiscal policy. Things are not quite so simple as that.

MONETARIST POLICIES

Monetarists do see monetary policy as the major means by which the government can influence national income and the price level. From their view that money matters—indeed, that maybe *only* money matters—they go on to take a possibly surprising position on macro stabilization policy.

Many monetarists argue that money is so powerful an influence on the short-run behavior of the economy that monetary policy is too dangerous a tool to be used as an anticyclical device!

Confusions between fiscal and monetary policy

Early discussions of fiscal and monetary policy did not make a sharp distinction between the two. Keynes himself simply advocated curing the depression by massive doses of deficit-financed government expenditure. Early Keynesians contrasted this kind of "fiscal policy" with the open market operations of monetary policy, in which the government attempted to influence aggregate expenditure by changing interest rates and banks' reserves.

It is now generally realized that Keynes's fiscal policies also contained a measure of monetary policy. Any government deficit has to be financed by increasing the supply of monetary assets—either bonds or money—in the hands of the public. Today economists would say that a *pure* fiscal policy is a change in government expenditure that does not cause a change in the supply of any monetary asset. This means that the expenditure must be a balanced budget change—that is, it must be accompanied by an equal change in taxes. A *pure* monetary policy is a change in the stocks of monetary assets held by the private sector of the economy that is not accompanied by any change in the government's propensities to spend or to tax out of national income. Such a change occurs, for example, when the Fed buys or sells bonds on the open market.

Mixed policies occur whenever the budget balance and the stock of monetary assets both change. Consider, for example, an increase in government expenditure unaccompanied by an increase in tax rates but financed by selling bonds to the Fed. In this case there will be an increase in the government deficit *and* an increase in the money supply. Both Keynesians and monetarists would predict expansionary effects on the economy; Keynesians are likely to put most emphasis on the expansion of expenditure, while monetarists are likely to put most emphasis on the increase in the money supply.

In the real world, fiscal and monetary changes often—indeed usually—go hand in hand, as the above example suggests. The reason for this is that if the government wishes to have an expansionary effect on the economy, there is no reason for it to limit itself to "pure" changes in either monetary or fiscal policy. This makes life easier for the government than it would be if it had to follow either a pure fiscal or a pure monetary policy. It does, however, make things more difficult for scholars trying to sort out the separate effects of each. This is one reason why empirical observations of the effects of particular policy moves have not finally resolved the debate about the relative effectiveness of pure monetary policy and pure fiscal policy.

They hold that although the money supply could conceivably be manipulated to stabilize national income, the exercise of monetary policy has in fact tended to destabilize the economy and that in practice it is unlikely to do otherwise. One reason for this pessimistic view follows from the monetarists' belief that the money supply exerts its powerful effects on the economy with time lags that are long and that vary for reasons not yet fully understood. Thus they argue that even the most enlightened attempt to use monetary policy as a

Congressional behavior, the consumption function, and the effectiveness of fiscal policy

We have considered the relative advantages of monetary and fiscal policy as seen by the monetarists and the Keynesians under the assumption that the macroeconomic policy makers could adopt whatever policy seemed desirable. Some practical considerations, however, have been important in the actual policy debate.

A monetarist critique of Keynesian proposals. Monetarists argue that the Keynesian theory of fiscal stabilization policy is naive in calling for prompt and precise adjustments in the budget balance to eliminate inflationary and deflationary gaps by changing either government expenditure or taxes. Monetarists argue that Congress is reluctant to change either taxes or government expenditure as a stabilizing measure, and for this reason monetary policy, which requires only the cooperation of the Fed, is much more flexible than is fiscal policy. They also argue that if fiscal policy is to be used, Congress tends to be even more reluctant to cut government expenditures as a stabilizing device than to cut taxes. Thus, as a matter of practical policy, the Keynesians' stabilization recommendations come down to levying temporary tax surcharges to remove inflationary gaps and giving temporary tax rebates to remove deflationary gaps.

At this point monetarists invoke the *permanent-income hypothesis* (see pages 566 and 885–889), which predicts that household consumption will vary only in response to income changes that are expected to be permanent. If Congress announces that changes in taxes are temporary, this may have little effect on households' views of their permanent incomes and thus the flow of consumption will be little affected. The changes in taxes will be mainly absorbed through changes in savings. Thus the monetarists argue that neo-Keynesian fiscal stabilization policy will have very little short-run effect on the economy. As evidence they point to the experience of 1968–1969 as one example of when a temporary tax surcharge did little to remove the inflationary forces in the economy.

A neo-Keynesian reply. Neo-Keynesians admit some of the force of the above arguments. Many of them would prefer to use government expenditure rather than taxes as a major stabilizing device. Efforts to persuade the Congress to delegate some standby authority to the Executive to make rapid changes in expenditure even within limits set by the Congress have so far failed. Thus tax changes may remain the more politically practical stabilization measure.

Neo-Keynesians deny, however, the monetarists' assertion that the permanent-income hypothesis necessarily implies the relative impotency of short-term changes in taxes. They argue that the permanent-income hypothesis does not easily predict the effect of short-term fluctuations in income on the *purchases* of consumers' durables. Say that a temporary tax rebate gives the Jones family an unexpected $500 increase in their income which they spend on a new refrigerator that lasts for ten years. The permanent-income theorists will say: "See, the Joneses are spreading their *consumption* of this extra income over a ten-year period." The neo-Keynesians would reply: "Notice that the *spending* that creates demand and employment occurred immediately after the tax rebate." Both would be right. The Keynesians' observation is, however, the relevant one for short-run stabilization policy. The ability of temporary tax reductions and rebates to raise aggregate demand, and thus to stimulate income and employment, depends on their ability to increase *expenditure*. The effect on current aggregate demand is the same whether the expenditure is on a nondurable that is consumed immediately or on a durable that is consumed slowly over the years.

The unresolved empirical question. The disagreement here rests upon the factual question as to the impact of short-term fluctuations in household disposable income on the purchase of consumer durable goods. If such expenditures are highly responsive to even temporary tax cuts or increases, fiscal policy may prove very effective; if they are not, fiscal policy may prove relatively ineffective as a practical matter.

short-run stabilizer of the economy may do more harm than good. By the time an anti-inflationary, contractionary policy begins to take hold, for example, the economy may already have turned into a downswing that will only be accentuated by the delayed effects of monetary policy. A second reason for their pessimistic view follows from their belief that the exercise of monetary policy by the Fed has been far from enlightened. They believe that the Fed tends to overreact to changes in the economy, first indulging in too much monetary restraint and then panicking at the resulting recession and indulging in inordinate monetary expansion that soon causes a severe inflation.

Thus monetarists feel that our ignorance of the behavior of the economy, our knowledge of the behavior of the Fed's decision makers, and our knowledge of the potency of the money supply all lead to the conclusion that decisions about the money supply should be removed from the Fed. The best results, they believe, would be obtained if the money supply were expanded at a constant rate year by year. The actual figure is itself subject to debate, but as a first approximation an expansion equal to the rate of growth of GNP (in constant dollars) is recommended. Thus, roughly, they would expand the money supply at about 4 percent per year. This would allow the money supply to expand to suit the needs of business as national income rose but would eliminate the disturbing effects of large short-term variations in the quantity of money.

The recommended absence of an active stabilization policy does not seriously worry the monetarists. They feel that their rule for monetary expansion will prevent both major declines in the money supply, such as the one that contributed so greatly to the severity of the depression in the 1930s, and too rapid increases in the money supply, such as those that contributed to the accelerating inflationary pressures of the early 1970s. They feel that their rule will put monetary policy in a neutral stance that will allow the economy's own self-regulatory powers to work, producing no more than relatively mild fluctuations around full-employment national income with neither serious inflations nor severe recessions.

NEO-KEYNESIAN POLICIES

Neo-Keynesians believe that an active stabilization policy is desirable and perhaps essential. They take a more eclectic view of monetary and fiscal policy than do the monetarists. They believe that money does matter somewhat and that monetary policy should be used as an anticyclical weapon in addition to fiscal policy. The neo-Keynesians believe that monetary policy can influence national income by its effects on interest rates. They tend to deny, therefore, that there is a serious conflict between monetary and fiscal policies; they see the policies rather as complements to each other. In the words of Walter Heller, "the 'new economics,' if you will, assigns an important role to *both* fiscal and monetary policy. Indeed, the appropriate mix of policies has been the cornerstone of the argument; . . . to anyone who fears that the 'new economics' is all fiscal policy, the record offers evidence, and the new economics assurance, that money *does* matter."

Neo-Keynesians tend, however, to place heavy emphasis on fiscal policy. They do this because they believe that monetary policy may be particularly weak in major depressions, when it is vitally important to have some policy intervention. In addition, they are disturbed by the uneven incidence of monetary policy. A restrictive monetary policy, for example, tends to hit especially heavily at homeowners, small businesses, and rapidly expanding firms that specialize in the production of new products—each of which is very vulnerable to tight money and rising interest rates. It is worth looking at each of these groups briefly.

When monetary restraints are applied, house building tends to be seriously affected because interest costs are a considerable part of the total expense of purchasing a house. Thus monetary policy affects the homeowner, particularly the homeowner with modest means who finds it difficult to arrange a mortgage in any case. Small firms tend to have more trouble acquiring credit than do large firms. Thus, it might be argued, the continual use of monetary policy reinforces the already strong tendencies for large firms to dominate the economy. New products are often produced by a host of small, new, and rapidly expanding firms. Since costs of production must be met before goods are sold, rapidly expanding firms usually find themselves in constant need of more and more credit to meet the gap between paying their costs and receiving money from the sale of their goods. These new firms are the source of much economic growth, but they are just the firms who are hardest hit—and sometimes driven into insolvency—by restrictive monetary policies that make it impossible for them to obtain the credit they need.

For all these reasons, neo-Keynesians call for an active stabilization policy with fiscal policy playing a major role and monetary policy playing a supporting role.

The significance of the debate

More or less intervention?

One major debate concerns whether we need more or less stabilization policy than we now have. Neo-Keynesians maintain that we could do more in controlling bouts of unemployment and rapid inflation than we do, and they call for a better informed and more rapidly adjusting set of stabilization policies. Monetarists feel that present stabilization policies are misguided and often accentuate cyclical swings in the economy. They call for a more neutral stance with respect to monetary policy in particular (but for fiscal policy as well) to give the economy's self-regulating powers a chance to work.

The neo-Keynesians call for more active monetary and fiscal policies; the monetarists call for more passive policies.

Which tools?

The debate on appropriate tools is also important. If it is agreed that intervention is required to remove an existing inflationary or deflationary gap, should the main burden fall on fiscal or on monetary policy? Monetarists tend to deride the neo-Keynesian's emphasis on fiscal policy and sometimes argue that, if any action is required, appropriate monetary policies are both necessary and sufficient.

Areas of agreement

Although these controversies between major groups of economists are important, it is possible to become too impressed with the differences between them and to forget the amount of agreement that does exist. If, for example, the economy were overwhelmed by a depression on the scale of the 1930s, there would be substantial agreement on what to do.

Everyone would agree on a number of policies designed to prevent panic in financial markets and fear-induced contraction in otherwise sound loans. Federal deposit insurance can prevent runs on banks. The willingness of the Fed to lend money to commercial banks when they require liquidity can avoid the banks' failing to make sound loans based on good security. Federal mortgage loan insurance can keep the construction industry from being forced to stop building.

Then, since almost no one believes that monetary and fiscal policy will cancel each other out, there would be fairly general agreement to use both. (There would no doubt be argument after the recovery as to which instrument should get most of the credit, but at least the debate would take place in a fully employed society rather than in one stagnating in the depths of a prolonged depression.)

A plausible scenario for the recovery would be as follows: The Fed expands bank reserves by buying government securities in the open market; it also cuts its discount rate and lowers legal reserve ratios. These actions lower interest rates and thereby stimulate the demand to borrow money and at the same time make it easy for the banks to lend to meet this demand. If the monetarists are right, this would be sufficient to set off a recovery phase. If the neo-Keynesians are right, these policies would not by themselves restore confidence in the future, and firms and households would be unwilling to go on a major spending spree financed by borrowed money. The government could then step into the breach and use newly created money to increase its spending. Thus the deflationary gap is removed by new government expenditure financed by monetary expansion; but the government increases its expenditure only insofar as private expenditure does not respond to the monetary incentives provided by the Fed. Once the recovery is well under way, confidence will return, and as private spending recovers, the government can reduce its own spending to prevent a serious inflationary gap from emerging.

As a practical matter, too much should not be made of the distinction between the efficacy of pure fiscal and pure monetary policies when the job of engineering a recovery from a serious depression could be done by a simple mixture of the two: Make money cheap and easily available and have the government spend it to the extent that the private sector refuses to do so.

The theories of both monetarists and neo-Keynesians predict that a combination of expansionary fiscal and monetary policies should be capable of removing any really serious and persistent deflationary gap that might emerge in the economy.

Summary

1. There is today a lively controversy over many aspects of macroeconomic theory and policy. Although there is a great variety of views, it is useful to identify two characteristic sets, which we label monetarist and neo-Keynesian.

2. Monetarists stress variations in the money supply as the major cause of cyclical fluctuations and inflations. Neo-Keynesians stress variations both in aggregate expenditure and in the money supply as causes of fluctuations and inflations. Neo-Keynesians argue that fluctuations in national income can, and usually do, *cause* fluctuations in the money supply.

3. Monetarists hold that the demand and supply of money is interest inelastic, while aggregate expenditure is interest elastic. Neo-Keynesians hold that the demand and supply of money is interest elastic, while aggregate expenditure is interest inelastic. The monetarist combination of elasticities makes monetary policy relatively effective and fiscal policy relatively ineffective. The neo-Keynesian combination makes fiscal policy relatively effective and monetary policy relatively ineffective.

4. Monetarists argue that the lags involved in monetary policy are long and variable and that monetary management has proven unenlightened. For both of these reasons, monetary policy proves to be a poor stabilization tool. They prefer a more or less automatic monetary policy in which the money supply is permitted to expand at a constant rate (say 4 percent per year). The natural forces of the economy can then be relied on to produce full employment without rapid inflation most of the time.

5. Neo-Keynesians argue that there is nothing to stop the economy from settling into a prolonged period in which actual national income is well below full-employment national income. In such situations an active stabilization policy is called for, with the major emphasis on fiscal policy and with monetary policy playing a supporting role.

6. Although there are serious differences between the monetarists and the neo-Keynesians, there are also large areas of agreement about how the economy works and how it might be controlled. In particular, both sides agree that a sufficient dose of monetary and fiscal policy would cure a really major depression.

Concepts for review

Monetarists and neo-Keynesians
Relation of changes in money supply to changes in national income, and vice versa
The effect of different assumptions about interest elasticities on the efficacy of fiscal and monetary policies.
The size of the crowding-out effect and the efficacy of fiscal policy
Combined monetary and fiscal policy actions

Discussion questions

1. A once fashionable theory involved a 50-year-long wave in business cycles. Recently an economist invoked it to predict that the U.S. economy was heading in the 1980's for another disastrous depression on the scale of the 1930s. If such an unfortunate event was to occur, what government policies would you advocate? Would you expect neo-Keynesians and Monetarists to be in sharp disagreement about whether to intervene? About what to do? About the mechanism by which a recovery would occur?

2. Suppose the following "facts" are accepted. Would any of them give substantial support to either the monetarists or the neo-Keynesians in their debate?
a. The U.S. has never had a recession without a concurrent decrease in the money supply.
b. Expanding the money supply during a recent deep depression led to falling interest rates, to increasing excess reserves, but aggregate spending continued to fall.
c. The recovery phases of each of the four most recent business cycles came to a halt shortly after the Fed slowed down the rate of monetary expansion.

3. The quantity equation of exchange, $MV = PY$ is used as part of the quantity theory of money (see Chapter 34). This theory states the quantity of money, M, times the velocity of circulation, V, equals the value of money national income. Could both monetarists and neo-Keynesians accept this equation as accurate? How might one use it to discuss the differing roles given by the two groups of economists to

monetary and fiscal policy in achieving full employment national income at stable prices?

4. In what ways might changes in the money supply be a cause of fluctuation in the GNP? In what ways might changes in aggregate demand be a cause of fluctuation in the GNP? Is it necessary to choose between either the money supply or aggregate demand as the cause of GNP fluctuations? If not, does it matter to the U.S. economy in the 1970s whether the monetarists or the neo-Keynesians are more nearly correct in their theories?

5. Relate each of the following to the shapes of the *LP, MEI,* and *AD$_r$* functions:
a. There is so much uncertainty about the future that a fall in interest rates does not lead to increased spending on goods and services.
b. Buying of houses, cars, and consumer goods on credit is greatly stimulated by new government policies providing loan insurance to lenders.

c. The government places a tax of 10 percent per month on bank reserves in excess of the reserves required by the Fed.
d. A reduced need for transactions balances due to development of a checkless society.

6. In a paper given to the Joint Economic Committee in 1958 Milton Friedman stated: "A steady rate of growth in the money supply will not mean perfect stability. . . . There are . . . serious limitations to the possibility of a discretionary monetary policy and much danger that such a policy may make matters worse rather than better." Did Friedman thus, in 1958, deny the monetarist position he holds in 1978?

7. "Whether or not the monetarists are correct in their criticism of neo-Keynesians depends critically upon the size of the crowding-out effect." To what extent is this correct? To the extent that it is correct, does it imply a simple empirical test that should solve the debate about relevant policies once and for all?

42

Conflicts among goals: unemployment versus inflation

The great economic policy debate of the 1930s concerned whether there was anything at all that the government might do to bring about a recovery from a depression that had lasted ten long years. The policy debate in the mid 1970s concerned how rapidly the recovery could be stimulated without setting off another bout of serious inflation, and how much inflationary risk it was worth taking in order to cut unemployment faster.

The change in the subject of the debate reflects both our accumulation of knowledge and our remaining ignorance. By and large, national-income theory is an impressive tool; through it we understand the workings of the economy far better than did most economists at the time of the Great Depression. Today, there is substantial agreement among economists on measures that will affect aggregate demand. A major and persistent depression can be fought with a mixture of monetary and fiscal policies whose combined efficacy most economists would accept. The extent of our remaining ignorance is reflected, however, in the lack of consensus among economists regarding the causes of and cures for the rising rates of inflation that have beset most countries during the 1970s. Today we wonder whether governments will dare to use their powerful tools to stimulate a higher level of economic activity for fear that in so doing they could set off a major bout of inflation. The inflation might then be difficult to bring under control without inducing an even larger recession than the one the government had set out to cure.

Indeed one of the most compelling policy problems in the 1970s concerns the extent to which satisfactorily low levels of inflation and unemployment can be achieved simultaneously. Some economic theories suggest that there is a permanent, long-term conflict between inflation and unemployment. Others suggest that in the very long term these policy goals do not come into conflict. Even the latter theories suggest, however, that there are shorter-term conflicts between these two objectives—conflicts that may persist over a time long enough to present serious problems for policy makers.

Conflicts arising from various types of inflation

Our first task in this chapter is to study how the twin objectives of full employment and relatively stable prices may come into conflict when the economy is experiencing various types of inflation.

DEMAND-PULL INFLATION

The traditional view of inflation is that it occurs when the economy is at its full-employment level of national income, Y_F, and an inflationary gap occurs. It is assumed that when the economy is already at this level of national income, output cannot be increased further. Thus if there is excess aggregate demand at full-employment national income, an inflation will necessarily ensue.

The L-shaped relation

Basic implications. The simplest view of demand-pull inflation follows from the L-shaped relation (see page 520) that underlies the analysis in Parts Eight and Nine of this book. This relation makes a sharp distinction between situations of unemployment and constant prices, on the one hand, and situations of full employment and inflationary pressure, on the other. The characteristics of this theory are illustrated in Figure 42–1, which is very similar to Figure 28–7. The L-shaped relation has stable prices up to the point at which full-employment national income is reached, and it permits inflation only if an inflationary gap develops at full employment.

The L-shaped relation implies that there is no conflict between the policies of maintaining full employment and maintaining stable prices.

If there is unemployment in the economy, aggregate demand can be raised until full employment occurs, without any consequent inflationary pressures. Inflation will result only if demand is increased in a situation in which full employment already exists. The economy can be kept in a position such as f in Figure 42–1 with full employment and stable prices. If the economy is at a with unemployment, then aggregate demand need only be expanded to move it to f; if the economy is at c with an inflation under way, then aggregate demand need merely be reduced until the inflation stops and the economy returns to f.

Microeconomic underpinnings of the L-shaped relation. The L-shaped relation requires two basic microeconomic assumptions. First, prices must be rigid downward in all markets. When the economy has heavy aggregate unemployment, all markets will have excess supplies, and hence there will not be any upward pressure on prices in any market. If prices were flexible downward in any significant number of markets, some prices, and thus the price level, would be falling. Because the price *level* is assumed not to fall, it follows that prices cannot fall in any significant number of markets. The second micro assumption is more important. It concerns the possibility of the economy really being at the point where full employment is combined with a stable price level. Full employment implies that there is no excess supply in any market; a constant price level implies that there is no excess demand in any market. Thus each and every market in the economy must be in equilibrium when the economy is at the point of full employment without inflation, which is indicated by the corner of the L-shaped relation.

Empirical relevance of the L-shaped relation. Each of these micro assumptions contradicts well-

Figure 42–1   The L-shaped relation

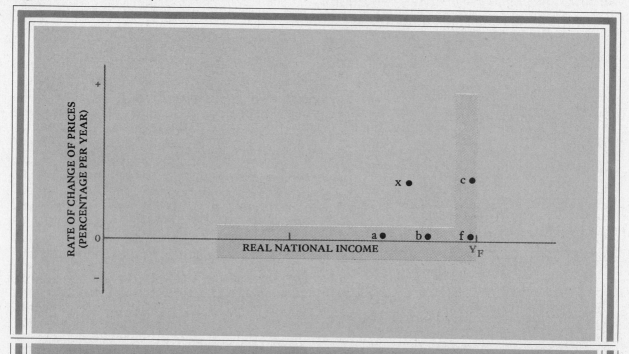

The L-shaped relation between real national income and the rate of inflation is such that there is no conflict between them.   Each point on the diagram indicates a level of Y (on the horizontal axis) and the accompanying rates of inflation or deflation (on the vertical axis). The point Y_F on the national income axis indicates the full-employment level of national income. Outputs above Y_F are assumed to be unattainable. According to the theory, all observations will be in the shaded band. When Y is less than Y_F, the price level will be approximately constant. A change in aggregate demand changes national income, moving the economy between, say, points a and b without causing significant change in the price level. Prices rise only when full employment exists, so all observations of inflationary price changes will be clustered in the narrow vertical band near Y_F. What is not allowed by the theory is a situation, such as that shown by point x, in which a significant degree of inflation is associated with a level of national income significantly below full-employment income.

established observations about the behavior of individual markets. First, although there are substantial downward rigidities in the prices of manufactured goods and unionized labor, a number of commodities and factors are sold on fairly competitive markets and their prices do fall during periods of low demand. Thus, when a slump is severe enough so that no individual prices are rising, the gen-

eral level of prices would be expected to be falling, albeit slowly.

Second, all of the markets of the economy cannot be expected to be in complete equilibrium relative to each other, displaying neither excess demands nor excess supplies. This is because the economy is continually being subjected to the disturbances that necessarily accompany economic growth. As productivity grows, the supplies of some commodities expand faster than others; and as real incomes grow, the demands for some commodities expand faster than others. A reallocation of resources is necessary to adjust to such changes. Such reallocations do not, however, happen instantaneously. Thus at any moment of time, some markets will exhibit excess demands while others exhibit excess supplies.

To see what follows from this situation, consider the economy during a major slump with heavy unemployment in all areas. Now let aggregate demand be increased; output will rise and unemployment will fall. Sooner or later, however, bottlenecks will develop in some markets while there are still substantial excess supplies in other markets. Thus inflationary pressures will develop at first only in isolated parts of the economy. As aggregate demand rises it will always be possible to squeeze a bit more output out of the economy, and thus output will rise as demand rises. But the higher the current level of output rises, the harder it is to produce still more, since an increasing number of industries are already producing at, or in excess of, full capacity. Thus further rises in demand will increasingly exert their primary effect on the price level rather than on output.

This argument suggests that the higher the level of aggregate demand, the greater is the short-term effect on price and the smaller is the effect on output and employment of yet further increases in demand.

The Phillips curve

The theory of the Phillips curve is based on two assumptions that are different from those implicit in the L-shaped relation: (1) At least some prices fall when there is excess supply and (2) all markets do not reach equilibrium simultaneously when aggregate demand is expanded toward its full-employment level.

These assumptions give rise to a relation between price changes and national income shown by the curve in Figure 42–2. This relation is called the **Phillips curve.**[1]

The relation between the level of national income and changes in the price level illustrated in Figure 42–2 shows prices falling slowly for low levels of real national income; at the full-employment level of national income, labeled Y_F, the price level remains steady; and the price level rises when national income exceeds Y_F. The higher the level of national income, the more rapid is the rise in prices, but it is always possible to obtain a further increase in national income (and hence a fall in unemployment) at the cost of a more rapid rise in prices.

With the Phillips curve, the economy does not move abruptly from a situation of underemployment of resources and constant prices to a situation of full employment with rising prices; instead, it moves by degrees from one situation to the other.

The Phillips curve not only slopes upward but is curved, indicating that the trade-off between more inflation and more output worsens as the level of output increases.

Given the Phillips curve relationship, minimizing inflation and minimizing unemployment are conflicting policy objectives.

Assume, for example, that the economy is at point *e* in Figure 42–2, with some measured unemployment of resources, due to frictional and structural causes and some inflation. In this situation, either the inflation can be

---

[1] The relationship between price changes and national income was first studied empirically by the late Professor A. W. Phillips, of the London School of Economics. Phillips drew graphs of British data from 1862 to 1958, showing the rate of change of *money wages* and the percentage of *unemployment*. Figure 42–2 shows the rate of change of prices and the level of national income. This has the effect of making the curve slope upward to the right instead of upward to the left as did Phillips's original curve. The basic behavior being described by the two curves is, however, identical. (Unemployment and national income are inversely related, while the rate of increase of money wages and money prices are directly related to each other.)

Figure 42–2 The Phillips curve relation

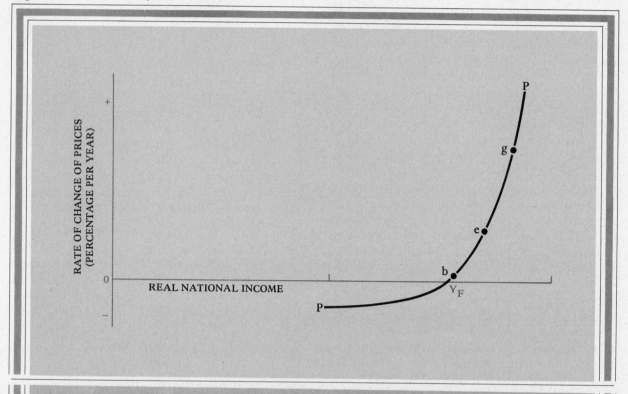

The Phillips curve relates the level of real national income to the rate of inflation in such a way that there is a trade-off between them. A movement along the Phillips curve caused by a rise in aggregate demand raises both national income and the rate of inflation. If, for example, excess demand were producing an inflation and a level of national income indicated by point *e*, a further rise in aggregate demand would raise the rate of inflation and raise national income to the level indicated by, say, point *g*.

slowed at the cost of decreased real income (less employment) or the level of employment can be increased—but only at the cost of a higher rate of inflation.

Empirical evidence. The theories of the L-shaped relation and the Phillips curve have been subjected to a great deal of testing over the last two decades. The testing of any interesting theory almost always raises complicated technical problems, but it is fairly clear

that the simple dichotomy implied by the L-shaped curve has not stood up well to testing. It appears that changes in aggregate demand usually cause changes both in output and in prices. The closer the economy is to full employment, the larger the change in prices and the smaller the change in unemployment for a given change in the flow of aggregate expenditure; the further the economy is from full employment, the more changes in expenditure will cause output variations and the less they will cause the price level to vary.

This is seen by even a superficial analysis of the U.S. data from 1947 to 1970, shown in Table 42–1. The data cover the period when a stable Phillips curve seemed to describe the employment–inflation relation in the United States. We shall soon look at what happened in the 1970s.

FROM DEMAND-PULL TO EXPECTATIONAL INFLATION: THE PHELPS-FRIEDMAN THEORY

Starting about a decade ago Professors Milton Friedman, of the University of Chicago, and Edmund Phelps, of Columbia University, mounted an attack on the theoretical under-pinnings of the theory of a stable Phillips curve. They argued that the curve describes a transitory relationship that cannot exist over the long term. According to their theory, if the economy were to settle down in some position such as *e* in Figure 42–2 with substantial inflation, people would soon come to realize that the inflation was permanent. Unions would then demand even larger wage increases, and others would also change their behavior to adjust to their expectations of continued inflation. This new behavior would accelerate the inflation. But once people came to accept the new higher rate as permanent, they would revise their behavior, and this would accelerate the inflation still further. Extensive empirical research over the first half of the 1970s has given support to the view that the Phillips curve would not remain stable if the economy were to operate at a low level of unemployment and a high rate of inflation for a sustained period.

This theory is a mixture of demand-pull and expectational inflation, and it has a number of important aspects which we must study in detail.

The short-term Phillips curve for zero expected inflation

In the Phelps-Friedman theory a critical role is played by inflationary expectations. We shall use the symbol P_e to refer to the rate of inflation that decision makers *expect* will rule over their planning period—say, the next year.

The pure demand-pull element of the Phelps-Friedman theory is illustrated in Figure 42–3 by the Phillips curve labeled $PP(P_e = 0)$. *This particular Phillips curve is drawn on the assumption that people expect a zero rate of inflation.* (This is indicated by the notation $P_e = 0$.) The curve shows that the higher

Table 42–1 Employment, unemployment, and inflation in the United States, 1947–1970

Unemployment[a]	Number of years	Average unemployment[a]	Average employment[a]	Average annual rate of inflation of CPI (percent)
Less than 4.0	9	3.5	96.5	4.8
4–4.9	5	4.4	95.6	2.5
5.0 or more	10	5.8	94.2	0.7

Source: Economic Report of the President, 1976.
[a] As a percentage of the civilian labor force.

On average, inflation and unemployment were negatively related over the years 1947–1970. Over this period higher levels of unemployment tended to be associated with stable or only slowly rising prices. Lower levels of unemployment tended to be associated with higher rates of inflation. These data are plotted in Figure 42–6.

Figure 42–3   The Phelps-Friedman theory of the Phillips curve

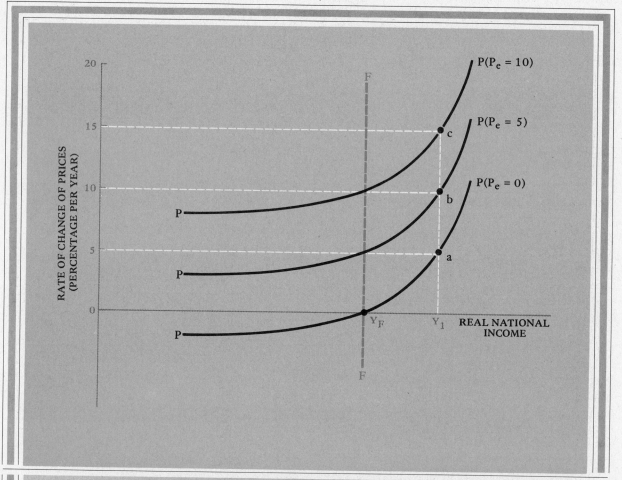

There is a separate Phillips curve for each expected rate of inflation.   The Phillips curve in Figure 42–2, shown here as $PP(P_e = 0)$, relates national income to inflation on the assumption that the price level is expected to remain stable. The actual rate of inflation depends upon national income and the expected rate of inflation. Thus for each expected rate of inflation the associated short-run Phillips curve lies above the $P_e = 0$ curve by the amount of the expected rate of inflation. Consider for example an inflationary gap with national income at Y_1. The actual rate of inflation will be 5 percent when the expected rate is zero (point *a*), 10 percent when the expected rate is 5 percent (point *b*), and 15 percent when the expected rate is 10 percent (point *c*).

In long-term equilibrium the actual rate of inflation must remain equal to the expected rate (otherwise expectations would be revised). This can only occur at the full-employment level of income Y_F, i.e., along *FF*. At Y_F there is no demand pressure on the price level; hence the only influence on actual inflation is expected inflation. Any stable rate of inflation (provided it is validated by the appropriate rate of monetary expansion) is compatible with Y_F and its associated natural rate of unemployment.

the level of national income (i.e., the higher the level of aggregate demand), the higher will be the associated rate of inflation. The point where the *PP* curve for zero expected inflation cuts the axis, labeled Y_F, indicates the level of national income at which there is no significant demand-pull inflation. The percentage of the labor force unemployed at Y_F is called the **natural rate of unemployment.** Because of frictional unemployment the natural rate of unemployment will certainly be positive; it may well be as high as 4 or 5 percent in the United States today.

Why does the Phillips curve for zero expected inflation cut the axis at Y_F? When national income is at its full-employment level, the Phelps-Friedman theory envisages all markets in the economy being in equilibrium, with demands equal to supplies. Thus, there is no market pressure on any price either to rise or to fall. In these circumstances all prices, and hence the price level, will remain stable.

Why does the Phillips curve for zero expected inflation show prices rising when national income exceeds its full-employment level and falling when national income is less than its full-employment level? Let the economy begin at full-employment income. Consider, first, the effects of a rise in aggregate demand. All individual demand curves shift outward, creating excess demands in all markets. Decision makers will respond in two ways: (1) they will increase their outputs (working overtime, extra shifts, etc.), and (2) they will raise their money prices, seeking thereby to raise their relative prices. Since this happens in all markets, there is an increase in national income combined with a rise in the price level. Next, consider what happens when there is a fall in aggregate demand with national income initially at its full-employment level. Decision makers respond by reducing output and by cutting money prices, seeking thereby to lower their relative prices. Since this happens in all markets, there is a

fall in national income combined with some downward movement in the price level.

Why does the price level continue to change as long as national income remains unequal to its full-employment level? When there is excess demand in all markets, we have seen that all decision makers raise their money prices, seeking thereby to raise their relative prices. But by definition *all* relative prices cannot rise. (It is impossible, for example, for rye whiskey to get more expensive relative to Scotch while at the same time Scotch gets more expensive relative to rye.) Thus, at least some decision makers will be frustrated in their attempts to raise their *relative* prices. To take a very simple example: If they all raise their money prices by 5 percent, seeking thereby to raise their relative prices by 5 percent, a 5 percent inflation will be generated; but they will not have succeeded in raising their own prices relative to other prices. As long as the excess demand persists, people will go on raising their money prices, thereby trying unsuccessfully to raise their relative prices. (Some may succeed, but everyone cannot.) Thus, general excess demand will be associated with a level of national income above its full-employment level and a *continuing* rise in prices.

An exactly parallel argument shows that when there is general excess supply, decreases in money prices by all decision makers, in an attempt to cut relative prices, will lead to a fall in the general price level, but many *relative* prices will not be decreased. Decision makers, therefore, will cut prices further. Because of these vain attempts to cut relative prices, national income below its full-employment level will be associated with a *continuing* downward pressure on prices.

In summary, the Phelps-Friedman theory holds, first, that general excess demand in the economy will be associated with national income above its full-employment level and with continuing inflation; and second, that general excess supply will be associated with national income below its full-employment level and with a continuing downward pressure on prices. In other words, the Phillips curve for zero expected inflation is upward sloping, and it cuts the axis at Y_F.

The actual inflation rate

The foregoing discussion of upward and downward pressure on the price level relied on the desire to raise relative prices when national income exceeded Y_F and to lower them when national income fell short of Y_F. Since decision makers' relative price is the relation between their own price and the general price level,[2] it follows that any decision to change relative prices means changing one's money price *relative* to what one *expects* the price level to be (over the time for which one's own price is being set). If a decision maker wishes to raise his or her relative price by 5 percent, this requires a 5 percent increase in the money price if no inflation is expected, a 10 percent increase in the money price if a 5 percent inflation is expected, and so on. If, on the other hand, the decision maker wishes to reduce his or her relative price by 2 percent, this requires a 2 percent reduction in the money price if no inflation is expected but a 3 percent *increase* in the money price if a 5 percent inflation is expected, and so on. In general, a decision to change a relative price by x percent requires a change in the money price by an amount equal to x percent *plus* the expected rate of inflation.

The above discussion explains what determines the actual rate of inflation in this theory.

According to the Phelps-Friedman theory, the actual rate of inflation is given by the demand-pull element, *plus* the expected rate of inflation.[3]

Thus, for example, if everyone expects a 5 percent inflation, prices and wages will be raised by 5 percent, *plus* the amount due to the pull of excess demand, which is shown by the Phillips curve for $P_e = 0$.

Another way of making the same point is to say that there is a separate Phillips curve relating actual inflation to national income for each expected rate of inflation. Each curve is defined for a particular expected rate of inflation, and each is called a short-run Phillips curve. (Each curve is short-run in the sense that the Phillips curve on which the economy is located will be given at any moment of time but will change whenever P_e changes.) This point is illustrated for three levels of expected rates of inflation in Figure 42–3.

The relation between actual and expected inflation

Actual inflation is equal to expected inflation *plus* an allowance for demand pressure.[4] It follows that actual inflation will exceed expected inflation when national income exceeds Y_F because demand pressures are then positive. When national income equals Y_F, demand pressures are zero, and actual inflation will equal expected inflation. When actual national income is less than Y_F, demand pressures are negative, and actual inflation will be less than the expected rate. [40]

The expected rate of inflation

People are assumed to base their expectations about the inflation rate in the immediate future on the actual rates that have occurred over the past two or three years. Thus whenever actual rates of inflation exceed expected rates, expectations will catch up—but with a lag. For example, if people are expecting a 5 percent inflation but continue to experience a 7 percent inflation, they will sooner or later revise their expectations upward and come to

[2] That is, a relative price is p/P where p is the individual price in question and P is the general price level (which is an average of the economy's prices).

[3] In symbols: $P_a = PD + P_e$ where P_a is the actual rate of inflation, PD is the inflation rate caused by demand pressure, and P_e is the expected rate of inflation.

[4] The allowance is positive when Y exceeds Y_F and negative when Y falls short of Y_F.

expect a 7 percent inflation. Conversely, if people are expecting a 7 percent inflation but are only experiencing a 5 percent inflation they will sooner or later revise their expectations downward and come to expect only a 5 percent inflation.

IMPLICATIONS OF THE PHELPS-FRIEDMAN THEORY

Accelerating inflation

A first important implication of the Phelps-Friedman theory is that if national income is *kept* above Y_F, the rate of inflation will accelerate continuously. Say the economy starts in full-employment equilibrium at stable prices—that is, at the point where the Phillips curve for $P_e = 0$ cuts the axis. Now let aggregate demand increase. Excess demand is created; national income increases; and the economy moves up its short-run Phillips curve to a higher level of national income and, say, a 5 percent inflation. This is shown by point *a* in Figure 42–3. This inflation occurs because people are trying to adjust their *relative* wages and prices upward in response to excess demand. No one expects an inflation. If the inflation persists, however, it will eventually come to be expected. People will then add a catch-up factor of 5 percent to any wage and price change they plan to make. When they do this the rate of inflation will then accelerate to 10 percent (point *b*). Sooner or later this will come to be expected, and the rate of inflation will then accelerate to 15 percent (point *c*), of which 10 percent is to keep ahead of expected inflation and 5 percent is a response to excess demand.

According to the Phelps-Friedman theory, whenever the economy has a level of national income above full-employment income (or, what is the same thing, a level of unemployment below the natural rate of unemployment) the actual rate of inflation will eventually accelerate. How fast it accelerates depends on how fast current inflationary expectations adjust to past actual rates.

It follows that if the government tries to maintain excess aggregate demand in the mistaken view that it can increase real national income above Y_F (i.e., lower unemployment below its natural rate) at the cost of a stable rate of inflation, it is in for a nasty shock. For a while people may not expect the inflation to continue; as a result inflation will proceed at a stable pace. Sooner or later, however, people will come to expect the inflation to continue; they will revise their inflationary expectations upward, and this will cause the inflation rate to accelerate. Later the new higher rate will come to be accepted; expectations of future inflation will be revised upward and the actual rate of inflation will once again accelerate.[5]

The long-run Phillips curve is vertical

When national income equals Y_F in the Phelps-Friedman theory there is no excess demand pressure on inflation. *Thus the only inflation that can occur when $Y = Y_F$ is expectational inflation.* If everyone expects 5 percent inflation, then all prices will be raised by 5 percent and an actual inflation rate of 5 percent will occur. If the money supply is increased by 5 percent to validate this inflation, then full-employment income and the natural rate of unemployment can be maintained indefinitely with a 5 percent expected and a 5 percent actual inflation. But the same argument could be repeated for 10 percent or for any other rate of inflation (or deflation).

In general, since at the natural rate of unemployment there is neither upward nor downward pressure on prices due to excess demand, the only cause of inflation arises from attempts to try to keep up with whatever rate of inflation is expected. [41] Thus full-

---

[5] Of course, as we saw in Chapter 40, the government will have to induce ever more rapid rates of monetary expansion to validate an ever-accelerating inflation rate. But if the government does try to hold national income above Y_F, it will induce, according to this theory, an ever-accelerating rate of inflation that will *have to be validated* by ever-increasing rates of monetary expansion.

employment national income and its associated natural rate of unemployment is compatible with *any* actual rate of inflation, provided that, first, the inflation is expected and second, that it is accompanied by the appropriate rate of monetary expansion.

The long-run Phillips curve that relates national income to a stable rate of inflation is vertical at full-employment income.

Policy implications

The Phelps–Friedman theory has a number of implications for economic policy. If the theory turns out to be substantially correct, these policy implications will be extremely important. A first implication has already been discussed.

Attempts to reduce unemployment below its natural rate will eventually cause the rate of inflation to accelerate.

A second implication concerns the natural rate of unemployment.

It is essential to discover the natural rate of unemployment because it is the only acceptable target for long-run stabilization policy.

To see why knowing the natural rate of unemployment is so important, assume that the economy has functioned satisfactorily for some time at an average unemployment rate of 5 percent and that the inflation rate has shown no tendency to accelerate. Policy makers will conclude that 5 percent is the natural rate of unemployment. Now assume, however, that unbeknown to the policy makers the natural rate of unemployment rises to 7 percent. If they go on trying to stabilize the economy around a 5 percent unemployment rate, the first indication they will have that something has gone wrong is that the inflation rate will begin to accelerate. It may take some time before policy makers conclude that the acceleration is not due to some transient cause but represents a genuine tendency for continual acceleration. By the time they reach that conclusion and decide to stabilize the economy around a higher level of unemployment, a very rapid inflation may already exist and may have been built into people's expectations. Thus, if the Phelps–Friedman theory is correct, quick and accurate determination of the natural rate of unemployment must be an important part of any effective anti-inflationary policy.

Once an expectational inflation is under way, policy makers may have to take account of a third important policy implication.

A period of excess demand and accelerating inflation will lead to accelerating inflationary expectations. A prolonged period with unemployment above the natural rate may be required before inflationary expectations are revised downward sufficiently to permit the actual inflation rate to fall.

This implication is illustrated in Figure 42–4. An increase in inflationary expectations moves the economy to a higher short-term Phillips curve. This increases inflationary pressures. To offset this a decline in national income is required, which moves the economy downward and to the left along any given short-term Phillips curve. This decreases inflationary pressure. In the early stages of a contraction in national income that is designed to bring an *accelerating* inflation under control, the effect of accelerating expectations may dominate the effect of declining demand and output. As a result, falling national income and rising unemployment may be associated with constant or even rising rates of inflation. When this occurs the economy is often said to be suffering a **stagflation**—the coexistence of high rates of inflation and high rates of unemployment.

An inflation-unemployment cycle[6]

The way in which changes in unemployment and inflation may work out over the longer period of a whole cycle is illustrated in Figure 42–5. To understand this possibility in a simple example, consider what happens (ac-

---

[6] This section may be omitted without loss of continuity.

Figure 42–4 Falling real national income and rising inflation (stagflation)

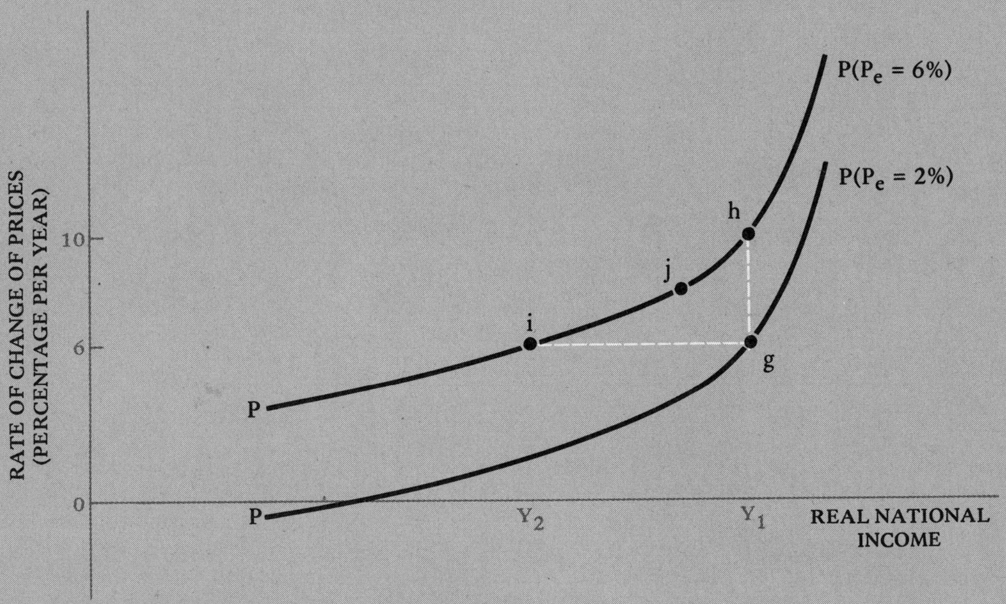

If the expected rate of inflation is rising, a fall in national income can easily be associated with a rise in the actual rate of inflation. The economy is at point *g* with a level of national income of Y_1, an expected rate of inflation of 2 percent, and an actual rate of 6 percent. Since the actual rate exceeds the expected rate, expectations will be revised upward. Suppose people come to expect a 6 percent inflation in the next period. If national income is held constant at Y_1, the economy will move to point *h* and the actual rate of inflation will accelerate to 10 percent. In order to offset this increase in inflationary expectations and hold inflation to 6 percent, national income must be reduced all the way to Y_2 (point *i*). If national income *falls* to any amount less than Y_1 but greater than Y_2, the economy will move to some point such as *j* where *falling* real national income is associated with *rising* inflation.

cording to the Phelps–Friedman theory) when the government first expands aggregate demand to induce a higher degree of resource utilization and then slams on the brakes by sharply lowering aggregate demand in an attempt to eliminate the resulting inflation. The type of path that can be expected from this sequence of events is shown in black in Figure 42–5.

In this example the economy starts at point *k* with full-employment national income and stable prices. An expansion of aggregate demand then takes the economy to point *a* with national income of Y_1 and a 5 percent inflation rate. As long as people go on expecting a zero inflation rate (i.e., they do not expect the existing 5 percent rate to persist) the economy remains at *a*. Once inflationary expectations

Figure 42–5   An inflation-unemployment cycle

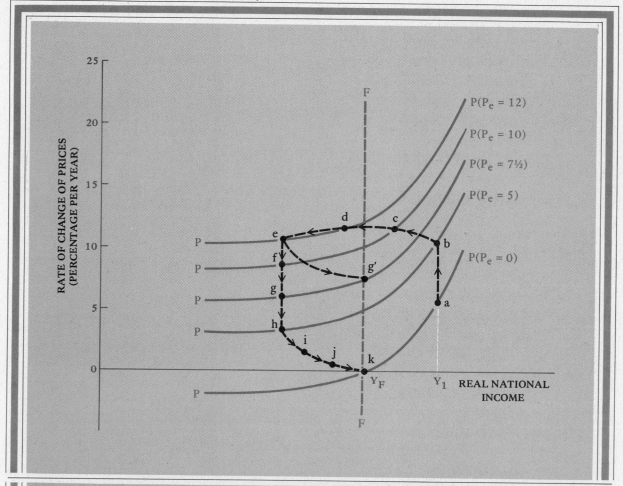

Removing entrenched inflationary expectations may require a prolonged bout of low national income combined with high rates of inflation.   An economy with an inflationary gap (actual income in excess of Y_F) may build a head of steam in terms of rising rates of actual and expected inflation. (See the path from point *a* to point *b*.) If aggregate demand (and hence national income) is then reduced in order to restrain the inflation, a period may ensue in which the inflationary effects of rising inflationary expectations more than offset the deflationary effects of falling national income. (See the path from points *b* to *d*.) Sooner or later, however, the deflationary effects of falling national income will predominate and the actual rate of inflation will begin to fall. (See the path from points *d* to *e*.) Inflationary expectations will now be revised downward and the actual rate will fall without further reductions in national income being necessary. (See the path from points *e* to *h*.) Once inflationary expectations are low enough, a cautious expansion towards full-employment income should be possible without setting off a new bout of demand-pull or expectational inflation. (See path from *h* to *k*.)

are revised upward the relevant Phillips curve shifts upward. The actual rate of inflation accelerates. When the expected rate of inflation has reached 5 percent the economy is at point *b* with a 10 percent actual rate of inflation.

At this stage suppose the government decides to do something. Perhaps the monetary authorities now refuse to increase the money supply enough to validate the inflation fully. Actual *Y* now falls, but the expected rate of inflation goes on accelerating and the two opposing forces take the economy to point *c* with a 10 percent expected inflation and an actual rate of 12 percent. The continuing nonvalidation of the inflation causes national income to fall further, but if the expected rate rises to 12 percent, the economy moves to point *d*. If the expected rate of inflation now holds constant at 12 percent, the nonvalidation of the actual inflation forces the economy down the $P_e = 12$ percent Phillips curve to some point such as *e*. Now at last the actual rate of inflation is falling and, even more important, it is below the expected rate.

The period of rising prices and rising unemployment may finally be at an end. The expected rate will now be revised downward, and if the government keeps the rate of monetary expansion in line with the actual rate of inflation, the economy can move through points *f*, *g*, and *h* as the expected rate falls to 10, 7.5, and 5 percent. Indeed if the government is careful, it can at some point begin stimulating aggregate demand again. As long as the inflationary effects of increases in demand are less than the deflationary effects of decreases in expectations, the economy can move through points *h*, *i*, and *j* back toward point *k*, where both full-employment income and a stable price level are achieved.

Note however that if the economy is restimulated too quickly, say from *e* to *g'*, it may reach the full-employment level of income when there are still substantial inflationary expectations in the system. The government then has the choice of validating the inflation to hold *Y* at Y_F or allowing another recession to occur to lower the actual rate of inflation and, after a lag, causing a lowering of inflationary expectations.

COST-PUSH AND PRICE-PUSH THEORIES

So far we have discussed the conflict between inflation and unemployment that arises from demand-pull and expectational inflation. We now consider conflicts that can arise from any of the other types of inflation. We shall concentrate on cost-push inflations, but the same argument applies to price-push inflations.

The most important proposition is that, unless validated by increases in the money supply, any cost-push, price-push, (or, for that matter, any expectational inflation) will be brought to a halt by ever-rising levels of unemployment. (See page 752.) When this automatic restraining mechanism starts to work, however, the government is presented with a major dilemma. An unvalidated inflation leads to a fall in national income and to a rise in unemployment. The standard cure for rising unemployment is an expansionary monetary and fiscal policy. But if the government indulges in a monetary expansion so that it is possible to return to full employment at the new higher price level, then the automatic restraining forces that eventually halt the inflation are frustrated. The way is then set for a new round of cost-push inflation: once again prices rise; once again the level of unemployment rises; once again the government validates the inflation by expansionary monetary policies in order to remove the unemployment.

Clearly this type of cost-push inflation can go on without end as long as the government continually validates the inflation. The government might do this in order to avoid the rise in unemployment which is part of the automatic adjustment process by which an inflation not validated by an increase in the money supply is eventually brought to an end.

Thus, cost-push and price-push inflations can also produce a conflict between the control of unemployment and inflation.

Wage-price controls

Direct government intervention in wage and price setting has seemed to some to be an attractive method of avoiding the dilemma between controlling inflation and preventing major long-term or short-term lapses from full employment. Various countries, including the United States, have experimented with such controls. Do they work? The answer appears to be that it depends on the circumstances in which they are used. We shall look, therefore, at the influence of direct controls in various alternative circumstances.

WAGE-PRICE CONTROLS TO REGULATE DEMAND-PULL INFLATIONS

Governments that have been validating inflations by increasing the money supply have often been tempted to attack these inflations by direct control over wage and price setting.

Wage-price guidelines in the 1960s

The major peacetime experiment with wage-price controls occurred during the Nixon administration, but the wage-price guidelines of the 1960s represented an earlier such attempt. This attempt implied an extremely naive theory of inflation—that the price level is whatever firms and unions choose to make it and that by exhorting them to lower their wage and price demands the rate of inflation could be permanently affected.

The power of the executive branch of the government can go beyond mere exhortation, as was seen in 1962, when President Kennedy forced the major steel companies to retract an announced price rise, and in 1965, when President Johnson's threat to release the vast government stockpile of aluminum persuaded the aluminum industry to rescind an announced price increase. Both of these measures had a temporary effect on the rate of inflation, but it is doubtful that they had any lasting effect. Few economists would hold that the U.S. price level would have been any higher in 1970 or 1975 if Presidents Kennedy and Johnson had *not* taken their forceful actions.

Wage-price controls in the 1970s

In mid 1971 there was a large balance-of-payments deficit and both unemployment and the rate of inflation were high. Unemployment averaged 5.9 percent of the labor force in 1971, and the rate of inflation was 4.3 percent. Although this seems modest by the standards of subsequent years, it was well above the average rates for both the 1950s and the 1960s. It was feared that contractionary fiscal and monetary policies adopted to reduce inflation would cause a further rise in unemployment, so wage-price controls were introduced. The hope was to lower the rate of inflation without necessitating a further rise in unemployment.

The subsequent set of policies was divided into several phases. Phase I (which lasted for two months) imposed a complete freeze on virtually all wages and prices in the economy. Phase II (fourteen months) attempted to hold wage increases to 5.5 percent per year and price increases to no more than was necessary to cover any increase in costs. Phase III (five months) began in mid January 1973. At that time the economy was expanding rapidly and a need was recognized for a more flexible program that would permit substantial changes in relative prices.

When it became apparent that Phase III was not restraining inflation, a new freeze was introduced in June 1973 with the announcement that it was temporary and was to be followed by a further set of Phase IV controls. During Phase IV a number of sectors were "decontrolled" as an initial stage of returning to free markets. Lumber, copper, scrap, public utilities, and coal sold to utilities were immediately decontrolled. Industries producing basic commodities were also decontrolled since low domestic prices had produced an unwanted rise in exports. Rents were exempted because they are administratively difficult to enforce. Wages in the auto industry were allowed to rise once assurance had been given that the increases would not be reflected in prices. Decontrolled areas were gradually extended. Phase IV controls proved ineffective, however, and they gradually petered out. By April 1974, when Congress let the control authority expire, its later phases were acknowledged failures.

Extensive research into the effects of this experiment with wage-price controls suggests that the entire costly effort had little or no effect on wages but that it did hold down price inflation by perhaps as much as 2 percentage points. The restraint on prices was achieved by forcing a narrowing of profit margins. Not surprisingly, once the controls were lifted, profit margins were restored. Thus the episode had little or no lasting effect on the price level.

Lessons to be learned?

What can we learn from this saga of a long, and in the end unsuccessful, attempt to control a demand-pull inflation by wage-price controls? Any story of wage-price controls usually involves most of the stages in this sequence:

1. successful application of blanket controls on everything

2. the need to regulate price changes brought about by innumerable unavoidable circumstances, since it would be inviting chaos to freeze relative prices permanently

3. exemption of many wages and prices for seemingly valid special reasons

4. the spread of exceptions (since all prices and costs are interrelated), leading to a growing web of exceptions, complex regulations, and diminishing effectiveness in controlling overall price rises

5. the abandonment of the system, followed by a price explosion taking prices to about where they would have been in the absence of the entire effort at control.

The American experience of 1971–1974 was no exception to these general rules.

WAGE-PRICE CONTROLS AS A CURE FOR EXPECTATIONAL INFLATION

The strongest argument for temporary wage-price controls is that they may be a cure for an entrenched expectational inflation. Assume that the government wishes to stop an ongoing demand-pull inflation in which inflationary expectations are already well entrenched. It can put on the monetary and fiscal brakes and accept the kind of path shown in Figure 42–5. Or it can use wage-price controls to force the inflation rate down while contracting aggregate demand in an attempt to take the economy directly to full-employment income without going through a period of heavy unemployment. If the controls succeed in holding the inflation rate down, and *if* inflationary expectations are then revised downward, the economy could move directly to Y_F and a low rate of inflation. It will thus avoid the period of heavy unemployment and slack demand otherwise needed to induce people to revise downward their inflationary expectations.

When used in an attempt to restrain expectational inflation, wage-price controls seek to force actual inflation rates downward and to cause immediate downward revisions of expectations. This is meant to leave the government free to use fiscal and monetary policy to eliminate demand-pull inflation without having to worry that an unvalidated expectational inflation may cause the unemployment rate to rise.

This use of wage-price controls could be valuable if it worked, and it has been strongly advocated in recent times. The most important experiment was carried on in Canada from October 1975 until 1978. The government sought to cut a 10 percent inflation rate to 4 percent by using a combination of a contractionary monetary policy (to remove the demand-pull element) and a set of wage-price controls (intended to break heavily entrenched inflationary expectations). Whether the controls will be successful in breaking these inflationary expectations or whether there will be an outburst of expectational inflation once the controls are lifted still remains to be seen at this writing.

WAGE-PRICE CONTROLS TO COMBAT COST-PUSH AND PRICE-PUSH INFLATIONS

Some economists, including J. K. Galbraith, see monopoly power in the hands of large unions and large firms as a major cause of inflation. Firms and unions raise wages and prices and, rather than risk a large rise in unemployment, governments increase the money supply to validate the ensuing cost-push inflation. Economists of this school accept that the money supply must be increased to sustain an inflation, but they believe that the *primary* cause of inflation arises from the cost-price push. They see increases in the money supply as merely passive accommodations that occur when governments seek to avoid the unemployment that would result from an unvalidated cost-push inflation.

In this view wage-price controls are the only way to control inflation without encountering politically unacceptable bouts of unemployment. Unlike the use of controls to break expectations, this method calls for *permanent* wage-price controls. This would mean a major new incursion of government into the behavior of the market, and many economists —probably the majority—believe that the cure of long-term wage-price controls would be worse than the disease of inflation.

*A view from the outside of the inside of upside down**

On the 18th of October, 1971, I assumed responsibility for the Price Commission in the conduct of Phase II of President Nixon's Wage and Price Control program. . . . In coming to the task of Chairman of the Price Commission I was new to the economic policy "game" and certainly shared some of the popular delusions about the way in which the policy process worked. . . . I was under the impression that economic policy was conducted in a very precise fashion in a milieu somehow above the foibles of human nature. . . . I want to relate something about my view of policy-making at the national level. I want to explain why it is inherently a confused sort of occupation and I want to imbue the reader with a healthy skepticism for the ability of central control to solve economic problems.

One of the main reasons why the policy-making process in general and wage and price controls in particular are inherently difficult is because they are attempting to regulate the most sophisticated information system that the world has ever seen—namely the North American market economy. . . .

The information system is the network formed by free people buying and selling and the signals are the variations in and the levels of wages, prices, interest rates, rents and, unfortunately, taxes.

Very often the best way to determine the contributions of people or things to an

* This quotation is excerpted from an article entitled "A View from the Outside of the Inside of Upside Down," by Jackson Grayson, dean of the School of Business, Southern Methodist University, in M. Walker, ed., *The Illusion of Wage and Price Control*, Vancouver, B.C., The Fraser Institute, 1976.

ongoing process is to see what happens in their absence. . . . To the extent that the program was effective, it began to produce an astonishing variety of evidence on the job that the market mechanism had been performing.

Shortages of products (ranging from natural gas to molasses) began to appear as slow-to-rise controlled prices told producers "don't make more" and told consumers "buy more."

For example, log prices were not controlled, but the price of finished lumber was. Predictably, this led to a shortage of finished lumber, produced an array of artificial middlemen and active black markets. Ultimately, our efforts to control lumber prices led to reduced production and an increase in the export of lumber.

In short, most of the products and services that we take for granted in our everyday lives can be taken for granted only because there is a functioning price system. A system that, despite its imperfections, delivers just the right quantity of California lettuce to Montana or Alberta, Canada; and decides the relationship between raw log prices in California and the price of finished lumber in Boston. As we discovered when we tampered with, and effectively suspended, the operation of the price system, we could no longer rely on the system itself and were forced to get more and more involved with what were, before controls, essentially automatic functions.

The problem that policy-makers must cope with, if they are determined to control the system, is the endless detail that is involved in the operation of the system. To control the system and yet keep it running smoothly, the authorities must intercept all of the signals coming from the system (and there are hundreds of millions), interpret them, appropriately change them (assuming they know how) and retransmit them.

What we at the Price Commission continuously found was that everything is related to everything else and there was, accordingly, no such thing as one intervention. We were drawn inevitably and progressively deeper into the system and the temptation to limit the necessity for our involvement by arbitrarily changing the system was very great. Herein lies the real danger from centralized control, that is, that an inability to handle the overload of signals, both incoming and outgoing, may produce attempts to simplify the system and hence jeopardize its survival.

The difficulty of taking over the wage-price signalling mechanism is indicated by the fact that during the first three weeks of Phase II there were nearly 400,000 inquiries about the program. In terms of getting down to the nitty gritty, had the Dow Chemical Company and the Commission not agreed to an across the board increase of 2 per cent we would have had to examine nearly 100,000 submissions on different products for that company alone.

. . . Wage and price controls are, by nature, a bureaucratic nightmare. There is no easy way to proceed, no escape from the remorseless tide of detail that is the inevitable consequence of attempting to interrupt the normal current of economic affairs. There is also no escape from the conclusion that detailed regulation breeds a restiveness in those being regulated that eventually must lead either to the collapse of the controls or the adoption of more coercive measures.

Stagflation

We have seen that high inflation coexisting with high unemployment poses a serious policy problem. Figure 42–6 shows the extent of American stagflation in the 1970s. It is clear that inflation is no longer a phenomenon encountered only when the economy is fully employed. There are several explanations of stagflation, some of which compete with each other, while others may be complementary.

ALTERNATIVE EXPLANATIONS OF AMERICAN STAGFLATION

Stagflation caused by an expectational inflation following a demand-pull inflation

In this view inflationary expectations became firmly entrenched in the early 1970s as a result of excess aggregate demand that had built up throughout the world in the late 1960s and early 1970s. When aggregate demand fell in the mid 1970s, prices and wages went on rising in response to these expectations. This theory uses the standard Keynesian explanation of how aggregate demand affects national income and prices, and supplements it with the possibility of an expectational inflation. It predicts that the fall in aggregate demand that occurred beginning in mid 1974 would moderate the inflation once unemployment became high enough and persistent enough to force workers and employers to revise their inflation expectations downward.

Stagflation caused by a cost push or a price push independent of any inflation gap

This theory says that unions and monopolistic firms exercised their arbitrary power to raise wages and prices, thereby causing the inflation. Governments were then forced to choose, on the one hand, between validating the inflation by raising the money supply, and on the other hand, holding the monetary line and accepting the rise in unemployment needed to cause a voluntary reduction in cost-push and price-push pressures.

Because inflation was of the cost-push/price-push variety it occurred even though there was no excess demand in the economy. Thus stagflation is a manifestation of cost-push inflation—rising prices without heavy excess demand. In this view stagflation is not a transitory phenomenon but will be a persistent problem whenever unemployment is high because of the exercise of the cost push.

Stagflation reflects a rise in the natural rate of unemployment

According to this theory much of the measured unemployment in the 1970s is composed of three types of non-deficient-demand unemployment: search unemployment, structural unemployment, and voluntary unemployment that shows up in the statistics as involuntary unemployment. This voluntary unemployment arises because unemployment benefits and public welfare payments are more generous and easier to obtain than they were even a few years ago. The theory claims that many people respond to this not by seriously seeking work but by remaining unemployed voluntarily in order to collect their benefits, and searching seriously for a job only when their benefits are exhausted. The search unemployment arises because in multi-worker households (which are much more common today than they were in the past) it is relatively easy for one member to support another member in search unemployment. The (temporary) structural unemployment arises because of the changing composition of the labor force. For example, women's liberation has brought many more women into the labor force and the country's changing age structure has meant that an unusually large number of unexperienced persons have left school and college to enter the labor force in recent years. These are not always the kinds of job seekers for which there is sufficient demand even in periods of high economic activity.

If for any or all of these reasons the natural

Figure 42-6 U.S. stagflation in the 1970s

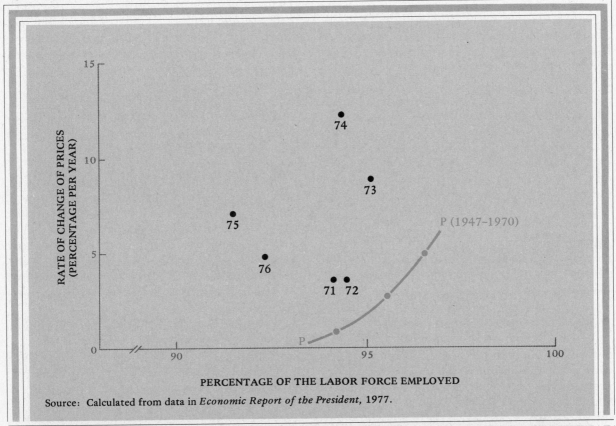

Source: Calculated from data in *Economic Report of the President, 1977.*

The 1970s have been unusual in combining high rates of unemployment with high rates of inflation. The three colored dots are plotted from Table 42–1. They show the average rates of inflation associated with the indicated rates of employment between 1947 and 1970. The colored curve is thus a rough Phillips curve for the economy of that period. The black dots show the rates of employment and inflation for each of the years 1971 to 1976. The year 1974 was the year of the most extreme stagflation. The employment rate fell from 95.1 to 94.4 percent while the rate of inflation rose from 8.8 to 12.2 percent! In 1975 the employment rate fell to its all-time low since World War II of 91.5 percent while the inflation rate remained at the high rate of 7 percent. In 1976 the inflation rate fell to under 5 percent while the employment rate rose to 92.3 percent.

rate of unemployment has risen, demand-pull inflations will set in at a higher level of measured unemployment than they did previously. According to this theory our inflation remains what it always has been: excess-demand inflation that sets in at or near full-employment income. Stagflation is merely a reflection of the fact that the natural rate of unemployment has significantly increased over the years.

AN EVALUATION OF STAGFLATION

The relevance of various explanations

There is little doubt that both the first and the third views just considered provide part of the explanation of stagflation. Certainly the path of the economy from 1973 to 1976 was consistent with the expectational explanation of stagflation. (Compare, for example, Figure 42–6 with Figure 42–5.) The inflation rate of 7 percent in 1975 was disturbingly high given an unemployment rate of 8.5 percent. However, the rate was also well below the rate of 12.2 percent in 1974 and was consistent with what would be predicted by a theory in which the expected rate of inflation adjusted to the actual rate with a lag. In 1976 the inflation rate fell yet further, to less than 5 percent, *and* real national income rose modestly. This too is consistent with a major reduction in inflationary expectations following on the experience of heavy unemployment and falling inflation rates over the recent past.

The explanation relying on an increase in the natural rate of unemployment is receiving a great deal of attention from economic researchers. Much current work is devoted to measuring by how much the natural rate of unemployment has increased in recent years. Until this work has been completed we cannot say much more than that it is unlikely that this will provide the whole explanation. Since there was clearly excess capacity of capital as well as unemployed labor in 1975 and 1976, it seems clear that the inflation was not exclusively the result of excess demand occurring while industry was producing at or near full capacity of capital (while the natural rate of unemployment of labor had risen).

There seems to be substantial evidence that the natural rate of unemployment has risen in the 1970s. The view that a major contributing factor is an increase in structural unemployment is given weight by the very uneven distribution of unemployment: while (for example) unemployment among heads of households was only 5.8 percent in 1975, it

was 8.0 for women 20 years and over, and 19.9 percent for persons between 16 and 19 years of age.

At least three questions remain: (1) How much of stagflation is explained by the two factors of expectational inflation combined with a rise in the natural rate of unemployment? (2) How important is each factor relative to the other? and (3) What other explanations, if any, are required to supplement these two factors? On the third question there is wide disagreement. Probably the majority of economists would not give major weight to the cost-push and price-push explanations discussed above. A significant minority, however, would make it *the* main explanation. Yet even the majority would agree that a cost push arising from external events such as the formation of OPEC and the severe winter of 1977 can exert a temporary but strong inflationary force.

The trouble with the cost-push theory as a principal explanation of inflation is that it does not easily explain the great acceleration in inflation in the 1970s. There is no evidence that the power of firms and unions to determine prices and wages independently of market conditions has increased over the last decade. Yet the rate of inflation in all Western countries rose sharply during that period. In order to show that this was caused by price and cost push it would be necessary to establish a theory of why this push accelerated so drastically over a single decade.

Is stagflation a crisis of contemporary theory?

Some commentators, including some economists, argue that stagflation is a phenomenon beyond the power of standard economics to explain. These people argue that the whole of macroeconomic theory is refuted by the existence of stagflation and that the theory should be abandoned. It should be clear from the foregoing discussion that we regard this view as hasty and extreme. Standard theory is able

The progress of economics

This chapter has discussed a number of current controversies about the behavior of the economy and the evidence relating to them that is now available. General acceptance of the view that the validity of economic theories should be tested by confronting their predictions with the mass of all available evidence is fairly new in economics. At this point you might reread the quotation from Lord William Beveridge given on the front endpapers of this book. The controversy that Beveridge describes was the one that followed the 1936 publication of Keynes's *The General Theory of Employment, Interest and Money*. Keynes work gave rise to the macroeconomics discussed in Part Eight and used so often in subsequent sections of this text. The question of how various parts of macroeconomic theory have been or could be tested has been raised at many points in this book; the student should reflect on how very different this approach to the problem of accepting or rejecting theories is from the approach described by Beveridge.

There is no doubt that since 1936 great progress has been made in economics in relating theory to evidence. This progress has been reflected in the superior ability of governments to achieve their policy objectives. The financial aspects of World War II were far better handled than those of World War I. When President Roosevelt tried to reduce unemployment in the 1930s, his efforts were greatly hampered by the failure even of economists to realize the critical importance of budget deficits in raising aggregate demand and in injecting newly created money into the economy. When the Vietnam War forced the government to adopt expansive fiscal and monetary policies, economists had no trouble in predicting the outcome: more involvement abroad was obtained at the cost of heavy inflationary pressure at home.

Such important policy areas as the running of wars, the curing of major depressions, and coping with inflations are where the general tone of theories is tested, even if all their specific predictions are not. In some general sense, then, economic theories have always been subjected to empirical tests. When they were wildly at variance with the facts, the ensuing disaster could not but be noticed, and the theories were discarded or amended in the light of what was learned. Our current inability to avoid the twin problems of inflation and unemployment is a case in point—and it is leading to intensive new research.

The advances of economics in the last forty years reflect economists' changed attitudes toward empirical observations. Today economists are much less likely to dismiss theories just because they do not like them and to refuse to abandon theories just because they do like them. Economists are more likely to try to base their theories as much as possible on empirical observation and to accept empirical relevance as the ultimate arbiter of the value of theories. As human beings, we may be anguished at the upsetting of a pet theory; as scientists, we should try to train ourselves to take pleasure in it because of the new knowledge gained thereby. It has been said that one of the great tragedies of science is the continual slaying of beautiful theories by ugly facts. It must always be remembered that when theory and fact come into conflict, it is theory, not fact, that must give way.

to provide a number of possible explanations of stagflation; these explanations are the subject of substantial current research.

One possible explanation that can be provided by standard theory for recent American stagflation runs as follows. The economy started from a trough in 1972 and then a boom developed that took the rate of inflation from 3.3 percent in 1972 to well over 10 percent in 1974. This was a conventional demand-pull inflation. Since the late 1960s the natural rate of unemployment had been drifting slowly upward, thereby raising the amount of unemployment that existed when excess-demand inflation set in. This explains why the boom of 1973–1974 that led to an inflation rate of over 10 percent got the unemployment rate only barely below 5 percent. By 1974 inflationary expectations had become firmly entrenched: both labor and management expected inflation to continue and, if anything, to accelerate. Wage and price contracts were thus drawn up on the assumption that a nominal 10 percent increase would be needed just to keep any price or wage in line with the average of all wages and prices. Added to this was a temporary cost-push inflation due to rising prices of oil, other energy sources, and some other basic commodities.

Then in the latter half of 1974 aggregate demand fell off; when it did, demand-pull pressures were removed. At this point the inflation became an expectational inflation with some added cost-push elements (due to such things as the continuing rise in energy prices). As a result wages and prices continued to rise until, in the face of a really severe slump, inflationary expectations were finally moderated. As this happened the actual rate of inflation began to fall as well.

It is too early to say how well this or similar scenarios will stand up to careful statistical analysis of what really happened. At this point of time there is no preponderance of evidence to suggest that the economy is involved in a brand new ball game where experience and theories developed in the past are completely irrelevant.

Those observers who have said that stagflation is the disease that killed contemporary macroeconomics are premature both in their issuance of a death certificate and in their assessment of the inability of macroeconomics to cope with this disturbing new phenomenon.

Summary

1. Policy conflicts between lowering unemployment (and thereby raising output and employment) and lowering inflation may arise for many reasons and over many different time horizons.

2. Excess aggregate demand is generally agreed to be a cause of inflation. When combined with the L-shaped relation the demand-pull theory involves no conflict between stable prices and full-employment national income. When combined with a *stable* Phillips curve the demand-pull theory does present a conflict, one which forces policy makers to choose between less inflation and more real national income and employment.

3. The Phelps-Friedman theory combines the demand-pull and expectational theories of inflation and predicts a trade-off between inflation and unemployment in the short term but not in the long term. In the long term only the natural rate of unemployment is compatible with a stable rate of inflation. This rate of unemployment is compatible with any stable rate of inflation, including zero inflation.

4. According to the Phelps-Friedman theory, if the government insists on holding unemployment *below* its natural rate (i.e., national income *above* Y_F), there will be a tendency for the inflation rate to accelerate.

5. The Phelps-Friedman theory also predicts that a prolonged period of demand-pull inflation will cause inflationary expectations to become entrenched. Even after the excess demand is removed, an expectational inflation may persist and a prolonged period of slump, with unemployment well above the natural rate, may be necessary before expectations are revised downward sufficiently that the economy can return to full employment and a low or zero rate of inflation.

6. Cost-push, price-push, and expectational inflations will all be brought to a halt by rising levels of unemployment unless they are validated by appropriate increases in the money supply.

7. Wage-price controls cannot be effective in permanently controlling demand-pull inflations. They have been advocated, however, to control cost-push and expectational inflations. The minority of economists who believe in persistent cost-push inflation advocate permanent wage-price controls. The theory of the use of wage-price controls to stop an expectational inflation calls for only a temporary use of controls. We do not yet have clear evidence of whether or not controls would be effective in breaking inflationary expectations.

8. During the 1970s stagflation has been a disturbing problem in a number of Western countries, including the United States. The major causes currently being investigated are that it is a transitory problem caused when an expectational inflation takes over from a demand-pull inflation during a recession, and that it reflects a rise in the natural rate of unemployment so that demand-pull inflation commences at a much higher level of unemployment than it did in earlier periods. There is also some debate regarding the extent to which cost-push factors have contributed to the inflation.

Concepts for review

The inflation-unemployment trade-off with the L-shaped
   relation and Phillips curve
Inflationary expectations and the Phillips curve
The natural rate of unemployment
Accelerating versus stable rates of inflation
Uses of wage-price controls
The meaning and possible causes of stagflation

Discussion questions

1. "Full-employment" was a policy goal of the 1930's. "Price-stability" was a goal during World War II. "Full employment *without* inflation" was a policy goal of the decade 1945–1955. "Full employment *or* inflation" was an apparent dilemma of the decade 1955–1965. "Is it possible to remove either unemployment or inflation?" is a current critical question. How has the behavior of the American economy led to these changes of policy emphasis? How has economic theory adapted to the changed circumstances? Is it not ironic that despite a half century of "growth" both in the economy and in economic knowledge, we face harder problems today than we did then?

2. The Congressional Budget Office recently suggested that a sufficiently rapid rate of real growth in the economy—say of 6% per year—would make it possible to achieve full employment, stable prices, and a balanced budget despite new social programs proposed by President Carter. How might growth mitigate the conflicts between unemployment and inflation? Will not the investment that growth requires necessarily add to aggregate demand and thus to inflationary pressures?

3. Leonard Silk, the New York Times economic reporter recently commented: "There are three major inhibitions on the Carter Administration's effort to stimulate the economy enough to cure unemployment. The first is the fear of reigniting inflation. The second is rising interest rates. The third is a large budget deficit." With respect to the first, is Silk's view consistent with the L-shaped relation, the Phillip's curve, and/or the Phelps-Friedman theory? With respect to the second and third "inhibitions" mentioned by Mr. Silk, why should they be treated as inhibitions?

4. Consider the following views of two leading Republican politicians on the unemployment-inflation tradeoff. Ronald Regan: "The long-range solution to unemployment is to bring an end to inflation which, in turn causes recessions." Gerald Ford: "Public works programs lead to large deficits, higher inflation and, ultimately, higher unemployment." What, are some of the theoretical linkages that leads from "more inflation" to "higher unemployment"? Does the existance of stagflation in the 1970's indicate that unemployment causes inflation? That inflation causes unemployment?

5. "It is necessary to discover the natural rate of unemployment if stabilization of prices is to be achieved." Explain why this is true in the Phelps-Friedman theory. What exactly is the "natural rate of unemployment"? What policies can increase it? What policies can decrease it? Are there reasons why a society might choose not to minimize this natural rate of unemployment?

6. "Economic man is not playing by the rule book again. It is awkward for professional economists when the laws of 'the dismal science' are flouted on the scale they have been in the recent recession, for it suggests psychologists may know more about the path to prosperity than the gentlemen with slide rules. The evidence is substantial:

—High inflation has gone hand in hand with high unemployment, although for years economists have claimed there was an inverse relationship between inflation and unemployment.

—Despite rapid inflation, the man in the street has been banking more money than ever before, apparently oblivious to the fact that its value is melting away, while the price of tangible goods is rising.

—Labor unions seek wage increases and businessmen price increases, despite unemployment and excess capacity.

—Budget deficits have not cured unemployment.

—OPEC raises prices above the free-market level."

Do each of these bits of evidence flout the laws of economics? Discuss carefully. To the extent that economics does not have satisfactory explanations for any or all of these phenomena, what is the solution?

PART TWELVE

ECONOMIC GROWTH AND COMPARATIVE SYSTEMS

43

Growth in developed economies

In Chapter 29 we saw that investment can be the culprit in causing economic fluctuations that vary in severity from mild disturbances to major upheavals. In the long run, however, investment has been a major cause of the economic growth that has raised living standards so rapidly over the last two centuries. Eightfold or tenfold increases in material living standards have occurred over the space of a single lifetime.

Investment affects growth because it affects the economy's ability to *produce* goods by changing both the quantity and the quality of the capital stock available. In other words, *investment increases the economy's potential, or full-employment, national income.*

The theory of economic growth concentrates on this effect of investment on full-employment national income. Contrast this with the theory of fluctuations, which concentrates on the effects of investment expenditure on aggregate demand and hence on the degree to which actual current national income falls short of, or exceeds, potential national income. Put another way, the theory of fluctuations is concerned with the degree of utilization of existing productive capacity, while the theory of growth is concerned with the growth of productive capacity.

The nature of economic growth

Economic growth has been one of the dominant forces in industiral nations over the last 200 years. It has been the source of industrialization's greatest triumph: the raising of the ordinary person's living standards to levels where leisure, travel, and luxury goods are, for the first time, within reach. It has produced standards of living in industrial nations that are the envy of the peoples of the rest of the world and has led many of them—with varying degrees of success—to strive to copy that performance. Economic growth has also been the source of spectacular failures—perhaps most notably pollution of the air, water, and land by chemicals, heat, and noise.

Members of developed societies have come to accept growth. Even when they worry about pollution and other concomitants of growth, they ask, How can we remove this or that side effect of growth? Few people ask, How can we stop growth? and even fewer people take those few seriously.

But growth, which seems inevitable to most of us, has not always been present, nor is it present everywhere today. There have been periods of increases in living standards in human history followed by long periods of no change. One of the latter was documented by Professor Phelps-Brown, of the London School of Economics, who showed that there was no significant increase in the real income of English building-trade workers between 1215 and 1798, a period of almost six centuries. Peasants in many underdeveloped countries today enjoy a living standard probably little different from that enjoyed by their ancestors a thousand or more years ago. (Provided, that is, that they are lucky enough not to have their "freedom" fought over by some of the more technologically advanced nations.)

Recent data show that world output has doubled in the last fifteen years. Despite dramatic population growth, output per person for the world as a whole has increased sharply. It was twice as high in 1975 as it had been in 1950.

These figures provide impressive evidence of the mastery of aspects of our environment, but they are enormously misleading in one respect: Most of this growth in output has occurred in countries that comprise only about one-fifth of the world's population, while much of the population growth has occurred in countries that have not experienced economic growth. For many countries, as well as for much of history, the phenomenon of growth is absent. In this chapter and the next one we ask why.

THE DEFINITION OF ECONOMIC GROWTH

In a country where GNP has increased tenfold in half a century, and where personal consumption expenditures per capita have doubled in real terms in less than thirty years, it is easy to recognize the phenomenon of growth. It is harder to measure because of a series of potential confusions. Because each of these is found in some contemporary discussions, it is worth bearing them in mind as you read of a particular country's spectacular achievements.

Capacity versus utilization. The growth in an economy's national income over three or four years reflects changes both in its productive capacity and in the percentage utilization of this capacity. Productive capacity can be measured by the concept of full-employment national income. As we saw in Figure 27–1, that capacity is often underutilized.

If there have been large decreases in unemployment, very high rates of increase in national income may be observed. But such increases will not be sustainable once full employment is reached.

American GNP increased by 50 percent between 1933 and 1936, but this reflected almost entirely increases in utilization of capacity from the depths of the Great Depression, not growth in full-employment national income.

For another example, some undeveloped countries start development with a large backlog of unused resources. Such countries can achieve very rapid rates of increases in income for as long as ten years and fail to distinguish this change in utilization rates from increases in capacity. In both Yugoslavia and Greece, much of the growth in national income during the 1960s was of this sort.

A great deal of confusion would be avoided if the term "growth rate" were used to refer only to the growth rate of full-employment national income and if comparisons of national income figures for one country over several years were divided into two parts:

changes due to such growth and changes due to variations in the utilization rates of existing productive capacity.

Money versus real output. Part of any increase in the money value of full-employment output may be due to a rise in prices rather than in output. Use of constant-dollar measures is essential in measuring growth and is now common practice of all major statistical agencies in reporting growth rates.

Output, output per capita, and output per man-hour. To determine a nation's growth in the context of its ability to wage war or to pollute its environment, it is necessary to look at total output. To measure living standards, per capita output is important; a country's average material living standard depends on output per person. (As an example of the relations between these concepts, a doubling of national output combined with a doubling of the population would mean no change in per capita output. As will be seen in Chapter 44, population growth is a problem plaguing many countries of the world.)

Output per person may grow at a different rate than the economy's productive capacity per person for a number of reasons. As an

economy grows, many people choose to spend a shorter portion of their days and lives at work. As standards of living rise, entry into the labor force tends to be delayed by increased schooling, work weeks are shortened to permit greater leisure, and the size of the older nonworking population rises because of both earlier retirement and longer life spans. Offsetting this may be increases in the labor force participation of women and of men who previously worked in nonmarket sectors of the economy.

In theoretical discussions of growth, it is useful to have an indicator of the ability of an economy to convert its resources into goods and services. A widely used summary measure of this is output per man-hour, often called simply **productivity.** It measures the average output per man-hour employed. Obviously, productivity depends not only on labor effort but also on the amount and kind of machinery used, the raw materials available, and so on. The focus of this measure is on the man-hour because special emphasis is put on output per unit of human labor.

THE CUMULATIVE NATURE OF GROWTH

A growth rate of 2 percent per year may seem rather insignificant, but if it is continued for a century it will lead to more than a sevenfold increase in real national income! Table 43–1 shows the large cumulative effect of small annual growth rates.

To see the significance of the cumulative effect of what seem like very small differences in growth rates, notice that if one country grows faster than another, the gap in their living standards will widen progressively. If two countries start from the same level of income and if country A grows at 3 percent while B grows at 2 percent per year, A's income per capita will be twice B's in 69 years. You may not think it matters much whether your economy grows at 2 percent or 3 percent, but your children and grandchildren will!

In order to dramatize the powerful long-

Table 43–1 The cumulative effect of growth

| YEAR | PERCENTAGE RATE OF GROWTH PER YEAR | | | | |
	1	2	3	5	7
0	100	100	100.	100	100
10	111	122	135	165	201
30	135	182	246	448	817
50	165	272	448	1,218	3,312
70	201	406	817	3,312	13,429
100	272	739	2,009	14,841	109,660

Small differences in growth rates make enormous differences in levels of potential national income over a few decades. Assume that potential national income is 100 in year zero. At a rate of growth of 3 percent, it will be 135 in 10 years, 448 after 50 years, and over 2,000 in a century. Compound interest is a powerful force!

run effects of differences in growth rates, we used to include a table that showed students of the 1960s that, if then-current growth trends continued, America would not long remain the world's richest nation, for Germany, Japan, and many others were growing much faster. Many readers of that era simply rejected the notion as a textbook gimmick; deep down they *knew* that the material standard of living of the United States was and would remain the highest the world had ever known. Such a table is no longer even interesting, for by 1976, four industrial countries (Switzerland, Sweden, Norway, and Denmark) had already passed the United States in terms of per capita national income and several more (West Germany, Canada, Belgium, and France) were within 10 percent of the U.S. level. In addition, Kuwait reported a higher average income than any other country.

BENEFITS OF GROWTH

Growth in living standards

A primary reason for desiring growth is to raise the general living standards of the population. A country whose per capita output is growing at 3 percent per year is doubling its living standards about every 24 years. (A helpful approximation device is the "rule of 72." Divide any growth rate into 72 and the resulting number approximates the number of years it will take for income to double.) [42]

The extreme importance of economic growth in raising income can be illustrated by comparing the real income of a father with the real income of the son who follows in his father's footsteps. If the son neither rises nor falls in the relative income scale compared with his father, his share of the country's national income will be the same as his father's. If the son is thirty years younger than his father, he can expect to have a real income nearly twice as large as that which his father enjoyed when his father was the same age. These figures assume that the father and son live in a country such as the United States

where the growth rate is about 2 or 3 percent per year. If they live in Japan, where growth has been going on at a rate of about 8 percent per yer, the son's income will be about 10 times as large as his father's.

For those who share in it, growth is a powerful weapon against poverty. A family earning $5,500 today can expect $8,200 within ten years (in constant dollars) if it just shares in a 4 percent growth rate. The transformation of the life-style of blue-collar workers in America as well as in Germany and Japan in a generation provides a notable example of the escape from poverty that growth makes possible. Of course, not everyone benefits equally from growth. Many of those who are poorest are not even in the labor force and thus are least likely to share in the higher wages that, along with profits, are the primary means by which the gains from growth are distributed. For this reason, redistribution policies will be required even in a growing economy if poverty is to be averted.

Growth and income redistribution

Economic growth makes many kinds of redistributions easier to achieve. For example, a rapid rate of growth makes it much more feasible politically to alleviate poverty. If existing income is to be redistributed, someone's standard of living will actually have to be lowered. If, however, there is economic growth, and if the increment in income is redistributed (through government intervention), it is possible to reduce income inequalities without actually having to lower anyone's income. It is much easier for a rapidly growing economy to be generous toward its less fortunate citizens—or neighbors—than it is for a static one.

Growth and life-style

A family often finds that a big increase in its income can lead to a major change in the pattern of its consumption—that extra money buys important amenities of life. In the same way, the members of society as a whole may find that some goods will be increasingly sought as income rises. For example, a country that is growing rapidly finds it desirable not only to produce more cars and highways but also to provide more recrea-tional areas for its newly affluent citizens. Indeed, concern about litter, pollution, and ugliness usually come only after basic needs of food, clothing, and housing have been met for a substantial majority of the population.

An open letter to the ordinary citizen from a supporter of the Growth-Is-Good School

Dear Ordinary Citizen:

You live in the world's first civilization that is devoted principally to satisfying *your* needs rather than those of a privileged minority. Past civilizations have, without exception, been based on leisure and high consumption for a tiny upper class, a reasonable living standard for a numerically small middle class, and hard work with little more than subsistence consumption for the great mass of people. In the past, the average person (who may or may not have been allowed the title "citizen") saw little of the civilized and civilizing products of the economy, except when he or she was toiling to produce them.

What is unique about the continuing Industrial Revolution is that it is based on mass-produced goods for consumption by the ordinary citizen. It also ushered in a period of sustained economic growth that has raised the consumption standards of ordinary citizens to levels previously reserved throughout the entire history of civilization for a tiny privileged minority. Reflect on a few examples: travel, live and recorded music, art, good food, inexpensive books, universal literacy and a genuine chance to be educated if you want to be. Most important of all, there is enough leisure to provide time and energy to enjoy these and myriad other products of the modern industrial economy.

Would any ordinary citizen seriously doubt the benefits of growth and wish to be back in the world of 150 or 500 years ago, in the same relative social and economic position? Most surely the answer is no. But we cannot say the same for persons with incomes in the top 1 to 2 percent of the income distribution. Economic growth has destroyed much of their privileged consumption position: They must now vie with the masses when visiting the world's beauty spots and be annoyed, while lounging on the terrace of a palatial mansion, by the sound of chartered jets carrying the ordinary people to holidays in far places. Many of the rich resent their loss of exclusive rights to luxury consumption. Some complain bitterly, and it is not surprising that they find their intellectual apologists.

Whether they know it or not, the antigrowth economists—such as Harvard's Ken Galbraith, Cambridge's Joan Robinson, and the LSE's Ed Mishan—are not the social revolutionaries they assume themselves to be. They are the counterrevolutionaries who would set back the clock of material progress for the ordinary person. They say that growth has produced pollution and wasteful consumption of

National defense and prestige

If one country is competing with another for power or prestige, rates of growth are important. If our national income is growing at 2 percent, for instance, while the other country's is growing at 5 percent, all the other country has to do is wait for our relative strength to dwindle. Moreover, a country will find the expenses of an arms race or a program of foreign aid easier to bear, the faster its productivity is growing.

More subtly, but similarly, growth has become part of the currency of international prestige, and countries that are engaged in persuading other countries of the might or right of their economic and political systems point to their rapid rates of growth as evidence of their achievements.

COSTS OF GROWTH

The benefits discussed above suggest that growth is a great blessing. It is surely true that, *ceteris paribus,* most people would regard a fast rate of growth as preferable to a slow one, but other things are seldom equal.

Social and personal costs of growth

Industrialization, unless carefully managed, causes deterioration of the environment. Unspoiled landscapes give way to highways, factories, and billboards; air and water become polluted; and in some cases unique and priceless relics of earlier ages—from flora and fauna to ancient ruins—disappear. Urbanization tends to move people from the simpler life of farming and small towns into the crowded, slum-ridden, and often darkly evil life of the urban ghetto. Those remaining behind in the rural areas find that rural life, too, has changed. Larger-scale farming, the decline of population, and the migration of children from the farm to the city all have their costs. The stepped-up tempo of life brings joys to some but tragedy to others. Accidents, ulcers, crime rates, suicides, divorces, and murder all tend to be higher in periods of rapid change and in more developed societies.

If an economy is growing, it is also changing. Innovation leaves obsolete machines in its wake, and it also leaves partially obsolete people. A rapid rate of growth requires rapid

---

trivia that contributes nothing to human happiness. But the democratic solution to pollution is not to go back to where so few people consume luxuries that pollution is trivial; it is to accept pollution as a transitional phase connected with the ushering in of mass consumption, to keep the mass consumption, and to learn to control the pollution that it tends to create.

It is only through further growth that the average citizen can enjoy consumption standards (of travel, culture, medical and health care, etc.) now available to people in the top 25 percent of the income distribution—which includes the intellectuals who earn large royalties from the books they write denouncing growth. If you think that extra income confers little or real benefit, ask those in the top 25 percent of the income distribution to trade income with the average citizen.

Ordinary citizens, do not be deceived by disguised elitist doctrines. Remember that the very rich and the elite have much to gain by stopping growth—and even more by rolling it back—but you have everything to gain by letting it go forward.

Onward!

I. Growthman

adjustments, and these can cause much upset and misery to the individuals affected. The decline in the number of unskilled jobs makes the lot of untrained workers much more difficult, and when they lose jobs they may well fail to find others, particularly if they are over 50. No matter how well equipped you are at age 25, in another 25 years you are likely to be partially obsolete. This is almost as true for a doctor or an engineer as it is for a mechanic.

An open letter to the ordinary citizen from a supporter of the Growth-Is-Bad School

Dear Ordinary Citizen:

You live in a world that is being despoiled by a mindless search for ever higher levels of material consumption at the cost of all other values. Once upon a time, men and women knew how to enjoy creative work and to derive satisfaction from simple activities undertaken in scarce, and hence highly valued, leisure time. Today the ordinary worker is a mindless cog in an assembly line process that turns out ever more goods that the advertisers must work overtime to persuade the worker to consume.

Statisticians and politicians count the increasing flow of material output as a triumph of modern civilization. Consider not the flow of output in general, but the individual products that it contains. You arise from your electric-blanketed bed, clean your teeth with an electric toothbrush, open with an electric can opener a can of the sad remnants of a once-proud orange, you eat your bread baked from super-refined and chemically refortified flour, and you climb into your car to sit in vast traffic jams on exhaust-polluted highways. And so the day goes, with endless consumption of high-technology products that give you no more real satisfaction than the simple, cheaply produced equivalent products consumed by your grandfathers: soft woolly blankets, natural bristle toothbrushes, real oranges, old-fashioned and coarse but healthy bread, and public transport that moved on uncongested roads and gave its passengers time to chat with their neighbors, to read, or just to daydream.

The slick magazines of today tell you that by consuming more you are happier. But happiness lies not in increasing consumption but in increasing the ratio of *satisfaction of wants* to *total wants*. Since the more you consume the more the advertisers persuade you that you want to consume, you are almost certainly less happy than the average citizen in a small town in 1900 whom we can visualize sitting on the family porch, sipping a cool beer or a lemonade, and enjoying the antics of the children as they play with discarded barrel staves and skipping ropes.

Today the landscape is dotted with countless factories producing the plastic trivia of the modern industrial society and drowning you in a cloud of noise, air, and water pollution. The countryside is despoiled by strip mines, petroleum cracking

The greatest effect is on those whose skills become completely outdated and unneeded.

It is often argued that costs of this kind are a small price to pay for the great benefits that growth can bring. Increasingly it is being rec-

plants, and dangerous nuclear power stations that produce the energy that is devoured insatiably by modern factories and motor vehicles.

Worse still, our precious heritage of natural resources is being fast used up. Spaceship earth flies, captainless, in its senseless orgy of self-consuming consumption.

Now is the time to stop this madness. We must stabilize production, reduce pollution, conserve our natural resources, and seek justice through a more equitable distribution of existing total income.

A long time ago Malthus taught us that if we do not limit population voluntarily, nature will do it for us in a cruel and savage manner. Today the same is true of output: If we do not halt its growth voluntarily, the halt will be imposed on us by a disastrous increase in pollution and a rapid exhaustion of natural resources.

Citizens, awake! Shake off the shackles of growth worship, learn to enjoy the bounty that is yours already, and eschew the endless, self-defeating search for increased happiness through ever-increasing consumption.

Upward!

A. Nongrowthman

ognized that some of these costs are not so small and, moreover, that they are very unevenly borne.[1] Indeed, many of those for whom growth is most costly (in terms of jobs) share least in the fruits of growth. But it is also a mistake to see only the costs—to yearn for the good old days while thriving on higher living standards that growth alone has made possible.

The opportunity cost of growth

In a world of scarcity, almost nothing is free. Growth usually requires an investment of resources in capital goods, in education, and in health. Such investments do not yield any *immediate* return in terms of goods and services for consumption. Growth, which promises more goods tomorrow, is achieved by consuming fewer goods today. For the economy as a whole this is a primary cost of growth.

A more rapid rate of growth may be purchased at the expense of of a lower rate of current consumption. Suppose the fictitious economy of USSA has full employment and is experiencing growth at the rate of 2 percent per year. Its citizens consume 85 percent of the GNP and invest 15 percent. The people of the USSA know that if they are willing immediately to decrease their consumption to 77 percent, they will produce more capital and thus shift at once to a 3 percent growth rate. This new rate can be maintained as long as they keep saving and investing 23 percent of the national income. Should they do it?

Table 43–2 represents the choice in terms of time paths of consumption. How expensive is the "invest now, consume later" strategy? On the assumed figures, it takes ten years for the actual amount of consumption to catch up to what it would have been had no reallocation been made. In the intervening ten

[1] The debate on growth versus the environment is discussed in Chapter 13; this issue continues to be one of the major issues of the 1970s.

Table 43–2 The opportunity cost of growth

IN YEAR	THE LEVEL OF CONSUMPTION		CUMULATIVE GAIN (LOSS) IN CONSUMPTION
	2% growth rate (A)	3% growth rate (A')	
0	85.0	77.0	(8.0)
1	86.7	79.3	(15.4)
2	88.5	81.8	(22.1)
3	90.3	84.2	(28.2)
4	92.1	86.8	(33.5)
5	93.9	89.5	(37.9)
6	95.8	92.9	(40.8)
7	97.8	95.0	(43.6)
8	99.7	97.9	(45.4)
9	101.8	100.9	(46.3)
10	103.8	103.9	(46.2)
15	114.7	120.8	(28.6)
20	126.8	140.3	19.6
30	154.9	189.4	251.0
40	189.2	255.6	745.9

Transferring resources from consumption to investment goods lowers current income but raises future income. The example assumes that income in year zero is 100, that consumption of 85 percent of national income is possible with a 2 percent growth rate, but that to achieve 3 percent growth rate, consumption must fall to 77 percent of income. A shift from A to A' decreases consumption the first 10 years but increases it thereafter. The cumulative effect on consumption is shown in the last column. The gains eventually become large.

years a good deal of consumption was lost, and the cumulative losses in consumption must be made up before society can really be said to have broken even. It takes an additional nine years before total consumption over the whole period is as large as it would have been if the economy had remained on the 2 percent path. [43]

Such a policy of sacrificing present living standards for a gain that one does not begin to reap for a generation is hardly likely to appeal to any but the altruistic or the very young. The question of how much one generation is prepared to sacrifice some of its living standards for its heirs (who are in any case going to be richer) is troublesome. As one skeptic put

it: Why should we sacrifice for them? What have they ever done for us?

Many governments, particularly those seeking a larger role in world affairs, have followed the route of forced diversion of resources from consumption to investment. The Germans under Hitler, the Russians under Stalin, and the Chinese under Mao Tse-tung adopted four- and five-year plans that did just this. Many less developed countries are using such plans today. Such resource shifts are particularly important when actual growth rates are very small (say, less than 1 percent), for without some current sacrifice there is little or no prospect of real growth in the lifetimes of today's citizens. The very lowest growth rates are frequently encountered in the very poorest countries (as will be seen), and this creates a cruel dilemma, discussed in Chapter 44 as the vicious circle of poverty.

GROWTH AS A GOAL OF POLICY: DO THE BENEFITS JUSTIFY THE COSTS?

Suppose that the members of a society want to increase their output of goods by 10 percent in one year. There are many ways they can do it.

1. They may be able to find idle and unutilized resources and put them to work.

2. They may be able to schedule extra shifts and overtime labor.

3. They may, by exhortation or by an appropriate incentive system, induce people to work much harder.

4. They may (if they have time) increase the supply of machines and factories.

5. They may discover new techniques that permit them to get more output from the same inputs.

In the short run, the first three of these approaches seem more promising than the last two; in fact, when nations face such crises as wars these devices are used to achieve rapid increases in output. But the gains to be achieved by utilizing unemployed resources, extending the hours of use of employed ones, or "working harder" are limited. Eventually they will be used up. When there are no longer unutilized resources or underutilized capacity, further increases in output become more difficult.

For the long-term increases in living standards that have eliminated the 14-hour-a-day, 6-day-a-week work load and brought leisure and high material standards of living within the reach of the bulk of North Americans and western Europeans, there is no substitute for economic growth. But do the already developed countries need yet more growth? Most people think they do. That poverty is now a solvable problem in the United States is a direct result of its enhanced average living standards. Clearly, people in the top quarter of the present income distribution have more opportunities for leisure, travel, culture, good whisky, and gracious living than have persons with much lower incomes. Most of those now in the bottom half of the income distribution would like these opportunities too. Only growth can give it to them.

Today, countries that have not yet—or only newly—undergone sustained periods of economic growth in modern times are desperately trying to copy those that have, in order to obtain the benefits of growth. There seems little doubt that most nations and most people will pursue the goal of growth for the benefits it brings, despite its costs.

How seriously the costs are taken depends in part on how many of the benefits of growth have already been achieved. With mounting population problems, the poor countries are becoming more and more preoccupied with creating growth; with mounting awareness of pollution, the rich countries are devoting more and more resources to overcoming the problems caused by growth—at the same time being understandably reluctant to give up further growth.

Indeed, a similar conflict can often be seen in the same country at the same time: one relatively poor community fighting to acquire a new paper mill for the employment and income it will create; another, relatively affluent community deploring the despoiling of its beaches and its air by an existing mill.

Theories of economic growth

Economists today recognize that many different factors may contribute to—or impede—economic growth. Although our present knowledge of the relative importance of these factors is far from complete, modern economists look at the problems of growth more optimistically today than did the classical economists of a century and more ago. Of particular importance is the nature and source of the investment opportunities that, when utilized, lead to growth. The differences between the classical and contemporary points of view can best be understood by considering a revealing though unrealistic case.

GROWTH IN A WORLD WITHOUT LEARNING

Suppose that there is a known and fixed stock of projects that might be undertaken and that nothing ever happens to increase either the supply of such projects or the knowledge about them. Whenever the opportunity is ripe, some of these investment opportunities are utilized, thereby increasing the stock of capital goods and depleting the reservoir of unutilized investment opportunities. Of course, the most productive opportunities will be used first. Such a view of investment opportunities can be represented by a fixed marginal efficiency of capital schedule of the kind met in Chapter 22. Such a schedule is graphed in Figure 43–1. It relates the stock of capital to the productivity of an additional

Figure 43–1 The marginal efficiency of capital schedule

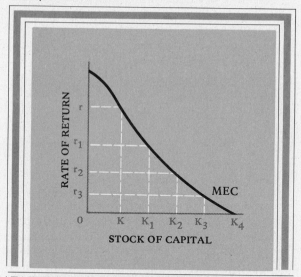

A declining *MEC* schedule shows that successive increases to the capital stock bring smaller and smaller increases in output and thus a declining rate of return. A fixed *MEC* schedule can represent the theory of growth in an economy with some unutilized investment opportunities but no learning. Increases in investment that increase the capital stock from K to K_1 to . . . K_4 lower the rate of return from r to r_1 to . . . zero. Because the productivity of successive units of capital decreases, the capital–output ratio rises.

unit of capital. The productivity of a unit of capital is defined as a rate of return by dividing the annual value of the additional output resulting from an extra unit of capital by the value of that unit of capital. Thus, for example, a marginal efficiency of capital of 0.2 means that $1 of new capital adds 20¢ per year to the stream of output.

The downward slope of the *MEC* schedule indicates that, with knowledge constant, increases in the stock of capital bring smaller and smaller increases in output per unit of

capital. That is, the rate of return on successive units of capital declines. This shape is a consequence of the law of diminishing returns.[2] If, with land, labor, and knowledge constant, more and more capital is used, the net amount added by successive increments will diminish and may eventually reach zero. Given this schedule, as capital is accumulated in a state of constant knowledge the society will move down its *MEC* schedule.

In a "nonlearning" world, where new investment opportunities do not appear, growth occurs only so long as there are unutilized opportunities to use capital effectively to increase output.

Growth, in a nonlearning world, is a transitory phenomenon that occurs as long as the society has a backlog of unutilized investment opportunities.

So far we have discussed the *marginal* efficiency of capital. The *average* efficiency of capital refers to the average amount produced in the whole economy per unit of capital employed. It is common in discussions of the theory of growth to talk in terms of the *capital-output ratio*, which is the reciprocal of output per unit of capital.[3] In a world without learning, the capital-output ratio is increasing.[4]

In a world without learning the growth in the capital stock will have two important consequences:

1. Successive increases in capital accumulation will be less and less productive, and the capital-output ratio will be increasing.

2. The marginal efficiency of new capital will be decreasing and will eventually be pushed to zero as the backlog of investment opportunities is used up.

---

[2] This hypothesis was discussed in detail on page 170.

[3] The capital-output ratio was first encountered in Chapter 20.

[4] This implies that the *marginal* efficiency of new capital is below the *average* of all past capital stock acquisitions. In a nonlearning world this will be the case if additions to capital stock have been going on for some time, since it will have been profitable to exploit first the most attractive opportunities.

GROWTH WITH LEARNING

The steady depletion of the country's growth opportunities in the previous model resulted from the fact that new investment opportunities were never discovered or created. If, however, investment opportunities are created as well as used up with the passage of time, then the *MEC* schedule will shift outward over time and the effects of increasing the capital stock may be different. This is illustrated in Figure 43–2. Such outward shifts can be regarded as the consequences of "learning" either about investment opportunities or about the techniques that create such opportunities. If learning occurs, it is impor-

tant to know how rapidly the *MEC* schedule shifts relative to the amount of capital investment being undertaken. Three possibilities are shown in Figure 43–2.

Gradual reduction in investment opportunities: the classical view

If, as in Figure 43–2(i), investment opportunities are created but at a slower rate than they are used up, there will be a tendency toward a falling rate of return and an increasing ratio of capital to output. The predictions in this case are the same as those given above (in color) for the world without learning, although the cause is different: too slow, rather than no, discovery of new investment opportunities.

Figure 43–2 Shifting investment opportunities: three cases

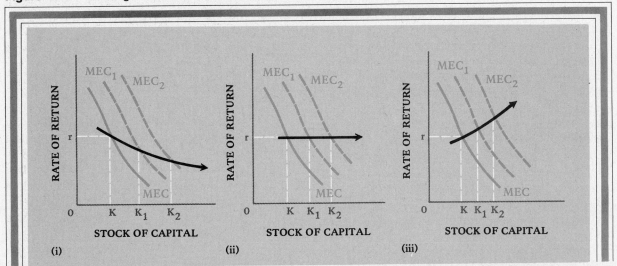

When both knowledge and the capital stock grow, the actual marginal efficiency of capital depends on their relative rates of growth. In each case, the economy at period 0 has the *MEC* curve, a capital stock of K, and a rate of return of r. In period 1 the curve shifts to MEC_1 and there is investment to increase the stock of capital by KK_1. In period 2 the curve shifts to MEC_2 and there is net investment of K_1K_2. It is the relative size of the shift of the *MEC* curve and the additions of the capital stock that are important.

In (i) investment occurs more rapidly than increases in investment opportunities and r will fall along the black curve. In (ii) investment occurs at exactly the same rate as investment opportunities and r is constant. In (iii) investment occurs less rapidly than increases in investment opportunities and r will rise.

This figure illustrates the theory of growth held by most economists of the eighteenth and nineteenth centuries. They saw the economic problem as one of fixed land, a rising population, and a gradual exhaustion of investment opportunities. These things, they believed, would ultimately force the economy into a static condition with no growth, very high capital-output ratios, and the marginal return on additional units of capital forced down toward zero.

Constant or rising investment opportunities: the contemporary view

The pessimism of the classical economists was due to their failure to anticipate the possibility of really rapid innovation—of technological progress that could push investment opportunities outward as rapidly or more rapidly than they were used up, as shown in parts (ii) and (iii) of Figure 43–2.

Because the facts (as will be seen in a moment) suggest that the classical economists' predictions are not confirmed, but rather that the economy generates new investment opportunities at least as rapidly as it uses up old ones, a general rethinking of the causes of growth has occurred, with attention devoted more to understanding the *shifts* in the *MEC* schedule over time and less to its shape under a nonlearning situation. The historical record suggests that it is the shifts over time that have led to the reality of sustained growth.

A CONTEMPORARY VIEW OF GROWTH

The classical economists had a relatively simple theory of growth because they viewed a single mechanism—capital accumulation—as being of decisive importance. Contemporary theorists begin by recognizing a number of factors that influence growth, no one of which is necessarily the dominant one. Half a dozen of them may be mentioned.

Quantity of capital per worker

Human beings have always been tool users, and it is still true today that more and more tools tend to lead to more and more output. As long as a society has unexploited investment opportunities, productive capacity can be increased by increasing the stock of capital. The effect on output per worker of "mere" capital accumulation is so noticeable that it was once regarded as virtually the sole source of growth. But if capital accumulation were the only source of growth, it would lead to movement down the marginal efficiency schedule and to a rising capital-output ratio and a falling rate of return on capital. The evidence does not support these predictions. The facts suggest that investment opportunities have expanded as rapidly as investments in capital goods, roughly along the pattern shown in Figure 43–2(ii). While capital accumulation has taken place and has accounted for much observed growth, it cannot have been the only source of growth.

Innovation

New knowledge and inventions can contribute markedly to the growth of potential national income, even without capital accumulation. In order to see this, assume that the proportion of the society's resources devoted to the production of capital goods is just sufficient to replace capital as it wears out. Thus, if the old capital were merely replaced in the same form, the capital stock would be constant and there would be no increase in the capacity to produce. But, if there is a growth of knowledge so that as old equipment wears out it is replaced by different, more productive equipment, national income will be growing.

Increases in productive capacity that inhere in the form of capital goods in use are called **embodied technical change.** The historical importance of embodied technical change is clearly visible: The assembly line and automation have transformed much of manufacturing, the airplane has revolutionized transportation, and electronic devices have come to dominate the communications industries. These innovations plus less well-known but no less profound ones—for example, improvements in the strength of metals, the productivity of seeds, and the techniques for recovering basic raw materials from the ground—tend to create new investment opportunities.

Less visible but nonetheless important changes occur through **disembodied technical change.** These concern innovations in the organization of production that are not embodied in the form of the capital goods or raw materials used. One example is improved techniques of managerial control.

Most innovations involve both embodied and disembodied changes: New processes require new machines, which make yet newer processes economical. Computerization promises many such changes in the decade ahead. One of these, which many regard with a mixture of awe and apprehension, is a cashless society in which banks become parts of vast information networks that receive one's pay, pay one's bills, and invest one's savings. But whatever the form of innovation, the nature of the goods and services consumed and the way they are made is continually changing as innovations occur. In 1968 *The New York Times* published a list of important innovations in the period 1860–1960 which is reproduced in Table 43–3. It is

Table 43–3 Important inventions and innovations, 1860–1960

1867	Reinforced concrete (Monier)	1913	Assembly line, for magnetos (Ford Motor Co.)
1867	Typewriter, practical (Scholes, C. Glidden, Soule)	1920	Continuous hot-strip rolling of steel (Tytus)
1869	Air brake (Westinghouse)	1923	Iconoscope electronic camera (Zworykin)
1870	Celluloid (J. W., I. S. Hyatt)	1926	Rocket, liquid fuel (Goddard)
1874	Barbed wire (J. Glidden)	1929	Coaxial carrier system (Espenschied, Affel)
1876	Telephone (Bell)	1931	Electron microscope (Knoll, Ruska)
1884	Linotype (Mergenthaler)	1931	Freon refrigerants (Midgley)
1884	Steam turbine (Parsons)	1931	Cyclotron (Lawrence)
1885	Transformer, power distribution (Stanley)	1932	Light polarizer (Land)
1886	Internal combustion engine, high speed (Daimler)	1935	Radar (Watson-Watt)
1886	Hand camera (Eastman)	1937	Jet engine (Whittle)
1888	Induction motor (Tesla)	1937	Nylon (Carothers)
1889	Electric elevator, commercial use in U.S. (Otis)	1938	Xerography (Carlson)
1893	By-product coke oven (Hoffman)	1938	Catalytic cracking of petroleum (Houdry)
1894	Kinetoscope parlor, movies (Edison)	1942	Nuclear chain reaction (Fermi)
1898	Radio, practical (Marconi)	1944	Mark I computer (Aiken)
1898	Submarine, practical (Holland)	1947	Transistor (Bardeen, Brattain, Shockley)
1903	Airplane, controlled, sustained, powered flight (W. and O. Wright)	1948	Long-playing record (Goldmark)
1904–1907	Vacuum tube (J. A. Fleming, DeForest)	1954–1960	Maser-laser (Townes, Shawlaw, Maiman)
1909	Bakelite (Baekeland)	1957	First artificial satellite
1911	Gyroscope (Sperry)	1958	Satellite communications
1911	Cellophane (Brandenberger)	1960	Birth-control pill (Pincus, Rock, Chang)

© 1968 by The New York Times Company.

In 1968 *The New York Times* made this selection of 44 of the most important inventions and innovations over the preceding century. Any list of this kind is arbitrary—for example, the *Times* does not regard the T-formation or color TV as worthy of mention. The list does illustrate the pace of inventions and innovations over the last century that have transformed material life beyond recognition in so short a period. Consider post-1960 inventions and innovations that you might add.

harder to judge recent contributions than more distant ones, but the decades of the 1960s and 1970s will, in retrospect, surely be found to have contributed significantly. The electronic memory chip seems to be one, and some scientists believe that the guidance and landing systems developed as part of the programs of space exploration will have major industrial applications.

The quality of human capital[5]

The "quality" of human capital has several aspects. One of these involves improvements in the health and longevity of the population. These things are, of course, desired as ends in themselves, but they have consequences for both the size of the labor force and its productivity. There is no doubt that they have increased productivity per worker-hour by cutting down on illness, accidents, and absenteeism. At the same time, the extension of the normal life span with no comparable increase in the working life span has created a larger group of nonworking aged that exercises a claim on total output. Whether health improvements alone have increased output per capita in the United States is not clear.

A second aspect of the quality of human capital concerns technical training, from learning to operate a machine to learning how to be a scientist. Training is clearly required to invent, operate, manage, and repair complex machines. More subtly, there are often believed to be general social advantages to an educated population. It has been shown that productivity improves with literacy and that, in general, the longer a person has been educated the more adaptable he or she is to new and changing challenges—and thus, in the long run, the more productive. But education may also increase feelings of alienation in a society that is thought to be arbitrary or unjust.

[5] Human capital is briefly discussed in Chapter 22 (page 369).

The quantity of labor

The size of a country's population and the extent of participation in the labor force are important in and of themselves, not merely because they affect the quantity of a factor of production. For this reason, it is less common to speak of the quantity of people available for work as a source of, or detriment to, growth than it is to speak of the quantity of capital or iron ore in this way. But, clearly, for any given state of knowledge and supplies of other factors of production, the size of the population can affect the level of output per capita. Every child born has both a mouth and a pair of hands; over a lifetime, each will be both a consumer and a producer. Thus, on average, it is perfectly possible to speak of overpopulated or underpopulated economies, depending on whether the contribution to production of additional people would raise or lower the level of per capita income.

Because population size is related to income per capita, it is possible to define a theoretical concept, **optimal population,** that maximizes income per capita. Such a concept is illustrated in Figure 43–3.[6]

Many countries have had or do have conscious population policies. America in the nineteenth century sought immigrants, as did Australia until very recently. Germany under Hitler paid bonuses for additional Aryan children and otherwise offered incentives to create Germans. Greece today is trying to stem emigration to western Europe. All of these activities bespeak a belief in insufficient population, although the motives are not in every case purely economic. In contrast, many of the underdeveloped countries of South America and Asia seek means to limit population growth. One of the most dramatic and controversial programs has been the mass

[6] The notion of an "optimal population," although purely technical, causes offense in some quarters. Kenya's President Kenyatta regarded as racists those who called for population control in his country in the interests of raising average income. How, he asked, could there be "too many" Kenyans when there were still foreigners in Africa?

sterilization of many males in India. The cogency of attempts to limit population growth are discussed in Chapter 44.

Social, religious, and legal institutions

Social and religious habits can affect economic growth. In a society in which children are expected to stay in their fathers' occupations it is more difficult for the labor force to change its characteristics and to adapt to the requirements of growth than where upward mobility is itself a goal. Max Weber argued that the ''Protestant ethic'' encourages the acquisition of wealth and is thus more likely to encourage growth than is an ethic that directs activity away from the economic sphere.

Legal institutions may likewise affect growth. The pattern of ownership of land and natural resources, by affecting the way in which such resources are used, may affect their productivity. If, for example, agricultural land is divided into very small parcels, one per family, it may be much more difficult to achieve the advantages of modern agriculture than if the land were available for large-scale farming. Many economists are thus concerned with patterns of land tenure.

Economists are interested in such relationships. If it is true that social, religious, or legal patterns make growth more difficult, this need not mean that they are undesirable. Instead, it means that the benefits of these things must now be weighed against the costs, of which the effect on growth is one. If people derive satisfaction from a religion whose beliefs inhibit growth, if they value a society in which every man owns his own land and is more nearly self-sufficient than in another society, they may be quite willing to pay a price in terms of growth opportunities foregone.

Some institutions inhibit growth without having wide appeal to the people. For example, the concentration of land ownership in the hands of a few absentee landowners who are not concerned to maximize their profits

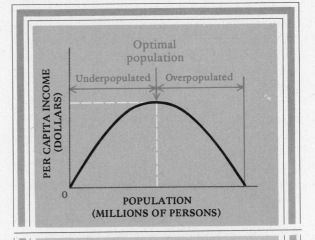

Figure 43–3   One concept of optimal population

The population that leads to the maximum per capita national income is sometimes called the optimal population. From the point of view of maximizing income per capita, one can have too few or too many neighbors (and children). The optimal size of population, in this sense, can be defined as in the diagram. The population that is optimal in other senses—considering religion, ecology, or the quality of life—may be different.

can be detrimental to growth. If the landlord's holdings are so vast that he can obtain all the income he desires without using his land effectively, he may have little motivation to introduce advanced techniques. In many societies in which this system of land ownership exists, land tenure reform (which usually implies the confiscation of land) becomes a necessary condition for growth. Not surprisingly, such reforms are resisted by existing governments, which tend to support the interests of the economically powerful. Land reform can often be accomplished only in the wake of a political revolution.

International trade and economic growth

The most important advantage that the existence of international trade confers on a growing country is that it allows it to escape from its own resource limitations, both natural and human, and concentrate its growth effort in the areas in which it has a genuine advantage. It can be very difficult for a small country to grow in all sectors at once, as would be required if it were a closed economy. With an open economy a small country is free to grow rapidly in sectors in which it enjoys a comparative advantage and to meet the rest of its requirements through foreign trade. The policy problem of choosing to foster either *balanced growth* in all sectors of the economy or *unbalanced growth* in some sectors is further discussed in Chapter 44.

The relative importance of particular influences

A complete theory of growth would do more than list a series of influences all of which affect the growth rate. It would include assessments of (1) their relative importance, (2) the trade-offs involved in having more of one beneficial influence and less of another, and (3) the interactions among the various influences. This poses a formidable empirical challenge to research that is just beginning to be accepted. While much remains to be learned, an important tentative conclusion of such scholars as E. F. Denison and Robert Solow is that improvements in the *quality* of capital, human as well as physical, have played a larger role than increases in the *quantity* of capital in the economic growth of the United States since 1900. Whether quality rather than quantity of capital is also the more important source of growth for countries with very different cultural patterns, more acute population problems, or more limited natural resources is a matter of continuing research.

ARE THERE LIMITS TO GROWTH?

Those opposed to growth argue that sustained growth for another century is unde-

sirable; some even argue that it is impossible. Of course all terrestrial things have an ultimate limit. Astronomers predict that the solar system itself will die as the sun burns out in another 6 billion or so years. To be of practical concern a limit must be within some reasonable planning horizon. Recent books by Jay Forrester [*World Dynamics* (1973)] and D. H. Meadows et al. [*The Limits to Growth* (1974)] predict the imminence of a growth-induced doomsday. Living standards are predicted to reach a peak about the turn of the century and then, in the words of Professor Nordhaus, a leading critic of these models, to "descend inexorably to the level of Neanderthal man."

Not surprisingly, this debate has received widespread attention in the popular press. Whatever the final verdict, there can be no doubt that the debate that has raged about these so-called doomsday models has helped to give needed awareness of, and attention to, problems of population growth, pollution, and exhaustion of the supplies of specific natural resources. While there is debate, on many matters there is also substantial consensus.

The increasing pressure on natural resources

The years since World War II have seen a rapid acceleration in the utilization of the world's resources, particularly the fossil fuels and the basic minerals. The world's population has increased from under 2.5 billion to over 4 billion in that period, which alone increases the demand for all of the world's resources. But the fact of population growth greatly understates the pressure on resources. Calculations by Professor Nathan Keyfitz of Harvard, and others, focus on the resource use by the so-called middle class, defined roughly as those who can claim a life style of the level enjoyed by 90 percent of American families. This middle class, which today includes about one-sixth of the world's population, consumes 15 to 30 times as much oil per

A case study of rapid growth: Japan, 1953–1971

The real national income of Japan was 5.4 times as large in 1973 as it was in 1953. Japan's economic growth rate was more than double the average rate in ten North American and European countries and greatly exceeded the rate in any of them. What accounts for the extraordinarily rapid growth of Japan's economy? To answer that question, two economists, Edward F. Denison and William K. Chung, analyzed and measured the sources of economic growth in Japan from 1953 to 1971 and compared the results with those for ten Western countries. They also measured the difference between levels of output per worker in the United States and Japan in 1970 and identified its sources and magnitude. Their results were published in 1976.★

They find that no single factor was responsible for Japan's high postwar growth rate. Rather, the Japanese economy benefited from several major sources of growth: an increase in quantity of labor, an increase in quantity of capital, improved technology in production, and economies of scale. Japan gained more in each of these respects than did any of the ten other countries studied. In addition, Japan had the greatest reallocation

★ Edward F. Denison and William K. Chung, *How Japan's Economy Grew So Fast: The Sources of Postwar Expansion* (Washington, D.C.: Brookings, 1976).

of labor from agriculture to industry of all the countries studied except Italy. Since productivity is generally higher in industry than in agriculture, a shift of this kind raises average productivity and thereby contributes to growth even without an increase in output per person in either sector.

The overall growth record of Japan is as good as it is partly because of a low *level* of productivity. It is easier to improve from a low base than a high one. At the end of the period productivity was still more than 40 percent lower in Japan than in the United States, even after eliminating the effects of differences between the countries in working hours, in composition and allocation of the labor force, in amounts of capital and land, in size of markets, and in the cyclical positions of the two economies. There is thus an obvious potential for still further Japanese growth relative to the United States.

Can Japan's growth rate be sustained? The authors stress the probability of a declining growth rate as various ways of securing fast growth by "catching up" are successively exhausted. Nevertheless, they consider a fairly high rate of long-term growth in Japan—between 5 and 8 percent per year—likely for the rest of this century. By that time Japan may well be enjoying the highest standard of living of any country in the world.

capita and, overall, at least five times as much of the earth's scarce resources per capita as do the other "poor" five-sixths of the population.

The world's poor are not, however, content to remain forever poor. Whether they

live in the USSR, Brazil, Korea, or Kenya, they have evidently let their governments understand that they expect policies that generate enough growth to give *them* the higher consumption levels that all of *us* take for granted. This upward aspiration is being fulfilled to a degree. The growth of the middle class has been nearly 4 percent per year—twice the rate of population growth—over the postwar period. The number of persons realizing middle-class living standards is estimated to have increased from 200 million to 500 million between 1950 and 1970. This growth rate is a major factor in the recently recognized or projected shortages of our natural resources: The increases in demand in the last two decades have outstripped discovery of new supplies and caused crises in energy and mineral supplies as well as food shortages. Yet the 4 percent growth rate of this middle class, which is too fast for our present resources, is too slow for the aspirations of the billions who live in underdeveloped countries and see the fruits of development all around them. Thus the pressure on our resources of energy, minerals, and food is likely to accelerate even if mere population growth is reduced.

Another way to look at the problem of resource pressure is to note that present technology and resources could not possibly support the present population of the world at the standard of living of today's average American family. Such a shift in level of living, if made overnight, would more than double the world's demand for resources. The demand for oil would increase fivefold to tenfold. Since these calculations (most unrealistically) assume no population growth anywhere in the world and no growth in living standards for the richest sixth of the world's population, the fact of insufficient resources is manifest. On all of this there is no serious disagreement among informed people.

Doomsday predictions

Those most alarmed about growth combine the undoubted acceleration of resource utilization with a series of assumptions: first, that there is no technical progress; second, that no new resources are discovered or rendered usable by new techniques; and third, that

there is no substitution of more plentiful resources for those that become scarce. Under these circumstances, exhaustion of one or more key resources is predictable. If, in addition, population growth continues at historical rates, this exhaustion will occur relatively quickly—certainly within the next century. And if the increasing production continues to pollute the atmosphere faster than the pollutants can be absorbed, the capacity to produce will be diminished and the quality of life further diminished.

These are the basic assumptions of the doomsday models. Doom can come in several ways (or in any combination of them): natural resources depletion, famine due to overpopulation, or an increasing and ultimately fatal pollution of the earth.

The many possible routes to disaster mean that no single restraint will suffice to prevent it. If both natural resource usage and pollution are controlled, doom results from overpopulation. Population control will prove self-defeating because it leads to an increase in the per capita food supply and in the standard of living—which in turn generates forces to trigger a resurgence in population growth. The only way to prevent disaster is to stop economic growth at once through a comprehensive plan to curtail drastically natural resource use (by 75 percent), pollution generation (by 50 percent), investment (by 40 percent), and the birth rate (by 30 percent). Since the countries of the world are not likely, within the next forty years, to agree on the stern measures needed to meet these targets, a descent down the slippery slope of declining living standards during our own lifetimes is inevitable—and disaster looms for our grandchildren.

A reply to doomsday

Critics reply that predictions of an imminent doomsday are as old as human life itself and about as reliable as predictions of the arrival of universal peace and goodwill on earth.

They recognize the pressures on the world's resources, and they concede that at present rates of utilization we would clearly run out of specific resources—particularly oil, gas, and certain minerals—in the foreseeable future.

But, they argue, all of our economic history shows the key assumptions of the doomsday models to be invalid. Nothing could be clearer than that technology is not constant and that people are ingenious in finding ways not only to economize on the use of scarce resources but also to substitute materials that are common for those that become scarce. Just as ample taconite replaced scarce iron ore in making steel, just as ample coal replaced scarce charcoal in making iron and steel, and just as synthetic rubber replaced natural rubber in making tires, so it is reasonable to expect new energy sources to be developed to replace fossil fuels. The potential supplies of nuclear and solar energy are inexhaustible, and we will one day be able to harness them.

Can it be doubted, they ask, that a society that has developed birth control pills and explored Mars can solve the problems of overpopulation and control of pollutants?

A tentative verdict

Most economists agree that conjuring up absolute limits to growth based on the assumptions of constant technology and fixed resources is not warranted. But this does not mean there is no cause for concern. Most agree that any barrier can be overcome by technological advances—but not in an instant, and not automatically. Clearly there is a problem of timing: How soon can we discover and put into practice the knowledge required to solve the problems that are made ever more imminent by growth in population, growth in affluence, and by the growing aspirations of the billions who now live in poverty? There is no guarantee at all that a whole generation may not be caught in transition, with social and political consequences that promise to be enormous even if they are not cataclysmic. The nightmare conjured up by the doomsday models may have served its purpose if it helps to focus our attention on these problems and their imminence.

Summary

1. Investment which causes short-term fluctuations in national income by affecting aggregate demand also makes possible long-term economic growth by increasing a nation's capacity to produce. Such growth is frequently measured using rates of change of potential real national income per person or per man-hour.

2. The cumulative effects of even small differences in growth rates become large over periods of a generation or more. (See Table 43–1.)

3. The most important benefit of growth lies in its contribution to the long-run struggle to raise living standards and escape poverty. Growth also makes more manageable the policies that would redistribute income among people. Economic growth can likewise play an important role in a country's national defense or in its struggle for international prestige.

4. Growth, while often beneficial, is never costless. The opportunity cost of growth is the diversion of resources from current consumption to capital formation. For some individuals who are left behind in a rapidly changing world the costs are higher and more personal. The optimal rate of growth involves balancing benefits and costs. Few wish to forgo the benefits growth can bring, but few wish to maximize growth at any cost.

5. Understanding growth involves understanding both the utilization of existing investment opportunities and the process of creating new investment opportunities. The source of economic growth was once thought to be almost entirely capital accumulation and the utilization of a backlog of unexploited investment opportunities. Today most economists recognize that many investment opportunities can be *created,* and much attention is given to the sources of outward shifts in the *MEC* schedule.

6. In addition to mere increases in quantity of capital per person, any list of factors importantly affecting growth includes the extent of innovation, the quality of human capital, the size of the working population, social and legal institutions, and the patterns of international com-

parative advantage and international trade. Current research is not yet at the point of a complete theory of growth, but the quality of capital seems to be at least as important as the quantity in contemporary growth.

7. The critical importance of increasing knowledge and new technology in sustaining growth is highlighted by the great drain on existing natural resources of the explosive growth of the last two or three decades. Without continuing new knowledge, the present needs and aspirations of the world's population cannot be met.

Concepts for review

The role of investment in increasing potential national income

The cumulative nature of growth

Benefits and costs of growth

Effects of capital accumulation with and without new knowledge

Embodied and disembodied technical change

Factors affecting growth

Limits to growth

Discussion questions

1. We usually study and measure economic growth in macroeconomic terms. But in a market economy who makes the decisions that lead to growth? What kind of decisions and what kind of actions cause growth to occur? How might a detailed study of individual markets be relevant to understanding economic growth?

2. Why is rising productivity a more significant contributing factor for economic growth than simply increasing the quantity of productive resources? Define *productivity*. List all the factors that increase the productivity of labor and the productivity of capital. Comment on the differences and similarities of the two lists.

3. The Overseas Development Council, in 1977, introduced "a new measure of economic development based on the physical quality of life." Its index, called PQLI, gives one-third weight to each of the following three indicators: literacy, life expectancy, and infant mortality. While countries such as the United States and the Netherlands rank very high on either the PQLI or on an index of per capita real national income, some relatively poor countries, such as Sri Lanka, rank much higher on the PQLI index than much richer countries such as Algeria and Kuwait. Discuss the merits or deficiencies of this measure.

4. "The case for economic growth is that it gives man greater control over his environment, and consequently increases his freedom." Explain why you agree or disagree with this statement by the economist Arthur Lewis.

5. Growth in income per capita is a necessary condition for a rising standard of living in a country. Is it also a *sufficient* condition for making everyone better off? Why may not everyone benefit from economic growth?

6. GNP in real terms in the United States doubled between 1957 and 1977. Over this period the annual percentage rate of increase in GNP in constant dollars was 3.5 percent per year. Evaluate this measure of growth with respect to how well it reflects changes in (a) the material well-being of the average resident of the United States and (b) the nation's capacity to produce goods and services. In each case suggest what additional information you would like to know.

7. You discover that a particular economy has achieved a rapid increase in the size of its capital stock over several decades with no appreciable change in the rate of return to capital. What, if anything, can you conclude about its rate of innovation? its rate of growth?

8. Consider a developed economy that decides to achieve a zero rate of growth for the future. What implications would such a "stationary state" have for the processes of production and consumption? What would be the rate of return to capital once this state is reached?

44

Growth and the underdeveloped economies

In our civilized and comfortable urban life, most of us lose sight of the fact that, in terms of the life span of the earth, it is a very short time since human beings lived as other animals, catching an existence as best they could from what nature threw their way. It is only about 10,000 years since human beings turned themselves from food gatherers into food producers, and it is only within the last few centuries that any significant proportion of the world's population could look forward to anything but unremitting toil in wresting an existence from a reluctant nature. The concepts of leisure and freedom from hunger as rights to be enjoyed by everyone are very new in human history

The uneven pattern of development

Table 44–1 will repay careful study. It shows how few people have made the transition from poverty to relative comfort. There are over four billion people living today, but the wealthy parts of the world, where people work no more than 40 or 50 hours per week and enjoy substantial amounts of leisure and a level of consumption at or above half of that attained by the citizens of the United States, contain only about 18 percent of the world's population.[1] Most of the rest struggle for their very subsistence. About two billion people exist on a level at or below that enjoyed by peasants in the more successful civilizations of five millennia ago.

There are many different ways to look at the inequality of income distribution among the world's population. One way is shown in Figure 44–1, which plots the Lorenz curve of the world's income distribution. The farther the curve bends away from the straight line, the greater is the inequality in income distribution. To give some perspective on the great

[1] The groups in Table 44–1 represent arbitrary groupings in which income doubles with each progression.

Figure 44–1 Lorenz curves showing inequalities among the nations of the world and within the United States

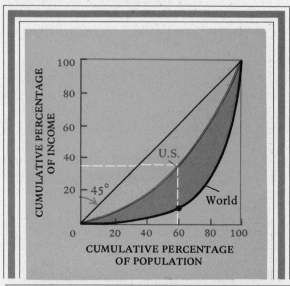

CUMULATIVE PERCENTAGE OF INCOME

CUMULATIVE PERCENTAGE OF POPULATION

The inequality in the distribution of income is much less within the United States than among all the nations of the world. In a Lorenz curve, a wholly equal distribution of income would be represented by the 45° line: 20 percent of the population would have 20 percent of the income, 50 percent of the population would have 50 percent of the income, and so on. The very unequal distribution of world income is shown by the black curve. For example, 60 percent of the world's population live in countries that earn only 10 percent of the world's income, as shown by the black dot. For contrast, the distribution of income within the United States is shown. The poorest 60 percent of the American population earn 36 percent of the nation's income. This is a far cry from equality, but it is much less unequal than the differences between rich and poor countries.

disparity in income among countries, the middle line shows the Lorenz curve of income distribution among people in the United States. It is much closer to equality than the world distribution.

Figures of the kind shown in Table 44–1 cannot be taken as accurate down to the last $100.[2] Nevertheless, the *development gap*—the discrepancy between the standards of living in countries at the two ends of the distribution—is very real and very large.

The consequences of underdevelopment

The human consequences of very low income levels can be severe. Someone studying the effect of variations in rainfall would find that for a rich country such as the United States, these variations would be reflected in farm output and farm income: for each inch of rainfall below some critical amount, farm output and income would vary in a regular way. In poor countries such as Zaire and India, variations in rainfall are reflected in the death rate. Indeed, many live so close to the subsistence level that slight fluctuations in the food supply bring death by starvation to large numbers. Other less dramatic characteristics of poverty include inadequate diet, poor health, low life expectancy, illiteracy, and—very important—an attitude of helpless resignation to the caprice of nature.

The fact that fluctuations that are measured in dollars in rich countries are often measured in lives in poor countries makes the problems of economic growth very much more press-

[2] There are many problems involved in comparing national incomes across countries. For one example, home-grown food is vitally important to living standards in underdeveloped countries, yet it is excluded—or at best imperfectly included—in the national income statistics of most countries. So is a warm climate. Such food and climate make it possible to survive on an income of $150 per year in Nigeria, although that would be quite impossible in most parts of the United States and Canada. But even though living on $150 per person per year in Nigeria is not like living on $150 in Washington, D.C., there is no doubt that the average Nigerian is at a low level of real income compared to an average American.

Table 44–1 Income and population differences among groups of countries, 1974

CLASSIFICATION (BASED ON GNP PER CAPITA IN 1974 U.S. DOLLARS)	Number of countries (1)	GNP (billions) (2)	Population (millions) (3)	GNP per capita (4)	PERCENTAGE OF THE WORLDS'		GROWTH RATE[a] (7)
					GNP (5)	Population (6)	
I Less than $175	26	$ 147	1,099	$ 134	2.7	28.6	1.2
II $175–349	20	320	1,075	298	5.9	28.0	3.5
III $350–699	27	95	191	497	1.7	5.0	3.1
IV $700–1399	20	384	378	1,016	7.0	9.8	3.8
V $1400–2799	16	910	406	2,241	16.6	10.6	3.9
VI $2800–5599	15	1,445	361	4,003	26.4	9.4	4.7
VII $5600 or more	11	2,172	331	6,562	39.7	8.6	3.0
Totals	135	$5,473	3,841	$1,425	100.0	100.0	

Source: International Bank for Reconstruction and Development, Economics and Social Data Division, *World Atlas 1976,* and unpublished data.

[a] Average annual percentage rate of growth of GNP per capita, 1960–1974.

Over half of the world's population live in poverty: many of the very poorest are in countries which have the lowest growth rates and thus fall ever farther behind. The unequal distribution of the world's income is shown in columns 5 and 6. Groups I–III, with over 60 percent of the world's population, earn only 10 percent of world income. Groups VI–VII, with 18 percent of the world's population, earn 66 percent of world income. Column 7 shows that the poorer countries are not closing the gap in income between rich and poor countries.

ing in poor countries than in rich ones, and reformers in underdeveloped countries often feel a sense of urgency not felt by their counterparts in rich countries. Many persons now living at the bare subsistence margin can look forward to improvements in their lot only if their country experiences an immediate and very rapid rate of economic growth. Yet, as the first row of Table 44–1 shows, the development gap for the very poorest countries has been widening. As will be seen, this is both an output problem and a population problem.

Incentives for development

Obviously "underdevelopment" is nothing new in the world. Concern with it as a possibly remediable condition, however, is recent. It has become a compelling policy concern only within the last half-century. Probably the dominant reason for this newfound concern has been the extraordinary success of planned programs of "crash" development of which the Soviet experience is the most remarkable (see Chapter 45) and the Chinese the most recent. Leaders in other countries ask, If they can do it, why not us?

"Demonstration effects" should not be underestimated. It has been said that the real secret of the atomic bomb was that it *could* be made, not how. Much the same is true of economic development. In the last quarter-century there have been many examples of rapid and more or less planned economic development. In a world that each year is made smaller by communication and transportation improvements, these developments are visible to everyone. It is bad enough to be poor, but to be poor when others are escaping poverty is intolerable. Suddenly people see that it is possible to achieve better things for themselves and their children, and they seek them.

A second push toward development has come from the developed countries which have fostered policies to aid underdeveloped countries. Some of these efforts, such as the Point Four program of the United States, have been ventures of a single developed country; others have been handled through such international organizations as the World Bank.

In any event, both from the inside and the outside have come pressures for faster economic development and a search for the causes of underdevelopment and techniques for overcoming them.

The meaning and measure of underdevelopment

Thus far the focus has been on per capita income as a measure of economic development. Is this the right measure? Clearly it is a reasonable measure of a people's command over purchasing power. It shows unmistakably that the countries classified in Table 44–1 in groups I, II, and III are desperately poor by U.S. standards. If one wishes to look instead at *developing* (i.e., growing) countries, it seems clear from comparative growth rates that countries in groups IV, V, and VI are undergoing more rapid growth than either the poorer countries in groups I, II, and III or the richer countries in group VII.[3]

[3] An unfortunate tendency of some politicians and economists is to use the terms "underdeveloped" and "developing" interchangeably, with the latter regarded as a more acceptable euphemism for *poor*. Clearly, *level* of income and *rate of change* are different things. Some contemporary commentators are distinguishing "developing nations" as a so-called third world and "economically troubled states" as a fourth world in which low levels of income are accompanied by little or no growth. (The first world in this vocabulary is the noncommunist industrialized nations; the second world, the USSR and the industrialized communist nations.)

But low per capita income can have many different causes. It could result either from the failure of a country to utilize its abundant natural resources or from the lack of resources to use. It may result from backwardness (lack of education and training, for example) of its people or from being underpopulated. Thus there are many dimensions to a country's stage of development, and many measures can be used: income per head, the percentage of resources unexploited, capital per head, savings per head, amount of "social capital" (i.e., roads, railroads, schools), and the degree of education of the working classes, to name a few.

Finding solutions to real problems is more important than arguing about definitions. Most often the "problem of underdeveloped countries" concerns their desire to overcome low levels of income by achieving a more rapid rate of growth. Obviously, the appropriate policies to foster development will be different in different cases. Raising the income of a country that has low capital per head, much unemployed labor, but few unexploited natural resources (Pakistan, say) is likely to require policies very different from those required to raise the income of a country such as Australia, which is underpopulated and has many unexploited natural resources. In some countries, India, Kenya, and Colombia, for example, limitation of population growth is probably *the* key element in promoting growth. In Greece, which has no problem of overpopulation, such policies are of no importance.

Barriers to economic development

If income per head is taken as a crude index of the level of economic development, a country may develop by any set of devices that causes its aggregate income to grow faster than its population. A growing population, a shortage of natural resources, or inefficiency in the way resources are used can each be an important barrier to development.

POPULATION GROWTH

Today many of the countries of the world have more national income, but they also have more mouths to feed. Thus their standard of living is no higher than it was a hundred or even a thousand years ago. The average Cambodian and the rural Ethiopian are as hungry as their great-grandparents were. The growth problem faced by these countries is how to get off the treadmill and onto the escalator. Will modest gains in the size of the capital stock eventually add up to enough to produce sustained growth? Not necessarily; it is the amount of output *per person* that determines whether living standards will rise, and there may be a race between output and population.

Population growth is a central problem of economic development. If population expands as fast as the national income, then per capita income will not increase. If population does expand rapidly, a country may make a great effort to raise the quantity of capital only to find that a corresponding rise in population has occurred, so that the net effect of its "growth policy" is that a larger population is now maintained at the original low standard of living. Much of the problem of the very poorest countries is due to population growth. They have made appreciable gains in income, but much of it has been eaten up (literally) by the increasing population. This is illustrated in Table 44–2.

The population problem has led economists to talk about the "critical minimum effort" that is required not merely to increase capital but to increase it fast enough so that the increase in output outraces the increase in population. The problem arises because population size is not independent of the level of income. If population control is left to nature, nature solves it in a cruel way. Population increases until many are forced to live at a subsistence level; further population growth is halted by famine, pestilence, and plague. This grim situation was perceived early in the history of economics by Thomas Malthus. In

Table 44–2   The relation of population growth in per capita GNP, 1960–1974 (percentages)

CLASSIFICATION OF COUNTRIES (GNP PER CAPITA, 1974 U.S. DOLLARS)			AVERAGE ANNUAL RATE OF GROWTH OF:			POPULATION GROWTH AS PERCENTAGE OF REAL GNP GROWTH
Group*a*	Income level	Percentage of population	Real GNP	Population	Real GNP per capita	
I	less than $175	28.6	3.6	2.4	1.2	66
II–IV	$175–1399	42.8	5.9	2.1	3.8	36
V–VII	over $1400	28.6	4.7	1.1	3.6	24

Source: International Bank for Reconstruction and Development, Economics and Social Data Division, *World Atlas 1976,* and unpublished data.

a Groups are defined in Table 44–1.

Growth in per capita real income depends upon the difference between growth rates of real national income and of population. The very poorest countries have *both* a relatively low growth rate of income and a relatively high growth rate of population. The middle group shows rising living standards despite large population growth by virtue of a high growth rate of income. The wealthiest countries owe much of their growth in living standards to a low rate of population increase.

Figure 44–2 World population growth

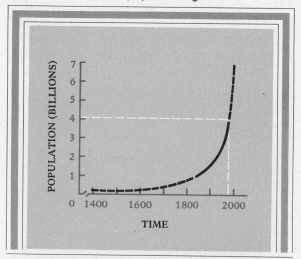

The current growth in the world's population is little short of explosive. The solid line reflects present measurements. The dashed line involves projections from observed trends. It took about 50,000 years from the emergence of modern human beings for the world's population to reach 1 billion. It took 100 years to add a second billion, 30 years to add the third billion, and 15 years to add the fourth billion. If present trends continue, the 1975 population of 4 billion will be doubled in 30 years.

some ways, the population problem is more severe today than it was even a generation ago because advances in medicine and in public health have brought sharp and sudden decreases in death rates. It is ironic that much of the compassion for the poor and underprivileged people of the world has traditionally taken the form of improving their health, thereby doing little to avert their poverty. We laud the medical missionaries who brought modern medicine to the savages, but the elimination of malaria has doubled the rate of population growth in Sri Lanka. Cholera, once a killer, is now largely under control. No one

would argue against controlling disease, but other things must also be done if the child who survives the infectious illnesses of infancy is not to die of starvation in early adulthood. In Mexico today the population is growing at a rate of more than 3 percent per year, and thus a rise in production of more than 3 percent per year is required for Mexico to "break even."

Figure 44–2 illustrates actual and projected population growth in the world today. The population problem is not limited to underdeveloped countries, but about seven-eighths of the expected growth in the world's population is in Africa, Asia, and Latin America, areas where underdevelopment is the rule rather than the exception.

RESOURCE LIMITATIONS

A country that has ample fertile land and a large supply of easily developed resources will find growth in income easier to achieve than one that is poorly endowed by nature with such resources. Kuwait has an income per capita above that of the United States, by the accident that it sits on top of the world's greatest known oil field. Lack of oil proved a devastating blow to many of the least developed countries when the OPEC cartel quadrupled oil prices during the early 1970s. Without oil their development efforts would be crippled; but to buy oil took too much of their scarce foreign exchange. Unlike many developed countries, which also bought oil, the least-developed countries were not markets in which the oil producers spent their new wealth.

Natural resource endowments are often the product of man as well as of nature. In fact, a nation's supplies of land and natural resources are often readily expandable in their effective use, if not in their total quantity. Badly fragmented land holdings may result from a dowry or inheritance system and thus limit the productivity of a nation. Lands left idle because of a lack of irrigation or spoiled by excessive irrigation or lack of crop rotation are well-known examples of barriers to development. Ignorance is another. The nations of the Middle East sat through recorded history alongside the Dead Sea without realizing that it was a substantial source of potash. Not until after World War I were these resources utilized; now they provide Israel with raw materials for its rapidly growing fertilizer and chemical industries.

Financial capital

Investment plays a vital role in economic growth, as was seen in Chapter 43. It may take as much as $10 of capital to increase full-employment national income by $1 per year. If this is so, it will take $58 *billion* of capital to raise average income per year by $100 in a country of 58 million people such as Mexico. Fifty-eight billion dollars is a lot of money in any country, but it is roughly as much as the whole GNP of Mexico. The shortage of investment funds is almost always a bottleneck on the road to development.

One source of financial capital is the savings of households and firms. The particular importance of banks and banking in underdeveloped or developing economies is that if they do not function well and smoothly, the link between private saving and investment may be broken and the problem of finding funds for investment greatly intensified.

Reliance on deposit money and on the good faith of bankers is limited to a small fraction of the world's economies. Many people in undeveloped economies do not trust banks, and they will therefore either not maintain deposits or periodically panic, draw them out and seek security for their money in mattresses, in gold, or in real estate. The tendency to flee from money is made stronger when, as in recent years, a sharp inflation threatens the value of money holdings. When this happens, increases in savings do not become available

for investment in productive capacity. If banks cannot count on their deposits being left in the banking system, they cannot engage in the multiple expansion of credit. Thus distrust of banks and of deposit money may impede economic development, even if private individuals are willing to refrain from current consumption.

Social-overhead capital

The progress of economic development is reflected in the increasing flow of goods and services from a nation's farms and factories to its households. But the ability to sustain and expand these flows depends on many supporting services, particularly transportation and communications, which are sometimes called the "infrastructure" of the economy. Their development is largely left for the government to accomplish.

Roads, bridges, railroads, and harbors are needed to transport people, materials, and finished goods. The most dramatic confirmation of their importance is in wartime, when belligerents always place high priority on destroying each other's transportation facilities.

Reasonable phone and postal services, water supply, and sanitation are also essential to economic development. The absence, whatever the reason, of a dependable infrastructure can impose severe barriers to economic development.

Human capital

A well-developed entrepreneurial class of persons motivated and trained to organize resources for efficient production is often lacking in underdeveloped countries. This lack may be a heritage of a colonial system that gave the local population no opportunity to develop; it may result from the fact that managerial positions are awarded on the basis of family status or political patronage; it may reflect the presence of economic or cultural attitudes that do not favor acquisition of wealth by organizing productive activities; or it may simply be due to the nonexistence of the quantity or quality of education or training that is required.

Poor health is likewise a source of inadequate resources. Less time is lost and more effective effort is expended when the labor force is healthy than when it is not. The economic analysis of medical advances is a very young field, however, and there is a great deal to learn about the quantitative importance of such gains.

INEFFICIENCY IN THE USE OF RESOURCES

Low levels of income and slower than necessary growth rates may result from inefficient use of resources as well as from scarcity of key resources.

Allocative inefficiency and X-inefficiency

It is useful to distinguish between two kinds of inefficiency. A man-hour of labor would be used inefficiently, for example, if a laborer was too hungry to concentrate on his or her task. It would also be used inefficiently if the worker, even though working at top efficiency, was engaged in making a product that no one wanted. Using society's resources to make the wrong products is an example of **allocative inefficiency.** In terms of the production-possibility boundary encountered in Chapter 1, allocative inefficiency represents operation at the wrong place on the boundary. If 2 tons of coal and 50 man-hours of labor are being used to make steel in the most efficient way, this may, nevertheless, be inefficient if this coal and labor could produce more national income by making electric power to be used to make aluminum. Allocative inefficiency will arise if the signals to which people respond are distorted—both monopoly and tariffs are commonly cited sources of distortions—or if market imperfections prevent resources moving to their best uses.

A second kind of inefficiency has come to be called X-inefficiency, following Professor Harvey Leibenstein. **X-inefficiency** arises whenever resources are used in such a way that even if they are making the right product, they are doing so less productively than is possible. If a worker, for example, is debilitated by disease, unmotivated, or inhibited by taboos, a man-hour of his labor may be singularly unproductive, even in its best use. Similarly, land or coal may be poorly used because of ignorance, indifference, or poor technology.

The distinction between allocative inefficiency and X-inefficiency is illustrated in Figure 44-3. While the two kinds of inefficiency can occur simultaneously, X-inefficiency is now believed to be far more important than allocative inefficiency in accounting for both the low levels of income and the difficulties in development of the less developed countries.

Sources of X-inefficiency

Both inadequate education and poor health may be important sources of X-inefficiency. As modern techniques are introduced, a large rise in the educational standards of the work force is necessary. A worker who cannot read or write or do simple calculations will be much less efficient in many jobs than one who can. A manager trained in modern methods of bookkeeping, inventory control, and personnel management is likely to be much more effective in getting the most output from a given input than one who is ignorant of these techniques.

Traditions, institutions, and habitual ways of doing business vary among societies, and not all are equally conducive to productivity. Often personal considerations of family, of past favors, or of traditional friendship or enmity are more important than market signals in explaining behavior. One may find a too-small firm struggling to survive against a larger rival and learn that the owner prefers to stay small rather than expand because expansion would require use of nonfamily capital or leadership. To avoid paying too harsh a competitive price for built-in inefficiency, the firms' owners may then spend half their energies in an attempt to influence the government to prevent larger firms from being formed or to try to secure restrictions on the sale of output—and they may well succeed. Such behavior is very likely to inhibit economic growth.

Whether a society's customs reflect cherished values or only such things as residual influences of a colonial history or an oligarchical political structure is important to the policy makers who must decide whether the cost in terms of efficiency should be paid. In any case, cultural attitudes are not easily changed. If people believe that who your father is is more important than what you do, it may take a generation to persuade employers to change their attitudes and another generation to persuade workers that things have changed. Structuring incentives is a widely used form of policy action in market-oriented economies, but this may be harder to do in a personalistic society than in a market economy. If people habitually bribe the tax collector instead of paying taxes, they will not be likely to respond to policies that are supposed to work by raising or lowering taxes. All that will change is the size of the bribe.

There is a lively current debate on how much to make of the significance of differing cultural attitudes. A widely held hypothesis is that traditional and cultural considerations dominate peasant societies to the exclusion of economic responses. While some recent research suggests that allocative inefficiency may be relatively small, many economists still believe that cultural considerations lead to massive X-inefficiency because managerial personnel are recruited from the wealthy, not the talented, and because there is no basic tradition that one ought to work hard.

Advocates of the position that cultural considerations play a major role in problems of developed countries point to what is called

Figure 44–3 Allocative versus *X*-inefficiency

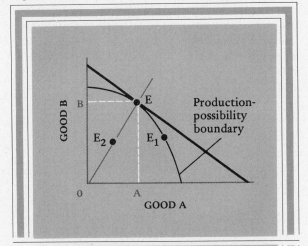

Allocative inefficiency places the society at the wrong point on its production-possibility boundary, while *X*-inefficiency places the society inside its boundary. The thinner black curve represents a society's production possibilities between two goods, A and B. The slope of the thicker black line represents the opportunity cost of good B in terms of good A. The efficient output of A and B is represented at point E. E_1 is inefficient in the allocative sense: Society is operating on its production-possibility boundary but producing too much A and too little B for the given opportunity cost. In contrast, at E_2 the proportions of B and A are the same as at E, but the society is operating within its boundary. This is *X*-inefficiency.

the *technology gap*—the fact that the same techniques of production prove less productive in underdeveloped countries than in developed ones. Achieving rapid growth should be easier in one respect for an underdeveloped than for a developed country. More modern techniques of production and distribution can be introduced without spending vast sums on research and development. An underdeveloped country can go a very long way merely by adapting techniques already in use in more developed countries.[4] But this requires imagination, informed personnel, an expansionary view of the future, and the motivation on the part of someone to do so. If these are lacking, the result will be to use a less efficient technology than is necessary or to use a given technique less productively than it is used in other countries.

Several empirical studies have shown enormous differences in productivity from country to country in particular industries using the same technologies of production. In some cases, great increases in productivity have been achieved simply by changing incentive systems. These facts suggest a large quantitative importance to X-inefficiency and a large payoff to overcoming it.

Fostering economic development

Economic development policy involves identifying the particular barriers to the level and kind of development desired and then devising policies to overcome them. Planners can seek funds for investment, and they can attempt to identify cultural, legal, social, and psychological barriers to growth. They can undertake the programs of education, legal reform, resource development, negotiation of trade treaties, or actual investment that smooth the way to more rapid growth. All of this is more easily said than done. Further, as the dozens of "development missions" sent out by the World Bank and other international, national, and private agencies have discovered, the problems and strategies vary greatly from country to country. Economic

development as a field of economic expertise is in its infancy. A few choices seem sufficiently pervasive that it is worth mentioning them here.

PLANNING OR LAISSEZ FAIRE?

How much government control over the economy is necessary and desirable? Practically every shade of opinion from "The only way to grow is to get the government's dead hand out of everything" to "The only way to grow is to get a fully planned, centrally controlled economy" has been seriously advocated. Such extreme views are easily refuted by factual evidence. Many economies have grown with very little government assistance; perhaps Great Britain and Holland are the best examples. Others, such as the Soviet Union and Poland, have sustained growth with a high degree of centralized control. In other countries, there is almost every conceivable mix of government and private initiative in the growth process.

What sense can be made of these apparently conflicting historical precedents? Probably the most satisfactory answer is that the appropriate action depends on the circumstances presently ruling in the country. Ineffective governments may have been interfering with the economy to the point of discouraging private initiative, in which case growth may well be enhanced by a reduction in government control over the economy. In other cases, where major quantities of social capital are needed or where existing institutional arrangements such as land tenure are harmful to growth, active intervention by the central authorities—planning, as it is called—may be essential to encourage growth. There are many possible mixes between state and private initiative that have been used successfully at various times and places. On the question of what is the best mix at a particular time and in a particular place, there is likely to be much disagreement.

---

[4] We use the term "adapting" rather than "copying" because an underdeveloped country will often have resource endowments, cultural traditions, and institutional arrangements different from those of a developed one and thus must or should use different techniques.

Government intervention and growth

The active intervention of the government in the management of a country's economy rests upon the real or alleged failure of the market forces to produce satisfactory results. The major appeal of such intervention is that it can accelerate the pace of economic development and change its direction.

Affecting the rate of growth. Any one of the barriers to development may be lowered by enlightened actions of the government. Consider, for example, the way that central authorities might seek to mitigate a shortage of investment funds. In a fully employed free-market economy, investment is influenced by the quantity of savings households and firms make, and thus the division of resources between consumption and saving is one determinant of the rate of growth.

When living standards are low, people have urgent uses for their current income. If savings decisions are left to individual determination, savings tend to be low, and this is an impediment to investment and growth. In a variety of ways, central authorities can intervene and force people to save more than they otherwise would have. Such compulsory saving has been one of the main aims of most of the "plans" of Communist governments. The justification offered by the planner for this compulsory sacrifice of the living standards of present generations for the benefit of future ones is that without it growth would be slow or nonexistent, inflicting a low living standard on all future generations.

The goal of the five-year plans of Russia, Poland, and more recently China is to raise savings and thus lower current consumption below what it would be, given complete freedom of choice. Extra savings may be the subject of planning even in less centrally controlled societies through tax incentives and monetary policies. The object is the same: increasing investment in order to increase growth, and thus to make future generations better off.

Affecting the direction of development. Although the rate of development is important and a desire to increase it might by itself lead to planning, planners are seldom content merely to do everything they can to achieve a more rapid growth rate. This is because they are aware that, as planners, they can choose among *alternative* plans of growth that hold different implications for their country's future. There may be both economic and non-economic reasons for choosing a different pattern of growth than the free market would provide. One role of planning is to direct growth in a different direction, one that society (or the group of planners) prefers.

One example concerns Greece, which in the period 1958–1965 was achieving rapid growth in income per capita largely because of a booming tourist trade and the emigration of many young Greeks to West Germany to work in factories there. The emigrants had been earning incomes in Greece that were substantially below the Greek average, and their remittances home to their families increased both domestic income and foreign exchange reserves. Although it was helpful to the Greek rate of growth to continue to rely on tourism and emigration as bulwarks of the economy, this policy threatened an image of life that visualized "Greece for the Greeks." Even at the prospect of some loss in growth, Greek planners recommended the restriction of emigration, the moderation of the size of the tourist role in the economy, and the development of new industry for the Greek economy.

EDUCATIONAL POLICY

Most studies of underdeveloped countries suggest that undereducation of various kinds is a serious barrier to development and urge increased expenditures on education. This poses a choice of whether to spend these educational funds on erasing illiteracy and increasing the level of mass education or on training a small cadre of scientifically and technically trained specialists. The problem is serious because education of any kind is very expensive and does not pay off quickly. Basic education requires a large investment in school building, in teacher training, and curriculum revision that will result in visible change in the level of education only after ten or more years and even less payoff to the economy in that time span in terms of greater productivity. Thus, with many urgent demands, the opportunity cost of such expenditures always seems high. Yet it is essential to make them *sometime* because the gains will be critical to economic development a generation later.

Many, perhaps most, developing countries have put a large fraction of their educational resources into training a small number of highly educated men and women—often by sending them abroad for periods of advanced study—because the tangible results of a few hundred doctors or engineers or Ph.D.s are relatively more visible than the results from raising the school-leaving age by a year or two, say, from age 10 to age 12. It is not yet clear whether this policy pays off, but it is clear that there are some drawbacks to it. Many of this educated elite are recruited from the privileged classes on the basis of family position, not merit; many regard their education as the passport to a new aristocracy rather than as a mandate to serve their fellow citizens; and, in addition, an appreciable fraction emigrate to countries where their newly acquired skills bring higher pay than at home. Of those who come home, many seek the security of a government job, which they may utilize merely to advance their own status in what is sometimes a self-serving and unproductive bureaucracy.

POPULATION CONTROL

The race between population and income has been a dominant feature of many underdeveloped countries. There are only two possible ways for a country to win this race. One is to make such a massive push that it achieves a growth rate well in excess of the rate of population growth. The second is to control population growth. The problem *can* be solved by restricting population growth. This is not a matter of serious debate, although the means of restricting it are, for there are considerations of religion, custom, and education involved.

Positive economics cannot decide whether population control is morally good or bad, but it can describe the consequences of any choice made. Both Sweden and Venezuela have death rates of about 10 per thousand population per year. The birth rate in Sweden is 14; in Venezuela it is 42. While the causes of variations in birth rates are complex, they have inescapable economic consequences. Thus in Venezuela the net increase of population per year is 32 per thousand (3.2 percent), but it is only 4 per thousand (0.4 percent) in Sweden. If each country achieved an overall rate of growth of production of 3 percent per year, Sweden would be increasing her living standards by 2.6 percent per year while Venezuela would be lowering hers by 0.2 percent per year. In 1975, Sweden's income per capita ($7,700) was three and one-half times as high as Venezuela's ($2,200)—and Venezuela is the wealthiest country in South and Central America. (This compares with the U.S. figure of about $7,000 and with the figure for India of about $150.) The gap will widen rapidly if present population trends continue.

Different countries have taken very different policy positions. China in 1954 initiated a national program of population control by promoting later marriages and exhorting parents both to have fewer children and to value daughters as well as sons. It has worked to a remarkable degree, and today the crude birth rate is about 20 per thousand, down from over 30 per thousand two decades ago. Kenya, with a birth rate of 50 per thousand, has rejected any serious national policy of population control.

ACQUIRING CAPITAL

A country can get funds for investment in three distinct ways: from the savings (voluntary or forced) of its domestic households and firms, by loans or investment from abroad, or by contributions from foreigners.

Capital from domestic saving: the vicious circle of poverty

If capital is to be created at home by the country's own efforts, it is necessary to divert resources from the production of goods for current consumption. This requires a cut in present living standards. If living standards are already virtually at the subsistence level, such a diversion will be difficult. At best, it will be possible to reallocate only a small proportion of resources to the production of capital goods. Such a situation is often described as the *vicious circle of poverty:* Because a country has little capital per head, it is poor; because it is poor, it can devote only a few resources to creating new capital rather than producing goods for immediate consumption; because little new capital can be produced, capital per head remains low, the country remains poor. France and the Soviet Union are notable examples of countries that have broken this vicious circle by their own efforts, France slowly over centuries and Russia rapidly over decades.

Imported capital

Another way of accumulating the capital needed for growth is to borrow it from abroad. If a poor country, A, borrows from a rich country, B, it can use the borrowed funds to purchase capital goods produced in B. Country A thus accumulates capital and needs to cut its current output of consumption goods only to pay interest on its loans. As the new capital begins to add to current production, it becomes easier to pay the interest on the loan and also to begin to repay the principal out of the increase in output. Thus income can be raised immediately and the major sacrifice postponed until later, when part of the increased income that might have been used to raise domestic consumption is used to pay off the loan. This method has the great advantage of allowing a poor country to have an initial increase in capital goods far greater than it could possibly have created by diverting its own resources from consumption industries.

However, many countries, developed or undeveloped, are suspicious of foreign capital for fear that the foreign investor will gain control over their industries or their government. The extent of foreign control depends on the form that foreign capital takes. If the foreigners buy bonds in domestic companies, they do not own or control anything; if they buy common stocks, they own part or all of the company; if they subsidize a government, they may feel justified in exacting political commitments. Whether foreign ownership of one's industries carries political disadvantages is a subject of debate. In Canada, for example, there has been a rising political opposition to having so much of Canadian industry owned by U.S. nationals who are presumably more open to pressure from U.S. central authorities than from Canadian authorities.

The economic differences, however, are quite clear. Accumulating a given amount of capital by domestic saving and accumulating it by foreign borrowing lead to different time paths of growth in living standards. The domestic method requires greater current sacrifice, but it pays a higher return later; foreign financing requires minimal present sacrifices, but it involves the commitment to hold living standards below what they might otherwise be later because of payments of interest to the foreign investors.

If both ways of financing are equally possible, the choice between them raises an important intergenerational question: To what extent should the sacrifices required to pay for growth be met now rather than ten years from now? One suspects that, political considerations aside, most people would prefer to postpone the cost by using borrowed capital.

Getting foreign capital is easier said than done in the early stages of development. America and Canada were once underdeveloped in the sense of being underpopulated and having many unused resources, but they were latent giants that held promise of rich returns to foreign investors. It is harder to see similar investment opportunities in Pakistan, say, where overpopulation has been a problem for centuries and where the soil is severely damaged by centuries of irrigation without proper drainage. The ability of such a country to borrow from private sources is small. Foreign capital is playing a role, but it is capital provided by foreign governments and international agencies, not by private investors.

Contributed capital

From the point of view of the receiving country, contributed capital would seem to be ideal. It has the advantage of enabling the country to shift to more rapid growth without either sacrificing consumption now or having to repay later. Investment funds for development are being received today by underdeveloped countries from the governments of the more developed countries acting both unilaterally (as in the U.S. Agency for International Development and a similar Soviet program) and through international agencies such as the World Bank and the Export-Import Bank.

Contributed capital has played a significant role in post-World War II economic development. For example, American foreign-aid expenditures in the decade after the war were $90 billion, and even today they amount to more than $3 billion per year. Much, though not all of this, was contributed capital. While in one sense $3 billion may seem small because it is less than one-quarter of 1 percent of our GNP and only a small fraction of our military expenditures, it is very important from the viewpoint of the recipients. The $3 billion amounts to more than 1 percent of the GNP of the two billion people who live in the most underdeveloped nations of the world.

The Soviet Union too has given substantial aid to less-developed countries. Russian aid to China in the 1950s was critical to that country's development of heavy industry. In addition to funds, the USSR transported capital in the form of over 150 complete plants and sent thousands of technician specialists to China to help plan, build, and run factories. China today is itself a significant donor to a few ideologically sympathetic countries, including Tanzania and Albania.

There is some significant resistance to accepting aid. The slogan "Trade Not Aid" reflected political opposition to U.S. economic aid in certain receiving countries. Yugoslavia turned down much aid proffered by the Soviets after 1948 and China has accepted no foreign aid since 1960. In 1975 Colombia made the decision to forego further U.S. aid on the grounds that "it breeds an unhealthy economic dependency." The primary explanation of this attitude lies in the country's noneconomic goals. It may suspect the motives of the givers and fear that hidden strings may be attached to the offer. Independent countries prize their independence and want to avoid either the fact or the appearance of being satellites. Pride—a desire to be beholden to no one—is also a factor. Economists cannot say that these fears and aspirations are either foolish or unworthy; they can only note that they do have a cost, for there is no doubt that economically it is better to receive than to give.

The motivations behind international giving have themselves become the subject of debate. Do developed nations give aid for humanitarian reasons, because it serves their political objectives, or because it is economically self-serving? Obviously all three can play a role, but which motive dominates?

Compassion versus political motivation. The Scandinavian Nobel Prize winning economist Gunnar Myrdal has argued that humanitarian considerations have played a large role. The evidence for the existence of humanitarian motives is, in part, the success of voluntary appeals in developed countries for food, funds, and clothes for persons in stricken areas of the world. Although this is not a new concern, as per capita incomes have risen in the Western world, so have contributions, private as well as public. It is the policy of the governments of most of the so-called Western democracies to devote some resources to alleviating poverty throughout the world.

Professor Edward S. Mason, among others, has argued that such aid as is given can be best understood by looking to political and security motives. He points to the substantial Congressional preference for military assistance over economic assistance, the denial of aid to countries such as Sri Lanka that traded with Communist countries, the fostering of Tito's Yugoslavia *because of* its anti-Soviet stand—all of which bespeak a strong political motive.

Patterns of development

Because planning can affect the direction of development as well as its rate, a country's economic planners face hard choices. To what extent should a developing country pursue the **balanced growth policy** of pushing expansion in all sectors of the economy rather than the **unbalanced growth policy** of pushing specialization in certain sectors? How should it decide how much effort to devote to increasing agricultural production, needed to feed its masses, and how much role to the industrialization that might change its role in the world economy? If it is to push industrialization, what commodities should it manufacture—those for which there is a large export market or those that will free it from the need to import?

COMPARATIVE ADVANTAGE: THE CASE FOR UNBALANCED GROWTH

The principle of comparative advantage provides the traditional case for the desirability of unbalanced growth. By specializing in producing those products in which it has the greatest comparative advantage, the country can achieve the most rapid growth in the short run. Since its potential for growth is certainly not the same in all sectors of the economy, balanced growth (pursued to the extreme of equal growth in all sectors) would result in a lower living standard than would result from some degree of specialization accompanied by increased international trade.

These are cogent reasons in favor of *some* specialization. China, for example, has a surplus of labor and a shortage of machinery. It specializes in producing rice (which uses much labor) and exports some of its rice crop in return for wheat (which requires more machinery and less labor than rice in production). But specialization involves risks, and these risks may be worth reducing even at the loss of some income. Specialization sometimes involves concentrating one's production in one or a few products. This makes the economy highly vulnerable to cyclical fluctuations in world demand and supply. When wheat is scarce and rice is cheap on world markets the Chinese economy suffers. Even more seriously, if technological or taste changes render a product partially or wholly obsolete, the country can face a major calamity for generations. Just as individual firms and regions may become overspecialized, so too may countries.

Which comparative advantages?

Unplanned growth will usually tend to exploit the country's *present* comparative advantages. A planned economy, through the planners, may well choose a pattern of growth that involves changing the country's *future* comparative advantage. One reason for doing so is the belief that the planners can evaluate the future more accurately than the countless individuals whose decisions determine market prices. Thus the distinguished Latin American economist Raúl Prebisch argues that underdeveloped countries are overspecialized in production of agricultural commodities that are sure to enjoy steadily worsening terms of trade relative to manufacturing outputs. Prebisch believes that current market prices fail to anticipate fully this worsening in the terms of trade for agriculture and thus the planners should intervene and shift the country out of what is sure to be an overreliance on agriculture in the long run.

Whether or not Prebisch is correct in the particular bias he identifies,[5] his concern is an example of a most important general point:

A country need not passively accept its current comparative advantages.

Many skills can be acquired, and the fostering of an apparently uneconomic domestic industry may, by changing the characteristics of the labor force, develop a comparative advantage in that line of production. The Japanese had no visible comparative advantage in any industrial skill when Commodore Matthew Perry opened that feudal country to Western influence in 1854, but they became a major industrial power by the end of the century. Soviet planners in the 1920s and 1930s chose to create an industrial economy out of a predominantly agricultural one and succeeded in vastly changing the mix between agriculture and industry in a single generation (see Chapter 45). These illustrations should serve

as cogent reminders that an excessive reliance on current comparative advantage may lead to an excessive defense of the status quo in the pattern of international specialization.

AGRICULTURAL DEVELOPMENT VERSUS INDUSTRIALIZATION

Visualize a country (such as Pakistan or India) with a very low level of income, a large and growing population, a historical reliance on agricultural production, and a chronic balance-of-payments problem. Suppose that its planners have reduced the myriad choices before them to a choice among three basic development strategies:

1. The country might choose to devote a major portion of its resources to stimulating agricultural production, say, by mechanizing its farms, irrigating land, and utilizing new seeds and fertilizers. If successful in these attempts, it might stave off the specter of starvation for its current population and even develop an excess over its current needs that would be available for export. This food surplus might earn foreign exchange that could be used to buy needed imports.

2. The country might attempt to reduce its reliance on foreign trade by using its resources to produce domestic substitutes for the goods it presently imports. If successful, it would reduce its imports and in that way improve its balance-of-payments deficit.

3. The country might seek to develop industrial export industries quickly in order to sell manufactured goods to the rest of the world. Like the previous strategy, this one contemplates industrialization, but with the intent of increasing, not decreasing, its foreign trade.

Any one of these strategies (or any combination of them), if successful, could lead to development. Each has been tried, and each has its advocates. None is without some successes, but none is without difficulties.

---

[5] A growing world food shortage and rising relative prices of food stuff may render some aspects of Prebisch's thesis obsolete as the terms of trade turn in favor of food producing countries, as they already have toward many raw material producing countries.

Agricultural development and the "green revolution"

India, Pakistan, and Taiwan, along with other Asian countries, have achieved dramatic results by the application of new technology —and particularly new seed—to agricultural production. Increases of up to 50 percent in grain production have been achieved, and it has been estimated that with adequate supplies of water, pesticides, fertilizers, and modern equipment, production could be doubled or even tripled. This has been labeled the "green revolution." When the Nobel Prize Committee gave the 1970 *peace* prize to the American plant pathologist Norman Borlaug, it recognized the potential importance of these developments in alleviating, for at least a generation, the shortage of food that the population explosion was expected to bring.

The possibilities of achieving such dramatic gains in agricultural output may seem almost irresistible at first glance, but many economists think they should be resisted—and they point to a series of problems.[6] One problem is that a vast amount of resources is required to irrigate land and mechanize production, and these resources alternatively could provide industrial development and industrial employment opportunities. Thus there is a clear opportunity cost. Critics of the agricultural strategy argue that the search for a generation free from starvation will provide at best only a temporary solution because population will surely expand to meet the food supply. Instead, they argue, underdeveloped countries should start at once to reduce their dependence on agriculture. Let someone else grow the food; industrialization should not be delayed.

A second problem with the agricultural strategy is that the great increases in world production of wheat, rice, and other agricultural commodities that the "green revolution" makes possible could depress their prices and not lead to increased earnings from exports. What one agricultural country can do, so can others, and there may well be a glut on world markets.

A third problem with the agricultural-development strategy has arisen (most sharply in India and Pakistan) where increasing agricultural output has been accompanied by decreasing labor requirements in agricultural production without any compensating increase in employment opportunities elsewhere in the economy. Requirements of labor per acre have dropped by one-half. Millions of tenant farmers—and their bullocks—have been evicted from their tenant holdings by owners who are buying tractors to replace them. Many have found no other work and are wandering around the country vainly seeking it. In other areas, unemployment is disguised rather than visible, but it is no less real. If 10 people work full time on a farm because they are all being supported by it and have nothing better to do, even though the same output could be achieved by only 6 people, then the marginal productivity of the last 4 workers is zero. It is as if 6 were gainfully employed and 4 were unemployed. None of the 10, of course, regards himself as an unnecessary worker.

Where there is visible or disguised unemployment, devoting resources to labor-saving innovations makes little sense unless at the same time there is development of new jobs for the displaced labor. Without such jobs, the potential increases in output that labor-saving techniques make possible will not be achieved.

IMPORT SUBSTITUTION

In the period since World War II, industrialization of underdeveloped countries has

---

[6] Myrdal and Prebisch are perhaps the most prominent exponents of this view. An excellent account of the issues barely touched in the text is C. R. Wharton, Jr., "The Green Revolution: Cornucopia or Pandora's Box?" *Foreign Affairs* (April 1969).

largely taken the form of producing for sale in the home market goods that were previously imported. Because these countries characteristically suffered from a significant comparative disadvantage in such production, it proved necessary both to subsidize the home industry and to restrict imports. A study of such policies in seven countries—Argentina, Brazil, Mexico, India, Pakistan, the Philippines, and Taiwan—concludes that

although there are arguments for giving special encouragement to industry, this encouragement could be provided in forms which would not, as present policies do, discourage exports, including agricultural exports; which would promote greater efficiency in the use of resources; and which would create a less unequal distribution of income and higher levels of employment in both industry and agriculture.[7]

These conclusions are controversial ones, and critics of them point to the fact that Taiwan, for example, represents one of the great successes of economic development: Its income per capita has averaged a rate of increase of over 6 percent during the whole of the last two decades.

The use of this import substitution strategy arose out of experience during the Great Depression, when the collapse in world agricultural prices caused the value of the exports of agricultural countries to decline drastically, and during World War II, when such countries found the manufactured goods they wished to import unavailable.

Implementing an import substitution policy is relatively easy because it can be done by imposing import quotas and by raising tariffs. Such tariffs and other restrictions on imports provide incentives for development of domestic industry by carving out a ready-made market and by providing a substantial price umbrella that promises high profits to suc-

cessful local manufacturers and to foreign investors who might enter with both capital and know-how. Subsidies, governmental loans, and other forms of encouragement have also been used in many cases.

Little, Scitovsky, and Scott concluded that policies of industrialization, accomplished by effective rates of protection that varied from 25 percent for Mexico to over 200 percent for Pakistan, aggravated inequalities in the distribution of income by raising the prices of manufactured goods relative to agricultural goods and by favoring profits over wages. Moreover, they found that productivity increased more than employment opportunities and that unemployment has grown because of the discouraging of such labor-using industries as textiles and the encouraging of the use of capital-intensive labor-saving processes.

In brief, the argument against these industrialization policies is that they have given too much attention to the advantages of self-sufficiency and too little to comparative advantage. Moreover, the opportunities for import substitution are limited: Once the country runs out of imports to substitute for, what then? Industrialization, these critics argue, ought to be encouraged, but along the lines where infant-industry arguments are truly valid: where, once the development period is past, the country will have a reliable industry that can compete in world markets.

INDUSTRIALIZATION

Obviously, if Tanzania or South Korea could quickly develop steel, shipbuilding, and manufacturing industries that operated as efficiently as those of Japan or West Germany, they, too, might share in the rapid economic growth that has been enjoyed by these industrial countries. Indeed, if a decade or two (or even three) of protection and subsidization could give infant industries time to mature and become efficient, the price might be worth paying. After all, both Japan and

[7] Little, Scitovsky, and Scott, *Industry and Trade in Some Developing Countries* (London: Oxford University Press, 1970), page 1.

Russia were underdeveloped countries within the memory of people living today.

The greatest problem with such a strategy is that there is no guarantee that it will succeed. Even if the country has the required basic natural resources, it may be backward enough so that it is unlikely to have the labor or managerial talent to achieve success within a reasonable time. India may create a steel industry and have its productivity increase year by year, but it must do more. It must catch up to the steel industries of other countries if it is to compete in world markets.

The catch-up problem is a race against a moving target. Suppose one is committed to having a given industry competitive in ten years. In such a situation, it is not sufficient to be making gains in productivity; they must be made at a rate fast enough to overcome a present disadvantage against an improving opponent. Suppose you must improve by 50 percent to achieve the present level of a competitor who is improving at r percent per year. If you want to catch him in ten years you must improve at $r + 4$ percent per year. [44] If r is 6 percent, you must achieve 10 percent. To achieve 6 percent or 7 percent may be admirable, but you will lose the race just the same.

Thus, while this route to development is available, it depends both on having required resources and on overcoming the things that contribute to X-inefficiency. This often means devoting resources for a long period to education, training, development of an infrastructure, and overcoming the various cultural and social barriers to efficient production. While this is hard, it is not impossible.

Brazil seems to be succeeding in this kind of development. Countries sometimes seek a short cut and pursue certain lines of production on a subsidized basis either for prestige purposes or because of a confusion between cause and effect. Because most wealthy nations have a steel industry, the leaders of many underdeveloped nations regard their

countries as primitive until a domestic steel industry has been developed. However, if a country has a serious comparative disadvantage in steel, then having a steel industry will make that country poor. Whether one really gains international prestige by having an uneconomic steel industry or a national airline is doubtful. It seems likely that, in the long run, prestige goes to the country that grows rich rather than to the one that stays poor but that produces at high cost a few prestigious commodities that are regarded as signs of wealth.

Summary

1. Sustained economic development is relatively recent in history and is highly uneven. About two-thirds of the world's population still exist at a level of bare subsistence. The gap between rich and poor is very large and is keenly felt.

2. While there are common problems in various groups of underdeveloped countries, there are also major differences. Because there is no single form of underdevelopment, there is neither a single barrier to development nor a single set of policies to employ in fostering development.

3. The transformation in less than half a century of Soviet Russia from a backward peasant economy to a major industrial power has had a powerful demonstration effect on the quest for economic development. This, along with the efforts of the World Bank and development agencies of the more developed countries, has fostered the conviction that backwardness can be overcome and development achieved.

4. Population growth, resource limitations, and inefficient use of resources are among the formidable barriers to economic development of particular underdeveloped countries. The race between output and population is a critical aspect of economic development in many countries, as recent trends in world population growth make clear.

5. Recent research suggests that X-inefficiency may be of major importance in accounting for low incomes and a slow rate of growth. X-inefficiency can be the product of

inadequate education, poor health, cultural attitudes, or ignorance. Consequently, adopting techniques used in more developed countries may prove disappointingly unproductive in less developed countries.

6. A basic choice of the policy maker is how much to intervene in the economy and how much to rely on the free market. History has demonstrated that growth is possible with almost any conceivable mixture of free market and central control. Planning can change both the pace of economic development and its direction.

7. Educational policy and population control, although vitally important to the long-run rate of economic development, yield benefits only in the future. As a result they frequently are bypassed in the search for more immediate results.

8. Acquiring capital for development is invariably a major concern in development. One source is domestic savings, but the vicious circle of poverty is the common problem of a country that is poor because it has little capital, but cannot readily forgo consumption to accumulate capital because it is poor. Importing capital rather than using domestic savings permits heavy investment during the early years of development, with much smaller sacrifices of current living standards. But imported capital is only available if the underdeveloped country has opportunities that are attractive to foreign investors. Much of the foreign capital for underdeveloped countries in the last two decades has come in the form of contributions by foreign governments and international institutions.

9. Selecting a pattern of development poses a number of difficult choices. The theory of comparative advantage provides the traditional case for unbalanced growth. There are, however, important reasons for not pushing specialization according to current comparative advantage too far, including the risks of fluctuations or declines in the demands for one's principal product and the overdependence on foreign trade. Furthermore, future comparative advantage may be different from current comparative advantage and may itself be affected by choice of development strategies.

10. Much of the current debate about development concerns the emphasis to give to (a) agricultural development, (b) reduction of dependence on foreign trade by development of import substitution industries, and (c) development of an industrial capacity that will create new export industries. None of the strategies is without problems and risks.

Concepts for review

Underdeveloped and developing economies
Critical minimum effort
Barriers to development
Allocative inefficiency and X-inefficiency
Balanced and unbalanced growth
Alternative development strategies
The role of government intervention in development

Discussion questions

1. Each of the following is a headline from a recent story in *The New York Times.* Relate them to the problem of economic development:
a. "Africa: Ferment for a Better Life"
b. "Poor Nations Are Spending a Fortune on Weapons for Prestige and Defense"
c. "Hungary Reforming Economy to Attract Tourists"
d. "Goodyear to Build Plant in Congo for $16 Million"
e. "Algeria's 4-Year Plan Stresses Industrial Growth"
f. "Volatile Prices Hurt Poor Lands"
g. "Foreign Banks to Finance New Guinea Copper Mine"
h. "Not All Benefit by Green Revolution"
i. "OPEC Nations Provide Loans to Undeveloped Nations to Pay for Oil Imports"

2. If you were a member of a U.S. foreign-aid team assigned to study needed development projects for a poor recipient country, to which of the following would you be likely to give relatively high priority, and why?
a. birth-control clinics
b. a national airlines
c. taxes on imported luxuries
d. better roads
e. modernization of farming techniques
f. training in engineering and business management
g. primary education
h. scholarships to students to receive medical and legal training abroad

3. Despite the record Chinese grain harvests the last few years, that nation still requires 5 million tons more each year just to keep up with its annual population growth of 17 million people. This is about five times Canada's wheat supply at present. What policy choices do these facts pose for the Chinese government? How should it resolve those choices?

4. "This natural inequality of the two powers of population and of production in the earth . . . form the great difficulty that to me appears insurmountable in the way to perfectability of society. All other arguments are of slight and subordinate consideration in comparison of this. I see no way by which man can escape from the weight of this law which pervades all animated nature. No fancied equality, no agrarian regulations in their utmost extent, could remove the pressure of it even for a single century" (T. R. Malthus, *Population: The First Essay,* Chap. 1, p. 6).

Discuss Malthus' "insurmountable difficulty" in view of the history of the past 100 years.

5. To what extent does the vicious circle of poverty apply to poor families living in developed countries? Consider carefully, for example, the similarities and differences facing a poor black family living in Arkansas and one living in Ghana, where per capita income is less than $200 per year.

6. How might each of the following affect a country's economic development?

a. a tradition that a man's land is divided equally among all of his children
b. a very unequal distribution of national income
c. specialization in a commodity in which it has a virtual world monopoly
d. a decision to be entirely self-sufficient

7. President Perez of Venezuela said recently: "The decision of OPEC members to raise petroleum prices should be applauded by all third-world countries. It represents the irrevocable decision to dignify the terms of trade, to revalue raw materials and other basic products of the third world." Which underdeveloped countries might be expected to have agreed? Which to have disagreed?

8. "High coffee prices bring hope to impoverished Latin American peasants" reads the headline. Mexico, Kenya, and Burundi, among other underdeveloped countries, have the right combination of soil and climate to increase greatly their coffee production. Discuss the benefits and risks to them if they pursue coffee production as the main avenue of their development efforts.

45

Comparative economic systems

Economics is concerned with these basic questions: What is produced? How is it produced? How is the product distributed? These and related questions have been examined in the context of a free-market economy in which private firms and private households interact in markets with some assistance and interference from the government. This kind of economy fits the pattern found in the United States, Britain, western Europe, and other areas of the world that together are inhabited by less than a quarter of the world's total population. This kind of economy has been studied for several reasons. First, this is the kind of economy that *we* live in. Second, it is the economic environment in which the serious study of economics was born and has grown. In science as in society, environment exerts a powerful influence on growing things.

Today, however, more than a billion people, a third of the world's population, live in the Soviet Union and China, countries that explicitly reject this kind of economic system. At least another third of the world's population live in countries whose economies have not yet developed to the point where the model of the free-market economy fits them closely; many of these countries are "uncommitted" economically as well as politically.

Can the same theories and measurements be used to study economies quite different from the free-market economy? So far as economics describes the ways in which people respond to incentives and mobilize scarce means to given ends, the same economic principles are applicable under a variety of different sets of assumptions about ends, means, or incentive systems.

All types of economies face scarcity, and all must decide how to allocate scarce goods; all may face problems of inflation or unemployment or balance-of-payments deficits or unsatisfactory rates of growth. So far as economic analysis concerns these things, it can have something to say even where familiar institutions are modified or absent. Furthermore, the study of a variety of different economic systems may provide clues to the strengths and weaknesses of different forms of economic organization.

Different economic systems

It is common to speak of the economic systems of "capitalism," "socialism," and "communism" as if they were the only three different paths to basic economic decisions. But this is at best a simplification and at worst a confusion. There are dozens of different economic systems in the world today, not three. Just as there are many differences among the United States, the United Kingdom, Germany, Sweden, Japan, France, Greece, and Brazil, so are there differences among the institutions of the Soviet Union, China, Poland, Bulgaria, Cuba, Czechoslovakia, and Yugoslavia. Different countries are dissimilar in many respects: in who owns resources, in who makes decisions, in the role of governmental planning, in the nature of the incentives offered to people, and in the way that the economy performs.

Which of these dissimilarities are the important ones? Differences of opinion here may lead to important differences in evaluation. Americans may see their economy as being responsible for their high standard of living and see in their cities' well-stocked stores proof of the superiority of free-enterprise capitalism; Russians may look at their economy and see, in its rapid and purposeful growth and the absence of urban unemployment, proof of its superiority to the American economy; Sweden's slum-free public housing, nationalized medicine, and high productivity in privately owned industry may lead Swedes to regard their "mixed" economy as very satisfying.

OWNERSHIP OF RESOURCES

Who owns a nation's farms and factories, its coal mines and forests? Who owns its railroads and airways? Who owns its streams and golf courses? Who owns its houses and hotels?

The answers to these questions differ in different countries. One characteristic of the system called capitalism is that the basic raw materials, the productive assets of the society, and the final goods are predominantly privately owned by individuals singly or in groups. By this standard, the United States is predominantly a capitalistic economy, although many of its resources are in fact held in public rather than private hands. In the United States there is public ownership of power, housing, and utilities as well as of many local transport systems and the postal system. Although a few observers see evidence of creeping or galloping socialism in such projects as the Tennessee Valley Authority (TVA), most people recognize that in the United States the pattern of ownership is predominantly private.

In contrast, theoretical socialism envisions a society in which the ownership of productive assets is public. Communism theoretically is opposed to any form of private property. Today there are no completely communistic or socialistic societies. In the Soviet Union, virtually all of the factories are state-owned and an attempt has been made to collectivize all the farms, but though the Soviets officially designate their economy as socialistic, there are three sectors of that economy—agriculture, retail trade, and housing—where some significant private ownership exists. If the USSR is not a pure socialist economy, it is sufficiently near the public-ownership end of the spectrum to distinguish it from the United States near the private-ownership end. Other countries fall between them on the spectrum. Great Britain has six times in this century elected Labor governments that have been officially committed to socialism to the point of nationalizing key industries: railroads, steel, coal, gas, electricity, atomic power, postal services, telephones, telegraphs, airlines, and some trucking. Although many key industries are publicly owned, the great bulk of industries producing goods and services for household consumption and capital goods for firms are under private ownership and control.

Ownership patterns are genuinely variable rather than of an either/or variety. Figure 45–1 illustrates this by showing the division of fixed investment between public and private sectors.

With respect to the ownership of resources and virtually every other dimension of an economy, it is worth remembering three basic points:

Every real economy is "mixed" rather than pure; among countries the mixture differs in ways that are appreciable and significant; over time, the mixture changes.

THE DECISION PROCESS (COORDINATING PRINCIPLES)

A distinction is sometimes made between two kinds of systems: a *market system,* in which decisions are made impersonally and in a decentralized way by the interaction of individuals in markets, and a *command system,* in which centralized decision makers decide what shall be done and issue appropriate commands to achieve the desired results.

Again, no country is found at either extreme, but it is true that some economies—those of the United States, France, and Yugoslavia, for example—rely much more heavily on market decisions than do the economies of East Germany, the Soviet Union, and Cuba. But even in the United States, the command principle has some

Figure 45-1 Estimated differences in ownership patterns for selected countries

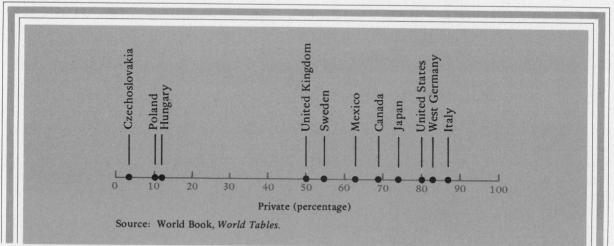

Source: World Book, *World Tables.*

Actual economies never rely solely on private or solely on public investment. These estimates are based on the percentage of gross fixed investment accounted for by the private sector. Such investment provides additions to the stock on productive capital. Private capital investment plays a role even in Communist countries, a public capital is a significant part of investment in all countries.

sway: minimum wages, quotas on some agricultural outputs, and wartime priorities are obvious examples. More subtle examples concern public expenditures and taxes that in effect transfer command of some resources from private individuals to public officials. (The extent of government interference with market forces was discussed in detail in Chapters 24 and 25.)

In the planned economies of the Soviet bloc, where plans and targets, quotas and directives are important aspects of the decision-making system, there is substantial command at work. But markets are used too. At the retail level, for example, people can spend their incomes with substantial discretion on a wide variety of goods.

Table 45–1 suppresses many subtle distinctions, but it focuses on important tendencies in certain twentieth-century economies by a simple classification according to ownership and decision patterns. Later in this chapter, the economic systems of the USSR and Yugoslavia, both of which are considered communist societies, will be examined more closely. The table suggests at once that they differ significantly from each other as well as from the United States.

Much economic behavior depends more on the decision pattern than on the ownership pattern. Thus, in the United Kingdom, although a large number of key industries are publicly owned, their control is vested in semiautonomous boards over which Parliament exerts very little control. By and large, the boards try to make their enterprises profitable, and, to the extent that they succeed, their behavior will be similar to that of profit-seeking privately owned firms. In predicting their market behavior, economic theorists need not concern themselves with the legal distinction between public and private ownership any more than they need concern themselves with the distinction between corporations and partnerships. By contrast, firms in Hitler's Germany were under a high degree of state control, even though technically they were privately owned. An attempt to predict their behavior using the profit-maximizing model would not have been successful because the central decision makers guiding their actions were concerned with goals quite different from that of profit maximization.

WHOSE VALUES?

In the market and command systems different

Table 45–1 Comparative economic systems: ownership and decision patterns

DECISION PATTERN	OWNERSHIP PATTERN	
	Predominantly private	*Predominantly public*
Predominantly decentralized with use of market	United States	Yugoslavia
Predominantly centralized with use of command principle	Nazi Germany	USSR

Each of these combinations of private and public ownership and centralized and decentralized control has actually occurred in practice. This table is a simplification that serves to highlight differences among economic systems. Ownership and decision patterns are *variables;* it would be an interesting exercise to use a grid that gives several, rather than just two, gradations for each variable and then attempt to place current and past economies in the appropriate cells.

groups make the relevant decisions, and it follows that different people's judgments will determine these decisions.

In a capitalistic market economy, dollars "vote." The demands of consumers for goods exert a major influence on the nature of the goods produced. Traditionally, this is spoken of as consumer sovereignty, but it should be noted both that the rich consumer has more say than the poor one and that firms have a great deal to say about what is and is not produced. In an unfettered market economy, the initial distribution of income and wealth influences the nature of economic decisions because it determines who has the dollars that exercise the effective demands. Mixed economies often use public policies to modify the decisions that would emerge from the uses of private purchasing power, but they are best regarded as supplementing rather than challenging the principle of consumer and producer sovereignty.

Early Marxists directly attacked the notion of a market-oriented value system. One of the great slogans of the utopian Marxists was "From each according to his ability, to each according to his need." Such a slogan does not solve the allocational problem: In a world in which desires for goods and services exceed the capacity to produce them, someone has to judge who needs what and then take steps to provide it for them.

In general, in command systems some group must decide what is to be produced and who is to get it. Because no one has yet devised a scheme by which everyone would automatically give according to his ability and in which everyone's needs would be clear to all, decisions have to be made. Whoever makes the decisions might do so on the basis of majority preferences, with each person having one vote, regardless of his or her share of the income. (Cooperatives operate on this principle, with each *member* having one vote. The contrast with a corporation, where each

share has one vote, is marked.) Alternatively, each decision maker might decide on the basis of his or her own preferences (autocracy) or those of a particular group, or the decision maker might decide on the basis of "what he or she thinks is good for the people."

The general point is that different systems are likely to reflect the values of different groups. Planned systems have tended to reflect the values of the central authorities somewhat more strongly than have market systems.

INCENTIVE SYSTEMS

Psychologists know that people (and most other living creatures) respond to reward and punishment. Incentives may be of two main kinds—the carrot or the stick—and of almost infinite varieties. Direct monetary rewards, in the form of wages or profits or bribes, are well understood. Indirect monetary rewards, such as special housing, vacations, or subsidized education, are not always as readily identified, but they can be effective. Nonmonetary "carrots" include praise, medals, certificates, and applause. Fines, prison terms, and other penalties are used to motivate behavior in all societies; in some societies coercion and fear provide even stronger motivation.

Capitalistic market economies put major reliance on monetary incentives. Monetary incentives to the individual in a socialistic society are not very different from those in a capitalistic economy. Differential earnings for different occupations are used in socialist economies, and piece rates are common. Gifts and bonuses of housing, cars, and other sought-after goods or privileges are used and are valued. Large accumulations of assets are not permitted, but the importance of this is in dispute. There are no millionaires in the Soviet Union, but the desire for power is perhaps as important as the desire for wealth in both capitalistic and socialistic societies.

The big difference in incentive systems is in whether those responsible for production respond to what it is *profitable* to produce or whether they respond to what they are directed to produce. In the first case, profits can provide their own reward in terms of bonuses, salaries, dividends, and perhaps the funds to permit growth and the accumulation of power. In the second case, it is necessary to provide incentives to managers and workers to achieve the assigned quotas.

Again, real economies are mixed. In the United States and in China, Cuba, and the Congo, examples of every form of incentive can be found. But the mixtures, the emphasis, and the social acceptability vary.

ENDS AND MEANS

Many, perhaps most, people in Western societies value the *means* of the free market and democratic processes even more highly than they value the *ends* of high and rising living standards. Most Americans distrust the agglomeration of central power and the loss of democratic institutions that accompany communism or any other form of centrally administered command economy. Many people believe that there is no need to choose between means and ends because they believe that the free market and democracy produce better results than do alternative systems in terms of both means and ends. But how many Americans would want to go over to the Soviet system, even if it could be *proved* that the Soviet system was certain to produce a higher growth rate than the American free-market one? In the 1930s it was believed that fascist dictatorships were more efficient than democracies. Mussolini, it was said, "made the Italian trains run on time." It is debatable that the belief was correct, but most people accepted it; yet only a handful of Americans

advocated that America become a fascist dictatorship.

In underdeveloped countries, the people often put more importance on the ends, higher living standards, than on the means of achieving them. They may regard a change of means per se as unimportant. The choice between a centralized and decentralized economy may seem to many to be merely one between which group will exploit them—government officials or powerful monopoly interests. The choice that many North Americans and Europeans see between political democracy or oligarchy they may see as one between oligarchy and oligarchy—the oligarchy in power now or the oligarchy that will manipulate an electoral system. If a highly planned communistic economy offers them a good chance of a 4 percent growth rate, while a democratically oriented market society offers 2 percent, they may well choose the planned society. To say to them that in so choosing they are throwing away their freedom is likely to evoke the reply, What has freedom meant to us in the past but the freedom to be hungry and exploited?

THE CHARACTERIZATION OF PARTICULAR ECONOMIES

Although no real economy is simple, it nevertheless often proves helpful to talk about and sometimes to analyze economies in terms of simple models. For example, it is sometimes helpful to characterize the American economy as one of private ownership, of market decision making, of consumer sovereignty, and of monetary incentives—with, in addition, a relatively large government sector that modifies the nature of economic decisions to some extent. This kind of capsule summary is useful in focusing on certain patterns that differentiate the United States from other real economies, two of which will be briefly discussed: the Soviet Union and Yugoslavia.

The economy of the Soviet Union

The modern *economic* history of the Soviet Union is usually taken to begin in 1928, eleven years after the Bolshevik revolution had wrested power for a small and militant minority from a small and decaying aristocracy. Russia at the time of World War I was a large and in most ways a backward country with an enormous, poor, and largely ignorant and illiterate peasantry, who were to prove as sullenly hostile to their new Bolshevik rulers as they had been to the Czars. Backward and poor though Russia was, by 1917 industrialization had been under way for three decades; the nucleus of heavy industry and of an industrial labor force already existed.

During its first decade of existence the new regime hung on by its teeth, contending with recurring famines, internal power struggles, and the invasion by the Western powers. By the late 1920s, Joseph Stalin had emerged as an effective strong man. Stalin had ruthlessly consolidated the Revolution and his personal power, and he was ready to undertake the economic task of lifting Russia from an underdeveloped giant to a major industrial power. Whatever the costs—and they have been enormous—the economic rise of the Soviet Union in four decades is a major economic achievement. Basically Stalin's economic policy was:

1. to consolidate management over all economic resources in such a way that they would respond surely and quickly to the needs of the regime;

2. to constrict consumption to an absolute minimum, so that the maximum possible rate of capital accumulation, and thus growth, could be achieved;

3. to channel growth into the areas of heavy industrial development required for a major military power.

Neither the current sacrifices that were imposed on the people as consumers nor the Herculean efforts that were asked of them as producers were borne without complaint or opposition. Stalin is perhaps best remembered for his "terrors," dramatized in the ruthless purges in which thousands met death or exile. Terror was pervasive in the omnipresent army, the police, and, above all, the notorious secret police. Whatever its primary purposes, this regime of terror had the twin economic effects of enforcing centralized power and providing a powerful if unpleasant set of incentives to carry out the orders of the regime.

The famous five-year plans, the first in 1928, began the rapid industrial development that was to transform the Soviet Union into a major military power by World War II and a major world power in the postwar period. The ninth five-year plan, covering the period 1971–1975, was the first to put major emphasis on production of consumer goods. Whatever the sacrifices were, both in privation and in terror, the Soviet Union today has a stable and relatively prosperous economy with butter as well as guns. It operates with a set of institutions that deals with the basic economic problems very differently from the way the American economy deals with them.

OWNERSHIP

With certain limited exceptions, the central government—the state—owns all land, all natural resources, all capital goods, all business enterprises, and most urban housing.

In the industrial sector, state ownership is virtually complete; in the retail fields, state stores make up about two-thirds of the total sales, with the bulk of the rest accounted for by rural cooperatives, but with a small amount of farm produce sold in free "farmers' markets." Most rural housing, and perhaps a third of urban housing, is privately owned (and officially restricted to personal use). The rest is publicly owned.

About a third of all agricultural production comes from farms (called sovkhos) that are owned, run, and managed by the state; another half of all production comes from collective farms, which, while nominally cooperatives into which peasants were once forced, are in fact so closely controlled by the state that their differences from the sovkhos are minor. A small part of the total agricultural output is produced by privately owned farms and by members of collective farms on garden plots that they are allowed to cultivate in their spare time.

Private enterprise is profitable where it is permitted—in agriculture and in personal services of various kinds from medicine to carpentry. The official figures probably underestimate the importance of the private sector by ignoring the existence of an illegal black market in privately produced goods and services.

The black market is a response by households (who are permitted to own savings deposits and personal possessions) to the restricted supply of officially available goods. They are glad to buy goods and services from others, who in turn are glad to earn the extra money by producing them.

THE ORGANIZATION OF PRODUCTION

In the industrial sector of the Soviet economy production is predominantly organized around individual plants that are managed by a "director" (appointed by the central authorities with the approval of the local Communist party group). Directors may appear omnipotent to the workers, but their orders with respect to how and what to produce and how and when to replace equipment or expand operations are actually handed down from higher up in the planning hierarchy. Directors are, in fact, more bureaucrat than entrepreneur.

Productive decisions are made in a highly organized pyramidal bureaucracy. The overall planning agency, the USSR GOSPLAN, develops broad plans that are translated into orders for regional GOSPLANs, which in turn hand down directives to particular ministries. Ministries may be either at the industry level or in control of a particular resource. Ministries' instructions ultimately take the form of orders to individual plant managers, who then do their best to carry them out.

The industrial firm's targets include quotas with respect to total output and output of individual commodities. A firm is often given maximum levels of inputs (such as number of employees, tons of coal). The wages a firm can offer are fixed by the government, and there is no open market on which the firm's manager can acquire scarce commodities. Within limits, workers are free to choose any job they are offered, and labor mobility is not really restricted—except that workers on collective farms have not been allowed to leave them at will. Despite rather large occupational wage differences, labor mobility has tended to be low.

Managers are exhorted to fulfill their quotas, and success is rewarded with bonuses, medals, and promotions. If managers are in danger of failing because, for example, they cannot acquire the labor they need, they can persuade their employees (by threat or promise) to work harder and longer, they can appeal to the appropriate ministry for an increase in permitted wages, or they can persuade someone to lower their quota. If they fail for what their superiors refuse to accept as good reasons, they may face demotion—or worse. While these firms are called enterprises, the manager is quite limited in the kind of enterprise he or she can show. Only since 1969 have managers been given the right to decrease their labor force by firing surplus labor and using the resulting savings to increase the pay of remaining employees.

Clearly, this part of the economy is governed by the rules of a command economy. Directives cover many aspects of a firm's operations, though they cannot, of course, cover all contingencies. *Within* the guidelines of the plan as it is sent down to the given firm, the firm is instructed and encouraged to be efficient and, where possible, to make "above-plan profits."[1] Planned profits go to the state; part of above-plan profits may be retained in the firm and used for the benefit of the employees. Thus there is some scope for maneuver, but the constraints are much tighter than they are for a typical firm in the American economy. A Soviet enterprise cannot usually experiment with new products or new methods of production without securing advance permission. Indeed, because there is such emphasis on meeting or exceeding plan quotas, *quantity* of output becomes more compelling than cost savings or quality.

Western observers, and Soviet ones, too, have often noted the many microeconomic inefficiencies that appear to result from the command principle. Among these are unreasonable stockpiles of some commodities, shortages of others, and low quality of many of the goods that are produced. Similar inefficiencies are often alleged to exist in such American activities as military procurement, where similarly centralized command systems are in use. This suggests that inefficiencies of these kinds may be inherent in overcentralized systems in which incentives are given in terms of fulfilling output quotas rather than earning profits.

Despite its inefficiencies, the system clearly works. The Soviets have produced a growing flow of armaments, goods, machines, and space vehicles. Soviet industry has proved adequate to the major demands placed on it: Its inefficiencies have been serious but not crippling. One of the sharpest critics of the inefficiencies of overcentralization is a Soviet professor, E. Liberman. As will be seen, Yugoslavia has responded to these criticisms

more than has the USSR, but there is currently within the Soviet Union a great debate on this very issue, and since 1965 there have been a number of decentralizing reforms. Governments, too, respond to incentives. If it is demonstrated that some practice is costing the Soviet Union too heavily in things its leaders value, one can be sure that they will change the offending practice.

One of the major problems of planned economies concerns innovation. Soviet managers have little incentive to innovate by experimenting with new products or new ways of producing old products. As long as the Soviet Union is catching up to the capitalist countries it can copy capitalist products and techniques. It is not so clear that a planned economy left on its own could produce as rapid a rate of innovation as is generated by a profit-oriented free-enterprise economy where decision making is effectively decentralized. One of the severest critics of the stultifying effects on invention and innovation exerted by a highly centralized economy has been the distinguished Soviet physicist and Nobel Prize winner A. K. Sakharov.

Agricultural production (which in 1928 absorbed 80 percent of the Soviet labor force and today absorbs about 40 percent) is almost as centralized as is manufacturing. The results have been much less successful than those in the industrial sector. The collective farms were designed to overcome the inability of Russian agriculture to provide cheap and adequate food supplies. But the compulsion required to bring unwilling individual peasants into the collective farms did not generate cooperative responses. Many observers believe that the lack of incentives and rewards is responsible. Meeting quotas of steel wins bonuses, medals, and praise—and pay raises —for the steelworkers; meeting grain quotas is likely to lead to yet higher quotas for the next period.

Collective farmers do not receive wages; rather, they share in the income of the farm.

---

[1] Because prices of everything are specified by the state and are spelled out in the directive, the firm can earn above-plan profits only by exceeding its output quotas. Many critics both outside and inside the system have noticed an overconcentration on physical output—on technological rather than economic efficiency.

But the government's policy, designed to keep food prices down by keeping farm prices low, has kept farm income low, too. In any case, low morale and forced labor (manifested in the refusal to permit farmers to leave the farms) have not led to high productivity, and agricultural production has been a chronic and continuing trouble spot in the Soviet economy.

THE DISTRIBUTION OF GOODS AND HOUSEHOLD INCENTIVES

Both the nature and the quantity of the goods to be produced are specified by the central planners. Those for consumers are placed in the state-owned shops or in cooperatives, to be sold at government-specified prices that include an important "turnover tax" (see below).

Households are free to spend their incomes on these goods. Here individual choice rather than "command" is at work, but even here the function of a market is restricted. If too many consumers want a particular item, for instance, it runs out, and there is no price rise to signal producers that there is a higher demand. The shortage is not an effective signal because producers are not motivated to respond to it. As a result there is no assurance that production will be increased. There is no automatic feedback of what consumers *want* and would buy that has an effect on the goods and services actually produced.

The use of the market, rather than direct allocation, in the distribution of consumer goods is explained by the need to avoid the impossible administrative burden of deciding who gets what, rather than by a philosophic desire to let consumers be sovereign. There is a difference between consumer sovereignty, which lets consumer choices help to determine *what is produced,* and consumer freedom to choose from among goods of *predetermined* quantity, quality, and price.

Until very recently Soviet planners had been reluctant to respond to such clear consumer signals as shortages of particular goods. The consumer riots in Poland in December 1970 seem to have changed this. Recently Soviet planners have begun to take account of shortages and surpluses of particular consumer goods at the existing prices in setting new production targets. To the extent that this occurs, consumer sovereignty is being introduced into the system.

These changes reflect Soviet growth. When the economy was very poor and very high investment levels were needed to stimulate growth, consumers had to be content with whatever crude goods were available. Now that a higher material living standard is being achieved, the variety of consumer goods is increasing greatly and at the same time consumers are becoming more selective. They no longer buy shoddy or unpopular goods automatically, and the resulting large inventories of unsold products are an embarrassment to the planners. As a result, there is much pressure for, and some experimentation with, a two-phase system. This allows the planners to decide what proportion of the nation's resources to devote to the production of consumer goods and then allows consumers, through a decentralized market-type decision mechanism to exert an influence on how these resources are allocated among all the various lines of production.

Household incomes come from the state principally in the form of wages and salaries. "To each according to his need" was the Marxian ideal, but in the Soviet Union scientists and engineers, ballet dancers, and athletes apparently need more than do laborers and teachers. Wage *differentials* are in fact very much larger than in the United States; skilled workers characteristically earn three or four times the amount earned by unskilled workers (in contrast to 50 percent more in the United States).

But wages are not the only determinant of the distribution of income. Many goods and services such as medical care, higher education, and old-age pensions are provided free to those who qualify. State housing is provided at very low cost. Large families receive special money allowances and special housing. Thus standards of living in the Soviet Union are somewhat less unequal than wage differentials suggest. In contrast to the United States, there are fewer extreme incomes at either end but a somewhat greater spread in the incomes of the middle- and upper-middle income groups.

Income distribution in the USSR is very much a matter of conscious policy decisions. Through wages, allowances, free and subsidized goods, and the turnover tax (which is like a sales tax but varies from product to product), the central authorities—the Party hierarchy—can effectively impress on the economy *their* views as to the appropriate pattern of goods and income distribution.

PLANNING IN THE SOVIET UNION

The Soviet economic system relies on public ownership, on the command principle, on private choices (within such limits as the central authorities choose to allow), and on a complex system of incentives that include differential wages, bonuses, and some compulsion and fear. Planners and the centralized decision makers play a leading role in the Soviet economy.

Two levels of planning warrant particular attention. These are the short-run (one-year) plans and the medium-range (usually five-year) plans. The medium-range plan is influenced by a yet longer-run "vision" of the society that motivates the leadership—a vision of what the economy promises its citizens twenty-five years hence. Stalin's vision was of a Russia become a full industrial and military power, and he lived to see it realized. Khrushchev began the transition to a vision that embraced more of the "good life," and the present Soviet leadership under Brezhnev

accelerated this change. Western living standards, once denounced as bourgeois decadence, are an increasingly visible goal.

Five-year plans

Five-year plans are, roughly, blueprints for later detailed implementation. They contain no orders to individual plants and no detailed quotas of goods to be produced, but they do prescribe both the level of aggregate income that is to be achieved and the *structure* of the economy by major sectors and industries.

Every five-year plan has included decisions about how drastically to curtail consumption to release resources for investment. Each has also decided how much effort is to be devoted to developing educational and technical resources that will be needed five to ten years in the future in order to have the technical labor force required to man the new plants spawned by the plan. Less global decisions are also required about such things as the form capital investment should take. How much should be invested in steel capacity, how much in cement, and how much in roads and railroads?

Once the structural goals of the plan are specified, it is necessary to spell out the year-by-year implications for particular industries and regions of the economy. Thus production of the Kiev steel industry may have to grow by X percent next year if other planned activities are not to encounter steel shortages. This kind of derived implication of a five-year plan becomes a control for next year's one-year plan.

One-year plans

Planning details are spelled out in the one-year plans. These are extremely complex and laborious exercises that work out the myriad microeconomic implications of certain broad objectives. By and large, the one-year plans translate the objectives of the five-year plans into detail sufficient to enable individual plants (or farms) to meet them and to ensure that the supplies of needed resources can be made available in the quantities required at the times needed. There is obviously an enormous coordinating job here, and the planners do not manage it perfectly, although they are saved from making an inordinate number of mistakes by a trial-and-error procedure in which tentative plans are sent down to lower bureaucratic levels for comments and suggestions before being issued as final orders. Actual quotas are to some degree negotiated between the directors at the operating levels, who have a strong desire to hold down the quotas expected of them, and the higher-level planners, who must achieve apparent miracles to satisfy the overall growth objectives. Over the years, an enormous amount of experience has been accumulated about the real limits of what is possible. Research by Professor Michael Manove suggests that because of this experience, the planning operation has proven quite successful in defining consistent and attainable plan quotas.

PRICES IN THE PLANNING PROCESS

Not all decisions can be made centrally by the planning agencies, and Soviet planners are increasingly using prices to assist in some kinds of allocational decision making. Two different sets of prices are now assigned as part of the planning process, one for production accounting, the other for sales to consumers and payments to factors.

Factor pricing

For internal productive use, "prices" of commodities or resources are designed to measure the scarcity value of the resources compared to alternative uses. If efficient use of resources is to occur, a tractor firm that uses steel should pay a price for steel that reflects its scarcity value if used in other products. Similarly, the charge for using the services of a carpenter anywhere should reflect the value of his or her marginal product elsewhere. So far

so good. But the state may wish to pay carpenters a higher wage than this either because it has embarked on some program of income redistribution in which carpenters are to be favored or because the state wishes to denote carpentry as a "prestige" occupation. The particular pattern of wage differentials built into the Soviet system may thus reflect the preferences of the central authorities as well as the system's current demands for labor. To avoid productive inefficiency, the planners assign *two* wage rates for carpenters. One of these is charged as a cost of production; the other (which may be higher or lower) is actually paid out to carpenters and becomes the source of their income.

With one important exception, this dual treatment of factor prices has been part of the Soviet planning procedure for a long time. The exception concerns the cost of capital. Mustering resources for capital investment has been hard, and brutal sacrifices in terms of curtailed consumption were imposed on Soviet citizens of the 1930s and 1940s. How should this scarce capital, whose opportunity cost was so high, be allocated efficiently among industries and regions?

The obvious answer was to assign a high interest rate that reflected the high opportunity cost of capital. But for many years an interesting doctrinal barrier prevented using this solution. Because "interest" is traditionally a payment to private owners of capital in capitalist societies, interest rates were odious to Marx and to early Marxist planners. But if those who use capital, a scarce resource, do not have to pay a price for using it that reflects its scarcity value, they will not be motivated to conserve it; and this is just what happened. Soviet planners were reluctant to assign a real scarcity value interest rate to funds allocated for investment until a series of studies showed that investment allocation was among the least efficient aspects of Soviet planning.

Recently dogma has yielded to the fact that acquiring the real resources to construct capital goods continues to be the greatest obstacle to further growth in the Soviet Union. Today, a number very much like an interest rate is used to measure the cost of capital.

Consumer prices and the turnover tax

Consumer prices are made up of two parts: the full cost of the good produced, using the correct internal accounting prices for factors, plus the **turnover tax.** The tax is in form an excise tax, and today the *average* turnover tax is about one-third of the price of the good. But the tax varies tremendously from commodity to commodity.

The size of the turnover tax is determined by the planners' idea of what goods people should be encouraged or discouraged to consume. In part this is a means for redistributing income. Goods consumed by low-income groups may have very low turnover taxes, for example.

Revenue from the turnover tax is used by the state for making new investment. By changing the average rate of the turnover tax, the planners can affect the relative size of consumption and investment. By varying the rate of the tax on different kinds of commodities, the state affects the relative sacrifice in consumption among different kinds of consumers. For example, if the turnover tax were raised on basic necessities and lowered on luxuries, it would increase the sacrifice of the lower-income groups. The pattern of the tax can be made regressive or progressive as the needs and desires of the planners dictate.

Allocation of the proceeds of the turnover tax is at the discretion of the planners. Investment funds produced by the turnover tax on steel might be reinvested in increasing steel output; they might also be diverted to capital investment in electric power, railroads, or the production of luxury goods.

Other sources of investment funds

The tax revenues of the Soviet state do not limit the amount it can spend for invest-ment—or for anything else. The central bank (GOSBANK) can expand the money supply and absorb any government deficit it is asked to absorb.

If it prints too much money, it will, of course, create an inflationary gap. With such a gap, there will be longer lines, more shortages, and more grumbling. These results could be avoided only by raising prices—by letting the inflation occur. Another aspect of the money supply is the ability of firms to borrow in order to expand. GOSBANK lends only to those enterprises whose expansion the planners want to encourage. It thus becomes a further device for implementing planners' objectives.

Unlike most Western central banks, GOSBANK is also a monopoly commercial bank with thousands of branches. As can be imagined, the central bank controls the commercial banking system completely; it does not need to use any of the indirect tools of control such as open market operations by which Western central banks seek to control the independent commercial banks.

COMPARATIVE PERFORMANCE: THE UNITED STATES VERSUS THE SOVIET UNION

In judging the performance of an economy, there are many different criteria and many different sets of eyes through which to view it. Moreover, comparing the actual performances of only two economies can be misleading. For example, during the last forty years the Soviet Union has experienced twice as great a growth rate as the United States. But before one concludes that this demonstrates a growth advantage of communism over capitalism, even higher growth rates achieved in West Germany and Japan—capitalistic countries—should be noted. With this warning in mind, we shall go on to compare elements of the economic performances of the United States and the Soviet Union.

The standard of living in the 1970s

Most national income accountants and students of the Soviet economy judge the level of real purchasing power per capita in the Soviet Union to be somewhat less than half that in the United States. This kind of statistic is difficult to interpret. Clearly, most Americans would feel very poor if their present incomes were cut in half. But American real incomes twenty-five years ago were half what they are today, and at that time the United States was the richest nation in the history of the earth. The adequacy of one's income depends on what everyone else's income is, and also on one's past and future expectations. The Soviet citizens' standard of living is so much higher than it was even a decade ago, and is rising so rapidly, that it probably seems comfortable to them.

It is nevertheless clear that Soviet citizens are poorer than their American counterparts. Not only is housing poorer and clothing in shorter supply and less elegant, but the average citizen has to work more hours to earn the cost of a pair of shoes or an evening dinner. When the Soviet Fiat became available in 1970, this appearance of an "economy car" was front-page news in the newspaper *Pravda*. The car was priced at about $9,000 in 1977 U.S. dollars. The Soviet worker buys less, works longer hours and has shorter vacations.

Notice, however, that these comparisons reflect in good part *our* social values. An observer might note that the Soviet citizen can see better chess, better gymnastics, and better soccer than an American counterpart—and can see them more cheaply. Yet another observer might note that Soviet citizens need not worry about their ability to provide medical and dental care for their families, the possibility of unemployment due to a severe economic slump, or providing for their retirement or for the support of their dependents after their own death. A comprehensive set of welfare programs covers all these contingencies for all Soviet citizens.

Growth

From 1928 to 1970 the Soviet Union achieved an overall rate of growth of more than 4.5 percent per year notwithstanding some unbelievable disasters, particularly the famines of the 1930s and the devastating impact of World War II. During the 1960s the Soviet rate of growth was twice the U.S. rate. In more recent times, however, the growth rate has declined (although it is still higher than the U.S. rate). Recent growth experience is detailed in Table 45–2.

As noted earlier, this remarkable growth record has not been costless. It was achieved by hard and conscious choice—by sacrificing current consumption for investment that led to greater production in the future. The relative prosperity of today's Soviet citizens is owed to their parents' forced forbearance, and to sustain this growth rate for another generation present-day citizens may well have to continue to forego many of the comforts available to Americans. There is little general enthusiasm for such policies, and the regime has lately chosen to ease the restrictions on the consumer sector even at the cost of its growth rate. But the Soviet economy has provided a most compelling demonstration to the world of how an underdeveloped country can develop in one lifetime, if it will pay the price and if it has the unexploited resources on which to base an expansion.

Economic stability

If growth has been the great triumph of the Soviet experience, employment stability has been a small one. A highly planned economy, if it is insulated from the outside world, need have no deficient-demand unemployment, no unintended inflation or deflation, and no cyclical phenomena. If it must engage heavily in foreign trade, it is not so easily insulated. In this regard the Soviet Union during its period of rapid growth has been fortunate. It is a large country with ample and varied natural resources (like the United States), and it has

Table 45–2   Estimates of growth of GNP in the USSR, by sector of origin

| | AVERAGE ANNUAL RATE OF GROWTH (PERCENT) | |
	1966–1970	*1971–1975*
Agriculture	4.5	−0.6
Industry	6.1	5.9
Construction	6.9	6.4
Transportation	6.6	6.4
Communications	8.9	7.4
Trade	8.2	6.2
Services	4.0	3.4
Other	4.5	3.1
Total GNP	5.4	3.9

Source: CIA, Research Aid, *Soviet Economy: Performance of 1975 and Prospect for 1976,* May 1976.

The rate of growth in virtually all major sectors of the Soviet economy slowed in the 1970s. Growth rates vary significantly from sector to sector, with agriculture showing the poorest growth performance. Although growth rates have fallen, they are still above those of the United States.

not had to rely heavily on foreign trade. Moreover, much of what it does need has been provided from within the Soviet system by the satellite countries of eastern Europe. Purchases from the West do require foreign exchange, but here pressures have not been serious, partly because the Soviet Union has been a major gold producer.

Years of crop failure have provided a significant exception to this generalization. Large purchases of grain have been made from the United States and Canada and the Soviet authorities have had to worry about earning sufficient foreign exchange to make those purchases.

Although unemployment due to deficient aggregate demand need not and does not occur in the Soviet system, frictional and structural unemployment can occur. The state's ability to control the movement of people away from the farms (through a system of work permits and internal passports) has led to much disguised unemployment in the agricultural sector. There is little

doubt that if people had been free to move from the farms, they would have moved in great numbers to the cities in search of the excitement and higher living standards there, and they would have moved at a faster rate than industry could have absorbed them. In a market economy, this would have led to substantial urban overcrowding and unemployment and would have served to depress the wages of those who were successful in finding work. The Soviet tendency has been to hold these people on the farms where they are underemployed and to allow them to move to the cities only as fast as they could be absorbed into jobs there. Again, the potential clash of values can be seen. Western observers are inclined to stress what to them is the severe loss of personal freedom, whereas Soviet observers tend to emphasize the gains to the economy of an orderly relocation of labor. In particular, they see the advantage to urban workers of not having their wages depressed by the unemployed migrants from the farm and the advantage to the farm dwellers in being detained on the farm, where they can be fed and housed at lower cost and in greater comfort until jobs are actually available in the city.

The Soviets have had less success in controlling inflation than in controlling unemployment. Like the princes discussed in Chapter 32, they found increasing the money supply too easy a way to finance public expenditures, particularly during the war. The high wartime expenditures resulted in a dangerously inflationary piling up of private money balances. But the response of a command economy can be quick and sure, if harsh. When monetary reform came, the state confiscated the bulk of private monetary balances and repudiated some of the public debt that workers had accepted in lieu of part of their wages. Thus workers who thought they had been saving found they really had been taxed.

This was the Soviet response to a problem that existed in all belligerent countries at the end of World War II. Wartime savings and deferred consumption created an enormous backlog of demand. After the war, this demand for goods was far in excess of the supply. The problem was complicated by the fact that any postwar production to meet this pent-up demand for consumer goods would create additional purchasing power. The Soviet response was to destroy the backlog of purchasing power by monetary reform; the Western answer was to allow people to try to exercise it and accept the inflation that inevitably followed and that reduced the real value of accumulated purchasing power to a level commensurate with the goods actually available to be purchased. Both systems produced the same end of reducing the real value of purchasing power to what was available. To Western eyes, the Soviet solution (confiscation) seems harsh and autocratic; to Soviet eyes, the Western solution (inflation) seems arbitrary and highly inequitable in its incidence.

Shortcomings of the Soviet economic experience

In at least two major ways, the Soviet-type economy compares unfavorably to a Western market economy. First, it is accompanied by a large number of microeconomic inefficiencies. So many small interdependent decisions have to be made that it is difficult or impossible to expect them to be made quickly, consistently, and efficiently by a centralized decision hierarchy. The shortages, gluts, misshipments, and shortfalls of key quotas that have annoyed Soviet industry and plagued Soviet agriculture are neither surprising nor wholly avoidable. They are periodically denounced as "planning errors" of a previous regime. Such errors, however, are apparently a cost of choosing to replace an automatic mechanism (whose implicit values the planners have chosen to reject) by a deliberate mechanism that permits the planners to introduce their own values. In recent years, some pressure has developed within Soviet-type economies to retreat from complete planning and to allow market or marketlike mechanisms to do more of the allocating.

A second deficiency has been in the detailed planning process itself, which is enormously demanding of time and energy. When labor was abundant, and when alternative uses of those with the planners' skills were not numerous, this "transaction cost" of planning was perhaps not serious. Increasingly, however, the Soviet bureaucracy has been absorbing a large quantity of valuable, highly trained manpower in plan formation and implementation, and the Soviets have come to recognize this as a real cost. The major surge of interest in techniques of mathematical programming, input-output analysis, and simulation reflects the effort of officials to substitute capital for high-priced labor in the "production function of planning." They hope both to save resources and to avoid some of the microeconomic inefficiencies and mistakes. Evaluation of how successful these techniques will prove must wait until there is more evidence. In principle, they should be able to assist in, if not to revolutionize, central planning, but the techniques are themselves in the developmental stages.

Source and costs of the achievements

A planned command economy has certain advantages over a market-oriented one: The leaders can set up whatever priorities they wish, and they can then use the full power of the state to give effect to them. In such economies, the power of the state has been used to achieve forced saving to permit capital formation and rapid growth. It has also been used to prevent widespread unemployment. It may well be that the Soviet growth record could not have been achieved if it had depended on popular or majority support, for it is by no means clear that the growth benefited the Soviet population of the 1930s and the 1940s.

This rapid growth has had costs—costs not only in current consumption foregone, but also the costs of coercing individuals, of their loss of freedom, and of substituting centralized for individual judgments. Because these things are not readily commensurable, the question of whether the benefits justify the costs is really a normative one, and the answer is a value judgment that each person must reach for himself. Different people would answer it differently. Most citizens of Western countries are content to have foregone both the benefits and the costs; contemporary Russians may feel they have been justified. Not surprisingly, different people and different governments in the "third world" come down on different sides.

Politically the present government is in many ways a monstrous and terrible tyranny—as has recently been emphasized by Aleksandr Solzhenitsyn. It is not necessary to assume, however, that this degree of tyranny *must* accompany any command economy. After all, the tradition of political tyranny in Russia stretches well back into the time of the Czars, and other command economies have had regimes less repressive than that of the USSR. Command economies do, however, by their very nature have to be more authoritarian than free-market economies. An important and still unsettled question concerns the minimum degree of repression of individual freedom that is consistent with a highly centralized planned economy of the Soviet type.

The economy of Yugoslavia

Yugoslavia emerged from World War II after a double war, the first one a long, highly organized and increasingly successful guerrilla war fought against the Germans from the time of their original conquest of Yugoslavia in 1941 until their eventual withdrawal in late 1944, and the second a desperate civil war. The victorious leader and military hero, Marshal Tito (Josip Broz), was a professed Communist, but he was not willing to be dominated by Stalin. The political break—the first within the Communist world—occurred in June 1948 and has played a significant role in the postwar political situation. The concern here is with its *economic* by-product: the emergence of a socialist market-type economy.

The economic theory of an economy in which the state owns the means of production but uses markets to allocate resources had been suggested a decade earlier by Oskar Lange and developed by Abba Lerner.[2] To

[2] The saying "truth is stranger than fiction" is illustrated in the story of Lange, a Polish economist, who was a professor at the University of Chicago when he wrote his celebrated essay "On the Economic Theory of Socialism" (1938). After the war, Lange returned to Communist Poland as a high official of the regime and remained there until his death in 1963. The Soviet-style economy of Poland never moved toward a Lange-type economy. Meanwhile, Yugoslavia, probably in ignorance of Lange's work, did move toward the kind of economy Lange had described—and was criticized by Poland for doing so.

put the Lange–Lerner theory in its simplest form, the business firm (owned by the state) would have a manager who was instructed to follow such rules as: "Take price as given to you and produce output up to the point at which price equals marginal cost" and "Taking wage rates as given, hire labor as long as the additional worker adds more to the value of output than his wages." Whether the prices and wages that were given to the firm came from the central planners (as in Lange's theory) or from markets where households buy goods and sell factor services (as in Lerner's theory) made no difference at the *firm* level. Marketlike forces determined what resources were used and where and how they were used.

When Yugoslavia turned away from the command economy and took the steps toward what was called the New Economic System, it did so not because it accepted this theory, but because in its break with the Soviet Union it needed all the economic success it could achieve, and it found some aspects of a controlled economy more expensive than it could afford.

The modern Yugoslav economic system evolved in two stages. The first (1952–1960) put major emphasis on decentralization and development of a market system for allocation of resources. The second, beginning with a series of political, economic, and constitutional reforms in 1961, put major emphasis on self-government of industrial enterprises.

In particular, Yugoslavians sought to avoid three features of the Soviet experience: (1) the inefficiencies and resulting disasters in agricultural production; (2) micro inefficiencies in industrial production; and (3) the burden of a large planning and administrative operation for which it lacked properly trained and motivated personnel.

The Soviet Union was by 1948 already an industrial power with a well-developed educational system. Yugoslavia was not. It emerged from World War II ravaged by years of struggle, a primitive agricultural society with very little industry, with few trained personnel, and with a low level of general education. Under these circumstances it could ill afford to waste its limited resources. Its realistic choices were to accept Soviet technicians, planners, and economic aid (and, realistically, political domination) or to go its own way. When, after 1948, it chose the latter course, it could not afford the luxury of avoidable inefficiencies.

What has emerged, often after substantial trial and error, is a reasonable approximation to a socialist market economy, with public ownership of most means of production, with substantially decentralized decision making through markets, but with a large role for planning and the public sector.

THE DECOLLECTIVIZATION OF AGRICULTURE

In the early postwar period, Yugoslavia had attempted to follow the Soviet pattern and create state farms or collective farms that would operate efficiently for the greater glory of the state. By the early 1950s, the program had gathered more than a quarter of the arable land under centralized control. The program met hostility and resistance at an increasing rate, however, and many of those who had been placed on collectives were unhappy and eager to leave. The Soviets had been obliged to use force and fear to create collectives and to use the police power of the state to maintain them. Faced with a similar bitter prospect, Yugoslavia, in 1953, abruptly reversed its stand. Not only did it stop collectivizing, it allowed farmers to leave the collectives and to resume personal ownership and operation of small farms. Today farmers can produce what they like and sell it where and when they wish. Since 1953, roughly half of the state acreage has returned to private operation, and the remaining state farms are run more nearly as cooperatives than as collectives.

The performance of Yugoslavian agriculture since the reversal in policy compares favorably with Russian performance. It has increased its output at a rate of 5 percent per year in the last decade, and it has not been plagued by any serious crisis. Moreover, it has not had to absorb scarce planning manpower in its management, which represents a gain compared to the Soviet experience over the same period.

LABOR-MANAGED ENTERPRISES

In the bulk of the nonagricultural sectors of the economy, public (state) ownership is retained, but management of the individual enterprises has been turned over to the workers, blue- and white-collar alike, who have virtually full authority over all operations and whose pay (above guaranteed minimum wages) is determined by the net income of the enterprise.

A characteristic arrangement might be for the workers in a plant to elect a workers' council, which in turn elects a management board. This board appoints a manager who is responsible to it, but who has a good deal of discretion. The local political party is consulted in the selection of the manager, and the manager is charged with upholding the state laws as they impinge on the operations of the firm. Any difference from a command system would be mere formality if the managers now received detailed orders from higher up, but they do not. Factors of production and goods are purchased on more or less free markets, and the firm can prosper or suffer. If it prospers it may, at its discretion, reinvest part of its profits, and it may borrow funds from banks and other firms for expansion.

The firm is subject to various taxes on its income, but beyond that its earnings are distributed to the workers. Nominally, workers receive only "profit sharing" and no wages, but the effect of a guaranteed minimum amount to each worker means that profit sharing comes into play only after minimal levels of income have been achieved.

Workers' managements appear to have several advantages for the Yugoslavian state. First, an enormous and demanding administrative burden is transferred from central planning to decentralized markets. Second, workers' morale, and their productivity, seems to have risen in response to their having a real and personal stake in their firm. Third, all sorts of incentives for efficient operation are created.

Along with these familiar advantages of a market-motivated system have come some of the familiar problems of market economies. Once the workers of a firm recognize that their income reflects the firm's profits, they may be tempted to increase those profits in any way they can. Indeed, because of the relatively small scale of most Yugoslavian industry, a potentially severe monopoly problem has arisen.

The earlier theoretical literature about the workings of a socialist market economy had visualized that the firm would act as a price taker and thus approximate competitive conditions. In Yugoslavia many firms have discovered that they need not be price takers and have (where allowed) increased prices and restricted output in textbook profit maximizing fashion. In a fully market oriented society, these monopoly profits would motivate new firms to enter the industry, and entry would continue until monopoly profits had been removed. In Yugoslavia, there is a more serious problem. Profits accrue to the workers in a firm, but who is motivated to organize the firm, in the first place? Sometimes the local community will do so if it has unemployed workers; more often it waits for some central official to decide that prices are rising too high and further firms should be encouraged or created.

As the last sentence suggests, unemployment has not been avoided in the Yugoslavian system. If one depends on the market mechanism to motivate resource movements, and if such movements are subject to immobilities and supply lags, pockets of unemployment may appear and persist in certain regions, industries, or occupations. "Structural unemployment" is discussed in Zagreb as well as in Seattle, and the Yugoslavs have been no more successful in preventing regional unemployment than have others who rely on market economies.

THE SCOPE AND ROLE OF PLANNING

The Yugoslav economy is somewhat less decentralized than the foregoing description may suggest. It retains many of the major planning functions of a command economy in the form of comprehensive five-year plans.

In some ways, these plans are not very different from those developed in nonsocialist countries such as Italy, France, and (more recently) Greece. A major part of any planning operation must identify general targets for development and work out the disaggregated implications of aggregate targets in terms of requirements for different products, services, factors of production, and raw materials. The reason these plans are more influential in the Yugoslav economy, where state ownership is common, is that more than two-thirds of all new investment is done by the state with money raised (largely) by taxation.[3] Because a rapid rate of growth and a consequent high level of investment have loomed large in Yugoslavian planning, the decisions with respect to whom to tax and where to invest have played a major role in the economy. These decisions have been made in a highly centralized way. For one example, a clear decision to give urban housing a very low priority relative to heavy industry and to tourist accommodations results in a situation of notice-

ably poor and dilapidated housing that not only distresses the Yugoslav people but is visible to the eye of even the casual tourist.

The success of the Yugoslavian experiment is shown by its growth rates: During the period of central planning, 1947–1952, before the new reforms were in effect, GNP increased at 2.3 percent per year. During 1952–1960, growth occurred at 9.8 percent per year, and since that date at approximately 6 percent per year. Although some of this apparent growth represents the utilization of previously unemployed resources, and although some of it represents the first, easy moves toward industrialization, it is nevertheless impressive. Yugoslavia has taken a significant step from the backward, Balkan peasant world into the world of developing countries. It has done so with a distinctive set of economic institutions that have developed pragmatically rather than in response to ideological considerations of either communism or capitalism.

Comparative systems: a final word

Perhaps the most important empirical observation about different economies is that a wide variety of different economic systems seem able to coexist and to show successes. No economic system seems to do all things better than any major competing system; indeed, each has its strengths and weaknesses relative to alternative systems. To talk of "better" and "worse" in this context may itself be misleading: different economic systems imply different choices between current and future consumption, between individual or collective choices, between degrees of freedom or coercion, between stability and growth.

The economic institutions of a society reflect in part its values, but they also reflect its

---

[3] The other one-third comes from reinvested enterprise earnings.

habits and traditions, experiments and inertia. These institutions change with time in given countries and vary at a given time among countries. In the variety of experience economists hope to find many clues as to which instruments achieve which ends.

In the contemporary experience, it looks as if the command principle makes the management of certain macro policies much easier than it is in a market system, but it also appears that it is less well suited than the market to handling micro allocations. While a command system can achieve great sacrifices in the short run, the growth evidence suggests no simple conclusion, for many countries with very different economic systems have achieved rapid growth. It is clear that markets are less personal than bureaucrats, and this makes them more acceptable to many people because they are less arbitrary and less subject to autocratic abuse.

Summary

1. Actual economies can differ from one another in a great variety of ways, and such capsule characterizations as "capitalism," "socialism," or "communism" represent simplifications of complex matters.

2. Among the important dimensions in which economies can differ from one another are (a) the pattern of ownership of goods and resources; (b) the nature of the decision process used, with a particularly important distinction concerning "command" versus "market" decision mechanisms; (c) whose values control the economy and how these values are articulated; (d) the nature of the incentive systems used; and (e) the relative concern about ends and means.

3. Central planning plays a major role in the Soviet economy. Long-term goals are given structure by a series of five-year plans, which in turn are implemented by highly detailed one-year plans. Most of the key decisions are made centrally by the various GOSPLANs, but prices are used both for internal accounting and to affect the distribution of goods and incomes.

4. The turnover tax is important in Soviet pricing. First, it is used as a weapon of distributive policy: as the size of the tax varies from commodity to commodity, the consumers of those commodities are differentially taxed. Second, in its average size the turnover tax determines the fraction of current production withdrawn from current consumption and returned to the state for reinvestment. Third, it takes reinvestment decisions out of the hands of individual industries and sectors and places them with the central authorities. The amount and pattern of investment is set by the planners directly through GOSBANK.

5. A comparison of relative performance between the United States and the Soviet Union reveals that the United States has higher levels of real output per capita but a much less impressive recent growth record. The Soviet Union has suffered less than the United States from unemployment but has not avoided inflationary pressures. Microeconomic inefficiencies have been numerous in the Soviet experience, and agriculture has proved to be a serious, chronic problem.

6. A major difference has been the use of force and coercion by the state. This has permitted the Soviet economy to achieve certain objectives, including extremely rapid capital formation, monetary reform, and the orderly mobility of labor from farm to city. To most Westerners, the costs in the form of coercion, loss of freedom, and the substitution of centralized for individual judgments seem to have been high. Most Russians today probably feel them to have been justified.

7. Yugoslavia is an example of a socialist market-type economy in which state ownership is combined with extensive use of markets for decision-making purposes. The Yugoslav system arose as a consequence of the political break with the Soviet Union in 1948.

8. The Yugoslavs have sought to avoid three features of the Soviet experience: (a) the inefficiencies and resulting disasters in agricultural production, (b) micro inefficiencies in industrial production, and (c) the burden of a large planning and administrative operation for which they lacked properly trained and motivated personnel.

9. The Yugoslavian economy exhibits three major differences from a Soviet-type economy: (a) the decollectivization of agriculture, (b) the decentralized management of industrial firms, and (c) the substantial managerial control given to workers. A very significant planning function remains to the Yugoslav central authorities because of the importance of the investment decisions that the state must make.

10. A wide variety of different economic systems seems able to coexist and to show successes. No economic system seems to do all things better than any major competing system; indeed, each has its strengths and weaknesses relative to alternative systems.

Concepts for review

Free-market and command economies
Alternative ownership and decision patterns
Central planning
Decentralized socialist economies

Discussion questions

1. In an economic report to the 25th Communist Party Congress in 1976, Soviet Prime Minister Aleksei Kosygin said that the crisis of capitalism was marked by inflation and unemployment, in contrast with the Soviet Union's full employment and stable retail prices. How does the Soviet Union avoid the problems of inflation and unemployment? In doing so, does it encounter problems not faced by capitalist countries?

2. According to the mayor of Moscow, that city could never have a crisis of the kind that plagues New York and other American cities. "In my country the city government owns and operates not only schools, hospitals, and other nonprofit enterprises but also such profitable enterprises as all the restaurants, stores, movie theaters, bakeries, food-processing factories, manufacturers of consumer goods, construction companies, and trucks in the city." These activities generate 80 percent of the revenues needed to run the city. The rest of the revenue is raised by taxes collected by the central government and paid to the city. Is a socialist country uniquely able to avoid or solve the problems of its biggest cities? Compare the things the U.S. government might do to help New York meet its deficit with those done for Moscow.

3. Capital is used in the heavy industries of both the United States and the Soviet Union, and in roughly equal amounts.

In what sense is the United States capitalistic and Russia socialistic? Who supplies the capital in a communist economy?

4. Russian consumers, believing they will get an inferior product for their money, tend to avoid purchasing TV sets and other products produced at the end of the planning period, when factories are rushing to fulfill their output targets. By the same token, American consumers are more reluctant to purchase a car produced either at the beginning or at the end of the model year. Thus, it seems that concerns about quality exist in both economies. Are these concerns generated by similar or by different factors? Discuss.

5. During World War II, the U.S. government (a) rationed steel, aluminum, and copper, (b) put price controls on most goods and services, but rationed only meat, sugar and gasoline, (c) used the draft to raise armed forces of 11 million, but deferred workers in key industries, (d) purchased about half of the goods and services comprising the GNP, (e) increased income taxes and introduced an excess-profits tax.

Would you classify the United States as a command economy at that time? Explain. Can you see reasons for each of the five measures outlined above, given the economic goals of the time?

6. How might the economies of the United States, the Soviet Union, and Yugoslavia attempt to achieve each of the following results? Which system would be likely to do it most easily?
a. achieve full employment
b. redistribute income from rich to poor
c. choose the appropriate mix between tractor production and residential construction
d. determine the relative pay of carpenters and school teachers
e. avoid a shortage or surplus of men's shirts
f. increase the rate of saving

7. "What the world of economics needs is an end to ideology and *isms*. If there is a best system of economic organization, it will prove its superiority in its superior ability to solve economic problems." Do you agree with this statement? Would you expect that if the world survives for another one hundred years, a single form of economic system would be found superior to all others? Why or why not?

APPENDIXES

appendix
to chapter 2

More on functional relations

The idea of relations among variables is one of the basic notions behind all science. Such relations can be expressed as functional relations.

FUNCTIONAL RELATIONS: THE GENERAL EXPRESSION OF RELATIONS AMONG VARIABLES

Consider two examples, one from a natural science and one from economics. The gravitational attraction of two bodies depends on their mass and on the distance separating them, attraction increasing with size and diminishing with distance; the amount of a commodity that people would like to buy depends on (among other things) the price of the commodity, purchases increasing as price falls. When mathematicians wish to say that one variable depends on another, they say that one variable is a function of the other. [45][1]

Thus gravitational attraction is a function of the mass of the two bodies concerned and the distance between them, and the quantity of a product demanded is a function of the price of the product.

One of the virtues of mathematics is that it permits the concise expression of ideas that would otherwise require long, drawn-out verbal statements. There are two steps in giving compact symbolic expression to functional relations. First, each variable is given a symbol. Second, a symbol is designated to express the idea of one variable's dependence on another. Thus, if G equals gravitational attraction, M equals the mass of two bodies, and d equals the distance between two bodies, we may write

$$G = f(M, d)$$

where f is read "is a function of" and means "depends upon." The whole equation defines a hypothesis and is read "gravitational attraction is a function of the mass of the two bodies concerned and the distance between them." The same hypothesis can be written as

$$G = G(M, d)$$

This is read in exactly the same way and means the same thing as the previous expression. Instead

---

[1] Reference numbers in color refer to Mathematical Notes, which begin on page 901.

of using f to represent "a function of," the left-hand symbol, G, is repeated.[2]

The hypothesis about the variables, desired purchases and price, can be written

$$q = f(p)$$

or

$$q = q(p)$$

where q stands for the quantity people wish to purchase of some commodity and p is the price of the commodity. The expression says that the quantity of some commodity that people desire to purchase is a function of its price. The alternative way of writing this merely uses different letters to stand for the same functional relation between p and q.

FUNCTIONAL FORMS: PRECISE RELATIONS AMONG VARIABLES

The expression $Y = Y(X)$ merely states that the variables Y and X are related; it says nothing about the form that this relation takes. Usually the hypothesis to be expressed says more than that. Does Y increase as X increases? Does Y decrease as X increases? Or is the relation more complicated? Take a very simple example, where Y is the length of a board in feet, and X is the length of the same board in yards. Quite clearly, $Y = Y(X)$. Further, in this case the exact form of the function is known, for length in feet (Y) is merely three times the length in yards (X), so we may write $Y = 3X$.

This relation is a definitional one, since the length of something measured in feet is defined to be three times its length measured in yards. It is nonetheless useful to have a way of writing relationships that are definitionally true. The expression $Y = 3X$ specifies the exact form of the relation between Y and X and provides a rule whereby, if we have the value of one, we can calculate the value of the other.

Now consider a second example. Let C stand for consumption expenditure, the total amount spent on purchasing goods and services by all American households during a year. Let DI stand for the total amount of income that these households had available to spend during the year. We might state the hypothesis that

$$C = f(DI)$$

and, even more specifically,

$$C = 0.8DI$$

The first expression gives the hypothesis that the total consumption expenditure of households depends on their income. The second expression says, more specifically, that total consumption expenditure is 80 percent of the total available for spending. The second equation expresses a very specific hypothesis about the relation between two observable magnitudes. There is no reason why it *must* be true; it may be consistent or inconsistent with the facts. This is a matter for testing. However, the equation is a concise statement of a particular hypothesis.

Thus the general view that there is a relation between Y and X is denoted by $Y = f(X)$, whereas any precise relation may be expressed by a particular equation such as $Y = 2X$, $Y = 4X^2$, or $Y = X + 2X^2 + 0.5X^3$.

If Y increases as X increases (e.g., $Y = 10 + 2X$), we say that Y is an *increasing function* of X, or that Y and X *vary directly* with each other. If Y decreases as X increases (e.g., $Y = 10 - 2X$), we say that Y is a *decreasing function* of X or that Y and X *vary inversely* with each other.

ERROR TERMS IN ECONOMIC HYPOTHESES

Expressing hypotheses in the form of functions is misleading in one respect. When we say that the world behaves so that $Y = f(X)$, we do not expect that knowing X will tell us *exactly* what Y will be, but only if it will tell us what Y will be *within some margin of error*. This error in predicting Y from a knowledge of X arises for two quite distinct reasons. First, there may be other variables that also affect Y. When, for example, we say that the demand for butter is a function of the price of butter, $D_b = f(p_b)$, we know that other factors will also influence this demand. A change in the price of margarine will certainly affect the demand for butter, even though the price of butter does not change. Thus we do not expect to find a perfect re-

---

[2] Any convenient symbol may be used on the right-hand side before the parenthesis to mean "a function of." The repetition of the left-hand symbol may be convenient in reminding us of what is a function of what.

lation between D_b and p_b that will allow us to predict D_b exactly from a knowledge of p_b. Second, variables can never be measured exactly. Even if X is the only cause of Y, measurements will give various Ys corresponding to the same X. In the case of the demand for butter, errors of measurement might not be large. In other cases errors might be substantial—as, for example, in the case of a relation between the total consumption expenditure of all American households and their total income. The measurements of consumption and income may be subject to quite wide margins of error, and various values of consumption associated with the same measured value of income may be observed, not because consumption is varying independently of income but because the error of measurement is varying from period to period.

When we say Y is a function of X, we appear to say Y is completely determined by X. Instead of the deterministic formulation

$$Y = f(X)$$

it would be better form to write

$$Y = f(X) + \epsilon$$

or

$$Y = f(X, \ \epsilon)$$

where ϵ, the Greek letter epsilon, represents an **error term.** Such a term indicates that the observed value of Y will differ from the value predicted by the functional relation between Y and X. Divergences will occur both because of observational errors and because of neglected variables. While economists always mean this, they usually do not say so.

The deterministic formulation is a simplification; an error term is really present in all assumed and observed functional relations.

This is true, by the way, not only of economics and other subjects dealing with human behavior, but of physics, chemistry, geology, and all other sciences. The old-time dichotomy between "exact" and "inexact" sciences is now abandoned; all theories and all measurements are subject to error.

appendix
to chapter 3

Graphing economic magnitudes

The popular saying "The facts speak for themselves" is almost always wrong when there is a large number of facts. Theories are needed to explain how facts are linked together, and summary measures are needed to assist in sorting out what it is that facts do show in relation to theories. The simplest means of providing compact summaries of a large number of observations is through the use of tables and graphs. Graphs play important roles in economics by representing both observed data and economic theories geometrically. Here both uses will be discussed.

GRAPHING ECONOMIC OBSERVATIONS

The surface of a piece of paper is a two-dimensional object, and a graph may readily be used to represent pictorially the interrelation between two variables. Flip through this book and you will see dozens of examples. Figure 3A–1 shows more generally how a coordinate grid can permit representation of any two measurable variables.

Economics is very often concerned only with the positive values of variables, and in such cases the graph is confined to the upper right-hand (or "positive") quadrant. Whenever either or both variables take on a negative value one or more of the other quadrants must be included.

The scatter diagram

The scatter diagram provides a method of graphing any number of observations made on two variables. In Chapter 3 data for income and meat purchases for a large number of American households were studied. To show these data on a scatter diagram, income was measured on the horizontal axis and meat purchases on the vertical axis. Any point in the diagram represents a particular income combined with a particular quantity of meat purchased. Thus each household for which there are observations can be represented on the diagram by a dot, the coordinates of which indicate the household's income and the amount of beef it purchases.

The scatter diagram is useful because if there is a simple relation between the two variables, it will be apparent to the eye once the data are plotted. Thus in Figure 3–1 (see page 33) meat purchases clearly tend to rise as income rises. It is also ap-

Figure 3A–1 A coordinate graph

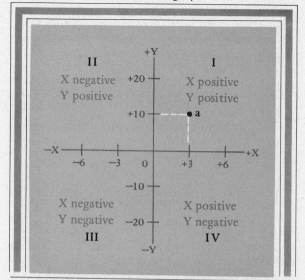

The axes divide the total space into four quadrants according to the signs of the variables. The upper right-hand quadrant is the one in which both X and Y are greater than zero and is usually called the *positive quadrant*. Point a in the figure has *coordinates* $Y = 10$ and $X = 3$ in the coordinate graph. These coordinates *define* point a.

parent that this relation is only approximately linear since, as income rises above $5,000 a year, beef purchases seem to rise less and less with further equal increases in income. The diagram also gives some idea of the strength of the relation: If income were the only determinant of beef purchases, all of the dots would lie on a single line; as it is, the points are somewhat scattered and particular incomes are often represented by several households, each with different quantities of beef purchased.

The data used in this example are **cross-sectional data.** The incomes and beef purchases of different households are compared over a single period of time. Scatter diagrams may also be drawn of a number of observations taken on two variables at successive periods of time. Thus, if one wanted to know if there had been any simple relation between personal income and personal

consumption in the United States between 1950 and 1975, data would be collected for the levels of personal income and expenditure per capita in each year from 1950 to 1975, as is done in Table 3A–1. This information could be plotted on a scatter diagram with income on the X axis and consumption on the Y axis to discover any systematic relation between the two variables. The data are plotted in Figure 3A–2 and do indeed suggest a systematic linear relation. In this exercise a scatter diagram of observations taken over successive periods of time has been used. Such data are called **time-series data** and plotting them on a scatter diagram involves no new technique: When cross-sectional data are plotted, each point gives the values of two variables for a particular unit

Table 3A–1 Income and Consumption, 1950–1975 (1972 dollars)

Year	Disposable personal income, per capita	Personal consumption expenditures per capita
1950	$2,386	$2,229
1951	2,408	2,219
1952	2,434	2,236
1953	2,491	2,283
1954	2,476	2,284
1955	2,577	2,391
1956	2,645	2,415
1957	2,650	2,421
1958	2,636	2,406
1959	2,696	2,493
1960	2,697	2,507
1961	2,725	2,516
1962	2,796	2,589
1963	2,849	2,649
1964	3,009	2,755
1965	3,152	2,872
1966	3,274	2,982
1967	3,371	3,035
1968	3,464	3,156
1969	3,515	3,234
1970	3,619	3,265
1971	3,714	3,342
1972	3,837	3,510
1973	4,068	3,642
1974	3,981	3,586
1975	4,012	3,588

Source: *Economic Report of the President,* 1976.

Figure 3A–2   A scatter diagram relating consumption and disposable income

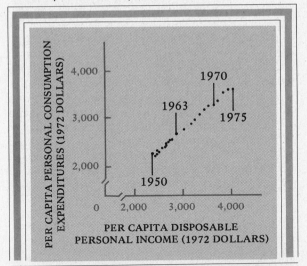

A scatter diagram shows paired values of two variables.   The data of Table 3A–1 are plotted here. Each dot shows, for a particular year, the values of per capita personal consumption and per capita disposable personal income. They show a close, positive, linear relationship between the two variables.

Figure 3A–3   A time series of consumption expenditures, 1950–1975

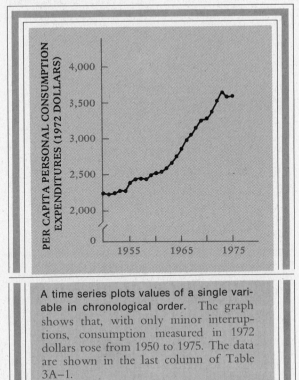

A time series plots values of a single variable in chronological order.   The graph shows that, with only minor interruptions, consumption measured in 1972 dollars rose from 1950 to 1975. The data are shown in the last column of Table 3A–1.

(say a household); when time-series data are plotted, each point tells the values of two variables for a particular year.

Time-series graphs

Instead of studying the relation between income and consumption suggested in the previous paragraph, a study of the pattern of the changes in either one of these variables over time could be made. In Figure 3A–3 this information is shown for consumption. In the figure, time is one variable, consumption expenditure the other. But time is a very special variable: the order in which successive events happen is important. The year 1965 followed 1964; they were not two independent and unrelated years. (By way of contrast, two randomly selected households are independent and unrelated.) For this reason it is customary to draw

in the line segments connecting the successive points, as has been done in Figure 3A–3. A chart such as this figure is called a time-series graph or, more simply, a time series. This kind of graph makes it easy to see if the variable being considered has varied in a systematic way over the years or if its behavior has been more or less erratic.

Ratio (logarithmic) scales

Often *proportionate* rather than absolute changes in variables are important. In such cases it is more revealing to use a ratio scale rather than a natural scale. On a **natural scale** the distance between numbers is proportionate to the absolute difference between those numbers. Thus 200 is placed halfway between 100 and 300. On a **ratio scale** the distance between numbers is proportionate to the absolute difference between their log-

Table 3A–2 Two series

Time period	Series A	Series B
0	$10	$ 10
1	18	20
2	26	40
3	34	80
4	42	160

Series A shows constant absolute growth ($8 per period) but declining percentage growth. Series B shows constant percentage growth (100 percent per period) but rising absolute growth.

arithms. Equal distances anywhere on a ratio scale represent equal percentage changes rather than equal absolute changes. On a ratio scale the distance between 100 and 200 is the same as the distance between 200 and 400, between 1,000 and 2,000, and between any two numbers that stand in the ratio 1:2 to each other. For obvious reasons a ratio scale is also called a **logarithmic scale.**

Table 3A–2 shows two series, one growing at a constant absolute amount of 8 units per period and the other growing at a constant rate of 100 percent per period. In Figure 3A–4 the series are plotted first on a natural scale and then on a ratio scale. The natural scale makes it easy for the eye to judge absolute variations, and the logarithmic scale

Figure 3A–4 The difference between natural and ratio scales

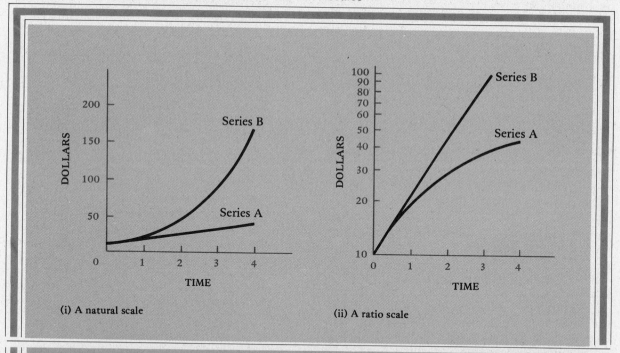

(i) A natural scale

(ii) A ratio scale

On a natural scale, equal distances represent equal amounts; on a ratio scale, equal vertical distances represent equal percentage changes. The two series in Table 3A–2 are plotted in each chart. Series A, which grows at a constant absolute amount, is a straight line on a natural scale but a downward-bending curve on a ratio scale because the same absolute growth is decreasing percentage growth. Series B, which grows at a rising absolute but a constant percentage rate, is upward-bending on a natural scale but is a straight line on a ratio scale.

makes it easy for the eye to judge proportionate variations.[1]

GRAPHING FUNCTIONS

Functions were discussed in the appendix to Chapter 2. Simple functions can be represented in the same two-dimensional space in which data can be graphed. When this is done we obtain a geometrical expression of the functions. Since economic theory is often expressed in terms of functions, graphing these functions is a way of providing a graphical representation of the theory.

Linear functions

Consider the functions

$$Y = 0.5X$$

$$Y = X$$

$$Y = 2X$$

These are graphed in Figure 3A–5. All of the Y functions are straight lines through the origin because if $X = 0$ in each of the above relations, Y also becomes 0. In the first equation, where $Y = 0.5X$, Y goes up half a unit every time X goes up by one unit, in the second equation, where $Y = X$, Y goes up one unit every time X goes up one unit; and in the third equation, where $Y = 2X$, Y goes up two units every time X goes up one unit. The straight lines differ only because of their slopes; each is a special case of $Y = bX$.

The symbol Δ is used to indicate a change in a variable. Thus ΔX means the value of the change in X, and ΔY means the value of the change in Y. In the first equation, if $X = 10$, then Y is 5, and if X goes up to 16, Y goes up to 8. Thus, in this exercise, $\Delta X = 6$ and $\Delta Y = 3$.

Next consider the ratio $\Delta Y / \Delta X$. In the above example, it is equal to 0.5. For any change made in X in the first equation, $\Delta Y / \Delta X$ is always 0.5. In the second, it is unity, and in the third, the ratio is

---

[1] Graphs with a ratio scale on one axis and a natural scale on the other are frequently encountered in economics. In the cases just illustrated there is a ratio scale on the vertical axis and a natural scale on the horizontal (or time) axis. Such graphs are often called *semi-log* graphs. In scientific work graphs with ratio scales on both axes are frequently encountered. Such graphs are often referred to as *double-log* graphs.

Figure 3A–5 Straight lines through the origin

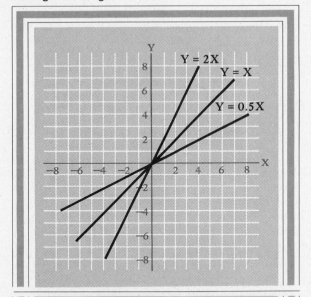

These straight lines differ only in their slopes. Each is a special case of $Y = bX$.

Figure 3A–6 Straight lines with slope of $+2$

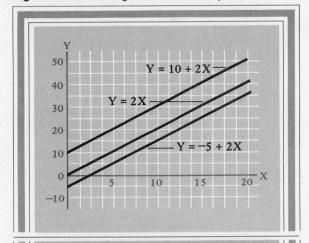

Parallel straight lines have the same slope but different intercepts. These straight lines differ only in their intercepts. Each is a special case of $Y = a + 2X$.

always 2. In general, if we write $Y = bX$, then the ratio $\Delta Y / \Delta X$ is always equal to b.

This ratio is defined to be the slope of a straight line. This slope gives the ratio of a change in Y to a change in X. The slopes of the three functions in Figure 3A–5 are 2, 1, and 0.5. Clearly, the greater the slope, the steeper the line.

Now consider the equations

$$Y = 2X$$

$$Y = 10 + 2X$$

$$Y = -5 + 2X$$

These are graphed in Figure 3A–6. It will be observed that all three lines are parallel—that is, they have the same slope; they differ only in their intercepts. Each is a special case of $Y = a + 2X$. In all three, $\Delta Y / \Delta X$ is equal to 2. Clearly, the addition of a (positive or negative) constant does not affect

Figure 3A–7 Three rectangular hyperbolas

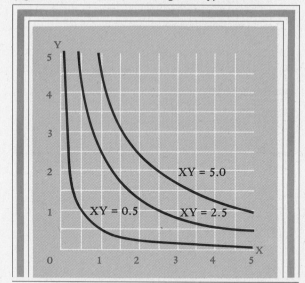

A rectangular hyperbola is an example of a nonlinear relation between two variables. Each of these hyperbolas is a member of the family $XY = a$. If a is also taken as a variable, the family of curves shows the interrelations among the three variables X, Y, and a.

Figure 3A–8 A parabola

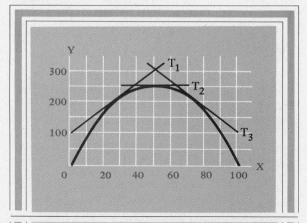

A parabola is an example of a nonlinear relation between two variables. The slope of a parabola, as with any nonlinear function, is not constant. The slope—how Y is tending to change as X changes—can be measured at any point on the function as the slope of a line that is tangent to the function at that point.

the slope of the line. This slope is influenced only by the number attached to X.

In general, the equation of a straight line may be written as

$$Y = a + bX$$

where b is the slope of the line and a is the value of Y when X is zero; a is called the Y intercept. The value of a does not affect the slope. [46] As the value of a changes it shifts the line upward or downward parallel to itself.

Each of the straight lines that has been drawn is upward sloping—it has a positive slope. A function such as $Y = 10 - 2X$, or, even more generally, $Y = a - bX$, will slope downward.

Figures 3A–5 and 3A–6 provide both the numerical grids which were used to plot the functions and the equations of the lines. Functions are often represented graphically, however, primarily in order to compare their general shapes. In such a situation both the numerical grid and the precise equation are often suppressed.

Nonlinear functions

Many of the relations encountered in economics are nonlinear. A nonlinear relation is expressed graphically by a curved line and algebraically by some expression more complex than the one for a straight line. Two common examples of nonlinear relations are expressed by the equations

$$Y = \frac{a}{X}$$

$$Y = a + bX + cX^2$$

The first equation describes what is called a rectangular hyperbola. Three examples are plotted in Figure 3A–7. The second equation describes a parabola that takes on various positions and shapes depending on the signs and magnitudes of a, b, and c. One example of such a parabola is given in Figure 3A–8.

Unlike a straight line, which has a constant slope, a variable slope is the essence of a nonlinear function. The slope of a nonlinear function changes from point to point, but it may be evaluated at any point. The slope of a curve at a point is

Figure 3A–9 A contour map of a small mountain

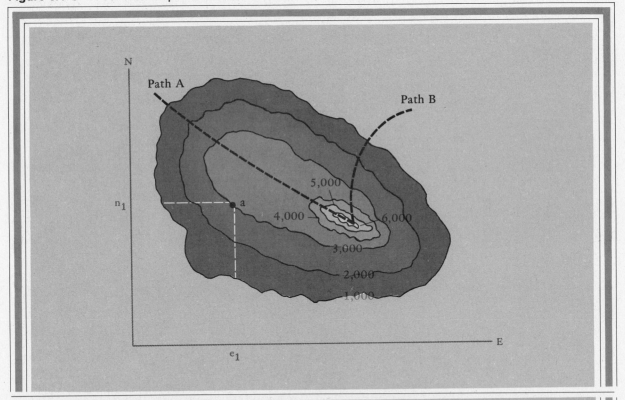

A contour map shows three variables in two-dimensional space. This is a familiar kind of three-variable graph, with latitude and longitude shown on the axes and altitude on the contour lines. The contour line labeled "1,000" connects all locations with an altitude of 1,000 feet, that labeled "2,000" connects those with altitudes of 2,000 feet, etc. Point a, for example, has a latitude n_1, a longitude e_1, and an altitude of 3,000 feet. Where the lines are closely bunched, they represent a steep ascent; where they are far apart, a gradual one. Clearly path A is a gentler climb from 3,000 to 4,000 feet on this mountain than path B.

defined to be the slope of the tangent to the curve at that point. For example, in Figure 3A–8, the slope of the function at $X = 30$ is the slope of the line T_1—that is, *is tangent to* (just touches) the function at that point. Line T_2 gives the slope of the same function at $X = 50$ and line T_3 at $X = 70$. When the curve is rising, the slope is positive; when the curve is falling, the slope is negative. When the slope is zero (as at $X = 50$), the function is neither rising nor falling.

Functions of three variables

Often in economics it is desirable to represent three variables on a two-dimensional graph. Consider the function $XY = a$, where X, Y, and a are all variables. Now look at Figure 3A–7, which plots this function for three different values of a. The variables X and Y are represented on the axes. The variable a is represented by the labels on the curves. A more familiar example of this sort of representation is the contour map of a mountain, where the vertical axis represents latitude, the horizontal axis longitude, and the contour lines are labeled to represent points of equal altitude. Such a map is shown in Figure 3A–9.

The important thing to notice about this map is that a *three*-dimensional mountain has been shown in a two-dimensional graph. Several examples of this kind of procedure occur throughout the book. (See, for example, indifference curves in Chapter 8 and isoquants in Chapter 11.)

appendix to chapter 6

Elasticity: a formal analysis

The numerical examples of elasticity computed and discussed in the text were measures of what is properly called **arc elasticity,** which is defined as the ratio of the percentage change in the quantity demanded to the percentage change in price for a discrete price change. Most theoretical treatments utilize instead a concept called point elasticity, which deals with infinitesimal changes in price and thus refers to a point on the demand curve. In this appendix we first consider arc elasticity formally and then treat point elasticity.

ARC ELASTICITY

For algebraic purposes it is convenient to use a different definition of elasticity than is used in the text. First, in Chapter 6 price and quantity were taken to be the average of the prices and quantities before and after the change being considered; for the more formal treatment in this appendix, it is more satisfactory to take price and quantity to be the ones ruling *before* the change being considered. The difference between taking p and q as original or average amounts diminishes, of course, as the magnitude of the change being considered becomes smaller.

Second, elasticity was defined as a positive number even though changes in price and quantity were of opposite sign. In formal analysis it is helpful to drop this simplification. The following symbols will be used.

$\eta \equiv$ elasticity of demand
$\eta_s \equiv$ elasticity of supply
$q \equiv$ the original quantity
$\Delta q \equiv$ the change in quantity
$p \equiv$ the original price
$\Delta p \equiv$ the change in price

The definition of arc elasticity can now be expressed in symbols

$$\eta = \frac{\Delta q/q}{\Delta p/p}$$

Inverting the denominator and multiplying results in

$$\eta = \frac{\Delta q}{q} \times \frac{p}{\Delta p}$$

Since it does not matter in which order multiplication is done (i.e., $q \times \Delta p \equiv \Delta p \times q$), the order

Figure 6A–1   A straight-line demand curve

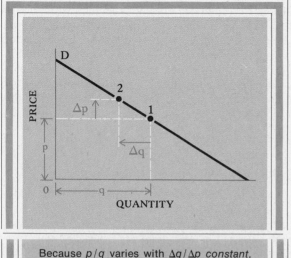

Because p/q varies with $\Delta q/\Delta p$ constant, the elasticity varies along this demand curve, being high at the left and low at the right.

Figure 6A–2   Two parallel straight-line demand curves

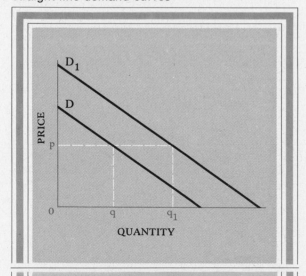

For any given price the quantities are different on the two curves; thus the elasticities are different on the two parallel curves, being higher on D than on D_1.

of the two terms in the denominator may be reversed and written

$$\eta = \frac{\Delta q}{\Delta p} \times \frac{p}{q} \qquad [1]$$

Elasticity has in equation [1] been split into two parts: $\Delta q/\Delta p$, the ratio of the change in price, which is related to the *slope* of the demand curve, and p/q, which is related to the *point* on the curve at which the measurement was made.

Figure 6A–1 shows a straight-line demand curve by way of illustration. To measure the elasticity at point 1, take p and q at that point and then consider a price change, say, to point 2, and measure Δp and Δq as indicated. The slopes of the straight line joining points 1 and 2 is $\Delta p/\Delta q$ (if you have forgotten this, refer to the appendix to Chapter 3, pages 861–862). The term in equation [1] is $\Delta q/\Delta p$, which is the reciprocal of $\Delta p/\Delta q$. Therefore the first term in the elasticity formula is the reciprocal of the slope of the straight line joining the two price-quantity positions under consideration.

A number of theorems relating to straight-line demand and supply curves may now be developed.

1. *The elasticity of a downward-sloping straight-line demand curve varies from zero at the quantity axis to infinity (∞) at the price axis.* First notice that a straight line has a constant slope, so the ratio $\Delta p/\Delta q$ is the same everywhere on the line. Therefore its reciprocal, $\Delta q/\Delta p$, must also be constant. The changes in η can now be inferred by inspecting the ratio p/q. Where the line cuts the quantity axis, price is zero, so the ratio p/q is zero; thus $\eta = 0$. Moving up the line, p rises and q falls, so the ratio p/q rises; thus elasticity rises. Approaching the top of the line, q approaches zero, so the ratio becomes very large. Thus elasticity approaches infinity as the price axis is approached.

2. *Comparing two straight-line demand curves of the same slope, the one farther from the origin is less elastic at each price than the one closer to the origin.* Figure 6A–2 shows two parallel straight-line demand curves. Pick any price, say, p, and compare the elasticities of the two curves at that price. Since the curves are parallel, the ratio $\Delta q/\Delta p$ is the same on both curves. Since elasticities at the same price are being compared on both curves, p is

the same, and the only factor left to vary is q. On the curve farther from the origin, quantity is larger (i.e., $q_1 > q$), and hence p/q is smaller; thus η is smaller.

It follows from theorem 2 that parallel shifts of a straight-line demand curve lower elasticity (at each price) when the line shifts outward and raise elasticity when the line shifts inward.

3. *The elasticities of two intersecting straight-line demand curves can be compared at the point of intersection merely by comparing slopes, the steeper curve being the less elastic.* In Figure 6A–3 there are two intersecting curves. At the point of intersection, p and q are common to both curves and hence the ratio p/q is the same. Therefore η varies only with $\Delta q/\Delta p$. On the steeper curve, $\Delta q/\Delta p$ is smaller than on the flatter curve, so elasticity is lower.

4. *Any straight-line supply curve through the origin has an elasticity of one.* Such a supply curve is shown in Figure 6A–4. Consider the two triangles with the sides p, q, and the S curve, and Δp, Δq, and the S curve. Clearly these are similar triangles. Therefore the ratios of their sides are equal; that is,

$$\frac{p}{q} = \frac{\Delta p}{\Delta q} \qquad [2]$$

Elasticity of supply is defined as

$$\eta_s = \frac{\Delta q}{\Delta p} \times \frac{p}{q} \qquad [3]$$

which, by substitution from [2], gives

$$\eta_s = \frac{q}{p} \times \frac{p}{q} \equiv 1 \qquad [4]$$

5. *The elasticity measured from any point* p, q, *according to equation* [1] *above, is in general dependent on the direction and magnitude of the change in price and quantity.* Except for a straight-line (for which the slope does not change), the ratio $\Delta q/\Delta p$ will not be the same at different points on a curve. Figure 6A–5 shows a demand curve that is not a straight line. To measure the elasticity from point 1, the ratio $\Delta q/\Delta p$—and thus η—will vary according to the size and the direction of the price change. This fifth theorem yields a result that is very inconvenient and is avoided by use of point elasticity.

Figure 6A–3 Two intersecting straight-line demand curves

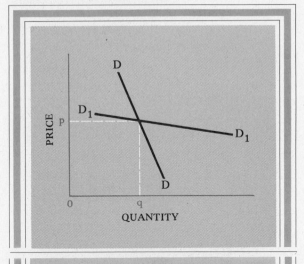

Elasticities are different at the point of intersection because the slopes are different, being higher on D than on D_1.

Figure 6A–4 A straight-line supply curve through the origin

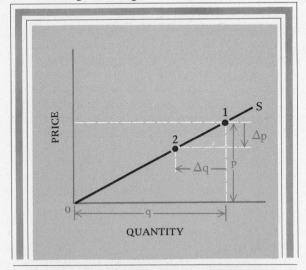

At every point on the curve, p/q equals $\Delta p/\Delta q$; thus elasticity equals unity at every point.

Figure 6A–5 Arc elasticities of demand

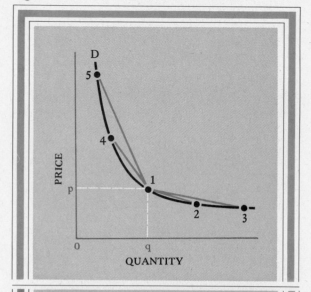

There are many arc elasticities measured from point 1 because the slope of the chord between 1 and every other point on the curve varies.

POINT ELASTICITY

To measure the elasticity at a point, it is necessary to know the reaction of quantity to a change in price at that point, not over a whole range. The reaction of quantity to price change at a point is called dq/dp, and this is defined to be the reciprocal of the slope of the straight line tangent to the demand curve at the point in question. In Figure 6A–6 the elasticity of demand at 1 is the ratio p/q (as it has been in all previous measures) now multiplied by the ratio of $\Delta q/\Delta p$ measured along the straight line, T, tangent to the curve at 1.

Point elasticity of demand is defined as

$$\eta = \frac{dq}{dp} \times \frac{p}{q} \qquad [5]$$

The ratio dq/dp, as defined, is in fact the differential calculus concept of the *derivative* of quantity with respect to price.

This elasticity is the one normally used in economic theory. Equation [1] may be regarded as an approximation to this expression. It is obvious from Figure 6A–6 that arc elasticity will come closer to the point elasticity the smaller the price change used to calculate the arc elasticity. The $\Delta q/\Delta p$ in equation [1] is the reciprocal of the slope of the chord connecting the two points being compared. As the chord becomes shorter, its slope becomes closer to that of the tangent T. (Compare the chords connecting point 1 to b' and b'' in Figure 6A–6.) Thus, considering [1] as an approximation to [5] the error will diminish as the size of Δp diminishes.

Figure 6A–6 Point elasticity of demand

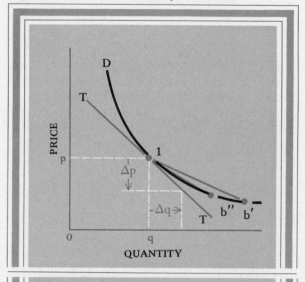

There is only one point elasticity measured from point 1 because there is only one tangent.

appendix
to chapter 8

___

Index numbers
and more on
indifference curves

This appendix is devoted to two quite distinct topics, both of which arise from the text discussion of Chapter 8: index numbers and the slope of the demand curve. In the first part of this appendix we deal with index numbers, discussing their use as summary measures of changes in economic variables and then, in more theoretical terms, their use in measuring changes in both household real income and household utility or satisfaction. In the second part of this appendix we take up the discussion of demand curves where we left it at the end of Chapter 8.

Index numbers

INDEX NUMBERS AS SUMMARY MEASURES

Economists frequently seek simple answers to questions such as How much have prices risen this year? or Has the quantity of industrial production increased this year, and, if so, by how much? There is no simple satisfactory answer to the first question because all prices do not move together, nor to the second because one cannot simply add up tons of steel, pieces of furniture, and gallons of gasoline to get a meaningful total. Yet these are not foolish questions. There *are* trends in prices and production—and thus there are real phenomena to describe. It is of no help to someone who asks about price changes over some period to be given a list of 4,682 individual prices and told, "See for yourself, they varied." **Index numbers** are statistical measures used to give a concise summary answer to the inherently complex questions of the kind suggested above.

Index numbers are *averages*. They point to overall tendencies or general drifts, not to single specific facts.

The two most important kinds of index numbers are price indexes and production indexes. While the basic principles are the same, the details are sufficiently different to warrant considering each briefly.

Index numbers of prices

Consider first the Consumer Price Index published regularly by the Bureau of Labor Statistics.

This index, known affectionately as the CPI of the BLS, measures changes in the prices paid by consumers and is an attempt to measure changes in the cost of living. What does it mean to say that the CPI for August 1975 was 162.8 (1967 = 100)? How did anyone come up with that figure? The statement seems to say that the prices paid by consumers were 62.8 percent higher in August 1975 than in 1967 and, in a very particular sense, it does say that. The phrase, 1967 = 100, means that prices are being compared to the average prices prevailing during the "base" period of 1967. Thus the index says that average prices to consumers were higher by 62.8 percent in August 1975 than in the base period.

But which consumers and which products, and where were the prices quoted? Surely consumers in New York City and in Oxford, Mississippi, paid different prices—as did the residents of Watts and of Beverly Hills, although not many miles apart. Is it significant that, on the average, public transportation prices rose by 54 percent while new car prices rose by 27 percent over this period? Need we know that costs of medical care rose by 71 percent, rent by 38 percent, costs of home ownership by 86 percent, and costs of food by 78 percent? Was the change in the level of consumer prices for a dieting homeowner who rides the bus to his frequent appointments with his doctor the same as for a healthy gourmet who drives her own (new) car from her rented apartment to her suburban office?

Because various prices change differently, it is necessary to report some average of price changes. The main problem in the construction of index numbers is how to *weight* different commodities whose prices change differently. To take the simplest example, suppose there are only two commodities, A and B, whose prices are as shown in Table 8A–1. Clearly their prices have both increased, B by 10 percent, A by 50 percent. The *average* percentage price increase is 30 percent

$$\text{Index} = \frac{150 + 110}{2} = 130$$

If some group buys A but not B, its prices have risen 50 percent; if another group buys only B, its prices have risen only 10 percent. If a third group buys one unit of A and one unit of B, its cost rises from $100 to $114—an increase of 14 percent.

When constructing an index of price changes we seek to weight different commodities by their economic importance and thus to find a representative "market basket" of commodities. It is hoped that the increase in the price of this fixed bundle of commodities will then reflect the effect of price changes on persons who consume that bundle.

Finding a representative group of commodities is not easy. To compare consumers' prices in 1930 and 1970, should a television set be included in the market basket? It was an important object of consumer expenditure in 1970, but it did not exist in 1930. The same was true of nylon stockings and hundreds of other commodities. Potatoes existed in both periods, but they represented a more important item in the consumer's budget in 1930 than in 1970. What is the correct market basket?

In one sense it is impossible to get a single correct market basket, because products change over time and tastes differ from person to person and change over time. Consider first the differences among people. While every individual differs in some ways from every other in what he or she likes to spend income on, highly systematic differences are known to be associated with household size, income, occupation, and place of residence. A Detroit auto worker with two children has different needs and wants than a semiretired Florida stockbroker or a rural Mississippi farm family with seven children and a mule. Obviously, it is impossible to provide a different index number for every possible group, but the BLS does attempt to define market baskets for particular economic groups (e.g., "urban wage earners and clerical workers"). For each such group the BLS first studies the consumption patterns of a sample of households to determine the proportions in which they allocate their expenditures

Table 8A–1   Prices of two commodities

Commodity	Period 0	Period 1	Relative price (P_1/P_0)
A	$10	$15	150
B	90	99	110

A relative price is the ratio of two absolute prices, multiplied by 100.

among different kinds of goods. These data lead to average *weights* which are then applied to price changes for individual goods. Thus individual goods and services are weighted by multiplying each price by a fraction reflecting the importance of the commodity or the group it stands for in actual consumer budgets in the "base" period. Given such weights, the arithmetic of index-number construction is straightforward. The total dollar cost of the specified market basket is computed for the base period and for the year in question. Suppose it is $120 for the base period and $150 for 1975. The index for 1975 is

$$\frac{\$150}{\$120} \times 100 = 125$$

This says that that bundle of commodities has increased in price by 25 percent since the base period.

In order to reflect geographic differences in the rates of change of prices, the BLS computes separate indexes for specified economic groups in each of 25 selected urban metropolitan areas, as well as an overall U.S. average.

Changing products and tastes over long periods of time present a more difficult problem. It would be hard to compare 1920 directly with 1970, for example, because products and tastes change so much in half a century. But it is not so difficult to compare 1970 to 1960, 1960 to 1950, 1950 to 1940, 1940 to 1930, and 1930 to 1920. In computing its index numbers, the BLS changes the weights about every ten years so that new products can be introduced and changes in relative importance recognized. The BLS thus attempts to choose roughly representative weights for commodities in each period.

Consumer prices are not the only prices of interest. Wholesale prices, prices received by farmers, and export prices are each important for different purposes. Index numbers of each are regularly computed in much the same way as the CPI.

The general procedure for computing a price index number may be summarized:

1. A representative set of products is chosen.
2. Their price changes are computed.
3. Individual price changes are weighted by the relative importance of the particular commodities and a total cost of the bundle is computed.

4. The value of the bundle of commodities in a given year is presented as the ratio to the value in some base (i.e., reference) period.
5. As a matter of convention, the computed ratio is always multiplied by 100, so the "base" index is 100.

Index numbers of physical outputs

There are many output indexes, and the Federal Reserve Board's Index of Industrial Production is one of the leading economic indicators. This index stood at 125.8 in June 1974 but had fallen to 110.0 in March 1975. In each case, 1967 was the "base" period for which the index was 100. This means that whatever the index measured was 25.8 percent higher in June 1974 than in the base period, but fell 15.8 points (approximately 13 percent) in the next three months. To the extent that the index is meaningful it measures both the growth of the American economy in the period 1967–1974 and the recession that was in progress in 1975. But what exactly does the index measure?

Like the price indexes discussed above, it is an average of the changes in production of thousands of individual items. It is not hard to measure the change in production of tons of steel from month to month or year to year, nor that of tires or TV sets. It is somewhat harder to measure the quantity of printing, of furniture, and of aircraft because the unit of output is less well defined, but these too can be approximated.

The compilers of the Index of Industrial Production first compute indexes of the change in quantity of output for individual industries and then combine them into an overall index by using the value of output in each industry as a weighting device. Table 8A–2 illustrates in simplified form the kind of computation for a two-industry world. The final computation says the index has increased by 29.2 percent between year zero and year 1. This is the weighted average of the 25 percent increase in production of industry A and the 50 percent increase in industry B. Nothing tangible increased by 29.2 percent. Yet this average reflects the fact that both industries expanded output and that industry A was in the aggregate five times as important as industry B. This procedure used in Table 8A–2 can be extended to include thousands of commodities and leads to an overall index of physical production. Compilers of index numbers

Table 8A–2   The calculation of a quantity index

	OUTPUT		QUANTITY RELATIVE	VALUE OF OUTPUT (BILLIONS OF DOLLARS)	
	Year 0 (Q_0)	Year 1 (Q_1)	Q_1/Q_0	V_0	$\frac{Q_1}{Q_0} \times V_0$
Industry A	40,000 tons	50,000 tons	1.25	\$10	\$12.5
Industry B	200,000 yards	300,000 yards	1.50	2	3.0
Total				\$12	\$15.5
Index value (year 0 = 100)				100	129.2

This quantity index weights quantity changes by the relative importance of the quantities in the base year. The increase in quantity in each industry is shown in the "quantity relative" column, Q_1/Q_0. Since industry A is much more important than B, as shown by V_0, it gets greater weight in computing the price index. The total value of output in year 0 was \$12 billion. The last column shows the increase in value of output caused by the increase in quantity, assuming that prices and relative importance of the two commodities did not change. This computed value is \$15.5 for year 1. The index for year 1 is $\frac{15.5}{12.0} \times 100 = 129.2$.

of physical output face many practical problems —which products to include, how to adjust for changes in quality of product, and which values to use as weights.

The accuracy and significance of index numbers

Index numbers of either price or output are by their very nature crude approximations. Given the changing nature of goods and products over time (a 1948 car is different from a 1975 car) and the changing relative importance of different commodities (the declining role of food in consumers' total budgets and the rising role of services), any fixed bundle of commodities becomes out of date very quickly. But if there is an important trend of prices or production underway, there is need to measure it approximately.

It would be foolish to make very much of the fact that the Consumer Price Index rose from 162.3 to 162.8 (1967 = 100) between July and August 1975, because an index number is the average of many other changes. Some prices rose and others fell; some rose a lot, others very little, and so on. When the net change is so small it may not mean very much by itself. This result, how-ever, taken in conjunction with similar or larger monthly increases in adjacent months (as shown in Table 8A–3) suggests an inflationary trend.

Index numbers are useful, then, as general indicators. People often become mesmerized by them and treat them as if they had an accuracy that their compilers do not claim for them. Being aware of their limitations should not lead one to neglect index numbers for the useful information they do show: average changes over time.

USE OF INDEX NUMBERS TO MEASURE CHANGES IN REAL INCOME

Price changes and real income

A proportional change in money prices enables one to say what has happened to the purchasing power of money and thus to real income. A doubling of money prices, for example, halves the purchasing power of money and thereby, if money income is unchanged, halves real income. But if prices do not all change in the same proportion, it is more difficult to characterize the effect on real incomes. In such cases we have to be more precise about what we mean by changes in the purchasing power of money and in real income. In practice it is usual to refer to the percentage change in the money income required to purchase a fixed bundle of commodities that was "representative" of consumers' purchases in the base period. If all prices change in the same proportion, it does not matter what bundle of commodities is selected since the costs of purchasing all bundles change by the same percentage. When different prices change in different proportions, however, the choice matters.

This problem is analyzed in Figure 8A–1. A budget line was previously used to show the alternative bundles of commodities available to a *single* household. Now we take three households having the same money incomes and facing the same money prices of food and clothing so that a single budget line shows the consumption possibilities open to all three. The three households are, however, assumed to have different tastes; when all three are presented with the same budget line they consume different bundles of commodities. The same set of price changes will therefore affect different households in different ways. For example, a very large rise in the price of clothing will have a great effect on a household that consumes a lot of that commodity and little effect on a household that consumes only a little. Thus the decrease in the real incomes of different households will be different. It follows that the magnitude and direction of the change in money income that would be needed to allow the original bundle of goods to be consumed at the new prices will depend on the proportions in which the two goods enter into the bundle of goods consumed by each household.

To the extent that an individual household's bundle differs from the "representative" bundle used in constructing the index number, the measured change in the purchasing power of income may inadequately reflect the actual changes for the particular household. Thus, if the typical bundle were that given by point 2 in Figure 8A–1(iii), the official index would show no change in the purchasing power of money even though household 1 would be able to buy less of both goods with a fixed income and household 3 would be able to buy more of both goods.

Purchasing power and household satisfaction

What does it mean to say that purchasing power is unchanged after a change in prices? By constant purchasing power we mean a situation in which a household can just purchase the identical bundle of goods both before and after the price changes. This useful notion of constant purchasing power utilized in the definition and measurement of price indexes is, however, not the same as "constant satisfaction" or "constant utility."

Figure 8A–2 illustrates the difference between purchasing power and household satisfactions. In Figure 8A–2(i) the changes in price leave the household just able to purchase its original bundle of goods but also make it possible to reach a higher level of satisfaction. Thus, although mea-

Table 8A–3 Monthly consumer price index, January 1975–January 1976

	CPI *1967 = 100*
January (1975)	156.1
February	157.2
March	157.8
April	158.6
May	159.3
June	160.6
July	162.3
August	162.8
September	163.6
October	164.6
November	165.6
December	166.3
January (1976)	166.7

The Consumer Price Index (CPI) during an inflationary year rose sharply. While the rise in the CPI in 12 months from 156.1 to 166.7 indicates no single specific price increase, it does highlight a strong inflationary trend. This trend is indicated by the fact that the index for each month is greater than it was for the preceding month. A look at more detailed data shows that the prices rose for all 18 major commodity groups that make up the CPI.

Figure 8A–1 The effect of changes in prices on three households with different consumption patterns

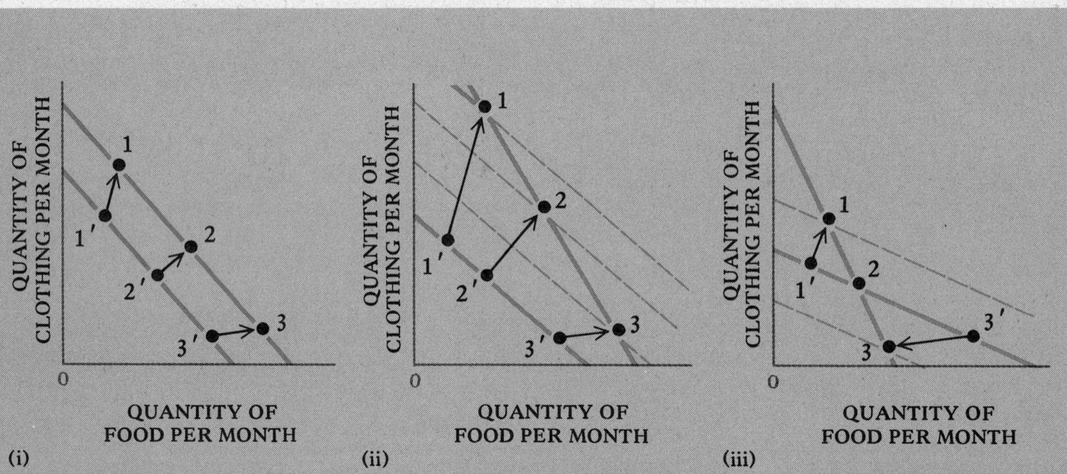

The same price changes affect different households differently. Three households all have identical budget lines, represented by the solid line. Because they have different tastes, the households reach three separate positions of equilibrium—1, 2, and 3 on the common budget line. Now consider three cases of changes in the prices of food and clothing:

(i) Both prices rise proportionately. This shifts the common budget line inward parallel to itself. The same percentage increase in money income would be required to restore each household to its original consumption position.

(ii) Both prices rise but in different proportions. The common budget line shifts inward to the line on which 1′, 2′, and 3′ are located. The purchasing power of money has fallen, but the magnitude of the fall differs among the households. The thin dashed budget lines show the shifts necessary to restore each household to its initial position at the new prices.

(iii) The price of clothing has risen and the price of food has fallen in such a way as to pivot the common budget line through point 2. Household 2 has no change in its purchasing power since it can just buy its original bundle at the new prices. Household 1 suffers a fall in its purchasing power because its budget line would have to shift outward to permit it to purchase its original bundle. Household 3 enjoys an increase in its purchasing power because it could buy the original bundle even if its income were reduced.

sured purchasing power is unchanged, satisfaction is increased. In Figure 8A–2(ii) the changes in prices are such that the household is unable to attain its original bundle, yet it can attain its original indifference curve and thus its original level of satisfaction.

Limitations on the usefulness of index numbers

Index numbers of prices can, at best, measure changes in purchasing power, not changes in sat-

isfaction. Because the household can substitute cheaper commodities for more expensive ones and leave its level of satisfaction unchanged, an index-number definition of change in real income that concentrates on changes needed to allow the household to buy an unchanged bundle of goods does not fully reflect the changes in real income caused by price changes.

Furthermore, because index numbers reflect a fixed bundle of goods they deal directly only with the purchasing power of groups for whom that bundle is representative. They are useful most often in dealing with average experience, not individual experience. You cannot tell exactly how much your standard of living changed just by knowing how your income changed and what happened to the Consumer Price Index—except in the unlikely event that your consumption pattern is the average consumption pattern.

You must not conclude from this that index numbers and other averages are useless. They are measures of typical situations and do not purport to represent perfectly the experience of each of many diverse households. While they can be used to give us interesting and useful information about changes in the cost of purchasing some fixed bundle of goods, they cannot be fully representative of the changes either in purchasing power or in satisfaction relevant to each of many households with differing tastes and consumption patterns.

More on indifference curves

DERIVATION OF DEMAND CURVES

To use indifference theory to derive the type of household demand curve introduced in Chapter 5 it is necessary to depart from the world of two commodities that we used for purposes of illustration in Chapter 8.

What happens to the household's demand for some commodity, say carrots, as the price of that commodity changes, *all other prices being held constant?* In Figure 8A–3 a new type of indifference map is plotted in which the quantity of carrots is represented on the horizontal axis and the value of all other goods consumed is represented on the vertical axis. The indifference curves give the rate at which the household is prepared to swap carrots for money (which allows it to buy all other goods)

Figure 8A–2   The difference between a change in purchasing power and a change in satisfactions

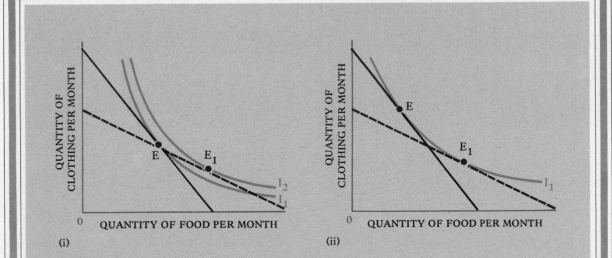

Purchasing power is measured by the ability to buy a specified bundle of goods; satisfaction is measured by the ability to achieve a specified indifference curve.

(i) A shift in the budget line from the solid black line to the dashed black line leaves the household's measured purchasing power unchanged but allows it to attain a higher level of satisfaction.

(ii) A shift in the budget line from the solid black line to the dashed black line reduces the household's measured purchasing power but leaves its level of satisfaction unchanged.

Figure 8A–3 The derivation of a demand curve

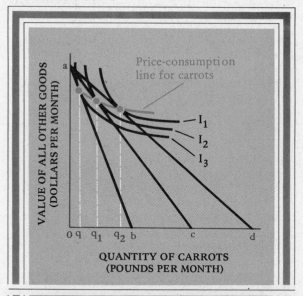

Note that Figure 8A–3 is similar to Figure 8–11. The axes are labeled differently and the price-consumption line in Figure 8A–3 is crowded into the upper part of the diagram, indicating that whatever the price of carrots, the household does not spend a large part of its income on them. Every point on the price-consumption line corresponds to one price and one quantity of carrots demanded. In the figure the quantity of carrots consumed increases as their price falls. These pairs of price-quantity values can be used to plot a conventional downward-sloping demand curve.

THE SLOPE OF THE DEMAND CURVE

We have derived from the indifference curve analysis of household behavior the information needed to plot a demand curve for a commodity—carrots in the example just considered. If plotted on a conventional price-quantity diagram the demand curve would be downward-sloping: the lower the price of carrots, the larger the quantity purchased. We now ask if that was an accidental or a necessary result.

The possibility that a commodity might have an upward-sloping demand curve has been discussed at length in demand theory. A good with such a demand curve is called a **Giffen good,** after the Victorian economist who is thought to have been first to observe such a case.

We must make a careful distinction between two concepts: the so-called **income** and **substitution effects.** A fall in the price of one commodity has something of the effect of a rise in income because it makes it possible for the household to have more of all goods. In indifference theory, the income effect is removed by reducing the household's income *until it can just attain its original level of satisfaction at the new set of prices.*

This is illustrated in Figure 8A–4. The original budget line is at *ab* and a fall in the price of carrots takes it to *aj*. The original equilibrium is at *E* with *q* of carrots consumed and the final equilibrium is at E_2 with q_2 of carrots consumed. To remove the income effect, imagine reducing the household's income until it is just able to attain its original indifference curve. In other words, shift the line *aj* inward toward the origin, parallel to itself, until it just touches the indifference curve that passes through *E*. In the figure, the new budget line is

Every point on the price-consumption line corresponds to both a price of the commodity and a quantity of the commodity demanded; this is the information required for a demand curve. The household has $a of income, and if it buys no carrots it can consume $a worth of all other goods. For each price of carrots there is a single budget line. As the price of carrots falls, the budget line pivots from *ab* to *ac* to *ad*, and the quantity of carrots demanded rises from *q* to q_1 to q_2. This leads to a downward-sloping demand curve for carrots.

at each level of consumption of carrots and of other goods. Given the money price of carrots and the household's income, a budget line can be obtained showing all those combinations of carrots and other goods that the household can consume for its given level of money income and the given price of carrots. Now assume a change in the money price of carrots. By joining the points of equilibrium, a price-consumption line can be traced between carrots and all other commodities in the same way that such a line was traced for food and clothing in Figure 8–11.

Figure 8A–4 The income effect and the substitution effect in indifference theory

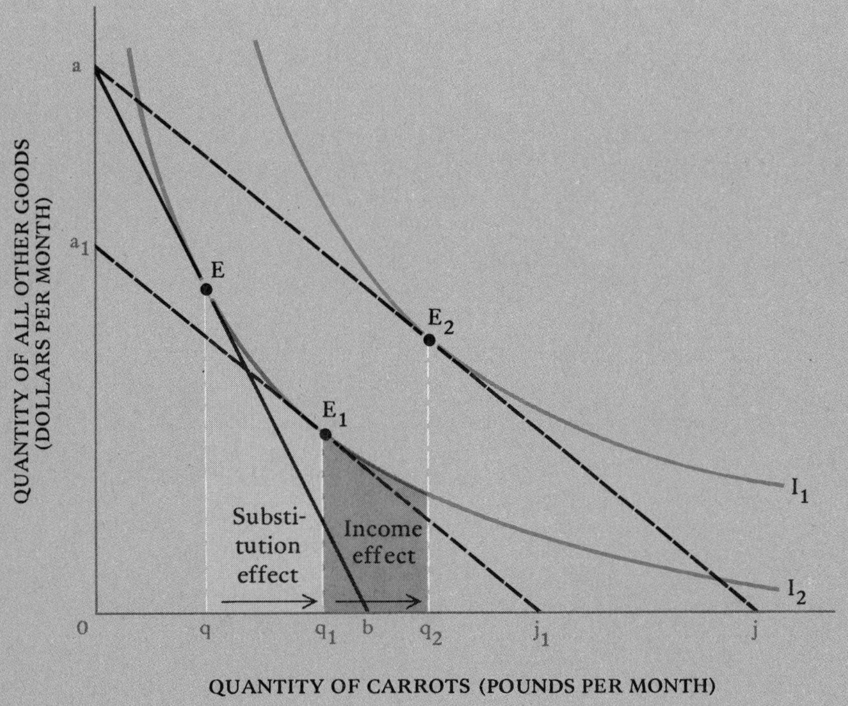

The substitution effect is defined by sliding the budget line around a fixed indifference curve; the income effect is defined by a parallel shift of the budget line. The original budget line is *ab* with equilibrium at E. A fall in the price of carrots takes the budget line to *aj* and equilibrium to E_2. The intermediate point E_1 divides the quantity change into a substitution effect qq_1 and an income effect q_1q_2. The intermediate budget line a_1j_1 just allows the household to attain its original level of satisfaction at the new prices.

a_1j_1 and the household would be in equilibrium on it at E_1, consuming q_1 of carrots and attaining the same level of satisfaction that it did at E.

It follows immediately from the convex shape of the indifference curves that more carrots are consumed at E_1 than at E. Thus the substitution effect is necessarily negative: price and quantity

move in opposite directions so that a fall in the price of carrots increases the quantity consumed.

We have said that the fall in the price of carrots would cause the household to move from E to E_1 on the *same* indifference curve. But this, of course, is not what happens when the price of carrots falls in the real world. No economic dictator reduces

Figure 8A–5 Negative income effects of a fall in prices in indifference theory

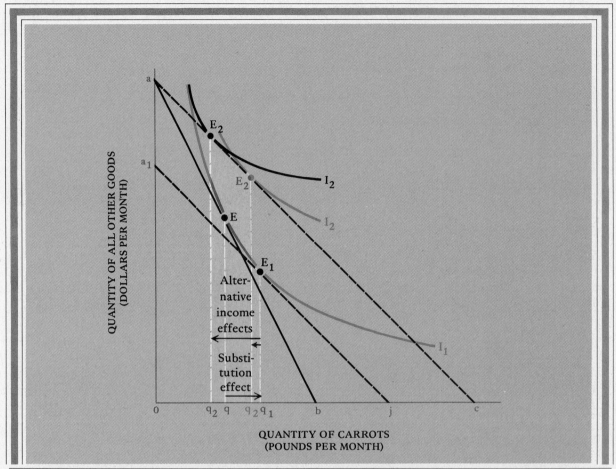

A large enough negative income effect can outweigh the substitution effect and lead to a decrease in consumption in response to a fall in price. Suppose the consumer is in equilibrium at E and the price of carrots decreases. The budget line shifts to ac. With inferior goods, the income effect is in the opposite direction from the substitution effect. Thus it is possible that the new equilibrium at E_2 will involve a smaller quantity of carrots than it did before the price decrease. Two cases are shown. The colored indifference curve I_2 lead to an increase in carrot consumption and thus a downward-sloping demand curve. The black I_2 leads to the black E_2, and an upward-sloping demand curve in which the quantity purchased decreases despite the price decrease. This is the so-called Giffen good case. Note that the two curves labeled I_2 are *alternatives;* they cannot exist simultaneously.

everyone's money income to ensure that they get no increase in utility from the price change. Instead, the budget line in Figure 8A–4 pivots from ab to aj and the equilibrium goes directly from E to E_2. To get from the intermediate position E_1 to the

final position E_2, we restore the household's income, keeping prices constant. This shifts the budget line outward parallel to itself from a_1j_1 to aj. As long as carrots are a normal good this increases their consumption—in the figure, the increase is from q_1 to q_2. This increase is an *income effect* since real income rises with relative prices constant.

In the actual world, when the price of carrots falls the budget line moves directly from *ab* to *aj* and the consumption of carrots goes from *q* to q_2. It was seen, however, that this movement can be broken up into a substitution effect that takes consumption from *q* to q_1 and an income effect that takes it from q_1 to q_2.

The change in quantity demanded for one commodity in response to a change in its price can be thought of as a composite of the income and the substitution effects. The theory predicts that the substitution effect is negative; thus a fall in the relative price of a commodity, with the level of satisfaction held constant, leads to a rise in the demand for the commodity. Unless an increase in income is expected to lead to a reduction in consumption of the commodity, because it is an inferior good, the theory gives the unambiguous prediction that more of the commodity will be demanded when its price falls.

A sufficient condition for theory to predict that the household's demand curve slopes downward is that the good in question should not be inferior. A decrease in its price will then lead to an increase in quantity demanded because of both substitution and the increase in real income.

In the case of an inferior good, however, a definite prediction about what will happen cannot be made. The income effect of a fall in price leads to a tendency for a decrease in the demand for the good. But the substitution effect still works for an increase in the quantity demanded. Thus the final result depends on the relative strengths of the two effects. Two cases of a negative income effect are shown in Figure 8A–5. The Giffen good case (an upward-sloping demand curve) occurs only when the negative income effect is large enough to offset the substitution effect.

We conclude from this analysis that the case of an upward-sloping demand curve for a product is a theoretical possibility. It requires a change in price to have a strong enough negative income effect to offset the substitution effect. A combination of circumstances that makes this possible is not often expected, and therefore an upward-sloping market demand curve must be expected to be an infrequent exception to the general prediction that demand curves will slope downward.

appendix
to chapter 10

___

Balance sheets,
income statements, and
costs of production:
two views

Accounting is a major branch of study in and of itself. Many students of economics will want to study accounting at some stage in their careers. It is not our intention to give a short course in accounting in this appendix, but rather to acquaint you with the kinds of summary statements that are used by both economists and accountants. **Balance sheets** report the picture of a firm *at a moment in time*. They balance in the sense that they show the assets (or valuable things) owned by the firm on one side and the claims against those assets on the other side. **Income statements** refer to a *period of time* (e.g., a year) and report in summary fashion the flows of resources through the firm in the course of its operations. Balance sheets thus measure a stock; income statements measure a flow.

In order to illustrate what balance sheets and income statements are, the same example will be treated from two points of view: that of the accountant and that of the economist.

AN EXAMPLE

Late in 1976, James Maykby, the second vice-president of the Acme Artificial Flower Corporation (at a salary of $25,000 per year), decided he would go into business for himself. He quit his job and organized the Maykby Leaf Company. He purchased suitable plant and equipment for $80,000 and acquired some raw materials and supplies. By December 31, 1976, he was in a position to start manufacturing. The funds for his enterprise were $40,000 raised as a bank loan on the factory (on which he is obligated to pay interest of $2,400 per year) and $55,000 of his own funds, which had previously been invested in common stocks. He also owed $5,000 to certain firms that had provided him with supplies.

Maykby, who is a trained accountant, drew up a statement of his company's position as of December 31, 1976. (See Table 10A–1.)

Maykby showed this balance sheet to his brother-in-law, an economist, and was very pleased and surprised[1] to find that he agreed that this was a fair and accurate statement of the po-

___

[1] He usually finds that he and his brother-in-law disagree about everything.

Table 10A–1 Maykby Leaf Company, balance sheet, December 31, 1976

Assets		Liabilities and equity	
Cash in bank	$ 5,000	Owed to suppliers	$ 5,000
Plant and equipment	80,000	Bank loan	40,000
Raw materials and supplies	15,000	Equity	55,000
Total assets	$100,000	Total liabilities and equity	$100,000

sition of the company as it prepared to start operation.

During 1977, the company had a busy year hiring factors, producing and selling goods, and so on. The following points summarize these activities of the twelve-month period.

1. The firm hired labor and purchased additional raw materials in the amount of $60,000, of which it still owed $10,000 at the end of the year.[2]

2. The firm manufactured artificial leaves and flowers whose sale value was $100,000. At year's end it had sold all of these, and still had on hand $15,000 worth of raw materials.

3. The firm paid off the $5,000 owed to suppliers at the beginning of the year.

4. At the very end of 1977, the company purchased a new machine for $5,000 and paid cash for it.

5. The company paid the bank $2,400 interest on the loan.

6. Maykby paid himself $10,000 "instead of salary."

AN ACCOUNTANT'S BALANCE SHEET AND INCOME STATEMENT

Taking account of all these things and also recognizing that he had depreciation on his plant and equipment,[3] Maykby spent New Year's Day, 1978, preparing three financial reports. (See Tables 10A–2, 10A–3, and 10A–4.)

[2] In this example all purchased and hired factors are treated in a single category.

[3] The tax people told him he could charge 15 percent of the cost of his equipment as depreciation during 1977, and he decided to use this amount in his own books as well. No depreciation was charged on the new machine.

These accounts reflect the operations of the firm as described above. The bookkeeping procedure by which these various activities are made to yield both the year-end balance sheet and the income statement need not concern you at this time, but you should notice several things.

First, note that some transactions affect the balance sheet but do not enter into the current income statement. Examples of these are the purchase of a machine, which is an exchange of assets—cash for plant and equipment—and which will be entered as a cost in the income statements of some future periods as depreciation is charged; and the payment of past debts, which entered the income statements in the period in which the things purchased were used in production.[4]

Second, note that the net profit from operations increased the owner's equity, since it was not "paid out" to him. A loss would have decreased his equity.

Third, note that the income statement, covering a year's operation, provides a link between the opening balance sheet (the assets and claims against assets at the beginning of the year) and the closing balance sheet.

Fourth, note that every change in a balance sheet between two dates can be accounted for by events that occurred during the year. (See the exhibits to the balance sheet, Table 10A–3.)

After studying these records, Maykby feels that it has been a good year. The company has money in the bank, it has shown a profit, and it was able to sell the goods it produced. He is bothered, however, by the fact that he and his wife have felt poorer than in past years. Probably the cost of living has gone up!

[4] Beginning students often have difficulty with the distinction between *cash* flows and *income* flows. If you do, analyze item by item the entries in Exhibit 1 in Table 10A–3 and in Table 10A–4, the income statement.

Table 10A–2 Maykby Leaf Company, accountant's balance sheet, December 31, 1977

Assets		Liabilities and equity	
Cash in bank (See Exhibit 1)	$ 32,600	Owed to suppliers of factors (See Exhibit 4)	$ 10,000
Plant and equipment (See Exhibit 2)	73,000	Bank loan	40,000
Raw materials and supplies (See Exhibit 3)	15,000	Equity (See Exhibit 5)	70,600
Total assets	$120,600	Total liabilities and equity	$120,600

Table 10A–3 Exhibits to balance sheet of December 31, 1977

Exhibit 1.   Cash

Balance, January 1, 1977	$ 5,000	
+Deposits		
Proceeds of sales of goods	100,000	$105,000
−Payments		
Payments to suppliers (1976 bills)	5,000	
Payments for labor and additional raw materials	50,000	
Salary of Mr. Maykby	10,000	
Purchase of new machine	5,000	
Interest payment to bank	2,400	− 72,400
Balance, December 31, 1977		32,600

Exhibit 2.   Plant and Equipment

Balance, January 1, 1977	80,000	
+New machine purchased	5,000	85,000
−Depreciation charged		− 12,000
Balance, December 31, 1977		73,000

Exhibit 3.   Raw Materials and Supplies

On hand January 1, 1977	15,000	
Purchases in 1977	60,000	75,000
Used for production during 1977		− 60,000
On hand December 31, 1977		15,000

Exhibit 4.   Owed to Suppliers

Balance, January 1, 1977	5,000	
New purchases, 1977	60,000	65,000
Paid on old accounts	5,000	
Paid on new accounts	50,000	− 55,000
Balance, December 31, 1977		$ 10,000

Exhibit 5.   Equity

Original investment	55,000
+Income earned during year (See income statement)	15,600
Balance, December 31, 1977	$ 70,600

AN ECONOMIST'S BALANCE SHEET AND INCOME STATEMENT

When Maykby's brother-in-law reviews the December 31, 1977, balance sheet and the 1977 income statement, he criticizes them in three respects. He says:

1. Maykby should have charged the company $25,000 for his services, since that is what he could have earned outside.

2. Maykby should have charged the company for the use of the $55,000 of his funds. He computes that had Maykby left these funds in the stock market he would have earned $5,500 in dividends and capital gains.

3. Maykby's depreciation figure is arbitrary. The plant and equipment purchased for $80,000 a year ago now has a *market value* of only $62,000. (Assume he is correct about this fact.)

The brother-in-law prepared three *revised* statements. (See Tables 10A–5, 10A–6, and the exhibit, Table 10A–7.)

It is not hard for Maykby to understand the difference between the accounting profit of $15,600 and the reported economist's loss of $10,900. The difference of $26,500 is made up as follows:

Extra salary	$15,000
Imputed cost of capital	5,500
Extra depreciation	6,000
	$26,500

What Maykby does *not* understand is in what sense he lost $10,900 during the year. In order to explain this his brother-in-law prepared the report shown in Table 10A–8.

Although Maykby spent the afternoon muttering to himself and telling his wife that his brother-in-law was not only totally lacking in any

business sense but unpleasant as well, he was observed the next morning at the public library asking the librarian whether there was a good "teach-yourself" book on economics. (We do not know her answer.)

Table 10A–4   Maykby Leaf Company, accountant's income statement for the year 1977

Sales		$100,000
Costs of operation		
Hired services and raw materials used	$60,000	
Depreciation	12,000	
Mr. Maykby	10,000	
Interest	2,400	− 84,400
Profit		$ 15,600

Table 10A–5   Maykby Leaf Company, economist's income statement for the year 1977

Sales		$100,000
Cost of operations		
Hired services and raw materials	$60,000	
Depreciation[a]	18,000	
Interest to bank[b]	2,400	
Imputed cost of capital	5,500	
Services of Maykby	25,000	110,900
Loss		$ (10,900)

[a] Market value on January 1 less market value on December 31.
[b] Because the bank loan is secured by the factory, its opportunity cost seems to the economist as properly measured by the interest payment.

Table 10A–6   Maykby Leaf Company, economist's balance sheet, December 31, 1977

Assets		Liabilities and equity	
Cash	$ 32,600	Owed to suppliers	$ 10,000
Plant and equipment	67,000	Bank loan	40,000
Raw materials, etc.	15,000	Equity (see Exhibit)	64,600
	$114,600		$114,600

Table 10A–8 Maykby's situation before and after

	(1) As second vice-president of Acme Flower Company	(2) As owner-manager of Maykby Company	Difference (2) − (1)
Salary paid	$25,000	$10,000	−$15,000
Earnings on capital, invested in stocks	5,500	0	− 5,500
Assets owned	55,000 (stocks)	64,600 (equity in Maykby Co.)	+ 9,600
Net change			−$10,900

Table 10A–7 Exhibit to balance sheet, December 31, 1977: equity of Mr. Maykby

Original investment		$55,000
New investment by Mr. Maykby		
Salary not collected	$15,000	
Return on capital not collected	5,500	20,500
		75,500
Less loss from operations		10,900
		$64,600

Summary

1. The balance sheet reports the assets and the claims against those assets at a moment in time. Balance sheets always balance because the equity of the owners is *by definition* the amount of the assets less the claims of the creditors of the company.

2. How large the "total assets" figure is depends on the valuations placed on them, and these can differ. The valuation problem arises over and over again—in the matter of inventories, patents, properties, and so forth, owned.

3. In order to avoid arbitrary, misleading, and even deliberately deceptive manipulation of accounts, accountants have developed certain normal and usual procedures of valuation. These may not in all cases reflect the economist's definition of the value of the resources.

4. The income statement reports the revenues and the costs that arise from the firm's use of inputs to produce outputs. It always covers a specified period of time. It also crucially involves the valuation problem: What is the value of the inputs used and outputs produced? Here again there are conventional accounting principles that may or may not be satisfactory for purposes of economic analysis.

5. The income statement of a firm may be important for several different purposes, and different principles of valuation may be required. For determining its income tax liability, the firm must use the valuations specified as permissible by the tax authorities. For determining its comparative performance compared to other companies, or to itself in other periods, it must use a consistent set of procedures, whatever the principle that governs them. For determining whether it has made the best use of the resources under its control, it must use valuations based on the alternative use of these resources. The economist's concept of opportunity cost is designed to do this job.

6. In general, it is the principles of valuation used and not the form of these statements that are important and decisive in interpreting the operations of the firm. Students of the firm who use the reported financial data as an aid to their analysis must be prepared to examine in detail whether the principles of valuation used are appropriate for their purpose and to adjust, correct, or recompute in cases where they are not appropriate.

appendix
to chapter 30

The permanent-income hypothesis and the life-cycle hypothesis

In the Keynesian theory of the consumption function, current consumption expenditure is related to current income—either current disposable income or current national income. Recent attempts to reconcile the apparently conflicting empirical data on short- and long-term consumption behavior have produced a series of theories that relate consumption to some longer-term concept of income than the income that the household is currently earning.

The two most influential theories of this type are the **permanent-income hypothesis (PIH)**, developed by Professor Friedman, and the **life-cycle hypothesis (LCH)**, developed by Professors Modigliani and Ando and the late Professor Brumberg. Although there are many significant differences between these theories, their similarities are more important than their differences, and they may be looked at together when studying their major characteristics. In doing this it is important to ask: What variables do these theories seek to explain? What assumptions do the theories make? What are the major implications of these assumptions? How do the theories reconcile the apparently conflicting empirical evidence? And what implications do they have for the overall behavior of the economy?

VARIABLES

Three important variables need to be considered: consumption, saving, and income. Keynesian-type theories seek to explain the amounts that households spend on purchasing goods and services for consumption. This concept is called *consumption expenditure*. Permanent-income theories seek to explain the actual flows of consumption of the services that are provided by the commodities that households buy. This concept is called *actual consumption*.[1] With services and nondurable goods, expenditure and actual consumption occur more or less at the same time and the distinction between these two concepts is not important. The consumption of a haircut, for example, occurs at

[1] Because Keynes's followers did not always distinguish carefully between the concepts of consumption expenditure and actual consumption, the word "consumption" is often used in both contexts. We follow this normal practice, but where there is any possible ambiguity in the term we will refer to "consumption expenditure" and to "actual consumption."

the time it is purchased, and an orange or a package of corn flakes is consumed very soon after it is purchased. Thus, if we knew purchases of such goods and services at some time, say last year, we would also know last year's consumption of these goods and services. But this is not the case with durable consumer goods. A screwdriver is purchased at one point in time, but it yields up its services over a long time, possibly as long as the purchaser's lifetime. The same is true of a house and a watch and, over a shorter period of time, of a car and a dress. For such products, if we know purchases last year, we do not necessarily know last year's consumption of the services that the products yielded.

Thus one important characteristic of durable goods is that *expenditure* to purchase them is not necessarily synchronized with consumption of the stream of services that the goods provide. If in 1970 Mr. Smith buys a car for $4,000, runs it for six years, and then discards it as worn out, his expenditure on automobiles is $4,000 in 1970 and zero for the next five years. His consumption of the services of automobiles, however, is spread out at an average annual rate of $666 for six years. If everyone followed Mr. Smith's example by buying a new car in 1970 and replacing it in 1976, the automobile industry would undergo wild booms in 1970 and 1976 with five intervening years of slump even though the actual consumption of automobiles would be spread more or less evenly over time. This example is extreme, but it illustrates the possibilities, where consumers' durables are concerned, of quite different time paths of *consumption expenditure,* which is the subject of Keynesian theories of the consumption function, and *actual consumption,* which is the subject of permanent-income type theories.

Now consider saving. The change in emphasis from consumption expenditure to actual consumption implies a change in the definition of saving. Saving is no longer income minus consumption expenditure; it is now income minus the value of actual consumption. When Mr. Smith spent $4,000 on his car in 1970 but used only $666 worth of its services in that year he was actually consuming $666 and saving $3,334. The purchase of a consumers' durable is thus counted as saving, and only the value of its services actually consumed is counted as consumption.

So much for consumption and saving. The third important variable in this type of theory is the income variable. Instead of using current income the theories use a concept of long-term income. The precise definition varies from one theory to another, but basically it is related to the household's expected income stream over a fairly long planning period. In the LCH it is the income that the household expects to earn over its lifetime.[2]

Every household is assumed to have a view of its expected lifetime earnings. This is not as unreasonable as it might seem. Students training to be doctors have a very different view of expected lifetime income than those training to become high school teachers. Both of these expected income streams—for a doctor and for a high school teacher—will be very different from that expected by an assembly-line worker or a professional athlete. One such possible lifetime income stream is illustrated in Figure 30A–1.

The household's expected lifetime income is then converted into a single figure for *annual* **permanent income.** In the life-cycle hypothesis this permanent income is the maximum amount the household could spend on consumption each year without accumulating debts *that are passed on to future generations.* If a household were to consume a constant amount equal to its permanent income each year, it would add to its debts in years when current income was less than permanent income and reduce its debt or increase its assets in years when its current income exceeded its permanent income; however, over its whole lifetime it would just break even, leaving neither accumulated assets nor debts to its heirs. If the interest rate were zero, permanent income would be just the sum of all expected incomes divided by the number of expected years of life. With a positive interest rate, permanent income will diverge somewhat from this amount because of the costs of borrowing and the extra income that can be earned by investing savings.

ASSUMPTIONS

The basic assumption of this type of theory, whether PIH or LCH, is that the household's

---

[2] In the PIH the household has an infinite time horizon and the relevant permanent-income concept is the amount the household could consume forever without increasing or decreasing its present stock of wealth.

actual consumption is related to its permanent rather than to its current income. Two households that have the same permanent income (and are similar in other relevant characteristics) will have the same consumption patterns even though their current incomes behave very differently.

IMPLICATIONS

The major implication of these theories is that changes in a household's current income will affect its actual consumption only so far as they affect its permanent income. Consider two income changes that could occur to a household with a permanent income of $10,000 per year and an expected lifetime of 30 more years. In the first, suppose the household receives an unexpected extra income of $2,000 *for this year only*. The increase in the household's permanent income is thus very small. If the rate of interest were zero, the household could consume an extra $66.66 per year for the rest of its expected lifespan; with a positive rate of interest the extra annual consumption would be more because money not spent this year could be invested and would earn interest.[3] In the second case, the household gets a totally unforeseen increase of $2,000 a year for the rest of its life. In this event the household's permanent income has risen by $2,000 because the household can actually consume $2,000 more every year without accumulating any new debts. Although in both cases current income rises $2,000, the effect on permanent income is very different in the two cases.

Keynesian theory assumes that *consumption expenditure* is related to current income and therefore predicts the same change in this year's consumption expenditure in each of the above cases. Permanent-income theories relate *actual consumption* to permanent income and therefore predict very different changes in actual consumption in each of these cases. In the first case there would be only a small increase in actual annual consumption, while in the second case there would be a large increase.

In permanent-income theories, any change in current income that is thought to be temporary will

[3] If the rate of interest were 7 percent the household could invest the $2,000, consume an extra $161 a year, and just have nothing left at the end of 30 years.

Figure 30A–1 Current income and permanent income

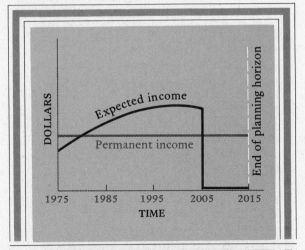

Expected current income may vary greatly over a lifetime, but expected permanent income is a constant amount. The graph shows a hypothetical expected income stream from work for a household that expects to live 40 years from 1975. The current income rises to a peak, then falls slowly for a while, and finally falls on retirement. The corresponding permanent income is the amount the household could consume at a steady rate over its lifetime by borrowing early against future earnings (as do most newly married couples), then repaying past debts, and finally saving for retirement when income is at its peak without either incurring debt or accumulating new wealth to be passed on to future generations.

have only a small effect on permanent income and hence on actual consumption.

Implications for the behavior of the economy

According to the permanent-income and the life-cycle hypotheses, actual consumption is not much affected by temporary changes in income. Does this mean that aggregate expenditure, $C + I + G + (X - M)$, is not much affected? *Not necessarily*. Consider what happens if households get a temporary increase in their incomes. If actual consumption is not greatly affected by this, then households must save most of the temporary increase in their incomes. But from the point of view of these theories, households save when they buy a durable good just as much as when they buy a financial asset such as a stock or a bond. In both cases actual current consumption is not changed.

Thus spending a temporary increase in income on bonds or on new cars is consistent with both the PIH and the LCH. But it makes a great deal of difference to the short-run behavior of the economy which is done. If households buy stocks and bonds, aggregate expenditure on currently produced final goods does not rise when income rises temporarily;[4] if households buy automobiles or any other durable consumer good, aggregate expenditure on currently produced final goods does rise when income rises temporarily. Thus the PIH and the LCH leave unsettled the question that is critical for the measurement of the size of the multiplier: What is the reaction of household *expenditures* on currently produced goods and services, particularly durables, to short-term, temporary changes in income?

The PIH and LCH theories leave unsettled the critical question of the ability of short-term changes in fiscal policy to remove inflationary and deflationary gaps.

Assume, for example, that a serious deflationary gap emerges and that the government attempts to stimulate a recovery by giving tax rebates and by cutting tax rates—both on an announced temporary basis. This will raise households' current disposable incomes by the amount of the tax cuts, but it will raise their permanent incomes by only a small amount. According to the PIH, the flow of actual current consumption should not rise much. But it is quite consistent with the PIH that households should spend their tax savings on durable consumer goods, the consumption of which can be spread over many years. In this case, even though actual consumption this year would not respond much to the tax cuts, expenditure would respond a great deal. Since current output and employment depends on expendi-

ture rather than real consumption, the tax cut *would be* effective in stimulating the economy. It is, however, also consistent with the PIH that households spend only a small part of their tax savings on consumption goods and seek to invest the rest in bonds and other financial assets. In this case the tax cuts may have only a small stimulating effect on the economy. It is important to note that PIH and the LCH do *not* predict unambiguously that changes in taxes that are announced to be only short-lived will be ineffective in removing inflationary or deflationary gaps.

A reconciliation of the data

The PIH and the LCH are able to reconcile the observation that the MPC appears equal to the APC in long-period data while it is less than the APC in short-period and cross-section data.[5] They do this by relating changes in observed income to changes in permanent income.

Long-term time-series data using decade-by-decade averages remove the effects of temporary fluctuations in income. The observed changes in Y mainly represent permanent increases in real income because of economic growth. Long-term time-series studies will thus tend to measure accurately the propensity to consume out of permanent income.

Now consider short-term data. A study covering 10 or 15 years at the most and using annual observations of C and Y will use an income series dominated by temporary changes caused by cyclical fluctuations. When a household loses employment because of a business recession it does not expect to remain unemployed forever; neither does it expect the extra income that it earns from heavy overtime work during a period of peak demand to persist. It may thus be assumed that households expect these cyclical changes in current income to be temporary and that they will thus have little effect on permanent income. Since consumption is assumed to depend on permanent income, it follows that the observed relation

[4] Except for any indirect effect through changes in interest rates.

[5] The short- and long-run time-series data are described in Chapter 27 (see pages 488–491). Cross-section data are for a number of households at one point in time and they show for that point in time how household consumption varies with household income. These data yield a consumption function similar to that obtained from short-term time-series data but with an even lower *MPC*.

between consumption and cyclical changes in income will tend to be smaller than the relation shown by the long-term time-series data. What this shows, however, is the lack of relation between changes in consumption and temporary changes in income, not any lack of relation between changes in consumption and changes in permanent income.

A similar analysis shows that cross-section studies are strongly influenced by the behavior of households whose incomes have temporarily departed from their permanent levels. Thus cross-section studies should be expected to yield a much lower observed marginal propensity to consume than that yielded by long-term time-series studies.

CONCLUSION

While permanent-income type theories succeed in reconciling various empirical observations of consumption functions, they leave ambiguous the multiplier effects of temporary increases in income. They are consistent with a constancy in both the *MPC* and the *APC* when *permanent income* changes (see Figure 27–3). They also suggest a high degree of stability of the actual flow of consumption in the face of temporary fluctuations in current income, which is consistent with an *APC* out of *current income* that varies inversely with current income, falling as income rises and rising as income falls (see Figure 27–4).

appendix to chapter 34

Money in the national income model

This appendix provides a model in which monetary and expenditure factors jointly determine the interest rate and the level of national income.

THE THEORY

Assumptions

The basic elements of the model are three. First, withdrawals and injections: There are two withdrawals, savings and taxes, and two injections, investment and government expenditures for goods and services. (We ignore foreign trade.) Second, the government sector: Tax rates are assumed constant throughout the analysis so that if consumption bears a stable relation to disposable income, it also bears a stable relation to national income. (This point was discussed in footnote 5 on page 488.) Government expenditure is not related to national income, and fiscal policy takes the form of varying the level of government expenditure with tax rates held constant. Third, the monetary sector: The money supply is set at any desired level by the monetary authorities and does not vary with either national income or the rate of interest; thus monetary policy takes the form of changing the money supply. The basic model is laid out and further described in Figure 34A–1.

The *IS, LM* representation of the model

It is awkward, although not impossible, to study the model in the form in which it is presented in Figure 34A–1. It is much more convenient to reduce it to a form first suggested by J. R. Hicks in his famous review of Keynes' *General Theory* entitled "Mr. Keynes and the Classics: A Suggested Interpretation." To do this, we derive from the four curves in Figure 34A–1 two new curves that relate the rate of interest to national income.

The IS *curve.* The *IS* curve is based on the Keynesian income-expenditure relations; *it shows all those combinations of national income and the rate of interest for which withdrawals equal injections.* An *IS* curve is plotted in Figure 34A–2(i). To understand this curve let us first determine one point on it. Start with a particular rate of interest, say r_1. This determines a level of injections (see Figure 34A–1 (iv)) where r_1 is associated with injections of e_1. Now find the level of income for which withdrawals equal these injections. If national income is too

Figure 34A–1 The basic assumption of a model integrating monetary and income-expenditure relations

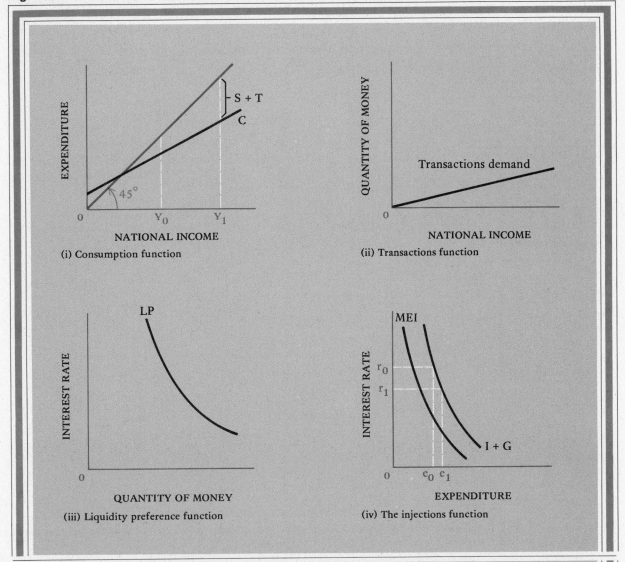

(i) Consumption function

(ii) Transactions function

(iii) Liquidity preference function

(iv) The injections function

The model includes both income-expenditure and monetary behavioral relations. Part (i) relates current consumption expenditure to current national income. The vertical distance between the C and the 45° line shows the amount of income *not* consumed (i.e., the amount devoted to saving and taxes).

Part (ii) shows the transactions demand for money rising as national income rises.

Part (iii) shows the speculative demand for money falling as the rate of interest rises (because the higher the rate of interest, the more willing the public will be to hold its wealth in the form of interest-earning assets rather than in the form of money).

Part (iv) shows desired investment expenditure (the *MEI* function) increasing as the rate of interest falls. The fixed amount of government expenditure is added to the variable amount of investment expenditure to obtain the total injections schedule ($I + G$). Since G is assumed constant, the $I + G$ curve has the same shape as the *MEI* curve (the injections schedule is obtained by shifting the *MEI* curve horizontally by G).

Figure 34A–2 The *IS* and the *LM* curves

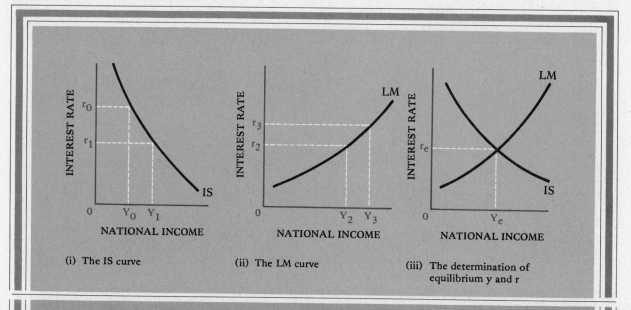

(i) The IS curve (ii) The LM curve (iii) The determination of equilibrium y and r

The *IS* and the *LM* curves reduce the four relations shown in Figure 34A–1 to the two relations shown here. Part (i) The *IS* curve slopes downward. A rise in income increases withdrawals, and a fall in the rate of interest is required to increase injections so that the equality of withdrawals and injections can be maintained.

Part (ii) The *LM* curve slopes upward. A rise in income increases the transactions demand for money, and a rise in the rate of interest is required to reduce the speculative demand so that the overall demand for money can remain equal to the unchanged supply.

Part (iii) Along the *IS* curve withdrawals equal injections. Along the *LM* curve the demand for money equals its supply. Only where the two curves intersect (Y_e, r_e in the figure) are both of these things true simultaneously. The equilibrium at Y_e and r_e is thus the combination of national income and the interest rate that satisfies the income and expenditure equilibrium condition ($W = J$) and also makes the demand for money equal to its supply.

low, withdrawals will be less than the given amount of injections; if national income is too high, withdrawals will exceed injections. At the level of income y_1, however, withdrawals as determined in Figure 34A–1(i) are just equal to the injections already determined in Figure 34A–1(iv) (i.e., the bracketed distance $S + T$ in (i) is equal to the distance e_1 in (iv)). This gives a particular combination of the rate of interest, r_1, and the level of income, Y_1, for which withdrawals are equal to injections. This combination is shown as a point on the *IS* curve in Figure 34A–2(i).

Now consider a lower level of income, say Y_0 in

Figure 34A–1(i). Withdrawals will be smaller than at Y_1, and if injections were constant, income could not be in equilibrium. But if the rate of interest is increased, investment and hence total injections will fall. If, as in Figure 34A–1(iv), the rate of interest rises to r_0, injections will be e_0 and they will equal the level of withdrawals associated with the lower level of income, Y_0. This new combination of national income and interest rate (Y_o, r_o) for which withdrawals equal injections is plotted as a second point on the *IS* curve in Figure 34A–2(i).

The argument can be repeated for alternative levels of income, and it leads to the following general statement: Since withdrawals (savings and taxes) vary directly with income and since injections vary inversely with the interest rate, withdrawals can be kept equal to injections if national income and the rate of interest vary in opposite directions. A rise in national income must, for example, be accompanied by a fall in the rate of interest to induce an increase in injections sufficient to match the increase in withdrawals caused by the rise in income. [47]

The *IS* curve, which shows all those combinations of national income and the rate of interest for which withdrawals equal injections, slopes downward because income and the rate of interest must vary in opposite directions if withdrawals are to be held equal to injections.

The LM *curve*. The second curve is derived from the monetary part of the model. This curve, the *LM* curve, *shows all of the combinations of national income and the rate of interest for which the demand for money* (as shown in parts (ii) and (iii) of Figure 34A–1) *is equal to the supply of money* (which is determined by the monetary authorities).

To understand the shape of this curve it is necessary to recall the modern theory of the consequences of an excess demand for or supply of money: When people have more money than they wish to hold (supply of money exceeds the demand for it) they seek to invest their surplus money in bonds; when people have less money than they wish to hold they seek to build up their money holdings by selling bonds. Attempts to buy or sell bonds on any large scale will lead to changes in the price of bonds and hence in the rate of interest.

Now let us start by assuming that the demand for money is equal to the supply of money at some level of national income and of the rate of interest, say Y_2 and r_2 in Figure 34A–2(ii). Now let income rise, say to Y_3. The transactions demand for money increases and, if the rate of interest were held constant, the demand for money would now exceed the supply. In an attempt to build up their money holdings people seek to sell bonds. But the attempt on everyone's part to sell bonds drives the price of bonds down and interest rates up. As the interest rate rises, less money is held for speculative purposes, so more is available for transactions

purposes. Indeed the rate of interest must rise until the demand for money has been reduced to the amount of the unchanged supply of money. This requires that the reduction in the demand for money caused by the increase in the rate of interest just offsets the increase in the demand for money caused by the rise in national income.

The argument can be repeated for a fall in income. As national income falls, less money is needed for transactions purposes. The supply of money will now exceed the demand for it. People will seek to convert their surplus money into bonds. This will raise the price of bonds and lower the rate of interest. As the rate of interest falls more money will be held for speculative purposes. The fall in the rate of interest needs to be such that people are just willing to increase their speculative balances by the amount that their transactions balances fell when national income fell. When this happens the demand for money will once again be equal to the unchanging supply of it.

This analysis leads to the following general conclusion: Since the demand for money varies directly with income and indirectly with the rate of interest, the effect on the demand for money of a change in national income must be offset by an opposite change in the rate of interest if the overall demand for money is to remain unchanged (so that it can remain equal to the unchanged money supply). For example, an increase in national income tends to increase the demand for money and an offsetting increase in the rate of interest is needed if the overall demand for money is to remain unchanged. [48]

The *LM* curve, which shows all combinations of national income and the rate of interest for which the demand for money equals the supply of money, slopes upward because income and the rate of interest must vary in the same direction if the overall demand for money is to be held equal to a constant supply of money.

Equilibrium income and the interest rate

The model has now been reduced to the two curves shown in Figure 34A–2. The intersection of the two curves indicates the only combination of national income and the rate of interest for which withdrawals are equal to injections *and* the demand for money is equal to its supply.

The intersection of the two curves thus gives the equilibrium levels of national income and the rate of interest in a model that combines both expenditure and monetary influences.

Shifts in the *IS* and *LM* curves

Figure 34A–3 shows the effects of particular shifts in the *IS* and the *LM* curves. This analysis leads to four general predictions:

1. A rightward shift of the *IS* curve raises national income and the rate of interest.

2. A leftward shift of the *IS* curve lowers national income and the rate of interest.

3. A rightward shift of the *LM* curve raises national income and lowers the rate of interest.

4. A leftward shift of the *LM* curve lowers national income and raises the rate of interest.

To go beyond mechanically shifting the two curves, it is necessary to derive predictions about how a change in anything included in the model shifts one of these curves. Once this is determined the four predictions tell us what should happen to national income and the rate of interest.

AN ANALYSIS OF FISCAL AND MONETARY POLICY

The representation of fiscal policy

An increase in G shifts the $G + I$ curve in Figure 34A–1(iv) outward to the right; a reduction shifts it inward to the left. What do these changes do to the *IS* schedule? Consider the position r_1 and y_1 on the curve *IS* in Figure 34A–3(i). Now let G increase. Injections are now increased and if income remains at y_1, injections will exceed withdrawals. To keep these two magnitudes equal it is necessary

Figure 34A–3   The effects of shifts in the *IS* and *LM* curves

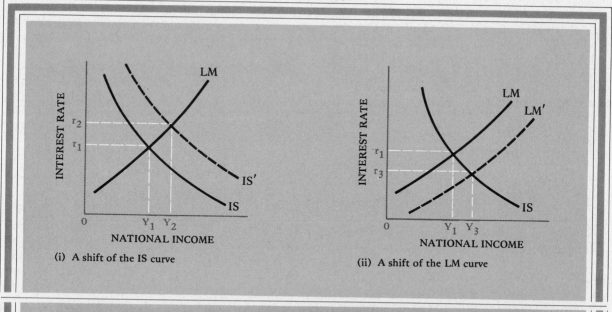

(i) A shift of the IS curve

(ii) A shift of the LM curve

Similar shifts in the *IS* and the *LM* curves have similar effects on national income and opposite effects on the rate of interest.   The initial levels of income and rate of interest are Y_1 and r_1 in both parts of the figure. In part (i) a rightward shift in the curve from *IS* to *IS'* raises national income from Y_1 to Y_2 and raises the rate of interest from r_1 to r_2. In part (ii) a rightward shift in the curve from *LM* to *LM'* raises national income from Y_1 to Y_3 and lowers the rate of interest from r_1 to r_3.

to increase withdrawals, which is done by increasing national income. In general the increase in G means that any given r is associated with a higher level of injections than previously. Thus the associated level of income at which injections equal withdrawals must also be higher than previously. The increase in G shifts the IS curve outward to the right, thereby indicating that each rate of interest must be associated with a higher level of national income than previously if withdrawals are to remain equal to injections. A reduction in G has the opposite effect.

A rise in G shifts the IS curve to the right and a fall in G shifts it to the left.

The representation of monetary policy

By monetary policy we shall here mean any deliberate change in the money supply engendered by the Fed. An increase in the money supply means that at any combination of Y and r, such as Y_1, r_1 in Figure 34A–3(ii), the supply of money exceeds the demand. If this excess supply of money is to be removed while holding the interest rate constant at r_1, it will be necessary to raise income, thereby raising the transactions demand for money. Thus any given rate of interest will be associated with a higher level of national income than previously if the demand for money is to be equal to the increased supply. The LM curve shifts outward to the right.

A reduction in the money supply means that at any combination of Y and r such as Y_1, r_1 in Figure

34A–3(ii), the demand for money exceeds the supply. If the excess demand for money is to be removed while holding the interest rate constant it will be necessary to lower income, thereby lowering the transactions demand for money. The LM curve then shifts inward to the left.

An increase in the quantity of money shifts the LM curve outward to the right; a decrease in the quantity of money shifts it inward to the left.

The effects of fiscal and monetary policy

If we combine these results about what monetary and fiscal policies do to the IS and LM curves with the result in the previous section, we obtain four basic predictions about the effects of monetary and fiscal policy.

1. An increase in G raises national income and raises the rate of interest.

2. An increase in the money supply raises national income and lowers the rate of interest.

3. A decrease in G lowers national income and lowers the rate of interest.

4. A decrease in the money supply lowers national income and raises the rate of interest.

These results represent what may be called the neo-Keynesian synthesis, in which both monetary and fiscal policies have an effect on national income and interest rates.

Much of the debate between the monetarists and the neo-Keynesians can be summarized by using the *IS* and *LM* curves introduced in the appendix to Chapter 34 (see page 886).[1] This is merely a more succinct way of summarizing the points of controversy analyzed in Chapter 41; anyone who has mastered the *IS, LM* apparatus can follow the argument in Chapter 41 using the form of analysis sketched out in this appendix.

THE REPRESENTATION OF MONETARY AND FISCAL POLICY

Fiscal policy

We did not explicitly incorporate the government sector into the *IS, LM* model developed in the appendix to Chapter 34. To do this, remember that government expenditure is an injection, as is investment, and that taxes are a withdrawal, as is saving. This suggests that we generalize the *IS* curve to become a *JW* (i.e., injections-withdrawals) curve; the curve shows all the combinations of national income and the rate of interest that will equate injections and withdrawals. (As a matter of convention the curve is called an *IS* curve no matter how many withdrawals and injections are included in the model.) Government expenditure is taken as a constant while taxes are a function of national income. The *IS* curve still slopes downward; this can be seen as follows. G is a constant, I varies with the rate of interest, while S and T vary with national income. As national income rises both withdrawals, S and T, rise and a fall in the rate of interest is necessary to induce sufficient extra investment to maintain equality between $I + G$ on the one hand and $S + T$ on the other.

Fiscal policy can now be shown by shifts in the *IS* curve. Figure 41A–1 shows the original *IS* and *LM* curves intersecting to determine a level of national income of y_1 and an interest rate of r_1. Now suppose that the government raises its expenditure, G, keeping tax rates constant. What does this change do to the *IS* curve?

Consider the position r_1 and y_1 in Figure 41A–1(i), which corresponds to the initial level of

*M*ore on monetary
versus fiscal policy

[1] Much of the debate between the two groups, however, depends on points of theory and measurement that are too advanced to be discussed in an elementary textbook.

Figure 41A–1 The effects of fiscal and monetary policy

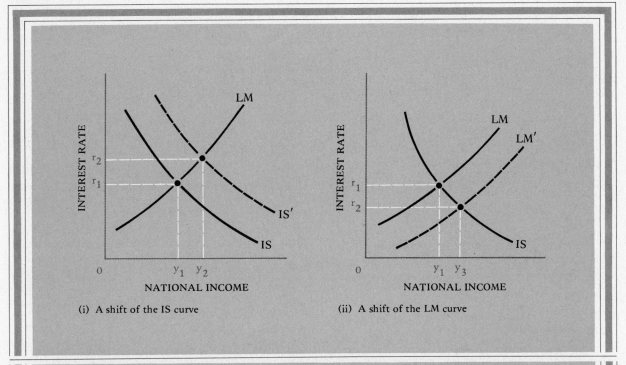

(i) A shift of the IS curve

(ii) A shift of the LM curve

Fiscal policy shifts the *IS* curve; monetary policy shifts the *LM* curve. The initial levels of income and rate of interest are y_1 and r_1 in both parts of the figure. In (i) an expansionary fiscal policy causes a rightward shift in the curve from *IS* to *IS'*, raises national income from y_1 to y_2, and raises the rate of interest from r_1 to r_2. In (ii) an expansionary monetary policy causes a rightward shift in the curve from *LM* to *LM'*, raises national income from y_1 to y_3, and lowers the rate of interest from r_1 to r_3. (Contractionary fiscal and monetary policies respectively shift the *IS* curve from *IS'* to *IS* and the *LM* curve from *LM'* to *LM*.)

G. The government now increases G. Injections are higher and *if* income were to remain at y_1, injections would exceed withdrawals at the rate of interest r_1. Holding the rate of interest—and thereby injections—constant, the equality between injections and withdrawals can be restored only if income—and hence withdrawals—increases. In general the increase in G means that *any given r* is associated with a higher level of injections than previously. Thus the associated level of income at which injections equal withdrawals must also be higher than previously. The increase in G shifts the *IS* curve outward to the right, indicating that each rate of interest must be associated with a higher level of national income than previously if withdrawals are to remain equal to injections. A reduction in G has the opposite effect.

A rise in government expenditure shifts the *IS* curve to the right and a fall shifts *IS* to the left.

Monetary policy

An increase in the money supply means that at any combination of y and r, such as y_1, r_1 in Figure 41A–1(ii), the supply of money exceeds the demand. If this excess supply of money is to be removed while holding the interest rate constant at r_1, it will be necessary to have a higher level of income, thereby raising the transactions demand for money. Thus any given rate of interest will be associated with a higher level of national income than previously if the demand for money is to be equal to the increased supply. The *LM* curve shifts outward to the right.

A reduction in the money supply means that at any combination of y and r, such as y_3, r_3 in Figure 41A–1(ii), the demand for money exceeds the supply. If the excess demand for money is to be removed while holding the interest rate constant, it will be necessary to lower income, thereby lowering the transactions demand for money. The *LM* curve then shifts inward to the left.

An increase in the quantity of money shifts the *LM* curve outward to the right; a decrease in the quantity of money shifts it inward to the left.

THE EFFECTS OF FISCAL AND MONETARY POLICY

The absolute effects of each

The effects of shifts in the *IS* and *LM* curves are shown in Figure 41A–1. The four policies—fiscal expansion, fiscal contraction, monetary expansion, monetary contraction—correspond to the four possible shifts in the *IS* and *LM* curves. The analysis in Figure 41A–1 of the effects of the four shifts yields the basic predictions concerning the effects of these policies.

1. An increase in government expenditure raises national income and raises the rate of interest.

2. An increase in the money supply raises national income and lowers the rate of interest.

3. A decrease in government expenditure lowers national income and lowers the rate of interest.

4. A decrease in the money supply lowers national income and raises the rate of interest.

These results represent what may be called the neo-Keynesian synthesis, in which both monetary and fiscal policies have an effect on national income and interest rates.

The relative effectiveness of the two

Although the neo-Keynesian synthesis holds that both monetary and fiscal policy can influence national income, many neo-Keynesians believe that monetary policy tends to be relatively ineffective compared to fiscal policy. Many monetarists hold the opposite view. Much of this debate turns around the assumed shapes of the *IS* and *LM* curves.

The shape of the IS curve. The monetarist case arises if investment is very sensitive to changes in the rate of interest. In this case a rise in income that increases withdrawals need only be accompanied by a small fall in the rate of interest in order to have injections expand by the same amount as withdrawals. This makes the *IS* curve relatively flat. The neo-Keynesian case occurs if investment is relatively interest inelastic. Then a large fall in interest rates is necessary to induce the extra injections to balance the extra withdrawals caused by a rise in income. This makes the *IS* curve relatively steep.

The shape of the LM curve. Both sides agree that the demand for money can respond to the level of income, but they disagree on the response to changes in the interest rates. The monetarist case arises when the demand for money is relatively unresponsive to the interest rate. In this case, a rise in income tends to raise the demand for money and a large rise in the rate of interest is necessary to keep the overall demand for money constant. This makes the *LM* curve very steep. In the neo-Keynesian case, the demand for money is interest elastic. When income rises and the transactions demand for money rises with it, only a small rise in interest rates is needed to restore the overall demand to its original level. This makes the *LM* curve relatively flat.

Fiscal versus monetary policy. The implications for fiscal and monetary policy of the assumed shapes in the *IS* and *LM* curves are analyzed in Figure 41A–2. The analysis of this figure yields the basic monetarist and neo-Keynesian predictions about the effects of these policies.

Figure 41A–2 The relative efficacies of fiscal and monetary policy

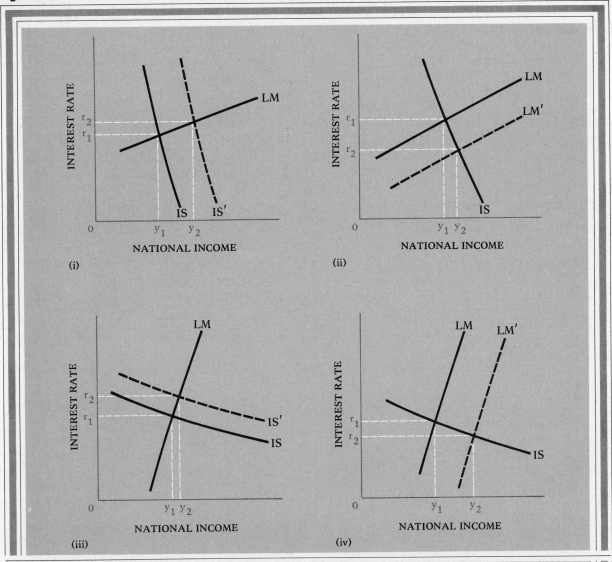

A neo-Keynesian view makes fiscal policy relatively more effective than monetary policy; a monetarist view reverses the relative efficacies of these two policies. In each of the four parts of the figure, the initial levels of national income and the interest rate are y_1 and r_1. The curve that shifts is indicated by a prime mark and the new levels of income and the interest rate are y_2 and r_2.

A neo-Keynesian view is shown in (i) and (ii). A relatively flat *LM* curve means that a shift in the *IS* curve has a large effect on income and only a small effect on interest rates. A relatively steep *IS* curve means that a shift in the *LM* curve has a large effect on interest rates and only a small effect on income.

A monetarist view is shown in (iii) and (iv). A steep *LM* curve means that a shift in *IS* has a large effect on the interest rate and only a small effect on income. A flat *IS* curve means that a shift in the *LM* curve has a large effect on income and only a small effect on interest rates.

Given the neo-Keynesian view of the shapes of the *IS* and the *LM* curves, the effects of fiscal policy are mainly felt in relatively large changes in the national income and relatively small changes in the rate of interest, while the effects of monetary policy are mainly felt in relatively small changes in national income and relatively large changes in the rate of interest.

Given the monetarist view of the shapes of the *IS* and *LM* curves, the effects of fiscal policy are mainly felt in relatively small changes in national income and relatively large changes in the rate of interest, while the effects of monetary policy are mainly felt in relatively large changes in the national income and relatively small changes in the rate of interest.

1. We are saying that many variables affect the quantity demanded. Using functional notation, the argument of the next several pages can be anticipated. Let Q^D represent the quantity of a commodity demanded and

$$T, \overline{Y}, N, Y^*, p, p_j$$

represent, respectively, tastes, average household income, population, income distribution, its price, and the price of the jth other commodity.

The demand function is

$$Q^D = Q^D(T, \overline{Y}, N, Y^*, p, p_j), j = 1, 2, \ldots, n$$

The demand schedule or curve looks at

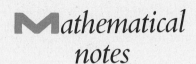

where the notation means that the variables to the right of the vertical line are held constant.

This function is correctly described as the demand function with respect to price, all other variables held constant. This function, often written concisely $q = f(p)$, shifts in response to changes in other variables. Consider average income. If, as is usually hypothesized, $\frac{\partial Q^D}{\partial \overline{Y}} > 0$, increases in average income shift $q = f(p)$ rightward and decreases in average income shift $q = f(p)$ leftward. Changes in other variables likewise shift this function in the direction implied by the relationship of that variable to the quantity demanded.

2. Continuing the development of the previous footnote, let Q^S represent the quantity of a commodity supplied and

$$G, X, p, p_j, w_i$$

represent, respectively, producers' goals, technology, price, price of the jth other commodity, and costs of the ith factor of production.

The supply function is

$$Q^S = Q^S(G, X, p, p_j, w_i), j = 1, 2, \ldots, n$$
$$i = 1, 2, \ldots, m$$

The supply schedule or curve looks at

$$Q^S = g(p) \Big|_{G, X, p_j, w_i}$$

This is the supply function with respect to price, all other variables held constant. This function,

Mathematical notes

often written concisely $q = g(p)$, shifts in response to changes in other variables.

3. Continuing the previous footnote, equilibrium occurs where

$$Q^D = Q^S$$

which *for specified values of all other variables* requires $f(p) = g(p)$. This condition is met only at the point where demand and supply curves intersect. Thus supply and demand curves are said to determine equilibrium price. A shift in any other variable, of course, will tend to shift the demand or supply curve and lead to a different equilibrium.

4. The "axis-reversal" arose in the following way. Marshall theorized in terms of "demand price" and "supply price" as the prices that would lead to a given quantity being demanded or supplied. Thus he wrote

$$p^d = D(q) \tag{1}$$

$$p^s = S(q) \tag{2}$$

and the condition of equilibrium as

$$D(q) = S(q) \tag{3}$$

When graphing the behavioral relations [1] and [2] Marshall naturally put the independent variable, q, on the horizontal axis.

Leon Walras, whose formulation of the working of a competitive market has become the accepted one, focused on quantities demanded and supplied *at a given price*. That is

$$q^d = D(p) \tag{4}$$

$$q^s = S(p) \tag{5}$$

and for equilibrium

$$D(p) = S(p) \tag{6}$$

Walras did not go in for graphic representation. Had he done so he would surely have placed p (his independent variable) on the horizontal axis.

Marshall, among his other influences on later generations of economists, was the great popularizer of graphical analysis in economics. Today we use his graphs, even for Walras's analysis. The "axis-reversal" is thus one of those accidents of history that seem odd to people who did not live through the "perfectly natural" sequence of steps that produced it.

5. The distinction made between an incremental change and a marginal change is the distinction for the function $Y = Y(X)$ between $\frac{\Delta Y}{\Delta X}$ and the derivative $\frac{dY}{dX}$. The latter is the limit of the former as ΔX approaches zero. Precisely this sort of difference underlies the distinction between arc and point elasticity, and we shall meet it repeatedly—in this chapter in reference to marginal and in cremental *utility* and in later chapters with respect to such concepts as marginal and incremental *product, cost,* and *revenue.* Where Y is a function of more than one variable—for example, $Y = f(X, Z)$—the marginal relationship between Y and X is the partial derivative $\frac{\partial Y}{\partial X}$ rather than the total derivative.

6. The relationship of the slope of the budget line to relative prices can be seen as follows. In the two-commodity example a change in expenditure (ΔE) is given by the equation

$$\Delta E = \Delta C p_C + \Delta F p_F \tag{1}$$

Along a budget line, expenditure is constant, i.e., $\Delta E = 0$. Thus, along such a line,

$$\Delta C p_C + \Delta F p_F = 0 \tag{2}$$

whence

$$-\frac{\Delta C}{\Delta F} = \frac{p_F}{p_C} \tag{3}$$

The ratio $-\Delta C/\Delta F$ is the slope of the budget line. It is negative because, with a fixed budget, to consume more F one must consume less C. In words, equation [3] says that the negative of the slope of the budget line is the ratio of the absolute prices (i.e., the relative price). While prices do not show directly in Figure 8–6, they are implicit in the budget line: its slope depends solely on the relative price, while its position, given a fixed money income, depends on the absolute prices of the two goods.

7. Marginal product as defined in the text is really "incremental product." A mathematician would distinguish between this notion and its limit as ΔL approaches zero. Technically *MP* measures the rate at which total product is changing as one factor is varied. The marginal product is the partial derivative of the total product with respect to the

variable factor. In symbols

$$MP = \frac{\partial TP}{\partial L}$$

Economists often use the term marginal product interchangeably with incremental product.

8. We have referred specifically both to diminishing *marginal* product and to diminishing *average* product. In most cases, eventually diminishing marginal product implies eventually diminishing average product. This is, however, not necessary, as the following figure shows.

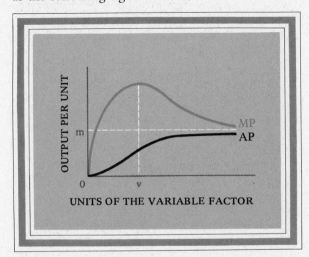

In this case, marginal product diminishes after v units of the variable factor are employed. Because marginal product falls toward, but never quite reaches, a value of m, average product rises continually toward, but never quite reaches, the same value.

9. Let q be the quantity of output and X the quantity of the variable factor. In the short run

$$TP = q = f(X) \qquad [1]$$

We now define

$$AP = \frac{q}{X} = \frac{f(X)}{X} \qquad [2]$$

$$MP = \frac{dq}{dX} \qquad [3]$$

We are concerned about the relation between these two. Whether average product is rising, at a maximum, or falling is determined by its derivative with respect to X.

$$\frac{d\frac{q}{X}}{dX} = \frac{X\frac{dq}{dX} - q}{X^2} \qquad [4]$$

This may be rewritten:

$$\frac{1}{X}\left(\frac{dq}{dX} - \frac{q}{X}\right) = \frac{1}{X}(MP - AP) \qquad [5]$$

Clearly, when MP is greater than AP, the expression in [5] is positive and thus AP is rising. When MP is less than AP, AP is falling, and when they are equal AP is at a stationary value.

10. The mathematically correct definition of marginal costs is the rate of change of total cost, with respect to output, q. Thus $MC = dTC/dq$. From the definitions, $TC = TFC + TVC$. Fixed costs are not a function of output. Thus we may write $TC = K + f(q)$, where $f(q)$ is total variable costs and K is a constant. And thus $MC = df(q)/dq$, which is independent of the size of the fixed costs.

11. This point is easily seen if a little algebra is used:

$$AVC = \frac{TVC}{q}$$

but

$$TVC = L \times w$$

and

$$q = AP \times L$$

where L is the quantity of the variable factor used and where w is its cost per unit. Therefore

$$AVC = \frac{L \times w}{AP \times L} = \frac{w}{AP}$$

Since w is a constant, it follows that AVC and AP vary inversely with each other, and when AP is at its maximum value, AVC must be at its minimum value.

12. Strictly speaking, the marginal rate of substitution refers to the slope of the tangent to the isoquant at a particular point while the calculations in Table 12–1 refer to the average rate of substitution between two distinct points on the isoquant. Assume a production function

$$Q = Q(K, L) \qquad [1]$$

Isoquants are given by the function

$$K = I(L, \bar{Q}) \tag{2}$$

derived from [1] by expressing K as an explicit function of L and Q. A single isoquant relates to a particular value at which Q is held constant. Define Q_K, and Q_L as an alternative, more compact notation for $\partial Q/\partial K$ and $\partial Q/\partial L$, the marginal products of capital and labor. Also let Q_{KK} and Q_{LL} stand for $\partial^2 Q/\partial L^2$ and $\partial^2 Q/\partial K^2$ respectively. To obtain the slope of the isoquant, totally differentiate [1] to obtain

$$dQ = Q_K dK + Q_L dL$$

Then, since we are moving along a single isoquant, set $dQ = 0$ to obtain

$$\frac{dK}{dL} = -\frac{Q_L}{Q_K} = MRS$$

Diminishing marginal productivity implies Q_{LL}, $Q_{KK} < 0$ and hence, as we move down the isoquant of Figure 12–4, Q_K is rising and Q_L falling, so the absolute value of MRS is diminishing. This is called the hypothesis of diminishing marginal rate of substitution.

13. Formally the problem is to maximize $Q = Q(K, L)$ subject to the budget constraint

$$p_K K + p_L L = C$$

To do this, form the Lagrangean

$$Q(K, L) - \lambda(p_K K + p_L L - C)$$

The first-order conditions for finding the saddle point on this function are

$$Q_K - \lambda p_K = 0; \quad Q_K = \lambda p_K \tag{1}$$

$$Q_L - \lambda p_L = 0; \quad Q_L = \lambda p_L \tag{2}$$

$$-p_K K - p_L L + C = 0 \tag{3}$$

Dividing [1] by [2] yields

$$\frac{Q_K}{Q_L} = \frac{p_K}{p_L}$$

i.e., the ratio of the marginal products, which is (-1) times the MRS, is equal to the ratio of the prices, which is (-1) times the slope of the isocost line.

14. For this note and the next one it is helpful first to define some terms. Let:

$$\pi_n = TR_n - TC_n$$

where π_n is the profit when n units are sold.

If the firm is maximizing its profits by producing n units, it is necessary that the profits at output q_n are at least as large as the profits at output zero. If the firm is maximizing its profits at output n, then

$$\pi_n \geq \pi_0 \tag{1}$$

The condition says that profits from producing must be greater than profits from not producing. Condition [1] can be rewritten

$$TR_n - TVC_n - TFC_n$$
$$\geq TR_0 - TVC_0 - TFC_0 \tag{2}$$

But note that by definition

$$TR_0 = 0 \tag{3}$$
$$TVC_0 = 0 \tag{4}$$
$$TFC_n = TFC_0 = K \tag{5}$$

where K is a constant. By substituting [3], [4], and [5] into [2], we get

$$TR_n - TVC_n \geq 0$$

from which we obtain

$$TR_n \geq TVC_n$$

On a per unit basis, it becomes

$$\frac{TR_n}{q_n} \geq \frac{TVC_n}{q_n}$$

where q_n is the number of units.

Since $TR_n = q_n p_n$ where p_n is the price when n units are sold, this may be rewritten

$$p_n \geq AVC_n$$

This proves rule 1.

15. Using elementary calculus, rule 2 may be proved

$$\pi_n = TR_n - TC_n$$

each of which is a function of output q. To maximize π it is necessary that

$$\frac{d\pi}{dq} = 0 \tag{1}$$

and that

$$\frac{d^2\pi}{dq^2} < 0 \qquad [2]$$

From the definitions

$$\frac{d\pi}{dq} = \frac{dTR}{dq} - \frac{dTC}{dq} = MR - MC \qquad [3]$$

From [1] and [3], a necessary condition of maximum π is $MR - MC = 0$, or $MR = MC$. For q_n to maximize profits requires $MR_n = MC_n$. Now

$$\frac{d^2\pi}{dq^2} = \frac{dMR}{dq} - \frac{dMC}{dq} \qquad [4]$$

From [2] and [4], a necessary condition of maximum π is

$$\frac{dMR}{dq} - \frac{dMC}{dq} < 0$$

which says that the slope of MC must be greater than the slope of MR. Taken with the previous result, it implies that, for q_n to maximize π, $MR_n = MC_n$ at a point where MC cuts MR from below.

16. Marginal revenue is mathematically the rate of change of total revenue with output dTR/dq. Incremental revenue is $\Delta TR/\Delta q$. But the term marginal revenue is loosely used to refer to both concepts.

17. To prove that, for a downward-sloping demand curve, marginal revenue is less than price, let $p = p(q)$. Then

$$TR = p \times q = p(q) \times q$$

$$MR = \frac{dTR}{dq} = q\frac{dp}{dq} + p$$

For a downward-sloping demand curve, dp/dq is negative by definition, and thus MR is less than price for positive values of q.

18. These propositions are easily proved using calculus. Let $p = a - bq$, which is the general equation for a downward-sloping straight line $(b > 0)$

$$TR = pq = aq - bq^2$$

and

$$MR = \frac{dTR}{dq} = a - 2bq$$

Comparison with the demand equation shows that the proof is complete.

19. The monopolist who produces in a single plant but sells in two or more markets will equate the marginal revenue in each market with his marginal cost. Thus $MC = MR_1 = MR_2$ is an equilibrium condition for a monopolist selling in two markets. But the ratio of price to marginal revenue is a function of elasticity of demand: the higher the elasticity, the lower the ratio. Thus equal marginal revenues imply a higher price in the market with the less elastic demand curve.

20. $p > MC$ follows at once from the two propositions that $MR = MC$ and $p > MR$ for a downward-sloping demand curve, proved in math note 17. $p > $ minimum ATC follows from the fact that it is equal to ATC where ATC is not a minimum.

21. Defining $TR = p \times q$

$$MR = \frac{dTR}{dq} = q\frac{dp}{dq} + p$$

At the kink in the demand curve, q and p are unambiguously determined but dp/dq, the slope of the demand curve, is very different in the upward and downward directions. Thus the level of MR must be different for increases and decreases in price at the same quantity.

22. The verbal argument in the text can be replaced by an easy proof:

$$MR = f(q)$$
$$MPP = g(q)$$
$$MRP = MPP \times MR = g(q) \times f(q)$$

By the hypothesis of diminishing returns, there is a level of output beyond which $g(q)$ declines. Hence, unless $f(q)$ rises, MRP will also decline. But $f(q)$ is constant or declining for all market structures identified. Therefore, MRP must have a declining section.

23. The proposition that the marginal labor cost is above the average labor cost when the average is rising is essentially the same proposition proved in math note 9. But let us do it again, using elementary calculus. The quantity of labor depends on the wage rate: $L = f(w)$. The marginal cost of labor is $d(wL)/dL = w + L(dw/dL)$. But w is the average cost of labor, and as long as the supply

curve slopes upward then $dw/dL > 0$, and thus $MC > AC$.

24. Let t be the tax rate applied to the profits, π, of the firm. The profits after tax will be $(1 - t)\pi$. If profits are maximized at output q^*, then by definition

$$\pi(q^*) > \pi(q_i)$$

where q_i is any other output. But

$$(1 - t)\pi(q^*) > (1 - t)\pi(q_i)$$

as long as

$$(1 - t) > 0$$

that is, for any tax rate less than 100 percent.

25. In the text we define the MPC as an incremental ratio. It is more convenient to define all marginal concepts as derivatives: $MPC = dC/dY$; $MPS = dS/dY$, and so on.

26. If $C = C(Y_d)$, and $Y_d = f(Y)$, then $C = C[f(Y)]$.

27. A constant APC necessarily implies the equality of APC and MPC:

$$APC = \frac{C}{Y}$$

If $\dfrac{C}{Y} = k$

then $C = kY$

and $\dfrac{\Delta C}{\Delta Y} = k = MPC$

28. In this economy, since $S = Y - C$, there is a simple relation between the propensities to consume and to save:

$$APC = \frac{C}{Y} = \frac{Y - S}{Y} = 1 - \frac{S}{Y} = 1 - APS$$

and

$$MPC = \frac{\Delta C}{\Delta Y} = \frac{\Delta Y - \Delta S}{\Delta Y} = 1 - \frac{\Delta S}{\Delta Y}$$
$$= 1 - MPS$$

Therefore, $APC + APS = 1$ and $MPC + MPS = 1$.

29. Proof: All that is needed for the stated result is that AD should always rise by less than income

and that it should exceed income when income is zero. Since in the Frugal economy $AD = C + I$ and we have assumed that I is constant and positive and that C is nonnegative at zero income, it follows that expenditure exceeds income at zero income and that

$$\frac{d\,AD}{dY} = \frac{dC}{dY}$$

The right-hand side is the marginal propensity to consume. The assumption given on page 490 ensures that $0 < MPC < 1$, which is what we require.

30. The equivalence of the two approaches is shown as follows: Approach 1:

$$AD \equiv C + I \quad \text{(defines desired expenditure)} \quad [1]$$

$$AD = Y \qquad \text{(states equilibrium condition)} \quad [2]$$

Approach 2:

$$C \equiv Y - S \qquad\qquad\qquad\qquad\qquad [3]$$

$$AD \equiv Y - S + I \qquad\qquad\qquad\qquad [4]$$

Substituting (4) into (2) gives

$$Y - S + I = Y, \text{ or } I = S$$

as the alternative statement of the equilibrium condition. Thus, $I = S$ if and only if $AD = Y$.

31. The total expenditure over all rounds is the sum of an infinite series. Letting J stand for the initiating expenditure and r for the marginal propensity to spend, the total expenditure for n rounds can be written

$$\Delta J\,(1 + r + r^2 + r^3 + \cdots + r^n)$$

If r is less than 1, the series in brackets converges to $1/(1 - r)$ as n approaches infinity. Total expenditure is thus $\Delta J/(1 - r)$. In the example in the box $r = .6$, therefore total expenditure is 2.5 times ΔJ.

32. The earlier discussion of expectations and profits can be related to the level of national income as follows:

The hypothesis that investment (I) is a function of expectations (e) is

$$I = I(e) \qquad\qquad\qquad\qquad\qquad\qquad [1]$$

If expectations are themselves importantly determined by the level of national income, that is, if

$$e = e(Y) \tag{2}$$

we can convert equation [1] into

$$I = I\,[e(Y)] = f(Y) \tag{3}$$

This says that investment is a function of the *level* of national income.

The hypothesis that investment (I) is a function of profits (π) is

$$I = I(\pi) \tag{4}$$

If aggregate profits are themselves largely determined by the level of national income, that is, if

$$\pi = \pi(Y) \tag{5}$$

equation [4] can be converted into

$$I = I[\pi(Y)] = g(Y) \tag{6}$$

In this form, the hypothesis says that investment is a function of the *level* of national income.

33. The accelerator may be stated as a general macroeconomic theory. Define I_n as the volume of net investment this year and ΔY as the increase in national income from last year to this year. The accelerator theory is the relationship between I_n and ΔY.

Assume the capital-output ratio is a constant.

$$\frac{K}{Y} = \alpha$$

or

$$K = \alpha Y$$

If Y is to change, K must be changed accordingly:

$$\Delta K = \alpha \Delta Y$$

But the change in the capital stock (ΔK) *is* net investment, so that

$$\Delta K \equiv I_n = \alpha \Delta Y$$

34. To see what happens to the budget deficit more generally, proceed as follows. Let Y be national income and $K = 1/w$ be the multiplier, where w is the marginal propensity to withdraw.

$$\Delta G = \text{initial deficit} \tag{1}$$

$$\Delta G - \Delta T = \text{final deficit} \tag{2}$$

and R is:

$$R = \frac{\Delta G}{\Delta G - \Delta T}$$

Let t = the marginal tax rate on national income. Thus

$$\Delta T = t\Delta Y \tag{3}$$

$$\Delta Y = K\Delta G = \frac{1}{w}\,\Delta G \tag{4}$$

Substituting gives

$$\frac{\Delta G}{\Delta G - \Delta T} = \frac{\Delta G}{\Delta G - \dfrac{t}{w}\,\Delta G} = \frac{1}{1 - \dfrac{t}{w}} = R$$

Since $0 < t < w$ we have $1 < R$, so that the initial deficit exceeds the final one. Only if taxes were the only withdrawal (i.e., if $t = w$) would the final deficit be zero.

35. This is easily proved. In equilibrium, the banking system wants sufficient deposits (D) to establish the legal ratio (r) of deposits to reserves (R). This gives $R/D = r$. Any change in D of ΔD will have to be accompanied by a change in R of ΔR of sufficient size to restore r. Thus $\Delta R/\Delta D = r$, so that $\Delta D = \Delta R/r$, and $\Delta D/\Delta R = 1/r$.

36. Proof: Let r be the reserve ratio. Let $z = 1 - r$ be the excess reserves per dollar of new deposit. If X dollars are deposited in the system assumed in the text, the successive rounds of new deposits are $X, zX, z^2X, z^3X, \ldots$. The series

$$X + zX + z^2X + z^3X \cdots$$
$$= X[1 + z + z^2 + z^3 + \cdots]$$

has a limit

$$X\,\frac{1}{1 - z} = X\left[\frac{1}{1 - (1 - r)}\right] = \frac{X}{r}$$

37. Suppose the public desires to hold a fraction, v, for any new deposits in cash. Now let the banking system receive an initial increase in its reserves of ΔR. It can expand deposits by an amount ΔD. As it does so the banking system suffers a cash drain to the public of $v\Delta D$. The banking system can only increase deposits to the extent the required reserve ratio, r, makes possible. The maximum is:

$$r\Delta D = \Delta R - v\Delta D$$

The left hand side gives the required reserves, the right hand side the actual reserves after the cash drain. From this,

$$r = \frac{\Delta R}{\Delta D} - v$$

or

$$\frac{\Delta D}{\Delta R} = \frac{1}{r + v}$$

38. The same argument can be developed using the quantity theory of money introduced in Chapter 34. We have $MV = PY$ where Y is real national income. If P is increased and M is held constant, then either V must rise or Y must fall. Although the velocity of circulation of money may rise somewhat, there are limits to how much it can rise. Thus sustained increases in P, unvalidated by sustained increases in M, must sooner or later be accompanied by falling Y.

39. Aggregate demand, AD, is hypothesized to be a function of both the level of national income, Y, and the rate of interest, r.

$$AD = AD(Y, r) \qquad [1]$$

Holding first r constant at $\bar{r}$ and then Y constant at $\bar{Y}$, we can derive two other functions:

$$AD_Y = AD(Y, \bar{r}) \qquad [2]$$

This is the one utilized in Chapter 27.

$$AD_r = AD(r, \bar{Y}) \qquad [3]$$

This is the one utilized in Chapter 41.

40. This is easily seen when we look at the relation $P_a = PD + P_e$ given in footnote 3 on page 770. It immediately follows that when $PD > 0$, $P_a > P_e$; when $PD = 0$, $P_a = P_e$; and when $PD < 0$, $P_a < P_e$.

41. The basic Phelps-Friedman relation is $P_a = PD + P_e$. When $Y = Y_F$ there is no excess demand inflation, so $PD = 0$. It follows immediately that we must have $P_a = P_e$ when $Y = Y_F$.

42. The "rule of 72" is an approximation derived from the mathematics of compound interest. Any measure X_t will have the value $X_t = X_0 e^{rt}$ after t years at a continuous growth rate of r percent per year. Because $X_t/X_0 = 2$ requires $r \times t = 0.69$, a

"rule of 69" would be correct for continuous growth. But 69 is an awkward number that is easily divisible only by 3 and 23. The number 72 is very close to 69 and is divisible by the integers 2, 3, 4, 6, 8, 9, 12, 18, 24, and 36. Thus it is convenient to use a "rule of 72" instead of 69. Probably the original reason for the use of 72 is that the rule was developed in the context of compound interest, and if interest is compounded only once a year the product of $r \times t$ for X to double is 0.72.

43. The time taken to break even is a function of the *difference* in growth rates, not their level. Thus, in the example, had 4 percent and 5 percent or 5 percent and 6 percent been used, it still would have taken the same number of years. To see this quickly, recognize that we are interested in the ratio of two growth paths: $e^{r_1 t}/e^{r_2 t} = e^{(r_1 - r_2)t}$.

44. The derivation of this result is as follows. Let X be your level and Y your competitor's.

$$X_0 = \frac{2}{3} Y_0 \qquad [1]$$

$$Y_{10} = Y_0 e^{10r} \qquad [2]$$

$$X_{10} = X_0 e^{10(r+a)} \qquad [3]$$

If $X_{10} = Y_{10}$ then

$$Y_0 e^{10r} = X_0 e^{10(r+a)} \qquad [4]$$

and

$$\frac{Y_0}{X_0} = \frac{3}{2} = e^{10a} \qquad [5]$$

for which $a = 0.04$.

45. Modern mathematicians distinguish between a correspondence and a function. There is a *correspondence* between Y and X if each value of X is associated with one or more values of Y. Y is a *function* of X if there is one and only one value of Y associated with each value of X. Mathematicians of an older generation described both relations as functional relations and then distinguished between single-valued functions (in modern language, functional relations) and multi-valued functions (in modern language, relations of correspondence). In the text we adopt the older, more embracing usage of the term functional relation.

46. The slope of $Y = a + bX$ is $dY/dX = b$, which is a constant. The slopes of the two functions shown in the section that follows in the text are not constant, they are $dY/dX = -a/X^2$ and $dY/dX = b + 2cX$.

47. If we assume that all relations describing behavior are linear, we can easily derive an algebraic equation for the *IS* curve using no more than high school algebra.

$$S = sY^d; \ 0 < s < 1 \qquad \qquad [1]$$

$$Y^d = Y - T \qquad \qquad [2]$$

$$T = tY; \ 0 < t < 1 \qquad \qquad [3]$$

$$I = h + iR; \ i < 0 < h \qquad \qquad [4]$$

$$G = \bar{G} \qquad \qquad [5]$$

$$S + T = I + G \qquad \qquad [6]$$

Upper case letters refer to variables: S is saving, Y^d is disposable income, Y is national income, T is total taxes, I is investment, R is the rate of interest and G is (constant) government expenditure (all of which is for the purchase of goods and services). Lower case letters refer to behavior: s is the marginal propensity to save out of disposable income, t is the marginal propensity to tax (all taxes are assumed to be personal income taxes), h is a constant and i relates the rate of interest to the amount of investment.

Equation [1] relates total saving to disposable income. Equation [2] relates disposable income to national income and taxes. Equation [3] shows how taxes vary with national income. Equation [4] shows how investment varies with the rate of interest. Equation [5] states that government expenditure is an exogenously determined constant (set at whatever level the government desires it to be). Finally, equation [6] states the condition that withdrawals, $S + T$, should equal injections, $G + T$.

Substitution of equations [1] through [5] into [6] produces

$$s(Y - tY) + tY = h + iR + \bar{G}$$

$$Y(s + t - st) = h + iR + \bar{G}$$

$$R = \left[\frac{s + t(1 - s)}{i} \right] Y - \frac{(h + \bar{G})}{i}$$

This is the equation of the *IS* curve. It is shown to be downward sloping since the restrictions on the various coefficients that describe behavior ensure that

$$\left[\frac{s + t(1 - s)}{i} \right] < 0$$

Since i is negative it follows that the increase in government expenditure, G, or in exogenous investment, h, shifts the *IS* curve outward.

48. The *LM* curve can be derived algebraically in a manner similar to the previous note on the *IS* curve. The linear version of the demand for money is

$$M^D = kY + lR; \ l < 0 < k \qquad \qquad [1]$$

where k is the transactions demand for money and l is the speculative demand. The money supply is an exogenous variable set at any level desired by the central bank. Hence

$$M^S = \bar{M}. \qquad \qquad [2]$$

Finally, in equilibrium

$$M^S = M^D \qquad \qquad [3]$$

Now substituting [1] and [2] into [3] yields

$$kY + lR = \bar{M}$$

or

$$R = -\frac{k}{l} Y + \frac{\bar{M}}{l}$$

This is the equation of the *LM* curve. Since l is negative but k/l has a negative sign in front of it, it follows that the slope of the curve is positive. To see the effects of a change in $\bar{M}$ notice that since l is negative, an increase in $\bar{M}$ shifts the *LM* curve downward and to the right.

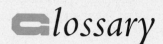
lossary

absolute advantage One nation has an absolute advantage over another nation in the production of a commodity if the same amount of resources will produce more of the commodity in the one nation than in the other.

absolute price A price expressed in money terms.

accelerator The theory that relates the level of investment to the rate of change of national income.

adjustable peg system A system in which monetary authorities peg (i.e., fix) the price of their domestic currency on the foreign exchange market but in which the price at which the currency is pegged can be adjusted (i.e., changed) from time to time.

ad valorem tax See *excise tax*.

aggregate demand (AD) function (or **aggregate expenditure function**) Relates aggregate desired expenditure to national income.

aggregate expenditure function See *aggregate demand function*.

allocative efficiency An allocation of resources in which price equals marginal cost in all industries and which is thus Pareto-optimal; it is often treated as a goal of economic organization.

allocative inefficiency The absence of allocative efficiency and the consequent absence of Pareto-optimality. Some consumers could be made better off by producing a different bundle of goods, without any being made worse off.

antitrust laws Laws designed to control monopolistic practices and monopoly power, including the Sherman Act (1890), the Clayton Act (1914), and the Federal Trade Commission Act (1914).

appreciation of the exchange rate A rise in the free-market value of domestic currency in terms of foreign currencies.

a priori Literally, "at a prior time" or "in advance"; knowledge that is prior to actual experience.

arbitrage The purchase of any commodity in markets where it is cheap in order to sell it in markets where it is dear, with the consequent effect of eliminating intermarket differentials.

arc elasticity of demand Elasticity of demand, for discrete changes in price and quantity. For analytical purposes, it is usually defined by the formula

$$\eta = \frac{\Delta q/q}{\Delta p/p}$$

An alternative formula often used where computations are involved is

$$\eta = -\frac{(q_2 - q_1)/(q_2 + q_1)}{(p_2 - p_1)/(p_2 + p_1)}$$

average cost (AC) Some measure of cost divided by the number of units of output.

average fixed costs (AFC) Total fixed costs divided by number of units of output.

average product (AP) Total product divided by the number of units of the variable factor used in its production.

average propensity to consume (APC) The proportion of total income devoted to consumption. Total consumption expenditure divided by total income ($APC = C/Y$).

average propensity to save (APS) The proportion of total income devoted to saving ($APS = S/Y$).

average revenue (AR) Total revenue divided by quantity. Where a single price prevails $AR = p$.

average tax rate The ratio of total tax paid to total income earned.

average total cost (ATC) Total cost divided by the number of units of output; the sum of average fixed costs and average variable costs. Also called *cost per unit, unit cost, average cost (AC)*.

average variable costs Total variable costs divided by the number of units of output. Also called *direct unit costs, avoidable unit costs*.

balanced budget A situation in which current revenue is exactly equal to current expenditures.

balanced budget multiplier The change in income divided by the tax-financed change in government expenditure that brought it about.

balanced growth policy Simultaneous growth in all sectors of the economy; a growth experience suitable to a closed economy.

balance-of-payments accounts A summary record of a country's transactions that typically involve payments or receipts of foreign exchange.

balance-of-payments deficit A situation in which a country's receipts on current and capital account fall short of its payments (ignoring transactions by monetary authorities).

balance-of-payments surplus A situation in which a country's receipts on current and capital account exceed its payments (ignoring transactions by monetary authorities).

balance of trade The difference between the value of exports and the value of imports of visible items (goods).

balance sheet A report showing a firm's assets and the claims against those assets at a moment in time. Balance sheets always balance because the owners' equity is defined as the amount of the assets less the claims of the creditors.

bank notes Paper money issued by commercial banks.

barriers to entry Legal or other impediments to entry into an industry. Patents, franchises, economies of scale, and established brand preferences may each lead to such barriers.

barter A system in which goods are traded directly for other goods.

base year A period chosen for comparison purposes, in connection with expressing or computing *index numbers* or *constant dollars*.

beggar-my-neighbor policies Policies designed to increase a country's prosperity (especially by reducing its unemployment) at the expense of reducing prosperity in other countries (especially by increasing their unemployment).

blacklist An employer's list of workers who have been fired for union activity.

black market A situation in which goods are sold illegally at prices above a legal maximum price.

bond An evidence of debt carrying a specified amount and schedule of interest payments, as well as a date for redemption of the face value of the bond.

bondholders Creditors of the firm, whose evidence of debt is a bond issued by the firm.

boycott A concerted refusal to buy (buyers' boycott) or to sell (producers' or sellers' boycott) a commodity.

bread-and-butter unionism A union movement whose major objectives are wages, hours, and conditions of employment rather than political or social ends.

budget line (isocost line) A line on a diagram showing all combinations of commodities that a household may obtain if it spends a given amount of money at fixed prices of the commodities.

built-in stabilizer Anything that tends to adjust government revenues and expenditures automatically (i.e., without an explicit policy decision) so as to reduce inflationary and deflationary gaps whenever they develop.

business cycles More or less regular patterns of fluctuations in the level of economic activity.

capacity The level of output that corresponds to the minimum level of short-run average total costs. Also called *plant capacity*.

capital A factor of production, defined to include all man-made aids to further production.

capital consumption allowance An estimate of the amount by which the capital stock is depleted through its contribution to current production. Often called *depreciation*.

capital deepening Adding capital to the production process in such a way as to increase the ratio of capital to labor and other factors of production.

capitalized value The value of an asset measured by the present value of the income stream it is expected to produce.

capital-output ratio The ratio of the value of capital to the annual value of output produced by it.

capital stock The aggregate quantity of a society's capital goods.

capital widening Adding capital to the production process in such a way as to leave factor proportions unchanged.

cartel An organization of producers designed to limit or eliminate competition among its members, usually by agreeing to restrict output in an effort to achieve noncompetitive prices.

categorical grants-in-aid Federal grants to state or local governments for specified categories of expenditures such as highways or welfare payments.

central authorities All public agencies, government bodies, and other organizations belonging to or under the control of government.

central bank A bank that acts as banker to the commercial banking system and often to the government as well. In the modern world the central bank is usually the sole money-issuing authority.

certificate of deposit (CD) A negotiable time deposit carrying a higher interest rate than that paid on ordinary time deposits.

ceteris paribus Literally, "other things being equal"; usually used in economics to indicate that all variables except the ones specified are assumed not to change.

clearing house An institution where interbank indebtednesses arising from transfer of checks between banks are computed, offset against each other, and net amounts owing are calculated.

closed economy An economy that does not engage in foreign trade.

closed shop A bargaining arrangement in which only union members can be employed. Union membership precedes employment.

coefficient of determination (r^2 or R^2) The coefficient showing the fraction of the total variance of the dependent variable that can be associated with the independent variables in the regression equation; r^2 is used for two variables and R^2 for three or more variables.

collective bargaining The whole process by which unions and employers arrive at and enforce agreements.

collective consumption goods Goods or services that, if they provide benefits to anyone, necessarily provide benefits to a large group of people or a community.

collusion An agreement among sellers to set a common price and/or to share a market. Collusion may be overt or secret. It may be explicit or tacit.

command economy An economy in which the decisions of the central authorities exert the major influence over the allocation of resources.

commercial banks Privately owned, profit-seeking institutions that provide a variety of financial services. They accept deposits from customers, which they agree to transfer when ordered by a check, and they make loans and other investments.

commodities Marketable items produced to satisfy wants. Commodities may be either *goods*, which are tangible, or *services*, which are intangible.

common-property resource A natural resource that is owned by no one and may be used by anyone.

common stock A form of equity capital usually carrying voting rights and a residual claim to the assets and profits of the firm.

comparative advantage (1) Country A has a comparative advantage over country B in producing a commodity, X, if it can do so at a lesser opportunity cost in terms of other products foregone. (2) As distinguished from absolute advantage: Comparing two countries, A and B, and two commodities, X and Y, country A has a comparative advantage in X if its margin of absolute advantage is greater in X than in Y.

comparative statics Comparative static equilibrium analysis; the derivation of predictions by analyzing the effect of a change in some exogenous variable or parameter on the equilibrium position.

competitive devaluations A round of devaluations of exchange rates by a number of countries each trying to gain a competitive advantage over the other and each failing to the extent that other countries also devalue.

complement A commodity that tends to be used jointly with the original commodity. Technically, a complement to a commodity is another commodity for which the cross elasticity of demand is nonnegligible and negative.

concentration ratio The fraction of total market sales (or some other measure of market occupancy) made by a specified number of the industry's largest firms. Four-firm and eight-firm concentration ratios are the most frequently used.

conglomerate merger See *merger*.

conscious parallel action See *tacit collusion*.

constant-cost industry An industry in which costs of the most efficient size firm remain constant as the entire industry expands or contracts in the long run.

constant dollars A series expressed in terms of the level of prices prevailing in a specified *base year*. Constant dollars are thus free of inflationary or deflationary trends. Used in contrast to *current dollars*.

constant returns A situation in which output increases proportionately with the quantity of inputs as the scale of production is increased.

consumption The act of using commodities to satisfy wants.

consumption function The relationship between consumption expenditure and all of the factors that determine it. In the simplest consumption function, consumption depends only on current income.

corporation A form of business organization with a legal existence separate from that of the owners, in which ownership and financial responsibility are divided, limited, and shared among any number of individual and institutional shareholders.

cost (of output) To a producing firm, the value of factors of production used up in producing output.

cost minimization Achieving the lowest attainable cost of producing a specified output. It is an implication of profit maximization that the firm will choose the least costly method available of producing any specific output.

cost-push inflation Inflation caused by increases in costs, mainly labor costs, not themselves associated with excess aggregate demand.

craft union A union organized according to a specified set of skills or occupations.

credit rationing Rationing of available funds among borrowers in a situation in which there is excess demand for loans at prevailing interest rates.

cross elasticity of demand A measure of the extent to which quantity of a commodity demanded responds to changes in price of a related commodity. Formula:

$$\frac{\text{percentage change in quantity of } x}{\text{percentage change in price of } y}$$

cross-sectional data Data referring to a number of different observations at the same point in time.

crowding-out effect A reduction in private expenditure as a direct result of an increase in government expenditure.

debt Amounts owed to one's creditors, including banks and other financial institutions.

decision lag A lag between obtaining relevant information about some problem and reaching a decision on what to do about it.

decreasing returns A situation in which output increases less than in proportion to inputs as the scale of production increases. A firm in this situation, with fixed factor prices, is an *increasing cost firm*.

deficient-demand unemployment Unemployment that is due to insufficient aggregate demand and that can be reduced by measures that raise aggregate demand.

deflationary gap The amount by which the aggregate demand schedule must be increased to achieve full-employment income.

demand There are several distinct but closely related concepts: (1) *quantity demanded;* (2) the whole relationship of the quantity demanded to variables that determine it, such as tastes, household income, distribution of income, population, price of the commodity, and prices of other commodities; (3) the *demand schedule;* (4) the *demand curve*. The phrase increase (decrease) in demand means a shift of the demand curve to the right (left) indicating an increase (decrease) in the quantity demanded at each possible price.

demand curve The graphic representation of the *demand schedule*.

demand deposit A bank deposit that is withdrawable on demand and transferable by means of a check.

demand for money The total amount of money that the public wishes to hold for all purposes.

demand-pull inflation Inflation arising from excess aggregate demand.

demand schedule The relationship between the quantity demanded of a commodity and its price, *ceteris paribus*.

deposit money Money held by the public in the form of demand deposits with commercial banks.

depreciation (1) The loss in value of an asset over a period of time; includes both physical wear and tear and obsolescence. (2) The amount by which the capital stock is depleted through its contribution to current production.

depreciation of the exchange rate A fall in the free-market value of domestic currency in terms of foreign currencies.

depression A period of very low economic activity with very high unemployment and high excess capacity.

derived demand The demand for a factor of production that results from the demand for products it is used to make.

devaluation of the exchange rate A downward revision in the value at which a country's currency is pegged in terms of foreign currencies.

dirty float Although foreign exchange rates are left to be determined on the free market, monetary authorities intervene in this market so as to influence exchange rates, but they are *not* publicly committed to holding their country's exchange rate at any announced "par value."

discount rate (1) In banking, the rate at which the central bank is prepared to lend reserves to commercial banks. (2) More generally, the rate of interest used to discount a stream of future payments to arrive at their *present value*.

discretionary fiscal policy Fiscal policy that is a conscious response (not according to any predetermined rule) to each particular state of the economy as it arises.

disembodied technical change Technical change that raises output without the necessity of building new capital to embody the new knowledge.

disposable income The income that households have available for spending and saving.

dissaving Negative saving; a situation in which household consumption expenditure exceeds disposable income.

dividends That part of profits paid out to shareholders of a corporation.

division of labor The breaking up of a task (e.g., making pins) into a number of repetitive operations, each one done by a different worker.

dollar standard (for international payments) International indebtedness between monetary authorities is settled in terms of dollars, which are not necessarily backed by gold or any other ultimate monetary base.

dynamic (or **disequilibrium**) **differential** A difference in factor prices caused by disequilibrium that will tend to lead to corrective movements of resources. In equilibrium these differentials will be eliminated. Observed because it often takes considerable time for equilibrium to be reached.

economic efficiency (in production) A method of producing some quantity of output is economically efficient when it is the least costly method of producing that output.

economic profits or losses (often simply **profits**) The difference in the revenues received from the sale of output and the opportunity cost of the inputs used to make the output. Negative profits are losses.

economic rent That part of the payment to a factor in excess of its *transfer earnings*.

effluent charge A fee, fine, or tax on a producer for polluting activity, usually on a per unit basis.

elastic demand The situation existing when for a given percentage change in price there is a greater percentage change in quantity demanded; elasticity greater than 1.

elasticity of demand A measure of the responsiveness of quantity of a commodity demanded to a change in market price. Formula:

$$\frac{\text{percentage change in quantity demanded}}{\text{percentage change in price}}$$

Conventionally expressed as a positive number, it is a pure number ranging from zero to infinity.

elasticity of supply A measure of the responsiveness of quantity of a commodity supplied to a change in price. Formula:

$$\frac{\text{percentage change in quantity supplied}}{\text{percentage change in price}}$$

embodied technical change A technical change that can be utilized only when new capital, embodying the new techniques, is built.

endogenous variables Variables explained within a theory.

envelope curve Any curve that encloses, by just being tangent to, a series of other curves. In particular, the *envelope cost curve* is the *LRAC* curve; it encloses the *SRAC* curves by being tangent to them but not cutting them.

equilibrium conditions The conditions that must be fulfilled for some economic variable, such as price or national income, to be in equilibrium.

equilibrium differentials Differences in factor prices that would persist in equilibrium, without any tendency for them to be removed. These differences may be associated with differences in the factor themselves or with the nonmonetary advantages of different employments.

equilibrium national income The level of national income at which aggregate expenditure equals total output.

equilibrium price The price at which quantity demanded equals quantity supplied.

equity capital Capital provided by the owners of a firm.

error term An expressed or implied variable in a functional relationship to allow for (1) omitted variables and (2) errors in measurement.

excess capacity (1) Production at levels below the output at which *ATC* is a minimum. (2) The difference between such actual output and capacity output.

excess-capacity theorem The proposition that equilibrium in a monopolistically competitive industry will occur where each firm has excess capacity.

excess demand A situation in which, at the given price, quantity demanded exceeds quantity supplied. Also called *shortage*.

excess reserves Reserves held by a commercial bank in excess of the legally required amount.

excess supply A situation in which, at the given price, quantity supplied exceeds quantity demanded. Also called *surplus*.

exchange rate The price in terms of one currency at which another currency, or claims on it, can be bought and sold.

excise tax A tax on the sale of a particular commodity. A *specific tax* is a fixed tax per unit of the taxed commodity. An *ad valorem tax* is a fixed percentage of the value of the commodity.

execution lag A lapse of time between the decision to do something and its actually being done.

exogenous variables Variables that influence other variables within a theory but that themselves are determined by factors outside the theory.

expectational inflation Inflation that occurs because decision makers raise prices (so as to keep their relative prices constant) in the expectation that the price level is going to rise.

externalities (also called **third-party effects**) Effects, either good or bad, on parties not directly involved in the production or use of a commodity.

factor markets Markets in which households sell the services of the factors of production that they control.

factor mobility The ease with which factors can be transferred between uses.

factors of production Resources used to produce goods and services to satisfy wants. Land, labor, and capital are three frequently used basic categories of factors of production. Sometimes used synonymously with *inputs*.

falling-cost industry An industry in which the lowest costs attainable by a firm fall as the whole scale of the industry expands.

federation In respect to labor unions, a federation is any loose organization of national unions.

fiat money Paper money or coinage that is neither backed by nor convertible into anything else but that is legal tender.

final products The economy's output of goods and services after all double counting has been eliminated.

firm The unit that makes decisions regarding the employment of factors of production and the production of goods and services.

fiscal drag The tendency for a deflationary gap to open up at full-employment income because tax revenues rise faster than government expenditure as full-employment income rises due to economic growth.

fiscal policy The deliberate use of the government's revenue-raising and spending activities in an effort to influence the behavior of such macro variables as the GNP and total employment.

fixed costs Costs that do not change with output. Also sometimes called *overhead costs*.

fixed exchange rate An exchange rate that is fixed or pegged within very narrow bands by the action of monetary authorities.

fixed factors Factors that cannot be increased in the short run.

floating exchange rate An exchange rate that is left to be determined on the free market without any attempt by monetary authorities to determine its value.

foreign exchange (foreign media of exchange) Actual foreign currency or various claims on it such as bank balances or promises to pay.

45° line In macroeconomic graphs, the line that joins all those points at which expenditure equals income.

fractional reserve system In contrast to a 100 percent reserve system, a banking system in which commercial banks are required to keep only a fraction of their deposits in cash or on deposit with the central bank.

freedom of entry and exit The absence of legal or other artificial barriers to entering into production or withdrawing assets from production.

free good A commodity for which no price needs to be paid because the quantity supplied exceeds the quantity demanded at a price of zero.

free-market economy An economy in which the decisions of individual households and firms (as distinct from the central authorities) exert the major influence over the allocation of resources.

free trade A situation in which all commodities can be freely imported and exported without special taxes or restrictions being levied merely because of their status as "imports" or "exports."

frictional unemployment Unemployment caused by the time taken for labor to move from one job to another.

full-cost pricing Pricing according to average total cost plus a fixed markup. Usually the costs and standard costs as defined by good accounting practice.

full-employment balance The budget deficit or surplus that would occur if national income were at its full-employment level.

full-employment GNP See *potential GNP*. Sometimes called *full-employment national income*.

function Loosely, an expression of a relation between two or more variables. Precisely, Y is a function of the variables $X_1, \ldots, X_n$ if for every set of values of the variables $X_1, \ldots, X_n$ there is associated a unique value of the variable Y.

functional distribution of income The distribution of income by major factors of production.

gains from trade The increased production that results from specialization and trade as opposed to a situation of self-sufficiency. It can be applied to persons, regions, or nations.

general equilibrium analysis The analysis of an interdependent set of markets or sectors with full regard for spillouts and feedbacks.

Giffen good An inferior good for which the negative income effect outweighs the substitution effect and leads to an upward-sloping demand curve.

GNP deflator See *gross national product deflator*.

gold exchange standard A monetary system in which some countries' currencies are directly convertible into gold while other countries' currencies are indirectly convertible by being convertible into the gold-backed currencies at a fixed rate. Under the Bretton Woods version only the U.S. dollar was directly convertible into gold.

goods Tangible commodities such as cars or shoes.

Gresham's law The theory that "bad," or debased, money drives "good," or undebased, money out of circulation because people will keep the good money and spend the bad money.

gross investment The total value of all investment goods produced in the economy during a stated period of time.

gross national income See *gross national product*.

gross national product (GNP) The sum of all values added in the economy. It is the sum of the values of all final goods produced and, which is the same thing, the sum of all factor incomes earned. Also called *gross national income*.

gross national product deflator The index number used to adjust the GNP measured in current dollars for price level changes so that it is measured in constant dollars.

holding company A company that holds the controlling shares of stock of another company.

horizontal merger See *merger*.

household All the people who live under one roof and who make, or are subject to others making for them, joint financial decisions.

human capital The capitalized value of productive investments in persons. Usually refers to investments resulting from expenditures on education, training, and health improvements.

hypothesis of equal net advantage The hypothesis that owners of factors will choose the use of their factors that produces the greatest net advantage to themselves and therefore will move their factors among uses until net advantages are equalized.

hypothesis of eventually diminishing returns The hypothesis that if increasing quantities of a variable factor are applied to a given quantity of fixed factors, the marginal product and average product of the variable factor will eventually decrease. Also called *hypothesis of diminishing returns, law of diminishing returns, law of variable proportions*.

identification problem The ambiguity introduced by attempting to use observations of prices and quantities actually exchanged to draw inferences about either supply curves or demand curves when shifts in both curves have occurred.

imputed costs The costs of using in production factors already owned by the firm, measured by the earnings they could have received in their best alternative employment.

income-consumption line A line connecting the points of tangency of a set of indifference curves with a series of parallel budget lines, showing how consumption of a good changes as income changes, with relative prices held constant.

income effect The effect on quantity demanded of a change in real income caused by a change in the commodity's price.

income elasticity of demand A measure of the responsiveness of quantity demanded to a change in income. Formula:

$$\frac{\text{percentage change in quantity demanded}}{\text{percentage change in income}}$$

income statement A financial report showing the revenues and costs that arise from the firm's use of inputs to produce outputs, over a specified period of time.

increasing returns A situation in which output increases more than in proportion to inputs as the scale of a firm's production increases. A firm in this situation, with fixed factor prices, is a *decreasing cost* firm.

incremental cost See *marginal cost*.

incremental product See *marginal product*.

incremental revenue See *marginal revenue*.

index numbers Averages that measure changes over time of variables such as the price level and industrial production. They are conventionally expressed as percentages relative to a base period assigned the value 100.

indifference curve A curve showing all combinations of two commodities that give the household equal amounts of satisfaction and among which the household is thus indifferent.

indifference map A set of indifference curves, each indicating a constant level of satisfaction derived by the household concerned, and based on a given set of household preferences.

industrial union A union organized to include all workers in an industry, regardless of skills.

industry A group of firms producing similar products.

inelastic demand The situation in which for a given percentage change in price there is a smaller percentage change in quantity demanded; elasticity less than unity.

infant-industry argument for tariffs The argument that new domestic industries with potential economies of scale need to be protected from competition from established low-cost foreign producers so that they can grow large enough to reap their own economies of scale and achieve costs as low as those of foreign producers.

inferior goods Goods for which income elasticity is negative.

inflation (1) A rising price level in the economy; (2) A phase of the business cycle in which price increases tend to be general and rapid.

inflationary gap The extent to which aggregate desired expenditure exceeds national income at full-employment national income.

injections Income earned by domestic firms that does not arise out of the spending of domestic households and income earned by domestic households that does not arise out of the spending of domestic firms.

innovation The introduction of inventions into methods of production.

inputs Materials and factor services used in the process of production. Sometimes synonymous with *factors of production*.

instrumental variables The variables that the central authorities can control directly; thus their instruments of policy.

interest The payment for the use of money.

interest rate The price paid per dollar borrowed per year. Expressed either as a fraction (e.g., 0.06) or as a percentage (e.g., 6 percent).

intermediate products All goods and services that are used as inputs into a further stage of production.

internalization A process that results in a producer taking account of a previously external effect.

invention The discovery of something new, such as a new production technique or a new product.

inventories Stocks of raw materials, or of finished goods, held by firms to mitigate the effect of short-term fluctuations in production or sales.

investment Expenditures on the production of goods not for present consumption.

investment goods Capital goods such as plant and equipment plus inventories; production that is not sold for consumption purposes.

invisibles All those items of foreign trade that are intangible; services as opposed to goods.

isocost line The graphic representation of alternative combinations of factors that a firm can buy for a given outlay.

isoquant A curve showing all technologically efficient factor combinations for producing a specified output; an iso-product curve.

isoquant map A series of isoquants from the same production function.

jurisdictional dispute Dispute between unions over which has the right to organize a group of workers.

kinked demand curve A demand curve with a corner, or "kink," at the prevailing price. The curve is more elastic in response to price increases than to price decreases.

labor A factor of production usually defined to include all physical and mental contributions to economic activity provided by people.

labor boycott An organized boycott to persuade customers to refrain from purchasing the products of a firm or industry whose employees are on strike.

labor force The number of people either employed or actively seeking work.

labor union See *union*.

laissez faire Literally, "let do"; a policy implying the absence of government intervention in a market economy.

land A factor of production, usually defined to include all gifts of nature, including raw materials as well as "land" conventionally defined.

law of diminishing returns See *hypothesis of eventually diminishing returns*.

law of variable proportions See *hypothesis of eventually diminishing returns*.

legal tender Anything that by law must be accepted for the purchase of goods and services or in discharge of a debt, and thus money.

life-cycle hypothesis (LCH) The hypothesis that relates the household's actual consumption to its expected lifetime income rather than, as in early Keynesian theory, to its current income.

limited liability The limitation of the financial responsibility of an owner (shareholder) of a corporation to the amount of money he or she has actually made available to the firm by purchasing its shares.

limited partnership Partnership with limited liability for partners not participating in management.

limit price The minimum price at which a new firm can enter a market without incurring a loss; equal to its minimum average cost. Existing lower-cost firms may be able to discourage new entrants by setting the price below this limit.

liquidity preference The demand to hold assets in the form of money rather than as interest-earning wealth.

liquidity preference schedule A schedule relating the amount of money held to the rate of interest. The amount held rises as the interest rate falls.

lockout The employer's equivalent of a strike, in which he temporarily closes his plant.

logarithmic scale A scale in which equal proportional changes are shown as equal distances. Thus 1 inch may always represent doubling of a variable, whether from 3 to 6 or 50 to 100. Contrasted with *natural scale*. (Also called *log scale* or *ratio scale*.)

long run The period of time long enough for all inputs to be varied, but in which the basic technology of production is unchanged.

long-run average cost curve (LRAC) The curve relating the least-cost method of producing any output to the level of output. Sometimes called *long-run average total cost* (*LRATC*).

long-run industry supply (LRS) curve The curve showing the relation of the quantity supplied to prices with quantities of all factors freely variable, and allowing time for firms to achieve long-run equilibrium.

Lorenz curve A graph showing the extent of departure from equality of income distribution.

L-shaped relation An assumed relation between the *rate of* inflation and the *level of* national income, showing the assumption that inflation will be zero when actual income is less than full-employment income and may be zero or positive where actual income equals full-employment income.

M₁ A narrow definition of money, as currency in circulation plus demand deposits.

M₂ A broader definition of money than M₁—currency in circulation, demand deposits, and savings deposits with commercial banks.

M₃ The broadest definition of money in widespread use—currency in circulation, demand deposits, and savings deposits with commercial banks and nonbank thrift institutions.

macroeconomics The study of the determination of economic aggregates, such as total output, total employment, and the price level.

managed float See *dirty float*.

marginal cost (incremental cost) The increase in total cost resulting from raising the rate of production by 1 unit; mathematically, the rate of change of cost with respect to output.

marginal efficiency of capital (MEC) The marginal rate of return on a nation's capital stock. It is the rate of return on one additional dollar of net investment, i.e., an addition of \$1 to capital stock.

marginal efficiency of capital schedule A schedule relating *MEC* to the size of the capital stock.

marginal efficiency of investment (MEI) schedule A schedule relating the total amount of desired investment expenditure to the rate of interest.

marginal physical product (MPP) See *marginal product*.

marginal product (MP) The increase in quantity of total output that results from using 1 unit more of a variable factor; mathematically, the rate of change of output with respect to the quantity of the variable factor. Also called *incremental product* or *marginal physical product* (*MPP*).

marginal productivity theory of distribution The implication from profit maximization that the use of a factor should be expanded until its marginal revenue product equals its price.

marginal propensity The ratio of the change of any flow to the change in income that brought it about.

marginal propensity to consume (MPC) The change in consumption divided by the change in income that brought it about ($MPC = \Delta C/\Delta Y$); mathematically, the rate of change of consumption with respect to income.

marginal propensity to save (MPS) The change in saving divided by the change in income that brought it about ($MPS = \Delta S/\Delta Y$); mathematically, the rate of change of saving with respect to income.

marginal rate of substitution (*in consumption*) The slope of an indifference curve, showing how much more of one good will just compensate in satisfaction the giving up of 1 unit of another good, expressed as a ratio of one to the other. (*in production*) The slope of an isoquant showing how much more of one factor of production must be used to compensate for the use of one less unit of another factor of production if production is to be held constant.

marginal revenue (MR) (incremental revenue) The change in a firm's total revenue arising from the sale of 1 unit more; mathematically, the rate of change of revenue with respect to output.

marginal revenue product (MRP) The addition of revenue attributable to the last unit of a variable factor. $MRP = MPP \times MR$; mathematically, the rate of change of revenue with respect to quantity of the variable factor.

marginal tax rate The fraction of an additional dollar of income that is paid in taxes.

marginal utility The additional satisfaction obtained by a buyer from consuming 1 unit more of a good; mathematically, the rate of change of utility with respect to consumption.

margin requirements The fraction of the price of a stock that must be paid in cash, while putting up the stock as security against a loan for the balance.

market A concept with many possible definitions. (1) An area over which buyers and sellers negotiate the exchange of a well-defined commodity. (2) From the point of view of a household, the firms from which it can buy a well-defined product. (3) From the point of view of a firm, the buyers to whom it can sell a well-defined product.

market structure Characteristics of market organization likely to affect behavior and performance of firms, such as the number and size of sellers, the extent of knowledge about each other's actions, the degree of freedom of entry, and the degree of product differentiation.

markup The percentage or amount added to cost to determine price.

medium of exchange Anything that is generally acceptable in return for goods and services sold.

merger The purchase of either the physical assets or the controlling share ownership of one company by another. In a *horizontal* merger both companies produce the same product; in a *vertical* merger one company is a supplier of the other; if the two are in unrelated industries, it is a *conglomerate* merger.

microeconomic policy Activities of the central authorities that alter resource allocation and/or income distribution.

microeconomics The study of the allocation of resources and the distribution of income as they are affected by the workings of the price system and by some government policies.

minimum efficient scale (MES) The smallest size of firm required to achieve the economies of scale in production and/or distribution. Also called *minimum optimal scale (MOS)*.

mixed economy Economy in which some decisions are made by firms and households and some by central authorities.

monetarists A group of economists who stress monetary causes of cyclical fluctuations and inflations, who feel that an active stabilization policy is not normally required, and who stress the relative efficacy of monetary over fiscal policy.

monetary policy An attempt to influence the economy by operating on such monetary variables as the quantity of money and the rate of interest.

money Any generally accepted medium of exchange.

money capital The funds used to finance a firm. Money capital includes both equity capital and debt.

money flow The flow of money payments from buyers to sellers in return for goods and services received.

money income A household or firm's income in the form of some monetary unit.

money rate of interest A rate of interest expressed in current dollars.

money substitute Anything such as a credit card or a charge account that permits the holder to purchase goods and services whether or not he or she possesses legal tender at the time.

money supply The total quantity of money existing at a point in time.

monopolistic competition A market structure of an industry in which there are many sellers and freedom of entry, but in which each firm has a product somewhat differentiated from the others, giving it some control over its price.

monopoly A market structure in which the output of an industry is controlled by a single seller or a group of sellers making joint decisions.

monopsony A market situation in which there is a single buyer or a group of buyers making joint decisions. Monopsony and monopsony power are the equivalent on the buying side of monopoly and monopoly power on the selling side.

multiplier The relation between the change in income and the change in expenditure that caused the change in income. In a model in which saving is the only withdrawal the multiplier is the reciprocal of the marginal propensity to save. More generally the multiplier is the reciprocal of the marginal propensity to withdraw funds from the circular flow—i.e., the slope of the withdrawals function.

national debt The current volume of outstanding federal government debt.

national income (1) The generic term referring to the total market value of all final goods and services produced in the economy over some period of time, and to the total value of all incomes generated over the same period of time. Also referred to as the *national product*. (2) A technical term used by national income accountants.

national income accounting The set of rules and techniques for measuring the total flows of outputs produced and inputs used by the economy.

natural monopoly An industry characterized by economies of scale sufficiently large that one firm can most efficiently supply the entire market demand.

natural rate of unemployment The rate of unemployment consistent (due to frictional and structural causes) with full-employment national income, Y_F. In the Phelps-Friedman theory this is the rate of unemployment at which there is neither upward nor downward pressure on the price level.

natural scale A scale in which equal absolute amounts are represented by equal distances.

near money Liquid assets easily convertible into money without risk of significant loss of value. They can be used as short-term stores of purchasing power but are not themselves media of exchange.

negative income tax (NIT) A tax system in which households with incomes below taxable levels receive payments from the government based on a percentage of the amount by which their income is below the minimum taxable level.

negotiable order of withdrawal (NOW) A checklike device for paying funds in one person's time deposit to another person.

neo-Keynesians Sometimes called Keynesians; a group of economists who stress changes in both aggregate expenditure and the money supply as causes of cyclical fluctuations and inflations, who feel that an active government stabilization policy is called for, and who stress the relative efficacy of fiscal policy over monetary policy.

net exports Total exports *minus* total imports $(X - M)$.

net investment Gross investment *minus* replacement investment.

net national income See *net national product*.

net national product (NNP) Gross national product *minus* a capital consumption allowance. Also called *net national income*.

net private benefit The difference between private benefits and private costs.

net social benefit The difference between social benefits and social costs. Where private production produces adverse externalities, it is net private benefit minus external costs.

neutrality of money The doctrine that the money supply affects only the absolute level of prices and has no effect on relative prices and hence no effect on the allocation of resources or the distribution of income.

nonprice competition Competition by sellers for sales by means other than price cutting. Advertising, product differentiation, trading stamps, and other promotional devices are examples.

nontariff barriers to trade Anything other than a tariff that tends to reduce the flow of international trade.

normal goods Goods for which income elasticity is positive.

normal profits A term used by some economists for the imputed returns to capital and risk taking just necessary to keep the owners in the industry. They are included in what the economist, but not the businessman, sees as *total costs*.

normative statement A statement about what ought to be.

NOW See *negotiable order of withdrawal*.

oligopoly A market structure in which a small number of rival firms dominate the industry. All forms are aware that they are interdependent.

open economy An economy that engages in foreign trade.

open market operations The purchase and sale on the open market by the central bank of securities (usually short-term government securities).

open shop A bargaining arrangement whereby a union represents its members but does not have exclusive jurisdiction. Membership in the union is not a condition of getting or keeping a job.

opportunity cost The cost of using resources for a certain purpose, measured by the benefit or revenues given up by not using them in their best alternative use.

optimal population The population for which per capita national income is largest.

organization theory In economics, a set of hypotheses in which the decisions of an organization are a function of its size and form of organization.

outputs The quantities of goods and services produced.

paradox of value The apparent contradiction in the observed fact that some absolute necessities to life are cheap in price while some relatively unimportant luxuries are very expensive.

Pareto-optimal An allocation of resources in which it is impossible by reallocation to make some consumers better off without simultaneously making others worse off. Also called *Pareto-efficient.*

partial equilibrium analysis Analysis within a particular market or sector neglecting effects on, or effects induced by feedback from, other sectors.

partnership A form of business organization with two or more joint owners, each of whom is personally responsible for all of the firm's actions and debts.

PE ratio (price-earnings ratio) Ratio of the price of a share of stock to the earnings per share of that stock, often written as *price/earnings* or simply P/E.

per capita GNP GNP divided by total population. Also called *GNP per person.*

perfect competition A market form in which all firms are price takers and in which there is freedom of entry into and exit from the industry.

permanent income The maximum amount that a household can consume per year into the indefinite future without reducing its wealth. (A number of similar but not identical definitions are in common use.)

permanent-income hypothesis (PIH) The hypothesis that relates actual consumption to permanent income rather than (as in the original Keynesian theory) to current income.

perpetuity A bond with no provision for repayment of the face value, but which pays interest in perpetuity.

personal income (PI) Income earned by individuals before allowance for personal income taxes paid or payable.

Phillips curve Originally a relation between the percentage of the labor force unemployed and the rate of change of money wages. It can also be expressed as a relation between the percentage of the labor force unemployed and the rate of price inflation, or between actual national income as a proportion of potential national income and the rate of price inflation.

picket lines Striking workers parading at the entrances to a plant or firm on strike. A picket line is a symbolic blockade of the entrance.

point elasticity of demand Elasticity calculated at a point, i.e., over an interval where changes in the variables approach zero. The formula for point elasticity of demand is (with or without a minus sign):

$$\frac{dq}{dp} \times \frac{p}{q}$$

point of diminishing average productivity The level of output at which average product reaches a maximum.

point of diminishing marginal productivity The level of output at which marginal product reaches a maximum.

policy variables The variables that the government ultimately seeks to control; the variables in whose behavior it is ultimately interested.

positive statement A statement about what is, was, or will be, as opposed to a statement about what ought to be.

potential GNP The GNP that could be produced if unemployment were held to 4 percent of the labor force. Also called *full-employment national income.*

poverty gap (or income gap) The number of dollars required to raise everyone whose income is below the poverty level to that level.

poverty level A measure of the minimum amount of annual income required to avoid poverty; approximately $5,500 in the United States for a family of four in 1975.

precautionary balances Money held in case of unexpected needs for money.

preferred stock A form of equity capital, with a preference over common stock to receipt of dividends, up to a stated maximum amount; may be voting or nonvoting.

present value (PV) The value *now* of a sum payable at a later date or of a stream of income receivable at future dates. PV is the discounted value of future payments.

price ceiling A maximum permitted price.

price-consumption line A line connecting the points of tangency between a set of indifference curves and a set of budget lines where one absolute price is fixed and the other varies, money income being held constant.

price discrimination The sale by a single firm of

the same commodity to different buyers at two or more different prices for reasons not associated with differences in cost. It may be systematic or unsystematic.

price-earnings ratio See *PE ratio*.

price floor A minimum permitted price.

price parity The ratio of prices farmers receive for products they sell to the prices they pay for products they buy, compared with some base period; a basic concept in U.S. farm policy.

price-push inflation Inflation caused by increases in prices brought about by the monopoly power of sellers and not associated with excess aggregate demand.

price taker A firm that acts as if it could alter its rate of production and sales without affecting the market price of its product.

principle of substitution The proposition that the proportions in which various inputs are used will vary as the relative prices of these inputs vary.

private cost The value of the best alternative use of resources used in production as valued by the producer.

private sector That portion of an economy in which principal decisions are made by private units such as households and firms.

producers' cooperative (producers' co-op) An organization of producers of a commodity usually formed to serve as a joint selling organization for the producers and often operated as a cartel.

product differentiation The process by which a seller makes its product different from its rivals' products. Brand names and special packaging are examples.

production The act of making commodities.

production function A functional relation showing the maximum output that can be produced by each and every combination of inputs.

production possibility boundary A curve on a graph that shows which alternative combination of commodities can just be obtained if all available productive resources are used. It is the boundary between attainable and unobtainable combinations.

productivity Output produced per unit of input; frequently used to refer to *labor productivity,* measured by output per man-hour.

productivity of capital The increase in production resulting from the use of capital, after allow-

ance for the maintenance and replacement of the capital.

product markets Markets in which firms sell their outputs of goods and services.

profit The difference between the value of output and the value of inputs. See also *economic profits or losses*.

progressivity of taxation The ratio of taxes to income as income increases. If the ratio decreases, the tax is termed *regressive;* if it remains constant, *proportional;* if it increases, *progressive*.

protectionism The partial or complete protection of domestic industries from foreign competition in domestic markets by use of tariffs or other means.

proxy A document authorizing the holder to vote one's stock in a corporation.

proxy fight A struggle between competing factions in a corporation to obtain the proxies for a majority of the outstanding shares.

public sector That portion of an economy in which principal decisions are made by the central authorities.

public utility regulation Regulation of prices and services of industries that have been deemed to be natural monopolies.

pump priming A short-term injection of government funds to eliminate a deflationary gap, on the theory that less than the whole of a deflationary gap needs to be filled by government expenditure. The assumption is that this will create such favorable expectations that private investment expenditure will rise to fill the remainder of the gap.

pure return on capital The amount capital can earn in a riskless investment; hence the transfer earnings of capital in a riskless investment.

quantity demanded The amount of a commodity that households wish to purchase in some time period. An increase (decrease) in quantity demanded refers to a movement down (up) the demand curve in response to a fall (rise) in price.

quantity supplied The amount of a commodity producers wish to sell in some time period. An increase (decrease) in quantity supplied refers to a movement up (down) the supply curve in response to a rise (fall) in price.

quantity theory of money A theory that predicts that the money value of national income (PY)

changes in proportion to changes in the money supply. (The changes will be all in prices, P, if national income, Y, is at its full-employment level, Y_F.)

random sample A sample chosen from a group or population in such a way that every member of the group has an equal chance of being selected.

rate base The total allowable investment to which the rate of return allowed by a regulatory commission is applied. The public utility may build into its prices the amount of profits so determined.

rate of return The ratio of profits earned by a firm to total investment capital.

rate of return on capital (Sometimes used synonymously with *rate of return*.) Frequently used to refer to a specific capital good. The annual net income produced by a capital good, expressed as a percentage of the price of the good.

ratio scale See *logarithmic scale*.

real capital (or **physical capital**) Physical assets, including plant, equipment, and inventories.

real flow The flow of goods and services from sellers to buyers.

real income A household's income expressed in terms of the command over commodities that the money income confers; money income corrected for changes in price levels, thus the purchasing power of money income.

real rate of interest A rate of interest expressed in constant dollars. It is the money rate of interest corrected for the change in the purchasing power of money.

recession In general, a downswing in the level of economic activity. The Department of Commerce defines a recession as occurring when real GNP falls for two successive quarters.

regression analysis (sometimes called *correlation analysis*) A quantitative analysis of the systematic interrelationships between two or more variables.

regression equation The mathematical equation describing the statistically determined equation of best fit between variables in regression analysis.

relative price The ratio of the price of one good to the price of another good; a ratio of two absolute prices.

rent (1) In macroeconomics, the proportion of national income going to the owners of the factor of production, land. (2) In microeconomics, a

shorthand for *economic rent*. (3) In everyday usage, the payment for rental housing.

required reserves In banking, the amount of reserves a bank must, by law, keep either in currency or in deposits with the central bank.

reserve ratio In banking, the fraction of deposits of the public that a bank holds in reserves.

resource allocation The allocation of an economy's scarce resources among alternative uses.

return to capital The total amount available for payments to owners of capital; the sum of pure returns to capital, risk premiums, and economic profits.

revaluation of the exchange rate An increase in the value at which a country's currency is pegged in terms of foreign currencies; the opposite of *devaluation*.

revenue sharing A noncategorical grant-in-aid, in which some of the revenue collected by the federal government is returned to state and local governments for unrestricted expenditure.

right-to-work laws State laws that give an individual the right to work in an organized plant without belonging to the union that is the collective bargaining agent of the workers. They are thus legislative prohibitions against closed or union shops.

rising-cost industry An industry in which the minimum cost attainable by a firm rises as the scale of the industry expands.

rising supply price A rising long-run supply curve, caused by increases in factor prices as output is increased, or by diseconomies of scale.

risk premium The return to capital necessary to compensate owners of capital for the risk of loss of their capital.

satisficing A hypothesized objective of firms, in contrast to maximizing behavior, whereby firms set target levels of satisfactory performance (e.g., profits) rather than seek to maximize some objective (e.g., profits).

saving Household saving is disposable income not spent on domestically produced or imported consumption goods and services. Firm saving is profits not distributed to owners.

scatter diagram A graph of statistical observations of paired values of two variables, one measured on the horizontal and the other on the vertical axis. Each point on the coordinate grid represents the values of the variables for a particular unit of observation.

search unemployment Unemployment caused by people searching for a good job rather than accepting the first job they come across no matter how poor it may be.

securities market See *stock market.*

selective credit controls Selective controls on credit imposed through such means as margin requirements, installment buying, and minimum down payments on mortgages.

services Intangible commodities, such as haircuts or medical care.

shop steward The representative of a local union in the shop or plant.

short run The period of time over which the quantity of some inputs cannot, as a practical matter, be varied.

short-run average cost See *average total cost.*

short-run equilibrium Generally, equilibrium subject to fixed factors; for a competitive firm, the output at which market price equals marginal cost; for a competitive industry, the price and output at which industry demand equals short-run industry supply and all firms are in short-run equilibrium. Either profits or losses are possible.

short-run supply curve The curve showing the relation of quantity supplied to prices, with one or more fixed factors; the horizontal sum of marginal cost curves (above the level of average variable costs) of all firms in an industry.

single proprietorship A firm consisting of one owner, where the single owner is solely responsible for the firm's actions and debts.

single-tax movement The movement headed by Henry George that advocated using only a tax on land values for financing government expenditures. It was designed to tap the "unearned increment" received by landholders.

size distribution of income The distribution of income by size class, without regard to source of income.

snake The agreement among several Western European countries to fix exchange rates among their own currencies and then to let them fluctuate in common against the U.S. dollar. Also called the *joint float.*

social cost (social opportunity cost) The value of the best alternative use of resources available to society, as valued by society.

special drawing rights (SDRs) Established in 1968, the Special Drawing Account of the International Monetary Fund provides additional international reserves for member countries. Subject to certain repayment provisions, members are able to treat SDRs in the same way as their own holdings of international currencies for financing balance-of-payments surpluses or deficits.

specialization of labor An organization of production in which individual workers specialize in the production of particular goods or services (and satisfy their wants by trading) rather than produce for themselves everything they consume (and thus be self-sufficient).

specific tax See *excise tax.*

speculative balances Wealth held in the form of money instead of interest-earning assets because of expectations that the prices of these assets may fall.

stabilization policy Any policy designed to produce full employment and a relatively stable price level. Attempts by the central authorities to remove inflationary and deflationary gaps when they appear.

stagflation The coexistence of high rates of unemployment with high, and sometimes rising, rates of inflation.

stockholders The owners of a corporation.

stock market (securities market) An organized market where stocks and bonds are bought and sold.

strike The concerted refusal of the members of a union to work.

strikebreakers Nonunion workers brought in by management to operate the plant while a union is on strike. (Derisively called "scabs" by union members.)

structural rigidity inflation The theory that downward inflexibility of money prices means that the adjustment of *relative* prices necessary in any changing economy will cause a rise in the average level of prices (i.e., an inflation).

structural unemployment Unemployment due to a mismatching between characteristics required by available jobs and characteristics possessed by the unemployed labor. (The sum of frictional plus structural unemployment may be measured by the number of unemployed when the total number of jobs available is equal to the total number of persons looking for acceptable jobs.)

substitute A commodity that satisfies similar needs or desires as the original commodity; technically, a substitute for a commodity is another commodity for which the cross elasticity of demand is nonnegligible and positive.

substitution effect The change in quantity of a good demanded resulting from a change in its relative price, eliminating the effect on real income of the change in price.

supply There are several distinct but closely related concepts: (1) *quantity supplied;* (2) the whole relationship of the quantity supplied to variables that determine it, such as producers' goals, technology, price of the commodity, prices of other commodities, and prices of factors of production; (3) the *supply schedule;* (4) the *supply curve.* The phrase increase (decrease) in supply means a shift of the supply curve to the right (left) indicating an increase (decrease) in the quantity supplied at each possible price.

supply curve The graphic representation of the *supply schedule.*

supply of effort (or **total supply of labor**) The total number of hours of work that the population is willing to supply.

supply of money See *money supply.*

supply schedule The relationship between the quantity supplied of a commodity and its price, *ceteris paribus.*

tacit collusion See also *collusion.* The adoption, without explicit agreement, of a common policy by sellers in an industry. Also called *conscious parallel action.*

takeover bid See *tender offer.*

tariff A tax applied on imports.

tax incidence The location of the ultimate burden of a tax; the identity of the ultimate bearer or bearers of the tax.

technological efficiency (sometimes called *technical efficiency*) A method of production is technologically efficient if the same output cannot be produced with fewer real resources.

tender offer (takeover bid) An offer to buy directly some or all of the outstanding common stock of a corporation from its stockholders at a specified price per share, in an attempt to gain control of the corporation.

terms of trade The relation between the average price of a country's exports and the average price of its imports.

third-party effects See *externalities.*

time deposit An interest-earning bank deposit, legally subject to notice before withdrawal (in practice the notice requirement is not normally enforced) and not transferable by check.

time-series data Data on variables where measurements are made for successive periods (or moments) of time. Contrasted with cross-sectional data.

time-series graph (sometimes simply *time series*) A graph of time-series data.

total cost Fixed costs plus variable costs at a given level of output; the sum of the opportunity costs of the factors used to produce that output.

total product The total amount produced during some period of time by all the factors of production employed over that time period.

total revenue (TR) The total receipts from the sale of a product; price times quantity.

total utility The total satisfaction resulting from the consumption of a given commodity by a buyer in a period of time.

trade union See *union.*

transactions balances Money held for day-to-day needs because the receipts and payments of firms and households are not perfectly synchronized.

transfer earnings That part of the payment to a factor in its present use that is just enough to keep it from transferring to another use.

transfer payment A payment to a private person or institution that does not arise out of current productive activity; typically made by governments, as in welfare payments, but also made by businesses and private individuals in the form of charitable contributions.

treasury bill The characteristic form of short-term government debt. A bill is a promise to pay a certain sum of money at some time in the early future (often one, three, or six months). It carries no interest payment; the lender earns interest because the price at which he or she buys the bill is less than its future redemption value.

turnover tax An excise tax levied on commodities and commonly used in socialist countries.

unbalanced growth policy Growth in only a few sectors of the economy with remaining needs met by international trade.

underemployment equilibrium An equilibrium of national income (withdrawals equal injections) where actual income is less than potential income, and as a consequence actual employment is less than full employment.

undistributed profits Earnings of a firm not distributed as dividends but retained by the firm.

union An association of workers authorized to represent them in bargaining with employers. Also called *trade union* or *labor union*.

union shop A bargaining arrangement in which the employer may hire anyone he chooses, but every employee must join the union within a specified period of time (often 60 days).

upper turning point The point at which a recession begins.

value added The value of a firm's output *minus* the value of the inputs that it purchases from other firms.

variable A magnitude (such as the price of wheat) that can take on a specific value but whose value will vary among times and places.

variable costs Costs whose total varies directly with changes in output. Also called *direct costs*.

variable factors Factors whose quantity used in production can be varied in the short run.

velocity of circulation National income divided by the quantity of money. Sometimes called the *income velocity of circulation*.

vertical merger See *merger*.

very long run The period in which even the technological possibilities open to a firm are subject to change.

visibles All those items of foreign trade that are tangible; goods as opposed to services.

wage-price policies The attempt by the government to influence wage- and price-setting—by methods ranging from guidelines to direct fixing of wages and prices by a governmental body—in an effort to control inflation.

wages and salaries Payments made for the use of labor services. Also called *wages*.

withdrawals Income earned by households and not passed on to firms in return for goods and services purchased, and income earned by firms and not passed on to households in return for factor services purchased.

X-inefficiency When resources are used less productively than is possible so that society is at a point *inside* its production possibility boundary.

Index

Absolute advantage, reciprocal, 686–688
Absolute cost advantages, oligopoly, 262
Absolute merit of government expenditures, 451
Absolute price, 121
Accelerator, 540
    interaction with multiplier, 544–545
    limitations of, 541–543
    numerical example, 540–541
Accelerator theory of investment, 540–543
Accord, treasury-Federal Reserve, 655, 657
Account, money as unit of, 600
Accountant
    balance sheet, 881–882
    income statement, 881, 883
Adjustable peg system, 714
    problems of, 715–718
Adjustments, miscellaneous, as income components, 470
Ad valorem tariff, 695, 699
Ad valorem tax, 436n.
Advertising
    as barrier to entry in oligopoly, 264–265
    corporate, 308
    role in economic analysis, 268
    trade-off with price, quality, and variety, consumer products, 267
Affluent Society, The (Galbraith), 451
AFL-CIO, 349
Agency for International Development, 822
Aggregate demand. See also Demand
    and demand for money, 637
    and employment, factors affecting, 568
    and equilibrium income, 514
    and 45° line at equilibrium, 498
    and government expenditure, 552–553
    and interest rates, 645–646
    and national income, 494
Aggregate demand function
    in Frugal economy, 492–493
    and taxes, 532
Aggregate desired expenditure and total output in Frugal vs. Governed economy, 505

Aggregate expenditure function, 493
Aggregate household behavior, 109
Agricultural development vs. industrialization, 824–825
Agricultural support policies, as built-in stabilizers, 563
Agriculture
    beneficiaries of success, 106
    competitive behavior and market structure, 234
    corporate farming, 102–103
    decollectivization, Yugoslavia, 847–848
    demand curve for products, 146
    farm policy since 1929, 100–101
    prices and incomes, 91–95
    problems of, 89
    production and prices, 68
    prospects for end of problem, 101–103
    stabilization and support plans, 97–100
    surpluses, 96
Agriculture Department, on crop production and prices, 68
AID. See Agency for International Development
Aid to families with dependent children (AFDC), 395
Airlines
    deregulation of fares, 304–305
    fares, as price discrimination, 249
Air pollution, 202
    alert, Pittsburgh, 207
Air quality-control standard, and low-sulfur vs. high-sulfur coal, principle of substitution, 191
Airplanes, spur for, 207
Alchian, Armen, 304
Alchian-Kessel hypothesis, 304
Alcohol
    drinking and heart attack, 129
    "nearly perfect" tax on, 455
Algeria, industrial growth plan, 828
All Brick Construction Co., and merger, 304
Allied Chemical Corp., 202, 205
    on profit, 320
Allis-Chalmers Corp., 280
Allocation
    of commodity in short supply, 84–85
    of factors, 333–335

Allocative efficiency, 286–287
Allocative inefficiency, 816
  vs. *X* - inefficiency, 816
Aluminum Company of America
    (ALCOA), 251, 311
  price discrimination, 246–247
Aluminum Company of America
    case, 295
American Automobile Association
    and Audubon Society suit to halt
    highway construction in
    Wisconsin, 207–208
  on rising insurance costs, 37
American Express credit card, as
    money, 611
American Federation of Labor (AFL),
    348
  beginnings, 353–354
American Motors Corp., and
    hypothesis that firms control the
    market, 320
American Stock Exchange, 380
American Telephone and Telegraph
    Co. (AT&T)
  antidiscrimination suit settlement,
    360
  shareholders, 312
  share of stock as money, 611
American Tobacco Co. case, 294
Amortization of loan, 538
Anchovy harvest and grain prices, 235
Ando, Albert, 885
Anheuser Busch, labor productivity,
    268
Annuity vs. perpetuity, 388
Antitrust, and profit as measure of
    monopoly power, 304
Antitrust laws, 291
Antitrust policy
  economics and law, 297–298
  and monopoly, 290–291
  nature of, 291–292
  sources of, 292–296
  success of, 297
Antonelli, Giovanni, 119n.
Appreciation of exchange rate, 680
A priori, 20
Arable land, 332
Arbitrage, 670
  and exchange rates, 671
Arbitrary decisions, 472–473
Arc elasticity of demand, 865–867
Armco Steel Co., 205, 425

Arnold, Thurman, 296
Artichoke wars, France, 282
Ash Commission, 302
Assembly line, spur for, 207
Assets and liabilities, commercial
    banks, 615–616
Asset value, 371–372
  and interest rate, 383
Assumptions, 23
Aswan Dam
  and investments in capital, 388
  private and social costs and
    externalities, 207
Athletes, professional, Jews vs. blacks
    among, 366
Atlas Co., investment opportunities,
    risk, and interest rates, 388
Atomistic competition, 257
Atom smashing, spur for, 207
Attitude survey, and utility, 118
Audubon Society, suit against
    Wisconsin and federal
    government to halt highway
    construction, 207–208
Austria, new gold coin, 611
Automation in printing industry,
    progress and problems, 208
Automobile(s)
  demand for vintage Edsels, 69
  gas-guzzling, and OPEC's reduced
    production of oil, 68
  market behavior and market
    structure, 234
  private vs. social costs of driving at
    55 mph, 207
  size, and hypothesis that firms
    control the market, 320
  vs. truck, depreciation method, 163
Automobile industry
  concentration patterns in, 252–253
  and consumer needs, 320
  effects of prohibitive tariffs on, 708
  in Israel, 191
  model changes, 268
  and perfect competition, 214
  Switzerland, automated techniques
    for, 191
  tire prices to, 321
Automobile insurance, AAA on cause
    of rise in costs, 37
Automobile retailing, as
    monopolistically competitive
    industry, 268

Automobile tires
  prices to car manufacturers, 321
  whitewall vs. blackwall, and
    market structure, 267
Average cost, 172
Average cost curve, 174
  long-run and short-run, 180–185
Average fixed costs, 172
Average income and quantity
    demanded, 57
Average product, 168
Average product curve, 169
  vs. marginal product curve, 171
Average propensity to consume, 488,
    489
  short run vs. long run, 505
  value of, 505
Average propensity to save, 491
Average revenue, 217
  and average variable cost, 212
  and elasticity of demand, 238
  and marginal revenue, 237
Average revenue curve for
    monopolist, 238
Average tax rate, 432
Average total cost, 172
  factors affecting, 176
Average variable costs, 172
  and average revenue, 212
Averch, Harvey, 301

Baby boom, microeconomic and
    macroeconomic effects, 49
Bain, Joe S., 243
Baker, Russell, on building Holiday
    Inn on Nantucket Island, 16
Balanced budget, 552
  vs. budget balance, 556n
  and national income, 559
Balanced budget multiplier, 556–557
  and crowding-out effect, 568
  size of, 558
Balanced growth, 804
Balanced growth policy, 823
Balance of actual payments, 670–
    676
Balance of desired payments, 676
Balance of payments, 675
  balance, and fixed exchange rates,
    683
  and foreign exchange market
    transactions, 683
Balance-of-payments account, 670

Balance-of-payments deficit, 674–676
  changing views of, 727
  and exchange rate, 681
Balance-of-payments surplus, 674
Balance of trade, 673
Balance sheet
  accountant's 881–882
  banks, as result of international trade, 670
  commercial banks, 616
  defined, 880
  economist, 883–884
  Federal Reserve Banks, 626
  monopoly bank, after credit expansion and cash drain, 624
  monopoly bank, and deposit money, 619–620
  multibank system, and deposit money, 620–621
  and open market purchases, 631, 632
  and reserve ratio, loaned-up banking system, 630
Ball Point Pen Co., 277
Baltic, pollution crisis, 207
Bangladesh
  pedicabs and wages in Dacca, 191
  vs. U.S., poverty in, 407
Bank(s). *See also* Central bank(s); Commercial bank(s); Federal Reserve System
  administration of interest rates, 374
  competition for deposits, 616–617
  in creating money, 608
  deposit money, 606–609
BankAmericard, 615
Bank credit cards, 615
Bank notes, 602–603
Bank of America, 613
Bank of Canada, 625
Bank of England, 625
Bank of Greece, 625
Bank of Zackville, and merger, 304
Barbers, inducements to long-haired youths, 282
Bargaining arrangements, unions, 349–350
Barriers to entry
  in monopoly, 241
  in oligopoly, 262–265
Barron's, and role of gold in international payments, 726–727

Barter, 39, 598, 599
Base year, 475
Baumol, William, 317
Beer industry, cost, efficiency, and concentration, 268
Beggar-my-neighbor policies, 712
Behavioral rules, profit-maximizing firms, 212–213
Berle, A. A., 313
Bethlehem Steel Corp., on taxes and capital formation, 549
Beveridge, Lord William, 783
Biased sample, 31
Bilateral trade agreements, 706
Bishop, R. L., 253
Blacklist, 350
Black market
  and price controls, 85–88
  Soviet, 837
Black market pricing and price ceiling, 84
Blacks
  discrimination in labor markets, 360–361
  poverty, 393–394
  vs. Jews, as professional athletes, 366
Blood banks, profit-making, 282
Blumenthal, Secretary of Treasury, on tax-rebate proposal, 568
Board of Governors, Fed, 628
Bond(s)
  as investment funds source, 379–380
  industrial, and interest rates, 388
  prices, and interest rates, 643, 644
  riskless, 382–383
  risky, 383
  speculative profits and money supply, 650
Bondholders, as investment funds source, 379–380
Boondoggle, 570
Borlaug, Norman, 825
Boycott
  and market price, 269–272
  coffee, 282
  grapes, 235
Brady, Robert, 307n.
Brand proliferation, as barrier to entry in oligopoly, 263–264
Brazil, effects of restricted coffee trade, 694

Bread-and-butter unionism, 351–352
Brennan's Restaurant, bidding at wine auction, 146
Bretton Woods system, 713–714
  collapse of, 718–721
  and role of gold in international payments, 726–727
Brezhnev, Leonid, 840
British Railways, 247
British Tennis Championships, prizes, and marginal productivity theory of distribution, 343
Brokerage commissions, SEC proposal on, 81
Brown, E. Cary, 570
Brumberg, Professor, 885
Buchanan, James, 451
Budgetary policy, contractionary, 572–573
Budget, balanced, and employment, 586–587
Budget balance
  actual vs. full-employment, 573
  vs. balanced budget, 556n.
Budget deficit, 513, 552
  size of, 554–555
Budget line
  and household choice, 119–122
  and indifference curve, 126
Budget surplus, 513, 552
  size of, 554–555
Building, cycle in, 546–547
Built-in stabilizers, 561–564
  examples, 568
  vs. fiscal drag, 587
Bundle of goods, 120, 123
Burger Court, 295
Burnham, James, 307n.
Burns, Arthur, 628
  on Carter's tax rebate proposal, 568
  and interest rates, 665–666
Business
  activity since 1870, 528–529
  conditions and interest rates, 374–375
  and predictability of human behavior, 28
  prediction of increased control of economy, 320
  profit as responsibility of, 320
  smallness vs. efficiency, 176
  starting up, 163

Business cycles
  causes, 526–527
  consensus on, 547
  and consumption function, 532
  elements of theory of, 543–547
  and GNP vs. pairs of series, 549
  and government policy to offset
    depression, 760
  historical record, 525–526
  monetarist views of, 744
  and money supply, 654
  neo-Keynesian view of, 744–747
  prices and incomes, agriculture,
    91–95
  stylized, 542
  terminology of, 543–544
  variety in, 546–547
Business fluctuations. *See* Business
  cycles
Business investment, "causes," 549
Business Statistics, 207
Butter vs. margarine
  demand for, 145
  elasticity of demand for, 81

California State Marketing Board,
  restriction of chicken and egg
  production, 282
Canada
  circulation of U.S. and Canadian
    coins, and Gresham's law, 611
  effect on dollar supply and demand
    of investors' purchase of shares
    on New York Stock Exchange,
    683
  exchange rates, vs. U.S., 684
  national tradition and tariff, 697
  railroad weekday vs. weekend
    rates, and price discrimination,
    249
  and U.S., GNP if countries were
    joined, 480
Canadian Olympic coins, demand for
  flawed pieces, 68–69
Cancer warnings and demand for
  cigarettes, 49
Capacity
  defined, 174–175
  vs. utilization, 789–790
Capital, 462. *See also* Factor(s) of
  production; Human capital;
  Investment; Investment funds;
  Money

acquisition, and economic
  development, 821–823
additional, firm's demand for,
  372–373
contributed, and economic
  development, 822–823
exit, and losses in competitive
  industry, 222
as factor of production, 155
factors affecting pure rate of return
  on, 388
interest and return on, 372–377
marginal efficiency of, 368–370
mobility of, 334
productivity of, 367–372
return on, 368–371
total supply of, 333
Capital account, 672, 674
Capital consumption allowance, 463,
  470
Capital deepening, 370, 543
Capital goods
  durability, and interest rates, 388
  investment in, 463
Capitalism, Socialism and Democracy
  (Schumpeter), 290
Capitalized value, 372
Capital movements and equilibrium
  exchange rates, 680
Capital-output ratio, 540, 798
Capital punishment, evaluating
  deterrent effects, 37
Capital stock, 368–369, 463
  and interest rates, 373, 539
  and rate of return on capital,
    808
Capital widening, 370, 542–543
Carey, Hugh, on New York urban
  crisis, 456
Carson, Rachel, 204
Cartel, 273
Carter, Jimmy, 575
Cash drain, commercial banks,
  624–625
Cash flow vs. income flow, 881n.
  and cost of improving postal
    service, 16
  and presidential economics, 568
  tax rebate proposal, 568
  on unemployment and industrial
    capacity, 16, 524
Cash, supply, and household
  spending, 666

Cashless society, and demand for
  money, 650
Categorical assistance in war on
  poverty, 395–396
Categorical grants-in-aid, 443
Caterpillar Tractor Co., 206
Celler-Kefauver Act (1950), 294
Central bank(s). *See also* Federal
  Reserve System; Monetary
  policy
  as banker to commercial banks,
    625–626
  as banker to government, 626–627
  discount rate changes, 630, 663
  and exchange rates, 722–723
  government borrowing, 552
  limits on issue of currency by,
    606–607
  and money supply, 627–633
  open-market operations, 630–633
  as regulator of money markets, 628
  as regulator of money supply,
    627–628
Certificates of deposit, 616
Ceteris paribus, 55n., 56
Chamber of Commerce of
  Southeastern Connecticut, and
  effects of shipyard strike, 524
Chateau Lafite-Rothschild, auction
  price, and demand curve for
  luxuries, 146
Chavez, Cesar, 350
Check clearing and collection, 614
Checkless society, 599
Chevron Oil Co., 426
Chicken and egg production,
  restrictions on, 282
China
  getting and giving contributed
    capital, 822
  population control, 820
  population and food supply,
    828–829
  specialization, 823
Choice of resources, 6–9
Chrysler Corp., 417
  and hypothesis that firms control
    the market, 320
Chung, William K., 805
Churchill, Winston, 170
Cigarette(s)
  consumer demand and cancer
    warnings, 49

and oligopoly theory, 279
private vs. social costs of smoking, 207
and WWII hyperinflation, 611
Cigarette industry
market structure, and smoking, 283
as monopolistically competitive, 268
Cincinnati Telephone Co., charge for directory-assistance calls, and drop in number of calls, 81
Circular flow of income
equilibrium, 503
in Frugal economy, 495
in general case, 502
injections into, 500
from microeconomics to macroeconomics, 44–46
as not completely closed system, 46–48
in Spendthrift economy, 460
withdrawals, 500–501; and injections, 47
Cities. *See* Urban crisis
large vs. small, number of specialists in, 49
property tax on rental property, 455
Civil Aeronautics Board and deregulation of airfares, 305
Clark, John Bates, 405
Clayton Antitrust Act (1914), 292–294, 295
and wage fixing vs. price fixing, 366
Clean Air Act (1970), 427
Clearing house, 614
Climax Molybdenum Co., 251
Closed economy, vs. open, 466
Closed shop, 350
Coal
and air quality-control standard, 191
monopoly in, 249
Coal industry, ease of exit and entry, and market behavior, 234
Coase, Ronald H., 423
Coase theorem, 423
Coefficient of determination, 33
Coffee
Brazil's restrictions, and gains from trade, 694
consumer boycott, 282

prices, and economy of underdeveloped countries, 829
Coinage. *See also* Money
debasing of, 601
and Gresham's Law, 605
Collective bargaining, 350–351
Collective consumption goods, 418
Collusion, 242
tacit, 243
Columbia Records, 139
Command economy, 42
in WWII, 851
Command system and decision process, 832–833
Commercial bank(s), 613–614. *See also* Central bank(s); Federal Reserve System; Money
cash drain, 624–625
central bank as banker to, 625–626
creation and destruction of deposit money by, 618–625
excess reserves, 624
interbank activities, 614–615
and money supply, 750
as profit-seekers, 615–617
reserves, 617–618
Committee of Twenty, 722
Committee on Constructive Consumerism, 305
Committee to Stamp Out Poverty in Wisconsin, and Audubon Society suit to halt highway construction, 208
Commodities suppliers, market behavior and market structure, 234
Commodity, 6
complement, 55
definition, and elasticity, 76
vs. factors, demand for, 326–327
in short supply, allocation of, 84–85
Commodity price and quantity demanded, 55
Common Market, 707. *See also* European Economic Community
Common-property resource, 203
Common stock, 379
prices, 383–385
Communist economy, sources of capital in, 851

Communist Party Congress, Kosygin report on U.S. vs. Soviet unemployment and inflation, 851
Company. *See* Business cycles; Competition; Firm
Comparative advantage
and development patterns, 823–824
and export of very high wage sector, 694
and gains from specialization, 687–688
and gains from trade, 688–689
and Uruguay's beef exports, 694
Comparative statics, 66
Compassion
and market failure, 420
vs. political motivation for contributed capital, 823
Competition. *See also* Monopolistic competition; Perfect competition
and economic discrimination, 363–365
innovation under, 289–290
laws promoting, 292–294
vs. monopoly, 282–290
movie theater prices, 249
noneconomic appeal of, 287–288
nonprice, 254, 261–264
Competitive behavior,
firm, 210
sectors of economy, 234
Competitive devaluations, 713
Competitive equilibrium, long-run, 231–233
Competitive firm, short-run vs. long-run equilibrium, 226
Competitive industry
incidence of excise tax in, 436–439
monopolization of, 285
Competitive labor market, union in, 345–346
Competitive market
exchange rate on, 678
factor price in, 335–341
Competitiveness of market structure, 210
Complement, commodity, 55
Complementarity and substitutability, 141
Concentration patterns in manufacturing, 252–253

Concentration ratios, 243
Conglomerate merger, 295
Congo, Goodyear builds plant in, 828
Congress
  consumption function, and fiscal
    policy, 756–757
  effect of restriction on cash supply,
    666
  effect of voting universal dividend
    financed from new money, 650
  Joint Economic Report, 106
  and presidential authorization to
    negotiate with foreign countries
    on tariff, 709
Congress of Industrial Organizations
  (CIO), 348
Conscious parallel action, 243
Conservative view on appropriate
  size of government, 452–453
Conspicuous consumption goods,
  138
Constant-cost industry, 226
Constant dollars, 475
  percentage increase of GNP,
    disposable income, and
    disposable income per capita in,
    481
Constant returns and long-run
  average cost curve, 182
Consumables, price index, 593
Consumer, Russian vs. American,
  concern about quality, 851
Consumer boycott
  coffee, 282
  grapes, 235
Consumer goods, durability, and
  interest rates, 388
Consumerism and New Industrial
  State, 310–311
Consumer needs, and automobile
  companies, 320
Consumer Price Index, 869–871
  monthly, 873
Consumer prices, Soviet, 842
Consumer products, trade-off of
  price, quality, variety, and
  advertising, 267
Consumers' surplus and price
  discrimination, 244
Consumption, 6
  actual, 885–886
  and disposable income, 529–532,
    859

personal, 466
and production, 199
shifts in, 527–529
and zero growth rate, 808
Consumption expenditures, 885–886
  and disposable income, 549
  time series, 859
Consumption function
  and business fluctuations, 532
  Congress, fiscal policy, and,
    756–757
  in Frugal economy, 488–491
  shape of, 505
Consumption-saving decisions in
  Frugal economy, 487–488
Consumption schedule, Frugal
  economy, 492
Continental Pen Co., 278
Contour map, 863
Contractionary monetary policy,
  652–653
Contributed capital and economic
  development, 822–823
Control
  of corporation, 311–312
  of credit, 662–664
  of currency, 627
  of government, 310
  of inflation, 739–740
  of interest rates, 373–374
  in managing fixed exchange rates,
    681
  of market, hypothesis of, 306–311
  mortgage, 663
  of national income, 652–653
  of pollution, 424–427
  of population, 820
  of unemployment, 735
  wage-price, 776–778
Coordinate graph, 858
Copper wire, monopoly in, 249
Corn laws, 685
Corporation. *See also* Business cycles;
    Competition; Firm; Industry
  advantages and disadvantages,
    150–151
  control of, 311–312
  defined, 149
  and departing from profit-
    maximizing behavior, 318
  farming, 102–103
  hypothesis of intercorporate
    control groups, 314

hypothesis of minority control,
  312–313
hypothesis of separation of ownership
  from control, 313–314
investment funds in financing, 379
profits, 470
rise of, 151–152
Corporation income tax
  incidence of, 439–440
  progressivity of, 433–434
Correspondent banks, 614
Corruption of value system in New
  Industrial State, 307
Cost(s). *See also* Opportunity cost
  of administering credit and interest
    rates, 377
  of buying house on time, 538
  with capital fixed and labor
    variable, 173
  concepts defined, 171–173
  decreasing, and long-run average
    cost curve, 180–182
  defined, 155
  definition, in natural monopoly
    regulation, 300
  and ease of exit and entry, coal
    industry, 234
  effect on price and quantity
    produced, 283–285
  factor prices, factor proportions,
    and, 189
  factors of production, and quantity
    supplied, 61
  of government activity,
    distribution of, 578–580
  of growth, 793–796; vs. benefits,
    796–797
  of land vs. high-rise construction,
    and principle of substitution,
    191
  and market structure, 288–289
  meaning and measurement of,
    155–156
  of money, 157
  private and social, 200; in allocative
    efficiency, 287; divergence
    between, 205–206
  and profit to firm, 155–162
  purpose in assigning, 156
  short-run variations in, 171–175
  short-run vs. long-run, 182–183
  and source of Soviet achievements,
    846

unproductive, and government regulation, 429
Cost advantage, absolute, oligopoly, 262
Cost curves
  and factor prices, 184
  shifts in, 183–184
Cost minimization, 177
  conditions for, 178–180
  and isoquants, 187–189
Cost-push inflation, 737
  and stagflation, 780
  and unemployment, 775–776
  and wage-price controls, 778
Cotton gin, spur for, 207
Council of Economic Advisers, 14, 483, 556, 561, 563
  chairman's proposal for government austerity program, 524
  and 1960s fiscal policy, 571–573
  and 1970s fiscal policy, 574–575
Council on Wage and Price Stability, and profit-making blood banks, 282
Cournot, A. A., 259
Craft union, 348
Crawford, Broderick, pay for commercial, and marginal productivity theory of distribution, 343
Creative destruction, process of, 290
Credit
  administrative costs, and interest rates, 377
  selective controls, 662–664
  terms, and demand for durable goods, 531
Credit cards
  American Express card as money, 611
  bank, 615
  Master Charge and sale of mink coats, 69
Credit crunch, 657
Credit rationing, 374
Criminal activity, competitive behavior and market structure, 234
Critical minimum effort, 813
Cross-classification table, 32–33
Cross elasticity of demand, 77–78, 130, 134

Cross-sectional data, 858
Crowding-out effect, 553
  and balanced budget multiplier, 568
  and fiscal policy, 752, 754
  and monetarists vs. neo-Keynesians, 761
  and opportunity cost of government expenditures, 578
Culpeper switch, 666
Cumulative movements and turning points, business fluctuations, 544–546
Currency
  elastic, Fed and creation of, 665
  limit on issue by central bank, 606–607
Currency control, 627
Current account, 672–674
Current dollars, percentage increase of GNP in, 481
Current Population Survey, 734
Curtailment of service in natural monopoly regulation, 301–302
Curves, movements along vs. shifts of, 506–508
Cut-off rates of return, 157
Cyclical fluctuations. *See* Business cycles

Dacca, Bangladesh, pedicabs and wages, 191
Dam
  Aswan, 207, 388
  opportunity cost of stopping, to preserve fish, 163
Data, analysis of, 32–34
DDT, externalities, 204
Death rate and income, poor countries, 810–811
Debasing of coinage, 601
Debt, 379. *See also* National debt
Debt policy, various organizations, 587
Decision errors, 35–36
Decision lag, 559–560
Decision makers, in market economy, 40–41
Decision making
  household, and demand theory, 136–137
  time horizons for, 166–167
Decision process and economic system, 832–834

Decision rules, 36
Declining industries, economics of, 228–229
Declining long-run supply curve, 230
Decollectivization of agriculture, Yugoslavia, 847–848
Decreasing costs and long-run average cost curve, 180–182
Decreasing returns, long-run, 182
Deduction and measurement, 26
Defense spending, effect of cuts in, 576–577
Deferred payments, money as standard of, 600
Deficient-demand unemployment, 733
Deficit
  balance of payments, 674–676, 681
  budget, 513, 552, 554–555
  and government sector, 564–565
Deficit financing, 552
  Great Depression, 570
Deflation. *See* Inflation
Deflationary gaps,
  and inflationary gaps, 519–523, 553–561
  and tax rebate, 568
Demand. *See also* Aggregate demand; Demand curve; Demand elasticity; Demand for money; Demand-pull inflation; Demand theory
  for additional capital by firm, 372–373
  arc elasticity, 865–867
  for butter vs. margarine, 145
  change in, 42–44
  for cigarettes, and cancer warnings, 49
  cross elasticities of, 77–78, 131, 133
  for durable goods, 531
  firm manipulation of, 306
  and gasoline prices, 81
  for grain, and price, 235
  and grape boycott, 235
  and identification problem, 134–135
  income elasticities of, 76, 95, 132–133
  measures of, 131–136

Demand *(Continued)*
for owner-occupied housing, and price of rental housing, 146; and mortgage interest rates, 146
perfectly competitive industry's long-run response to change in, 225–227
point elasticity, 868
price elasticities of, 131–132
and price of color TV, 69
and quantity demanded, 53–56; changes in, 58–59; effect of various factors on, 69
Demand and supply
determination of price by, 63–65
of labor, market fluctuations in, 399–400
Demand and supply schedules, 65
Demand curve, 56–57. *See also* Demand
vs. aggregate demand function, 493n.
for agricultural products, 146
and constant elasticity, 75
derivation of, 875–876
for dollars, 677–678
effect of shape of, 71
elasticity, 866–867
for factor, 326–327, 328
horizontal vs. vertical sum of, 129
household, 108–109, 115
kinked, 265–266
for luxuries, and price of wine, 146
for monopolist, 238
for perfectly competitive firm, 216
perfectly inelastic, 138–139
shifts in, 57–59
slope of, 876–879
straight-line, elasticity along, 74
for tape recorders, 69
Demand deposits, 608
and required-reserve ratio, 634
reserve requirement changes, 660
Demand elasticity, 70–72, 677. *See also* Demand
and average revenue, 238
calculation of, 73
determinants of, 76
examples, 81
for factor, 327
firm vs. market, 215
interpreting numerical values of, 73–74
necessities vs. luxuries, 116–117

price elasticity, 72–76
total revenue, marginal revenue, and, 237–239
and utility, 116–117
Demand for money, 636. *See also* Demand; Money
and aggregate demand, 637
and cashless society, 650
and interest rates, 373, 643–644
precautionary motive, 641–642
and quantity theory, 637
speculative motive, 642–643
transactions motive, 641
Demand-pull inflation, 736–737
and L-shaped relation, 763–765
and Phillips curve, 765–767
and stagflation, 780
and unemployment, 763–767
and wage-price controls, 776–777
Demand schedule, 56–57, 58
Demand theory, 52–53. *See also* Demand
and affordable housing, 142–143
and household decision making, 136–137
poverty, obesity, and 146
as way of saying anything can happen, 137–144
Demonstration effect, and development, 811–812
Denison, E. F., 804, 805
Deposit(s)
bank competition for, 616–617
in monopoly bank, 619–621
in multibank system, 621–622
multiple, in multibank system, 622–624
Deposit money, 606–609
creation and destruction by commercial banks, 618–625
Depreciation, 463
automobile vs. truck, 163
of exchange rate, 681
imputed cost, 159–160
and profits, 164
Depression,
in business fluctuation, 543
government policy to offset, 760
and short-run decisions, 176
Derived demand, 326
and factors of production, 343
Determination, coefficient of, 33

Devaluations
competitive, 713
of dollar, 719–720
of exchange rate, 681
Development
agricultural, vs. industrialization, 824–825
and competitive advantage, 823–824
and import substitution, 825–826
incentives for, 811–812
patterns of, 809–811
Development gap, 810
Diet, marginal vs. total utility of, 129
Differentials, dynamic vs. equilibrium, in factor prices, 343
Diminishing average productivity, point of, 168
Diminishing marginal productivity, point of, 169
Diminishing marginal rate of substitution, hypothesis of, 124–125
Diminishing marginal utility, hypothesis of, 110–111
Diminishing returns
hypothesis of, and depth of drilling for oil in Texas, 176
law of, 170
short run, vs. long-run decreasing returns, 182n.
Dirty float, 722
Discount from list price, as price discrimination, 249
Discount rate, 626, 661–662
changes in, 630, 663
Discretionary fiscal policy, 564–567
Discretionary monetary policy, Friedman on, 761
Discrimination
economic, 362–365
model of effect of, 362–363
and wages, 360–365
Disembodied technical change, 801
Disequilibrium
in foreign exchange market, 676
and net investment, 540
Disposable income, 474. *See also* Income; National income
and consumption, 529–532, 859
and consumption expenditures, factors affecting, 549
Disposable income per capita, in constant dollars, 476

Dissaving, 490
Distribution
  of goods and household incentives, Soviet Union, 839–840
  marginal productivity theory of, 328
  problems of, 322–325
Distribution theory, 325–326
  examples, 366
  and functional distribution of income, 405–406
  and just distribution of income, 404
  misconceptions about, 404–405
  and pay in government vs. universities, 343
  predictions of, 407
  relevance of, 398–403
  restated, 403–404
Dive for Cross, Epiphany ceremony in Greek harbor halted by pollution, 207
Dividends, 150, 462
Division of labor
  and hypothesis of diminishing returns, 171
  in market economy, 39
Doctors, supply and earnings, 357
Dollar(s). *See also* Exchange rates; Money
  constant, 475
  convertibility to gold, and usefulness as international medium of exchange, 727
  demand and supply curves for, 677–678
  devaluation of, 719–720
  as international reserves standard, 727
  speculation against, 718–719
Dollar standard, de facto, 721
Domestic savings and economic development, 821
Doomsday predictions, 806–807
Double counting, 461
Double-log graph, 861n.
Dow Jones index, 381
Dow Jones Industrial Index, data in updating, 388
Drinking and heart attack, 129
Drugs, prescription, tradeoff of price, quality, variety, and advertising for, 267

Dun and Bradstreet, 381
Du Pont de Nemours, E. I. and Co., 311
  price increase, and demand for man-made fibers, 68
Durable goods, demand for, 531
Duration and interest rates, 377
Dynamic differentials, factor price, 337

Earley, James, 315
Earnings
  and factor movement, 401–403
  and price, 382–387
Eastern Airlines, monopoly power, 249
East India Co., 151
Economic activity
  indicators, 530
  nonmarketed, and national income, 477
Economic analysis
  and economic policy, 12–15
  in deciding policy questions, 429
  role given to advertising in, 268
Economic development
  and acquisition of capital, 821–823
  and educational policy, 819–820
  factors affecting, 829
  and inefficient use of resources, 816–818
  New York Times headlines, 828
  and planning vs. laissez faire, 818–819
  and population growth, 813–814, 820
  and resource limitations, 814–816
Economic discrimination, 362–363
  and competition, 363–365
Economic efficiency vs. technological efficiency, 154, 155
Economic growth
  benefits of, 791–793
  defined, 789–790
  and government intervention, 819
  and international trade, 803–804
  Lewis on, 808
  in market economy, 808
  nature of, 788–789
  and poverty, 391
  price level, employment, and, 741
  production-possibility boundary, 11

theories of, 797–807
  Yugoslavia, 849
Economic objectives, 16–17
Economic policy
  and economic analysis, 12–15
  Stalin, 836
Economic problems
  classification, 9–11
  contemporary, 3–5
Economic profits, 160–161
Economic rent, 224
  pay for factor services as, 343
  and transfer earnings, 338–339
Economic Report of the President, 561
Economics
  cause of problems, 6
  of declining industries, 228–229
  defined, 5–12
  as developing science, 25–27
  flouting of laws of, 785–786
  and law, antitrust policy, 297–298
  monopoly power of professor of, 249
  positive and normative statements in, 19
  presidential, 568
  progress of, 782
  of superstar salaries, 330–331
  of urban decay, 446–450
Economic stability, U.S. vs. Soviet, 843–845
Economic stabilization program and multiplier, 524
Economic system
  and decision process, 832–834
  ends and means, 835
  and incentive systems, 834–835
  and ownership of resources, 831–832
  of Soviet Union, 836–846
  U.S. vs. Soviet, 842–846
  and values, 833–834
  Yugoslavia, 846–849
Economic theory
  and behavior consistent with it, 28
  and political realism, 566–567
  statistical testing of, 30–35
Economic well-being and GNP, effect on various factors, 481
Economies of scale
  and gains from trade, 691
  oligopoly, 262–263
Economist, balance sheet and income statement, 883–884

Economy
  chances for U.S. vs. Soviet Union
    and Yugoslavia to achieve
    various results, 851
  Closed, 466
  command, 42
  decision makers in, 49
  and defense spending, 576–577
  effects of social dividend financed
    from new money, 650
  fiscal impact on, 551–552
  Frugal, 462–464
  Governed, 464–467
  and government borrowing, 587
  government role in, 456
  interdependent, 410–417
  interest and return on capital in,
    373–376
  and money, 590–592
  Open, 466–468
  prediction of increased control by
    business, 320
  and principle of substitution,
    179–180
  real and money parts of, 590–592
  Spendthrift, 459–462
  stock market in forecasting, 37
  structure of, 250–253
  types, 41–42
  U.S., 468–473
Education
  average total cost, 176
  college, as monopolistically
    competitive industry, 268
  factor pay, mobility, and, 343
  factors, and diminishing
    productivity, 176
  higher, subsidizing of, 444–445
Educational policy and economic
  development, 819–820
EEC. *See* European Economic
  Community
Efficiency
  and competition vs. monopoly,
    285–287
  and smallness of business, 176
"Efficiency" defense, in illegal
  acquisition, 304
Effluent charge, 421
Effort, supply of, 329–332
Egalitarian U vs. Elitist Tech,
  salaries, 407

Ehrlichman, John, utility schedule,
  129
Elastic demand vs. inelastic demand,
  74
Elasticity. *See also* Demand Elasticity
  demand curve, 75, 866–867
  nomenclature, 79
Elasticity of demand. *See* Demand
  elasticity
Elasticity of supply, 80
Electric companies, variable
  consumption and rates, and price
  discrimination, 249
Elitist Tech vs. Egalitarian U,
  salaries, 407
Embodied technical change, 800
Emotional statements, rewording of,
  28
Empire State Building, and mobility,
  407
Employers' associations, as potential
  monopsonists, 348
Employment. *See also* Full
  employment; Labor;
  Unemployment; Unions
  and aggregate demand, factors
    affecting, 568
  effect of balanced budget on,
    586–587
  and fiscal policy, 587
  and L-shaped relation, 520–521
  in monopsonistic market, 347
  and paradox of thrift, 511
  price level, economic growth, and,
    741
  and union membership, 353
  and wages, 358, 400
Employment Act (1946), 14, 571
Employment opportunities
  shift from cities, 447
  in war on poverty, 395
Endogenous variable, 24
Ends and means, 12–14
Energy, inanimate, production of,
  194–195
Energy crisis and growth, 4–5
Energy shortage and long-run
  reduction of input per unit of
  output, 191
Energy use, tax vs. price rise on, 455
The Engineers and the Price System
  (Veblen), 163

Environment, TVA as threat to, 207
Entry and exit. *See* Freedom of entry
  and exit; Barriers to entry
Environmental policy, 427–428
Environmental Protection Agency
  (EPA), 427
Epiphany, Dive for Cross halted by
  pollution in Greek harbor, 207
Equal net advantage, hypothesis of,
  333
Equilibrium
  of firm and industry, 217–221, 223,
    240–241
  in Frugal economy, 494–499
  general, and price system, 414–417
  graphic illustration of, 498–499
  household, 113–115, 125–127
  monopolistically competitive
    industry, 255
  in terms of withdrawals and
    injections, 501, 503
Equilibrium conditions, 493
Equilibrium differentials, factor
  price, 337
Equilibrium exchange rate,
  determinants of, 678–680
Equilibrium income, 484
  and aggregate demand, 514
  in Frugal economy, 493–499
  vs. full-employment income, 496
  and interest rate, 893–894
Equilibrium interest rate for fixed
  capital stock, 373
Equilibrium national income, 484
  concept of, 505
  general graphical approach,
    503–504
  two countries with different
    injections and withdrawals, 505
  withdrawals-injections approach in
    general case, 499–503
Equilibrium output, firm in perfect
  competition, 217–218
Equilibrium price, 64–65
  agriculture, 98–99
  and ceiling price, 83–84
  marijuana, and legalization, 69
Equipment delivery, speedup, and
  short-run decisions, 176
Equity capital, 379
Error term, in economic hypothesis,
  855–856

Escalator clauses, and inflation, 595
European Economic Community
    (EEC), 707
    effect of drop in price of
        manufactured goods, 694
    snake, 721
Eventually diminishing average
    productivity, hypothesis of, 174
Eventually diminishing returns,
    hypothesis of, 170
Ever-normal granary, 97–98
Evert, Chris, 331
Excess capacity, 175, 255
    theorem, 256
Excess demand, 63, 64
Excess reserves, 617, 618
    commercial banks, 624
Exchange rates. *See also* International
    trade; Tariff
    and arbitrage, 671
    and balance-of-payments
        equilibrium, 717
    Canadian vs. American, 684
    and central banks, 722–723
    on competitive market, 678
    factors affecting, 683
    fixed, 680–682, 721; vs.
        fluctuating, 682
    flexible, and unemployment, 727
    and foreign exchange market
        transactions, 683
    management of, 723–724
    nature of, 668–670
    and prices, 677–678
    Smithsonian agreements, 720–721
    and speculation on foreign
        exchange markets, 683–684
Excise tax
    in discouraging use of product,
        455
    incidence in competitive industry,
        436–439
    regressivity of, 432
Execution lag, 565
Exogenous variables, 24
Expansionary monetary policy, 653
Expansion or recovery in business
    fluctuation, 543–544
Expectation, and investment in plant
    and equipment, 537, 539
Expectational inflation, 736–737
    Phelps-Friedman theory, 767–775

and stagflation, 780
and wage-price controls, 777–778
Expenditure and final output in
    Frugal economy, 464. *See also*
    Government expenditure
Experiment, uncontrolled, 31
Exploitation doctrine, tariff, 700–701
Export(s)
    domestic supply price and
        equilibrium exchange rate, 679
    as injection into circular flow, 500
    and national income, 509
    net, 467
    and tariffs, 702
Export-Import Bank, 822
Externalities, 202–204
    Aswan Dam, 207
    blame for, 204–205
    and Coase theorem, 423

Factor earnings
    and market conditions, 398–401
    and mobility, 407
Factor(s) of production, 6. *See also*
    Capital; Factor price; Labor;
    Land
    allocation to particular uses,
        333–335
    availability, and slope of isocost
        line, 191
    cost and quantity supplied, 61
    demand for, 326–329
    and derived demand, 343
    earnings, and market conditions,
        398–401
    firm, 152–155
    fixed, 166
    hired and purchased, as
        opportunity cost, 157
    and isoquant shape, 191
    market for, 41
    mobility, 334–335
    response to changes in earnings,
        401–403
Factor pay, mobility, and education,
    343
Factor payments, division between
    economic rent and transfer
    earnings, 339
Factor-payments approach
    to GNP, 469
    income components, 470

in Spendthrift economy, 462
in U.S. economy, 469
Factor price. *See also* Factor(s) of
    production; Price(s)
    in competitive markets, 335–341
    and cost curves, 184
    costs, factor proportions, and, 189
    differentials, 335–338
    dynamic vs. equilibrium
        differentials in, 343
    and income in competitive market,
        325
    and long-run industry supply
        curves, 227–230
    and marginal productivity theory
        of distribution, 343
    and output, 191
    theory of, 325–326
    transfer earnings and economic
        rent, 338–339
Factor pricing, Soviet, 841–842
Factor proportions, factor prices, and
    costs, 189
Factor services
    in market economy, 39
    payment as economic rent vs.
        transfer earnings, 343
Factor supply, 329–333
    theory of, 404
    and wages, 340–341
"Failing company" defense, in illegal
    acquisition, 304
Fair return, in natural monopoly
    regulation, 301
Fair-trade laws, 88–89
Falling-cost industry, 231
Families. *See also* Household; Income
    distribution
    income, 323
    Lorenz curve of income, 324
    poverty among, 392
Fast-food restaurants in Greenville's
    "gut row," 283
FCC. *See* Federal Communications
    Commission
FDIC (Federal Deposit Insurance
    Corp.). *See* Federal Reserve
    System
Featherbedding, 359
Federal Communications
    Commission, 251
Federal Farm Board, 100

Federal funds market, 617n.
Federal income tax, 440–443
Federal Reserve Bank of New York, 655
    president's statement on inflation and international trade, 684
Federal Reserve Bulletin, 612
Federal Reserve notes
    vs. gold certificates, 634
    as money, 611
Federal Reserve System, 612, 613. *See also* Central bank(s); Monetary policy; Money supply
    and bank failures, Great Depression, 744
    Board of Governors, 628
    and creation of elastic currency, 665
    Culpeper facility, 666
    and currency control, 627
    decrease in money supply and speculative profit on bonds, 650
    monetary policy weapons and purposes, 666
    and money supply, 746
    Open Market Committee, 629, 655–656
    required reserve ratios, 629–630, 659
    requiring general equilibrium analysis of events, 428
    Reserve banks, 628–629
Federal Trade Commission Act (1914), 293, 294
Federal Trade Commission and antitrust policy, 292
Federation of unions, 349
Feedback and impact, General Motors strike, 416–417
Female-male differentials, labor markets, 361–362
Fertilizers, chemical, and water quality, 16
Fiat money, 604–606
Fidrych, Mark, 330–331
Final output and expenditure in Frugal economy, 464
Final products, 462
Financial capital and economic development, 815
Financial holdings, motives for, 650
Financial institutions, loans as investment funds source, 380

Fine tuning
    fiscal policy, 559–560
    vs. removing persistent gaps, 561
Finley, Charles O., and baseball player's salary, 343
Firestone Tire and Rubber Co., 321
Firm. *See also* Business cycles; Competition; Corporation
    age, and ease of entry into industry, 235
    behavior, and market structure, 210–211
    in circular flow, 46
    competitive behavior, 210
    cost and profit to, 155–162
    criticism of economist's concept of, 314–319
    demand for additional capital, 372–373
    economic efficiency, 155
    economic theory, and productive decisions of nonprofit organizations, 163
    factors of production, 152–155
    hypothesis of control of market, 306–311
    and industry, equilibrium, 217–221, 223, 240–241
    and information, 314–316
    input decisions, isoquants in analysis of, 184–190
    invention and innovation as exogenous to, 196, 198
    kinds, 153
    manipulation of demand, 306
    in market economy, 40
    measurement of opportunity cost by, 156–160
    motivation of, 316–319
    organization of, 316
    payments and expenditures approach to income statement of, 471
    as price taker, 213
    production function, 167–168
    profit maximization motive, 152
    raw materials monopoly, vs. union shop contract, 366
    sensitivity to market pressures, 308–311
    size, and monopsony power, 348
    in standard economic theory, 305

time horizons for decision making, 166–167
Fiscal drag, 572, 574
Fiscal policy
    after WWII, 571–575
    alternative, 557, 559
    before 1946, 570–571
    built-in stabilizers, 561–564
    Congress, consumption function, and, 756–757
    defined, 550
    discretionary, 564–567
    effects of, 898–900
    effect of taxes and government spending on, 552–557
    and employment, 587
    fine tuning, 559–560
    future, 575–577
    and inflation, 574
    on interest rates and durability of goods, 388
    monetarist view of, 752–754
    vs. monetary, 755
    and national debt, 581–586
    in national income model, 894–895
    neo-Keynesian view of, 753, 754
    1970s, 573–575
    removal of persistent gaps, 560
    representation of, 896–897
    theory of, 551–552
Fish, demand and quantity demanded, effect of various factors on, 69
Fisher, Irving, 119n.
Fishing and externalities, 203
Fishmeal scarcity and grain prices, 235
Fixed costs, 171
Fixed exchange rates, 680–682
    and balance of payments, 683
    breakdown of, 721
    vs. fluctuating, 682
Fixed factors, 166
Flat Earth Society, freedom of speech and equal network time, 16
Floating exchange rates, 680, 721–722
    and IMF, 724–725
Flow variables, 24
Fluctuating exchange rates, 682
Fluctuations. *See* Business cycles
Food supply and population, China, 828–829

Ford, Gerald, 448, 575
  and presidential economics, 568
  on unemployment-inflation
    tradeoff, 785
Ford, Henry, II, 305
Ford Motor Co., 311, 417, 426
  and hypothesis that firms control
    the market, 320
  motive for holding payroll account
    in local bank, 650
Foreign aid to underdeveloped
  countries, priorities for, 828
Foreign borrowing to finance
  government activity, 580–581
Foreign entanglements and free trade,
  708
Foreign exchange, 669. *See also*
  Exchange rates; International
  trade
Foreign exchange market
  and arbitrage, 684
  demand and supply curves for
    dollars, 678
  disequilibrium in, 676
  factors affecting dollar supply and
    demand on, 683
  quote from *New York Times* about
    gold prices on, 727
  speculation, and exchange rates,
    683–684
Foreign ownership and economic
  development, 821
Forrester, Jay, 804
Fortune, 277
  report on labor productivity in beer
    industry, 268
45° line, 489
  and aggregate demand at
    equilibrium, 498
  and total expenditures vs. total
    income, 505
Fractionally backed paper money,
  603–604
Fractional reserve system, 617, 618
France
  artichoke wars, 282
  trade war with U.S., 709
Freedom of entry and exit, in perfect
  competition, 212
Freedom of speech, and equal time on
  TV, 16
Free good, 113

Free-market economy, 41–42
Free trade. *See also* International trade;
  Tariff
  defined, 696
  and foreign entanglements, 708
  vs. no trade, 698
Frictional unemployment, 485, 732
Friedman, Milton, 14, 88, 551, 566,
  744
  on discretionary monetary policy,
    761
  on OPEC, 282
  and Phelps-Friedman theory,
    767–775
Fringe benefits vs. wages, 359–360
Frisbee, spur for, 207
Frugal economy, 462–464
  aggregate demand function in,
    492–493
  aggregate desired expenditure and
    total output in, 505
  circular flow of income, 495
  consumption function in, 488–491
  consumption-saving decisions in,
    487–488
  equilibrium income, 493–499
  expenditure and final output in, 464
  income-expenditure approach to
    equilibrium in, 493, 494, 496
  investment in, 463
  investment decisions in, 487
  output-expenditure approach in,
    463–464
  saving in, 463
  saving function in, 491–492
  saving-investment approach to
    equilibrium in, 497–499
Fruits and vegetables, retail, market
  behavior and market structure,
  234
FTC. *See* Federal Trade Commission
Full-cost pricing, hypothesis of,
  315–316
Full employment. *See also*
  Employment; Unemployment;
  Unions
  and inflation, 785
  meaning of, 485
  and modified quantity theory, 639
  and money supply, 637–638
  and prices, L-shaped relation,
    763–765

Full-employment balance, 556, 573
Full-employment GNP, 483
Full-employment income
  and fiscal drag, 587
  vs. equilibrium income, 496
Full-employment national income
  and investment, 788
Full-employment surplus, 571, 572
Function, 24–25
  of three variables, 864
Functional distribution of income,
  322–323, 405–406
Functional forms, 855
Functional relations, 24–25, 854–855
Fundamental disequilibrium, 716, 717

Gains from trade, 685, 686
  and Brazilian coffee, 694
  and comparative advantage, 688–689
  and economies of scale, 691
  graphic representation, 692–693
  and learning by doing, 691
  sources, 686–691
Galbraith, John Kenneth, 14, 305,
  451, 778, 792
  concept of New Industrial State,
    306–311
  on tax rebate and deflationary gap,
    568
Gaps, inflationary and deflationary,
  519–523, 553–561
Gasoline prices and demand, 81
Gas stations, full-service vs.
  self-service, 163
General Agreement on Tariffs and
  Trade (GATT), 706–707
General case
  circular flow of income in, 502
  income-expenditure approach in,
    503
  withdrawals-injections approach
    in, 499–503
General Electric Co., 202, 205,
  279–280
General equilibrium analysis,
  feedback of events requiring,
  428–429
General equilibrium and price system,
  414–417
General Motors Corp.,
  and bargaining with raw materials
    monopolist vs. union, 366

General Motors Corp. *(Continued)*
and bigness vs. badness, 304
and hypothesis that firms control
the market, 320
1970 strike, 415–417
*General Theory of Employment, Interest
and Money, The* (Keynes), 522,
553, 743, 745
Genevra de Benci (da Vinci), sold to
National Gallery, and utility
theory, 129
George, Henry, and single-tax
movement, 340–341
George V, King, 512
Ghettos, formation in inner cities,
447, 450
Giffen, Sir Robert, 138
Giffen good, 137–138, 876
GNP. *See* Gross national product
GNP deflator, 475
Gold
Austria's new coin, 611
dollar convertibility, and usefulness
as international medium of
exchange, 727
as medium of exchange, 611
and paper money, 602
quote from *New York Times* on
foreign exchange market prices,
727
role in international payments,
726–727
Gold certificates vs. Federal Reserve
notes, 634
Gold exchange standard, 714
Gold leaf and price of gold vs. labor, 191
Gold flow, 711–712
Gold points, 711
Gold standard, 602, 711–712
and inflation, 727, 741
1920s failure of, 712
and role of gold in international
payments, 726–727
Golf, marginal vs. total utility of, 129
Gompers, Samuel, 353
Good(s), 6
allocation, 9–10
conspicuous consumption, 138
distribution, Soviet, 839–840
Giffen, 137–138, 876
production, 9–11
and services, government
purchases of, 467

Good Old Brick Co., Zackville,
and merger, 304
Goodyear Tire and Rubber Co., 321
and bargaining with raw materials
monopolist vs. union, 366
builds Congo plant, 828
unproductive costs and
government regulation, 429
GOSBANK, 842
GOSPLANs, USSR, 837
Governed economy, 464
aggregate desired expenditure and
total output in, 505
government expenditures in, 466
transfer payments in, 465–466
Government
action in resolving grievances, 429
agricultural price supports, 98, 99
appropriate size, 452–453
beneficial or adverse effects of
various actions, 429
borrowing, and central bank, 552
borrowing, and economy, 587
case for and against action in
various areas, 429
central bank as banker to, 626–627
control of, 310
control of interest rates, 373–374
debt policy, 587
effect on dollar supply and demand
of grant to Peru for purchase of
U.S. farm machinery, 683
events that may require
intervention, 429
expenditure, and jobs, 587
intervention, and economic
growth, 819
intervention to internalize an
externality, 423
in market economy, 40–41
and paradox of thrift, 511–512
policy on old-age pensions, 16
policy to reduce inflationary gap,
549
progressivity of taxation policies,
435–436
purchases of goods and services,
467
regulation, and unproductive costs,
429
revenue sharing vs. categorical
grants-in-aid for state and local
governments, 456

role in economic problems, 5
services, rising demand for,
445–446
stabilization of farmers' revenue by
open market purchases and sales,
98–99
subsidy of particular industries or
regions, 568
vs. universities, pay, and
distribution theory, 343
Government activity
alternative means of financing,
578–581
opportunity cost of, 577–578
Government expenditure
and aggregate demand, 552–553
and business cycles, 527
evaluating, 450–453
in Governed economy, 465
as injection into circular flow, 500
and national income, 509
in selected countries, 551
and taxes, 552–557
types, 441–446
WWII, 571
Grants-in-aid
categorical, vs. revenue sharing,
456
and crisis of cities, 443–446
examples, 455
Grape boycott and demand, 235
Graphing
of economic observations, 857–
861
function of three variables, 864
linear functions, 861–862
nonlinear functions, 863–864
Grayson, Jackson, 778n.
Great Atlantic and Pacific Tea Co.,
311
Great Depression
and agricultural prices and receipts,
92–93
agriculture vs. industry, 94
bank failures and money supply,
744
end of, 745
fiscal policy, 570
and monetary system
experimentation, 712–713
and paradox of thrift, 511–512
and pump priming, 557
unemployment, 10, 570

Greece
  government intervention in
    direction of development, 819
  pollution cancels Epiphany Dive
    for Cross in harbor, 208
Green, Tom, loses job and exists on
  savings, 505
Green Bay Packers, lifetime pass to
  football games as money, 611
Green revolution and agricultural
  development, 825
Greenspan, Alan, on business
  recovery, 549
Greenville, South Carolina, fast-food
  restaurants on "gut row," 282
Gresham, Thomas, 602
Gresham's law, 602, 605
Greyhound Corp., 103
Grimsby household, invests in
  wildcat oil drilling venture, 505
Gross investment, 463
Gross national income, 464
Gross national product (GNP), 464
  actual and potential, 484
  business cycles, pairs of series, and,
    549
  if Canada and U.S. were joined as
    one country, 480
  in current and constant dollars, 475,
    476
  and disposable income, 474
  and economic well-being, effect of
    various factors on, 481
  factor-payments approach to,
    469
  fluctuations in, causes of, 761
  and foreign trade, 705
  in Governed economy, 465
  Great Depression, 570
  growth, USSR, 844
  and investments, 533
  and money supply, 761
  and NNP, output-expenditure
    approach to, 468
  to Open economy, 466, 468
  per capita, 476, 813
  percentage increase in current and
    constant dollars, 481
  potential and actual, opposite
    movement of, 505
  productive acts not in, 480–481
  and real gross private investment,
    534

real growth vs. growth in constant
  dollars, 808
and transfer payments, 466
Gross private domestic investment,
  466–467
Gross private investment, 535
Growth. *See also* Development;
  Economic development
  contemporary view of, 800–804
  costs of, 793–796; vs. benefits,
    796–797
  cumulative nature of, 790–791
  and energy crisis, 4–5
  and income distribution, 791
  Japan, 805
  with learning, 799–800
  and life-style, 791–792
  limits to, 804–807
  in living standards, 791
  and national defense, 793
  open letter from supporter of,
    792–793
  and prestige, 793
  products, and innovation, 207
  U.S. vs. Soviet, 843–846
  in world without learning, 797–798
Guaranteed annual-employment
  contract, and short-run
  decisions, 176
Guggenheimer, Elinor, on coffee
  boycott, 282
Gulf & Western Industries, 384
Guns, private vs. social costs of
  private ownership, 207

Haberler, Gottfried, 527
Hall, Charles Martin, 197
Hammer, Armand, purchase of
  Rembrandt's *Juno* as marginal vs.
  total utility, 129
Hammerstein, takes to wine, women,
  and song when wife leaves, 505
Hand, Learned, 292
Hansen, Alvin, 526, 527
Hardcrust, Homer, advises
  government austerity program,
  524
Harris, Mrs. Henry, subsists by
  clipping coupons on bonds, but
  won't touch capital, 505
Harrod, Sir Roy, 228–229
Hart-Scott-Rodino Antitrust
  Improvement Act (1976), 294

Hawtrey, R. G., 744n.
Hayek, F. A. von, 86n., 744n.
Heart attack, and smoking and
  drinking, marginal vs. total
  utility, 129
Heller, Walter, 573, 743
Hickman, Bert, 527
Hicks, Sir John R., 116, 890
Higher education, subsidizing of,
  444–445
Hills, Carla A., 143
Holding company, 312
Holiday Inn on Nantucket Island,
  Baker on, 16
Hollister, Donald, and long-lasting
  light bulb, 282
Hoover, Herbert, 94
Horizontal merger, 295
Hotelling, Harold, 259
Hours worked and total supply of
  labor, 331
Household
  choice, and indifference curve
    analysis, 119, 122–128
  in circular flow, 44
  decision making, and demand
    theory, 136–137
  demand curve, 108–109, 115
  equilibrium, 113–115, 125–127
  expenditures and income, 49
  incentives, Soviet, 839–840
  income, and quantity demanded,
    54–55, 139–141
  income decrease vs. spending
    increase, 129
  marginal utility theory of behavior,
    109–119
  in market economy, 40
  reaction to change in income, 127
  reaction to change in price, 127–128
  satisfaction, and purchasing power,
    873–874
  supply of cash and spending, 666
Housing
  affordable, and demand theory,
    140–141
  mobile home sales, interest rates,
    and construction of, 549
  no-frill, taste vs. price and income,
    145
  owner-occupied, and mortgage
    interest rates, 146; and price of
    rental housing, 146

Housing *(Continued)*
rental allowance for poor, 407
Hudson's Bay Company, 151
Hull, Cordell, 706
Human behavior
and economic theory, 28
predictability of, 20–22; and
business, 28
Human capital, 369. *See also* Capital
and economic development,
815–816
quality of, 802
Human welfare and national income,
477–479
Hume, David, 685
Hungary, economic reform to attract
tourists, 828
Hunter, Robert, on poverty, 352
Hyperbola, 862
Hyperinflation, 596–597
and U.S. cigarettes as money
during WWII, 611
Hypothesis, 23–25
decision to reject or accept, 35–36
vs. law and prediction, 66
proof as true or false, 35

IBM Corp., 251
effect on dollar supply and demand
of moving dollars to Paris bank,
683
Icebergs, opportunity cost of towing
to Saudi Arabia, 163
Identification problem and demand,
134–136
Illegal activities and national income,
477
Impact of GM strike, 415–417
Import(s)
quota vs. tariff, 709
restrictions, and tariffs, 708–709
and tariffs, 702–703
as withdrawal from circular flow,
501
Imported capital and economic
development, 821–822
Import schedule and national income,
510
Import substitution and
development, 825–826
Imputed costs, 157, 159–160
Incentive systems and economic
systems, 834–835

Income. *See also* Income distribution;
National income
after-tax, factors affecting size
distribution of, 342–343
and circular flow, 46–48; in
Spendthrift economy, 460
components, 466–467, 470
decrease, vs. spending increase,
129
and factor price in competitive
market, 325
functional distribution of,
322–323, 405–406
future, present value of, 370–371
household reaction to change in,
127
vs. money, 49
personal, 473–474
and population among groups of
countries, 811
vs. price and taste, and no-frill
houses, 145
and prices, agriculture, 91–95
of proprietors, 470
real and money, 122
rental, 470
size distribution of, 323–325
ICC. *See* Interstate Commerce
Commission
IMF. *See* International Monetary
Fund
Income-consumption curve, 78
Income-consumption line, 127
Income distribution. *See also* Income;
National income
changes in, 531–532
functional, 405–406
and growth, 791
households, and quantity
demanded, 54–55
and national debt, 587
rich and poor, 389–391
Soviet, 839–840
and tax-exempt municipal bonds,
455
and tax policy, 431–436
U.S. and world, 809–810
Income distribution theory and just
distribution of, 404
Income effect and price, 878–879
Income elasticity of demand, 76, 95,
132–133
and price elasticity, 81, 146

Income-expenditure approach
to equilibrium in Frugal economy,
493, 495, 496
in general case, 503
Income flow vs. cash flow, 881n.
Income levels, households, and
quantity demanded, 54
Income redistribution and inflation,
598
Income statement
accountant, 881, 883
economist, 883
firm, payment and expenditures
approaches to, 471
Income tax
corporation, 433–434, 439–440
negative, 396, 434–435
personal, 432–433, 440–443
Increasing costs and long-run average
cost curve, 182
Increasing returns, long-run, 181
Incremental cost, 173
Incremental product, 168
Incremental utility, 110n.
Index numbers, 475
accuracy and significance, 872
limitations, 874–875
to measure changes in real income,
872–874
of physical outputs, 871–872
of prices, 869–871
Index of Industrial Production, 871
India, agricultural development and
unemployment, 825
Indifference curve, 122–124
Indifference curve analysis and
household choice, 119, 122–128
Indifference map, 125
Indifference theory, derivation and
slope of demand curve, 875–879
Indirect business taxes, 470
Individuals
federal transfer payments to,
442–443
protection of, 419
Industrial bonds, interest rates on,
388
Industrial capacity and
unemployment, Carter on, 16,
524
Industrialization and development,
824–827
Industrial union, 348

Industry. *See also* Business cycles; Competition; Corporation; Firm
  characterized by few large firms, 251
  constant-cost, 227
  declining, economics of, 228–229
  defined, 211
  ease of exit and entry, 234, 235
  and firm: equilibrium in monopoly, 240–241; short-run equilibrium, 217–221
  freedom of entry and exit in perfect competition, 212
Industry supply curve, perfect competition, 219–220
Inelastic demand and agricultural prices and incomes, 91–93
Inelastic demand vs. elastic demand, 74
Infant-industry argument for tariffs, 698, 700
  as valid for world as economic unit, 709
Inferior goods, 76
Infinite elasticity, 75
Inflation
  actual vs. expected rate of, 770–771
  anticipated, 595–597
  in business fluctuation, 544
  control of, 739–740
  cost-push, 737, 775–780
  and deflation, importance of, 592–593
  demand-pull, 736–737, 763–767, 776–777, 780
  dominant cause, 738–739
  effect on various groups, 611
  expectational, 736–737, 765–778, 780
  experience of, 740
  and fiscal drag, 587
  and fiscal policy, 574
  and full employment, 785
  and gold standard, 727, 741
  and interest rates, 374–375
  and international trade, 684
  losers by, 597–598
  monetarist view of, 747
  and money supply, 658
  neo-Keynesian view, 747
  price-push, 737, 775–780
  and purchasing power, 10–11

and real national income, L-shaped relation, 764
reasons for concern of policy makers, 736
statements about, 28
structural rigidity, 737
unanticipated, 593–595
and unemployment, 4, 772–775; Ford and Regan on tradeoff between, 785; Soviet, 844–845
validated and unvalidated, 739–740
writers' focus of attention on, 741
Inflationary gaps
  and deflationary, 519–523, 553–561
  government policy in reducing, 549
  and monetary policy, 659
  post-WWII, 571
Injection
  into circular flow, 47, 48
  and equilibrium national income, 505
  and national income, 509
  and withdrawals, compensating changes in, 512–513
Injection schedule, shift in, 508–509
Innovation, 196
  and growth, 800–802
  and invention, 196, 198
  and investment in plant and equipment, 537
  in monopoly vs. competition, 289–290
  and product growth, 207
  Soviet, 838
  spur for, 207
Input, 153
Input decisions, firm, isoquants in analysis of, 184–190
Installment credit, selective control, 663
Instrumental variables
  monetary policy, 652
  money supply vs. interest rates, 654–655
Interbank activities, commercial banks, 614–615
Intercorporate control groups, hypothesis of, 314
Interdependence, oligopolistic firms, 260

Interdependent economy, 410–413
  and general equilibrium, 414–417
  and market that works well, 413–414
Interest, 157, 462
  factors affecting market rate of, 388
  on national debt, 467
  net, 470
  and return on capital, 372–377
Interest elasticity, 748
  monetarist and neo-Keynesian views of, 748, 749
Interest inelasticity, 748
Interest rates, 157
  actual vs. nominal, 378
  and aggregate demand, 645–646
  and asset value, 371–372
  average, 661
  bank administration of, 374
  and bond prices, 643, 644
  and capital stock, 373, 539
  as credit control, 663–664
  and demand for money, 373, 643–644
  and durability of capital goods and consumer goods, 388
  future profits, present value, and 388
  government control of, 373–374
  home construction, mobile home sales, and, 549
  on industrial bonds, 388
  and inflation, 374–375
  and investment in inventory, 536
  and investment in plant and equipment, 539–540
  investment opportunity, risk, and, 388
  monetarist view of influence, 747–749
  monetary policy in controlling, 652
  and money supply, 646, 654–655
  and mortgage, 537, 538
  vs. national income as policy variables, 653–654
  neo-Keynesian view of influence, 749–750
  New York vs. London, and foreign exchange markets, 683
  and residential construction, 537
  shift away to money supply as monetary policy variable, 657
  variety of, 376–377

Interlocking directorates, 314
Intermediate products, 462
Internalization, 421
International Harvester case, 294, 295
International Monetary Fund (IMF),
    714–715
  and exchange rate management,
    723
  and floating exchange rates,
    724–725
  loans, and OPEC oil prices, 727
  and new international reserves, 724
International Nickel Co., 251
International Telephone and
    Telegraph Co. (ITT), 103, 318
International trade. *See also* Exchange
    rates; Tariff
  bank balance sheet as result of, 670
  defined, 668
  and economic growth, 803–804
  and GNP, 705
  and inflation, 684
  and national wealth, 694
Interstate Commerce Commission,
    251
Invention, 196
  causes of, 196–197
  and innovation, 196, 198;
    1860–1960, 801
  spur for, 207
Inventory, 463
  investment in, 534–536
Inventory cycle, 526, 546
Investment, 532–534
  accelerator theory of, 540–543
  in capital goods, 463
  factors affecting, 549
  and full-employment national
    income, 788
  gross and net, 463
  gross private domestic, 466–467
  as injection into circular flow, 500
  in inventories, 463, 534–536
  and opportunity cost, 164
  in plant and equipment, 537–540
  and profit, 164
  reasons for changes in, 534
  in residential construction,
    536–537
  and saving at equilibrium, 498–499
  and saving in Frugal vs. Governed
    economy, 505
  shifting opportunities, 799–800

Investment decisions in Frugal
    economy, 487
Investment expenditures and national
    income, 509
Investment funds
  bonds and bondholders, 379–380
  in financing corporation, 379
  reinvested profits, 380
  sources of, 377–379
  Soviet, 842
  from stock and stockholders, 379
Investment goods, 463
Investment opportunities, interest
    rates, and risk, 388
Invisibles, 673
Ireland, money during bank strike,
    611
IS curve, 890–893, 894
  and fiscal vs. monetary policy, 898
Isocost line, 120, 187–188
  slope, and availability of factors of
    production, 191
Isoquant
  and cost minimization, 187–189
  map, 187
  single, 185–187
  slope, and production, conditions,
    191
Israel, auto industry in, 191

Japan, growth, 805
Jews vs. blacks as professional
    athletes, 366
Jobs and public expenditure, 587
Job security vs. wages, 358–359
Jockey, prize money, and marginal
    productivity theory of
    distribution, 343
John Hancock Life Insurance Co.,
    103
Johnson, George, 362
Johnson, Harry, 700, 722
Johnson, Harvey, 301
Johnson, Lyndon B., 776
Joint Economic Committee, and
    Friedman on discretionary
    monetary policy, 761
Joint profit maximization, oligopoly,
    260–261
Jones and Laughlin Steel Co., 416
Jouvenal, Bertrand de, 86
Judicial interpretation, antitrust,
    294–295

Juno (Rembrandt), marginal vs. total
    utility of Armand Hammer's
    purchase, 129
Jurisdictional disputes, 348–349
Justice Department and antitrust, 292,
    295–296
  and "failing company" vs.
    "efficiency" defense of illegal
    acquisition, 304
Just prices, 117, 119

Kahn, David, 277
Kaiser, Henry, 253
Kaldor, Nicholas, 746n.
Kauper, Thomas, 296
Kennedy, John F., 571, 707, 776
Kennedy Round, 707
Kenya Meat Commission and meat
    prices, 106
Kessel, Reuben, 304
Keyfitz, Nathan, 804
Keynes, John Maynard, 522, 743,
    745. *See also* Neo-Keynesians
Khalid, king of Saudi Arabia, on
    increasing oil production to
    lower prices, 16
Khan, Abdul, pedicab driver in
    Dacca, and wages, 191
Khrushchev, Nikita, 840
Kindleberger, Charles P., on Bretton
    Woods, 713–714
Kinked demand curve
  and oligopoly, 265–266
  and state of mind vs. market
    conditions, 268
Kinked demand theory, and price,
    268
Klein, Lawrence, 14
Knights of Labor, 353
Koppang, Bob, sale of shredded
    currency, and utility theory, 129
Kosher King Meat Products, and
    marginal vs. total utility of liver,
    129
Kosygin, Aleksei, on Soviet vs. U.S.
    unemployment and inflation,
    851

Labor, 462. *See also* Employment;
    Factor(s) of production; Full
    employment; Labor market;
    Unemployment; Unions
  and change in demand, 43

division of, 39; and hypothesis of
   diminishing returns, 171
earnings and market conditions,
   399–400
effect of cost on trade, 694
as factor of production, 155
vs. gold, price, and principle of
   substitution, 191
market fluctuations in demand and
   supply of, 399–400
mobility of, 334–335, 336
poverty and urge to organize,
   351–352
productivity, Anheuser Busch,
   268; factors, 808; in theocracy,
   611
quantity of, 802–803
response to changes in earnings,
   402–403
specialization of, 38
and tariffs, 701–702
total supply of, 329–332
turnover, 485
Laboratory sciences, testing theories
   in, 29–30
Labor boycott, 350
Labor force
   participation in, 330–331
   union membership growth, 354
Labor-managed enterprises,
   Yugoslavia, 848–849
Labor market. *See also* Labor
   black-white differentials, 360–361
   female-male differentials, 361–362
   institutions, 348–351
   monopoly elements in, 400–401
Labor unions. *See* Unions
Laissez faire, 413
   and economic development,
   818–819
Lake Nasser and Aswan Dam, 207
Land, 462. *See also* Factor(s) of
   production
   earnings and market conditions,
   398–399
   as factor of production, 155
   mobility of, 334
   response to changes in earnings,
   401–402
   taxes and urban values, 341
   total supply of, 332
Landlords and payment of property
   tax, 436–437

Lange, Oskar, 846, 847
Large numbers, law of, 21–22
   in making economic statements
   testable, 37
Law(s)
   antitrust, 291
   of diminishing returns, 170
   and economics, antitrust policy,
   297–298
   fair-trade, 88–89
   Gresham's, 602, 605
   of large numbers, 21–22
   vs. prediction and hypothesis, 66
   promoting competition, 292–294
   right-to-work, 355
   of variable proportions, 170
Lawyers, supply and earnings,
   357–358
Learning
   growth in world without, 797–798
   growth with, 799–800
Learning by doing, and gains from
   trade, 691
Legal institutions, and growth, 803
Leibenstein, Harvey, 816
Leisure
   and MEW, 478–479
   and national income, 477–478
Lerner, Abba, 846, 847
Levitt, Bill, 142
Lewis, Arthur, on economic growth,
   808
Lewis, John L., 354, 358
Liability, limited, 150
Liberal view of appropriate size of
   government, 453
Liberman, E., 838
License fees, 439
Licorice candy, monopoly in, 249
Life-cycle hypothesis, 566
   assumptions, 886–887
   implications, 887–889
   variables, 885–886
Life insurance, and predictability of
   human behavior, 28
Life-style and growth, 791–792
Lifetime income, 566
Limited liability, corporation, 150
Limited partnership, 150
Limit price, 262
Linear functions, graphing, 861–862
Ling-Temco-Vought (LTV), 377
Liquidity preference, 644

Liquidity preference schedules, 643,
   644
   flat, and steep marginal efficiency
   of investment schedule, 650
Literary Digest, forecast of 1936
   election results, 37
Little, Ian M., 826
Liver, chopped, marginal and total
   utility of, 129
Living standards
   and capital acquisition, 821
   growth in, 791
   and inflation, 595
   and tariff, 697–698, 702–703
   U.S. as two nations or as combined
   North American nation, 694
   U.S. vs. Soviet, 843
LM curve, 893, 894
   and fiscal and monetary policy, 898
Loans
   from financial institutions, as
   investment funds source, 380
   to friend, opportunity cost of, 163
   sharing of, 614–615
Local government
   categorical grants-in-aid vs.
   revenue sharing for, 456
   rising relative cost of services, 446
Loch Ness monster, question as to
   existence of, 37
Lock box, bank service, 616–617
Lockout, 350
Logarithmic scale, 859–861
Logrolling, 453
Long run
   cost curves in, 180–182
   in decision making, 167
   detailed analysis of, 223–233
   input decisions in, 177–180
   in outline, 221–223
Long-run average cost curve, 180–185
   and short-run curve, 191
Long-run average total cost, lowest,
   and average cost curve, 182
Long-run competitive equilibrium,
   231–233
Long-run consumption function,
   488–490
Long-run costs vs. short-run costs,
   182–183
Long-run equilibrium, 221–233
   monopolistically competitive firm,
   255

Long-run industry supply curve, 227–231

Long-run profit maximization, hypothesis of, 317–319

Long-term capital in capital account, 674

Long-term disequilibria and adjustable peg system, 716–717

Lorenz curve, 324
U.S. and world income distribution, 809–810

Losses, 160–161
in competitive industry, and exit of capital, 222

Lower turning point in business fluctuation, 545–546

L-shaped relation, 520–521
and demand-pull inflation, 763–765
and inflation-unemployment tradeoff, 785
and modified quantity theory, 638
unemployment, industrial capacity, and, 524

LTV. *See* Ling-Temco-Vought

Lump-sum taxes, incidence of, 439

McCracken, Paul, 14

McGovern, George, on New York urban crisis, 456

McKean, Roland, 451

McLaren, Richard, 296

Macroconcentration, 291

Macroeconomic policy
diagnosis of problem, 743–747
extreme views of, 742–743
goals of, 730–731
instruments of, 747–754
recommended, 754–758
significance of debate over, 758–760

Macroeconomics, 11
and circular flow, 44–46
vs. microeconomics, 459
overview, 46–48

Malthus, Thomas, 813
insurmountable difficulty, and China's population and food supply, 828–829
Managed float, 722
Manipulation of demand, 306
Manove, Michael, 841

Manufacturing. *See also* Corporation; Firm; Industry
competitive behavior and market structure, 234
concentration patterns, 252–253

Margarine vs. butter
demand for, 145
elasticity of demand for, 81

Marginal cost, 172–173
and marginal revenue, 212–213
in monopsony, 346
and price, 284

Marginal cost curve, 174
perfectly competitive industry, 219–220

Marginal disutility, 112

Marginal efficiency of capital, 368–370

Marginal efficiency of capital schedule, 369–370, 646n., 798

Marginal efficiency of investment schedule, 645–646
steep, and flat liquidity preference schedule, 650

Marginal net private benefits, 413

Marginal net social benefits, 413

Marginal physical product, 328

Marginal product, 168–169

Marginal product curve, 169
vs. average product curve, 171

Marginal productivity, diminishing, 169

Marginal productivity theory of distribution, 328, 403
and factor price, 343
as inhumane, 404–405

Marginal propensity to consume, 488, 489, 508
long run vs. short run, 505; value of, 505

Marginal propensity to save, 491

Marginal rate of substitution, 124–125, 185–186

Marginal revenue, 217
and average revenue, 237
and marginal cost, 212–213
total revenue, elasticity of demand, and, 237–239

Marginal revenue curve for monopolist, 238

Marginal revenue product, 328

Marginal revenue product curve of factor, 404

Marginal tax rate, 432

Marginal utility
curve, 112
defined, 110
and demand elasticity, 117
schedule, 111
vs. total utility, choices involving, 129

Marginal utility theory of household behavior, 109–119

Margin of error, 855

Margin requirements, as credit controls, 662–663

Marijuana, legalization, and equilibrium price, 69

Market
automobiles and hypothesis of firm control of, 320
and change in demand, 42–44
and change in supply, 44
competitive, factor price and income in, 325
coordination of, 411–412
defined, 41
firm sensitivity to pressures of, 308–310
household view of, 211
how it works, 42–44
hypothesis of firm's control of, 306–311
imperfections, 417–418
need for, 412–413

Market conditions, and factor earnings, 398–401

Market demand curve vs. household demand curve, 108–109

Market economy, 38–41
economic growth in, 808

Market failure
coping with, 420–421, 424
and government intervention, different countries, 456
optimal correction of, 424
and pollution control, 424–427
sources of, 417–420

Market incentives in overcoming market failure, 421, 424

Market price
and boycott, 269–272
and demand and revenue curves, 217

Market structure
and cost, 288–289
and firm behavior, 210–211

illegal aspects, 304
mixture, and oligopoly theory, 280–281
significance of, 211–212
and whitewall vs. blackwall tires, 267
Market system decision process, 832–833
Market value, growth in, 458
Markup, 315
Marshall, Alfred, 77n., 224
on economics, 6
Marshall Plan, 707
Marx, Karl, 307n., 322, 576
Mason, Edward S., 823
Master Charge, 615
and sale of mink coats, 69
Meadows, D. H., 804
Means, Gardiner, 313
Means and ends, 12–14
Meany, George, 349
Measurement and deduction, 26
Measure of economic welfare (MEW), 478–479
Meat boycott (1973) and market price, 269–272
Medallions, New York taxicabs, factors affecting price, 407
Medicaid, 395
Medical services, market behavior and market structure, 234
Medicare, 395
Medium of exchange
money as, 598–599
need for, 611
stones vs. gold and paper money as, 611
various items, 611
Mellon Bank, 37
Merger
conglomerate, 295
"failing company" vs. "efficiency" defense of, 304
WREDD Brick Co., 304
Merit, absolute, of government expenditures, 451
Metropolitan Museum, purchase of Picasso painting, and investments in capital, 388
MEW. *See* Measure of Economic Welfare
Michigan State University, head coach's pay for not coaching, and

marginal productivity theory of distribution, 343
Microeconomic policy
defined, 430
and L-shaped relation, 763
overview of, 453–454
and public expenditure, 441–453
and rule making, 420–421
Microeconomics, 10
and circular flow, 44–46
vs. macroeconomics, 459
overview, 42–44
Middle classes, disenchantment with cities, 447
Mine safety standards, coal industry, and market behavior, 234
Minimum efficient scale, 263
Minimum prices, setting, 88–89
Minimum wages, 89
effects of, 106
Mink coats, and Master Charge, 69
Minority control of corporation, hypothesis of, 312–313
Mishan, Ed, 792
Mitchell, Wesley, 527
Mixed economy, 42
Mobile home sales, home construction, and interest rates, 549
Mobility of factors, 334–335
and earnings, 407
pay, education, and, 343
Mobil Oil Corp., monopoly power, 249
Modigliani, Franco, 566, 855
Monetarists
factors in debate with neo-Keynesians, 760
and quantity theory of money, 760–761
recommended macroeconomic policies, 754–758
significance of debate with neo-Keynesians, 758–760
view of cyclical fluctuations, 744
view of fiscal policy, 752–754
view of inflation, 747
view of influence of interest rates, 747–749
view of monetary policy, 750–752
view of stabilization policy, 743
Monetary expansion, trend of, 659

Monetary History of the United States, A, 1867–1960 (Friedman and Schwartz), 744
Monetary objectives, conflicting, 666
Monetary policy. *See also* Central bank(s); Federal Reserve System; Monetary systems; Money
contractionary, 652–653
in controlling interest rates, 652
in controlling national income, 652–653
discount rate, 626, 630, 661–663
effects of, 898–900
and exchange rates, 680
expansionary, 653
vs. fiscal, 755
instrumental variables, 652
monetarist view of, 750–752
and money supply, 647, 649, 657
moral suasion, 664
in national income model, 895
national income vs. interest rate in, 653–654
policy variables, 651–652
quantitative effectiveness of, 648
representation of, 897–898
reserve requirements, 660–661
and stabilization, 664
and Treasury–Federal Reserve Accord, 655, 657
variability, 657–659
Monetary systems
Bretton Woods, 713–714, 718–721
current, 721–725
experimentation period, 712–713
gold standard, 711–712
International Monetary Fund, 714–715
Money. *See also* Capital; Central bank(s); Commercial bank(s); Demand for money; Dollar(s); Exchange rate(s); Inflation; Interest rates; Investment; Monetary policy; Money supply; Quantity theory of money
banks in creating, 608
and bank strike in Ireland, 611
as cause of fluctuations in national income, 745–747
commercial banks in creating, 634
cost of, 157
defined, 598
deposit, 606–609, 618–625

Money *(Continued)*
economy, 590–592
vs. income, 49
limits on issue of currency by
central bank, 606–607
in market economy, 39
as medium of exchange, 598–599
metallic, 600–602
modern view of role, 640–641
in national income model, 890–895
near, 609–610
neutrality of, 592
paper, 602–606
price level changes, 592
purposes, 611
relative size of M_1, M_2, and M_3, 634
stock of, 613
as store of value, 599–600
and theocracy, 611
as unit of account, 600
various items as, 611
Money balance, and velocity of
circulation, 640
Money capital, 379
Money flow, 46
Money income
and budget line, 120
and poverty level, 407
vs. real income, 122
Money markets, central banks as
regulators of, 628
Money output vs. real output, 790
Money price, 121
Money rate of interest vs. real rate of
interest, 374–375
Money substitutes, 610
and Irish bank strike, 611
Money supply, 612. *See also* Demand
for money; Money; Quantity
theory of money
and bank failures, Great
Depression, 744
and central banks, 627–633
changes related to inflation and
unemployment, 658
and commercial banks, 750
factors affecting, 634
and GNP, 761
and inflation, 741
vs. interest rates, as instrumental
variables, 654–655
and monetary policy, 647, 649, 657

and national income, 646–647,
746–747
and reserve requirements, 666
and speculative profits on bonds,
650
and unemployment, 638
weapons and purposes, 666
Money values vs. real values, 475
Monopolia, movie theater prices, 249
Monopolist
revenue curves, 236–239
selling at single price, 236–241
supply curve, 240
Monopolistic competition. *See also*
Competition; Perfect
competition
controversy over, 258
defined, 253–254
importance of theory, 256–257
predictions, 256–258
theory of, 254–255
Monopolistically competitive
industry, 267–268
equilibrium of, 255
examples, 267–268
Monopolization of competitive
industry, 285
Monopolized market, profit
maximization in, 239–240
Monopoly. *See also* Oligopoly theory
and antitrust policy, 290–291
attempts in perfectly competitive
industries, 272–277
barriers to entry in, 241
vs. competition, 282–290
defined, 236
equilibrium of firm and industry in,
240–241
innovation under, 289
labor market elements, 400–401
vs. perfect competition, satisfaction
of nonmonetary aims in, 304
public policy toward, 290–298
public utility regulation, 298–302
raw materials, vs. union shop
contract, 366
Monopoly bank
balance sheet after credit expansion
and cash drain, 624
single new deposit in, 619–621
Monopoly firm, price and elasticity of
demand, 249

Monopoly power
bases of, 249
economics professor, 249
measures of, 242–243
nature and extent of, 241–242
profit as measure of, 304
Monopsonist(s)
employers' associations as
potential, 348
unions as potential, 348–349
Monopsonistic labor market
union in, 347–348
without union, 346–347
Monopsony, 345
Moody's, 383
Moral suasion, 664
Mortgage and interest rates, 537,
538
Mortgage control, 663
Mortgage loans, market behavior and
market structure, 234
Motion pictures, spur for, 207
Motivation of firm, 152, 316–319
Motorcycle, noise pollution, 429
Motor oil, synthetic, sales and price,
146
Movie theater prices, Monopolia vs.
Competitia, 249
Mrs. Weinberg's Kosher Chopped
Liver Co. and marginal vs. total
utility of liver, 129
Mueller, Paul, 204
Multibank system
deposit in, 621–622
multiple deposits in, 622–624
Multiple-regression analysis, 35
Multiplier
defined, 515
and economic stabilization
program, 524
factors affecting, 524
graphic representation, 517–519
interaction with accelerator,
544–545
intuitive statement on, 515, 517
numerical approach to, 516–517
size of, 519
Multiplier effects, location of, 564
Mundell, Robert A., 711
Municipal bonds, tax exempt, effect
on income distribution and
resource allocation, 455

Murphy, Aristotle, movie theaters and prices, 249
Murphy, Thomas, on bigness, 304
Muscovy Company, 151
Myrdal, Gunnar, 823, 825n.

Nader, Ralph, 305
Namath, Joe, 330
Nantucket Island, Russell Baker on building Holiday Inn on, 16
Narragansett Electric Co., hand delivery of bills after postal rate increase, 81
NASA, innovations and average total cost, 176
National Cash Register Co., 251
National debt, 581–586
    and income distribution, 587
    interest on, 467
    relative significance of, 584
    and secular stagnation, 575
    trends in, 583
National defense
    and growth, 793
    and tariff, 697
National Farmers Organization, 273
National Gallery of Art, purchase of da Vinci's *Genevra de Benci,* and utility theory, 129
National Health Service (Britain), and supply and demand theory, 106
National income. *See also* Gross national product (GNP); Income; Income distribution; National debt; Tax(es) and taxation
    and aggregate demand, 494
    alternative method of deriving basic predictions, 513–514
    and balanced budget, 559
    compensating shifts in injections and withdrawals, 512–513
    concept of, 459
    definitions and assumptions of theory, 483–486
    and disposable income, 532
    effect of taxes and government expenditures on, 553–554
    evaluation of measures, 479
    factors affecting, 524
    in Frugal economy, 462–464, 487–499
    in Governed economy, 464–466

gross vs. net, 464
by industry of origin, 60
vs. interest rate as policy variables, 653–654
and investment in plant and equipment, 540
and measure of housewife's value, 481
monetary policy in controlling, 652–653
money as cause of fluctuations in, 745–747
money in model of, 890–895
and money supply, 646–647, 746–747
money values vs. real values, 475
and movements along curves vs. shifts in curves, 506–508
and multiplier, 514–519
omissions from, 476–479
in Open economy, 466–468
output-expenditure approach to, 459–462
predictions of theory, 509–510
related measures of, 473–474
shift in injection schedule, 508–509
shift in withdrawal schedule, 509–512
in Spendthrift economy, 459–462, 486–487
and tariffs, 702–703
in theocracy, 611
total output vs. per capita output, 475–476
in U.S. economy, 468–473
National income accounting, 459
National income statistician, 458
National traditions and tariff, 697
National Urban League, on unemployment, 741
National Wildlife Federation, 427
Natural gas shortage, 106
Natural monopoly
    problems of implementing regulation theory, 300–302
    regulation theory, 299–300
Natural rate of unemployment, 769
Natural resources, 332
    and growth, 844–846
Natural scale, 859
Near money, 609–610
    and Irish bank strike, 611

Negative income tax, 396, 434–435
Negotiable order of withdrawal (NOW), 608–609, 612n.
Neo-Keynesians, 743
    factors in debate with monetarists, 760
    and quantity theory of money, 760–761
    recommended policies, 758
    significance of debate with monetarists, 758–760
    view of cyclical fluctuations, 744–747
    view of fiscal policy, 753–754
    view of inflation, 747
    view of influence of interest rates, 749–750
    view of monetary policy, 751, 752
    view of stabilization policy, 743
Nessen, Ron, on New York urban crisis, 456
Net excess reserves, 657n.
Net exports, 467, 468
Net interest, 470
Net investment, 463
Net national income, 464
Net national product (NNP), 464
    and GNP, output-expenditures approach to, 468
Net private benefit, 413
Net social benefit, 413
Neutrality of money, 592
New Deal
    and development of unions, 354
    farm policy, 100–101
New Economic Policy
    1960s, 571–573
    1971, 720
New Guinea, financing of copper mine, 828
New Industrial State, Galbraith's concept of, 306–311
New Jersey Development Council, and factor mobility, 343
Newspapers, local, monopoly in, 249
New York City, comments on crisis, 456
New York Stock Exchange, 380
    effect on dollar supply and demand of Canadian investors' purchase of shares on, 683

New York Times, 102, 270, 801
  headlines, relation to economic
    development, 828
  on interest rates, 665–666
  letter on inflation and gold
    standard, 741
  quote on gold prices, 727
Nile Delta and Aswan Dam, 207
Nixon, Richard, 720
Noise pollution, motorcycle, 429
Nonlaboratory sciences, testing
  theories in, 30
Nonlinear functions, graphing,
  863–864
Nonmarketed economic activities and
  national income, 477
Nonmarket goals, neglect of,
  419–420
Nonprice competition, 254
  oligopoly, 261–264
Nonprofit organization
  productive decisions, and
    economic theory of firm, 163
  vs. profit-maximizing firm,
    production costs, 191
Nontariff barriers to trade, 707
Nordhaus, William, 478, 479
Normal curve of error, 21
Normal goods, 76
Normal profits, 161
Normative statements
  on inflation, 28
  vs. positive statements, 17–19
Northica, standard of living if U.S.,
  Mexico, and Canada were
  combined into, 694
NOW account, as money, 611
Nuclear bomb, spur for, 207
Nuclear power
  peaceful, United Nations warning
    of hazards, 207
  spur for, 207
  Time on need for, 16

Oakland Athletics baseball team, pay
  of star player, 343
Obesity and poverty, 146
Oil, reduced production, and
  decreased demand for
  gas-guzzling cars, 68
Oil companies, pros and cons of
  vertical disintegration, 304

Oil drilling
  and externalities, 203
  offshore, private vs. social costs,
    207
  in Texas, and hypothesis of
    diminishing returns, 176
Oilman, bidding at wine auction, 146
Oil prices
  and IMF loans, 727
  King Khalid on increasing
    production to lower prices, 16
  and monetary systems, 723–724
  and OPEC, 282
  OPEC disagreement about rise in,
    268
Okun, Arthur, 14
Old-Age and Survivors Insurance
  Program, 563
Old Age Assistance (OAA), 395
Old-age pensions, U.S. policy on, 16
Oligopolistic behavior, 260–262
  and model changes in automobile
    industry, 268
Oligopoly, 252
Oligopoly theory, 258–259
  and assuming how firms react,
    259–260
  and barriers to entry, 262–265
  and cigarettes, 279
  generalizing from hypotheses
    about observed behavior,
    260–262
  and mixtures of market structures,
    280–281
  need for, 279–281
  and price inflexibility, 265–266
  and steam-turbine generators,
    279–280
OPEC. *See* Organization of
  Petroleum Exporting Countries
Open economy, 466–468
Open Market Account, 655
Open Market Committee, Fed, 629,
  655
  policy formulation by, 656
Open market operations, 630–633
Open shop, 349–350
Opportunity cost, 6–7. *See also*
  Cost(s)
  defined, 156
  factors as, 157
  and gains from trade, 689–691
  of government activity, 577–578

of green revolution, 825
of growth, 795–796
and investment, 164
of loan to friend, 163
measurement by firm, 156–160
of money balances, 636
of politician being fined and
  imprisoned, 163
and productive decisions of
  nonprofit organizations, 163
of stopping dam that would destroy
  fish, 163
of towing icebergs to Saudi Arabia,
  163
Optimal population, 802–803
Organization of firm, 316
Organization of Petroleum Exporting
  Countries (OPEC), 280, 281
  disagreement about oil price rise,
    268
  and economic development, 814
  loans to underdeveloped nations to
    pay for oil imports, 828
  and monetary systems, 723–724
  oil price increase, and need for IMF
    loans, 727
  and price of oil, 282; principle of
    substitution, 191
  reduced oil production, and
    decreased demand for
    gas-guzzling cars, 68
  Venezuela's President Perez on
    prices, 829
Outboard motors, monopoly in, 249
Output, 153, 790
  with capital fixed and labor
    variable, 168
  cost, and isoquant and isocost
    slope, 191
  determining least-cost method of,
    188
  and factor prices, 191
  physical, index numbers of,
    871–872
  and price discrimination, 245–246
  and price fluctuations, 90
  total vs. per capita, 475–476
Output-expenditure approach
  in Frugal economy, 463–464
  to GNP and NNP, 468
  income components, 466–467
  in Spendthrift economy, 459–462
Output per capita, 790

Output per man-hour, 790
Overseas Development Council,
    index of physical quality of life,
    808
Over-the-counter markets, 380
Ownership
    of corporation, hypothesis of
        separation from control,
        313–314
    patterns, selected countries, 832
    of resources, and economic system,
        831–832
    in Soviet Union, 836–837

Paarlberg, Don, on agricultural
    production and prices, 68
Paige, Satchel, 360
Pakistan, agricultural development
    and unemployment, 825
Palmer, Arnold, 331
Paper money
    evolution of, 602–603
    fiat, 604–606
    fractionally backed, 603–604
    as medium of exchange, 611
Parabola, 862
Paradox of thrift, 510–512, 551
Paradox of value, 108, 115–116
Pareto, Vilfredo, 119n.
    studies of income inequality, 323
Pareto-optimal, 286n.
Paris, rent control in, 86–87
Partial equilibrium analysis, 414
Partial equilibrium vs. general
    equilibrium, 415
Partnership, 149–150
Patent, and incentive to innovate, 290
Patent monopoly, decline and fall of,
    277–278
Payment(s)
    in balance-of-payments account,
        670
    deferred, money as standard of, 600
    single future, value of, 370–371
    value of infinite stream of, 371
Peak, in business fluctuation, 544
Pedicabs and wages, Dacca, 191
Penicillin, spur for, 207
Penn Central Railroad, 308
Pepsi-Cola Co., monopoly power,
    249
Per capita GNP, 476
    and population growth, 813

Per capita output vs. total output,
    475–476
Perez, Venezuelan president, on
    OPEC prices, 829
Perfect competition. *See also*
    Competition; Monopolistic
    competition
    as alternative to monopoly,
        286–287
    assumptions of, 213–215
    equilibrium output of firm in,
        217–218
    vs. monopoly, satisfaction of
        nonmonetary aims in, 304
Perfectly competitive firm
    demand and revenue curves for,
        216–217
    equilibrium output of, 217–218
    short-run profitability, 220–221
    supply curve, 218–219
Perfectly competitive industry
    attempts to monopolize, 272–277
    characteristics, 234
    ease of exit and entry, 234
    and grain prices, 235
    long-run response to change in
        demand, 225–227
    supply curve, 219–220
    and technology, 231
Perfectly competitive market
    structure, sectors of economy,
        234
Perfectly inelastic demand curves,
    138–139
Permanent-income hypothesis (PIH),
    566, 756
    assumptions, 886–887
    implications, 887–889
    variables, 885–886
Perpetuity, 382–383
    vs. annuity, 388
Personal consumption, 466
Personal consumption expenditures,
    53
Personal costs of growth, 793–795
Personal income, 473–474. *See also*
    Income; National income
Personal income tax
    incidence, 440–443
    progressivity, 432–433
    Richville vs. Uniontown, 455–456
Peru, anchovy harvest, and grain
    prices, 235

Petulama, California, chicken and egg
    production, 282
Phelps, Edmund, 767
Phelps-Brown, Professor, 789
Phelps-Friedman theory, 767–771
    implications of, 771–775
    and natural rate of unemployment,
        785
Phillips, A. W., 765n.
Phillips curve
    and demand-pull inflation,
        765–767
    and inflation-unemployment
        tradeoff, 785
    Phelps-Friedman theory of,
        767–769
Physical quality of life, Overseas
    Development Council index of,
        808
Picasso painting
    and investment in capital, 388
    as money, 611
Picket line, 350
Pipeline, trans-Canada, effect on
    foreign exchange markets, 683
Pittsburgh, air pollution alert, 207
Planning, 167
    and economic development,
        818–819
    scope and role, Yugoslavia, 849
    Soviet, 840–842
Planning decisions, 167
Plant
    beer industry, efficient size, 268
    and equipment, investment in,
        537–540
Point elasticity of demand, 868
Policy
    pervasiveness of decisions, 12
    proposing and evaluation, 13–14
Policy variables
    monetary policy, 651–652
    national income vs. interest rate as,
        653–654
Polio vaccine, spur for, 207
Political motivation vs. compassion,
    as basis for contributed capital,
        823
Political objectives, 14–15
Political realism and economic
    theory, 566–567
Politician, fined and imprisoned,
    opportunity cost of, 163

Politics and AFL-CIO, 349
Pollution
  of air, 202
  Baltic crisis, 207
  cancels Epiphany Dive for Cross in
    Greek harbor, 207
  control of, 424–427
  influence of alleged facts on control
    policy, 429
  Pittsburgh alert, 207
  and progress, 3–4
  of water, 200–202
Poor. *See also* Poverty
  defined, 391–392
  reasons for being, 392–393
  rental allowance for, 407
  and rich, income distribution
    between, 389–391
Population
  and food supply, China, 828–829
  and income among groups of
    countries, 811
  optimal, 802–803
  size, and quantity demanded, 54
  and total supply of labor, 329
Population growth and economic
  development, 813–814, 820
Portman, John, on New York urban
  crisis, 456
Positive statements
  about inflation, 28
  vs. normative statements, 17–19
Posner, Richard, 302
Postal rates and hand delivery of bills,
  81
Postal service, cost of improving, 16
Post Office production and average
  total cost, 176
Potential GNP, 483–484
Pound, speculation against, 718
Poverty
  Arkansas vs. Ghana, 829
  black, 393–394
  and labor's urge to organize,
    351–352
  and movement of labor, 403
  and obesity, 146
  problem of, 389–391
  vs. scarcity, 16
  scope and adequacy of programs,
    396–397
  and unemployment, 407
  in U.S. vs. Bangladesh, 407

vicious circle of, 821
  waging war on, 394–396
  and wealth, 3
Poverty (Hunter), 352
Poverty gap, 390
Poverty level, 389
  omissions in establishing, 407
  percentage below, 390
Prebisch, Raúl, 824, 825n.
Precautionary balances, 641–642
Precautionary motive, demand for
  money, 641–642
Prediction, 25
  vs. law and hypothesis, 66
  modified quantity theory, 639
Preference, and quantity demanded,
  54
Preferred stock, 379
Present value
  of future income, 370–371
  future profits, interest rates, and,
    388
  and interest rates, 644
Prestige and growth, 793
Price(s). *See also* Factor price
  bonds, and interest rates, 643, 644
  and budget line, 121
  color TV, and supply and demand,
    69
  common stock, 383–385
  and consumer boycott, 282
  and demand for grain, 235
  determination by demand and
    supply, 63–65
  and earnings, 382–387
  and elasticity of demand,
    monopoly firm, 249; railroad
    passenger travel, 81
  and exchange rates, 677–678
  of exports, and equilibrium
    exchange rate, 679
  flexibility, oligopoly, 261
  and full employment, L-shaped
    relation, 763–765
  gold vs. labor, and principal of
    substitution, 191
  and grape boycott, 235
  of haircuts, 275–277
  household reaction to change in,
    127–128
  and income, agriculture, 91–95
  and income effect, 878–879
  index numbers of, 869–871

just, 117, 119
  and kinked demand theory, 268
  maximum, 83–89
  and milk co-op, 273–275
  and monopolization, 288
  and monopoly vs. competition,
    movie theaters, 249
  and output, 92, 520
  and production, agriculture, 68;
    Great Depression, 94
  and quantity demanded, 55–56,
    72–76, 137–139, 141, 283–285
  and quantity supplied, 60–62
  and real income, 872–873
  of rental housing, and demand for
    owner-occupied housing, 146
  rise vs. tax on energy use, 455
  and sales, synthetic motor oil, 146
  setting of, 320
  seven centuries of, 593, 594
  single, monopolist selling at,
    236–241
  on stock market, 381–382
  vs. taste and income, and no-frill
    houses, 145
  tradeoff with quality, variety, and
    advertising, consumer products,
    267
  and unemployment, 486
Price ceiling, 83
Price-consumption line, 127, 128
Price controls
  setting maximum prices, 83–88
  setting minimum prices, 88–89
Price discrimination, 243–244
  consequences of, 246–247
  normative aspects, 246
  positive effects, 245–246
  systematic and unsystematic,
    246–248
  and transportation and electricity
    rates, 249
  when it is possible, 244–245
  why it pays, 244
Price-earnings ratio (P/E), 384
Price elasticity, 72–76
Price elasticity of demand, 131–132
  and income elasticity, 81, 146
Price expectations and demand for
  durable goods, 531
Price fixing vs. wage fixing, and
  Clayton Act, 366
Price floor, 88

Price index, consumables, 593, 594
Price inflexibility and oligopoly, 265–266
Priceless vs. worthless, 129
Price level
  changes in, 592
  economic growth, employment, and, 741
  and equilibrium exchange rates, 679–680
  mechanism, gold standard, 711–712
  and money supply. *See* Quantity theory of money
Price parity, 93
Price-push inflation, 737
  and stagflation, 780
  and unemployment, 775–776
  and wage-price controls, 778
Price supports, agriculture, 98, 99
Price system
  as coordinating mechanism, 44
  and coordination of markets, 411–412
  and general equilibrium, 414–417
  as social control mechanism, 42
Price-taking firm, 213
  revenue curves for, 217
  supply curve for, 219
Price theory, applications of, 282
Pricing
  full-cost, 315–316
  regulatory commission strategy, 300
  and Soviet planning process, 841–842
Primitive society, stones as medium of exchange in, 611
Principal of substitution, 180
  discussion questions, 191
Principle of substitution, 180
  and economy, 179
  and isoquants, 189–190
Principles of Economics (Marshall), 77n., 224
Printing industry, automation, progress and problems, 207
Private cost vs. social cost, 200
  in allocative efficiency, 287
  Aswan Dam, 207
Private enterprise, Soviet, 837
Private expenditure, crowding-out effect, 553

Private goods, as complement to public goods, 429
Private sector, 42
Private valuations vs. social valuations, 417
Producers' cooperative, 273–277
Product differentiation, 254
Product growth and innovation, 207
Production, 6
  and consumption, 199
  and division of labor, 39
  goods and services, 9
  organization in Soviet Union, 837–839
  and price, agriculture, 68; Great Depression, 94
  and profit, 164
  value added through stages of, 461
  and zero growth rate, 808
Production costs, profit-maximizing firm vs. nonprofit organization, 191
Production factors. *See* Factor(s) of production
Production function and short, long, and very long run, 167–168
Production possibilities, 7–9
Production-possibility boundary, 8
  and allocative vs. *X*-inefficiency, 817
  and economic growth, 11
  and unemployment, 10
Production-possibility curve, 8
Productive acts not in GNP, 480–481
Productive capacity, growth of, 11
Productivity, 193–194. 790
  of capital, 367–372
  diminishing, 168–169
  and economic growth, 808
  and 4-day week, 207
  increasing, 194–198
  labor, at Anheuser Busch, 268
  past and future growth, 198–199
  and progress, 191–193
Product market, 41
Profit(s), 462
  Allied Chemical Corp. on, 320
  of commercial banks, 634
  corporate, 470
  and cost to firm, 155–162
  and depreciation, 164
  and ease of entry into industry, 235
  economic, 160–161

  and entry of capital in competitive industry, 222
  future, and present value, 388
  and invention, 197
  and investment in plant and equipment, 539
  as measure of monopoly power, 243
  and production and investment, 164
  reinvested, as investment funds source, 380
  and resource allocation, 162
  as responsibility of business, 320
  speculative, on bonds, and money supply, 650
  undistributed, 150
Profitability and economic discrimination, 364–365
Profit maximization
  as firm's motivation, 152
  long-run, 317–319
  in monopolized market, 239–240
Profit-maximizing firm
  behavioral rules for, 212
  vs. nonprofit organization, production costs, 191
Profit-maximizing price, monopoly firm, 249
Program Planning and Budgeting Systems (PPBS), 451
Progress
  desirability of, 199
  and pollution, 3–4
  and productivity, 192–193
Progress and Poverty (George), 340
Progressive tax, 432
Progressivity
  concept of, 431–432
  of corporate income tax, 433–434
  of government policies on taxation, 435–436
  of personal income tax, 432–433
  of tax system, 434
Property tax
  on central city rental property, 455
  payment of, 436–437
  regressivity of, 432
Proportional tax, 431–432
Proprietors, income of, 470
Proprietorship, single, 149
Protectionism and tariff, 696–698

Proxmire, William, report on
  Culpeper switch, 666
Proxy, 312
Proxy fight, 313
Public employees, right to strike, 366
Public expenditure, as tool of
  microeconomic policy, 441–453
Public finance and taxation, 430–441
Public goods, as complement to
  private goods, 429
Public interest and New Industrial
  State, 310–311
Public Interest Research Group in
  Michigan (PIRGIM), study of
  jobs and public expenditure, 587
Public officials and control of market,
  306–307
Public sector, 42
Public utility
  competitive behavior and market
    structure, 234
  regulation, 298–302; vs.
    competitive market, 304
Publishing, textbook, as
  monopolistically competitive
  industry, 268
Pullman Co., 308
Pump priming, 557, 559
  Great Depression, 570
Purchases
  of goods and services, examples,
    455
  on open market, 631–632
Purchasing power
  and household satisfaction, 873–874
  and inflation, 10–11
Pure profit, tax on, 439–440
Pure return on capital, 368
Pure return on invested capital and
  service charge on unpaid balance
  in store, 388
Purex Corp., 103
Pyramids, and mobility, 407

Qualified joint profit maximization,
  oligopoly, 260–261
Quality, tradeoff with price, variety,
  and advertising, consumer
  products, 267
Quantity demanded
  and average income, 57
  and demand, 58–59; effect of
    various factors on, 69

determinants of, 54–56
and household income, 54–55,
  139–141
nature of, 53–54
and price, 55–56, 137–139
and price change, 72–76
and price of other commodities,
  142
Quantity equation of exchange, 760
  and taste, 54, 143–144
Quantity index, calculation of, 872
Quantity produced and price, effect of
  cost on, 283–285
Quantity sold and revenue, 237
Quantity supplied
  and commodity price, 60–62
  determinants of, 59–61
Quantity theory of money, 601–602
  assumptions of, 637
  classical vs. modern, 637n.
  defined, 635–636
  formal statement of, 639
  and full employment, 637–638
  modified, 638–640
  and monetarists vs.
    neo-Keynesians, 760
  and transactions demand, 636–637
  and unemployment, 638

Radar, spur for, 207
Railroads
  Canada, weekday vs. weekend
    rates, and price discrimination,
    249
  price and elasticity of demand for
    passenger travel, 81
Rainfall and death rate, 810
Ralston Purina Co., 103
Random sample, 31
Rate base, in natural monopoly
  regulation, 300–301
Rate of return, 300
Rate of return on capital, 368
  and capital stock, 808
  at zero growth rate, 808
Rationing in allocating scarce
  commodity, 84–85
Ratio scale, 859–861
RCA Corp., 384
Real capital, 379
Real estate, central city property tax
  on rental property, 455
Real flow, 46

Real gross national product
  annual changes in, 525–526
  effect of various events on, 481
Real gross private domestic
  investment, 535
Real gross private investment and
  GNP, 534
Real income
  vs. money income, 122
  and price, 872–873
Real national income
  and inflation rate, L-shaped
    relation, 764
  Japan, 805
Real output vs. money output, 790
Real rate of interest vs. money rate,
  374–375
Real values vs. money values, 475
Receipts
  and demand, 93
  Great Depression, 94
Recession, in business fluctuation,
  544
Reciprocal absolute advantage,
  686–688
Reciprocal trade agreements, 706
Regan, Ronald, on
  inflation–unemployment
  tradeoff, 785
Regression analysis, 33
Regression equation, 33
Regressive tax, 432
Regulation W, 663
Regulation X, 663
Relative prices and budget line,
  121–122
Religious institutions and growth,
  803
Rembrandt, *Juno,* Armand
  Hammer's purchase as marginal
  vs. total utility, 129
Rent, 462
  controlled vs. free-market, 88
  economic, 224; and transfer
    earnings, 338–339
Rental allowances for poor,
  arguments on, 407
Rental income, 470
Rent controls, 13
  in Paris, 86–87
Republic Steel Co., 204–205
Republican party, freedom of speech
  and equal network time, 16

Required reserve, 618
Required reserve ratio, 629–630, 659
   and demand deposits, 634
Resale, and price discrimination, 245
Resale-price maintenance, 88
Reserve, commercial banks, 617–618
Reserve banks, Fed, 628–629
Reserve Mining Co., 199, 200–201, 204
Reserve ratio, 618
   and balance sheet, loaned-up banking system, 630
   changes, 660–661
Reserve requirements, 660–661
   and money supply, 666
   and possibility of panicky runs on banks, 634
   Wall Street Journal questions need for, 634
Residential construction, investment in, 536–537
Resource(s)
   and allocative efficiency, 287
   and change in demand, 43
   inefficient use, and economic development, 816–818
   limitations, and economic development, 814–816
   ownership, and economic system, 831–832
   utilization, 10
Resource allocation, 9
   and advertising in economic analysis, 268
   and inflation, 593–594
   and profits, 162
   and tax-exempt municipal bonds, 455
   and tax structure, 436–441
Restaurant operation, as monopolistically competitive industry, 268
Retail outlets, optimal number, 267
Retail stores, service charge on unpaid balance, and pure return on invested capital, 388
Return on capital, 368–371
   and interest, 372–377
Return to capital, 368
Revaluation of exchange rate, 681
Revenue
   ability to collect, 418–419
   and quantity sold, 237

Revenue Act (1932), 570
Revenue curve
   monopolist, 236–239
   for perfectly competitive firm, 216–217
Revenue sharing, 443
   vs. categorical grants-in-aid, 456
Reynolds, Milton, and ball point pen, 277–278
Reynolds International Pen Co., 277–278
Ricardo, David, 322, 685, 688
   and concept of economic rent, 338
Rich and poor, income distribution between, 389–391
Richville vs. Uniontown, local personal income tax, 455–456
Right-to-work laws, 355
Rising-cost industry, 230
Rising supply price, 230
Risk
   and common stock prices, 384
   and interest rates, 376–377
   investment opportunities, interest rates, and, 388
Riskless bond, 382–383
Risk premium, 368
Risk taking, imputed cost, 160
Risky bond, 383
Robinson, Joan, 792
Rockefeller, John D., 246
Rod and Gun Club of Wisconsin and Audubon Society suit to halt highway construction, 208
Roman Catholic Church relaxation of ban on eating meat on Friday, and demand for fish, 69
Roosevelt, Franklin, 94, 511–512, 570
   and antitrust, 296
   and balanced budget, 586–587
Roosevelt, Theodore, and trustbusting, 296
Roper poll, forecast of 1948 election results, 37
Rubber, synthetic, spur for, 207
Rule making and microeconomic policy, 420–421
Rule of capture, in oil fields, 203
Rule of reason, 294
Rural crisis, 4

Safire, William
   on coffee boycott, 282
   on natural gas shortage, 106

Sakharov, A. K., 838
Salaries
   baseball player, 343
   Egalitarian U vs. Elitist Tech, 407
   Michigan State University's head coach, for not coaching, 343
   professors vs. teaching assistants, and principle of substitution, 191
   superstars, economics of, 330–331
Sales
   on open market, 632–633
   and price, synthetic motor oil, 146
Sales maximization, hypothesis of, 317
Sales taxes, regressivity of, 432
Sample, in statistical testing, 31–32
Sampling and forecasts of 1936 and 1948 election returns, 37
Sam's Used Car Lot, and merger, 304
Samuelson, Paul, 14, 743
Sand and gravel, market behavior and market structure, 234
Satisficing, hypothesis of, 316–317
Saudi Arabia
   King Khalid on increasing oil production to lower prices, 16
   opportunity cost of towing icebergs to, 163
Saving
   compulsory, and government planning, 819
   domestic, and economic development, 821
   in Frugal economy, 463, 491–492
   and inflation, 10–11
   and investment at equilibrium, 498–499; in Frugal vs. Governed economy, 505
   as withdrawal from circular flow, 500
Saving-investment approach in Frugal economy, 497–499
Savings and loan associations (S&Ls), competition for deposits, 616
Saving schedule
   Frugal economy, 492
   and national income, 510
Scabs, 350
Scale advantages, oligopoly, 262–263
Scarcity
   and marginal utility, 113
   in market economy, 39–40
   of resources, 6

Scatter diagram, 32, 857–859
Schedules, movements along vs.
    shifts of, and national income,
    524
Schultz, Henry, 131
Schultze, Charles, 737n.
Schumpeter, Joseph, 527, 744n.
    on process of creative destruction,
    290
Schwartz, Anna, 744
Science
    laboratory vs. nonlaboratory, 37
    natural vs. social, 20
Scientific inquiry, 19–20
Scitovsky, Tibor, 826
Scott, M., 826
Search unemployment, 733–734
SEC. *See* Securities and Exchange
    Commission
Secular boom, 577
Secular stagnation, 575–577
Securities and Exchange Commission
    (SEC), 386
    proposal on brokerage
        commissions, 81
Securities market, 380–382
Selective credit controls, 662–664
Seller's preference in allocating scarce
    commodity, 84
Semi-log graph, 861n.
Service charge on unpaid balance and
    pure return on invested capital,
    388
Services, 6
    curtailment in natural monopoly
        regulation, 301–302
    production, 9
Shaw, George Bernard, 15
Sherman Antitrust Act (1890), 292,
    293
Shop steward, 351
Short run
    duration of, 176
    in decision making, 166–167
Short-run consumption function,
    490–491
Short-run cost curves, 173–174
    family of, 175
Short-run cost vs. long-run cost,
    182–183
Short-run decisions, and guaranteed
    annual-employment contract,
    176

Short-run equilibrium
    firm and industry, 217–221
    firm in monopolistic competition,
        254
Short-run equilibrium price, 220
Short-run profitability, perfectly
    competitive firm, 220–221
Short-run supply curves
    of one firm, 218–219
    of one industry, 219–220
Short-term capital, in capital account,
    624
Short-term fluctuations
    and adustable peg system, 715–716
    prices and incomes, agriculture, 91
Silent Spring (Carson), 204
Silk, Leonard, 14
    on inhibitions to Carter efforts to
        stimulate economy, 785
Simon, Herbert, 316
Simpson, O. J., 330
Single proprietorship, 149
Single-tax movement, 340–341
Size, of government, 452–453
Size distribution of income, 323–325
    after tax, factors affecting, 342–343
Skeeter, Inc., future profits, interest
    rates, and present value, 388
Slope of curve, 508
Small Business Administration, 380
Small firms, sectors of economy with
    many, 251
Smiling Sam, and repair of used car
    that breaks down, 164
Smith, Adam, 42, 115, 283, 322, 685
    and connection between national
        wealth and foreign trade, 694
Smith (A. O.) Co., 416
Smithsonian agreements, 720–721
Smoking and heart attack, and
    marginal vs. total utility, 129
Snail darter, opportunity cost of
    stopping dam construction to
    preserve, 163
Snake, 721
Social control mechanism, 42
Social cost, 199–200
    Aswan Dam, 207
    of growth, 793–795
    vs. private cost, 200; in allocative
        efficiency, 287
Social dividend financed from new
    money, effect on economy, 650

Social institutions and growth, 803
Social insurance
    as built-in stabilizer, 563
    in war on proverty, 395
Socialist party, freedom of speech and
    equal network time, 16
Social obligations and market failure,
    419–420
Social-overhead capital and economic
    development, 815
Social security, as built-in stabilizer,
    563
Social Security Act (1935), 395
Social Security Administration
    measure of housewife's value, 481
Social valuations vs. private
    valuations, 417
Solow, Robert, 804
Solzhenitsyn, Aleksandr, 846
Southern California Edison Co., 199
Soviet Union
    chances of achieving various
        results, 851
    contributed capital, 822
    distibution of goods and household
        incentives, 839–840
    grain purchases, and price rise, 235
    organization of production,
        837–839
    ownership in, 836–837
    planning in, 840–841
    shortcomings of economic
        experience, 845–846
    as socialistic economy, 851
    source and costs of achievements,
        846
    vs. U.S., comparative
        performance, 842–846
    use of capital in heavy industry, 851
Soybeans, market behavior and
    market structure, 234
Special Drawing Rights (SDRs), 716,
    724
Specialists, number in large vs. small
    cities, 49
Specialization
    China, 823
    gains, and opportunity costs, 690
    gains with absolute vs. comparative
        advantage, 687
    of labor, 38
    and surplus in market economy,
        38–39

Specific tax, 436
Speculation
  against dollar, 718–719
  on foreign exchange market, and
    exchange rates, 683–684
  against pound, 718
Speculative balances, 642
Speculative crises and adjustable peg
  system, 717–718
Speculative motive, demand for
  money, 642–643
Speculative swings, 385–386
Spending increase vs. income
  decrease, 129
Spendthrift economy, 459–462
  factor-payments approach in, 462
  national income in, 486–487
  output-expenditures approach in,
    459–462
Spillout, GM strike, 416
Stabilization
  and monetary policy, 664
  and support plans, agriculture,
    97–100
Stabilization policy, monetarist and
  neo-Keynesian views, 743
Stafford, Frank, 362
Stagflation, 574, 772
  evaluation of, 782–784
  explanations of, 780–783
  and unemployment, 785
Stalin, Joseph, 836, 840
Standard of deferred payments,
  money as, 600
Standard Oil Co. case, 294
Statics, comparative, 66
Statistical Abstracts of the United States,
  207
Statistical analysis, 29
Statistical testing, 34–35
Steam-turbine generators, and
  oligopoly theory, 279–280
Stigler, George, 88, 302, 421
Stock and stockholders, 379
Stock market
  in forecasting economy, 37
  as investment funds source,
    380–381
  as investment marketplace vs.
    gambling casino, 386–387
  prices on, 381–382
  speculative swings, 385–386
Stock variables, 24

Stone, Richard, 131
Stones as medium of exchange, 611
Store of value
  money as, 599–600
  need for, 611
  various items, 611
Strike, 350
  GM (1970), 415–417
  Irish banks, and money, 611
  public employees' right to, 366
  at Southeastern Connecticut
    shipyard, effects of, 524
  worker days lost by, 355
Strikebreaker, 350
Structural rigidity inflation, 737
Structural unemployment, 733
Structure of interest rates, 377
Students, standby air fares as price
  discrimination, 249
Subsidy
  of higher education, 444–445
  of particular industry or region,
    568
  for various community needs, 429
Substitutability and
  complementarity, 141
Substitute, commodity, 55
Substitution
  of factors, 327
  principle of, 179–180
Sunk costs, 159
Superstars, economics of salaries of,
  330–331
Supply
  change in, 44
  and demand, 63–67
  of effort, 329–332
  elasticity of, 80
  of factors. *See* Factor supply
  of money. *See* Money supply
  theory of, 59
  union restriction to increase wages,
    356–358
Supply curve, 61–62
  for dollars, 678
  effect of new entrants on, 222
  elasticity, 80, 867
  monopolist, 240
  shifts, 62–63
Supply schedule, 61–62
  alternative, 63
Supreme Court and antitrust,
  294–295

Surplus
  agricultural, 96
  balance-of-payments, 674
  budget, 513, 552, 554–555
  consumers', and price
    discrimination, 244
  and specialization in market
    economy, 38–39
Survey of Current Business, 388
Sweating of coins, 601
Sweden vs. Venezuela, population
  growth, 820
Sweezy, Paul, 265
Switzerland, auto industry and
  automated techniques, 191

Tacit collusion, 243
Taft-Hartley Act (1948), 350, 355
Taft, William Howard, 727
Takeover bid, 318
Tape recorders, demand curve for, 69
Tariff
  defined, 695–696
  duties, by commodity classes, 709
  and free trade, 696
  and import restrictions, 708–709
  vs. import quota, 709
  presidential authorization to
    negotiate with foreign countries
    on, 709
  prohibitive, effects on auto
    industry, 708
  and protectionism, 696–698
  selected commodity groups, 699
  and trade, 698–704; international
    agreements on, 705–707
  U.S., 704–705; trade war with
    France, 709
Taste
  and equilibrium exchange rate, 679
  vs. price and income, no-frill
    houses and, 145
  and quantity demanded, 54,
    142–144
Tax(es) and taxation. *See also*
    National income; Tariff
  and aggregate demand function,
    532
  as built-in stabilizers, 562, 563
  cases for and against, 455
  double, of corporate income, 151
  and government spending,
    552–557

Tax(es) and taxation *(Continued)*
  increase, 1968, 572
  indirect business, 470
  land, and urban land values, 341
  lump-sum, 439
  marginal, 432
  and national income, 553–554
  vs. price rise, on energy use, 455
  and public finance, 430–441
  rebate, and deflationary gap, 568
  on tobacco and alcohol, 455
  welfare benefits, supply of effort,
    and, 331–332
  as withdrawal from circular flow,
    500–501
Tax cut, 571–572
  and national income, 559
Taxicabs, New York, medallion
    prices for, 407
Tax incidence, 436
Taxing authority, single, case for, 455
Tax policy and income distribution,
    431–436
Tax rates
  vs. government expenditures in
    discretionary fiscal policy,
    564–565
  and national income, 510
Tax Reduction Act (1975), 574
Tax revenues, cities, 444–445
Tax structure
  allocative effect, 441
  and resource allocation, 436–441
Tax system progressivity, 434
Technical change, embodied vs.
    disembodied, 800–801
Technological efficiency vs.
    economic efficiency, 154, 155
Technology
  and perfectly competitive industry,
    231
  and quantity supplied, 60
Technology gap and economic
    development, 817–818
Teledyne, Inc., 384
Television
  broadcasting, market behavior and
    market structure, 234
  color, effect of supply and demand
    on price, 69; spur for, 207
  programs, tradeoff of price,
    quality, variety, and advertising,
    267

Tenants, and payment of property
    tax, 436–437
Tender offer, 318
Tenneco Oil Co., 103
Tennessee Valley Authority, as threat
    to environment, 207
Terms of trade, 691
Theocracy and money, 611
Theory
  contradictory observation in
    disproving, 37
  deduction and measurement, 26
  definition and testing of, 22–25
  testing techniques, 29–30
Theory of the Leisure Class, The
    (Veblen), 138
Third-party effects, 202–203
Thrift, paradox of, 510–512
Time, and labor mobility, 335
Time
  on need for nuclear power, 16
  on OPEC price war, 282
Time deposits, 608–609
Time lags in discretionary fiscal
    policy, 565
Time series, 23
Time-series data, 858
Time-series graph, 859
Tito, Marshal (Josip Broz), 846
Tobacco, "nearly perfect" tax on, 455
Tobacco Institute on smoking and
    health, 282
Tobin, James, 14, 478, 479, 743
Tokyo Round, 707
Toronto taxicab medallion, vs. New
    York, 407
Total cost, 171
Total cost curve, 174
Total expenditures
  and elasticity of demand, 74–76
  and 45° line, 505
Total income and 45° line, 505
Total output
  and aggregate desired expenditure
    in Frugal vs. Governed
    economy, 505
  and national income, 494
  vs. per capita output, 475–476
Total product, 168
Total product curve, 169
Total revenue, 216
  and elasticity of demand, 74–76;
    and marginal revenue, 237–239

Total supply of factors, 329–333
Total utility, 110
  vs. marginal utility, choices
    involving, 129
Total utility curve, 112
Total utility schedule, 111
Trade
  effect of labor cost on, 694
  gains, and comparative advantage,
    688–689
  interpersonal, interregional, and
    international, 685–686
  percentages with U.S., 706
  and specialization, 38
  and tariffs, 698–704; international
    agreements on, 705–707
  wholesale and retail, competitive
    behavior and market structure,
    234
Trade Agreements Act (1934), 706
Trade unions. *See* Unions
Trade war, France vs. U.S., 709
Trailways Bus Co., "opportunity-
    fare" tickets to Detroit
    unemployed, and factor
    mobility, 343
Transactions, in balance-of-payments
    account, 670
Transactions balances, 636–637
Transactions demand for money,
    641
  and quantity theory, 636–637
Transfer earnings
  and economic rent, 338–339
  pay for factor services as, 343
Transfer payments, 467
  examples, 455
  federal, to individuals, 442–443
  in Governed economy, 465–466
Transportation, competitive behavior
    and market structure, 234
Treasury bill, 552
Treasury notes, reasons for high
    yield, 587
Treaty of Rome, 707
Trough, in business fluctuation, 543
Truck vs. automobile, depreciation
    method, 163
Truman, Harry S., 727
Trustbusting, 296
Tuition
  law students vs. history students,
    price discrimination, 249

out-of-state students, price
discrimination, 249
Turner, Donald F., 296
Turning points and cumulative
movements in business
fluctuations, 544–546
Turnover, labor, 485
Turnover tax, Soviet, 842

UFOs, question as to existence of, 37
Ultra-Keynesians, 746n.
Unbalanced growth, 804
Unbalanced growth policy, 823
Uncertainty and common stock
prices, 384
Uncontrolled experiments, 31
Uncoordinated markets vs.
unplanned markets, 411–412
Underdeveloped countries
barriers to economic development,
812–818
development patterns, 823–827
effect of coffee prices on economy
of, 829
foreign aid priorities, 828
fostering economic development
in, 818–823
and OPEC oil prices, 829
uneven pattern of development,
809–812
vs. U.S., poverty in, 407
Underdevelopment
consequences of, 810–811
meaning and measure of, 812
Underemployment disequilibrium,
745
Underemployment equilibrium, 745
Undistributed profits, 150, 463
Unemployment. *See also*
Employment; Full employment;
Labor; Unions
and agricultural development, 825
as concern of policy makers,
731–732
control tools, 735
and cost-push inflation, 775–776
deficient-demand, 733
and demand-pull inflation,
763–767
experience of, 735–736
and flexible exchange rates, 727
frictional, 485, 732
Great Depression, 10, 570

and industrial capacity, Carter on,
16, 524
and inflation, 4, 772–775; Soviet,
844–845
and job security, 358–359
measured and unmeasured,
734–735
and modified quantity theory, 639
and monetary policy, 657–659
and money supply, 638
and movement of labor, 403
move to full employment in WWII,
16
natural rate of, 769
Phelps-Friedman theory of
inflation and, 767–775
post-WWII rate, 735–736
and poverty, 407
and price-push inflation, 775–776
and prices, 486
and production-possibility
boundary, 10
search, 733–734
and short-run decisions, 176
and stagflation, 780–784
structural, 733
and tariffs, 703
voluntary vs. involuntary, 731
and world aggregate demand, 713
writers' focus of attention on, 741
Yugoslavia, 848–849
Unemployment insurance, as built-in
stabilizer, 563
Unions
competing goals, 358–360
in competitive labor market,
345–346
craft vs. industrial, 366
effect on wages, and size of
membership, 366
equal pay demand between plants
vs. between men and women,
366
evolution of, 351–352
historical development, 353–356
monopsonistic labor market
without, 346–347
in monopsonistic market, 347–348
as potential monopsonists,
348–349
requirements for success, 352–353
in restricting supply to increase
wages, 356–358

union shop contract vs. firm's raw
materials monopoly, 366
and wage determination theory, 28
Union shop, 350
Uniontown vs. Richville, local
personal income tax, 455–456
Uniroyal Inc., 416
Unitas, John, 330
United Airlines and deregulation of
airfares, 304
United Automobile Workers, 351,
358
and bargaining with raw materials
monopolist vs. union shop
contract holder, 366
and GM strike (1970), 415–417
United Farm Workers Organizing
Committee, 350
United Mine Workers, 354, 358
United Nations
debt policy, 587
warns of hazards of peaceful nuclear
power, 207
United Shoe Machinery Corp., 251
United States
business activity since 1870,
528–529
and Canada, exchange rates, 684;
GNP if countries were joined,
480
as capitalist economy, 851
chances of achieving various
results, 851
as command economy in WWII,
851
contributed capital, 822
economy, 468–473
effect of drop in price of
manufactured goods in
Common Market, 694
percentages of trade with, 706
vs. Soviet Union, comparative
performance, 842–846;
unemployment and inflation,
851; urban crisis, 851
standard of living as two nations or
as combined North American
nation, 694
stock of money, 613
tariff, 704–705
trade war with France, 709
vs. underdeveloped countries,
poverty in, 407

U.S. economy
   factor-payments approach, 469
   reconciliation of expenditure and
      payments approaches, 471–473
U.S. Steel case, 294
U.S. Steel Corp., 348, 427
U.S. v. Socony-Vacuum Oil Co., 295
Unit elasticity, 75
Unit of account
   money as, 600
   need for, 611
   various items, 611
Universities vs. government, pay,
   and distribution theory, 343
Unplanned markets vs.
   uncoordinated markets, 411–412
Unrealistic assumptions, visualizing
   situations with, 28
Upper turning point in business
   fluctuation, 544, 545
Urban crisis, 4
   and economics of decay, 446–450
   and grants-in-aid, 443–446
   New York City, 448–449
   policy alternatives, 450
Uruguay, beef exports and
   comparative advantage, 694
Usher, Abbot Payton, 196
USSR GOSPLAN, 837
Utility
   and demand elasticity, 116–117
   marginal vs. total, 115–116
   maximizing, 112–115
   regulation of, 298–302
Utility schedules and graphs,
   111–112
   John Ehrlichman, 129
Utility theory
   and priceless vs. worthless, 129
   and sale of da Vinci painting, 129
   and sale of shredded currency, 129
Utilization vs. capacity, 789–790

Valuations, private vs. social, 417
Value
   of asset, 371–372
   and cost, 155
   and economic system, 833–834
   of housewife, 481
   of leisure, 478–479
   of marginal propensity to consume
      and/or average propensity to
      consume, 505

money as store of, 599–600
money vs. real, 475
paradox of, 108, 115–116
present, of future income, 370–371
   of single future payment, 370–371
urban land, and taxes, 341
in use vs. in exchange, 115–116
Value added
   defined, 461–462
   through stages of production, 461
Value and Capital (Hicks), 119
Value system, corruption in New
   Industrial State, 307
Variable(s), 22–23
   functional forms, 855
   functional relations, 854–855
   life-cycle hypothesis, 885–886
   relations among, 23–24
Variable costs, 171–172
Variable factors, 166
Variable proportions, law of, 170
Variety, tradeoff with price, quality,
   and advertising, consumer
   products, 267
Veblen, Thorstein, 130, 307n.
   argument that financing and
      pricing are superfluous, 163
Velocity of circulation and money
   balances, 640
Venezuela vs. Sweden, population
   growth, 820
Verdoorn, P. J., 700
Vertical merger, 295
Very long run, in decision making,
   167
Vicious circle of poverty, 821
Viner, Jacob, famous error, 183
Vineyards, crops and profits, 106
Visibles vs. invisibles, 673
Von's Grocery case, 295
Von Stackelberg, H., 259
Vote for 17-year-olds, marginal vs.
   total utility of, 129

Wage(s)
   between plants vs. between men
      and women, 366
   determination in competitive labor
      market, 345–346
   determination in monopsonistic
      market, 347–348
   differentials, Soviet, 839
   and discrimination, 360–365

and employment, 358, 400
and factor supply, 340–341
vs. fringe benefits, 359–360
vs. job security, 358–359
minimum, effects of, 106
New England vs. South Carolina,
   and principle of substitution, 191
and pedicabs, Dacca, 191
and quantity of factor supplied,
   340–341
and salaries, 462
and tariffs, 701–702
union effect on, and size of
   membership, 366
union's restriction of supply to
   increase, 356–358
Wage determination theory and labor
   unions, 28
Wage fixing vs. price fixing, and
   Clayton Act, 366
Wage-price controls
   and cost-push inflation, 778
   and demand-pull inflation,
      776–777
   and expectational inflation, 777–778
   and price-push inflation, 778
Wagner Act (1935), 354
   and right of public employees to
      strike, 366
Wallich, Henry, 628
Wall Street Journal on reserve
   requirements, 634
Walters, Barbara, 330
   pay as economic rent vs. transfer
      earnings, 343
War
   and business cycles, 527
   and future potential GNP, 505
   who pays for, 582
War on poverty, 394–396
Warren Court, 295
Washington, George, Farewell
   Address, 708
Water monopoly, price and elasticity
   of demand, 249
Water pollution, 200–202
Water quality and chemical fertilizers,
   16
Water Resources Research Bill (1964),
   453n.
Wealth
   national, and international trade,
      694

and poverty, 3
redistribution, and inflation, 594–595
Wealth of Nations, The (Smith), 42, 283
Wealthy
  flight from cities, 446–447
  on motives of firms and households, 49
  and poor, income distribution between, 389–391
Welfare, expenditure for, 397
Welfare benefits, taxes, and supply of effort, 331–332
Welfare services, as built-in stabilizer, 563
Welmesfelder, W., 700
Westinghouse Electric Corp., 280
Wetbacks and minimum wage, 106
Wharton, C. R., Jr., 825n.
Wheat farmer, and perfect competition, 214–215
Wheel, spur for, 207
WHO. *See* World Health Organization
Wholesale price index, 90, 591
  Germany, post-WWI, 596
Wicksell, Knut, 744n.
Williams, Ted, marginal and lifetime batting average, 172
Wine, auction price, and demand curve for luxuries, 146

Winter 1977, production levels and average total cost, 176
Wisconsin, Audubon Society suit to halt highway construction in, 207
Withdrawal(s)
  from circular flow, 46
  and equilibrium national income, 505
  and injections, compensating changes in, 512–513
  and national income, 510
Withdrawal curve and multiplier, 518
Withdrawal schedule, shift in, 509–512
Withdrawals-injections approach, in general case, 499–503
Women
  and labor market differentials, 361–362
  traditional occupations and employment opportunities, 366
  in work force, 343
Work force, participation vs. composition, 343
Workweek, 4-day, and productivity, 207
World Bank, 818–822
World Health Organization (WHO), 204

World War II
  hyperinflation and U.S. cigarettes, 611
  move from unemployment to full employment in, 16
Worthless vs. priceless, 129
WREDD Brick Co., potential merger, 304

Xerox Corp., monopoly power, 249
X-inefficiency, 816–818

Yarvard Law School, excess demand and admission criteria, 106
Yugoslavia
  chances of achieving various results, 851
  decollectivization of agriculture, 847–848
  economic system, 846–847
  labor-managed enterprises, 848–849
  scope and role of planning, 849

Zero elasticity, 75
Zero growth rate, production and consumption at, 808
Zero profit, 161
Zero-profit equilibrium, 222
  in monopolistic competition, 255, 256

79 80 9 8 7 6 5 4

An index of wholesale prices in the U.S. 1785–1975 (1967 = 100)

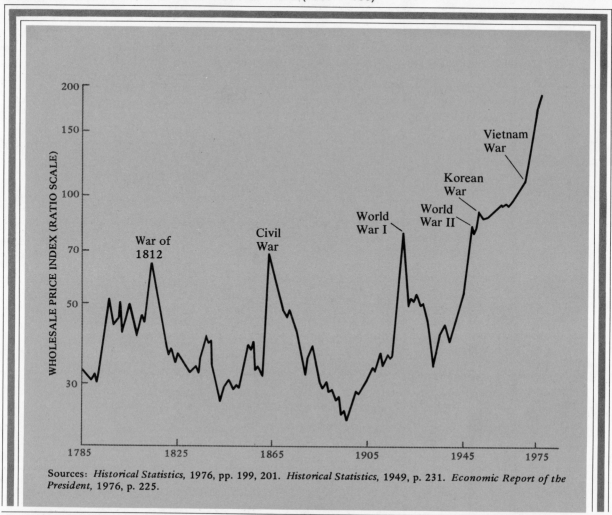

Sources: *Historical Statistics*, 1976, pp. 199, 201. *Historical Statistics*, 1949, p. 231. *Economic Report of the President*, 1976, p. 225.

Inflation is a major concern of Americans in the 1970s. This graph shows that inflation is not a new phenomenon in America. The War of 1812, the Civil War, and World War I were all accompanied by sharp inflations. However, each of these inflations was followed by a deflation that brought the price level more or less back to its prewar level.

As with all past wars World War II was accompanied by a major inflation but, unlike all past wars, there was no significant postwar deflation. The Korean War brought another unreversed rise in price level. After a short period of stability, the price level began to creep upwards in the late 1950s and early 1960s, but by the late 1960s the trend of inflation began to accelerate. In the 1970s the inflation rate increased, and America entered into the most rapid period of peace-time inflation ever recorded in its history.

The study of inflation in this book poses such problems as:

Who gains and who loses from inflation?

Why do inflations occur?
    Are the unions to blame?
    Are the great corporations to blame?
    How much responsibility lies at the feet of the government?

How can inflation be brought under control?

What are the costs and benefits of income policies that attempt to control inflation through direct government intervention?

ECONOMICS

$14.65 F1